WYOMING
ALMANAC

Phil Roberts
David L. Roberts
Steven L. Roberts

Wyoming Almanac/Skyline West Press
Cheyenne
6th Edition, Revised
2010

ISBN: 978-0-914767-32-9
Wyoming Almanac/Skyline West Press
P. O. Box 20052
Cheyenne WY 82003-7001
(307) 745-8205 (Laramie)
E-mail: philwyo@yahoo.com; srobden@bresnan.net
Webpage: www.wyomingalmanac.com

This is a Wyoming-made book. All production and printing of Wyoming Almanac was done in Wyoming.
Published by Wyoming Almanac/Skyline West Press and printed by Pioneer Printing, Cheyenne.

Introduction to the Sixth Edition

Five earlier editions of Wyoming Almanac have been published since 1989. This edition includes much new information and lists as well as updated materials from earlier editions.

All lists and entries in this book relate directly to Wyoming. All incidents noted took place prior to July 10, 2010 (coincidentally, the 120th anniversary of Wyoming statehood). Even with these criteria, the subjects are simply too overwhelming to summarize and categorize in these few pages. We do not presume that it is either complete or entirely accurate (although care has been taken to limit the number of mistakes and to correct some errors made in earlier editions). The subjects for the lists and their contents were chosen completely by authors' whim. Many of the categories reflect the personal interests of the authors. For instance, Steven L. Roberts developed many of the lists in the sports area. David L. Roberts suggested inclusion of the topics of books, movies and television. Phil Roberts added a fascinating (to him) new section in this edition on taxes. We believe no book can do more than provide a glimpse and feel for a unique place in this country and the few hardy souls who live here. This edition was compiled with all of them in mind.

Many of the lists may change frequently. Consequently, Wyoming Almanac has a web site where updates will be posted from time to time. The web site is: www.wyomingalmanac.com

Special thanks to Michael Vann Gray for the cover illustration of the bison, to the capable staff of Pioneer Printing in Cheyenne who printed the book, and to the many people who provided special lists, stories and suggestions since the last edition. Many provided key facts and entries for various categories, both in the course of their employment and through their genuine interest in and love for our state. Again, we thank the hundreds of people who have provided suggestions, offered advice on categories, helped correct the record on various points, and generally enlivened the contents of this edition. Of course, any inaccuracies are solely those of the authors.

Phil Roberts
David L. Roberts
Steven L. Roberts
July 10, 2010

ADVERTISING
Some Interesting Wyoming Ads

1. "Individual Towels"

Sign, posted in 1868, promoting one of the best features of a hotel in Benton, now a ghost town in Carbon County. Other less exclusive establishments did not make such claims.

2. **"Since man to man has been unjust**
I scarcely know what man to trust.
I've trusted so many to my sorrow—
So pay today and I'll trust tomorrow."
—Poetic sign over Belander's Butcher Shop, Carbon, 1880s

3. "All you prospector boys, drop in and get a map of your mugs."
Newspaper ad for Ferris Photo Shop, *Dillon Doublejack*, 1900

4. "St. Jacobs Oil"

Sign painted on rocks before 1900 and visible to railway passengers from trains crossing the Dale Creek trestle in southeastern Wyoming. Advertising space on the nearby Ames Monument was once offered for sale at $20 per square foot or $160,000 annually, but not by the Union Pacific, who put a quick stop to the deal.

5. "Twist the Grey Mule's tail and take the elevator."

Bill Nye's sign at the bottom of the stairs leading to his second floor office of the *Laramie Boomerang* (named for a mule). The main floor of the building, located on the southwest corner of 3rd and Garfield, housed a livery stable.

6. "Wagner's Pants Are Down"

When editor Bill Nye sought an ad from Laramie dry goods merchant Henry Wagner, the merchant told Nye he didn't think advertising worked. Nye, the intrepid ad salesman, noticed that Wagner had a sale on pants. He wrote up the sale as a "news item" in his paper the next morning. The pants sold out quickly and Wagner became a believer in newspaper advertising. When Nye founded his own paper, Wagner backed it financially.

7. "Grit, Gumption and Get There"
Newspaper slogan of early day *Worland Grit* editor Tom Daggett.

8. "Home of Rock Springs Coal—Welcome"

The sign, erected about 1930, spanned C Street in Rock Springs. Half of the cost was paid by coal mine operators and the rest through popular subscription. The sign was moved to Western Wyoming College in 1980.

9. "Welcome to Fort Laramie—Population 350 Good People and 6 Soreheads"

Signs are on the eastern and western edges of the town of Fort Laramie and updated every ten years to reflect the change of population and, presumably, the number of soreheads.

10. "Drink Sweetwater Beer and Be Healthy"

Ad for the Sweetwater Brewing Company, Green River, it appeared in many newspapers, including the *Wyoming Industrial Journal*, July, 1907.

11. "Butch's Taxidermy—Butch Mounts Anything"
Sign advertising a Fort Bridger business.

12. "Everybody's—Members Only"

The contradictory sign was on the door of "Everybody's," an after-hours club popular

When Dan Radon was convicted in Thermopolis of the murder of Marko Ragnovich on Sept. 25, 1931, he was sentenced to hang. He appealed the case, however, claiming that the jury was drinking liquor during his trial.

with Laramie residents in the 1950s and 1960s. In theory, only members were served, but "membership cards" were available for purchase at the door.

13. "Find Yourself in Wyoming"

Wyoming Travel Commission sign near the entrance to Lincoln Tunnel, New York City, in October, 1987. In 1989, television ads starred the cartoon character, Bullwinkle Moose. The moose told national TV viewers, "If the last moose you watched was on Saturday mornings, it's time to find yourself in Wyoming." In early 1992, the travel commission admitted making a mistake with the slogan, "A Great Land Outdoors" after many residents complained it didn't make sense. The original slogan, "The Great Land Outdoors," would not fit within the sign space. In the 1990s, the commission's slogan was "Wyoming: Like No Place on Earth."

14. "Ten miles from water, 20 miles from timber and no grub in the house. God bless our home."

The words, painted on a cracker box nailed above a cabin door, were seen by President Chester Arthur's party between Fort Washakie and Yellowstone in 1883.

15. "Somewhere West of Laramie"

One of the most famous advertisements of all time, the ad was written by Edward S. Jordan, co-founder and owner of the Cleveland-based automobile manufacturing firm using the ad. The Jordan car was priced at about $2,500 when the lowest priced Ford was selling for about $500. The car was selling badly so Jordan took a train ride to the West Coast, hoping he could come up with a plan to sell more vehicles. As Jordan's train passed through southern Wyoming, Jordan watched a beautiful young woman ride her horse alongside the train for a short distance. The sight impressed Jordan so much that he turned to a companion and asked where they were. "Somewhere west of Laramie," was the reply. Back home, Jordan sketched out an ad with the slogan. The ad first ran in *Saturday Evening Post* in June, 1923. Sales of the Jordan cars picked up immediately. Soon, other auto makers were using the new form of "image advertising." Despite the strong sales resulting from the ads, the Jordan company eventually failed, a victim of the Great Depression. Nonetheless, the ad became legendary. In 1945, *Printer's Ink* magazine readers voted it the third greatest ad ever created.

16. "Dalton Motors--Clean Comfortable Ladies"

The ad accidentally omitted the words "rest rooms" at the end of the line. *Wyoming Eagle*, 1927. Years later, publisher Tracy McCraken laughed that such an error made an editor "wish he were moving to Fiji."

17. "Summer petticoats, made of Everett, Zephr and Mercerized ginghams, extremely well made and very wide."

Laramie Sentinel ad, 1872.

18. "No skinning or hanging in the park."

Sign in the Kaycee City Park, 1999.

19. "Oysters R In"

The sign hung outside the Palace Meat Market in Evanston, starting about September 15 each year, notifying customers that fresh oysters from Baltimore had arrived. Oysters were shipped in by train over the transcontinental route.

20. "Wanted: 100 Enterprising Young Men...."

The ad, placed by William Ashley and Andrew Henry who were forming a fur-trading firm, appeared in St. Louis newspapers in March, 1822. Among those responding to the ad were Jim Bridger, Jedediah Smith and David E. Jackson.

In an episode of the animated series, The Simpsons, in 1994, the story centered around a brand of cigarettes called Laramie.

21. **"Eat American lamb, 10 million coyotes can't be wrong"**
Statement painted on signs in sheep-raising areas of Wyoming in the 1990s.

22. **"Anything, everything from a needle to a threshing machine"**
Ad for A. G. Rupp General Merchandise in *Worland Grit,* 1906.

Some TV-Magazine Ads Filmed in Wyoming or Mentioning Wyoming

1. Marlboro
Ads for the cigarettes have been shot in western Wyoming during the 1960s and 1970s. Wyomingite Darrel Winfield was one "Marlboro man" featured in print and television ads. Several of the ads were shot on the Teton Valley Ranch near Jackson.

2. Levi Dockers
A February, 1991, TV ad for the jeans included the statement that an individual's luggage had been sent to Cheyenne, Wyo., apparently a disaster for Levi jean wearers.

3. Seabreeze Skin Cream
Although not filmed in Wyoming, a 1991 ad for the product featured two women who claimed to be from Wyoming and who credited the product with giving them "gorgeous skin."

4. Redman Chewing Tobacco
The company used locations around Rawlins, Saratoga and Hanna as backdrops for a 1986 ad.

5. Budweiser Beer
Anheuser-Busch's ad agency filmed a Budweiser beer television commercial in northwest Wyoming in 1988. Other beer companies have used Wyoming locations. Miller, for instance, filmed in the state in 1984; Genessee Beer in the same year. Torrington auctioneer Lex Madden appeared in a beer advertisement in 1993.

6. Old Milwaukee Beer
Dan Woodward, an employee of the Jackson National Fish Hatchery, appeared as a flyfisherman in the ad, filmed at Oxbow Bend in Grand Teton National Park. The two other actors in the 30-second segment were "Breck O'Neill, a stuntman, and his downstairs neighbor, Todd Link," according to a detailed description of the production of the ad written for a historic resource study for the NPS by William H. Goetzmann..

7. Toyota Corolla
Various Wyoming locations were used for a 1984 ad for the Japanese car company.

8. Jeep Cherokee
An ad was filmed at Devils Canyon Overlook near Lovell in May 1990, for the Jeep Cherokee. An ad appearing on television in 2006 showed the vehicle parked in front of Ames Monument, the 60-foot-high pyramid off I-80 between Cheyenne and Laramie

9. General Motors
A General Motors safety ad televised in February 1992, noted: "Some guy from Wyoming could be driving that car." The meaning wasn't made clear.

10. Saturn automobiles
In July, 1996, Pinedale was featured on a national television ad for Saturns. The narrator tells about being flown 250 miles to the nearest Saturn dealership in Salt Lake City. Main street of Pinedale is shown as well as the local post office.

The largest neon tube display sign in the state in June 1932 advertised the Park Hotel in Rock Springs. It contained 187 feet of neon tubing.

11. Chevrolet

During the 1997 All Star baseball game, a Chevrolet rolled onto the TV screen, the driver's side door opened and the whole Teton Range flowed out—"Like a Rock.". .

12. Honda

The TV ad in 2000 showed a driver parking in front of Jackson Drug in Jackson and, as he got out of the vehicle, his dog sneaked a drink from his soft-drink cup. The town square and other parts of Jackson are shown in the background.

13. Other automobiles

Two car companies filmed commercials along the Beartooth Highway in northwest Wyoming during the summer of 1996.

14. Prelude Cigarettes

The British-owned firm was one of several foreign companies who used Wyoming locations for advertising spots in recent years.

15. Danon Yogurt

The 1987 ad was one of many made by food companies using Wyoming backdrops.

16. Amtrak

The passenger rail service was criticized when it utilized a backdrop of the Grand Tetons in a televised commercial promoting the "great scenery" along the Amtrak route. The ad appeared on television a few months after Amtrak pulled its trains from the route across southern Wyoming, electing to use what they called a "more scenic route through Colorado." Of course, neither line passes anywhere near Jackson Hole or the Tetons.

17. Bank advertising

Numerous regional bank television commercials have been made with Wyoming backdrops. Credit card companies also have utilized Wyoming scenes.

18. Microsoft

A two-page magazine advertisement for the computer software giant in February, 1995, carried the following heading: "NPR changed the station in Chugwater, Wyoming and things haven't been the same since." The ad was selling Microsoft Word. In 1998-99, Microsoft ran a series of national TV ads featuring residents of Lusk and how computers had changed their operations. One such ad ran during the 1999 Super Bowl.

19. Cub Cadet lawnmower

In March, 1997, the company featured an ad showing a man riding a lawnmower with the statement made that "Wyoming could use a trim."

20. Metamucil

The company advertised the "regularity" of its laxative by showing a park ranger surreptiously dumping a bottle down Old Faithful Geyser in Yellowstone, implying that is how the geyser remains "regular." The ad met controversy from park officials who said the ad encouraged vandalism of the natural features. The company added a written statement, flashed on the screen under a scene, noting that the ad was a simulation only.

---

5 Names Suggested for Wyoming*

1. Cheyenne	3. Platte	5. Lincoln
2. Arapahoe	4. Sweetwater	

Wyoming, the name finally agreed upon, was not indigenous to the region. The name, given to a valley in Pennsylvania, was a Delaware Indian word meaning "large plains." The above listed names were submitted by residents or proposed by congressmen prior to or during the course of Congress' 1868 attempt to apply a name to the territory before it was created.

AFRICAN AMERICANS

1st African American in Wyoming: Probably, Jim Beckwourth, the mountain man, who came in 1825. Big Horn Basin pioneer Edward Rose, a mountain man whose presence in Wyoming dates to at least 1808, was part Black.

1st African American legislator in Wyoming: W. J. Hardin, (b. Kentucky, c. 1830), elected in Laramie County (1879)

1st Black church in Wyoming: Allen Chapel, AME Church, Cheyenne (1875)

1st Black church in Casper: Grace AME Church, formed in 1917 by Rev. James Otto Minor. First meetings were held in a house on C Street, a half-block from the later church site on North Grant Street. Rev. Minor's daughter, Marie Davis, was an opera singer, reared in Casper. In 2004, she was a delegate to the Democratic National Convention. She was living in Foster City, Calif.

1st African American woman elected mayor of a Wyoming town: LaVertha Gotier, elected mayor of Worland in 2000.

The "Cheyenne League of Colored People" was organized on Aug. 15, 1918.

Some Well Known Wyoming African Americans

1. Edward Rose

Rose, the son of a white father who was a trader among the Cherokees and a half Black/Cherokee mother, was born in Kentucky. He had a checkered reputation. According to Washington Irving, Rose "belonged to a gang of pirates who infested the islands of the Mississippi River." They operated both on land and the river and it is said they robbed and killed many travelers. Rose went up the river in 1807 or 1808 with the Manuel Lisa company and helped them build Fort Raymond at the mouth of the Big Horn river in Montana. He later joined with the Crow Indians and decided to live with them. Some accounts say that he built a cabin in the Big Horn Basin about this time--if correct, it would have been the first non-Native American structure built in Wyoming. According to Irving's account in *Astoria*, Rose offered to guide the Hunt party in 1811, but his offer was refused. In 1812 he worked for the Missouri Fur Company. An interpreter on Ashley's expedition in 1823 at the Aricaras village where they stopped to trade, Rose warned Ashley of the Indians' behavior. Ashley, however, did not trust Rose and did not take precautions, thus leading to a battle on May 2-3, 1823. Later, Rose joined Col. Leavenworth's expedition with the rank of ensign and, in 1825, he was on the Atkinson/O'Fallon expedition up the Missouri River. He died sometime after and, according to accounts, he is buried on the banks of the Missouri River nearly opposite the mouth of the Milk River.

2. Jim Beckwourth, Mountain Man

Born in Fredericksburg, Virginia, Beckwourth, a mulatto, was one of the first non-Native people to visit what is now Wyoming. He probably came to the area in 1825. He was employed by Ashley's Rocky Mountain Fur Company and trapped across Wyoming from the Laramie Plains to the Green River in 1825. Just before his death in 1866, he was hired as a scout and messenger at Fort Laramie.

3. Janisse, Explorer

The only African American to travel with the Fremont expedition, Janisse, who was entrusted with carrying the barometer to the summit, was one of the men to witness, on Aug. 15, 1842, the raising of the first American flag over Wyoming, the 26-star flag made by Fremont's wife. Some mountaineer historians claim the climb was not of Fremont Peak, but what is now Mount Woodrow Wilson in the Wind River Range. Janisse has been called the first African-American mountain climber.

4. Lucretia Marchbanks, Crook County, Rancher

Marchbanks, born a slave in Tennessee in 1832, bought Crook County ranch in 1885. Before the Civil War, her father purchased her freedom for $700 and she went west to

California. Later, she moved to South Dakota where she ran a hotel in Deadwood for many years. Known as "Aunt Lou," she died in 1911 and was buried in Beulah.

5. Barney Ford, Cheyenne, Hotel Operator

Ford owned and operated the Occidental Hotel in Cheyenne, in its time, the most luxurious hotel in the territory. President U. S. Grant stayed at Ford's hotel during an official visit west in 1875. Later, Ford moved to Denver where he also operated a luxury hotel. Born in 1822, he died in 1902. A stained-glass window in the Colorado State Capitol honors his contributions to that state.

6. W. J. Hardin, Cheyenne, Legislator

Hardin, a Cheyenne barber, was elected to the state legislature in 1878. He was the first Black member of that body. Born in Kentucky of free Black parents, he went to California with the gold rush and finally settled in Denver where he became known as an orator and an employee of the U. S. Mint. A scandal erupted in 1873 in which a Black woman from Kentucky found him in Denver and charged him with having fathered her child and abandoning them in the 1850s. Hardin denied the charge, but he lost his job at the mint and, with his reputation in ruins, moved to Cheyenne. Six years later, he was elected to the Wyoming legislature where he distinguished himself as a orator. He was re-elected in 1880 and was the only incumbent who won. He did not run for a third term. According to historian Roger Hardaway, Hardin left Cheyenne about 1884, perhaps moving to Utah or Colorado. The place and date of his death is not known. *Source: Roger Hardaway, "William Jefferson Hardin, Wyoming's 19th Century Black Legislator," Annals of Wyoming 63 (Winter 1991).*

7. Nate Thaxton, Lovell, Storekeeper

Little is known of Thaxton who operated Lovell's first meat market. He came to the area with the cattle drives from Texas in the 1880s. He ran the first store in the area from his cabin near the Big Horn River ferry.

8. Louis Brown, Dubois area, Tie Hack

Louis and his brother Bill worked with primarily Swedish tie hacks in the mountains near Dubois. Both men spoke excellent Swedish. When a newcomer heard Brown speak Swedish, he asked what nationality he was. Brown replied, "I'm a sunburned Swede."

9. Vernon J. Baker, Soldier

Baker, a native of Cheyenne, led an all-Black army unit against a German outpost in Italy in 1945. One of the army's first Black officers, Baker was a second lieutenant in the 370th Regiment. On January 13, 1997, President Bill Clinton awarded Baker the nation's highest military honor, the Congressional Medal of Honor, in White House ceremonies. The award to Baker and six other Black soldiers was recommended in June, 1996, by the Department of Defense. Baker was the only one of the seven surviving, thus becoming the first African-American to be awarded the Medal of Honor for World War II acts of bravery. He died in St. Maries, Idaho, on July 13, 2010.

10. Edward L. Baker, Jr., Soldier

Edward Baker, born Dec. 28, 1865, (no relation to Vernon Baker, above), was the first Wyoming-born recipient of the Congressional Medal of Honor. He was born at Fort Laramie and enlisted in 1882 in Cincinnati, Ohio. A sergeant-major in the 10th Cavalry, he earned the award in the Spanish-American War at Santiago, Cuba, on July 1, 1898.

11. Elizabeth Byrd, Cheyenne, Legislator

The first African American woman to serve in the Wyoming legislature, the long-time elementary school teacher was elected to the House in 1980 from Laramie County. Later, she was elected to the State Senate. She served in the legislature until 1991.

12. James Byrd, Cheyenne, Law Enforcement Officer

Born in New Jersey in 1925, Byrd first came to Wyoming with the U. S. Army. Following his marriage to a Wyoming native, Elizabeth Byrd (previously noted), he became an officer with the Cheyenne Police Department in 1949. He became chief of police in 1966 and served until his retirement in 1975. He was the first African-American to hold that post. During the Carter administration, he was U. S. Marshal for Wyoming (1977-1981). Byrd died in December 2005.

13. Matt Campfield, Casper, Natrona County Coroner
    Campfield, who opened a barber shop in Casper soon after his arrival in 1888, was twice elected county coroner. He died in 1897 during his second term in office.

14. Dick Sparks, Cowboy
    Sparks was the first African-American in the Big Horn Basin. He came there as a cook on the first cattle drive in 1879. He continued to work for the Carter Ranch until 1887 when he was caught in a Christmas blizzard en route from the ranch to Trail Creek. He died in the storm.

15. Cheryl Johnson, Cheyenne, Miss Wyoming 1973
    The 20-year-old college student became the first African American crowned "Miss Wyoming." She represented her native state in the Miss America Pageant in 1973.

16. Rev. J. Crossley, Evanston, Pastor
    The Rev. Crossley was the first minister in Evanston. He preached at the Evanston Baptist Church from 1871 to 1874 and from 1876 to 1877. During that time, he also managed the Rocky Mountain Hotel in Evanston.

17. Isom Dart, Brown's Park, Rancher
    Dart came to Wyoming from Texas in 1882 as trail boss for a large cattle outfit. One of the best riders in the area, Dart operated a small ranch in Brown's Hole. In October 1900, he was ambushed and killed. Stock detective Tom Horn was suspected in the case although he was never formally charged with Dart's murder.

18. Flynn Robinson, University of Wyoming, Basketball Player
    Robinson starred with the Cowboys from 1962 to 1965. He scored 2,049 points during his collegiate career, the most of any player in UW history to that point and second all-time. Later, he played professional basketball in the NBA, playing eight seasons with the Cincinnati Royals, Chicago Bulls, Milwaukee Bucks, Baltimore Bullets, and the Los Angeles Lakers. On March 27, 1968, he scored 41 points to lead the Chicago Bulls against the Lakers to the team's first-ever NBA playoff game victory. He later played for the Lakers and retired from basketball after playing on the Lakers' 1972 NBA title team.

19. Joby Wright, UW Basketball Coach
    Wright, born in Georgia in 1950, coached at the University of Wyoming from 1993 to 1996. As a collegian, he played basketball at Indiana University and, later, served as assistant coach for ten years. After graduation, Wright was drafted as the fifth pick in the 1972 NBA draft by the Seattle Sonics. He played three years of professional basketball. Before coming to UW, he coached at Miami University (O.) He coached four years at UW, but had no winning seasons, resigning in 1997. He moved to Cincinnati where he served as a coach and sports consultant for a new basketball league franchise. His daughter Cara played basketball for the University of Dayton from 2004-06.

20. John Wideman, Laramie, Author/Academician
    Wideman, a former Rhodes scholar and collegiate basketball star at the University of Pennsylvania, taught English at the University of Wyoming from 1974 to 1987. His several novels included *Sent for You Yesterday* for which he received the prestigious PEN-Faulkner award in 1981. In 1987 he left UW to teach in Massachusetts. He now teaches at Brown.

Boxer George Foreman was pictured on television the morning after his fight against Evander Holyfield on April 20, 1991, wearing a University of Wyoming T-shirt. The shirt was a gift from a sparring partner who had played football at Wyoming and had maintained Wyoming connections.

21. LaVertha Gotier, Mayor

LaVertha Gotier and her husband Roy moved to Worland in 1976. In 2000, she was elected mayor of Worland, the first African-American woman elected mayor of any Wyoming city. In 2010 she was chair of the Washakie County Democratic Party.

Incidents of Discrimination in Wyoming

1. Cheyenne World War II incident

In downtown Cheyenne during the Christmas holidays, 1943, several African-American soldiers were told they could not patronize a downtown cafe and bar. Sparked by the blatant bigotry, a fight ensued. Windows were broken and several people were injured in the violence. Publicity about it was kept to a minimum in the interest of the "war effort.

2. Moose Lodge baby contest

In November, 1947, the Casper Moose Lodge came under national criticism for refusing to allow "two Negro babies" entry into their "beautiful baby" contest. After national bad publicity, a lodge spokesman blamed the policy on an "out-of-state promoter."

3. Black 14 incident, University of Wyoming

The October, 1969, incident involved 14 African-American football players who sought permission to wear black armbands in that week's game against Brigham Young University as protest of the policy of the LDS church on banning Blacks from the priesthood. Other coaches had allowed such actions at universities in Arizona, Texas and Washington, but Wyoming coach Lloyd Eaton angrily refused to let them wear the armbands. He kicked them off the team. The university president and trustees backed Eaton's action. The incident ended in litigation, but the after-effects were disastrous to University of Wyoming football fortunes for the next decade. *For a complete story of the incident, see Clifford Bullock, "Fired by Conscience: The Black 14 Incident at the University of Wyoming and Black Protest in the Western Athletic Conference," in Readings in Wyoming History, 3rd ed. (Laramie: Skyline West, 2000); and a response by James A. Barrett, Wyoming's attorney-general at the time, "The Black 14: Williams v. Eaton," in the same volume.*

4. Newspaper comments about Filippinos, 1934

"Following the arrest of five American girls and six Philippine boys at a party on West Midwest Avenue last week, Franz G. Schreck, chief of police, declared that public cooperation is needed in the handling of the problem of mixed racial gatherings in Casper. About 25 couples were at the party, but all but 11 of them escaped. One of them was the mother of two of the girls. When questioned she remarked that 'I don't care. I think that the Filippinos are gentlemen compared to the white boys.'" *Quoted directly from a news account in the Wyoming Eagle, April 6, 1934, p. 12.*

5. Advice to Avoid Discrimination

John Cullen, Ohio Oil Company executive, wrote in his journal, July 31, 1946: "Thomas Dumis, a colored engineer, Northwestern University, Iowa State, Masters Degree in Architectural Engineering, 32 years old, wants job in foreign country." Cullen advised that he felt prejudice was not as great in the "foreign field, as in the United States." Cullen wrote that he told Dumis "we had no foreign connections, but the Standard of New Jersey, Standard of California, Texas Company, and Shell, all had connections." He recommended that Dumis contact people in those companies.

The 25th Infantry bicycle corps, an all-Black unit, followed the Burlington route across Wyoming during their 1,900-mile ride from Fort Missoula to St. Louis. They made the trip in 41 days in the summer of 1897, spending the 4th of July at Fort Robinson, Neb., and making it to St. Louis on July 24

AGRICULTURE AND RANCHING

1st farmers in Wyoming: Indians who raised pumpkins and maize along the Powder River hundreds of years before Columbus

1st cattle in Wyoming: A fur trade party brought five cattle to the Wind River Rendezvous in 1830. Farm-raised cattle accompanied emigrants' wagon trains west to Oregon, beginning in 1843.

1st sheep in Wyoming: "Uncle" Dick Wooton and Kit Carson brought 13,000 sheep from New Mexico to Fort Laramie and then west along the Oregon-California trail to San Francisco in 1853 where they sold the sheep to miners for $5.50 a head.

1st sheep brought to Wyoming (not passing through): Thomas F. and John H. Durbin brought several hundred head into the territory in the fall of 1870. The same year, William Tweed brought 200 head to Red Canyon, Fremont County.

1st garden vegetables grown by Euro-Americans in Wyoming: Beans, peas, carrots grown by Mormons at Deer Creek Station (now Glenrock) in 1853.

1st irrigation farming in Wyoming: Near Fort Laramie, conducted by Mexicans who worked at the fort, 1855. In 1997, 1,719,463 acres were irrigated on 5,306 ranches and farms.

1st potatoes, wheat and oats grown in Wyoming: Mormons at Fort Supply, 12 miles southwest of Fort Bridger, 1854.

1st sugar beets grown in Wyoming: Probably those grown experimentally by Rufus Snell, Sr., near Lovell in 1901. Earlier attempts were made to raise them on the Laramie Plains.

1st cattle received for sale at Union Stockyards, Omaha, 1884: 531 longhorns shipped from Medicine Bow.

1st cattle shipped from Gillette on Burlington Railroad: Aug. 12, 1891. More than 3,400 cars of longhorns were shipped from there in the following three months.

Brands: The Wyoming Livestock Board registers brands. In 2010, more than 28,000 were registered.

Oldest Wyoming brand still in use: M Hook, recorded by Uinta County rancher John W. Myers and used by descendants more than a century later.

Most brands registered to one individual: 28 by A. R. Converse, Cheyenne banker for whom Converse County was named. He held the brands in the 1880s. The Swan Land and Cattle Company owned so many brands that it published a brand book for the benefit of company foremen.

1st Herefords in Wyoming: Probably those brought by the Swan brothers about 1880. Alexander Swan organized the Wyoming Hereford Association in 1883.

Last herd trailed from Texas to Montana on the Texas Trail through Wyoming: A herd of XIT cattle which passed Jay Em Creek in east central Wyoming on June 17, 1897.

Total number of cowboys in Wyoming (1995): 2,840 statewide. Cowboys are defined as "beef cattle workers" who are paid a wage for more than 150 days of work per year. Another 4,079 cowboys were classified as seasonal. Average hourly wage was $7.48.

Average annual value of all agricultural crops sold: $95,712 (2002), down from $97,327 (1997).

Losses to rustlers (1993): The value of cattle rustled was estimated at $567,000.

Crops in order of value: Hay, sugar beets, beans, barley. State ranked **43rd** of the 50 states in total value of agriculture crops, $289 million (1993).

Sheep lost to predators (1995): 66,000 sheep and lambs compared to losses of 96,000 in 1994. Coyotes accounted for 73 percent of the losses with weather, disease, poison, lambing and old age accounting for the rest, according to the Wyoming Agricultural Statistics Service, March 10, 1996.

Wool production in Wyoming (1994): 7.34 million lbs., worth an estimated $6.17 million, placing Wyoming as the second largest wool producing state.

1st sheep sheared by steam-shearing method: By Mrs. J. B. Okie, 1894, near Casper. She could shear a sheep in less than four minutes.

No. of commercial aquaculture (fish) farms in Wyoming (2002): 17

Nut, fruit and berry farms in Wyoming (2002): 11

Bee colonies in Wyoming (2007): 45,633, 15th in the nation among the states

Scenic easements: By the end of 1995, the Nature Conservancy had preserved 50,000 acres of land in Wyoming in 53 easements. Their three other easements in Jackson Hole on 464 acres were transferred to the Jackson Hole Land Trust that also held 9,791 acres in 91 projects in 1999.

Cowbelles organized: The organization was formed in 1940 in a meeting at the Noble Hotel in Lander. Among the founders were: Charlotte Snodgrass, Mrs. Pat Quealy, Lilian Cross and Miriam "Mim" Jenkins Barlow.

Highest price paid for a Wyoming ranch: A ranch sold to H. Ross Perot's Hillwood development company in Jackson Hole probably sold for in excess of $100 million in 2004 although the exact price was not disclosed. The 1990s record was $52 million paid by Tennessee businessman John Thornton in 1997 for the Crescent H Guest Ranch, south of Wilson in Teton County. The 1,300-acre ranch was sold as part of a bankruptcy settlement in June, 1997. In Sheridan County, Chevron/Texaco sold the 26,000-acre Bar 6 Bar Ranch near Story in 2005 for an undisclosed price. The ranch had been listed for sale at $36.5 million. By 2008, prices had escalated dramatically and many properties sold for in excess of that price.

Wyoming had **136** farms and ranches subject to Farmers Home Administration (FHA) foreclosure due to delinquent loans (1992).

1st University of Wyoming Livestock Judging Team: 1920.

Total Cattle in Wyoming

2007: 1,311,799 (24th among the states) **1910:** 959,000
2005: 1,350,000 (25th among the states) **1885:** 2,000,000
1997: 1,297,000 (24th among the states) **1870:** 8,143

Ranch Lands, Cattle Prices and Ranches in Wyoming

Total cattle ranches in Wyoming: 5,282 ranches raised cattle in 2002; 5,526 in 1997.

Wyoming ranks **48th** among the states in the **average value of land per acre**. In 2002, the average was $290 per acre; $300 per acre in 2004. In 1994, average land value was $169 per acre; in 1997, the value had risen to $222 per acre. Average for irrigated land (2004) was $1,150 per acre.

Average value per farm/ranch: $1,080,195 in 2002, up from $808,346 in 1997.

Cattle: average value per head (1994): $655.

June average price paid for beef cattle--
1994- $62; **1995-** $60; **1996-** $53.80; **1997-** $61; **1998-** $65.10; **2000-** $67.00, **2005-**$98.30

Average age of Wyoming ranchers/farmers (2007): 56 years old

Average grazing rates charged on private land in Wyoming (2003): $13.40 per animal unit month (aum).

Wyoming ranks **48th** in the average value of land per acre. In 1994, average land value was $169 per acre; in 1997, the value had risen to $222 per average acre.

Total ranches of more than 1,000 acres: 3,235 (2002); 3,592 (1997)

No. of ranches raising more than 1,000 cattle (2004): 350 ranches

No. of ranches raising fewer than 50 cattle (2004): 2,300 ranches

Total ranches with more than 1,000 acres: 3,592 (1997)

Total Acres of Wyoming Owned by Foreigners: 92,336 (1988)

11 Pioneers of the Wyoming Livestock Industry

1. Jack Robertson (1834)

Robertson, a Bridger Valley pioneer, raised cattle. He settled near Black's Fork in 1834.

2. Seth E. Ward (1852)

Ward, the post sutler at Fort Laramie, wintered several hundred work cattle on the Chugwater River.

3. Alexander Majors (1854)

A partner in the famed transport firm of Russell, Majors and Waddell, Alexander Majors wintered cattle along the Chugwater River in 1854, a practice he continued for almost a decade.

The post surgeon at Fort Sanders, near Laramie, in 1869 wrote that the 25-acre post garden produced 840 bushels of potatoes, 300 bushels of turnips and beets, and 1,200 heads of cabbage that year.

4. Nelson Story (1865)

Story brought the first herd north to Wyoming on the Texas Trail. The longhorns wintered south of the North Platte River before continuing on the Bozeman Trail to Montana the next year.

5.-6. W. G. Bullock and B. B. Mills (1868)

Bullock, post sutler at Fort Laramie, and his partner Mills brought the first permanent ranch herd to Wyoming. The herd grazed near Fort Laramie after being brought in from Kansas, Iowa and Missouri.

7. Alexander Swan (1880)

The organizer of the famous Swan Land and Cattle Company, Swan and his brother brought the first Herefords to Wyoming. In 1883, Alexander Swan founded the Wyoming Hereford Association.

8. Amos W. Smith (1878)

Smith was perhaps the first white person to winter in what is now Sublette County. In 1878, he trailed cattle from the Ruby Mountains of Nevada into the area, becoming one of the largest landowners in western Wyoming in the 19th century. He died in 1918.

9.-10. Eugene Bigelow Willson and George Luther Willson (1880)

Eugene came to Wyoming from his native Illinois in 1870. His brother followed the next year. After work with a survey crew, they invested in an Iowa farm, sold it in 1876 and returned to Wyoming where they established the Running Water Ranch in present Niobrara County in 1880, beginning with 1,500 sheep. They remained lifelong business partners. George died in 1931; Eugene in 1935. *Source: Anne Willson Whitehead. Willson Brothers Running Water Ranch (1999)*

11. Edwin L. Patrick (1883)

Patrick ran the Rawhide Butte stage station in 1880. He bought a nearby homestead and began ranching in 1883. The ranch, now about 22,000 acres about 16 miles north of Lingle, is operated by Patrick's descendants.

Earliest Ranchers in Southeast Wyoming

1. John W. Iliff

Iliff, who lived in Cheyenne from 1868-1874, later became Colorado's biggest landowner. He began his career running a meat market in a small Kansas town. In February 1868, he brought longhorns to the Cheyenne vicinity.

2. W. G. Bullock and B. B. Mills

The two men brought 250 cows and a few bulls from the Midwest to the vicinity of Fort Laramie in October 1868.

3. Hi Kelly

The site of the Kelly ranch was first used by Alexander Majors to winter cattle from 1854-1864. The railroad construction crews were just arriving in Wyoming when Kelly took possession. Later, Kelly built a beautiful home in Cheyenne. Now demolished, the home was located across what is now Carey Avenue from the State Capitol. The new state parking garage stands on the location.

4. John Phillips

Phillips gained fame for making a famous ride from Fort Phil Kearny to Fort Laramie in the wake of the Fetterman fight in 1866. In 1870 Phillips established a ranch on Chugwater Creek, and six years later, built a hotel there for travelers on the Cheyenne-Black Hills

The 28,865-acre Thunderbird ranch was purchased by the Wyoming Game and Fish Department in 1991 for $7.5 million

stage line, en route to the gold rush. In 1878, he sold his ranch and moved to Cheyenne, where he lived until his death in 1883.

5. J. K. Moore

Moore's properties included the JM Ranch north of Lingle. The community of Jay Em is named for the ranch. Moore's widow married pioneer rancher R. S. Van Tassell.

10 Earliest Ranches in the Big Horn Basin

1. Pitchfork Ranch (1878)

The ranch was founded by Otto Franc, who brought 1,200 cattle from Montana to the ranch in 1879 via Idaho, Green River and South Pass to avoid Indian difficulties. Franc, a native of Germany, came to America, following his two brothers who were the first to introduce bananas to the United States (from Panama). Following Franc's death by accidental shooting in 1903, the ranch was bought by L. C. Phelps, a Chicago capitalist. Phelps died in 1922 while filing a deed in the Park County Courthouse. Later, the ranch was managed by Phelps' son-in-law, famed photographer Charles Belden. *Source: Bob Edgar and Jack Turnell, Brand of a Legend, 39-40.*

2. Owl Creek Ranch (1878)

The ranch was founded by Big Horn Basin pioneer J. D. Woodruff whose cabin was the first building in what is now Hot Springs County.

3. Carter Ranch (1879)

Founded by Fort Bridger post sutler William A. Carter, the ranch was managed for many years by L. C. McCulloch. The first herd of cattle in the Big Horn Basin was brought there from Fort Bridger by 1879. Area landmarks, Carter Mountain and McCulloch Buttes, are named for the two pioneers.

4. Two Dot Ranch (1879)

Founded by John Chapman on Pat O'Hara Creek, the ranch was owned by H. V. "Bob" Skogland, Minnesota Vikings owner and insurance executive, in the 1960s. Later, it was bought by Geneva-based banker Yves Burrus who, in February, 1999, sold it to Egyptian-born fund manager Fayez Sarfim for approximately $25 million.

5. Belknap Ranch (1880)

Located on the South Fork of Stinkingwater (now the Shoshone River), it was founded by Englishman H. Belknap.

6. M L Ranch (1880)

Founded by Henry C. Lovell, the "M" stood for his partner Anthony L. Mason, a Kansas City capitalist who furnished the money for the enterprise. Original ranch buildings still stand. The town of Lovell is named for Henry C. Lovell.

7. Quarter Circle Y Ranch (1880)

Located on Gooseberry Creek, the ranch was started by A. McDonald.

8. L U Ranch (1881)

George W. Baxter, who became a controversial territorial governor in later years, founded the ranch on Grass Creek. David Dickie incorporated the ranch in 1899. (Dickie is buried on a hill overlooking the main ranch house). Since the mid-1930s, the ranch has been owned by the Healy family. Originally, the ranch ran both sheep and cattle, but the last of the sheep were sold in 1984 and the ranch shifted entirely to a cattle operation.

9. Wilson Ranch (1881)

Andrew B. Wilson began the ranch located on Meeteetse Creek.

10. Hoodoo Ranch (1881)

Founder was Englishman Richard Ashworth. William R. Coe bought the ranch in 1919. E. V. Robertson managed the ranch for many years until he was elected to the U. S. Senate. During the presidential campaign of 1948, Robertson hosted a dinner at the ranch in honor of Republican candidate Thomas E. Dewey. About 700 people attended. The ranch was leased to Texas oil billionaire H. L. Hunt in 1948 and is now owned by a management company controlled by the Hunt family. A movie titled *Hoodoo Ranch* was released January 22, 1926, starring Buddy Roosevelt and Jay Wilsey.

3 Pioneer Albany County Ranchers

1. Thomas Alsop

Alsop (b. England, 1832) came to Wyoming as foreman for Edward Creighton's bull trains in 1860. (Creighton was a pioneer telegraph builder and capitalist, for whom Creighton University in Omaha is named). While returning on a trip from Salt Lake to Omaha in 1863, he got caught in a blizzard east of present Laramie. He left his oxen, returning in spring to find them surprisingly alive and fat. In 1868, with the backing of Creighton, he returned to ranch eight miles southwest of Laramie. He brought 3,000 sheep to the area from Iowa in 1870. In the 1880s, his Morgan horses pulled Omaha streetcars. Alsop died in 1889 while driving sheep to a Laramie buyer.

2. Charles Hutton

Hutton (b. Canada, 1832) is recognized as the first rancher to locate on the Laramie Plains. In 1868 he was awarded the meat contract for Fort Sanders, at the south edge of present-day Laramie. Hutton favored Texas cattle because they took less feed than short-horns. Besides cattle ranching, Hutton was involved in other enterprises in Laramie. He died at Fort Sanders in 1899.

3. Phil Mandel

Mandel (b. France, 1834) had the first recorded land filing on the Laramie Plains, filed in Dakota Territory in 1864, five years before Wyoming Territory was created. Formerly stage manager at the Little Laramie River station, he purchased foot-sore cattle from passing freighters. He spent his entire life ranching near Laramie. He died in Laramie in 1917.

5 Texas Trail Markers in Wyoming

1. West of Moorcroft. The stone monument was erected by Edward Burnett, a pioneer northern Wyoming rancher.

2. Pine Bluffs. The marker was dedicated Aug. 1, 1948.

3. Torrington   **4. Lusk**   **5. LaGrange**

4 Ranches Along the North Platte River in 1872

1. Goose Egg, west of present Casper   **3. CY Ranch**, near Casper

2. Fiddleback Ranch, near Douglas   **4. VR Ranch,** east of Casper on Deer Creek

Farms/Ranches in Wyoming: Number and Average Acres

Year	No.	Acres	Year	No.	Acres	Year	No.	Acres
2008:	11,000	2,736	1974:	8,018	4,274	1920:	15,748	7,501
2004:	9,200	3,743	1969:	8,838	4,014	1910:	10,987	778
2002:	9,422	3,651	1964:	9,038	4,100	1900:	7,915	1,333
1997:	9,232	3,692	1959:	9,038	3,715	1890:	3,125	586
1993:	9,200	3,742	1954:	11,402	3,069	1880:	457	272
1987:	9,205	3,650	1950:	12,614	2,729	1870:	175	25
1982:	8,861	3,781	1940:	15,018	1,866			
1978:	8,040	4,182	1930:	16,011	1,469			

Wyoming Counties with Most Ranches/Farms

1. Fremont (983)
2. Goshen (688)
3. Laramie (615)
4. Park (588)
5. Sheridan (568)

Wyoming Counties with Fewest Ranches/Farms

1. Teton (104)
2. Hot Springs (147)
3. Sweetwater (160)
4. Washakie (205)
5. Weston (233)

Source: USDA, 1997 Census of Agriculture

Average Acres in Ranches/Farms (By County)

1. Natrona (9,025)
2. Sweetwater (8,881)
3. Carbon (7,360)
4. Converse (7,228)
5. Johnson (6,767)
6. Hot Springs (6,423)
7. Albany (6,103)
8. Weston (6,097)
9. Niobrara (5,785)
10. Campbell (5,544)
11. Crook (3,393)
12. Uinta (3,133)
13. Sheridan (2,831)
14. Laramie (2,810)
15. Platte (2,787)
16. Fremont (2,664)
17. Washakie (2,195)
18. Sublette (2,152)
19. Goshen (1,840)
20. Park (1,720)
21. Big Horn (896)
22. Lincoln (810)
23. Teton (504)

Source: Census of Agriculture, 1997.

Early Sheep Herds in Wyoming

1. Flag Ranch (1871)

Pioneer Albany County rancher Robert Homer brought the sheep to the Laramie Plains in 1871.

2. Ike Miller Ranch (1875)

Miller brought sheep to Carbon County in 1875. By 1888, his herds numbered more than 40,000 sheep.

3. Warren Livestock Company

The company, owned by Wyoming Sen. Francis E. Warren, was an early purebred breeder of Warhill sheep.

4. King brothers

The brothers were early breeders of Rambouillets.

5. Moncrieffe Ranch

The Sheridan County ranchers were early breeders of Corriedales.

6. J. M. Wilson (b. 1854, d. Douglas, 1925)

Dr. Wilson began sheep ranching in Carbon County. He was present at the formation of the Wyoming Wool Growers Association. When the association was formally organized in 1905, Wilson became its first president.

Sheep in Wyoming

In 2007, Wyoming ranked 4th in numbers of sheep.

Leading Sheep-producing counties, 2004-2005

	2004	2005
Converse:	61,000	60,000
Uinta:	42,500	43,000
Johnson:	32,500	34,000
Lincoln:	33,500	32,000
Campbell:	31,500	32,000

State Total:

1890:	420,000
1900:	3.3 million
1990:	837,000
1994:	870,000
2000:	1.1 million
2005:	340,000
2007:	412,814

Total sheep ranches in Wyoming: 966 ranches raised sheep in 2002; 1,112 in 1997.

7. Henry Reed and Calvert Hargreaves (1879)

The two men ran the first sheep herd north of the North Platte River.

6 Early Ranches in Niobrara County

1. Runningwater Ranch
2. O. W. (Converse Cattle Company)
3. Tom Swan Ranch
4. T. B. Hord Ranch
5. Emmons and Brewster Ranch
6. Frank S. Lusk Ranch

1st Livestock Raisers in Uinta County

1. Jack Robertson (1st rancher in Wyoming, ran cattle on Black's Fork, 1834)
2. Samuel Smith   6. Philip Maas
3. Charles Ragan   7. Moses Byrne
4. Isaac Edwards   8. William A. Carter
5. John Vagar   9. John W. Myers

Farm and Ranch Firsts in Fremont County

1st farm: W. A. Barrett farm on Barretts Creek, near Red Canyon, 1869. Barrett sold vegetables to area residents.

1st commercial sugar beets: Marshal Graham, William Madden, J. A. Delfelder, L. O. Kelley, Bonalli and Farrell, C. D. Brown, L. C. Nelson and Arapahoe Farm were first growers in Fremont County in 1917.

10 Well-Known Ranches

1. TE Ranch

Buffalo Bill Cody owned the ranch on South Fork southwest of Cody. Following Cody's death, the property was purchased by F. S. Groves, Jr., of Philadelphia, a former owner of Campbell Soup Company. When Groves died in 1930, the ranch was sold to Paul Patton of Kansas City. Patton, after a political scandal in Missouri, was forced to sell the property. The next owner was Robert Woodruff (b. 1889, d. 1985), then-president and, later, board chairman of Coca Cola. In 1972, Woodruff sold the ranch to Charles Duncan (b. 1926), coffee company heir and Coca Cola executive who later became Energy Secretary in the Carter Administration..

2. Bradford Brinton Memorial Museum and Ranch

The ranch near Big Horn in Sheridan County was established as the Quarter Circle A by William Moncreiffe who built the house in 1892. (Moncreiffe's brother Malcolm founded the Polo Ranch nearby). Bradford Brinton bought the place in 1923 and built many additions to the house to accommodate his large art collection. He died in 1936 and his sister lived there during the summers until 1960 when it became a museum under the terms of Brinton's will.

7 Leading Cattle-Producing Counties

	2002	2003	2004	2005
1. Goshen	140,000	123,000	124,000	121,000
2. Platte	110,000	97,000	108,000	114,000
3. Fremont	110,000	100,000	90,000	93,000
4. Carbon	90,000	83,000	93,000	90,000
5. Campbell	88,000	79,000	88,000	80,000
6. Laramie	87,000	64,000	68,000	69,000
7. Sheridan	85,000	70,000	80,000	70,000
State Total:	1,470,000	1,320,000	1,400,000	1,350,000

3. Palette Ranch

Artist and writer A. A. Anderson (1847-1940) owned the ranch for many years. On it, he established the first golf course in the Big Horn Basin. The first superintendent of the Yellowstone Forest Reserve (now Shoshone National Forest), Anderson was acquainted with all of the well-known American progressives of the time as well as many European artists. In his youth, he spent several years studying art in Paris and returned there frequently for visits. In the 20th century, the ranch was incorporated into the nearby Hoodoo Ranch. Ernest Thompson Seton's book, Biography of a Grizzly (1899), was dedicated to the memory of the days Seton spent at the Palette Ranchy.

4. Swan Land and Cattle Company

The firm was organized in Edinburgh, Scotland, in 1883 and capitalized for $2 million. The company owned several ranches in southeast Wyoming. The firm's most familiar brand was the Two Bar, which was carried by more cattle in Wyoming in the 1880s than any other brand. The Swan's herds were decimated by the blizzard of 1886-87, but the company was reorganized and continued in operation until Dec. 20, 1951. John Clay managed the ranch from 1888 to 1896. In 1915, Curtis Templin became the manager and remained in that position after the firm liquidated much of its holdings. Later, Russell Staats was manager.

5. Wyoming Hereford Ranch

Founded east of Cheyenne in 1883 by Alexander Swan, the ranch was bought by a succession of owners following Swan's bankruptcy in 1889. The ranch is the oldest Hereford breeding operation in North America. The ranch has been owned for the past 30 years by Dr. Sloan and Anna Marie Hales.

6. Careyhurst Ranch

The Converse County ranch was the home of former Senator and Gov. Robert Carey, son of the ranch founder J. M. Carey, also a former governor and senator. In the 1920s, Robert Carey raised grains experimentally on the ranch, many of which gained international recognition. One year, he raised 45 different varieties of small grains.

7. Oxford Horse Ranch

Founded by an Englishman in the 1880s, the Oxford became known for breeding thoroughbred horses. As many as 1,000 at a time grazed in ranch pastures in Albany County. Some of the horses won national awards. Cincinnati streetcars were pulled by Oxford horses in the 1880s. The ranch was purchased in 1992 by Dick and Kris McGuire. The huge 160 x 50-foot log barn, built in 1887, is on the National Register of Historic Places. In 1988, a herd of Cashmere goats was brought to the ranch. The herd numbered 500 (2008).

8. Diamond Ranch

Built near Chugwater in 1878 by George Rainsford, the ranch was home to Rainsford's famed horses. One horse, his stallion Spartan, won first prize at a Madison Square Garden show in the 1880s. He also raised prize-winning Clydesdales. Rainsford was architect for many Cheyenne homes. An entire historic district in Cheyenne is named the "Rainsford District" in homage to the many homes Rainsford designed in that downtown neighborhood.

9. Arapahoe Ranch

Established in 1940, seven ranches comprise some 595,000 acres. The ranch is owned by the Arapahoe tribe. There are three ranch units on each side of the Owl Creek Mountains along with the headquarters ranch located 18 miles northwest of Thermopolis near

---

A 1997 article in Worth magazine listed R. Earl Holding as the 14th largest landowner in the U.S. He owned 500,000 acres in Wyoming and elsewhere. The True family was 28th on the list with 225,000 acres. Philip Anschutz was 38th with 200,000 acres, including 140,000 in Carbon County. His father Fred had 75,000 acres in the 1950s in Utah and Wyoming.

Hamilton Dome. In 1999, the ranch ran about 4,000 cattle and had an annual budget of $1.5 million. In 2009, the ranch ran 3,500 cows and 2,000 head of yearlings. In the 2000s, the ranch contracted with Whole Foods to be the sole supplier of organic, grass-fed beef for sale in the company's stores in the West.

10. 4J Ranch

The 4J brand was held by Adams and Glover until it was bought in 1888 by Oscar Keeline. The 4J Ranch was established at the head of Caballo Creek, 18 miles southwest of Gillette, in 1893. Keeline sold the brand in 1900. He sold the ranch to A. M. Mankin in 1923.

Some Well-Known "Ranchers" in Wyoming

1. Harrison Ford

The famous actor lives on a $47 million ranch near Jackson. He had purchased the ranch with his then-wife author/screenwriter Melissa Matheson. When they divorced after 16 years of marriage in the early 2000s, Matheson received half of the value of the 800-acre ranch along with one of seven large building lots on the ranch property. Ford donated 389 acres as a conservation easement to the Jackson Hole Land Trust.

2. James Baker

The former Secretary of State (in the Bush administration) and his wife own a 1,500-acre ranch next to the Wind River range in Sublette County.

3. Fayez Sarfim

The Houston billionaire money manager purchased the 145,000-acre Two Dot ranch in Park County from Geneva-based banker Yves Burrus in February, 1999. Sarfim paid an estimated $25 million for the ranch

4. Sen. Herb Kohl

The Wisconsin senator owns a 1,200-acre cattle ranch in Jackson Hole. Nearby, he owns a smaller ranch where he raises quarterhorses and maintains guest cabins. Heir to a merchandising fortune and owner of the Milwaukee Bucks basketball team, Kohl was elected to the U. S. Senate as a Democrat in 1988. He was reelected in 1994, 2000 and 2006.

Facts About Wyoming Crops

1. Barley

The 2005 production was about 5.6 million bushels. Barley was planted on 75,000 acres. Yield was 94 bushels per acre. This compares with the 1998 production was approximately 7.31 million bushels with a yield of 86 bushels per acre. In 1996 Wyoming ranked 7th in production of barley with 10 million bushels. In 1990 the total was 9.3 million bushels with an average yield of 74 bushels. About 150,000 acres were planted annually in the 1990s. Park County led in barley in 1990. The average per bushel price in 2004 was $3.45 per bushel. In Dec. 1990, prices were: $2.24 bushel for feed barley, $3.41 for malting barley. The all-time high price: $3.99 (all barley)was set in November, 1985. All-time low price: 22 cents per bushel, 1933.

2. Oats

Wyoming farmers produced 600,000 bushels of oats in 2005 and 795,000 in 2004. It was 1.92 million bushels in 1999. Some 30,000 acres was planted in oats in 1999. Record yields of 64 bushels per acre were set in 1995, 1998 and 1999. Oat production was 2.1 million bushels in 1995; average price per bushel in 1995 was $1.90, up from $1.55 in 1993. The 2004 average was $1.60 per bushel.

3. Wheat

Producers planted 127,000 acres in wheat in 2007, down from 160,000 acres of wheat planted in 2004. Average price per bushel in 2004 was $3.20. In 1995, it was $4.50; $3.55 in 1994. The price had fallen to nearly $2.50 per bushel in the summer of 2000. Lowest price in Wyoming history was 14 cents per bushel in 1931.

4. Beans

Acreage planted in beans in Wyoming declined to just 34,000 acres in 2005. During 1998, about 37,000 acres was planted in beans in the state with an average yield of 2,180 pounds per acre. Wyoming farmers harvested 43,000 acres of beans in 1994 with an average yield of 1,910 pounds per acre.

5. Corn

Corn was planted on just 37,000 acres in Wyoming in 2004, down from 55,000 acres in 1999.. About 60,000 acres in Wyoming was planted in corn in 1998. Average yield in 1998 was 127 bushels per acre. Corn plantings totaled 85,000 acres statewide in 1992.

6. Sugar Beets

In 2007, sugar production was 664,000 tons with an average yield of 24.5 tons. In 2005, 37,000 acres in Wyoming was planted in sugar beets at 181 farms. Average yield in 2005 was 21.9 tons per acre. In 1999, farmers planted almost 57,000 acres in Wyoming in sugar beets. Average yield was estimated at 20 1/2 tons per acre in 1999. More than 1.1 million tons of sugar beets were grown in Wyoming in 1994. Average price in 1994 was $34.60 per ton, down from $37.30 per ton in 1993.Wyoming ranked **7th** nationally in sugar beet production, 1,238,000 tons in 1997.

7. Alfalfa Hay

Alfalfa was planted on 28,000 acres in Wyoming in 2004. Record production was attained in Wyoming in 1999 with 1.86 million tons. Yields topped 2.9 tons per acre, up from 2.6 tons per acre in 1998. The previous record yield had been 2.7 tons in 1995 and 1997.

Source: Wyoming Agricultural Statistics Service and USDA, National Agricultural Statistics Service

Misc. Agricultural Items

* Of the more than 50,000 cattle brought into Wyoming during 1885, some 9,964 cattle were brought north from Texas. About 15,000 came from New Mexico and Oklahoma territories.

* Susan Jane Quealy (1870-1956) was the first woman member of the Wyoming Stockgrowers Association and the only woman to serve on the organization's executive committee.

* Joe Watt, Moorcroft, owner of the Triangle T Ranch and UW trustee, was the first recipient of the "Wyoming Stockgrower of the Year" award, presented by the Wyoming Stockgrowers Association in 1972.

* The Holly Sugar factory at Torrington began processing sugar beets Oct. 10, 1926. In the first year, the plant processed 21,000 tons. The Sheridan beet factory opened Oct. 23, 1915.

* A Lusk rancher reported growing a turnip weighing 21 lbs. in 1887.

* Dry farming proponent Dr. V. T. Cooke came to Wyoming in 1904 as director of "state experiments in dry farming." He had been a dry farmer for 25 years in eastern Oregon.

* Col. E. J. Bell grew more than 1,000 acres of field peas on his land on the Laramie Plains in 1909.

* A Holstein cow named "Mountain Maid," owned by Cheyenne mayor Archie Allison, produced 34,000 pounds of milk in one year (1934).

* In 1995, the Padlock Ranch near Dayton was cross-breeding Polled Herefords and Red Angus, the hybrid called "Baldies," and then having them bred to shorthorns.

* Triplets were born to a cow owned by Craig Sandlin of Jay Em. All three calves in the unusual birth were born alive in March 1992.

Presidents, Wyoming Stock Growers Association

1873-75: M. V. Boughton	1946-47: Oda Mason	1979-81: Gerald Palm
1876-81: Alexander Swan	1947-50: Clarence Gardner	1981-83: Ken Kirkbride
1882: N. R. Davis	1950-51: Manville Kendrick	1983-85: Charles Kane, Jr.
1883-88: Joseph M. Carey*	1951-53: Lloyd Taggart, Sr.	1985-87: G. A. "Jim" Berger
1889: Col. A. T. Babbitt	1953-55: Clifford P. Hansen*	1987-89: Robert L. Wright
1890-95: John Clay, Jr.	1955-57: Norman Barlow	1989-91: Wally Ramsbottom
1896-1911: William Irvine	1957-59: Bryan Patrick	1991-93: Ed Weppner
1912-13: John B. Kendrick*	1959-61: Frank C. Mockler	1993-95: John Eyre, Lyman
1914-17: Robert Carey*	1961-63: Ernest R. May, Jr.	1995-97: Stan Flitner
1917-19: James C. Shaw	1963-65: Joe H. Watt	1997-99: Nels Smith
1920: J. C. Underwood	1965-67: Lloyd Van De Burg	1999-01: Rob Hendry
1921-29: John L. Jordan	1967-69: Carl Jorgensen	2001-03: Jack Turnell
1930-32: J. Elmer Brock	1969-71: Van Irvine**	2003-05: Philip Ellis
1932-35: Dugald R. Whitaker	1971-73: Bruce von Forell	2005-07: Lois Herbst
1936-39: Sam C. Hyatt	1973-75: Walt Reynolds	2007-09: Jon Kirkbride
1940-42: Charles A. Myers	1975-77: Kim Krueger	2009-10: Frank Shepperson
1943-45: George A. Cross	1977-79: Jim Daly	

Wyoming governor
***Irvine's grandfather, W. C. Irvine, served as WSGA president from 1896-1911.*

Executive Secretaries, WSGA

W. L. Kuykendall, 1873-75	B. F. Davis, 1923	Dean Prosser, 1963-84
Thomas Sturgis, 1876-87	Minnie Haas, 1924-30	Bob Budd, 1984-93
Thomas B. Adams, 1888-90	Russell Thorp, 1930-50	Cindy Garretson-Weibel, 1993-98
H. B. Ijams, 1891-95	Robert D. Hanseworth,	*Jim Magagna, 1998-
Alice Smith, 1896-1922	1950-63	*The office is now known as executive vice president.*

Presidents, Wyoming CowBelles*

Name was changed from Wyoming CowBelles to Wyoming CattleWomen in 1972.

Susan J. Quealy	Mary Cross	Lois Morel	Dixie Mathisen
Charlotte Snodgrass	Elizabeth Johnson	Laural Krueger	Mary Engebretsen
Elizabeth Whitaker	Evelyn Grieve	Betty Percival	Marilyn Werner
Mary Ellen O'Neill	Beth Brown	Margery Masters	Eleanore JOnes
Lillian Cross	Inice Mill	Helen Allemand	Laura Salisbury
Laura Jordan	Ethel Jewett	Virginia McIntosh	Pat Frolander
Miriam Barlow	Julia Hunt	Glenna Hirsig	Sandy Eike
Rouene Hyatt	ardath Van De Burg	Gaynell Park	Katie Smith
Arlene Watt	Harriet Sanford	Alice Renner	Terry Henderson
Lillian Kane	Rubie Dover	Better Bergner	Martha Cooper
Mary Patrick	Goldie Graham	Wilma Baldwin	Kay Wright
Margaret Boice	Maxine Kellogg	Barbara Werner	Darla Griffin
Virginia O'Neill	Elaine Barton	Clara Rankine	Dianne Kirkbride
Nelda Barton	Myra Holmes	Myra Lou Drake	Martha Hellyer
Clara Fuller	Doris Floyd	Flossie Moulton	

Leading Counties in Harvested Croplands*

1. Goshen (172,562 acres)   2. Laramie (159,739)   3. Carbon (112,744)
4. Crook (108,391)   5. Fremont (98,450)

State total: 1,717,027 acres (1987). Source: Census of Agriculture, 1987.

Rocky Squirrel and Bullwinkle Moose, cartoon characters in the 1960s, bought the "Lazy J Ranch" near "Squaw's Echo, Wyoming," in one episode.

Presidents of the Wyoming Wool Growers Association

Wyoming Woolgrowers Association was formed in 1903 with 41 charter members.

1903-11, 1916-25: Dr. J. M. Wilson, Douglas
1912-13: J. A. Delfelder, (b. Kansas, d. Riverton, 1921), Riverton
1914-15: James Mulford Rumsey (b. Ohio, 1862, d. 1937), Rawlins
 (Rumsey also served as Wyo Banker's Assoc. president in same years)

1927-28: Kleber H. Hadsell, Rawlins
1929-36: Thomas Cooper, Casper
1937-46: John A. Reed, Kemmerer
1946-48: Reynold A. Seaverson, Rawlins
1948-53: Harold Josendahl, Casper
1954-56: Leonard Hay, Rock Springs
1957-58: Howard Flitner, Shell
1959-60: J. Norman Stratton, Rawlins
1961-63: Joe M. Donlin, Casper
1963-64: Adolph Magagna, Rock Springs
1965-66: M. Joseph Burke, Casper
1966-67: Vern Vivion, Rawlins
1968-71: E. D. Moore, Douglas
1971-72: William P. Mau, Rock Springs
1973-74: John Burke, Casper
1975-76: Don Meike, Kaycee
1984: Stan Smith, Cheyenne

1985: John Etchepare, Cheyenne
1986: John J. Hines, Gillette
1987: Jim Magagna, Rock Springs
1988: Lee Coffman, Casper
1989: Bill Taliaferro, Rock Springs
1990: Pat Litton, Gillette (1st woman pres).
1991: Brad Palm, Elk Mountain
1992-95: Frank Moore, Douglas
1995-97: Truman Julian, Kemmerer
1997-99: Frank Philp, Shoshoni
1999-01: Brad Boner, Glenrock
2001-03: Bob Innes
2003-05: Jerry Dilts
2005-07: Jw Nuckolls
2007-09: Dave Julian
2009-11: Gene Hardy

Executive Director: Bryce Reece has been in that position since 1993. Carolyn Paseneaux served in the position from 1982-1993. J. Byron Wilson was executive director from 1918-62.

Value of Agricultural Products, Wyoming (2007)

Product	Total Sales	State Rank
1. Cattle	801,833,000	17th
2. Hay crops	130,888,000	24th
3. Grains, dry beans, peas	72,618,000	37th
4. Sheep and goats	34,292,000	6th
5. Hogs and pigs	41,923,000	25th
6. Horses, mules, donkeys	24,631,000	15th
7. Dairy products	22,331,000	46th

Source: 2007 Census of Agriculture, USDA

Acres in Agricultural Crops, Wyoming (2008)

Top Crop Items (acres)

1. Forage land	1,192,000	4. Barley for grain	52,457
2. Wheat for grain	127,051	5. Corn for silage	32,146
3. Corn for grain	54,567		

Q: Why would old-time settlers choose homestead lands on which sagebrush grew in preference to lands having greasewood?
A: They knew that if soil is too saline, sagebrush will not grow on it—nor will agricultural crops. Greasewood thrives in such soil, however.

Value of Agricultural Products, Wyoming (2002)

Product	Total Sales	% of sales	No. of farms
1. Cattle	$643,123,000	74.4	4,997
2. Hay crops	$86,027,000	10.0	2,298
3. Grains, dry beans, peas	$44,522,000	5.2	886
4. Sheep and goats	$28,853,000	3.3	1,019
5. Hogs and pigs	$23,057,000	2.7	247
6. Horses, mules, donkeys	$12,400,000	1.4	1,555
7. Dairy products	$ 7,473,000	.9	81

Source: 2002 Census of Agriculture, USDA

Historic Levels of Cattle Prices in Wyoming

Year	Cows	Ster/Heifer	Calves
1998	34.80	71.80	84.90
2000	39.70	87.50	107.00
2002	38.00	79.50	92.60
2004:	47.10	92.50	118.00

Source: Wyoming Agricultural Statistics Service

UW Experiment Stations

1.First Stations, 1891

After the state received federal lands and authority to use the proceeds for expansion of land grant agricultural college work, the university organized six experiment farms in 1891 at various locations: Laramie, Lander, Saratoga, Sheridan, Sundance, and Wheatland. The 140 acres of the Lander station, six miles southwest of Lander, was donated by the Business Men's Club of Lander. The 40 acres for the Saratoga station, one mile northwest of town, also were donated. The Sheridan Board of Trade donated the 50 acres for the Sheridan site in May 1891. Locatl citizens gave the 49 acres for the Sundance farm, located 1 1/2 miles east of town, to the university.

2. Torrington

The experiment station opened between 1912-15 just to the west of Torrington. The University sold the property in 2002 and moved all operations to a new center south and west of Lingle.

3. Sustainable Agriculture Research and Extension Center (Sarec), Lingle

The university purchased 3,467 acres south and west of Lingle in 2003. The station opened the following year. It has 1,522 acres of dry land cropland. The center was named in honor of long-time state legislator James Hageman in December 2006. Hageman died in August 2006.

4. Afton

The Afton Experiment Station closed in June 1998.

5. Sheridan Experiment Station

The UW station was formed as the Sheridan Experiment Farm in May 1891 about 12 miles southeast of Sheridan. In recent years, the station employees worked with 15-20 varieties of grapes on parts of the 320-acre facility.

6. Archer Experiment Station

Sold in early 2000s, the activities were shifted to the new facility near Lingle..

7. Powell Research and Extension Center

The Seed Analysis Laboratory, opened at the center in 2002, was named in honor of Denny Smith, a state legislator from Powell who strongly supported the UW College of Agriculture programs.

BLM/Forest Service Grazing Fees*

Year	BLM	Forest Service			
1992	$1.92	$2.25-$3.42	2006	$1.56	$1.56
1993	$1.87	$2.04	2007	$1.35	$1.35
1999	$1.92	$1.92			

*Per Animal Unit Month (AUM). An AUM is the amount of forage needed to sustain one cow and her calf, one horse, or five sheep or goats for a month. The fees apply to 16 Western states on public lands administered by the BLM and the Forest Service. The Rock Springs Grazing Association holds the largest BLM permits in terms of total acreage of any company in America..

8 Large Wyoming Landowners

1. Earl Holding, 400,000 acres

Ranking 16th nationally is R. Earl Holding who owns some 400,000 acres in Wyoming and elsewhere in the region. Holding also owns Little America and Sinclair.Oil Company as well as Sun Valley resort. He was 77th richest on the Forbes 400 list with a fortune of about $4.6 billion.

2. True family, 255,000 acres

The True family held down the 27th spot nationally with 255,000 acres in Wyoming, including the historic LAK ranch near Newcastle and the family's first purchase in 1957, the Double Four Ranch near Laramie Peak. Along with True Oil Company, the family also has extensive interests in other businesses, including Black Hills Trucking,.

3. Philip Anschutz, 225,000

In 1997, Worth Magazine had Philip Anschutz as the 38th largest landowner with 225,000 acres. In the 2008 report, he had dropped to 59th place. Some 140,000 acres of Anschutz' land was the historic Overland Trail Ranch, founded by Richard Savage in the 19th century and bought by Anschutz in 1995. The ranch stretches for 22 miles along the North Platte river and the property has it four historic stage stations from the Overland Stageline that crossed the area in the early 1860s. Anschutz listed the ranch for sale in 2006 at a price of $47.5 million, but in 2009, he still owned the property. A wind farm is being developed on part of the property south of Rawlins. His father Fred Anschutz owned 75,000 acres in Wyoming during the 1950s.

5. Homer Scott family

Scott (1904-1993) began with Peter Kiewit Construction Company. He moved to Sheridan in 1937. In 1943, he bought the Padlock Ranch near Sheridan. He was appointed to the Kansas City Federal Reserve Bank, serving two terms as chairman. He bought the Bank of Commerce in Sheridan in 1968 and retired from Peter Kiewit two years later. His family is the 55th largest landowner in the US.

6. Mark and Gary Booth

The Booths are 73rd. In 1985, they bought what would eventually become a 13,000-acre ranch north of Bosler..

7. Reese family

Their Rockin 7 ranch is near Shawnee in southeastern Converse County. They operate a hunting lodge where they specialze in antelope and deer hunting, but also offer buffalo, pheasant and coyote hunting.. They are 84th on the list.

8. Stan Kroenke

Kroenke is based in Colorado, but has some land holdings in Wyoming. He is 10th nationally with 600,000 acres.

Sources: *Worth Magazine (1998); The Land Report 100, published by The Land Report:: The Magazine of the American Landowner (2008).*

AIRPLANES

1st airplane flight in Wyoming (1911): Denver-built airplane piloted by George W. Thompson appeared at Gillette's Fourth of July celebration.

2nd airplane flight in Wyoming (1912): St. Louis-built airplane piloted by W. S. Adams flew at the rodeo grounds, along Park and across what is now Federal Blvd., Riverton

1st airplane built in Wyoming: The plane was built in Cheyenne by Harold Brinker and flown at Frontier Park, possibly in 1911. Brinker also drove the "Thomas Flyer" automobile across Wyoming in the "Great Race."

1st transcontinental airmail flight across Wyoming: Sept. 8, 1920. The DeHavilland biplane, piloted by Buck Heffron, carried 400 pounds of mail on its westbound flight.

1st licensed pilot in Wyoming: Lt. Boyd Briggs, Wyoming National Guard, with "International Aeronautique" license number 511.

1st Wyoming resident to own his own airplane (1920): Reed Hollister, a Cheyenne motorcycle dealer, bought the plane but he had no license to fly it. He hired an experienced air ace to fly the plane for him.

1st round-trip transcontinental passenger flight (July 29-August 22, 1920): The airplane landed at several airports in southern Wyoming.

1st official passenger of transcontinental passenger flight: John Goldstein, a New York newspaper reporter.

1st public parachute jump in Wyoming: Probably the jump from a hot-air balloon made by a Dr. Haddon during the 4th Cheyenne Frontier Days (1900)

1st commercial airplane landing in Casper: Landed Sept. 29, 1919, 3:55 p.m. Bert L. Cole, pilot, and Jay Y. Stock, passenger and plane owner, who bought the plane to set up an aerial service in Casper. The flight took 3 hours, 15 minutes from Denver.

1st crash of airplane based at Casper: Jan. 14, 1920. Pilot Bert Cole was injured and passenger Maud Toomey killed in the crash landing.

1st parachute jump in Casper: May 20, 1920, 6 p.m., Frank E. Hansen, leaped out of upside-down airplane, 5,000 feet above Casper with 5,000 people watching from the airfield. On a July 2 ascension made in a similar fashion, the parachute didn't open. Hansen plummeted to his death.

Air service, Cheyenne-Los Angeles (1934): Passengers could leave Cheyenne at 11:25 p.m., daily with arrival in Los Angeles at 6:15 a.m., the next morning.

Commercial passenger boardings in Wyoming: 782,803 (2004); 376,483 (1998); 374,738 (1997).

Busiest airport in Wyoming: Jackson Hole Airport, 431,918 (2004); 199,536 emplanements (1998)

Federal "essential air service" subsidies to Wyoming: $1.35 million (1999) for service to three locations: Laramie, Worland and Rock Springs. By 2007, Laramie and Worland continued to be among the 145 communities nationwide receiving these federal DOT funds.

Fastest round-the-world flight: In February 1996, former Casper resident and cable TV magnate Bill Daniels' white Learjet circled the globe in less than 48 hours.

Total landing strips/airfields (2005): 119

Some Significant Events in Wyoming Aviation History

1. First airplane flight in Wyoming, Gillette (July 4, 1911)

2. First airplane built in Wyoming flown in Frontier Park, Cheyenne. The builder was Harold Brinker who had been a driver in the 1908 "Great Auto Race" across Wyoming and the West. (1911)

3. Lillian Gatlin, the first woman transcontinental passenger in a mailplane, landed in Cheyenne and Rock Springs (Oct. 8, 1922)

4. Cheyenne airport hangar burned destroying seven airplanes (Nov. 8, 1924)

5. Air passengers were accepted by airlines, but forced to sit on mail sacks or carry them in laps because mail had top priority (1927)

6. Boeing Air Transport Co., a subsidiary of United Airlines, began flying as the first airline to carry passengers on regular schedules for distance flights, first to fly passengers at night on regular schedule and first to fly trimotor airplanes (June 30, 1927)

7. Charles Lindbergh flew his "Spirit of St. Louis" into Cheyenne for a two-day visit.

Before he became famous, he flew the transcontinental mail, landing often at Cheyenne (Sept. 1-2, 1927)

8. Four major air transport firms merged to form United Airlines (July, 1931)

9. 1st commercial airline route entirely within Wyoming began operation. The company, owned by Joe and Dick Leferink, had two planes. One, a Stinson 4-passenger, departed from Sheridan to Casper (April 13, 1931)

10. Donald Travis, 17, a sophomore at Sheridan High School, became the youngest licensed pilot in Wyoming after flying solo (September 1932)

11. Government officials announced Wyoming had 53 airports (1934)

12. Cheyenne-based pilot Elrey Jeppesen sold first air charts, 50 for $10 (1934)

13. United Air Lines moved repair facilities to Cheyenne; city called "air transportation center of the West" (1934)

14. More than 20,000 people attended dedication ceremony for new Casper airport, largest crowd to attend any public event in Casper to that time (Aug. 26, 1934)

15. Three major airlines offered service to Wyoming in all four directions, as many as 12 flights went in each direction from Cheyenne (1935)

16. First star mail delivery route in Wyoming was established. R. J. Riggans was the mail contractor. The pilot, A. A. Bennett of Jackson, made first airmail delivery between Jackson and Pinedale. Landing, with mail and two passengers, was on "hard snow" west of town as plane was equipped w ith skis. The trip took 45 minutes. Bennett had been "the first pilot to carry mail by plane in Alaska." (January 1935) Sources: "Pinedale Gets First Cargo of Air Mail," Wyoming Eagle, Jan. 11, 1935, p. 12; Wyoming Eagle, Dec. 14, 1934, p. 12.

17. First airplane landed within Yellowstone National Park (Sept. 30, 1935)

18. United Air Lines, unhappy with the perception of ill treatment from Cheyenne officials, accepted Denver offer to route east-west flights through Denver (May, 1937)

19. Pilot E. V. Hogan picked up airmail from all post offices in Niobrara County, the first county in U. S. to have total airmail service (May 20, 1938)

20. National Airmail Week celebrated with airmail service to many rural post offices. Mary June Reed, a Cheyenne student, won airmail week essay contest and William Wallace, Rock Springs, won the poster contest (May 15-21, 1938)

21. United Airlines flight training division, established a decade earlier in Cheyenne, moved to Denver (1942)

22. Casper Army Air Base established for final phase of four-engine bomber training for World War II airmen (summer, 1942)

23. Army Air Corps began phasing in the new B-24s at Casper Army Air Base, to replace Boeing B-17 Flying Fortresses. First christened the "Diane" (April 1943)

24. Wyoming Aeronautic Commission established (1945)

25. Army airfield at Casper deactiviated (March 7, 1945)

26. Wyoming Air National Guard founded (Aug. 10, 1946)

27. United Airlines Stewardess School moved to Cheyenne (1947)

28. Fort F. E. Warren turned over to the U. S. Air Force, renamed F. E. Warren Air Force Base (1947)

29. Aeronautics commission announced more than 90 commercial and 40 private airfields were in use in Wyoming (1948)

30. Federal government gave Casper Air Base to Natrona County (1952)

31. First regular airmail pickup from Fremont County began (Dec. 17, 1953)

Diavolo, famed air show dare-devil and stunt man, was performing in an air show in Cheyenne in 1923. His parachute failed to open and he plummeted to his death. The accident happened near the Cheyenne airport.

32. Air Force 90th Strategic Missile Wing activated at Warren Air Force Base with 200 Minuteman missiles (June 30, 1965)

33. Pitts aerobatic airplane, designed by Curtis Pitts and built by Aerotech (now Aviat) in Afton, helped U. S. aerobatic team win first-ever world title (1972)

34. President Ronald Reagan announced MX missile system would be located in southeastern Wyoming (Nov. 22, 1982)

35. First ten MX missiles put on operational status (December, 1986)

36. MX Peacekeeper missiles officially deactivated by the Air Force (Sept. 17, 2005)

3 Wyoming Air Museums

1. Warbirds Museum, Casper

The museum, located in Hangar #1 of Natrona County International Airport, features the eclectic tastes of founder Jim Good. Along with displays of airplanes, the collection includes antique aircraft instruments, practice bombs used at Casper Air Base in the 1940s, airplane engines and various military weapons.

2. Aerial Firefighting Museum, Greybull

An aerial fire-fighting museum is located near South Big Horn County Airport, Greybull. The museum was begun in the summer of 1992 and closed in 2006. Hawkins and Powers, the operators of the museum, went out of business and more than 60 of the aircraft were sold in 2006.

3. Call Air Museum, Afton

The museum began at Call Air headquarters, but in 2002, the airplanes and other items of air manufacturing in the Star Valley was moved to the Afton civic center.

Some Fatal Air Crashes in Wyoming

1. The first person killed in an airplane crash in Wyoming was 1st Lt. Edwin V. Wales. His co-pilot, Lt. William C. Goldsborough, narrowly escaped serious injury. Wales and Goldsborough were participating in the army's "First Transcontinental Reliability and Endurance" contest when their Army DH-4 mail plane crashed west of Cheyenne in a snowstorm. (Oct. 9, 1919).

2. Maud Toomey became the first passenger killed in an airplane crash in Wyoming when she died and pilot Bert Cole was injured in a crash landing at Casper (Jan. 14, 1920).

3. Airmail pilot John F. Woodward became the third person killed in an airplane accident in Wyoming when his DH-4 mail plane crashed into Red Buttes near Tie Siding in heavy fog (Nov. 6, 1920)

4. Airmail pilot Walter Bunting died when his plane exploded and crashed shortly after taking off from Rock Springs airport (1921)

5. Major D. P. Wardwell, 34, World War I veteran pilot and organizer of Wyoming Airways for whom Casper's first airport was later named, killed in crash near Casper with two Worland men, Al Holz and George Cameron. Plane erupted in flames while in the air above the Casper airfield (Aug. 8, 1929)

6. Paul Andert of Cheyenne was killed when his US Airlines mail plane crashed on a mountain 80 miles west of Green River near Knight, Wyoming. He was en route to Cheyenne with 500 pounds of mail when he encountered a fierce blizzard. (Feb. 7, 1932)

7. Herbert Hunter and Lloyd Collenberg, both of Cheyenne, were killed when Collenberg's plane, piloted by Hunter, crashed at Collenberg's private airstrip, nine miles east of Cheyenne (May 24, 1932)

8. Henry Halkjar, Evanston pilot, and passenger Charles McCraig, 22, died when the plane dived into the ground in Evanston, just missing the home of H. J. Gewecke. (Sept. 25, 1932)

9. Eight people were killed when a United Airlines tri-motor crashed in the mountains on the Wyoming-Utah border. Among those killed was the mayor of Benton Harbor, Mich. (Feb. 23, 1934)

10. Lt. A. R. Kerwin and Lt. F. L. Howard, Army Air Corps pilots flying the airmail route and practicing night flights, killed in Cheyenne crash (March 9, 1934)

11. 2d Lt. H. G. Richardson of Cheyenne, an army airmail pilot, killed when plane crashed three miles west of Cheyenne airport (March 17, 1934)

12. Pilot Henry Pabst of Ucross and passenger Agnes Nedeff, 17, of Sheridan, were killed in an airplane crash near Burlington Lake, Gillette (Sept. 5, 1934)

13. Three Indianapolis residents were killed when their private plane slammed into Laramie Peak (Aug. 16, 1935)

14. Beechcraft biplane crashed 60 miles northeast of Sheridan, killing three--oil executive Lloyd Terry, pilot E. E. Dildine and company secretary Margaret "Patsy" True of Shelby, Mont., formerly of Cheyenne (Sept. 26, 1935)

15. Veteran pilot Al Lucas of Wyoming Air Service killed in crash near Glendo (April 27, 1935)

16. United Airlines passenger twin-engine Boeing piloted by H. A. Collison, a veteran pilot, crashed northwest of Cheyenne, killing all nine passengers and crew of three, including the pilot and stewardess Leona Mason of Kemmerer (Oct. 7, 1935, 2:17 a.m.)

17. United Airlines transport plane crashed five miles south of Cheyenne, killing company chief test pilot M. T. Arnold, Sheridan pilot Hanley Cohn who was "just along for the ride" and company employees Edward Yantis and Harold Kaufman, both of Cheyenne, (Oct. 30, 1935, 7:40 p.m.)

18. Bomber from Casper Air Base crashed north of Casper, seven crew members killed (Jan. 13, 1943)

19. Casper-based bomber crashed near Douglas, killed crew of 10 (March 2, 1943)

20. Bomber crashed in Big Horn Mountains, eight killed. The site was renamed "Bomber Mountain" (June 16, 1944)

21. United Airlines transport with 21 aboard, en route from Seattle to New York, crashed on Elk Mountain during a storm. Victims were 12 servicemen returning home to New York from the war, six civilians and a crew of 3. Search crews were hampered by blowing snow and -40 degree temperatures (Jan. 31, 1946, 3 a.m.)

22. 1st Air National Guard accident in Wyoming and first fatality--pilot Cary Alburn killed east of Cheyenne (May 22, 1948)

23. Pilot Henry Dobnik of Diamondville and passenger Robert Lampeck were killed when plane, flying low, hit pole and crashed into front porch of Pete Kirkwood home, Diamondville (Aug. 15, 1948)

24. Chartered DC-3 airplane carrying religious group hit Mount Moran in the Tetons. The bodies of the 21 victims were not recovered until the following spring. (Nov. 11, 1950)

25. Two men were killed near Lusk when their plane crashed while hunting coyotes (1952). In August, 1964, Charles Fairchild told Milwaukee police he had caused the accident by shooting the pilot before the plane crashed.

26. Two killed when plane crashed in Uinta Mountains (March 30, 1955)

27. Pilot killed in light plane crash near Rock Springs (May 18, 1955)

28. Two killed in airplane crash near Alva (July 21, 1955)

1st reported non-crash-related injuries suffered in a commercial airliner in Wyoming: a United Airlines DC-10 hit severe turbulence at 39,000 feet over Boysen Reservoir at 10:40 a.m., 50 passengers injured as they bounced over seats and against the ceiling in a jolt that lasted about one minute. (July 16, 1982)

29. Air National Guard pilots Ralph Van Horn, Thomas Tucker and Leland Palmer killed when F-80 collided with T-33 near Torrington (Sept. 18, 1955)

30. Two people killed in crash of light plane near Leo (Sept. 22, 1955)

31. Seven killed in crash near Burns (Sept. 24, 1955)

32. Worst airline crash in Wyoming history, United DC-4 from Denver, bound for Salt Lake City, struck below the top of Medicine Bow Peak in the Snowy Range. All 66 people aboard were killed. (Oct. 6, 1955)

33. Two Californians killed in crash near Keystone, wreckage found later (1955)

34. Two killed when C-45, based at Hill AFB, Utah, crashed on Wyoming-Utah border, ended worst year in Wyoming aviation history with a total of 91 fatalities (Dec. 1, 1955)

35. F86L crashed east of Cheyenne killing veteran pilot Jack Ziemer (April 8, 1958)

36. F86L piloted by Dale Knochenmuss crashed near Slater, pilot killed (Nov. 9, 1958)

37. Cheyenne teacher/Air Guard pilot Charles Place killed in crash near Utah border (Oct. 23, 1959)

38. Cessna wandered into path of Air National Guard F86. Cessna pilot killed in collision, F86 pilot ejected as plane crash landed in race track south of Cheyenne. None of 24 armed rockets exploded even though plane destroyed. (Winter, 1959)

39. Campbell County pilot Quentin Marquiss, 42, was killed when his plane struck a hillside while he was flying low "herding" antelope toward a motion picture crew, B Bar B rnach, 15 miles north of Wright (Feb. 21, 1964)

40. Army C-47 transport crashed in Cheyenne, five crewmen died (April 26, 1971)

41. An advance-man for the elite Air Force "Thunderbirds" precision flying team was killed when his plane, a T-38 jet trainer, careened into the grandstand and injured a Cheyenne Central High School bandsman cleaning up the grounds, Frontier Park, Cheyenne. The crash also killed two rodeo bulls. (July, 1978)

42. McCue family of Cheyenne killed in Jackson Hole crash (Jan. 4, 1981)

43. Two Pinedale residents, Truman Miley and Ben Chapin, Jr., were killed when their twin-engine Cessna crashed into Sheep Mountain, 25 miles north of Kemmerer (Oct. 23, 1982)

44. Lee Crawford, 26, rodeo cowboy from Greybull, killed with two others when plane hit a power line west of Columbus, Montana, and fell into the Yellowstone River (October, 1991)

45. Game and Fish biologists Kevin Roy and Kirk Inberg and pilot Ray Austin killed in crash of single-engine Maule in South Absarokas (Oct. 16, 1991); wreckage not discovered, despite intensive search, until Sept. 23, 1995, when two hunters came upon burned wreckage.

46. Mark Powers and Charles Renneison, veteran pilots who had flown numerous fire-fighting operations in the West, were killed when a plane they were ferrying from Arizona crashed in a heavy storm en route to Greybull, early 1992.

47. A Casper Life Flight air ambulance helicopter crashed in a snowstorm southwest of Emigrant Gap Ridge, 12 miles west of Natrona County International Airport. Killed in the crash were patient Hank Williamson of Riverton, pilot Tom Rickert, Wyoming Medical Center paramedic Dennis Patrick, and emergency room nurse Tom Wolf. All three crewmen received the Pete Vase Outstanding EMT award posthumously in Sept. 1993. (April 6, 1993)

48. Seven-year-old Jessica Dubroff, Pescadero, Calif., her father Lloyd Dubroff, and her flight instructor Joe Reid were killed a few minutes after take-off from Cheyenne airport in a storm. She was trying to break the record of the youngest person to pilot an airplane coast-to-coast when the Cessna 177B crashed one mile north of Cheyenne airport, near corner of Sunset and Kornegay (April 11, 1996)

49. Eleven crewmen flying equipment out of Jackson Hole, following the summer visit of President Clinton, were killed when their plane crashed into a hillside (August, 1996).

Air Corps chief Gen. Hap Arnold visited Casper Air Base on July 12, 1943.

50. Gillette Police Chief/pilot Jeff Pfau, 44, and passenger Vicky Lunbock, 37, were killed when the small plane crashed near Yellowtail Dam (Jan. 5, 1997).

51. Jackson wildlife filmmaker Kenneth "Chip" Houseman, 35, and author Helen Gramme, 28, killed with 99 others in air crash in Thailand while en route to film a wildlife documentary (Dec. 11, 1998)

52. Four relatives attending a family reunion were killed six miles north of Newcastle. The plane, piloted by John McDill, hit a power line. (August 17, 1999).

53. The aerial firefighting firm, Hawkins and Powers Aviation of Greybull, had two fatal airplane crashes in 2002 fire season. The first on June 17 in Calif., killed the two members of the crew. On July 18, an accident in Colorado also killed two crewmen.

54. On June 27, 2005, John Walton, heir to a part of the Wal-Mart fortune, died when his ultra-light experimental aircraft crashed shortly after take-off from the Jackson Hole airport. Walton, a decorated Vietnam War veteran and experienced pilot, was 58 years old. At the time of his death, he was the wealthiest Wyomingite and listed 11th on the *Fortune* list of 400 wealthiest Americans with a worth of some $20 billion.

55. On August 13, 2005, Evanston resident Julia Bond died making her first skydive near Ogden, Utah. In the tandem dive, her instructor was seriously injured in the fall.

*List compiled from numerous sources. Many incidents and dates provided or verified by historian Mel Duncan (b. 1931, d. 2007), author and veteran Air National Guardsman, Cheyenne, who was an authority on the history of Wyoming aviation.

4 Airplanes Built in Wyoming

1. Call-Air A2, A5

The only production passenger aircraft with a braced wing, the plane was designed in 1939. Only 50 of the planes were built.

2. Call-Air A9

Call Air began producing crop dusters in Afton in the 1930s. An agricultural dusting plane, several hundred of the A9's were manufactured between 1963 and 1965. The design was sold to North American Rockwell (now Rockwell International) who then sold it to a Mexican company.

3. Christen Husky A-1

The U. S. Border Patrol bought 12 of the Afton-built planes in 1987. The multi-purpose plane has been used by Alaska bush pilots for years.

4. Pitts S-1-11B

Probably the most powerful "competition" airplane ever built, its 300-horsepower engine can power the craft to 212 mph with a thrust-to-weight ratio of 1-1 and capable of climbing 4,140 feet per minute. Aviat, the builder, was purchased by Stuart Horn from Malcolm White in late 1995.

History of Some Wyoming Airports

1. Cheyenne Regional Airport

First planes landed on a dirt strip prepared for the transcontinental airmail in the summer of 1920 by the U. S. Postal Service. Later, Cheyenne became the primary maintenance

---

Airplanes had been flying over and landing in all parts of Wyoming by 1935. Yet, in that year, an airplane landed for the first time within the borders of Yellowstone National Park. Pilot Herman C. Underhill of San Francisco made an emergency landing on the northeast shore of Yellowstone Lake on Sept. 30, 1935, when the plane's engine began to fail. The craft was not damaged, but there is no word as to how Underhill removed his plane from the site. No airfield existed in the park.

hub for United Airlines. During World War II, the B-17 bomber modification center was located at the airport. It also was home base for United Airlines' stewardess school until it moved to Chicago in 1961. In 2004, the current name was adopted from Cheyenne Airport and on June 18, 2004, the field was named "Jerry Olson Field" in honor of 13-year airport manager Jerry Olson who died of cancer earlier that year.

2. Jackson Hole Airport

A dirt landing strip was used in the early 1930s. The current site was selected and leased in 1939. The first commercial air service began in 1941 with Western Airlines. The airport was incorporated into Grand Teton National Park in 1950 when Jackson Hole National Monument on which the airport stood was incorporated into the Park. It remains the only airport in the US located within the boundariees of a national park. Western Airlines left in 1959 and Frontier Airlines began service the same year. After considerable controversy over noise levels, the National Park Service authorized Frontier to begin landing 737s at the airport in June 1981.

3. Rock Springs-Sweetwater County Airport

Once located on the site of the current fairgrounds in north Rock Springs, the current site was established in 1942. Among those landing at the original air strip was Amelia Earhart who landed there in June 1931.

4. Worland Municipal Airport

Originally a dirt landing strip, it was paved in 1949.

5. Laramie Regional Airport

The airport was located on the current site in 1934. The original hangar was still standing in 2010. The current name was adopted in 1992, the airport previously known as Brees Field, named in honor of General Herbert Jay Brees, (b. 1877, d. 1958) a Laramie native and University of Wyoming graduate (1897) who served in the army from 1898 until his retirement as commanding officer of the Third Army in October 1940. The current terminal was constructed in 1959 and remodeled in 1994.

6. Other Wyoming airports

An airplane census in Wyoming in 1932 showed there were 67 total airplanes in the state. 49 pilots, 67 mechanics. 28 landing fields—11 municipal, two commercial, 12 intermediate and three auxiliary. In 1933, the federal government started funding construction and paving of airports in nearly 50 Wyoming communities. Former Casper newspaper manager J. Kirk Baldwin ((1894- 1967) directed the federal program. Later, he became the first Democrat ever elected Wyoming state treasurer (1935-39).

Airport Codes for the 10 Wyoming Commercial Airports

1. Jackson (JAC)*	5. Laramie (LAR)	9. Gillette (GCC)
2. Casper (CPR)	6. Worland (WRL)	10. Riverton (RIW)
3. Cheyenne (CYS)	7. Cody (COD)	
4. Rock Springs (RKS)	8. Sheridan (SHR)	

Source: Official Airline Guide (Dun and Bradstreet, July, 1987). Oddly, there are no direct flights between most Wyoming towns. The "hub system" practiced by airlines causes passengers to travel to Denver, Salt Lake City, and other out-of-state locations for transfer to flights to Wyoming cities. The Jackson airport recorded 53 percent of all Wyoming boardings in 1998.

The Cheyenne airport tower was shown in the movie thriller "Turbulence" starring Lauren Holy and Ray Liotta.

Some Unusual Incidents in Wyoming Aviation History

1. William Heath, a Rawlins locomotive painter, developed a pilotless flying machine "powered by a kerosene engine and with a dragon-fly inspired body." (1880s)

2. Jack Copman, a ranch employee on Upper Shell Creek, Big Horn County, designed an airship about 1882. The take-off point was to be a 500-foot cliff near the Lovell ranch. Copman told friends the cliff would be his tomb if his flight failed, but there is no evidence he ever tried to fly the plane from the cliff. A man who saw it reported years later that Copman's plane would have flown "if he had had a gasoline engine to furnish the power." The cliff became known as "Copman's Tomb," although Copman died, not from flying, but from a stroke in 1907.

3. Dr. E. C. Steele of Jackson Hole claimed to have invented an airplane from which it was "impossible for aviators to fall." The long, narrow craft had a rudder set on top of its frame. Four canvas wings were set in pairs, one pair directly behind the other. A newspaper reported, "Steele styles his invention an aeromobile," but the term didn't catch on.

4. Former World War I flying ace Eddie Rickenbacker crashed his airmail plane when it hit a ditch at the end of the runway, Cheyenne (May, 1921)

5. Airmail pilot Randy Page, Cheyenne-eastbound, "bombed" an Iowa town with rolls of toilet paper after the townspeople complained to the post office department about being bothered by Page's low-flying plane. Page once consumed two quarts of whiskey on his Omaha to Chicago run, but it is not known if the toilet paper incident occurred on the same flight. (1920s)

6. Slim Lewis, a pilot in the airmail service, landed in the pasture of Wyoming Hereford Ranch, his plane hitting and killing a prize bull. Postal authorities, when presented with a bill amounting to several thousand dollars, asked Lewis why he had to crash "into an entire herd"!

7. Airmail pilot Hal Collison, on a stormy December night, took off in four airplanes at Cheyenne in rapid succession. All four planes came down one-half mile from the airport when their carburator jets froze. Collison was uninjured in all four crash landings. (1920s)

8. Airmail pilot Jimmie Murray crashed in a blizzard at Sand Lake in the Snowy Range. He walked to Arlington, 17 miles away, in heavy snow. (Oct. 18, 1920)

9. Airmail pilot Bob Ellis' plane struck a down-draft shortly after take-off from Rock Springs. He was attempting to cross White Mountain, but when he realized the plane would not clear the mountain, he eased back on the stick and cut the engine. The plane hit the ground and slid backward 50 feet, stopping at an 80-degree angle on the mountain side. Ellis, uninjured, rolled the mail sacks 1,500 feet down the mountain. He then loaded the sacks into a backup plane which he flew on to his destination. (1920s)

10. Profiting from a favorable tail wind, airmail pilot Jiggs Chandler flew from Rock Springs to Cheyenne in one hour, 32 minutes. After he landed in Cheyenne, he could not take off again. The 80-mph wind gusts were so strong that it took a dozen men to keep the plane from blowing off the runway. (Jan. 31, 1921)

11. Boeing Air Transport Co., a subsidiary of United Airlines, began flying on June 30, 1927. It was the first airline to carry passengers on regular schedules for distance flights, the first to fly passengers at night on a regular schedule and the first to fly trimotors. The company's transcontinental route passed through Wyoming. (1927).

12. First airplane flights made for extension courses, University of Wyoming. Professors Mallory, Reusser and Bloomfield visited classes by air, leaving Laramie before noon on Friday and returning Sunday after more than 1,000 miles in the air. Classes were held in Wheatland, Sheridan, Buffalo. (Fall, 1931)

Ralph Seney owned the first airplane in Buffalo (1926). He gave land for the airport in 1938.

13. An airplane census in Wyoming showed there were 67 airplanes in the state, 49 pilots, 67 mechancis and 28 landing fields. Two of the fields were commercial, 11 were municipal and 12 were listed as intermediate. The remaining three were auxiliary. Source: Green River Star, Feb. 19, 1932, p. 7.

14. Ray Varney a Thermopolis-born stunt pilot, appeared at an air festival in Vallejo, Calif. (May 1933)

15. Plane crashed but no one injured when airplane hit a gopher hole on take-off from Cody airfield, June 1933. Both men from Michigan. See "Park Visitors Nose Plane over at Cody", Cody Enterprise, June 28, 1933, p. 1.

16. George Hopkins, a stunt parachutist, jumped from an airplane and intentiionally landed on top of Devils Tower. After six days of national intrerest in his plight, Hopkins was rescued by climbers led by Jack Durrence who endured rain and ice to save him. (October 1941)

17. Wyoming fighter pilot Lt. Bob Milliken became last pilot to achieve "ace" status with a P-38 Lightning airplane in northern Europe in World War II when he shot down his fifth German plane in one-on-one aerial combat (1945)

18. Casper resident and Casper College alumnus Paul "Bob" Streich and six others survived seven days on the ice of Antarctica after his Otter airplane crashed during Operation Deep Freeze. Streich is credited with making the first night flight over the Antarctic. (1956)

19. Pioneer resident Ed Arnold took an airplane ride on first commercial airline to land in Lusk (Frontier). He also was present to see the first train come into Lusk in 1886. (Sept. 26, 1958) Source: Lusk Herald, Oct. 2, 1958.

20. Three Cheyenne-based engineers, working on construction of the missile silos, were passengers in a plane piloted by 56-year-old Edgar Van Keuran when, about 50 miles east of Cheyenne, the pilot suffered a fatal heart attack at the controls. The three engineers, in their 30s, were "talked down" by a veteran pilot in the Cheyenne airport tower. (Jan. 28, 1963)

21. Sixty-nine-year-old Bill Hackworth, a former airmail mechanic at Rock Springs, flew a 50-year-old open cockpit plane along the original airmail route (1968)

22. James E. Barrett, Wyoming Attorney General, was a passenger in a state-owned airplane piloted by veteran pilot George Kealey, 54, en route from Cheyenne to speak to a convention in Riverton. Somewhere over Bairoil, Kealey suffered a cerebral hemorrhage at the controls. Even though Kealey was unconscious and gripping the stick, Barrett, who had no flight training, was able to turn the plane around and fly toward Rawlins. Kealey soon died and Barrett circled the plane over Rawlins, unable to gain communication with the ground. The plane ran out of gas and crashed east of Rawlins. Barrett survived but with back and facial injuries. Later, Barrett was named to the federal bench as a judge on the 10th Circuit Court of Appeals. (Dec. 4, 1969)

23. A Boeing 737 carrying 100 passengers, Western Airlines Flight 44 from Denver to Sheridan, landed at Buffalo on the 4,500-foot runway. Pilot Lowell Ferguson claimed he mistook the Buffalo airport for the larger Sheridan one. (July 31, 1979)

24. The town of Buffalo celebrated "Lowell Ferguson Day" in honor of the pilot who mistakenly landed the jetliner there the previous year. The pilot and everyone else named "Lowell Ferguson" were honored guests. The event being commemorated likely would not be duplicated. Western Airlines had discontinued flights to Sheridan in July. (1980)

25. Pioneer pilot Clyde Ice of Pinedale flew three airplanes on his 100th birthday (1989). The veteran pilot for whom the Spearfish, S. D., airport was named, died in Jackson in 1992 at the age of 103.

26. Jet carrying pilot and two passengers, including actress Sandra Bullock, slid off end of Jackson Hole Airport runway; no one hurt (Dec. 20, 2000)

27. Afton-born Olympic wrestler Rulon Gardner and two companions survived the crash of a small plane into Lake Powell (Feb. 25, 2007)

Worst Casper Army Air Base Accidents, 1942-1945

1. On Feb. 22, 1943, a B-17 on a training mission crashed 28 miles northwest of Glenrock. Ten airmen were killed.

2. B-24 based at Casper crashed 25 miles east of Gunnison, Colorado, on July 19, 1943, killing 10 crewmen.

3. B24J crashed on Sept. 24, 1944, just three miles west of the Casper base. Nine crewmen died.

4. Eight died when a B-17 stationed at Casper Army Air Base crashed on May 30, 1943, near Covelo, California.

5. B-24 crashed four miles southwest of the base on Jan. 30, 1944, killing all eight crewmen.

6. On March 3, 1944, a B-24 crashed 25 miles east of the base. Eight crewmen died.

7. B-24 crashed on Casper Mountain, 12 miles southeast of the base, on June 19, 1944, killing eight crewmen.

8 B-24J crashed on the airfield killing seven crewmen on Oct. 22, 1944.

9. B-17 crashed Jan. 13, 1943, in New Mexico, killing seven crewmen.

Source: Gerald Adams, "The Casper Army Air Field in World War II, Annals of Wyoming, Summer/ Fall, 1992, 23. Adams counted 21 fatal accidents.

Wyoming Encounters by Some Famous Aviators

1. Amelia Earhart

Earhart flew over Rock Springs on July 26, 1932, in her red Lockheed Vega. Some 13 months earlier, she landed in Rock Springs while on a cross-country flight. Later, on a competition flight across country, she stopped in Cheyenne and laid in a crawl space under an airport building until she recovered from air sickness. *Wyoming Eagle* photographer Francis Brammar shot a picture of her later, once she was able to stand. At the time she disappeared over the Pacific Ocean in 1937, she was having a cabin constructed as a summer home near Meeteetse.

2. Charles Lindbergh

Aviator Charles Lindbergh once landed his plane on the flats east of Gillette and rode to town on a pony he borrowed from a boy living on a nearby ranch. **3. Eddie Rickenbaker**

The famous World War I aviator was flying the transcontinental mail route. On May 26, 1921, his attempt to set a coast-to-coast speed record ended abruptly when his plane crashed at the Cheyenne airfield while attempting a night landing. He was uninjured but the plane was destroyed and he cancelled the rest of the trip.

4. Chuck Yeager

Yeager, assigned to Casper Air Base as a flight officer, crashed his P-39 about 15 miles west of Casper in October 1943. He bailed out safely but the fighter plane was destroyed. He later gained fame as the nation's top test pilot.

5. Elrey B. Jeppeson

Jeppeson, for whom the terminal at Denver International Airport was named in 1991, served as an airmail pilot across Wyoming. In 1930, he began flying for Varney Airlines, headquartered in Cheyenne. There, he began creating flying charts for use by pilots who, previously, had to rely on regular highway maps or follow roads or rail tracks to determine a course. The pioneer pilot/chartmaker met his future wife, one of the first airline stewardesses, while he was living in Cheyenne.

Fifteen survivors of the crash of United Airlines DC-10 in Iowa on July 19, 1989, were from Wyoming. More than 100 people died when the airplane lost its hydraulic system and had to make an emergency landing in Sioux City. Seven of the survivors were from Moorcroft; three from Laramie; two each from Pine Bluffs and Cheyenne; one from Casper.

Inductees, Wyoming Aviation Hall of Fame*

1. Ralph S. Johnson (1906-Jan. 10, 2010)

Johnson was chief test pilot for United Airlines when the company was headquartered in Cheyenne. He developed the stabilized approach as well as use of various life-saving devices still in use.

2. Slim Lewis (1894-1945)

Lewis was a pioneer airmail pilot who flew the mail from 1919 to 1927. Later, he became Boeing's chief test pilot for the Model 40-A.

3. Samuel Phillips (1921-1990)

Phillips headed the Apollo space program at its peak in 1969. A graduate of the University of Wyoming, he entered the air corps in 1942, ultimately reaching the rank of four-star general.

4. W. Dillard "Pic" Walker (1911-1993)

Walker helped develop the Civil Air Patrol, served as Wyoming's first wing commander and directed civilian pilot training programs during World War II.

Inductees by Year

1996: Gene Powers, Greybull.
1997: Reuell T. Call, Afton
1998: Carle B. (C.B.) Jackson, Worland
1999: Melvin Christler, Greybull
2000: Lester A. Larsen, Lander
2001: James P. Murray, Cheyenne
2002: E. H. (Herb) Andersen

2003: C. L. (Bud) McHolland
2004: Robert T. Johnson, Cheyenne
2005: William A. Monday, Cody
2006: Barlow H. Call, Afton
2007: Roy E. Cooper, Cheyenne
2008: William Maxwell, Cheyenne
2009: Don Veal, Laramie
2010: Robert Gose, Sundance

The first four were inducted in 1995. The Hall of Fame is headquartered at the Cheyenne airport.

3 Gliding Flights

1. Kevin Christopherson of Casper has flown the longest glider flights in the world from Whiskey Peak. He set the gliding record of 287 miles from Whiskey Peak to Kyle, S. D., on Aug. 3, 1989, beating a mark he had set on June 28, 1989, of 245 miles from the peak to Buffalo Gap, S. D.

2. On Dec. 21, 1995, 14-year-old Mikhail Schork of Jackson became one of the 50 youngest people in America to solo in a glider. The flight lasted about 15 minutes.

3. On July 16, 2006, paraglider Josh Riggs of Wilson launched his paraglider from the tiny Teton County town, and in five and-a-half hours, touched down behind a Lander junior high school, setting a new state paragliding record of 120 miles in the process.

"It was luck I landed in Lander," Riggs told the *Wyoming State Journal* in Lander. Riggs estimated it was 110 degrees as he flew over Fremont County.

In the spring of 1912, former Wyoming Gov. W. A. Richards purchased a 150-acre farm about 110 miles from Melbourne, Australia. On July 25, 1912, he attended a banquet in honor of Elwood Mead, the former Wyoming state engineer who had been in Australia rewriting the country's water code. Mead was returning to the U. S. the following day. "The men left together and walked around the city," according to the *Cheyenne State Leader*. Richards felt ill and returned to his hotel. In the morning, still ill, he was taken to a private hospital. There, he died that morning. Meanwhile, Mead left for America, not knowing of his friend's illness and death until he arrived back in the States. Services for Richards were held in the Baptist Church, Cheyenne, after his body lie in state at the Capitol rotunda. Burial was in Lakeview Cemetery, Cheyenne, on August 20, 1912.

ANIMALS

State Mammal: American bison, designated by the 1985 legislature.
Oldest existing mammal native to Wyoming: Pronghorn antelope
Rarest mammal in Wyoming: Black-footed ferret. It is the only ferret native to North America. The ferrets were rediscovered near Meeteetse in September 1981. Fewer than 150 of the animals existed in about 20 prairie dog colonies, but soon after their rediscovery, a distemper epidemic nearly wiped them out. A Wyoming Game and Fish captive breeding program has been successful in bringing the number back. By the time the population was reintroduced into the wild, the total population in existence numbered around 300. In July, 1992, the first two wild-born ferret kits were spotted among a group of 49 animals reintroduced in Shirley Basin in the fall of 1991. In February, 1996, the U. S. Fish and Wildlife Service took over the cost of rearing captive black-footed ferrets, saving the state about $250,000 annually. In 2007, an estimated 750 lived in the wild with an additonal 250 living in zoos.

19 Mammals Living in Wyoming

1. Bats (16 species)
2. Shrews (9 species)
3. Mole
4. Opossum
5. Beaver
6. Porcupine
7. Squirrels (16 species)
8. Cats (3 species)
9. Mice (27 species)
10. Pika
11. Bears (2 species)
12. Raccoons (2 species)
13. Weasels (13 species)
14. Borids (bison, mtn goat, sheep—3 species)
15. Deer, including moose (3 species)
16. Hares and rabbits (7 species)
17. Pocket gophers (4 species)
18. Dogs (coyote and grey wolf—5 species)
19. Pronghorn (only horned animal to shed horns annually)

In total, seven orders and 117 species live in Wyoming of the 18 orders and 4,200 species. *Source: Tim W. Clark and Mark R. Stromberg. Mammals of Wyoming. (Lawrence: University of Kansas Museum of Natural History, 1987).*

5 Wyoming Mammals Depleted by Man

1. Audubon's bighorn sheep
Now extinct, the animal was once common in the Black Hills.

2. Wolves
More than 10,000 bounties were paid in Wyoming for wolves from 1897-1908. In the two years, 1897-1898, 4,281 bounties for wolves were paid in eastern Wyoming. According to some experts, by 1910, the wolf was eradicated from Wyoming although others believe some packs lived in the Yellowstone area. Wolf reintroduction in the 1990s brought hundreds back into the Wyoming wilds.

3. Pronghorn antelope
In 1492, an estimated 45 million pronghorn roamed North America. The number in Wyoming was reduced to just 14,000 by 1924. Since then the population has continued to grow. More pronghorn live in Wyoming than in any other state. Were Congress ever to adopt "one pronghorn, one vote," Wyoming would have the electoral clout of California. In the 1930s, Wyoming pronghorn were sent to zoos in Europe, some by airship to Germany.

4. American bison
An estimated 75 million bison occupied North America at the time the Pilgrims landed at Plymouth Rock in 1620. In 1868, William F. Cody got his nickname of Buffalo Bill by

In July 1992, a moose belly-flopped into an empty swimming pool at the Circle EW Guest Ranch near Moose. The pool had been drained for cleaning. The moose was unhurt and walked out on a ramp provided by rescuers.

killing 4,250 buffalo in an eight-month period for meat for the Union Pacific workers in Kansas. By 1895, only 800 bison were still living in the wild and that number declined to just 25 free-ranging in Yellowstone in 1905. More than 500,000 now live in the United States today. Some 5,000 live in Wyoming, many on private ranches, but others are in herds in the national parks. The herd in the Greater Yellowstone area has been estimated at 3,500 in 2009. The state maintains a herd at Hot Springs State Park. A small natural herd existed in the Red Desert until it died out in the mid-1960s.

5. Lynx

In the past 140 years, there have been only 262 sightings of lynx in Wyoming.

Animal Speeds (in order from fastest)

1. Pronghorn antelope: 70 miles per hour

The fastest animal in North America. Of all world animals, only the cheetah is faster. (The world mark for man is about 27.8 miles per hour).

2. Quarterhorse: 47 1/2 miles per hour

3. Elk: 45 miles per hour

4. Coyote: 43 miles per hour (short distances only)

5. Buffalo: 30 miles per hour (a good bit of speed for an animal weighing up to 2,400 pounds)

Animal Weights

1. Bear

Abner Forrester killed a 1,700-pound grizzly near Savery in Carbon County in November, 1888. Harry S. Yount, a former Yellowstone game keeper, claimed he once tracked a grizzly near Laramie Peak for seven years before finally shooting it in 1880. He said it weighed 1,600 pounds. Hank Mason of Weston County killed a nine-foot grizzly in 1894 near his ranch home. He died from the effects of being mauled by the animal.

2. Coyote

The heaviest coyote ever weighed in the United States tipped the scales at 74.8 pounds. It was shot near Afton on Nov. 19, 1937. It measured 63 inches tip to tip.

3. Mountain lion

A mountain lion was killed near Laramie in December, 1877, after it killed 54 sheep. The animal measured more than seven feet in length and weighed about 200 pounds.

3 Incidents Involving Wyoming Pronghorn

1. Pronghorn Aboard the Hindenburg (1936)

Charles Belden, a photographer and manager of the Pitchfork Ranch in Park County, sent antelope to zoos around the world. Usually, the animals were sent by airplane, but in 1936, Belden sent two antelope to Germany aboard the airship Hindenburg. The trip broke a speed record for sending animals that distance—60 hours from the Pitchfork Ranch to Berlin. The same year, Belden supplied antelope to zoos in Milwaukee and Detroit. All of the animals arrived at their destinations safely and in good condition.

2. Antelope Shut Off From Winter Range (1983-1984)

Taylor Lawrence, a Carbon County rancher, gained national notoriety during the harsh winter by erecting a 28-mile-long fence which kept the antelope from crossing his land to their grazing areas on public lands. Hundreds of antelope died and game proponents

> Two-thirds of all pronghorn on earth live in Wyoming. So do two-thirds of all sage grouse worldwide.

in Wyoming and elsewhere were outraged. A court injunction forced him to remove the fence. He appealed the action to the U. S. Supreme Court which ruled on Dec. 5, 1988, that the injunction was proper.

3. Thirsty Pronghorn (1935)

Art McIntyre of Gillette was hunting west of town in October, 1935. He stopped at his car to pour himself a drink of water when he felt something lick his hand from behind. A young antelope, thirsty for water, was standing there looking at McIntyre. The would-be hunter let the animal drink from his cup and then took it back to Gillette--alive--and provided it with feed and more water.

3 Items about Wyoming Bats

1. Bats in the Fort Laramie Belfry

National Park Service personnel report that brown bats have a nursery colony near the old fort in eastern Wyoming. The animals help control the mosquito population that thrives on the Laramie River. One colony of bats reportedly consumes 3 million mosquitoes per hour. (Where were they the last time I went fishing?) The Park Service has constructed "stilt houses" to keep the animals away from the historic buildings. Each of the structures can hold up to 100 or more bats.

2. Mine Reclamation and Bats

Efforts by the federal government in the 1980s to close abandoned mines in the state resulted in threats to bat colonies in the mines.

3. Bats in Flight

"Friendly" bats occupy ranch buildings and cabins throughout Wyoming. They are extremely valuable for insect control. Occasionally, bats wake up unexpectedly during daylight hours. In the summer of 1993, a conference was held at the University of Wyoming Research Center on the shores of Jackson Lake. Cool temperatures caused conference organizers to start the fireplace. A minor smoke back-up "awakened" the resident bat mascot which hung from the ceiling of the main conference center. It swept down from the ceiling, past the speaker and over the audience before deciding it was time to return to its perch. Conference participants, if they had been dozing earlier, stayed alert for the rest of the sessions!

16 Bear Stories

1. Tracking for Seven Years

Harry S. Yount (b. 1847, d. 1923) once tracked a bear he called "Old Big Foot" for seven years. The animal ranged the Laramie Peak area for many years. When Yount finally shot it, the bear weighed 1,600 pounds. Yount, a former Yellowstone gamekeeper from 1880-1882, killed 57 grizzlies during his career as a hunter. In the early 1870s, he hunted pheasants and mountain lions for the Smithsonian.

2. Reattaching an Ear

Jedadiah Smith, the mountain man, survived a grizzly mauling in the Powder River country in September 1823. The bear tore off one of his ears and scratched him severely. One of Smith's men sewed his ear back on and, for the rest of his life, Smith wore his hair long to cover the deep scars.

3. Helping a Bear

Peno, a Canadian trapper in the Powder River country in the early 19th century, once pulled a sliver from a grizzly's paw. A bull buffalo gored his horse and broke his leg. A hungry bear happened on the scene. Peno noticed the bear was limping and, recognizing the futility of escape from the beast, he bravely coaxed the bear into allowing him to remove a sliver from the paw. The grateful bear did not hurt him.

4. Roping a Bear

"A cowboy in Uinta County has discovered by actual experience that there is a great difference between roping a cow and a bear. He roped the bear all right, but the bear killed his pony and badly injured him, and then escaped to the mountains, dragging the lariat." —*Cheyenne Weekly Sun,* Sept. 10, 1891.

5. Devouring Roast Beef

Mrs. Emma Bictoll cooked a roast beef for dinner in a grading camp just east of the summit between Laramie and Cheyenne in 1867. A yearling grizzly ambled into her tent-kitchen, grabbed the roast off the warming oven, and disappeared outside. Mrs. Bictoll, thinking the culprit was a large dog, gave chase. She knocked the roast from the animal's mouth with an axe handle, chastised it for its impertinence, and shooed it away. Only later when she told camp workers about the "ugly dog" did she discover the true identity of the roast-rustler.

6. In the Chops

Ned Frost, pioneer Cody outfitter, was once attacked in camp by a grizzly. The bear mauled Frost, but he was able to hit the bear in the face with a frying pan, driving it away. Frost was able to escape, injured but not critically.

7. Bathing with a Bear

A Rawlins newspaper published a story in 1874 about Captain Lang, a Rawlins man who owned a pet bear. He would take the bear to a Rawlins pond occasionally because the bear enjoyed swimming. The paper tells the rest of the story: "...the captain arrayed in his Sunday best, walked down to the pond, holding the lariat firmly in his hand. Just as he reached the water, the animal made a lunge forward. Our friend was helped out of the water, but his new silk tie has not yet come to the surface."

8. Saratoga Bear Hunt

In June, 1918, a bear wandered into the city limits of Saratoga. His presence set off a bear hunt in which the animal was "pursued by hunters armed with rifles, shotguns, pistols and bowie knives," according to the *Saratoga Sun.* Raymond Ault, using a six-shooter, shot the bear a few miles east of town.

9. First White Sighting of a Wyoming Bear

"There were many bears in the neighborhood drawn by the wild cherries and the other fruits that there are here. The banks of the river are covered with bear dung as the approaches to a stable are with cattle manure." *Journal of Francois Larocque, first European visitor to Wyoming, August, 1805.*

10. Electrocuted

Three young grizzly males were killed in August, 1995, when they came into contact with a downed power line in the Hayden Valley area of Yellowstone. Power had not been disrupted and when linemen checked for the cause, they found the dead animals.

11. Giving the Warden Cold Feet

Fern K. Nelson wrote of Herb Whiteman, a Jackson Hole pioneer, who continued to trap bears even after it was made illegal. One day, he trapped a bear and was skinning it when he spotted a game warden coming his way. After three attempts to shake off the warden by circling around on skis in the snow, back to skin out the bear, Whiteman concluded it wasn't worth the $50 bounty to go to jail. He went home and to bed. The warden, meanwhile, after following Whiteman for three times in the circle, decided to sit near the bear and wait for the poacher's return. He never did. The warden nearly froze his toes and fingers as he waited most of the night in the freezing cold to no avail. *Source: Fern K. Nelson, This Was Jackson's Hole. (Glendo: High Plains Press, 1994).*

12. Old "Griz"

"The oldest grizzly bear in the Yellowstone ecosystem lived to be 27 years old," according to Jack Hanna's *Animal Adventures* television program on Feb. 3, 1996, which featured the Grizzly Discovery Center in Yellowstone.

13. Charging Bears

A large bear and her three cubs encountered hunters Doyle and Brandon Ward of Riverton in September, 1995, in the Teton Wilderness. The largest grizzly and one other charged at the pair, but stopped less than ten feet away, rose on hind legs and growled. They then abruptly turned and ambled away. According to Wyoming Game and Fish bear expert Dave Moody, the Wards did the right thing by not shooting at the bears during a "bluff charge." A shot, Moody said, would have caused the bears to charge with potentially serious results for all parties.

14. Meeteetse Grizzly

In 2000, a 900-lb. grizzly was killed near the Hoodoo Ranch, west of Meeteetse. The 11-year-old male, with an unusual blond coat, had been killing livestock in the area over the previous six years.

15. Photographed Bear

The often photographed 12-year-old grizzly bear, designated by Park authorities as #264, was killed by a motorist 22 miles south of Mammoth in Yellowstone National Park on June 14, 2003.

16. Stuffed Bear

Bear "104" was hit by a car on Cody road to Yellowstone in May 2001. The bear had lived near Pahaska Teepee and was a crowd favorite. The stuffed animal is on display in the Draper Museum of Natural History, BBHC, Cody.

Yellowstone fatalities, 1981-1986*

1. Automobile deaths (17)   3. Homicides (2)
2. Killed by grizzlies (3)   4. Climbing falls (2)

*According to historian Lee H. Whittlesey, during the period from 1839 to 1993, more than 300 people died violent deaths in Yellowstone, not counting individuals killed in car and snowmobile accidents. In the period from 1987 to 1994, Whittlesey listed four drownings, three people killed in falls, two victims of airplane crashes, two killed by avalanches and one who died in a hot spring. Source: *Lee H. Whittlesey, Death in Yellowstone: Accidents and Foolhardiness in the First National Park. (Boulder: Roberts-Rinehart, 1995).*

5 Items About Bison

1. Getting Up Close

It is illegal to walk within 25 yards of a bison in Yellowstone National Park. Nonetheless, every year, individuals are injured because they get too close to one of the animals.

2. Injuries

During the period from 1983-1994, there were a reported 75 injuries to people from bison in Grand Teton National Park and Yellowstone National Park. During the same period, four deaths from buffalo were reported in the parks. *Source: Todd Wilkinson, Jackson Hole News, July 20, 1994.*

3. Thermopolis herd

William Clayton of Thermopolis paid $40,000 for a herd of 200-250 buffalo sold by D. R. Turner of Fort Garland, Colo., in March 1919. Turner had acquired the herd from "General Palmer who bought the first ones at Goodnight, Texas," according to a news account of the purchase. Clayton apparently broke up the herd and sold small numbers to parks throughout the United States. Source: *Worland Grit,* March 13, 1919.

4. Privately-owned herd

The Marquiss family purchased buffalo from the South Dakota buffalo "rancher" Scotty Phillip on Feb. 5, 1923. For years, the Marquiss herd, ranging on their ranch south of Gillette, was the only privately owned herd in the state.

5. Largest private herd

The Durham Buffalo Ranch located south of Gillette, has been owned since the middle 1960s by the Flocchini family. The original bison came from the Yellowstone National Park herd in the late 1950s. In 2010, the ranch was home to 2,500 bison making it the largest private herd in Wyoming. Much of the meat produced from the herd is sold to supermarkets and restaurants hroughout the Western United States by Sierra Meat Company, located in the San Francisco bay area.

3 Items About Beavers

1. Pelt Prices

The average pelt price in 1980 was $25 and in 1990, the price had dropped to $12. In 1980, 1,005 trappers caught 19,253 beaver in Wyoming; in 1990, 362 trappers caught 4,131 beaver.

2. Dam Builders

The Bureau of Land Management trucked beaver into the Rock Springs area in 1983 so that the animals might build dams and stop soil erosion.

3. Yellowstone Lodges

In 1991, there were 140 beaver lodges in Yellowstone.

13 Items Involving Coyotes

1. White One

Of the thousands of coyotes seen from 1915 to 1945, only one was an albino.

2. Coyote Harvests

Trappers harvested huge numbers of coyotes around the turn of the century. The Hardesty brothers trapped 84 coyotes, 15 bobcats and a wolf along the Upper Greybull River in December, 1909. "Coyote" Smith, best remembered as a Glenrock photographer, gained his nickname and his livelihood from coyote trapping from 1900-1920.

3. Ranging far from home

Coyotes have been known to move as far as 100 miles in one season. One coyote was found just north of Saratoga one year and four months after it had been tagged in Sweetwater County near the Colorado border.

4. Swimming

Coyotes have been seen swimming in various Wyoming streams. A rancher once watched a coyote swim across the Green River south of Black's Fork.

5. Begging for Food

In the summer of 1947, two coyotes made news for begging along the main road in Yellowstone, 10 miles from Old Faithful. Normally, bears monopolized such activities.

6. Chasing a Bobcat

Ranchers in the Independence Rock area often see coyotes chase bobcats.

In a journal entry for August 30, Charles Preuss, accompanying the Fremont expedition in 1842, described finding a skunk south of present-day Glenrock. "A polecat! Last night a stinker was killed, and we ate it this morning for breakfast. I never thought such a foul-smelling beast could taste so good. During the attack, it squirted right into Badeau's face; the fellow still smells of it." Yum....

7. Carrying a Companion

In 1941, a Yellowstone naturalist watched a coyote carry a dead (but still warm) coyote some 28 yards up a steep 30 percent slope "at a dead run."

8. Living to Old Age

Wyoming coyotes can live to be more than 18 years old. The harsh environment in which they live allows few to make it beyond the age of 10.

9. Walking with a Badger

Geologist Samuel Aughey reported watching a badger and coyote walk together in 1884. "The coyote would go in front of the badger, lay its head on the latter's neck, lick it, jump into the air, and give other expressions of unmistakable joy...the badger seemed equally pleased," Aughey wrote.

10. Predator losses

In 2005 an estimated 4,000 cattle and calves were killed by predators. An estimated 800 were killed by wolves; 2,100 from coyotes. Almost 24,000 sheep and lambs were killed by predators in 2005. (Losses had been 66,000 in 1995). Coyotes accounted for 31 percent of all sheep/lamb losses. Weather, disease, poison, lambing and old age accounted for remainder. *Source: Wyoming Agricultural Statistics Service, Annual Report.*

11. Rare human bite

Charlotte Stewart of Cody was bitten on the arm by a coyote Oct. 2, 1992, while surveying on the Sylvan Pass road.

12. Ski hazard

On Jan. 4, 1990, a coyote knocked down and attacked a cross-country skier in the Old Faithful area. The animal had been fed regularly by humans.

13. Chasing Antelope through Town

On December 12, 1891, the Laramie newspaper reported that an antelope was seen being chased through town by a pack of coyotes.

10 Coyote Calls*

1. Sunrise serenade	5. Domain call	8. Distress call
2. Female invitation	6. Challenge call	9. Lost mate call
3. Roundup call	7. Love call	10. Attack call
4. Interrogation call		

Identified by coyote authority Bill Austin (b. 1946, Rawlins).

4 Items about Wyoming Sled Dogs

1. Hauling the mail

Many Jackson Hole pioneers used dog sleds to haul freight and passengers. Slim Lawrence used a dog sled in the 1930s to bring mail from the end of the mail sleigh road at Moran to his home eight miles north of there. His wife Verba made canvas booties for the team of Irish setters to keep their feet warm.

2. Malamutes at home

Geraldine Lucas, the first woman to climb the Grand Teton, received a team of Alaskan malamute sled dogs in the early 1920s from her son, a commander in the Coast Guard stationed in Alaska. They kept her from being snowbound all winter at her home north of Jenny Lake.

3. Annual races

In the 1930s, annual sled dog races were held in Jackson on Washington's birthday.

4. 450-mile dog race

The Rocky Mountain Stage Stop Sled Dog Race, modeled after Alaska's Iditerod, was started by Frank Teasley and Jane Ottman. First run in February 1996, the course started in Moran, looped toward Kemmerer and turned north back to Alpine. The route has varied over the years, however. Proceeds from the event go to charity.

1996: Rick Swenson   **2004:** Blayne "Bud" Streeper, Ft. Nelson, B.C.
1997: Hans Gatt, Altin, B.C.   **2005**: Hernan Maquieira, Ushuaia, Argentina
1998: Hans Gatt   **2006:** Melanie Shirilla
1999: Jeff King, Denali, Alaska   **2007:** Wendy Davis, Lander
2000: Hans Gatt   **2008**: Melanie Shirilla
2001: Hans Gatt   **2009**: Melanie Shirilla
2002: Melanie Shirilla, Lincoln, Mont.   **2010:** Blayne "Bud" Streeper
2003: Gwen Holdman, Alaska

Source (Items 1-3): "Dogs of the North," Teton Magazine, Winter-Spring, 1973. Used with permission of publisher Gene Downer.

7 Famous Wyoming Dogs

1. Woofer D. Coyote

Woofer holds the distinction of being the first canine candidate for the U.S. presidency. The dog ran against Ronald Reagan in 1984 and based his independent campaign on promises to "outlaw the use of poison bait traps against coyotes" and "to ban the use of animals in medical experiments." Woofer lost. In late July of 1985, Woofer died of injuries received from being hit by a car. The dog's campaign manager in the 1984 election was Al Hamburg of Torrington.

2. Thornburg

Thornburg was a great friend of teamsters and other personnel at Fort Bridger in the early years of the post. He guarded the fort and, on one occasion, saved an emigrant child from drowning in a nearby creek. His owner was freighter Buck Buchanan. Following Thornburgh's death on Sept. 27, 1888, as a result of being kicked by a mule, he was buried on the post. A gravestone, restored in 1993, marks his resting place on the fort grounds. It reads: "Man never had a better, truer, braver friend. Sleep on old fellow. We'll meet across the range."

3. Grease-ball, the Wonder Dog

Owned by Lee A. Pearson and his daughter, the Crook County dog uncovered the murder weapon in the "celebrated Beulah Limerick case" in Washington, D.C. The story about the case appeared in *True Detective* magazine. Grease-ball gained additional fame when he performed tricks at President Franklin D. Roosevelt's Christmas party for children in 1936.

4. Bingo

Bingo, a border collie, was a finalist for "Dog Hero of the Year" in 1987. In April of 1987, when Bingo's owner, State Rep. Marlene Simons, was injured in a freak pickup accident, Bingo helped her maintain consciousness by licking her, barking and jumping in and out of the cab. Because of Bingo's encouragement, Simons was able to drive back to her ranch house. She was hospitalized for broken ribs and a damaged spleen following the wreck, but recovered.

5. Mandy

The brindle greyhound retired from the Colorado race tracks and was adopted by a Laramie family. Mandy escaped from her new owners and stayed at large for almost a year from May, 1991, to April, 1992. The animal survived by eating from area garbage cans while she frustrated local animal control officers trying to recapture her. Mandy was finally captured near Washington Park, examined by a veterinarian and then returned to her Laramie home.

6. Coup

Coup, a black Labrador, was the first North American avalanche rescue dog to find a buried skier. She became famous in 1992 when she found skier Drew Dunlap who was buried for 90 minutes in a Green River Bowl avalanche. Jackson Hole ski patrolman Jerry Balint was Coup's owner. In Feb. 1993, Coup was trampled to death by a moose cow, and buried near Jackson in a ski patrol ceremony.

7. Jim, the Wonder Dog

The dog was well-known in the 1930s for his "psychic powers." When the dog, from Marshall, Missouri, performed with his owner in Kemmerer, the local newspaper gave the dog his nickname, "the Wonder Dog." A statue of the dog stands in downtown Marshall, noting that Jim received his nickname in Wyoming.

6 Items About Elk

1. Jackson Elk Herd

The largest elk herd in America lives in Wyoming. The Jackson elk herd numbered 10,000 in 1990 and 11,600 in 2010. Wyoming ranked fifth in U. S. elk population with 71,000 in 1987.

2. Poachers

Rangers arrested a man in Yellowstone in 1902 for poaching 25 pairs of elk antlers. Soon after, the B.P.O.E. Elks abolished antlers as the emblem for their clubs because poachers often sold their illegal gains to local lodges.

3. Antler Sales

Since 1967, elk antlers retrieved from the National Elk Refuge have been sold by Boy Scouts. The scouts keep twenty percent of the proceeds while the rest goes back to the elk refuge. The sale averaged 50 cents per pound. In 1989, the record price of $14.07 per pound was reached. Purchasers included collectors, hobbyists and some Asians who sell ground up antlers in the Far East as aphrodisiacs. There were 111 bidders from 25 states and one foreign country in 1995 who bought 9,567 pounds for $93,295. The 9,335 pounds sold in 1996 brought in $91,684 or $9.82 per pound.

4. Wendell, the Trophy Elk

"Wendell" hangs on the wall of the Chugwater soda fountain. The trophy elk, named for the hunter who shot him, is a town favorite--so much so that if the fountain ever closes, Wendell goes to the local museum.

5. World's Largest Elkhorn Arch

Arching over Main Street in Afton, it is a favorite photo spot.

6. Sale of Elk Antler Arch, Jackson

One of the elk antler arches on Jackson Town Square was sold at auction on May 22, 2007. Purchaser was Jerry Johnson of Jackson who outbid a Salt Lake City interior designer by paying $51,000 for the arch. Proceeds of the sale went to the Rotary Club. A new arch, assembled from antlers purchased from the Boy Scouts, was put in its place.

3 Cases of "Moving" Elk

1. Game wardens made the first attempt in Wyoming to relocate elk in 1910 when a shipment of elk was made to the Big Horn Mountains from Jackson Hole. Of the 28 elk

---

Myrtle Gunderson owned Tie Siding for 41 years. She bought the "town" in 1922 when it was moved one mile west of its original location. She sold Tie Siding in 1963 to L. P. Westbrook who then sold the town in 1974.

loaded in railroad cars for the trip from St. Anthony, Idaho, to Sheridan, all but three survived the three-week journey.

2. In 1911, elk were transplanted from Jackson Hole to the Glendo area and to northern Albany County. Others were sent to the Black Hills of South Dakota in December of 1913.

3. From 1892 to 1938, 4,914 Yellowstone elk were shipped to zoos, Indian reservations, private ranches and game preserves in 38 states. Thirty-one elk were sent to the National Zoo in Washington, D.C., four to the national zoo of Argentina, and several hundred to Canadian provincial parks.

Sightings of Black-Footed Ferrets (Mustela nigripes)

1. One was captured near the Cheyenne train depot (1877)

2. Two were found near Cheyenne, another near Newcastle (1895)

3. Several were seen near Beulah, Manville, Lusk and Laramie (1920s)

4. A dead ferret was found near Leo, Carbon County (1972)

5. A Meeteetse woman, Lucille Hogg, noticed that her dog was carrying the carcass of a dead ferret. From there, a ferret colony was found near Meeteetse (September, 1981)

4 Zoos with Wyoming Black-footed Ferrets (1993)

1. Cheyenne Mountain Zoo, Colorado Springs (18 ferrets)

2. Louisville Zoo, Kentucky (22)

3. Henry Doorly Zoo, Omaha, Nebraska (49)

4. Phoenix Zoo, Arizona (12)

In September, 1991, black-footed ferrets were reintroduced into the wild by the Wyoming Game and Fish Department. The first release site was in the Shirley Basin area. A number of reintroductions followed, including one in northwestern Colorado by the U. S. Fish and Wildlife Service in October, 1998.

Four Places Where Black-footed Ferrets Were Reintroduced into the Wild

1. Conata Basin, S. D., 250 animals (2008)

2. Two areas in Wyoming, 223.

3. Aubrey Valley, Ariz., 100.

4. Grasslands National Park, Saskatchewan, Canada, 34.

Famous Wyoming Cats

1. Monster

A frequent visitor to Jackson's Town Square, Monster was famous for trying to keep the square dog-free. Born in Ohio, Monster was owned by Michael Dettmer. In 1995, the cat was diagnosed with a brain tumor. After operations and medical expenses that exceeded $4,000, Monster died just short of his 15th birthday on Sept. 18, 1995.

2. Cubby

A cat found by Phil Roberts in Medicine Bow became the official mascot of the *Wyoming Almanac* in 1989. Cubby, a large black, polydactyl cat, enjoyed riding in motor vehicles. He rode round-trip to Seattle several times and made frequent trips around Wyoming. He died at the age of 17 in 2003.

"The grey wolf and coyote abound, the latter coming close to the camp at night in search of offal. Game is abundant, immense herds of antelope and elk can be found within a few miles of the fort and black-tailed deer and mountain sheep are also plentiful." Post Surgeon's report, Fort Fred Steele, 1870

HORSES

1st wild horse refuge in U. S: Pryor Mountain Wild Horse Range, north of Lovell., established 1968.
1st Wyoming-owned horse to run in the Kentucky Derby: Lusty Latin, 2002. The horse was owned by Joey and Wendy Platts of Lyman.

Some Famous Wyoming Horses

1. Dapple Dan
The gray horse from Company C was the only army survivor of the Fetterman Fight near Fort Phil Kearny in December, 1866.

2. Grey Eagle
The other horse figuring in the Fetterman Fight, Grey Eagle, was owned by Col. Henry Carrington, commander at Fort Phil Kearny. According to myth, Grey Eagle carried John "Portugee" Phillips from Fort Phil Kearny to Fort Laramie in freezing cold in December, 1866. The horse was said to have died in front of Old Bedlam at Fort Laramie on Christmas night at the end of the grueling 240-mile ride. In actuality, Grey Eagle probably never left Fort Phil Kearny. In fact, he was ridden by Col. Carrington two days after Phillips' departure. No single horse carried Phillips the entire distance. Records show he changed horses several times at ranches and stage stations along the route.

3. Old Blue
A popular children's book was written about this dependable old cow pony. The horse worked on ranches in Laramie County. The marker on his grave on the Wyoming line between Cheyenne and Fort Collins reads: "Erected to the memory of Old Blue—the best old cow pony that ever pulled on a rope, by the cowpunchers of the 7XL outfit. Rest in peace."

4. Muggins
Also a working cow pony, Muggins later appeared in several silent western films. The Wyoming horse died in Los Angeles and was buried at the Los Angeles Union Stockyards where a marker was erected to his memory. Years later, his remains were dug up, his head removed and stuffed by a taxidermist. The head is now part of the permanent collections of the Wyoming State Museum.

5. Steamboat
One of the best known bucking horses of all time, Steamboat was known as the "horse that couldn't be ridden." He is said to have been the inspiration for the emblem on the Wyoming license plate. Raised by Frank Foss, the animal struck his nose while he was being branded and broke a small piece of the bone. Sam Moore of the Swan Company bought the horse, trimmed away the protruding bone and the horse was left with a peculiar whistle. Jimmy Danks told a Swan foreman that the animal "sounds like a steamboat," hence the name. Ironically, Danks' brother Clayton Danks won the world championship at Cheyenne Frontier Days in 1907 by riding Steamboat. The horse made his first public appearance in a Denver rodeo in 1901. Steamboat performed at an Irwin Brothers show at Salt Lake City in 1914. A lightning storm spooked the horses held in a wire enclosure after the show. In the melee, Steamboat was cut by the wire. He was returned to Cheyenne, but the injury caused blood poisoning from which he died.

6. Midnight
The legendary bucking horse was known as the hardest bronc to ride during the 1930s. It is said that the horse had been raised by a female schoolteacher who had ridden him to

---

Khadefy Skoal, an 11-yr-old gelding, was the top bareback bucking horse at 1994 National Finals Rodeo held in Las Vegas. The horse was owned by Hank and Lori Franzen, Wright, Wyo.

school daily before selling him to rodeo stockmen Vern Elliott and Ed McCarty. After a long career on the rodeo circuit, Midnight was retired in 1933, but reactivitated soon after for a rodeo season which included shows in England. He died in 1937. Buried near Platteville, Colo., the horse's body was exhumed in 1966 and reburied on the grounds of the Cowboy Hall of Fame in Oklahoma City.

7. Five Minutes to Midnight

Another great bucking horse, Five Minutes to Midnight was once called the "greatest athlete I've ever seen" by Curt Gowdy, Wyoming-born sportscaster. The horse's bucking career began when he was a four-year-old. The times he was ridden can be counted on one hand. Pete Grubb rode him successfully at Cheyenne Frontier Days in 1939. At the horse's last appearance at Cheyenne in 1942, he was ridden to the buzzer by Ralph Collier. Five Minutes to Midnight remained active on the rodeo circuit for a total of 17 years until his retirement in 1945. He died in 1946 and was buried next to Midnight near Platteville, Colo. Like his predecessor, Five Minutes to Midnight's body also was reinterred at the Cowboy Hall of Fame in the middle 1960s.

8. Rip Van Winkle

The greatest bucking horse in the history of Sheridan County, Rip Van Winkle was owned by Don Iddings. It is said that the legendary horse was "never rode."

9. Ragalon

Renamed "Wyoming" by owner Theodore Roosevelt, Ragalon was a gift to the president from citizens of Douglas. Roosevelt rode the horse on his celebrated ride from Laramie to Cheyenne in 1903. The horse was shipped East after the ride to pastures near the president's home on Long Island.

10. Teddy

Teddy, a Cody area horse, won the Evanston-Denver horse race in 1907. A working cow pony, Teddy was regionally famous for his endurance.

11. Sir Barton

Sir Barton was a thoroughbred horse that was the first-ever Triple Crown winner (Kentucky Derby, Preakness, Belmont Stakes), in 1919. Born in Lexington, Ky., in 1916, the horse was sold to Cmdr. J. K. L. Ross of Canada in 1918. When he was a three-year-old in 1919, he won the Triple Crown, eight more races and was named "Horse of the Year." He was the last Triple Crown winner until 1930. After being defeated in a match race in 1920 against the younger Man o' War, Sir Barton was retired and sold back to an American. In 1933, he ended up at Fort Robinson, Neb., as stud for army horses. There, he was purchased by Dr. Joseph Hylton of Douglas who brought Sir Barton to his ranch on LaPrele Creek. The horse remained there until his death in 1937 at age 21. A statue, depicting Sir Barton, stands in Washington Park, Douglas, near where the remains were transferred from the burial site on Hylton's ranch.

12. Brigham

Buffalo Bill Cody named his first horse, c. 1868, for Mormon leader Brigham Young. Years later, Cody rode two other horses in his shows. One was named Isham. The other, Cody's last horse, was named McKinley, in honor of President William McKinley.

13. Sitting Bull's gray circus horse

William F. Cody presented the handsome gray horse to Sitting Bull when the Sioux medicine man left Cody's Wild West Show in the late 1880s. On Dec. 15, 1890, when Indian police came to Sitting Bull's home to arrest him for his part in the so-called "ghost dances," gunfire erupted. As legend has it (even though evidence for it does not exist), trained to respond to the sound of rifle shots, the horse went to his haunches and began performing tricks while Sitting Bull and seven of his followers died in the hail of bullets. Six police also died in the gun battle.

14. Gypsy

The name belonged to a long series of horses ridden over a 50-year period by pioneer eastern Wyoming stockman R. S. Van Tassell. He was still riding a "Gypsy" when he was in his 80s.

15. Babe

The black and white Shetland, owned by Velda and Wayne Childers, Goshen County, lived to the age of 52, a record age for a horse. Born in April 1906, in South Dakota, the horse was bought by the Childers' in 1936 from an owner who had abused her. They nursed Babe back to health. She lived until June 14, 1958.

16. The Spanish Mustang (breed)

The first registry for the line of horses was founded by Bob Brislawn and Larry Richard in Crook County in 1957. The Spanish Mustang Registry was still being kept by Brislawn at the time of his death in 1979.

17. Foolish Pleasure

The 1975 winner of the Kentucky Derby was purchased by Ron Vanderhoef in 1993. The horse was brought to Vanderhoef's Horseshoe Ranch near Dayton where the 19-year-old horse enjoyed retirement until his death in 1994. At the height of his fame, Foolish Pleasure finished second at both the Belmont Stakes and the Preakness following his Derby win. As a two-year-old colt, he ran a match race against Ruffian in which Ruffian broke her leg and had to be destroyed.

5 Famous Wyoming Rides

1. John "Portugee" Phillips' ride to Fort Laramie, 1866

Born Manuel Felipe Cardoso in the Azores, Phillips came from Montana to Fort Phil Kearny in September, 1866. A prospector, he intended to winter there and then return to the Big Horns to hunt for gold. On Dec. 21, 1866, Capt. William Fetterman and 80 others were lured into an ambush at Lodge Pole Ridge near the fort. Post commander Col. Henry Carrington hired Phillips and another man, Daniel Dixon, to ride the 240 miles to Fort Laramie for help. Even though he was riding under a full moon, probably the brightest at any point during the century, the snow and cold temperatures forced Phillips to change horses frequently along the route. He arrived at his destination four days later on Christmas Day, at 10 a.m. The ride became legend and in 1922, the first reference was made to Phillips' use of a single horse, Grey Eagle. Evidence shows, however, that Grey Eagle, Carrington's horse, never left Fort Phil Kearny during those four days.

2. Joe Rankin's ride to Rawlins, 1879

Rankin guided the army expedition from Fort Fred Steele to the White River Ute Reservation in Colorado, the site of an Indian uprising. After the two companies of soldiers were surrounded and their commander, Major T. T. Thornburgh, was killed, Rankin rode through the Indian lines for help. His own horse had been killed so he took a cavalry mount and completed the 150-mile trip in 27 1/2 hours. Soon after Rankin brought word of the troubles, soldiers lifted the siege. Nathan Meeker, the reservation agent, was among the victims in the incident. Along with working as a guide, Rankin operated a livery stable in Rawlins with his brother. In 1890, Rankin was appointed U. S. Marshal for Wyoming. He served four years, moved to Ogden, Utah, and then, to California. He died in San Diego in 1919.

3. Frank Buchanan's ride to Casper, 1889

Buchanan was a cowboy employed along the Sweetwater River when he witnessed the lynching of James Averell and Ella Watson (Cattle Kate) on July 20, 1889. The masked lynchers spotted Buchanan who had watched from hiding 100 yards away. He managed to elude capture and rode to Casper to report the incident to law officers. Three days after the lynching, six men were arrested and charged with the crime, but they were released soon after because the chief witness, Buchanan, had mysteriously disappeared. Some people believed Buchanan was kidnapped while others thought he was paid off to leave the territory. No trace of him was ever found.

4. Jack Flagg's ride to Buffalo, 1892

Flagg, a Buffalo rancher, was in a buggy with his son on their way to a political convention in Douglas when they happened on the Invaders' siege of the KC ranch cabin. The Invaders had Nate Champion and Nick Ray trapped inside and were shooting at the cabin. Flagg and his young son unhitched the horses from the buggy and eluded attempts by riders to stop them. They raced back to Buffalo to spread the alarm. By the time the Invaders had killed Ray and had set fire to the cabin, smoking out Champion and shooting him to death, the citizens of Buffalo were armed and ready to repulse the Invaders. Flagg bought a paper in Buffalo and, later, sold his interest. He moved to Nevada where he died in 1925.

5. "Jimmy the Tough's" ride, Tubb Town's main street, c. 1889

"Jimmy" was one of the wildest prostitutes in the wide-open town. She rode down Main Street in the middle of a summer day clad only in her long hair. She apparently made the ride to win a substantial bet. Tubb Town was established in 1889, but residents soon moved to the thriving nearby town of Newcastle and Tubb Town disappeared.

Two Mountain Lions

1. Sublette County mountain lion

In October, 1995, John Stach of Pinedale wounded a bull elk near Mulligan Park in Sublette County. As he reached the elk, he noticed large tracks in the snow. While he was dressing the elk, he looked around and saw a mountain lion staring at him from about ten feet away. He fired a warning shot and lion kept moving toward him. Fragments from a second shot killed the animal. Strach had the carcass of the 180-pound mountain lion stuffed and displayed in the Museum of the Mountain Man in Pinedale.

2. Sheridan area mountain lion

In January, 2000, a mountain lion weighing 81 pounds was killed near the Sheridan airport. The animal was approximately two years old.

One Famous Wyoming Mule

Bill Nye's mule is the only animal known to have a Wyoming newspaper named for him. Boomerang was so named because every time Nye tried to get rid of him, he kept coming back. The *Laramie Boomerang* claims the distinction of being the only newspaper in America named for a mule.

Two Pig Stories

1. Art Brozett, a Frenchman, worked as a harness and saddlemaker for Jack Kirwin in Douglas in 1919. He fashioned a set of miniature harness for a team of pigs, trained two pigs to the harness and hitched them to a tiny wagon. The unusual team and wagon was a big hit at the Wyoming State Fair of 1919 and it was frequently photographed.

2. "The county commissioners authorize us to say that they will pay a bounty of $1 each for every hog caught running at large in the streets of this city, which shall be driven into the yard back of Wright's Harness shop on 2nd Street." --*Laramie Sentinel, 1872.*

The annual Jake Clark's Mule Days auction and rodeo in Ralston, Park County, hosted visitors from 28 states in 2009. The event started in 1997 as an all-mule rodeo. By 2010, the five-day festival included mulemanship classes and various competitive events.

Prairie Dogs

1. During the fall and winter of 1934, officially sanctioned "prairie dog hunts" were held in six Wyoming counties with bounties from the animals used to pay "poor relief" to the nearly one-fifth of the state's population on welfare. Such drives were held in Laramie, Platte, Converse, Niobrara, Campbell and Crook counties. In Natrona, Converse, Carbon, Sweetwater, Lincoln and Campbell counties, ground squirrel drives were held during this same years to supplement relief.

2. "Lander Lil" is the name of the weather-predicting prairie dog--the western equivalent of Pennsylvania's "Punxsutawney Phil." Like Phil, Lander Lil predicts on Feb. 2.

One "Rabbit Race"

As part of Medicine Bow Days in Medicine Bow, wild rabbits were caught, put under cardboard boxes and then released in a circle chalked onto the ground. The rabbit running outside the circle first was the winner. All returned to the wild. The event was terminated in the late 1980s as a result of protests from animal rights' groups.

Three Wyoming Encounters with Whales

1. Narrow Escape

In April, 1996, Casper attorney Frank Chapman and his two children were fishing in Mexican waters when their chartered boat was smashed by a gray whale. The three and two crew members had minor injuries. The boat, although damaged, did not sink. A fishing boat rescued them a few minutes after the mishap.

2. Arctic Tragedy

Four bicyclists, Sharon Kava, Brad Humphrey, Michael and Daniel Moe, had just become the first ever to cycle across the Barnes Ice Cap in the Arctic when the boat in which they were riding was overturned by a whale. Kava and the Moe brothers were from Laramie; Humphrey was from Douglas. All died in the freak mishap in the Arctic Ocean.

3. Whale of San Clemente

The 1,286-lb. embalmed animal was displayed in Rock Springs Aug. 22-23, 1932. It took 38 barrrels of embalming fluid to preserve the animal. The railroad fare to haul the whale carcass equalled the fare for 18 1/2 people.

8 Wolf Stories

1. Wolf Carnage

The Thorn brothers of Sundance killed 79 wolves in one week in May, 1897. Employed as wolfers by the Standard Cattle Company, the two men earned $4 per pelt in bounties. In the two-year period, 1897-1898, the state paid bounties on 4,281 wolf pelts. In the 11 years to 1908, an additional 10,819 bounties were paid. Wolves were extinct in most of Wyoming by 1910.

2. Hungry Wolves

The winter of 1897 was difficult for wolves in the Big Horn Basin. Heavy snows made hunting difficult and the animals were left to picking off dogs from area ranches. On January 18, rancher Shap O'Mara rode from Shell Creek to Hyattville. Just as he emerged from a draw, two immense wolves were staring him in the face. He stopped his horse to look more closely and seven more wolves appeared just below the hill from him. He dismounted and threw a large rock at them. As the rock tumbled down the hill, the wolves snapped at it, but it did not divert their attention from O'Mara and his frightened horse. The wolves followed him for three miles until finally giving up.

3. Up a Telegraph Pole

A trainman on the Saratoga-Encampment run in 1900 came upon a man clinging to a telegraph pole and waving his arms frantically. The conductor stopped the train and discovered the man was a trackwalker who had been chased by five large wolves. The trackwalker claimed the animals were right at his heels when he reached the pole. "I don't know how I got up the pole," he said. "It was wet and smooth, but I got there and would have been there yet if the engine hadn't come along." The newspaper report of the incident called it "one of the most clever feats in western pole climbing."

4. Oregon Traveler's View

Hastings' 1845 *Emigrants Guide to Oregon and California* described the wolves in Wyoming: "The cause of there being such an abundance of all the different kinds of wolves is, perhaps, that they are never killed...[travelers] do not kill them, because they are entirely worthless, and because the people in that country have not a superabundance of ammunition. In traveling through the valleys of this section, you will pass many hundreds of them during the day, which appear to evince no timidity, but with heads and tails down, in their natural crouching manner, they pass within a few rods of you."

5. Dubious Wolf Story

An old trapper told about his experience with wolves. He claimed that a pack of wolves sent him up the closest tree. The trapper claimed he waited all night while the two dozen wolves circled the tree, quarreling among themselves. As time passed, they began devouring one another. Soon, two dozen were reduced in number to a dozen and then to just six. When morning came, there was only one wolf left standing below the tree. "He was so fat from eating up the ones who had eaten the others, etc., that I didn't even have to run to get away from him," the trapper asserted.

6. Ouch!

Jackson Newell came to Wyoming in 1876 to trap and prospect in the Laramie Peak area with his brother. Newell had a long, flowing, gray beard. One day while trapping wolves and beaver near Horseshoe Creek, he was setting the trap when it suddenly snapped shut, catching his whiskers. Unable to release himself, he walked six miles to his home carrying the trap in one hand and his rifle in the other, muttering some strong words. *Source: Guy Newell, Sr., as told by Vera Dunham in Pages from Converse County's Past. (Casper, 1988), p. 422*

7. Wolf reintroduction in Yellowstone

In 1995 U. S. Fish and Wildlife Service officials captured 29 wolves in Canada and released 14 of them in Yellowstone (and the rest in Idaho's Frank Church Wilderness Area). The wolves were released from two pens in the Lamar Valley. The two Yellowstone packs had a combined total of nine pups born during 1995. One of 14 reintroduced wolves from Canada was found dead on a highway near Daniel on Feb. 11, 1996. By the summer of 1996, of the first 29 wolves reintroduced into the Yellowstone area, one had been shot and another had been run over by a delivery truck in Yellowstone. In 1996, more wolves were transplanted to Yellowstone from Canada and released from the Lamar Valley site and from two new release pens at Black Hill Plateau and from near Nez Perce Creek.

8. Wolf sightings in Yellowstone, pre-reintroduction

More than 160 people reported seeing a wolf in Yellowstone during 1993. A Yellowstone biologist said, however, that when physical evidence was present--in 33 reports--it turned the park visitors saw coyotes, not wolves. In 1992, 60 reports were filed and 24 reports were made in 1991. By 2000, reports were common.

Of the 4,522,000 sheep on Wyoming ranges in 1907, 723,426 grazed on lands in Natrona County.

ARCHAEOLOGY

Most sites excavated in Wyoming by an archaeologist: Probably Dr. George Frison, University of Wyoming professor of anthropology. Former state archaeologist. Dr. George Gill, current state archaeologist Dr. Mark Miller, and Dr. Charles Reher of the university have excavated numerous Wyoming sites, too.

Some Significant Archaeological Sites in Wyoming

1. Agate Basin site (Niobrara County)

Discovered by rancher William Spencer in 1916, the site was excavated by the Smithsonian (1942 and 1961) and the University of Wyoming (1959, 1975-80). The site contains several related paleo-Indian temporary camps.

2. Altithermal Sand Dune site (Sweetwater County)

Excavations were made by archaeologists from Western Wyoming College in the early 1980s. The site was a plant collecting and processing site used up to 7,000 years ago.

3. Black's Fork site (southwestern Wyoming)

Found in the early 1930s by area ranchers, the site was studied by Denver archaeologist E. B. Renaud who found thousands of artifacts on top of the ground from 1935 to 1939. Because the artifacts were found on the surface and not excavated, some experts argue that the sites do not reveal a clear date of origin.

4. Wardell site (Sublette County)

The site, northeast of Big Piney, provided the first evidence of box and arrow use in bison hunting from around 500 A. D. E. B. Renaud, who studied the Black's Fork site, excavated the Wardell site in the late 1930s.

5. Casper site (Natrona County)

Discovered by two couples (Dave and Jamie Egolf, Mr. and Mrs. Roderick Laird), the site is on the west edge of Casper near the Interstate highway. A bison trap used by people for killing and butchering some 10,000 years ago, it was excavated by the University of Wyoming in the early 1970s.

6. Colby site (Washakie County)

Mammoth remains were found at the site as early as 1907, but the site was first investigated by archaeologists from the University of Wyoming in 1974-75. Evidence of human habitation as long ago as 11,000 years was discovered as well as 463 mammoth bones. Site materials, many excavated by Dr. George Frison, are featured in the new Washakie County Museum and Cultural Center opened May 14, 2010 on the eastern edge of Worland.

7. Finley site (Sweetwater County)

The site near Eden was discovered in the 1930s by O. M. Finley. In the spring of 1940, Harold J. Cook of Agate, Nebraska, found several Yuma points at the site, the first time they had been found in situ. Twenty-four projectile points, called "Eden" points, were found with Pleistocene mammal bones. University of Pennsylvania and Nebraska State Museum scientists also excavated the site. Archaeologists from the University of Wyoming found materials at nearby locations from 1971-73.

8. Frederick-Hell Gap site (Platte County)

The Guernsey area site was found by a University of Wyoming student in the 1950s

---

The Washakie County Museum and Cultural Center was dedicated on May 14, 2010. The Worland museum contains significant exhibits of archaeological sites in the Big Horn basin as well as historical displays on early Worland and county history.

who found a projectile point in a gully and reported the find to the State Archeologist. Cynthia and Henry Irwin, archaeologists form Harvard, studied the site from 1958 to 1965. On March 3, 1988, it was named a state archaeological site, marking the occupation of a community of nomadic people who lived there about 12,000 years ago.

9. Hanson site (Big Horn County)

Milford and Imogene Hanson of Cody discovered the site in the late summer of 1973. Flint tools, probably used for woodworking and butchering, were found by University of Wyoming archaeologists there in the middle 1970s.

10. Horner site (Park County)

James Allen of Cody found the site east and north of town on July 1, 1939. The bison kill site was occupied on a short-term basis by nomadic peoples more than 10,000 years ago. Princeton and Smithsonian teams excavated from 1949 to 1952 and a University of Wyoming group did additional excavation in 1978-79.

11. Lawrence site (Teton County)

Slim Lawrence of Jackson found the site, one of 300 identified in the area as having been occupied by Sheepeater Indians. No site indicates habitation later than 1640 A. D. Now submerged under the north end of Jackson Lake, the site was excavated in 1977 when Jackson Lake was very low due to extreme drought.

12. Medicine Lodge Creek site (Big Horn County)

Humans frequented the site for more than 10,000 years. Layers indicate almost continuous habitation. Petroglyphs on nearby sandstone cliffs tell stories. The site, still being excavated, is owned by the State of Wyoming.

13. Medicine Wheel (25 miles west of Burgess Junction, US 14A)

First discovered by present-day people in the 1880s, the Medicine Wheel, at an elevation of almost 10,000 feet, has been the subject of numerous theories. Some Wyoming archaeologists believe the 75-foot diameter "wheel" of stones was done about 1770 as a monument to an unknown chief. Others say the 28 spokes indicate the ancient builders meant it for a calendar. Still others contend it is remnants of an Indian celebration site. Theories about construction by Druids, Aztecs and extraterrestrial beings have been discounted by most experts. Astronomer John Eddy showed that the wheel is aligned to the position of the rising sun at the summer solstice. In 1970, the site became a National Historic Landmark. In the early 1990s, Native American groups lobbied for a 2 1/2 mile boundary around the site to protect it from timbering encroachment. At the same time, Forest Service officials planned a visitors' center at the urging of community boosters in nearby Lovell. The Indian groups asked the Forest Service to withdraw the multiple use status of nearby lands. On Dec. 6, 2001, a federal judge ruled in favor of a historic preservation plan for the site. The 10th Circuit Court of Appeals upheld the judge's decision.

14. Mummy Cave (Park County)

Discovered by Bob Edgar of Cody, the site is west of Cody along the North Fork of the Shoshone River. In 1963, Edgar was joined by Dr. Harold McCracken and W. R. Wedel in excavating the site. Work continued the next year with funding from the National Geographic Society. Excavations show the site has been inhabited as long as 9,000 years. The cave, cut into the wall of Blackwater Creek, contained the desiccated body of an adult male interred 1,230 years ago, wrapped in a mountain sheepskin garment.

Dr. Douglas Owsley is a forensic anthropologist for the Smithsonian. A graduate of the University of Wyoming and a former resident of Lusk, he has worked at Historic Williamsburg and at other historic locations and has been featured frequently in such publications as Smithsonian and National Geographic. A book about his career, No Bones Unturned, was wrritten by Jeff Benedict.

15. Obsidian Cliffs (Yellowstone National Park)

Artifacts made from the material at the site have been identified as far east as Ohio and Michigan and as far south as Oklahoma, indicating a lively village-to-village trade in the unusual stone. Dr. James B. Griffon of the University of Michigan conducted neutron activation tests on such items and conclusively proved that the artifacts from far afield originated at Obsidian Cliffs.

16. Spanish Diggings (Platte-Goshen-Niobrara Counties)

Cowboys and travelers in the 19th century discovered the site, mistakenly believing it was Spanish in origin, hence the name. In actuality, the site was where prehistoric people quarried stone for arrow tips.

17. Torrington site (Goshen County)

A highway blasting crew detonated a blast in 1938 at the site and discovered human bones protruding from the crevices. Much of the site was destroyed by the blast but remains of four individuals, apparently from the Pleistocene period, were recovered. W. W. Howells and colleagues excavated the site in the late 1930s.

18. Union Pacific Mammoth Kill site (Carbon County)

Ivan Hayes was operating a dragline on the Union Pacific right-of-way in 1960 when he uncovered huge bones. Later, the University of Wyoming Anthropology Department received funds from the National Geographic Society to conduct field work at the site where prehistoric people killed and skinned huge mammoths. Many of the materials were located by archaeologists Henry and Cynthia Irwin and are on display in the Peabody Museum, Harvard.

19. Vore Buffalo Jump (Crook County)

Discovered by interstate highway surveyors in 1969, the site was donated to the University of Wyoming by the Vore family in 1989. The site is the resting place of the bones of more than 20,000 bison that were stampeded off the cliffs by Native people as early as 3,500 years ago. It is one of the largest bison kill sites in the United States. The site was featured in *National Geographic Magazine*. A foundation opened the first phase of a visitor center at the site in 2009. (Fund-raising continues for site improvements. For information, write: P. O. Box 369, Sundance, WY 92729).

20. Yellowstone National Park sites

More than 500 prehistoric archaeological sites have been identified in Yellowstone, including several in Norris Geyser Basin and Lower and Upper Geyser Basins. A fire hearth dating to 2,950 B. C. was found at Rigler Bluffs near Corwin Springs.

2 Books About Wyoming Archaeology

1. Prehistoric Hunters of the High Plains. *(New York: Academic Press, 1978)*

Written by Wyoming's pre-eminent archaeologist George Frison, the book was issued in a second edition in 1991.

2.   Medicine Lodge Creek: Holocene Archaeology of the Eastern Big Horn Basin, Wyoming. *(Albuquerque, Clovis Press. 2007)*

The book was edited by George C. Frison and Danny N. Walker.

The Wyoming Archaeologist is a journal published by the Wyoming Archaeological Society. The journal began publication as *The Smoke Signal,* a monthly newsletter ,in 1958 . In 1961, it became a quarterly and, in 1982, semiannual journal. Members receive the journal as a benefitr of membership.of the Wyoming Archaeological Society, organized in 11 chapters around the state. Dale Wedel was society president in 2010 and Danny Walker was the managing editor of the journal.

ARCHITECTURE

1st non-native log cabin in Wyoming: Robert Stuart cabin, Bessemer Bend near Casper, built by the "reverse Astorians" in October, 1812.

1st building (non-log) in Wyoming: Portuguese houses, built by Antonio Mateo (Montero) between 1828 and 1834, 12 miles east of present-day Kaycee.

Oldest standing structure in Wyoming: "Old Bedlam," the bachelor officers' quarters at Fort Laramie, built in 1849.

Tallest structure in Wyoming (excluding communications towers): The chimney serving the first three units of the Dave Johnston Power Plant near Glenrock stands 500 feet high. The wind turbine near Medicine Bow, 262-foot tower and 391 feet high when blades are in vertical position, was constructed by Hamilton-Standard Company in 1982. The smokestack of the Holly Sugar factory in Torrington, 257 feet high, was the tallest in pre-World War II Wyoming.

Largest log structure in the world: Old Faithful Inn, built in 1904. The stone fireplace reaches a height of 85 feet, one of the tallest in America.

Most expensive home sold in Teton County: A log home near Jackson was listed in 2009 for $69.5 million. It was among Zillow's ten most expensive homes for sale in the United States. A house south of Wilson sold in 1995 for $7.5 million, a record for the county and the state to that time, but easily eclipsed during the next decade. Ten percent of all single-family homes sold in Jackson Hole in 1995 went for $1 million or more, up from six percent in 1994 and just one percent in 1991. By 2008, the average sale price for existing family home in Teton County was $457,326, up from the 1999 average of $374,882. There were 180 new homes built in 2006 and the average cost was $732,600.

1st escalator in Wyoming: 1st National Bank of Casper, 1958. In 2010, it was still the only operating public escalator in the state.

Marching Skyward: The Tallest Buildings in Wyoming

8 stories

The Gladstone Hotel, Casper, held the distinction as the tallest building in Wyoming from 1924 to 1965. The tallest man-made structure, however, was the 257-foot-high smokestack at the Holly Sugar factory in Torrington, constructed in the early 1920s.

12 stories

Two dormitories on the campus of the University of Wyoming are 12 stories tall and held the height mark until 1972. Official measurements indicated that even though both had the same number of floors, McIntyre Hall was a bit less than a foot taller than neighboring White Hall.

14 stories

The enclosed building housing the Jim Bridger Power Plant in Sweetwater County has been the tallest building in the state since 1972. The smokestacks are considerably taller.

1st Permanent Buildings in 5 Wyoming Towns*

1. Cheyenne

Built in July, 1867, by Judge J. R. Whitehead, the first permanent structure was located on the corner of what is now 16th and Pioneer.

Thomas Molesworth (1890-1977) is known for his distinctive furniture made in a Western style. In 1931 he started the Shoshone Furniture Company in Cody.

2. Sundance

Phil Falbaugh's cabin, built in 1879, was the first building.

3. Casper

The Demorest Home Restaurant was the first permanent structure in Casper. The restaurant was built on Center Street in 1888.

4. Rock Springs

Rock Spring Stage Station, built as a stage "swing" station for the Overland Stageline in 1862, existed before the town was established.

5. Buffalo

Ed O'Malley operated a lively place south of the site of Buffalo known as "Six Mile Ranch." He opened the "Lone Star" dance hall about 1879. The Johnson County Courthouse is on the site of O'Malley's Lone Star. The Trabing store was constructed of logs in the fall of 1879, the structure used for the next 30 years. In 1880, the first Occidental Hotel was built.   *Excluding military structures.*

Some Wyoming Structures Built by the PWA*

1. Arts and Sciences Building, University of Wyoming

2. Student Union Building, University of Wyoming

3. Natrona County Courthouse (1940)

4. Hot Springs County Courthouse (1938)

5. Guernsey State Museum

6. U. S. Post Office, Lusk

7. U. S. Post Office, Powell

8. U. S. Post Office, Riverton

9. Wheatland City Hall (built as the U. S. Post Office)

10. Fort Caspar complex (reconstruction)

11. Casper Mountain Road

12. NCHS Stadium, Casper

13. Anna Miller Museum, Newcastle (built as National Guard cavalry barn)

14. Muncipal golf course shelter, Buffalo

Thirty-three public schools in the state were built by the Public Works Administration as well as rodeo grounds, fences, roads, parks and other civic structures. The PWA was an integral part of Franklin Roosevelt's New Deal attempts to bring America out of the Great Depression. The construction costs were a welcome infusion into local economies.

Eileen Starr's Favorite Wyoming Historic Buildings from An Architectural Perspective*

1. Old Faithful Inn, Yellowstone

The inn, the largest log structure in the world, was designed by Seattle architect Robert Reamer.

2. Union Pacific Depot, Cheyenne

Designed in 1886 by Henry Van Brunt and Frank Howe of Kansas City, the building faces the State Capitol down Capitol Avenue in Cheyenne. Railroad president Charles Adams commissioned the structure's construction.

3. Sheridan Inn

Designed by Thomas Kimball of Omaha, the inn opened in 1893.

4. Natrona County High School, Casper

Designed by structural engineer Arthur Garbutt and draftsman-partner C. T. Weidner, the building was considered by some to be extravagant even though it was built when Casper was experiencing an oil boom. Stock scenes of the building appear on TV shows.

5. Cell Block A and the Administration Bldg., State Penitentiary, Rawlins

Cell Block A is definitely the scariest building in Wyoming! The design has been attributed to Walter E. Ware. The Salt Lake City architect also designed Laramie's Ivinson mansion.

6. Blyth and Fargo Store, Evanston

A great example of manufactured architecture-iron front.

The next four are examples of Folk/Vernacular Architecture (great craftsmanship):

7. Motley Barns, Albany County

The double barns are mirror images of each other where Motley, a crazed remittance man, attempted to domesticate elk so they could pull his sleigh and wagons. The interior of one of the barns has beautiful hand-crafted stalls supposedly constructed for the elk. Architecturally some of the barns on the Laramie Plains are rather unusual, if not rare, because of their piece-sur-piece construction and these barns are great examples of p-s-p construction.

8. New Fork Dance Hall, Sublette County

The false-front building was originally called the "Valhalla Dance Hall" following its construction in 1909.

9. Our Father's House, Ethete

The log church is located on the Wind River Indian Reservation.

10. Bath Ranch, Albany County

Also known as the Stone Ranch, the house was restored by members of the Bath family. The work earned a preservation prize from the Wyoming State Historical Society in 2004.

*Eileen Starr is the author of *Architecture in the Cowboy State, 1849-1940: A Guide. (Glendo: High Plains Press, 1992).* Formerly architectural historian, State Historic Preservation Office, State of Wyoming, Starr was a doctoral student in historic preservation at George Washington University when she compiled this list. She now lives and works in Kentucky.

Architects' Choice:
Best Designed Modern Buildings in Wyoming*

Public Buildings:
1. All-Events Center, Casper
2. Big Horn Canyon National Recreation headquarters, Lovell
3. Herschler State Office Building, Cheyenne
4. Sweetwater County Courthouse, Green River
5. Visitors' Center, Jackson

Commercial Buildings:
1. Guaranty Federal Savings and Loan, Casper
2. Husky Oil office building, Cody
3. Jackson State Bank, Jackson
4. Wyoming Machinery Company, Casper

Chain Canyon, north of Lovell, is said to have been a hideout for outlaws including Butch Cassidy.

Private Homes:

1. Quinn Blair house, Cody (only home in Wyoming designed by legendary architect Frank Lloyd Wright)
2. Dr. W. T. Close home, Big Piney (Close, a world authority on the Ebola disease, is the father of film star Glenn Close)
3. Governor's Mansion, Cheyenne (some other critics compare the modern design of the $800,000 structure to that of a chain motel complex)
4. F. E. Warren home, south of Cheyenne

Most Innovative Design:

1. Arena-Auditorium, Laramie
2. Big Horn Canyon National Recreation Area headquarters, Lovell
3. Cheyenne Obstetrics and Gynecology, 421 E. 17th St., Cheyenne
4. Westridge Elementary School, Rock Springs

Most Beautiful Buildings:

1. Buffalo Bill Historical Center, Cody
2. Cheyenne Civic Center
3. Herschler State Office Building, Cheyenne
4. Husky Oil headquarters, Cody
5. State Capitol, Cheyenne
6. Southwest Counseling Service office, Rock Springs
7. State Sanitarium, Basin
8. Visual Arts Building, Casper College
9. Young-at-Heart Senior Citizen Center, Rock Springs

The poll of Wyoming architects was conducted by Capitol Times magazine in 1983. The names of several buildings have been changed since the poll was taken.

8 Famous Demolished Buildings

1. Cheyenne Club

Built shortly after the club was organized in 1880, the structure was practically synonymous with the cattle baron era of the 1880s. After the disastrous winter of 1886-87, membership declined as fortunes evaporated. Ownership of the building went to the Cheyenne Industrial Club in 1909. In 1927 the organization changed its name to the Cheyenne Chamber of Commerce. The chamber's historic home was torn down in 1936 and replaced by a nondescript single-story brick office building.

2. Goose Egg Ranchhouse

The stone home, built in the 1880s, served as headquarters for the famed ranch. Author Owen Wister stayed there and the main ranch building was described in his fiction. The home was bulldozed in the summer of 1951.

3. Frewen's Castle

Built by British cattleman Moreton Frewen six miles east of Kaycee, it was modeled after Eastern hunting lodges. Like the Cheyenne Club, the building was a victim of declining fortunes. Following the severe decline in cattle prices and the winter of 1886-87, Frewen returned to England. The house eventually fell into ruin.

The American Heritage Center, designed by Santa Fe architect Antoine Predock, was featured on the cover of the December, 1993, issue of *Architecture* magazine. The writer said of the design: "Predock's building, which intensifies the landscape and Indian associations, seamlessly merges with them, becoming Wyoming rather than just about Wyoming and the West." The structure won another design award in 2000.

4. Hi Kelly House, Cheyenne

One of the numerous homes built in Cheyenne by "cattle barons" during the late 19th century, the ornate structure once stood across the street from the State Capitol. The site is now a parking lot.

5. Castle Dare

Built for cattleman Alexander Swan as a gift to his daughter on her marriage to R. S. Van Tassell, the house was designed by J. P. Julien. (Julien designed the macabre "Julien gallows" on which Tom Horn was hanged). When Swan was hit with financial reverses before the final payment was made, Julien took the house back and sold it to Cheyenne photographer/banker/con-man D. D. Dare. The high-living Dare occupied the house briefly before moving to San Diego to set up a second bank. When both Dare's Cheyenne bank and his San Diego one failed in 1892, allegedly as a result of Dare's swindles, Dare fled to the Middle East where he built a railroad in Palestine and sold rugs in Athens. He is said to have been killed by bandits in Armenia while he was buying rugs there about 1915. The house, which continued to carry Dare's name, eventually became the home of the Odd Fellows Lodge. It was razed in the 1960s, but the carriage house remained as offices for the county health department. In the summer of 1993, the county commission contracted with an out-of-state "house mover" to move the structure to make room for the new addition to the city-county building. Following countless unexplained delays and inept attempts at lifting the rock building, the county commission allowed the "house-mover" to tear the building down—and keep the moving fee!

6. Mondell House, Newcastle

The house was built in 1892 for Frank Mondell, long-time Wyoming congressman. Builders were Kilpatrick Brothers and Collins, pioneer Newcastle contractors. The only mansion in Newcastle, the structure was demolished to make way for the Weston County Hospital in the early 1950s. That hospital structure is now senior housing.

7. Woodruff Cabin, Hot Springs County

Built in 1871 of cottonwood logs, the structure was home to J. D. Woodruff (b. New York, 1846, d. Shoshoni, 1926), the first resident of what is now Hot Springs County. The first cabin built in the Big Horn Basin, the structure was located on what would become the headquarters of the Embar ranch, 26 miles west of Thermopolis on Owl Creek.

8. Leek's Lodge, east shore of Jackson Lake

Stephen N. Leek, photographer and naturalist, built the lodge between 1925 and 1927. He was a pioneer guide in the area and key figure in saving the Jackson elk herd. In 1996, the Park Service decided to demolish the lodge because it had fallen into severe disrepair.

11 Well-Known Wyoming Architects

1. George Rainsford

Rainsford came to Wyoming from New York. Trained as a civil engineer and architect, he designed more than 30 private homes in Cheyenne. He was best known as the architect of the Cheyenne Club (1881). He also designed the buildings for his Diamond Ranch near Chugwater which he built in 1878. Along with practicing architecture, Rainsford raised champion Morgan horses.

2. William Dubois (b. Cheyenne, 1879, d. 1953)

Dubois designed the east and west wings of the State Capitol, the Laramie County Courthouse, the main State Hospital building at Evanston, the Albany County Courthouse and the Half Acre Gym (both in collaboration with Wilbur Hitchcock), Hoyt and Merica

---

The University of the Wilderness bought the main lodge and several cabins at Snowy Range Camp, 40 miles west of Laramie on Wyo Highway 130, for $100 in 1981. The seller was the University of Wyoming.

Halls on the University of Wyoming campus, the orphanage at Torrington, the State Supreme Court building and high schools at Cheyenne (Old Central), Rawlins, Lander and Riverton.

3.-4. Leon Goodrich and Karl Krusmark

Goodrich worked for William Dubois until 1917 when he moved to Casper during the oil boom. A foundier of the Wyoming Chapter, American Institute of Architects, Goodrich designed the National Guard Armory in Casper and the Paul Stock house in Cody (1944). He collaborated with fellow Casper architect Karl Krusmark on schools and on the Natrona County Courthouse. Krusmark came to Casper as architect for the Midwest Oil Company.

5. Wilbur Hitchcock

When Hitchcock arrived in Laramie from his native South Dakota, he was seeking relief for his asthma. He had with him a hammer, a saw and $1 in his pocket. Following graduation from the University of Wyoming, he won the 1922 design competition for the original University of Wyoming Library (now the Aven Nelson building). Hitchcock designed three other campus buildings: the Engineering Building, McWhinnie Hall (former'ʸ called Graduate Hall) and, in collaboration with William Dubois, Half Acre Gym. A his best known works are the Ivinson Home for Ladies, the Cooper house and th   ʸy Range Lodge. Hitchcock was killed in a car accident in 1930 and his sons, C   ₁ and Eliot, carried on the architectural practice.

6. Frederic H. Porter

Porter's best known works were the First Presbyterian Church and the Boyd Building, both in Cheyenne, and the Carbon County Courthouse in Rawlins. Outside his architectural work, Porter was active in civic activities including the Cheyenne Little Theatre, where he designed and built elaborate stage sets.

7. F. W. Cooper

One of the state's first architects, Cooper owned a pioneer Cheyenne firm. He designed many Cheyenne homes in the 1870s and 1880s. His best known work was the Cheyenne Opera House, built in 1882 and destroyed by fire in 1902.

8. J. P. Julian

Julian was actually a civil engineer, but he designed a number of homes including "Castle Dare" in Cheyenne. Also, he invented the complicated gallows arrangement known as the "Julian gallows" on which many Wyoming criminals were executed.

9. Robert C. Reamer (b. Ohio, 1873, d. Seattle, 1938)

Reamer, a Seattle-based Pacific Northwest architect, gained fame for several important buildings in Yellowstone National Park. Old Faithful Inn (1902), Canyon Hotel (1910), and Roosevelt Arch (1902) near Gardiner, Montana, are his best known works. Later, he was architect for significant structures in Seattle where he practiced until his death in 1938.

10. D. W. Gibbs

Gibbs won the design competition for the Wyoming State Capitol. Despite the commission, Gibbs never lived in Wyoming. He was principal in an important architectural firm in Toledo, Ohio.

11. A. A. Anderson (b. 1846, d. 1940)

Born in New Jersey, Abraham Archibald Anderson came to Wyoming about 1883 from New York. Educated in private schools and in Paris, Anderson married Elizabeth Milbank (1850-1921), the daughter of a wealthy railroad tycoon. She became a renowned philanthropist for public health causes. An avid hunter and conservationist, Anderson was a friend of President Theodore Roosevelt who appointed him superintendent of the Yellowstone "forest reserves" in 1902. He had limited experience as an architect (his primary skill was painting), but he designed his own Palette Ranch headquarters, now known as Anderson Lodge, William Cody's Pahaska Teepee and a beaux arts building in New York.

Significant Wyoming Buildings Made of Logs

1. Gymnasium, Cowley

Built by the Public Works Administration (PWA) in 1936 as the community building, it is made of logs cut in the Pryor Mountains.

2. Willson Cabin, Lusk

The small cabin, donated to the DAR, was moved to the City Park and dedicated Oct. 10, 1929. It is one of the oldest buildings in Niobrara County, built by the pioneer Willson family about 1880.

3. Old Timer's Cabin, Douglas

The log structure was built by popular subscription in 1926 on the grounds of the Wyoming State Fair.

4. Old Faithful Inn

The biggest "log cabin" in the world, it was built in 1902 for $200,000.

5. Morris Cabin, South Pass City

In the summer of 1992, archaeologists continued to search for the foundation of the original cabin. The existing structure is a reconstruction of how Esther Hobart Morris' cabin might have looked. She was the world's first woman judge.

6. Charles Carter Cabin, Cody

Built in 1879, the structure may be the oldest standing building in the Big Horn Basin. It is among more than two dozen buildings moved since 1967 by Bob Edgar to Trail Town, west of Cody.

7. Pahaska Teepee, East Entrance to Yellowstone

"Longhair's Lodge" is a two-story structure made of lodgepole pine built for William F. Cody in 1903 as his hunting lodge. Among the famous visitors was the Prince of Monaco who stayed there during a hunt in the area in 1913.

8. Cunningham Cabin, Jackson

The cabin, the oldest standing building in Jackson Hole, was built in 1889 by James P. Cunningham. In 1893, a posse shot down horse thieves as they emerged from the cabin. The National Park Service restored the building in 1956. The cabin is located six miles south of Moran Junction.

9. Robert A. Miller Cabin, Jackson

Miller, the first supervisor of the Teton Division of the Yellowstone Timberland Reserve, built the cabin about 1900. The structure served as headquarters for the National Elk Refuge from 1912 to 1942.

10. Maude Noble Cabin, Menor's Ferry

The cabin was the site of the July 26, 1927, meeting which led to the creation of Grand Teton National Park.

11. Wapiti Ranger Station, Park County

The first ranger station built in the United States, the building served as headquarters for the oldest national forest in the United States, now Shoshone National Forest, created in 1891. The log headquarters was built by forest supervisor W. H. Pierce and remained in use throughout the 20th century.

12. Frank Chatfield Cabin, Sunlight Basin

Chatfield built the first cabin in Sunlight Basin in 1884. Remains of the cabin are still visible.

The main administration building at Tulane University is built of stone taken from a quarry south of Rawlins. The same stone was used to build the original main building at the Wyoming State Penitentiary, now the Wyoming Frontier Prison, in north Rawlins.

13. Quadra Dangle Square Dance club building, Laramie

Originally built in 1928 as a Union Pacific Railroad employees' clubhouse and named "Gray's Gables" for the company vice president Carl Gray, the structure was once on the eastern edge of Laramie. The structure was officially dedicated on May 20, 1929, by the Union Pacific Athletic Club. The Quadra Dangle dance club bought the building in 1949. By the late 1970s, the building was surrounded by housing. The street in front is called "Gray's Gables Road." The building was badly damaged by a tornado in 2008, but rebuilt.

14. Ranch A Lodge, Crook County

The log lodge, built at a cost of $300,000, with log outbuildings on 680 acres south of Beulah, was built by Chicago publisher Mo Annenberg. He first saw the site while on a fishing trip nearby and bought the 2,000 acres in 1932. In 1936, he heard about the Philadelphia Enquirer being up for sale while he was fishing at Ranch A. Later, after conviction for tax evasion, Annenberg was forced to sell the property when he was sent off to prison. His son Walter, rarely stayed at Ranch A. He later made a fortune publishing such magazines as *TV Guide*. Sold to former Gov. Nels Smith, Ranch A was later purchased by the federal government and used as a fish hatchery until 1980. In 1996, legislation transferred ownership to the State of Wyoming.

Some Interesting Wyoming Houses

1. Robert Stuart cabin, Bessemer Bend

What some have called the first building constructed by white Americans in Wyoming, the cabin was erected in October, 1812, by Stuart's party traveling east from Fort Astoria, Oregon. The roof of the structure was made into a raft the next month. Nothing remains of the structure.

2. "Old Bedlam," bachelor officers' quarters, Fort Laramie

The oldest frame building in Wyoming still standing, it was built in 1849, the year the army bought the fort. The house was nicknamed because of the wild antics of junior officers housed there. Capt. Charles King, a 19th century novelist, named one of his 50 novels, "Queen of Bedlam," after the old house. The two-story structure was restored during the past 50 years by the National Park Service.

3. "Big Teepee," Lost Cabin

The home of pioneer sheepman J. B. Okie, the structure was a modern mansion built miles from any large town. Starting in 1900, Okie built the 16-room mansion with the latest in refinements including flush toilets, tooled leather interior trim, chandeliers and tapestries. An aviary on the grounds housed rare birds. Flowers bloomed year-round in the greenhouse. The complex later included an oak-floored roller rink and a movie house. Okie drowned in 1930 in a nearby reservoir while he was hunting ducks. The house was occupied by Okie's son Van until 1945 when it was sold to the Spratt family. Burlington Resources purchased the property in late 1998 and, by 2010, the entire town was owned by Conoco/Phillips. In 1998, the firm built a gas plant nearby. In June 2010, part of the gas plant was leveled by an explosion and fire.

4. J. C. Penney house, Kemmerer

The restored single-story frame house where Penney lived at the time he began his first store, it has been restored and is open to the public. It is located along "the triangle" in downtown Kemmerer.

5. Trail End, Sheridan

Now a state historic site, the mansion, designed in Flemish revival style by Glenn Charles McAlister, was completed in 1914. Begun in 1908, the house was home to Sen.

The National Historic Trails Center overlooking Casper from north of the city was dedicated Aug. 9, 2002.

John B. Kendrick who made a fortune in ranching and oil, served as governor and, at his death, was completing his third term in the U. S. Senate.

6. Bradford Brinton Ranch, near Big Horn

Built for Malcolm Moncrieffe, the house is an example of a home built for English noblemen. Since 1960, the ranch has served as an art museum and gallery. The two-story frame house was built in 1893 and was home for Moncrieffe and his brother for 30 years. They sold horses to the British Army and raised highly regarded polo ponies. In 1923, businessman Bradford Brinton bought the ranch, expanded the house and added other buildings to house his extensive art collection. After his death in 1936, the ranch was owned by his sister. When she died in 1960, her will stipulated that it become a museum, open to the public. The museum holds some 600 works, including paintings by John James Audubon, Charles Russell, Frederic Remington and Bill Gollings.

7. Ivinson Mansion, Laramie

Edward Ivinson, pioneer Laramie banker, had the home built the year he ran for governor of Wyoming (1892). The structure served as a girls' school from 1921-1958. Later, it stood empty until 1972 when it was sold by the Episcopal diocese to the Laramie Plains Museum, Association, for $110,000. It became the main building housing the collections of the Laramie Plains Museum.

8. Cooper House, Laramie

The unusual Mission Revival-style home of a wealthy English family who held extensive ranching and mineral properties in Wyoming was built in 1921. It became the property of the University of Wyoming in the early 1980s and was in danger of demolition for a parking lot and Commerce and Industry building expansion. The building was saved and it now houses the University's American Studies program. An outbuilding, which once housed a raquetball court, served as the University's Visitor Center until June 2009.

9. Nagle Mansion, Cheyenne

One of the last examples of the "cattle baron" homes, once numerous in Cheyenne, the house was actually built for Erasmus Nagle, a prosperous merchant. For many years, it housed the local YWCA.

10. Lacey-Whipple House, Cheyenne

The building was owned successively by a merchant, a lawyer and a Greek social club. The structure was restored in the early 1980s and housed a restaurant.

11. Brooks Home, Casper

The home was built for B. B. Brooks, stockman and former governor (1905-1911). Constructed in 1923, the 12-room home remains a private residence.

12. Wolfensohn house, Jackson Hole

The 10,000-square-foot home of James Wolfensohn, the president of the World Bank from 1995-2005, was designed by architect Cesar Pelli and completed in the early 1990s.

13. LAK Ranchhouse, east of Newcastle

The "castle-like" stone building occasionally is occupied by the True family who own the ranch. The original ranch house began as a cabin constructed about 1877 which housed the ranch headquarters until 1924. The original owner of the ranch, J. C. Spencer, named the ranch for the initials of three Chicago investors who put up money for him to buy his first herd. Their names were Lake, Allerton and King.

14. A. A. Anderson Lodge

Built as a studio by the famed artist in 1890, six miles west of his Palette Ranch headquarters, restoration of the structure was begun in 1995 by the U. S. Forest Service. The building was featured on the PBS series *This Old House* in 1996. Because of the house's location, reconstruction had to be done solely with hand tools because no power tools were allowed in the wilderness area.

15. Elinore Pruitt Stewart Homestead, near Burnt Fork

The author of letters, later published as *Letters from a Woman Homesteader*, lived on a homestead near Burnt Fork. The original homestead building, constructed about 1909, still stands. It is on private land.

16. Brinkerhoff Lodge, Grand Teton National Park

Built as a vacation home, the structure was designed by Jan Wilding just at the end of World War II. Furnished with dozens of pieces of Thomas Molesworth furniture, in the years since it opened in 1946, it has achieved prominence as a vacation hideaway for public officials. In September 1978, President Jimmy Carter and his wife stayed there for six nights.

17. Ferris Mansion, Rawlins

The 21-room brick house, designed by Barber and Kluta of Knoxville, Tenn., was built in 1903 for George Ferris, successful miner and developer of the Grand Encampment Mining District in southern Carbon County. Ferris died in an accident before the house was completed, but his widow lived in the house until 1931.

18. Sullivan House, Casper

One of Casper's oldest and largest mansions, the three-story Sullivan house was built in 1909 for sheep rancher Patrick Sullivan. Sullivan received three lots on which to build the house from Joseph M. Carey, owner of the CY, with the stipulation that he build a house to attract other home owners. Sullivan was U. S. Senator from Wyoming in 1929.

19. Henning House, Casper

The house was built about 1920 for Welker F. Henning, a Kentucky-born plumber, who came to Casper in 1909 and is said to have been Casper's first millionaire. His wife and housekeeper lived there,, but Henning lived in the Henning Hotel in downtown Casper.

20. Historic Governors' Mansion, Cheyenne

Located on the corner of 21st and House Avenue, the building was designed by Omaha architect Charles Murdock in Colonial Revival style. Completed in the fall of 1904, the 2 1/2-story house with full basement and a separate carriage house, completely furnished, cost $33,253.29, including $3,000 for the lot and $2,036 for landscaping. From 1905-1976, the house was home for 19 Wyoming governors and their families. B. B. Brooks' family was the first to occupy the house; Ed and Casey Herschler were the last residents. In July, 1977, following completion of the present Governors' Mansion, the historic home became a museum administered by the State of Wyoming. Furnishings include a round pedestal table of inlaid woods made by rancher Johnnie Gordon for the Wyoming exhibit in the 1904 St. Louis World's Fair and numerous pieces of Molesworth furniture, brought to the mansion in the 1950s by Gov. Milward Simpson.

21. UW President's House

From 1947 to 1995, the UW president was housed in a university-owned home on the corner of 13th and Ivinson, across the street from Coe Library. In 1995, the trustees authorized the sale of the home to G. F. and Amy Williamson. President Terry Roark built his own home and received a housing allowance. Soon after Philip Dubois was named UW president in 1997, he constructed his own home on the corner of 30th and Reynolds, receiving a housing allowance from the university for the residence. Tom Buchanan, the next UW President, lived on Dover Street in the northeast part of Laramie.

22. Eugene Halone House, Thermopolis

Halone was a Finnish immigrant who built the house on the corner of Second and Amoretti in Thermopolis. The house features an attached Finnish sauna. Halone, an expert

---

The old Federal Courthouse at 10th and Center, Evanston,was sold and the spaces became retail shops on the ground floor and a dance company on the second floor.

stone mason, also built the Catholic and Lutheran churches, the Elks Building and stone fence around the fairgrounds, all of native stone, in Thermopolis.

23. Linford House, Laramie

Built in 1999 by Gary and Shirley Linford, both physicists and inventors, the home is of Tudor-style design. The house and accompanying two-story carriage house has 18,000 usuable square feet. The structures stand on a 36-acre parcel south of Corthell Hill in Laramie.

24. 305 N. Durbin Street, Casper

Oldest standing residence in Casper, it is now an apartment house once known as the Durbin Hotel, built in 1888.

G. E. Kidder Smith's Significant Buildings in Wyoming*

1. Ames Monument

Located on the summit between Laramie and Cheyenne, the monument honors brothers Oakes and Oliver Ames who were principal investors in the construction of the Union Pacific Railroad. Both men were implicated in the "Credit Mobilier" scandal in which the government was defrauded of millions of dollars by railroad builders. Nonetheless, friends and family members honored their work with the pyramid-shaped structure built at the highest point on the transcontinental railroad. The monument was designed by H. H. Richardson who also designed the New York State Capitol, Trinity Church in Boston and Harvard Law School. It is farther west than any Richardson-designed structure. "This is perhaps the finest memorial in America," wrote Henry-Russell Hitchcock, *The Architecture of H. H. Richardson and His Times.* (New York, 1936). Completed in 1882, the 60-foot-high pyramid featured nine-foot stone medallions made by Augustus St. Gaudens. The structure cost $65,000.

2. State Capitol

Several architects designed various portions of the building. Despite admiration for the structure from many people, it had the dubious distinction of winning the most votes for "ugliest" state capitol building in America in a nationwide poll of architects some years ago. Poll respondents noted that even county courthouses in many states had more "class" than the Wyoming State Capitol building.

3. Old Main, University of Wyoming, Laramie

The building has been significantly altered since its construction as the first building on the university campus in 1887. The structure was designed by Frederick Albert Hale. It was substantially remodeled in 1938-1939 and again in the 1950s.

4. Sheridan Inn, Sheridan

Designed by Thomas Kimball, the structure has 69 gables. It was built by the railroad. It was falling into disrepair when it was purchased by Neltje Kings in 1967 and restored. *(See Famous Wyoming Hotels, below)*

5. Union Pacific Depot, Cheyenne

In the 1990s, the structure was sold to a foundation to refurbish it as a transportation museum. The building faced the State Capitol at the other end of Capitol Avenue.

6. First Methodist Church, Cheyenne

Designed by J. P. Julien, the structure was completed in 1890.

7. Old Faithful Inn

8. Fort Laramie

Abandoned by the army in 1890, many buildings on the post have been restored since 1938. It is a national historic site.

*The Architecture of the United States by G. E. Kidder Smith.(NY: Doubleday, 1981).

19 Well Known Buildings That Moved

1. Jim Baker's Cabin

The old mountain man's home was built near Savery in the mid-1800s. It was moved to Frontier Park in Cheyenne in 1917, but returned to Savery in 1976. The building has been dismantled twice and moved four times since it was first built.

2. Mandel Post Office

Located behind Trail End in Sheridan, the cabin was built in 1883. It was Sheridan's first store, first law office and first home of the First National Bank of Sheridan. It also served as the town's first school, taught by Clara Works. It was moved five times during its existence, the final time in 1977 as a Bicentennial project by the Colonial Dames.

3. Daddy Payne Cabin

Built in Basin in 1907, the cabin was moved in 1979 to the old cemetery.

4. Buffalo Bill's birthplace

Cody was born in the house on Feb. 26, 1846. The home was purchased by Ralph Budd, president of the CB&Q, for $150. The two-story home was moved by the railroad from its original site in LeClaire, Iowa, to Cody on June 9, 1933. It was cut in pieces and shipped on two freight cars. The railroad gave the structure to the Buffalo Bill Memorial Association in 1947 and the building was placed next to the first Buffalo Bill Museum (now Cody Country Art League). In 1969 the building was moved across the street onto the grounds of the Buffalo Bill Historical Center.

5. Owen Wister's Cabin

Originally constructed in the national forest near Jackson, the summer home of the Western author was dismantled and moved to Medicine Bow in 1976.

6. Gro Vont Post Office

Big John Emory built it in 1907 for Jim and Nan Budge and it housed the post office from 1907 to 1934. In 1955, federal officials ordered its destruction or removal because it was inside the boundaries of Grand Teton National Park. The Turner family moved it to their Triangle X ranch where it is now the home of John and Mary Kay Turner. The structure, one of the oldest in Jackson Hole, was used in scenes in the film *Jubal*, starring Glen Ford and Rod Steiger.

7. Tie Siding Post Office

Actually, the entire town of Tie Siding moved one mile west of its original site in 1931. The post office was the principal building in the "town."

8. Hanna Episcopal Church

The structure was built in Cheyenne, but was soon outgrown. Railroad cars carried the church in pieces to Hanna, 100 miles away, where it was reassembled in 1900.

9. Inyan Kara Methodist Episcopal Church

The "first country church in Wyoming" was built in July 1891, southeast of Sundance by the Rev. O. B. Chassell. The building was moved to Sundance, 15 miles away, about 1947 and converted into a private residence.

10. Jenney Stockade

Built in 1875 as a log fort for an expedition headed by Prof. Walter P. Jenney, the structure was later used as a stop-over for goldseekers en route to the Black Hills. One of the two cabins within the stockade became a part of the headquarters house for the LAK Ranch. The cabin was moved from the original site on the LAK ranch, east of Newcastle, to the courthouse grounds and, later, to the grounds of the Anna Miller Museum.. It is the oldest standing building in the Black Hills.

11. Finnish meeting house

Built in the town of Carbon by Finnish coal miners, the two-story structure was moved to Hanna just after the turn of the century. Miners moved it by hand, rolling it on logs the seven miles from the old location to the new. The building, converted to an apartment house in the 1960s, burned in 1979.

12. Pleasant Valley schoolhouse

Built about 1886, the building served the first school district in Converse County. The schoolhouse was moved to the State Fairgrounds in Douglas in 1930.

13. Lusk newspaper office

The Main Street building housed newspaper offices for many years, most recently for the *Lusk Free Lance* in the 1950s. The front of the building was moved to its present location in the Stage Coach Museum complex in 1972. A log school from Cheyenne River was moved to the complex in 1976.

14. Slash Ridge fire lookout tower

When the structure was moved to the Encampment Museum complex in 1988, it became the 15th historic building moved to the site.

15. Van Tassell Carriage House

The building, designed by George Rainsford, was built behind the Van Tassell home in Cheyenne. When the house was demolished in 1960, the building was moved to Holliday Park where it housed the Cheyenne Artists Guild.

16. Lady of Fatima Chapel, Casper

The structure was built on Casper Army Air Base and moved into town after the base closed in 1944.

17. Trail Town

The complex, west of Cody, contains cabins and ranch buildings from throughout the Big Horn Basin which have been moved to the site over the years. The "town" was assembled by Bob Edgar..

18. Fort Sanders Community Center/Children's Museum

The building in Laramie's LaBonte Park was originally constructed at Fort Sanders, south of present-day Laramie. After the fort was abandoned in 1882, the structure was moved into town. In 1965, it was moved to its present location where, since the late 1990s, it has housed a children's museum. Parts of other fort buildings were used by area ranchers for various structures over the years.

19. Conrad Schwiering home

The log home, built in 1959 at the base of Shadow Mountain in Grand Teton National Park, narrowly escaped from the path of a wildfire in 1994. The next year, the building was purchased by contractor Ken Hake and moved 97 miles to Pinedale.

Average Sales Price for
Existing Single-Family Homes* (1999)

Wyoming Community Development Authority, "2009 Wyoming Profile of Demographics, Economics and Housing"

State Aver.:	$98,760	Uinta:	$87,911
Teton:	$374,882	Natrona:	$81,521
Park:	$148,047	Washakie:	$79,433
Albany:	$115,603	Converse:	$77,723
Laramie:	$109,518	Goshen:	$71,735
Campbell:	$105,490	Carbon:	$68,157
Sweetwater:	$105,356	Hot Spr.:	$66,044
Sublette:	$104,375	Platte:	$64,230
Johnson:	$102,678	Crook:	$61,906
Sheridan:	$101,160	Weston:	$57,462
Lincoln;	$99,065	Big Horn:	$51,945
Fremont:	$96,154	Niobrara:	$41,077

Some Famous Wyoming Hotels

1. Irma Hotel, Cody

Built by William F. Cody in 1902, the two-story stone structure was named for Cody's daughter Irma. Among the honored guests at the grand opening on Nov. 18, 1902, was artist Frederic Remington who sketched "Irma at the Irma," a portrait of a young woman on horseback arriving at the hotel.

2. Plains Hotel, Cheyenne

From the time of its opening to the 1960s, the Plains was the "unofficial state capitol" where legislators stayed, conducted business and met with lobbyists. Among the hotel's features are the first bathroom fixtures ever installed in the United States in a color other than white. Among the numerous famous guests over the years have been Harry Truman and Richard Nixon.

3. Sheridan Inn, Sheridan

The magnificent hotel was designed by Thomas R. Kimball of Omaha to resemble a Scottish inn. Ripley's "Believe It or Not" once called it the "House of 69 Gables." The inn was built in 1893 and from 1894 to 1896, it was owned by William F. Cody. Neltje Doubleday Kings bought the inn in 1967, saving it from demolition. It reopened in August 1969. In 1985 it became the property of the Children's Hospital Foundation of Denver.

4. Virginian Hotel, Medicine Bow

Built in 1911 in the busy cattle-shipping center, the hotel was named for the Owen Wister book published a decade earlier which was set in Medicine Bow. Wister never stayed at the hotel although many notables have been guests there, including John Madden, sportscaster and former Oakland Raider football coach.

5. Wolf Hotel, Saratoga

Built for $6,000, the Wolf has been a Saratoga landmark since 1893. The orginal owner was Frederick G. Wolf, for whom it was named. Owners Doug and Kathy Campbell began extensive restoration in 1977.

6. Parco Inn, Sinclair

The hotel was built by the Producers and Refiners Oil Company (PARCO) when Sinclair, then known as Parco, was a company town. The structure was designed to resemble a Spanish monastery. The building was abandoned for several years and in the early 2000s, purchased by a religious group.

Average Sales Price for Existing Single-Family Homes* (2008)

Wyoming Dept. of Administration and Information, Div. of Economic Analysis

State Aver.	$256,045	Uinta:	$197,390
Teton:	$1,829,237	Fremont:	$197,173
Sublette:	$296,638	Converse:	$187,131
Lincoln:	$246,253	Crook:	$170,602
Sweetwater:	$242,470	Carbon:	$151,093
Campbell:	$242,341	Platte:	$134,896
Sheridan:	$240,270	Washakie:	$133,754
Albany:	$222,151	Hot Spr.:	$133,421
Johnson;	$220,549	Goshen:	$131,037
Park:	$215,692	Weston:	$129,108
Natrona:	$204,154	Big Horn:	$109,295
Laramie:	$202,304	Niobrara:	$ 98,935

The state average sales price is down some three percent from the record high average sales price in 2007 of $265,044.

7. Old Faithful Inn, Yellowstone National Park

The largest log structure in the world, approximately eight stories high at the center, the Inn has 356 bedrooms and 196 baths. It is the best known of the hotels which have served visitors coming to the park. Others were the Lake Yellowstone Hotel, Roosevelt Lodge, Canyon Hotel and Mammoth Hot Springs Hotel.

8. Jackson Lake Lodge, Grand Teton National Park

On his first trip to the area in the 1920s, John D. Rockefeller, Jr., stayed at the "original" Jackson Lake Lodge, then known as the Amoretti Inn. The "new" lodge, built by Rockefeller, was dedicated on June 11, 1955. It was sold to CSX Corporation of Richmond, Va., in 1986. The lodge is a frequent convention center for national meetings as well as a tourist destination. Other well known lodges in the area are Signal Mountain Lodge and Jenny Lake Lodge.

9. Noble Hotel, Lander

Under construction from 1917-19, the Noble first housed a bank on the ground floor along with the hotel rooms above. Harold Del Monte, a former bank cashier, bought the hotel in 1930. He hired noted Montana artist J. K. Ralston to paint sketches throughout the building, including 23 panels depicting the life of Chief Washakie. Del Monte sold the hotel in 1969 to D. L. Petersen who later sold it to the present owner, the National Outdoor Leadership School, for its offices.

10. Connor Hotel, Laramie

The hotel was built in 1911-1912 by Frannie Connor, the widow of John W. Connor, former Laramie mayor and real estate investor. Connor had died of injuries in the great San Francisco earthquake of 1906. Later, the building was owned by Frannie's granddaughter, Pinkle Murrell, a Miami, Florida, attorney.

11. Pahaska Teepee

The hotel and hunting lodge was built by William F. Cody in 1901 and designed by A. A. Anderson. Constructed two years after completion of Cody's Irma Hotel, the still-unfinished building was headquarters for a ten-day hunt in the winter of 1904 when Cody hosted Gen. Nelson Miles and a party of wealthy Englishmen. Sold by the Cody estate at his death in 1917, the lodge passed through a succession of owners until 1946 when it was purchased by Henry H. R. Coe whose family still owns the lodge.

12. Wort Hotel, Jackson

Built by John and Jess Wort, the hotel opened Sept. 5, 1941. The red stone was quarried along the Gros Ventre River, loaded on boats and then trucked into Jackson. The Silver Dollar Bar was added in 1950 with 2,032 uncirculated 1921 silver dollars. The hotel was damaged by fire on Aug. 5, 1980, and one fireman was killed fighting the blaze.

13. Hotel Townsend, Casper

Built in 1923 for Charles H. Townsend, a banker and businessman, the hotel was one of three on the corner of 2nd and Center Streets. The building was placed on the National Register in November, 1983.

14. Little America

S. M. Covey was herding sheep in western Sweetwater County in the 1890s. He vowed that someday he would build a hotel in the area for the comfort of travelers. In 1932 he built Little America, naming it because he had read about Adm. Richard Byrd's expeditions in the Antarctic. In 1950, the inn was rebuilt when the highway was re-routed. Earl Holding became manager in 1951 and, eventually, became owner. Covey died in 1959.

Holliday Park in Cheyenne was named for Cal Holliday who was mayor from 1930-1932. For many years, the Van Tassell carriage house, moved to the park, served as the gallery and headquarters for the Cheyenne Artists' Guild.

15. Trail Hotel, Torrington

Built in 1922, for many years the Trail Hotel was the only place in Torrington other than the police station that was open 24 hours. Its original function ended in March, 1968, when the hotel furnishings from the 55 rooms and the lobby were auctioned off.

16. Hotel LaBonte, Douglas

Built for $55,000, it was opened January 16, 1914. First managers were Mr. and Mrs. H. O. Emery. For many years, the LaBonte was the hotel of choice for State Fair visitors and dignitaries visiting Douglas.

17. Hotel Evanston, Evanston

Built in 1912 by partners Downs and Tisdel, the hotel was social center for the community. Pete Downs chained a pet brown bear outside the front of the bar. One night a brakeman stumbled out of the saloon and into the bear pit where he found what he thought was a warm, furry place to sleep. Awakening to his predicament about the same time that the bear did, the brakeman howled in fear and sobered up quickly as he ran down the street. *Source: Evanston Walking Tour.*

18. Ranger Hotel, Lusk

The population of Lusk jumped from 400 to 1,200 in 1918 with the discovery of oil at nearby Buck Creek. During the winter, accommodations were so scarce that people paid 50 cents per night for a chair to sit on in a hotel lobby or pool hall. In the summer of 1919, construction began on the Ranger, a large four-story hotel.

Construction on the hotel began in 1919, but the building was not finished when the oil boom ended the following year. It finally opened in the early 1920s. In recent years, the structure has been converted from a hotel to senior housing.

Other Hotels

Many hotels have had important local significance. Some still serve their original function such as the Hotel Higgins in Glenrock, the Hotel Teton in Riverton and the Kemmerer Hotel. Others have been torn down in recent years including the Hotel Washakie, a Worland landmark, demolished in 1994 to make way for a parking lot.

4 Unusual "Homes" in Wyoming

1. Crystal Castle, near Buford

Henry Widholm built the unusual home between 1962 and 1964, using 35,000 formaldehyde bottles from mortuaries in three states. Some of the bottles are still partially filled with the embalming fluid.

2. Daellenbach home, near Cheyenne

Built for $1.5 million by the U. S. Air Force as an Atlas missile silo, F. Daellenbach bought it for $3,116 in 1966. He transformed the underground silo into a comfortable private home which has no need for a "fallout shelter."

3. Bendel home/company office, near Chugwater

In 2006, former Lockheed Martin propulsion engineer Tim Bendel and his wife moved into a former nerve center of a missile silo, 30 feet below the ground. Bendel, president of Frontier Aeronautics, ran his business from the silo. It was appropriate, given that his company developed rockets for eventual use in space tourism. The firm's rocket testing facility is located there.

Richard Savage, a Canadian, came to Wyoming as a buffalo hauler. Later, he provided meat to the UP Railroad crews working across Wyoming. In the early 1890s, he established what became the Overland Trail ranch southeast of Rawlins and built the Savage Mansion, a large stone house.

4. Fossil Cabin, Como Bluff

The "oldest cabin in the world" is made of 26,000 pieces of fossils taken from Como Bluff, the world-class dinosaur "graveyard." The cabin, constructed in 1933 by Thomas Boylan (b. Calif., 1863, d. Laramie, 1947), was featured by Ripley's "Believe It or Not" on April 16, 1938. Boylan had homesteaded on the site and collected the bones for 16 years prior to giving up on a dream of reassembling dinosaurs from the bones and turning the pile into a building.

5 Unusual Buildings in Wyoming

1. Green River Brewery

The brewery, located across from the Union Pacific tracks in Green River, is modeled on the European style. Built of stone in 1900 by Hugo Gaensslen, the building housed a bottling plant for non-alcoholic beverages during Prohibition.

2. South Superior Union Hall

Six United Mine Workers locals combined to build the structure in 1921. Architectural historians have called it the "only parallelogrammatic structure in the state." The trapezoid structure's ruins have been stabilized and made part of an innovative interpretive historical site.

3. Power House, Heart Mountain Relocation Center

The structure is one of a few still standing on the site where more than 10,000 Japanese-Americans were interned during World War II. Most were housed in the 450 barracks that were quickly constructed to accommodate the internees, most of whom were brought from the West Coast. The site was abandoned after the war and many of the buildings were either demolished or moved to nearby farms. An old barracks building was dismantled, shipped to Los Angeles and reassembled for the Japanese American National Museum in 1994.

4. Powder House, Fort Fred Steele

The native stone, windowless structure is one of the few buildings still standing from the old fort, established in 1868 and abandoned in 1886.

5. Casper Clubhouse, Casper

The structure was built in 1924 by Midwest Oil Co., designed by the local architectural firm of Garbutt and Weidner. The building went on the National Register in 1983.

Wyoming and Comics: 1. The American Heritage Center, University of Wyoming, holds the collections of Stan Lee, creator of Spiderman, Marvel Comics. 2. Karl Erickson, a Jackson artist, wrote a book on the art and business of cartooning titled It's Super Comix. It was published in 1994.

ART

1st art in Wyoming: Petroglyphs dating back to 1500 B. C. (and before) drawn by native people.
The Wyoming Arts Council was established in 1967.
Best known artist who was born in Wyoming: Jackson Pollock, born in Cody in 1912 *(see biography below)*
Wyoming ranked **28th** among the states in per capita appropriations for state art agencies, 66 cents per person annually.
Casper Artists' Guild was founded in 1924 by Lin and Ruth Joy Hopkins, Leo Goodrich, Tom and Eva Carrigen.

First Artists in Wyoming

1. Alfred Jacob Miller (b. Baltimore, 1810, d. 1874)

The Baltimore-born artist accompanied Capt. William Drummond Stewart, a Scottish nobleman, to the Green River Rendezvous in 1837. He made sketches and, after his return East, full-length paintings of the area. Several of his drawings were of Fort Laramie, then a privately-owned fur trading post. The paintings are described in Robert Warner, *The Fort Laramie Paintings of Alfred Jacob Miller.* (Laramie: University of Wyoming, 1979), and some are on display in the American Heritage Center, UW.

2. Father Nicholas Point (b. 1799, d. 1868)

Point illustrated Father Pierre DeSmet's travel narrative, published in 1843. The drawings were based on sketches Point made in Wyoming in 1841.

3. Charles Preuss (b. 1803, d. 1854)

A cartographer educated in Germany, Preuss accompanied the John C. Fremont expedition into Wyoming and illustrated Fremont's report to Congress. He also drew maps. Suffering from depression throughout his life, he died, a suicide, in Washington, D. C.

4. George Wilkins Christy

A New Orleans lawyer, Christy accompanied Stewart in 1842 and made sketches along the way.

5.-6. Monsieur P. Pietierre, Stedman R. Tilgham

The two men accompanied Capt. William Drummond Stewart in 1843. Miller declined the offer to make a second trip with the Scottish nobleman. Tilgham, a recent medical school graduate, sketched many landmarks including Devil's Gate.

Some Famous Artists with Wyoming Affiliations

1. A. A. Anderson (b. New Jersey, 1846, d. 1940)

Anderson studied art in Paris. He owned a ranch west of Meeteetse and served as the first superintendent of what is now Shoshone National Forest. Among his works are portraits of O. O. Howard and Thomas Edison.

2. Thomas Hart Benton (b. Missouri, 1889, d. 1975)

Benton came to Wyoming in the summer of 1930, accompanying his student Glen Rounds to the Fourth of July rodeo in Saratoga. After the trip, he painted numerous scenes of cowboys and rodeos. His American West mural in the Whitney Gallery, New York, incorporates some of the Wyoming sketches.

3. Albert Bierstadt (b. Germany, 1830, d. 1902)

Bierstadt made three trips west to Wyoming. In 1859, he accompanied Frederick W. Lander with his surveyors in the Wind River mountains. In 1863, he made a brief trip to southern Wyoming and in 1881, he visited Yellowstone. He is best known for spectacular mountain landscapes, many of which are held in the collections of the Buffalo Bill Historical Center, Cody.

4. Edward Borein (b. California, 1873, d. 1945)

Between 1925 and 1927, he traveled in Wyoming and sketched western scenes. He painted a series of panels at the Bradford Brinton ranch near Big Horn. Most of his work was done in the Southwest.

5. James Boyle (b. New Castle, Pa., 1910, d. Laramie, 1996)

Known more as an art educator than for his own art work, Boyle taught at the University of Wyoming from 1946 until his retirement in 1979. He was the first head of the university's Department of Art.

6. John Clymer (b. Washington, 1907, d. 1987)

Clymer lived and worked at Teton Village. Most of his paintings are scenics or historical scenes. Many are on display at the Whitney Gallery of Western Art, Buffalo Bill Historical Center, Cody.

7. Bill Gollings (b. Idaho, 1878, d. 1932)

Gollings painted in the Sheridan area for many years. A working cowboy, he had been trained in art in Chicago. He captured the authenticity of cowboy life in paintings, some of which hang in the State Capitol in Cheyenne. He also made many etchings and pencil sketches, many of which are in private collections around Wyoming. Some of the best known are his "Christmas card" drawings he sent annually to friends.

8. Nick Eggenhofer (b. Germany, 1897, d. 1989)

Eggenhofer came to the United States in the 1920s and studied art in New York. Fascinated by the West, he lived for many years in Cody. He produced an estimated 30,000 Western illustrations in all media.

9. Sanford Robinson Gifford (b. New York, 1823, d.

A prominent member of the Hudson River school, Gifford came west in 1870 with the Hayden expedition. The previous year, he painted in Egypt. He had studied art in Europe in the 1850s and traveled extensively during his career. He became famous as a landscape artist. He died in New York City in 1880. His paintings include "Valley of the Chug Water."

10. William H. Jackson (b. New York, 1843, d. 1942)

Jackson first traveled west as a bullwhacker in 1866. He sketched along the Oregon Trail. Later, he started a photo studio in Omaha and in 1871, accompanied the Hayden survey to Yellowstone. On this trip, he photographed extensively. Later, he moved to Detroit and worked for a photographic company, returning annually to Wyoming until two years before his death.

11. Frank Tenney Johnson (b. Iowa, 1874, d. 1939)

Johnson studied art and worked in Milwaukee. In the 1930s, he made frequent trips to Wyoming where he often visited his cousin, Mildred Martin, who owned the Rim Rock Ranch near Cody. He was best known as an illustrator.

12. Roy Kerswill (b. 1924, d. 2002}

The Jackson area artist painted in oils and watercolors. He did landscapes, portraits, historical scenes and still-lifes. In the 1990s, he was commissioned to do a 28-piece series on the Oregon Trail which appeared in the book, *A Pictorial Story of the Oregon-California Trail*, published in 1996.

13. Hans Kleiber (b. Germany, 1887, d. Sheridan, 1967)

Kleiber owned a studio in Dayton, Wyo., for many years. Self-taught, he is known for his watercolors and etchings. He was known as "etcher of the Rockies."

14. W. H. D. Koerner (b. Germany, 1878, d. 1938)

One of the best known illustrators of his age, Koerner made frequent trips west. On one trip in 1924, he and his family camped out on the North Fork of the Shoshone River above Cody. Many of his works are on display at the Whitney Gallery of Western Art, Buffalo Bill Historical Center.

15. Thomas Moran (b. England, 1837, d. 1926)

The first artist in Yellowstone National Park, Moran accompanied the Hayden expedition in the summer of 1871. His paintings of the wonders of Yellowstone helped convince Congress to set aside the area as a national park in 1872.

16. Jackson Pollock (b. Jan. 20, 1912, d. Aug. 11, 1956)

The originator of "abstract expressionism," Pollock was born on the Watkins ranch near Cody. The fifth son of Cody area farmers, Pollock moved with his parents when he was ten months old to their new home in San Diego. Later, the family moved to Phoenix. In 1930 young Jackson Pollock went to New York, studied with Thomas Hart Benton, Diego Rivera and others, and developed his own unique painting style. By the 1950s, he was the most influential artist in New York--perhaps in America. He died at the height of his fame in an automobile accident on Aug. 11, 1956, in New York. He was 44 years old.

17. Garrett Price (b. Kansas, 1896, d. Norwalk, Conn., 1979)

Reared in Saratoga, Price attended UW briefly and then Chicago Art Institute. He began as a staff artist for *Chicago Tribune* and, in 1920, moved to New York, becoming a free-lance artist. His illustrations appeared in *Life*, *Esquire*, *Colliers* and *Ladies Home Journal*. He was best known for illustrating covers for the *New Yorker*. He died in 1979.

18. Frederic Remington (b. New York, 1861, d. 1909)

Remington was a frequent visitor to Wyoming. A friend of William F. Cody, he attended the grand opening of the Irma Hotel in 1902 and made sketches.

19. Carl Rungius (b. Germany, 1869, d. 1959)

Rungius is best known for his paintings of big game animals. He made his first trip to Wyoming in 1895 and returned frequently. He often visited in the Pinedale area and painted extensively in the Wind River Range. Many of his works are on display at the National Wildlife Art Museum in Jackson.

20. Conrad Schwiering (b. Boulder, Colorado, Aug. 8, 1916, d. 1986)

Schwiering's work is most closely identified with the Tetons. His father, Dr. Oscar Schwiering, was principal of Cheyenne schools (1912-16), and superintendent in Douglas and Rock Springs, prior to becoming professor and later dean of education at the University of Wyoming (1924-54). Conrad Schweiring graduated from Laramie High in 1934 and UW in 1938. He studied art in the east following graduation. After military service in World War II, he was discharged with the rank of lieutenant colonel in 1946 and moved to Antelope Flats near Jackson where he built a home and studio in 1947. He is best known for his distinctive oil paintings of the Tetons. His mountain scene was used for the Wyoming centennial commemorative stamp issued by the U. S. Postal Service in February 1990.

21. Joseph H. Sharp (b. Ohio, 1859, d. 1953)

Sharp visited frequently in northern Wyoming. He is best known for his paintings of Indians but he also painted numerous Wyoming landscapes.

22. Ernest E. Stevens (b. Aplington, Iowa, 1872, d. Torrington, 1938)

Stevens was trained in art and began his career executing patent drawings in Washington, D. C. Later, he moved to Van Tassell and, in 1935, to Torrington where, among his paintings, are the murals in the Torrington High School lobby (moved from their original location on the auditorium walls, now demolished).

23. Allen True (b. Colorado, 1881, d. 1955)

True primarily worked in Colorado, but his best known illustration is the bucking horse on the Wyoming license plate. He executed the drawing on commission from Secretary of State Lester Hunt who originated the idea of a license plate logo. Wyoming's was the first of any state. True also painted Indian scenes and Western landscapes including a number of paintings in the Colorado State Capitol in Denver.

24. James Bama (b. New York, 1926)

The long-time resident of Wapiti initially gained fame over 22 years as an illustrator of book covers and posters. They included the "Cool Hand Luke" poster and covers for many James Bond paperbacks. Later, after moving to the Cody area in 1968, he turned to painting and became known for his Western art.

Some Well-Known Wyoming Murals

1. Greybull Post Office mural

The six-by-ten foot mural depicts a group of cowboys singing around the campfire. Artist Manuel Bromberg (b. Centerville, Iowa, 1917) was chosen in 1939 by the Federal Works Commission from among 1,475 entrants to paint the work. Later, he was on the faculty at North Carolina State and, until his retirement, a small New York college.

2. Torrington High School murals

Painted in 1935-36 by area artist E. E. Stevens (b. Aplington, Iowa, 1872, d. Torrington, 1938), the works were removed from the wall of the old auditorium prior to demolition of the old high school building. The four murals are now displayed in the lobby of the present high school, built on the same site.

3. University of Wyoming Student Union mural

The mural depicts the "kidnapping" of President A. G. Crane in 1922 when he was ceremonially welcomed to the campus to begin his term. The 20 by 7-foot mural was done by Lynn Fausett of Salt Lake City in 1940. The mural once decorated the main stairwell in the Union building. It was stored away in 1992 and placed on the west wall of the Yellowstone Ballroom after the Student Union building was remodeled in the early 2000s.

4. Wyoming State Capitol murals

The works were painted by Allen True, the Denver artist who also drew the famous bucking horse design for the Wyoming license plate.

5. Cody LDS Church murals

The works are among the best known paintings by famed artist Edward Grigware (b. Michigan, 1889, d. 1960), who also painted a mural in the lobby of the Education Building at the University of Wyoming.

6. Skyline Drive-In mural, Laramie

John Guthrie, Jr., of Laramie and Rock River painted a giant mural titled "Tom Mix Transcending the Vail" on the screen of the abandoned outdoor theater during the summer of 1991. The mural, meant as a temporary work of art, was painted over in 1992. The mural captured the attention of motorists along Skyline Drive, but it also could be seen from Interstate 80.

7. Greybull Elevator mural

The 900 square-foot painting done on the side of the large grain elevator was the work of Karyne Dickson. A western scene picturing a cowboy on a horse and a buffalo, the mural was commissioned by elevator owners David and Jeanne Van Gelder. It can be seen from ground level for three blocks. A second mural of a Shoshone Indian on a horse was painted on another side of the elevator in 1992.

8. Torrington downtown mural

Donna D. Peterson painted the old West scene on the south wall of the Coast-to-Coast store on Main Street in Torrington.

9. Kennedy Center for the Performing Arts, Washington, D. C.

Grade school art students from Sheridan executed the "Wyoming mural" in the Wash-

A WPA-commissioned painting was loaned to the Laramie Junior High School in the 1930s. The painting finally was returned to the owner, the General Services Administration, in 2010.

ington, D. C., center. Sponsored by the PTA, the mural was done by students of Thelma Maydew who traveled to the nation's capital for the dedication of the mural in October, 1969.

10. Wheatland City Park mural

In July 1993, area children under the direction of Holly Jones, a freelance artist, painted a mural in Lewis City Park, Wheatland, on a 55-foot-long wall.

11. Service Men's Club, Casper Air Base

Four enlisted men, Cpl. Leon Tebbetts, Private David Rosenblatt, Sgt. J. P. Morgan, Sgt. William Doench, executed the paintings depicting the story of pioneers and their efforts to conquer Wyoming and the west. Twenty-one episodes in the state's history are depicted, according to an article in the base newspaper, the *Slip Stream*, June 30, 1944. Painted in June 1944, the murals are preserved in the building once owned by Natrona County and leased to a square dance club, but now the Wyoming Veterans Museum.

12. Cheyenne Fire Station mural

The mosaic scene, created by S. R. Elliott, shows old Cheyenne with a building aflame and the horse-drawn fire engine being used to put out the blaze. The mural is on the southeast side of the building on 19th and Bent, Cheyenne.

13. Jackson Lake Lodge murals

From 1957 to 1959, artist Carl Roters (b. New York, 1898) completed 11 panels, each of about eight feet high, for placement in Jackson Lake Lodge. The Rockefeller family commissioned the art works.

14. Wayne Martinez memorial mural

Commissioned by friends of Martinez, a correctional officer at the Wyoming State Penitentiary who was murdered by three inmates in an attempted escape in 1997, the mural is on the walls of a highway underpass in Rawlins.

15. Murals, downtown Lander

The murals were done by artist J. Antolik who also painted murals in Shoshoni.

16. Lincoln School murals, Laramie

The mural depicts the contributions of Latino culture to Wyoming history. It was executed by Stevan Lucero, a Laramie-born artist living in Denver. The work was dedicated in May 2010.

Record Prices for "Wyoming" Art

1. Pollock paintings

The most expensive painting ever done by a Wyoming artist was sold at Sotheby's in New York on May 2, 1989, for $10.55 million. The artist was Cody native Jackson Pollock. A second Pollock sold at the same auction for $3.6 million. In May, 1988, "Search" by Pollock sold at Sotheby's for $4.8 million.

2. Moran paintings

In 1994, a painting by artist Thomas Moran titled "Cliffs of Green River, Wyoming," sold at Christie's in New York for $2.75 million. In December 1991, two other paintings by Moran were auctioned. Moran's 1899 oil called "In the Teton Range," sold for $385,000. A second painting, a 1912 view of the Grand Canyon by Moran, remained unsold at a Sotheby's auction. Moran is the best known artist of Yellowstone National Park.

Critics objected to the first state seal designed for the 1st legislature in 1891. The design showed a nude woman with chains hanging from each of her arms, pointing one hand to a star. The next legislature ordered the woman "clothed." The seal was totally changed in 1921.

Arts Proposals

1. "Canyon of the Chiefs" (1969)

The proposal was for 25-foot statues of 20 Native American chiefs to be carved along the west wall of Wind River Canyon, seven miles south of Therm-opolis. On the east side of the canyon, plans called for an amphitheater, a library and an Indian history museum. The plan was revived by Jeremy Hayek, director of the Thermopolis Chamber of Commerce, in 1991 as "Canyon of the Spirits."

2. "Copper Buffalo" (1992)

An organization called the Great Buffalo Herd Monument Foundation retained New York sculptor Robert Berks to build 1,000 life-sized bronze buffalo on federal land near Beaver Rim, southeast of Lander. Local opposition arose and the plan was (at least, temporarily) shelved in 1993.

3. Art on Cattle

Pip and Duane Brant and Sue Thornton, Pinedale artists, received $4,000 from the Rockefeller Foundation, the Warhol Foundation and the National Endowment for the Arts for a "moving exhibit" along County Road 353, 12 miles southeast of Pinedale. The artists painted words from Phyllis Luman Metal's journal on the sides of cattle, one word for each of 70 head.

4. 40-foot Neon Cowgirl (1999)

While critics didn't consider it "art," a proposal was offered in the winter of 1999-2000 that a huge neon sign be placed on top of the Cheyenne Transportation Museum (formerly the Union Pacific Depot) in the shape of a cowgirl on a horse. The proposal was rejected.

7 Well-Known Wyoming Art Museums

1. Whitney Gallery of Western Art, Cody

Part of the Buffalo Bill Historical Center, the Whitney Gallery contains paintings by most of the best-known Western artists including Charles Russell and Frederic Remington. Studios of W. H. D. Koerner and Remington are reconstructed. Works include those by George Catlin, Thomas Moran and Albert Bierstadt.

2. University of Wyoming Art Museum, Laramie

The museum has a wide-ranging collection from contemporary art to European impressionist works. It is housed in the UW Centennial Complex.

3. Nicolaysen Art Museum, Casper

Housed in what was once a power plant, the museum specializes in contemporary art, but shows have included a collection of works by "old masters." The museum contains seven different gallery spaces including a children's museum.

4. National Museum of Wildlife Art, Jackson

The museum, north of Jackson on a hill across from the elk refuge, holds more than 250 paintings and sculptures of wildlife. The largest such museum collection in the world, it houses works by such important artists as Karl Bodmer, George Catlin and Carl Rungius.

5. Fine Arts Center, Rock Springs

First formed with WPA funds during the New Deal, the museum holds works by Grandma Moses, Norman Rockwell, Hans Kleiber and others.

6. Bradford Brinton Memorial Ranch, Big Horn

The museum holds some 600 works, including paintings by John James Audubon, Charles Russell, Frederic Remington and Bill Gollings

7. Art Gallery, Wyoming State Museum, Cheyenne

Among the gallery's many holdings is the original sketch for the bucking horse on the Wyoming license plate.

ASIAN AMERICANS

Evanston Joss House: Evanston residents, as a state centennial project in 1990, built a replica of the town's "joss house" in Depot Square. The original "joss house" (burned Jan. 26, 1922), for the numerous Chinese who lived in southwestern Wyoming, was one of only three such temples of worship in the United States.

Not a Citizen: The Wyoming attorney-general ruled in May 1932 that Kohei Sunuda, born on a Japanese ship Manila Maru when his mother was traveling to Japan on Dec. 8, 1926, from San Pedro, Calif., to Yokahama, Japan, was not a citizen. His five siblings were all born in America and U. S. citizens. Because of the ruling, he could not be admitted to Green River schools unless his family made a "tuition" payment. Source: Green River Star, May 20, 1932, p. 1.

Some Well-Known Wyoming Asian-Americans

1. Bill Hosokawa, Journalist/Editor

Born in Seattle in 1915, Hosokawa was sent to Wyoming as an internee at the Heart Mountain Relocation Center during World War II, where he served as editor of the camp newspaper, the *Heart Mountain Sentinel*. Later, he became an editor for the *Denver Post*. Following retirement, he taught journalism at the University of Wyoming. He died in

2. Grant Ujifusa, Author/Editor

Ujifusa is a native of Worland. A graduate of Harvard College, he worked as senior editor for Macmillan. He is co-author (with Michael Barone) of the *Almanac of American Politics,* published every two years by *National Journal*.

3. Tosh Suyematsu, Attorney

Born in Oakland, Calif., in 1918, he moved with his family to Casper in 1919. A veteran of the 442nd Regimental Combat Team, the much decorated Japanese-American unit during World War II, he returned to practice law in Wyoming. He served as assistant U. S. Attorney from 1969 to 1989. He died in a traffic accident in 1994.

4. Mormon Charlie

The Chinese man, a local vegetable dealer, was a popular fixture in Evanston from the turn of the century until his death in 1939.

5. Sam Sling

Sling began work as a section hand on the Union Pacific near Evanston. Later, he became general assistant to the railroad superintendent. When the Oregon Short Line was built, Sling became storekeeper and stationery clerk for the company. After serving as manager of Chinese exhibits at the World's Columbian Exposition in Chicago in 1893, he returned to work for the Union Pacific as a passenger agent headquartered in Chicago. Later, he moved back to Hong Kong and worked on railroads there.

6. Norman Mineta, Secretary of Commerce

Born in San Jose, Calif., in 1931, Mineta spent three years as an internee at Heart Mountain Relocation Center in Park County during World War II. His Japanese-American parents were relocated from their California home. At the camp, he met fellow Boy Scouts outside the camp, including Al Simpson from Cody. Years later, Mineta served as mayor of San Jose. In 1974, he was elected to Congress from California, serving 20 years. President Bill Clinton appointed him Secretary of Commerce, the first Asian-American in a Cabinet post, June 28, 2000. On Jan. 2, 2001, he was named Transportation Secretary by Pres. George W. Bush. He was the only Democrat in Bush's Cabinet.

7. Winberg Chai, UW Professor and Author

Born in Shanghai in 1932, Chai's parents were educated in the United States. Chai, who holds the Ph.D. from New York University, has taught at UW since 1988. Prior to coming to UW, he was vice president at the University of South Dakota. He is author of more than 20 books and a recognized specialist on government and politics in Asia.

AUTOMOBILES

1st car in Wyoming: Built in Laramie during the winter of 1897-1898 by Elmer Lovejoy from pieces ordered from various manufacturers, the vehicle weighed 940 pounds. The "little iron buggy wheels cut into the soft places so that progress was very slow," the *Laramie Boomerang* reported, adding that Lovejoy had ordered pneumatic tires which had not yet arrived in time for the first "test drive" on May 7, 1898. The car had two speeds, one of five miles per hour and other of ten miles per hour—and no reverse.

1st auto accident in Wyoming: Happy Jack Road, Laramie County, 1906. The car, owned by a man named Sapho of Cheyenne, overturned and a passenger, Billy Rich, sustained a broken leg. When Boyd Frye tried to salvage the car, he hitched his team and wagon to it, but when the team started pulling, the wagon overturned, breaking Frye's leg. Only 11 cars were registered in Laramie County at the time.

1st fatal automobile accident in Wyoming: Rawlins, Nov. 4, 1906. The victim was the young son of William Weightman, a Rawlins market owner. He was hit by a car on a Rawlins street and died at the scene.

1st auto dealership in Wyoming: Probably, the partnership of Frank V. Wright and Robert Lawson. The two started selling bicycles at 1711 Ferguson, Cheyenne. In 1906 they began selling the Smith automobile.

1st automobile to enter Yellowstone National Park: June 2, 1902, a 1897 Winton driven by Henry G. Merry of Electric, Mont., was turned away by troops, then serving as rangers, just a few yards into the park.

1st automobile legally driven into Yellowstone National Park: July 31, 1915, a Ford driven by K. R. Seiler of Red Wing, Minn., was the first vehicle legally allowed into the park. Of the first seven vehicles, five were Fords, one was a Buick and one, a Haynes.

1st transcontinental automobile race across Wyoming: 1903. Tom Fitch and Marcus Kraarup drove a single-cylinder Packard from San Francisco to New York in 61 days. They followed the Union Pacific route across southern Wyoming. There were no improved roads across the state.

1st automobile on the Meeteetse to Cody road: Eugene Phelps' "Grout Steamer" in 1907.

1st organized automobile race in Wyoming: Aug. 17, 1909. The event was held at Frontier Park in Cheyenne. Such races were held annually and drew such famed racers as Barney Oldfield. The sport was banned in 1923 after a serious car accident. Also, the Frontier Days committee worried about damage to the horse race track.

1st uniform license plates on cars required by law: 1913. Before that, owners designed their own.

1st police car in Wyoming: Purchased in March 1912 by the Cheyenne Police Department.

1st state speed limit law passed: 1913. The limit was 12 mph in towns. The speed limit was raised in 1924 to 35 mph on the highway. At the time, there were 30 miles of paved roads statewide.

1st automobile equipment required: 1913. A red lamp was required on the rear of any motor vehicle.

1st highway signs erected in the state: 1920

1st highway completed through Wind River Canyon: Jan. 22, 1924.

1st license plates with a county number designation: 1929. The order was determined by each county's assessed valuation for the previous year and the numbers have remained the same since.

1st Wyoming Highway Patrolman hired: 1933.

1st arrest by Wyoming Highway Patrol: Dan Pappos, 18, Cheyenne, no tail light, June 10, 1933.

1st drivers' licenses issued by the state: 1947. Wyoming was one of the last states requiring that drivers be licensed.

1st interstate highway contract awarded: Sept. 26, 1956, for a 10.13 mile section of I-25 north of Cheyenne (Torrington interchange to the Whitaker Road interchange). The surfacing was completed on the last section on July 8, 1985, a 10.1-mile section of I-90 between Ranchester and the Montana state line. The section was opened concurrently with a 22-mile Montana section on Oct. 10, 1985. Duration of the Interstate construction program was 29 years, 2 weeks.

1st personalized license plates issued: 1969.

1st downtown parking garage in Wyoming opened: Casper, completed in 1979 for 443 cars.

1st mandatory seat belt law in Wyoming: 1989.

Bus fares in Wyoming towns (1940): Casper, 5 cents; Cheyenne, 7 cents in town and 10 cents to ride to Fort Warren.

Worst mass collision in Wyoming history: 36 vehicles involved and seven people killed on I-80, three miles west of Buford, on August 19, 2004, when heavy fog limited visibility.

Most common color of cars involved in fatal accidents: Red. In daylight hours, 15.1 percent of cars in such mishaps are red. After dark, the most common color is two-toned, according to a 1982 study. In 2003, there were **619,864** total vehicles registered in Wyoming. Of this total, 385,053 were trucks. In 1993, more than **558,000** motor vehicles were registered in Wyoming. The state led the nation in **per capita registrations** with 1,187 registrations for every 1,000 persons.

Wyoming had 742 **licensed drivers** per 1,000 population in 2004, **6th per capita** in the United States. The 2008 **highway fatality rate** in Wyoming was **29.85 deaths per 100,000** population, more than double the national average of 12.25 per 100,000.

Speed limits: On Dec. 8, 1995, the speed limit in Wyoming was raised to 75 miles per hour on interstates and 65 on most other highways. The 55-mile-per-hour limit had been in effect on non-interstates since President Richard Nixon had it set in 1974 as a fuel conservation measure. The interstate limit had been reduced to 55 in the Reagan administration in 1987.

2 Vehicles Named for Wyoming Places
1. Plymouth Sundance   2. Chevrolet Cheyenne

1st Car Owners in Wyoming Towns

1. Laramie (1898): Elmer Lovejoy *(see 1st car in Wyoming, above)*

2. Rawlins (1900): Dr. John Osborne, a medical doctor and sheep rancher who had served as Wyoming governor and congressman, owned the first car in town.

3. Sheridan (1901): O. P. Hanna began an "auto-stage line" between Sheridan and Buffalo in late October 1901. The first car, driven from Omaha on a trip which took almost ten days, had a capacity of nine passengers. Earl Eaton owned a 20-horsepower Cadillac in 1906. By 1909, more than 30 locally owned cars negotiated Sheridan streets.

4. Cheyenne (1903): Dr. W. W. Crook brought the first car to Cheyenne, a single-cylinder, curved-dash Oldsmobile on Sept. 1, 1903. The vehicle cost him $750.

5. Douglas (1905): A chain-driven, two-cylinder Rambler owned by Friday Nelson was the first car. Nelson sold rides in it for 50 cents. Four years later, there were 13 cars owned by Douglas residents.

6. Weston County (1905): The first car driven into the county was owned by T. V. Garlock of Custer, S. D., who drove it to the county fair in 1905. The first local owner was John Sedgwick, a sheepman, whose Model N Ford was delivered in a large box wrapped in heavy paper. Sedgwick had to assemble the $1,150 car from the instructions included in the kit. According to a local newspaper account: "[The machine] literally flys, making the distance between town and the Sedgwick ranch in 30 minutes... He tried to climb a telephone pole one day and got stalled halfway up. At another time he tried turning a corner at a 40-mile clip and as a consequence, turned several somersaults before landing. Dr. Johnson attended him." Another report noted that Sedgwick's first trip ended when he swerved to avoid hitting a small child and struck a telephone pole. The damage to the car took two weeks to repair. The second trip concluded with the county's first injury from an auto accident. The car overturned, pinning Sedgwick under it. The driver was not injured, but passenger Dr. Johnson suffered a sprained ankle. Sedgwick sold the car in 1910. Other early cars included a Ford Roadster owned by E. R. Maris, the railway agent. J. C. Baird owned a Studebaker touring car which he drove from Denver in two days, prompting a newspaper to report: "He is considered one of the best drivers in the West." Dr. S. W. Johnson owned an International and John E. Meade drove a Wayne runabout.

7. Buffalo (1906): The car was a high-wheel Holzman owned by Frank Gatchell, the county surveyor. Eight cars were owned by Buffalo residents by 1909.

8. Lander (1906): F. W. Thomas, county clerk, owned the car, make unknown. The car was shipped in before the railroad arrived. By 1909, 12 cars were in Lander, eight owned by T. J. McMasters, a garage owner who rented them out.

9. Wheatland (1906): The first car was a Lambert, owned by sheep rancher/banker William Ayers. The same year, Glede Noble and Dr. Wood Phifer purchased cars.

10. Evanston (1906): Probably, Dr. J. L. Wicks owned the first car in town. A newspaper item described his experience with his new machine: "Dr. J. L. Wicks used his McIntyre for one year. It is a buggy-type with solid tires and the vibration is so noticeable that the doctor has determined to give it away at a raffle to be held soon." Later issues of the paper do not report a raffle winner, if one was held. There were six cars in Evanston by 1909.

11. Lusk (1906): A 1905 Cadillac owned by Hans Gautschi was brought to town in 1906. The engine was still used as late as 1961 as part of a well drilling rig in Niobrara County.

12. Sundance (1908): First car was a Ford Model N roadster owned by John Sedgwick of Newcastle, driven to Sundance to the rodeo in the early summer of 1908. People paid $1 each to ride in it. The first locally owned car was an 18-horsepower Ford owned by Dr. R. Knode. Jesse Driskill and Walter Wellman purchased cars in the early years. Wellman's vehicle was a 40-horsepower Studebaker.

13. Thermopolis (c. 1908): The first two cars were Oldsmobiles brought overland from Denver via Rawlins and Lander and used to haul passengers between town and the hot springs. Later owners included W. B. Garrett, Dr. J. R. Richards, and banker Ira E. Jones. Seven cars were locally owned in 1909.

14. Casper (1908): J. P. Cantillion, a local railroad official, was the first car owner in Casper. He had a 20-horsepower Pope-Toledo. First car in town, however, was J. B. Okie's touring car, shipped by railroad and driven to his Lost Cabin home.

15. Rock Springs (c. 1908): Within a year, there were 17 cars in Rock Springs, six of which were owned by the Wyoming Auto Transit Company.

16. Jackson Hole (1911): At least five cars made it into the valley during the summer of 1911. One, an EMF driven by Charles Caughlin of Idaho Falls, drove over Teton Pass, the first automobile to make the harrowing trip. Part of the trip was assisted by horses and buggies giving an occasional pull. Caughlin planned to sell rides for 25 cents, but he hadn't counted on competition from other cars.

17. Torrington (1912): Early car owners included Dr. C. H. Platz, J. T. Snow and Joe Amery.

18. Saratoga (c. 1912): The first car was a two-cylinder Peerless owned by D. E. Winsor.

19. Star Valley: Early car owners included Dr. Grooms (Afton), A. C. McCombs (Grover), A. C. Toland (Auburn), Barton M. Cranney (Etna). Eugene Weber brought the first tractor to Star Valley in 1912.

Highway Fatalities

1988: 129	1994: 144	2000: 152	2006: 195
1989: 113	1995: 170	2001: 186	2007: 149
1990: 105	1996: 143	2002: 176	2008: 159
1991: 122	1997: 137	2003: 165	2009: 131
1992: 118	1998: 154	2004: 164	
1993: 120	1999: 189	2005: 170	

Highest ever was 264 killed in 1981.

Counties with Greatest Number of Fatalities (2008)

1. Fremont (14)   **6.-8.** Albany, Teton, Uinta (6 each)

2.-3. Natrona and Sweetwater (10 each)   **9.** Park (5)

4-5: Big Horn and Campbell (9 each)   **10.** Carbon (4)

More than 45 percent of all vehicles sold in Wyoming in 1997 were light trucks, according to the Wyoming Automobile Dealers' Association. That year, there were 164,000 passenger cars registered in Wyoming and 290,000 light trucks.

3 Unusual Wyoming Automobiles

1. Lee Doud's Whippet, Casper

Doud, a roadster dealer, drove one of his Whippets up the steps of the Natrona County Courthouse in 1927 as a publicity stunt.

2. Ed Hadley's "postage stamp" car, Casper

The vehicle, covered entirely with stamps, was featured in "Ripley's Believe It or Not" in 1936.

3. Len Austin's 1972 "postage stamp" Volkswagen Bug, Laramie

Austin was coordinator of the Center for Academic Advising at the University of Wyoming. He applied more than 6,000 stamps to his car as an alternative to a new paint job. Austin said the car was frequently photographed because it had such an unusual appearance. The car was estimated to be worth more than $12,000 in 1991.

11 Auto Speed Records

1. Lee Doud's Whippet

Doud drove from Casper to Rawlins, Cheyenne and Lavoye in 24 hours, setting an average speed mark of 62.5 miles per hour in the early 1920s.

2. Martin Fletcher's Oldsmobile

On Aug. 17, 1909, Fletcher set a world record of 58 1/2 miles per hour for a 200-mile race on a circular dirt track. Fletcher completed the race in 3 hours, 39 minutes, 47 seconds. The first auto speed race in Wyoming, it was held at Frontier Park, Cheyenne.

3. David Kidd's Thomas Flyer Steamer

Kidd's steamer broke down during the 45-mile trip from his ranch to Casper. It was pulled into town by horses, arriving 12 hours after he left the ranch.

4. Henry Joy's Packard Touring Car

Joy and his party crossed Wyoming in three days in 1915 in the "twin-six" Packard averaging 7 1/2 miles per gallon of gasoline (more than 60 gallons required for the 450-mile trip). The car also consumed five gallons of oil. A monument noting Joy's dedication to auto travel is located along I-80, west of Rawlins.

5. Will Goodale's car, Laramie

"Will Goodale of Laramie...has established the record for the round-trip from Fort Collins, 72 miles in six hours, 40 minutes. The roads were in fairly good shape and Mr. Goodale left Laramie at 2:20 in the afternoon, reaching the garage on the return trip at 9. He took one passenger to Fort Collins and returned alone." *Laramie Sentinel*, Oct. 5, 1909.

6. Billy Irwin's Ford Runabout

"Billy Irwin, a druggist in Spearfish, S. D., made a trip to Sundance, a distance of 35 miles, in a case of sickness, in an hour and 40 minutes in a Ford Runabout." Crook County newspaper report, c. 1908.

7. George T. Beck's car, Cody

Beck made an auto trip from Pahaska to Cody in October 1911. He drove the 56 miles in two hours, 23 minutes, fast enough to gain newspaper mention.

8. Norman DeVaux's Buick

DeVaux drove the 22-horsepower, two-cylinder car from New York to California in 24 days in the summer of 1906. Among the five passengers were two newsmen and a mechanic. "We ran into mud across Wyoming, but we had a tackle to pull us out of the holes," he told a *Spokane Evening Chronicle* reporter at the end of the journey. "We got off the trail time and again in the sagebrush country, and would wind up in a ravine. We were compelled to do a lot of scavenging around to find roads at times, and often they were so bad we were compelled to make it the best we could over the sagebrush."

9. Dr. Lathrop's speedy runabout, Casper

The Casper physician owned one of Casper's first cars. He sped so fast on Casper streets that city officials, concerned for pedestrian safety, "installed speed bumps to slow him down," according to the late Edness Kimball Wilkins who remembered Dr. Lathrop's first automobile.

10. C. M. Elgin's touring car, Casper

In 1909 Casper bought a car in Denver and then drove it home to Casper. He made it from Denver to Cheyenne in five hours, 45 minutes in actual driving time. The Cheyenne-Douglas leg took almost ten hours and he managed the final stretch into Casper in about three hours. As a local newspaper reported, "the many hours spent along the road when the car was not in operation were deducted." The trip took four days.

11. C. A. Taylor's Ford, Casper

In the summer of 1919, Taylor, the district court reporter, drove from Casper to Denver via Alcova. He set a new record. He left Casper at 3 a.m., on a Sunday morning and arrived in the Colorado capital city at 7:30 p.m. that evening.

The Bucking Horse on the License Plate

Artist Allen True received $75 for painting the bucking horse logo, commissioned by Secretary of State Lester Hunt in 1934. True, born in Colorado in 1881, had painted eight large murals in the State Capitol, commissioned in 1917. He died Nov. 8, 1955.

The debate continues as to the name of the horse and the rider depicted on the license plate. Hunt contended it was meant as a "composite." Others believe it depicts the great bucking horse, Steamboat, being ridden by either Stub Farlow or Clayton Danks. Still others contend that the design was not original to True and Hunt, but had come from a logo designed for Wyoming National Guard vehicles in World War I.

When the design was added to the license plate in 1935, Wyoming was the first state to have anything except numbers on the plates. Soon, other states started using license plates for advertising slogans or state logos.

Laramie attorney Nellis Corthell was so certain that the logo was intended as an advertisement for Cheyenne Frontier Days that, not wanting to promote the rival town, he covered it up on his license plate with masking tape.

In 1994, the Automobile License Plate Collectors Association chose the Wyoming plate as third best in the United States. Only the plates from North Dakota and Indiana received more votes from the association's members. Devils Tower was added as background on the new plates issued for 2001.

County Designations on License Plates

1 Natrona	9 Big Horn	17 Campbell
2 Laramie	10 Fremont	18 Crook
3 Sheridan	11 Park	19 Uinta
4 Sweetwater	12 Lincoln	20 Washakie
5 Albany	13 Converse	21 Weston
6 Carbon	14 Niobrara	22 Teton
7 Goshen	15 Hot Springs	23 Sublette
8 Platte	16 Johnson	

Numbers were designated according to each county's assessed valuation in 1929. (Population was not the basis). Similar measures today would yield a different numerical order. For example, Campbell likely would move from 17 to 1 or 2 and Niobrara would drop from 14 down to 22 or 23.

Holders of License Plate Number 1-1*

1. Jacob Schwoob, Cody

When the legislature made state licensing of motor vehicles mandatory in 1913, Schwoob was the President of the State Senate. The Park County senator's work promoting highway improvements was recognized when he retired from the Senate. The legislature awarded him auto license number 1-1. When each county was given a designation in 1929, based on the county's assessed valuation, Natrona County was assigned number 1. Nonetheless, Schwoob retained his 1-1 plate and the law gave Park County the right to assign 1-1 for the next 25 years.

2. Mrs. Mabel Laird Schwoob Robertson, Cody

Mrs. Robertson was Schwoob's widow and she retained the number after her husband's death. In the 1930s, she married Sen. E. V. Robertson, who had been widowed about the same time.

3. Fremont and Tina Michie, Casper

The special assignment to Park County expired in 1954 and, the next year, the plate number was returned to Casper where it was assigned to the Michies until 1957.

4. Dick Jones, Powell

In 1957, the Department of Revenue and Taxation was established to collect revenues for all agencies. Previously, the Highway Department handled its own funds. At that time, the old licensing law was re-enacted and Park County was again granted the number 1-1 for yet another 25 years. Jones represented Park County in the State Senate at the time and he offered to give the number to another Park County resident, then Gov. Milward Simpson. The governor declined the offer so Jones retained the plate number until 1969.

5. Burke Sheep Company, Natrona County

The 40th legislature in 1969 passed several laws relating to automobile licenses. In one law, the legislature struck from the books the special provision which had given 1-1 to Park County. As a result, the plate number went to Natrona County for assignment. Burke Sheep Company received the number. The company retained the plate annually until 1988 when the number was registered to John and Mary Burke. They still held the number in 1999. *Sources: Letter from Tom Jones (son of Dick Jones) to authors; the Natrona County Treasurer's Office, Auto Licensing Division; Wyoming Session Laws.*

New Hampshire Cowboy

In September, 1885, the Cheyenne Daily Sun reprinted what the editor claimed was Bill Nye's "interview" with a young man from New Hampshire who had come to Wyoming for the first time.

According to Nye, the young man said he first thought it was important to dress like someone from Wyoming. "I got one of those Chicago sombreros with a gilt fried cake twisted around it for a band. Then I got a yellow silk handerchief on the ten-cent counter to tie around my neck. Then I got a suit of smoke-tanned buckskin clothes and a pair of moccasins. I had never seen a bad, bad man from Chi-enne, but I had seen pictures of them and they all wore moccasins. The money I had left I put into a large revolver and a butcher knife with a red Morocco sheath to it. The revolver was too heavy for me to hold in one hand and shoot, but by resting it on a fence I could kill a cow easy enough if she wasn't too blamed restless. I went out to the stockyards in Chicago one afternoon and practiced with my revolver. One of my thumbs is out there at the stock yards now."

Nye then quotes the young man about his arrival in Cheyenne. First, he encountered the desk clerk at the Interocean Hotel: "'You are from New Hampshire, are you not?' the desk clerk said. I told him not to give it away, but I was from New Hampshire. Then I asked him how he knew. He said that several New Hampshire people had been out there that summer and they had worn the same style clothes and revolver, and generally had one thumb done up in a rag."

BALLOONS

11 Japanese "Balloon-Bombs" Found in Wyoming

The Japanese in 1944 sent large paper and rubberized silk balloons aloft in a last-ditch effort to cause panic in the United States. Detonating devices attached to the balloons were set to explode on impact. Many of the balloons drifted in the jet stream over the United States, but only one caused any fatalities—five children and one woman near Klamath Falls, Oregon. Eleven of the devices were found in Wyoming.

1. Thermopolis (Dec. 6, 1944)

Only the third discovery of a balloon in the United States, the device was found 15 miles southwest of Thermopolis where it was seen exploding in the air about 6 p. m. Federal officers sealed off the area and refused to divulge details of the discovery. They asked news reporters not to publicize the finding because of the potential threat to national security.

2. Manderson (Dec. 19, 1944)

A 12-square-foot fragment of a paper balloon bomb was found near town. No explosion device or other parts were found.

3. Worland (Jan. 28, 1945)

Parts found might have come from the balloon-bomb which fell in December near Thermopolis.

4. Newcastle (Feb. 8, 1945)

Ranchers found the balloon 25 miles west of Newcastle as it drifted to the ground about 6 p.m. The bomb did not explode and the ranchers turned the balloon over to federal authorities. The story of the incident is told in "Bombs on the Prairie" by Liz Barritt in *Wyoming History Journal*, Spring, 1996.

5. Casper (Feb. 9, 1945)

Only a fragment was found.

6. Kirby (Feb. 22, 1945)

Local residents watched the balloon hit the ground near town. The complete balloon was recovered by federal officials.

7. Powell (Feb. 22, 1945)

Two local residents reported watching a balloon explode in the air. Fragments were recovered, including the remains of a 25-pound bomb which caused no damage.

8. Glendo (Feb. 22, 1945)

Residents watched the balloon land. The complete balloon and bomb were recovered intact along with two sandbags, one of which weighed six pounds.

9. Gillette (March 21, 1945)

A fragment only.

10. Basin (March 22, 1945)

A fragment only.

11. Casper (April 6, 1945)

Fragments only.

The first Riverton Rendezvous Balloon Rally was held in 1980.

BANKS AND FINANCE

1st bank in Wyoming: Probably, the Iliff and Company bank at South Pass City, managed by Amos Steck, 1869.

Oldest bank still operating in Wyoming: First Interstate Bank of Laramie, began as the Wyoming National Bank of Laramie, chartered as a national bank on May 17, 1873. Edward Ivinson received the first charter. The bank merged in 1895 with the Laramie National Bank, becoming the First National Bank of Laramie.

1st insurance company organized in Wyoming: Wyoming Life Insurance Company, incorporated March 23, 1911, in Cheyenne.

1st cooperative health care organization: Fetterman Hospital Association, organized by cowboys and cattlemen in present Converse County in April, 1885.

1st drive-in bank window in Wyoming: Wyoming National Bank of Casper, opened Feb. 10, 1950. Someone "tested" the bullet-proof window by firing a bullet at the window 11 days before the facility officially opened. The bullet did not penetrate the glass. The window passed the test. A newspaper reported the shot was fired by someone "whose motives were believed to have been purely selfish."

Scrip payment: The Laramie town council issued scrip to city employees for two months in 1932. The action was not popular with city employees or local merchants. The city ended the practice and, in September, 1933, redeemed $600 of the $1,115 in scrip issued that spring.

No. of banks in Wyoming (1910): 88 (30 national banks, 55 state banks and 3 private banks.

Only Wyoming county named for a banker: Converse County, named for Amasa Converse, Cheyenne banker and stockman.

First bank opening in Wyoming since middle-1980s: Oregon Trail Bank of Chugwater, opened Jan. 2, 1993, a branch of Guernsey-based Oregon Trail Bank.

World Bank president: James Wolfensohn, president of the World Bank, owned a home in Jackson Hole. He was named head of the organization in June 1995 and served until June 30, 2005.

1st Banks in Wyoming Towns

1. Casper

Later known as the W. A. Denecke Company Bank, it opened in 1888. The name was later changed to Bank of Casper. Ironically, the bank became the first in Casper history to fail when it went out of business in 1903.

2. Lander

The first bank in town was opened by Eugene Amoretti in 1875. It was named Amoretti Bank.

3. Torrington

The North Platte Valley Bank was issued a charter on March 1, 1903. According to Robert C. Muhm, banking historian, there is no record that the bank opened. The first verifiable bank was the private bank, Snow and Clarke Bank, opened in December 1904. A year later, the bank became Torrington State Bank and with issuance of a national charter in 1908, it became First National Bank of Torrington. It closed permanently on Dec. 16, 1924.

The number of trucks passing through Wyoming ports of entry reached three million for the first time in 2005. In the same year, trucks accounted for 28 percent of all the vehicle miles traveled on Wyoming highways and roads.

4. Afton

In the early days of the community, the W. W. Burton Mercantile Company served as an informal bank. Later, Senator Allen, a U. S. Senator from Nebraska, established the first actual bank. Allen's son-in-law, D. D. Lynch, was the cashier.

5. Lost Springs

The first bank was called the "State Bank of Lost Springs." Started in 1911, it occupied the corner of a building that also housed the local billiard parlor. The bank closed in 1927.

6. Jackson

Robert Miller organized Jackson State Bank in 1914. He served as president and Harry Wagner was first cashier.

7. Buffalo

The first bank operated from the south end of the log structure built by the Trabing brothers and moved piece by piece from Crazy Woman to Buffalo in 1879. The First National Bank of Buffalo was chartered February 2, 1885, to replace the privately-owned older bank.

8. Sundance

The predecessor to the present Sundance State Bank, chartered in 1895, was the first state bank in the northeast part of Wyoming to gain a charter. The bank moved from a frame structure to a stone building in 1914.

7 Banks in Founded beforeWyoming Statehood and Still Operating in 1989*

1. First Interstate Bank of Laramie (May 17, 1873)
2. Wyoming National Bank of Cheyenne (1882)
3. Key Bank of Rawlins (1883)
4. First National Bank of Buffalo (1885)
5. State Bank of Green River (1887)
6. First Interstate Bank of Casper (1889)
7. Central Bank of Lander (1890)

    Source: Wyoming Bankers Association, 1989.

County Rankings by Per Capita Personal Incomes (1990)

1. Teton	9. Park	17. Converse
2. Campbell	10. Carbon	18. Albany
3. Natrona	11. Crook	19. Big Horn
4. Sheridan	12. Hot Springs	20. Lincoln
5. Sweetwater	13. Johnson	21. Goshen
6. Niobrara	14. Washakie	22. Fremont
7. Laramie	15. Platte	23. Uinta
8. Sublette	16. Weston	

In the spring of 1933, the City of Laramie was unable to make the payroll to city workers. Consequently, the town council authorized issuing scrip to employees, in lieu of money for their monthly salaries. After $1,115 in scrip was issued and only $600 was redeemed, the city terminated the experiment.

Wyoming Bank Profile

In May 2010, there are 34 banks in the State of Wyoming. 25 are state chartered institutions and 9 are national institutions. There are 185 branch banks: 58 state bank branches; 21 national bank branches; 48 interstate state bank branches; and 61 interstate national bank branches (branches of banks chartered in states other than Wyoming). One Wyoming state bank had an interstate branch in Nebraska.

In July, 2000, there were 50 banks in Wyoming. Of that 50, 29 were state-chartered and 21 had national charters. Additionally, there were 114 branch banks in the state, 38 affiliated with state-chartered banks, 54 connected to nationally-chartered banks and 22 were interstate national bank branches.

Ten years earlier, in 1990, Wyoming had 32 national banks and 39 state banks. The national bank with the most money in deposits in 1990 was Wyoming National Bank of Casper ($175.6 million in 1991). In that year, the state bank with the most in deposits: 1st Interstate Bank of Commerce, Sheridan ($262.2 million in 1991). *Source: Wyoming Department of Audit, July 2000, May 2010.*

18 Wyoming Bank Failures, 1983-1990

1. Western Bank of Lovell (June 24, 1983)
2. Western National Bank, Casper (1984)
3. State Bank of Mills (1984)
4. Saratoga State Bank (October 1985)
5. Yellowstone State Bank, Lander (November 1985)
6. American Bank of Casper (January 1986)
7. First National Bank of Douglas (February 1986)
8. Security Bank of Glenrock (June 6, 1986)
9. First National Bank of Sheridan (July 1986)
10. Medicine Bow State Bank (August 1986)
11. American National Bank of Casper (August 1986)
12. Valley State Bank, Baggs (October 1986)
13. Guaranty Federal Savings of Casper (Dec. 12, 1986)
14. American National Bank of Evanston (Aug. 20, 1987)
15. Stockman's Bank and Trust, Gillette (Sept. 18, 1987)*
16. First State Bank of Shoshoni (Dec. 20, 1987)
17. Bank of Casper (1988)
18. First Savings Bank of Diamondville (June, 1990)

The Stockman's failure was the biggest in Wyoming history. The bank had assets of $150 million and, at the time of its failure, it was the fourth largest bank in the state.

17 Wyoming Bank Failures, 1920-1923

1. Bank of Arvada, June 1920 (1st bank failure in Wyoming since 1903)
2. Bank of Lusk
3. State Bank of Meeteetse (Dec. 22, 1920)
4. Garland State Bank (1921)
5. Guernsey State Bank (1921)
6. Moorcroft Bank (Aug. 5, 1921)

> 1931 commodity prices in Wyoming: Wheat: 14 cents per bushel. Oil: 19 cents per barrel (price at Salt Creek). Cattle: $4.14 per hundred.

7. Powder River State Bank (Oct. 20, 1921)
8. Citizens' State Bank of Upton (Oct. 27, 1921)
9. Citizens' State Bank of Gillette (Oct. 1921)
10. People's Bank of Moorcroft (Oct. 29, 1921)
11. Big Horn County Bank, Basin (May 15, 1922)
12. Platte County State Bank, Wheatland (Feb. 1, 1923)
13. Stockmen's State Bank of Medicine Bow (March 1923)
14. First National Bank of Rock River (June 14, 1923)
15. Stockgrowers State Bank of LaGrange (June 14, 1923)
16. Marbleton State Bank (July 5, 1923)
17. First National Bank of Manville (Dec. 11, 1923)

25 Wyoming Bank Failures in 1924*

1. Weston County Bank (Feb. 2)
2. First National Bank of Lusk (Feb. 7)
3. First National Bank of Lingle (March 19)
4. Torrington National Bank (March 19)
5. Powell National Bank (March 27)
6. Clearmont State Bank (April 23)
7. Citizens' State Bank of Sheridan (May 15)
8. Manderson State Bank (May 25)
9. Thermopolis State Bank (June 10)
10. First National Bank, Newcastle (June 12)
11. Osage State Bank (June 12)
12. First National Bank of Basin (June 14)
13. Bank of Carpenter (July 9)
14. Bank of Upton (July 9)
15. Cowley State Bank (July 9)
16. Hillsdale State Bank (July 9)
17. First National Bank, Cheyenne (July 9)
18. Bank of Keeline (July 10)
19. Citizens' Bank of Cheyenne (July 21)
20. Johnson County Bank, Buffalo (Sept. 10)
21. First National Bank, Kaycee (Nov. 24)
22. Lingle State Bank (Dec. 10)
23. Cheyenne State Bank (Dec. 10)
24. Commercial State Bank, Guernsey (Dec. 10)
25. First National Bank, Torrington (Dec. 16)

FDIC-Insured Financial Institutions That Failed, 1991-2010

1. Westland Federal Savings and Loan, Rawlins, July 26, 1991
2. Bank of Wyoming, Thermopolis, July 10, 2009

James R. Robinson (b. Casper, 1932, d. Slovenia, 1995), headed the international division of Bank of America. Later, he helped restructure the central banks of Hungary, Czechoslovakia, Poland, Romania and Slovenia.

County Rankings by Per Capita Personal Incomes (2007)

1. Teton County, $132,728*
2. Sublette, $61,411 (26th nationally)
3. Natrona, $52,543 (61)
4. Sheridan, $50,669, (76)
5. Campbell, $47,151 (110)
6. Sweetwater, $46,195 (123)
7. Park, $44,060 (161)
8. Crook, $43,462 (169)
9. Laramie, $43,351 (173)
10. Uinta, $42,621 (191)
11. Converse, $42,602 (192)
12. Weston, $41,992 (207)
13. Washakie, $40,781 (239)
14. Johnson, $40,462 (249)
15. Lincoln, $40,373 (254)
16. Carbon, $40,123 (265)
17. Hot Springs, $39,168 (302)
18. Fremont, $35,512 (531)
19. Niobrara, $35,128 (573)
20. Albany, $34,983 (589)
21. Platte, $34,480 (655)
22. Goshen, $32,906; (852)
23. Big Horn, $28,519 (1,659)

* In 2007, Teton County had the highest per capita income of any of the 3,112 county/state sub-divisions in the United States. Number in parentheses is the county's ranking nationally among all counties in the U. S.

Wyoming Bankruptcies, 1991-2009

1991--1,500 bankruptcy petitions were filed in Wyoming.
2005—3,300 bankruptcies in Wyoming.
2008--   866
2009-- 1,400

6 Well-Known Wyomingites Who Went Bankrupt

1. Alexander Swan

Swan once controlled the largest cattle operation in Wyoming, the Swan Land and Cattle Company. The ranch's herds were decimated by the blizzard of 1886-1887 and Swan, who had borrowed substantial sums from British banks and investors, was forced into bankruptcy. Reorganized, the firm survived until 1950.

2. Moreton Frewen

Frewen, a British gentleman, established the 76 Ranch in the Powder River Basin in the 1870s. He built a substantial house called "Frewen's castle" and entertained lavishly both at his ranch and his Cheyenne home. Among the guests were his in-laws, the Randolph Churchills, the parents of the future Prime Minister Winston Churchill. Like Swan, the cattle "bust" and the hard winter put an end to Frewen's ranching career in Wyoming.

3. DeForest Richards

Richards served as governor of Wyoming from 1898 until his death in 1903. A pioneer Douglas banker, Richards had once owned a tannery in Alabama where he had gone shortly after the Civil War from his native New Hampshire. The business proved to be a disaster and Richards was forced into bankruptcy. He worked for two years as a shoemaker, turning the tannery skins into a useful product, and paid back his debts. He came to Wyoming in 1886 after working for a year in his brother's Chadron, Nebr., bank.

Joe Leiter, Chicago millionaire, like to play faro and other gambling games at the Turf Exchange, Sheridan..During a gambling evening in 1904, he was at one point $72,000 in the hole, but. managed to win $4,000 by end of the game. .

4. Carl Garver

Garver owned and operated the "Maverick Bank" of Douglas in the early 1890s. When making loans, he took anything for security including spurs, saddles and revolvers. After the bank failed in 1893 and he was forced into bankruptcy, Garver returned to Des Moines, Iowa, where he was elected mayor years later.

5. C. H. "Dad" Worland

Worland (the man for whom the town of Worland was named) declared bankruptcy on April 16, 1910, following serious reverses in the hotel business. He lost ownership of his "Worland Hotel" but apparently continued as manager for a short period. *Source: John W. Davis, Sadie and Charlie: The Lives and Times of Sadie and Charlie Worland. (Worland: Washakie Publishing, 1989), p. 22.*

6. Ed Herschler

Governor Herschler became the first sitting governor of Wyoming to declare bankruptcy. In September 1985, after his partnership in the Yellowstone Ranch in west-central Wyoming ran into financial difficulty, he was forced into the move. After his third term as governor, a record, he did not seek re-election in 1986. He died in February 1990.

Some Supposedly "Lost" Treasure Troves in Wyoming

Numerous accounts exist of lost treasure in various corners of Wyoming. Most of the stories have little or no foundation, but they include:

1. Outlaw treasure near Baggs

Legend has it that Butch Cassidy's gang hid loot from train robberies in the Baggs area.

2. Butch Cassidy's treasure near Smoot

Another legendary hiding place for train robbery loot.

3. Ezra Lay's lost treasure near Rock River

4. Jack Slade's lost treasure near Guernsey

Slade, a stage company manager for the Overland Stageline, operated out of Virginia Dale, Colo. He was hanged by vigilantes in Montana. It seems curious that any of his "treasure" would have been buried near Guernsey.

5. Cold Springs stage robbery treasure, near Newcastle

The loot was removed from a coach on the Cheyenne-Deadwood stageline in 1877. Much of it was rumored to have never been recovered and, thus, perhaps buried in the area of the robbery.

6. Outlaw treasure near Fort Laramie

7. Dead Train Robber's treasure near Rock Springs

8. Rock Creek "treasure"

Ruben Stockwell and Jess White found a real "lost treasure" on Aug. 7, 1909. The two men found a jar in a basement of an abandoned building in Rock Creek. The jar contained $4,000 in 20-dollar gold pieces. William Taylor, the owner of the property, contested their "find," contending that he had buried the coins years earlier. The dispute went into court. In 1915, the Wyoming Supreme Court found in favor of Taylor's claim.

On Sept. 1, 2008, a Worland gambler at the Araphaho-owned Wind River Casino hit a jackpot of nearly $390,000, one of the casino's biggest recorded jackpots. Wind River Casino policy prohibits identifying jackpot winners. Jimmy Valdez of Cheyenne won $470,000 in June, 1992, at Wyoming Off-Track Betting by picking the correct choices for consecutive races. Several Wyomingites have won the top prize in the Colorado lottery. The first Wyoming person to win money on iWon.com was Laura Claunch of Casper who won $1,000 on June 17, 2000.

BETS

1. Harry Yesness on the Dempsey-Willard Fight

Yesness had opened a small tailoring business in Casper and, in July 1919, he was slowly going broke. He saw one opportunity to stay open by betting successfully on the outcome of the world heavyweight championship fight between champion Jess Willard and challenger Jack Dempsey on the Fourth of July, 1919, in Toledo. Yesness bet heavily on Coloradoan Dempsey who knocked out Willard in the third round. From the winnings, Yesness was able to stay in business. Soon, he was able to finance the opening of a second shop.

2. Julia Carey on the outcome of a legislative act

The wife of Gov. Robert Carey bet six pairs of gloves that she could get the bill passed to authorize Saratoga Hot Springs reserve. Judge T. Blake Kennedy, dubious about the bill's prospects, accepted the bet. The judge saluted Mrs. Carey's lobbying skills and paid up when the legislature passed the act in its next session.

3. Buffalo Bill and others on a poker game

George T. Beck, Jake Schwoob, William F. Cody and others played poker together frequently in 1900. One evening the betting seemed particularly fierce. Cody, noting the size of one pot, commented that the winner should donate his take to the Episcopal Church building fund drive, then in progress. When Beck won, he announced he would follow Cody's suggestion and donate the money to the church. The Episcopal Church, "built on a bet," was dedicated in 1902.

4. Buffalo brewer on a rooster

Joe Sharp, a barber in Buffalo, raised and trained fighting bantam roosters. In the summer of 1885, Fischer, the local brewery owner, heard that Sharp had been "bragging up" his tiny fowl. The brewer owned a huge rooster and he told Sharp the rooster would show his chicken how to fight. Fischer, a novice at cockfighting, did not know that the bantam had sharp spurs attached to his legs. In the "fight" that followed, his rooster was reduced to ribbons. Sharp claimed the bet. Fischer paid up, muttering about the relative unfairness of "arming" a chicken.

5. Gambling at the Wort

In 1933, Wilbur Woodrow, who had lost money gambling, sued Charles and Jesse Wort and Otto Johns for running a speakeasy, retail liquor business and gambling house out of the Wort Livery Stable in Jackson during Prohibition. His case was unsuccessful and Woodrow was allegedly later pistol-whipped by the defendants.

6. Walter Heacock on "Five Minutes to Midnight"

The rodeo cowboy arrived too late to participate in the 1935 Cheyenne Frontier Days rodeo. Confident that he would have won had he been able to ride in the bronc-riding competition, Heacock bet Pete Knight, the bronc-riding champion, that he could ride "Five Minutes to Midnight," the famed bucking horse. Heacock got thrown almost immediately. He unsaddled his own horse, walked over and presented it to Knight and walked out of the arena.

7. Dr. W. C. Cunningham keeping his eye on the cards

Cunningham was an early-day Uinta County dentist who had lost an eye due to an infection and had a glass eye fitted in the socket. He was a serious poker player and, one night when a game with big stakes was in progress, he was called away from the table to perform an emergency tooth extraction. All of the players agreed to hold their cards until

> Item in Thermopolis newspaper, Aug. 2, 1907: "Thermopolis area cowboy won a high stakes poker game. As he was cashing in his chips--pushing the chips across the table--he died of a heart attack."

he returned. To ensure that no one cheated, Dr. Cunningham laid his cards face down on the table and removed his glass eye. He placed it on the cards, reminding his fellow players that it was there to "watch these so-and-so's until I return."

8. Nurse Hits the Jackpot

Jackson historian Jack Huyler, in his book And That's the Way It Was in Jackson's Hole, tells of watching a huge bet once in the late 1930s. A nursing convention was in Jackson and one of the nurses walked into the Log Cabin Saloon and straight up to the roulette wheel. She put $1,000 down on 'red' without a word to anyone. "We all held our breath," Huyler wrote. The marble fell in 'red' and she walked out with the winnings.

7. Numerous bets in the wide-open gambling parlors, Jackson, 1950s

In the early 1940s, slot machines were a common sight in Jackson, even though gambling was against state law. Jackson mayor Harry Clissold could often be found at the card tables in the lobby of the Wort Hotel. The first official crack-down on illegal gambling in the town took place in 1951. The practice re-emerged and, in 1956, Gov. Milward Simpson ordered action to be taken against gambling in Teton County. Four bars lost their liquor licenses as a result of official attempts to end gambling.

Gambling Stories

In 1901 the Wyoming Legislature made gambling illegal in the state. Before then, a number of notorious episodes resulted from poker games and roulette.

When gambling was legal in Wyoming in the 19th century, few stories appeared in the newspapers about it. It was only when some desperado robbed a gambling house or a cheat was discovered that it was news.

In 1890, the year of Wyoming statehood and just a few years after Casper was founded, a crooked gambler known only as "Black Dick" stole a pile of silver dollars off a saloon card table while a game for higher stakes was going on nearby. When it was discovered that the money was missing and so was Black Dick, nearly everyone in the saloon gave chase.

The entire town was searched but somehow, Black Dick had given the vigilantes the slip. But the next morning, the sheriff caught him boarding a train at Glenrock. When he was brought back to Casper, some people were so incensed at the gravity of his crime that they wanted to lynch him. Instead, he was given a 90-day jail sentence and told to leave town when he was released.

Casper newspapers in those days seemed to measure prosperity by the extent of gambling activity. The *Wyoming Derrick* reported in 1894: "The town is the liveliest in the state. Business of every kind is good and as a further evidence of our prosperity, there are four poker games in full blast."

Just before gambling was outlawed, two men were caught in Casper operating a crooked roulette wheel. The newspaper reported: "The men left town just before the people could deal with them in accordance with their feelings." The editor concluded: "A man who would cheat at a gambling table is considered the worst kind of a cheat."

It may be that these types of incidents prompted the legislature to outlaw gambling in 1901.

C. W. Jeffrey died in 1974, at the age of 90. Born in Osceola, Nebr., he came to Wyoming in 1916, worked for the Union Pacific Railroad and later homesteaded near Riverton. After service in World War I, he attended medical school at the University of Illinois, graduating at the age of 27. He returned to Wyoming and practiced medicine in Rawlins. In the 1930s, he loaned $5,000 to oilman A. B. Cobb who was drilling for oil near Cutbank, Montana. Jeffrey gained a fortune when Cobb's well hit a gusher. Jeffrey went on to underwrite uranium exploration and, consequently, the uranium town of Jeffrey City was named in his honor.

Small Investors Lost in Wyoming Cattle Collapse

European investors sunk hundreds of thousands of dollars in the cattle industry in Wyoming in the 1880s. Many of these investors were Scots, mostly from the cities of Edinburgh, Glasgow and Dundee. A substantial number were "small investors."

According to Board of Trade records of "dissolved companies" held in the Scottish Public Record Office in Edinburgh, wealthy investors, many of whom were bankers and industrialists, put money into the ranch companies during the initial stages in the early 1880s. By the middle of the decade, however, many were selling small numbers of shares to middle class investors.

The famous Swan Land and Cattle Company was incorporated in Scotland on March 30, 1883, with 60,000 shares, each share valued at ten British pounds. The largest initial investor was not a Scottish resident, but A. R. Converse, Cheyenne banker, who held some 10,500 shares. Company organizer Alexander Swan was the second largest stockholder and eleven other American investors held substantial amounts, including several Chicago bankers. Converse and most of the Americans sold all of their shares in 1884 while 533 Scottish and English shareholders retain their interests in the firm. By the spring of 1886, the number of shareholders had risen to more than 840 and included editors of two Edinburgh newspapers.

Prices for cattle declined in the middle 1880s as supply overtook demand. Nearly a million cattle ranged over the public lands in Wyoming in 1886. Following a dry summer, the cattle were not in condition for the terrible snowstorms that started in November and continued until April of 1887. Thousands of cattle were lost. While many of the bigger investors sold their shares in the spring of 1887, apparently after receiving news of the bad range conditions, Swan and most of the smaller shareholders hung on. Predictably, the stock declined in value.

In April, 1889, Swan forfeited his shares. Others sold at huge losses. Nonetheless, the firm stayed in operation. A resolution passed by shareholders at an extraordinary meeting in Edinburgh in March, 1889, read: "Notwithstanding the statement made by directors in their report to the annual meeting of shareholders held today, that it appears to them that one-half of the paid-up capital of the company is lost, the company shall not be dissolved and wound up." Despite the optimism, company fortunes continued to erode.

In late March of 1892, the company shareholders held another extraordinary meeting in Edinburgh, declaring that 600,000 pounds of capital had been lost. Paid up capital was reduced substantially. Apparently, ranch manager John Clay, then the president of the Wyoming Stockgrowers Association, attended the Edinburgh meeting. Due to the importance of the meeting to the company's fortunes, it is not surprising that Clay was out of the country at the time the Johnson County Invasion force was setting off early that next month.

After reorganizations, the Swan managed to survive. Many other firms that had once attracted capital from hundreds of excited European investors left little but unrealized hopes and worthless stock certificates in their wake.

The main house on the Flag Ranch, south of Laramie, was built by Robert Homer in 1890, In Nov. 1933, the house was destroyed by fire. At the time, the ranch was.owned by Fred Klink, Sr., the wealthy owner of a Denver packikng house. His son, Fred Klink, Jr., manager of the ranch, had died in an auto accident between Denver and Cheyenne on Oct. 29, 1932.

BIRDS

Wyoming's best known "birder": Probably Dr. Oliver Scott of Casper. The rancher/doctor had a lifetime list of 720 species by the end of 1994. He helped found the Casper Audubon Chapter in 1954 and was one of the originators of the annual "Christmas count" in 1947. He was the Wyoming reviewer for the classic, *A Field Guide to Western Birds.*

1st clinic to specialize in treatment of falcons: Dave and Cheryl Remple sold their Laramie animal hospital and moved to Dubai in 1983 where they started the world's first falcon clinic. A story of the clinic appeared in the *Wall Street Journal*, April 12, 1990.

State Bird Farm: Established in 1937, the facility is located three miles south of Story on 50 acres. More than 10,000 pheasants are raised there annually.

One Ornerythologist's Concatenation of Wyoming's 10 Most Fascinating Feathered Friends
(in evolutionary order)
By Phil White

1. White Pelican

These ancient birds have nine-foot wingspans, second only to the California condor among North American birds. Seeing their black-tipped wings aloft over Yellowstone Lake is one of the most sublime sights in all of nature. Besides, "an amazing bird is the pelican; its beak can hold more than its belly can."

2. Trumpeter Swan

The mid-continent population of trumpeters was saved from destruction primarily because Yellowstone Park provided refuge from irresponsible hunters. They are North America's largest waterfowl and the world's tallest swan. Look for them at Christian Pond in Grand Teton or on Flat Creek near Jackson. They feed on potamogeton. Doesn't everybody?

3. Osprey

The fish eagles dine on fish exclusively. In summer, follow flying ospreys to their large stick nests on rock towers deep in the Grand Canyon of the Yellowstone.

4. Peregrine Falcon

Once extirpated from most of their range by pesticide poisoning, these bullets in the air are making a tentative comeback. A number of captive-bred birds have been released in the wild in Northwest Wyoming in recent years. We hope these "wanderers" will return to Wyoming to raise young in wild eyries.

5. White-tailed Ptarmigan

A tough, grouse-like resident of the harsh alpine rocks around Medicine Bow Peak west of Laramie, its pure white plumage in winter and mottled color in summer make it very hard to find. Its feathered toes are built-in snowshoes.

6. Whooping Crane

Forty-five years ago only about 15 wild whoopers were left and extinction appeared certain. But protection of their Canadian nesting grounds and their Texas coast wintering area has helped these giant white birds to make a very slow recovery. In the mid-1970s, Canadian and American biologists began placing wild and captive-produced whooper eggs in the nests of sandhill cranes at Gray's Lake National Wildlife Refuge just west of Freedom. For several years, some of the whoopers raised by the sandhill crane foster parents have chosen to spend their summers in Wyoming. It would be thrilling and fitting if Wyoming, the last redoubt of so many creatures on the brink, becomes the site of the first successful nesting by members of this new flock.

7. Burrowing Owl

A small owl with long legs and a quizzical look that nests in rodent burrows on the prairies. Urbanization has eliminated a number of nesting colonies near Cheyenne and Casper.

8. Horned Lark

My personal nomination for state bird. Though it is probably the most numerous, widespread and often-seen native bird in Wyoming, most state residents could not identify it. It is the only lark native to North America and its spring "skylarking" performances are inspiring. Unlike some state birds I know, the horned lark does not abandon Wyoming in the winter.

9. Water Ouzel (or dipper)

Slate-gray, stubby-tailed denizens of river cascades and waterfalls. Ouzels build mossy nests behind a waterfall and walk in and under rushing water to find insects. They do deep knee bends incessantly when out of the water. John Muir writes of their glorious song, but I never can hear anything but the waterfall.

10. Rosy Finch

A resident of the alpine, these birds nest near the permanent snowfields where they harvest seeds and insects. Males have rosy wings and rumps. In winter, they move to the valleys.

(**An apology:** Each of the 371 species of birds that has been seen in Wyoming is ineffably fascinating in its own way. Limiting me to ten was a cruel stroke by the editors. I chose some endangered ones, some less known and unappreciated ones, some grandly beautiful ones or comical ones.

I have purposely left out our state bird, the meadowlark. I think meadowlarks are wonderful, but five other states have also chosen the meadowlark as their state bird. Wyoming's state bird should be a unique, memorable symbol of this state alone. No state has chosen the trumpeter swan, the golden eagle, the osprey, the peregrine falcon, the prairie falcon, the whooping crane, the western tanager, the violet-green swallow, the horned lark. Any of these would make a better avian symbol for Wyoming than our fairweather friend, the meadowlark).

Editor's Note: *Phil White, Laramie lawyer, writer and naturalist, wrote this list for our first edition of Wyoming Almanac. By popular demand, it is reprinted in this edition.*

Misc. Stories About Birds

1. Cassie Allen's white owl

The Allen family lived in the northern part of Jackson Hole near Moran in the early 1900s. Young Cassie was crossing through a cemetery one evening where two of her brothers were buried (one from drowning and the other in a horse accident) when, suddenly, something large, soft and white drifted down toward her from the trees. Cassie thought it was a ghost, but it turned out to be a great snowy owl.

2. The Pigeon Question

Amidst talk of the need to poison the M Street Underpass pigeons considered a nuisance by some, the Rock Springs City Council in May 1987, designated the pigeon as the official city bird. In early 1989, however, the City Council de-designated the pigeon and hung a ceramic owl at the underpass in an effort to frighten the birds. The pigeons were not much impressed, but were relieved nonetheless when someone stole the ceramic owl a few weeks later.

3. Film Delivery

In the late 1980s, homing pigeons were used to deliver film to a photography lab in

Jackson. Photographer Ken Beale shot scenes on raft trips, tied the film to a pigeon and sent it flying off to land at Rod Lewis' lab.

4. Bird Count

The Audubon bird count is conducted annually by Murie Audubon Society of Casper. As an example of the variety of birds in the area in winter, on Dec. 20, 1992, counters recorded 46 species in Casper and 43 species in Bates Hole. Included at Bates Hole were 40 golden eagles and a saw-whet owl.

5. Bird hospital

The first Wyoming "bird hospital" was organized in 1971 by Frank and Lois Layton in Casper. By 1998, bird hospitals also operated in Cody and Gillette.

5. Sage Grouse

The numbers of sage grouse in Wyoming have declined markedly since the 1970s. A 1996 Game and Fish estimate put the numbers at 40 percent of the 1970s total. Causes for the decline include encroachments of civilization, drought and severe winters. On March 5, 2010, the Department of the Interior announced that the sage grouse would not be listed as an endangered species, but careful observation would be kept on their numbers in the event that the declines continued

4 Facts About Trumpeter Swans in Wyoming

1. Trumpeter Swans in Jackson Hole

Once reduced to just 66 birds in the United States in 1933, the trumpeter swans now number more than 1,500 in Wyoming, Montana and Idaho. About 300 live in Jackson Hole and another 200 elsewhere in the state.

2. Only Existing Trumpeters in Early 1900s

The Greater Yellowstone population is the only nesting group in the lower 48 states that was not eliminated by the early 1900s as the species neared extinction.

3. Total Trumpeters in Greater Yellowstone Area

When surveyed in September 2008, all breeding groups in the western United States contained only 459 trumpeters, including 408 adults and 51 cygnets. Of these, 427 (379 adults and 48 cygnets) summered in Greater Yellowstone, 12 (9 adults and 3 cygnets) in Oregon, and 20 (20 adults with no cygnets) in Nevada.

4. Rarest Birds in the Rockies

With less than 70 nesting pairs in the entire west, trumpeter swans are one of the rarest native breeding bird species in the western United States. From 2004-09, there has been an average of 56 nesting pairs in Greater Yellowstone.

4 Most Common Areas to Sight Trumpeter Swans

1. Flat Creek, north of Jackson
2. Oxbow of Snake River, south of Highway 89-287, 30 mi. north of Jackson
3. Madison Junction, Yellowstone
4. Red Rocks National Wildlife Refuge (Idaho)

Plans for construction of the Buffalo Bill Museum and Whitney Gallery of Western Art were announced on Feb. 13, 1957.

BOOKS

1st book printed in Wyoming: *Dictionary of the Sioux Language* compiled by Lts. J. K. Hyer and W. S. Starring, published at Fort Laramie in December, 1866. No more than 50 copies were printed. Examples are held in collections of the Huntington Library and Newberry Library. In the summer of 2005, a copy was brought to *Antiques Roadshow* while the show was filming in Tampa, Florida.
2nd book printed in Wyoming: Also a dictionary, *A Vocabulary of the Snake, or Sho-Sho-Nay Dialect* compiled by Joseph A. Gebow, published at Green River in 1868.
Most expensive new book published in Wyoming: Ferdinand LaFrentz's *Cowboy Stuff,* a book of poems. Ten copies were sold for $5,000 each as a fundraiser for charity in the 1890s.
1st book to describe what is now Wyoming: *The Adventures of Captain Bonneville* by Washington Irving, published in 1843.

Best-Loved Books on Wyoming

Pat Hall of Cheyenne conducted a centennial-year poll to determine what 100 Wyomingites believed were their favorite books about Wyoming. The poll results were released in October, 1990. The respondents listed a total of 224 titles. The books receiving the most mentions were:

History of Wyoming by Dr. T. A. Larson
Banditti of the Plains by Asa S. Mercer
Wyoming: A History by Dr. T. A Larson
The Virginian by Owen Wister
The Solace of Open Spaces by Gretel Ehrlich
Red Wind of Wyoming by Peggy Simson Curry
Letters of a Woman Homesteader by Elinore Pruitt Stewart
The War on Powder River by Helena Huntington Smith
Rising from the Plains by John McPhee
Wyoming Place Names by Mae Urbanek

Wyoming in Fiction

1. Ghosts of Wyoming by Alyson Hagy (2010)
The work is the fourth collection of short stories written by Hagy who teaches creative writing at the University of Wyoming.
2. Junkyard Dogs by Craig Johnson (2010)
Johnson is the author of five previous books featuring "Absaroka County," Wyoming, and its sheriff, Walk Longmire. Johnson lives in Ucross.
3. Gather My Horses by John D. Nesbitt (2010)
The 25th novel by Nesbitt, a professor of English and Spanish at Eastern Wyoming College, Torrington.
4. Hard Evidence by Roxanne Rustand (2007)
The 16th novel by the prolific romance novel author.
5. Angel's Fall by Nora Roberts (2006)
Roberts wrote more than 160 novels. This book, like many of her earlier works, was made into a movie, *Angels Fall* (2007), starring Heather Locklear.
6. Try by Lily Burana (2006)
Burana is a New York-based writer. who writes of a young artist who is the heroine of the story, returns to Cheyenne, meets a rodeo cowboy and goes away with him.
7. The Next Mrs. Blackthorne by Joan Johnston (2005)
The ninth book in Johnston's Bitter Creek Series.

8. A Home of Her Own by Cathleen Connors (2005)
Harlequin Romance written by a prolific author.

9. An Unfinished Life by Mark Spragg (2005)
The book, set near Cody, was made into a film starring Robert Redford.

10. The Cold Dish by Craig Johnson (2005)
Johnson lived in Ucross and this was the fourth in his mystery series.

11. Night Thunder by Jill Gregory (2004)
The author, based in Michigan, wrote more than 30 romance novels, many set in Western locales.

12. Vow of Vengeance by Lewis B. Patten (2004)
Initially published in 1975, this book was one of more than 100 novels written by Patten, a Denver-based writer who died in 1981. Three of his novels became movies: *Red Sundown, Death of a Gunfighter,* and *The Undefeated.*

13. Wyoming Wedding by Nancy J. Parra (2004)
The romance novel by the Chicago-based former journalist was published by Avalon Books.

14. Trial by Ice and Fire by Clinton McKinzie (2003)
McKinzie, a native of Santa Monica, Calif., graduated from the University of Wyoming College of Law. His first book, *Edge of Justice*, was published in 2002. He works as deputy district attorney in Colorado.

15. Wyoming Trucks, True Love and the Weather Channel by Jeffe Kennedy (2003)
The book, published by the University of New Mexico Press, was the Laramie-based author's first book of essays.

15. Black Hat Butte by John D. Nesbitt (2003)

16. Under Cottonwoods by Stephen Grace (2003)
The first novel published by the Laramie-based author.

17. The Wages of Genius by Gregory Mone (2003)
The story by the Long Island-based author is about a young scientist who was born in the mythical town of Ionia, Wyoming.

18. Cassidy by Wayne D. Overholser (2003)
Overholser, who died in Boulder, Colo., in 1996 at the age of 89, wrote numerous novels under his own name and many pen names, including Dan J. Stevens, Joseph Wayne, and John S. Daniels. He was a graduate of the University of Oregon who taught in public schools before turning to writing full time in 1945. Cassidy was the reissue of a book first published in 1973.

19. Fire Flight by John J. Nance (2003)
The book, about aerial fire-fighting in Yellowstone, was one of many written by the Texas-based attorney and author.

20. Wyoming Widow by Elizabeth Lane (2003)
A Harlequin romance set in Wyoming.

21. Spirit Warrior by Cassie Edwards (2002)
Story of firefighters engaged in their work in Yellowstone National Park.

22. Wyoming Wind: A Story of Tom Horn by Jon Chandler (2002)
Chandler's great-grandfather was a Tom Horn friend. Chandler, a 4th-generation Coloradoan who lived in the Denver area, also was known as a songwriter and musician.

23. Dream Country by Luanne Rice (2002)
The New York City-based writer used Wyoming as a setting in her romance novels.

Gardner Cowles, owner and publisher of the *Des Moines Register*, visited his daughter, Mrs. James D. LeCron, in Cheyenne in December, 1912.

24. Storm Clouds over Chantel by Colleen L. Reece (2002)

The author wrote inspirational/religious novels.

25. Edge of Justice by Clinton McKenzie (2002)

In this, his debut novel, McKenzie introduced the character that would appear in later novels, Antonio "Ant" Burns: agent of the Wyoming Division of Criminal Investigation and amateur rock climber.

26. Kelly and the Three-Toed Horse by Peter Bowen (2001)

Bowen, who lived in Livington, Montana, wrote about Yellowstone Kelly in a series of historical novels.

27. Day Star Rising by Louise Lenahan Wallace (2001)

"A tale of healing love against slander and suspicion in Wyoming territory," is noted as a sub-title.

28. Girl Beside Him by Cris Mazza (2001)

Mazza taught writing at the University of Illinois, Chicago. The novel features a wildlife biologist's adventures in Wyoming.

29. Click by Dan Whipple (2001)

The first novel by the former Casper journalist who wrote for many magazines and websites.

30. Half-Moon and Empty Stars by Gerry Spence (2001)

The first novel by Spence, a famed Wyomng trial lawyer wrote numerous non-fiction works, features a small-town lawyer, Abner Hill, who is asked to defend a Native American charged with murder.

31. Wyoming Wildflower by Pam Crooks (2001)

The romance writer, now based in Omaha, once lived in western Nebraska.

32. In the Snow Forest by Roy Parvin (2000)

A woman finds herself snowbound in a Wyoming town.

33. Black Mountain by Les Standiford (2000)

The Florida-based author usef Wyoming as a setting for a wilderness trip by a New York governor in this suspense thriller.

34. Wyoming by Barry Gifford (2000)

The story of a mother and 9-year-old son traveling through the Midwest in the 1950s by car, the two don't have any destination in mind. In their hearts, Wyoming symbolizes a retreat, anonymity. But they never make it there.

35. Close Range: Wyoming Stories by E. Annie Proulx (2000)

The Pulitzer Prize-winning author wrote the book while she was living in Centennial in the late 1990s. She won the Pulitzer for fiction in 1994 for *Shipping News*.

36. Best Man in Wyoming by Margot Dalton (2000)

The book is a Harlequin romance.

37. Miss Wyoming by Douglas Coupland (1999)

The book was published by Pantheon.

38. Letters from Yellowstone by Diane Smith (1999)

The novel is about a young medical student and botanist who becomes the sole woman on a Smithsonian-backed expedition to Yellowstone National Park in 1898.

39. Wyoming Born and Bred by Cathleen Galitz (1999)

The author has taught junior high and high school. The book is one of a series published by Silhouette Romance.

Tom Clancy, *Clear and Present Danger* (New York: Berkley, 1989): "'And he'd be the richest guy in Cody, Wyoming,' Mike Schratz observed. 'But the wrong people got a sniff. I wonder what tipped them off? What did our friends say?'"

40. Grave Victory by Gregory Bean (1998)

A novel about the only two police officers in Victory, Wyo., who become involved with the investigation of the murder of a young research assistant at Laramie's "agricultural college."

41. The Ranch by Danielle Steel (1997)

A novel by the well-known romance author is about three women who met while working on a Wyoming ranch. They reconnect 20 years later and share their stories.

42. Shifting Stars by Page Lambert (1997)

Lambert, who lives in northeastern Wyoming, writes of a woman Indian warrior in Wyoming Territory in 1850. She moved to Wyoming in 1985 and lives near Sundance. She also wrote *In Search of Kinship: Modern Pioneering on the Western Landscape* (1996).

43. Windmill: Essays from the Four-Mile Ranch by David Romtvedt (1997)

The book was published by Red Crane Books. Romtvedt also wrote *Crossing Wyoming* (1993).

44. Amnesia Moon by Jonathan Lethem (1996)

The novel is described as a "funny post-apocalytic road noir tale of Chaos, an introverted occupant of an abandoned movie theater in Hatford, Wyoming, who is surrounded by mutant locals and living on canned food."

45. Twin Rivers by John D. Nesbitt (1995)

Nesbitt's first novel was "One-Eyed Cowboy Wild." Nesbitt teaches at Eastern Wyoming College in Torrington.

46. Shameless by Judy Collins (1995)

At a July 1995, book-signing in Denver, singer Judy Collins pointed out to *Almanac* co-author Steve Roberts that Wyoming is mentioned in her first fictional novel. The book's main character notes her Wyoming travels (Jackson Hole, the Tetons, along the Continental Divide) toward the end of the novel. Collins, a folk singer and actress from Colorado, has recorded 27 albums with copy sales in the millions. Her 1995 album, also titled "Shameless," was recorded especially for the debut of the novel and a CD version is included with hard-cover editions. It is rare for a novel to have its own soundtrack.

47. A Day of Reckoning by Kurt Arnusch (1995)

The western novel written by Arnusch, a Torrington resident, tells of two brothers in Wyoming and the West in the 1870s.

48. Wendigo Border by Catherine Montrose (1995)

Montrose, who was reared in Laramie, published her earlier work under her maiden name of Catherine Cooke. She taught writing at the University of Colorado, Denver. The Wyoming prairie is the setting for the novel.

49. Sky's Witness: A Year in the Wind River Range by C. L. Rawlins (1994)

Rawlins worked with the Forest Service from 1977-92 as a firefighter, range rider, and field hydrologist. Active in environmental organizations, he lives near Jelm in Albany County. He served as president of the Wyoming Outdoor Council in 1997-99. He also was visiting writer at the University of Wyoming.

50. Ten Sleep by Sarah Andrews (1994)

The book deals with the adventures of Em Hansen, a fictional woman geologist. Trained as a petroleum geologist in Coloardo, Andrews worked for the USGS and Amoco as a geologist in Wyoming. The book became the first of a "forensic geology mystery series." Andrews now teaches and writes in northern California.

51. The Dark Half by Stephen King (1989)

The town of Fort Laramie and Yellowstone National Park are sites mentioned in the novel by the famous author of horror stories. The book had the second-highest sales of any book in 1989, just behind *Clear and Present Danger,* a book in which Cody, Wyoming, is mentioned. Oddly, when the movie version was released, starring Timothy Hutton, Wyoming references were omitted.

52. Murphy's Rainbow by Carolyn Lampman (1993)

Riverton writer Carolyn Brubaker uses the Lampman nom de plume. Her historical romance novel won the National Readers' Choice Award for best historical series romance for 1993. Her first novel, the first part of a trilogy, it is set in Wyoming Territory.

53. Murder in Jackson Hole by J. Royal Horton (1993)

The murder mystery was published by Homestead Publishing, Jackson. "Detective Tommy Thompson uncovers underworld of wealth, influence, drugs and corruption while investigating a series of murders in the shadow of the Grand Tetons in Jackson Hole, Wyoming."

54. Doc Wyoming by Sharon Brondos (1993)

The book is a Harlequin Romance novel. "Wyoming author Sharon Brondos was inspired to write *Doc Wyoming* because of the growing shortage of primary physicians in her home state," the back cover announces.

55. Wyoming Giant by John S. McCord (1992)

The story is about Luke Baynes, a New York lawyer, who was appointed a federal judge in Wyoming territory. McCord is a retired army lieutenant colonel.

56. Drinking Dry Clouds by Gretel Ehrlich (1991)

Ehrlich is a Californian who moved to northern Wyoming to operate a ranch until a lightning accident prompted a return to the West Coast. Her first book was the critically acclaimed *The Solace of Open Spaces* (1986), which won the American Academy and Institute of Arts and Letters prize of $5,000 awarded in 1986. She also wrote *Heart Mountain* (1989) and *Islands, the Universe, Home* (1991).

57. Whiskey Creek by Gary McCarthy (1992)

California-born McCarthy wrote four novels set in Wyoming. The others are *Wind River* (1984), *Last Buffalo Hunt* (1985), and *Powder River* (1985). Much of the action of the novel is set in the mythical town of Whiskey Creek, Wyoming.

58. Prairie by Anna Lee Waldo (1988)

The fictional account of the life of Wyoming rancher and showman Charlie Irwin was written by novelist Waldo whose first book, *Sacajawea*, was also based on a Wyoming character. It was published in 1987.

59. Cord: Paradise Valley by Owen Rountree (1986)

The book, one of a series written by joint authors William Kittredge and Steven Krauzer under the pseudonym, was set in the Cody area. The Cord series of Westerns began in 1982.

Fictional Wyomingites

1. Paul Bartling

The title character in the 1936 novel by K. Smith Albert about Wyoming's oil boom and Casper's growth. The author was a former Casper engineer.

2. Clyde Pickett

The trigger-happy young man shot and killed a young Indian woman and, as a result, was "skinned alive" in the *Legend of the Rawhide* by Eva Lou Bonsell (1946). The story was dramatized annually from 1946 to 1966. After a 20-year hiatus, the pageant was revived in 1986 and presented annually at Lusk.

3. Singletree

The title character of a 1990 novel by Jack Ravage about an African American and a Native American teaming up to defeat unsavory men in 19th century Medicine Bow.

4. Jose Maria Sisnoris

A good guitarist, he played so well that the music put to sleep the sheriff who had come to arrest him near Laramie. He is the main character in the short story, "A Wyoming Night's Entertainment" written by Marion Hamilton Carter and published in *Colliers*, Jan. 13, 1912, pp. 12-13, 30.

5. The Virginian

The title character in the Owen Wister classic, he had no other name.

6. Joe Pickett

Pickett is the game warden main character in the series of novels by C. J. Boxx. Boxx's first Pickett novel was *Open Season* (2001).

7. Sheriff Walt Longmire

Longmire is the central character in a series of mysteries written by Craig Johnson, including *The Dark Horse* (Viking, 2009).

8. Burns brothers

The fictional brothers are primary characters in the mysteries written by Clinton McKinzie, a UW law graduate and Denver-based prosecutor.

Nonfictional Wyomingites in Fiction

1. M. C. Brown, Laramie lawyer and first mayor

Brown was president of the Wyoming Constitutional Convention in 1889. From 1900 to 1905, he was a federal judge in Alaska and is said to be the prototype for a character in Rex Beach's novel, *The Spoilers*. Brown died in Laramie in 1928, on the same day as Edward Ivinson, banker and also former mayor.

2.-3. Richard and Marjorie Cooper, Laramie

Richard Cooper, a close friend of Ernest Hemingway, fished and hunted with the famed author. Hemingway frequently visited the Coopers in Laramie. The Coopers are said to have been the models for the couple about whom Hemingway wrote in his short story, "The Short and Happy Life of Francis Macomber."

4. C. B. Irwin, Laramie County rancher and showman

Prairie by Anna Lee Waldo is a partially fictionalized account of Irwin's life. The book was published by Berkley Books in 1986.

5. "Buffalo" Jones, ranger and outdoorsman

Zane Grey told Jones' story in his 1911 novel, *Last of the Plainsman*.

6. "Uncle Nick" Wilson, pioneer outdoorsman

The man for whom the town of Wilson was named came to Jackson Hole in 1889. He spent his childhood years with Shoshone Indians. He's the hero in the H. R. Driggs novel, *The White Indian Boy or Uncle Nick Among the Shoshones* (1919).

7.-8. Dr. Frances Lane, Cody physician, and George T. Beck, Cody founder

Dr. Emma Harpe, the title character in Caroline Lockhart's sensational book about the town of Cody, *Lady Doc*, is modeled after Dr. Lane. The character is portrayed, however, as a blackmailer and quack. In fact, Dr. Lane was a prominent citizen for whom a memorial window in the Cody Episcopal Church was dedicated in May, 1939. A second character, Andy P. Symes, is said to have been modeled after George T. Beck, Cody founder. The characterization is uncomplimentary—"he was the sort of man who is nearly, but not quite, a gentleman." The book was published by Lippincott in 1912.

9. Sen. Lester C. Hunt

The former Wyoming governor, secretary of state and senator committed suicide in his U. S. Senate office in 1954. The Allen Drury novel, *Advise and Consent*, includes a U. S. senator whose death is similar. Oddly, the Wyoming senator in the Drury novel is the villain and the character who committs suicide in the novel is the senator from Utah.

10.-11. Charles and Alice Moncini, Sheridan

The Sheridan trucker and his wife became the models for the characters in Ernest Hemingway's short story, "The Wine of Wyoming" (1928).

Books for Children and Young Adults Set in Wyoming or by Wyoming Authors

1. Cubby in Wonderland (1932)

The story of a bear cub named Cubby was written by Frances Joyce Farnsworth (1881-1962) who lived in Riverton at the time the book was published. The book, set in Yellowstone National Park, was published by the University of New Mexico Press.

2. Noodles, Sheep Security Guard (1988)

The book about a Hungarian komondor dog was written by Sharon O'Toole who lives in the Savery/Baggs area of Carbon County. The dog guards flocks of sheep at a Wyoming ranch.

3. Purvi and the Bright Star, Purvi and the Rainbow Marble, others

The books about a marble and his friends were written by Jeff Glandt, a Cheyenne East High School and University of Wyoming graduate who wrote the books while teaching in South Dakota.

4. Sarah, Plain and Tall

Author Patricia MacClachlan was born in Cheyenne in 1938. The award-winning book, published in 1986, was made into a film.

5. Wyoming (2000)

The book by Carlienne Frisch was published by Lerner Publications.

6. Bow Wow!: Wyoming Dogs in History, Mystery, Trivia, Legend (1999)

Author is Carole Marsh.

7. Beauregart the Bear (2009)

The book by Kathryn Phylarry, published by Homestead Publishing, is about a Yellowstone bear.

8. Dinosaur Hunter (2003)

The book, written by Elaine Marie Alphin, is an adventure story about a young boy finding remains of dinosaurs on his father's ranch in the 1880s.

9. Secret of the Black Widow (2002)

The book by Eugene M. Gagliano is set in Wyoming about the time of statehood.

10. Adventure in Wyoming (2000)

The book by Bob Schaller is the story of how a family interrupts a vacation to help find a friend who was in an airplane that crashed somewhere in Wyoming.

11. Red Dog by Bill Wallace (1994)

Wallace, a former teacher in Chickasha, Okla., wrote dozens of books for young readers. *Red Dog* is a historical novel set in the wilderness of Wyoming in the 1860s.

Wyoming Autobiographies

1. A Bride Goes West. *By Nannie T. Alderson. (Farrar and Rinehart, 1942).* Alderson was reared on a plantation in the South, and met her husband, Walt, in Kansas. The two ranched in Wyoming. Alderson's memoir, *A Bride Goes West*, was first published in 1942. According to some sources, "she spent her last 30 summers on a ranch outside of Sheridan, Wyoming."

2. The Sage of Bellyache Flats. *By Emory J. Anderson. (Jackson: Pinon Pine, 1988).* Ohio-born and educated Anderson moved to Wyoming to work at the *Northern Wyoming Daily News* in Worland. Later, after ranch and farm jobs, he became editor of the *Jackson Hole Guide*. The book describes his Wyoming adventures.

3. Fair Fights and Foul: A Dissenting Lawyer's Life. *By Thurman Arnold. (New York: Harcourt Brace, 1951).* The Laramie-born lawyer served as the head of the Anti-Trust Division of the Department of Justice and founded one of the nation's largest and most prestigious law firms. Prior to his government service, he practiced law in his home town, served as mayor and was elected to a term in the legislature.

4. Jackson Hole Journal. *By Nathaniel Burt. (Norman: University of Oklahoma Press, 1983).* The reminiscences of the son of writers Struthers and Katherine Burt.

5. Diary of a Dude Wrangler. *By Struthers Burt. (New York: Scribners, 1924).*
Burt began ranching near Moran in 1908 and the book is an account of his adventures in his adopted region.

6. Frontier Trails. *By Frank Canton. (privately printed, 1930).* Wanted for murder in Texas shootout in 1874, Canton drifted to Wyoming where he became a range detective for the Wyoming Stockgrowers Association. From 1882 to 1886, he was sheriff of Johnson County. He participated in the Johnson County Invasion (on the side of the Invaders) and continued to work as a stock detective and gunman. Canton wrote his autobiography after serving nine years as Oklahoma's first adjutant general.

7. Bill Carlisle, Lone Bandit. *By Bill Carlisle. (Pasadena, Calif.: Trail's End Publishing, 1946).* Carlisle robbed trains and gained the name of the "Gentleman Bandit" because he would not steal from women passengers. He was caught, sentenced to a long prison term, escaped, was recaptured and released after more than 20 years behind bars. He managed a motel east of Laramie in his later years.

8. My Army Life and the Fort Phil Kearny Massacre. *By Frances Carrington. (New York: Lippincott, 1910).* The second wife of Col. H. B. Carrington, commander of Fort Phil Kearny during the Fetterman Fight, Frances Carrington was the widow of Capt. William Grummond, who died in the battle.

9. Ab-sa-ra-ka, Home of the Crows. *By Margaret Carrington. (New York: Lippincott, 1868).* The first wife of Col. Carrington wrote this book about the Indians, their habits and their country.

10. South Pass, 1868. *By James Chisholm, edited by Lola Homsher. (Lincoln: University of Nebraska Press, 1960).* The Chicago newspaperman reported on his trip west on the railroad and then by horse to the gold mining fields of South Pass City. His published columns and letters to friends tell the story of a rough, lawless country. Miss Homsher was first director of the Wyoming State Archives and Historical Department.

11. My Life on the Range. *By John Clay. (Chicago: Antiquarian Press, 1961).*
Clay managed the famous Swan Company ranches in the late 1800s.

12. A Doctor's Story: From City Surgeon to Country Doc. *By Dr. William Close. (Ivy Books, 1996).* Close served for many years as a medical doctor in sub-Saharan Africa. He moved to Big Piney and practiced medicine there until his death in 2009. One of the world's foremost experts on the Ebola disease, he is also author of *Ebola: A Documentary Novel and Its Explosion (1995).* His daughter, Glenn Close, is a well-known actress.

13. They Call Me Dirty. *By Conrad Dobler and Vic Carucci. (New York: Putnam, 1988).* Dobler formerly played football in the National Football League where he gained a reputation as the "dirtiest player in football." He played college football at the University of Wyoming and, following his retirement from the pros, returned to live in Wyoming. Playing football took a heavy toll on the Chicago native. He had nine knee replacement surgeries in his later years as a result of football injuries.

14. Sagebrush Dentist. *By Will Frackelton. (Chicago: McClurg & Co., 1941).* The author (1870-1943) lived in Sheridan and practiced dentistry in Sheridan County.

15. Under the Ten Sleep Rim. *By Paul Frison. (Worland: privately printed, 1972).*
Frison's reminiscences tell the story of a covered wagon trip from Colorado at the turn

of the century, the fights between big cattle companies and homesteaders, and the violent "sheep wars" of the early 1900s.

16. Wyoming Cowboy Days. *By C. A. Guernsey. (New York: Putnam's, 1936).* Guernsey tells of open range days in the southeastern part of the state. The town of Guernsey is named for this cowboy-autobiographer.

17. Letters from Honeyhill: A Woman's View of Homesteading, 1914-1931. *By Cecilia Hennel Hendricks. (Boulder: Pruett Publishing, 1986).* Mrs. Hendricks and her husband raised bees in the Shoshone Valley after their marriage in 1914. The journal letters were written to a friend in Indiana.

18. Life of Tom Horn. *By Tom Horn. (Chicago: privately printed, 1904).* Horn wrote the book in his Laramie County Jail cell while he was awaiting execution for murder. After his death, publication of the manuscript was underwritten by Horn's friend and former employer, John Coble.

19. Time Exposure. *By William H. Jackson. (New York: Putnam's, 1940).* The recollections of the famous photographer who was the first man to take pictures of Yellowstone National Park. He drove a herd of horses west through Wyoming in 1866, photographed along the Union Pacific in 1870, and accompanied the Hayden expedition to Yellowstone in 1871.

20. Memoirs of a Pioneer. *By George Lathrop. (Lusk: privately printed, 1920).* The book contains recollections of one of the last stagecoach drivers of the Old West. Lathrop's memory is honored by a marker near Lusk.

21. Wyoming Peace Officer. *By Joe LeFors. (Laramie: privately printed, 1953)* The famous lawman wrote of his years as U. S. Marshal and the highlights of a career, including the arrest of Tom Horn for the murder of young Willie Nickell.

22. Tim McCoy Remembers the West. *By Tim McCoy. (Garden City: Doubleday, 1977).* The life story of the Michigan-born cowboy who became Wyoming adjutant general and motion picture star.

23. Growing Up with Wyoming. *By Fremont Miller (as told to Eugenia Christensen). (Lander: Mortimore Publishing, 1998).* After his plane crashed in the North Sea after a bombing run over Germany in World War II, Miller survived 76 hours in the cold water. He returned to his native Fremont County, raised bees, and served in civic and political offices, including the Wyoming legislature.

24. Wapiti Wilderness: The Life of Olaus and Margaret Murie in Jackson Hole, Wyoming. *By Margaret Murie. (Boulder: Colo. Assoc. Univ. Press, 1985).* The autobiography of the famous naturalists who lived and worked in Alaska and Jackson Hole.

25. Black Elk Speaks: The Life Story of a Holy Man of the Oglala Sioux. *Edited by John Neihardt. (New York: Little, Brown, 1932).* Black Elk, a native of the Powder River Basin, is the best known Wyoming autobiographer. A classic, the book frequently is required reading in school classes.

26. Ranch on the Laramie. *By Ted Olson. (Boston: Little, Brown, 1973).* The veteran newspaperman wrote about his boyhood on a Wyoming ranch and his career in journalism.

27. The Other Side of Time: A Combat Physician in World War II. *By Dr. Brendon Phibbs. (New York: Little, Brown, 1987).* Dr. Phibbs practiced medicine in Casper from 1952-1971. He moved to Tucson in 1971 where he was professor of cardiology at the University of Arizona Medical School. The book tells of his experiences as a combat surgeon. He also wrote *The Human Heart: A Consumer's Guide to Cardiac Care*, in 1982.

28. Letters of a Woman Homesteader. *By Elinore Pruitt Stewart. (Lincoln: University of Nebraska Press, 1961).* The book first appeared as a series of articles in *Atlantic Monthly* in 1913-1914. In 1979, the book was made into the acclaimed film, *Heartland*. A second book, *Letters on an Elk Hunt by a Woman Homesteader,* was published in 1979 by Nebraska Press.

29. Wyoming Scientist: Horses to Space Ships. *By Emerson M. Pugh and Ruth Edgin. (Pompano Beach, Fla.: Exposition-Phoenix, 1979).* The Evanston-born Pugh told of his early life in Wyoming and career in science.

30. Pony Trails in Wyoming. *By J. K. Rollinson. (Caldwell, Idaho: Caxton, 1941).* The autobiography of a pioneer cowboy in Goshen Hole country who later ventured into the Big Horn Basin and became a forest ranger. He tells of game hunts with Buffalo Bill, chasing outlaws in Sunlight Basin, and rounding up cattle on the open range before fences.

31. Journal of a Trapper. *By Osborne Russell. (Lincoln: U. of Nebr. Press, 1955).* The journal was kept by a mountain man who frequented the Wyoming wilderness in the 1830s.

32. Gerry Spence: Gunning for Justice. *By Gerry Spence and Anthony Polk. (Garden City: Doubleday, 1982).* The story of the 12-month period during which Spence prevailed in four important lawsuits including the famous Cantrell murder trial and the Karen Silkwood case. Spence has written three other books.

33. Heart and Sole. *By David Stewart. (Glendale, Calif.: White/Boucke, 1994).* The book is about his 1,600-mile walk (1988) from Wyoming to Nashville, Tennessee, where his dream of singing on stage at the Grand Ole Opry came true.

34. My People of the Plains. *By Bishop Ethelbert Talbot. (New York: Harpers, 1906).* Talbot was Episcopal bishop of Wyoming when he wrote of his life and the lives of his parishioners in Wyoming after the turn of the century.

35. Tales and Irreverencies of a Country Parson. *By Eugene F. Todd. (Cheyenne: Western Americana Publishing, 1997).* This is the memoir of a Wyoming ranch child (b. near Ucross, 1928) who went on to become a controversial Episcopal priest. After graduation from theology school and a term as campus pastor in South Dakota, Todd returned to his native Wyoming in 1961 to serve a parish in Green River. In 1965, he moved to St. Mark's Church in Cheyenne where he served as rector until he retired in 1992.

36. Courage of a Conservative. *By James G. Watt. (New York: Simon and Schuster, 1985).* Watt, a native of Lusk, served as Secretary of the Interior during the first three years of the Reagan administration. The book is less memoir than it is a statement of political philosophy.

37. Brothers and Keepers. *By John E. Wideman. (New York: Penguin, 1984).* The true story of two brothers on two paths. The author was a University of Wyoming professor. His brother, Robbie, was in prison in Pennsylvania, serving a life sentence as an accomplice to a murder. Wideman, who is well known as a novelist, also wrote a memoir.

38. As I Remember. *By Margaret L. Creemens Carr. (1993).* Carr, who died in 2002, wrote about pioneer life in northeastern Wyoming.

39. Rock Springs: Growing Up in a Wyoming Coal Town, 1915-1938. By Thomas P. Cullen. (Portland, 1985).

40. Riding the Edge of an Era: Growing Up Cowboy on the Outlaw Trail. *By Diana Allen Kouris. (High Plains, 2009).* The book is a memoir of growing up in Brown's Park on the Utah-Colorado-Wyoming border.

41. Claiming Ground: A Memoir. *By Laura Bell. (Knopf, 2010)* . After graduating from college in 1977, Bell decided to move west where she became a sheepherder. She lives near Cody where she now works for the Nature Conservancy.

Biographies of Some Well-Known Wyomingites

1. Steamboat: Legendary Bucking Horse. *By Candy Vyvey Moulton and Flossie Moulton. (Glendo: High Plains, 1992).* The book tells of the famous bucking horse, but also about the cowboys who "tried to tame him."

2. First Ladies of Wyoming. *Edited by Mabel Brown. (Cheyenne: Wyoming Commission for Women, 1991).* Brown, a former president of the Wyoming State Historical Society and publisher of the magazine "Bits and Pieces", and 12 other writers researched and wrote biographies of all of the women who have served as the state's "first lady."

3. Goliaths of the World. *By John Bonar. (Laramie: Jelm Mountain, 1981).* Bonar wrote about Glenrock area people and incidents about early life in Converse and Natrona counties. He died in 2006.

4. Gold Buckle Dreams: The Rodeo Life of Chris LeDoux. *By David G. Brown. (Boston: Quinlan Press, 1987).* LeDoux, a former rodeo cowboy who composes and sings, lives and works in Kaycee.

5. E. E. Stevens, Prairie Artist. *By Florence Canfield Burden. (Torrington: privately printed, 1983).* Stevens painted murals for numerous public buildings during the first half of this century. He lived in Goshen County.

6. Finn Burnett, Frontiersman. *By Robert B. David. (Glendale, Calif: Arthur H. Clark, 1937).* Burnett's adventures read almost like fiction. He explored Wyoming as a trapper, scout and teamster in the 19th century.

7. Malcolm Campbell, Sheriff. *By Robert B. David. (Casper: privately printed, 1932).* The legendary sheriff lived in the most exciting days of the Old West. The author, the son of a pioneer stock manager, lived in Casper for many years.

8. Washakie. *By Grace Raymond Hebard. (Glendale, Calif.: Arthur H. Clark, 1930).* Dr. Hebard, the long-time Western historian at the University of Wyoming, wrote biographies of the Shoshone chief and of *Sacajawea* (published in 1933, by Arthur H. Clark).

9. Rising from the Plains. *By John McPhee. (New York: Farrar, Straus, Giroux, 1986).* The book tells the story of Wyoming from its geology and the life of one of the state's best known geologists, David Love. The book began as a series of articles in the *New Yorker.*

10. Wyoming in Profile. *By Jean Mead. (Boulder: Pruett Publishing, 1982).* A collective biography of numerous significant figures in Wyoming government, the arts, and industry, it was written by Mead, a Casper writer.

11. Hans Kleiber, Artist of the Big Horn Mountains. *By Emmie D. Mygatt and Roberta Carkeek Cheney. (Caldwell, Ida.: Caxton, 1975).* Kleiber was a well-known artist. His paintings and etchings are scenes of the Big Horns near his Sheridan County home.

12. Boswell: The Story of a Frontier Lawman. *By Mary Lou Pence. (Cheyenne: privately printed, 1979).* Boswell was a pioneer Albany County lawman.

13. Caspar Collins. *By Agnes Wright Spring. (New York: Columbia University Press, 1927).* Mrs. Spring, who died in 1988, served as State Historian for Wyoming and, later, for Colorado, during her long career. Her biography of Collins, for whom Casper was named, remains the standard work.

14. Stories of Early Days in Wyoming. *By Tacetta Walker. (Casper: Prairie Publishing, 1936)* The book contains biographies of notable Big Horn Basin pioneers.

15. Aven Nelson of Wyoming. *By Roger Williams. (Boulder: Colorado Associated Press, 1984).* Nelson, one of the first members of the University of Wyoming faculty, taught physical science courses at UW for many years. The well-known botanist later served as university president, but returned to teaching.

16. Moreton Frewen's Western Adventures. *By L. Milton Woods. (Laramie: American Heritage Center, 1986).* The story of the Englishman who operated a ranch in the Powder River Basin in the heyday of the open range.

17. Buffalo Bill, His Family, Friends, Fame, Failures, and Fortunes. *By Nellie Snyder Yost. (Chicago: Sage Books, 1979).* One of many biographies of the famed showman. Yost, a Nebraska historian, focuses on his North Platte, Nebr., days.

18. Tom Horn: Killing Men is My Specialty. *By Chip Carlson. (Cheyenne: Beartooth Corral, 1991).* Carlson also wrote a biography of Joe LeFors published in 1995.

19. Samuel Howell "Doc" Knight, Mr. Wyoming University. *By Frederick W. Reckling and JoAnn B. Reckling. (Laramie: UW Alumni Assoc., 1998).* Knight, born in Laramie in 1892, was appointed to the UW faculty in 1916. He served as department chair, state geologist and founder of the UW Science Camp. He retired in 1963 and died in 1975. In 1999, he was chosen "Wyoming Citizen of the Century" in balloting conducted by the American Heritage Center.

20. William F. Cody's Wyoming Empire: The Buffalo Bill Nobody Knows. *By Robert Bonner. (Norman: University of Oklahoma Press, 2007).* Bonner, a native of Powell, was a retired history professor at Carlton College before returning to his native county.

21. Losing Matt Shepard. *By Beth Loffreda. (Columbia University Press, 2001).* The author, who teaches writing at the University of Wyoming, wrote about the tragic murder case of gay student Matthew Shepard in 1998.

Some Well-Known Novelists Associated with Wyoming

1. Katherine Newlin Burt (1882-1957)

Once fiction editor of *Ladies Home Journal,* Burt wrote several novels.

2. Struthers Burt (1882-1954)

Burt began ranching in Wyoming in 1908 following graduation from Princeton. He wrote two books of poetry, several novels, and a number of non-fiction works. Until 1938, he operated the Bar BC Ranch in Jackson Hole. *Diary of a Dude Wrangler* (1924) is his best known work. He was married to Katherine Burt *(above).*

3. Hal Evarts (1887-1935)

His best known work, *Silent Call,* was set in Wyoming. Later, the story was scripted into a movie. Before he was a famous writer, Evarts started a "skunk fur farm" on the North Fork of the Shoshone River in 1915 with a partner. The fur had little appeal and Evarts' business failed soon after he left for World War I service.

4. Zane Grey (1875-1939)

Although Grey visited Wyoming only briefly, he frequently used the state as a setting in his novels. Among his better works set in Wyoming are *The U. P. Trail* (1918) and *Last of the Plainsman* (1911). Even his most loyal fans would agree that *Wyoming*, republished in 1988, is one of his worst novels.

5. Ernest Hemingway (1899-1961)

Hemingway wrote part of *A Farewell to Arms* while he was a guest at the Sheridan Inn in 1928. In July of that year, he was fishing along Shell Creek and met novelist Owen Wister for the first time who happened to be the only other fisherman on the stream. His short story, "The Wine of Wyoming," was written in 1930. That year, he fished in the Clark's Fork north of Cody and proclaimed it "the best fishing spot on earth." He married his third wife, author Martha Gellhorn, in Cheyenne on Nov. 21, 1940. In July, 1944, his fourth wife, Mary, became ill during a trip across the state. She had surgery in the Casper hospital. Shortly before his death by suicide in Idaho, he was returning from a medical treatment at the Mayo Clinic when he attempted to step into the airplane propeller blade at the Casper airport. He was restrained by the pilot.

The longest title of any booklet published in Wyoming may be the 121-word title of a book by Arthur Ernest Hatheway, the contents of which are summarized in the title: "The Case of Arthur Ernest Hatheway, a British subject, who, induced by the promises of quick profits in the West, settled at Big Horn City, Wyoming Territory, U. S. October 6, 1884, and after more than four months continuous residence there, being wholly innocent of any offence against the law, was, on Feb. 20, 1885, at nightfall, arrested by United States Soldiers, manacled and shackled, charged with being a deserter and horse-thief, carried away from his home and business, and unjustly imprisoned at Fort McKinney, for a whole month, and part of the time in solitary confinement, and subjected to many indignities and great hardships and in peril of his life, after which he was tried by court martial and honorably acquitted"

6. Emerson Hough (1857-1923)

A graduate of the University of Iowa Law School, Hough practiced law in Whiteoaks, New Mexico. He spent the winter of 1895 in Yellowstone National Park. Later, he was instrumental in promoting laws to protect buffalo and other wildlife. His books about Wyoming and the West include *The Story of the Cowboy* (1897), *North of 36*, and *The Covered Wagon*, made into a movie in 1922.

7. Charles King (1844-1933)

A cavalry officer stationed at Fort Laramie for five years, King wrote more than 50 novels in his career. *Laramie or the Queen of Bedlam* (1911) is representative of the military Western for which he is best known.

8. Caroline Lockhart (1875-1962)

An Illinois native, Lockhart started in writing as a reporter for a Boston newspaper. She came to Wyoming in 1905 and became editor of the *Cody Enterprise*. During her stormy editorship, which was punctuated by a landmark libel suit filed against her by the county attorney, Lockhart wrote several novels. Her first, *Me—Smith*, was published in 1911. The next year, Cody residents enjoyed trying to decipher what local people were models for the thinly disguised fictional characters in her *Lady Doc*. Other novels were *Full of the Moon* (1914), *Man from the Bitter Roots* (1915), *Fighting Shepherdess* (1919), *The Dude Wrangler* (1921), and *Old West and New* (1933). She retired to her ranch on Dryhead in Big Horn County on the Montana-Wyoming line. She died in 1962.

9. John Masters (1914-1983)

Author of numerous novels about British India, Masters ranched in the Absarokas near Cody. He was born in Calcutta, India, a fifth-generation English colonialist in that country. Following graduation from Sandhurst, he served in various units of the Indian army, including a unit of the famous Gurkha Rifles. He retired in 1948, moved the United States, and became a U. S. citizen in 1954. Most of his numerous books are set in India including the autobiographical novel, *Bugles and a Tiger* (1956). Masters died in Santa Fe, New Mexico, in May 1983.

10. Mary O'Hara (1885-1980)

O'Hara lived at the Remount Ranch, west of Cheyenne, from 1930 to 1946. She wrote several novels set in Wyoming. They were *My Friend Flicka* (1943), *Thunderhead* (1943), *Green Grass of Wyoming* (1946), and *Wyoming Summer* (1963). She was married to rancher Helge Stuve-Vasa in 1922, but they divorced in 1947.

11. Elizabeth Page (1889-1969)

A native of Vermont, she was author of *Wagons West* (1930). Page lived in Basin for five years, beginning in 1927. During her residence there, she researched and wrote *Wild Horses and Gold: From Wyoming to the Yukon* (New York: Farrar and Rinehart, 1932). The book was based on a true story.

12. Vladimir Nabokov (1899-1977)

The author of *Lolita* and 16 other novels came to Wyoming with his wife in the 1950s to chase butterflies in the Snowy Range. He was an avid collector.

13. Mary Roberts Rinehart (1876-1958)

Rinehart was a Pennsylvanian who vacationed in Wyoming. She came for the first time in 1915 and continued as a regular summer guest at the Eaton Ranch at Wolf, Sheridan County. She wrote *Tenting Tonight* (1917), followed by two books about ranch life in Wyoming, *Breaking Point* (1924), and *Lost Ecstasy* (1927).

14. Robert Roripaugh (1930-   )

Roripaugh, a retired professor of English at the University of Wyoming, has written

---

Equality State Book Festival was held for the first time in Casper in 2006. The annual event features readings by Wyoming authors and poets as well as workshops for writers.

several books of poetry as well as novels. *Honor Thy Father* is his novel set on the Wind River Indian Reservation, near where Roripaugh's family ranched. In 1995, Gov. Jim Geringer named Roripaugh the state poet laureate and he served in that post to 2003.

15. Owen Wister (1860-1938)

Wister, born in Pennsylvania and educated at Harvard, vacationed in Wyoming for many years. He owned a summer cabin in Jackson Hole. His best known work, *The Virginian* (1902), is set in the Medicine Bow area. On July 21, 1885, Wister found himself in Medicine Bow with no room vacancies in the only hotel. Consequently, he slept on the counter of the general store. The novel, written 15 years after his visit, was a smashing best seller, going through 15 printings in eight months. The book was dedicated to Wister's friend, Theodore Roosevelt.

16. Stephen Covey (1932-)

A former management professor at BYU, Covey wrote *The Seven Habits of Highly Effective People*. Published in 1989, the book stayed on best-seller lists for four years. Covey is a native of Utah, but his grandfather, S. M. Covey, was a Wyoming sheepman and founder of Little America in Sweetwater County.

17. Anna Proulx (1935-)

Born in Connecticut and a long-time resident of Vermont, the Pulitzer Prize-winning novelist spent part of each year near Centennial. She won the Pulitzer Prize for fiction in 1994 for her novel, *The Shipping News*, set in Newfoundland. The book also won the 1993 National Book Award. Her novel, *Postcards*, won the PEN/Faulkner award in 1993. She also wrote *Close Range: Wyoming Stories*. One story from the book was the basis of the film *Brokeback Mountain* (2005).

18. W. Michael Gear (1955-)

The Way of Spider is one of the novels by Gear who lives and writes on a ranch near Thermopolis. His first novel, *The Warriors of Spider*, was published by DAW Books in 1988. In later years, Tor Books published his work including *Long Ride Home* (1988). His wife, Kathleen O'Neal Gear, is also a well-known novelist *(below)*. Both lived near Dubois prior to purchasing the Thermopolis area ranch.

19. Kathleen M. O'Neal (1954-)

O'Neal, a California native, once was an archaeologist for the Bureau of Land Management. She wrote numerous best-selling "pre-history" books and novels including *An Abyss of Light, People of the Fire*, and *People of the Wolf*. She lives on a ranch near Thermopolis with her husband, W. Michael Gear *(above)*. They write books and raise bison. In 2009, she took a break from their successful series, "First Native Americans and Anasazi mysteries," to write a novel for young readers titled *Children of the Dawnland* (Starscape, 2009).

20. Tim Sandlin

Born in Duncan, Okla., Sandlin came to Jackson with his family each summer where his father was a seasonal ranger. Following graduation from the University of Oklahoma, Sandlin moved to "the valley" permanently. Known as the "literary voice of grunge," he is author of *Sex and Sunsets, Sorrow Floats, Social Blunders* and *The Pyms: Unauthorized Tales of Jackson Hole*.

21. Ed Bryant (1945-)

Bryant was reared in Wheatland. He graduated from the University of Wyoming in 1967 and earned a master's degree in English from UW the next year. Bryant received the Nebula award for the best science fiction short story from the Science Fiction Writers of America in 1979. His books include *Wyoming Sun* (1980), *Cinnabar* (under the pen name of Lawrence Talbot in 1976), *Phoenix Without Ashes* (1975), and *Among the Dead and Other Events Leading up to the Apocalypse* (1973).

22. G. Edward Pendray (1901-1987)

Born in Nebraska, but reared in the tiny town of Van Tassell, Wyoming, Pendray graduated from the University of Wyoming. He was science editor of the *New York Herald-Tribune* from 1925 to 1932. Pendray advocated manned space travel and rocket power as early as the 1920s. He was a founder of the American Rocket Society and served as assistant to the president of Westinghouse Electric. Classified as "science fiction" when they were written, Pendray's several books were predictive of man's conquest of space.

23. Dee Linford (1915-1971)

Born in Afton, Linford served as editor of Wyoming Wildlife magazine in the 1940s when he was author of the book, Wyoming Stream Names. His best-selling novel, Man Without a Star (New York: Morrow, 1952) was later made into a movie starring Kirk Douglas and Jeanne Crain.

24. John Wideman (1941-   )

Wideman taught English at the University of Wyoming. He received the PEN-Faulkner award in 1984 and again in 1990, the only writer to win the award twice. He was awarded the MacArthur genius award in 1993. In 2010, he was teaching at Brown University and living in New York City.

25. George Clayton Johnson (1929-   )

Born in Cheyenne, Johnson was co-author (with William F. Nolan) of *Logan's Run,* a science fiction novel that also became a movie. Johnson also wrote the book, *Writing for the Twilight Zone.* He worked as a writer for the original *Twilight Zone* TV series as well as parts of the 1983 *Twilight Zone* movie.

26. Ron Franscell (1957-   )

A native of Casper, Franscell's first "true crime" book, published in 2007, was based on a 1973 murder near Casper. Titled *The Darkest Night*, it tells the story of the two Thomson sisters. who were thrown by two abductors into a deep canyon from a remote Wyoming bridge. He also wrote several fiction novels. His first book, *Angel Fire*, gained critical acclaim in 1998. The second, titled *The Deadline*, was a mystery. He is a former Gillette journalist who later moved to San Antonio, Texas.

27. C. J. Box

Box, a native of Casper, began writing novels while working as a reporter for the *Saratoga Sun* in the 1990s. His first published novel was *Open Season* (2001), a book about the adventures of Wyoming game warden Joe Pickett. The mystery series continued through the decade with his sixth novel, *In Plain Sight,* published in 2006.

27. Mark Spragg

Spragg's best-known novel was *An Unfinished Life* (Knopf, 2004), He and his wife Virginia co-wrote the screenplay by the same name for the film starring Robert Redford. In 2008 Spragg wrote a prize-winning memoir titled *Where Rivers Change Direction.* He also wrote *The Fruit of Stone* (2002) and *Bone Fire* (2010). Spragg was reared along the Northfork of the Shoshone River, west of Cody.

28. Alexandra Fuller (1969-   )

Her first book titled *Don't Let's Go to the Dogs Tonight* (2002) was a memoir of growing up in Rhodesia (now Zimbabwe) and elsewhere in Africa. Following her marriage to Charles Ross, the couple moved from Africa back to Ross' home state of Wyoming. In a book set in Sublette County, she explores the life and death of a young oil worker who fell from an oil rig in February 2006. The book is titled *The Legend of Colton H. Bryant.*

Wyoming is home to many travel writers. One of the best known is Mark Jenkins (1958-)who has written three well-received travel adventure books *Off the Map (1993), To Timbuktu: A Journey Down the Niger (1998)* and *The Hard Way (2003).* He also writes for outdoor and other magazines. He and his family live in Laramie.

Wyoming Authors Less Known for Writing Than for Other Endeavors

1. Richard Cheney

Elected U. S. Vice President in 2000, Cheney formerly served as Wyoming's representative in Congress, and as Secretary of Defense in the elder Bush administration. In 1983, he co-authored with his wife Lynne, *Kings of the Hill: Power and Personality in the House of Representatives.* (New York: Continuum, 1983). The book surveyed the impact Speakers of the House had on American history and on Congress. Lynne Cheney was director of the National Endowment for the Humanities in the Bush years. In 2000, the Cheneys lived in Dallas, Texas, where he was chief executive officer of Halliburton until being named Republican vice presidential nominee by George W. Bush on July 25, 2000.

2. William P. Cooke

Cooke taught statistics at the University of Wyoming from 1969 to 1986. He wrote two mystery novels, *The Nemesis Conjecture* (1980) and *Orion's Shroud* (1981). In 1986, he accepted a professorship in statistics at Baylor University where he continued to write mystery novels as an avocation.

3. Gale McGee

McGee represented Wyoming in the U. S. Senate from 1959 to 1977. A former professor of history at the University of Wyoming, he held a doctorate degree in history. He wrote T*he Founding Fathers and Entangling Alliances* (Chicago: University of Chicago Press, 1947). Following his defeat for re-election, he was named U. S. Ambassador to the Organization of American States. He died in Washington, D. C., in 1992.

4. Frederic Remington

Known mostly as an artist and sculptor, Remington wrote several books. He collaborated with Theodore Roosevelt on a book about Western ranching. He also wrote a novel, *John Ermine of the Yellowstone* (1903).

5. Warren Richardson

The Cheyenne author, father of three businessmen/philanthropists, wrote the forgettable novel, *Dr. Zell and the Princess Charlotte*, published by L. Kabis and Company of New York in 1892.

6. Charles E. Winter

A lawyer, politician and business promoter, Winter wrote the words to the official state song. He also wrote a novel, *Grandon of Sierra* (1907). Winter served three terms in Congress from Wyoming, 1923-1929.

Books with Wyoming Connections

1. Photographic histories

Arcadia Publishing released a series of paperback books from 2005-10 on various places in Wyoming, authored by local residents and historians. Published were histories of Buffalo, Cheyenne, Cody, Evanston, Green River, Hot Springs County, Kemmerer, Laramie, Pinedale, Platte County, Powell, Rock Springs, Sheridan, Sweetwater County, and Yellowstone National Park.

2. Civil War Day by Day

Author E. B. Long taught Civil War history at the University of Wyoming. He was a national authority on the war, having once been chief researcher for the Bruce Catton series on the Civil War. *The Civil War Day by Day* was published during the time Long taught at Wyoming. His book about the Mormons and the Civil War, *Saints and the Union*, was posthumously published.

3. Crane manuscript

An original manuscript by Stephen Crane was found in the collections of the American Heritage Center at the University of Wyoming in 1991. The discovery, made by a student researcher, was an article titled "The Devil's Acre."

4. The Dinosaur Heresies

Author Robert T. Bakker is professor of paleontology at the University of Colorado. He is one of the world's foremost experts on dinosaurs. *Dinosaur Heresies* includes information about the discovery of dinosaurs at Como Bluff, near Rock River. The book was published in 1986. Bakker has helped in the development of the Rock River Museum.

5. Food Finds

The second edition of *Food Finds* by Allison Engel and Margaret Engel featured America's best local foods and the people who produce them. Published in 1991 by HarperCollins, the second edition includes Chugwater chili, Queen Bee Honey Taffy of Lovell and Grandma Pat's Soup Mixes of Albin. During the research for the book, Margaret Engel came to Wyoming where she spoke to University of Wyoming journalism classes. She was a *Washington Post* reporter and director of the Alicia Patterson Foundation which grants journalism fellowships.

6. Home Town News: William Allen White and the Emporia Gazette

Author Sally Foreman Griffith, the daughter of former state auditor and state treasurer James Griffith, praised her hometown of Lusk, in the foreword to her 1989 study of Kansas editor William Allen White. Griffith also praises the community values of the *Lusk Herald* and its former publishers Gerald and Jane Bardo. Griffith's father and grandfather also were *Herald* publishers. For many years, she was professor of history at Villanova University near Philadelphia.

7. Prolific author of Western novels

Bob Kammen had written 30 Western novels (1992). A former postmaster in Minnesota, Illinois and North Dakota, he moved to Casper in 1990. His books include *Guns Along the Yellowstone*, *Death Rides the Rockies* and *The Watcher*.

8. The Lincoln Highway

The Complete Official Road Guide of the Lincoln Highway was published in 1916 by the Lincoln Highway Association. It had information about towns and travel experiences along the highway based on three transcontinental inspection trips by association officers. The highway, proposed by Carl Fisher in 1912, became the first U. S. transcontinental highway, stretching from New York, through Wyoming, to San Francisco. Lyn Prottteau, a highway historian from Sacramento, Calif., who traveled what was left of the route in her 1941 Chevrolet in 1984, had the guidebook re-published in 1984.

9. Nuclear Highway

Tad Bartimus and Scott McCartney wrote *Trinity's Children, Living Along America's Nuclear Highway* (1991). Interstate 25 is called the nuclear highway because of the weapons factories and missile silos along the 1,000-mile-long stretch from Buffalo, Wyoming, south through Cheyenne, and Colorado to Las Cruces, New Mexico. People in the Cheyenne and Chugwater areas are featured.. The authors were Associated Press journalists.

10. Owen Wister Out West

Author Frances Kemble Wister Stokes was the daughter of the famous Western novelist. Stokes accompanied her family to the Wister cabin in Jackson Hole during vacations early in the century. She died in 1992 at the age of 90.

11. Subcortical Dementia

Dr. Jeffrey L. Cummings, Los Angeles, a 1966 graduate of Basin High School and a 1970 graduate of the University of Wyoming, wrote the scientific treatise, *Subcortical Dementia*, in 1990. The book was the fourth written by Cummings.

12. Wall Street Words and Libraries

Freelance writer Richard Maturi of Laramie specializes in business writing. Among his books are *Wall Street Words: The Basics and Beyond* (1991) and *Cultural Gems: An Eclectic Look at Unique United States Libraries* (co-authored with Mary Buckingham Maturi in 1995). Featured is the Lusk Carnegie Library.

13. Watts Riot

Author Robert E. Conot in *Rivers of Blood, Years of Darkness: The Unforgettable Classic Account of the Watts Riot* (New York: William Morrow, 1968), describes the incident leading up to the tragic 1965 Los Angeles riot. The central character, an African American named Marquette Fry, was reared in Hanna, Wyoming. He left in 1957 when he was 13 and moved with his family to Los Angeles.

14. Newbery Award Winner

Author Patricia MacClachlan, born in Cheyenne in 1938, was presented the award from the American Library Association for writing the most outstanding children's book in 1986. It is the most prestigious award in the area of children's literature. She won for her best-selling book, *Sarah, Plain and Tall.*

15. March of Dimes Poster Child

Author Emily Rapp writes about her early life in Poster Child: A Memoir. (Bloomsbury USA, 2007). Rapp was born with a congenital defect in her foot and when she was four, her foot was amputed below the ankle. She became a March of Dimes poster child, a skilled skier, and won a Fulbright to study in Korea. She went on to earn the MFA from the University of Texas and now teaches writing at Antioch University. A native of Nebraska, she was reared in Laramie where her father served as a Lutheran minister.

16. Almanac of American Politics

The popular reference book, an essential work for political junkies, was first published in 1971 with new editions released every two years. The book includes biographical information and voting data for every state and every congressional and gubernatorial election. Grant Ujifusa, a native of Worland and graduate of Worland High School (1960), came up with the idea for the book while he was on the staff of the *Harvard Crimson* in 1971. He and fellow journalist Michael Barone co-authored the first edition, published the following year, and the subsequent 20 editions. Editions after 1984 were published by *National Journal*. He also served as senior editor of *Reader's Digest*.

17. Classic Black-and-White Scenic Photography

One of the finest recent photographic "cover-table" books about Wyoming was compiled by Michael McClure, former chief photographer for the *Casper Star-Tribune* and widely acclaimed freelance photographter. The book, *Artifact: A Cultural Geography of Wyoming* (Wigraf Publishing, 2008), showcases McClure's photos of the open spaces of Wyoming. McClure died Nov. 28, 2008, shortly after the book was published.

18. Chinese Family Saga

UW political science professor Winberg Chai and his daughter, May-Lee Chai, wrote about the lives of Winberg's parents, Ruth and Charles Chai in *The Girl from Purple Mountain: Love, Honor, War and One Family's Journey from China to America.* (Thomas Dunne Books, 2001). Ruth was one of the first women admitted to a Chinese university.

Read More About It: Wyoming and Authors (if you need to know more about the following topics, here is where you may find it)

Animals and Insects:

Douglas Crowe. *Furbearers of Wyoming* (1986). The book published by the Department of Game and Fish features information about 26 animals in the state.

Tim W. Clark. *Mammals of Wyoming* (1987).

Jeffrey A. Lockwood. *Locust: The Devastating Rise and Mysterious Disappearance of the Insect that Shaped the American Frontier* (2004); and *Six-Legged Warriors: Using Insects as Weapons of War.* (2009).

Ghosts:

Debra D. Munn. *Ghosts on the Range: Eerie True Tales of Wyoming* (1989). Munn lived in Powell; the ghosts "live" everywhere in the state.

History:

Randy Adams and Craig Sodaro. *Wyoming, Courage in a Lonesome Land* (1990); and *Frontier Spirit: The Story of Wyoming* (1986). The histories are for school students. Adams taught in Torrington. Earlier histories of Wyoming for school students were written by Grace Raymond Hebard, Velma Linford, Virginia Cole Trenholm and Clarice Whittenburg.

Gay Day Alcorn. *Tough Country: A History of the Saratoga and Encampment Valley* (1984).

Alice Antilla. *History of the Upper Hamsfork Valley.* (1974). Antilla also wrote a book about coal-mining in the Kemmerer area, published just before her death in 2007.

Gladys B. Beery. *The Front Streets of Laramie City* (1990). A resident of Laramie from 1956 to 1993, she died in Greeley, Colo., Jan. 28, 2008.

William F. Bragg. *Wyoming Rugged but Right* (1979). Bragg, public information officer in state government and for Casper College, served in the Wyoming legislature. He died in May 1988.

Robert A. Campbell. *Discovering Wyoming,* (1989). Campbell taught social studies at University School in Laramie until his retirement in 1999.

Harry E. Chrisman. *1001 Most-Asked Questions about the American West* (1982). A Kansas journalist and hstorian, Chrisman died Dec. 17, 1993, at the age of 87

Barbara Windom Costopoulos. *Sunrise Silhouettes Shadows from the Shafts: Sunrise, Wyoming People and Places 1900 to 1980* (2006).

Lavinia Dobler. *I Didn't Know That About Wyoming* (1984). The author, whose father was an early settler of Riverton, worked as an editor in New York for many years before returning to her native state. She died in 2005.

Lewis Gould. *Wyoming From Territory to Statehood* (1989). The author was a professor of history at the University of Texas, Austin. An earlier version was published in 1968 by Yale University Press.

T. A. Larson. *History of Wyoming* (1965; revised second edition, 1991). Larson, "Mr. Wyoming History," taught at the University of Wyoming from 1936-76. Earlier Wyoming histories were written by C. G. Coutant (1899) and Ichabod S. Bartlett (1918).

Gladys Powelson Jones. *"Cheyenne, Cheyenne..." Our Blue-Collar Heritage* (1983). Author Jones, an artist and historian, wrote about the south side of Cheyenne. She died in Washington in 2004.

Mark E. Miller. *Hollow Victory: The White River Expedition of 1879 and the Battle of Milk Creek.* (1997). Miller is Wyoming State Archaeologist.

Ester Johansson Murray. *A History of the North Fork of the Shoshone River.* (1996). Historian Murray has written extensively on Cody area history.

John H. Ostrom. *Marsh's Dinosaurs: The Collections from Como Bluff* (2000)

Phil Roberts, ed. *Readings in Wyoming History* (six editions).

Lylas Skovgard. *Basin City* (1988). Basin's town history from 1896 to 1918. Skovgard died in 1993.

Eileen Starr. *History of Wyoming Architecture.* (1992). Starr was architectural historian for the State Historic Preservation Office (SHPO). In 2010, she was an architectural historian living in Bowling Green, Kentucky.

Mae Urbanek. *Wyoming Place Names* (1967). Urbanek, also a poet, ranched near Lusk. She was state poet laureate in the 1950s. The author of 14 books, she died in 1995.

Wyoming State Historical Department. *Wyoming Historical Blue Book.* 6 vols. (various dates, editors were Marie Erwin, Virginia Trenholm, Jim Donahue, Loren Jost, and Phil Roberts).

Humor/Essays:

Bob Budd. *Send Fresh Horses* (1987); and *A Wide Spot in the Road* (1990). Budd was executive director of the Wyoming Stock Growers Assoc. until 1993.

Sandra E. Guzzo. *Chickens in the Greenhouse and Other Wyoming Escapades* (1986). A collection of short stories by the Laramie author and columnist.

T. A. Larson, editor. *Bill Nye's Western Humor* (1975). Nye was a nationally known humorist in the late 19th century who founded the *Laramie Boomerang.*

Jerry Palen. *Mad Bull and Other Stuff,* and other books. He is best known, however, for his cartoons which feature rural agricultural life.

David L. Roberts. *Sage Street* (1991). A collection of newspaper columns by the former Medicine Bow editor and co-author of *Wyoming Almanac.*

Donna Smith. *Etc.: Firsthand Observations and Offhand Opinions.* (1999) Smith was a former newspaper writer, ad agency owner and journalism professor. She also published *A Legendary Feather and Her Tail* (2002), a book for young readers.

Bill Sniffin. *The Best Part of America* (1993). The book contains 60 of his best columns he wrote over 23 years as *Wyoming State Journal,* Lander, editor. In the 2000s, Sniffin wrote a weekly syndicated column appearing in many Wyoming newspapers.

Minerals:

Mel Duncan. *Medicine Bow Mining Camps* (1991). Duncan owned a summer home in the area which prompted his interest in the history of the camps. He retired from the Air National Guard. He was also a specialist on aviation history. He died Oct. 11, 2007, in Cheyenne.

A. Dudley Gardner and Verla R. Flores. *Forgotten Frontier: A History of Wyoming Coal* (1989). Another good reference work for coal mining in Wyoming is the 1940 classic, *History of the Union Pacific Coal Mines* by the company.

Marion Huseas. *Sweetwater Gold: Wyoming's Gold Rush, 1867-1870.* (1991). Huseas is a former curator in the Wyoming State Museum. She lives in Cheyenne.

Stanley A. Kuzara. *Black Diamonds of Sheridan.* (1977). The author, born in Dietz in 1906, died at the age of 93 on Jan. 4, 2000.

Mike Mackey. *Black Gold: Patterns in the Development of Wyoming's Oil Industry.* (1997). Mackey also edited a volume on civil rights in Wyoming.

Robert Righter. *Making of a Town, Wright, Wyoming* (1985). Righter formerly taught history at the University of Wyoming. He and his wife, historian Sherry Smith, maintain a summer home near Moose.

Movies:

William R. Huey. *In Search of Hollywood, Wyoming* (1985). Huey was a former resident of Lusk who lived and worked in Cheyenne.

People:

Susan Anderson. *Living in Wyoming, Settling for More* (1990). Photos by Zbigniew Bzdak. Anderson, a former state legislator from Natrona County, worked as a television journalist in Casper. From 1998, she edited *Casper Journal* until she became an advisor to Gov. Dave Freudenthal..

Dale Bardo. *Mrs. Barriers.* (1993). A profile of his wife Helen and her efforts for handicapped accessibility. Long-time Lusk residents, both died in 2000.

Mabel Brown. *Inga and Harry.* (1995). The lives of the Thorsons of Newcastle, written by one of Wyoming's best known historians. She died in Cheyenne Oct. 3, 2008.

Elnora L. Frye. *Atlas of Wyoming Outlaws at the Territorial Penitentiary* (1990). Frye lives in Laramie.

John Ace Bonar. *Goliaths of Glenrock.* (1981).

Gordon Hendrickson, ed.. *Peopling the High Plains: Wyoming's European Heritage* (1977).

Dollie Iberlin. *The Basque Web* (1981). About the Basque people living in the Buffalo area.

Mark Junge. *Wyoming: A Pictorial History* (1989). The pictorial work, done for the centennial anniversary, is the second photo book by Junge. His first featured photography of J. E. Stimson.

Mike Mackey. *Remembering Heart Mountain.* (1999)

Victoria Murphy, ed. *Wyoming: A 20th Century History of the Citizens, Businesses and Institutions.* (1999)

L. Douglas Nelson. *Heart Mountain* (1974). Nelson is director of the Annie E. Casey Foundation, one of the world's largest. He holds the MA from UW.

Geoffrey O'Gara. *What You See in Clear Water* (2000) Story of how water rights litigation on the Wind River impacted the people on the reservation.

Larry Pointer. *In Search of Butch Cassidy* (1977).

Virginia Cole Trenholm. *The Shoshonis, Sentinels of the Rockies* (1964); *The Arapahoes: Our People* (1970); and other books. Author Trenholm died in 1993. Her Arapaho-given name was "Ha-The-Da-He"—"narrator" or "storyteller" in Arapaho.

Mary Ann Trevathan. *More Than Meets the Eye: Wyoming Along I-80.* (1993). A journey along I-80 with profiles of people and history of places.

Lawrence M. Woods. *Wyoming Biographies* (1991). Woods also wrote *British Gentlemen in the Wild West: The Era of the Intensely English Cowboy* (1989) and a biography of rancher Moreton Frewen. He is former CFO of Mobil Corporation and lives in Washakie County.

Places:

Edward C. Bryant. *Hat Creek and Hard Times* (1988). An account of the community north of Lusk where Bryant, a government economist, was reared.

Robert H. Burns, A. S. Gillespie and W. G. Richardson. *Wyoming's Pioneer Ranches* (1955).

Julianne Crouch. *Jackrabbits and Jackalopes: A Wyoming Bar Tour.* (2008.

John Galvin. *The Meadow* (1992). A 100-year history of a meadow on the Wyoming-Colorado border. The author lived near Tie Siding.

Mary Alice Gunderson. *Devils Tower: Stories in Stone* (1988).

Cathy Killean. *To Save a Mountain* (1997). Story of attempts by a community to save Bessemer Mountain from a rock quarry.

Geoffrey O'Gara. *A Long Road Home* (1989). A journey through America's present in search of America's past, starting in Lander, and ending in the state. O'Gara lives in Lander and worksas a producer and host for Wyoming Public Television in Lander..

Nancy Heyl Ruskowsky. *Two Dot Ranch: A Biography of Place.* (Pronghorn Press, 2009). A ranch history with biographical accounts of ranch owners and workers.

Anne Willson Whitehead. *History of Manville, Wyoming and the Manville Ranching Community* (1998). Whitehead's grandparents were Niobrara pioneers.

Poetry:

Betsy Bernfeld, editor. *Sagebrush Classics* (1990). A collection of poetry by 40 poets associated with Wyoming. *(See Poetry)*

The first ferry over the North Platte near Saratoga on the Cherokee (Overland) Trail used a cable made of twisted buffalo hide from which the vessel was towed back and forth across the river.

Travel Guidebooks:

Winfred Blevins. *Roadside History of Yellowstone Park* (1989).

Orrin and Lorraine Bonney. *Guide to Wyoming Mountains and Wilderness Areas.* (revised ed., 1977).

Nathaniel Burt. *Wyoming* (1991). Part of the "Discover America" travel guide series published by Compass American Guides, Oakland, Calif.

Susan Carlson. *Wyoming Historical Markers at 55 MPH.* (1994). Carlson describes 164 historical markers and monuments along Wyoming's highways.

Gregory W. Franzwa. *The Oregon Trail Revisited (1997).*

Bill Hunger. *Hiker's Guide to Wyoming (1992).* Seventy-five hikes are featured in this guidebook for Wyoming back country trails.

Mike Jording. *A Few Interested Residents: Wyoming Historical Markers and Monuments.* (1992). Jording, a Newcastle resident, was president of the Wyoming State Historical Society, 1999-2000.

Mark Junge. *Wyoming: A Guide to Historic Sites* (1976).

Dan Lewis. *8,000 Miles of Dirt:A Backroad Travel Guide to Wyoming* (1988).

Catherine Mealey. *Best of Wyoming* (1990). Guide to Wyoming attractions.

Candy Moulton. *Roadside History of Wyoming* (1995). A guidebook containing brief historical sketches on sites along Wyoming's highways.

Don Pitcher. *Wyoming Handbook* (1991),

Agnes Wright Spring, editor. *WPA Guide to Wyoming.* First published in 1941 as part of the WPA American Guidebook Series, the book was reissued in 1981.

D. Ray Wilson. *Wyoming Historical Tour Guide* (1990).

Wyoming Division of Vocational Rehabilitation. *Wyoming Travel Guide for the Person with a Handicap* (1991).

University of Wyoming

Emmett D. Chisum. *Memories: University of Wyoming Centennial* (1987). A compilation of photographs with accompanying text written by the long-time reference librarian and historian at the university. He died in October 2009.

Wilson Clough. *A History of the University of Wyoming, 1887-1964.* (1964). Clough was a well-known faculty member who wrote numerous books during his career as an English professor at the university. He died in 1991.

Deborah Hardy. *Wyoming University: The First 100 Years, 1886-1986.* (1986). Published by the university during its centennial year, the book was written by Hardy, now a retired professor from the Department of History.

Ralph McWhinnie. *"Those Good Years at Wyoming U."* (1965). A collection of stories by many people about their UW experiences. McWhinnie served as university registrar for many years. He died in 1995.

Writers:

Jean S. Johnson. *Wyoming Centennial Imprints: A Bibliography (1992).*

Roy A. Jordan. *Wyoming: A Centennial Bibliography (1988).*

Eva Floy Wheeler. *A History of Wyoming Writers* (1940; revised edition, 1981). The compiler received a master's degree from the University of Wyoming. The book lists hundreds of Wyoming writers and short biographical sketches.

In 1918, Josephine Collins, the sister of Lt. Caspar Collins who was killed at Platte Bridge station in 1865, donated $100 to the Episcopal Church of Casper for purchase of a gold and silver communion set.

Some Wyoming Books with Unusual Titles

1. Mooching Moose and Mumbling Men (1963)

This humorous book is one of several by Joe Back who lived near Dubois.

2. "...the damned elk et my broom!" (1976)

The book of stories by Charles B. Beck is subtitled "Facts, Folks, and Fables of the Frontier."

3. A Tale of Dough Gods, Bear Grease, Cantaloupe, and Sucker Oil: Marymere/ Pinetree/ Mae-Lou/AMK Ranch (1986)

The unusual book is by three Jackson Hole authors, Kenneth L. Diem, Lenore L. Diem and William C. Lawrence.

4. Never Pet a Rabbit if His Nose is Running (1991)

Author Richard Dumbrill of Newcastle wrote the book of autobiographical sketches of ranch life in Crook County in the 1930s and 1940s.

5. Wind Pudding and Rabbit Tracks (1989)

The history of Goshen County is titled for the comment made by a young homesteader to his wife on their arrival in Goshen County when she looked around the "homestead" and asked what they were going to live on. He replied, "Wind pudding and rabbit tracks, my love, there's plenty for the taking."

6. Wrinklebelly (1999)

The book, a biography about her parents and Goshen County early in this century, was written by Goshen County writer/historian Sally Vanderpoel (b. Jan. 9, 1921, d. Feb. 1, 2010).

Ten Book Presses in Wyoming

1. Agathon Books, Lander
2. Alpine Press, Mills
3. Crazy Woman Creek Press, Cheyenne
4. High Plains Press, Glendo
5. Homestead Publishing, Moose
6. Narrative Press, Torrington
7. One-Eyed Press, Cody
8. Pronghorn Press, Greybull
9. Twin Souls Publishers, Lusk
10. Skyline West Press, Laramie

Source: International Directory of Little Magazines and Small Presses. Edited by Len Fulton. (Paradise, Calif.: Dustbooks, 2009). Editor Fulton is a graduate of the University of Wyoming.

In August 2008, a film crew from Discovery Channel visited the old prison at Rawlins to film the gas chamber. Former warden Duane Schillinger was interviewed in the segment on the technology of the gas chamber for the series on the history of the death penalty in the world. Schillinger wrote *Wyoming: Attitudes, Short Ropes and Long Falls, Prison Walls* (2003) and *In Wyoming's Prison Hungry Men May Become Vicious Men* (2004).

BRIDGES

1st paint used on the Brooklyn Bridge, New York: "Rawlins Red," a mineral paint from a mine near Rawlins, was used to paint the bridge in the late 1880s.

Some Famous Wyoming Bridges

1. Fort Laramie Iron Bridge

The bowstring truss bridge, built over the North Platte River by the U. S. Army in 1875, is the oldest existing military bridge west of the Mississippi River and the oldest standing bridge in Wyoming. In July, 1977, it was dedicated as a historic landmark.

2. First Platte River Bridge

Built in 1853 near present Evansville by John Richard (Reshaw), the toll bridge supplanted the Mormon Ferry which began crossing the river nearby in 1847. Richard charged tolls of 50 cents per person or animal and $5 per team and wagon to recoup the bridge construction cost of about $25,000. The bridge was destroyed by army troops in 1866 who used the materials to expand Fort Caspar, six miles upriver.

3. Second Platte River Bridge

Louis Guinard built a toll bridge over the Sweetwater River below Independence Rock in the early 1850s. In 1859, he moved to the Mormon Ferry site and built a 1,000-foot bridge of cedar logs. The 13-foot wide bridge rested on cribs filled with stone. Built for $60,000, it was the most notable of its kind west of the Missouri River. The "Platte Bridge Station," (later Fort Caspar and, still later, Casper) was named for Guinard's bridge.

4. Wind River Diversion Dam Bridge

The bridge is the longest highway truss bridge in Wyoming. Built for $58,000 for the Wyoming Highway Department by Taggart Construction Company in 1924, the bridge is located in Fremont County.

5. Fishing Bridge, Yellowstone

The famous bridge was designed by H. M. Chittenden who also laid out the park road system between 1899-1906. Chittenden, a famed author and historian, later supervised construction of the Lake Washington Ship Canal in Seattle from 1906-1910. He died in 1917 at the age of 59.

6. Dale Creek Trestle

Completed April 23, 1868, at a cost of $200,000, the first Dale Creek Trestle was 720 feet long and 135 feet above the creek. At the time of its completion, it was the highest railway bridge in the world. In 1876, the wooden structure was replaced by an iron bridge. The railway right-of-way was moved south in 1898 where it crossed the creek over a huge landfill. The site was placed on the National Register of Historic Places in May 1986.

7. Wind River Bridge

The first bridge over the Wind River was constructed by the Department of the Interior in 1887.

8. Sunlight Creek Bridge

The bridge on State Highway 296 over Sunlight Creek north of Cody is the highest bridge in Wyoming, 280 feet above the creek. It was constructed in 1986.

9. Bryan Stock Trail Bridge

The bridge over the North Platte River at Casper collapsed and fell into the river in August 1961.

10. Cole Creek Bridge

The railroad bridge near Glenrock was washed out by a violent rainstorm on Sept. 27, 1923. Soon after the bridge failed, a CB&Q passenger train hurdled into Cole Creek, killing 30 of the 66 passengers. It was the worst train wreck in Wyoming history. The railroad paid a total of $60,000 in settlements to the relatives of the victims.

11. Swinging Bridge, Hot Springs State Park

Built in 1916, the bridge was declared unsafe and torn down in August 1991 by the Wyoming National Guard. The pieces were auctioned off in December 1991, the funds used to build a new bridge dedicated Aug. 19, 1992.

12. Trona Bridge, Green River

The bridge was built with funds provided by area trona companies and constructed over the Green River at Expedition Island as part of the city's greenbelt trail. The bicycle-pedestrian bridge opened in 1995.

13. Garfield Street pedestrian bridge, Laramie

Plans were drawn up in May, 1929, by the Union Pacific Railroad for the railroad overpass bridge. It was completed the next year for a cost of $35,000 as part of the University Street Viaduct project, the expense shared by the railroad and the city of Laramie. Crossings over the tracks at Grand, Fremont and Lyons were closed by city ordinance on May 6, 1930.

3 Natural Bridges

1. Ayers Natural Bridge

The rock arch, 20 feet high and 90 feet across, passes over LaPrele Creek ten miles west of Douglas. First photographed by William H. Jackson in 1870, the formation is named for Alva Ayers, who established a ranch near the site in the 1880s.

2. Blackwater Natural Bridge

The rock arch is located at an elevation of 10,800 feet, about six miles south of Blackwater Lodge along the Cody Road to Yellowstone, Park County.

3. Moose Lake Natural Bridge

It is the best known of several natural bridges in the Tetons.

BICYCLES

Memorable Events Concerning Bicycles

1. High-Wheeler

Thomas Stevens, an Englishman, rode an "Ordinary" or high-wheel bicycle from San Francisco to Boston in 1884, making the journey in 104 1/2 days. The bicycle had a huge wheel in the fornt, over which the rider sat and pedaled and a small wheel at the rear. The journey took Stevens across southern Wyoming. The 100th anniversary of the trip was commemorated in the summer of 1984 by cyclist Jack Castor of Phoenix, Arizona, and other riders on high-wheel bicycles.

2. Yellowstone Tour

W. O. Owen, Charles Greenbaum and Walter Sinclair toured Yellowstone National Park by bicycle in the fall of 1883. They were the first bicyclists in Yellowstone.

3. Cross-State Record

The state record for crossing Wyoming by bicycle, 402 miles, is 20 hours, 24 minutes by Jim Byrnes, Laramie, set in October 1992. He started on the border near Evanston and rode east to Pine Bluffs.

4. Across Russia

Several Wyoming cyclists have traversed Russia in recent years. One of the first to cross Russia was Laramie cyclist Mark Jenkins. In 1990, Howard Cooper, a self-described "former Cowboy," toured Russia by bicycle. During the 7,400-mile trip, he went through seven rims, 40 tires and 200 spokes. In 1991, Kathy Sherin, Todd Borth and Ted Holtz, all of Laramie, were bicycling in Russia at the time of the Aug. 19, 1991, coup.

BUSINESS

1st business in Wyoming: Traders attending the first annual rendezvous near present-day Daniel on July 1, 1824, were the first white businessmen conducting business in Wyoming.

1st employee of a business in Wyoming: John Colter, commissioned by Manual Lisa to trade with the Crow Indians in northwestern Wyoming, 1807.

1st sale of a business in Wyoming: Rocky Mountain Fur Company sold by William Sublette, Jedadiah Smith and David Jackson to the partnership of Thomas Fitzpatrick, Milton Sublette, Jim Bridger, Henry Fraub and J. Gervais. The firm changed hands at the Wind River Rendezvous in July 1830.

1st business in a permanent location: Fort Laramie, a fur-trading post before it was purchased by the U. S. Army in 1849, was founded by William Sublette and Robert Campbell in 1834. Another early entry was Fort Bridger, established by Jim Bridger and business partner Louis Vasquez in the 1830s.

1st mercantile establishment: Probably, the partnership of John S. Tutt and Lewis B. Dougherty, the post sutlers at Fort Laramie from 1849 to 1857.

1st filing for a business corporate charter in Wyoming: Atlantic City and South Pass City Wagon and Toll Road Company, filed May 23, 1869. The corporation's principal office was in Atlantic City, Wyoming.

1st recorded unpaid debt: The sutler's store charges rung up by gambler Robert Lawrence from the Tutt and Dougherty store at Fort Laramie in 1849.

1st "help wanted" advertisement: Although it did not appear in a newspaper published in Wyoming, the advertisement placed by William Ashley in the *Missouri Republican* on March 22, 1822, should qualify as the oldest solicitation for workers in Wyoming. The ad asked for "enterprising young men" interested in the fur trade. Jim Bridger, among others, answered Ashley's famous advertisement.

1st K-Mart in Wyoming: Casper, opened Nov. 5, 1964, the 77th store in the national chain.

Total business establishments in Wyoming with employees (1993): 16,259

Total business establishments in Wyoming with employees (2006): 21,100

5 Oldest Corporations in Wyoming (still active)

1. United Presbyterian Church of Laramie, chartered Oct. 7, 1871.
2. Pioneer Canal Company
3. First Baptist Church of Cheyenne
4. Wyoming Stock Growers Association
5. Cheyenne Lodge No. 1, I.O.O.F.

2 Regional Chains with Headquarters in Wyoming

1. Taco Johns

The chain, headquartered in Cheyenne, was founded by John Turner as one small taco shop on East Lincolnway in 1968. His partner was Harold Holmes who operated a trailer/camper business and provided the first prefabricated buildings. In 1969, Jim Woodson joined the partnership and the firm was formally named "Taco Johns." It grew into a national chain by the 1990s.

On March 28, 1906, the concentrating mill used for the refining of copper ore burned to the ground in Encampment. The fire marked the end of the "boom years" for mineral production in the area. Disappointed investors included Col. William F. "Buffalo Bill" Cody who suffered from poor investments during his long show-business career.

2. Mini-Mart

Founded by Rodney Kinskey, the chain began as a side venture of Jersey Creamery in Sheridan. By 1971, the new company had four stores in Cheyenne. By 1982, the company had expanded to 75 stores and by 1989, the number jumped to 120 Mini-Marts throughout the region. In 1998, the company headquarters was moved from Casper to Pueblo, Colo., following a merger with Dillon Enterprises, a Kansas corporation and wholly-owned subsidiary of Krogers..

Well-Known Business People Associated with Wyoming

1. J. C. Penney, chain store founder

Born in Missouri in 1875, Penney moved to Denver for health reasons when he was 22. After a short stint as a store clerk, he opened a butcher shop in Longmont. It soon failed. He accepted a job with the Colorado firm of Johnson and Callahan and sent to Evanston to manage the firm's branch mercantile store. After two years there, he borrowed money and opened his own store, a "cash only" mercantile store in Kemmerer, on April 14, 1902. Soon, the store was so successful that he opened branch stores in Rock Springs and Cumberland. By 1912, Penney owned a chain of 34 "Golden Rule" stores. He changed the name of the firm to J. C. Penney in 1919. By the time he died in 1971 at the age of 95, the company had nearly 2,000 stores throughout the country. In May 1992, the J. C. Penney corporation held its annual shareholders' meeting in Kemmerer. More than 500 executives and shareholders attended the sessions held in the Kemmerer High School auditorium.

2. W. Edwards Deming, management expert

A graduate of Powell High School and the University of Wyoming, Deming (b. Nebr., 1900) worked for the U. S. Department of Agriculture from 1927-1939. He earned a Ph.D. from Yale in 1928. Following World War II, he was a consultant to Japanese industry. He is credited with that country's reindustrialization and is fondly referred to in Japan as the "American father of Japan." The prestigious Deming Prize is given annually to the Japanese corporation demonstrating "general excellence" in management and product quality. Deming died in New York in 1994.

3. C. H. King, banker and merchandiser

King came to Wyoming from Pennsylvania in 1885, opening a store at the town of Fetterman, Converse County. When the new town of Douglas was laid out, King owned the first store. In 1886, he established one of the first stores in Casper. In 1902, with partner DeForest Richards (who was Wyoming governor), King formed the Lander Transportation Company. He owned several banks in Wyoming, a lumber company and general merchandise stores at the time of his death in California in the 1930s. From 1974 to 1976, King's grandson, Gerald R. Ford, was President of the United States.

4. Henry G. Hay, treasurer, U. S. Steel

An Indiana native, Hay came to Cheyenne about 1870 to be assistant U. S. land surveyor. Later, he went into partnership with merchant I. C. Whipple in his grocery and freighting enterprises. Hay owned ranches, served as a bank president and was elected to the state's constitutional convention in 1889. In 1894, he was elected state treasurer and held that position until September 1903, when he resigned to accept a position with U. S. Steel Corporation in Gary, Indiana. He was company treasurer when he died in 1919.

John S. Harper, chief clerk in the surveyor's office in Cheyenne, left town in June, 1895, following the death of Maud Vest, a young girl employed as a maid in the home of the State Attorney General. Officials said she died from the effects of a botched abortion. Harper's role in the incident was not directly stated. "This act caused great astonishment," a newspaper noted. "He resigned his position and left for California with his wife."

5. Richard Trimble, secretary-treasurer, U. S. Steel

Trimble was born in New York in 1857 and educated at Harvard. From 1882 to 1887, he was a partner with Harvard classmates H. E. Teschemacher and Frederick deBillier in a Wyoming ranch. The ranch failed as a result of huge winter losses in 1886-87. Trimble returned to New York. When U. S. Steel was formed in 1901, he was the corporate secretary, a position he held until 1922. He died in New York Cityin 1924.

6. Ferdinand Lafrentz, board chairman, American Surety Co.

Born in Germany in 1859, Lafrentz came to Wyoming in the 1870s to serve as treasurer of the Swan Land and Cattle Company. A graduate of New York University Law School, he practiced law in Wyoming, New York and Utah. In 1888, he was elected to the territorial legislature from Laramie County. When the cattle business went into decline because of the harsh winters and wild speculation, Lafrentz returned to New York and became president of American Surety Company. He was board chairman at his death in 1954.

7. Arthur "Frank" Cooper, entrepreneur

In the 1870s, Cooper began the first successful means of freezing and transporting beef by rail. He sold his Laramie-based "Pacific Meat Market" and returned to his native England in 1904 where he died in 1927. Sons Richard and John and daughter Barbara remained in America and watched over ranching and oil properties the family had acquired. Richard built a house (now known as the Cooper House) in Laramie and spent hunting holidays in exotic places with hunting companions such as Ernest Hemingway. Barbara lived in the Cooper House until her death in the early 1980s.

8. Charles Boettcher, Denver financier

Born in Germany in 1852, Boettcher came to the United States in 1869 and opened a hardware store in Cheyenne. In 1872, he moved to Denver where he later organized the Great Western Sugar Company, Ideal Cement Company and the Denver Tramway Company. He died in Denver in 1948.

9. F. L. Joslin, department store founder

Joslin owned and operated a mercantile store in Cheyenne in the 1870s. He moved to Denver late in that decade and founded Joslin Dry Goods Company which became a major regional chain.

10. William R. Coe, insurance executive/philanthropist

Coe was born in England in 1869 and educated there. He came to the United States in 1883 and began work in the insurance industry in New York. From 1916 to 1943, Coe was board chairman of the New York firm of Johnson and Higgins, a major insurance underwriter. Throughout his career and retirement, Coe maintained close ties to Wyoming. He owned a home in Cody and when he died in March 1955, his will provided a substantial sum for construction of the University of Wyoming library which was named for him. The families of his descendants remained active in Wyoming business and politics.

11. Robert Woodruff, board chairman, Coca-Cola Company

Born in Georgia in 1889, Woodruff ran the Atlanta-based national soft drink firm for almost 40 years until his retirement in 1955. Although he maintained residences in Georgia and Ohio, he often spent summers on his ranch south of Cody. There, he entertained other business executives and film stars. He died in Atlanta in 1985 and much of his estate was willed to Emory University, Atlanta. In 1996, another Coca-Cola CEO, Summerfield K. Johnston, Jr., bought two ranches south of Buffalo. He purchased his first ranch in the area, the X Bar X, in the early 1980s from the Peter Kiewit family. He later sold it. By 1996, he owned 30,000 acres in the county.

12. George A. Tomlinson, shipping executive

Born in 1869, Tomlinson was the last and largest single owner of freighters on the Great Lakes. He spent two years as a cowboy on a Wyoming ranch. Later, he was a bronc rider for Buffalo Bill's Wild West Show and a newspaper reporter in Detroit before he entered the Great Lakes shipping business. He owned 17 freighters at the time of his death in 1942.

13. John S. Bugas, vice president, Ford Motor Company

Bugas was vice president of Ford from 1946 to 1960 when he became head of the firm's international division. He retired from Ford in 1968 and died in 1982. Born in Rock Springs in 1908, he graduated from the University of Wyoming College of Law in 1934. He joined Ford after serving in the Federal Bureau of Investigation. He owned ranches in Sunlight Basin and made numerous donations to the University of Wyoming over the years.

14. William R. Howard, CEO, Piedmont Airlines

Born in Wheatland in 1922, Howard was reared in Scottsbluff, Neb. He graduated with a law degree from George Washington University. Following World War II service as a pilot, he became associated with commercial air carriers. From 1983 to 1987, he was CEO of Piedmont, at that time the third largest air transport firm in the country. He also was CEO of TWA. Howard was the only Wyoming native listed in Forbes' 800 chief executive officers of America, published in the June 15, 1987, issue of the magazine. After he left Piedmont in the summer of 1987, Howard led a group which tried to purchase United Airlines. He died in Gainesville, Ga., Jan. 19, 2009.

15. H. P. "Bob" Skogland, co-owner, Minnesota Vikings

A Minneapolis insurance executive and football team owner, Skogland owned the Two Dot ranch north of Cody.

16. H. L. Hunt, founder, Hunt Oil Company

Hunt's name became synonymous with oil-rich Texas. A native of Illinois, Hunt, in the 1960s, owned several ranches in the Cody area.

17. Glenn Nielson, founder, Husky Oil Company

Born in Aetna, Alberta, Canada, in 1903, Nielson operated a sheep ranch in his native province until 1935 when he came to the United States. He organized Husky Oil Company in 1937 and served as company president from 1938 to 1967. He became board chairman in 1967 and held that position until he sold his majority interest in the firm in 1979. Nielson was a director of the American Petroleum Institute and held numerous important positions in the LDS (Mormon) Church. He died Oct. 19, 1998, in Cody.

18. H. A. "Dave" True, founder, True Oil Company

A Cheyenne native (b. 1915), True worked for several oil companies before forming his own firm in 1951. True, who lived in Casper, was an officer in numerous petroleum organizations and from 1965 to 1977, he was a member of the University of Wyoming Board of Trustees (and board president from 1971-1973). True's companies included Black Hills Trucking and True Ranches, the largest private landowner in the state. He died in 1994.

19. John T. Leithead, president, Peabody, Cluett Company

Born in Lovell in 1907, Leithead was president of the company whose best known product is Arrow shirts.

20. J. Oliver Crom, president, Dale Carnegie and Associates

A native of Alliance, Nebr., (b. 1933), Crom was reared and educated in Cheyenne. He graduated from the University of Wyoming in 1955. In 1978, he was named president of the Garden City, New York, firm which specializes in educational training and self-improvement. He was named vice chairman of the board in 2000. His mother-in-law, Dorothy Carnegie, owned a ranch in Wyoming during the years she ran the company named for her husband.

21. Jerry Buss, sports team owner, Los Angeles Lakers

Born in Kemmerer in 1933, Buss graduated with a B. S. degree in chemistry from the University of Wyoming. He went on for graduate training at the University of Southern California where he received a Ph.D. After several years teaching at the college level and working for McDonnell-Douglas, Buss became active in real estate investment in the Los Angeles area. In 1979 he bought the Los Angeles Lakers NBA basketball team and, in 2010, appeared on television June 17, 2010, to receive the NBA championship trophy following the Lakers win 93-89 over the Celtics in game 7 of the series. He also owned the Los Angeles Forum basketball arena and once held a majority interest in the Los Angeles Kings of the National Hockey League.

22. Stanley Resor, ad agency president

Born in 1879, Resor was a pioneer in the field of advertising. He was president of J. Walter Thompson agency from 1916 to 1955 and board chairman until his death in 1962. A founder of the American Association of Advertising Agencies, he originated numerous ad campaigns. Resor spent summers working and entertaining guests on his ranch in the Jackson area.

23.-24. John and Charles Arbuckle, coffee magnates

The Arbuckle brothers developed the first pre-ground coffee packed in cans. John Arbuckle was president of the Royal Horse Association in 1871. Soon after, the brothers bought the PO ranch in Laramie County. John died in March, 1912.

25. Henry A. Blair, Chicago financier

Blair was a Chicago financier who controlled the Merchant's National Bank of Chicago. He consolidated the Chicago transit railways. In the early 20th century, Blair owned the Hoe Ranch in the Powder River Basin.

26. Curt Gowdy, media owner

Gowdy, known primarily as a sportscaster, owned a number of broadcast stations. A native of Green River, he lived in retirement in Florida until his death in 2006 .

27. Al Wolfe, president, DDB Needham Worldwide

Born in Wyoming in 1932, Wolfe received a B. A. degree in psychology from the University of Wyoming in 1958. He was named president of the Chicago-based advertising agency in 1987. In the 1990s, he served as president of the University of Wyoming Foundation.

28. Rodney Kinskey, founder, Mini-Mart stores

Kinskey came to Wyoming in 1964 from his native Ohio and purchased the Jersey Creamery in Sheridan. As a side venture, he opened a small convenience market that evolved into the regional chain store operation he now heads. He sold the Sheridan creamery in 1974, but continued to expand the chain.

29. John T. Dorrance III, heir, Campbell Soup Company fortune

Dorrance, born in 1944, lived near Devils Tower in Crook County. In 1989, *Forbes Magazine* listed him as the 107th richest person in America with an estimated wealth of $660 million. In the early 1990s, he was locked in a legal battle with the Wyoming Game and Fish Department over his desire to import exotic animals onto his ranch.

30. L. Milton Woods, Mobil Oil Company executive/publisher

Woods, born in Manderson in 1932, graduated from the University of Wyoming in 1953. He was employed by Mobil in 1956 and, in 1966, he was named head of the North

James (Jim) Corbett, co-founder of the Sanctuary movement, was born in Wyoming in Casper, Oct. 8, 1933. A rancher, writer, philosopher and human rights activist, he was best known as the co-founder of the movement in which churches sheltered illegal aliens in the southwest in the 1990s. Corbett died in Benson, Arizona, in August 2001.

American division of the company. He was executive vice president from 1977 to 1985. Woods holds both a law degree and a Ph.D. degree. He is the author of several books on Wyoming and Western history.

31. Herbert B. Woodman, board chairman, Interchemical Co.

Woodman, born in Cheyenne, served as board chairman of the New York-based firm of Interchemical company. A 1925 graduate of the University of Wyoming, he was named a Rhodes scholar in 1927. He returned to graduate from Harvard Law School. He became president of Interchemical in 1947 and retired in 1978 as board chairman. In 1961, as president of New York's Economics Club, he presided at a dinner the club gave for Soviet Premier Nikita Khruschev. He died at the age of 87 in June 1991.

32. S. M. Covey, founder, Little America

Born in Salt Lake City, Covey came to Wyoming as a sheepherder in the 1890s. In 1932, he built Little America, near where he had been lost in a snowstorm when he was herding sheep more than 40 years earlier. Known more as a sheep rancher than hotelier, his sheep ranch ran more than 20,000 sheep in 1959, the year of his death at the age of 89.

33. Donald Kendall, CEO, Pepsico

Kendall (b. Sequim, Wash., 1921), was PepsiCo CEO from 1971-86. He owns a ranch in Sublette County.

34. Reuel J. Call, founder of Maverik stations

Call started his first gas station in Afton in 1928. Gradually, he opened more stations and, eventually, they became convenience stores. Call died in 1994, but the chain continued to grow, operating in seven Western states. In October 2009, the firm opened its 200th store. At the time, the firm, headquartered in Salt Lake City, was owned and managed by the third generation of the Call family. Reuel Call's nephew, O. Jay Call, founded another discount gasoline station/convenience store chain in 1968. He named it Flying J. O. Jay Call was killed March 18, 2003, when the company plane he was piloting crashed in Salt Lake City. The privately-held firm was reorganized after bankruptcy in 2008 and many of its stations were purchased by Pilot Travel Centers in July 2009.

35. Foster Friess, fund manager

Friess (b. 1940, Rice Lake, Wisc.), moved to Jackson Hole in the 1990s. He made millions as a fund manager for the firm he founded in 1974, selling his interests in 2001. Friess became known for funding the Republican Party and as an influential philanthropist for evangelical Christian causes.

Unusual Products Made by Businesses in Wyoming

1. Aerobatic aircraft

Manufactured in Afton by Aviat, formerly Aerotek, Inc.

2. Compasses

In the 1990s, Brunton Optics of Riverton was the only United States maker of compasses. The firm, founded in 1971, also manufactured digital readout pocket transits, binoculars and Lakota cutlery.

3. Native seeds

Wind River Seed, based in Manderson, was featured in the *Wall Street Journal* in June 1992 and on *NBC Nightly News* in July. The firm was founded in 1987 by Claire and Richard Dunne. The company provided seed for revegetation projects, but the firm that generated $1.5 million in 1992 also sold wildflower seeds.

"Missionaries lately arrived in Cheyenne, are assigned to duty at Chi-nan-foo and Ningpoo, China. They might possibly be the humble instruments of doing much good by remaining in Cheyenne." --Denver Times, Sept. 26, 1876.

4. Honey candies and taffy

Queen Bee Gardens of Lovell, owned by the Clarence Zeller family, began making honey candy in 1976. Bessie Zeller developed the main recipe for honey candy when her son's optomotrist suggested that he not be fed candy with sugar, but he could have honey. The firm was featured in a 1984 book on America's best local foods written by Allison and Margaret Engel and published by Harper and Row. The company nearly went out of business when a fire destroyed the firm's factory in 1993. With help from the community and Mormon groups around the country, the firm moved to a former Safeway Store and was back in operation 30 days after the fire.

5. Cat litter

Bentonite plants near Worland, Colony and Lovell produce most of the cat litter used in the U.S. The American Colloid company, headed by John Hughes, bought an Illinois-based cat litter company in 1988. Three years later, the company was granted a patent for clumping cat litter made from Wyoming-mined bentonite. During the 1990s, more than four million tons were produced annually in the state.

6. Baking soda

Church and Dwight Company, founded in 1846, produces baking soda, washing powder and carpet deodorizer at their Green River area facility. A majority interest in the parent company of the firm, makers of "Arm and Hammer" brands, was purchased in 1988 by the late Armand Hammer (b. , 1898, d. 1990). In 2001, the company began expanding into consumer products. The company stock is traded on the New York Stock Exchange.

7. "First Day" covers

The world's largest producer of "First Day" stamp covers collected worldwide by philatelists is Unicover Corporation, Cheyenne. The company was formed by James Helzer (b. Cheyenne, 1946, d. Denver, March 7, 2008), in 1968 after he graduated from Yale.

8. Pepper spray

The product, a self-defense spray to be used against attackers, was made by Defense Technology Corporation, Casper, the nation's leading manufacturer of such sprays. The company was sold in the summer of 1996 to Armor Holdings.

9. Hockey sticks

Isofiber Company moved to Laramie from California in the summer of 1992. Among the company's products are hockey sticks, wind surfer masts and golf club shafts. In 1995 the firm was sold and operations moved to Heber City, Utah.

10. Mountain bicycles

Victor Wieburg and Rick Lorenz owned a company, Battle Mountain Bikes, that made mountain bike frames of composite materials. It was headquartered in Encampment.

11. Teaching guides

Bob Codner owned and operated Mathematics Criterion Center Publications, founded in 1988, to publish curriculum materials for high school and college teachers. The firm was located in Evanston.

12. Hunting bows

Hunting bows were made by T&J Bows of Worland, started in 1991 by Terry Jundt and John Pitz of Worland.

One evening, soon after Edward Ivinson opened his first business in Laramie, he was walking home when several men coming from the direction of Fort Sanders asked Ivinson to reopen the store so they could buy some rope. He complied but the men did not buy any because, acccording to Ivinson years later, "they said I had no rope of the proper size." It was soon after three men had been hanged by vigilantes and the men visiting Ivinson's store needed additional rope for more hangings.

13. Belt Buckles

Western Heritage Company, established in Encampment by Pat Lynch in 1976, made official belt buckles for the U. S. Forest Service as well as some 400 other designs.

14. Bottom-ash into pavement

Gillette-based Consolidated Engineers and Materials Testing developed a way to turn a by-product of coal firing into an aggregate for pavement repair. The firm, headed by James P. Murphy, won a U. S. Small Business Administration award in Oct. 2000.

15. Water cleaning products

ET Ventures, Inc., Thermopolis, developed products from bentonite that remove toxic hydrocarbons from streams. The State of Wyoming (through STEA) invested funds in the operation in February, 1996.

16. Mars Space Probe

In July, 1998, NASA hired Detection Limit of Laramie, manufacturers of spectroscopic instruments, to develop a Mars space probe to seek signs of life there.

17. Quilts

Big Horn Quilts began as the first business to sell quilts and fabrics over the internet Started initially by Julie Owens (b. Michigan, 1941) from her home in Greybull, in the early 2000s, the business expanded to a building in downtown Greybull. The company also sells fabrics online.

18. Wine

The first commercial vineyard established in Wyoming since before Prohibition, Table Mountain Vineyards, Huntley, was started in 2004 by Patrick and Amie Zimmer who won a business plan competition with their idea while students at UW.

19. Rollers for Treadmills

Star Tech of Riverton began as a small machine shop and has since grown to become the primary supplier of rollers to the world's largest manufacturer of treadmills. In 2009, they were producing more than two million rollers a year for treadmills alone.

20. Teaching English to Foreign Speakers

The firm initially started in Ten Sleep in 2006, but the headquarters relocated to Cody in 2009, Eleutian Technology used the internet to teach English to Korean, Japanese, and Chinese students through video conferencing. In 2010, the firm employed more than 50 teachers who worked part-time for the firm.

21. Bamboo fishing rods

The Double Hook Rod Co., Rozet, manufactures custom bamboo fishing rods. The firm, run by John Jones, makes 12-15 per year, selling them for $1,000 to $1,800 each.

22. Chili mix and chili powder

As a means of revitalizing their hometown, five couples organized a company in 1986 to produce chili powder for prize-winning chili. Their enterprise was Chugwater Chili Company. A local chili cook-off has drawn contestants from throughout the country over the years. The couples were: Jan and Karl Wilkerson, Ginny and Mark Kaufman, Marcelyn and Jim Brown, Viola and Louis Voight, and Teresa and Dennis Baker.

In the late 1800s a Wyoming rancher named William Taylor sent some of the clay that he found on his ranch to the University of Wyoming to be studied. He first dubbed the clay "taylorite," but soon thereafter changed the name to "bentonite" because he had found it near Fort Benton. In the early 1900s that deposit became one of the first commercial bentonite mines in the world. The substance was originally mined from the earth's surface by horse and wagon, shipped to Chicago, milled into a fine powder, and processed into a skin-wrinkle cream called "Denver Mud"--the clay was still a chief ingredient in beauty mask products in the 1990s.

CAVES

1. Bates Creek Ice Cave
Ice inside does not melt even during the summer heat in this 238-foot-long cave in the Shirley Basin area.

2. Big Horn Caverns
Discovered in 1961, the cave may be the longest in the state at 21,754 feet (four miles). The entrance of the cave lies just north of the Wyoming line. In 1968, cavers discovered that it linked with the massive Horsethief Cave.

3. Casper Mountain Cave
208 feet long.

4. Cave Creek Cave
One of the most impressive of Wyoming's caves, it is located in the Shirley Mountains of Carbon County. Surveyed at 2,048 feet, the cave contains a room called "History Hall" which is 15 feet high, 30 feet wide and 300 feet long.

5. "Captain Bonneville's Marvelous Cave"
Reported and described by W. O. Owen in a Laramie newspaper in 1890, the cave supposedly was found and explored by Capt. B. L. E. Bonneville, one of Wyoming's first white visitors. Owen described Bonneville's adventure and his cave although contemporary cavers report no similar cave in the Wind River area.

6. Columbine Crawl
The longest cave in North America, cavers have taken it far below the Tetons, but it may stretch much farther, according to experts.

7. Darton's Cave
Photographed by N. H. Darton in 1898, the gypsum cave near Sundance is 456 feet long and contains a waterfall. "Graffiti Crawl" is a 100-foot stretch that has suffered vandalism in recent years, hence its name.

8.-9. Dead Man's Cave and Dead Man Cave
The two caves with similar names are located in opposite ends of the state. Dead Man's Cave, in Sybille Canyon near Bosler, gained its name from a miner who, in 1900, walked to Laramie from a nearby mine. On his return, he was caught by a March snowstorm and took refuge in the cave. The storm lasted longer than he did. His body was found and carried across the creek from the cave. Dead Man Cave, a 289-foot cave in Big Horn County's Cottonwood Canyon, is named for a sheepherder who, in the 1920s, fell in and broke his leg. He was unable to crawl back out and died in the cave. His body was later found and removed.

10. Deer Creek Canyon Cave
One of the most dangerous caves in Wyoming, it contains numerous straight drops of up to 50 feet in its descent 212 feet below the earth's surface. The writer of an article for a magazine in 1953 called his exploration of it "Descent into Wyoming's Cave of Terror." The first exploration was made in the 1930s. The University of Wyoming Outing Club mapped the cave in 1961.

11. Grand Vedauwoo Caverns
Just 43 surveyed feet in length, the cave is located in the state recreation area between Cheyenne and Laramie.

12. Holmes Cave
E. B. Holmes found the cave in 1898 and mapped it in 1905. The 410-foot-long cave contains 50-million-year-old tropical swamp debris and several waterfalls.

13. Horsethief Cave
The cave is 21,400 feet in length, making it a bit shorter than the more recently dis-

covered Big Horn Caverns. Horsethief Cave is located in Little Mountain east of Lovell. The government installed a gate at the entrance in 1972 after a Montana caver was lost inside for several days. Like most of Wyoming's caves, permission to explore must be gained from the landowner or government officials if the cave is on public land.

14. La Caverna de los Tres Charros

Located near Dry Medicine Lodge Creek in the Big Horns, the cave remains cold and damp year around. Several waterfalls may be found within its 2,277-foot length.

15. Monsson's Mud Hole Cave

The Shirley Basin area cave is named for George Monsson, one of Wyoming's first cavers.

16. Relatively Long Dark Ugly Tight Cave

The 158-foot-long cave with the unusual name is located near Bosler.

17. Rendezvous Peak Cave

The Tetons cave is one of the most dangerous in the state because it drops 511 feet in its 1,360-foot length at a steady 20-30 degrees.

18. South Fork Ice Cave

Ranchers once used the 474-foot -long cave in Big Horn County as a natural freezer for meat.

19. Spence Cave

The 2,388-foot cave on Burlington Northern land in Big Horn County was designated a county fallout shelter in the 1950s.

20. Spirit Mountain Caverns

First named "Frost Cave" for Ned Frost who discovered the caverns in November 1908, the caverns were designated a national monument by President Taft in 1909 as "Shoshone Caverns National Monument." The cave, measured to 4,044 feet, descends to the level of the Shoshone River some 1,100 feet below its entrance into Cedar Mountain, west of Cody. The national monument was abolished in 1955 and the ownership was turned over to the city of Cody. They were then leased to Claude Brown and the name was changed from Shoshone Caverns. In the late 1980s, the property reverted to the Bureau of Land Management.

21. Table Mountain Cave

Surveyed length of 600 feet, located in the Laramie Range.

22. Tongue River Cave

The cave stretches underground for more than 6,500 feet. One of the most visited caves in the state, it is also one of most badly vandalized. Natural features include the "Wind Tunnel" and the "Sled Room." Located near Dayton, a caver died inside, apparently of natural causes, in early 1989.

23. Upper and Lower Kane Caves

Both caves meander underground for more than 1,000 feet. Inside the upper cave some 450 feet, a stream flows much of the year.

24. Wind Cave

The most spectacular entrance of any Wyoming cave, the 1,000-foot cave in the Tetons' Darby Canyon has an opening of 75 feet high and 30 feet wide.

Sources: Chris Hill, Wayne Sutherland and Lee Tierney. Caves of Wyoming. (Geological Survey of Wyoming, March 1976); press reports; interviews of cavers.

Well-known Montana caver, James Chester,was born in Lusk in May 1944. A graduate of Montana State University, he took up cave exploration and, by 2010, was known as the "maestro of Montana caving." An army veteran, he is a member of the Explorers Club and National Speleological Society. He worked 28 years as a rural mail carrier for the U. S. Postal Service.

CHURCHES

1st church service in Wyoming: Aug. 13, 1835, Hoback Canyon, conducted by the Rev. Samuel Parker, a Presbyterian minister en route to Oregon.

1st Catholic mass celebrated in Wyoming: July 5, 1840, Fort Bonneville, by Father Jean Pierre DeSmet.

1st Eastern Orthodox Church in Wyoming dedicated: Sept. 6, 1925, Rock Springs.

1st Jewish congregation in Wyoming: Congregation Emanuel, organized in March 1888, in Cheyenne

1st Jewish synagogue in Wyoming: Mt. Sinai Synagogue, Cheyenne, constructed in 1915.

1st separate Catholic diocese of Wyoming created: Aug. 9, 1887.

1st Roman Catholic bishop assigned to Wyoming diocese: Rev. Maurice F. Burke, (b. Ireland, 1845)

1st Church of God organized: Thermopolis, July 31, 1932. Earlier that month, the state organization was formed following a revival meeting in Thermopolis.

1st Lutheran services in Niobrara County: Keeline, 1909.

1st African Methodist Episcopal Church in Wyoming: Allen Chapel, Cheyenne, 1875.

1st YMCA building constructed in Wyoming: Sunrise, early 1900s.

1st brick LDS church in Wyoming: Evanston, corner of 7th and Main, built in 1890.

Oldest non-profit corporation in Wyoming: United Presbyterian Church of Laramie, charter filed under the Territory of Wyoming's general corporation law on Oct. 7, 1871.

Papal visit in Denver: Jeremy Aycock of Evanston and Susan Kinsella of Jackson were chosen by computer lottery to be among the 100 people who attended a special mass during World Youth Day in Denver in 1993 when the Pope visited the US. Just two students were chosen from each state.

Senate guest chaplain: Rev. Carl Beavers, St. Mary's parish, Cheyenne, was guest chaplain for the U. S. Senate on June 16, 1992.

Design: The Episcopal Church in Jackson, designed by architects John and Nancy Carney, has been considered one of the most tastefully designed modern buildings in Teton County. Another distinctive design is that of the First United Methodist Church of Laramie. From various angles, the exterior looks like the hull of a large ship.

Organ from Television: The Episcopal Church in Rock River received an organ as a result of the appearance of local resident Dorothy Hall on the popular daytime program "Queen for a Day" in the 1950s. Hall told of the need Mrs. Mallory of Rock River had for an organ. When the organ was given as a prize, Mrs. Mallory donated it to the church.

Church "Firsts" in Wyoming

1. Basin

The Baptist Church was built in 1899. Additions were made to the building over the years, but the original portion has remained in use.

2. Buffalo

The Rev. Addison Blanchard organized the Union Congregational Church on Oct. 10, 1884. The original frame structure was built in 1886 on a steep hill. The building was moved onto the present foundation in 1911.

3. Casper

Congregational Tabernacle, completed in the summer of 1889, was the first church in Casper. The structure served as the community's first schoolhouse. It was located on the southeast corner of First and Wolcott. In 1891, the first Episcopal church in Casper was built for $700 on the northeast corner of Second and Wolcott. The structure was moved to the fairgrounds in 1953.

4. Douglas

The first church services in Douglas were conducted by two theology students in a saloon in May 1886, when Douglas was still a "tent town."

5. Ethete

St. Michael's Mission was established in 1887 as a small log church to serve the Northern Arapaho tribe. In 1910 receipt of a large endowment, furnished by Mrs. Baird Cooper, allowed the mission to expand into stone buildings.

6. Evanston

The Baptist Church was the first in town, built in 1871 on the corner of Center and 9th. The Rev. J. Crossley, an African American, was the first minister.

7. Hulett

The Baptist Church, first in town, was dedicated Oct. 30, 1904.

8. Jackson

The LDS meeting house was constructed about 1905.

9. Kemmerer

The first church, the Catholic Church, was dedicated about 1898. The first resident priest was Father Casey.

10. Lander

Father Moriarity built a Catholic church from stone in 1881.

11. Laramie

The Episcopal church was the first formed in Laramie. First services were conducted on Sept. 13, 1868. The first Episcopal Sunday school in Laramie was held in July 1868, in a small building on the southwest corner of Third and Grand. The oldest standing church in Albany County is the former First Scandinavian Evangelical Trinity Lutheran Church in West Laramie. The church was founded Aug. 13, 1884, and the building finished in July 1885.

12. Lusk

The First Congregational Church started holding services in a tent at the townsite in the spring of 1887.

13. Newcastle

The Episcopal Church cornerstone was laid Oct. 11, 1890. Built for about $2,500 on donated land, it still stands, the oldest church building in Weston County.

14. Pinedale

The Congregational Church was the first church in town, organized Sept. 15, 1907. The first resident pastor was the Rev. J. W. Naylor in 1910. The first church building, constructed for $4,000, was dedicated Aug. 29, 1915.

15. Powell

The Presbyterian Church was the first to hold services in town on Feb. 14, 1909. The church was dedicated May 11, 1911. St. Barbara's Catholic Church, dedicated July 20, 1910, was built for $3,500. The first priest was Father N. J. Endres.

16. Sheridan

The first sermon preached in Sheridan was by a Congregational minister, the Rev. Probert, in the spring of 1884.

17. Star Valley

LDS church structure completed in the late 1870s was the first church in the Star Valley.

18. Sundance

The Methodist Church was built in 1886.

19. Washakie County

The first church in the county was the Methodist Church at Ten Sleep, founded March

14, 1901. Built at a cost of $900, the first building was dedicated Jan. 8, 1905. The structure was moved to its present site on the Circle J Methodist Church camp, east of Ten Sleep, in 1975.

20. Wheatland

The first was the Union Congregational Church, formed July 7, 1895.

5 Rural Churches in Wyoming

1. Inyan Kara Methodist Episcopal Church

The first "country church" in Wyoming, the Inyan Kara church was built in 1891 north of Inyan Kara Mountain, ten miles southeast of Sundance. Formally dedicated Feb. 7, 1892, the structure was moved to Sundance in 1947 where it was converted into a private residence. A plaque, placed in August 1950, marks the original site.

2. Church of St. Hubert the Hunter

The Episcopal church is in the Fall River Basin above Hoback Canyon in Teton County.

3. Chapel of the Transfiguration

This Episcopal chapel near Moose is pictured in many features on the Tetons. The view from the chapel is one of the most spectacular in the country.

4. St. Stephens Mission

Founded May 20, 1884, as a mission school for Indians, the first mass was celebrated that day by Father John T. Jutz who started the mission. The main building, a Georgian Mansion-style structure, was built in 1889-90.

5. St. Thomas Catholic Church

Built in the mining town of Monarch in 1923, the church served a parish of Polish miners who worked nearby. The church closed in 1958 after mines closed in the area. The Sheridan County site is now a ghost town.

Bishops of the Roman Catholic Diocese of Cheyenne

1. Maurice F. Burke (1887-93)
2. Thomas F. Lenihan (1897-1902)
3. James J. Keane (1902-1912)
4. Patrick A. McGovern (1912-Nov. 8, 1951)
5. Hubert M. Newell (1951-1978)
6. Joseh Hart (1978-2001)
7. David L. Ricken (2001-2008)
8. Paul D. Etienne (2008-   )

Memberships of Church Denominations in Wyoming*

1. Roman Catholic, 13.1%
2. Latter-Day Saints (Mormon), 8.6%
3. Lutheran, 3.9%
4. Baptist (all), 3.8%
5. Methodist, 3.2%
6. Presbyterian, 2.2%
7. Seventh Day Adventist, .5%
8. Jewish, .1%

*1980 figures. Wyoming had 361 churches and a total confirmed (full) membership in all denominations of 60,950. Adherents totaled 158,198 or 47.6 percent of the population. Some denominations have age requirements while others count even small infants in their membership. These are representative percentages. Source: New Book of American Rankings. (Facts on File, 1984)

Grace A. M. E. Church, formed in 1917 by Rev. James Otto Minor, was the first Black church in Casper. First meetings were held in a house on C Street, a half-block from the later church site on North Grant Street.

Frontier Footwear: A Painful Ordeal

Movie and television Westerns usually portray the frontier soldier as a cavalryman mounted on a swift Army-regulation brown horse. The truth is that infantry regiments were as common as cavalry companies at most frontier posts.

At Fort Laramie, for example, cavalry troops rarely outnumbered infantry. Even at the time of Custer's defeat at the Little Big Horn in June, 1876, more foot soldiers than horse troops were stationed at Fort Laramie.

Proper footwear was as important to the infantryman as a good horse and saddle was to his cavalry counterpart. An army may travel on its stomach, but the infantryman usually had to walk.

Frontier military footwear was made at the military prison at Fort Leavenworth, Kansas. Construction was neither careful nor skillful. One frontier surgeon reported: "The shoes were of very coarse leather, upper fastened to the sole by brass screws." The two-piece construction of the shoe was not all that made them uncomfortable. Rights and lefts were indistinguishable. The right shoe might well have fit the left foot better than the designated left shoe.

The heels on the shoes, often called "bootees" to distinguish them from boots when requisitioning, were very short. Many a foot soldier found them not high enough to keep trousers out of the mud during spring marches.

The shoes did not wear well. One writer asserts that it was the exceptional man who could make one pair last for six weeks. It is little wonder that many troops wore citizen's boots rather than the issued footwear. Regulations, however, were stiff and there had to be a good reason why the issue shoes were not being worn.

The *Manual of Military Hygiene* described how foot soldiers could make their shoes comfortable: "Soak them in water until quite soft and pliable; put them on, while wet, over a thick pair of socks and take a long walk; remove them, pack them tightly with oats and set aside to dry slowly, the swelling of the oats preventing shrinkage of the leather; when dry, rub on several coats of neatsfoot oil."

As another precaution against blisters, soldiers often rubbed soap on feet and socks before making a long march. The added benefit was that when they washed their feet in the evening, they didn't need to get soap from their packs.

Despite such care, foot disorders were common among Fort Laramie infantrymen. The post surgeon in May, 1869, reported that the major problems were "cuts, bruises, sprains and ulcers." In 1868 a private was discharged because of a bruise on the bottom "of the left foot which ulcerates on the slightest pressure and prevents him from wearing a boot or shoe."

A recently-arrived recruit in 1870 was discharged when it was discovered that he was lame due to a fractured tibia. Flat feet allowed a Private Cahill to be released from Fort Laramie service in 1871, although the Medical History gives no clue as to how his difficulty was discovered and diagnosed.

The shoes had to stand up in all kinds of weather. The frontier troops were not issued overshoes. A private in the 18th Infantry reported that burlap sacks were "at a premium" at Fort Laramie during the winter of 1866-67. "We wrapped them around our shoes to keep from freezing," he wrote, adding that "there were no overshoes or rubbers to be had at the fort."

Military issue boots were often no less comfortable than the shoes. They were frequently oversized and the square toes failed to conform to the foot's shape.

The cavalryman had to wear the ill-fitting boots, too, but he didn't have to walk in them. His toes may have been pinched, but his parts in contact with the murderous McClellan saddle received the pain from service on the Wyoming frontier.

CITIES AND TOWNS

County with fewest incorporated towns: Teton County (1) Jackson

County with most incorporated towns: Carbon County (10) Rawlins, Medicine Bow, Saratoga, Baggs, Dixon, Elk Mountain, Encampment, Hanna, Riverside, Sinclair.

Wyoming has 99 incorporated cities and towns. Of these, 19 are listed as "first class cities." Only three have the council-manager form of government (Casper, Laramie, Rawlins). The remaining 95 have the mayor-council form. Henry Rolfe was Casper's first city manager (1958).

SMSA: Casper is the 4th smallest metropolitan statistical area in the United States of 363 cities qualifying for such designation; Cheyenne is 11th smallest with an estimated 2008 population of 86,750. The Casper SMSA has a population estimated at 72,799 in 2008. The total in 2000 was 66,258, placing Casper as the 3rd smallest SMSA among the cities with SMSA designation. In 1990, its population was 61,226, down from 71,856 in 1980 when Casper ranked 275th of 281 SMSA cities. The 14.8 percent drop over ten years from 1980 to 1990 was the most population loss of any metro area in the United States for that period.

Beautification Award: The city of Gillette was awarded the National Arbor Day Foundation's Lady Bird Johnson award in 1991 for planting 810 trees along major roads from 1984-1991.

Tree City USA: 40 Wyoming communities and Warren AFB have been so designated. Cheyenne has been designated for 27 years; Green River, 26; Torrington, 25; Worland, 24; Buffalo, 22 years. Sheridan was designated in 2010, the latest Wyoming Tree City.

Wyoming town with the most common name: Probably Fairview, west of Afton. According to Rand McNally, the United States has 121 "Fairviews."

Number of entries in the Montreal, Quebec, telephone book with the last name of "Laramee": 288 in 1992 (two entries for Jacques Laramee)

Sister Cities: Several Wyoming towns have "sister cities." Casper has two: Hsi Chih, Taiwan, and San Pedro, Belize. Jackson's relationship with Leinz, Austria, began in 1969. In 1994, the town considered a similar arrangement with San Martin de los Andes, Argentina. Cody has such a relationship with Lanchkhuti in the nation of Georgia.

All-America City Award: The award, presented to ten cities nationwide each year by the National Civic League, was initiated in 1948. Designated in 1958, Sheridan was the first city in Wyoming to be so honored. Powell received the honor in 1994.

Ownership issue: In the 1940s, the City of Cody took over operation of the Buffalo Bill Historical Center and operated the museum for four years. The non-profit Buffalo Bill Memorial Association took it back after a lawsuit. Later, in 1952, the city took ownership of Shoshone Caverns.

Counties without any county zoning ordinances (Sept. 1993): Big Horn, Crook, Hot Springs, Johnson, Niobrara, Weston and Washakie.

1st woman mayor in Wyoming: Susan Wissler, elected mayor of Dayton, began serving May 9, 1911. Owner of a dress shop, she served two terms.

Deep Hole: If one were to dig straight through the earth from the center of Wyoming, he would come out the other side somewhere in the Indian Ocean west of Australia.

Sale of First Lots in Wyoming Towns

1. Douglas

The first town lot was sold to DeForest Richards for $1,250. He built the First National Bank on the property. Later, Richards was elected governor of Wyoming.

2. Evanston

First surveyed lot was sold Dec. 16, 1868, to Dr. F. H. Harrison for $200. The Federal building now stands on the lot.

3. Gillette

The railroad chose the site for the new town, naming it for their locating engineer. The

---

6 Towns Named for Brands

1. Kaycee	3. Keeline	5. Ucross
2. Jay Em	4. Pitchfork	6. Embar

first lots were sold in July, 1891, at a rate of $1.25 per acre. The next month, the Burlington railroad tracks were laid to the new town.

4. Ranchester

Platted in 1894 by a land company, the first town lot was sold for $130 to J. A. Hartman who built a store on the lot.

5. Newcastle

First lots were sold September 10, 1889. The town was located on the first tract of land in the United States to be patented under the placer mining laws as an oil placer. Town lots sold in the main business district for $1,000 to $1,400 each and all were snapped up on the first day.

6. Sheridan

Surveyed on May 16, 1882, the first lots were sold for $2.50 each. Buyers of one lot could buy a second one for an additional 50 cents.

7. Afton

Afton was surveyed in 1886 by Henry M. Harmon who used ropes and a carpenter's square. He laid out 30 blocks, each containing ten acres. One-quarter block sold for $1.

8. Casper

In July, 1889, prices of the first town lots in Casper depended on type and location within a block. The corner business lots sold for $250; inside business lots, $200. Corner residential lots went for $125; inside lots, $100. The first business lot had sold in 1888 on the northwest corner of Second and Center Streets.

9. Evansville

The first town lots, 222 of them, sold from March-August, 1922.

10. Jackson

Maggie Simpson purchased a 40-acre tract from the government for $90. She patented the land in 1900 and, in 1901, sold ten acres of it for $90 to Grace Miller. The town of Jackson was platted on that ten acres.

11. Mills

Charles Hawks homesteaded the town site in 1906 and sold it in 1919. The town was founded in 1921 by three brothers, Thomas, James and William Mills, who owned Mills Construction Company. The brothers had the lots platted and the streets laid out, but left the naming of the town to a vote of the residents. *Source: Jo Mills, letter to Casper Star-Tribune, July 9, 1996.*

12. Sundance

The first town lot was sold in 1884 to Meyer Frank (1854-1911) who helped lay out the town of Newcastle in 1889. Frank built a store on the Sundance lot.

13. Powell

The federal government began selling lots in Powell on May 25, 1909. The first 45 lots brought $13,450. The town was incorporated on May 10, 1910, and by the end of that year, a total of 62 lots had been sold with proceeds of $17,375 going into the federal reclamation fund.

14. Lusk

On July 20, 1886, the first 43 town lots were sold for a total of $9,000.

7 Unusual "Ghost Towns"

1. Carbon

Once one of the largest towns in Wyoming, the town boasted important mines along the Union Pacific in the 1870s. Fires and the railroad's decision to open mines near Hanna and rebuild the main line away from Carbon turned the place into a ghost town by 1900.

2. Sampo

The coal mining town near Hanna existed from 1907 to 1912. The town had a large Finnish population, according to William L. Hewitt in a 1981 community profile, *Sampo, Wyoming: The Community People Forgot.*

3. Shirley Basin

The townsite was officially closed June 15, 1992, by Pathfinder Mines, the owner of the 12-acre site. In the early 1980s, the town boasted a population of 800 people (living in more than 200 mobile homes) until the uranium industry on which the town depended, went into decline when yellow cake prices dropped from $43 to $8 per pound. The town was started by Pathfinder, Kerr-McGee and Getty Petroleum as a "permanent" town. Miners were moved from an earlier site, Teton Camp, ten miles from where Shirley Basin was constructed.

4. South Pass City

The roaring gold mining town of the late 1860s and early 1870s was a county seat and home to Esther Hobart Morris, the nation's first woman justice of the peace. When the mines played out, residents departed. In 1967, the State of Wyoming purchased the town as a historic site. The state purchased the nearby Carissa mine and mill in 2000.

5. Arland

The town, located two miles north of Meeteetse, lasted for 13 years. Victor Arland, who founded the town in 1884, shot, in self-defense, Broken Nose Jackson in 1888. Arland was himself shot to death in 1890 in a Red Lodge saloon while playing cards by Bill Landon in retaliation for shooting Jackson.

6. Kirwin

The town was founded soon after William Kirwin found gold nearby in 1883. The town land was bought by a dude ranch after the turn of century when the town no longer existed. The ranch sold the land in the 1960s to a copper mining company. In 1992, a foundation bought the site and donated it to the Forest Service.

7. Cambria

The Weston County town was thriving into the 1920s. The coal vein on which the mines depended had become depleted. The last shift at the mine ended at noon, March 15, 1928. The company closed down the town.

2 Unusual Cases of Town Incorporation

1. Kaycee

The town of Kaycee was incorporated in 1906 in order to keep the town saloon. The legislature passed a law that only incorporated places could have saloons. In order to be incorporated, the town had to have a population of at least 150 residents. Kaycee fell far below that number, but town incorporators were undeterred. They extended the corporate limits 20 miles on every side, encompassing enough ranch families and cowboys to swell the "town population" above the 150 people required by the law.

2. Lost Springs

When the residents decided to incorporate in the fall of 1911, it was discovered that a minimum of 30 voters was needed within the town's limits. The lines were extended one mile in each direction to include enough voters from area ranches to meet the legal limit.

Author Norman Crampton listed two Wyoming towns as two of the best small towns in America in 1993. Lander was fifth on his list; Douglas was 27th. Elko, Nevada, was his first choice in his book, "The 100 Best Small Towns in America."

7 Towns Located on Ranches

1. Casper

Joseph M. Carey's CY Ranch occupied much of the land on which Casper was later built. A major street in Casper, CY Avenue, is named for the ranch.

2. Lander

Frank Ecoffey's ranch was located on the site of Lander in the late 1870s.

3. Ucross

The town was located on the Wesley Copps ranch with the Leiter estate nearby.

4. Lusk

The site was once part of Frank S. Lusk's horse ranch, established in 1883.

5. Sundance

The town was built on what had been the Albert Hogg ranch in the late 1870s.

6. Edgerton

Founded in 1922 about 47 miles north of Casper on the Kiefer homestead, the homes and offices were moved to the site from Lavoye and Salt Creek. The town was incorporated in 1925 with Mike Keifer as the first mayor.

7. Meeteetse

In 1893, the town was started on part of the 160 acres William McNalley homesteaded. McNalley paid a $6 filing fee for the entire quarter section.

Mythical Wyoming Places

1. Muskrat

Willis G. Emerson proposed the location as the site for the state capitol in 1904 during the heat of the contest between Cheyenne, Lander and Casper for location of the permanent state capitol. Emerson, an Encampment area promoter, said the site was "ideal" for the capital because it was in the exact center of the state, between Casper and Lander. The name came from the creek flowing in the area. Voters did not take Emerson's suggestion seriously. If they had, Wyoming would have been the only state with a capital named for a rodent!

2. Absaroka

In the 1930s, some Northern Wyomingites proposed separating their area from Wyoming and joining it to southern Montana to create a new state named "Absaroka." When the state responded to local needs, the movement ended.

2. Buzzard's Breathe

When Pittsburgh Steeler linebacker Jack Lambert introduced himself to a national TV audience before a Monday Night Football game in the late 1960s, he claimed his hometown was "Buzzard's Breathe, Wyoming."

3. Fractured Jaw

The Wyoming town in the Raoul Walsh spoof of Western movies, *The Sheriff of Fractured Jaw*, made in 1959.

4. Normal

The Wyoming town in the 1992 film, *Leaving Normal*. Some of the scenes were filmed in real-life Superior in Sweetwater County.

5. Sagebrush Center

H. L. Mencken called it one example of a "joke town" to which local people might

Soon after R. O. Graham and Charles Peterson each deeded ten acres of land to the Pinedale Townsite Company, an individual would be given a lot for free if he promised to either build a business structure or a home on it.

refer in jokes and stories. *Source: Mencken, The American Language, edited by Raven I. McDavid, Jr., (New York: Knopf, 1963), p. 420.*

6. Sublette City

Name given to "town" in Hollywood film, *The Legend of Earl Durand*, starring Peter Haskell and Martin Sheen.

7. Whiskey Creek

The title town in the 1992 novel by Gary McCarthy.

8. Wolf City

The Wyoming town where the action in the film *Cat Ballou* occurred.

9. "Old Cheyenne"

Euro-Disney theme park near Paris, France, has a replica of the "Old Cheyenne Hotel," a modern facility with 1,500 rooms. The building contains exact copies of the bunk beds used at the Remount Ranch west of Cheyenne.

10.-11. Benson and Faith

In the television film *Without Warning* (CBS, 1994), the town of Benson, Wyoming, was the site of where UFOs had landed. The 3,000 citizens of the town of Faith, Wyoming, had been "swallowed up" by the alien beings.

4 Towns That "Moved"

1. Alpine

The town "moved" only on maps—into Idaho when the post office moved across the street in February, 1943. Because the state line runs down Main Street, mail reached Alpine with both state names, the actual designation changing whenever the post office site changed.

2. Esterbrook

Once part of Albany County, residents petitioned successfully for the town's inclusion into Converse County in 1956.

3. Lavoye

The Ohio Oil Company claimed it owned the federal government lease to the land where Louis Lavoye had laid out the townsite. After a three-year court battle, the company's claim was upheld in 1925. The company forced the town's residents to either pay them for the land or move. The town, 48 miles north of Casper, had a population of 1,000 at the time of the court suit, but it soon dried up to nothing.

4. Acme

The original townsite sat over a rich coal deposit. When the company needed the coal, the town moved.

Towns Cut Off from Wyoming

1. Alta, Teton County

The Teton County town of about 240 residents is only five miles from Driggs, Idaho, but 45 miles to Jackson. The lone Wyoming town in Idaho's Teton Valley, residents must either take skis or a horse to reach Wyoming without passing through a part of Idaho.

2. Colony, Crook County

Alzada, Montana, and Belle Fourche, S. D., are closest towns via highway, US 212.

3. Henry, Nebraska

While it is not exactly "cut off" from Wyoming (it is a Nebraska town, after all), residents of Henry live very close to the state line. Several residents of the border town live in Wyoming. In one case, the state line runs down the middle of a family home.

3 Underwater Communities

1. Kane

When Yellowtail Dam was completed in 1966, the townsite was covered by the waters of Big Horn Lake which formed behind the dam. During drought years in the early 2000s, outlines of the former townsite again could be seen.

2. Marquette

The store, post office and other buildings were submerged by the waters of Buffalo Bill Reservoir in 1910.

3. Pick Ranch

The home of early-day guide Boney Ernest, the ranch was covered by 100 feet of water when Pathfinder Dam was completed in 1908. From the ranch, Ernest had guided British royalty on hunting trips in 1879.

1st 10 Names Drawn for Lots in Riverton*

1. Hans Berlin, Laramie
2. Edwin F. Buck, Basin
3. Thomas Bly, Fairplay, Colo.
4. William Brunning, Cheyenne
5. Charles F. Overkamp, Lyons, Iowa
6. Robert L. Barley, Silex, Missouri
7. James A. Morrow, Lewistown, Mo.
8. Orion N. Gibson, Trenton, Mo.
9. Bernard Frommel, Thermopolis
10. Henry Schoel, Cheyenne

Drawing made ten days before the entry on Aug. 15, 1906. Thirty days later the train arrived in the new town.

3 Unusual Town Surveys

1. Cody (1897)

When George T. Beck and Charles Hayden were surveying the lots for the new townsite of Cody, a sudden gust of wind blew the survey map out of their hands and carried it away. The map was not retrieved. Cody's first plat was not "filed" in a courthouse.

2. Glendo (1916)

The town was laid out in 1916 by Fred McDermott and one small boy. They used only a tape measure and a yardstick to accomplish the task.

3. Sheridan (May 10, 1882)

J. D. Loucks, the surveyor, drew the plan for Sheridan streets and lots on a sheet of brown wrapping paper. He named it for his Civil War commander, Gen. Philip Sheridan.

Some Company Towns in Wyoming

1. Sinclair (Parco)

(See "Some Wyoming Name Changes")

2. Hanna

Town was named by Union Pacific officials for Sen. Mark Hanna of Ohio, a powerful congressional supporter of the railroad.

3. Sunrise (1903)

The town was founded by Colorado Fuel and Iron Corporation. The iron ore deposits were first brought to the company's attention in 1898 and, three years later, the firm purchased 72 claims. The town is now abandoned.

4. Superior, South Superior (1905)

The town was started by the Union Pacific Coal Company. At one time, the town had a population of nearly 5,000. As the mines closed down in the 1950s, the company sold or demolished the 300 company houses in town. The company pulled out in the early 1960s and in 1966, the high school closed. In January, 1996, the town had about 280 residents.

5. Midwest

The Midwest Oil Company was formed in 1911. In 1920, Standard of Indiana bought one-eighth of the firm. Established on land owned by the Stock family and known as "Home Camp," the name was changed Jan. 1, 1924, to distinguish it from a camp at Salt Creek to the southeast. Midwest Oil was dissolved in 1932 and the operations, including the town, sold to Stanolind, a Standard of Indiana subsidiary. Houses were sold to the residents in 1960. In 1975, no longer company-owned, the town was incorporated. First mayor was Elwanda Burke.

6. Cambria (1889)

The town was established by Kilpatrick Brothers and Collins, the firm that was hired to construct stretches of the Burlington railroad into the area and provide coal for its locomotives. Liquor was never legally sold in the town during its 40 years of existence as a privately owned mining town. The town closed down with the mines in 1928.

7. Wright (1976)

The town was laid out and constructed by ARCO. The town was dedicated on July 8, 1976, at a ceremony attended by numerous state officials. It was incorporated in 1985 as an independent town, no longer company-owned.

8. Bairoil (1916)

The place was named for the Bair Oil Company, the firm named for Charles Bair, former sheep rancher who entered the oil business about 1916 and founded the town. A post office was located there in 1924. The town was incorporated in 1980.

9. Diamondville (1894)

A sharp dividing line existed between Kemmerer, operated by the Kemmerer Coal Company, and Diamondville, established by the Diamond Coal and Coke Company. The Diamondville mines had been opened by Thomas Sneddon in 1894. With head offices in Anaconda, Mont., the firm also operated mines at Oakley and Glencoe. The company owned the mines, the light plant, houses, and the store, and it hired the town's doctor.

10. Rudefeha (1896)

A copper mining town, owners outlawed liquor in the town. The miners were undeterred. They started the non-company competing town of Dillon. The name of Rudefeha came from the first two letters of the last names of its four founders- John Rumsey, Robert Deal, George Ferris and Ed Haggerty.

11. Kooi (1907)

The town was built by the Kooi Coal Company, operated by Peter Kooi (b. Chicago, 1866- d. Denver, 1935). Kooi came to Wyoming in 1904 to work for the Wyoming Mining Company at Monarch, also a company town. Kooi went into business on his own, locating his town two miles west of the town of Monarch, 12 miles northwest of Sheridan. The Kooi post office opened in 1907 and closed in 1925. At its peak, the town had a population of 500. Kooi sold the company and town to the Sheridan-Wyoming Coal Company in 1920.

Some Wyoming Name Changes

1. "Rawlins Springs"

Originally named for Gen. John A. Rawlins, the "springs" portion was dropped early in the town's existence. The same thing happened to the "city" behind the names of Laramie and Green River in the 19th century.

2. "Shoshone Dam"

Renamed "Buffalo Bill Dam" in 1946, the dam was the highest in the world when it was completed in 1910. Col. Cody was a strong proponent of irrigation and the dam on the Shoshone River was renamed in his honor.

A 1961 study commissioned by Pacific Power predicted that Wyoming's population by 1980 would be at least 700,000. "Wyoming has virtually every requisite except population to become one of the greatest industrial states in the nation," the report said. The 2000 census showed just 493,782 Wyoming residents.

3. "Stinkingwater River"

The river was officially renamed the "Shoshone River" by legislative act in 1901, to the relief of Cody area residents who thought the original name might not be healthy for the tourist industry.

4. "Charger"

The name was applied, briefly, to a community in Sheridan County that originally had been called "Cedar Rapids" after the Iowa hometown of promoters. In November, 1916, the name was changed from Charger to Ucross, for the cattle brand of the nearby Leiter Estate.

5. "Doggett"

The Carbon County town was renamed "Riverside" in the 1890s.

6. "Pilot Knobs"

Peter Skene Ogden changed the original name of "Pilot Knobs," which originated with area fur trappers, to Grand Tetons about 1825. The new name for the landmark peaks derived from French—"trois tetons" or "three teats."

7. "Pease County"

The county was named in 1875 in honor of Dr. E. L. Pease, a Uinta County resident. When young attorney E. P. Johnson of Cheyenne died on Oct. 3, 1879, the legislature renamed the county in his memory, effective Dec. 13, 1879.

8. "Carter County"

Originally named in 1867 in honor of Fort Bridger judge and post trader William H. Carter, it was renamed "Sweetwater County" on Dec. 13, 1869.

9. "Parco"

Named for the Producers and Refiners Corporation when it was laid out in 1925, the planned town of Parco became Sinclair in December, 1942. The original company fell on hard times during the Great Depression and the refinery and company townsite were sold in a bankruptcy sale from the steps of the Carbon County Courthouse on April 12, 1934. The entire package (town, refinery, pipeline) went for $1,775,000 to Consolidiated Oil Company, which later became Sinclair Refining Company. The firm sold most of the townsite to local residents in 1967 and the refinery became part of Atlantic Richfield when Sinclair merged with that company in 1970. After a series of complex mergers and sales, the present Sinclair Oil Company purchased the refinery in July, 1976.

10. "Home-on-the-Range"

Originally named for postmaster Beulah Peterson's highway cafe and store, the site was renamed "Jeffrey City" for Dr. Charles W. Jeffrey, Rawlins physician and philanthropist, who held uranium investments in the area.

11. "Spanish River"

Originally named by trappers who recognized that the river flowed south toward Spanish territory, it was renamed "Green River" by William H. Ashley in 1824. It is said that Ashley named it for a St. Louis partner and not for the characteristic green color of the river.

12. "Camp Brown"

The name was changed Dec. 30, 1878, to Fort Washakie, in honor of Chief Washakie. During the previous year, the Shoshone chief reluctantly agreed to allow the government to move several hundred Arapahoes onto the reservation as a "temporary measure."

13. "Eustis Lake"

The lake was named for William Eustis, President James Madison's secretary of war,

---

The population of the coal-mining town of Monarch went from 500 to 29 in the year following closure of the mines in May, 1953.

by William Clark from information provided to him by John Colter, the first white American to see the lake and the Yellowstone area. Later, the name was changed to Sublette Lake and then to Yellowstone Lake in 1839.

14. "Alamo"

The town was renamed Manderson in 1889 by railroad officials in honor of Burlington Railroad's general counsel.

15. "Snake Lake"

Named by trappers for the early Indian tribe inhabiting the area, the name was changed to "DeLacy's Lake" in 1863 by the area's first mapmaker, Walter DeLacy. In 1872, the Hayden expedition named it "Shoshone Lake."

16. "White City"

Founded about 1900, the coal mining town's name was changed to Reliance by officials of the Union Pacific Coal Company because the coal beds near there were "reliable" producers.

17. "Merino"

The original name for Upton, the Burlington Railroad changed the name in 1901-02 after the post office complained that the name was confusing because it was the same as a town in northeast Colorado. The new name honored railroad surveyor George S. Upton.

Some "New" Towns

1. Wright

Constructed by ARCO, the town was dedicated on July 8, 1976.

2. Pine Haven

The community was an "improvement district" for 12 years until it was incorporated in 1987. It is located near Keyhole Reservoir, Crook County.

3. Mountainaire

The new town was proposed in January 1994, for the neighborhood north of Rock Springs occupied by approximately 2,000 residents.

5 Incorporated Places with Fewer Than 100 People

1. Lost Springs 1

The population in 1990 had been four times the 2000 count--4 people.

2. Frannie 6

The population of Frannie has been in steady decline since 1970 when the town boasted a population of 36. Only 17 were counted in 1980. The 1990 count showed six residents.

3. Van Tassell 18

The 1990 population was just 8 people.

4. Kirby 57

Kirby and the nearby ghost town of Gebo were once home to coal miners working the rich veins in the area. Kirby's population shrank by nearly half from 1980 when the Census Bureau counted 129 residents to 59 in 1990 and then to 57 in 2000.

5. Hartville 78

Founded in 1881, Hartville had at least ten saloons in the early 1880s. A few years after the first copper boom ended in 1884, the mines in the area switched to production of iron ore. The town was incorporated by vote of the residents on May 31, 1900.

Postal authorities were not pleased with the name chosen for their town by residents of "Never Sweat" in the middle 1880s. They insisted the name be changed to "Dubois."

Wyoming Cities by Population (1990, 2000)

(1990 U. S. Census ranking)

1. Cheyenne 50,008 (1)	53,011	46. Ranchester 676 (44)	701
2. Casper 46,742 (2)	49,644	47. Dayton 565 (46)	678
3. Laramie 26,687 (3)	27,204	48. Shoshoni 497 (48)	635
4. Gillette 17,635 (5)	19,646	49. Cowley 477 (53)	560
5. Rock Springs 19,050 (4)	18,708.	50. Byron 470 (55)	557
6. Sheridan 13,900 (6)	15,804.	51. Alpine 200 (74)	550
7. Green River 12,711 (7)	11,808	52. Lingle 473 (54)	510
8. Evanston 10,903 (8)	11,507	53. Cokeville 493 (50-51)	506
9. Riverton 9,202 (10)	9,310	54. Rolling Hills 330 (61)	449
10. Cody 7,897 (11)	8,835	55. Encampment 490 (52)	443
11. Jackson 4,472 (17)	8,647	56. LaBarge 493 (50-51)	431
12. Rawlins 9,380 (9)	8,538	57. Sinclair 500 (47)	423
13. Lander 7,023 (12)	6,867	58. Big Piney 454 (56)	408
14. Torrington 5,651 (14)	5,776	59. Hulett 429 (57)	408
15. Powell 5,292 (15)	5,373	60. Midwest 495 (49)	408
16. Douglas 5,076 (16)	5,288.	61. Hudson 392 (58)	407
17. Worland 5,742 (13)	5,250	62. Meeteetse 386 (60)	351
18. Buffalo 3,302 (18)	3,900	63. Baggs 272 (64)	348
19. Wheatland 3,271 (19)	3,548	64. Thayne 267 (65)	341
20. Thermopolis 3,247 (20)	3,172	65. LaGrange 224 (72)	332
21. Newcastle 3,003 (22)	3,065	66. Ten Sleep 311 (62)	304
22. Kemmerer 3,020 (21)	2,651	67. Burns 254 (67)	285
23. Mills 1,574 (28)	2,591	68. Medicine Bow 389 (59)	274
24. Lovell 2,131 (24)	2,281	69. E. Thermopolis 221 (73)	274
25. Evansville 1,403 (30)	2,255	70. Wamsutter 240 (70)	261
26. Glenrock 2,153 (23)	2,231	71. Burlington 184 (79)	250
27. Lyman 1,896 (26)	1,938	72. Kaycee 256 (66)	249
28. Afton 1,394 (31)	1,818	73. Superior 273 (63)	244
29. Greybull 1,789 (27)	1,815	74. Chugwater 192 (77)	244
30. Saratoga 1,969 25)	1,726	75. Fort Laramie 243 (69)	243
31. Lusk 1,504 (29)	1,447	76. Rock River 190 (78)	235
32. Pinedale 1,181 (34)	1,412	77. Glendo 195 (76)	229
33. Wright 1,236 (32)	1,347	78. Pine Haven 141(81)	222
34. Basin 1,180 (35)	1,238	79. Elk Mountain 174 (80)	192
35. Sundance 1,139 (37)	1,161	80. Deaver 199 (75)	177
36. Mountain View 1,189 (33)	1,153	81. Edgerton 247 (68)	169
37. Pine Bluffs 1,054 (39)	1,153.	82. Yoder 136 (82)	169
38. Guernsey 1,155 (36)	1,147	83. Pavillion 126 (83)	165
39. Dubois 895 (41)	962	84. Granger 126 (84)	146
40. Bar Nunn 835 (41)	936	85. Albin 120 (85)	120
41. Hanna 1,076 (38)	873	86. Clearmont 119 (86)	115
42. Upton 980 (40)	872	87. Manderson 83	104
43. Moorcroft 768 (43)	807	88. Opal 95	102
44. Marbleton 634 (45)	720	89. Manville 97	101
45. Diamondville 864 (42)	716	90. Bairoil 228 (71)	97

COAL

1st coal used in Wyoming: Early man used coal for fires thousands of years ago.

1st report of coal in modern times: John C. Fremont wrote in his 1843 journal: "Coal made its appearance occasionally in the hills and a gap through which we passed to make our encampment on Little Muddy Creek." Fremont probably referred to the Cumberland area near Kemmerer.

1st use of coal by white Americans in Wyoming: Overland stage employees burned coal for fuel and blacksmithing at the stage stop at Rock Creek Crossing (near present-day Rock River) in 1865. The coal was from "Coal Bank Hollow."

1st modern commercial coal mine in Wyoming: Opened at Carbon in 1867.

1st labor strike in Wyoming: Miners at Carbon went out on strike in 1870.

1st electric mine locomotive built in the United States began operating: Rock Springs No. 7 mine, 1892.

1st strip mining in Wyoming reported: The method was noted in the State Mine Inspector's Report, 1925, but the location was not specified.

1st union organized in northern Wyoming: United Mine Workers at Dietz, 1903.

1st shipment of Powder River Basin coal made to Europe: May 1991, 62,000 tons were sent to Spain by the Spring Creek Coal Co. The Antelope Coal Company sent regular test shipments to Spain. Both firms were owned by NERCO.

Heavy use: Use at the Jim Bridger Power Plant averaged six million tons per year since 1986. In some years, the power plant burned up to seven million tons of coal.

Largest unbroken concentration of coal in the United States: Wyodak bed, centered in Campbell County, penetrates the surface along a line 120 miles long. It has a thickness of 25-150 feet and runs to a depth of 200 feet. The bed has an estimated 15 billion tons of usable coal, 20 times the entire United States output. To a depth of 2,000 feet, the bed contains an estimated 100 billion tons of coal.

Coal by area: Sub-bituminous coal lies under more than 40,000 square miles of Wyoming. The coal dates from the Cretaceous Period (16-135 million years ago) when the area was a lush, humid tropical forest.

Coal production: Wyoming leads the nation in coal production with an average of about 3 million tons mined per week.

Coal production from federal lands in Wyoming: 370.7 million tons (83.2% of all coal produced in Wyoming) was mined on federally-owned lands (2006)

Wyoming led nation in coal production on federal lands each year since 1994. In 1994, 214.7 million tons (73 percent of U. S. total); royalties, $159.2 million; in 2006, 370.7 million tons.

Wyoming's share of coal lease bonuses: The Minerals Management Service, Dept. of the Interior, collects bonuses from coal producers who are issued coal leases on federal lands. The leases are granted after competitive bidding and payable in five annual installments. Wyoming receives 50 percent of the bonus payments or $207.7 million in 2006.

State severance tax rate on coal: 7 percent, payable on the value where the production process is complete (at the mine), before processing and transportation.

Average Market Prices for Coal

1. Low sulfur coal

At the mine site, the price in 2008 averaged $11.39 per ton. The cost did not include transportation or other processing costs. The severance tax is assessed on the cost at the mine. In 2000, the price was between $3.50 to $6 per ton. If the coal is produced on federal land, mines pay an average of 8-10 percent for the federal mineral royalty.

In 1998 Wyoming coal was shipped to electric power utilities in 25 states, Canada and Spain. More than 140 million tons (46%) went to utilities in southern and southeastern states; 126 million tons (41%) went to Midwest utilities. Utilities in the Rocky Mountain and Pacific Northwest states used just 35.6 million tons (12%) while Spain and Canada combined received 2.2 million tons (1%). Source: U. S. Department of Energy

2. All Wyoming coal

The price in 1982 reached $12.75 per ton. The next year, 1983, coal hit a record price of $13.14 per ton. In 1992, AMAX estimated the price was $7.70 a ton (as an average of spot price and contract prices). Spot market prices dropped to less than $4 per ton in 1992, remaining in that range to the end of the decade. The average price in 2007 was $10.33 per ton, rising to $11.39 per ton in 2008.

3. Coal employment

Coal employment dropped from 6,020 employees in 1982 to fewer than 4,600 in 1993. Employment fell again in 1999 and severance taxes were reduced while production continued to increase. By 2008, employment in the coal industry had risen to 6,760.
Source: Wyoming Mining Association, 2010.

Wyoming Coal Production Marks

1985: Black Thunder mine in Campbell County in June set a national record (it has since surpassed) by producing two million tons of coal in a single month.

1988: Wyoming led the nation in coal production.

1990: Wyoming mines produced 184 million tons. Campbell County's 15 surface mines produced 154 millions tons with the rest coming from mines in six other counties. Wyoming had 27 surface mines and four underground operations in 1990.

1992: The 190 million tons produced in the state accounted for 20 percent of the national total.

1993: Wyoming continued to lead all states in coal production for the fifth consecutive year. Total mine production was nearly 210 million tons.

1995: Wyoming coal production passed 263 million tons during the year, once again, placing Wyoming as the leading coal-producing state in the nation.

1998: Wyoming mines set a new production record of 314.5 million tons.

1999: Wyoming mines produced 334 million tons, leading the nation for the 11th consecutive year. More than 93 percent of the total came from the 14 producing mines in Campbell County.

2000: Production increased slightly to 339 million tons while employment fell slightly to 4,414.

2004: Total state production set another mark at 395 million tons and employment increased to more than 5,300 for the first time since the "boom years."

2005: For the first time, annual coal production topped 400 million tons.

2008: Another annual record was set for production--466.3 million tons produced, with the coal used in 37 states to generate power.

2009: 433.5 million tons, a reduction of 8.5% from 2008, the first year-to-year decline in two decades. Nonetheless, Wyoming accounted for 40 percent of the US supply of coal.

Some Large Wyoming Mines*

1. Black Thunder, Wright

The mine, 12 miles southeast of Wright, was operated by the Thunder Basin Coal Company LLC. Initially, it was operated by an ARCO subsidiary until it was purchased

---

The biggest truck in the world began service in Wyoming on Nov. 12, 1998, at the Black Thunder mine, Campbell County. The truck, built by Liebherr Mining Equipment Co., of Baxter Springs, Kansas, was a T282, 360-ton haul truck. It had a 21 ft., 6-inch wheel base and the diesel engine puts out 2,700 hp. The cost of one was $3 million.

in 1998 by Ark Land Company. It was the biggest coal mine in Wyoming and the nation, in terms of production, in 2003 and 3004, regaining the top spot the following two years and then dropping to second spot to North Antelope/Rochelle in 2007.   In 2008, the mine produced 88.6 million tons of coal. Black Thunder employed 1,083 people in 2008. The mine provided coal to 116 power plants in 25 states in 2010. Arch Coal, owner of Black Thunder and nearby Coal Creek mine is the biggest private employer in Campbell County with nearly 2,000 employees. On March 9, 2009, Arch Coal announced the purchase of Rio Tinto's Jacobs Ranch mine adjoining Black Thunder for a reported $761 million.

2. North Antelope/Rochelle Mine

Owned and operated by Peabody Coal subsidiary, Powder River Coal Company, this mine took the top spot for coal production in 2007 with 91.5 mllion tons, an increase from 88.5 million tons in 2006. It retained the mark in 2008 with 97.6 million tons and, in 2009, 98.3 million tons. Until 2007, the mine employed an average of 800 people, but that number increased to 935. By 2009, 1,188 workers were employed at the North Antelope/ Rochelle mine.

2. Jacobs Ranch, Wright

The mine was purchased by Black Thunder Coal, an Arch sudsidiary, on March 9, 2009. Previously, Jacobs Ranch had been bought by Kennecott, Inc., in 1998 and then sold to Rio Tinto Energy America. The mine produced 42.1 million tons of coal in 2008 and employed 643 people.

3. Belle Ayr and Eagle Butte, Gillette

Both mines, now operated by Alpha Coal West, a unit of Alpha Natural Resources, a firm organized in 2002 and publicly traded since 2005. The mines were once run by Cyprus/AMAX, sold in 1999 to REG Coal International, a German-based company, and then to Alpha Coal West. The Belle Ayr mine produced 28.7 million tons of coal in 2009 and employed 352 while Eagle Butte produced 21.5 million tons and had 280 workers.

5. Cordero/Rojo, Gillette

Operated by Cloud Peak Energy, LLC, the mine complex produced 39.4 milion tons in 2009. The mine complex employed 634. Cloud Peak, a "carve-out of Rio Tinto," went public in Nov. 2009 as the third largest coal producer in the United States.

6.-7. Rawhide and Caballo, Gillette

Exxon Coal USA Inc. once owned both mines, but in 2009, both were owned by Powder River Coal Company, a subsidiary of Peabody Coal. Rawhide produced 15.8 million tons of coal in 2009. It employed 226 workers, up from 199 working there in 1991 Caballo produced 23.3 million tons in 2009, up from 14.4 million in 1994. Peak production was 32.7 million tons in 2006.

8. Antelope Mine, Converse County

The mine, owned by Cloud Peak Energy, produced 34 million tons in 2009 through the efforts of 488 employees.

In December, 1917, the U. S. Fuel Administrator, charged to see that there was efficient use of fuel resources in the country, received a complaint from coal operators in Hot Springs County that "the saloons at the coal mines were open day and night, demoralizing the labor force and causing a decrease in production." County authorities passed regulations that required saloons to be closed from 11 p.m. to 7 a.m. and all day on Sundays. As a contemporary observer wrote: "This had the desired effect for a time but it was necessary to continuously guard against the abuse of liquor causing a decrease in production. The mines in Hot Springs County are located in a bleak and desolate section, practically a desert, and opportunities for amusement and recreation are limited."

8. Jim Bridger, Point of Rocks

The mine is owned by MidAmerican Energy/Berkshire Hathaway. The coal from the mine fuels the Jim Bridger Power Plant, operated by Pacificorp (bought by MidAmerican Energy in March 2006) and Idaho Energy Resources. Production is both surface and underground. In 2009, the mine produced 5.2 million tons of coal and employed 422.

9. Black Butte, Point of Rocks

The mine produced 3.9 million tons in 2009. It employed 178 workers. Black Butte Coal Company was formed in 1974 and began shipping coal in 1979. The company operates the mine as a joint venture with Anadarko Petroleum.

10 Shoshone Mine, near Hanna

Located in Carbon County near Hanna, Shoshone was opened in the early 1970s by a Union Pacific subsidiary and partner. Cypress Coal bought the mine in 1987. Later, it was purchased by RAG Shoshone Coal Company. The mine reopened in the 1990s, producing 2.8 million tons in 1997, its peak year at this stage when it employed more than 140 workers. In 2000, Shoshone produced 1.2 million tons and employed 67 workers. Production dropped to zero the following year. It closed for a second time (and permanently) on Aug. 30, 2000.

11. Seminoe II

The mine, opened by Arch in the 1970s, closed in 1988 due to poor demand and low coal prices. It reopened a couple of years later when demand returned. After peak years in the 1980s, the mine briefly came back in 1997 with production of 601,000 tons. Employment varied between 27 and 45 for the next several years, but the mine permanently closed in 2005 when just four employees were retained at the mine. The mine underwent final reclamation from 2006-09.

12. Medicine Bow, Carbon County

The mine produced closed to 2 million tons through the 1990s and employed nearly 80 workers. Production and employment at the mine dropped dramatically in the early 2000s. No coal was produced at the mine in 2005 and only 26 million tons was extracted the following year.

13. Grass Creek mine, Big Horn Basin

A tiny mine by Wyoming standards, the production began in 2005 with 6,200 tons mined by four employees. After a production drop to just 167 tons in 2008, production jumped rapidly in 2009 to 12,700 tons. Still a tiny operation in comparison with mines in the Powder River Basin, the Grass Creek mine is the first in the Big Horn Basin to open since the mine at nearby Gebo closed a half century earlier.

14. Kemmerer Mine, Kemmerer

Operated by the Pittsburg and Midway Coal Company, production has remained stable at about 4 million tons since the 1980s. The mine employees have averaged around 300 over the life of the mine.

15. Dave Johnston Mine, Converse County

For many years, the mine produced all of the coal firing the power plant by the same name at Glenrock. In 2000, the mine was closed when it became more economical dto ship coal in from the Powder River mines than to mine it near the power plant.. In 2006 reclamation of the mine site began, continuing to 2010.

Mountain Home Coal Mine, Converse County, began burning below ground about 1921. The site became a favorite for picnickers. The cracks from which flames came were as wide as a foot in places. At night the flames could be seen for miles. By 1950, the fire covered an underground area of about 60 acres. The federal government sent fire crews to extinguish the flames, contracting with the Isbell Brothers of Riverton to do the job in the summer of 1950.

16. Dry Fork

The mine serves one customer—the Laramie River Power Station.

Production figures and ownership courtesy of the Wyoming Mining Association. When offices in Cheyenne were forced to move about 2005, many of the WMA's historical records were donated to the American Heritage Center, University of Wyoming, and made available to researchers.

14 Mine Disasters in Wyoming*

1. Hanna, June 30, 1903, 169 killed.

Highest death toll in Wyoming coal mining history, 46 escaped the explosion in No. 1 mine, caused by coal gas ignition.

2. Kemmerer, Aug. 14, 1923, 99 killed.

Only 135 of 250 workers were in the Frontier No. 1 mine because of a holiday. The explosion and fire apparently started when a fire boss attempted to relight his flame safety lamp with a match. It ignited the coal gas. A group of 21 barricaded themselves from the flames until they were rescued.

3. Red Canyon, March 1895, 62 killed.

The mine was located near Almy in Uinta County. When the mine exploded, the sound was heard seven miles away in Evanston.

4. Hanna, March 28, 1908, 59 killed.

Eighteen miners died in the initial explosion at the same site as the 1903 disaster. Forty-one rescuers, including the state mine inspector, died in an unsuccessful attempt to reach trapped miners at 10:30 p.m., the night of the initial explosion. Only 32 bodies were recovered. The rest were left inside and the mine sealed. A monument was erected over the site in 1933.

5. Sublet, Sept. 16, 1924, 39 killed.

An explosion was caused by gas ignited by an arc from the locomotive trolley in Sublet No. 5 mine.

6. Almy, March 4, 1881, 38 killed.

The first major mining mishap in Wyoming history, the resulting fire also destroyed buildings on the mine surface.

7. Diamondville, Feb. 26, 1901, 26 killed.

Suffocation caused the deaths following a cave-in deep in the mine.

8. Diamondville, Oct. 1901, 22 killed.

The disaster was a repeat of the February incident. Rescuers could not reach the miners trapped beneath the cave-in.

9. Diamondville, Dec. 2, 1905, 18 killed.

An explosion during the night shift "destroyed cement and stone stoppings 18-24 inches thick." The site was Diamondville No. 1 mine, the same site as the 1901 tragedies.

10. Almy, Jan. 12, 1886, 13 killed.

Among the victims were two young boys.

Gebo #1 mine closed June 1, 1933, putting more than 300 miners out of work. According to reports of the closure in the *Thermopolis Independent Record,* May 19, 1933, p. 1., the mine, owned by Owl Creek Coal Co., had been open for more than 25 years.

11. Sublet, July 26, 1920, 6 killed.

The magazine exploded when a miner hit a powder keg with a mallet.

12. Cumberland, January, 1912, 6 killed.

Along with the six killed, 20 other miners were injured when coal dust exploded in No. 4 mine, known as the "Susie mine."

13. Cumberland, April 30, 1914, 5 killed.

A coupling broke on mine cars, dropping seven of the cars back down the mine shaft. Many men jumped to safety as the cars careened downward.

14. Deadman Creek, Feb. 11, 1938, 5 killed.

The accident occurred at Vail truck mine, 78 miles from Afton and at an elevation of 8,200 feet. The mine foreman's wife skied through four feet of snow to a ranch to get help. *State Mine Inspector's Reports. The U. S. Bureau of Mines defines a mine "disaster" as an accident killing five or more miners at one time.*

4 Coal Miners' Memorials

1. Sheridan

A coal miners' memorial at the Visitor's Center east of Sheridan was dedicated in 1973 to the underground miners working area underground coal mines, open from 1891 to 1951. The statue is by John Kuchera, a former area miner.

2. Cambria

Just a year before coal operations ceased at the mining town in Weston County, Cambria coal company officials developed plans for a recreation complex as a memorial to the miners. It opened in 1929, a year after the mines at Cambria closed, leaving the town a ghost town. The memorial, located along US 85, is now operated as a restaurant and lounge.

3. Hanna

The Hanna Basin Historical Society dedicated a miners' memorial on May 27, 1984, on which is listed the names of all miners who died in the area mines from 1870 to 1982. A separate memorial, situated south of the present Hanna school, marks the site of the state's largest coal mine disaster.

4. Superior

A monument to the generations of area miners was dedicated in 1992 and located inside the trapezoid-shaped Union Hall, the ruins of which are preserved.

Five Casper area men claimed to have seen a UFO near Casper in March 1951. On July 10, 1947, a flying saucer was reportedly seen near Chugwater. The strangest UFO case in Wyoming involved Carl Higdon who was elk hunting south of Rawlins in October 1974. While following some elk, he happened on a strange man who gave him a pill and ordered him into a seven-foot square cubicle. He claimed he was transported to a huge tower and, after a short visit there in what seemed to be a spacecraft, he was returned to the ground unharmed.

COUNTIES
Unusual Facts About Courthouses

1. Uinta County Courthouse

The Evanston building was constructed in 1874 of brick which had been dyed red from the blood taken from the slaughterhouse near the brickyard.

2. Weston County Courthouse

The Antlers Hotel in downtown Newcastle served as the county courthouse from 1890 until 1894.

3. Lincoln County Courthouse

Legal business was conducted in the First National Bank building from 1913 until 1925 when the new courthouse building in Kemmerer was completed.

4. Park County Courthouse

The courthouse clock, donated to the county by philanthropist and local resident William R. Coe, was too heavy for the roof. In the 1920s, the clock fell through the ceiling into the room below. No one was injured, but the timepiece left a large dent in the floor.

5. Johnson County Courthouse

The site for the downtown Buffalo building was purchased in 1881. On the lot was the Lone Star Dance Hall, demolished to make way for the new courthouse. Built by Edward and James Curran for $81,650 in 1884, the structure is the oldest courthouse in Wyoming retaining its original character and still being used for its original purpose. Except for the removal of the bell tower, the exterior has not changed. The bricks were made of clay taken from south of the Buffalo City Park.

6. Niobrara County Courthouse

The statue of justice topped the Lusk building until 1930 when it was removed because of the heavy weight it placed on the roof. The statue was stored in a mine cave until World War II when it was added to the scrap metal drive.

7. Natrona County Courthouse

County offices occupied two rooms on the second floor of Robert White's saloon on Center Street from 1890 to 1895. White received $450 a year in rent. Court was held in the town hall.

8. Carbon County Courthouse

During the first term of court in Rawlins in June 1870, court was held in a tent erected in the middle of a downtown street. The clerk, Frank Edmunds, also served as county clerk, treasurer, probate judge, U. S. court commissioner, and deputy U. S. revenue assessor.

Some Interesting Items Relating to Counties

1. Brother commissioners

Alvin Robinson and his brother Reynold lived on the same street in Freedom in 1933. Nonetheless, each served as county commissioner—in two different counties in two different states. One brother lived in Lincoln County, Wyoming, while the other who lived across the street, resided in Caribou County, Idaho.

2. In the same house, not the same county...

George, William and Lizzie Stoll were all born in different territories. That fact, in

> "The county commissioners authorize us to say that they will pay a bounty of $1 each for every hog caught running at large in the streets of this city, which shall be driven into the yard back of Wright's Harness shop on 2nd Street." --Laramie Sentinel, 1872

itself, is not unusual except that all three were born in the same house—and the house never moved! George Stoll was born April 18, 1857, at Fort Bridger, Utah Territory. Eleven years later on April 3, 1868, his brother William was born in the same house, only this time it was in Fort Bridger, Dakota Territory. When sister Lizzie (Kirkendall) was born on June 8, 1871, in the house, it was located in Fort Bridger, Wyoming Territory. *Source: This story first appeared nationally in Ripley's Believe It or Not, Sept. 26, 1930.*

Proposed New Counties

1. Hanover County

C. F. Robertson, first mayor of Worland, tried for years to have the legislature create a separate county for his hometown. He represented the Hanover Canal Company, the firm responsible for much of the agricultural development in the area. Consequently, when a new county was authorized in 1911, initially, it was given the name "Hanover County." Seven days later, the name was changed to Washakie County. Clason, a Denver map company, hurriedly published a map showing the new counties in 1911, but the firm's draftsmen had neglected to make the name change. The firm's Wyoming map for 1911 is a collector's item.

2. Waconda County

Residents of the Shoshoni area proposed creation of a new county to be carved from the northern part of Fremont County in 1911. Suggested names for the new county were Waconda and Shoshone. In 1913, a bill creating Shoshone County passed the legislature, but was vetoed by Gov. Joseph M. Carey.

3. Golden Prairie County

Residents of eastern Laramie County proposed the new county in 1913 with Burns to be the county seat.

4. Iron County

Goshen County legislator Tom Powers introduced a bill into the 1917 legislature to create "Iron County," the north part of Platte County containing the iron ore mines at Sunrise. Residents in the north part of Platte County were unable with the county's refusal to accept sites in Guernsey for the site of the county courthouse. The Powers bill was defeated by a vote of 12-10 in the State Senate.

5. Elk County

Star Valley residents proposed a new county for their area in 1913. Afton was to be the county seat. Residents were unhappy about Kemmerer running the county.

6. Battle County

Some residents of eastern Carbon County tried to form "Battle County" in the late 1970s. Medicine Bow was the proposed county seat.

7. "Wyoming" County

While no county within the state of Wyoming is named "Wyoming," there are Wyoming counties in New York, Pennsylvania and West Virginia.

8. Colter and Barrett counties

In the 1969 legislative sessions, Ed Whitehead and Thomas J. Carroll, both Laramie County Democrats, introduced a bill into the legislature to merge Teton and Sublette counties and call the new county "Colter County." Also the bill called for merging Weston and Niobrara and calling it "Barrett county," after Gov./Sen. Frank Barrett from Lusk. The bill, HB 280, didn't pass.

Only one Wyoming county has a "county administrator." The position is in Teton County. In 1996, Gary Debus was the first person appointed to the position.

6 County Seat Contests

1. South Pass City v. Green River (1873)

South Pass City, the first county seat of Sweetwater County, was a thriving mining town in the first years of Wyoming Territory. When the railroad town of Green River challenged the more remote place for the courthouse, the Wyoming legislature authorized the move despite violent protests from South Pass residents. Currently, South Pass City is not even in Sweetwater County, but in Fremont County where the town never was made the county seat.

2. Casper v. Bessemer (1890)

Bessemer won the election by a vote of 677 to Casper's 304. The county commissioners, however, determined that most Bessemer voters had cast two or more ballots, so they awarded the courthouse to Casper.

3. Basin v. Otto v. Cody (1896)

Cody was a late entrant in the race for the county seat of Big Horn County, at that time the entire Big Horn Basin. The town of Basin won by 30 votes over Otto, the runner-up, because Cody's entry drew "west county" votes from Otto.

4. Douglas v. Lusk (1888)

The two young towns vied for county seat of Converse County. Douglas won the election narrowly. Partisans claimed Lusk voted "children, canary birds and poodle dogs." But shenanigans were not limited to one side. After 69 "O'Briens" had signed for ballots, a Douglas election judge (whose name just happened to be O'Brien) yelled, "No more O'Briens today!" There were but 16 people by that name in the entire county, according to the census.

5. Sheridan v. Big Horn v. Dayton (1888)

Sheridan won the election with 486 votes to Big Horn's 248. Dayton came in third with 224.

6. Jackson v. Kelly (1922)

In the closest county seat election in Wyoming history, Jackson won the Teton County seat over neighboring Kelly by just two votes.

During the Carter administration, the US Bureau of Reclamation constructed two giant wind turbines near Medicine Bow to test the potential for wind power. When the administration changed, the Reagan USBR had one of the turbines dynamited and hauled off for scrap. Built for $10 million, the remaining structure was sold in 1989 to Medicine Bow resident Bill Young. The huge wind turbine of Young's tower "blew apart" on January 14, 1994. One tip of the giant blade hit the tower and threw the entire mechanism out of balance momentarily, but long enough for the other tip to be sheared off when it came into contact with the tower. A Casper couple watched as the machine's propeller disintegrated. Young repaired the damage and the machine returned to operation. In the following years, more than a dozen smaller machines were erected nearby and, in 2000, all were producing power. By 2010, huge wind farms were either operating or under construction in three directions from Medicine Bow.

DAMS

24 Significant Wyoming Dams (by completion date)

1. Corbett Dam, Park County (1908)
A concrete dam on the Shoshone River, 18 feet high and 938 feet long at the crest, its primary purpose was to provide irrigation water for area farmers.

2. Pathfinder Dam, Natrona County (1909)
A granite masonry arch dam, Pathfinder is 214 feet high and 432 feet long at the crest. Named for John C. Fremont, the "Pathfinder,"dam construction began in February 1905. The million-dollar dam holds about one million acre-feet of water. It is located 47 miles southwest of Casper.

3. Buffalo Bill Dam, Park County (May 16, 1910)
Originally known as Shoshone Dam, the concrete arch on the Shoshone River was the highest in the United States at the time it was completed. The dam, now 350 feet high, gained 25 additional feet in 1991 although the increase in height still did not bring it up to the world's highest. The dam is 200 feet long at the crest.

4. Eden Dam, Sweetwater County (1910)
The dam was rebuilt in 1959 as part of the Eden Project on the Little Sandy. Located seven miles north of Farson, the present dam is 25 feet high and 3,500 feet long at the crest.

5. Boysen Dam (1st), Fremont County (1911)
Completed in October 1911, by Asmus Boysen, the dam cost its builder nearly $3 million. Faced with lawsuits from the railroad and the state, Boysen tried to raise it from its original height of 35 feet to 50 feet. He lost the cases and in 1913, he lost another suit in which the dam was declared a menace to other river users. Badly damaged by the flood of 1923, the structure was abandoned. (See #14 below).

6. Jackson Lake Dam, Teton County (1911)
The first rock-filled crib dam on the Snake River site was built in 1907, but was washed out in 1910. The present concrete gravity dam was completed in 1911 and raised in 1966. It is 65 1/2 feet high and 4,920 feet long at the crest.

7. Willwood Dam, Park County (1924)
Located on the Shoshone River, Willwood Dam is 70 feet high and 476 feet long. It provides irrigation water for the Willwood Irrigation Project.

8. Pilot Butte Dam, Fremont County (December, 1926)
Made up of three earthfill embankments, the dam is 51 feet high. The three portions extend 5,900 feet along the Wind River, 22 miles northwest of Riverton.

9. Guernsey Dam, Platte County (July 1927)
Technically known as a "diaphragm-type earthfill," Guernsey Dam on the North Platte River is 135 feet high and 560 feet long. The lake behind the dam is a popular state park and recreation area.

10. Alcova Dam, Natrona County (Feb. 8, 1938)
The 265-foot high dam on the North Platte, 30 miles southwest of Casper, was part of the Kendrick irrigation project. It was completed at a cost of $23 million just before the beginning of World War II. The dam is 763 feet long at the crest. The reservoir is popular with water skiers and fishermen.

The Dam Bar and Cafe was destroyed by fire in August 1963. The structure stood at the south end of the Wind River canyon tunnels for more than 20 years. It was named for its proximity to Boysen Dam.

11. Grassy Lake Dam, Teton County (1938)

The 30-foot-high zoned earthfill dam is 1,170 feet long at the crest. Located 25 miles northwest of Moran on Grassy Creek, the dam's weather observation point receives state record snowfall during the winter months.

12. Seminoe Dam, Carbon County (April 1, 1939)

Often mispronounced "Seminole" as in the Florida Indian tribe, Seminoe was named for a local pioneer ranching family who owned land now covered by its reservoir. Located 31 miles northeast of Rawlins, the dam is a concrete arch measuring 530 feet long at the crest and 295 feet high.

13. Kortes Dam, Carbon County (Feb. 6, 1950)

The dam was built but two miles below Seminoe in the Black Canyon of the North Platte. The concrete gravity dam is 244 feet high with a crest length of 440 feet.

14. Boysen Dam (2nd), Fremont County (October 1951)

The second dam to occupy the site (see #5 above), Boysen Dam is 220 feet high and 1,143 feet long at its crest. A zoned earthfill dam, it holds back the waters of the Wind River just before the river enters Wind River Canyon, 20 miles south of Thermopolis.

15. Keyhole Dam, Crook County (Feb. 12, 1952)

The zoned earthfill dam, 168 feet high and 3,430 feet at its crest, is on the Belle Fourche River, 17 miles northeast of Moorcroft.

16. Big Sandy Dam, Sweetwater County (May 13, 1952)

The zoned earthfill dam, located ten miles north of Farson, was part of the Eden Project. The structure is 85 feet high and runs 2,350 feet at its crest.

17. Glendo Dam, Platte County (1958)

The most recently built dam on the North Platte River in Wyoming, Glendo is 190 feet high and 2,096 feet long at its crest. Another zoned earthfill dam, its reservoir is popular with water skiers and boaters.

18. Anchor Dam, Hot Springs County (November 1960)

Anchor Dam is the least known dam in Wyoming—and for good reason. The multi-million dollar Bureau of Reclamation structure on Owl Creek, eight miles west of Embar, often holds no water. Soon after the 208-foot high, 660-foot long concrete arch was completed, sinkholes developed in the reservoir immediately behind the dam. Attempts to plug them with concrete failed. Closed by the bureau to the general public, unmarked on maps and difficult to find, the dam stood high above the trickle of water from Owl Creek, flowing unimpeded downstream through one of the Bureau's biggest embarrassments. In the summer of 1993, engineers reported they had succeeded in keeping water in the reservoir for the first time in 32 years. An aberration? Stay tuned.

19. Gray Reef Dam, Natrona County (1961)

Built two miles below Alcova Dam, the 36-foot high, 650-foot long dam is another segment of the Kendrick project.

20. Fontenelle Dam, Lincoln County (April 1964)

The dam is 139 feet high and more than a mile long at its crest (5,421 feet, to be exact). The earth-filled structure is located on the Green River, 24 miles south of LaBarge. In recent years, concern has been expressed about leaks which have developed in the dam, weakening the structure.

21. Meeks Cabin Dam, Uinta County (1971)

Located just two miles north of the Utah state line southwest of Fort Bridger, the dam is zoned earth and rock fill. It is 184 1/2 feet high and 3,162 feet long. According to the Bureau of Reclamation, seepage problems developed at the site during the spring of 1971 when the reservoir was filling. Fearing internal erosion of the dam, the Bureau started on repair work in the spring of 1993. Estimated costs of the corrections were $9.1 million. *Source: Uinta County Herald, May 7, 1993, p. B4.*

22. Sulphur Creek Dam, Uinta County (May 1988)

The dam is located nine miles southeast of Evanston. Although it is privately owned, the dam holds water for the Evanston municipal water supply. State funding was granted to the project from the water development accounts. Water was made available by the increased allocations received by Wyoming as a result of revisions made in 1992 to the Bear River Compact.

23. Sandstone Dam, Carbon County

In 1993, the legislature authorized $30 million for construction of Sandstone Dam to be built on Savery Creek and Big and Little Sandstone Creeks about 30 miles west of Encampment and 10 miles north of Savery. The dam would hold up to 23,000 acre-feet of water. Critics of the dam charged that it would destroy moose, deer and elk habitat as well as thousands of cottonwood trees.

24. Tie Hack Dam, Johnson County

The $8.7 million project was designed to augment Buffalo's municipal water supply. The dam, 520 feet long and 130 feet high, was built at the confluence of Sourdough Creek and South Fork of Clear Creek with construction completed in the fall of 1997.

3 Out-of-State Dams with Reservoirs Extending into Wyoming

1. Flaming Gorge Dam, Utah (1963)

The concrete arch dam on the Green River, 31 miles south of the border in Utah, is 502 feet high and 1,285 feet at its crest. Just 15 percent of the reservoir is outside Wyoming. The reservoir is the largest man-made lake in Wyoming, even after subtracting out the portion in Utah. With nearly 3.8 million acre-feet of water, the reservoir exceeds the capacity of Seminoe and Pathfinder combined.

2. Yellowtail Dam, Montana (1966)

The concrete thin-arch dam on the Big Horn River has a height of 525 feet and lengh of 1,480 feet. The dam backs up the river into "Big Horn Lake" which extends into Wyoming. When the reservoir was filled in 1966, the Wyoming town of Kane was among the sites inundated by its waters.

3. Stateline Dam, Utah (1979)

Built just 1/2 mile south of the Wyoming border, the dam is 134 feet high and 2,900 feet in length. The dam is on the east fork of Smiths Fork, 28 miles south of Fort Bridger.

Buffalo Bill Dam, known as Shoshone Dam until 1946, was one of the first arch dams to be designed using a mathematical method of analysis. Edgar Wheeler, the consulting engineer, considered changing water surface elevations, variation in temperatures and deflection issues. Daniel Webster Cole was the project chief engineer. The dam was completed in 1910.

DEATHS

Deaths in work-related accidents: 33 people died of workplace-related injuries in Wyoming (2008). Between 2000 and 2009, there were 351 workplace deaths in the state.
Death rate: 3,847 deaths were recorded in Wyoming in 1998, a death rate of 8 per 1,000 population. Death rate the previous year was 7.8 per 1,000 (total of 3,740).

Some Well-Known Wyomingites Killed in Car Accidents

1. Charles Miller, Hulett

Miller owned the first car in Hulett and on Jan. 1, 1913, he became the first person killed in an automobile accident in Crook County.

2. Winfield S. Collins, Basin founder

In November 1916, the 68-year-old Collins was a candidate for Big Horn county attorney. He was in a car with four other candidates enroute to a Republican rally in Burlington. Three miles east of Otto, the steering wheel loosened, the car missed a curve and turned over. Collins was pinned under the car. The others escaped with minor injuries, but Collins died at a local hospital a few days after the accident.

3. Dr. J. S. Newland, Kemmerer doctor

The 72-year-old doctor was killed in late March, 1919, in a car accident while en route to treat a patient. He had practiced medicine in Wyoming for 47 years.

4. James Ambrose Ross

The son of two Wyoming governors, William B. and Nellie Tayloe Ross, young Ross died in a car accident near Saratoga in December 1928.

5. Wilbur Hitchcock, Laramie architect

Hitchcock's first wife died in 1925, leaving four children. In November 1930, he married Verna Johannesen, an employee of the University of Wyoming Extension Service. Just 11 days after their marriage, Hitchcock was killed in an auto accident in California where they were honeymooning.

6. Art Royce and daughter, Cody

Royce and his daughter, 3 1/2 years old, died in August 1933, when the car plunged 225 feet into Shoshone Canyon, coming to rest just 25 feet from the power house at the bottom of the canyon next to the dam.

7. Dyer Hayes, Assistant U. S. Attorney

Hayes, 35, was killed in a car accident ten miles south of Wheatland on Sept. 4, 1933.

8. Charles D. Carey, rancher

Carey, son of Joseph M. Carey and brother of the then-U. S. Senator Robert D. Carey, was killed with his wife in an automobile accident on the outskirts of Cheyenne on Jan. 6, 1935. The Careys were returning from Sunday dinner at the ranch home of Helge Sturve-Vasa when their car struck the center abutment of the underpass of the Colorado and Southern Railroad, west of Cheyenne. Carey was 53; his wife Julianne was 36.

9. C. B. "Charlie" Irwin, rancher/showman

The corpulent stockman and Wild West Show owner died in March 1934, after his Buick Coupe blew a tire, skidded on an icy highway near Cheyenne and flipped over. Legend has it that Irwin held a piece of the steering wheel in his hand when his body was pulled from the car. He weighed 500 pounds at the time of his death and it took ten men to

---

In July 1933, Roy Ferguson, 45, a Goshen County farmer, was injured in a fight with a neighbor over irrigation water. When Ferguson died a week later from being struck over the head with a shovel, the neighbor, Albert Nietfeldt, was charged with second-degree murder.

carry his casket. More than 2,000 people jammed a Cheyenne school auditorium to attend his funeral. Irwin is the subject of the Anna Lee Waldo novel, *Prairie*, published in 1986.

10. Roger W. Toll, Yellowstone official

Toll was superintendent of Yellowstone National Park when he was appointed to a commission to determine the feasibility of a joint U. S.-Mexico peace park. While attending committee meetings in New Mexico, he was killed in a traffic accident on Feb. 25, 1936.

11. Mrs. Justus F. Soule, Laramie

Mrs. Soule was killed in an auto accident in Sept. 1938, as she and her husband, an original faculty member at the University of Wyoming, were celebrating their 50th wedding anniversary. Dean Soule died in October 1939.

12. Ashby Howell, Worland pioneer

Howell, for whom a street in Worland is named, died Nov. 9, 1940, from injuries suffered in a car crash. The vehicle in which Howell was riding hit a patch of black ice near Emblem and overturned. Howell operated a dry goods store in Worland and served on the first town council. More than 1,000 people attended his funeral.

13. Eugene Phelps, rancher

Born in 1884, Phelps owned the Pitchfork Ranch near Meeteetse. He and future brother-in-law Charles Belden, the noted photographer, took the first automobile tour of Russia in 1909. In 1944, Phelps' car struck a bridge over the Wood River. He died later in the Cody hospital.

14. E. O. "Ted" Huntington, editor

Huntington had been editor of the *Lovell Chronicle* for many years. He was killed in an auto wreck southeast of Lander on Dec. 6, 1954.

14. Jackson Pollock, artist

Born in Cody Jan. 20, 1912, Pollock was killed in a single-car accident in New York on Aug. 11, 1956. The nation's most famous artist, he was just 44 at the time of his death.

15. Ernest May, rancher

The former president of the Wyoming Stockgrowers Association died at the age of 55 when his Corvette hit a patch of ice and slammed into the Wood River bridge southwest of Meeteetse in June, 1966.

16. Nancy Wallace, legislator

A state representative from Uinta County, Wallace was elected in 1968. She was killed in a car accident in March 1971. She was serving in the legislature at the time of her death.

17. Dr. Robert H. Burns, wool expert/author/historian

Burns, a professor at the University of Wyoming, was an international wool expert, author, and historian. He died in a car accident eight miles west of Laramie on Interstate 80 on June 13, 1973. He was returning from assisting National Geographic writers with research on area ranches when his car overturned.

18. Harry Thorson, businessman/political leader

Thorson, an important figure in Republican Party politics and in the oil and bentonite industries, died soon after his car was struck as he pulled onto the highway at Newcastle on Sept. 26, 1976. The car rolled over, pinning Thorson beneath it. He died eight hours later in a Casper hospital. He was 74.

19. Stephen Naegle, master painter/art teacher

The well-known young Casper artist and art teacher was killed in a car accident in 1981. He had a short but prolific career. 300 of his pieces are in Casper collections.

20. Bruce Kennedy, publisher

Kennedy, a leading figure in Wyoming journalism, died in a one-car rollover about one-half mile east of Shell (19 miles east of Greybull) in June 1992. At the time of his death, he was publisher of the *Gillette News-Record, Cody Enterprise, Green River Star,*

Douglas Budget, Greybull Standard and *Whitefish* (Mont.) *Pilot.* His column was the longest running in the state.

21. Dr. Steven Heymann, psychology professor

The popular University of Wyoming professor died in an accident in Denver. Exact details of the accident may never be known, but Heymann apparently fell or was pushed from a moving car as it traveled along Interstate 70 in Denver.

22. Sarah Gordon, environmental activist

Gordon was a director and board secretary for *High Country News* Board of Directors and a leading member of the Wyoming Outdoor Council. She was killed in August 1993, near Buffalo when she was struck by a pickup while jogging. She was 37.

23. Tosh Suyematsu, attorney

Former Assistant U. S. Attorney, he was reared in Casper and served with famed 442nd Regimental Combat team in World War II. He was killed in June 1994, near his home in Carpenter after a tire blew out on his van and the vehicle overturned.

24. Steven Johnson, public defender

Johnson, senior public defender in Campbell County, died June 3, 1994, when his car overturned near Encampment. At the time of the accident, he was returning home to Gillette from the annual public defenders' seminar held in Saratoga.

25. Cordelia Peck, businesswoman/civic leader

The wife of State Sen. Robert Peck, Cordelia Peck was killed Feb. 17, 1996, when her car overturned on Interstate 80, six miles west of Elk Mountain. Mrs. Peck was active in Riverton community activities and with the *Riverton Ranger*, published by her husband.

26-27. Grant and Priscilla Sanders, civic leaders

The Sanders were killed in an auto accident on April 20, 1997, between Lovell and Greybull. Grant Sanders, a former legislator, was superintendent of schools in Byron at the time of his death.

28.-36. Cody Brown, Kyle Johnson, Josh Jones, Justin Lambert-Belanger, Morgan McLeland, Kevin Salverson, Nick Schabron, & Shane Shatto, students and members of the University of Wyoming cross-country team

The eight young men were returning from Colorado on Highway 287 near Tie Siding, 17 miles south of Laramie, when their vehicle was struck by a pickup driven by a drunk driver. The eight cross-country team members all died in the accident on Sept. 16, 2001. The driver of the pickup, Clinton Haskins, who was a UW student, was sentenced to prison.

37.-38. Dr. Tom Thorne, wildlife expert, and Dr. Beth Williams, professor/researcher

The Laramie husband and wife died on Dec. 29, 2004, in an auto accident on Highway 287 just south of the Wyoming line. Thorne had retired the previous year as acting director of the Wyoming Department of Game and Fish. Williams, like her husband a veterinarian by training, was an expert on chronic wasting disease. The year after their deaths, the Sybille research center, north of Laramie, was renamed in their memories.

39.-40. Carol L. MacNee, 59, and Susan M. McCabe, 54, UW nursing professors

The two women died Dec. 18, 2008, in a multi-vehicle crash about 10 miles south of the Colorado-Wyoming border. Both women taught nursing at the University of Wyoming.

41. Willie Neal, 19, ski champion/political activist

Neal, from Wilson, was in Maine training on June 21, 2009, on roller skis when a car struck and killed him. He had won eight straight Nordic ski titles in high school. He was the youngest Obama delegate from Wyoming to the Democratic National Convention.

42. John Alden, 24, young historian

Alden died in an accident south of Laramie on Jan. 3, 2010. A student at the University of Wyoming and employee at the Wyoming Territorial Park, Alden was killed when another driver coming in the opposite direction attempted to pass a snowplow.

Deaths from Animals

1. Alfas Kalby

The Turkish man was crushed to death by an elephant May 25, 1903. The incident occurred when Kalby, the trainer, became wedged against the inside of a freight car carrying the circus animal. The train stopped at Medicine Bow where Kalby's body was taken from the train and buried in the local cemetery. He appears to be the only person to have been killed in Wyoming by an elephant, at least in modern times.

2. Philip Vetter, Meeteetse

Vetter's death at the hands of a grizzly bear was not altogether uncommon in early-day Wyoming. Vetter lived in a log cabin on the Greybull River near present-day Meeteetse. In 1892, a sudden rainstorm forced a local man to seek shelter in Vetter's cabin. On the cabin floor, the man found Vetter's body. Beside it was a note written on an old newspaper in Vetter's own blood. "All would have been well had I not gone down to the river after supper," Vetter had written. A later message simply said, "I'm dying." His jammed rifle was found nearby as well as signs of a furious battle with a grizzly. His grave is in Trail Town, west of Cody.

3. Hank Mason, Weston County

Mason was a pioneer of Weston County who died from a grizzly mauling. Apparently, he stumbled across the bear near his cabin and managed to fire several shots when the animal attacked him. The bodies of Mason and the bear, one of the largest seen in the area, were found together by neighbors a short time later.

4. Martha Hansen, Yellowstone visitor

The 45-year-old woman surprised a grizzly as she was leaving her Yellowstone cabin on Aug. 22, 1942. She was mauled by the bear and died four days later in a nearby hospital.

5. Harry Walker, Yellowstone visitor

Walker was visiting Yellowstone in June 1972 when he was attacked and mauled by a bear that was eating food at his campsite near Old Faithful Inn.

5. Brigitta Fredenhagen, Yellowstone camper

A bear dragged the woman from her tent, pitched on the south end of White Lake in Yellowstone in July 1984.

4. William J. Tesinsky, Montana photographer

Tesinsky was one of three people who died from bear maulings in Yellowstone between 1981-1986. While photographing a grizzly, he apparently came too close to the animal. The incident occurred between Canyon and Lake in October 1986.

5. George Ferris, mining entrepreneur

Ferris, co-discoverer of the rich Ferris-Haggerty lode near Encampment, died in a road accident near Saratoga in August 1900. His wagon was upset by a runaway team, he was thrown out and killed.

6. Tom O'Day, outlaw

O'Day was killed in South Dakota in 1930 when a runaway team flipped the wagon in which he was riding.

7. Otto Gramm, Laramie businessman

Gramm was riding in a parade when his horse spooked, throwing him off. He died of a fractured skull.

8. Alvah Ayres, Douglas rancher

Ayres was a pioneer Converse County rancher on whose land the "Ayres natural bridge" was located. He died Aug. 13, 1918, as a result of injuries received on a trip from his ranch to Douglas. A car frightened his team of horses. They ran away, upsetting the wagon and killing Ayres.

9. Phil Yoder, rodeo rider

Yoder, winner of Cheyenne Frontier Days bronc riding and steer roping titles in 1921, was injured in a serious steer roping accident at Douglas in 1929. Disabled by the accident, he died in 1941.

10. Harold "Hardluck" Bursch

Bursch, who gained his nickname in childhood after falling under a train and losing his arm, was a cowboy for the Spear Ranch in Sheridan County. On Oct. 5, 1932, he was killed in an accident while performing with a wild west show in Memphis, Tenn.

11.-12. Afton "Sonny" Thayer, Maurice Fulton

The two young Park County men died in separate accidents with horses in 1933. Fulton, a 24-year-old rodeo rider from Powell, was killed by a bucking bronc in Cody on Oct. 4. Thayer, a school boy, died July 5. He had participated the previous day in the Stampede Days cowboy races. Source: *Cody Enterprise*, July 5, Oct. 4, 1933.

13.-16. Sharon Kava, Brad Humphrey, Michael and Daniel Moe

The four bicyclists had just become the first ever to cycle across the Barnes Ice Cap in the Arctic when the boat in which they were riding was overturned by a whale. Kava and the Moe brothers were from Laramie; Humphrey was from Douglas. All died in the freak mishap in the Arctic Ocean.

17. Mary Hansen Mead Steinhour, rancher/politician

Mead was the Republican nominee for governor in 1990. She died on her 61st birthday on June 21, 1996, when the horse she was riding, a spirited four-year-old named Little Joe, fell with her while she was helping move cattle near the family ranch in Jackson Hole. She was the daughter of Clifford P. Hansen, former governor and U. S. Senator.

18. Erwin Evert, Cody

The 70-year-old Cody man was the first person to be killed by a grizzly in Wyoming in some 25 years. He went hiking from his cabin on Kitty Creek and was mauled by a grizzly about five miles outside the east boundary of Yellowstone National Park on June 17, 2010. Bear researchers had examined a bear in the area earlier in the day.

19. Nicolas Gillett, Cody bronc rider

The 20-year-old cowboy was riding a bronc when his left spur caught on the saddle on his way out of the chute at the Jackson Hole Rodeo June 23, 2010. He died from a fractured skull.

Some Wyomingites Who Died by Accidental Shooting

1. Otto Franc, rancher

Count Otto Franc von Lictenstein, the first rancher in the Big Horn Basin and founder of the Pitchfork Ranch in 1878, died from a gunshot he sustained from his own rifle. It discharged while he was climbing through a barbed wire fence Nov. 30, 1903, killing him instantly. An accident was presumed although not definitively established, given there were no eyewitnesses to the incident.

2. Kitty Chatfield Davis, rancher

Mrs. Davis was wounded by a gunshot fired in a Cody hotel in 1909 and died from the injuries. Kitty Creek, a tributary of the Shoshone River, was named for her. She ranched with her husband in the Sunlight Basin area.

3. Jim Bridges

Not to be confused with Jim Bridger, Bridges had the bad habit of pulling a gun to scare people. On Aug. 11, 1881, he argued with another tenant at dinner in the rooming house in which he stayed. Apparently, the two were quarreling over who should get the last of the mashed potatoes. When Bridges reached for his gun, the other man was faster and

Bridges was shot dead. *Source: Sharon Lass Field, Fort Fetterman Cemetery. (Privately printed, 1970).*

4. George Vincent Hamilton Gordon, British tourist

The second son of Gen. E. H. Gordon, Gordon was a student at Oxford, when he came West to hunt antelope on the Laramie Plains. On Sept. 15, 1887, he and a companion were hunting antelope on a ranch southwest of Laramie when the other hunter mistook him for an antelope. Apparently, the mistake resulted from the bright sunshine reflecting off his clothes in sagebrush country. Gordon died and his body was buried in the Green Hill Cemetery, Laramie. He had been in America but two weeks at the time of his death.

5. George L. Bruce

The 25-year-old principal of schools in Smoot died Oct. 3, 1932. He returned home from a hunting trip and as he entered the house, he accidentally dropped his shotgun. The weapon discharged, striking Bruce and killing him.

6. Boyd Wilson, Cowley valedictorian

The 17-year-old accidently shot himself while cleaning a rifle on May 17, 1933, days before he was due to graduate as the school's valedictorian.

7. Jack Mann, Casper journalist; Justin Bryan, Casper student; Melvin Erickson, Laramie

The 18-year-old reporter for the *Casper Tribune-Herald* died while practicing target shooting with a friend on July 21, 1933. Bryan, 17, died in an unrelated accidental shooting that same day at his family's home in Casper. Erickson, 23, also died on the same day near Laramie when his gun accidentally discharged while he was hunting gophers.

Some Wyoming Poisonings

1. Annie Richey, convicted horse thief

The Lincoln County woman died at her home just before she was to begin serving a six-year prison sentence for rustling. In 1919, law officers in Omaha found 23 hides from cattle owned by rancher Bill Davidson. Richey had sold them and on this evidence, she was tried. In 1922, following her conviction by the district court, Richey and her helper, a man named Otto, ate some stew. Both died from poison placed in it. It was not known if the poisoning was suicide, accidental or the result of foul play.

2 James Bruce, Star Valley

Bruce died on March 21, 1907. An autopsy revealed that he had been poisoned, apparently by eating a plum pie laced with a toxic substance. His daughter, Annie Bruce, was charged with poisoning her father, convicted of manslaughter and sentenced to four years in prison.

3. Several guests, Hardpan Ranch, Park County

Sam Aldrich operated the lodge known as "Aldrich Lodge" 26 miles west of Cody in the 1920s. In July 1924, four guests at a cocktail party at his lodge became ill and died as a result of eating tainted olives. Among them were Mrs. Paul S. Asche and her son of Pittsburgh who had planned to stay for the summer. Mr. Asche, who did not accompany his family to the lodge, was a prominent oil man.

4. Joe McCarthy rally, Dubois

Although no one died as a result, several hundred people developed food poisoning from eating tainted ham at an outdoor rally featuring a speech by Wisconsin Senator Joseph M. McCarthy at Dubois in 1953. Critics of McCarthy's talk pointed out that "poison" of two types had been handed out that afternoon.

Harry Glicken, a volcano expert who had done extensive work in Wyoming studying extinct varieties, was killed in the eruption of Japan's Mount Unzen in June 1991.

5. Clara Hamilton, student, Casper

The *Natrona Tribune* noted the death on April 4, 1895, of Clara Hamilton, 17, the daughter of the paper's editor, who died of trichinosis "from eating raw sausage." The item appeared next to an ad for Sommers' Meat Market.

Deaths of Some Wyomingites in Snowstorms

1. Peter LeMieux and Charles Comer

The two men were snowshoeing into the mountainous country near Encampment in January 1903, checking downed telephone lines. A sudden avalanche crashed down on them. Their bodies were not found until later in the spring.

2. Mr. and Mrs. Robert Miller, Laramie

A severe late season snowstorm stranded the couple's car in the hills northeast of Laramie in May 1927. The couple left their two passengers, Glenn Holder, 11, and George Holmes, 13, and tried to reach help at a nearby ranch. They died three miles from their destination. The two boys in the car were found late the next day by Undersheriff Robert E. Welliever. They had been kept awake and able to resist the cold by their pet dog.

3. Amasa Bybee, South Pass City

The 72-year-old mail carrier was caught in what was the worst blizzard ever recorded between Atlantic City and South Pass City in early April, 1920.

4. Jim Forsling, Casper Mountain

During the winter of 1942, Forsling was on his way to his home on Casper Mountain from Casper. He became lost in a strong blizzard and died in the storm.

5. Fifteen members, Willie's Handcart Company

The Mormon emigrants started too late in the season on their journey to Salt Lake. They were caught by an October blizzard in 1856 and 15 members of the company froze to death about eight miles southeast of present-day Atlantic City. They ranged in age from 6 to 67. Of the 404 people in the caravan, 77 died before help arrived, the survivors reaching Salt Lake City in early November 1856.

6. Dick Sparks, Big Horn Basin

Sparks, the first African-American in the Big Horn Basin, was a cook on the first cattle drive in 1879. During Christmas week, 1887, Sparks died when he was caught in a sudden storm while riding from the Carter ranch to Trail Creek.

7. Storekeepers in Kirwin

The mining town, west of Meeteetse, was founded in 1891. In 1907 the Tewksbury Store was destroyed by an avalanche in 1907. Three people were killed and the incident is said to have ended the mining district's life.

8. Dr. Agnes Wergeland, UW professor

Wergeland, the first Norwegian woman to earn a Ph.D. in any field, fell on the ice one evening in front of Old Main en route home from a class. She died a few days alter on March 6, 1914.

9. Fred E. Demmell, Dell F. Yoakum, Dillon McKinnon, hunters

The three men disappeared in a fall snowstorm in the Big Horn mountains in 1932. They froze to death sometime around Oct. 17, 1932, but two of the bodies were discovered at the end of the month. One body was not found until the following summer. Demmell was from Sheridan; Yoakum, from Columbine, Wyo. McKinnon, a 17-year-old, was from Greybull.

10. Uheiga Namba and Usaburo Namba, Cherokee

The two Japanese-Americans, Uheiga, 31, and his 53-year-old uncle Usaburo died of exposure on Feb. 10, 1932, after leaving Rawlins and getting caught in a blizzard en route home to Cherokee, Wyo. Within two miles of the Cherokee airstrip, their car became stuck. The two left the car where Uheiga's wife and two young children remained, and tried to walk for help.

11. Junius Burrington, Powell

In 1933, Junius Burrington froze to death in McCullough Peaks near Powell. He was helping his uncle move sheep on a mild late winter day when a sudden snowstorm hit. The high school student, clad in shirtsleeves, missed meeting his uncle at the planned meeting spot. A search showed he had tried to start a fire but his frozen hands had made the task impossible. His body was found the next day, frozen, near Roan Wash bridge.

12. Dan Sullivan, Lander

Sullivan, an employee of Yellowstone Sheep Co., froze to death within 100 yards of a stalled car on April 26, 1933. He and a Thermopolis couple were en route to Rawlins when their car was stuck in the snow 40 miles southeast of Lander. The couple managed to reach a nearby ranch where they were stranded for four days. The storm was said to be one of the worst late spring storms in memory in that region.

13. Rick Hutchinson and Diane Dustman, Yellowstone

The two seismic geologists were monitoring a geyser basin in the southern part of Yellowstone National Park in March, 1997. They were caught in an avalanche on Factory Hill above Heart Lake. The bodies were found five days later.

14. Michael Heinrich, Laramie snowmobiler

The 33-year-old man was found dead after his snow machine went into Libby Creek, west of Centennial, and he was unable to free it. His body was found on the fifth day of search, Dec. 31, 2003.

15. Dr. Margie Zamudio, UW sociology/Chicano Studies professor

Zamudio slipped on ice on her porch, fell and struck her head on Christmas Eve, 2009. Due to the heavy snowfall, her body was not found until the following day.

Some Wyomingites Who Drowned

1. Hiram M. Cook, Cheyenne mayor

The first mayor of Cheyenne in 1867, Cook moved further west in 1869. He drowned while crossing the Green River in Ledore Canyon on June 18, 1869.

2. J. B. Okie, stockman

Okie was duck hunting near a private reservoir on his ranch at Lost Cabin in November 1930, when he apparently slipped into the water and drowned.

3. Loren Loomis, Jackson Hotel owner

Loomis bought a ranch near Moran in 1917. That summer, he worked on the Jackson Lake Dam, earning extra money to pay the mortgage on the ranch. He disappeared without a trace in the summer of 1917. Some searchers believed he had drowned in the Snake River but his body was never found. An unfamiliar car was seen in the area the night of his disappearance and some speculated he might have left the area—and his mounting debts.

4. Robert S. Wilson, Rock Springs publisher

Wilson, editor/publisher of the *Rock Springs Rocket,* drowned while trying to resuce his five-year-old son who had fallen into Half Moon Lake on July 26, 1931. The boy was saved by others in the party.

5. Charles Lindsay, historian

Author of *History of the Big Horn Basin*, Lindsay held a doctorate from the University of Nebraska. He was a dean at a Nebraska college when he drowned in the river while visiting family members near his hometown of Byron, in 1931.

6. Richard Cooper, sportsman/capitalist

Cooper, a frequent hunting companion of Ernest Hemingway, owned Laramie's "Cooper House," which now houses the University of Wyoming's American Studies program. Cooper drowned in 1950 while bird hunting on his African estate.

7. Seymour Sharp, scholar/surveyor

A Platte Valley engineer for 30 years, Sharp was a University of Wyoming graduate who had been a Rhodes scholar at Oxford. He was carrying surveying instruments and attempting to ford the North Platte River near Saratoga when he slipped into the water and drowned on the Fourth of July, 1953.

8. Ed Synakowski, football player

He had just completed his sophomore season as quarterback for the University of Wyoming football team when he drowned in a boating accident at Lake Hattie in 1972.

9. Hill Logan, Cheyenne pioneer

The father of Ernest Logan, stagecoach driver and entrepreneur, Hill Logan drowned in 1876 when he fell through the ice on Lake Minnehaha near Cheyenne. The lake, created in 1873, claimed its first drowning victims in the summer of 1874. Four people drowned when their sailboat capsized during a windstorm.

10. Mol Carshier, Thermopolis tourist

Carshier camped at the Hot Springs where, one morning, he went out to "coat" specimens--a favorite pastime of tourists who would place blocks of wood in water near the hot springs where, a short time later, they would have a mineral coating. While collecting the wood, above the falls where the water flows into the Big Horn River, he lost his balance, tumbled over the side and, because he was wearing a heavy overcoat, drowned. His body was buried in "Smoky Row" cemetery in Hot Springs State Park.

11. Seven loggers, North Fork of the Shoshone River, June, 1906

The Wallop-Moncrieffe Lumber company brought experienced river runners to float logs from the upper North Fork downstream to the company sawmill. In attempting to dislodge a logjam, a boat carrying 11 men overturned. Seven drowned. *Source: Ester Johansson Murray. A History of the North Fork of the Shoshone.*

12. Don Wagoner and Clarence Martin, Cody area men

The two men from South Fork drowned on Irma Lake near Coe Lodge on Oct. 16, 1932, when their canoe upset in cold water. Source: Cody Enterprise, Oct. 18, 1932.

Sports Deaths in Wyoming

1. Football

Harold Mathews, the 13-year-old son of W. G. Mathews of Laramie, died of injuries received in a football game between high school and the younger boys at the University of Wyoming in November, 1914. It was the first death from football recorded in Wyoming.

2. Track and Field

Frederick H. Buchanan, 13, of Thermopolis, died April 29, 1933, as a result of injuries sustained in track practice earlier that week. He complained of pain in his hip after landing hard on his heels in broad-jump practice, an event he was due to compete in that week.

One Well-Known Wyomingite Killed in an Earthquake

1. John W. Connor, Laramie

Connor, a real estate developer and a former mayor of Laramie (1876), visited San Francisco in 1906. Soon after he arrived, the famous San Francisco earthquake and fire devastated the city. Connor was killed by falling debris. His widow returned to Laramie and built the Connor Hotel (1911).

Wyomingites Killed in Falls

1. Frank N. Hammitt, Forest Ranger

Hammitt, one of the nation's first U. S. Forest Rangers, fell with his horse to their deaths from a cliff in Sunlight Basin on July 25, 1903. Born in Denver, he had worked as chief of cowboys for Buffalo Bill's Wild West Show for three trips to Europe. He knew eight languages fluently and had studied for the priesthood prior to becoming a ranger in 1898. He was stationed at the Old Painter Ranch ranger station. Buried near where he died, the CCC marked his grave in 1938 with a 4'x6' pole fence and the legend "Forest Ranger on Guard." *Source: Cody Enterprise, April 15, 1939.*

2. Gilbert Leigh, Irish nobleman

Leigh fell off a limestone cliff in Ten Sleep Canyon on Oct. 23, 1883, when he became lost in a sudden snowstorm. Up to eight inches of snow had fallen the night before. Leigh, who had been working as a cowboy at the Home Ranch since July, thought it was an ideal time to hunt big horn sheep. Clouds thickened during the day and, by afternoon, snow was falling again. Leigh apparently tied his horse to a tree at the top of the canyon and, blinded by the snow, did not realize how close he was to the edge. His body was found hundreds of feet below about two weeks later. A 150-pound marble slab was shipped to the site and erected there by Leigh's friends.

3. Ralph Goodrich, retired UW dean of engineering

Two years after he retired from UW in 1948, he was hired as the engineer for the Upper Colorado Commission. He moved to Grand Junction, Colo. On Aug 4, 1961, he was inspecting a building under construction on the campus of Mesa College. He fell and was seriously injured. He died on Aug. 17 without regaining consciousness. In 1918, he was in China helping design the grand canal in Shantung. He came to UW in 1927 as an engineering professor before being appointed the college dean.

4. Craig Arnold, poet

Arnold (1967-2009) taught in the MFA Program at the University of Wyoming. His first book of poetry, *Shells*, won the 1998 Yale Series of Younger Poets award. He was working on a book about volcanoes when he apparently fell to his death on Kuchinoerabu-jima, a remote Japanese island in April 2009.

Some Wyoming Suicides*

1. E. B. Carling, army officer

Carling, an army colonel, founded Camp Carlin (named for him) near Cheyenne. Until it closed in the 1880s, it was the largest supply depot in the United States. The colonel, a veteran supply officer, had been an officer in the Civil War and served in Indian campaigns in the West. He committed suicide in July 1875, at Fort Sanders, near Laramie, where he was stationed.

2. J. S. Collins, Cheyenne banker

When the Cheyenne National Bank failed in the panic of 1893, Collins was accused of fraud and mismanagement. Rather than face possible legal entanglements, he committed suicide March 3, 1892, with a pistol in a San Diego hotel room while officers waited

In 1896, humorist Bill Nye died on Feb. 22. Exactly four years to the day later, Chief Washakie died. Even more unusual, however, prominent Laramie banker Edward Ivinson died on April 10, 1928, the very same day as Melville C. Brown, Laramie's first mayor. Famed Cheyenne photographer C. D. Kirkland, active in Wyoming from 1877 to 1895, shot numerous scenes of roundups and cowboys on the range. He died on Aug. 23, 1926, the same day as silent screen star Rudolph Valentino.

in the next room to take him to jail. His partner, D. D. Dare, absconded, turning up years later selling rugs in Athens.

3. George L. Beard, Cheyenne banker

Beard was cashier in Collins' bank in Cheyenne. He shot himself at his home soon after the bank failed.

4. F. O. Sawin, surveyor

The Kansas-born surveyor was hired in 1886 by Francis E. Warren, the territorial governor, to select the university's "land grant" lands. Sawin, the older brother of a UW mathematics professor, had come to Wyoming in 1872. He prospected for gold in Colorado and Wyoming and began surveying for the Wyoming Central Land and Improvement Co. On Aug. 11, 1892, he committed suicide after walking away from a stagecoach that had stopped at a ranch near Saratoga, shooting himself with a revolver. His young daughter was with the 57-year-old man at the time.

5. William T. Shafer, Evanston editor

Shafer, the founder of the *Uinta Chieftain*, published newspapers in Evanston for 50 years. He died by suicide in December 1923.

6. John Coble, rancher

Coble, a rancher and former employer of gunman Tom Horn, provided funds for Horn's defense. After Horn's executiion, Coble underwrote the publication of Horn's autobiography. A decade later, after suffering financial reverses in the ranching business, Coble committed suicide in the lobby of a hotel in Elko, Nevada, in December 1914.

7. Robert Brayton, Sheridan student

The 18-year-old high school student died, a suicide, in March 1935. Press accounts indicated that one cause may have been his removal as manager of the school basketball team.

8. Annie Richey, convicted horse thief

Her death may have been homicide or accidental. *(See "Poisonings.")* Richey was born in 1890 southwest of Kemmerer. Her original name was Anna Byers.

9. George P. Mullin, cowboy actor

The 32-year-old Platte County cowboy had appeared in several western movies. His death was ruled a suicide in April 1933.

10. William Cody Bradford, nephew of Buffalo Bill

Apparently despondent over poor health, the 60-year-old former president of the Buffalo Bill Historical Association died at his Casper home on Sept. 3, 1933. He had been a rider with Cody's Wild West show.

11. Lester C. Hunt, U. S. Senator

The senator, formerly Wyoming governor and secretary of state, died of a self-inflicted .22 rifle shot in his U. S. Senate office on June 19, 1954. Failing health was cited as the apparent reason for the suicide.

12. Charles J. Belden, rancher/photographer

Belden died in St. Petersburg, Florida, Feb. 1, 1966, of a gunshot wound. Apparently, it was self-inflicted.

13. California couple

A man and his wife, both in their 30s, bought funeral plans from a Laramie mortuary and burial plots in Medicine Bow in March 1988. Sellers did not know that the woman was suffering from incurable cancer. Once arrangements were made, the couple drove to an isolated area in northern Albany County and committed suicide. Their only connection to the area had been a brief visit to Medicine Bow and its museum.

14. Jim Fagan, Casper attorney

Fagan (b. Casper, 1926) was a well-known Casper attorney and former congressional aide. He was a strong defender of the Bill of Rights and favored "death with dignity" legislation. When he became terminally ill, he decided on suicide on Feb. 12, 2003.

Wyoming Suicide Rate for Selected Periods

2007: 21.8 per 100,000 (national average was 10.82)
2004: 17.6 per 100,000
2002: 21 per 100,000, the highest rate of any state in the union.
1999-2005: 20 per 100,000, the 9th ranking cause of death in the state during the period.
1992-96: 19.7 per 100,000. National average was 12 per 100,000.
The teen suicide rate in Wyoming was twice the national average from 1985-95. According to a University of Wyoming study, one in 13 students in Wyoming schools attempted suicide in 1994.

Well-Known Visitors Who Died in Wyoming

1. Wilbert L. Gore, businessman
The outdoorsman and founder of the company that manufactures the waterproof sporting goods fabric, Gore-Tex, died of an apparent heart attack while backpacking in the Wind River Range in August 1986. He was 74.

2. Charles "Bet-a-Million" Gates, financier
Born in Chicago in 1876, Gates became nationally famous as a stockbroker and financier. He was secretary-treasurer of two railroads and founder of banks, power companies and milling operations. In the fall of 1913, he visited the Cody area and while vacationing there, died at the age of 37. Many people suspected his Cody doctor had mis-prescribed medication which led to his premature demise.

3. W. W. Piper, architect
Piper was a respected Portland, Oregon, architect who designed numerous Northwest structures including the first Oregon state capitol building. While returning for a visit to his birthplace in the East, Piper either jumped or was pushed from a moving passenger train as it passed through Medicine Bow. A coroner's jury concluded his death was a suicide, but his sister suspected foul play.

4. William Barrow Pugh, church official
Pugh (b. New York, 1889) was Stated Clerk of the General Assembly of the Presbyterian Church, U.S.A., when he was killed Sept. 14, 1950, in a car accident in Wind River Canyon, 15 miles south of Thermopolis.

5. Miss Marks, Rodeo Rider
"Miss Marks, a bareback rider with Robinson's circus, while jumping through a hoop stuck full of butcher knives at Laramie last week, was so badly injured that she died before reaching Rock Springs." *Rowdy West (Douglas), July 4, 1887, 2.*

6. Dr. Norman A. Welch, President of the American Medical Association
Dr. Welch, a Boston internist, was preparing to address the annual meeting of the Wyoming Medical Society on Sept. 2, 1964, at Jackson Lake Lodge when he collapsed in his hotel room with a cerebral hemorrhage. Despite the efforts of specialists, Welch died the next day in St. John's Hospital, Jackson.

7. Judy Tyler, Actress
Miss Tyler died in a car accident on July 3, 1957, near Rock River while returning to New York with her husband, Greg Lafayette, who also died in the crash. She had just completed the filming of *Jailhouse Rock* with Elvis Presley. Also, she had made appearances on television programs, including *Howdy Doody*.

8. Walter W. Granger, Paleontologist

Granger (b. Vermont, 1872) led paleontological expeditions in the U. S., Egypt, China and Mongolia. He discovered the Bone Cabin Quarry near Como Bluff in 1897 and quarried fossils of more than 60 dinosaurs from the site over the following eight years. He died in Lusk on Sept. 6, 1941, of heart faulure while on a field expedition.

Premature Deaths of Some Wyomingites

1. Alvah Unthank, traveler, 19

Unthank traveled west on the Oregon Trail with companions from Wayne County, Indiana, in the spring of 1850. On June 23, Unthank carved his name on Register Cliff, near present-day Guernsey. Five days later, the party made camp along the North Platte River near present-day Glenrock. There, Unthank died of a sudden illness and was buried along the trail.

2. Caspar Collins, soldier, 20

The son of Col. William O. Collins for whom Fort Collins, Colo., is named, Caspar Collins was killed by Indians at Platte Bridge Station on July 26, 1865. Fort Caspar and, later, the city of Casper was named for the young soldier.

3. Matthew Shepard, University of Wyoming student, 21

Shepard died Oct. 11, 1998, five days after having been tied to a fence on the outskirts of Laramie and beaten by two Laramie men. Found 18 hours later by a passing biker, he died in a Fort Collins hospital without regaining consciousness. The death of Shepard, who was openly gay, led to national media coverage of "gay-bashing" incidents and his death sparked renewed calls for "hate-crime" legislation.

4. Henry Gilbert, Jr., airman, 22

The Lovell, Wyoming, airman (b. Okla., 1919) was the youngest member of the famed "Flying Tigers" squadron in World War II. He was also the first to die in combat when on Dec. 23, 1941, his P-40 was hit by a cannon shell, crashing into the East Asian jungle.

5. Lucinda Rollins, traveler, 24

Rollins (b. Ohio) was traveling west on the Oregon Trail when she died June 11, 1849. Her body was buried along the trail, south of present-day Guernsey on the south bank of the North Platte River.

6. John Grattan, soldier, 24

Grattan, an army lieutenant, was killed Aug. 19, 1854, with 28 members of his command near Fort Laramie while attempting to arrest Indians for stealing a cow from Mormon travelers.

7. Joseph Jacobucci, writer, 25

Jacobucci, editor of the University of Wyoming *Branding Iron*, was expelled from the University in 1936 by unsmiling administrators who were offended by the witty satire in the so-called "Yellow Sheet," the April Fool's issue. Jacobucci had completed 29 chapters of a book on the history of Wyoming newspapers at the time of his death in 1939 from meniingitis.

8. Ella Watson ("Cattle Kate"), rancher, 27

Watson was lynched along the Sweetwater River in 1889 along with her companion, James Averell.

9. John Bozeman, trailblazer, 27

Bozeman was killed by Indians soon after originating the "Bozeman Trail" to Montana across "Indian lands" in the Powder River country.

10. T. V. McCandlish, editor, 29

The first editor north of the North Platte, McCandlish founded the *Buffalo Echo* in 1883. He died on March 5, 1885.

11. William J. Fetterman, soldier, 31

Born in Connecticut in 1835, Fetterman reported for duty at Fort Phil Kearny on Nov. 3, 1866. On December 21, he and 81 members of his command died in a battle near the post. It was the worst Army defeat until the Little Big Horn battle.

12. Jedadiah Smith, mountain man, 32

Smith was killed by Indians in present-day western Kansas in 1831. He had trapped extensively in Wyoming and knew the country well.

13. Dr. Edwin Payson, professor, 34

Payson was a botany professor for six years at the University of Wyoming. He died suddenly in 1927.

14. Asa Dobbins, first weather observer in Wyoming, 34

Dobbins, born in New Jersey in 1849, arrived in Cheyenne on Oct. 15, 1870, to open the first weather office in Wyoming. His first recorded observation was made on Nov. 1, 1870, from the office at 16th Street and Capitol Avenue. He served in Cheyenne until Dec. 1877. He died Aug. 19, 1883, in Los Angeles from a tumor under his jaw.

15. Crazy Horse, warrior, 36

Born in the Powder River Basin about 1841, Crazy Horse was killed by soldiers in the guardhouse at Fort Robinson, Nebr., in September 1877. Probably the most famous person ever born in Wyoming, his life is legendary. (See "Native Americans" for a biography).

16. George Cox, Cheyenne mayor, 37

Born in Cheyenne in 1932, Cox had a law degree from Denver University. He served in the legislature from 1963-69 when he became mayor of Cheyenne. Cox made a trip to the Pentagon with three other civic leaders to lobby for Minuteman missile deployment at Cheyenne when on Aug. 11, 1969, he suffered a heart attack and died in the Arlington, Va., hospital. He was 37. A 540-space, $2.8 million parking garage, opened in March, 1995, was named in his honor.

17. Rev. James Reeb, minister/civil rights activist, 38

A graduate of Natrona County High School in the mid-1940s, Reeb was ordained in the Presbyterian Church in 1953. He served as a pastor in Philadelphia, Washington, D. C., and Boston. In March 1965, he joined a civil rights march in Selma, Alabama. Although Reeb was white, apparently he was recognized as a civil rights worker because on his first evening in Selma, he was attacked and killed by white ruffians on a city street.

18. Billy Miller, Weston County sheriff, 40

Miller was killed in the Lightning Creek Fight on Oct. 31, 1903. Some historians consider him to be the last white man killed in the "Indian wars" in the United States. Others consider his death to have been in the line of duty as part of his law enforcement work. He was attempting to arrest the Indians for poaching.

19. Keith Thomson, Senator-elect/Congressman, 41

Thomson died of a heart attack Dec. 9, 1960, just one month and a day after he was elected to the U. S. Senate. He had served in the U. S. House of Representatives from 1955 until his death. His widow, Thyra Thomson, served as Secretary of State for 24 years, 1963-1987.

20. Donald P. Musso, forest ranger, 42

Musso (b. 1942) was district ranger on the Clarks Fork District of the Shoshone National Forest from 1977-1984. Following his death in 1985, a marker was placed in his memory along the steep edge of Clark's Fork River in Sunlight Basin.

21. William H. Barton, historian/editor, 42

Barton edited *Annals of Wyoming* and headed the Research and Publications Division of the State Historical Department until he died in 1986.

22. Jack O. Horton, Jr., government official, 43

A Sheridan native, Horton was a Rhodes scholar. He entered government service and from 1973 to 1977, he was assistant secretary of the interior for land and water. He died of cancer in 1981.

23. Amasa Converse, banker, 43

Converse, for whom Converse County was named, served as territorial treasurer. He had extensive interests in livestock ranches and banks. In June 1885, he died in New York City while visiting there on business.

24. Wilbur Knight, geologist, 44

Knight, born in Illinois in 1858, graduated from the University of Nebraska in 1886. Until 1893, he was superintendent of a mining company. He joined the faculty at the University of Wyoming as professor of mining engineering in 1893. He taught geology and established the geology museum. The herbarium originated from a Knight field trip in 1894. He died suddenly July 28, 1903, at the age of 44. One daughter and three sons survived him, including Samuel Knight who became a legendary professor of geology at the University of Wyoming.

25. Dr. Gary Weiss, cardiac surgeon, 45

The Casper doctor died suddenly on March 7, 1997.

26. Bill Nye, humorist/editor, 46

Nye founded the *Laramie Boomerang*. Later, he became a nationally known lecturer. He died in North Carolina in February 1896.

Last Words of Some Famous/ Infamous Wyomingites

1. *"It's not night yet. The house is all fired. Goodbye boys, if I never see you again."* — Nate Champion, words he is said to have written just before he was killed by the Johnson County Invaders, April 9, 1892, KC Ranch cabin.

2. *"Joe, they tell me you're married now. I hope you're doing well. Treat her right."* —Gunman Tom Horn to T. Joe Cahill, just before Horn was hanged inside the Laramie County Jail, Nov. 20, 1903.

3. *"Do you really think it's too bad?"* (to doctor who advised him he had but a short time to live, to which the doctor replied: *"Yes."*) Then, to brother-in-law: *"Well, let's forget about it and play high five."* Later, to his adopted son: *"I wish Johnny would come."* —William F. Cody (Buffalo Bill), Denver, Jan. 1917.

4. *"Beautiful weather we're having, isn't it?"* —U. S. Senator Lester C. Hunt, approximate words to a Capitol watchman on the morning of Saturday, June 19, 1954, on his way to his Senate office where he then committed suicide. The watchman did not recall the exact words of what seemed a normal greeting.

5. *"I wish you'd hurry up. I want to get to hell in time for dinner."* —Convicted murderer Bill Booth before his 11:30 a.m., execution in Buffalo on Feb. 26, 1886.

6. *"...and when I saw Bob Devine along there with his gun held down behind his leg, I thought I'd better get to shooting or I'd be dead. But I guess I'll be dead anyway."* —Bob Smith, suspected rustler, to his wife. He was killed by R. M. Devine in the "Hole-in-the-Wall Fight" west of Buffalo on July 22, 1897.

7. *"Hurrah for Jeff Davis and the Southern Confederacy."* —A man known only as Jennings who was hanged for murder at Fort Halleck, May 22, 1865.

Burial Places of Some Well-Known Wyomingites

1. John Colter. Died: Nov. 1813, Dundee, Mo. Buried: Family farm near Dundee. Colter was the first Anglo-American to step foot in Wyoming.

2. Pinckney Sublette. Died: 1828. Buried: On Fontenelle Creek, southwest of LaBarge.

One of the five famous fur trading Sublette brothers, his heirs filed a lawsuit in St. Louis to establish the relationship to Solomon Sublette, one of the brothers. Pinckney's bones were exhumed, taken to St. Louis to establish his death, and for the next 40 years, shunted about in the county clerk's vault. Finally, a court ordered the bones returned. His remains were reburied July 4, 1936, in Sublette County near the site of DeSmet's "Prairie Mass."

3. Robert Stuart. Died: 1848 in Detroit, Mich. Buried: Elmwood Cemetery, Detroit. The discoverer of South Pass and leader of the first west-to-east overland expedition along what became the Oregon Trail, Stuart served as Michigan Superintendent of Indian Affairs from 1845-1848. In 1965, the Sublette County Historical Society lost a court battle to move Stuart's remains to Pinedale when Stuart's descendants contested the action.

4. Frederick Lander. Died: March 2, 1862, near Paw Paw, Va., of illness while preparing for an attack on the Confederate forces occupying Winchester, Va. He had been wounded in a battle at Edward's Ferry on Oct. 22, 1861, and probably died from the long-term effects of the injury. Buried: West Tomb, Broad Street Cemetery, Salem, Mass.

5. Ah-no-ap-pa ("Wheat Flour" but also translated as "Falling Leaf." She is often referred to simply as "Spotted Tail's daughter.") Died: Spring, 1866, in the Powder River country. Buried: Body placed on a scaffold in the Indian tradition in the post cemetery, Fort Laramie, with full military honors. In 1879, her body was reburied at Rosebud Agency.

6. Caspar Collins. Killed in battle of Platte Bridge Station, July 26, 1865. Buried: Fort Caspar until March 1866, when his remains were moved and reburied in the family cemetery at Hillsboro, Ohio, on July 24, 1866.

7. Capt. William Fetterman. Killed Dec. 21, 1866, near Fort Phil Kearny. Buried: Five days after his death in the Indian fight, Fetterman's remains and those of two officers were buried on the battle site. Next to them, in a 50-foot-long trench, the bodies of 67 soldiers and two civilians were buried. With the exception of Lt. Grummond's body which had been reburied in the East early the next spring, all remains were moved to Custer Battlefield National Cemetery and reburied on June 24, 1896.

8. Crazy Horse. Killed Sept. 6, 1877, Fort Robinson, Nebr., guardhouse. Buried: Unknown location. Family members claimed the body of the Wyoming-born warrior and it is unknown where burial took place. Local lore has it that the grave site is on the side of one of the steep cliffs which overlook Fort Robinson on the north.

9. Jim Bridger. Died July 17, 1881, Westport, Mo. Buried: Mount Washington Cemetery, Independence, Mo., where the remains were moved in 1902 from the original burial site one mile north of Dallis, Mo.

10. John "Portugee" Phillips. Died Nov. 18, 1883. Buried: Lakeview Cemetery, Cheyenne. The tall obelisk is one of the more imposing monuments in the old part of the cemetery.

10. Sacajawea. Died: Wyoming claimants assert she died April 9, 1884, on the Wind River reservation. North Dakotans, however, contend she died near Fort Manuel, N. D., at the age of 25 years old about 1815. Buried: Either one mile northwest of the Shoshone Episcopal Mission, Fort Washakie, Wyo., or near Fort Manuel, N. D., depending on which claim one accepts.

11. Amasa Converse. Died: New York City, June 9, 1885. Age 43. Buried: City Cemetery, Three Rivers, Michigan. A Laramie County banker and rancher, he never lived in what is Converse County, the county created on May 21, 1888, and named for him. He had been born in Hinsdale, Mass., on March 26, 1842.

12.-14. James Averell and Ella Watson ("Cattle Kate"). Lynched July 21, 1889, along the Sweetwater River. Buried: The two were buried in shallow graves near where they were lynched. Natural elements and coyotes caused the graves to disappear.

15. John C. Fremont. Died: July 13, 1890, California. Buried: Hills of Eternity Cemetery, Coloma, Calif. Fremont, who never actually lived in Wyoming, explored the area extensively in the 1840s. A county, a dam ("Pathfinder") and numerous natural features in Wyoming are named for him. His death came just three days after Wyoming was admitted as the 44th state.

16. Bill Nye. Died Feb. 22, 1896. Buried: Calvary Churchyard, Fletcher, N. C. Nye, a nationally known humorist, wrote for the *New York World* after gaining fame with the *Laramie Boomerang*, which he founded and edited, 1881-1884.

17. Chief Washakie. Died Feb. 22, 1900, Fort Washakie. Buried: Old Military Cemetery, Fort Washakie, Wyo. The chief, who may have been more than 100 years old at his death, was buried with military honors at the post named for him.

18. John "Jeremiah" Johnson. Died Los Angeles. Buried: Los Angeles. His remains were removed to Old Trail Town near Cody for reburial on June 8, 1974. He had died in obscurity in California. Robert Redford, who played Johnson in the film, *Jeremiah Johnson,* attended the reburial.

19. Tom Horn. Executed Nov. 20, 1903, inside the county jail, Cheyenne. Buried: Columbia Cemetery, Boulder, Colo. Following his hanging, the hired gunman's body was claimed by his brother Charles, a Boulder businessman.

20. Frederic Remington. Died Dec. 26, 1909, New York. Buried: Evergreen Cemetery, Canton, N.Y. Remington's studio is now part of the collections of the Buffalo Bill Historical Center's Whitney Gallery of Western Art in Cody.

21. William F. Cody (Buffalo Bill). Died: 12:05 p.m., Jan. 20, 1917, 2932 Lafayette St., Denver. Buried: Buffalo Bill Memorial Museum and Grave, Lookout Mountain, Colo. Cody was nearly penniless at his death and the *Denver Post* owners Bonfils and Tammon paid Cody's widow for the right to bury the famous scout and showman on the Colorado site even though Cody himself had expressed a desire to be buried atop Cedar Mountain west of Cody. When the rumor reached Denver that irate Wyoming friends of the colonel planned to dig up the grave and remove the coffin to the Wyoming site, *Post* officials ordered numerous truckloads of concrete poured onto the deeply buried coffin, entombing it forever above the Colorado capital city.

22. C. H. "Dad" Worland. Died: Chula Vista, Calif., March 21, 1933, age 89 (b. Feb. 1844, Montgomery City, Missouri). Buried: Glenn Abbey Memorial Park, Chula Vista, Calif. He was founder of Worland.

23. Dr. Grace Raymond Hebard. Died: 1936, Laramie. Buried: Greenhill Cemetery, Laramie, between her sister Alice (b. 1859, d. 1928), and close friend Agnes Wergeland (1857-1914). In the same plot is the grave of Charles Bocker (b. 1848, d. Nov. 20, 1929), an Oregon Trail pioneer, stage driver and buffalo hunter.

24. Jackson Pollock. Died: August 11, 1956, New York. Buried: Green River Cemetery, East Hampton, Long Island, N.Y. Pollock, born in Cody, left the state as a child. He was educated in Arizona and California and spent much of his life in New York. He is credited as the originator of abstract expressionism.

25. J. C. Penney. Died: Feb. 12, 1971, New York. Buried: Woodlawn Cemetery, Bronx, N.Y. Penney, born in Missouri, started his first store in Kemmerer.

26. Nellie Tayloe Ross. Died: Dec. 19, 1977, Washington, D. C. Buried: Lakeview Cemetery, Cheyenne. Mrs. Ross, the first woman elected governor of any state, was buried next to her husband who also was Wyoming governor. She was 49 years old at the time she was inaugurated in 1925 and she died at the age of 101. Her birthday, Nov. 29, is a state holiday.

Oregon Trail traveler Quiintina Snodderly died, possibly from an accident, on June 25, 1852. She was buried along the trail, ten miles east of present-day Casper on the north bank of the North Platte River. The grave was found accidentally during road construction in 1974. After the remains were studied by anthropologists, the body was reburied in 1987.

8 Unusual Tombstones

1. Miners' Monument, Hanna

The marker, chiseled by Hugh Renny, marks the grave of 27 miners whose bodies were never recovered from No. 1 mine following explosions on June 20, 1903, and March 28, 1908. The monument, on a hill southeast of town near the new high school, was dedicated in 1933.

2. Vandehei tombstone, Lakeview Cemetery, Cheyenne

The marker was once the base for the watering fountain, from which horses drank, which stood for many years in the middle of Capitol Avenue in front of the Union Pacific Depot, Cheyenne.

3. Pike's tombstone, Douglas cemetery

Pike was a well-known local character in early-day Douglas.

"Underneath this stone in eternal rest
Sleeps the wildest one of the wayward West
He was a gambler and sport and cowboy, too,
And he led the pace in an outlaw crew.
He was sure on the trigger and staid to the end
But was never known to quit a friend.
In the relations of death all mankind's alike
But in life there was only one George W. Pike."

4. Unknown and Crazy

Natrona County historian A. J. Mokler in 1923 reported seeing a grave about three miles west of Alcova along the trail with the following legend scratched on the flat stone above the grave:

"The Deep Sleep - He Was Crazy."

No date, no name nor any other identifying facts were given.

5. Mattie Culver's grave

Culver, the wife of the winter keeper of Fountain Flats Hotel in Yellowstone National Park, died in childbirth in 1888. She was buried in Yellowstone near the Nez Perce crossing of the Old Faithful-Madison road. For years, Culver was the only person buried in Yellowstone National Park.

6. Caroline Todd's grave

The 18-year-old Oregon Trail traveler climbed to the top of Devils Gate and fell off to her death about 1860. Her gravesite near where she died had the following inscription:

"Here lies the bones of Caroline Todd
Whose soul has lately gone to God.
'Ere redemption was too late,
She was redeemed at Devils Gate."

7. Miss Kate Arnold

A housekeeper at Sheridan Inn in the early 1900s, when Miss Arnold died, her ashes were buried within the wall of her room in the Inn. Her ghost is said to occupy the building.

8. David Dickie's Hill-top Grave

Dickie, a pioneer Hot Springs County sheep rancher, is buried in a maausoleum placed on a mountain top overlooking his ranch, the LU, and can be seen from the ranch. He died in Chicago Jan. 4, 1935. The casket was hauled by truck to the site.

John Marzel, Wyoming state geologist, was hit by a train while visiting in Cleveland, Ohio, in March 1933.

Causes of Death in Frontier Wyoming

1. Cause of Death of the 162 Recorded to Have Died in 1880 in Wyoming

Disease (or other "natural causes"): 148

Coal mine mishaps: 6

Weather deaths (freezing): 4

Murders: 3

Killed by Indians: 1

2. Cause of Death of 10 Decedents at Atlantic City, 1870

Killed by Indians: 7 Killed by a horse: 1 (a 2-year-old girl)

Heart disease: 1   Murdered: 1 (a 42-year-old gold miner)

3. Cause of Death of 5 Decedents at Fort Laramie, 1870

Heart trouble: 2   Accidental gunshot: 1

Suicide: 1   Murdered: 1

Causes of Death in Wyoming, 2006

1. Heart disease, 983, (24.2%)

2. Cancer, 922 (22.7%)

3. Lung ailments, 343

4. Stroke, 231

5. Auto accidents, 157

6. Other unintentional mishaps, 138

7. Various infections, 127

8.-9. Suicide, pneumonia, 116 each

10. Alzheimers, 113

In 2006, nine people died of homicide. Suicide is the second most common cause of death of those between 15-24 years old behind only auto accidents.

Deaths by County of Residence* (1998)

1. Laramie (621)
2. Natrona (513)
3. Fremont (342)
5. Sheridan (322)
6. Sweetwater (240)
7. Park (212)
8. Albany (184)
9. Carbon (146)
10. Big Horn (136)
11. Campbell (135)
12. Goshen (134)

13. Washakie (95)
14. Lincoln (87)
15. Converse (86)
16.-17. (tie) Johnson, Uinta (84)
18. Weston (69)
19. Teton (62)
20. Hot Springs (60)
21. Crook (55)
22. Sublette (52)
23. Niobrara (24)
*State Dept. of Health, Vital Statistics, 1998.

The petrified body of a man, purportedly that of Montana Territorial Gov. Thomas Meagher, was hauled by wagon to Yellowstone Park in 1899 by a man who sold it for $2,500 to Arthur Mills who put it on display in Upper Geyser Basin. Mills charged each viewer 25 cents to see the 356-pound remains. No explanation was given as to how the remains became petrified or why they were dragged 700 miles overland rather than being placed on display near where Meagher had drowned.

DENTISTS

Total dentists in Wyoming (1990): 263

Total dentists in Wyoming (1993): 287. The state ranked 22nd nationally in dentists per capita.

Total dentists in Wyoming (1996): 292

Total dentists in Wyoming (2008): 462 dentists, according to the Wyoming Board of Dental Examiners, but only 254 were in active practice. There were 439 dental hygienists.

Dentists per capita in Wyoming (2008): .49 per 1,000 population. Teton county has the highest per capita total of 1.04 per 1,000 people.

1st law requiring dentists to register qualifications with the state: 1893. Each dentist was required to file an affidavit as to their qualifications. From 1893 until formal licensing was required in 1905, 45 dentists filed under the 1893 statute.

1st dentist in Wyoming: According to the Wyoming Dental Association, the first actual dentist in Wyoming was Dr. A. F. Thode who opened a practice in Carbon in 1876, later moving to Rawlins in 1881.

1st dentist to be licensed in Wyoming: Dr. Peter J. Appel (b. Green River, 1880) was awarded license #1 when the Board of Dental Examiners was created and licensing began in 1905. He practiced dentistry in Cheyenne.

Wyoming Cities with the Most Dentists*

	1993	1996	2008
1. Cheyenne	46	48	37
2. Casper	44	44	35
3. Sheridan	19	19	15
4. Laramie	16	17	13
5. Rock Springs	15	15	11
6. Gillette	11	13	14
7. Jackson	14	12	14
8. Riverton	10	12	9
9. Cody	12	11	8
10. Green River	-	-	8
11. Lander	10	10	6

2008 figures from Wyoming Healthcare Commission. According to the commission, there was at least one dentist in every Wyoming county except Niobrara.

First Dentists in Wyoming Towns

1. Buffalo

Dr. R. E. Hollbrook opened a practice in Buffalo in 1883.

2. Evanston

Dr. W. C. Cunningham opened a practice in Evanston in 1900. He was the third dentist to be licensed statewide when the law required dental licensing in 1905. The story is told that whenever he had to remove a particularly difficult tooth, he would pull out a huge bear tooth that he always kept in his pocket, leading the patitent to believe that the gigantic tooth had been the troublesome one removed during the procedure.

2. Riverton

Dr. Ralph J. Inman was the first dentist to open a practice in Riverton.

3. Basin

Dr. C. W. G. Dodge opened his Basin dental office in the summer of 1906.

Cheyenne butcher Harry Rhine, 49, was killed in September, 1935, when the carcass of a beef he had just slaughtered fell off the packing company overhead trolley, fracturing his skull.

DINOSAURS

Most dinosaurs per capita: Wyoming holds the distinction. Dinosaurs from the state are displayed worldwide. An estimated 1/10 of 1 percent are displayed in Wyoming.

1st dinosaur discovered in Wyoming: The Agathaumas sylvestris, a horned dinosaur, was 30 feet in length and weighed six tons. It roamed the earth more than 65 million years ago.

1st discoverer of a dinosaur fossil in Wyoming: Edward Drinker Cope, a noted paleontologist from Philadelphia, came across the fossilized remains of the Agathaumas sylvestris in the Laramie formation near the Black Butte railroad station in western Wyoming Territory in 1872.

Most common locations for fossils in Wyoming: Fossils have been found throughout the state in such diverse locations as the Big Horn Basin, near Upton, Rock Springs, Saratoga, Centennial, Douglas, Pine Bluffs and numerous other locales.

"Oldest building" in Wyoming: The Como Bluff Fossil Cabin, made of dinosaur bones found at Como Bluff, was built by Thomas Boylan in 1933. He operated a service station at the location. "Ripley's Believe It or Not" called it the world's oldest building because of the dinosaur bone and mortar from which it was made.

Largest dinosaur skeleton displayed at the University of Wyoming Geological Museum: The Brontosaurus, one of the largest dinosaurs which was 75 feet long, 15 feet high and weighed 30 tons. The skeleton was excavated from the Morrison formation near Sheep Creek in Albany County by the Carnegie Museum in 1901 and obtained by UW in 1956.

Largest lizard that ever lived: A fossil of the mosasaur was found by Charles Bass of Jay Em at a site 50 miles northeast of Lusk. It is on display at the UW Geological Museum.

1st diplodocus ever found: It was dug up at Como Bluff by two railroad company employees. The two men contacted famed Yale paleontologist O. C. Marsh who came to Wyoming in 1878 to supervise the important dig.

1st rhinoceros (yes, rhinoceros!) ever to live in Wyoming: Fossilized remains of the creature are common in Wyoming. The earliest rhinos lived in Wyoming about 50 million years ago. The state was home to crocodiles, the remains of which have been taken from the Morrow Creek area near Farson. A small three-toed horse, mesohippus, has been found near Lusk. The only skull of a Myopterygius americanus ever discovered was found near Osage.

Only Wyoming golf course on which dinosaurs have been found (but not playing the game): Torrington's Cottonwood Country Club was the site of a dinosaur dig by a team headed by Dr. Eric Schlaikjer of Harvard in 1939.

Big bucks for dinosaur fiction: Dr. Robert Bakker, University of Colorado paleontologist who researched extensively at Como Bluff, was paid $650,000 as an advance for his first novel on dinosaurs. He wrote numerous non-fiction books.

Dinosaurs Native to Wyoming

1. Allosaurus

This medium-sized, flesh-eating dinosaur was about 35 feet long and lived 130 million years ago. It was capable of killing the much larger brontosaurus. In 1991, an Allosaurus skeleton was found on Bureau of Land Management property near Shell. Named "Big Al," the world's most complete skeleton of the dinosaur was mounted in the University of Wyoming Geological Museum and dedicated Jan. 26, 1996.

2. Diplodocus

This dinosaur was the largest known. A skeleton at a Pittsburgh museum reaches 87 1/2 feet in length. It lived about 124 million years ago, and spent most of its life in water, according to some experts. Bones of this dinosaur were first discovered at Como Bluff near Medicine Bow.

3. Brontosaurus

The brontosaurus lived 125 million years ago. It reached lengths of 65 feet.

BLM workers recovered one dinosaur bone weighing 500-lbs., a leg bone of a Brontosaurus, near Rock River on Aug. 24, 1995.

4. Orintholestes

This small, flesh-eating dinosaur measured about six feet in length, and lived 125 million years ago. Its name means "bird stealer."

5. Stegosaurus

This plant-eating dinosaur stayed on dry land and was equipped with an appearance of armor plates running along its backbone. It was about 20 feet long and nine feet tall and lived 120 million years ago.

6. Tyrannosaurus

The largest of the flesh-eating dinosaurs, it was 50 feet long and stood about 20 feet tall. Probably, it was the most fierce creature ever to live on earth. It lived in what is now Wyoming some 70 million years ago.

7. Triceratops

One of the last dinosaurs to roam the earth, it lived 60 million years ago. Most probably, it measured 20 to 30 feet in length.

8. Drinker nisti

A 20-pound, plant-eating dinosaur, remains of the reptile were found by James Siegwarth and Jim Filla in 1989 near Como Bluff. The first part of the name honors Edward Drinker Cope while the second part honors the National Institute of Standards and Technology, the agency for which Seigwarth and Filla were working at the time of the find. Pieces of the fossil had been found by Dr. Robert Bakker and his wife near Rock River in 1974 and 1977, but their significance was not recognized at the time. Three other small dinosaurs were found near the same site by teams working with Bakker in 1989 and 1990. All lived in Wyoming about 130 million years ago when the area was swampland.

9. Shoshonius copperi

Four unusually complete skulls of the mouse-sized primate were found in the Wind River Basin between 1984 and 1987 by paleontologists Dr. Richard K. Stucky of the Denver Museum of Natural History, and Drs. K. Christopher Beard and Leonard Krishtalka, both of the Carnegie Museum of Natural History. The fossils are thought to be more than 50 million years old, pushing the record of pre-simian mammals back millions of years. The area had first been explored for fossils a century ago.

10. Batodonoides

The fossilized remains of the world's smallest mammal were found in north central Wyoming in the late 1990s by a University of Michigan team. Existence of the 65-million-year-old fossil was announced to the public on Oct. 1, 1998.

Unusual Dinosaur Finds in Wyoming

1. Edward Cope found his first dinosaur near Point of Rocks in 1872 while his rival, Othniel Marsh, made early discoveries in the Como Bluff area. The rivalry became so intense that the former friends became bitter enemies. Marsh did name something for his former friend—fossilized dinosaur manure!

2. The first "mummy-dinosaur" ever discovered was found near Lusk by George P. Sternberg in 1908. The skin impression of the trachodon annecteus was preserved over most of the body of the fossil. The specimen became part of the collection in Dinosaur Hall, American Museum of Natural History, New York.

3. Dr. Samuel Knight found a fossilized Ichthyosaur in Niobrara County. The reptile had an articulated paddle and could swim well.

4. Petrified rhinoceros, monkeys, anteaters and rodents have been found in the Grizzly Buttes, Uinta County, and in Dinosaur Butte National Historic Site near Kemmerer.

5. Remains of the Eohippus, a rabbit-sized horse, have been recovered from several sites in Wyoming. Specimens are on display at the Geology Museum, University of Wyoming.

6. Fossils were so common in the Como Bluff area in 1881 that government surveyors used them for corner stones. In 1933, the area was proposed as a "natural museum."

7. A National Geographic Society team conducted field studies into the environment of the dinosaurs near Rock River. They conducted the research during the summer of 1974.

8. The massive skull of a Triceratops was found in a gulch near Lusk in 1979. The skull was six feet long, four feet wide, three feet high and weighed 1,000 pounds. The dinosaur had lived 70 million years ago.

9. In June 1991, the remains of a dinosaur skeleton were found near Cottonwood Beach at Alcova Reservoir. Later, a second dinosaur turned up while the first was being excavated.

10. John Bell Hatcher, formerly an assistant to O. C. Marsh, sent 50 skulls of Triceratops back east from a site near Lance Creek, Niobrara County, between 1889 and 1892. Displays of the skulls appear in museums around the world including the Bavarian state collections in Germany.

11. Dinosaur expert Robert Bakker told a Laramie audience in 1999 that Wyoming had a sufficient supply of dinosaurs to have "one dinosaur museum within 20 miles of every Wyoming grade school student--and it should have that many."

Weight of Fossils Taken from Como Bluff, 1898-1903

1898: 141 specimens shipped in 100 boxes weighing 60,000 pounds
1899: 132 specimens in 70 boxes, 40,000 pounds
1900: 87 specimens, 27 boxes, 21,000 pounds
1901: 54 specimens in 44 boxes, weight not known.
1902: 48 specimens in 23 boxes weighing 15,000 pounds
1903: 21 specimens, 11 boxes, 10,000 pounds.
The total: 483 specimens shipped in 275 boxes with a total weight of more than 146,000 pounds.

Edward Drinker Cope, professor at the University of Pennsylvania from 1888-1897, was one of two men leading expeditions to find dinosaur remains at Como Bluff. In 2000, a painting of Cope hanging in a building on the Penn campus was stolen. A bronze bust of him, stolen from another campus location in 1996, was retrieved in 1999.

DUDE RANCHES

1st dude ranch: Eaton Ranch, Wolf, Sheridan county, 1904. Before opening their Wyoming ranch, Howard, Willis and Aldon Eaton started the first dude ranch in the country at Medora, Montana, in 1892.

1st dude ranch to operate entirely as a dude resort: Holm Lodge, Park County, 1907. Built by Tex Holm, the lodge was an overnight stopping place for people en route to Yellowstone. It never was a "working" ranch.

1st visitor to be guided on a Wyoming game hunt: Sir George Gore of Ireland. Gore spent two years hunting big game in Wyoming in the 1850s. Gore and his 40 servants stayed at Fort Laramie during the winters. An earlier visitor was Sir William Drummond Stewart who came in 1834.

1st visitors to be guided in Jackson Hole: One unnamed hunter stayed at the ranch home of Elwood Hoffer in Jackson Hole in the fall of 1888 and Hoffer guided him on a successful big game hunt.

First woman dude wrangler: Probably, Katherine Yokel, Jackson, 1920s.

12 Well-Known Dude Ranches

1. JY Ranch, Jackson Hole

The first dude ranch in Jackson Hole, it was started by Lou Joy in 1905. Later, he sold the ranch to author Struthers Burt.

2. Valley Ranch, South Fork of the Shoshone River

Bought in 1915 by Winthrop Brooks (of Brooks Brothers suits fame) in partnership with I. H. (Larry) Larom, the ranch was known as "Valley Ranch School for Boys" from 1922 to 1934. Larom became the sole owner in 1926. Guests included actresses Tallulah Bankhead and Joan Crawford. Larom sold the ranch in 1969, four years before his death.

3. CM Ranch, Dubois

The ranch was founded by Charles Moore as a boys camp in 1906. The first camp was held the next July. Moore, who was reared on the Wind River reservation and educated in the East, had practiced law before returning to ranching in Wyoming. The first "dudes" were parents of boys camp students who came to stay in cabins specially built for them by Moore in 1920. In 1925, Jimmy and Elliott Roosevelt were sent to the camp by their parents, Franklin and Eleanor Roosevelt. Eleanor accompanied the boys to the ranch and stayed several days. Jimmy returned in 1935. Moore sold the ranch in 1952.

4. Eaton's Ranch, Wolf

Brothers Howard, Willis and Alden sold their Montana ranch and started the Wyoming dude ranch in 1903. It was the first dude ranch in the state. In fact, it is believed that the term "dude" was first applied by the Eatons to mean a paying guest from the East.

5. HF Bar Ranch, Saddlestring

Founded by Frank Horton about 1902 as a working ranch, the place started accepting guests about 1915. Nonetheless, the ranch continued to run cattle commercially. Horton was elected to the state legislature and, in 1938, he was elected to one term in the U. S. House of Representatives. He died in Sheridan in 1948.

6. Teton Camp for Boys

Stephen Leek and Dillon Wallace established the camp about 1926. The camp hosted 25 boys each summer for a fee of about $600 each. It closed in 1934.

7. One Bar 11 Ranch, Carbon County

The ranch was "boys only" during the 1930s. It was operated by Paul Holmes.

3 Common Questions Asked by Dudes

1. "What time do the moose turn into elk?"
2. "What color of uniforms do cattle guards wear?"
3. "This is the Yellowstone entrance. Where is the exit?"

8. Remount Ranch

Homesteaded in 1886 by Thomas Gunston, he sold the ranch in 1923. Seven years later, the ranch was sold again, this time to Helge and Mary Sture-Vasa. Mrs. Sture-Vasa is better known as Mary O'Hara, the novelist who wrote *My Friend Flicka, Thunderhead, Green Grass of Wyoming* and *Wyoming Summer* while living at the ranch. The name of the ranch came from the business of raising horses there for purchase by the U. S. Cavalry. The Sture-Vasas also operated a boys camp at the ranch. In 1946, the ranch was sold to John and Carol Knox who built it into a guest ranch, hosting such celebrities as Arthur Godfrey and Pat Boone. It was sold again in 1962. In 1970, the Remount Ranch was purchased by the Ostlund family and they sold it in 1996.

9. R Lazy S Ranch

Established near Moose by author Owen Wister in 1911, the cabin from the 151-acre place was dismantled and moved to Medicine Bow in 1976. The dude ranch encompassing Wister's original homestead was started in 1948.

10. Pitchfork Ranch

The working ranch began accepting guests in 1907. Russell Crane operated the property until 1915, when L. G. Phelps bought it. Initially, it was managed for Phelps by Carl Dunrud. In 1922, Charles Belden, who was married to Phelps' daughter, managed the ranch. During the next two decades, Belden gained his greatest fame as a photographer of ranch and Western scenes.

11. Gros Ventre Lodge

The Sublette County lodge was built in 1897 by William (Billy) Wells who operated it until 1906. It was famous as a hunting lodge hosting big game hunters from Europe and the East Coast. Called "Dog Ranch" by local residents because of Wells' foxhounds he kept for hunting, the ranch had the first wooden bathtub in western Wyoming. The ranch closed in 1906. Game laws made it unprofitable to continue operating.

12. White Grass Dude Ranch

Built as a cattle ranch during World War I, it was converted to a dude ranching operation in 1919.

13. Darwin Ranch

The ranch was started by trapper Fred Darwin in the early 20th century near what is now the Gros Ventre Wilderness. For many years, the ranch kept weather records. The site set the coldest temperature ever recorded in Wyoming during the month of November, -46 degrees, on Nov. 27, 1976.

14. Bar BC Ranch

The second-oldest dude ranch in Jackson Hole, the ranch was started in 1912 by author Struthers Burt and Horace Carncross. Acquired by the Park Service in 1986, some 45 structures remain although the site no longer functions as a dude ranch.

The Dude Ranchers Association was formed in 1925 with Larry Larom as its first president. He served for 19 years. By 1929, Wyoming ranches hosted more than 10,000 guests annually. In that year, 21 guest ranches operated in Teton and Fremont counties, many of them in the Dubois area. By 1947, there were more than 100 such ranches in the state and they continue to thrive.

EARTHQUAKES

Predicted eruption: A 1991 report by University of California geologist Dr. Don DePaolo predicted a giant eruption in Yellowstone within 100,000 years. Such eruptions have occurred 2 million, 1.3 million and 630,000 years ago. The eruption would occur in the giant caldera, an area 40 by 25 miles containing hot springs and geysers, DePaolo said.

Moving: Just north of Yellowstone Lake, the earth's surface is rising at a rate of .9 inch per year. Wyoming ranks **ninth** among the states in the number of reported earthquakes in recent decades. The state is **seventh** if Alaska and Hawaii are not included, according to the U. S. Geological Survey. Earthquakes have been recorded in every Wyoming county. Three counties--Weston, Crook and Platte--have experienced just one each. Just two were ever felt in Goshen and Laramie counties.

Earthquake advice: On Jan. 17, 1994, the Los Angeles area earthquake was the focus of all press attention. Peter Jennings, ABC News, noted there was humor shown by scientists in the aftermath. He said one had a poster that had this advice: "Before an earthquake, place yourself in a safe place... like Wyoming."

Shaky Park: More than 1,200 earthquakes were reported in Yellowstone in 1995, up from 800 the previous year and just 179 in 1993.

Strongest Earthquakes Felt in Wyoming Since 1959
(by Richter scale)

7.1: Aug. 17, 1959. Actually centered just outside Wyoming at Hebgen Lake, Montana, this major earthquake struck just before midnight, killing 28 and causing $11 million in damages. The earthquake caused Old Faithful eruptions to slow slightly from an average of once every 61 minutes to once every 65 minutes. Some 18,000 people were vacationing in Yellowstone at the time. The quake was felt statewide and throughout the West, cracking walls and cement sidewalks throughout the state. As of 2000, the quake was the 13th largest ever recorded in the contiguous states.

6.4: June 30, 1975. The earthquake knocked out Yellowstone telephones and was felt throughout the Western United States.

5.9: Feb. 3, 1994, 2:05 a.m. The quake had an epicenter just east of Auburn. No injuries, but some damage to structures. Three other shocks at about the same time exceeded 4.0 on the Richter. The first one, at 12:15 a.m., Feb. 3, was 4.5. At 4:19 a.m., after the biggest one, a 4.7 struck. At 7.42 p.m. on Feb. 3, a 5.2 aftershock was measured. Another 4.0 aftershock was felt at 8:10 p.m.

5.5: Oct. 18, 1984. Centered about 25 miles southeast of Casper, this earthquake struck at 9:30 a.m. Slight damage was reported at Medicine Bow, Douglas, Casper, Shirley Basin, McFadden, Rock River and Guernsey.

5.1: Sept. 7, 1984. Centered about 30 miles southeast of Buffalo, minor damage reported.

5.1: May 29, 1984. This earthquake occurred at 2:18 p.m., centered about 25 miles west of Gillette.

5.1: Dec. 9, 1976. Centered in Yellowstone. Slight damage reported.

5.0: Nov. 3, 1984. One of five earthquakes reported in Wyoming in 1984, this one rocked the Lander area, causing some damage. It struck at 2:30 a.m. and was centered about 20 miles southeast of Lander.

4.8: April 21, 1973. This earthquake struck at 11:07 p.m., rocking Jeffrey City, but causing minor damage.

4.8: Aug. 21, 1986. Just after midnight, this strong earthquake was felt in the Jackson area. It was centered about 20 miles south of Jackson.

4.7: Feb. 6, 1983. Another Yellowstone area earthquake, this one hit at 1:25 p.m., centered northeast of Old Faithful.

4.7: Largest earthquake in Wyoming in 1993, the quake rocked eastern Teton County on Dec. 28, 1993. There were 21 earthquakes in Wyoming measuring over 2.9 during 1993, the most in ten years.

4.6: Sept. 6, 1985. This morning earthquake (9:27 a.m.) caused rock slides which temporarily closed Highway 89 in Snake River Canyon south of Jackson. It was centered about 15 miles south of Jackson.

A Definition of the Richter Scale*

Earthquake magnitude, first defined by Charles F. Richter in 1935, is the measure of an earthquake's size. For each unit of magnitude the amplitude of ground motion (or seismic waves) increases by a factor of ten. Thus, a magnitude 6 earthquake produces ground motions that are ten times greater than those from a magnitude 5 earthquake. The energy released as seismic waves increases even faster, a factor of 33 increase for each unit of magnitude. *From Earthquakes and Volcanoes. USGS publ., Vol. 20, #2 (1988), p. 42.*

30 Wyoming Earthquakes Reported Before 1980

1. October, 1870. The first record of an earthquake in Wyoming, it was noted by the Post Surgeon at Fort Laramie. Apparently, it caused little or no damage.

2. November, 1882. A strong earthquake rocked the Big Horn Basin on the evening of election day. The tremor caused some springs to go dry in what is now Hot Springs County and reportedly caused some cooling of the world's largest mineral hot spring at Thermopolis.

3. June 25, 1894. The earthquake rocked Casper and caused the North Platte River to run thick with mud.

4. Nov. 14, 1897. The Grand Central Hotel in Casper was damaged by this earthquake centered near Casper.

5. July 25, 1910. A moderate earthquake shook houses in Rock Springs and was felt by miners working underground.

6. May 8, 1915. North central Yellowstone.

7. March 23-April 12, 1923. Thirteen minor shocks felt at Kelly.

8. Nov. 17, 1925. Strong earthquake rocked Big Horn in Sheridan County and was felt statewide.

9. Feb. 13, 1928. Shook Thermopolis and felt elsewhere in the Big Horn Basin.

10. June 12, 1930. The estimated 5.8 quake cracked walls in Grover.

11. Aug. 24-Dec. 22, 1930. Long series of minor shocks felt in Yellowstone.

12. Jan. 26, 1932. South of Yellowstone. The quake awakened residents of Jackson and was felt as far away as Dubois and Lander.

13. c. August 10, 1934. Lusk.News reports said it occurred "sometime last week."

14. Nov. 23, 1934. Light damage at Lander, also felt at Atlantic City and Rock Springs.

15 October, 1935. Sheridan area felt the quake centered near Helena, Mont.

16. Jan. 14, 1936. South entrance of Yellowstone.

17. Aug. 5, 1942. Thumb Ranger Station, Yellowstone.

18. Feb. 23, 1943. Jackson.

19. Jan. 20, 1954. Felt at Albany, Centennial and Laramie and strongly felt at Fox Park and Jelm. A light after-shock was felt five hours later.

20. July 4, 1954. This 12:40 a.m. earthquake was felt by tourists in Yellowstone and awakened residents of Mammoth.

21. April 28, 1958. Old Faithful.

22. Aug. 17, 1959. Yellowstone. 7.1 magnitude. The strongest earthquake felt in Wyoming to date, actually centered just outside the state line in Montana. At least 28 people died from effects of the quake destroying a dam in Montana. Old Faithful's eruptions slowed slightly after the earthquake that was felt as far away as eastern Wyoming.

23. Feb. 25, 1963. This strong 4.3 quake was felt at Fort Washakie.

24. March 27, 1964. Van Tassell, Niobrara County.

25. Aug. 21, 1964. A second, stronger quake near Van Tassell, measured 4.5. Like the earlier March earthquake, shaking was felt in Lusk and as far away as western Nebraska.

26. Dec. 8, 1972. 4.1 magnitude earthquake struck near Thermopolis.

27. April 21, 1973. 4.8 magnitude struck at 11:07 p.m., between Lander and Jeffrey City.

28. Aug. 30, 1974. Yellowstone. The strong quake was felt at Norris, Old Faithful and West Yellowstone. Numerous after-shocks followed.

29. June 30, 1975. A 6.4 earthquake in Yellowstone caused rockslides that blocked traffic in various parts of the Park. After-shocks continued for several weeks.

30. Jan. 27, 1976. A small earthquake was felt near Rawlins.

Sources: Carl von Hake, Earthquake Information Bulletin, 10, (July-August 1978); local newspaper accounts; notes from history sources.

Some Earthquakes Reported in Wyoming, 1983-2008

Feb. 6, 1983.	Northeast of Old Faithful, 1:25 p.m., 4.7.
Feb. 13, 1983.	Medicine Bow, 6:45 a.m., 4.0.
Nov. 2, 1983.	Jackson, 1:04 p.m., 3.5.
Nov. 9, 1983.	Dubois, 6:53 a.m., 3.6.
Nov. 15, 1983.	Casper, 5:33 a.m., 3.0.
Dec. 20, 1983.	Jackson, 3:52 p.m., 4.5.
Dec. 22, 1983.	Jackson, 11:56 a.m., 3.4.
Jan. 5, 1984.	Jackson, 1:10 p.m., 3.0.
May 29, 1984.	West of Gillette, 2:18 p.m., 5.1.
Sept. 7, 1984.	Southeast of Buffalo, 7 p.m., 5.1.
Oct. 18, 1984.	25 miles southeast of Casper, 9:30 a.m., 5.5.
Nov. 3, 1984.	20 miles southeast of Lander, 2:30 a.m., 5.0.
June 17, 1985.	30 miles north of Old Faithful, 3.5.
Aug. 13, 1985.	3 miles northwest of Rock Springs, 2:57 p.m., 3.5.
Aug. 16, 1985.	15 miles southeast of Riverton, 12:05 a.m., 4.3.
Aug. 23, 1985.	Jackson, 12:06 a.m., 4.8.
Aug. 30, 1985.	Jackson, 3:08 p.m., 4.3.
Sept. 6, 1985.	South of Jackson, 9:47 a.m., 4.6.
Jan. 16, 1986.	Yellowstone, 3.4.
April 18, 1986.	Northwest Yellowstone, 7:18 a.m., 3.2.
Nov. 14, 1986.	Yellowstone, 5:57 a.m., 3.4.
Nov. 17, 1986.	20 miles south of Jackson, 1:34 a.m., 3.9.
June 6, 1987.	10 miles south of Old Faithful, 6:40 a.m., 4.0.
Jan. 13, 1988.	Northwest of Norris, Yellowstone, 3.4.
June 24, 1989.	Five miles north of Jackson, 3:25 a.m., 4.1.
March 4, 1990.	Southeast of Jackson, 11:51 p.m., 3.9.
Aug. 7, 1991.	Southwest of Thermopolis, 6:49 a.m., 3.4.

Jan. 31, 1992.   Lander area, 5:02 a.m., 2.8.

April 3, 1992.   Felt on Wyoming-Idaho border. 6:30 p.m., 4.2.

July 20, 1992.   Yellowstone area, 1:04 a.m., 3.7.

Aug. 30, 1992.   Kaycee, Barnum, 7:40 p.m., 3.6.

Oct. 10, 1992.   Felt in Lander, no injuries or damage, 9:41 a.m., 4.0.

Nov. 10, 1992.   In Idaho but felt at Freedom, Afton, 3:46 a.m., 4.8.

Nov. 15, 1992.   Centered in Idaho but felt at Alpine, 7:32 p.m., 3.4.

Dec. 28, 1993.   Largest earthquake in Wyoming in 1993, the quake rocked eastern Teton County, 4.7.

Year, 1993: There were 21 earthquakes in Wyoming measuring over 2.9 during 1993, the most in ten years.

Jan. 30-Feb. 3, 1994. 47 earthquakes of various intensities were felt in the Star Valley area. Epicenters of only 16 of them were in Wyoming, however. The rest were in Idaho. The largest (5.9 on the Richter scale), 2:05 a.m., Feb. 3, 1994, had an epicenter just east of Auburn. No injuries were reported, but some damage was caused to structures, including the Auburn Fish Hatchery. The first one, 12:15 a.m., Feb. 3, was 4.5. At 4:19 a.m., after the biggest one, a 4.7 was recorded. At 7:42 p.m., on Feb. 3, a 5.2 aftershock was noted and another 4.0 aftershock struck at 8:10 p.m.

Sept. 24, 1994. 3.6 quake shook Yellowstone.

Feb. 3, 1995. At 8:26 a.m., seismographs measured a 5.4 shake 18 miles west of Green River. Trona miners were trapped underground at Solvay and one man died. Initial reports indicated the cause was an earthquake, but investigators later determined that the seismograph actually measured a cave-in at the mine, mistaking it for an earthquake.

June 29-July 10, 1995. A series of 550 small earthquakes rattled Yellowstone. Some were as high as 3.1 on the Richter scale. Most were centered in Mount Haynes area, east of the town of West Yellowstone.

Aug. 28, 1995. Centered five miles south of Yellowstone, 9:16 p.m., 4.5.

Oct. 6, 1995. More than 100 earthquakes began shaking Yellowstone, one with a magnitude of 4.3 on the Richter. Centered near Mount Sheridan and Lewis Lake in the southern part of the park.

Sept. 28, 1998. A series of 100 small shocks rumbled through Yellowstone, followed on Sept. 30 by a 3.2 earthquake at 6:59 a.m., and a 3.1 at 11:09 a.m.

April 5, 1999. The 4.2 temor struck at 6:41 p.m. and caused minor damage in Baggs and Wamsutter. Epicenter was 35 miles southwest of Rawlins.

May 26, 2000. Bairol in Carbon County was shaken by a 4.0 quake at 3:58 p.m.

Nov. 24, 2000: A 4.6 magnitude quake struck in Yellowstone at 4:20 a.m. It was felt as far away as Cody.

April 21, 2001. A magnitude 5.4 struck at 5 p.m., at a depth of 1/2 mile. .Northwestern Wyoming.

Jan. 7, 2004. At 7:51 a.m., the Jackson area was shaken by a magnitude 5.0 earthquake that occurred some 1.9 miles in depth.

Jan. 9, 2007.. Five miles east of Thermopolis, 3.5.

March 25, 2008. At 11:59 a.m., a magnitude 4.5 earthquake (at a depth of just 0.2 mi) struck in Yellowstone.

The Weekly World News, supermarket tabloid, stated in the June 10, 2003, issue that a "space alien baby" had been found in Casper. Casper officials had no knowledge of the sensational claim. No "Phil Merleson" was listed in the Casper directory, supposedly the person reporting the baby's existence. The same publication had accused Sen. Al Simpson of being an "extraterrestrial" in 1992 and again in 1994.

ELECTRICITY

1st electricity generated in Wyoming: By Brush-Swan Electric Light Company, Cheyenne, in 1882. Cheyenne had 1,000 incandescent lights by the next year.

1st interior-lighted building in Wyoming: Cheyenne Club, 1884.

1st hotel in the world lighted by an electric light in each room: Inter Ocean Hotel, Cheyenne

1st electric-powered flour mill in Wyoming: Laramie Milling and Elevator Company, 1888.

1st electric typewriter in Wyoming: A machine in the offices of the *Wyoming State Tribune*, Cheyenne, first used on June 20, 1925.

1st electric lights in Sheridan: May, 1893, when electricity generated by a coal-fired threshing machine engine lighted the bulbs in the Sheridan Inn and nearby buildings. When a whistle blew at midnight, it was the signal that electricity to the 200 lights was about to shut down for the night and the engine was turned off.

1st electric lights in Newcastle: 1898, brought to town by Peter Kinney who also started the first telephone company in town.

1st electric lights in Casper: June 12, 1900, 10 p.m., when 20 businesses and 150 homes first received power from the Casper Electric Company plant

1st electric lights in Riverton: Turned on for the first time on Dec. 5, 1914, at 3:40 p.m.

1st electric lights in Lyman: 1927, following purchase of Delco light plant by Ray Blackner and lines run by Al Stewart and Jim Ellingford.

Lowest cost producer of electricity of any U. S. power plant: The Laramie River Station near Wheatland, operated by Basin Electric Power Cooperative, held the mark for the period 1986-90 with an average cost of $10.20 per net megawatt hour.

1st large wind power project in Wyoming: Foote Creek Rim near Arlington, Carbon County, dedicated April 22, 1999, 61 are owned by PacifiCorp (80%) and Eugene (Oregon) Water and Electric Board (20%), generating 41.4 megawatts. A total of 105 turbines were operating on the site in early 2000.

Long Blackout: In October 1998, an early fall snowstorm and strong winds brought down both main power lines into Lusk. The town was without electricity for five days.

5 Significant Wyoming Power Plants

1. Dave Johnston Power Plant, six miles east of Glenrock

Ground was broken for the coal-fired steam electric plant on June 30, 1956, and the excavation of the site began Oct. 22, 1956. The plant was named for W. D. "Dave" Johnston, a long-time Pacific Power and Light Company official who retired in 1956 as company vice president (d. June 6, 1975). He attended the groundbreaking ceremonies. The first 100,000 kilowatt generating unit went on line in October, 1958. Three more units were added in the next 14 years. The second unit was finished in 1960, the third in 1964 and the fourth in 1972. Combined with design improvements made in 1977, the plant's capacity was increased to 810,000 kilowatts. The plant, on a 400-acre site on the north bank of the North Platte River, employs about 240 full-time workers.

2. Laramie River Station, Basin Electric Power Cooperative, Wheatland

The plant, six miles east of Wheatland, has a generating capacity of 1,650 megawatts. Construction began July 12, 1976, and the entire project cost was $1.6 billion. In October, 1978, a federal judge ruled that the environmental impact statement was inadequate as to

Robert and Helen Lynd, pioneer sociologists who wrote famously of "Middletown," had a Wyoming connection. Robert Lynd was sent as a minister in training, in 1920, to the Elk Basin oil camp in the northern Big Horn Basin. He not only preached but also worked as a laborer during his almost two years at the camp. Later, he and his wife relocated to Muncie, Indiana, where they began their path-breaking sociological studies.

the water. Two months later, the plant builder, Missouri Basin Public Power, signed an agreement with Nebraska and contributed $7.5 million to a fund used to protect waterfowl habitat. The first unit on the 650-acre plant site went on line in 1980, followed by Unit 2 in 1981 and Unit 3 on Nov. 1, 1982. Water for the plant comes from Grayrocks Reservoir, six miles east of the plant. Grayrocks Dam, 100 feet high and 2,500 feet long, holds 104,000 acre-feet of water. The plant is fueled by about 7 million tons of coal annually, most coming from Dry Fork Mine in the Powder River Basin. About 350 people are employed at the plant and mine. Plant operator, Basin Electric Power Cooperative, is headquartered in Bismarck, N. D., and serves 117 rural electric member systems in eight states.

3. Jim Bridger Power Plant, 35 miles northeast of Rock Springs

The coal-fired plant has a generating capacity of 2,080,000 kilowatts per hour. Unit 1 went on line in November 1974; unit 2 in Dec. 1975; unit 3 in Sept. 1976; and unit 4 in Dec. 1979. Each generates 520 kilowatts. Nearly 500 people work at the power plant. The mine, four miles northeast of the plant, opened in May 1974. It employs an additional 359 people. Water for the plant comes from the Green River through a 40-mile-long steel pipeline. The plant was a joint project of Pacific Power and Light and Idaho Power Company. Nearly 5,000 people were employed in the construction phases.

4. Naughton Power Plant, Kemmerer

Located southwest of Kemmerer, the plant has 200 full-time employees. Unit 1 generates 160 kilowatts and it went into operation in May 1963. The second unit of 210 kilowatts, produced commercial electricity for the first time in October 1968. The third unit, 330 kilowatts, opened in October 1971. Water for the plant comes from the Hams Fork River. The mine adjacent to the plant is operated by Pittsburgh and Midway Coal Mining Co., Englewood, Colo.

5. WyoDak Power Plant, Gillette

When the plant was built in the 1970s, it was the world's largest air-cooled power plant. It began operating on Sept. 18, 1978, as a joint project of Pacificorp (80 percent) and Black Hills Power and Light (20 percent). The Neil Simpson plant, adjacent to the WyoDak plant, was the first air-cooled power plant in the United States. Nearly 125 people are employed at the plant. The mine, from which the coal comes to fire the plant, is just 1,000 feet from the plant entrance.

One fall afternoon in the early 1980s, Medicine Bow Post editor David Roberts (co-author of this book) was driving his car, a late model Nova, through the Sybille to Wheatland when he noticed a deer next to the road. He stopped, got out of the car, leaving the door open and started to take a photograph of the animal. The deer kept moving closer and closer and Roberts had to keep changing the focus. Finally, the deer was right at the car, trying to climb in. Roberts had to push the would-be hitchhiker away from the car, wondering what passing motorists were thinking of the unusual scene. In the summer of 2000, the press reported a similar incident happening at a Dubois bookstore. A deer came in to the store, perhaps seeking to purchase a Wyoming Almanac?

FESTIVALS AND FAIRS

1st Wyoming State Fair: The "Wyoming Industrial Convention" was held in Sheridan in 1903. It has often been called the first "state fair."

2nd Wyoming State Fair: Casper, 1904.

3rd Wyoming State Fair: Douglas, 1905. Douglas became the permanent location for the fair which was held there every year, except for the Depression years of 1935 and 1936, 1937 because of a polio outbreak, and 1943-1945 because of World War II.

1st St. Patrick's Day celebration in Wyoming: March 17, 1868, by members of the Fenin Brotherhood of Cheyenne who organized a street parade and dance to commemorate the event. Probably, it was the first organized parade in Wyoming history.

Some Distinctive Events in Wyoming

1. Saratoga Fish Fry

The first such event was held Aug. 28-29, 1907.

2. International Night, Rock Springs

The first multi-national celebration was held in 1924.

3. Gift of the Waters Pageant, Thermopolis

The pageant tells the story of how the public received the world's largest mineral hot spring as a gift from the Indians. The pageant, written by Marie Montabe Lindstrom, premiered in 1925.

4. Jackson Pole, Peddle and Paddle Race

Each contestant must downhill ski, then switch to cross-country skis, ride a bicycle the next 19 miles, get in a canoe and paddle for ten more miles. The race destination was Astoria Hot Springs. In April 1981, more than 700 contestants were entered in the event.

5. Pioneer Days, Lander

The first annual rodeo was held in 1893. The Lander rodeo holds the distinction of being the first organized in Wyoming, four years older than Cheyenne Frontier Days. A rodeo was held later in the summer of 1893 in Dayton, Sheridan County, making it the second ever organized in the state.

6. Legend of the Rawhide Pageant, Lusk

The pageant depicts the origins of the name of Rawhide Butte, a local landmark. The premiere showing was on Aug. 24, 1946. Held annually until 1965, the event was revived in 1986.

7. Powder River Basin Air Festival, Gillette

The first such event was held in August 1986.

8. Riverton Rendezvous Balloon Rally

The first rally was held in 1980.

9. Grand Teton Music Festival

Founded in 1962 by a group headed by Baroness Consuela von Gontard of Melody Ranch, the permanent music hall was completed in 1974. The event annually attracts top international musicians. In 1989, the New York Philharmonic played there. Ling Tung served as music director for 20 years. In July, 1996, Aije Oue, conductor of the Minnesota Orchestra, was named full-time music director.

10. Shoshoni Old Time Fiddle Contest

The annual event, usually held in May, was started in 1973.

11. Tobacco-spitting contest, Riverton

The event was held annually in March at Central Wyoming College

12. Cheyenne Frontier Days

"The Daddy of 'em All" began with a one-day rodeo in September 1897. Today, the event is held annually the last full week in July. More than 300,000 people attend the sessions and thousands more watch the parades through town. Jean Nimmo Dubois was crowned in 1931 as the first "Miss Frontier."

13. All-American Indian Days

The Indian Days festival was organized by three area residents, F. H. Sinclair, Don Diers and Donald Deernose in 1951 following the selection of a Crow woman, Lucy Yellowmule, as queen of the Sheridan Rodeo. The new event was first held in Sheridan in 1952, highlighted by the crowning of Miss Indian America. Twenty-eight were crowned during the event's run at Sheridan. In 1984, the event was moved to Bismarck, North Dakota, where it was to remain for five years. *(Source: Dale E. Kinley, Sheridan, Wyoming)*

14. Woodchoppers' Jamboree, Encampment

The first jamboree was held in 1960, celebrating the skills of old time woodchoppers and tie hacks who were once active in the nearby woods.

15. Green River Rendezvous, Pinedale

Green River Rendezvous has been held annually in Pinedale since 1936.

16. Buffalo Bill's Birthday, Cody

The "birthday party" was held on the anniversary of William F. Cody's birth on Feb. 26, 1846. The event included dances at the Cody Auditorium and special programs at the Buffalo Bill Historical Center. In the 1970s, a large fiberglass buffalo statue was installed on top of Cedar Mountain on the site Cody chose for his grave. Following his death in 1919, his wish was not honored. His grave is on Lookout Mountain in Colorado.

17. Rabbit Races, Medicine Bow

The event was an attraction of Medicine Bow Days. It originated after organizers were asked to come up with an encore to a one-time tortoise race. Since "hares" are more abundant in the area than tortoises, promoters substituted wild rabbits. The "race" was held annually until 1987 when it was dropped following complaints from animal protection advocates. Medicine Bow Days has been held annually since 1959.

18. Fort Bridger Rendezvous, Fort Bridger

The "mountain man" event was first held in 1974. It grew to become the second largest visitor event in Wyoming. Held during Labor Day weekend, the rendezvous drew large enough crowds to make the town of Fort Bridger, temporarily, the state's largest city.

19. Oktoberfest, Worland

The festival, imported from Germany, was first celebrated in Worland in October 1969. It was held annually during that month for the next 18 years. The area has many residents who have German or Russian-German ancestry.

20. "Meteor Day"

The Casper event was held in 1958. A helicopter flew over a downtown street and released thousands of ping-pong balls, some redeemable for special prizes. "Meteor Day" apparently was a one-time event.

21. Tom Browning Day

The designation of Sept. 20, 1988, honored the Casper native, a major league pitcher for the Cincinnati Reds, for the perfect game he pitched three days earlier.

22. Northwest Jazz Festival, Powell

Northwest College has hosted the annual event since 1983. Jazz concerts feature musicians ranging from professionals to high school students.

23. Fossil Discovery Days, Fossil Butte National Monument

The event, held at the national monument near Kemmerer, was first held in the summer of 1987.

24. Crimson Dawn celebration, Casper Mountain

The annual Midsummer's Eve celebration on Casper Mountain was first held in 1928 when festival founder Mrs. Neal Forsling invited children of friends to join her children to hear mountain legends. Held on the summer solstice at her home on the mountain in Crimson Dawn Park, the festival was attended by as few as six and as many as 3,000 people over the years. Mrs. Forsling, a talented writer, had short stories and poetry published in the 1930s and 1940s. In 1973, she deeded her 94 acres to the Natrona County Parks Dept. Her cabin became a museum. She died in 1977. Each year, the trek begins at the Crimson Dawn museum then moves east through the park, ending with a bonfire on Red Butte.

25. Powder River Sheepherders Fair, Powder River

The event tests the skills of working sheepdogs and the skills of sheep people. It has been held annually at Powder River since 1984. Previously, the fair headquarters was the Big Horn Hotel in Arminto until the structure burned in 1984.

26. International Basque Festival

The annual event, attended by Basques from throughout the world, has been hosted on two occasions by Buffalo--in 1988 and again in 1995.

27. Laramie Jubilee Days

The first running of the annual event was held on July 10, 1940, to celebrate the 50th anniversary of Wyoming statehood. It was first called "Equality Days," but renamed Jubilee Days in 1941.

28. Hulett Ham and Jamb

An offshoot of the nearby Sturgis, S. D., motorcycle rally, Ham and Jamb was started in 1989 by Jim Delancey, proprietor of the Rodeo Bar. Some 250 motorcyclists came to the first event. It was continued by later owners Ron and Maria Waugh. An estimated 30,000 people attended the 1999 event.

Some Fairs in Wyoming Counties

1. Johnson County

The first county fair in Wyoming was held near Buffalo in 1885.

2. Big Horn County

The first was held in Basin in October, 1897.

3. Converse County

The first county fair was held at Manville in 1891. The town, now part of Niobrara County, hosted the Converse County Fair again in 1898.

4. Carbon County

The first county fair was held in Saratoga in September 1910.

5. Niobrara County

The first fair in what is now Niobrara County was at Manville in 1891, but after the county was created in 1911, the first fair was held at Lusk in September 1913.

Wyoming's energy boom prompted some counties to recruit workers form Michigan in the 2006. At least 800 people looking for jobs attended Wyoming presentations at job fairs held in Michigan early in 2006 after automakers in that state announced plans to lay of tens of thousands of workers.

FIRES

1st volunteer fire department in Wyoming: Probably, the Pioneer Hook and Ladder Company, founded in Cheyenne in 1868. The company did "little more than purchase hats for its 75 members." Each Wyoming military post had its own fire fighting company. Technically, they were not "volunteer."
1st paid fire department in Casper: 1917
1st motor-driven fire truck in Casper: May 3, 1910
Fire business: Hawkins and Powers Aviation of Greybull (organized in 1969) was one of largest aerial firefighting companies in the United States. The firm closed and the fleet of about 60 airplanes was liquidated in 2006.

Monuments to Wyoming Firefighters

1. Fallen Firefighter Memorial
   The monument was erected on the grounds of the Wyoming Fire Academy in Riverton. Envisioned by Larry L. Lee, Fremont County fire warden, and designed by Ken Metzler, the monument was dedicated in 1990.
2. Fire Fighters Memorial
   The memorial, dedicated Aug. 20, 1939, is located 35 miles west of Cody. It honors the 15 men who died in the "Blackwater fire" on Aug. 21, 1937, a few miles away. Thirty-nine others were injured when a gale whipped up the fire, trapping the men at two locations. Ten who died were CCC enrollees. Other signs and markers away from the highway indicate the exact spots at which the men died as well as fire camps and first aid centers that were located along the trail.
3. Fire Fighters Monument
   Also dedicated to the victims of the "Blackwater fire," this monument is located near Meadowlark Lake in the Big Horns, far from the fire scene. It was built in September 1937 by the men from a CCC camp located near Ten Sleep.

Significant Fires in Wyoming Cities

1. Casper (1867; October 1891; June 17, 1921; several dates in 1953; 1996)
   Fort Caspar, abandoned by the army, was burned by Indians who also set fire to the Platte River Bridge in 1867. (The present replica of Fort Caspar was built on the foundations of the original fort in 1936). In 1891, the town's first jail burned when an inmate, Dr. Joe Benson, set fire to his cell. Dr. Benson, also known as "Joe Riley," died in the fire. The most spectacular fire in Casper history occurred on June 17, 1921, when lightning ignited seven tanks in the Midwest Oil Company's tank farm overlooking the city. The fire burned steadily for 60 hours and consumed more than a half million gallons of oil. Several buildings burned in 1953 in a series of seven fires set by an arsonist. In 1996, the VFW building in downtown Casper burned by a fire set by an arsonist.
2. Cheyenne (Jan. 11, 1870; Jan. 9, 1875; Dec. 31, 1916; Dec. 28, 2004)
   Two city blocks were wiped out in the 1870 fire. Almost 80 buildings burned. Following the fire, merchants rebuilt many structures using brick as the primary building material. The Officer's Quarters at Fort D. A. Russell burned in the 1875 fire. The most spectacular fire in Cheyenne history occurred on New Year's Eve, 1916, when the Interocean Hotel, a downtown landmark, went up in flames. The 2004 fire destroyed several buildings between Carey and Capitol on 16th Street, including a structure built in 1882 that once housed Warren Mercantile.
3. Carbon (June 19, 1890)
   Most of the business district burned. The fire started when a Scranton House hotel guest knocked over a kerosene lamp while fighting bedbugs. At one time, one of the most important cities in Wyoming, the town never regained its prominence after the fire.

4. Dayton (1903)

Fire destroyed an entire city block. The town was incorporated in 1906.

5. Encampment (March 28, 1906)

The concentrating mill used for copper refining burned to the ground. The fire marked the end of the "boom years" for mining in the area.

6. Cody (Dec. 1, 1907; February 1965; May 1974)

Cody's history is marked by several serious fires. The earliest in 1907 burned seven downtown stores. The Cody Trading Company and other Sheridan Avenue (Main Street) stores burned in 1965. A third serious blaze killed fire chief Bob Moore and a *Cody Enterprise* photographer when the newspaper plant burned in an arson-set blaze in 1974.

7. Rawlins (July 18, 1912)

Prisoners rioted at the state penitentiary and burned the broom factory on the prison grounds. In the ensuing melee, 27 prisoners escaped and one Rawlins citizen was killed · by an escapee. It was the most serious prison riot in state history.

8. Sheridan (Jan. 14, 1915)

The Sheridan Commercial Company building was consumed in one hour, 45 minutes. The company rebuilt the store later in the year. The only Sheridan fireman killed in the line of duty was Fire Chief Fred W. Tossie who died fighting a house fire on Jan. 22, 1929.

9. Powell (February 12, 1915; Sept. 11, 1918)

The 1915 fire began in a hardware store on the main street and soon, it destroyed nine businesses. The fire prompted local residents to establish a volunteer fire department the following December. The offices and printing plant of the *Powell Tribune* were destroyed in a 1918 fire. Other nearby buildings were damaged. In the days of linotypes which required molten lead, fires were a hazard in the newspaper business. A few years after the *Tribune* fire, a blaze destroyed the offices of the *Lovell Chronicle* in nearby Lovell.

10. Douglas (Oct. 10, 1915)

Many downtown buildings were destroyed or damaged in the fire.

11. Evanston (Sept. 11, 1917; Jan. 26, 1922, May 7, 2007)

The original State Hospital building burned in 1917. In 1922, the Chinese joss house in Evanston, one of just three such ceremonial houses in America, burned to the ground. A fire in 1879 burned the offices of the *Uinta County Chieftain*. The 2007 fire destroyed the Strand Theater, a downtown landmark built in 1918.

12. Lingle (Fall 1920)

The town's first laundry burned to the ground, killing its owner, "Grandpa" Story. On the night of the fire, money was collected to begin the Lingle Volunteer Fire Department.

13. Gillette (Nov. 24, 1921)

Several downtown stores burned in an overnight blaze.

14. Hulett (Jan. 4, 1925)

Fire destroyed the bank, hotel, pool hall and the Odd Fellows Hall, a large portion of the downtown business district.

15. Riverton (Jan. 22, 1927; Feb. 20, 1951)

The Golden Rule store and Holden Cafe in the downtown burned in the 1927 fire. In 1951, fire destroyed the Ben Franklin store building and several adjacent structures. A barber died in the blaze that broke out in sub-zero weather.

16. Sinclair (April 5, 1927)

An explosion ripped through the oil refinery and, with the ensuing fire, 16 people died. In terms of loss of life, it was the worst fire in Wyoming history.

The first "state fire tournament" was held in Rock Springs in August, 1891.

17. St. Stephens (Jan. 20, 1928)

The mission burned to the ground, but there were no injuries.

18. Fort Bridger (Dec. 20, 1931)

The historic home of Judge William A. Carter was destroyed by fire.

19. Thermopolis (Feb. 4, 1932)

Fire destroyed the Washakie Hotel.

20. Torrington (Dec. 7, 1933)

One man died and four were injured in an explosion and fire in the old bank building, downtown. The explosion, caused by a gas leak, occurred at 6:05 p.m.

21. Gillette area (1934)

In the spring of 1934, "20 tents" of Civilian Conservation Corps (CCC) workers, many from New Mexico, were brought to the Gillette area to help extinguish the long-burning coal fires deep beneath the ground. The crews extracted the burning coal and filled in the resulting holes. Their "tent city," first occupied on May 4, 1934, was in an area south of Gillette, west of the 4J Road.

22. Laramie (April 14, 1948; June 20, 1989)

In 1948, some 30 businesses were destroyed in a raging inferno which leveled the buildings of the Holliday Furniture Company. The fire, visible for 40 miles, started in the elevator shaft of the Holliday company store, a building the firm had occupied for 76 years. The blaze was reported at 1:45 a.m., but it raged out of control for 15 hours before fireman finally subdued it. The 1989 fire destroyed one business, the Country Woods Furniture Store on Second Street, and damaged several others.

23. Centennial (1952, 1992)

The Old Corral in Centennial, a popular restaurant known for steaks, first opened in 1946. The structure was destroyed in a fire in 1952 and rebuilt by long-time owner Pat Self (b. 1914, d. 1993). Soon after Self sold the business in 1992, the building burned again. The new owners rebuilt it, extensively expanding its size. No one was hurt in either fire.

24. Fort Fred Steele (Dec. 31, 1976)

Two sets of the original enlisted men's barracks at the historic Carbon County fort were destroyed by a fire set by vandals on New Year's Eve.

25. Rock Springs (March 15, 1978)

Our Lady of Sorrows Catholic Church was extensively damaged by fire, apparently set by a transient.

26. Jackson (Aug. 5, 1980)

The Wort Hotel fire cost the life of a Jackson fireman, Cecil Lynch.

27. Buffalo (Aug. 16, 1988)

In the worst fire in the history of Buffalo's downtown, five buildings were damaged by the fire during the hottest summer in memory.

28. Cave Gulch (Aug. 13, 1998)

A natural gas well blew out and caught fire at the oil field 50 miles northwest of Casper. The fire burned for months before it was extinguished through a combination of relief drilling operations and luck.

29. Newcastle (Dec. 18, 1998)

Four century-old buildings were destroyed on Newcastle's Main Street. A fire in 1893 destroyed four buildings behind a downtown bar and one woman, Mary Miller, was killed. In 1975, the old elementary school in town burned.

30. North Fork, Shoshone River (March 19, 2004)

The main lodge of Crossed Sabres Guest Ranch was destroyed by fire.

Meadowlark Dam in the Big Horn mountains was built by the CCC in 1936.

Firefighters Killed in the Line of Duty in Wyoming*

1. John S. Federhen, Cheyenne, Sept. 10, 1920
2. Fred W. Tossie, Sheridan, Jan. 22, 1929
3. Henry Larsen, Rawlins, Feb. 23, 1930
        Blackwater fire, Aug. 21, 1937**
4. C. K. Coltrane, Casper, Jan. 16, 1949
5. Edward Archer, USFS, Sept. 7, 1950
6. Michael T. Sullivan, Cheyenne, March 13, 1952
7. Elsie Christensen, Weston County, Oct. 23, 1952
8. Floyd L. Travis, Campbell County, July 24, 1960
9. Ike Roberts, Rock Springs, Sept. 15, 1962
10. Galen M. Northrop, BLM, Aug. 14, 1969
11. Wayne A. Garkie, Sept. 3, 1969
12. David L. Stoudt, Avery Aviation, Sept. 3, 1969
13. John E. Bastian, Aug. 18, 1970
14. James R. Elgin, Aug. 18, 1970
15. Robert C. Moore, Cody, May 20, 1974
16. Kenneth D. Double, Warren AFB, July 21, 1976
17. Cecil Lynch, Jackson, Aug. 8, 1980
18. Gene Ahrendt, Sept. 3, 1983
19. Douglas Cuzzort, Bighorn Airways, Sept. 3, 1983
20. Steven L. Huitt, Warren AFB, April 21, 1988
21. Darrell D. Staley, Evanston, July 4, 1988
22. Merrin Rodgers, BLM, Aug. 19, 1988
23. Donald Kuykendall, USFS, Sept. 11, 1988
24. Edward L. Hutton, BLM, Oct. 11, 1988
25. Alan L. Mickelson, Gillette, Jan. 31, 1989
26. James E. Dame, Natrona County, March 7, 1991
27. Wilbert Hansen, Laramie, Nov. 11, 1993
28. Bruce Honstain, Powell, Sept. 10, 1996
29. James Burnett, Aug. 11, 2000
30. Roger "Bo" Rathbun, Crook County, Nov. 8, 2000
31. Anndee Huber, Newcastle, May 22, 2003
32. Robert Henderson, Evanston, April 18, 2005
33. Jacob Cook, Evanston, April 18, 2005

Names listed on the Firefighters Memorial, Wyoming Fire Academy, Riverton. The memorial was dedicated in 1990.

**15 died in the Blackwater fire in Park County on Aug. 21, 1937--12 from the Civilian Conservation Corps. They were: William Whitlock, Will C. Griffith, Rubin D. Sherry, John B. Gerdes, Earnest Seelke, Ambrocio Garza, Mack T. Mayabb, George Rodgers, Roy Bevens, Clyde Allen, James Saban, Paul E. Tyrrell. Killed in the same incident were Billy Lea (BLM), Rex A. Hale, (USFS), and Alfred G. Clayton (USFS)*

Civilian Fire Deaths in Wyoming*

1991:	12	1993:	6	1995:	3
1992:	3	1994:	5		

Source: Wyoming State Fire Marshal's office

Forest Fires

1. Shoshone National Forest (Aug. 21, 1937)

Fifteen men died in this forest fire 36 miles west of Cody along the North Fork of the Shoshone River. The victims included forest ranger Alfred G. Clayton and ten members of the CCC. The men were fighting the forest fire when it unexpectedly changed direction, trapping them against a sheer cliff. A monument next to the highway, dedicated August 20, 1939, points to the location of the disaster, the second worst fire in Wyoming history in terms of lost lives.

2. Yellowstone National Park (Summer 1988)

The most spectacular fires in Wyoming history were also the most destructive to forest lands. More than a third of the land in the 2.2 million acre national park was charred by flames. Including fires in adjacent areas to the park, more than 1.2 million acres went up in smoke. The fires caused huge smoke clouds which blew east and south across the state, limiting visibility in many areas. The fires received national attention and called into question the National Park Service's controversial "let-burn" policy toward fire caused by natural forces. Casper firefighter Ed Hutton, 25, was killed by a falling tree when he was mopping up the fire near Crandall.

Noteworthy Wyoming Explosions

1. Rock Springs (July 17, 1891; Oct. 29, 1935)

In the summer of 1891, two drunks with rifles fired shots into a barrel of blasting powder next to a powder house containing another 1,200 kegs of the substance and 700 pounds of dynamite. The powder house (and the drunks) disappeared in the blast. Two other men in a nearby building at the time of the explosion also died. In 1935, five young boys, ages 7 to 12, were playing in a vacant lot when one boy shot his .22 rifle into a wooden explosives box. The resulting blast killed all five of them.

2. Cody (December 16, 1964)

An explosion ignited the main natural gas line leading into Cody. The accident killed Art Manorgan, a gas company workman, and left the town without natural gas. The night temperature dropped to -31 degrees and the heavy demands placed on electricity caused blackouts. The date is remembered as the "night Cody froze."

3. Cheyenne

On June 8, 1992, an explosion rocked the Frontier Refinery in Cheyenne. In the blast and fire, one workman was killed and six others were injured.

4. Cody

In February 1996, a natural gas explosion demolished an apartment house in Cody. Eleven people were injured when gas, leaking from a cracked gas line under the building, ignited.

5. Douglas

Two downtown Douglas buildings were demolished and third condemned for structural damage after a natural gas explosion April 1, 1996. No one was injured in the explosion that leveled a sheet metal company and damaged the Converse Hotel.

During the Great Depression when unemployment was more than 25 percent in Wyoming, the legislature in February 1937, debated, but defeated an act that would have required all working wives to be fired so that men could get those jobs..

FLOODS

1. Bitter Creek, Rock Springs, April 4-5, 1924; July 11, 1937

No deaths or serious injuries resulted but many were left homeless in the 1924 flood caused by a sudden thaw. In 1937, heavy rains filled Killpecker Creek. The next day, a cloudburst caused Bitter Creek to overflow. Crews of volunteers, including CCC boys, built dikes to avoid heavy damage.

2. Clear Creek, Buffalo, August 1895; June 11, 1912

The 1895 flood swept away the city hall. The entire business district was swamped in the 1912 flood caused by a sudden cloudburst that hit just after supper. The current was so strong that the concrete bridge crossing the creek was washed out. A jeweler's bench was seen floating in the street "with a diamond ring sitting undisturbed on it." An area cowboy panicked when he saw a form floating past him. Through quick thinking and skill from roundups, he was able to lasso the figure. To his surprise, he had rescued a clothing store mannequin.

3. Gillette flood, 1912

The "Burlington ditch" running through town overflowed its banks, flooding several downtown businesses. The Daly Brothers' store, the oldest business in Gillette, suffered the loss of $1,200 in damaged prunes. The firm sued, collecting $1,000. They redried the prunes and resold them.

4. Sheridan flood, September 1923

More than six inches of rain fell in three days, putting Main Street under a foot of water and washing out telephone and power lines. The bridge over Powder River at Arvada was washed out.

5. Thermopolis flood, July 20-27, 1923

Hot Springs State Park and much of the town was flooded by rains from a huge storm. On July 25, the Big Horn River was reported to have risen three feet higher than at any time in the previous 30 years. Two people were drowned.

6. New Fork Dam flood, late 1920s

The Sublette County dam went out early one morning. According to an observer, the water was "probably three feet high just rolling along about a mile wide." Cattle and horses were lost and ranches damaged.

7. Powder River, 1890s

Joe Davis of Gillette told a WPA interviewer in 1936 about the flood: "When the ice was breaking up in the river, a flood came in the night. We were awakened by a huge chunk of ice bumping against the house." Swift-flowing water was more than three feet high and area ranch buildings were damaged.

8. Garden Creek flood, Casper Mountain, 1906.

In the spring of 1906, a heavy rain caused the normally placid stream to become a raging river. Water came down the creek in a wall eight feet high.

9. Gros Ventre earth slide and flood, 1925 and 1927

The earth slide on June 23, 1925, caused a natural dam which then burst on May 18, 1927, wiping out the town of Kelly and drowning eight residents. A 75-ton steel bridge was carried 1/4 mile downstream by the force of raging waters.

Louis "Copenhagen" Corish, a Cody area rancher, had a problem in the spring of 1932 when flood waters kept him from shopping for supplies in Cody. He ran out of "snoose." Not to be deprived, he called Cody pilot Bill Monday who made an emergency air drop of several cans tied in a bundle. As the newspaper reported, "He retrieved it from a sagebrush....and went on a solitary chewing binge."

10. Midwest-Edgerton, 1926

The Fourth of July flood washed out five houses at "Canadian camp," along with a highway bridge and a railway bridge. High waters put the Midwest Oil Company's field out of commission for days.

11. Cheyenne floods, 1883, 1896, 1904, 1985

A June rainstorm in 1883 carried away stores close to Crow Creek. In July 1896, the creek overflowed from 4 1/2 inches of rain falling in less than three hours. In 1904, a 25-foot-high wall of water carried away two children. The 1985 flood was the most costly. Twelve people died and 70 injured. Before the flood, a state record 6.06 inches of rain fell in three hours, 3 1/2 inches from 7-8 p.m.

12. Antelope Coal Mine flood, June 14, 1965

The mine, 55 miles north of Douglas, was opened on state land in 1931. Production was fairly small as it was a one-person operation and called Best Coal Company, in later years. On June 14, 1965, at about 11 p.m., a 60-foot wall of rushing water filled the mine pit and washed away nearby buildings. Mine owner Kenneth Brannan died in the flood.

13. Kaycee, August 27, 2002

A four-foot wall of water swept down the Middle Fork of Powder River and through the town. A total of 52 structures were made uninhabitable, including 19 trailer houses, 22 houses and 12 of the town's 15 businesses. Following the flood, the Kaycee Flood Prevention Project was organized to provide flood protection to the 239 residents of the town.

14. Floods along Wind, Popo Agie, North Platte, Laramie Rivers, June 12-21, 2010

Heavy spring rains added to extensive run-off to swell the Little Wind River and Popo Agie River to the highest levels in memory. Numerous homes and businesses were damaged by the flood and at least one important bridge was swept out. Elsewhere in Wyoming, water levels hit record highs. The Laramie River overflowed its banks in Laramie and flooded the greenbelt walkway and homes and businesses on the West Side. Saratoga homes and businesses were flooded by the North Platte and water levels filled reservoirs all along the North Platte system in Wyoming.

Reunion of Two Brothers

The covered wagons were stopped at the Green River, near the present site of the town of Green River sometime in the 1840s or 1850s. The ferry boat to take the wagons across the river had washed out a day or two before and the travelers had to camp there until the new one was put in place.

One afternoon, a group of Indians came into camp. They told of a white man that was "very sick" at their camp some miles up the Green River. They were uncertain how to treat the man so they asked if the travelers would help.

John Baker and several others went with the Indians back to their camp where they found the white man delirious and unable to talk or move. After a while, Baker and two other men elected to stay until the man was well enough to proceed on his own. Baker said he could catch up to the wagon train within a few days.

A while later, the sick man began to improve. He was able to move a bit and, finally, to talk. Baker asked the man his name and where he was from. The answer came as a shock. The sick man turned out to be Baker's brother, Jim Baker, a mountain man who had lost contact with his eastern family many years earlier.

John Baker didn't return to the wagon train. Instead, he joined his brother in the fur-trapping business and later became his partner in a cattle ranch on the Snake River near present-day Baggs, Wyoming. He never did see Oregon.

FOOD

1st flour mill in Wyoming: Said to be a mill built at the mouth of Wolf Creek Canyon in Sheridan County by Tim Hersey

1st cannery in the Big Horn Basin: Big Horn Canning Company opened at Cowley in 1926, canning 5,600 cases of canned vegetables in the first season. The firm ventured into quick-frozen foods in 1946.

Boiling temperature of water at Laramie: 198 degrees F. Water at sea level boils at 212 degrees F., but at 7,200 feet (Laramie's elevation), the boiling temperature is lower. Consequently, cooks suggest that to make good cake and breads, one should add flour, cut back on yeast and sugar and increase the oven temperature.

Memorable Meals

1. Duncan Hines' "best meal"*

In July 1899, Hines was hired to take a Wells Fargo wagon to Cheyenne from Denver. The 19-year-old Kentuckian became lost along the way and went two days without food. When he finally reached Cheyenne, it was the Fourth of July. He went to Harry Hynds' restaurant and ordered a $5 plate of ham and eggs—a huge meal in those days. Years later, after Hines became famous as a food critic, he recalled the meal as the "best" he had ever eaten. "I have eaten many exotic foods in many expensive restaurants since that day in Cheyenne," he wrote, "but nothing has since tasted as good as that plate of ham and eggs."

The story is told in Hines' autobiography.

2. Tex Eastwood's best meal

Eastwood, a LaBarge pioneer and trapper, was attacked by Indians during the summer of 1878 while trapping. He wandered for 15 days, subsisting on nothing but sagebrush and greasewood. Finally, two other trappers found him and "treated" him to a meal of dried elk meat gruel and a small cup of tea. Until his death in 1894, Eastwood spoke of it as his most memorable meal.

3. Stagecoach passenger on the Overland Trail, 1862

The stage stations served as food stops for stagecoach passengers who would eat while the horses were changed. At one station, the operator cut off a huge slab of greasy salt pork and offered it to a cultured gentleman. "I never eat that. Do you have something else?" the finicky passenger said. "Well, then, help yourself to the mustard," the station operator replied.

4. Jim Kelsey's potato meal*

Kelsey, a Lovell man, stopped by the home of colorful Crooked Creek settler Frank Sykes to rest and feed his horse. Kelsey had no intention of staying for dinner, having heard that Sykes ate only one thing at a meal, usually fried in rancid bear grease. When Sykes asked him to pull up a chair, Kelsey said he'd have only coffee. "Nonsense," said Sykes, "here, have some potatoes." Kelsey reluctantly agreed to have a small portion. When he finished choking down the grease-coated potatoes, Sykes offered more. "No thanks," Kelsey said, looking up into the barrel of a .45. "Go ahead and finish the whole works," his host said, "because you're going to eat potatoes just like that horse of yours is eating my hay."

Story told in Rosa Vida Bischoff Black, Lovell—Our Pioneer Heritage. (Salt Lake City: Olympus, 1984), p. 225.

5. Gordon Wright's load of snuff*

Wright, who ranched near Laramie in the 1880s, also carried freight to Centennial and the mines in the vicinity. He hauled to the timber company store in Keystone a solid 2,000-lb. load of Copenhagen snuff, "quite a lot of snuff even for Scandinavian timber workers who could also handle a lot of liquor." *Story told in Burns, Gillespie and Richardson, Wyoming's Pioneer Ranches. (Laramie, 1952).*

6. FDR's Antelope Steaks

When President Franklin D. Roosevelt traveled through southern Wyoming in September, 1935, he was presented with packages of antelope steaks at Cheyenne. When his train arrived in Green River, he received another package of antelope steaks. Later in the day, at Evanston, local officials also presented him with a gift representative of the area-- more antelope steaks!

7. Fort Laramie dinner, supper, breakfast....

The supply train to the fort was late in 1849. By the time it arrived, the 58 men and five officers had been reduced to eating wild onions and water cress for every meal. Almost two decades later, the conditions at the post had improved considerably. An inventory taken in August 1868 showed a store of 282 bottles of whiskey, two barrels of beer, 72 quart bottles of brandy, 231 bottles of sherry and 27 quarts of port.

8. Mrs. Holm's ham sandwiches

In the 1906 Cody Stampede Days parade, Mrs. Tex Holm rode on a float. She depicted a woman making ham sandwiches. From time to time, she would toss a sandwich to the parade watchers. It was said to have been one of the most popular floats ever to appear in the annual Fourth of July parade.

9. Abner Luman's pancakes

Upper Green River valley pioneer rancher Abner Luman stopped at a cow camp. The cowboys had run off cattlemen but Luman made up his mind it wouldn't happen to him. The cowboys told him he could stay with them but he had to do the cooking. The first night the cowboys put Luman's socks into the sourdough jug. The next morning he couldn't find his socks so he wore his boots without them. When he went to make the pancakes, he found the socks in the dough, fished them out and scrapped off the dough. He then made the hotcakes as the cowboys watched, confining themselves to coffee that morning! *Source: Phyllis Luman Metal, Cattle King on the Green River. (Wilson: Sunshine Ranch, 1983), p. 131.*

2 Unusual Wyoming Recipes

1. Calamity Jane's 20-Year Cake*

25 eggs, beaten separate	2 1/2 lbs. butter	pint of brandy
2 1/2 lbs. sugar	2 oz. mace	1/4 oz. cloves
2 1/2 lbs. flour	2 oz. nutmeg	1/2 oz. cinnamon
7 1/2 lbs. seeded raisins	1 tsp. yeast powder or 2 tsps. soda and	
1 1/2 lbs. citron cut fine	3 tsps. cream of tartar	5 lbs. currants

Bake the cakes and pour the pint of brandy over them while they are still warm. Seal in a tight crock. Makes three cakes, each weighing eight pounds. The cakes should keep for up to 20 years.

*Recipe from Nolie Mumey, Calamity Jane, 1852-1903. (Denver: Range Press, 1950).

2. Cowpuncher's sandwich

One large red onion, sliced

A bowl of equal parts ice water and vinegar

Soak the onion slices overnight in the water-vinegar solution. Drain and put between slices of bread. Presto. A cowpuncher's sandwich.

*"Recipe" given to authors by their grandfather Rulo G. Roberts of Hat Creek, Niobrara County, who ate cowpuncher's sandwiches most of his life. Some recipes mention oregano although he never used the spice in his version.

Winners, 1st Annual Chugwater Chili Cook-off* (1987)

1. Doc's Chili

Made by Dr. Charles Kilgore of Wheatland, the chili won first place in both the taste and the showmanship competition.

2. Amigo Chili

Runner-up in the taste competition, the chili was Cheyenne-made.

3. Tillie's Chili

Runner-up in showmanship, the chili was made by Tillie, the cook at the Diamond Guest Ranch near Chugwater.

*All chili at the event was judged on the basis of aroma, consistency, taste, aftertaste and color. A second chili cooking event, the Overthrust Cook-off in Evanston, was held for the first time in June 1981.

Other Wyoming Food Facts

1. Salad dressings

Betty Havens made and sold "Betty's Salad Dressing" from her shop in Shoshoni.

2. Steak sauces

"Johnny Midnite" Steak Sauce, made in Buffalo, won acclaim at the International Fancy Food and Confection Show in New York in 1991. Called "Johnny Midnite Black Peppercorn Steak Sauce," it was made by Sauce Sensations, Buffalo.

3. Chocolate Fantasy Cookbook

The more than 100 recipes containing chocolate in various forms was collected from patrons at libraries in Cody, Powell and Meeteetse. The book was published by friends of the library in 1994.

4. Chocolates

Meeteetse cowboy Tim Kellogg, during the off-season from rodeoing, began making chocolates using a recipe from his grandmother in 2004. Within a few years, he opened "Meeteetse Chocolatier" in downtown Meeteetse.

5. Honey

In 2010 Wyoming had about 65 bee farms, with about 32,000 hives. About 2 million pounds of honey were produced per year, according to the website Bee Natural run by Dennis Murrell. In 1998, the Wyoming Beekeeper Association.president was Terry Booth, Cheyenne. Gross sales for Wyoming beekeepers $2.6 million in 1996; $1.7 million in 1997.

6. Horse Meat

The price of horse meat in Europe rose to 80 cents a pound in May 1993. In 1989, a good saddle horse could be found for about $500 when horse meat, a delicacy in Europe, was selling for about 35 cents per pound. Sales of the meat are most common in Belgium and France. The minimum price by May 1993 was around $1,000 per horse.

7. Malts

Travelers to the Big Horn Basin from the south may stop at the Yellowstone Drug Store in Shoshoni for one of the "world's best malts." Art and Doris Zube purchased the legendary "Best Malts and Shakes in Wyoming" store on March 1,1977, from Leon Palmer. In 1994, the drug store served 34,624 malts and shakes. The number in 1999 was 64,694. The daily record was said to be 710, set in the early 2000s. In 2007, the store's lease was not renewed by the Odd Fellows' Lodge that owned the Yellowstone Drug building. Pur-

---

Cowboys on the Wyoming range used to use Blue Parrott brand tomatoes from a can as a sunscreen.

chased by Rachael Goff, the business moved a block east and across the street in a modern building. It was reopened in 2008 under the name of Yellowstone Malt Shop.

8. Burgers and Fries

The "Shamrock," a double cheeseburger on french fries, is a specialty of Grub's Drive-in, Rock Springs. In the summer of 1946, the family of Nick "Grub" Skorup opened the diner in order that Nick would not have to go to work in the mines. His only brother died in a coal-mining accident at the age of 14. Skorup, his mother and his nine sisters established the hamburger stand and other family members have worked there and it has remained in continuous operation under family management since. "Grub" Skorup died in 1992, but his son and widow now operate the business along with "Grub's" sister, 84-year-old Manda Tomicich (who, to 1996, had worked in the cafe for 50 years), and "Grub's" cousin Mary Karpan who had worked there for 20 years. Grub's celebrated its 50th anniversary in July, 1996, with a gala celebration attracting some 3,000 people. *Source: Katherine Collins, Casper Star-Tribune, July 10, 1996.*

9. Ice Cream

Wyomingites have local favorite ice cream stores. Many people enjoy stopping at Little America where vanilla twist cones sell for 50 cents each. Originally, in the 1950s, the cost was a nickel, rising to a quarter by the 1980s and 35 cents in the late 1990s. One ice cream store widely known in Wyoming is the Farson Mercantile. The store briefly closed in the mid-"oughts," but reopened in 2008. Many long-time Laramie residents remember purchasing ice cream from the University of Wyoming dairy farm through its outlet store on the UW campus. The store, equipped with a drive-up window, was on Lewis Street, behind the College of Agriculture building. The store also offered cheese and other dairy products, depending on the production from the dairy. The store was closed down in the early 1980s.

2 Most Common Brands of Coffee on the Range (1880s)

1. Lion's coffee

2. Arbuckle's coffee

The Arbuckle brothers, John and Charles, established their coffee company in 1871. The company was the first to sell ground coffee in cans. John (b. 1852, d. 1912) bought a Laramie County ranch with some of the profits.

"...compared to the great region of dry desert land which produces little besides sagebrush, saltbush and cactus. A colony of bees would starve on a million acres of such range. No one has attempted to keep bees in the mountains, as the snowfall is heavier, the winters colder, and the seasons shorter than at lower elevations. While there are many wild flowers it's doubtful if they would yield a surplus."--John Lovell, Honey Plants of North America. (1926, reprinted in 1999)

HATS
Some Famous Wyoming Hats

1. William F. Cody's Stetson
Cody's hat, described by the Stetson Company as "a soft felt sombrero of quite generous proportions," was a size 7 1/8.

2. Wild Bill Hickok's hat
The hat he had on when he was shot and killed in a Deadwood saloon on Aug. 2, 1876, was sent to a close friend, Major John Talbot of Cheyenne, who reported receiving it Aug. 15, 1876. It later was in the Wyoming State Museum.

3. Sitting Bull's hat
The "white sombrero, size 8" was given to the Sioux medicine man by William F. Cody in 1887. A tiny American flag was attached to the hat band.

4. Caspar Collins' cap
Lieutenant Collins gave the cap to Private James B. Williamson, telling him he did not expect to return alive from a mission against the Indians on July 25, 1865. His premonition came true. Williamson kept the cap for the rest of his life.

5. Max J. Meyer's "Ten-Gallon Hats"
Meyer, a New York native, moved to Cheyenne in 1884 and opened a clothing business which he ran for the next 61 years. He invented the "Ten-Gallon Hat."

6. Mike Sullivan's battered Stetson
Gov. Sullivan wore the dilapidated 11-year-old hat during his first campaign for governor in 1986. It became a trademark. "It was at one time a businessman's Stetson," Sullivan once told reporters. "Everybody used to wear one to the legislature. I wore mine fishing, gardening, doing branding work with my friends...it just sort of deteriorated."

7. Little Shield's "fireman's hat"
The Arapaho chief's portrait became the trademark for the Plains Hotel in Cheyenne when the building opened in 1911. In 1966, the hotel was remodeled and the painting was "updated" to match the decor of a firehouse. Consequently, a new portrait of Little Shield was painted, showing the chief in a fire hat. A public uproar ensued and the original painting was rehung in December 1966.

8. "Mr. Ten-Gallon Hat"
A Kemmerer area man was saluted in Ann Landers' column in August 1987, for stopping to assist a stranded motorist. The man did not identify himself to the letter writer who called him "Mr. Ten-Gallon Hat" in her letter of thanks, carried in the nationally syndicated column.

9. Caroline Lockhart's hat
Lockhart, the colorful writer and *Cody Enterprise* editor, wore a hat with a band of two strands of multi-colored beads. She also used a large hat pin to keep it on her head.

10. Sen. E. V. Robertson's "Triple X" beaver hat
Robertson, who operated the Hoodoo Ranch in the Cody area, was U. S. Senator from 1943-49. He wore the Stetson beaver hat for more than 20 years.

11. Daze Bristol's hats
Bristol, a newspaper columnist, was known as the "first lady of Cheyenne Frontier Days." She wore magnificent hats. She died at the age of 105 in 1983.

12. Percy Metz's Stetson
Metz, famed district judge in the Big Horn Basin, always wore a Stetson hat. His biography, written by Vera Saban and published in 1980, is titled *He Wore a Stetson*.

In the early winter of 2004, astronomers at the University of Wyoming discovered a star cluster in the constellation Aquila. They named it the "Cowboy Cluster."

HISTORY

True or False Tales from Wyoming History

"It is better not to know so much than to know so many things that ain't so." --Josh
Billings

1. "Women suffrage stems from Esther Morris' tea party."

As Dr. T. A. Larson, Wyoming's foremost historian, has shown, the alleged tea party, at which Mrs. Morris was purported to have extracted election promises from legislative candidates to introduce the suffrage act, never took place. Morris, had little, if anything to do with the introduction of the suffrage bill. Much of the credit should go to legislator William Bright, possibly his wife Julia, Gov. John A. Campbell and Territorial Secretary Edward M. Lee.

2. "Portugee Phillips rode War Eagle all the way to Fort Laramie."

Phillips indeed made the celebrated ride from Fort Phil Kearny to Fort Laramie in the deep of winter to seek reinforcements for the post after the Fetterman fight. The mythical part relates to his horse. Almost certainly, he did not ride Col. Carrington's prize Kentucky thoroughbred. Even more certainly, he changed mounts at numerous points during the 235-mile ride. He did not ride just one horse the entire distance.

3. "All known copies of Banditti of the Plains were burned."

Copies of the book were neither banned nor burned. According to historian Pat Hall who conducted extensive research on the myth, the confusion resulted from the impounding of issues of the newspaper edited by A. S. Mercer, the *Banditti* author, as a result of debt disputes at the time the serialized version of George Dunning's confession was being published in Mercer's newspaper. The book was not involved in that action nor at any later point. Copies do exist in most libraries.

4. "Butch Cassidy did not die in Bolivia."

Even though Larry Pointer argued in his 1977 study that Cassidy did not die in Bolivia, historians Dan Buck and Anne Meadows disagree. In an article published in *True West* in 1996, the couple provided evidence of Butch's demise in South America. They dismissed William Phillips' claims to being Butch Cassidy as contrary to all evidence.

5. "Sacajawea lived to a ripe old age on the Wind River reservation."

The dispute over Sacajawea's date of death and burial place continue. William Clark's diary indicates that Sacajawea died in what is now South Dakota early in the 19th century when she was still a young woman. On the other hand, Dr. Grace Hebard and others have argued that Sacajawea died in 1884 on the Wind River reservation. Her name at the time was "Porivo." The evidence strongly favors the South Dakota location and Clark's record of her death date.

6. "The Virginian was modeled after my grandfather" [or another of the teller's close relatives]

Owen Wister, author of the book, frequently told reporters that he had no particular person in mind when he described the arch-type Westerner in his 1902 novel. The character, he said, was a composite of many people he had met.

7. "Edison invented the electric light on the shores of Battle Lake."

The myth was perpetuated on the Wyoming highway map and by a historic marker near the lake in Carbon County. The story can not be accurate. Edison did vacation at the site, but when he returned to his Menlo Park, N. J., laboratory, it was more than a year before he came across a substance suitable for a lightbulb filament. The story of his purported "discovery" in Wyoming, where he supposedly watched the ends of a bamboo fishing pole glow when it had fallen into the campfire, was not told until nearly three decades after it was supposed to have occurred. Edison never mentioned such an incident in his lifetime.

8. "Rawlins got the pentitentiary and Laramie got the university because Rawlins had first choice."

Dr. T. A. Larson points out the folly of the suggestion in his *History of Wyoming* (1965), p. 145: "There is no truth in the legend because Laramie had more influence than Rawlins or Evanston."

9. "Chili was invented in Wyoming."

Denver Post columnist Red Fenwick humorously claimed that chili was invented by a Wyoming sheepherder to keep the feet of his sheep dogs warm on cold nights. The sheepherder sent some to a Texas friend who ate it by mistake, "which Texans have been doing ever since." Although there is no evidence favoring Fenwick's claim, neither has it been refuted....

10. "The Medicine Wheel was built by extraterrestrials."

Astronomer John Eddy has shown that the Medicine Wheel is aligned to the position of the rising sun at the time of the summer solstice. Archaeologists view this as additional evidence of the formation of the wheel by prehistoric Indians. Its construction by people from outer space has few proponents.

11. "Winston Churchill narrowly missed being born in Wyoming."

This statement is inaccurate. The only recorded time that Churchill's parents vacationed in Wyoming, at Moreton Frewen's ranch in the Powder River country, they left their 10-year-old son Winston at home in England.

12. "The novel 'The Virginian' was not written by Owen Wister."

When Washakie County historian Paul Frison was a young man in the early 20th century, Basin newspaper editor Tom Daggett was claiming he had given much of the story to Wister with only two strings attached: that the book be called "The Virginian" in honor of a long-dead fiance from that state and that Wister write a plausible conclusion to newly completed story. Daggett's claim, however, cannot be confirmed.

Wyoming History Newspaper Columns

1. In Old Wyoming by John Charles Thompson

The column began in the *Wyoming State Tribune* on July 28, 1938. The last column was published July 14, 1950. Thompson, the long-time editor of the *Tribune*, also served on the state landmarks commission. During his long career in Wyoming journalism, Thompson had covered many of the stories which became a part of the state's history. For instance, he wrote an eyewitness account of the execution of Tom Horn. Thompson died Feb. 7, 1952.

2. Ye 'Good Old Days' by W. S. Kimball

The column was written by the Casper pioneer editor in the 1940s and appeared as a regular, popular feature in the *Casper Tribune-Herald*. Kimball's daughter, Edness Kimball Wilkins, served in the Wyoming legislature for many years.

3. Wyoming--From the Archives by Lola Homsher and others

The column, syndicated by the Wyoming State Archives and Historical Department, ran in numerous Wyoming newspapers in the 1950s and 1960s. Homsher was the first director of the department and an organizer of the Wyoming State Historical Society. She died in Arizona in 1986.

4. Buffalo Bones: Stories from Wyoming's Past by Phil Roberts and others

The column, syndicated by the Wyoming State Archives, Museums and Historical Department, first appeared in July, 1978, with a feature on the life of mountainman John

Hoback. The last column in the series was published in July, 1994, although it was revived briefly in 1991. Columns were compiled into four books. Burton Thompson, the son of John Charles Thompson (above), furnished the name for the column. A former Associated Press reporter, Burton Thompson was then editor of *Credit/Edit*, a publication of the State Examiner's office.

5. Other history columns

Numerous history columns produced by the staffs of local museums are published by Wyoming newspapers. Larry Brown, a volunteer in the State Museum, frequently produces history columns for the *Casper Star-Tribune*. Others include regularly appearing columns in the *Thermopolis Independent-Record, Newcastle Newsletter Journal* and *Weston County Gazette*, among others. Many papers also run columns which include extracts from past issues over the years. The *Lusk Herald* and *Buffalo Bulletin*, among others, regularly run these columns. Eleven newspapers in Wyoming published a column based on the contents of this book from 1992-1999. The column also was called *Wyoming Almanac*.

4 Wyoming History Publications

1. Bits and Pieces

The quarterly magazine of history was published for many years by Wyoming historian Mabel Brown of Newcastle. The magazine contained articles about the history of Wyoming and the Black Hills area of South Dakota.

2. Wind River Mountaineer

The journal, initially published in conjunction with the Pioneer Museum, Lander, was edited by Tom Bell. Later, Loren Jost, director of the Riverton Museum, became editor. The quarterly focuses on Fremont County history.

3. Annals of Wyoming/The Wyoming History Journal

Published by the Wyoming State Historical Society, the journal began in the 1890s as the *Miscellanies*, published by a state agency. The modern *Annals* dates from 1923. In 1995, Dr. Celeste Colgan, director of the State Department of Commerce, (formerly the Wyoming State Archives and Historical Department), evicted the State Historical Society from state offices. The society began publishing its own journal, *Wyoming History Journal*, with a volunteer staff. Colgan claimed the *Annals* still belonged to the State, but the journal wasn't published for the next year. Colgan resigned to accept a position with Halliburton in Texas in the spring of 1996. In the summer of 1996, the society and the Department of Commerce agreed to merge the two journals under the society's direction. Rick Ewig and Phil Roberts, founders of the *Journal*, became co-editors of the newly constituted *Annals*. From 1997-2003, it was edited by Phil Roberts, UW history professor. From 2003 to 2010, the editor was Rick Ewig, associate director of the University of Wyoming's American Heritage Center. .

4. Wyoming History News

The newsletter of the Wyoming State Historical Society was edited by Loren Jost for more than a decade. Later, Rose Wagner edited the journal and, in 2007, Linda Fabian, executive director of the Wyoming State Historical Society, assumed the editorial duties. The newsletter, along with Annals of Wyoming, is a benefit of membership in the Wyoming State Historical Society.

When S. D. Perry, the founding publisher of the *Gillette News*, first came to Gillette in 1904, he rode in an emigrant car on the train. With him was his printing equipment and one pig. Why the pig? In order to "qualify" for travel in an emigrant car, he had to be traveling with at least one farm animal in his possession.

The 10 Most Significant Events in Wyoming History

According to historians Randy Adams and Craig Sodaro, authors of Frontier Spirit: The Story of Wyoming. (Boulder: Johnson Books, 1986), a textbook used in many Wyoming schools. They compiled the following list for a series of programs sponsored by the Wyoming Council for the Humanities in 1988.

1. Discovery of South Pass (1812)

The Robert Stuart expedition, returning from the Pacific Coast, came through South Pass, the gentlest break in the Continental Divide. The discovery, although not immediately exploited, did lead to Oregon Trail migration through the state.

2. Construction of the transcontinental railroad (1867-1869)

The railroad brought the first large permanent population to the state and caused the establishment of most of the towns along the southern tier of counties, including Cheyenne, Laramie, Rawlins, Green River and Evanston

3. Women's suffrage (1869)

When Gov. John A. Campbell signed the bill on Dec. 10, 1869, giving Wyoming women the right to vote, the state became the first in the nation to give women the franchise. From this act, the state gained its nickname, the "Equality State," as well as international fame.

4. Minerals boom (intermittently from the 1950s-1983)

Mineral exploration and exploitation brought rapid population growth and great wealth to the state. The severance taxes assessed on such minerals have underwritten construction of many public schools and civic structures. With the development, however, came adverse changes such as increases in crime, domestic violence and environmental degradation.

5. Indian wars (1840s-1890)

The U. S. Army purchased Fort Laramie in 1849 to protect travelers along the Oregon Trail. Later, other posts were established along the Cherokee (Overland) Trail, along with the railroad right-of-way and north along the Bozeman Trail into Montana. Army operations against native tribes led to numerous clashes.

6. Fur trade (1807-1840s)

Fur trappers and traders were the first permanent white residents in Wyoming. The first rendezvous of fur trappers was held in Wyoming near Daniel on July 1, 1824, some 17 years after John Colter first entered the state to trade with Crow Indians for his boss, Manuel Lisa.

7. Discovery and establishment of Yellowstone National Park (1872)

The park's wonders were known to prehistoric Indians and to early fur trappers. Not until the Hayden expedition of 1871 returned East with stories of its grandeur did the area become nationally renowned. The photographs of William Henry Jackson and the spectacular paintings of Thomas Moran helped convince Congress to set aside the area as the nation's first national park.

8. Statehood (July 10, 1890)

The population was below the normal standard for admission to statehood. Besides, not everyone in Congress believed any state should be admitted which had given women the right to vote. Despite the obstacles, a constitutional convention met in 1889 and in 25 days, drew up the state's constitution. President Benjamin Harrison signed the bill on July 10, 1890, making Wyoming the 44th state.

On Aug. 25, 1995, Hillside Geyser, located near West Thumb Geyser Basin, erupted for the first time in 40 years. Castle Geyser is probably the Park's oldest--4000 years old.

9. Development of the cattle industry (1830s-1887)

Much of Wyoming was settled by cattlemen who brought herds north from Texas or east from Oregon in the heyday of the cattle barons. Despite the great blizzard of 1886-87 which decimated the herds and threw foreign-owned firms into bankruptcy, the cattle industry remained the state's main industry for a century, only recently overtaken by mining and tourism.

10. Johnson County War (April 1892)

It is the oft-told story of out-of-state gunmen hired by owners of large ranches and sent to Johnson County to liquidate the small ranchers. A century later, the incident remains controversial.

Phil Roberts' 17 Most Significant Events in Wyoming in the 20th Century*

1. First motion picture made in Wyoming, Rock River (1904)
2. Devils Tower National Monument established (1906)
3. First paved highway in Wyoming opened, north of Casper (c. 1915)
4. Prohibition began, law enforcement modernized as result (June 30, 1919)
5. Colorado River Compact negotiated (1922)
6. Largest gasoline-producing refinery in the world opened at Casper (1922)
7. 25 Wyoming banks failed, Depression deepened statewide (1924)
8. Bucking horse symbol added to Wyoming license plates (1935)
9. First community college in Wyoming opened, Casper College (1945)
10. UW football team invited to Gator Bowl; beginning of "big-time" sports (1951)
11. School district consolidation continued (1950s)
12. First television broadcast made in Wyoming (March 21, 1954)
13. Atlas missiles placed in Wyoming silos (1958)
14. Severance tax passed on minerals (1969)
15. State minimum wage set at $1.60 per hour; same level 28 years later (1972)
16. For first time, Wyoming gained less from federal funds than paid in (1977)
17. Wyoming led the nation in coal production (1988)

* Some items aren't important in themselves, but represent the beginning of a trend or industry that became important. List is by year, not significance.

Two Yoder area people were driving down a country road in Prohibition-era Goshen County when the passenger told the driver to stop the car. He pointed toward the ditch. "There's Grant Jepson's teeth." Jepson was happy to have them when his dentures were returned. He apparently had lost them en route home from a dance the previous Saturday night and, because of overindulgence or "bad hooch," he hadn't noticed they were missing. He must have had a pretty distinctive smile for his dentures to be recognized in a dtich from a moving car. *Source: Wrinklebelly. By Sally Vanderpoel. (Casper, 1999).*

George Bird Grinnell: A Profile

George Bird Grinnell was a young student at Yale when he first visited Wyoming in 1870. He came West with the expedition that discovered dinosaur fossils at Como Bluff near present-day Medicine Bow.

Grinnell, impressed by the vastness of the land and the plentiful supply of big game, returned to hunt elk. In 1882, he and a partner bought a ranch in Shirley Basin where they raised livestock—mostly horses. He left the daily ranch management in the hands of his partner, however, making only occasion visits to oversee the operations. During those visits, he gathered material for a book he wrote about area Indians. The book was published as *The Fighting Cheyennes*. He retained an interest in gathering fossils, too, but his career was taking him far from the hills of northern Carbon County.

In 1886, he was editing the national magazine known as *Forest and Stream*. (The magazine was later renamed *Field and Stream*.) In the same year, he helped found the Aububon Society.

Following the disastrous winter of 1886-87, in which his ranch partnership lost hundreds of cattle, Grinnell had little reason to maintain an interest in the Wyoming property. At some point in the decade, he sold out to his partner.

He went on to become nationally known as a proponent for the rights of Native Americans. His work in natural resources gained him the nickname of "father of American conservation." How many of the lessons might he have learned in Wyoming—looking for fossils at Como Bluff and raising horses and cattle in Shirley Basin?

4 Professors of Wyoming History, UW

1. Dr. Grace Raymond Hebard, 1908-1936

Dr. Hebard (b. Clinton, Iowa, 1861) served on the University Board of Trustees in the early 1890s. She taught a course at the university for the first time in 1894, a class in constitutional history. Wyoming history was not offered until 1908.

2. Dr. T. A. Larson, 1938-1976

Dr. Larson (b. Wakefield, Neb., 1910, d. Santa Ana, Calif., Jan. 26, 2001) returned from a year of conducting research in Europe in his specialty, medieval history, and took over the History of Wyoming course. His book, History of Wyoming, is the foremost history of the state. After he retired from 40 years' teaching at UW, he served in the Wyoming legislature from 1977-85.

3. Dr. Robert Righter, 1976-1988

Dr. Righter resigned to accept an appointment to the history faculty at the University of Texas at El Paso where his wife, Sherry L. Smith, also had a faculty appointment. They now live in Dallas, Texas, and maintain a summer home in Teton County.

4. Dr. Phil Roberts, 1990-present

One of the authors of this book, Roberts (b. Lusk, 1948) received his Ph.D. in history from the University of Washington. He was the first native of Wyoming ever to serve on the faculty of the Department of History, UW.

When a man named John Thompson was convicted in Gillette in May, 1981, of running over assorted vehicles and causing miscellaneous damage of more than $200,000 with a D-9 Caterpillar tractor, he said to authorities: "If I'd had a four-wheel drive, they'd never caught me." His antics, conducted while intoxicated, inspired the following bumper sticker seen around Gillette in the early 1980s: "When D-9s are outlawed, only outlaws will have D-9s."

WYOMING HOLIDAYS
Schools and State Offices Closed

New Year's Day
*Martin Luther King, Jr., Wyoming Equality Day: third Monday in January (set by legislative act in 1990)
*Washington's and Lincoln's Birthday: observed the third Monday in February
Memorial Day: the last Monday in May
Independence Day
Labor Day: the first Monday in September
*Veterans Day: November 11
Thanksgiving Day: fourth Thursday in November
Christmas Day
Other Days: "Any date appointed or declared by the president of the United States as an occasion of national mourning, rejoicing or observance of national emergency," upon declaration by the governor.
*Schools remain open unless the local school board orders.

Other Significant Holidays

Arbor Day: last Monday in April (requires the state forester to plant a tree on state grounds in a simple ceremony, act originally passed in 1888)
Columbus Day: the second Monday in October (until 1990, it was a state holiday for state employees, but was eliminated when Martin Luther King, Jr., Wyoming Equality Day was designated an official state holiday)
Statehood Day: July 10. Wyoming was admitted to statehood July 10, 1890.
Native American Day: third Friday in September (set by legislative act in 1987)
Nellie Tayloe Ross' Birthday: Nov. 29 (set by legislative act in 1978, the day commemorates the birth of the first woman governor in the United States who was elected Wyoming's chief executive in 1924)
Wyoming Day: Dec. 10 (commemorates the signing of woman suffrage act in 1869 by Gov. John A. Campbell, the first such enactment in the world. The legislature designated the observance in 1935)
"Day of Memorial": In 1990, Gov. Mike Sullivan designated March 11 of that year to honor the memory of the Rev. James Reeb, a former Casper resident who was murdered 25 years earlier following a civil rights march in Selma, Alabama. He was 38. The day after Reeb's death, President Lyndon Johnson proposed the Voting Rights Act as a result of what had happened to Reeb.

28 Events That Happened in Wyoming on the Fourth of July

1. Missionary Marcus Whitman led patriotic prayer service at South Pass en route to Oregon—the first recorded Fourth of July observance in Wyoming **(1835)**

Measuring Water
1 cubic foot = 7.48 gallons (62.4 lbs.)   1 acre-foot= 43,560 cubic feet
1 cubic foot per second= 448.83 gallons per minute or 26,930 gallons per hour.

2. 1st official meeting of Masonic Lodge in Wyoming, Independence Rock (**1862**)

3. The army abandoned Fort Halleck, Carbon County (**1866**)

4. Cheyenne named by Gen. Grenville Dodge (**1867**)

5. First recorded holiday baseball games in Wyoming, South Pass v. Atlantic City; "Wyoming Club" of Fort Sanders beat the Laramie City team 43-26 (**1870**)

6. Bates Battle fought near the Big Horn Mountains between 268 soldiers and Shoshones against about 400 Arapahoes and allies (**1874**)

7. First bicycle in Laramie demonstrated to the curious public (**1876**)

8. General George Crook and staff, hiking in the Big Horns, awoke to find frost covering the ground and ice formed on standing water (**1876**)

9. Six-horse stagecoach robbed one mile inside the north border of Yellowstone on the way to Mammoth (**1887**)

10. English novelist Rudyard Kipling rode into Yellowstone Park in a stagecoach (**1888**)

11. Converse County rodeo rider "Jerky Bill" rode the meanest bronc in the area to a standstill, Glenrock (**1888**)

12. First climb made of Devils Tower, witnessed by 800 people at a picnic below (**1893**)

13. First climb made of Devils Tower by a woman, Mrs. William Rogers (**1895**)

14. Duncan Hines, a Wells Fargo agent (later, a renowned food critic) ate what he described as "most memorable meal" at Harry Hynds' cafe in Cheyenne (**1899**)

15. First automobile made its appearance in Lusk. The driver sold rides for 25 cents. "The chuck-chuck got away with a large and juicy bundle of filthy lucre," the *Lusk Herald* reported (**1906**)

16. The Comet, the first steamboat to operate on the Green River, launched at Green River (**1908**)

17. The first airplane flight in Wyoming, Gillette (**1911**)

18. Buffalo Bill statue by Gertrude Vanderbilt Whitney dedicated in a ceremony, Cody (**1924**)

19. 6,000 people heard performance by Madame Ernestine Schumann-Heink, Wagnerian contralto, Wyoming State Fairgrounds, Douglas (**1924**)

20. A flood near Edgerton washed out five houses at "Canadian camp" as well as a highway bridge and a railroad bridge (**1926**)

21. A pageant of historic events to celebrate the 50th anniversary of Laramie was performed in the field owned by Maggie Couglin, just north of town. Thousands watched, many from cars parked on the brow of the hill just beyond W hill (**1928**)

22. Oregon Trail Centennial celebrated at Independence Rock (**1930**)

23. Artist Thomas Hart Benton attended Saratoga rodeo with student Glen Rounds and told organizers he was *Denver Post* reporter so he could get close to the action. He later painted scenes of the rodeo (**1930**)

24. Lost Springs, the nation's smallest town designated a "Bicentennial Community," celebrated the Fourth and a British Broadcasting Company film crew recorded the event (**1976**)

25. Harry Jackson's statue of Sacajawea unveiled, Cody (**1980**)

26. One-third of an inch of snow fell at Yellowstone Lake (**1983**)

27. Dedication held of reconstruction of "Old Fort Bridger" (**1987**)

28. Snow fell in Laramie, accumulations in nearby mountains (**1993**)

In 1985 the Wyoming legislature finally repealed a law which required any person wanting to open a pool hall in Wyoming to present a petition to the county commission bearing the names of a majority of voters within two miles of the proposed location or he could not open such a business.

HOT SPRINGS
Some Wyoming Hot Springs

1. Saratoga Hot Springs

Fenimore Chatterton, who later was Wyoming governor, surveyed the townsite for Saratoga in 1886. He named the hot springs for the spa in New York. Previously, the place had been called "Warm Springs." Hobo Pool, a main spring in the system, has a water temperature of 118 degrees. In 1911 water from springs was bottled, advertised as "radioactive mineral water" and sold nationally. The State of Wyoming acquired the springs and created the park in 1917. Later, Hobo Pool was deeded to the Town of Saratoga.

2. Douglas Warm Springs

The 86-degree spring is seven miles south of Douglas on the Esterbrook Road. The waters were used by Oregon Trail travelers. In 1926, the spot became a popular bathing area. "Jackalope Plunge" was built there in 1961.

3. Kendall Warm Springs

· The 85-degree water coming from the springs provides the only known habitat for the Kendall Warm Springs dace, a very rare fish species. Barely two inches long when fully grown, the fish spends its entire life in the spring pools. At breeding time, the males are purple and the females are green. The springs are located 26 miles north of Cora in Sublette County.

4. Hot Springs of Thermopolis

The world's largest mineral hot spring and four other springs created "Rainbow Terraces" and two large "teepee" cones. The 133-degree water is used by the state bathhouse and five commercial establishments. The first white report of the springs was made by Dr. Thomas Maghee in 1876 who wrote: "An unfortunate rattlesnake had fallen into the reservoir and was thoroughly cooked." He had visited the springs on August 15, 1874, while accompanying an army group escorting surveyors laying out the boundaries of the Wind River reservation. The springs were obtained from the Shoshone tribe in 1896. An annual pageant, "The Gift of the Waters," commemorates the acquisition.

5. Auburn Hot Springs

The 150-degree water was used for swimming until 1945 when the pool building was destroyed by fire. The commercial facility at the springs, located 2 1/2 miles south of Auburn in Lincoln County, was built in 1946.

6. Alcova Hot Springs

Once a well-known stopping point for bathers, the springs are now covered by Alcova Reservoir.

7. DeMaris Hot Springs

First described by John Colter in 1806-7, the immediate area was dubbed "Colter's Hell" because of the prevalence of springs and geysers. Used for a resort for the first time in 1894, the springs hosted such well-known bathers as John D. Rockefeller. Located two miles west of Cody, the 90-degree springs were named for Charles DeMaris who became the owner of the springs in the early 1880s.

8. "Immigrant's Wash Tub"

John C. Fremont described the 70-degree springs in 1842. Located three miles southwest of Guernsey, across the North Platte River, the site gained its name from Oregon Trail travelers who used the waters for washing trail-soiled clothes.

9. Fort Washakie Hot Springs

Located 3 1/2 miles west of Ethete on the Wind River reservation, the springs had been used by native people for generations. Water temperature remains at a steady 111 degrees. The springs were first reported in the 1830s by Capt. B. L. E. Bonneville. In 1881, President Chester Arthur stopped at the springs en route to Yellowstone. A pool and commercial bathhouse occupied the site for many years, but the facility fell into disrepair and was closed in 1991. The Shoshone tribe authorized $200,000 for renovations in 1995. Soon after, the pool reopened.

10. Astoria Springs

The springs were first reported by the 1872 Hayden expedition. In 1906, a commercial bathhouse was built at the spring which provides 99-degree water. The spring is located 17 miles south of Jackson on U. S. Highway 26.

11. Huckleberry Hot Springs

Known for many years as "Flagg Ranch Hot Springs" for the ranch located 1 1/2 miles to the south, the springs were leased by the Forest Service to various commercial operators. The spring water temperature is 142 degrees as it comes from the ground.

12. Granite Hot Springs

The springs are 26 miles south of Jackson on Highway 189, 12 miles up Granite Creek. The CCC built the pool at the site in 1933. Since 1960, the Forest Service has leased out the 106-degree springs for a fee.

Some Facts Involving Yellowstone Hot Springs

1. DNA From Yellowstone's Hot Springs

DNA, used in countless criminal cases and in wildlife biology "evolved from Yellowstone's geothermal microorganisms," according to Michael Finley, park superintendent. In the 1960s, the discovery of one cigar-shaped microorganism led to the revolutionizing of the study of blood and led to DNA "fingerprinting." That find alone earns a Swiss drug company $100 million annually. The company paid nothing in fees or royalties to Yellowstone.

2. Geothermal Features in the Park

Yellowstone contains 60 percent of the earth's geothermal features. The park has 80 percent of the world's geysers.

3. Bioprospecting Agreements

In 1997, Yellowstone entered into a unique "benefit-sharing" bioprospecting agreement with Diversa Corp. of San Diego under which they would share revenue from park research and pay $35,000 annually for five years in search fees. However, the agreement was challenged almost immediately by the Edmonds Institute, the International Center for Technology Assessment, the Alliance for the Wild Rockies, and a Montana citizen. In April, 2000, U. S. District Judge Royce Lamberth ruled the agreement was proper and did not conflict with the park's mandate.

The "Teepee Fountain" at the entrance to Hot Springs State Park dates from 1907-11 when Jacob Paulus was park superintendent. When a hot water distribution line was laid, it was discovered that with it came heavy back-pressure in the pipes. Consequently, a standpipe was built in a gulch and Paulus had a rock base built to support it. Travertine deposits built up over the years, eventually covering the pipe and the base.

HUMORISTS

1. Jim Bridger, Mountain Man

Bridger once told about finding a petrified forest. He said he tried to jump across a gorge in the forest, but found it was too wide. He claimed he would have fallen to his death had he not been supported "by petrified air."

2. Bill Nye, Newspaperman, 1876-1883

—On summer: "The surprised and indignant agriculturist [can be] caught in the middle of a July day with a terrific fall of snow, so that he is virtually compelled to wear snowshoes all through his haying season."

—On wealth and eccentricity: "I have been thinking the matter over seriously and I have decided if I had my life to live over again, I would like to be an eccentric millionaire. I have eccentricity enough, but I cannot successfully push it without more means."

3. Merris Clark Barrow ("Bill Barlow"), b. Pa., 1857, d. Douglas, 1910

Barrow was founder and publisher of *"Bill Barlow's Budget"* (later, the *Douglas Budget*). He worked for newspapers in Laramie and Rawlins from 1879 to 1885 before setting up his paper in the new town of Douglas in 1886. Barrow also served as Douglas mayor and as a delegate to the Constitutional Convention. He founded a "wit and humor" magazine known as *Sagebrush Philosophy.*

4. Jack Chenery, Riverton editor

Chenery edited the *Riverton Review* and wrote a column called the "Big Bend Bazoo" in the early 1900s. His humor was topical with a local flavor.

5. George R. Caldwell, Lander columnist

From 1886 to 1906, Caldwell's columns appeared in various Wyoming newspapers. He was known as the "lurid liar of Lander."

6. Jack Gage, State Official/Lecturer, b. Neb. 1899, d. 1970

Gage served as state superintendent of public instruction from 1931-1939 and Secretary of State from 1959-1961 when he became acting governor. When he left office in 1963, he began six years on the professional lecture circuit. He once spoke in Cheyenne at a dinner honoring football star Boyd Dowler and the Green Bay Packers. Bill Nation, the mayor of Cheyenne, presented the players with "keys to the city." Gage told them to regard the honor dubiously because "until you boys hit town, we haven't had to lock anything up." He told the graduating class at Cody High School in 1965 that he had graduated "ninth in my class" at Ten Sleep High School. He paused and then added, "Yup. That was a good class—five girls and four boys."

7. Bob Budd, Author/Columnist

Budd, formerly the executive director of the Wyoming Stock Growers Association, wrote a monthly column in *Cow Country*, the association's magazine. Many of the columns were witty looks at how cowboys "struggle against the often-seeming absurdities and miscalculations of this curious lifestyle- business of being a cowboy." Some of his columns were collected and published in a book, *Send Fresh Horses* (1987).

8.-9. Al Simpson, U. S. Senator; Pete Simpson, Professor/Historian

Senator Simpson gained fame in Washington, D. C., for his humorous remarks and clever witticisms. Apparently, it is a family trait because his brother, Dr. Peter K. Simpson, former legislator and former vice president for development at UW, also is well-known as a popular and entertaining speaker. A distinguished professor at UW, Pete Simpson teaches popular courses on Wyoming politics.

The Half Fast Diner was located in downtown Byron.

9. Burton Thompson, editor of Credit/Edit, 1979-1985

A former Associated Press reporter and public relations man, Thompson wrote a popular column in the newsletter of the State Examiners' Office. In it, Thompson often took a humorous look at financial activities in Wyoming, ranging from the "buffalo overshoes" sold by the Fort Bridger post sutler to the odd trade items Indians received under the terms of the Fort Laramie treaties.

10. Sandra Guzzo, Laramie columnist

A columnist for the *Laramie Boomerang* until the late 1990s, she frequently used humor. She wrote *Chickens in the Green House*, a book of columns.

11. Bill Jones, Lander poet

Jones wrote the 1991 book, *There Ain't Much Romance in the Life of Us Cows*. In a poem called "The Mule Ropin' Doctor" about a doctor friend who needed to go to mule-roping school, Jones concluded the poem with these lines: "Another thing we'd tell Doc, (If he should ever ask us), Hang that rope up on a nail, And stick to Family Practice."

12. Doug Hecox

Hecox, a University of Wyoming journalism graduate, worked as a congressional aide and in several federal government agencies. In the 2000s, he performed as a stand-up comic in Washington, D.C., and elsewhere. He writes a regular syndicated humor column appearing in many regional dailies.

Wyoming Columns—Some Extracts

My Mine
By Bill Nye

I located a claim called the Boomerang. I named it after my favorite mule. I call my mule Boomerang because he has such an eccentric orbit and no one can tell just when he will clash with some heavenly body....

Those who have never been wakened from a sweet, sweet dream by the low sad wail of a narrow-gauge mule, so close to the ear that the warm breath of the songster can be felt on the cheek, do not know what it is to be loved by a patient, faithful, dumb animal.

Nye wrote one of the best known resignation letters in Wyoming history when he quit as postmaster of the Laramie post office in 1883. In those days, every postmaster was a political appointee and when the presidency changed from one party standard-bearer to another, all postmasters became patronage casualties.

Nye wrote to the new President: "I beg leave at this time to officially tender my resignation as postmaster of this place and in due form deliver the great seal and the key to the front door. The safe combination is set on the numbers 33, 66 and 99, though I do not remember at this moment which comes first, or how many times you turn the knob..."

He made sure the President was aware of the location of other items important in operating the post office. "You will find the postal cards that have not been used under the distributing table and the coal down in the cellar. If the stove draws too hard, close the damper in the pipe and shut the general delivery window."

After a few other instructions to the President on details of running the office, Nye concluded: "Tears are unavailing. I once more become a private citizen, clothed only with the right to read such postal cards as may be addressed to me personally and to curse the inefficiency of the post office department."

The nationally broadcast program, "Bill Nye, the Science Guy," features the Seattle-based scientist/entertainer who is a distant relative of Laramie's famed 19th century editor, Bill Nye.

Decisions, Decisions
By Sandra E. Guzzo (From "Chickens in the Greenhouse")

At first, I thought it was the Wyoming high altitude going to my head. I have had this problem lately. I think it's called the toxic indecisiveness syndrome. I find it difficult to use two of the simplest words in the English language—yes and no.

[Her son asks for a new toy].

I paused from folding the bath towels and said in the firmest manner I could muster, "No, you may not!"

His response surprised me.

"Okay," he said. "I just wanted to know."

He's right, my son. He deserved a definite answer. I, too, want to know. I want to know that my decision is the right one. Only it's just not that simple...

—Guzzo, a Laramie resident, wrote a regular column in the Laramie Boomerang. This selection is from her book also titled "Chickens in the Greenhouse."

Blood, Sweat and Tears (A Sports Column)
By David L. Roberts, Medicine Bow Post

First a left, then a right, then another left. The punches flew amidst cheers from the crowd. A left hook was followed by a right jab, followed by a left punch to the nose, followed by a nose bleed.

Then I decided it was time to leave the newspaper office and cover the boxing match at the high school gym.

—David Roberts was founder/publisher of the Medicine Bow Post from 1977-1989 when the paper was given to the University of Wyoming as a workshop publication for students enrolled in the community journalism program. The University closed the newspaper and suspended the program in 1994.

7 Ways to Tell You're Really a Wyoming Native
By "Sagebrush Sven," Buffalo Bulletin

1. You prefer car keys to Q-tips when you clean the wax out of your ears.

2. You took a beer to your last job interview.

3. Six dogs died when the front porch on your house collapsed.

4. The only thing your parakeet can say is, "Open up! Police!"

5. Your stereo speakers came from the Sunset Drive-In Theater.

6. You get a sunburn on a 75-degree day the first part of April and know that you'll probably lose calves in a blizzard two days later.

7. You know the names of four of the best saddle bronc riders in the country, but you don't have a clue who the "Final Four" were.

Alfred W. Lawson, inventor of twin-engine airplanes, told the Wyoming Eagle that he was developing a "super airliner" capable of carrying 100 passengers and traveling at 100 mph. The ten-motor plane would fly non-stop coast-to-coast, transferring passengers by chute to smaller planes in flight for intermediate stops. (March 28, 1926).

INSECTS

1st entomologist in Wyoming: William Wood, Jr., who crossed southern Wyoming with the army expedition led by Lt. F. T. Bryan in July 1856.

1st collector of Wyoming butterflies (specimens still existing): Constantin F. Drexler, who traveled west as a medical orderly (even though he was a taxidermist by training) in 1859-1860.

Modern collecting: A team led by Karolis Bagdonas of the University of Wyoming collected more than 30 species of moths and butterflies in the Absarokas from 1985-87 which previously had not been known in Wyoming.

Insect species named for Wyomingites: Robertomyia lavignei is named for Robert Lavigne, UW professor of plant, soil and insect sciences, who found two previously undescribed "robber flies" while in Somalia from 1985-88. A species, the Ascogaster Shaw, is named for UW entomology professor Scott Shaw.

Insect genus named for Wyomingite: A New South American genus and species of wasp was named for UW entomology professor Scott Shaw in 1993. The scientific name is "Shawius braziliensis." It may be extinct. It is the first insect genus to be named for a University of Wyoming professor.

Grasshopper expert: Robert E. Pfadt (b. Pa., 1915), a retired UW professor, is the acknowledged expert. He wrote *Field Guide to Common Western Grasshoppers*, published in 1988, identifying 75 species of the insect.

Author-collector: Vladimir Nabokov (1899-1977), the author of *Lolita* and 16 other novels, came to Wyoming with his wife in the 1950s to chase butterflies in the Snowy Range. He was an avid collector.

Insect museum: The University of Wyoming Insect Museum was started in 1894 by Prof. Frank Niswander. Harold Gilbert ran the museum from 1930-43. Over the years, the collection grew to more than one million specimens. Scott Shaw was the first permanent curator, hired in 1989.

Flea collection: UW Insect Museum received a large flea collection from J. S. Wiseman in 1955.

Mosquito collection: Dr. William Owen donated his collection to the Insect Museum in 1971.

Large donation of butterfly collection to a Wyoming museum: Maurice L. Howard of Pueblo, Colo., gave his 6,000 butterflies, moths and other various insects to the University of Wyoming in 1991. He had collected the specimens for more than 30 years.

1st extension entomologist in Wyoming: Ted Robb, 1944.

Annual meeting, International Lepidopterist Society: The organization, dedicated to research and interest in butterflies and moths, held its annual meeting in Laramie in 1984.

Two books on influence of insects on history: Jeffrey A. Lockwood, UW, has written *Locust: The Devastating Rise and Mysterious Disppearance of the Insect that Shaped the American Frontier* (2004); and *Six-Legged Soldiers, Using Insects as Weapons of War* (2009).

Noteworthy Early Butterfly Collectors in Wyoming

1. William Wood, Jr.

2. Constantin F. Drexler

3. Several officers with the Wheeler expedition, U. S. Army Corps of Topographic Engineers, late 1860s

The products of their collecting went to W. H. Edwards of Coalburgh, W. Va., for study. He named a number of the previously unknown varieties.

4. Joel Asaph Allen (b. 1838, d., 1921)

Allen collected in Wyoming in 1871. From that year until 1885, he was affiliated with Harvard University. He was appointed curator of mammalogy and ornithology at New York's American Museum of Natural History in 1885.

5. Thomas Luttrell Mead

Mead collected widely in Wyoming after 1871. The son-in-law of William Edwards, he founded the New York Entomological Society and named a number of butterflies.

Source: Clifford D. Ferris and F. Martin Brown, eds. Butterflies of the Rocky Mountain States. (Norman: University of Oklahoma Press, 1981).

Hutton Lake National Wildlife Refuge, 12 miles southwest of Laramie, consists of 1,968 acres. It was set aside on Jan. 28, 1932.

INVENTORS

1st patent issued to a person living in Wyoming: 1867, Anson Mills for an "improvement to the cartridge belt"
Patents Issued to Wyoming residents (to 2010): 4,259
Wyoming inventors holding patents (to 2010): 3,264

Some Wyoming Inventors

1. Anson Mills, Fort Bridger (August 20, 1867)
Mills was a captain stationed at Fort Bridger when he patented an "improvement to the cartridge belt."

2. S.W.Y. Schimonsky, Cheyenne (August 25, 1868)
Schlmonsky lived in Cheyenne when it was still in Dakota Territory on the date that his patent was issued for an improved railroad car-brake.

3. George C. Choate, Wyoming Station (April 12, 1870)
Choate was awarded the first patent issued to a resident of the Territory of Wyoming. The Albany County man patented an improvement in shovel-handles.

4. Frank Freund, Cheyenne (1876-82)
The well-known pioneer gunsmith received 11 patents during the period for innovations on firearms.

5. William Pratt, Fort Laramie (1883)
Pratt invented a "broken-shell extractor" which he patented in June 1883, while he served at Fort Laramie.

6. Alfred A. Lambrigger, Big Horn (1883)
Lambrigger's device, an improved car-brake for railroad cars, was patented less than six months after Pratt's invention.

7. Samuel Benson, Evanston (1883)
Benson's inventions also related to the railroad industry. A "journal-box," the device was patented the same year as Pratt's and Lambrigger's inventions.

8. James Candlish (1880s)
Candlish owned a Rawlins blacksmith shop in the late 19th century. There, he is said to have built the world's first sheepwagon. He held two patents, one for a bridle and another for a bolt cutter, but none for the sheepwagon.

9. James N. Farlow, Lander (Nov. 11, 1890)
Farlow received the first patent issued to a resident of the State of Wyoming. He patented a new and improved friction-wrench.

10. Benjamin Staunton, Douglas (May 26, 1891)
Staunton, a citizen of Great Britain, was the first foreign national living in Wyoming to receive a patent. He gained the patent for a "rotary index and photograph album."

11. Myrtle M. Wallin, Rock Springs (Dec. 25, 1900)
Wallin became the first Wyoming woman to receive a patent. She received it for a "work-holder."

12. J. D. Carmichael, Shoshoni (1907)
Carmichael claimed to have invented a process to make rope from sagebrush. His claim was published by the *Wyoming Industrial Journal,* July, 1907, but there is no evidence that his invention became commercially successful. No patent was issued for the invention.

13. Elmer Lovejoy, Laramie (1918)
Lovejoy invented an automatic door opener, patented in March 1918. He also invented the tracks for mounting the ceiling-type garage door opener, patented in March 1921. Lovejoy was the builder of Wyoming's first car which he drove on Laramie streets in May

1898. He invented other devices, including the steering mechanism still used in today's cars. Unable to afford the $350 costs associated with getting a patent for the idea, he traded the steering mechanism invention to the Locomobile Company for a new car in 1905.

14. Burt C. Buffum, Worland (1908)

Buffum, a University of Wyoming agronomist from 1891-1900, was co-founder of the Rocky Mountain Herbarium on the campus at Laramie. He invented a hulling machine, built mills for flour and breakfast food production and developed beardless black winter wheat from 1908 to 1916 while operating a seed firm at Worland. In 1916, Buffum moved to Denver where he retired from agronomy and inventing three years later.

15. Arthur Gwynn, Lucerne (1915)

Gwynn patented a cattle guard for use on railroad tracks.

16. John D. Pedersen, Jackson (1909-1944)

Pedersen patented nearly 70 inventions from the period 1909 to 1944. Many were innovations on firearms. He still holds the mark as Wyoming's most prolific inventor in respect to patents he held.

17. C. O. Bunten, Rawlins (1924)

The Rawlins dentist invented the "Bullseye BB Launcher" in 1924. The toy had a tubular magazine holding No. 6 lead pellets that could kill flies from 10 feet away but couldn't even break a light bulb or a window. The pistols were assembled in the old Osborne Building in Rawlins. The toy, using rubber bands as "propellant," sold for $2.

18. Andy Matheson, Lander/Shoshoni (1923. 1926)

Matheson invented an "alligator lug picker" that he patented in 1923 and a sugar beet topper, patented three years later. In the late 1920s, Lander businessmen invested in the Matheson Pneumatic Beet Planter Company, according to an article about the company in the *Wind River Mountaineer*, April 23, 1931.

19. Judson E. Gibbs, Rock River (1928)

Gibbs patented an animal heater used to provide heat for survival of newborn or young livestock on the range. A year later, he patented a detonating device which regulated explosive sounds mainly to frighten coyotes from sheep ranges. The patent office called it "a method and means for producing intermittent flares." Examples of both devices are on display at the local museum in Medicine Bow.

20. William Linn Culbertson, Worland (1930)

Culbertson invented a system of raising submerged ships. He was serving in the U. S. Navy at the time the patent was granted.

21. D. H. Inloes and Walter Tanner, Lander (1931)

The two men invented a paring knife, made by a Denver company.

22. Emerson Pugh, Evanston (1940)

Pugh invented and designed large electromagnets. Born in Ogden, Utah, he was reared in Evanston. For many years, he was a professor of engineering at Cal Tech and Carnegie Tech. His autobiography was published in 1979.

23. Daniel D. Love, Saratoga (1944)

Love is one of perhaps thousands of American inventors who patented a "better mousetrap." The patent for his trap was registered on March 7, 1944.

24. Eugene R. Anderson (1947)

The then 21-year-old chemistry teacher at Superior in February 1947, claimed to have

Top 10 Assignees for Wyoming Patents, 1867 – 2003	
1. Standard Oil Company, 49	6.-7. Marathon Oil Company, 15
2. General Electric, 36	6.-7. Atlantic Richfield, 15
3. Brunton Company, 27	8. Foresight Industries, 14
4. FMC Corporation, 26	9. Western Research Institute, 13
5. University of Wyoming, 23	10. Woodworker's Supply Inc., 12

invented an internal combustion engine which would run on water. There is no record that he patented such a device.

25. Frank B. Odasz, Jr. (1960, 1961, 1962)

Odasz filed four patents for rubberized blown asphalt. Three of the four patents were jointly filed with a Canadian co-inventor and the invention was assigned to Husky Oil Company.

26. William R. Van Deburg, Jackson (1965)

He invented a steam-cleaning apparatus, the patent for which was registered on May 25, 1965.

27. Norman J. Hayes, Cody (1967-1991)

Hayes was granted 16 patents during the period, most involving identification tags for livestock animals.

28. Thomas E. Osborne (1960s)

Osborne, a native of Meeteetse, invented the first commercial desktop electronic calculator, marketed by Hewlett-Packard in the 1960s. A 1957 University of Wyoming graduate, Osborne held more than 60 patents.

29. Bruce Wampler (1981)

Wampler, a 1970 graduate of Kelly Walsh High School in Casper, first developed the computer program, Grammatik, in 1981. It was later bought by Wang Labs. Later, he formed a new company and developed Grammatik 3 which checked subject, verb agreement and parts of speech. In 1992 his company was sold to WordPerfect for $19 million. Following the sale, Wampler taught at the University of New Mexico and wrote about computer programming.

30. Corri Anne Rabidue, Rock River (1988)

Rabidue was one of 19 elemenary school *Weekly Reader* National Invention contest winners in 1988. She invented a safety lock faucet to prevent injuries from hot water.

31. Fred Hopkin, Lovell (1989)

Hopkin invented a device that will automatically feed calves and lambs by dispensing milk into a pipe from which the young animals can suck it through rubber nipples. The inventor claimed to have first thought of the invention in 1976 while selling feeders in California.

32. Randy Lewis, Laramie (1989)

Lewis, a molecular biologist, worked with a team of University of Wyoming researchers. They isolated a gene from a spider gland that makes silk. They also found a second protein required to make the silk. The silk is waterproof, five times stronger than steel and twice as elastic as nylon, able to stretch up to 130 percent of its length. *Discovery* magazine featured the research in May 1992. As of 2008, Lewis held six patents.

33. Mark Hunter, Afton (1989)

Hunter designed and built the "Vision Clip," a high-tech clipboard which can be wiped clean with an attached magnetic eraser. The device is used by highway patrolmen and even by NBA coaches, including Jerry Sloan of the Utah Jazz who diagrammed plays using the clipboard in the 1990s.

34. Larry Goddard, Torrington (Oct. 22, 1991)

Goddard, a Torrington optometrist, invented a device that can be attached to an eye drop bottle for people having trouble using eye drops.

35. Russ Huson (1992)

Huson, a 1954 graduate of Johnson County High School, is an expert on super-conductivity. He invented a device to make trains travel at 300 miles per hour by levitating them by giant magnets a few inches above the tracks. Also, he has invented improved MRI equipment which will make scans of the entire body in a matter of seconds. Huson retired in January 1992, as director of the Texas Accelerator Center.

36. Lee Christiansen, Meeteetse (1992)

Christiansen invented a machine that lets people know when and what pills they need to take. When it is time for the pills to be taken, they fall from their container to a small drawer and an alarm sounds, continuing until the person takes the pills out of the drawer.

37. Ronald Ericsson, Gillette (1990s)

The inventor of a process to help ranchers pick the sex of livestock, he also has invented a male birth control pill and an at-home male fertility test. Born in South Dakota, Ericsson has lived since the 1970s on a 17,000-acre ranch in Crook County.

38. John Frederick Ackerman, Cheyenne (1985-2001)

Ackerman was either sole patent holder or joint holder with others on at least 24 devices, many assigned to General Electric.

39. Leon Hirsch, Sublette County (1990s)

Like Ericsson, Hirsch owns property and lives in Wyoming. He invented the surgical staple years earlier while living in another state. He was a founder and CEO of U. S. Surgical.

40. Vern Gilbert, Kaycee (June 29, 1993)

Gilbert invented and patented a fluid filter.

41. Ron Schlagle, Torrington (1995)

Schlagle designed a machine allowing farmers to till the soil and make planting rows in one pass instead of two. He began producing the machines with manufacturer Harold Weis in 1995.

42. Edmond A. Cook, Lusk (2005, 2006)

Cook patented a vertically and horizontally swinging gate, filing two patents on aspects of the invention.

43. G. F. Williamson, Laramie (April 27, 2010)

Williamson received a patent for a system of burial in vertical positions as a means of increasing the capacity in crowded cemeteries.

Other Wyoming Inventions:

Numerous Wyomingites have either patented devices or participated in their design and invention. The above list, like other lists in this book, is merely a sample and is not meant to be inclusive.

Researchers in the University of Wyoming Department of Electrical Engineering invented the world's first working digital hearing-aid in 1983. Two years later, department researchers invented the first such device using a microprocessor.

Two Teton County men, Richard C. Greig and Frank Werner, hold numerous patents for improvements on golf clubs and equipment.

Many early-day Wyoming "inventors" never formally filed applications for protection of their inventions. Among them was Isaac Tippetts of Lovell who invented such devices as apple pickers and sugar beet loaders.

Top 6 Wyoming Patent-holders*

1. John D. Pedersen, Jackson, 68 patents.
2. Robert F. Deike, Cheyenne, 32 patents.
3. Frank D. Werner, Jackson, 26 patents.
4. John Frederick Ackerman, Cheyenne, 24 patents.
5. Chang Yul Cha, Laramie, 20 patents.
6. Joan D. Sherida, Cheyenne, 20 patents.

Source: Wyoming Inventors Database compiled by the Wyoming State Library, http://cowgirl.state.wy.us/inventors

LABOR

1st organized labor union in Wyoming: Knights of Labor organized in the coal mines at Carbon and Rock Springs in 1871.
1st labor strike in Wyoming: By miners at Rock Springs and Carbon in 1871, after coal operators decided to unilaterally cut pay. The strike did not succeed. The companies, with the help of federal troops from Fort Steele who set up camps in both cities, fired the striking workers and replaced them, mostly with immigrant labor including Chinese.
1st Wyoming Miners' Hospital: Rock Springs, the first building was destroyed by fire on Jan. 4, 1897.
1st mob violence against Asian workers: On Sept. 2, 1885, 28 Chinese were killed by white miners. The incident, known variously as the "Rock Springs massacre" and "Chinese massacre," was precipitated by company policies designed to break up labor organizing efforts
Largest union membership in proportion to industrial population: Wyoming in 1940 led the nation. The state had 200 locals with nearly 15,000--half were railroad employees or coal miners.
Total non-farm employment in Wyoming (2007): 215,615
Number of Wyomingites working for state and local government (2008): 59,238, of these 52 percent (30,986) were in education.
Basic minimum wage: $5.15 per hour tied with Georgia for the lowest hourly minimum wage in the nation (2010)
Personal income per capita in Wyoming (2009) was $45,275, ranking the state at 6th per capita among the states. In 1994, it was $20,436 and Wyoming ranked 27th among the states in per capita income.
Wyomingites living below the poverty line (2008): 9.5%, compared to national average of 13.2% In 1993, the rate in Wyoming was 13 percent of the population living below the poverty line, 25th per capita.

Significant Labor Strikes in Wyoming before 1940

1. Brotherhood of Locomotive Engineers, Laramie (1869)
According to labor historians, the first strike in Wyoming occurred in 1869 at Laramie by the Brotherhood of Locomotive Engineers.
2. Union Pacific miners' strike (1871)
The strike failed. All strikers were fired and replaced with Scandinavians at reduced wages.
3. Rock Springs miners (1875)
Strike against the Union Pacific for increase of wages from $1 to $1.25 per ton of coal mined. More than 500 miners were involved. The strike failed and Chinese miners replaced the strikers.
4. Rock Springs massacre (1885)
The incident in which 28 Chinese died was sparked by a labor strike during which many of the strikers were replaced by Chinese. On Sept. 2, 1885, a fight broke out in the mines over who should be mining a specific area. Mine officials closed for the day, but miners adjourned to the bars. Some white miners, mostly immigrants themselves, raised a mob that viciously attacked Chinese rather than considering the source of tlabor problem.
5. Switchmen (1888, 1890)
The 1888 strike in Cheyenne succeeded but the Rawlins strike two years later failed.
6. Railroad laborers, Gillette (1892)
Laborers went on strike to increase pay from $1.75 to $2 per day. The strike was successful.

On Oct. 14, 2008, Gov. Dave Freudenthal, UW President Tom Buchanan and GE executives signed an agreement to build a $100 million High Plains Gasification Advanced Technology Center in Wyoming. Both GE and the State agreed to contribute $50 million to the project.

7. Sheepshearers' Union, Casper (1895)

Strike was against sheep companies attempting to force shearers to live in designated rooming houses.

8. Machinests and Boilermakers, Cheyenne (1899)

Successful strike to increase wages from 32 1/2 cents to 35 cents per hour.

9. Deliverymen, Cheyenne; Laundry workers, Sheridan; Teamsters (1912)

All three strikes succeeded.

10. Laundry workers, Rock Springs (1917)

Strike was successful after local Trades and Labor Council threaten to set up a cooperative laundry.

11. Culinary workers, Casper (1923, 1926)

Both strikes failed.

12. Most strikes in any year (1928)

Although fewer workers were on strike than during nationwide rail and coal strikes earlier in the century, four unions went on strike in Wyoming in 1928: culinary workers in Sheridan; painters in Casper; bakers in Casper; and barbers in Sheridan.

13. Coal miners, southern Wyoming (1928)

The region-wide strike for wage increases failed.

14. Tie and Timber Workers, Fox Park (1936)

Successful strike for increased wages.

15. Mine workers, statewide (1939)

The general strike, called to enforce acceptance of a new agreement reducing hours and increasing wages, was successful. *Source: "Wyoming Labor History," by Keith Henning, Wyoming State AFL-CIO, July 1984.*

11 Miscellaneous Items about Wyoming Labor

1. Labor statutes involving women

A 1922 law required that women who are on their feet on the job must have two rest periods of at least 15 minutes twice per day, one in a.m., one after lunch. A 1937 labor law made it illegal for women between ages of 16-18 to work before 5 a.m. or after midnight of any one day.

2. Shutting off the lights

The organizational meeting of the United Mine Workers in Kemmerer was held in a saloon by candlelight. The coal company, in an attempt to halt the meeting, cut off electricity to the saloon.

3. Mine union organizations

The first Wyoming chapter of the United Mine Workers was organized in Sheridan County in 1900. The union organized in Rock Springs a few months later.

4. Eight-hour day

United Mine Workers won a statewide agreement which included a clause establishing an eight-hour workday for miners. The agreement was signed Sept. 1, 1907. When the agreement expired a year later, the coal companies proposed reducing wages. Miners statewide went on strike. The two sides reached a settlement after four weeks.

5. CIO organized in Wyoming

The C. I. O. was organized in Wyoming in 1937 mostly through the efforts of the United Mine Workers. Locals organized workers in a Laramie creosote plant, the iron

Charles Bellamy (1851-1934) was the first licensed professional engineer anywhere. Wyoming was the first state to require licensure for engineers. His wife Mary (1861-1955) was the first woman elected to the Wyoming legislature (1910).

mine at Sunrise, the reclamation plant in Cody, dairymen and warehouse workers in Rock Springs, and oil workers around Wyoming. The State CIO Council headquarters was first in Rock Springs but later in Parco. The CIO merged with the American Federation of Labor in 1955 to form the AFL-CIO.

6. Theater workers organize

In 1934, ushers, doormen and cashiers in Cheyenne theaters organized. It was the first such union in the Rocky Mountain West.

7. Labor holidays

A day during the first week of April was always set aside as a holiday in Rock Springs to commemorate the United Mine Workers' long-time crusade for the eight-hour day, begun in the 1890s. Ten and 12 hours were standard before then. Labor Day picnics, parades, baseball games and union rallies were commonplace in many Wyoming towns between 1900 and World War II. It was celebrated the first Monday in September.

8. Sheepherders' Union (1911)

In 1911, attempts were made to organize sheepherders into an international union to be called the Stock Helpers' International Union. The attempt was unsuccessful.

9. 1st locals in Wyoming towns

In the World War I period, bartenders locals were organized in Newcastle, Thermopolis and Cody. They were the first unions formed in those towns.

9. Severe unemployment

A 1988 needs assessment survey taken on the Wind River reservation showed an unemployment rate of 70.5 percent.

10. Lost jobs during "national prosperity"

Wyoming's economy often seems counter-cyclical in relation to the rest of the country. During the "roaring '20s," Wyoming suffered from a severe economic depression which included a record number of bank failures in 1924. From 1983 to 1989, the state of Wyoming suffered from an even greater economic downturn. More than 30,000 jobs were lost during the period.

11. Hospital workers (1999)

The first non-federal hospital staff in Wyoming to unionize was at Platte County Memorial Hospital on Aug. 16, 1999. The Union of Operating Engineers was chosen as bargaining agent by a vote of 70-62. At the time of the vote, the staff had the lowest average salary of any hospital in Wyoming.

12. Workers' Compensation

In 1910, the United Mine Workers union began a drive to establish the Workers' Compensation program in Wyoming. In Nov. 1914, Wyoming voters approved an amendment to create such a system. Flat-rate charges of employers were made until it was changed to an experience-rated system in 1986.

Total Claims: 1980— 32,304   **1988**— 15,318   **1992**—20,036
2002-- 15,400 compensable injuries

Wyoming lost the bid for the location of the superconducting supercollider in 1988. The project was awarded to a site in Texas and the project was terminated in 1993. The proposed location in Wyoming was near Burns in Laramie County. In the early 2000s, Wyoming had better success when NOAA announced that a Cheyenne area site had been chosen for construction of a site for the world's fastest supercomputer. NOAA, other federal officials, University of Wyoming and state officials held the ground-breaking in mid-June 2010.

Some Licensed Occupations in Wyoming

1. Certified Public Accountant*
2. Education Administrator*
3. Nursing Home Administrator
4. Architect*
5. Artificial Inseminator of Animals
6. Audiologist
7. Barber
8. School bus driver
9. Social worker*
10. Chiropractor*
11. Claims adjuster
12. Cosmetologist ("must be 16")
13. Dental hygienist
14. Dentist*
15. Education program specialist*
16. Electrician
17. Embalmer
18. Emergency medical technician
19. Engineer
20. Professional guide
21. Hearing aid specialist
22. Law enforcement officer
23. Lawyer*
24. School librarian
25. Mine examiner ("must be no younger than 23")

26. Mine foreman
27. Mine inspector ("must be at least 35 years old")
28. Marriage and family therapist*
29. Licensed practical nurse
30. Nurse practitioner*
31. Optometrist*
32. Outfitter ("must be at least 19")
33. Pharmacist*
34. Physical therapist*
35. Physician*
36. Physician assistant
37. Podiatrist*
38. Psychologist*
39. Radiation technician
40. Insurance salesperson
41. Real estate salesperson
42. Surveyor
43. Special education teacher*
44. Teacher*
45. Veterinarian*

Minimum requirements include a college degree

Source: "Directory of Wyoming Licensed Occupations," compiled by Curtis Krause. State of Wyoming Department of Labor.

Some Famous People Once Employed in Wyoming

1. Ralph Nader, 2000 Presidential candidate/lawyer/activist (b. Conn., 1934)

Like hundreds of other students from around the country, Nader worked in Yellowstone National Park during the summers of his college years. In 1996, Nader was a presidential candidate and, in 2000, he again was nominated as the Green Party candidate. He spoke on the campus at UW in the spring of 2000.

2. Glen Campbell, popular singer (b. Ark., 1938)

During the late 1950s and early 1960s, before he gained popularity with such songs as Wichita Lineman and Galveston, Campbell played in small nightclubs throughout the West. Years later, he claimed that his career hit bottom when he was fired by a nightclub owner in Cody. The experience caused him to return to Albuquerque, N. M., where he

Much was made of the three-decade feud between two "grand old men of Wyoming politics," Francis E. Warren and Joseph M. Carey. According to a mutual friend of both men, however, the longstanding feud was civil. In his memoirs, U. S. District Judge T. Blake Kennedy said he only heard Carey make one comment about Warren in all the years the men knew one another. "Warren always did wear good-looking vests," Carey once said of his rival, according to Kennedy. The federal judge also commented on the reason for Warren's incredible success. He served as U. S. Senator from Wyoming for more than 37 years. At election time, Kennedy remembered, Warren always had "enthusiasm for his itinerary." Kennedy noted that the other senator from Wyoming at the time, C. D. Clark, "would whine," while U. S. Representative Frank Mondell would "want to change it." Warren was the only one, according to Kennedy, who truly "loved politics."

was hired in a well-known club, "discovered" by record producers and began his rise to stardom.

3. Dr. Francis E. Townsend, social theorist (b. 1867, d. 1960)

Originator of the "Townsend Plan" for pensions in the 1930s, Dr. Townsend opened a medical practice in Hulett, Wyoming, in 1908. Later, he moved his practice to Belle Fourche, S. D., before relocating to Long Beach, Calif., in 1931 where he gained fame for his political ideas. .

4. Gerald Ford, U. S. President (b. Neb., 1913)

In the summer after he graduated from the University of Michigan, Ford worked as a summer park ranger in Yellowstone. In 1974 when Ford became president on the resignation of Richard Nixon, his son Jack was employed in Yellowstone on a fire lookout tower.

5. Jerry Voorhies, California congressman (b. 1901, d. 1982)

Chiefly remembered for losing his congressional seat to political novice Richard Nixon in the 1946 election in a southern California district, Voorhies was director of "Dray Cottage Home for Boys" in Laramie from 1926-1927.

6. Arthur MacArthur, military officer (b. 1845, d. 1912)

The father of General Douglas MacArthur, Lt. Gen. MacArthur was a captain when he commanded a company at Fort Sanders, near Laramie, in 1867. The next year, he was sent to Fort Bridger. In the fall of 1873, he was transferred to Fort Fred Steele where he stayed for a year. He was unmarried at the time.

7. J. C. Penney, chain store founder (b. Mo., 1875, d. 1971)

After an unsuccessful attempt at operating a retail store in Colorado, Penney was hired by a Colorado firm to manage its store in Evanston. Later, Penney started his own "cash-and-carry" store in Kemmerer which became the first of more than 2,000 in the famous Penney store chain.

8. George Bird Grinnell, naturalist (b. N. Y., 1849, d. 1938)

Grinnell owned a ranch in Shirley Basin in the 1880s. From 1876 to 1911, he edited *Field and Forest* magazine. Known as an editor and author, Grinnell came to Wyoming for the first time in 1874 as naturalist with the Custer expedition. He sold his ranch after suffering numerous reverses on account of hard winters.

9. Elwood Mead, engineer (b. Ind., 1858, d. 1936)

Mead was territorial and state engineer from 1888 to 1899. He pioneered the Wyoming water allocation system. In 1924, he became Commissioner of the U. S. Bureau of Reclamation. Lake Mead, on the Colorado River, is named for him.

10. Gen. Mark Clark, military officer (b. 1896, d. 1984)

In the early years of his career, Clark served at what is now F. E. Warren Air Force Base in Cheyenne. Clark gained fame for his military leadership during World War II and in Korea.

11. Duncan Hines, restaurant critic/author (b. Ky., 1880, d. 1959)

From 1899 to 1902, Hines worked for Wells Fargo in Cheyenne. Following his marriage to a Cheyenne woman, Hines became a printing salesman in Chicago. In 1935, he began writing his restaurant reviews which made his name a household word. "Duncan

---

A Wyoming court was asked to decide, "When is a dude ranch not a dude ranch?" The issue was raised in a 1940 case involving registration for an unemployment tax exemption which was available to dude ranches but not to other establishments. The judge decided that the ranch in question, Pahaska Teepee at the East Entrance to Yellowstone, had ceased to be a dude ranch on July 1, 1938, "even though it was impossible to tell exactly," and, therefore, not entitled to the exemption.

Hines-approved" became a by-word for quality food. The dry cake mix was named for him in 1949.

12. Damon Runyon, sports writer (b. 1880, d. 1946)

Although he spent little time in Wyoming, Runyon served as president of a Denver-based baseball league in 1910 which included a Cheyenne team. The other teams in the eight-club circuit were Denver, Colorado Springs, Pueblo, LaJunta, Cripple Creek, Trinidad and Fort Collins.

13. John F. Kennedy Jr., magazine publisher (b. 1960, d. 1999)

When Kennedy was 17 years old, his mother, former first lady Jacqueline Kennedy Onassis, with help from Wyo. Cong. Teno Roncalio, lined up a job for him on the ranch of Sublette County rancher John Perry Barlow. The two men became life-long friends, visiting and communicating regularly. One of the last e-mail messages Kennedy sent before his tragic death in an airplane crash on July 17, 1999, was a message of condolence to Barlow on the death of Barlow's mother.

Labor Relations on the Ranch

1. Unique hiring practice

Henry C. Lovell, the northern Wyoming rancher for whom the town is named, asked prospective employees two questions: "Do you smoke?" and "Do you wear suspenders?" If the answers were "yes" to the first question and "no" to the second, Lovell would not hire the man. "He would spend most of his time rolling cigarettes and the rest pulling up his pants," he said.

2. Not exactly a pink slip

R. S. Van Tassell, Laramie County rancher for whom the town is named, once told a ranch hand to go out and dig a hole four feet deep, four feet wide and eight feet long. When the man finished digging, he came back into the ranch house and asked Van Tassell, "Now, what do you want me to do with the hole?" The irascible old rancher snapped, "Drop into it and cover yourself with dirt, you worthless son-of-a-bitch. You move like you're dead anyway."

3. Health coverage

Cowboys and cattlemen organized a health care cooperative in what is now Converse County in 1885. The cooperative opened a hospital, brought Dr. Amos Barber from Pennsylvania as the cooperative's contract physician, and assessed "subscribers" $1 per month for coverage. Although it eventually closed because of the collapse of the cattle industry in the late 1880s, the "Fetterman Hospital Association" was the earliest organized health care cooperative in the United States.

William Hale Thompson served as mayor of Chicago in the 1920s. He spent several of his teen years working on Wyoming ranches. When he arrived in Laramie County in the 1880s, the only job available was for a cook on a nearby ranch. Thompson assured the rancher that he was skilled in the kitchen so he was hired as a cook for the Hunter Ranch on Horse Creek. His cooking career lasted exactly one meal. The quality of the meal betrayed his inexperience as a cook and the cowhands were ready to revolt if the rancher didn't get him away from the chuckwagon. He was fired, but the rancher felt sorry for the lad and kept him on as a cowhand, much to the young man's delight. He remained a cowboy for a couple of seasons, returning to his native Chicago and, eventually, becoming the city's mayor in 1917.

LAW

1st lawyers in Wyoming: Several are known to have crossed Wyoming on the Oregon Trail.

1st meeting of the Wyoming State Bar: The organizational meeting was held Jan. 28, 1915, in the U. S. District Courtroom, Cheyenne

1st president of the Wyoming State Bar: C. P. Arnold of Laramie

1st woman admitted to law practice in Wyoming: Dr. Grace Raymond Hebard of Laramie was admitted on Dec. 22, 1914. (She had been admitted to practice before the district court in Laramie on Nov. 18, 1898). The first woman to actually practice law in Wyoming was Mrs. Grace McDonald Phillips, Newcastle/Casper, who was admitted to the bar on April 19, 1920.

1st woman to argue a case before the Wyoming Supreme Court: Laura Bicknell Harris of Casper in 1927.

1st law school in Wyoming: University of Wyoming College of Law, first classes conducted in September 1920.

1st University of Wyoming College of Law graduate named to a district judgeship: Glenn Parker in 1949.

1st UW law graduate named to State Supreme Court: Glenn Parker, 1955.

1st woman appointed to the Wyoming Supreme Court: Marilyn Stebner Kite, (b. Laramie), appointed in March, 2000.

Youngest person in the United States to serve as a district judge: Percy W. Metz was 29 years old when he was elected district judge in the Big Horn Basin in 1913. Five years earlier, he set the mark for becoming the youngest county attorney in the country at the age of 24. He died at the age of 80 in 1964.

1st law school club established: Potter Law Club formed by Thurman Arnold, 1922.

Disbarred lawyers: From March 1990-June 1, 1994, ten lawyers in Wyoming were disbarred by the State Bar and 33 were suspended for rules violations.

Lawyers in the Attorney General's office: In 2010, the office employed 24 assistant AGs, 41 senior assistant AGs, five Deputy AGs and a chief deputy. Bruce Salzburg was attorney general.

1st county court judges in Wyoming: (1979) Franklin Mockler and Robert W. Allen, Laramie County; Stephen Davidson and Michael J. Krampner, Natrona County.

First Lawyers in Wyoming Towns

1. Cheyenne

Judge J. R. Whitehead and W. W. Corlett. In 1867, Whitehead had been at Fort Laramie, awaiting a military escort to the north when he heard about the Union Pacific plan for a town. The two men formed a partnership in a tent on July 2, 1867, two days before the city of Cheyenne was named. Corlett "bought into the partnership" for one $5 greenback.

2. Sheridan

Tom Cotton, who had an office in one corner of the cabin which also had housed Sheridan's first school, first store and first bank. The building stands on the grounds of Trail End State Historic Site.

3. Douglas

Winfield S. Collins, who came to Douglas in 1886. Later, he surveyed the town site of Basin and drilled the first oil well in the Big Horn Basin.

4. Gillette

Elwood Anderson moved to Gillette in 1911 as superintendent of schools. He was admitted to the Wyoming Bar July 22, 1912, and became the first practicing attorney in Campbell County. Anderson, who had a fondness for cigars, practiced in Gillette until his death in 1955.

By May 11, 1870, two years to the day when the first train came to Laramie, four lawyers had well-established practices. They were: M. C. Brown, E. L. Kerr, L. P. Corey, and Stephen Downey.

Legal Firsts

1. First civil case brought before the Wyoming Supreme Court

Western Union Telegraph Co. v. Monseau (1870) was the first civil case heard by the three-member court. Monseau claimed the telegraph company breached a contract with him in which he had agreed to supply 754 telegraph poles at $2.50 per pole. The company claimed the man who had entered into the contract with Monseau in the company's name was not its authorized agent. E. P. Johnson, the man for whom Johnson County was later named, represented Monseau. The court affirmed the lower court judgment in Monseau's favor.

2. First criminal case heard by the Wyoming Supreme Court

Territory of Wyoming v. Anderson (1869) was the first criminal case appealed to the Supreme Court. Anderson was indicted in September 1869 for "keeping a disorderly house." He was found guilty and fined $300. His appeal was based on a technicality—absence of witnesses' names on the indictment. The court, however, affirmed his conviction without issuing a formal opinion.

3. First personal injury case brought in a Wyoming court

Union Pacific Railroad v. Silas Hause (1870) was the first personal injury case brought in any Wyoming court. Hause was sitting on top of the caboose of a Union Pacific train when the car went off the track at Sherman, midway between Cheyenne and Laramie on the summit. As Hause jumped off the caboose, "a barrel of molasses burst through the side of the car and struck Hause, fracturing his leg." The trial court returned a judgment award of $10,000 for Hause, but the Supreme Court remanded the case back to district court because "damages granted were in excess of actual damages."

4. First appeal from a death sentence

Kinsler v. Territory of Wyoming (1873) was the first appeal from a death sentence handed down by a Wyoming court. Toussaint Kinsler had been found guilty of killing a Cheyenne man. His death sentence was affirmed by the court and he was hanged for the crime.

5. First women on a jury

Laramie was the first place anywhere in America where women were allowed to serve on a jury. Six women were called to petit jury service: Eliza Stewart, Mrs. Amelia Hatcher, Mrs. G. F. Hilton, Mrs. Mary Mackel, Mrs. Agnes Baker and Mrs. Sarah Pease.

6. First libel case

Territory v. Wilson (1873) was the first libel case filed in a Wyoming court. Posey S. Wilson wrote a letter to the *Omaha Herald* commenting on the unfitness of a local judge. The judge had him fined for contempt of court and criminal libel. Various aspects of the case continued to occupy the Supreme Court's time during 1873 and 1874. A 47-page brief by Jason B. Brown, Wilson's attorney in the case, is held in the collections of the National Archives.

7. First case brought in Esther Hobart Morris' court

Morris v. James W. Stilman (1870) was the first case filed in the court in which the first woman justice of the peace in the world presided. Morris herself brought the suit to force Stilman, her predecessor, to turn over the court's official records to her. The case was dismissed when Morris discovered she lacked jurisdiction to hear her own case.

8. First woman charged with murder

Mrs. Jennie Berry of Fort Laramie was charged with the murder of Robert Rice, her 35 year-old bachelor employer in June 1887. She was charged along with three co-defendants, David Lewis, Edward Everst and Robert Sanderson, when Rice's body was found three months after he was reported missing. She was convicted in March 1888 of being an accessory to murder and sentenced to two years in prison. Her sentence was commuted in January 1889 by the acting governor of the state.

9. First divorce brought in a Wyoming court

The first divorce granted in what is now Wyoming was Nicholas Walke from Anna W. Walke on Nov. 14, 1866, at Fort Bridger, then a part of Utah Territory.

Some Courtroom Stories

1. First Day of Court, Buffalo, 1879

Sheriff Nat James, a former cowboy, opened the first court session in Johnson County history. He had been nervous about doing it. Judge Jacob Blair, who was presiding, advised James not to wear chaps and gave him a piece of paper on which was written what he should say as he opened the session. The hour came and Jones shouted, "O, yea! O, yea! O, yea!" He stopped, stammered, and started again. Still unsuccessful at remembering what to say next, he put his hand in his vest pocket, looked at the judge and said in a trembling voice, "What the hell did I do with that paper you gave me?"

2. Looking Down a Gun Barrel, c. 1880*

Judge Jacob Blair, like other Supreme Court justices in the territorial period, rode circuit as a district court judge when the Supreme Court was not in session. He was presiding over a murder trial and a gunsmith was called to the witness stand. As the man sat on the stand, holding the defendant's revolver, the judge turned to spit tobacco into a nearby cuspidor. He noticed immediately that the gun was pointed right at him.

"Mr. Witness, is that gun loaded?" Blair asked.

"Yes, your honor," the gunsmith-witness replied.

"Point it toward the lawyers. Good judges are scarce."

The story was told by pioneer lawyer A. C. Campbell in a 1931 interview published in Annals of Wyoming in 1947.

3. Tears and Doubt

Lander attorney Douglas Preston may have been Wyoming's most famous trial lawyer in the early days. In one case, he shed tears as he described to the jury how his client had been so falsely accused of horse theft. The jury, after drying their eyes, acquitted his client. As the prisoner was being released, Preston admonished him not to do it again. "You know damn well you stole that horse," Preston told him. The client replied, "Well, Doug, I always thought I stole that horse, but after hearing your plea to that jury, now I've got my doubts about it."

4. "My Client, the Liar"*

Prohibition-era Lusk lawyer Thomas Fagan had a particularly difficult case to defend in the 1920s. His client had been arrested for bootlegging when a still was found and authorities believed it belonged to the man on the strength of his "confession"--bragging to anyone who would listen that it was his. Fagan put witnesses on the stand who attested to his client's complete lack of honesty. In his closing argument, the lawyer concluded that his client's story was simply another of his far-fetched falsehoods. The jury agreed; the man went free.

Story told to the authors by a lawyer who practiced in a nearby town during the same period.

5. Card Game in the Jury Room

During the second court term in Carbon County in 1870, court was held in a billiard room in downtown Rawlins. The "jury room" was separated from the court by a thin partition. A particularly controversial assault case went to the jury and, after several ballots, it was clear that the jurors could not agree on a verdict. There were several card tables in the room so one juror suggested they play some cards and take another vote later. Soon, the card game became so interesting that the jurors forgot about the case. Meanwhile, the judge could hear every word from the other side of the partition. He waited to bring the jury back in and while the 12 card players filed back into the courtroom, the judge turned to the clerk. "Enter up a fine of two dollars each against the jury for trying to arrive at a verdict by playing cards." He added to the sheriff, "They will stand committed until the fines are paid," whereupon he slapped on his hat and walked out of the courtroom-billiard parlor. *The story was told by Rawlins pioneer John Friend, who said he was one of the jurors.*

6. No Judge in His Pocket

Charles Clay was appointed the first justice of the peace in Douglas in 1886. One of the first defendants brought before him was a bouncer for a local dance hall accused of beating up a local cowboy. "I guess I'm guilty, your honor," the bouncer said, after the complaint had been read.

"The court fines you $100...."

The bouncer interrupted, "Here it is." He threw the money on the grocery counter serving as the bench.

"...and six months in jail," the judge continued. "Have you got that in your pocket, too?"

Later that evening, several of the bouncer's friends threatened Clay with tar and feathers. He quietly walked behind the counter which had served as his judge's bench and pulled out a revolver. "This gun will always be here to make the sentence good," he warned. *The story is told in Robert B. David, Malcolm Campbell, Sheriff. (Douglas, 1951).*

7. Naturally Offensive

An arrogant young attorney entered the courtroom of an early-day Wyoming judge. After exchanging some heated words about respective lack of legal knowledge (and confirming the young man's lack of common sense in arguing with a judge), the exasperated judge finally said to the lawyer, "Young man, you are extremely offensive." The young attorney showed bad sense, again. "As a matter of fact, we both are," he told the judge, "but I'm trying to be and you can't help it."

8. Legal Insurance

During a 15-year period, Converse County gambler/outlaw George W. Pike made no fewer than two court appearances for various offenses each year. He once bragged that he hired local attorney Fred Harvey to keep him out of jail by paying him an annual retainer to do the job.

9. Double Jeopardy

An Irishman named Murphy was justice of the peace in Laramie in the 1880s. He was very proud of his position and so was his wife. One day, their young daughter asked her mother, "Are we all justices of the peace?"

"No, dearie," Mrs. Murphy replied, "Only me and your pa."

10. "Move Your Rocks"

Murphy, the Laramie justice of the peace, discovered that Ames Monument had been built by accident on public land that was open to homesteading. Murphy immediately filed on the land, hoping the builder of the monument, the Union Pacific Railroad, would pay him off to settle the surveying discrepancy. When railroad lawyers failed to respond, Murphy sent them the message, "Gentlemen, please move your rocks." The railroad had no intention of caving in to Murphy's claim and, certainly, they did not plan to move the monument off the plot. The railroad lawyers found out that Murphy was extremely proud

In 44 years on the Wyoming Supreme Court (1919-1963), Fred Blume wrote 660 opinions.

of his judicial post so they threatened to have him impeached for "improprieties" in the filing. Murphy, fearing he might lose his judgeship, traded his claim for several Laramie building lots. The railroad's "rocks" stayed in place.

11. Where's the Washing Machine?

In 1876, William Sloan was elected county commissioner of Uinta County. His election was challenged, however, because it was contended that he was not a bonafide resident of Wyoming because his wife lived in Salt Lake City. A Uinta County judge ruled that Sloan was, indeed, a legal resident of the state. The court agreed with Sloan's argument that a man is "entitled to hold office wherever he had his washing done." Later, Sloan ran unsuccessfully for a seat in the territorial council (senate).

12. Continuances ad infinitum

"When the angel Gabriel blows his horn, a vast array of lawyers will rise up and from sheer force of habit, move for a continuance of the cases before the court." —*Cheyenne Daily Leader*, 1880.

13. Beyond Court's Jurisdiction

"The name of William D. Foster was next called. The case was one appealed from the Justice Court, and for a time, the officers were at a loss to know what had become of the offender, when it was remembered that Foster was dead and had passed beyond the jurisdiction of the court." —*Wind River Mountaineer (Lander), Dec. 14, 1906.*

14. Pig under the Bed

Soon after the county was established, the Campbell County attorney visited a woman accused of stealing a neighbor's pig. The only furniture in the tiny homestead shack was a bed and the woman sat on it as she declared her innocence. Her story soon was contradicted, however, when the pig, bound and gagged under the bed, began thrashing about violently, nearly pitching the woman off of the bed.

Lawyers in Wyoming Towns*

	2005	2000	1996	1994	1989	1977
1. Cheyenne:	494	438	416	395	353	186
2. Casper:	221	218	203	195	185	121
3. Jackson:	144	103	98	85	51	19
4. Laramie:	132	130	129	106	91	56
5. Sheridan:	77	69	62	61	55	36
6. Gillette:	72	63	61	55	46	19
7. Cody:	49	46	43	34	35	20
8. Rock Springs:	45	49	42	38	36	19
9. Lander:	41	32	28	24	19	16
10. Riverton:	34	37	38	37	31	21
11. Evanston:	31	30	33	31	27	8
All other Wyo.	264	269	231	218	221	144

*Members of the Wyoming State Bar. Lawyers counted include bar members who are retired, inactive, employed as house counsel for business or in government, judges, law professors and full-time holders of political offices. Information is courtesy of the Wyoming State Bar, Cheyenne.

On Feb. 9, 1996, a Gillette teenager splashed a woman and her young child by driving his car fast through a mud puddle as they walked on an adjacent sidewalk. He was arrested and charged with "assault with an icy puddle."

States with the Most Wyoming State Bar Members

	2005	2000	1996	1994	1989		2005	2000	1996	1994	1989
1. Colo.	368	325	267	241	160	8. Idaho	33	32	22	16	4
2. Calif.	76	87	72	62	57	9. Florida	32	21	22	17	12
3. Utah	66	52	45	34	24	10. Va.	28	19	24	24	29
4. Texas	51	40	41	38	40	11. Nebr.	19	23	21	18	7
5. Mont.	47	40	30	22	26	12. D. C.	24	17	22	23	22
6. Ariz.	45	40	33	33	31	13. Nevada	21				
7. Wash.	34	20	17	12	10						

Unusual Ordinances

1. Lovell (1909)

A city ordinance made it illegal for persons to tie horses to growing trees without the tree owner's permission.

2. Rock Springs (1940s)

An ordinance made it illegal for more than two children to sip a soft drink from the same bottle.

3. Green River (early 1900s)

The council made rock-throwing illegal and punishable by a $50 fine. The fine for shooting up the town was only $25.

4. Buffalo (1931)

An ordinance made it illegal to ride into town and leave your horse untied. Another ordinance made it illegal to carry a sling-shot or a blow-gun in the city.

5. Casper (1889)

An ordinance prohibited women from "using vile, profane, or indecent language, or from acting in a boisterous manner." (The rule didn't apply to men). Also, it was illegal for women to smoke cigars, cigarettes or pipes in public.

6. Torrington (c. 1913)

Ordinances established the automobile speed limit at 12 miles per hour in town, six miles per hour at railroad crossings.

7. Burns

A restrictive covenant, first imposed on homeowners in 1907, forbade the sale of alcohol on all town lots. To 2009, the covenants were still in effect.

8. Newcastle (1890)

"It shall be unlawful for any female person to frequent, remain in or loiter about any saloon, sample room, ale house in the town of the City of Newcastle between the hours of 6 a.m. and 8 p.m." According to the *Newcastle Journal*, Dec. 12, 1890, "Marshal Bond has given notice that...the ordinance of the city will be strictly enforced." The fine was between $5-$25.

9. Sheridan (1884)

A town ordinance established the speed limit on city streets at six miles per hour. Another ordinance stipulated that animals could be "parked anywhere but must be attended."

10. Sheridan (1919)

On April 3, 1919, the Sheridan City Council passed an ordinance making it illegal to make either "a sale or gift of tobacco to boys under the age of 18." Conviction of the misdemeanor would result in a possible fine of $100. Curiously, nothing was said about tobacco and girls...probably assumed they wouldn't want to engage in such a habit.

Costs of Justice

1. Two Bits for Beer

Cheyenne's first justice of the peace was Luke Murrin, a saloonkeeper who added an extra 25 cents to each fine for "purchase of liquid refreshment" for the court. Also, he consistently ordered a $10 fine against any person shooting at another person in the city limits "whether he hits anyone or not."

2. An Unabridged Dictionary

An unusual legal fee was charged by lawyer/humorist Bill Nye who had represented a Laramie client in a land case. When the case was settled, Nye was on a speaking tour in the East with poet James Whitcomb Riley. The client wired Nye about the fee and he received a telegram back from Nye that it would be "one unabridged dictionary." The humorist explained that Riley had stolen the only one Nye owned.

3. Horses and Saddle

In May 1893, a Natrona County jury entered a not guilty verdict in favor of a man accused of stealing horses. The next day the man was caught with a stolen saddle and several stolen horses—all the property of a man who had been on the jury!

4. $50

The story, unsubstantiated, is told about a particularly unscrupulous defense lawyer in Wyoming territorial days. After the first day of testimony, the defense lawyer knew his case was not going well. If his client were given a new trial, he would do much better, he thought. Consequently, during a break in the trial, he offered a jury member $50 if the man would "hang the jury," forcing a new trial. The case went to the jury. The lawyer became concerned because the jury stayed out for many hours. Finally, the jury returned, announcing it had been unable to reach a verdict. The lawyer was delighted and relieved. Later, the juryman came to his office for the payoff. The lawyer peeled off the $50 and thanked the man again. "That was one tough job," the juror admitted. "It was all I could do to keep those damn fools from bringing in a verdict of not guilty!"

Some Nationally-Publicized Trials

1. Fanny Kelly v. Sarah Larimer

Kelly filed suit against Larimer in Kansas in October 1870, accusing the Wyoming woman of stealing a manuscript and publishing it under her own name. *The Capture and Escape or Life Among the Sioux* by Larimer was released just weeks before Kelly's book, *Narrative of My Captivity Among the Sioux Indians*, was published in 1871. Both women had been kidnapped by Indians about 80 miles west of Fort Laramie in July 1864. Larimer managed to escape after two days, but the 19-year-old Kelly and her five-year-old adopted daughter were not rescued until December 12 at Fort Sully, miles from their capture. Following the ordeal, Mrs. Kelly returned to Kansas with her husband. He died of cholera in July 1867, and Mrs. Kelly accepted an invitation to stay with the Larimers in Cheyenne where Larimer was a photographer. While there, Mrs. Kelly finished her book. She alleged that in May 1869, Mrs. Larimer secretly took her manuscript to a Philadelphia publisher and had it printed under her own name. Kelly won a judgment of $5,000 from a trial court, but the judgment was reduced to $286.50 in damages and $2,000 in court costs on appeal. The judgment also required Larimer and her printer to destroy all copies of the book. Mrs. Kelly later became a federal government employee. She died in Washington, D. C., in 1904.

2. State v. Frank Canton et al

Canton and the rest of the Johnson County "invaders" were rescued by the army at the TA Ranch in April 1892. Later that month, they were escorted to Cheyenne to face trial.

The venue change allowed the "prisoners" to enjoy hospitable quarters at Fort Russell and never spend a day in jail for their crimes. Because of the projected expenses of such a trial, Johnson County officials decided not to prosecute and all of the prisoners were released.

3. Race Horse Case

Race Horse, a Bannock chief during the so-called "Indian War of 1895" in Jackson Hole, was convicted of violating state game laws. His conviction was appealed to the Wyoming Supreme Court. The court ruled that "a state has jurisdiction over the game within its borders."

4. Teapot Dome "Annulment Trial"

The federal government attempted to annul the leases to lucrative federal oil reserve lands at Teapot Dome near Midwest. The leases had been granted to several oil companies on the authority of Interior Secretary Albert Fall who was later convicted of accepting bribes in exchange for the leases. The trial, held in federal district court in Cheyenne from March 7-27, 1925, gained national publicity.

5. City of Green River v. Fuller Brush Company

The city of Green River became the first in the United States to pass a law requiring "peddlers" to be licensed and banning them from soliciting during particular hours. The Fuller Brush Company violated the law and the Green River city attorney had the company representative prosecuted. The case went to the federal courts where, in April, 1935, the court said the so-called "Green River ordinance" was a legitimate exercise of municipal power.

6. U. S. v. 63 Draft Resisters

The largest mass trial in Wyoming history, 63 Nisei young men from Heart Mountain Relocation Center were charged with failure to report for pre-induction physicals. The men were protesting the condition of Americans of Japanese descent who were being held in detention without trial and without any charges being brought against them. In the trial before Judge T. Blake Kennedy, the 63 were found guilty on June 26, 1944, and sentenced to as long as three years in federal prison.

7. State v. Richard and Deborah Jahnke

Richard Jahnke, 16, and his sister Deborah were accused of the murder of their father, an IRS agent who, the children claimed, had abused them for the many years. The man was shot by his son with a 12-gauge shotgun while he was opening the garage door at his home north of Cheyenne in 1983. A Laramie County jury found him guilty (and his sister guilty of being an accessory). The State Supreme Court upheld the verdicts. Gov. Ed Herschler commuted Richard Jahnke's sentence from a long prison term to time in the boys' school until he turned 21. The case gained national attention on CBS's *60 Minutes* and became the subject of a best-selling book and made-for-television movie.

8. Coastal Corp. v. Occidental Petroleum

The case, heard in federal court in Cheyenne, involved an oil contract dispute between two industry giants. When the verdict was handed down in November 1976, Coastal was awarded a judgment of $549 million, the third largest civil judgment ever awarded in an American court at the time. Michael L. Beatty (b. 1948), a former University of Wyoming law professor, was Coastal's general counsel who won the case.

9. Davis v. Alioto

In the middle 1960s, 199 ranchers hired Joseph L. Alioto, former mayor of San Francisco, and his son to bring suit against Safeway, A&P and Kroeger grocery chains, alleging the firms were conspiring to drive down cattle prices. The Aliotos selected six ranchers, including C. C. Davis of Cheyenne, to bring the test case. Little was done for three years, then Safeway and Kroeger each settled for $85,000, the settlement monies to be used to continue the suit. Instead, the Alioto firm kept most of the money. Years later, the suit against A&P was settled for $10.6 million, the Alioto firm receiving $5.2 million in fees. Davis filed suit against the firm in July, 1976, alleging legal malpractice. After litigation lasting for years, the Wyoming Supreme Court in July, 1984, upheld a judgment against the Alioto firm for $3.55 million, the largest legal malpractice award in state history.

10. State v. Dr. John Story

In April 1985, Lovell physician Dr. John Story of Lovell was convicted on six counts of sexually assaulting several of his patients over a number of years. His case was the subject of a CBS' *60 Minutes* episode and two books. The Wyoming Supreme Court upheld his conviction and sentence in 1990.

11. U. S. v. Imelda Marcos

Wyoming attorney Gerry Spence represented Mrs. Marcos when she was charged for racketeering in connection with the looting of the Philippine treasury. The case went to trial in March 1990, and Mrs. Marcos was found not guilty. Mrs. Marcos was famous for her huge collection of shoes. A New York newspaper photographer had taken pictures of her shoes each day of the trial. When the verdict was announced, the paper ran small separate photos of each pair she had worn and headlined the photo spread, "Imelda Walks."

12. State v. Woodbury (1990)

A 38-year-old Los Angeles area freelance commercial artist told authorities about incidents of sexual abuse she had suffered at the hands of her father some 30 years earlier. As a result of her testimony, authorities brought charges against her father in district court in Rawlins in 1990. The incidents had occurred in Carbon County in the 1950s and early 1960s. The father pleaded guilty in December 1990 to the charges and was sentenced to five years' probation. It was one of the oldest cases ever prosecuted in Wyoming because there was no statute of limitations for the offense. It was unusual, too, because even though there was no physical evidence, several people agreed to testify for the victim.

13. Mogensen v. Aetna Casualty and Surety Company (1992)

The jury returned a verdict for $15 million in compensatory damages and $18.5 million in punitive damages against the insurance company in a Bakersfield, Calif., court. The $33.5 million judgment was the biggest jury verdict for insurance fraud in U. S. history. Jackson attorney Gerald Spence represented Mogensen who had been made a quadriplegic in a 1970 auto accident and had been convinced by an Aetna claims representative to sign an invalid release of liability while he was hospitalized. The verdict was appealed.

14. Virginia Military Institute case (1996)

The State of Wyoming intervened on the side of the institute when the college was challenged for its all-male policy. Attorney General Bill Hill defended his decision to allow Wyoming to file on the side of the college while Secretary of State Diana Ohman and former Secretary of State Kathy Karpan criticized the decision for seeming to contradict Wyoming's Equality State image. In June, 1996, the U. S. Supreme Court ruled against VMI with only Justice Scalia dissenting.

15. Armstrong v. Day (1957)

Saratoga area rancher Kenneth Day, to thwart fishermen from coming upstream on the North Platte River where it flowed through his land, built a barbed wire fence and stretched it across the river. Fisherman challenged his action and fishermen in a boat cut the strands of the fence and floated upstream to fish. Day had them arrested for trespassing. The State Supreme Court determined that Day could not bar the fishermen from fishing on Wyoming waters because the state not only owns the water, but the law would not allow a private landowner from interfering with navigaton. As long as the fishermen did not get out of the boat, they could fish on the river passing through Day's ranch. B. B. Lummis' name appeared first on the case, but he died before it reached trial. Consequently, the case was heard by the Wyoming Supreme Court as Armstrong v. Day.

Court Decisions Make Interesting Reading:
Two Wyoming Examples

1. Greenwood v. Wierdsma

A footnote in the August 1987, Wyoming Supreme Court decision: "After painstaking deliberation, we have decided that we like the word 'conclusory,' and we are distressed by its omission from the English language. We now proclaim that henceforth 'conclusory' is appropriately used in the opinions of this court. Furthermore, its usage is welcomed in briefs submitted for this court's review. Webster's, take heed!" *741 P.2d 1079 (1987) at 1086.*

2. Compass Insurance Company v. Cravens, Dargan and Company

Justice Walter Urbigkit wrote the opinion in the 1988 case which contained several extremely long sentences. One was 113 words. It was followed by this intriguing sentence: "Factually and procedurally, this litigation is sufficiently strange so that, at least in contemplation of a standard for future litigation, we could leave its precedential value in a fashion akin to the paraphrased comment as Justice Felix Frankfurter once related in dissent, and I would find here similarly to be perceived, as the flying Dutchman known only as a floating hulk once briefly observed upon the silent sea to surely disappear as having been a temporary mirage in the ocean of law." Later, in the same opinion, Urbigkit continued the analogy: "To the contrary, if the rule of the case is considered to be its real issue of the right of subrogation of a property-damage carrier against its mutual insured's liability carrier, then we find ourselves not only in the Sargasso Sea attendant to the hulk of Frankfurter's perception, but flailing water by the teaspoonful when faced with a typhoon by challenging the weight of general law denying a right of subrogation." *748 P.2d 724 (1988) at 731, 736.*

Some Well-Known Lawyers from Wyoming

1. Willis Van Devanter (b. Indiana, 1859, d. 1941)

The only United States Supreme Court justice to be appointed from Wyoming, Van Devanter served from 1910 to 1937. He came to Cheyenne in 1884 to open a law practice and four years later, he was chief justice of the territorial supreme court. A close associate of Sen. Francis E. Warren, Van Devanter went to Washington in 1897 as an assistant attorney general. From 1903 to 1910, he served as a judge on the 8th Circuit Court of Appeals. After nearly three decades on the Supreme Court, Van Devanter resigned, citing ill health. The resignation came during the controversy over President Franklin Roosevelt's "court-packing" plan. A court opponent of New Deal legislation, Van Devanter's departure from the court diminished the importance of court enlargement as the balance swung toward support for the constitutionality of New Deal measures. Van Devanter was replaced by Hugo Black.

2. Thurman Arnold (b. Laramie, 1891, d. Nov. 1969)

The son of a lawyer, Arnold was born in Laramie. He graduated from Harvard Law School in 1914, practiced law in Chicago and Laramie, and served as dean of the University of West Virginia Law School from 1927 to 1930. Arnold taught law at Yale from 1930 until he was appointed head of the Anti-Trust Division of the Justice Department in 1938, a position he held until 1943. After a brief term as a federal judge, Arnold joined with Abe Fortas and Paul Porter to form what became the largest law firm in the world in the 1960s.

"While trying to escape from a savage wolf which was pursuing him, Dan Chalfant received a cold bath. In jumping the creek, the ice gave way, placing Dan in the water to his neck, but he escaped further harm by remaining under the ice until the wolf lost his trail and does not feel any worse for his adventure." --Lusk Herald, Jan. 31, 1907.

Now known as Arnold and Porter, the firm is one of the most prestigious in Washington, D. C. He was a skilled trial lawyer, but Arnold is also known for his legal scholarship. He wrote six books including *The Folklore of Capitalism*. Arnold's son George taught labor law at the University of Wyoming for several years after a long career as a labor attorney in California. George Arnold died in 1993.

3. Gerry L. Spence (b. Laramie, 1929)

Spence, a native of Laramie, is nationally known as a personal injury lawyer who represents plaintiffs. In 1995, he started hosting his own television program on CNBC. Formerly a prosecuting attorney in Fremont County and an unsuccessful candidate for Congress, Spence won trial verdicts for the estate of Karen Silkwood against Kerr-McGee and for a former Miss Wyoming in a suit against *Penthouse Magazine*. He successfully defended former Rock Springs lawman Ed Cantrell in a murder trial in 1979. In a rare departure from his usual representation for the defendant in criminal cases, he served as special prosecutor in the trial of Mark Hopkinson for the Vehar murders. In the five books he wrote (to 1993), the reader was given behind-the-scenes accounts of some of his most celebrated cases and frequent exposure to his often unconventional views on the legal system. He speaks frequently at national conventions and appears regularly on television programs dealing with legal issues. In 1987, for instance, he debated fellow attorney Richard "Racehorse" Haynes on ABC's *Nightline*. In a dramatization of *The Trial of Lee Harvey Oswald*, a television program in 1988, he played the role of defense attorney. In 1990, he made national news for successfully defending former Philippine first lady Imelda Marcos in a New York court.

4. James Neal (b. Sumner Co., Tenn., 1929)

Neal came to the University of Wyoming on a football scholarship, graduating in 1952. He earned a law degree from Vanderbilt Law School in 1957. Neal practiced law in Tennessee. He became nationally known during the Watergate scandal as associate special prosecutor. In 1984, he was named a UW distinguished alumnus.

5. Michael L. Beatty (b. 1947)

A former University of Wyoming law professor, Beatty won a $549 million judgment for Coastal Corporation against Occidental Petroleum over a gas contract dispute in November 1986. It was the third largest civil judgment ever awarded in an American court. He joined Coastal in 1981 after leaving the University of Wyoming and he became the firm's general counsel in 1985. The case was heard in federal court in Wyoming.

6. Larry EchoHawk (b. Cody, 1948)

EchoHawk graduated from the University of Utah Law School in 1973. After private practice in Utah, he became general counsel to the Shoshone-Bannock tribes in 1977, serving in that capacity until 1985. Elected to the Idaho House of Representatives in 1982, he served until 1986 when he became prosecuting attorney for Bannock County, Idaho. In 1990, he was elected Idaho Attorney General, the first Native American in the United States to be elected attorney general of any state. He ran for governor in 1994 but lost in the general election. On May 20, 2009, the U. S. Senate confirmed his nomination and on May 22, he was sworn in as head of the Bureau of Indian Affairs in the Obama administration's Interior Department.

The number of drinks in a pint of whiskey has been established by a court ruling in the state of Wyoming. In one of the more unusual statements of law ever made in a decision of the Wyoming Supreme Court, Judge Fred Blume defined the exact number. "A pint of whiskey contains 12 good drinks served in the usual (and not small) whiskey glass," the judge wrote in the case of Eagan v. Wyoming. The judge didn't state how he arrived at the measurement. The case involved the murder of a woman by her husband in a Casper apartment in 1940. At issue was the defendant's possible intoxication and his veracity.

7. Leslie Lawson (UW class of 1972)

Lawson graduated from the University of Wyoming College of Law in 1972. Six years later, while practicing law in Denver, she won the nation's first sexual harassment case. Later, from 1986-1989, she served as a Denver district judge.

8. M. Margaret McKeown (b. Casper, 1951)

A judge on the United States Court of Appeals for the Ninth Circuit, she was appointed to that position in 1998 by President Bill Clinton. Judge McKeown graduated from the University of Wyoming in 1972.

Wyoming Supreme Court Justices, 2000-2010

Larry Lehman (b. Iowa City, 1945), appointed July 8, 1994, died Dec. 10, 2004.
Richard V. Thomas, (b. Superior, Wyo., 1932), appointed Dec. 30, 1974
*Richard J. Macy (b. Saramac Lake, NY, 1930), appted Dec. 2, 1985, ret., June 2, 2000.
Wyoming Supreme Court Justices, 2010
Michael Golden (b. Enid, Okla., 1942), appointed June 30, 1988
William U. Hill (b. Montgomery, Ala., 1948), appointed Nov. 3, 1998
Marilyn Stebner Kite (b. Laramie, Oct. 22, 1947), appointed March 30, 2000
Barton R. Voigt (b. Thermopolis, 1949), appointed March 29, 2001
E. James Burke, appointed January 2005 (b. 1949)
Retired in 2000. Kite was his replacement.

Federal Judges in Wyoming, 1890-2000

U. S. Supreme Court
Willis Van Devanter *(see biography)*
Circuit Court of Appeals Judges
Willis Van Devanter (b. Marion, Ind., 1859; d. D. C. 1941), 8th Circuit, 1903-10
John Pickett (b. Ravenna, Neb., 1896; d. Cheyenne, 1983), 10th Circ., 1949-83
James E. Barrett, (b. Lusk, 1922), 10th Circ., 1971-retired in January, 2000
Wade Brorby (b. Omaha, Neb., 1934), 10th Circuit, 1988-
Terrence L. O'Brien (b. Lincoln, Neb., 1943)

U. S. District Court Judges
John Riner (b. Ohio, 1850; d. Cheyenne, 1923), U. S. District Judge, 1890-1921
T. Blake Kennedy (b. Mich., 1874; d. Cheyenne, 1955), Dist. Judge, 1921-1955
Ewing T. Kerr (b. Bowie, Texas, 1900; d. Cheyenne, 1992), 1955-1992
Clarence Brimmer (b. Rawlins, 1922), U. S. District Judge, 1975-
Alan B. Johnson (b. Cheyenne, 1939), U. S. District Judge, Jan. 1986-
William Downes (b. Boston, Mass., 1946), U. S. District Judge, July 5, 1994-
Nancy Roan Freudenthal (b. Cody, 1954), U. S. District Judge, June 1, 2010-

---

Famed trial lawyer Clarence Darrow passed through Wyoming by train on July 30, 1907, en route to defend Harry Orchard, the man accused of murdering the governor of Idaho. When the jury was selected for that high-profile trial in Boise, an odd coincidence occurred. O. V. Seeburn, formerly a rancher in Goshen Hole in Wyoming, had moved to Idaho where he was seated on the Orchard jury. It turned out that he was a veteran juror. In 1903, when he was still living in Wyoming, he had served on the jury that convicted Tom Horn in Cheyenne.

Wyoming State District Court Judges, 2010*

by judicial district

1st Dist. Peter G. Arnold
       Michael K. Davis
       Thomas T. Campbell
2nd Dist. Jeffrey A. Donnell
       Wade E. Waldrip
3rd Dist. Dennis L. Sanderson
       Jere A. Ryckman
       Nena R. James
4th Dist. John G. Fenn
5th Dist. Robert E. Skar
       Steven R. Cranfill

6th Dist. Dan R. Price II
       John R. Perry
       Michael N. Deegan
7th Dist. W. Thomas Sullins
       David B. Park
       Scott W. Skavdahl
8th Dist. John C. Brooks
       Kenneth G. Kautz
9th Dist. Nancy J. Guthrie
       Norman E. Young
       Marvin L. Tyler

Presidents, Wyoming State Bar, 1922-2010

1922: Roderick Matson	1953-54: R. D. Wallace	1983-84: Harry L. Harris
1923: R. B. West	1954-55: J. O. Spangler	1984-85: Thomas S. Smith
1924: D. A. Preston	1955-56: Edwin Magagna	1985-86: James Hettinger
1925: W. L. Wells	1956-57: Oliver Steadman	1986-87: William S. Bon
1926: C. A. Zaring	1957-58: Thomas Miller	1987-88: D. Carmichael
1927: N. R. Greenfield	1958-59: James O. Wilson	1988-89: John M. Daly
1928: G. R. Hagens	1959-60: Charles Crowell	1989-90: Richard Davis
1929: Erle H. Reid	1960-61: John P. Ilsley	1990-91: Richard Day
1930-31: L. E. Armstrong	1961-62: George Sawyer	1991-92: David Uchner
1932-33: E. E. Enterline	1962-63: George Millett	1992-93: Eric M. Alden
1933-34: Thomas Hunter	1963-64: Jerry Housel	1993-94: L. Galen West
1934-35: J. R. Sullivan	1964-65: R. R. Bostwick	1994-95: Kermit Brown
1935-36: Glenn Kinsley	1965-66: Elmer J. Scott	1995-96: Gerald Mason
1936-37: P. W. Spaulding	1966-67: George F. Guy	1996-97: H. MacMillan
1937-38: A. McCulloch	1967-68: Henry Burgess	1997-98: Paul J. Hickey
1938-39: C. R. Ellery	1968-69: Ed Herschler*	1998-99: Tim Kirven
1939-40: Lewis H. Brown	1969-70: James Zaring	1999-00: Paul J. Drew
1940-41: C. O. Brown	1970-71: Ross Copenhaver	2000-01: Cath. MacPherson
1941-42: H. Harnsberger	1971-72: Joseph Sullivan	2001-02: Timothy C. Day
1942-43: L. A. Bowman	1972-73: Houston Williams	2002-03: Richard Honaker
1943-44: M. S. Reynolds	1973-74: Thomas Morgan	2003-04: Thomas Lubnau II
1944-45: Spencer Lewis	1974-75: William Kirven	2004-05: Mark W. Harris
1945-46: G. McConnell	1975-76: Charles Kepler	2005-06: Warren Lauer
1946-47: Lloyd Sampson	1976-77: Lawrence Yonkee	2006-07: Joseph Bluemel
1947-48: William Wehrli	1977-78: G. Joseph Cardine	2007-08: Gay Woodhouse
1948-49: R. Diefenderfer	1978-79: William Schwartz	2008-09: Richard Lavery
1949-50: Alfred M. Pence	1979-80: Thomas Lubnau	2009-10: William Hiser
1950-51: Archie McClintock	1980-81: Carl L. Lathrop	*only Bar president later*
1951-52: Burton S. Hill	1981-82: H. McDaniel, Jr.	*elected governor of Wyoming*
1952-53: Edward Murane	1982-83: William R. Jones	

Bill Barlow's Budget (Douglas) published the following paragraph in 1890: "An old lawyer used to say a man's requirements for going to law were ten in number, and he summed them up as follows: Firstly, plenty of money; secondly, plenty of patience; thirdly, a good case; fourthly, a good lawyer; fifthly, plenty of money; sixthly, a good counsel; seventhly, a good witness; eightly, a good jury; ninthly, a good judge; tenthly, plenty of money.'"

LAWMEN AND OUTLAWS

Cost of housing prisoners in state prison system: $119 per day or $43,500 per year per prisoner (2009). In 1996, the cost was $49.40 per day or $18,031 per year. In 1999, the cost had risen to $82 per day or $30,000 per year.

Total prisoners in Wyoming prisons (incarcerated): 2,033 average population in all state facilities, but 722 housed in non-state facilties (2009).

In 2010, the prisoner count at Rawlins was 758. Male prisoners numbered 1,483 in 1996, an increase of 34.9% from 1991. In August, 1999, 900 men were held at Rawlins, 50 prisoners were held for the state in county jails around Wyoming and 148 were incarcerated in a private prison in Olney Springs, Colo.

Wyoming men's prisons: In 1980, a 500-cell facility was opened south of Rawlins. The $54 million new prison facility, located next to the 1980 penitentiary south of Rawlins opened July 21, 2001, with a capacity of 404, but the older facility was closed the same day due to structural problems. The new Medium Security Institution at Torrington was dedicated on Jan. 6, 2010, to accommodate 720 prisoners.

Total number of women in prison in Wyoming: 191 in 2010. In 1999, 151 women were imprisoned in Wyoming.

Total state corrections officers: 1,149 (2008). The total was 429 in 1982; 919 in 2005.

1st prison for women in Wyoming: The Wyoming Women's Center founded on June 20, 1977, originally housed on the grounds of the State Hospital at Evanston. The facility was opened in Lusk in 1984.

Wyoming Public Defender Program founded: July 1, 1978.

1st jail in Afton: The town set aside $250 for construction of a jail on the lot purchased for $40 in 1904.

1st man arrested in Campbell County: In 1912, soon after the county was established, the Rev. C. W. Harris, a Baptist minister, was arrested and charged with carrying a gun.

1st woman deputy U. S. Marshal: Esther A. Duerksen, 1950.

1st woman officer of the Wyoming Highway Patrol: Bonnie Coppock, commissioned in 1979.

Wyoming Highway Patrol canine unit organized: 2000 with four drug-detection Labrador dogs.

Profile of a Wyoming murder: most likely to occur in the spring, be committed with a handgun, involve a victim between the ages of 20 and 29 who is acquainted with his/her assailant.

Murders, 2008: 14; four committed with handguns. In 2004, 11 people were murdered in Wyoming. In 1998, there were 26 homicides, the most since 1986. In 1992, there were murders in Sweetwater, 5; Laramie and Natrona, 3 each; Sublette and Teton, 2 each; one each in Fremont and Campbell. There were no murders in the other 16 counties during 1992.

Wyoming hate crimes: 19 were reported in 1995; 12 in 2008

Driving While Intoxicated (2008): 7,159 arrested statewide for the offense

Armed Robberies (2008): 35

All violent crimes: 633 arrests made in 2008.

All property crimes: 3,073 arrests made in 2008.

Biggest prison escape in Wyoming history: On October 11, 1912, following a prison riot at the State Penitentiary in Rawlins, 27 prisoners escaped. Three were killed in the outbreak and one local man was killed. All but two prisoners had been recaptured by the end of the year. The leader, Burt Dalton, was captured near Big Piney on Dec. 27, 1912.

Some Famous Jail Inmates

1. Jesse James

According to some accounts, Sheriff Nate Boswell of Laramie once arrested and jailed James and several other men on suspicion of horse theft. The men were released before James was recognized. It is said that James once used a hideout near Sheridan in the 1870s. Even though the man's name was "Jesse James," it is not likely that the individual was the notorious Missouri outlaw, however.

2. James Averell

An inmate in the Carbon County Jail in Rawlins when the 1880 census was taken on Aug. 29, Averell was doing time for "shooting with intent to kill." Nine years later, Averell and Ella Watson ("Cattle Kate") were lynched near their homesteads on the Sweetwater River.

3. Alferd Packer

The "Colorado cannibal" was arrested at Emanuel "Crazy Horse" George's cabin on Latham Creek, a tributary of Wagon Hound Creek, near Fort Fetterman in 1883 by Sheriff Malcolm Campbell. Packer was accused of devouring five companions when the party became stranded in a Colorado blizzard earlier that winter. Packer was held briefly in the local jail and taken to Colorado for trial.

4. Phil Watson

With a partner, Watson was arrested for stealing horses in September, 1889. He was serving as Casper town marshal at the time. He was convicted and sentenced to five years in prison. He was the first public official in Wyoming to be sentenced to the penitentiary.

5. Butch Cassidy

From July 15, 1894, to Jan. 19, 1896, Cassidy was a prisoner in the Wyoming State Penitentiary in Laramie. He had been convicted in Fremont County of stealing 60 horses from the Padlock Ranch. When asked for proof of ownership by Deputy Sheriff Bob Calverly near Afton, Cassidy produced a forged bill of sale. His defense lawyer was Douglas Preston; the prosecutor was William Simpson. Cassidy, 27 years old at the time of sentencing, was pardoned by Gov. William A. Richards. The term in the Laramie prison was the only jail time Cassidy ever served.

6. Red Cloud

The Sioux chief and his son were both jailed in Casper in 1895 for poaching.

7. Tom Horn

The range detective and hired gunman was held in the Laramie County Jail from January, 1902, until his execution on Nov. 20, 1903. On Aug. 9, 1903, Horn and fellow prisoner Jim McCloud escaped from jail. They were recaptured a few blocks away.

8. Doc Middleton

The notorious Nebraska outlaw, who later became a peaceable saloonkeeper in South Dakota, was serving a short sentence in the Converse County Jail for disturbing the peace in 1913. He died in jail on Dec. 27 from stab wounds suffered from being knifed in a fight in an Orin Junction saloon before his incarceration.

9. Earl Durand

Durand, a reclusive "mountain man," was arrested and sentenced to six months in the Park County Jail in 1939 for poaching. He escaped one morning by striking deputy sheriff Noah Riley over the head with a milk bottle and taking Riley's keys. Following a crime spree which included the murder of four law enforcement officers, Durand was shot and killed at the front entrance of the First National Bank of Powell minutes after he robbed the bank and killed the bank teller.

10. George Sitts

In South Dakota, Sitts murdered the Butte County sheriff and a special agent near Spearfish on Jan. 24, 1946. After hiding out for a few days in the locked cellar of the Deadwood police chief (unknown to the chief), Sitts stole a car and escaped into Wyoming. He took back roads and, near Arminto, the car skidded into the ditch. A passing motorist recognized him from the broadcast description and called police. Sitts was arrested near Lysite when deputies found his car stalled on a dirt road. Jailed briefly in Casper, he was returned for trial in South Dakota.

11. Charles Starkweather

The Nebraska man went on a killing spree across Nebraska and Wyoming with his

---

Crimes reported in Casper, 1922: liquor law violations, 161; gambling, 55; auto theft, 34; attempted murder, 3; murder, 2; one for confidence operations; one for embezzlement; "eight I.W.W.'s arrested."

young girlfriend Carol Fugate in 1958. The two were finally captured near Douglas and held in the county jail. Starkweather was returned to Nebraska for trial where he was convicted of the crimes and executed. Fugate was also convicted. In the late 1980s, it was reported that she had been released.

12. Randy Kehler

The Encampment resident was imprisoned but he was not an outlaw. A peace activist who opposed war on moral grounds, he was coordinator of the Nuclear Freeze movement. In February, 1970, he was sentenced to two years in federal prison for resisting the draft. He was the first Wyomingite so sentenced during the Vietnam War era. In recent years, Kehler made the news again when he refused to pay the portion of his income taxes which would be used for military spending.

13. Howie Wolke

Wolke and Dave Foreman started the environmental organization, Earth First! in 1980 in a Jackson Hole bar. Wolke served six months in the Sublette County Jail in 1985 for removing survey stakes from an oil rig road. In the 1990s, Wolke quit Earth First! believing it had strayed from its original goals. In 1995, he operated a back packing guide service headquartered in Hamilton, Montana.

14. Bobby Seale

While he was being transferred from California to the "Chicago 7" trial in 1968, the well-known Black radical was housed overnight in the Laramie jail. He was the only prisoner. He remembered the jail as "the best I ever stayed in."

Wyoming and the FBI 10 Most Wanted List, 1950-88*

1. Harry Burton (b. 1902)

Wanted for questioning in a robbery-murder in Los Angeles in October, 1947, Burton had a long arrest record before the incident. His name was placed on the FBI Most Wanted List on Feb. 18, 1951. Following a feature about him on a "True Detective" radio broadcast, he was recognized and arrested at a Cody auto dealership where he had worked for several weeks. He had spent four years in the Cody area, changing jobs frequently. He was extradited to Los Angeles. A jury found him not guilty of the robbery-murder and he was set free.

2. Everett Krueger (b. Laramie, 1922)

Krueger had a long criminal record including a sentence for burglary in Casper in 1942. Following honorable discharge from the U. S. Army in 1946, he returned to his criminal career with another burglary conviction. Following his release, he was arrested in Jackson in 1952 again for burglary and for aiding and abetting an escape. While in jail, awaiting trial, Krueger and two others overpowered a jailer on May 8, 1953, and escaped in a stolen vehicle into Idaho. The two accomplices were captured but Krueger evaded arrest. He was put on the FBI Most Wanted List on Jan. 25, 1954. Three weeks later, he was arrested in Las Cruces, N. M., Krueger apparently was the only Wyoming native ever listed by the FBI.

3. Richard Hunt (b. Oregon)

A military policeman during the Korean War, Hunt went AWOL. A series of crimes in Montana led to his imprisonment there in 1954. In 1958, he was released from prison and began stealing cars in Wyoming and elsewhere. On March 24, 1958, he kidnapped an Oregon police chief. While in pursuit, another policeman was critically wounded by Hunt's gunfire. His name was added to the Most Wanted List on May 27, 1959. A few days later, Hot Springs County Sheriff Eddie Todorovich noticed the wanted poster and recognized Hunt as a man he had met some months before, working at a Thermopolis area ranch.

Hunt was arrested at the ranch June 2, 1959, tried for his Oregon crimes and sentenced to a life term.

4. Chester McGonigal (b. Colo.)

McGonigal attempted to murder his wife in an Aspen, Colo., bar in April, 1961. His name was added to the FBI Most Wanted List in August, 1961. He was arrested in Denver on Aug. 17. During the four months he was at large, McGonigal worked on a ranch near Elk Mountain.

5. Willie Hughes

Wanted for a Detroit murder in 1961, Hughes worked briefly on a Wyoming ranch before he was arrested in Pocatello, Idaho.

6. Robert Leroy Lindblad

Lindblad, whose name was added to the Most Wanted List July 11, 1968, was charged with the murder of two Jackson Hole businessmen in a "murder-for-hire" scheme involving a partner of the two victims. Lindblad, the "trigger man" allegedly hired by the third partner, killed the two partners near Dayton, Nevada, in August, 1967. He surrendered to authorities in Nevada in October, 1968.

7. Lohman Mays, Jr. (b. Texas, 1943)

Mays was in prison for a murder conviction in North Carolina when he escaped July 1, 1984. He robbed two banks in two states and was listed by the FBI on Feb. 15, 1985. On Sept. 23, 1985, Mays was arrested in Wyoming.

*Source: The FBI Most Wanted: An Encyclopedia. By Michael and Judy Ann Newton. (New York: Garland, 1989). According to the authors, the Most Wanted List was first used March 14, 1950. Until mid-1988, 420 fugitives had been listed.

30 Wyoming Executions, 1865-1991

1.-3. Chief Little Thunder, Two Face, Walks-under-the-Ground, Fort Laramie, 1865
The three Native Americans were hanged on the order of post commander Col. Thomas Moonlight. who later became Wyoming territorial governor.

4. Mr. Jennings, Fort Halleck, May 22, 1865

The record does not reveal Jennings' first name. He was executed by the army for murdering a man at the military post near present-day Elk Mountain.

5. John Boyer, Cheyenne, April, 1871

Boyer was the first person legally hanged by order of a Wyoming court. He killed two men, James McClusky and William H. Lowry, near Fort Laramie on Oct. 26, 1870. He was tried in Cheyenne March 21, 1871, with Chief Justice J. H. Howe as circuit judge. He was hanged April 21, 1871, by Sheriff T. Jeff Carr.

6. William "Tousant" Kensler, Cheyenne, November, 1874

In July, 1873, the Wyoming Territorial Supreme Court heard his appeal, the first appeal from a death sentence in Wyoming history. The court upheld the lower court's conviction and the execution proceeded. Kensler shot and killed rancher Adolph Pena at Pena's ranch on the Sybille. Captured by the army, he escaped from the guardhouse at Fort D. A. Russell and fled to Nebraska. He was again arrested by soldiers at Red Cloud Agency in a gunfight, leaving him shot in both legs. Transported by army ambulance back to Cheyenne, Kensler went on trial in November, 1972. He was convicted and hanged on Nov. 19, 1874, in Cheyenne.

7. LeRoy Donovan, Rawlins, 1884

Donovan was the first man legally executed in Rawlins. ("Big Nose" George Parrot was sentenced to hang in 1881, but following an abortive escape attempt, he was lynched by Rawlins citizens fearing he would escape before being hanged). Donovan, also known as John Lee (and supposedly the son of Mormon John D. Lee of Mountain Meadows massacre fame), killed a 40-year-old Rock Springs barber with a hammer in a robbery attempt at Rock Springs. The trial was held in Rawlins on a change of venue. Donovan was convicted in October, 1883, and hanged on Jan. 18, 1884.

8. George Cook, Laramie, Dec. 12, 1884

Cook, a 30-year-old Englishmen working for the railroad at Medicine Bow, went into Laramie to celebrate Thanksgiving Day, 1883. He and his brother-in-law, James Blunt, went on a two-day drinking spree. The two quarreled, Cook pulled a .45 and shot Blunt in the head on Front Street, Laramie. Convicted, Cook was hanged Dec. 12, 1884.

9. William Booth, Buffalo, March 5, 1886

Booth is the only person ever legally executed in Johnson County. The 25-year-old Booth worked on a ranch six miles from Buffalo. He was convicted of murdering his employer, rancher Jake Schmerer. Booth was captured by Sheriff Frank Canton on June 12, 1885, and convicted of first degree murder on July 8. He was hanged March 5, 1886, at Buffalo by Sheriff Canton.

10. Ben Carter, Rawlins, October 26, 1888

Carter, born in Texas in 1850, shot and killed James Jeffreys, a 17-year-old cowboy, on Oct. 4, 1886, while at a cattle roundup camp northeast of Rawlins. Captured at the Sun Ranch, Carter stood trial for murder in May, 1887. He was convicted. After a stay of execution pending appeal and a temporary reprieve from the governor, he was executed Oct. 26, 1888, in Rawlins.

11. George Black, Laramie, February, 1890

Black was convicted of the May, 1889, murder of Robert Burnett, an eccentric, 60-year-old rancher at Burnett's ranch 15 miles east of Laramie at Pole Mountain. Black shot Burnett and he and a colleague burned the body. Three months later, neighbors found the ashes of the man and brought them in to the Albany County sheriff. The two men were arrested in August, 1889. Black's colleague confessed and testified that Black was the killer. The 27-year-old Black was hanged in Laramie on Feb. 26, 1890, by Sheriff Charles Yund.

12. Charles E. Miller, Cheyenne, April 22, 1892

The youngest person ever executed in Wyoming (16 years, 7 months), he was the first person executed on the "Julian gallows." Miller, then just 15, shot and killed two St. Joseph, Missouri, men, Waldo Emerson and Ross Fishbough, while they slept in a boxcar at Hillsdale. Convicted and sentenced to hang, Miller suffered from various ailments while awaiting execution and escaped twice. In his second escape, Miller was recaptured with a companion in Pine Bluffs. A third escapee, William Kingen, a Nebraska cattle rustler, froze to death. Miller was hanged April 22, 1892, by Sheriff A. D. Kelley.

13. Frank Howard, Rawlins, Dec. 7, 1894

On New Year's Eve, 1893, Howard shot and killed Charles Horn at Dixon in a jealous rage. After trial in June, 1894, the Wisconsin native was sentenced to hang. The execution was carried out at the Carbon County Jail on Dec. 7, 1894.

14. James Kieffer, Lander, Sept. 25, 1903

Kieffer was convicted of killing 60-year-old D. J. Warren, a horse tender at the Derby stage station, 18 miles east of Lander. The motive was robbery and Kieffer got from the victim just 50 cents. Kieffer claimed insanity, but witnesses told of his bragging of killing 17 men in 17 states prior to coming to Wyoming in 1901. He was convicted in July, 1902. On Sept. 25, 1903, he became the first and only person legally executed in Fremont County. The hangman's knot was in the Pioneer Museum, Lander.

15. Tom Horn, Cheyenne, Nov. 20, 1903

The notorious stock detective, convicted of the ambush murder of 14-year-old Willie Nickell, died on a gallows specially designed by Cheyenne architect J. P. Julian. The complicated device supposedly allowed a prisoner to "hang himself" through a complex system of pulleys, ropes and escaping water. The mechanism was dismantled from where it was used inside the Laramie County Jail, sent to Rawlins and reassembled. It was used in the next nine executions. The site of Horn's hanging is near the present location of the elevator in the City-County Building. As one wag observed, "You and I have the option of going up or down on the spot where Horn could go only one way."

16. Joseph Seng, Rawlins, May, 1912

Seng was convicted for killing a Union Pacific watchman in Evanston in the fall of 1910. Following Horn's execution, the law required that all executions be carried out at the State Penitentiary in Rawlins. Seng had been catcher for the prison baseball team. As a teammate wrote: "The ball team didn't amount to much after they hanged the catcher."

17. J. Warren Jenkins, Nov. 14, 1913

As if Jenkins didn't have enough problems, the judge who sentenced Jenkins to death also ordered him to pay a fine of $1,000. The Cheyenne man was convicted of murdering his wife at home in the so-called "Indian club murder case." The Jenkins home site is the parking garage of Memorial Hospital, Cheyenne.

18. Millard Flanders, June 16, 1916

Convicted of the murders of Mr. and Mrs. Sam Aultz, neighbors near his Red Canyon ranch in Sheridan County, Flanders was convicted and sentenced in Sheridan. The 50-year-old Flanders had been a prominent railroad engineer and 32nd degree Mason.

19. Wilmer P. Palmer, Aug. 11, 1916

The 33-year-old Natrona County waiter was convicted of murder and sentenced in May, 1915, but the Wyoming Supreme Court delayed his first execution date until the next summer.

20. Oscar White, Oct. 20, 1916

The 26-year-old laborer became the third man executed in 1916, the most in one year in Wyoming history. He had been convicted in Natrona County of first-degree murder in October, 1913.

21. Yee Geow, March 11, 1921

The 24-year-old cook had been convicted in Laramie County the previous year of first-degree murder.

22. George Brownfield, March 10, 1930

At 54 years old, Brownfield was the oldest man executed in Wyoming. A sheep rancher from Colony, he was convicted in February, 1930, in Crook County of murdering a man near his sheep wagon and assaulting the dead man's wife in July, 1929. Brownfield was executed before 33 witnesses.

23. Charles Aragon, May 14, 1930

The 23-year-old ranch hand was sentenced in December, 1928, in Fremont County for first-degree murder.

24. Talton Taylor, May 11, 1933

Taylor was the last person executed by hanging in Wyoming. He was convicted in Johnson County of first-degree murder.

25. Paul H. Carroll, Aug. 13, 1937

The first man executed in the Wyoming gas chamber, the 37-year-old fireman was convicted for the murder of a railroad official in Laramie County.

26. Stanley S. Lantzer, April 19, 1940

The 36-year-old Colorado man was convicted two years earlier of killing his wife in August, 1938, in Cheyenne. According to historian Carol Bowers who has written an article about the case, Lantzer's crime seemed no more heinous than others where the convicted persons were not executed. Gov. Nels Smith was asked to commute the sentence to life in prison on the scheduled day of execution. He denied the request. He delayed the decision because he was recovering from having had a tooth pulled the previous day. *Source: Carol Bowers, "Loving Cecile: The Strange Case of Stanley Lantzer," in Readings in Wyoming History (2000).*

27. Cleveland Brown, Jr., Nov. 17, 1944

The 26-year-old transient railroad worker had been convicted of rape and murder in Lincoln County the previous year. His last request was for a bottle of whiskey, but the wish was denied.

28. Henry Ruhl, April 27, 1945

Ruhl, a transient and federal prisoner, was convicted of killing a Cheyenne man. As he was blindfolded before being placed in the gas chamber, he laughingly told onlookers, "Hell, I thought I was going to see something."

29. Andrew Pixley, Dec. 10, 1965

The last person executed in the Wyoming gas chamber, Pixley was a 22-year-old laborer who was convicted of killing a 12-year-old Chicago area girl in a Jackson motel. The girl's eight-year-old sister had been killed, too, but Pixley was not tried for her death. He was convicted by a jury in Worland where the case had been moved on a change of venue from Teton County.

30. Mark Hopkinson, Jan. 22, 1991

The 42-year-old Fort Bridger man was the first (and, at this writing, the only) person executed in Wyoming by lethal injection. He was convicted of ordering, from his prison cell, the murder of another man. At the time, he was serving a life sentence for his role in the 1977 bombing deaths of Evanston attorney Vincent Vehar, Vehar's wife and son.

*Sources for the territorial executions include Elnora Frye, Atlas of Wyoming Outlaws at the Territorial Penitentiary (Laramie: Jelm Mountain, 1990); Larry Brown, You Are Respectfully Invited to Attend My Execution (Glendo: High Plains, 1998); various newspaper articles.

Norton Moses' List of Noteworthy Wyoming Lynchings*

1. Cheyenne, 1868

Five men were lynched. (I don't want to refer to these men as "victims" of lynching because that would attach too much sympathy to four murderers and a horse thief).

2. Dale City, 1868

A day's ride west of Cheyenne, three more men received "Judge Lynch's" supreme penalty.

3. Laramie, 1868

In what may have been Laramie's first lynching, vigilantes dispatched "the Magician" in May, 1868. A man named "The Kid" wore the hemp necktie in August. Robbery ran him afoul of the vigilantes. Four more got the rope in Laramie in October, 1868. Mayor Asa Moore and two "deputy town marshals" were shot and then hanged. The next day, Long Steve Young declined an order to leave town and was strung up. When a vigilante tried to speed Young to Hell by jerking his legs, the rope broke. A man stomped on his face before the vigilantes put him back on a pole for the rest of the hanging.

Fremont County did not enjoy a reputation for "law and order" in the 1890s. In his memoirs, long-time Wyoming lawyer A. C. Campbell wrote that he once prosecuted a doctor for murdering a Lander druggist. "During the trial, the doctor threatened to kill me," Campbell wrote. "After he had been acquitted, I told the foreman of the jury that if I had an enemy that I desired to get rid of, I would lure him into Fremont County."

4. Soldier, 1877

In December, 1877, a member of Company A, 3rd Cavalry, was lynched by the other men in his unit because he had murdered a sergeant.

5. Carbon, 1879

Dutch Charlie Burris, a fellow bandit of Big Nose George, was hanged from a pole in Carbon. One story avers that the sister-in-law of a deputy sheriff killed by Dutch Charlie kicked the barrel from under him at his hanging.

6. Rawlins, 1881

In what was probably Wyoming's second most infamous lynching, Big Nose George Parrott swung from a pole in Rawlins in 1881. The hanging itself was remarkable because he freed his hands as he was strangling and made several efforts to climb the pole and avoid death. The aftermath was even more noteworthy--Dr. John Osborne tanned Parrott's skin and made a bag and a pair of shoes. The doctor gave the top of the outlaw's skull to his assistant, Lillian Heath Nelson, who used it variously as a pin tray and a door stop.

7. Laramie, 1885

Si Partridge was lynched. Laramie maintained its leadership in mob justice.

8. Sweetwater River, 1889

Wyoming's most notorious lynching was a "double-event": the hangings of Ella Watson ("Cattle Kate") and her lover/partner James Averill near the Sweetwater River in July, 1889. Controversy about her status--prostitute and accomplice of rustlers?--and the fact that cattlemen murdered a woman have kept up interest in the story.

9. Casper, 1902

Charles Woodward was lynched on the scaffold built for his legal hanging in Casper, 1902. He had killed the Natrona County sheriff. After the Wyoming Supreme Court stayed his execution, a mob made sure justice was not further delayed.

10. Newcastle, 1903

One man's grudge apparently led to William Clifton's arrest for a double murder and his lynching in Newcastle in 1903. A mob noosed "Diamond L Slim's" neck, tied the rope to the Little Owl Creek bridge, and threw him over the side. When the rope snapped taut, it ripped the head off his body.

11. Basin, 1903

When stays of execution benefited two murderers in 1903, lynchers broke into the jail, killed a deputy sheriff in the process, and shot the convicted killers in their cells. One wonders about lynchers' murder of a law officer in their pursuit of "justice."

*Norton Moses teaches history at Montana State University, Billings. He is author of Lynching and Vigilantism in the United States: A Bibliography *published by Greenwood Press. He would appreciate a letter if any reader has citations to books or articles (but not newspaper stories) about the following lynchings: J. S. Bedford, Big Horn, Oct. 1892; John Martin, Laramie, Aug. 1904; Frank Wigfall, Rawlins, Oct. 1912; Wade Hampton, Rock Springs, Dec. 1917; Edward Woodson, Green River, Dec. 1918.*

Larry Brown's List of Female Felons*

1. 1st woman prisoner

Nettie Wright-Stewart was the first woman to be imprisoned at the Wyoming Territorial Penitentiary in Laramie. Charges against her were subsequently dropped and she was never assigned a convict identification number.

The Brady law affected Wyoming gun sales. In March, 1994, the first month of the new law, 33 illegal gun buyers were stopped-- 14 were convicted felons or wanted by the law. More than 1,000 Wyomingites applied for permits to purchase handguns in the first month.

2. 1st woman prisoner with ID number

The first woman to be formally lodged and assigned a prisoner identification number in the Territorial Prison was Mary "Mollie" Wrisinger (#10). She and Belle Jones (#11) were imprisoned at the same time, but Molly was processed first. Incidentally, Molly was the stepdaughter of Robert Black, who was the last person legally executed in Wyoming before the territory became a state.

3. In Laramie and Rawlins

Pearl Smith and Gertie Miller were the only women to serve time in both the Territorial Penitentiary in Laramie and the State Penitentiary in Rawlins.

4. Repeat offender

Carolyn Winfield (#126)-Hayes (#365) was the only woman recidivist convict in either the Territorial Penitentiary or the State Penitentiary in Rawlins. She was first convicted of arson. After she was released, she married before being convicted again, this time for theft.

4. Kleptomania as a defense

The first criminal case in which kleptomania was used in Wyoming as a legal defense involved Stella F. Gatlin (#271), an assistant to her postmaster husband at the Myersville stage station. Stella was convicted of stealing from the United States mails.

5. Married couples sentenced

Pete (#270) and Minnie (#271) Snyder, who were convicted of murder, were the only husband and wife to be imprisoned at the Laramie facility. Minnie, the daughter of the founder of Hulett, Wyoming, subsequently served more than twice as much time as any other woman to be imprisoned there or at the Rawlins institution. Joe (#781) and Lenora (#780) Nash, who were convicted of forgery, were the only married couple to serve time at the Rawlins penitentiary.

Larry K. Brown is a historian and author. He has written several books including The Hog Ranches of Wyoming *(Glendo: High Plains, 1995), and* You Are Respectfully Invited to Attend My Execution *(Glendo: High Plains, 1998).*

Unusual Law and Order Stories

1. Executions

Since 1940, only four people have been executed in Wyoming. Three forms of execution have been allowed in Wyoming history. The first, hanging, was the accepted mode until 1935 when the gas chamber was authorized for execution. In the middle 1980s, lethal injection replaced execution by gas. To date, just one person has been executed by lethal injection in Wyoming.

2. Slavery in the Equality State

Slavery did not touch Wyoming like it did many other states. Nonetheless, the institution was not unknown in the area. In 1847, Brigham Young's party brought three slaves across Wyoming to Utah. They were Hark Lay, Oscar Crosby and Green Flake. Prior to 1863, a Black slave was kept at the Rock Ranch, upriver from present-day Torrington.

3. Last Lynching in Laramie

Joe Martin, an African-American prisoner being held in the Albany County Jail, was lynched in Laramie from a telephone poll in front of the home of Judge Carpenter, across

---

Wyoming was ranked the 44th most dangerous state in the U.S., in 2009 (or one of the six least dangerous). Nevada was the most dangerous state from 2006 to 2009. To determine the most dangerous states, rates for six crime categories—murder, rape, robbery, aggravated assault, burglary, and motor vehicle theft—are compared to the national average for a given crime category.

Grand Avenue from the County Courthouse on August 28, 1904. Source: *Rock Springs Miner*, Sept. 1, 1904, p. 1.

4. Window-shopping

Goshen County had no jail during its early years. The county hired a man to guard the prisoners, walking them along Torrington's streets during the day and putting them up in a local hotel at night.

5. Census Count

Casper's Sand Bar brothels employed nearly 2,000 prostitutes during their peak in 1920.

6. First Case

Milward Simpson was graduating from Harvard Law School when he received word that his father had been charged with murder in Park County. He graduated, returned to Wyoming and joined the defense team for his father.

7. Murdered in 1973, Died in 1992

Rebecca Thomson Brown died July 30, 1992, when she either fell or jumped from the Fremont Canyon bridge, 108 feet above the water. Friends said she had "died" two decades earlier. In September 1973, Brown survived a savage attack in which two men raped her, threw her off the Fremont Canyon bridge and killed her 11-year-old step-sister, also throwing her off the bridge. Brown was 18 years old at the time of the crime and she was seriously traumatized by the incident. A jury convicted two men, Ronald Kennedy and Jerry Jenkins, in April 1974. They were given life sentences in the state penitentiary. Casper-born author Ron Franscell wrote about the case in a book titled *The Darkest Night*, published in 2007.

8. Death Threats

Two Gillette junior high school students were subjects of Secret Service investigations in February, 1996, after they apparently made death threats against President Clinton on the Internet. On Oct. 13, 1964, Wyoming papers reported that two Casper youths, one 17 years old and the other 16, had threatened the life of President Lyndon Johnson while the President was visiting in Wyoming.

9. Water Murder

The *Cheyenne Daily Leader*, May 25, 1894, reported the following: "James Widdep, an old settler, was shot and killed Monday on Burnt Fork, southern Uinta County, by Willard Blodgett, in a dispute over water rights. His son, Thomas Widdep, was also shot, but not fatally. Blodgett escaped."

10. Football game murder

On Oct. 21, 1947, a 14-year-old Daniel boy pulled a knife and stabbed to death 18-year-old Richard Doyle as Doyle was moving the chains during the fourth quarter of a football game between Pinedale and Big Piney high schools. Doyle, a former star athlete, had graduated the previous year and was working on the family ranch. The game was called off; the community was shocked by the crime.

11. Armed Robbery of State Treasurer

On the night of Nov. 2, 1964, two armed men came to the home of State Treasurer Everett T. Copenhaver, took him captive and forced him to accompany them to the State Treasurer's office. When they could not gain access to the Capitol Building, they returned to Copenhaver's home where they tied him up with electrical cord and stole $45 and a $80 gold watch before fleeing.

On Dec. 21, 1921, the Natrona County sheriff's office, on a tip, sent three deputies to a grocery store which the informant claimed was to be robbed. Soon, two men entered the store in masks, attempting a robbery. Both were killed by the concealed deputies.

12. Murder of Episcopal Priest

Rev. David Duncombe, the Episcopal vicar at St. Michael's mission in Ethete, was murdered April 24, 1976. His assailant, a 16-year-old Shoshone boy, claimed to have had no memory of the crime. The prosecution charged that the boy committed the act while heavily intoxicated. Prior to coming to the Wind River reservation as priest in 1970, Duncombe had served parishes in New York and Reno, Nevada. He was survived by a wife Patricia and five children.

Unwelcome Radicals

1. Dr. Hiram Wesley Evans

Evans, the imperial wizard of the Ku Klux Klan, made a hasty exit from Casper in 1925 after parishioners of the First Christian Church refused to allow him to use the building for a rally.

2. Green River Klansmen

In February, 1926, the Green River school board meeting was interrupted by a dozen men wearing white Klan robes. A contemporary newspaper report claimed the men only "wanted to present the board with an American flag."

3. David Johnson

Johnson, leader of a Glendale, Calif., based white supremacist group, moved to Casper a few weeks before the 1989 special election for the House seat vacated by Richard Cheney. Johnson gained enough signatures to have his name on the ballot, but he received fewer than 500 votes statewide.

4. KKK Rallies

Radical groups, including the KKK, have had little luck spreading their message in Wyoming. In 1989 the group held a small rally in Casper on Martin Luther King's birthday. A similar gathering was held in January, 1996, when 16 Klan members and supporters (none from Wyoming) demonstrated in front of the State Capitol on Martin Luther King, Jr/ Wyoming Equality Day.

5. Rev. Fred Phelps, Kansas

The pastor of the Westboro Baptist Church led a small group picketing the funeral of slain gay University of Wyoming student Matthew Shepard in front of a Casper church on Oct. 16, 1998. Civic and religious leaders deplored the vicious anti-gay, hate-filled signs and chants. Phelps and his group returned to Kansas.

Arrests in Wyoming

UCR FBI figures, Uniform Crime Reports

1990—25,267	1998--36,262
1995—33,755	1999--34,250
1996—33,553	2008--40,979

Handguns contributed 50 percent of the violent crime in the state; rifles and shotguns were 38.9 percent. 44 percent of murder victims in 1996 were killed by an acquaintance, 17 percent by a spouse. Only 11 percent were killed by strangers. In 1998, there were 26 homicides in Wyoming, the most since 1986.

According to figures from the Southern Poverty Law Center in 2005, there were five active hate groups operating in Wyoming that year. The center listed them as: one Neo-Nazi group each in Cheyenne and Douglas; Racist Skinhead groups in Newcastle and Cheyenne; and one "Other" group (Women for Aryan Unity--no listing of specific town). For Wyoming, there were no "active" Ku Klux Klan groups, Christian Identity groups, Neo-Confederate groups, or Black Separatists groups.

Names on Wyoming Peace Officers' Memorial, Douglas

Bill Stanford, Cheyenne PD 2007
Dennis Schuck, Cheyenne PD 2006
Chris Logsdon, WHP 1998
Del Dixon, Rawlins PD 1996
Steve M. Crerar, Fremont Co. SO 1995
Ryan F. Weltman, NPS, YNP 1994
Robert E. Mahn, Jr., NPS, YNP 1994
Harley Mark, Torrington PD, 1993
Kay Henri Bowles, Wyo. G&F 1992
Kirk Inberg, Wyo. G&F 1991
Robert A. VanAlyne, Jr., Lar. Co. SO 1985
Jon R. Hardy, Gillette PD 1983
Craig L. Schulte, Campbell Co. SO 1983
Clifford D. Stevens, Wyo. G&F 1983
Pete Visser, WHP 1981
Dwain Hardigan, Albany Co. SO 1979
George W. Henderson, Wyo DCI 1973
Francis Gradert, WG&F, 1973
Boyd L. Hall, Teton Co. SO 1972
William Edwards, Teton Co. SO 1972
William Barnett, WHP, 1965
Allan St. Clair, Ft. Wash. PD-BIA 1965
Charles Calvert, WG&F, 1965
Norbert E. Tuck, Laramie Co. SO 1961
Edward Phillips, Sweetw. Co. SO 1955
Jack N. Jernigan, Cheyenne PD 1954
Anthony B. Nelson, Powell PD 1950
Clifford E. Smith, Glenrock TM 1946
Bill Lakanen, Wyo. G&F 1945
Don Simpson, Wyo. G&F 1945
John Alderdice, Greybull PD 1945
Arthur A. Argento, Park Co. SO 1939
Orville H. Linaberry, Park Co. SO 1939
D. M. Baker, Park Co. SO 1939
Charles Lewis, Powell PD 1939
Charles Gatza, Laramie Co. SO 1934
Ed Goodfellow, Hot Spr. Co. SO 1927

Frank McFarlane, Hot Spr. Co. SO 1927
C. M. Cosby, Albany Co. SO 1927
Arthur E. Osborn, Laramie Co. SO 1927
George F. Radden, Casper PD 1925
William McPherren, Sheridan Co. SO 1921
George E. Price, Hot Springs Co. SO 1921
Tom Majors, Natrona Co. SO 1919
John Buxton, Wyo G&F 1919
Hugh C. Petrie, Cheyenne PD 1919
Frank B. Roach, Laramie Co. SO 1916
Tom Harris, Rock Springs PD 1915
William H. Veach, Sheridan Co. SO 1914
Daniel Hanson, Cokeville TM 1912
Alfred H. Bath, Albany Co. SO 1909
C. Henry Edwards, Cheyenne PD 1907
John Baxter, Rawlins PD 1903
Thomas King, Rawlins PD 1903
William H. Miller, Weston Co. SO 1903
Louis Falkenberg, Weston Co. SO 1903
W. C. Ricker, Natrona Co. SO 1902
Charles B. Holden, Uinta Co SO 1901
Josiah Hazen, Converse Co. SO 1899
George A. Wellman, U. S. Marshal 1892
Charles S. Gunn, Lusk Constable, 1887
Edward L. Lloyd, Johnson Co. SO 1886
H. H. Vinson, UPRR, 1878
Robert Widdowfield, Carbon Co. SO 1878

Abbreviations: SO (Sheriff's Office); PD (Police Department); WHP (Wyoming Highway Patrol); TM (town marshal); Wyo G&F (Wyoming Game and Fish Department); NPS (National Park Service).
*Officers who died in the line of duty, regardless of cause. List was provided by Sonja Erickson, Admissions Div., Wyoming Law Enforcement Academy, Douglas.

16 Wyoming Law Officers Killed in the Line of Duty*
*41 Wyoming officers, including five county sheriffs, have died in line of duty.

1. Deputy Sheriff Robert Widdowfield, Carbon County

Widdowfield was killed along with railroad detective Tip Vincent while the two were trailing outlaws who had tried to rob the Union Pacific train near Medicine Bow in August 1878. Big Nose George Parrott and "Dutch Charley" Burris were captured separately and returned to Carbon County to stand trial. Dutch Charley was lynched from a telegraph pole in Carbon before he could be tried. Parrott was found guilty, sentenced to hang, and attempted to escape from the jail. Rawlins residents, fearing he might succeed in getting away before the execution could be carried out, dragged him from the jail and lynched him on March 22, 1881. In May, 1996, a controversy arose in Rawlins over plans to place a marker on the spot where he was executed. Descendants of Widdowfield argued that Widdowfield and Vincent were more properly owing plaques, given that they were the first law officers killed in the line of duty in Wyoming history.

2. Sheriff Joe Hazen, Converse County

Hazen, an Illinois native who had come to Wyoming in 1877, was shot in a gunfight with train robbers he and his posse cornered 40 miles north of Casper on June 5, 1899. The identities of the robbers, who escaped, were not known. There was speculation that Butch Cassidy and his gang might have been the culprits.

3. Charles S. Gunn, Lusk Town Constable

On Jan. 15, 1887, less than a year after Lusk was founded, Constable Gunn entered the Waters Saloon where he was shot by Bill McCoy.. As Gunn fell to his knees, he dropped his revolver, but while trying to retrieve it, McCoy shot him a second time, in the head at point-blank range, killing him instantly. McCoy was convicted of murder and sentenced to hang, but he escaped from jail before the sentence could be carried out. He was never apprehended after his escape.

4. Sheriff Charles Ricker, Natrona County

Ricker was shot and then clubbed with his own gun by outlaw Charley Woodard in Casper in 1902. Woodard was captured by officers, convicted and sentenced to hang. The night before his scheduled execution, Woodard was taken from his jail cell by an angry crowd and lynched.

5. Deputy Sheriff Earl Price, Big Horn County

Price was killed in the melee when in September 1903, a mob stormed the jail and shot two outlaws, Jim Gorman and J. P. Walters, who were awaiting trial.

6. Sheriff William H. Miller, Weston County

Miller died in the Lightning Creek Raid along with five others, four of whom were Indians, on Oct. 31, 1903. It was the last Indian-White violent encounter in Wyoming and involved illegal hunting.

7. Sheriff Al Bath, Albany County

Bath died while pursuing a murder fugitive on May 29, 1910. Elmer Lovejoy drove Bath out to the Woods Landing area where Bath took a horse into the heavily forested area after the outlaw, Tom Summers. Bath was ambushed, shot and killed.Summers fled and never stood trial for the crime.

8. Deputy Sheriff Tom Majors, Natrona County

Majors was shot and killed Nov. 2, 1919, during a shoot-out following a Prohibition raid on a Casper house. Two men were charged but found not guilty after a change of venue to Converse County was granted.

9. Sheriff Charles Crosby, Albany County

Crosby was killed by outlaw Frank Bray near the city springs on April 21, 1927. Bray was kllled by Robert Welliever, Crosby's deputy sheriff.

10. Prohibition Agent James Capen

Capen was killed while attempting to arrest Mike Septick, a suspected bootlegger, 20 miles southwest of Kemmerer on May 10, 1928. Septick also died in the shootout.

11. George Trabing, Prohibition Agent in Seattle

Trabing, a Laramie native, was accidentally killed while working with the Prohibition Bureau in Seattle, Washington, in 1931.

12.-13. Charles Lewis, Powell Police Dept., D. M. Baker, Park County deputy

The Powell policeman was killed March 15, 1939, while attempting to arrest Earl Durand who had escaped from the Park County Jail. Baker was killed later in the week when law enforcement officers tried to trap Durand in Sunlight Basin. They attempted to "rush" him during the night. Later, Durand was killed in a shootout after he robbed the Powell bank. During the course of the incident, two other men, deputized in the manhunt, also were killed. They were Arthur Argento and Orville Linaberry.

14. Michael Rosa, Rock Springs undercover officer

On July 14, 1978, the Rock Springs public safety director Ed Cantrell shot and killed undercover policeman Michael Rosa while both men sat with other officers in Cantrell's police car in the parking lot of the Silver Dollar Bar. Cantrell, who shot Rosa between the eyes, claimed self defense and the jury acquitted him.

15. Pete Visser, Wyoming Highway Patrol officer

Vissler became the first patrolman to be killed in the line of duty in the history of the Wyoming Highway Patrol. The patrol was created in 1933. He was investigating a traffic accident west of Rawlins on I-80 in October 1981, when he was struck and killed by a pickup driven by a drunk driver.

16. Lt. Steve Crerar

Crerar, a Fremont County sheriff's employee, was shot and killed April 30, 1995, by John M. Sides, 17, Lander. Crerar was driving Sides to Worland where he was to be held at the State Training School. Sides freed himself from his handcuffs as Crerar drove up to the school, took Crerar's revolver and shot the officer in the head. Sides pleaded guilty and was given two life sentences for the crime.

First Officers in Wyoming Highway Patrol

Began operations June 1, 1933

1. Capt. George Smith, Douglas
2. Roger McCall, Riverton
3. Frank McCue, Laramie
4. Leslie Waters, Lovell
5. Leroy Mankin, Gillette
6. Mike Maher, Green River
7. Louis Cooper, Torrington

Directors, Wyoming Highway Patrol

1. George Smith
4. Bill Bradley, 1941-1965
5. Fred Wickam, 1965-75
6. Stan Warne, 1975-81
7. W. O. "Fred" Oyler, 1981-84
8. Everette Ayers, 1984-98
9. John Cox, 1998-2005
10. Sam Powell, 2005-2010
11. *Jess Oyler, 2010-
*Jess Oyler is the son of Fred Oyler.

Wyoming Towns with Most Police Officers, 2007*

1. Cheyenne: 99
2. Casper: 92
3.-4. Gillette: 47
3.-4. Laramie: 47
5. Rock Springs: 44
6. Green River: 30
7. Sheridan: 28
8. Evanston: 27
9-10. Jackson: 22
9.-10. Riverton: 22

2007 figures, sworn officers only.

Law Enforcement by Government Unit*

1. County:	301
2. State:	154
3. Municipality:	603

sworn officers, 1994

By comparison, the Los Angeles Police Department had 845 sworn officers; New York City had 1,561.

Wyoming Peace Officers of the Year

The award is made annually by the Wyoming Peace Officers Association.

1957: John J. Terrill, SO, Rawlins
1958: Louis E. Cooper, SO, Casper
1959: George M. Nimmo, SO, Green River
1960: Lenard F. Meacham, SO, Buffalo
1961: C. A. "PeeWee" McDougall, SO, Lander
1962: James Black, SO, Worland
1963: Eddie Todorovich, SOe, Thermopolis
1964: LaVell C. Brinkerhoff, SO, Basin
1965: Earl Ellsworth, SO, Kemmerer
1966: Morris C. Horton, SO, Pinedale
1967: Frank Slagle
1968: E. E. Peters
1969: James Stark, SO, Green River
1970: Darrell R. Ketcham, HP, Worland
1971: Duel Price, SO, Riverton
1972: Jim Johnston, GF, Thermopolis
1973: Boyd Hall, SO, Jackson (posthumous)
1974: Charles W. Ogburn, SO, Rawlins
1975: Robert B. Warne, HP, Buffalo
1976: Jack Matheny, PD, Gillette
1977: Pete Muchmore, GW, Medicine Bow
1978: Ernest L. Johnson, LEA, Douglas
1979: Margie M. Meacham, JP, Rawlins
1980: D. B. "Spike" Hladky, SO, Gillette
1981: Bill Brewer, SO, Cody
1982: Delaine Roberts, USMS, Cheyenne

1983: Fred Van Horn, PD, Mills
1984: H. Stephen Smith, GF, Cheyenne
1985: Robert A. VanAlyne, Jr., SO, Cheyenne (posthumous)
1986: Stan Warne, HP, Cheyenne
1987: Robert D. Coorough, PD, Powell
1988: Paul D. Breed, GF, Sheridan
1989: Thomas J. Pagel, DCI, Cheyenne
1990: DeLoyd Quarberg, SO, Thermopolis
1991: Kevin C. Hughes, DCI, Gillette
1992: Dan Dyer, HP, Laramie
1993: Peggy Parker, PDt, Jackson
1994: Jeffrey M. Pfau, PD Gillette
1995: John Harrison, SO, Cheyenne
1996: Mont L. Mecham, PD Green River
1997: William R. Miller, NPS, Moose
1998: Kim Clark, SO, Cokeville
1999: Scott Hughes
2000: Delaine Baldwin, HP
2001: Steve Miller
2002: Byron Oedekoven, SO, Gillette
2003: Juel R. Leuis, HP
2004: James "Mike" Reed, PD, Rawlins
2005: John Fanning, SO, Albany County
2006: Lin Bashford, GF
2007: Mike Picerno

Abbreviations: SO (Sheriff's Office); PD (Police Department); HP (Wyoming Highway Patrol); TM (town marshal); GF (Wyoming Game and Fish Department); NPS (National Park Service); DCI (Division of Criminal Investigation); JP (Justice of the Peace); LEA (Wyoming Law Enforcement Academy), *List to 1998, courtesy Dean Parks, Secretary, Wyoming Peace Officers' Assoc., 1999.

Wyoming Game & Fish Wardens/Chief Wardens, 1899-2010*

1888-1891	Louis Miller	1938-1942	Lester Bagley (Game)
1891-1913	Gustave Schnitger	1939-1943	James R Simon (Fish)
1913 -1915	D. F. Hudson (Game)	1944-	+Lester Bagley
1913-1919	John J. Lenihan (Fish)	1943-1944	Jim Simpson
1915-1919	Nate P. Wilson (Game)	1945	R. R. Rousseau
1919-1921	William T Judkins (Game)	1946-1947	Archie Pendergraft
1919-1921	Charles Morgareidge (Fish)	1948-1952	Charles Hanscum
1921-1923	William t. Judkins	1953-1958	Norbert Faass
1923-1924	Frank S. Smith	1959-1963	James White
1925-1926	A. A. Sanders	1964-1965	Earl Thomas
1927-1930	Bruce Nowlin	1966-1972	Howard Robinson
1931-1937	Robert Hocker	1972-1989	Rex Corsi
1937-1939	Andrew Martin (Game)	1989--	Jay Lawson
1937-1939:	Frank Crook (Fish)		

* The State Game Warden has been in charge of wildlife management and enforcement in the State of Wyoming. Over time the position name has changed, but duties have remained essentially the same. Currently, Jay Lawson, the Chief Game Warden, is head of the Wildlife Division for the WGFD. Source: Wyoming Blue Book; Wyoming Game and Fish Dept.

+ Bagley was the first person desginated State Game and Fish Commissioner

In 1899, the state paid bounties of $20 for each wolf or mountain lion; $1 each for coyotes.

Misc. Facts about Game and Fish Regulation

1. Game and Fish laws

The first Wyoming territorial legislature passed laws protecting and regulating fish and game in 1869. In 1871, the legislature made it illegal to waste game and restricted killing of elk. Non-residents were prohibited from killing game in 1886. Non-residents licenses were allowed for first time in 1895, and non-resident guides were required in 1899. Resident licenses for hunting were not required until 1903. The first appropriation by the state for feeding game was made in 1909.

2. State Game and Fish Commission

While individuals were hired as "game commissioners" and "fish commissioners" in the territorial period (before 1890), the first State Game Commission was established in 1911. It became the Game and Fish Commission in 1921. Initially, the legislature determined hunting and fishing seasons. The powers were given to the Game and Fish Commission in 1929.

3. Game wardens

The state's first game warden, Albert Nelson, was paid $1,200 per year, but he had to pay the $3 per day for any deputy state game wardens he needed from his own salary. Game wardens were required to pass oral and written exams as a conditon for hiring only after 1937. There was no standard enforcement uniform for wardens until 1941, the same year that the pronghorn insignia of the agency was designed by Ten Sleep Game Warden Archie Pendergraft. In 1964, a college degree became a requirement for employment.

4. Game warden numbers

Game wardens numbered fewer than a half dozen statewide until after World War II. By 1952, their number had grown to 31. In 1965, Game and Fish employed 44 game wardens and the number rose to 50 only in 2008.

5. Fish

The first "fish commission" was created in 1879. Its jurisdiction was extended to include game in 1895. The first state fish hatchery was built in 1885.

6. Good Games?

A woman from Newcastle called state game warden in February 1935. She first asked if he was the state game warden. He said he was and she said she'd had difficulty reaching him, but she needed his help. "I'm having a birthday party for my son this afternoon, and I wondered if you wouldn't suggest some good games."

1st Murders in Wyoming Places

1. 1st murder in Casper

Committed by a man in Lou Polk's dance hall in Sept. 1890, Polk is said to have furnished the gun to the murderer.

2. 1st murder in Washakie County (county organized 1911)

On Dec. 29, 1913, Tom McIntyre shot and killed Louis Cloud in a Worland bordello operated by Jewell Mills. McIntyre had been a cook there but had been fired and returned, drunk and angry, to settle some old scores. McIntyre, who admitted shooting Cloud three times, pleaded guilty to second degree murder and was sentenced to a life term in Rawlins.

3. 1st murder in Thermopolis

In August, 1901, Mrs. A. L. Hoover, a widow from Otto, was camped at Hot Springs

As of 2002, 4.1% of the voting population of Wyoming were disenfranchised as a result of having been convicted of a felony. The national average is just 2 percent.

State Park, taking the baths. A man named Walters accosted her and when she demanded he leave, he drew a .32 caliber pistol and shot her twice. He then shot himself. Mrs. Hoover had operated a general store in Otto. She left three children.

8 Notorious Houses of Prostitution

1. Southern Mansion and Fannie Bell's, Casper

They were the best known of the Casper Sand Bar district houses during the oil boom of the early 1920s. Later, Van Rooms became equally notorious.

2. Cora Gray's, Rock Springs

The house on a Rock Springs hill operated openly until the middle 1920s.

3. Yellow Hotel, Lusk

The brothel was run by Dell Burke until the 1970s. It is said that Burke managed to keep the place open because she held most of the town's water bonds.

4. Black and Tan, Cheyenne

The place catered to soldiers stationed at Fort Warren during World War II. It was located in west Cheyenne on 18th and Snyder Avenue, almost exactly halfway between Fort Warren and the railroad yards. The building still stands.

5. Ida Hamilton's House of Mirrors, Cheyenne

The fashionable brothel operated in the heyday of the cattle barons, some of whom stayed at the Cheyenne Club and frequented Hamilton's downtown brothel. The Cheyenne Club never operated as a brothel, but the "Cheyenne Social Club" in the film of that name resembles Ida Hamilton's place.

6. Front Street brothels, Laramie

From the 1880s intermittently through the 1960s, Laramie's Front Street was a haven for prostitution. The various establishments operated under a number of names. Periodically, the houses would be closed during "clean up" campaigns. In the 1950s, the University of Wyoming administration urged closure, fearing that adverse publicity of the existence of the Front Street establishments frightened parents of university students and threatened enrollments.

7. Willis House, Encampment

The structure was built in 1899 to house Madame Willis' thriving business. Local residents "asked" her to leave town before the building was finished and it stood empty until 1931.

8. Kemmerer area brothels

Several brothels operated intermittently in Kemmerer. In 1903, the city government "fined" each house $3 per month, raising the "fine" later to $5 per month. As long as the fines were paid, the houses were allowed to stay open. An additional gambling "fine" of $8 was assessed those establishments whose owners did not wish to pay the "annual gambling license fee" of $75.

Some Wyoming Homicides

1. Charlotte Shepard ("Mother Featherlegs")

Shepard operated a house of prostitution along the stageline south of present-day Lusk from about 1876 until her murder three years later. She was known as "Mother Featherlegs" because she wore ruffled lace underwear that flapped in the breeze when she rode her horse. She often held valuables for cowboys in the area and, apparently, became the victim of a robbery. In the summer of 1879, Mrs. O. J. Demmon, the wife of a local

James Brown, age 64, was convicted of forgery in Carbon County in 1900 and sent to prison. He was released 34 years and 8 months later, soon after his 99th birthday.

rancher, rode to Mother Featherlegs' for a visit, having no one else to talk to. She discovered the madam's murdered body lying beside the spring; apparently she had been killed while filling a bucket with spring water, and had been dead for two or three days. Tracks in the area indicated that a man known locally as "Dangerous Dick" may have murdered her and fled with the money and jewels she was holding for local bandits. Mother Featherlegs was buried quietly on the spot. The crime was not definitively solved. On May 17, 1964, a marker was placed to mark her burial place, the only known monument in the United States in memory of a prostitute.

2. William Milne

On April 3, 1895, Joel J. Hurt, Natrona County state senator and former mayor of Casper, shot and killed Milne, a sheep rancher, on Center street in front of a saloon. The shooting was the result of a scandal involving Milne and Mrs. Hurt. After the shooting, Hurt was taken to jail and charged with manslaughter. The case went to trial in May, 1895, and a jury found Hurt not guilty. After gaining his freedom, Hurt divorced his wife and moved to Omaha, Nebraska.

3. Willie Nickell

Hired gunman Tom Horn was convicted of the murder of the young boy after a 16-day trial in Cheyenne in October 1902. Horn was hanged Nov. 20, 1903.

4. Jessie Root Jenkins

The press called it the "Indian club" murder. Charged was J. Warren Jenkins, a 33-year-old Cheyenne carpenter who married Jessie Root, a wealthy Denver woman, in June 1911. Two days after the marriage, Mrs. Jenkins drew up a will giving most of her property to her new husband in the event of her death. They were married less than a year when Mrs. Jenkins' body was found in the dining room of the couple's home on House Avenue. (The site is now occupied by Memorial Hospital's parking garage). She had been struck numerous times with an Indian club (an exercise barbell) found near the scene. When Jenkins could not explain why buttons to his clothes and underwear were found among ashes in the kitchen stove, he was charged with the murder. The prosecution claimed he burned the clothes because they were covered with blood after the attack. Jenkins was convicted and executed on Nov. 14, 1913.

5. Frank Brown

Horace Adams was charged with killing rancher Frank Brown at Silver Crown on June 6, 1921. Adams, who inherited the Silver Crown mine from his father, frequently shot at "trespassers." He contended Brown was "claim-jumping " on his mine property. Cheyenne lawyer William B. Ross, who lost the Jenkins case in 1913, defended Adams who was found not guilty by a Laramie County jury. Two years later, Ross was elected governor of Wyoming.

6.-7. Edna Mae Richards Jenkins and Thomas Jenkins

The recently married couple was found dead in late September, 1911. Mrs. Jenkins, the daughter of former Wyoming Gov. W. A. Richards, had married the young military officer in Cheyenne and the couple went to Gov. Richards' ranch on the Red Bank near Ten Sleep for their honeymoon. Their bodies were found Sept. 24, Mrs. Jenkins in a bed at the ranch house and Jenkins, outside, a few yards from the building. Some speculated the case was murder-suicide although others believed it was a double murder. The case was never solved.

8. Ed Rains

On Sunday, Aug. 19, 1923, a Cody barber attacked prominent attorney William Simpson on a Cody street, knocking him down. Simpson returned to his law office, got a gun from a desk drawer and returned to confront Rains. He found Rains in the pool hall and a fight ensued. During the fight, Simpson shot Rains and the barber died of his wounds later that night. Simpson was charged with murder. County attorney Ernest Goppert, the prosecutor, asked for a manslaughter conviction. Simpson was represented by prominent attorney E. E. Enterline, Casper, who claimed Simpson had acted in self-defense. Assisting Enterline was Simpson's son, Milward, a recent law school graduate. It was Milward Simpson's first case. The jury trial was held in Basin and in April, 1924, the jury returned with a deadlocked verdict. Eventually, the charges were dropped.

8. Mrs. B. J. Minor and four children

One of Torrington's leading citizens, Baptist minister Rev. B. J. Minort also a police judge and manager of a grain company, killed his wife and four children and himself in December 1926. He had previously served time in a Missouri prison for 2nd degree murder of a miner.

9. S. S. Combs, Casper attorney

Mrs. Hazel Combs jailed for murder of husband, former Casper city attorney S. S. Combs. On the morning of June 11, 1934, the bullet-riddled body of the prominent Casper attorney was found at the wheel of his automobile, to one side of the road within view of their ranch house. He had been shot five times in the back and head. Four days later, at the scene of the murder, Mrs. Combs was arrested and charged with the slaying. She pleaded not guilty. From the day of her arrest she maintained her innocence and expressed astonishment that the authorities should even consider her a suspect. On Jan. 6, 1935, the day before her trial was to begin in Rawlins, she hanged herself in her cell in the Carbon County Jail, Rawlins.

10.-11. Charles C. Barnard and R. H. Fasen

The 55-year-old superintendent of the Wyoming Division of the Union Pacific Railroad was murdered in the UP Depot, Cheyenne, on Oct. 27, 1935, by P. H. Carroll, 36, who had been fired earlier from his job as a switch tender. Carroll was later convicted and executed, the first to die in Wyoming's gas chamber. Ironically, on the day Barnard became superintendent, Oct. 13, 1933, a similar incident occurred in which Keith Bellairs, a disgruntled former employee, shot and killed R. H. Fasen, UP shop superintendent, in Cheyenne. In that case, Bellairs was tried, found not guilty by reason of insanity and sent to the State Hospital.

12. L. J. Schiller

The Hulett mill owner was murdered in September, 1933, apparently for the $100,000 he held in a strong box. Seven people faced charges stemming from his beating death. Jim Vines was convicted in the trial in Sundance in April, 1934, and sentenced to death. The execution was stayed on appeal. Richard Reel and Lloyd Wilkerson were given life sentences. The others were charged as accessories. Ironically, Schiller's mill was destroyed by fire in August, 1934, the same month during which Vines' execution had been scheduled.

13. Warren Moody

Moody, the city attorney for Shoshoni was murdered July 20, 1906, by someone who ambushed him outside his home. As reported in the *Wind River Mountaineer*, July 27, 1906, Moody was killed about 11:30 p.m. that Friday night, just 30 feet from his home. A later report, Sept. 14, 1906, indicated that Marshal Joe LaFors was on trail of suspect in South Dakota. Was the case ever solved? The sources are silent.

14. Robert Meyers

Anson Eddy, a reclusive Park County rancher, was arrested and charged with the murder of Meyers (b. 1919), an artist who was Eddy's neighbor. The victim had been shot

---

The Wyoming Law Enforcement Academy began in 1973, but moved into its present facility northwest of Douglas in 1984. The $8 million facility includes state of the art firing ranges as well as computer classrooms.

down while opening a gate at his ranch on the South Fork near Cody. After a long and widely reported trial, the Park County jury found Eddy not guilty of the crime. Meyers had been a well-known New York illustrator prior to moving to the Cody area in 1960 when he turned to Western art.

15. Michael Rosa

Ed Cantrell was a law enforcement officer in Rock Springs. In July 1979, he was arrested and charged with the murder of undercover police officer Michael Rosa. Rosa was seated between two other police officers who were also involved in the undercover operation in the back seat of Cantrell's car. The police car was parked outside a Rock Springs club. Cantrell, who later claimed he could sense that Rosa was "going for his gun." turned from where he was sitting in the driver's seat and shot Rosa between the eyes. The trial was held in Pinedale. Cantrell's lawyer, Gerry Spence, persuaded the jury that Cantrell shot Rosa in self-defense. The defense claim was that Cantrell could draw a gun faster than almost anyone alive. When he saw "in Rosa's eyes" that Rosa was going for his gun, Cantrell's draw was so fast that Rosa was dead, reportedly before he could move even a finger from the wine glass he was said to have been cupping with both hands. In 1980 Rosa's widow filed a $6 million wrongful death lawsuit against Cantrell, two police officers, and the city of Rock Springs. The suit was settled in 1984 out of court for $100,000. Cantrell died in June 2004 at the age of 76. The story was the subject of a TV documentary on "City Confidential" in its third season. In the spring of 2010, a film was planned on the case tentatively titled "Quick Draw: A True Story."

16. Lisa Marie Kimmel

Lisa Marie Kimmell (b. 1969), was kidnapped and murdered while on a trip home from Colorado to Billings, Montana, in 1988. In the summer of 2002, investigators researching cold cases came across Kimmell's rape kit, and a DNA profile was then developed from that evidence. Police entered the DNA profile into law enforcement database and it matched the profile of Dale Wayne Eaton, 57, of Moneta, who, at the time, was incarcerated in Englewood federal prison at Littleton, Colo., on an unrelated weapons charge. The case was further cracked when neighbors living near Eaton's property reported to investigators that they had seen him digging a large hole on his land shortly after Kimmell's murder. The place was about an hour's drive from where Kimmell was last seen alive. When the site was excavated, Kimmell's Honda CRX was unearthed and pulled from the ground, still bearing her distinctive "LIL MISS" license plate. Eaton was charged with eight crimes connected to the Kimmell case. He was tried and found guilty of all charges and sentenced to death on March 20, 2004. The court turned down his appeal. Scheduled to be put to death in February 2010, he gained a stay of execution in December, 2009. As of June 2010, Eaton was the only inmate on Wyoming's death row.

17. Emma Lou McCoid, Kyle Baumstarck, Arthur Taylor

The three were murdered in the Little Chief Lounge, a Worland bar/gas station on Jan. 20, 1997. Martin Olsen was sentenced to life in prison for the crime.

18. Christin Lamb

Lamb, an eight-year-old Laramie girl, was visiting her grandparents in Powell when she disappeared July 19, 1998. Her body later was found and a 22-year-old neighbor was convicted and sentenced to life in prison for the crime.

19. Wayne Martinez

Martinez, a correctional officer at the Wyoming State Penitentiary, was jumped by

President Bill Clinton and prosecutor Kenneth Starr shared *Time* Magazine's "Man of the Year" choice for 1998, but the person receiving the most votes for the designation from *Time* readers was Matthew Shepard, gay UW student whose murder in Laramie brought national attention to hate crimes.

three prisoners who killed him in a botched escape attempt. All three men were convicted of murder. James Martin Harlow was sentenced to death by a jury in November, 1998.

20. Matthew Shepard

Shepard, a gay college student at the University of Wyoming, died after being robbed, beaten and tied to a fence east of Laramie on the night of Oct. 6-7, 1998. Shepard was found by a passing dirt bike rider some 18 hours after he was tied and beaten. He died the next week in a Fort Collins hospital without regaining consciousness. Two Laramie men, Russell Henderson and Aaron McKinney, were charged in the crimes. Henderson pleaded guilty in April, 1999, and was sentenced to two life terms in the Wyoming State Penitentiary. McKinney's case went to trial in October, 1999, and a jury found him guilty on Nov. 3, 1999. Before the penalty phase of the trial began, at which consideration of the death sentence could have been made by the jury, Shepard's mother asked that McKinney's life be spared and he be sentenced to life in prison. The judge complied. The incident and the trial gained international publicity.

21. Amber Carlson and Adam Towler

On July 16, 2006, the two college students were murdered by a third sudent, Justin Geiger, 19, who then killed himself. Carlson, 19, was a UW student from Denver. Towler, 20, attended Emory University in Atlanta, but was home in Laramie for trhe summer. Geiger, also a UW student, had a history of run-ins with authorities, including a charge of minor under the influence of alcohol, but no motive was given.

22. Brenda Davila

The 22-year-old Lovell mother of two was shot by her husband after a domestic dispute in front of the home of her parents. The house was next door to a grade school and the shooting occurred in mid-afternoon during recess at the school. Immediately following the shooting on Nov. 6, 2007, Stephen Lopez, the shooter, turned the gun on himself.

Other Law and Order Stories

1. Domestic Violence

Domestic violence cases in Wyoming increased from 2,293 reports and 640 arrests in 1988 to 3,320 reports and 1,334 arrests in 1994.

2. Teardrop Tattoo--A Giveaway

A woman who escaped from prison after being convicted of murder in Missouri was identified by a teardrop tattoo in Green River in February, 1996. An acquaintance of the woman had seen the description featured on the television program, *America's Most Wanted*.

3. Guilty Cowboy

Herbert Brink was the only cowboy ever convicted for involvement in a sheep raid. He was sentenced to a term in Rawlins in 1909 for participating in the so-called Spring Creek Raid, in which three sheepherders were murdered. John Davis' book, *A Vast Amount of Trouble*, tells the story of the famous incident.

4. Dead Shot

In the middle 1920s, Fred Van Gordon was killed by Sheriff Albert Peyton in a shoot-out in the LaBonte Hotel in Douglas. Van Gorden had murdered his wife and son in Casper. He had been a Camp Perry marksman.

5. We Want a Radio!

During a murder trial in Thermopolis in September 1933, the judge honored the jurors' request for a radio "so that they could get the latest baseball scores."

6. Coat Inside Out

A Douglas cowboy was playing cards and drinking in a Gillette saloon. He left and a few minutes later, returned with his coat turned inside out to rob the place. After forcing

Ralph Nader spoke on the UW campus in April 2000 during his campaign for the U. S. Presidency.

the saloonkeeper to empty the till, he went back outside, turned his coat back right side out and returned to the saloon to play cards.

7. Dynamite Plot?

In August 1934, Rev. Oscar Autritt, a Russian-born clergyman and former Mississippi college professor, told authorities that he had unmasked a plot "by Communists to dynamite Sheridan and Lander churches " Residents in the two towns said the statements are "exaggerated." Authorities found no evidence to back up the pastor's claims.

8. Monkey in the pokey

An item in the October 12, 1913, issue of the *Laramie Boomerang* provides some interesting facts but only enough to tantalize. The article explains that a man was sent to jail for "mutilating an actress' clothes." Not only was the man sent to jail but accompanying him to the pokey was a monkey.

9. Marijuana arrests

In 2002, 1,928 arrests were made in Wyoming for marijuana possession. Of those, 526 were in Laramie County; 324 in Natrona County; 190 in Campbell; 149 in Sweetwater; 121 in Albany,;105 in Carbon; and 104 in Sheridan. No marijuana-related arrests were made in Goshen or Sublette counties during 2002.

Sentence Commutations by Governors, 1975-98*

Gov. Ed Herschler	**Gov. Mike Sullivan**
1975-86: 956	1987-94: 213
Gov. Jim Geringer	**Gov. Dave Freudenthal**
1995-2002: 12	2003- : less than 50 to 2009.

Herschler commuted 132 sentences in both 1983 and 1984. He commuted 123 in 1985 and 134 in 1986. The state penitentiary was severely overcrowded in those years and, given that the commutation recipients had been convicted of non-violent crimes, the number was not criticized. His most controversial commutation was for the prison sentence given Richard Jahnke, a 16-year-old Cheyenne boy, convicted as an adult for the murder of his father in 1983. Due to Jahnke's youth and some extenuating circumstances in the case, Herschler commuted the sentence to imprisonment in the boys' school until Jahnke reached the age of 21.

Geringer rarely issued a commutation even though the prison system was very crowded during his eight years in office. Some prison experts criticized the policy for making it more difficult to control prisoner conduct by not providing incentives for better behavior.

Freudenthal's most controversial commutation was made in 2007. The governor commuted the lengthy sentence given to Jeffrey Reichert, 44, a Torrington businessman who defrauded farmers of more than $1 million and pleaded guilty in November 2004. The commutation made him eligible for parole in order that he could receive additional treatment for lung cancer. Freudenthal said he was reluctant to commute Reichert's sentence and requested that the Legislature provide the option of a temporary medical parole. The legislature passed the law, called "medical parole" act, in 2008.

*Source: Joan Barron, "Governors differ on commutations," Casper Star-Tribune, July 5, 1992, p. 1; Star-Tribune, March 12, 1995; Dec. 20, 1998; Nov. 1, 2009.

Earth First! activist Howie Wolke was sentenced to six months in jail in 1986 for pulling up surveyor's stakes at a controversial oil well site in Sublette County. The justice of the peace who sentenced Wolke received hundreds of letters either protesting the sentence or angrily demanding to know why a tougher sentence wasn't meted out. Wolke later operated a guide service near Livingston, Montana.

LECTURES

Lectures in Wyoming by Some Well-Known People

1. The Rev. Sheldon Jackson, Missionary

Jackson preached in Cheyenne in 1869. According to Territorial Gov. John A. Campbell's diary, Jackson was disappointed by the turnout. Not one Cheyenne resident is said to have attended the scheduled sermon! Jackson became famous for his missionary work in Alaska where a college still bears his name.

2.-3. Susan B. Anthony and Elizabeth Cady Stanton, Suffragists

Wyoming women already had the right to vote when Anthony came to Wyoming to lecture for the first time in June 1871. Elizabeth Cady Stanton also lectured in Wyoming in the summer of 1871.

4. Alexander Kerensky, Russian president

Kerensky (b. 1881, d. 1970) was the head of the Russian government before the Bolsheviks took power in 1917. He spent the summer of 1949 as a guest lecturer at the University of Wyoming. Students who took his class remember the constant presence of his armed bodyguards. Dr. Robert M. Hutchins, president of the University of Chicago, also lectured on campus that summer.

5. Robert Kennedy, U. S. Senator/Presidential Candidate

Bobby Kennedy spoke at several locations in Wyoming during 1968 when he was seeking the presidential nomination. His two brothers also spoke in Wyoming. When Ted Kennedy came to the state to campaign for his brother John in 1960, he rode a bucking bronc in a Sheridan rodeo. He spoke in Casper in October 1972. President John F. Kennedy spoke to a crowd of 12,500 people at War Memorial Fieldhouse on Sept. 25, 1963, less than two months before he was assassinated. It was the largest crowd ever to hear a speaker in Wyoming.

6. Robert Frost, poet

The San Francisco-born poet, known for his poems about New England, lectured at the University of Wyoming on April 20, 1939. The poetry library in Hoyt Hall, UW's collection of works of poetry and literature, is named for him.

7. Hubert H. Humphrey, U. S. Vice President

Humphrey became the first non-Wyomingite to address a joint session of the state legislature when he spoke in the House chambers on Feb. 8, 1965. A native of South Dakota and long-time senator from Minnesota, Humphrey came to Wyoming many times. When he was a presidential candidate in 1968, he made campaign stops in the state and spoke at the Democratic State Convention in Rawlins.

8.-9. Vachel Lindsay, poet, and Hamlin Garland, author

Lindsay gave a reading of his poetry at the University of Wyoming in 1920. According to Wilson Clough's *History of the University of Wyoming*, his "efforts to enlist audience cooperation in his readings were long remembered, especially the picture of Dean and Mrs. Soule in the front row, roaring like lions at his bidding." Garland spoke at Laramie on April 30, 1923.

10. Oscar Wilde, English author/playwright

The English author toured America in 1882. He made a brief stop and speech from the depot platform in Cheyenne on March 23, 1882.

11. Bill Haywood, Labor Activist

Haywood, exonerated after being tried for involvement in the death of a former Idaho governor, spoke in Cheyenne on Sept. 12, 1911. According to an account of the speech in a Cheyenne newspaper, a "sizeable crowd" attended.

12. Roy Wilkins, Director, NAACP

Wilkins lectured at Casper in 1965 in honor of a former Casper man, the Rev. James Reeb, killed in Selma, Alabama, while in a civil rights march.

13. Joseph R. McCarthy, Wisconsin Senator

The Wisconsin Republican, who gained notoriety in the 1950s for claiming Communists occupied numerous key government posts, spoke to audiences in Riverton, Worland and Dubois in 1952. At his Dubois speech, several members of the audience became ill from eating contaminated ham served before the address.

14. Henry Kissinger, Secretary of State

He was a former Secretary of State when he spoke at UW on Feb. 4, 1976.

15. Byron R. White, Supreme Court Justice

The U. S. Supreme Court justice spoke at dedication ceremonies for the new University of Wyoming College of Law building in September 1977.

16.-17. Sam Donaldson and Al Simpson

Donaldson, the ABC news commentator, and Simpson, Wyoming senator and U. S. Senate whip, debated the role reporters should have in covering the lives of public officials. They appeared together in September 1988, at the annual meeting of the Wyoming State Bar in Cheyenne. Donaldson also spoke at UW at a later time.

18. William Jennings Bryan, Presidential Candidate

Bryan, defeated three times in presidential elections, spoke often in Wyoming during his life. During his first campaign in 1896, he spoke at several towns along the Union Pacific, including an address to a large crowd from the station platform at Laramie. He vacationed in the Saratoga area.

19. Charles Dickens Jr., Lecturer

As the Cheyenne newspaper on March 3, 1888, reported his visit: "A large, fashionable and appreciative audience greeted Charles Dickens, Jr. ...The literary people of the community regarded the opportunity to hear the talented son read the works of his gifted father as a great privilege and embraced it."

20. Norman Thomas, perennial Socialist candidate for President

Thomas made speeches in Laramie and Cheyenne in October, 1932.

21. Martin Luther King III

The son of the famed civil rights leader spoke in Laramie in February 1991.

22. Earl Warren, California Governor/Chief Justice, U. S. Supreme Court

Warren was governor of California when he addressed the 1947 commencement at the University of Wyoming.

23. Kwame Ture (Stokely Carmichael), Black activist

Ture, then a resident of Guinea, spoke on the campus of the University of Wyoming in March 1994. In the 1960s, he was a Black Power activist and the "prime minister" of the Black Panther Party.

24.-25. Walter Prescott Webb and Bernard DeVoto, Historians

Webb, the well-known Western historian from the University of Texas, and DeVoto, the Utah-born journalist/historian, taught history classes at the University of Wyoming summer school in June 1937.

26. Al Gore, Vice President of the United States

Gore spoke on Aug. 17, 1997, at Mammoth in Yellowstone in a ceremony commemorating the 125th anniversary of the park.

27.-28. George W. Bush, presidential candidate; Dick Cheney, running mate

The two spoke at Natrona County High School on July 25, 2000, after Bush designated the former Wyoming congressman his vice presidential running mate.

29. George McGovern, former U. S. Senator and Presidential candidate

McGovern and former Sen. Al Simpson appeared jointly in a conversation about civility in American politics. The event, part of the UW Simpson Lecture series, was held in the Education Auditorium, UW, in March 2003.

30. Sandra Day O'Connor, Supreme Court Justice

Justice O'Connor participated in several events at UW in March 2004. She spoke to a large crowd at UW on March 16, 2004, as a Simpson series lecturer..

31. Johnny Cochran, trial lawyer

Cochran, principal attorney in the O. J. Simpson case, spoke in Laramie Feb. 10, 2000. Cochran died March 25, 2005.

32. Angela Davis, activist

Davis was keynoter at UW on Jan. 18, 2006, for Martin Luther King Jr. Day..

33. Barack Obama, presidential candidate

Obama spoke to one of the largest crowds ever to attend an indoor speech in Wyoming on March 7, 2008, at the Arena-Auditorium in Laramie. An estimated 10,000 people heard the speech. The event was held the night before the Wyoming Democratic Party county caucuses. Obama overwhelmed his closest rival, Hillary Clinton, to win the majority of Wyoming's convention delegates.

34. Bill Clinton, former President

Clinton made several speeches in Wyoming in March 2008. He was campaigning for his wife Hillary who was a primary election candidate. He spoke in Casper, Riverton and in the multipurpose gym, UW.

35. Chris Matthews, TV commentator

Matthews, host of MSNBC's "Hardball," spoke at the Arts and Sciences Auditorium, UW, on April 11, 2009. Pete Williams and David Broder previously lectured at UW.

36. Dick and Lynne Cheney

The Cheneys were speakers at the dedication for the Cheney International Center at the University of Wyoming on Sept. 10, 2009. The Cheneys donated $3 million for the center and an additional $3.4 million to support international scholarships and study-abroad programs.

37. William Ayers, education theorist

Ayers, a professor in Chicago, was invited to speak at UW by the Social Justice Research Center. In the 1960s, Ayers co-founded the Weather Underground, an anti-war group that conducted nonfatal bombings at locations including the Pentagon. He had tenuous ties to candidate Barack Obama and the connection became an issue in the 2008 campaign. Ayers was scheduled to speak on April 5, 2010, but the research center withdrew the invitation to speak. University officials said the speech was cancelled, citing security concerns. When he was invited by student Meg Lanker to speak at the multipurpose gym, UW refused to allow it. Lanker sued, alleging First Amendment violations. U. S. District Judge William Downes sided with Lanker and ordered UW to allow the speech. On April 28, 2010, more than 1,100 heard Ayers speak on campus. He spoke without incident.

A summer American Studies lecture series was popular with University of Wyoming students in the post-World War II years. During the summer session of 1949, the guest lecturer was Alexander Kerensky, the Russian president who headed the Russian government before the Bolsheviks took power in 1917. Students who took his class remember the constant presence of his armed bodyguards. Although he was never attacked and died of natural causes in 1970, his paranoia probably was justified, given that Joseph Stalin, Soviet dictator at the time, had a long memory. Stalin had ordered the ice-pick assassination of arch-rival Leon Trotsky in August, 1940, even though Trotsky was living in exile in Mexico.

LIBRARIES

1st county library in the United States: Laramie County Library (1886)

Only library in Wyo designated "Patent and Trademark Depository" by U. S. Dept. of Commerce: Natrona County Library, Sept. 1993.

Public Libraries in Wyoming held a total of 2,416,716 volumes (1993) or 5.33 volumes for each person in the state. *Source: American Library Directory. (Bowker, 1993-1994).*

1st Libraries in Wyoming Towns

1. Casper

Women's Christian Temperance Union formed a library in 1902, housed on Center Street between First and Second. The Natrona County Library Association was formed in 1903. The first building, built in 1910, contained 15,000 volumes.

2. Cody

Formed in 1906, the library received Carnegie funds in 1915.

3. Douglas

The Pleasant Valley Schoolhouse, now on the State Fairgrounds, served as the town's first library in the 1920s.

4. Gillette

The first library opened in an attic room in the old courthouse on May 5, 1928, and served patrons every Saturday. George Amos, who had come to the Gillette area in the 1880s and worked as foreman for the 4-J Ranch, died in December, 1929. He left his estate amounting to $21,000 for construction of a Gillette library. The structure was completed in December, 1941, and named the George Amos Memorial Library. The current library building on 4J Road, constructed at a cost of $3.5 million, opened in the summer of 1983. It was renamed the Campbell County Public Library, but the bronze statues in front of the building are a reminder of Amos' contribution to his community.

5. Sheridan

The first library was housed in the YMCA in 1903 after H. A. Coffeen donated 4,000 volumes as the initial collection. Two years later, in August, 1905, the Carnegie library opened, much of the construction paid for by philanthropist Andrew Carnegie. In 1971, Henry B. Fulmer pledge $300,000 for construction of a new library in the memory of his wife Margaret. While he was examining the prototype of the building on May 19, 1972, Fulmer died of a heart attack at the age of 81. The Sheridan County-Fulmer Library opened in August 1974. New additions were built in 1986 and 1995.

6. Laramie

The "Wyoming Library and Literary Association" was formed Sept. 20, 1871. Within four years, the library contained more than 1,000 volumes. The Carnegie Library was dedicated Jan. 22, 1906. The structure now houses county offices. The present Albany County Library opened July 12, 1981.

7. University of Wyoming

The original library, consisting of 300 books donated by Charles Clay in 1887, was located in a room in Old Main. In 1922, the first library building was completed. The building, no longer housing a library, is known as the Aven Nelson Building. The present main library was built in 1956 and named for William R. Coe whose estate gave $1.8 million toward its construction. The Science Library, located in the Science Complex, was opened in 1968. An additional wing was added in 1977. On Nov. 19, 2009, a new wing was dedicated, adding almost 100,000 square feet to the library. It was part of a $50 million library renovation and expansion project.

8. Fort Laramie

The post surgeon reported in 1870: "There is a post library in the adjutant's office containing about 300 old, nearly worn-out books; a number of papers and periodicals are subscribed for from the post fund and kept in the library room, to which the enlisted men have access. The hospital library also comprises about 300 volumes, a majority of which are religious works."

9. Fort Bridger

Post sutler William A. Carter is said to have maintained a personal library of perhaps 10,000 books. One-sixth of the books eventually came to the University of Wyoming many years after Carter's death in 1881.

10. Jackson

In the 1930s, a community effort led by Edith Mercill, Stella Watson and Helen Benson established a library in the north wing of the American Legion Building. The first librarian, Juliane Tanner, was hired in 1938. In 1940 the library moved into the log building on King Street, built through community solicitations and from a donation from the Dr. Charles Huff Memorial Fund.

11. Pinedale

The Sublette County Library first opened in Worl's Ford Garage in 1951, through the efforts of Sally Mackey and Ethelyne Worl. In 1953, the Town of Pinedale let the library use a log house next to the fire station. Marie Meyer was the first paid librarian. In 1958, the county commission established the Sublette County Library and Big Piney Branch. The new Pinedale library opened in 1970 and Big Piney in 1971. Sublette was the last county to have a county library.

12. Kemmerer

First opened March 4, 1926, in the Legion building, the library was moved to a Justice of the Peace courtroom in the courthouse in October, 1926.

13. Powell

The first library, organized by the Ladies' Union in 1910, consisted of four shelves of books in the home of A. P. Libby. Later as the number of books increased, the library moved to Lewellen's Drug Store, then to the Wyoming Hotel, and to the basement of the Baptist Church. In 1921, the community bought the old Fairview School, moved it to the corner of 3rd and Clark, and turned it into the library. Finally, in 1934, a building specifically designed for a library, became the town's library.

Growth of the University of Wyoming Library*

1887:	300	1958:	275,000	1993:	1,046,163
1897:	5,600	1966:	390,000	2000:	1,250,000
1904:	17,000	1972:	446,000	2009:	1,400,000
1917:	39,000	1978:	600,000		
1923:	50,000	1988:	913,346		

*Source: "The Development of the University of Wyoming Libraries and Special Collections," by Emmett D. Chisum. Annals of Wyoming, Spring 1982. The 1988 and 1993 figures are from the American Library Directory, 1988-89; 1993-94; UW, 2010.

National Advocacy Honor Roll

Honored for library service by the American Library Association, 2000, 2005

Wayne Johnson	*James G. Crawford	*Mabel Wilkinson
Agnes Milstead	*Harry Fulmer	Floyd Esquibel
Denice Wheeler	*Dr. Grace Raymond Hebard	Carol McMurry
Cherry Williams	*Rose Mary Malone	Jack Mueller
		*posthumous award

3 Overseas Libraries Holding 'Wyoming Almanac'

1. University of Edinburgh (Scotland)

As of 1999, the Scottish institution was the only university library in Britain listed as holding the book.

2. American University in Cairo Library (Egypt)

The AUC Library is the only one in Egypt (or Africa) with *Wyoming Almanac* in its holdings. The Great Library of Alexandria opened in the summer of 2000. The new library will have a copy of this new edition, just as its predecessor is said to have held one copy of every book (papyrus scoll) in existence before it faded away in the Middle Ages.

3. Khazar University Library, Baku, Azerbaijan

The library is one of two located in former Soviet states having a copy of the *Almanac*.

A Wyoming Explorer in Siberia

Throughout the 19th century, explorers tried unsuccessfully to reach the North Pole. One expedition had a Wyoming connection.

Nelse Iverson arrived in Laramie in 1873 at the age of 22 from Greenland where he had been a miner. For six years, he worked in a Laramie meat market as a butcher, but in the spring of 1879, he went to San Francisco to sign on to an expedition to the North Pole.

With the DeLong expedition, he set sail for the North, but their ship became stuck in the ice floes off the coast of Siberia. When the ice finally started melting, the ship sunk. It was the spring of 1881, but they were so far north that warm weather was weeks, perhaps months, away.

Far from shore, the crew divided into three parties in three small boats, 12 men in each boat. One boat was lost at sea while a second hit land after a few weeks and five of its crew were saved. Iverson was on the third boat, along with the expedition commander, a naturalist, an engineer, a minister, a medical doctor, an African American hunter, a cook and three sailors.

Their boat struck land near the Lena River and the crew abandoned the craft and started walking up the river, hoping to hit civilization. There was no let-up in the cold and snow. After 40 days, only Iverson and the expedition commander were still alive, but according to the commander's diary, Iverson died of cold and starvation, too.

The next year, a search party located the crew's bodies along the banks of the Siberian river, frozen solid in snow and ice. Iverson, just one in a long series of unsuccessful North Pole explorers, was buried in a New York cemetery, far from his Wyoming home.

During the "Johnson County Invasion," newspaperman E. H. Kimball of Glenrock suspected what was happening. Not involved in the plot, his curiosity caused him to try to find out as much as he could about it. The "invaders" were sending telegraph messages which were being received at the Glenrock depot. Kimball enlisted his brother-in-law, Charles Rollins, to crawl under the station platform and try to decipher, undetected, the Morse code messages audible from there. Rollins, a well-dressed man who disliked having to maintain the position in the dirt under the platform, did his duty, but not happily. At one point, one of the men inside the depot came out on the platform and urinated over the side. The angry eavesdropper didn't move despite his unfortunate predicament. Source: J. R. Slaughter in *Pages from Converse County's Past.* (Casper, 1988), p. 326.

LIGHTNING

Deaths from lightning: From 1990-2003, Wyoming counted 14 people killed by lightning. Wyoming ranks 21st among the states in total lightning fatalities.

Per capita deaths from lightning: Wyoming ranks 1st in the nation, according to NOAA figures, with 2.02 people per million dying annually from being struck by lightning.

Most common victims: Hikers above timberline and mountain climbers were most at risk. Riders on horses and fishermen were next in risk of being struck.

National leader in total people killed by lightning, Florida leads the nation with 126 poeple killed by lightning from 1990-2003.

Weather-related injuries: A 1992 study showed that 17 people were killed in Wyoming by lightning between 1979 and 1990. An additional 73 were injured from lightning strikes. No other weather event is as deadly.

Worst Months for Lightning Injuries and Deaths in Wyoming, 1959-1983

Month*	Injured	Killed
June	32	4
August	21	6
July	17	7
Sept.	6	2
May	4	2
Total:	**80**	**21**

None in any other month.

Some Wyomingites Struck by Lightning

1. Private Edward T. Diffley, 4th Infantry

The 24-year-old soldier was killed by lightning at Fort Laramie on the afternoon of May 25, 1881. It is one of the earliest recorded deaths by lightning in Wyoming. Lightning strikes were a common cause of death among range cowboys and soldiers who stayed outside in storms, unfamiliar with the dangers it presented in the somewhat treeless terrain.

2. E. W. Whitcomb

Whitcomb, a pioneer rancher, was killed by lightning in 1915. The 77-year-old owner of a large herd of Shetland ponies, Whitcomb was riding his quarterhorse near his Laramie County ranch when he was struck.

3. Steamboat

Although the famous bucking horse did not die directly from a lightning strike, he was in a pasture when lightning hit a nearby post. The noise so frightened the animal that he leaped against the barbed wire and seriously cut himself. He later died from blood poisoning sustained in the injury. The incident occurred in Salt Lake City, but Steamboat was returned to the Cheyenne area where veterinarians unsuccessfully tried to save him.

4. Posse chasing the Wilcox train robbers

Two members of the posse were struck in June 1899, while tracking the robbers near Laramie Peak. Neither man died. The chase yielded no suspects.

5. Other reported deaths

A Sundance man, Dave Coward, was killed by lightning on July 8, 1887. A horse and rider were reported killed near Medicine Bow by lightning on Aug. 30, 1916. On Sept. 19, 1920, the president of a Moorcroft bank was struck and killed near that northeast Wyoming town. A man herding sheep on Copper Mountain near Thermopolis was killed by lightning on July 25, 1923. Jimmy Viney, 14, a Midwest Boy Scout, was struck and killed by lightning at "Camp Carey," near Glenrock, on June 28, 1926. Pete Urruity, 22, was killed by lightning while herding sheep south of Buffalo on June 10, 1931.

6. Flagger Hit by Lightning

A Dubois woman working as a highway flagger on a state highway, 10 miles west of Dubois, was struck in the left wrist by lightning on June 29, 1993. The lightning strike exited through her nose, knocking her to the ground. She survived.

7. Seven Bighorn Sheep

The seven sheep were among a group of some 60 bighorns ranging on Mount Everts in Yellowstone National Park during the summer of 1999 when they were struck and killed by lightning. Yellowstone has fewer than 180 bighorn sheep ranging within its borders.

8. Waiting for Old Faithful

Over the years, lightning has struck numerous people while they waited for the eruption of Old Faithful. One incident in June 2005 left 11 people injured. Another strike on June 1, 2010, injured nine, including serious injuries to a Florida man.

9. Talking on a Cell Phone

In order to get reception on his cell phone, 70-year-old Robert Gurney of Torrington walked up a hill near Upper Sunshine Reservoir in Park County where he and his son had been fishing. There, on June 20, 2010, he was struck and killed by a bolt of lightning.

10. Long-distance Runner

David Westlake, 63, of Sheridan, known as a long-distance runner, was struck and killed by lightning on July 12, 2010, along a forest service road near Sheridan.

Number of Entries for "Wyoming" in Various Libraries

1. University of Wyoming Coe Library

In June, 1992, the entries numbered 9,565. In June, 1996, it was 15,562. The number was 47,217 in June 2010. There were 3,147 entries for "Colorado" in 1996; 14,524 in June 2010.

2. Colorado State University Library

The library had 3,507 entries for "Wyoming" in 1996. By June 2010, it was 6,926.

3. Denver Public Library

A total of 1,966 entries were listed under "Wyoming" in June, 1996; 3,902 in June 2010.

4. Chicago Public Library

Just 306 entries for "Wyoming" were listed in June, 1996. By June 2010, the number was 1,290.

5. America Online NetFind

In January 1999, requesting the subject of "Wyoming" yielded 79,214 matches. Google, in June 2010, had an estimated 71,000,000 matches for "Wyoming."

6. American University in Cairo (Egypt)

"Wyoming" entries numbered 35, two of which were *Wyoming Almanac*!

On Aug. 8, 1997, more than 250,000 books from the Colorado State University Library were moved to the Laramie Cold Storage building in Laramie. The move was necessitated by a flash flood that swept through the partially completed Fort Collins library soaking many books. The books were moved to Laramie in preparation for freeze-drying and restoration in a Texas facility.

LIQUOR

1st beer brewery in Wyoming: Probably, the small brewery opened at the mining town of Atlantic City in 1868.

Passage of prohibition in Wyoming: Election of November 1918. The amendment passed by a 3-1 margin and was to become effective on Jan. 1, 1920. The legislature, however, passed a measure in February 1919, which made prohibition effective six months earlier, midnight on June 30, 1919. Wyoming was the last state in the region to adopt prohibition.

Prohibition repealed: Election of November 1932, a referendum to repeal prohibition passed with 71.5 percent of the voters approving. Hard liquor sales resumed in Wyoming in April 1935.

Alcohol tax: 2 cents per gallon, the lowest rate of any state except Nevada.

Alcohol consumption: 8th greatest in the U.S. (2009). Beer, 264.9 cans per person per year; wine, 9.1 bottles per person annually; spirits, 2.7 gallons per person annually (2009).

1st operation of State Liquor Commission: June 1, 1935. After the first six months of operation, the commission reported profits from the sale of liquor of more than $137,800. The first commission director was O. O. Natwick.

1st legal serving of liquor above the ground floor of a building: Sky Room of the Gladstone Hotel, Casper, 1953.

Wyoming was the last state to raise the legal drinking age to 21 on July 1, 1988. The state would have lost $8.2 million in highway funds had the legislature not passed the act.

1st micro brewery in Wyoming: Otto Brothers Brewing Co., of Wilson, established in 1989.

1st distillery in Wyoming: Kolts Fine Spirits in Sheridan, founded by brothers Justin and Jason Koltiska and their uncle Rob Koltiska. The product, Koltiska Original, the slightly sweet, amber-colored liqueur "with hints of extracts and spices," is distilled and bottled in Sheridan. The 60-proof liquor (30 percent alcohol by volume) debuted in April 2005.

1st legal bourbon distillery in Wyoming: Wyoming Whiskey, Inc., Kirby. In 2009, the firm built a 5,500 square foot distillery in Kirby that will produce 1,000 barrels a year. Distilling operations began July 4, 2009. According to CEO Bradford Mead, all ingredients come from Wyoming.

Microbreweries/brew pubs in Wyoming: 23 (1999)

1st Wyoming winery: Terry Ranch Cellars, established in 1994 near Cheyenne.

1st Wyoming vineyard: Table Mountain Vineyards, near Huntley, established by Patrick Zimmerer and his sister Anne in 2001. It became a full-scale winery in August 2004.

Liquor licenses in Wyoming: 1,360 total licensees, including 738 retail, 276 restaurant, 23 bar and grill, 121 limited retail, 73 county malt beverage, 31 malt beverage wholesalers, and 12 microbreweries,

Some Wyoming Breweries

1. City Brewery, Cheyenne

Opened in June 1870, it was the first of several breweries in the capital city. An earlier operation, known as the Pacific Brewery, was opened at Hazard Station, six miles west of town, in January 1869.

2. Sheridan Brewing Company

The largest brewery in the state until Prohibition, the brewery began operations about 1885, just a year after the town of Sheridan was platted. The first building burned and a second began operation on Feb. 21, 1889. It was incorporated Dec. 20, 1890, by Peter Demple, Gothard Paul and Wilhelminim Demple, but the firm changed ownership several times over the years. It acquired the Coca-Cola franchise in 1921 which enabled the firm to weather Prohibition. The first bottle brewed after Prohibition came off the line on June 15, 1933. The firm made 60,000 barrels of beer annually until 1954. After brewing ceased, the firm became the first in the U. S. to introduce the flat-top soft drink canned beverage. The "Can-a-Pop" was introduced in July 1953.

3. Fischer Brewery, Buffalo

The brewery operated for more than a decade in the late 1800s. It closed when Fort McKinney was shut down. The original building, occupied for many years by a flour mill, was demolished in 1974.

4. Casper Brewing Company

The firm brewed Hillcrest Beer in the early 1940s.

5. Becker Brewery, Evanston

The company opened in Odgen, Utah, in 1888. When Utah "went dry" in 1917, the firm started the Evanston brewery. Owner G. L. Becker was credited with being the "good example" of a responsible brewer. He influenced Utah legislators to repeal Prohibition in 1933. The firm reopened in both locations after repeal and sold "Becker's Beer" and "American Pilsener" for the next decade.

6. Sweetwater Brewery, Green River

Started in 1872, German immigrant Karl Spinner bought the business in 1879. He sold to Hugo Gaensslen in 1891. In 1900 the firm moved into the ornate building which still stands in downtown Green River.

7. Wyoming Beer Company, Rock Springs

The small local brewer operated from 1900 to 1912. Almost every Wyoming town had a local brewer before Prohibition.

8. Otto Brothers Brewing Co., Wilson

Established in 1988, brands include "Teton Ale," "Old Faithful Ale" and "Moose Juice Stout." The firm, licensed for beer sales in 1987, was the first commercial brewing operation to open in the state since the Sheridan brewery closed in 1954. The firm also established the first deposit program for returnable bottles in Dec. 1992. The operation was started by Charlie and Ernie Otto and Don Frank.

9. Medicine Bow Brewing Company, Cheyenne

10. The Library Brew Pub; Bowman Brew Pub, both in Laramie

By early 1996, brew pubs were being established in other Wyoming towns including Pinedale and Sheridan, indicating a resurgence in local brewing for the first time in a generation. The Library Brew Pub opened in the Minidome Mall across from the Washakie Center complex in Laramie, thus letting students say they'd spent the night "in the library." Bowman Brew Pub, in downtown Laramie, closed in 1997. In 1999, another brew business, Altitudes, opened at the location.

11. Sweetwater Brewing

The first brew pub to open in Casper, Sweetwater Brewing opened for business on East C Street in October, 1995.

12. Bootleggers Brewery, Casper

The brew pub opened on the site of the former Wonder Bar on Center Street in Casper in 1996.

Unusual Liquor Trivia

1. "Kemmerer Moon"

The potent potable was distilled in the Kemmerer area during Prohibition. The premium illegal booze could be purchased in speakeasies from coast to coast.

2. "Booze block"

Before Prohibition, Casper city officials allowed only one block on Center Street between 1st and 2nd, for saloons. Six were located there: the Mint, Grand Central, Elkhorn, Caledonian, Wyoming and the Parlor Car.

3. Do As We Say....

In the territorial legislative session of 1884, legislators were lectured by a traveling temperance advocate. Soon after, on April 13, the entire body left by train for a junket to Salt Lake City. The local newspaper noted that en route, they were provided with "generous servings of spirituous beverages."

4. First building—first saloon

The first structure in Kaycee was a saloon opened in 1897. The town was incorporated in 1906 in order to keep it open. Only incorporated places could have a saloon, according to legislative acts that year. In order to be incorporated, the town had to have at least 150 residents. To include a sufficient number, the corporate limits of Kaycee were extended 20 miles on every side.

5. Swallow for President

The Prohibition Party presidential candidate in 1904 with the unlikely name of Silas C. Swallow polled 217 votes in Wyoming.

6. Stiff competition

In July 1876, newspapers counted 65 saloons operating in Cheyenne. Just eight years later, their number had been reduced to 29—still a sizable number for a city of fewer than 10,000 residents.

7. Name Appropriation

Hornell Brewing Company of Brooklyn, N. Y., was criticized for selling Crazy Horse Malt Liquor in 14 states and D. C. Indian officials accused the company of using the legendary Wyoming-born warrior's name to get Indians to buy the malt liquor.

8. Liquor in Burns

The Burns Town Council approved the town's first liquor license in 40 years in February 1993. No ordinances prohibited liquor sales, but no such outlets operated. The new ordinance disallowed sales on Sundays.

9. Wyoming Wineries

At least two fully-functional wineries operated in Wyoming in 2010. The oldest was Table Mountain Vineyards, near Huntley, established by Patrick Zimmerer and his sister Anne in 2001. It became a full-scale winery in August 2004. Another, Irvin Cellar Winery in Riverton, was founded in 2008 by Kathy Irvin and her husband Terry.

10. Liquor Sales

The Wyoming Liquor Commission is wholesaler for wine and spirits in Wyoming. In 2009, the case sales were 58% spirits and 42% wine.

11. "Set 'em up!"

The officials of Tubb Town, located near present-day Newcastle, passed an ordinance in 1889 requiring anyone passing through town "to pay a sufficient toll to set 'em up for the bunch" in the local saloon In contrast, the Kilpartrick brothers, founders of the nearby town of Cambria, banned liquor from the town.

12. By Prescription

One loophole existed in the Prohibition laws, in Wyoming as well as the rest of the country. An individual could be prescribed alcohol for "medicinal purposes." Military hospitals, for instance, kept supplies and they had to come in from government sources. In April 1922, it was reported that A. T. Wentz , the Burlington Railroad agent at Gillette, had been arrested the the theft the previous Dec. 3 of "25 cases of bottled-in-bond whiskey being shipped from a St. Louis government warehouse to a point in Montana for medicinal purposes." His case was not unique. Drugstore employees occasionally were accused of providing alcohol to individuals without asking to see a prescription.

13. "Taxi! Taxi!"

In April 1922, a Cheyenne taxi driver was found guilty of violating the Prohibition law when "Policeman Thompson and Special Agent B. P. Hodge got a taste of liquor from a spill" on the floor of the cab where a bottle had broken. The 20-year-old cab driver, James Hefferon, claimed that the bottle belonged to a fare who had been visiting a "south side dance club" that night. He was fined $25 and sentenced to 30 days in jail.

In May 1929, Cheyenne police arrested a 14-year-old boy for bootlegging. The 8th grader worked on a 50 cents per pint commission, selling for a neighbor who made the illegal booze.

14. Bullet holes

Wyoming's U S. District Judge John Riner asked his clerk to come down to the garage next to the federal building to see bullet holes in his car. The previous night, the judge was returning from a judicial conference in Denver when an unmarked car, apparently driven by Colorado Prohibition agents, chased the judge's new black Buick. As the judge was out-running them to the Wyoming state line, they fired shots at the car. Colorado had prohibition at the time and Wyoming did not. Riner claimed he had no idea why he was being pursued and shot at.

6 Prohibition-Era Wyoming Scandals

1. Laramie, 1919

Frank Jennings, a 33-year-old Bosler rancher, was murdered while driving north of Laramie toward home one Sunday night in September 1919. A few days later, John Cordillo, the head of a state prohibition bureau strike force, confessed that he and his two partners had mistaken Jennings for a bootleg and shot him while he was "attempting to flee" from their unmarked car. It had been one of the first raids in the new bureau's history. Cordillo and the others were convicted of manslaughter and sentenced to long prison terms. The director of the Prohibition Bureau, who had hired Cordillo and the others, resigned.

2. Casper, 1923

In a raid on a home on West F Street in November, 1923, police found loose-leaf notebooks containing lists of payoffs to police officers for "protection." A police captain was charged with aiding and abetting a bootlegging ring, but the case was dismissed because the notebooks, the main evidence in the case, had been seized without a search warrant. Four other officers were fired for their roles in the racket. In the same year, a Casper city councilman was fined $400 and sent to jail for four months for keeping a cache of illegal booze in his warehouse.

3. White Mule Boomerang, 1926

In a mimeographed sheet printed on Easter Sunday, 1926, unnamed accusers claimed that UW President Arthur G. Crane had ignored illegal drinking on campus and should have taken action against the wrongdoers. An investigation revealed that the sheet had been printed at the Methodist Church. Three students from Sheridan and the pastor of the church, Rev. Raymond H. Laury, confessed to making the charges. Just three years earlier, Crane had fired the chair of the Department of Mathematics for suspicion of illegal drinking.

4. Cheyenne and Thermopolis, 1929

Will Irving, the State Law Enforcement Commissioner, was indicted along with his assistant and others on May 17, 1929, for accepting pay-offs from bootleggers. Irving was convicted and sentenced to prison. In a related case, the mayor of Thermopolis and nine other town officials pled guilty to aiding a bootleg ring.

5. Rock Springs, 1930

Thirteen city officials, one county officer and 38 others were charged May 18, 1930, with violating the Prohibition laws. All were acquitted in federal court on July 2, 1930.

6. Casper, 1933

The mayor, the county sheriff, the police chief of Casper and 37 others were tried in federal court for conspiracy to bootleg liquor. After eight days of testimony and two days of jury deliberation, the jury returned a not guilty verdict for all defendants.

They look like huge beehives. They are the remains of five huge charcoal kilns built near Piedmont by Moses Byrne in 1869. Wood was sealed inside and burned slowly to make charcoal. Three of the structures, each measuring about 30 feet high, still stand.

LOST

Some Lost People in Wyoming

1. Alf Landon, Politician

Landon, the former Kansas governor who lost to Franklin Roosevelt in a landslide in the 1936 presidential election, came to the Big Horns to fish in August 1948. After a long pack trip to the Lake Solitude area, Landon became separated from the party and remained lost in the woods for most of one day in the vicinity of Cliff Lake. Neither Landon nor his outfitter wanted to divulge the tale at the time. The incident occurred in a presidential election year. Landon is said to have wanted to avoid the inevitable newspaper puns about "Landon, lost again."

2. Jim Bridger, Mountain Man

For once in his life, Bridger found himself lost while guiding the Raynolds expedition through the Jackson Hole country to Yellowstone. The party wandered for almost two weeks until Bridger finally realized they were in Pierre's Hole, far to the west of where he thought they were.

3. Dr. Mortimer Jesurun, Douglas stockman/physician

Jesurun, born in 1860 on Curacao Island off the coast of South America where his father was U. S. Consul, came to the Fort Fetterman area of present Converse County in 1878. He operated a large ranch, returning to New York to receive a medical degree in 1892. He returned to Douglas, entered a ranch partnership and went deeply in debt. On Feb. 19, 1905, Dr. Jesurun was seen at the Union Pacific station in Council Bluffs, Iowa, enroute home to New York. He dropped from sight. He had been carrying a substantial sum of money and many suspected foul play in his disappearance. In the 1920s, a Masonic charm was found in Chanute, Kansas. When inquiry was made of lodge headquarters about the identity of the owner, it reportedly belonged to Dr. Jesurun who was then working in Chanute in the commission business under an assumed name. He fled the town and disappeared again until 1935 when the death of his mother was reported in Los Angeles, indicating he had died a few years earlier. He had been in the drug store business. Why he "disappeared" remained a mystery. *Source: John R. Pexton, Pages from Converse County's Past. (Casper, 1986), pp. 311-312.*

4. George Hopkins, Stunt Parachutist

Hopkins' condition is more precisely described as "marooned"—on top of Devils Tower. He parachuted from an airplane and intentionally landed on the famous landmark on Oct. 1, 1941. After six days of national publicity about his plight, Hopkins was rescued by climbers led by Jack Durrence who endured rain and ice to save him.

5. Connie Smith, Granddaughter of Gov. Nels Smith

The 10-year-old girl disappeared from a girls' summer camp in the east in 1956. No trace of her was ever found.

6. Mae Wardell, Gillette

The 83-year-old Wardell made national news in October, 1995, when she survived for eight days after her car became stuck in the mud on an isolated road 15 miles west of Midwest. Wardell had been in Casper visiting her sister and headed home to Gillette only to become lost. She survived on fruit juice and the frost she scraped from the hood of her car. Temperatures had dropped into the 20s. She was found by two hunters.

Swan Land and Cattle Company manager Finlay Dun had an idea in the middle 1880s. To keep from counting the same animal twice in the herd of 123,000 animals, he decided to paint each one. The plan was not followed.

7. Craig Williamson

The husband of a Cody woman, Williamson was "found" by having his story featured on the television program, *Unsolved Mysteries*. His wife Christine Reinhard of Cody, believing he might be dead, called in her story to the TV program in 1994. Living in California, he saw a rerun of the program in 1995, found his wife (who had moved to Cody after his disappearance) and made contact. The couple later divorced.

8. Dale Hauger

The Greybull man disappeared while hunting near Ten Sleep in October, 1970. In 1993, more than 23 years after his disappearance, his skeleton, rifle and personal effects were found near Leigh Creek in the vicinity of where he was last seen alive.

9.-10. Lt. A. Ray Krogman, Worland, and Staff Sgt. Steven H. Adams

The two men are among the estimated 2,500 American servicemen missing in action in Vietnam. Krogman, on an Air Force mission over Laos, was last heard from on Jan. 17, 1967. Adams' plane was shot down over the Gulf of Tonkin on Oct. 18, 1966. Adams' brother, Dr. Bruce Adams of Laramie, is Wyoming state coordinator for the National League of POW/MIA Families. *(See below for additional MIAs from Wyoming).*

11. Lynn Knievel Bush

The 26-year-old Casper woman was last seen at 5:30 p.m., on Dec. 8, 1990, buying groceries at a Buttrey's grocery store in Casper. Her pickup truck was found in the store parking lot with the recently purchased groceries inside along with her keys and identification. The vehicle door was open. No trace of her was found.

12. Amy Wroe Bechtel

The 24-year-old Lander resident was last seen July 24, 1997, southwest of Lander where she had gone running on the Loop Road between Sinks Canyon and South Pass. A massive search failed to uncover any clues to her disappearance.

9 Wyomingites Missing in Action in Korea

(for list of Wyomingites killed in action in Korea, see p. 338)

1. Clifford E. Baker, Army lieutenant, Big Horn County
2. Joseph G. Garcia, Army corporal, Carbon County
3. Bill Elsom, Air Force captain, Cheyenne
4. John David Hoke, Air Force lieutenant, Cheyenne
5. John L. Horn, Air Force captain, Cheyenne
6. Robert A. Finch, Army lieutenant, Fremont County
7. Demaret Kirtley, Army PFC, Johnson County
8. David H. Kuiper, Army PFC, Sheridan County
9. John A. Swanson, Air Force lieutenant, Torrington

6 Wyomingites Missing in Action in Vietnam

(for list of Wyomingites killed in action in Vietnam, see pp. 338-339)

1. Harry B. Coen, Riverton, May 12, 1968
2. Orville Dale Cooley, Range, Nov. 8, 1967
3. Lawrence G. Evert, Cody, Nov. 8, 1967
4. Joseph L. Hart, Afton, Feb. 25, 1967
5. Alva Ray Krogman, Worland, Jan. 17, 1967
6. Thomas W. Skiles, Buffalo, Dec. 19, 1971

.After train robber Bill Carlisle was captured, 128 claimants came forward in March 1917 for the reward of $6,500 the railroad offered for his capture and arrest.

"Lost" Documents

1. Fort Laramie Register of Oregon Trail Travelers

Numerous diarists noted they signed the big leather-bound book at Fort Laramie while on their way west on the Oregon Trail. The book apparently disappeared at the time the army abandoned the post in 1890.

2. Nate Champion's Diary

When Nick Ray and Nate Champion were killed by the "invaders" at the KC Ranch cabin in April 1892, Champion supposedly kept a detailed record of their ordeal, crudely written with a pencil while the action was unfolding. Chicago newspaper correspondent Sam Clover claimed he found the notes on Champion's body shortly after he was shot down in an attempt to escape. The account was published widely, but the "original" diary was never seen after Clover transcribed it to his own notes. Did it "blow away with the wind" or was it "lost" in the offices of Clover's editor in Chicago? It remains missing.

3. "The Man from the Bitterroots"

Cody Enterprise editor Caroline Lockhart completed the manuscript in her hotel room in Honduras where she had gone to hunt jaguar. She left the manscript in her room one day, returning from the hunt to discover that the building had burned to the ground. With it, her manuscript also went up in flames. It was the only copy, but Lockhart was not deterred. She spent the next year reconstructing the manuscript from memory.

4. Town Plat for Cody

Charles E. Hayden and George T. Beck platted the town site on a windy afternoon in 1896. Just as they were completing the job, a sudden gust of wind blew the plat map skyward and the two men were unable to retrieve it. Beck's son told an interviewer years later that his father always said that Cody's was the only town plat "filed up above."

5. Caspar Collins' Journals

The young lieutenant was said to have kept daily accounts of his activities and impressions of the countryside. Following his death at the hands of Indians at Platte Bridge Station in July 1865, no journals were found.

6. "Mountaineering in the Tetons"

Fritioff Fryxell and Philip D. Smith completed the mansuscript for the book during World War II, but it was not immediately published because of paper shortages. In 1946, their updated manuscript, the third one they had written, was destroyed in a house fire.

7. Autographed Picture of Alexander Graham Bell

Casper High School history teacher V. Y. Russell took the photograph to a Telephone Pioneers Association meeting in the Townsend Hotel, Casper, in March 1947. It vanished. Russell's widow started searching for the photograph 49 years later in February, 1996.

First Emigrant Fatality on Oregon Trail

The first fatality of the Oregon Trail migration across Wyoming was a nine-year-old boy. According to the diary of one eyewitness of the death of young Joel Hembree, "He fell off waggon tung and both wheels run over him." Most likely, he was riding on the tongue between the two animals, with a hand on each of them when he fell between them.

The accident occurred July 18, 1843, but young Hembree lived for another day until the wagon train was camped along LaPrele Creek. He died the next afternoon and was buried nearby, with the drawer of an oaken dresser used to cover the upper part of his body.

According to historian Gregory Franzwa, the gravesite was excavated and the skeleton moved to higher ground in 1961 because a local rancher in the area was building a dam on the creek and the original site was slated for inundation.

MAGAZINES

A Representative Sample of Wyoming Magazines

1. Alumnews

Published by the University of Wyoming Alumni Association eight times yearly, the publication began in the early 1950s. Editor (2010) was Julianne Couch.

2. American Cowboy

A national magazine about cowboy life, past and present, initially, it was headquartered in Sheridan. The magazine began publishing in 1994. Jesse Mullins was editor from its inception until July 2009

3. Annals of Wyoming

Published by the Wyoming State Historical Department (now part of the Department of Commerce), *Annals* began in the 1890s as the *Miscellanies*. The modern *Annals* dates from 1923. The current magazine format was adopted in 1979. Since the 1950s, the editors have included: Lola Homsher, Katherine Halverson, William H. Barton, Phil Roberts, Rick Ewig, Mark Junge, and Loren Jost. In the spring of 1995, Dr. Celeste Colgan, director of the State Department of Commerce, the agency in charge of the journal, questioned the state's support for the Wyoming State Historical Society and its journal. As a result, the society was "evicted" from offices in the department and the organization was forced to publish its own journal as the successor to *Annals of Wyoming*. Members Rick Ewig and Phil Roberts edited the quarterly *Wyoming History Journal* for four issues until the summer of 1996. Colgan resigned to accept a position in Texas. The Department of Commerce and WSHS contracted for a return to publication of a merged *Annals* and *Journal* in June, 1996. Roberts and Ewig continued to edit the publication until 1998 when Roberts became sole editor. Ewig returned as sole editor in 2003.

4. Bits and Pieces

The quarterly magazine of history was published for many years by Mabel Brown of Newcastle. It contained articles on the history of Wyoming and western South Dakota.

5. Wyoming History News

The official newsletter of the Wyoming State Historical Society, the first issue appeared in 1953. Current editor is Linda Fabian, also WSHS executive secretary.

6. Capitol Times

A city magazine in newsprint form was published in Cheyenne from 1981-1984. It contained articles on politics, the arts and personality features.

7. Frontiers

The general interest magazine, published by University of Wyoming students, began in 1989. *(See list of first dozen editors, following page)*

8. In Wyoming

Published from 1967 to 1980, the magazine offices were in Casper. Contents included current events, personality profiles and features. In the spring of 1996, the files of the publication were donated to the American Heritage Center, University of Wyoming. Russ Fawcett was publisher.

9. Owen Wister Review

The review, a nationally-acclaimed literary and arts magazine, has been published since 1978 by the University of Wyoming Student Publications.

Bill Nye, editor of the *Laramie Boomerang*, told his readers about the army surgeon who carelessly dropped a live cigar stub on a keg of gunpowder. "They never found anything but his false teeth. They buried these with military honors," Nye wrote. He reported that above the grave, the following inscription was placed: "Not dead, but spontaneously distributed."

10. Wind River Mountaineer

The magazine is published by the Fremont County Museums. Editor in 2010 was Loren Jost, Fremont County historian and director of the Riverton Museum.. The editor in 2000 was Tom Bell, founder and long-time editor of *High Country News* until the magazine was sold and moved to Paonia, Colorado.

11. Quill

A University of Wyoming literary magazine, *Quill* appeared periodically from the 1930s. Well-known publisher/poet Alan Swallow edited the magazine when he was a student at the university in the middle 1930s.

12. Cow Country

The magazine is the official publication of the Wyoming Stockgrowers Association. In 2010, Kosha Olsen was editor.

13. The Paintbrush

Published by inmates of the Wyoming State Penitentiary, *Paintbrush* is the successor to a publication called *Best Scene*.

14. Wyoming Magazine

The full-color, well-designed slick magazine was published in Jackson in the late 1990s.

15. Wyoming: The Featured Discussion Magazine of the Equality State

Published from 1956-1958, the Casper-based magazine was edited by Mike Leon who also edited the *Democratic Spokesman*, a newspaper for Wyoming Democrats, in the mid-20th century.

16. Wyoming Archaeologist

Published by the Wyoming State Archaeological Society, the magazine was initially called *Smoke Signals*. It has been published since 1958.

17. Wyoming Horizons Magazine

The magazine was published as a monthly supplement to the *Casper Star-Tribune* from 1981-1986. In 1991, the concept was revived by the *Star-Tribune* by publication of a weekly broadsheet section called "Wyoming Weekend." In 1995, the feature section was suspended.

18. WREN

Wyoming Rural Electric News enjoys a huge circulation among rural electric users both on ranches and in Wyoming small towns. Established in 1954, WREN is published 11 times annually and has a circulation of 39,000 (2010). Editor in 2010 was Kris Wendtland.

19. Wyoming Trucker

The official magazine of the Wyoming Trucking Association, it was first published in 1945. The association was formed in 1939.

20. Wyoming Wildlife

The official publication of the Wyoming Game and Fish Commission, the first issue was published in January, 1936. Dan Greenburg was the first editor of what was then mimeographed sheets printed on coarse paper. Publication was suspended from 1944-Janu-

Frontiers Magazine Editors

Frontiers is a general interest magazine published by University of Wyoming students.

1989: Michele Fugere	1994: Alisha Short	1999: RyAnne Scott
1990: Pam Sax	1995: Todd Chatman	2000: John Harte
1991: Kris Kerr	1996: Molly Hand Schedler	
1992: Stephanie Silsby	1997: Marc Ethier	
1993: David Coleman	1998: RyAnne Scott	

ary, 1946, because of World War II. After publication resumed, *Wyoming Wildlife* gained national acclaim from conservation publishing organizations under a succession of editors who included Dee Linford, George Sura and George Padget. Chris Madson became editor in 1983 and, as of 2010, remained in the post, serving longer than any editor in the magazine's history. LuRay Parker, the publication's award-winning wildlife photographer, retired in 1995 after 25 years in that position.

21. Bad taste

University of Wyoming students attempted to start a humor magazine in 1954 but it was banned by university officials on the basis of bad taste.

Editors of Owen Wister Review, UW Literary Magazine

1978: Andi Dunn and Ted Duncombe
1979: Steve Johnson and Catherine Copello
1980: Clay Hutto and Janet Sue Craven
1981: Jack William Burden and Bill Bryant
1982: Karen Mobley and Robert Waggener
1983: Will Guthrie
1984: Sheri Hoem
1985: Carolynn Wolff
1986: Carolynn Wolff
1987: Brad Schaedler
1988: Peter Anderson
1989: Laura White Schuett
1990: Erika L. S. C. Knudson
1991: Erika L. S. C. Knudson
1992: Jon Forrest Glade
1993: Spence Keralis

1994: Georgette Hartley
1995: Walter Domes
1996: Cari Taplin
1997: C. C. Russell
1998: Christy Stillwell
1999: Tony Contento and C. C. Russell
2000: Sammi M. Smith
2001: Pony Smith
2002: Brian M. Van Hise
2003: Lindsay Wilson
2005: Robert K. Townsend
2006: Joan Bolander
2007: Ken Steinken
2008: Zach Parrie
2009: Joshua Watanabe

In September, 1981, a Bremerton, Washington, psychic dreamed about a busload of school children struck by a train with considerable loss of life. She phoned the Wyoming Highway Patrol and described the crossing, presumably in the Casper area. Believing there was such a spot in Mills, police there were especially alerted. The psychic claimed she "saw" a little girl reading a newspaper dated Nov. 11, when there supposedly would be a blizzard. When the fatal date came and went, the Casper Journal reviewed the incident and printed a photo of the dangerous Mills crossing. The deaths of two teenaged Kemmerer girls in a railroad crossing accident in December, 1981, were not related to the mishap envisioned by the psychic because faulty brakes were the cause--not bad weather--and the two killed were not "small children" as the psychic had "seen."

MARRIAGE AND DIVORCE

The median age of a Wyoming bride: 21.2 years
The median age of a Wyoming groom: 23.7 years
1st marriages for brides: 54.9% of Wyoming brides marry for the first time
1st marriages for grooms: 57.3% are marrying for the first time
Wyoming ranked 3rd in per capita divorces in 2002 with 6.1 per 1,000 population. Divorces numbered more than 2,900 in Wyoming for the year. Only Nevada and Arkansas had higher rates. In 1990, Wyoming was 5th in the nation in per capita divorces with 3,095 or 6.6 divorces per 1,000 population.
Divorce state: Between 2005 and 2009, a total 13,547 couples divorced in Wyoming. Of these, 2,619 couples divorced in Laramie County during the five years, 19 percent of the total. On average, 500 couples divorce every year in Laramie County.
Splitsville: The national magazine, *Men's Health*, in June 2010, referred to Cheyenne as "Splitsville" because it had the highest per capita divorce rate of any city in the United States.
Wyoming ranked 7th in per capita marriages in 2001 with 10.3 per 1,000 population. In 1990, Wyoming ranked 16th in per capita marriages with 4,843 or 10.3 per 1,000 population.

First Weddings in Wyoming Places

1. Laramie: Henry G. Morgan and Lizzie Jones, June 21, 1869.
2. Fairview: Caroline Campbell and Eli Sprague, c. 1885.
3. Weston County: Charles Dow and Orpha May Nelson, Oct. 11, 1891.
4. Salt Creek oil fields: Mr. and Mrs. Clarence Swanger, 1922.
5. Hot Springs County: Nels Mikkelson and Sylvia Cheney, 1884.

Some Noteworthy Marriages in Wyoming

1. Steve McQueen and Ali McGraw

The well-known motion picture stars were married July 13, 1973, next to "Big Boy" in Holiday Park, Cheyenne. Justice of the Peace Arthur Garfield officiated. McQueen's last film, *Mr. Horn*, was loosely based on a Wyoming subject, gunman/stock detective Tom Horn. McQueen died of cancer soon after the film was released.

2. Ernest Hemingway and Martha Gellhorn

Justice of the Peace F. A. Stennett officiated at the Nov. 21, 1940, ceremony held in the courtroom of the city-county building in Cheyenne. It was the third marriage for the 42-year-old groom; the first for his 28-year-old bride, a magazine writer. Hemingway wore a "brown tweed suit" and Miss Gellhorn was attired in "a gray suit and red blouse." Witnessing the ceremony were Cheyenne lawyer W. E. Mullen and Mrs. F. A. Wilson. After their wedding, the couple dined at the Union Pacific Dining Room, stayed overnight at the Plains Hotel and departed for New York. More than 1 1/2 inches of snow fell during the day of the wedding and the high temperature was just 23 degrees. Wyoming figured in Hemingway's fourth and final marriage in March 1945. When he married Mary Walsh in Havana, Cuba, his best man was Richard Cooper of Laramie. The ceremony was held in Cooper's Havana vacation home.

3. J. C. Penney and Berta A. Hess

Following their marriage in Cheyenne on Aug. 24, 1899, the Penneys took the train back to Kemmerer where Penney had opened a general merchandise store. The couple lived in the back of the store and then moved to small house nearby. The business expanded into a national chain. Mrs. Penney died in 1910, before the firm's success.

4. Duncan Hines and Florence Chaffin

Hines was a young employee of Wells-Fargo in Cheyenne in 1899 when he met his future bride, the daughter of the Laramie County assessor. They were engaged in 1900, but broke off the marriage when Florence's mother objected to the match. A short time later,

Florence married a young army lieutenant, but the marriage did not last. Meanwhile, Hines had accepted a job in Canaea, Mexico, but corresponded with Florence who continued to live in Cheyenne following her divorce from the lieutenant. When her parents moved to New Rochelle, N.Y., she moved there with them. In September 1905, Hines left Mexico, arriving in New York where he and Florence were married. They moved to Chicago where Hines worked as a printing company salesman. After years of national travel, he compiled a list of "best places to eat" at Florence's suggestion in 1935. Florence died four years later, but Hines' guides became nationally renowned. Later, a prepared cake mix was named for him. He died in 1959.

5. Wild Bill Hickok and Agnes Thatcher Lake

Cheyenne Methodist Church minister W. F. Warren officiated at the ceremony held on March 5, 1876, in the home of saloonkeeper S. L. Moyer. (The site is now a vacant lot on the south side of 18th street between Pioneer and Thomes). The marriage was Wild Bill's first. His bride, a world-renowned trick rider and lion tamer, was the widow of a circus manager who had been killed 14 years earlier. Rev. Warren was not convinced that the match between Wild Bill and Agnes was a good one. He wrote in the marriage record: "I don't think he meant it." Following the ceremony, the couple honeymooned in Cincinnati for two weeks and then Wild Bill returned to Cheyenne alone to make arrangements for a trip to the South Dakota gold fields. He was killed in a Deadwood saloon in August. A year later, his widow came west to lay a wreath on his grave. In Cheyenne, she married her escort, a man 15 years her junior. She died in New Jersey in 1907.

6. Bill Nye and Clara F. Smith

Nye, the *Laramie Boomerang* editor and nationally known humorist, married Miss Smith on March 7, 1877, in Laramie. The newspaper report of their marriage noted that he "thought there were too many Smiths and he owed a duty to society to reduce their number as much as possible."

7. Fred J. Benzer and Frances Serenker

Their marriage was a featured event at the second Cheyenne Frontier Days, held in September 1898. The marriage ceremony for the young Denver couple was performed directly in front of the grandstand "on a specially erected altar, under a bevy of flowers and attention."

8. Herman Wellnitz and Nettie Faber

Chief Justice H. V. S. Groesbeck presided over the first wedding held in the State Capitol Building. Wellnitz, a Cheyenne resident, married Faber, from Mendota, Illinois, on June 24, 1891. The evening ceremony was held in the governor's office.

9. Ursula Thiess and Robert Taylor

Actor Robert Taylor married Miss Thiess of Pacific Palisades, Calif., in a civil ceremony aboard the Wort Hotel's boat in Moran Bay on Jackson Lake on May 24, 1954. Justice of the Peace Russell Robinson officiated. The best man was the pilot of Taylor's plane. Only three other guests were present. The next day, the couple left by plane for Cloverdale, Calif., where Taylor started on another film.

10. Bruce and Alina McCampbell

The Powell couple were featured in an Associated Press story in May 1996. The couple met through a Russian-American firm specializing in arranging marriages between Americans and Russians. Alina saw an ad for the firm, applied, and met Bruce who had traveled to Russia for a prospective bride in 1995.

Gov. Dave Freudenthal, in the closing months of his second term as governor, received a gift from his family, a .454-caliber Casull handgun, made by Freedom Arms in Wyoming and engraved with his name and term as governor.

3 Marriages/Receptions in the Governor's Mansion*

1. Elisa Nila Hunt and Lt. Russell H. W. Chadwick, January 18, 1945

Ellsa, who was the daughter of Governor Lester C. and Emily Hunt, and her husband, an army officer, were not married in what is now the Historic Governor's Mansion in Cheyenne, but the reception was held there after the wedding.

2. Theresa Sullivan and J. R. Twifford, summer of 1993

Just as in the case of the Chadwick-Hunt wedding, the wedding for Twifford and the daughter of Governor Mike and Jane Sullivan was not held in the mansion, but the reception that followed was held in the Historic Governor's Mansion.

3. Crystal Lee Borchert and Robert Geringer, Aug. 12, 1995

The Borchert-Geringer wedding was the first to be held in the new Governor's Mansion. Robert Geringer's father, Jim Geringer, had been inaugurated as governor the previous January.

*Source: Tim White, curator, Historic Governor's Mansion, Cheyenne.

10 Noteworthy Divorces in Wyoming History

1. William F. Cody from Louisa Frederici Cody

The divorce action was filed in 1905 and the case was heard in both Sheridan and Cheyenne. Mrs. Cody accused her famous husband of traveling in Europe with the Wild West Show and in the company of several younger women. Cody filed his own petition for divorce accusing Mrs. Cody of trying to poison him. Neither was approved and the Codys remained married until his death in 1919.

2. George Baggs from Maggie Baggs

Baggs, for whom the town in Carbon County is named, started a ranch at what is now Baggs in the early 1880s. He had met his wife Maggie in Chicago where she worked in a dance hall. She was a shrewd businesswoman, but she also had "roving eyes." After a number of torrid liaisons with ranch cowboys, Maggie became infatuated with one of them, a younger man named Mike Sweet. This affair was too much for her patient husband who sued for divorce. Maggie received half of the proceeds from the sale of the ranch cattle and she and her new beau moved to California. Years later, the two were said to have operated a rooming house in Galveston, Texas. George sold the ranch to William Swan in 1882 and returned to New Mexico.

3. Dorothy Ayer Gardner from Leslie L. King, Sr.

King, the son of prominent Casper and Riverton banker C. H. King, married Gardner Sept. 7, 1912. Following a stormy 15-month marriage and the birth in Omaha of one son, the couple divorced Dec. 19, 1913. The former Mrs. King took her son and moved to Grand Rapids, Mich., where she soon remarried. The child, Leslie King, Jr., was adopted by his mother's new husband and assumed the name of his adoptive father, Gerald R. Ford. Young Ford, of course, became President of the United States in 1974.

4. Mary O'Hara from Heige Sture-Vasa

The couple owned the Remount Ranch west of Cheyenne where O'Hara wrote many of her novels including *My Friend Flicka*. In March 1947 the couple divorced after 24 years of marriage. O'Hara claimed marital troubles began as early as 1930 at the Remount when

Jackson Hole resident and well-known film actor Harrison Ford married actress Calista Flockhart June 15, 2010, on the grounds of the Governor's Mansion in Santa Fe, N.M. News reports indicated that the couple would split time between Ford's 800-acre ranch near Jackson and a home in Los Angeles. It was Ford's third marriage.

Sture-Vasa began paying "conspicuous attention to other women—very young women." The ranch was sold after the divorce and O'Hara moved to Connecticut.

5. J. B. Okie from Jeanette Okie

The well-known central Wyoming sheepman and his wife were married in Rawlins in 1887. After more than 20 years of marriage, Okie filed for divorce in order to marry Clarice Lovett, the ex-wife of a Casper telephone company manager. Jeanette received a $50,000 cash settlement in the divorce action. Okie and Clarice were divorced in October 1921, when Okie alleged her "great beauty and attentiveness to younger visitors" caused her to begin "straying." In 1923, Okie met the daughter of a former president of Mexico and the following years, they became parents of two children. He died in 1930.

6. Malcolm Forbes from Roberta Laidlaw Forbes

Mrs. Forbes, who ranched near Jackson, was granted a divorce in Teton County in November 1985. Her husband of nearly 40 years had been Malcolm Forbes, the publisher of *Forbes Magazine*, who died in February 1990. Their son, Steve Forbes, ran for the Republican presidential nomination in 1996.

7. Nicholas Walke from Anna W. Walke

The divorce, granted Nov. 14, 1866, at Fort Bridger, is considered the earliest granted in Wyoming.

8. Francis Weed Hubbell from E. S. Hubbell

Mrs. Hubbell, heiress to the Weed tire chain fortune, divorced E. S. Hubbell, Encampment dude rancher and legislator (1927-1929), in September, 1935. E. S. Hubbell was known as the "father of Wyoming's aviation laws."

9. Marietta Panos and Peter Panos, Superior

"In the district court last week Marietta Panos of Superior appeared and asked the court to annul her marriage to Peter Panos, saying both were intoxicated when they got married. The court did not think they were drunk enough, however, not to understand what they were doing, although undisputed testimony showed both were intoxicated. Judge Tidball refused the sought-for annulment decree." (*Rock Springs Rocket, Jan. 7, 1927, p. 1*).

10. French Wallop from former Sen. Malcolm Wallop

The wife of former Sen. Wallop announced their divorce in 1998 by sending out an engraved change-of-address card, illustrated with a picture of a woman's boot, that read, "French Wallop regrets to inform you that due to a significant indiscretion on the part of her husband of 16 years, he may now be reached at the following address." The announcement was published in *The Washington Post*. On April 28, 2004, the Wyoming Supreme Court upheld the couple's property settlement. Wallop had married French Goodwyn May 26, 1984, during his second term in the Senate. It was the senator's third marriage and his bride's second.

2 Daughters of Wyoming Senators Married to Generals

1. Frances Warren to John J. Pershing, 1905

Frances, the daughter of U. S. Senator Francis E. Warren, met the dashing young major at a dance at Fort Myer, Virginia, in December, 1903. Even though she returned to Cheyenne for much of the following year after Pershing was assigned to posts in the Southwest, they did see each other occasionally. The two were engaged on Christmas Day, 1904, in Washington, D. C. They planned to marry the following June but soon after the engagement, Pershing learned he had orders to the Far East. They chose to marry the next month. On January 26, 1905, in a full-scale Washington blizzard, the couple exchanged vows at the Church of the Epiphany. More than 500 guests attended. The U. S. Senate adjourned so that members could go. Cheyenne society treated the couple to a "lavish reception" on their brief visit the following week. A few days later, Pershing went alone to his next station in Japan, Frances joining him only after his next duty assignment. The couple visited Cheyenne frequently over the next ten years as the young major rose in rank to general. In 1915, Pershing was sent to border duty in Mexico, leaving his wife and family at home at the Presidio in San Francisco. A disastrous fire broke out in the home, killing Frances and three of their four children. Funerals and burial were in Cheyenne. Pershing went on to become General of the Army, the highest rank attainable in the U. S. Army. He commanded Allied forces in World War I. Pershing died in 1948.

2. Rosa Maye Kendrick to Hubert Reilly Harmon, 1927

Rosa Maye, the daughter of U. S. Senator John B. Kendrick, met Harmon in Washington, D. C., where he was stationed and where she lived with her family while her father was serving in the U. S. Senate. Harmon, a native of Chester, Pa., had graduated from West Point in 1915. (One of his classmates was Dwight D. Eisenhower). Hubert Harmon and Rosa Maye Kendrick married in 1927. He went on to service in World War II and, following the war, accepted assignment in the newly created U. S. Air Force. In 1955, he was appointed the first superintendent of the U. S. Air Force Academy near Colorado Springs. He died two years later. Rosa Maye died in 1979.

5 Most Common Marriage Months in Wyoming (2006)

1. July (729) 3. June (665) 5. May (336)
2. August (675) 4. September (543)

Least common month is January with just 202 marriages in 2006. Most popular marriage months vary by county. June was the most common marriage month in Laramie County while July was the most common in Teton and Sweetwater counties. August was most common in Albany and Park. No couple married in either Johnson or Niobrara county in the month of April, 2006. *Source: Wyoming Dept. of Public Health, Division of Vital Statistics*

Marriages by County (2006)

1. Laramie 875
2. Natrona 624
3. Teton, 520
4. Campbell, 338
5. Sweetwater, 327
6. Fremont, 297
7. Sheridan, 273
8. Park, 268

9. Albany, 216
10. Uinta, 187
11. Carbon, 144
12. Lincoln, 124
13. Converse, 103
14.-15. Goshen,
   Sublette, 80 each
16. Johnson, 78

17. Big Horn, 62
18. Weston, 61
19.-20. Hot Springs,
   Washakie, 53 each
21. Platte, 50
22. Crook, 44
23. Niobrara
Total Marriages in Wyoming: 4,873

Divorces by County (2006)

1. Laramie 598
2. Natrona 393
3. Teton, 94
4. Campbell, 213
5. Sweetwater, 221
6. Fremont, 156
7. Sheridan, 148
8. Park, 141

9. Albany, 102
10. Uinta, 109
11. Carbon, 87
12. Lincoln, 65
13. Converse, 58
14.-Goshen, 46
15. Sublette, 34
16. Johnson, 40

17. Big Horn, 31
18. Weston, 25
19.-Hot Springs, 26
20. Washakie, 43
21. Platte, 49
22. Crook, 20
23. Niobrara, 12
Total Divorces: 2,691

400 workers lost their jobs in 1983 when the Atlantic City iron ore mine and mill closed.

Famous Cheyenne Trunk Maker

William H. Vanderhoff came to Cheyenne in 1904 to open the "Cheyenne Trunk Factory." His firm manufactured all lines of luggage as well as smaller items such as leather billfolds and pocketbooks.

The handmade trunks were well constructed and popular with local people as well as with soldiers at nearby Fort Warren. Vanderhoff prospered but in 1922, he was forced to sell his business due to ill health. He sold the "factory" to Joseph J. Barbian who managed to keep the firm going even in the depths of the 1920s depression.

According to an article by Mariann McCormick in a 1988 issue of *Annals of Wyoming*, the factory closed soon after Barbian died in an accident. He was working on his 1928 Chrysler coupe in a closed garage in the spring of 1932 and died of carbon monoxide poisoning. With his death, the company folded.

The trunks made by the firm are valued by owners, not only for their quality but for their rarity. Is there one in your closet or attic?

Asmus Boysen: Dam Builder

Iowa businessman Asmus Boysen applied for a permit on August 15, 1906, to build a dam on the river just as it entered Wind River Canyon. His company, the Big Horn Power Company, planned to produce and market electricity generated by the structure.

The State Engineer allowed him to build the dam, but nearly half as tall as his projected plan. Two years later, Boysen amended the plan to include a substantial superstructure, including a wagon roadway along the crest of the dam.

The permit was granted, but the next summer, the deputy state engineer inspected the project and discovered substantial deviations from the original plans. Alarmed that the increased height of the dam would cause damage to its tracks in times of high water flow, the Chicago, Burlington and Quincy Railroad asked the State Engineer to withdraw the permit.

In a case that finally was decided by the Wyoming Supreme Court in June, 1915, Boysen's company was ordered to dismantle the offending roadway along with the concrete support columns that apparently caused logs and other debris to lodge and then back water up above the height of the dam's crest.

The reduced height of the dam diminished its profitability. The remainder of Boysen's structure was carried away by a record-breaking flood in 1923. The present dam, named for Boysen, was completed in 1951.

In October, 1995, a judge sentenced 34-year-old Felix Urioste to one year in jail in Utah. Urioste, posing as a woman named "Leasa," had married a 35-year-old Wyoming man in Lyman, Wyoming, in 1991. Urioste's "husband" claimed he did not know that Urioste was a male. Urioste was arrested in June, 1995, after running up charges of more than $50,000 on a credit card in the "husband's" name. At that time, police unmasked his true identity to the surprise of the "husband."

MEDICINE

1st surgical operation performed in Wyoming: Dr. Marcus Whitman removed an arrow from Jim Bridger's back, Aug. 12, 1835. *(See below).*

1st plastic surgery practiced in Wyoming: Dr. Thomas Maghee, Rawlins, 1886. *(See Famous Medical Treatments, below)*

1st nurse registered by the Wyoming State Board of Nurse Examiners: Miss Amy Miller, Rock Springs, 1911.

1st doctor licensed by the State of Wyoming: Dr. George P. Johnston, Cheyenne, in 1899, soon after the medical licensing law took effect.

1st X-ray machine in Wyoming: Brought to Sheridan by Dr. Marcus A. Newell.

1st public health nurses in Wyoming (1936): Eliene Goodall, Laramie; Penelope Gordon Johnson and Ethel Moss, Sheridan; Lillian Retzloff, Casper.

1st sperm bank in Wyoming: Opened by Dr. C. W. "Buzz" Ely, Jr., in March 1982, in Jackson. It was the first sperm bank in the West.

1st medical doctor to use an automobile regularly on his rounds: Dr. W. W. Crook, Cheyenne. He owned one of the first cars in Cheyenne.

Total hospitals in Wyoming: 26 in 2008. Of the total, three were for-profit hospitals. In 2010 there were 17 certified rural health clinics in the state.

Total acute care facilities in Wyoming: 26. Of these, 22 are operated by a government unit.

Total licensed physicians in Wyoming (2007): 2,532, of which 940 lived in Wyoming.

Number of medical doctors in Wyoming (non-federal): 1,237 in 2008. Of these, 547 were primary care physicians. The total number of actively practicing physicians in 1992 had been 725.

Actively practicing medical doctors in Wyoming: 480 (1995); 940 (2007).

No. of physician's assistants in Wyoming: 172 (2007). There were 34 in 1995.

Total number of graduates from the Wyoming Family Practice Centers: Casper Family Practice Center had graduated 79 students by 1991. The Cheyenne center had graduated 59.

Opening of UW Nursing School: Fall, 1951.

1st health care cooperative in the United States: Fetterman Hospital Association, formed by ranchers and cowboys in Converse County in 1885.

Health insurance (2007): 60% of residents had employer-provided health insurance; 10% purchased their own health insurance; and 12% were under Medicaid. The rest were uninsured.

Uninsured residents: In 2008, more than 100,000 Wyoming residents had no health insurance. The state ranked 24th per capita in uninsured residents. A State Department of Health survey in 2004 showed that 19 percent of the state's population had no health insurance.

Patients treated, Wyoming emergency rooms (2007): 228,000, according to the Wyo. Hospital Assoc.

Total surgeries performed in Wyoming hospitals (2007): 39,000

Total patients staying at least one night in a Wyoming hospital (2007): 52,000

National Health Policy: Dr. Paul Ellwood headed the "Jackson Hole Group," an informal organization of health care experts who spent months deliberating plans for a national system of health care. Meetings in Jackson Hole were well away from the media spotlight. The proposals were considered by the Clinton administration in the process of developing its health care plan in 1993-94.

Emergency Medical Services "Physician of the Decade, 1980-1990": Dr. Richard Campbell, Torrington, named in April 1992. The next award was made in 2001.

1st trained flight nurse in the U. S.: Geraldine Brier, Cheyenne, during World War II. She helped evacuate the wounded from the beaches on D-Day.

1st person to be fitted with a new myoelectric arm: Jonathan Goldman, 14, of Laramie, who was born without a left arm below the elbow, was fitted with the new device in January 1992, by its inventor, Tom Haslam of Houston.

1st artificial limb purchased by State Compensation Department for injured worker: Artificial leg for Dan Daniels, Jr., of Winton, a coal miner injured April 15, 1935, when he caught his leg in a duckbill loading device in a Union Pacific mine.

Average daily cost of one night's stay in a hospital: The figure is virtually impossible to find. Nationally, the average cost in 2009, depending on the nature of the treatment, ranged from $3,000-$5,000.

1st formal charge of malpractice: One of the earliest on record is the case brought by the Casper Town Council against Dr. J. L. Garner for "attending a case of diphtheria and claiming it was some other disease" in January 1896. A jury found in favor of Dr. Garner.

Births: Wyoming ranked **33rd** nationally in the number of births per capita with 14.6 per 1,000 people. In 2007, there were 7,200 babies born in Wyoming up from 6,801 babies in 1991. In 1997, Wyoming ranked **5th** nationally in percentage of low birth-weight babies (9 percent).

Death of Children: In 1998, Wyoming ranked **9th** nationally in per capita deaths of children, 1-4 years old, with 31 per 100,000 children. The national average was just 25 per 100,000. In 1989, Wyoming was **8th** per capita with 38.51 per 100,000 children.

Buffalo Bill's personal physician: Dr. Daniel Quigley was Cody's doctor. His granddaughter, Jane Alexander, an actress, was director of the National Endowment for the Humanities (1995-97).

Adult regular smokers: 21% of the state's population smoked (2006-08). Wyoming ranked 18th per capita among the states for number of smokers in the population.

Obesity: In 2009, Wyoming ranked 38th per capita among the states for adult obesity. In that year 24.3% of the population was classified as obese.

Only five cases of **tuberculosis** were reported in Wyoming in 2009. Wyomng had the fewst such cases of any state in the union.

Top Ten Most Likely Places to Catch a Cold: Vicks, the cold-remedy manufacturer, conducted a survey of 1,700 medical professionals nationwide in 1995, and Casper was listed in the top ten. Such varied locations as San Diego, Indianapolis, and Hartford, Conn., also were included on the list.

10 Famous Medical Treatments

1. Dr. Marcus Whitman, surgeon; Jim Bridger, patient, Aug. 12, 1835.

In the first recorded medical operation by a trained professional in Wyoming, Dr. Whitman removed an arrow from Bridger's back. The operation, done without anesthesia, was performed at the Green River Rendezvous at a site in present-day Sublette County.

2. Dr. Thomas Maghee, surgeon; an unnamed sheepherder, patient

Dr. Maghee, a former army surgeon who was practicing in Rawlins, reconstructed the nose and face of a sheepherder. The patient, who had attempted suicide by firing a shotgun blast from below his chin, reconsidered the matter when the shot was not fatal and he survived without a nose or lower face. Dr. Maghee used celluloid for the base and grafted skin from the man's legs and arms onto the reconstructed nose and face. The effort was one of the first reconstructive surgical operations in medical history.

3. Chief Washakie, the "surgeon"; Chief Big Robber, the "patient"

Although not exactly surgical, Chief Washakie is said to have removed the heart from the Crow chief Big Robber after prevailing in a hand-to-hand fight to settle a dispute over hunting rights in the area of what is now Crowheart Butte, named for the episode.

4. Lou Polk's Nose

Lou Polk, a Casper dance hall "hostess," was kidnapped by her jealous house mate Dagae Lee and taken on a ride near Casper. To keep her from gaining the attentions of other men, Lee cut off Lou's nose. Attempts to sew it back on were unsuccessful, so doctors constructed a wooden nose which was held on Lou's face by her eyeglasses. After that, Lou always wore a heavily veiled hat whenever she appeared in public.

5. Big Nose George's Skull and Skin

After the notorious outlaw was hanged in Rawlins in 1879, his body was taken to the offices of Dr. John Osborne who sawed off the skull cap in an experimental attempt to discern what may have caused his aberrant behavior. At the same time, Dr. Osborne removed enough skin from the outlaw's body to make a lamp shade and a pair of shoes. The skull cap later became a pin tray and doorstop in the Rawlins home of Osborne's assistant, Dr. Lillian Heath Nelson. The shoes are on display in Rawlins.

6. Double Lung Transplant

Lance Borden of Newcastle (b. Casper 1959) became the first double-lung transplant recipient in Colorado history on March 15, 1994. He received the lungs at University

Frank Wigfall, an African-American man, was lynched inside the state prison on Oct. 2, 1912.

Hospital in Denver because cystic fibrosis had destroyed his own. Borden worked to help others cope with the problems of transplantation until his death on June 22, 2000.

7. Snake Removed from the Stomach of a Green River Woman

Two well-known Laramie physicians Drs. Harris and Finfrock supposedly performed an unusual operation in Laramie, according to the April 1, 1874, issue of the *Laramie Daily Sentinel*. The woman was reported to have told the doctors she believed something alive was crawling in her stomach. When they operated, they removed a large snake, the paper said. The April Fool's joke was reprinted as fact by other newspapers who failed to notice the odd coincidence between the incredible operation and the day it was reported.

8. Swallowed a silver dollar?

A Meeteetse man, involved in a car accident on Sept. 9, 1935, told the sheriff in Red Lodge, Mont., near where the accident occurred, that he went off the road because he was biting down on a silver dollar and it suddenly slid down his throat. Doctors in Billings removed the coin. Later, the sheriff arrested the man for drunk driving.

9. An Artist's Broken Leg

In the 1890s, when famous animal artist Carl Rungius (b. 1869, d. 1959) was on a pack trip to the Green River headwaters, he broke his leg. A medical doctor arrived, but was under the influence of alcohol and set the leg incorrectly. After the man left, Rungius noticed it was not set straight so he asked his colleagues to "straighten it out." Two of them sawed off the first cast and ground it back into powder. Without any pain killer, he endured having the leg stretched and repositioned. The realignment worked. Rungius sent a painting to his "leg-straightener." *Source: Fern K. Nelson, This Was Jackson's Hole. (Glendo: High Plains, 1994).*

10. Burying Nate Champion in the Mud

Champion, who died with Nick Ray in the "Invaders'" attack on the Kaycee ranch cabin in the Johnson County War of 1892, suffered from rheumatism. Sometimes, he would be bedridden with the condition. According to a story told years later by a pioneer named Settle, Champion was taken by two friends to the Hot Springs near present-day Thermopolis. Helpless by the time he arrived, Champion was carried by the two men to a likely hole where they laid him down and silently began covering him with warm mud. "Thinking his time had come, Champion plead like a good fellow for his life." They continued to pack mud onto him, leaving only his head sticking out, and walked away. When they returned a few hours later, Champion's condition improved. The treatment was continued until he was again able to walk. *Source: Tacetta Walker, Stories of Early Days in Wyoming. (Casper, 1936).*

1st Medical Doctors in Wyoming Places

1. Big Horn Basin

Dr. C. Dana Carter, (b. 1874) came to Basin in 1896. He also opened the first hospital in Basin in 1911.

2. Douglas

Dr. Amos Barber, who had come to the territory as the physician for the Fetterman Hospital Association, opened a private practice in the new town of Douglas in 1886. He did so with the permission of the association.

3. Kemmerer

Dr. Charles M. Field started a practice there in the fall of 1897.

4. Laramie

Dr. Frank H. Harrison opened a practice on May 1, 1868. Dr. J. H. Finfrock practiced at nearby Fort Sanders before Harrison's arrival.

5. Lovell

    Dr. Clymer built the first hospital in town, a log structure, in 1902.

6. Star Valley

    Dr. Arthur V. Stoughton located in the valley in 1889. Dr. G. W. West arrived in 1903 and continued to practice for the next half century. The first permanent dentist in the valley, Dr. L. C. Proctor, who arrived in 1905, also practiced for a half century.

7. Torrington

    Dr. C. H. Platz began practicing in Torrington in 1903, just two years after the first businesses were established in town. In 1912, he was one of the first owners of an automobile in Torrington.

8. Jackson

    Dr. Charles W. Huff came to Jackson in 1913, the first trained physician to locate in the Hole. In 1916, Royal Balcomb, the Episcopal minister, asked fellow residents, "Why don't we build Dr. Huff a hospital?" Citizens dragged logs from Cache Creek in order to build the hospital named "St. Johns." The building was enlarged in 1919 and again in 1925 when an elevator was installed which ran on a piston driven by water pressure. Huff died in 1937.

9. Sundance

    Dr. Charles Fowler was the first medical doctor in town. Notice of his arrival was printed in the *Sundance Gazette*, March 7, 1885.

10. Buffalo

    Although she was not a medical doctor, Mrs. D. A. Sonnesberger served as the county's first physician, moving to the area in the late 1870s. She had studied medicine at Monmouth College in Illinois prior to coming to Wyoming, but did not complete the program.

6 Early-Day Woman Doctors in Wyoming

1. Dr. Lillian Heath Nelson, Rawlins

    The first woman in Wyoming to be licensed to practice medicine, Dr. Nelson graduated from a medical school in the Midwest. A native of Rawlins, she returned to her hometown in 1893 and practiced there until 1909. Although she did not practice full-time, she retained her medical license, the fifth ever issued in Wyoming, until her death in 1962.

2. Dr. Flora Hayward Stanford, Sundance

    Dr. Stanford moved to Crook County from the Black Hills of South Dakota, where she had been practicing for several years, in 1897. She homesteaded near Sundance and died in 1901.

3. Dr. Frances M. Lane, Cody

    Born in Ohio, Dr. Lane was the daughter of a nationally renowned architect. She graduated from medical school in Chicago in 1900 and moved to Cody two years later. From 1905 to 1910, she served as contract physician to the U. S. Bureau of Reclamation on the Shoshone (Buffalo Bill) Dam project. A former chair of the National Women's Party, she campaigned strenuously for the National Woman Suffrage amendment. Although she had many admirers, her feud with Cody editor Caroline Lockhart resulted in Dr. Lane becoming the title character in Lockhart's novel, *Lady Doc*. It was not a flattering portrayal.

4. Dr. Caroline Amelia Daniels Mills, Evanston

    Born in Provo, Utah, Mills was one of the first graduates of what is now Brigham Young University. She taught school. Following her marriage to Frank Mills in 1882, she moved to Evanston where he was a store clerk. In the early 1890s, Mills attended medi-

---

The town of Dayton was not named for the Ohio city. Dayton was the middle name of rancher Joe Thorn, a pioneer resident in the fall of 1882 when the town was established.

cal school in Iowa City, Iowa. She was the mother of five children, the second-youngest born while she was a medical student. After graduation in 1895, she opened a practice in Evanston where her husband was receiver in the Land Office. Later, she moved her practice to Cokeville where her husband opened a general store. In 1910, they moved to Salt Lake City, but after her husband's death four years later, she returned to Wyoming, practicing medicine in the Bridger Valley. She retired from medicine in 1928 after marrying James Davis and moving to Salt Lake City. She died Aug. 24, 1934. *Source: Kathaleen Kennington Hamblin, Bridger Valley: A Guide to the Past (1993).*

5. Dr. June Etta Downey, Laramie

Although not a physician, Dr. Downey was a psychologist who pioneered research in the field. Born July 13, 1875, in Laramie, she graduated from the University of Wyoming in 1898. In 1907, she was granted the Ph.D. from the University of Chicago. She taught for many years at the University of Wyoming where she became the first woman in the United States to chair a psychology department. She remained on faculty until her death on Oct. 10, 1932, while visiting a sister in Trenton, N. J. A campus dormitory is named for her.

6. Dr. Florence Patrick, Rock River

Dr. Patrick began her practice in the Albany County community soon after the turn of the century. Along with practicing medicine, she helped form the local civic club, the American Legion Auxiliary, and Camp Fire group. She was state chair of the American Women's Hospitals in World War I. She retired in the 1930s and spent the rest of her life near the community of Garrett, Wyoming.

AIDS Cases in Wyoming

Progression of AIDS cases in Wyoming

1. To the end of 2007, **242** cumulative cases in Wyoming. 19 new cases were reported in 2004; 11 new cases in 2005. Of the total, 156 had died during the period, (1981-2005). Just 18 died of the disease between 2001 and 2005, compared to 29 between 1996 and 2000.

2. As of June 30, 2004, **218**, 28 of whom were women.

2. As of June 30, 2000: **178**, 21 of whom were women. 109 people had died.

2. As of Sept. 30, 1995: **125**. At that date, 75 had died—66 men, nine women.

3. As of June 1, 1993: **85**

4. As of Sept. 30, 1991: **51**. Another 63 people were reported HIV positive. As of the same date, 27 people had died of AIDS in Wyoming.

5. As of Jan. 1, 1990: **36**

Counties with Most AIDS Cases, % of State Total (1984-July, 2000)

	AIDS	HIV	% state		AIDS	HIV	% state
1. Laramie Co.:	45	15	(25.3%)	**6.** Sweetwater Co.:	13	1	(7.3%)
2. Natrona Co.:	26	6	(14.6%)	**7.** Fremont Co.:	10	9	(5.6%)
3. Albany Co.:	14	8	(7.9%)	**Includes 8 AIDS, 3 HIV in State Penitentiary.*			
4. Carbon Co.:	14*	3	(7.9%)	Most AIDS cases reported 1 year: **31** in 1990.			
5. Teton Co.:	13	5	(7.3%)	New cases, 2005: **11.**			

A 23-year-old California man enrolled in the Civilian Conservation Corps (CCC) and assigned to "Hot Springs camp" near Jackson suffered from an abdominal pain. Assuming he could cure the affliction himself, he performed self-surgery with a pocket knife and a bottle of iodine. Results were unsatisfactory and the professional help of a Jackson doctor was required to keep the man from bleeding to death. (Sept. 1935)

Some Disease Epidemics in Wyoming

1. Typhoid epidemic

Three died in the epidemic that swept through the new town of Douglas in October 1886. The only other serious disease outbreak in town occurred in 1937 when a polio outbreak caused cancellation of the State Fair.

2. Fort Fred Steele Surgeon's Report, 1870

"Bowel afflictions are prevalent during the months of July, August and September on account of alkali washed by rains from the plains into the river; at such times the water is a milky hue." The report showed that of the 247 men at the post in 1869, there had been 83 cases of dysentery, 14 of venereal diseases, 97 "catarral afflictions" (pneumonia, pleurisy, bronchitis), and 106 cases of "malarial fevers."

3. Scarlet fever

Three died from an epidemic of scarlet fever in Cheyenne in December 1913. Santa Claus was forbidden to appear in public because of the outbreak.

4. Scurvy cure

The post surgeon at Fort Laramie in 1858 indicated that scurvy could be avoided if the following diet were followed: pickles, at least four times a week; dried apples; molasses; vinegar; and cactus juice. "It is impossible to get the companies as such to use the cactus juice...it is only practicable to get the men to take the cactus juice when mixed with whiskey."

5. Diarrhea cure

The post surgeon at Fort Laramie on July 26, 1868, wrote that the condition could be "relieved by one or two days' rest at the hospital, the administration of mercury and rhubarb and abstinence from the use of coffee."

6. Smallpox epidemic

The disease was a serious problem for Oregon Trail travelers and Indian tribes in the West of the 19th century. In 1876, the wife and eight children of "Beaver Dick" Leigh died of smallpox in Jackson Hole. Jenny Lake is named for Leigh's wife.

7. Rheumatism and Arthritis

Denver Mud, an early name for bentonite, was said to have beneficial properties in the treatments of rheumatism and arthritis. Bentonite from northeast Wyoming was used for the "cure."

8. General ailments

Benjamin F. A. Kueny of Cheyenne formulated what he called "the celebrated Kueny whiskey cure" in the late 1800s. Several other Wyomingites provided products for the patent medicine industry during the same period.

9. Rabies

In 1992, Wyoming had the fourth highest per capita incidence of rabies in the United States with 83 cases reported. In 1998, there were 68 cases. All but six were reported in wild animals: 52 were skunks; 8 were bats. There were 32 cases reported in animals in 2008. In 2009, of the 40 reported cases, all but six were skunks.

10. Meningitis

A severe outbreak occurred in Casper in May 1898. Schools dismissed early for the summer and church services were suspended. The epidemic ended in less than a month, but it caused the city council to adopt sanitary ordinances including restrictions against pig pens and corrals within the city. A diphtheria epidemic in Casper claimed the lives of many children two years earlier.

By mid-July 2008, 304 wind turbines had been erected in Wyoming and were generating electricity. An additional 2,000 were projected by 2011.

11. World War I flu epidemic

The 1918 influenza pandemic caused thousands of deaths in the United States. In Wyoming, the epidemic was so serious that public events were cancelled, schools were dismissed, and businesses closed. In Thermopolis, the disease caused so many deaths in December, 1918, that the local undertaker was unable to furnish enough caskets.

12. Hantavirus

Eight cases were reported in Wyoming between 2000 and 2009. Four people died of the disease. The first to die from it was Irene Pedersen, 64, of Lander, who died of the disease in August 1993. In August 1999, a 35-year-old man died after cleaning his mobile home. Hantavirus was thought to have caused the deaths of two Carbon County residents in 2008.

13. Tick diseases

Number of Lyme disease cases diagnosed in Wyoming (1982-99): 55 total cases. There was one case reported in 1998 and three in 1999.

During 1995, five cases of Rocky Mountain spotted fever were reported in Wyoming. There were 16 cases of Colorado tick fever reported. All three diseases are caused by tick bites.

14. Plague

The disease was first found in Wyoming in a ground squirrel in 1936. Outbreaks among animal populations include one in the 1990s among prairie dogs that spread to the black-footed ferrets, further endangering the rare animal.

15. West Nile Virus

The disease, transmitted by mosquitoes, was first reported in Wyoming in the late summer of 2002. In 2009, 12 cases were reported in Wyoming of the 663 recorded nationally. Wyoming ranked 11th among the states in actual West Nile cases.

Source: Wyoming Department of Health

Disciplinary Actions Brought Against Wyoming Doctors

Number of serious actions (2002): 12 or 11.87 per 1,000 doctors, ranking Wyoming the state with the highest per capita actions among the states. (Total practicing physicians was 1,011). The state also ranked first in 1994 with 12.41 actions per 100,000 physicians, but as low as 39th in 2001 and 31st in 1996. In 1991, the Wyoming Medical Board brought disciplinary actions equivalent to 6.81 per 1,000 doctors. Wyoming's was the 9th highest in the country The higher the number and ranking, the more diligent the state licensing board acts, according to the report.

Causes for Disciplinary Action, 1989-94	Number
Criminal conviction	1
Sexual abuse or misconduct with patient	1
Misprescribing or overprescribing drugs	2
Drug or alcohol abuse	3
Action by another state or agency	1
Other offenses	9
Total	**17**

Source: Questionable Doctors, Public Citizen Health Research Group Report, March 1996; Public Citizen website, 2010 (www.citizen.org)

"The state of Wyoming enjoys the enviable distinction of being the home of a smaller number of insane and feeble-minded persons than any other state." --Bill Barlow's Budget, Jan. 22, 1914, noting there were 105 males and 57 females in the categories. Wyoming's total of 162 was considerably below the next lowest state, Nevada with 230.

4 "Medical" Governors

1. Dr. John W. Hoyt (1878-1882)

Dr. Hoyt, appointed territorial governor by President Rutherford Hayes, was both a medical doctor and a lawyer. Hoyt graduated from the Ohio Medical College and the Eclectic Medical Institute. Later, he was professor of chemistry at Antioch College and editor of an agricultural journal in Wisconsin prior to his appointment as territorial governor. When the University of Wyoming was established in 1887, Hoyt was named its first president. Hoyt was founder of both the Wisconsin and Wyoming Academies of Science, Arts and Letters. He was elected to the Wyoming Constitutional Convention in 1889. Later, he lobbied Congress, unsuccessfully, for creation of a national university in Washington, D. C.

2. Dr. Amos Barber (1890-1893)

A graduate of the University of Pennsylvania medical department, Barber came to Wyoming in 1885 as contract physician for the Fetterman Hospital Association, the first health care cooperative in the United States. When local cattlemen suffered serious financial reverses in the blizzards of 1886-87, Barber was given permission to open a private practice in the new town of Douglas. In 1890, Barber was the successful candidate for Secretary of State. He became acting governor 17 days after he took office when Francis E. Warren resigned the position to go to the U. S. Senate. After Barber's term expired, he was assistant surgeon of the U. S. Army during the Spanish American War. Later, he set up private practice in Cheyenne which he ran until his death.

3. Dr. John Osborne (1893-1895)

Osborne, a medical graduate from the University of Vermont, came to Rawlins in the early 1880s as a surgeon for the Union Pacific Railroad. Along with his medical practice, Osborne operated a sheep ranch, a dry good store and a drug store. He was elected mayor of Rawlins in 1888 and, five years later, he was elected governor. In 1896, he won election to the U. S. House of Representatives where he served one term. He remained active in politics, losing a Senate race against Francis E. Warren by 1,000 votes in 1918. Previously, he had been first assistant Secretary of State, appointed to that position by President Woodrow Wilson in 1913.

4. Dr. Lester C. Hunt (1943-1949)

A graduate of St. Louis University College of Dentistry, he came to Wyoming in 1917 to both practice dentistry and play semi-professional baseball. Shortly after he passed the Wyoming dental examination and began practice in Lander, he was called to service in the Army Dental Corps during World War I. He returned to Lander where he practiced until 1934 when he was elected Secretary of State. During his first term in that position, he commissioned the "bucking horse" logo for the state license plate. In 1942, he was elected Wyoming governor. He was elected to the U. S. Senate in 1948, serving until his death by suicide in 1954.

*Acting Gov. C. J. "Doc" Rogers received his medical nickname from an adoptive uncle. He was not associated with the medical or dental professions.

Some Well-Known Wyoming Doctors

1. Dr. George P. Johnston (1863-1956)

The holder of the first medical license issued in the state of Wyoming, Dr. Johnston was one of three doctors responsible for the licensing act that passed the legislature in 1899. A graduate of the Medical College of Ohio, he studied surgery at the University of Vienna in the early 1900s. He was the first doctor in Wyoming to perform an appendectomy as well as the first to do an abdominal section. He brought the first registered nurse to Wyoming. During his more than 50 years of practice in Cheyenne, he delivered more than 11,000 babies. At the time of his death in 1956, Dr. Johnston was the oldest member of the American Medical Association's House of Delegates, representing Wyoming in that body for more than 30 years.

2. Dr. Thomas Maghee (1842-1927)

Dr. Maghee performed the first "plastic surgery" in Wyoming. He came to the territory as post surgeon at Camp Brown near Lander in 1873. The next year, he was cited for gallantry in action in the Bates Battle against the Indians. He resigned from the army in 1878 and set up practice in Green River. Elected to the territorial legislature from there, he later moved to Rawlins where he continued to practice until 1905. In that year, he returned to Lander where he organized the Wyoming State Training School and served as its first superintendent.

3. Dr. William A. Hocker (1847-1919)

Hocker was a physician in Evanston for more than 25 years. He served as first superintendent of the Wyoming State Hospital (then known as the State Insane Asylum). He had served in the legislature during the session in which the hospital had been authorized and he was instrumental in passage of the enabling act.

4. Dr. C. Dana Carter (1894-1945)

Dr. Carter was the first physician in the Big Horn Basin when he came to Basin in 1896, the year the town was established. He opened a hospital there, the first in the Big Horn Basin. In 1912, he moved to Thermopolis where he built the Carter Hotel and sanitarium near the world's largest mineral hot spring. He practiced medicine for more than 42 years.

5. Dr. W. W. Crook (1836-1920)

Dr. Crook was the first physician in the state to use an automobile while visiting his patients. His car, a 1908 Olds, was one of the first owned by a Wyoming resident. A graduate of the University of Iowa, he wrote articles for medical journals along with operating a thriving capital city practice.

6. Dr. Don MacLeod (1905-1983)

Born in Colorado, MacLeod graduated from the University of Colorado Medical School in 1932. When Jackson pioneer physician Dr. Charles Huff died in 1937, MacLeod moved from Sheridan to Jackson. Until his retirement in 1964, he had delivered 2,500 babies in Jackson Hole and treated countless victims of accidents and disease. He was very active in civic affairs, serving as a founding member of the Teton County Historical Society and one of a group of businessmen who promoted the Snow King ski area.

7. Dr. Nathan E. Wells (1876-1962)

A third-generation medical doctor, Wells came to Newcastle in 1905, accepting a position as company physician at the nearby coal-mining town of Cambria. He relocated to Newcastle in 1911, but continued to treat Cambria patients from his new offices until the mines closed in 1928. He practiced medicine in Newcastle until the 1940s, frequently filling in for other doctors in later years. A brief autobiography, *Just Another Country Doctor*, was published in 1954.

According to army records, frostbite of the appendages was a frequent wintertime problem at Wyoming forts during the frontier period.. Often it resulted in the loss of fingers or toes, but occasionally, it led to death as the recorded cases of Private Hugo Brown in 1872 and a Private Smith in 1874 illustrate. Both came down with severe frostbite while on patrol in the vicinity of Fort Laramie and both died from the affects.

Some Early Wyoming Hospitals

1. Cheyenne hospital

Dr. George P. Johnston and Dr. W. A. Burgess purchased the H. G. Hay mansion on Carey Avenue in Cheyenne and converted it into a private hospital in 1906.

2. Laramie

The Catholic Sisters of Charity of Leavenworth established a hospital in Laramie in 1876. Just before World War I, banker Edward Ivinson offered to donate $50,000 and give the land for construction of a new hospital in Laramie. The cornerstone of Ivinson Hospital was laid on June 7, 1916. At the same time, William R. Coe donated almost $4,000 to the new hospital for the purchase of a Studebaker ambulance. The present Ivinson Hospital was completed in 1973. The old building housed the University Police and the UW computing center until 2009 when the police moved to the former credit union building on North 15th and the new computer center on Sorority Row opened in 2009.

3. Powell

Dr. John R. Whitlock opened a privately-operated 18-bed hospital in 1917. He operated the hospital until selling it in 1936 to Dr. Robert Siddle. Following Siddle's death about 1946, the hospital continued to operate with equipment obtained from the hospital, recently closed, at Heart Mountain Relocation Center. During the post-World War II years, community leaders raised funds for a new community hospital, constructed as War Memorial Hospital and dedicated in 1952.

7 Counties with the Most Physicians

1. Laramie 123	3. Fremont 63	5. Albany 43	7. Teton 32
2. Natrona 119	4. Sheridan 48	6. Sweetwater 37	

7 Counties with the Most Health Professionals per capita

1. Teton (4.1 doctors per 1,000 people)   **5. Fremont** (2.1)
2. Park (2.81)   **6. Sheridan** (2.02)
3. Laramie (2.38)   **7. Albany** (1.94)
4. Natrona (2.37)

The state average (2007) was 1.94 doctors per 1,000 people; the national average was about 2.81 per 1,000. Lowest was Weston County with .59 per 1,000. Next lowest were Crook, Niobrara and Carbon counties. Source: Wyoming Health Care Commission report (2008)

Lanacane Dry Itchy Skin Index, announced Dec. 6, 1998, showed three of the top four "itchy cities" were in Wyoming. Laramie led the list with an itchiness rating of 94 percent. Cheyenne was second with 93 percent. Lander was fourth with 62 percent, behind third place Colorado Springs, Colo. The index, calculated by the Lanacane Itch Information Center and the Univ of Delaware's Center for Climactic Research, was begun in 1996. Wind, temperature, humidity, and the environment inside a heated home were elements in the index.

Presidents, Wyoming Medical Society*

1900: George P. Johnston	1936: J. F. Replogle	1972: William G. Erickson
1901: Ernest E. Levers	1937: Victor R. Dacken	1973: Donald lF. Mahnke
1902: G. G. Verbryck	1938: J. D. Shingle	1974: Paul R. Yedinak
1903: S. B. Miller	1939: J. H. Goodnough	1975: Donald B. Hunton
1904: J. H. Wichs	1940: P. M. Schunk	1976: Patrick Nolan
1905: ?	1941: R. H. Reeve	1977: James E. Stoetzel
1906: W. A. Wyman	1942: R. H. Reeve	1978: Kent Christensen
1907: A. C. Godrey	1943: G. H. Phelps	1979: James Alexander
1908: C. E. Stevenson	1944: Earl Whedon	1980: John C. Budge
1909: G. L. Strader	1945: Thomas J. Riach	1981: Richard G. McCleery
1910: No President	1946: J. D. Shingle	1982: William A. Fogarty
1911: A. G. Hamilton	1947: W. A Steffan	1983: Archie P. Kirsch
1912: Amos Barber	1948: E. W. DeKay	1984: Walter G. Saunders
1913: Amos Barber	1949: DeWitt Dominick	1985: Arnold N. Krause
1914: A. G. Hamilton	1950: Karl Krueger	1986: Howard T. Willson
1915: ?	1951: John W. Cline	1987: Lee K. Hermann
1916: R. W. Hale	1952: Paul R. Holtz	1988: Meade O. Davis III
1917: W. V. Gage	1953: Edward J. Guilfoyle	1989: Jeffrey R. Balison
1918: G. P. Johnston	1954: James W. Sampson	1990: John A. Barrasso
1919: W. V. Gage	1955: B. J. Sullivan	1991: Charles Lyford
1920: G. P. Johnston	1956: R. I. Williams	1991-92: Gregory McCue
1921: H. R. Lathrop	1957: J. S. Hellewell	1992-93: Timothy P. Hallinan
1922: E. A. Kell	1958: H. B. Anderson	1993-94: Thomas E. Spicer
1923: G. A. Fox	1959: L. Harmon Wilmoth	1994-95: John Babson
1924: J. D. Lewellen	1960: Benjamin Gitlitz	1995-96: Jay Swedberg
1925: A. B. Hamilton	1961: Francis A. Barrett	1996-97: Jack A. Larimer
1926: John L. Linn	1962: F. H. Haigler	1997-98: Mark S. Wurzel
1927: V. J. Keating	1963: S. J. Giovale	1998-99: J. Richard Hillman
1928: A. P. Kimball	1964: John H. Froyd	1999-00: Lawrence Kirven
1929: F. A. Mills	1965: Howard P. Greaves	2000-01: J. Stephen Sloan
1930: C. W. Jeffrey	1966: Thomas Nicholas	2001-02: Marion Smith
1931: E. L. Jewell	1967: Ray K. Christensen	2002-04: Stephen Brown
1932: R. H. Sanders	1968: Laurence Greene, Jr.	2004-06: Robert Monger
1933: F. L. Beck	1969: Henry N. Stephenson	2006-08: Michael Jording
1934: H. L. Harvey	1970: John J. Corbett	2008-10: Reed Shafer
1935: J. L. Wicks	1971: Fenworth M. Downing	2010- +Geraldine Gardner

*The Society was founded in 1903. Presidents are elected to one-year terms, starting each June.

+1st woman elected Wyoming Medical Society president

Exec. Director: Richard W. Johnson, Jr., served in that post from 1984-97. Wendy Curran served in that position from 1997 until she became health care policy advisor to Gov. Freudenthal in 2009. Sheila Bush was appointed executive director in January 2010.
.

A Sheridan lawyer limped into a doctor's office in September, 1935, for treatment of a badly sprained toe he had received from kicking a horse.

LATINOS/MEXICAN-AMERICANS

4 Early-day Hispanic Pioneers

1. Louis Vasquez

Vasquez was born in St. Louis, Oct. 3, 1798. His father, born in Galacia, Spain, came to St. Louis in 1770 when the area was Spanish territory. His father died when Louis was 12. He went West with the fur trade in his early 20s. He went into partnership with Henry Fraeb and Jim Bridger in 1840 in a fur post along the Green River. Fraeb was killed the next year and Vasquez continued his partnership with Bridger by establishing Fort Bridger in the summer of 1843. He often returned east to bring supplies back to the post. Francis Parkman encountered Vasquez at Fort Laramie on June 15, 1846, on one of Vasquez's trips for supplies. He married a Kentucky widow in 1846 and opened a store in Salt Lake City in 1849. He severed his interests with Bridger in 1855. Four years later, his nephew opened a grocery store in Denver in which Vasquez held an interest although he apparently remained in Missouri. He died in St. Louis in September, 1868. He was survived by his widow, seven children and two stepchildren.

2. Antonio Montero, Portuguese trader, Powder River country

Montero (or "Mateo") built a trading post about 1834 using hand-hewn logs. The log stockade, 100 feet square and ten feet high, contained within its walls trade goods and a huge press for beaver pelts. The press was made from the native cottonwood trees. Montero left "Fort Antonio" briefly in 1838, returned in 1839, then abandoned the place because of its remote location from prime trapping areas. His so-called "Portuguese houses," among the first permanent buildings in the state, were seen by early travelers. The site is ten miles east of present Kaycee.

3. Manuel Armenta

Armenta owned the "Jack Pot" ranch in western Natrona County in the 1880s. Soon after the Burlington railroad line was built through the area some 58 miles west of Casper, the company established a station they named "Arminto." They changed the last letter of the name, however. Armenta later served as deputy sheriff and, in 1905, was involved in the capture of "Black Mike" Smith, an outlaw who shot at another deputy after he attempted to cash a forged check at a Wolton saloon.

4. John "Portugee" Phillips

A native of the Azores, Phillips prospected for gold in California and Colorado before deciding to try his luck in the newly opened Montana goldfields in 1866. He happened to be at Fort Phil Kearny at the time of the Fetterman fight. When the post's commanding officer sought volunteers to ride to Fort Laramie, 236 miles away, to take word to the army about the disaster , Phillips accepted the challenge. Riding day and night, he changed horses fsrequently, made it to Deer Creek Station (Glenrock) where he sent a message by telegraph to the fort. In order to ensure that the message was received and to deliver a personal message from the Phil Kearny post commander, he continued on to Fort Laramie. It is still considered the greatest ride in Wyoming history. Phillips later ranched near Chugwater.

Speaking Spanish

According to the 1990 census, Spanish was the primary language spoken in more than 13,800 Wyoming homes. In 2000, 6.4% of the population communicated at home in a language other than English. According to the 2008 estimates, 7.7% of the state's population was Latino or Mexican-American.

MILITARY FORCES

1st American flag raised over Manila in the Spanish American War: Raised by 1st Battalion, Wyoming volunteers, on Aug. 13, 1898, over Luneta Barracks in Manila. E. G. Guyer of Sheridan was one of the flag raisers.

1st shot fired by an American in World War I: Fired by Rock Springs native Michael B. Chockie, a Marine corporal, who was a member of the boarding party from the U. S. S. Supply, fired across the bow of an Imperial German navy launch in Guam harbor in the Pacific on April 6, 1917. The German ship later was captured. Chockie returned to Rock Springs and, later, lived in Colorado. He died in Denver in 1980 at the age of 91.

1st Wyomingite killed in World War II: Charles William Jones of Casper, who was killed in the bombing of Pearl Harbor on Dec. 7, 1941.

Killed in action: 203 servicemen killed in World War II were ex-University of Wyoming students.

1st Wyomingite killed in the Vietnam War: Carlton J. Holland, 1965.

1st ICBM placed in service in Wyoming (Atlas missile): October, 1959.

Wyoming has the fewest defense installations of any state with a total of one with 5,866 acres. California has the most (nearly 80). During World War II, the state had three facilities: Fort Warren (now F. E. Warren Air Force Base) at Cheyenne, Casper Air Base, and the prisoner of war camp at Douglas. The War Relocation Authority operated the Heart Mountain Relocation Center in Park County.

Number of veterans: With a total of 49,000 living veterans (July 1, 1994), Wyoming ranks 48th among the states. Only Alaska and Vermont have fewer veterans.

Most Marine Corps recruits per capita in World War II: Casper

Highest percentage of population of any U. S. county in the service during World War I: Washakie County, where ten percent of the population was in uniform.

Most officers: During World War II, Wyoming furnished 22.2 officers per 100 enlisted men, the highest percentage of officers in service from any state.

Oldest living Marine in the United States: Art Hansen of Casper held that distinction in 1991. A World War I private, he led the Fourth of July parade in Casper in 1991 at the age of 99. He celebrated his 100th birthday on April 18, 1992.

1st Wyomingite killed in El Salvador (1991): Army helicopter pilot Daniel Scott, 39, of Ranchester, died when his helicopter was shot down in January 1991.

Only Wyoming resident killed in the Persian Gulf War: Army Spec. 4 Manuel Davila, Gillette, killed Feb. 28, 1991, just hours before the cease fire.

1st Wyomingite killed in Iraq War: Lt.,Therrel Shane Childers, Powell, USMC, killed on the opening day of the Iraq invasion, March 21, 2003.

World War I soldiers' benefits: Wyoming authorized a $2,000 tax exemption for World War I veterans (passed by the 1921 legislature). The 1917 legislature had authorized bronze medals for each soldier.

World War II soldiers' benefits: The 1945 legislature passed ten bills for various types of veterans' benefits including a $2,000 tax exemption.

Wyoming ranked **5th** among the states in the proportion of veterans in its population: 14.1% (2004). The national average is 12.1%. Only Alaska, Montana, Maine and Virginia have higher proportions.

Potential draft pool in Wyoming: On Aug. 1, 1989, 28,735 males were registered in Wyoming with the Selective Service. Laramie County had the most with 5,277. *(For Vietnam era draft, see p. 288)*

Total defense payroll in Wyoming (Sept. 1995): 4,025, of which 3,511 were active duty Air Force personnel.

Civil War Generals with Wyoming Places Named for Them

1. Philip Kearny

The major general, a nephew of Gen. Stephan Watts Kearny, was killed Sept. 1, 1862, in the battle of Chantilly, Virginia. Fort Phil Kearny in northern Wyoming was named for him. It was burned by Indians after the Fort Laramie Treaty of 1868 closed the Bozeman Trail. The location is now a state historic site.

2. Jesse L. Reno

Major General Reno died at South Mountain, Maryland, on Sept. 1, 1862.

3. David A. Russell

Brig.Gen. Russell was killed at Winchester, Va., on Sept. 19, 1864. Until 1930 when the name was changed to Fort Warren and later to F. E. Warren Air Force Base, the military installation near Cheyenne was named Fort Russell.

4. William P. Sanders

The fort near Laramie was named Fort Sanders in honor of Brigadier General Sanders who was killed near Knoxville, Tenn., on Nov. 19, 1863.

5. William T. Sherman

Now a ghost town between Laramie and Cheyenne, the town was once a stop on the Union Pacific Railroad named for General Sherman, Civil War and frontier army general.

6. Philip Sheridan

The largest Wyoming town named for a Civil War general is Sheridan named for Philip Sheridan, the commanding officer of one of the town's founders. Sheridan, born in Albany, N.Y., died Aug. 5, 1888. He is buried in Arlington National Cemetery.

7. Henry Halleck

Fort Halleck, where soldiers were stationed to protect the Overland Stageline, was named for General Halleck. Ironically, many of the troops stationed at the post were "galvanized Yankees"—Confederate prisoners of war who volunteered out of POW camps to serve on the frontier.

8. Frederick Lander

The town was named for Gen. Frederick Lander who surveyed the "Lander road" in the 1850s. Gen. Lander served in the Civil War and died March 2, 1862, near Paw Paw, Va., of illness while preparing for an attack on the Confederate forces occupying Winchester, Va. He had been wounded in a battle at Edward's Ferry on Oct. 22, 1861, and probably died from the long-term effects of the injury.

9. John A. Rawlins

Rawlins, a native of Galena, Illinois, was acquainted with U. S. Grant long before the Civil War. When Grant became commander of Union forces, Rawlins became his adjutant. Later, when Grant was U. S. President, he appointed Rawlins as his Secretary of War, but he served less than a year before he died from tuberculosis Sept. 6, 1869.

10. Fred Steele

A fort in Carbon County was named for the New York native who had graduated from West Point and served in the Mexican War. A major general in 1862, he retired from the service in 1867 and died Jan. 12, 1868.

19th Century Soldiers with Wyoming Connections

1. Charles B. Stambaugh

A private in Co. H, Ohio Cavalry, Stambaugh was a first lieutenant on May 4, 1870, when he was killed by Indians near Miner's Delight. The post in Fremont County was named for him.

2. Howard Stansbury

Stansbury explored Wyoming with the U. S. Topographical Engineers. He retired in 1861 as a major general and died April 17, 1863. A coal mining town in Sweetwater County, an area he explored in 1849, was named for him.

3. Albert Sidney Johnston

Johnston commanded "Johnston's Army," the expedition sent west to Utah in 1858 against the Mormons. The Kentucky-born West Point graduate later resigned from the army to accept a generalship in the Confederacy. He was killed in battle April 6, 1862.

4. H. M. Chittenden

Chittenden was an engineer assigned to duty in Yellowstone at the turn of the century where he laid out the modern road system for the park and designed many of the bridges. He had graduated third in his West Point class and spent his entire career in the Corps of Engineers. After leaving Yellowstone, he designed the Chittenden Locks, Seattle.

5. John A. Campbell

The first territorial governor of Wyoming, Campbell had seen Civil War service at Shiloh and Stone River, among other battles. When the war ended, Campbell was a brigadier general of volunteers. He was appointed territorial governor by President U. S. Grant, his commanding officer during the war. Campbell died July 15, 1880.

6. John A. McKinney

The post near Buffalo was named for McKinney, a Tennessee-born West Point graduate who, as a first lieutenant in the frontier army, was killed Nov. 25, 1876, on the North Fork of Powder River.

7. John L. Grattan

Grattan led a party to investigate the disappearance of a Mormon cow near Fort Laramie on Aug. 19, 1854. He and his entire command died, perhaps as a result of miscommunication between area Indians and the soldiers. Grattan was newly arrived at Fort Laramie, having graduated from West Point two years earlier. He was a 2nd Lieutenant in the 6th Infantry.

8. John Buford

The first post near Laramie was named for Buford but renamed Fort Sanders soon after because another post had the same name. A gas station stop on I-80 between Cheyenne and Laramie retains the name, however. Buford, a native of Kentucky, served as major general of volunteers in the Civil War. He was killed Dec. 16, 1863.

9. George Crook

Born in Dayton, Ohio, in 1829, Crook graduated from West Point and began a distinguished military career, mostly with service against the Indians. He died March 21, 1890, in Chicago. During his career, he frequently served in Wyoming.

Wyoming POW Camps

1. Douglas

The camp, located one mile west of Douglas, held about 2,500 prisoners from Germany and Italy. It opened in 1943 and closed two years later.

2. Timber camps

About 600 German POWs cut timber in the Medicine Bow National Forest from 1943-1945. Of that number, 300 lived at the former CCC camp at Ryan Park while the other half lived in cabins along Mullen Creek near Centennial.

3. Goshen County area

POWs held in the prisoner of war camp near Scottsbluff, Neb., were brought to some Goshen County communities during the later years of the war where some lived in converted CCC camps while all worked on area farms.

4. Heart Mountain

Not a prisoner of war camp, Heart Mountain imprisoned Americans of Japanese descent who had been removed from West Coast cities and forcibly placed in camps in the interior. In October 1942, the camp had a population of 10,872, making it the third largest city in the state. By February 1945, the number had declined to 8,663.

A soldier at a Wyoming fort was given a can of field rations in 1890 on which was stamped the date of its canning—1863. The contents of the can, 27 years old, were older than the soldier who had opened the can!

Some Representative Wyomingites
Who Were Prisoners of War*

1. John D. Stevenson, Laramie

Born in Laramie in 1914, Stevenson graduated from Laramie High and after three years at the University of Wyoming, entered West Point where he graduated in 1937. Early in World War II, he served with air units in England and North Africa. Soon after he was made commander of the 27th Fighter Bomber Group, he was shot down over Europe and captured by the Germans in August, 1943. He spent the duration of the war in POW camps. After the war, he resumed his military career as director of development for atomic weapons. He retired in 1966 with the rank of major general. He died in 1995.

Robert W. Adams, Rawlins

A prisoner in Germany from April 29, 1944 until April 2, 1945, Adams later became an investor in uranium. He was executive for a company that built the first mill in Wyoming at Jeffrey City in July 1957.

2. Carl Otto, Yoder

A bomber navigator, Otto had been shot down over Germany and held as a war prisoner for 18 months. After his release, he returned to Goshen County where he ranched and served in the state legislature.

3. Warren Keiffer, Torrington

Keiffer was a prisoner of war in the Philippines following Japanese capture of the islands in 1942.

4. John Winterholler, Lovell

Winterholler had been a star athlete in four sports at the University of Wyoming prior to his Marine Corps service in World War II. He was captured while in the Philippines. From 1942-1945, he was a POW held by the Japanese during which time he became permanently paralyzed from the waist down.

5. Theodore Gostas, Cheyenne

Gostas, a University of Wyoming graduate with a degree in English, is a well-known artist and writer. During the Vietnam War, he was taken prisoner during the Battle of Hue and remained in confinement in Hanoi for more than six years.

* Numerous others were POWs. This is a representative listing only.

Wyomingites in War

War	Active Duty	Killed	Surviving (1988)	(1994)
World War I	12,000	468	fewer than 100	>10
World War II	35,000	1,095	19,000	13,000
Korean War	10,965	55	11,000*	8,000
Vietnam War	5,700**	137	26,000***	17,000
Service between				
Korea and Vietnam	8,000	-	7,000	6,000
After Vietnam	5,000	-	4,500	4,000
Gulf War	3,000	1	3,000	3,000
Iraq/Afghanistan	-	19++	-	-

+ *The Department of Veteran Affairs reported an estimated 53,000 veterans in Wyoming in 1992. The number on July 1, 1994, was 49,000. Projected total in 2040 is about 23,000.*
*Includes 1,000 who also served in World War II.
** Service in Southeast Asia. Active service includes thousands more.
***Service between August 1964 and May 1975.
++ Total to July 1, 2010

7 Recent Wyoming War Memorials

1. Wyoming Vietnam War Memorial

Located on the grounds of the Veterans Administration Medical Center, Cheyenne, it was dedicated on Memorial Day, 1983.

2. Vietnam War Memorial

The monument in Cody was dedicated on Veterans Day, 1986. Names of the 137 Wyomingites killed in Vietnam are inscribed on the memorial which is designed like the national Vietnam memorial in Washington, D. C.

3. Uinta County War Memorial

The marker, which includes recognition of Korean War veterans, was dedicated June 13, 1987. It stands next to the World War I Doughboy statue on the grounds of the Uinta County Courthouse, Evanston. Five Uinta County residents were killed in the Vietnam War.

4. Crook County War Memorial

Dedicated Nov. 11, 1989, the memorial honors all veterans from Crook County. The World War II memorial had been dedicated in 1945. The new memorial, in the courthouse square, contains the names of 1,718 veterans from the county who served in American wars.

5. Persian Gulf War Memorial

Dedicated July 4, 1992, in Rock Springs, the memorial was executed by John C. Rodiak and dedicated to 158 Sweetwater County residents who took part in the war and Manuel Davila, the only state resident killed in the war.

6. Niobrara County War Memorial

The memorial, on which is listed the names of more than 400 deceased Niobrara County war veterans from the Civil War to Vietnam, was dedicated May 30, 1994. It is located at the north edge of the Lusk Cemetery.

7. Campbell County War Memorial

More than 500 people attended the dedication of the memorial on May 30, 1994, to the 62 veterans from Campbell County who died in all wars. The black granite slabs on which the names were inscribed is located in Lasting Legacy Park. A previous county war memorial in front of the George Amos Memorial Library had only names of veterans killed from World War I to the Korean War.

Congressional Medal of Honor Winners from Wyoming

1. Edward L. Baker, Jr., Sgt. Major, 10th Cavalry

Baker, a Laramie County native, was recognized for service in Santiago, Cuba, during the Spanish American War. He "left cover and, under fire, rescued a wounded comrade from drowning."

2. Charles DuVal Roberts, 1st Lieutenant, U. S. Army

Roberts, a West Point graduate, won the Medal of Honor at El Caney, Cuba, during the Spanish American War. According to his citation, he "gallantly assisted in the rescue of the wounded from in front of the lines under heavy fire from the enemy." Roberts was born in 1873 at Fort D. A. Russell, according to his West Point record. Other sources, however, list his birthplace as the Cheyenne Agency of South Dakota.

An early accessions record for the Wyoming State Museum in 1920 indicated that among the museum's holdings was "an unexploded shell from the Custer Battlefield." It's not known if the ammunition article is still there and so listed.

3. Charles F. Carey, Jr., Tech. Sgt., 379th Infantry, 100th Inf. Div.

Carey enlisted in the army when he was a resident of Cheyenne. He commanded an anti-tank platoon near Rimling, France, on Jan. 8-9, 1945, when the unit was attacked by an enemy company and 12 tanks. Carey attacked a house filled with enemy snipers and captured 16 prisoners by himself. Later, in that area, he was killed by sniper fire.

4. William Hampden Sage, Major General, U. S. Army

Sage served as commander of Cheyenne's Fort D. A. Russell in 1922 where he died. The only Fort Russell commander to win the nation's highest medal, Sage received it for duty in the Philippines against the Moros in the early 1900s.

5. Vernon J. Baker, 2nd Lt., 370th Regiment, U. S. Army

Baker, a native of Cheyenne, led an all-black unit against a German outpost in Italy in 1945. One of the army's first black officers, Baker was a second lieutenant in the 370th Regiment. In June, 1996, the Department of Defense recommended that Baker and six other black soldiers be awarded the nation's highest military honor, the Congressional Medal of Honor. Baker, the only one of the seven surviving, became the first African-American to be awarded the Medal of Honor for World War II service in White House ceremonies on Jan. 13, 1997. His memoir, *Lasting Valor,* was published later that year. Baker died in St. Maries, Idaho, on July 13, 2010.

A number of soldiers serving in the Indian Wars of the 1870s received the Congressional Medal of Honor for acts of heroism while on duty in Wyoming. None, however, had any other connection to the state. Joe Foss, a long-time resident of Beulah, won the Medal of Honor in World War II as a fighter pilot. He served from South Dakota and is "credited" to that state. Several Wyomingites received the Medal of Honor during the Civil War, but the terms of its award were less stringent at that time. They include Francis E. Warren and Capt. Frederick Phisterer, who established Camp Brown on the site of present Lander on June 19, 1869. Source: "Medal of Honor Recipients, 1863-1973," Committee on Veterans' Affairs, United States Senate Document, 1973.

Some Well-Known Wyomingites in the Military Services

1. Emory S. Land, Navy rear admiral (1879-1971)

Land, a native of Colorado, graduated from the University of Wyoming in 1898. From there, he went to the Naval Academy after which he was commissioned an ensign in 1902. He retired as a rear admiral in 1937. The next year, he came out of retirement to chair the U. S. Maritime Commission, following Joseph P. Kennedy in that position when Kennedy became U. S. ambassador to Great Britain. In 1942 Land was named admiral of the War Shipping Administration, a post he held until 1946. In 1953, the University of Wyoming established the Admiral Land Award, presented annually to the student who makes the greatest contribution to university athletics. Land died in 1971 in Washington, D. C.

2. Lloyd R. Fredendall, Army general, (1883-1955)

Fredendall, a native of Cheyenne, was appointed to West Point in 1900. He stayed just two years, entering the army as a lieutenant in 1902. He rose in rank to brigadier general by the time Pearl Harbor was bombed. At the age of 60, he was given command of II Corps in North Africa in 1942. His army was the center force in a three-pronged offensive and his troops captured Algiers. The army had no training in desert warfare and the Wyoming-born general had no experience in such fighting. In a smashing counter-offensive, German Field Marshal Erwin Rommel's Afrika Corps routed the Allied army at Kasserine Pass

---

In the original group photograph of Marines raising the flag over Iwo Jima was Wyoming Marine Louis Charles. The first photo was taken by SSgt. Lou Lowery. A later photograph, made by Joe Rosenthal, became famous. No Wyomingite was pictured in the second shot. The Rosenthal photograph was the inspiration for the design of the Marine Memorial in Washington, D. C.

in February, 1944. One of the worst defeats ever inflicted on U. S. troops to that point in history, superiors placed much of the blame on Fredendall whose relaxed discipline was said to have made the army "soft." His successor, Gen. George C. Patton, was particularly critical of Fredendall's leadership. Fredendall was reassigned to a training post in the United States and, soon after, he retired from active service.

3. Victor Krulak, Marine Corps general, (1913-2008)

Born in Denver, Krulak moved to Cheyenne with his parents in the 1920s. A graduate of Cheyenne High School, Krulak was appointed to the Naval Academy where he graduated in 1934. After service in China, Krulak commanded Marine units in the South Pacific during World War II. He was chief of staff of the 1st Marine Division in Korea. Following Marine retirement in 1968, he became managing editor of San Diego's largest newspaper, the *San Diego Union*. He retired from the newspaper in 1979. In 1995, his son, Charles C. Krulak (b. Quantico, 1942) was named USMC assistant commandant and, later, its commandant.

4. John J. Pershing, General of the Armies, (1860-1948)

Evidence of Pershing's residence in Wyoming is unclear. The 1910 census lists the Missouri native as living at Fort D. A. Russell, now F. E. Warren Air Force Base. Pershing's wife was the daughter of Sen. Francis E. Warren. She died in a fire at the Presidio in San Francisco before World War I with two of their children. Pershing commanded all Allied forces in Europe during World War I. A street in Cheyenne and streets in other towns memorialize this war hero and "in-law" of Wyoming.

5. Samuel C. Phillips, Air Force general (1921-1990)

Born in Arizona in 1921, Phillips attended public schools in Cheyenne where his father was an electrician for Cheyenne Light, Fuel and Power Company. A graduate of Cheyenne High School in 1938, Phillips received a degree in electrical engineering from the University of Wyoming in 1942. He was a pilot in Europe during World War II. In 1961 he was named director of the Minuteman missile program. Promoted to major general in 1964, Phillips became director of the Apollo lunar landing program of NASA in October of that year. He directed the program when the first landing was made on the moon. In 1968 he was promoted to lieutenant general. He retired in 1975 and died Jan. 31, 1990.

6. Herbert J. Brees, Army general (1877-1958)

Brees, a Laramie native and West Point graduate, served in Torrey's Rough Riders, the Wyoming National Guard unit in the Spanish American War and, later in the Regular Army. He received his brigadier general's star in 1930. Lake Hattie, west of Laramie, was named for Brees' mother, Hattie Richards Brees, and until the 1990s, the Laramie airport was named for him. Local officials changed the name to Laramie Area Regional Airport after they received complaints about the bad impression on tourists who thought the airport was a testimonial to area "wind."

7. Francis X. McInerney, Navy admiral (1899-1956)

Born in Cheyenne, McInerney graduated from the Naval Academy in 1920. During World War II, he commanded the allied destroyer force in the Battle of Coral Sea. Later, he served on Admiral Halsey's staff and late in the war, he commanded the battleship U.S.S. Washington. During the Korean War, he was in charge of the U. S. Navy amphibious forces in the Far East. He retired from the Navy in 1955 with the rank of Vice Admiral and died a year later at the age of 57. A guided missile frigate was named for him in 1978.

8. K. L. Tallman, Lieutenant General and Supt. of the Air Force Academy

Born in Omaha in 1925, Tallman moved to Cheyenne with his parents and graduated from Cheyenne High School in 1942. He was appointed to West Point, graduating in 1946. In June, 1977, he became the 8th superintendent of the Air Force Academy, serving in that position until his retirement in 1981. He died March 6, 2006.

9. Paul "Bob" Streich, Navy aviator (c. 1928-1999)

Streich, a graduate of Natrona County High School (1946) and Casper College (1948), was a decorated aviator and advisor to the U. S. Joint Chiefs of Staff. He served many years as adventurer Adm. Richard Byrd's pilot. The international Explorers' Club honored Streich for his exploration activities in Antarctica. In 1956, during Operation Deep Freeze, his Otter airplane crashed in the Antarctic. He and six crewmen survived seven days on the ice. He made the first night airplane flight over Antarctica. One of 13 people designated Distinguished Alumni of Casper College, Streich died in Colorado Springs, Colo., in August, 1999.

10. James Herdt, Master Chief Petty Officer, U. S. Navy (1947-)

Herdt, a graduate of Natrona County High School, Casper, became only the ninth sailor in history ever to hold the rank of Master Chief Petty Officer. He was the highest ranking enlisted man in the Navy in 1998. Herdt joined the Navy soon after high school graduation in 1965.

11. Peter J. Schoomaker, General, U. S. Army (1946-)

Schoomaker, a native of Detroit and a former UW football player, graduated from the University of Wyoming in 1969. As a ROTC graduate, he was commissioned and assigned to an armor unit. In 1977, he was assigned to the "Green Berets," the army special forces unit. On Oct. 24, 1997, he was promoted to general. In 2000 he retired after serving as commanding general in charge of the U. S. Special Operations Command headquartered at MacDill AFB, Florida. Called out of retirement, on Aug. 1, 2003, he was sworn in as the 35th Chief of the Joint Chiefs of Staff, the highest rank in the armed forces. He stepped down as chief of staff and retired for a second time from the army on April 10, 2007.

12. Susan L. Pamerleau, Major General, Air Force

Pamerleau was the highest ranking woman in the U. S. Air Force at the time of her retirement in September 2000. In her 32-year career in the Air Force, she served primarily in personnel resources posts. Her last duty asignment was as director of personnel force management stationed in Washington, D. C. She graduated from the University of Wyoming with a degree in sociology in 1968.

13. Neil L. Eddins, Major General, Air Force (1931-)

Eddins, born in Afton in 1931, graduated from Star Valley High School in 1950. After a semester at UW, he joined the Air Force and was commissioned in 1954. From 1959-1961, he was slot man for the Thunderbirds, the precision flying team. Following 100 combat missions over North Vietnam, he returned in January 1967 as the Thunderbirds' commander and lead pilot. He retired as a major general in 1984 after serving as chief of the U. S. Military Training Mission to Saudi Arabia.

14. Dennis K. Jackson, Major General, Army

Jackson graduated from the University of Wyoming in 1968. A native of Cheyenne, he was named Army chief of ordnance and commanding general of the ordnance training schools in November, 1998. In 2004, he was awarded for service as Director for Logistics, J-4, United States Central Command, MacDill Air Force Base, Florida. He led the massive logistics efforts in Operation Enduring Freedom (Afghanistan) and Operation Iraqi Freedom. He retired in 2004 after a 35-year career in the Army.

15. Dennis G. Haines, Major General, Air Force

Haines earned the B.S. degree in business administration from the University of

On Nov. 13, 1997, Tracy Ritchie, 41, born in Sheridan, educated in Gillette, an employee of Union Texas Petroleum Co., was murdered by terrorists along with three other company employees and their local driver when their car was ambushed in Karachi, Pakistan. He had worked for the company for 15 years. He had a UW degree in accounting.

Wyoming in 1968 and the M. S. degree in the following year. After serving as director of logistics for various Air Force commands, he was assigned as commander of the Warner Robins Air Logistics Center in Georgia, in 2000. He retired in April 2002.

16. Carla Hawley-Boland, Major General, Army

General Hawley-Boland became the first female physician to achieve the rank of general in the U. S. Army Medical Corps. In August 2006, she began service as chief of the U. S. Army Medical Corps. Born in Casper, she graduated from Natrona County High School in 1970. Her undergraduate degree is from CSU. She graduated from Creighton University School of Medicine in 1978.

Oldest National Guard Units in Wyoming

1. Cheyenne Rangers (1873)

The volunteer militia was formed to fight Indians in the vicinity of the capital city. The company consisted of men who furnished their own horses, equipment and firearms.

2. Laramie Home Guards (1874)

3. Carbon (1876)

4. Wyoming Rangers, Lander (1876)

5. Laramie Grays (1888)

The unit was officially designated "Company A" of the Wyoming militia.

6. Cheyenne Guards (1888)

The unit was also known as "Company B" of the Wyoming militia.

7. Company C, Buffalo (1890)

8. Company D, Rock Springs (1890)

9. Company E, Green River (1890)

10. Company F, Douglas (1891)

The unit included the "Douglas Cornet Band."

11. Company G, Sheridan (1891)

12. Company H, Evanston (1892)

13. 1st Artillery Battery, Rawlins (1893)

The organization included the "Rawlins Brass Band."

Wyoming National Guard Summer Training Camps

1. Camp Barber (1891)

The site, 1 1/2 miles east of Laramie, was the first organized camp for all companies of the national guard which consisted of 145 officers and men. The site had two names. One was Camp Barber in honor of the acting governor of the state, Dr. Amos Barber. It also was called "Camp Kabis" after the commanding officer at the time.

2. CY pasture near Casper (1904)

A ten-day encampment in which 287 officers and men participated, the pasture is now part of the city of Casper. The Lander contingent included a cornet band and the entire unit marched to and from the camp, 150 miles each way.

3. State Fairgrounds, Douglas (1905)

Six companies participated in the encampment held with the Wyoming State Fair.

4. Pole Mountain (1906)

The site, orginally a wood reserve, was first a target range for Fort D. A. Russell soldiers in 1903. In 1906, National Guardsmen trained jointly with soldiers from the fort.

The first polo match west of the Mississippi was played at Fort Fetterman, near Douglas, in 1886. A polo club was organized at Fort Russell, now Warren AFB, in the late 1800s.

5. Fort D. A. Russell Maneuver and Target Area (1908)

Maneuvers also were held at Camp Crawford, a temporary post 14 miles from Dale Creek station along the Union Pacific Railroad. The following year the Fort Russell site was renamed "Pole Mountain Maneuver Area."

6. Camp E. S. Otis (1910, 1912)

The Wyoming National Guard had 698 enlisted men and 52 officers in 1910. The site was the same as the 1908 encampment, but the name of the camp had been changed. In 1912, Guard units participated in the filming of *Charge of the Light Brigade*. The Edison Company shot the film at what is now the Terry Bison Ranch, south of Cheyenne.

7. Camp J. M. Carey (1911)

The camp was one mile west of Wheatland. The entire guard moved from the site to "Carey Heights" near Cheyenne for several days to participate in Frontier Days. Both sites were named for Gov. J. M. Carey.

8. Camp Merritt (1913)

Same as Camp Otis, the site was renamed for the 1913 encampment.

9. Four camps (1915)

Sheridan, Douglas, Cody and Cheyenne hosted units for first regional encampments.

10. Basin (1920)

11. Fort D. A. Russell (1923)

12. Pole Mountain (1924-1937)

The site, first used in 1908, was between Cheyenne and Laramie. A federal appropriation of $25,000 was used to build a mess hall, kitchen and officers' mess in 1923. Except for 1933, the camp was held there annually until 1936. Airplanes were first used in maneuvers there in 1925. Primarily, cavalry maneuvers were held there, however. Guard units participated in the filming of *The Plainsman* in 1936. The camp was moved from the site because of federal rules requiring "all-weather" access to the camp--something not possible for a camp located at nearly 8,000 feet in the Laramie mountains. The site was abandoned in 1937 and turned over to the U. S. Forest Service in 1959. *Source: Christi Hutchison, "Pole Mountain: A Military Maneuver Zone," 2000.*

13. Camp Guernsey (1938-present)

Recommendations for the site were made as early as 1931. Temporary buildings were used the first year of the camp's operation while construction on the permanent facilities continued into 1940. The training camp for the Wyoming National Guard, it also hosts guard units from other states.

Wyoming at West Point

1. Verling K. Hart, Class of 1889

The first Wyomingite appointed to the Military Academy, Hart was the son of a former commander of Fort McKinney. His mother, Juliet W. Hart, once owned the townsite of Buffalo. He graduated 41st in a class of 49 and retired as a captain. He managed the Plains Hotel in Cheyenne until his death in June, 1914.

2. Alfred E. Kennington, Class of 1896

Born in Wyoming, Kennington was appointed from Washington. A cavalry officer in Cuba and the Philippines, he died while on active duty in Texas in 1931.

3. Charles DuVal Roberts, Class of 1897

Roberts was born at Fort Russell in 1873. (Some sources give his birthplace as Cheyenne Agency, South Dakota). A Congressional Medal of Honor winner in Cuba, he went on to become a brigadier general and retired at that rank in 1937. He died in 1966.

4. Pierce Ambrose Murphy, Class of 1897

Murphy, a Wyoming native, was appointed from Washington. Following graduation, he taught at the academy and later served as commanding officer of an infantry regiment in World War I. At the time of his death in 1928, he was a colonel stationed at Fort Hayes, Ohio.

5. Guy Kent, Class of 1902

Born in 1877, Kent served in the Quartermaster Corps throughout most of his career. He retired in 1941 and died in 1959.

6. William Morse Nichols, Class of 1903

Nichols, who graduated in the same class as Douglas MacArthur, did not make the army a career. He resigned his commission in 1905 and in 1907, he returned to Wyoming to work for the Yellowstone Park Company. He was made president of the firm in 1931. He died in Yellowstone in 1957.

7. Innis Palmer Swift, Class of 1904

Born at Fort Laramie in 1882, Swift was appointed from Illinois. He served as commanding general of the 2nd Cavalry Brigade from 1939-1941, and commanding general of the 1st Cavalry Division in the South Pacific from 1941-1944. He directed the assault leading toward recapture of Admiralty Island in 1944 and then commanded the 1st Army Corps in New Guinea and the Philippines until the close of the war. He died in Texas in 1953.

8. George Bowditch Hunter, Class of 1904

Hunter was born at Fort Fetterman in 1879, the son of a career army officer. An honor graduate of the academy, he served in the aviation section of the Army Air Corps during World War I. He taught at the Army War College in the post-war years. A brigadier general during World War II, he commanded the New Orleans Embarkation depot where he retired in 1944.

9. George Dillman, Class of 1905

Dillman served as chief of staff of the 8th Artillery during World War II. He retired as a colonel in 1942 and died in Texas 12 years later.

10. Charles J. Taylor, Class of 1906

Taylor was the distinguished cadet in his second academy year. He was in the engineers during World War I. After the war, he was ROTC director at the University of Illinois. From 1942 until his death in 1943, he headed ROTC at LSU.

11. James Irwin Muir, Class of 1910

Muir was born at Fort Russell in 1888. Like many Wyoming natives, Muir rose to the rank of major general. He died in 1964.

12. Bradford Chynoweth, Class of 1912

Born at Fort Russell just ten days after statehood, Chynoweth received his West Point appointment from Wisconsin. From 1941 to 1942, he was a brigadier general, commanding the Visayan Force of the army in the Philippines. When the Philippines was abandoned by American forces, he and the men of his unit were made prisoners of war where they remained until the close of the war. He died in California in 1985.

13. William F. Heavey, Class of 1917

Although he was born in Georgia, Heavey was appointed from Wyoming. A brigadier general during World War II, he received the Distinguished Service Medal, the Legion of Merit and numerous other medals for his wartime service. He commanded the engineer brigade in the South Pacific from 1942 to 1946. He retired in 1948 and died in 1974.

14. John Dudley Stevenson, Class of 1937

Stevenson, born in Laramie in 1914, served as a colonel in the Army Air Corps during World War II. His plane was shot down and he spent two years as a prisoner of war. Fol-

---

Niobrara County Memorial Hospital ceased operations as a hospital on May 31, 2000, but reopened five years later.

lowing his retirement from the Air Force in 1966 as a major general, he directed mission operations for NASA from 1966 to 1971. He died Nov. 3, 1995.

15. William McGregor Lynn, Jr., Class of 1938

Lynn graduated 11th in his class and, by the end of World War II, had attained the rank of lieutenant colonel. An artillery officer during the Korean War, he retired as a major general in 1968.

16. Keith G. Lindell, Class of 1943

Lindell was born in Montana but reared near Opal, Wyoming. He was a pilot in the Pacific, rising to the rank of major at the close of World War II. He taught mathematics at the academy from 1949 to 1952 and retired with the rank of colonel in 1963. He died in January 1981.

First Wyomingites at the Naval Academy

1. Russell Willson (entered the academy in 1902)

The first Wyoming-appointed midshipman at the Naval Academy, Willson was a New York native who spent summers with family members in Crook County. He graduated from the academy in 1906 and spent the next 36 years in naval service. During his career, he was superintendent of the academy (1941), naval chief of staff (1942), and deputy commander of the U. S. Fleet (1942). When he retired in 1942, he was a vice admiral, the 16th senior-ranking officer in the navy. He died in 1948 and is buried on the grounds of the academy.

2. Charles Talley Blackburn (1903)

Blackburn (b. 1885) was the first Wyoming native appointed to the Academy.

3. James Bruin Howell (1903)

An ensign, he was assigned to duty as an instructor at the Naval Academy in 1910.

4. John Borland (1903)

A Wyoming native like Blackburn and Howell, Borland resigned from the academy after his first year.

5. Franklin Harper Fowler (1904)

Fowler was born in Wyoming in 1887.

6. John B. Okie, Jr. (1907)

The son of pioneer Fremont County sheepman J. B. Okie, the younger Okie graduated from the academy, but resigned from the navy in 1912.

7. John C. Thom (1907)

Thom retired with the rank of commander in 1937 after serving nearly 30 years in active service.

8. Lawrence K. Forde (1908)

As an ensign, he was dismissed from the Navy on Jan. 11, 1916.

9. Beriah Magoffin Thompson (1908)

Thompson retired in 1933 at the rank of lieutenant commander.

10. Clarence C. Riner (1909)

Riner entered the U. S. Marine Corps on academy graduation.

11. Marion Bell Humphrey (1909)

Like classmate Riner, Humphrey elected to take a Marine Corps commission on graduation. He retired from the corps in 1942 as a colonel.

12. Bert Franklin Clark (1909)

Corrina Lankford, arrested in Haiti for kidnapping in 2010, graduated from Campbell County High School in 1986. She lived in Middleton, Idaho, at the time of the incident. Her 18-year-old daughter also was charged.

13. Walter E. Doyle (1913)

A Laramie native, Doyle graduated from Cheyenne High School in 1908 and went to the academy in 1909. As a submariner, he commanded the Submarine School, New London, Conn., in 1928. He was executive officer to Adm. Chester Nimitz (1937-40), and commanded the 9th Division of submarines stationed at Manila during World War II. Later, he commanded of all submarines in Asiatic waters. He retired in 1947 as a captain.

Tough Times at Fort Halleck, 1862

1. Capt. John O'Ferrell, commander of Fort Halleck, 1862

O'Ferrell was the first commander of the post on the Overland Trail in present-day Carbon County. He resigned from the army and returned to "civilized life" in his native Ohio after he discovered he had become infected with lice at the post.

2. Capt. F. W. Shipley, commander of Fort Halleck, 1862

Shipley was O'Ferrell's successor. Shipley resigned from the army after it was discovered that he had cheated the garrison of $12,000 in soldiers' pay.

Lottery Numbers for Selective Service, 1969-1972

The Congress authorized a draft lottery system in 1969 to draft men born between 1944-1953. The Selective Service System was charged with administering the lottery. Each date was drawn in random order. The drawing of the first ten numbers in December, 1969, was televised nationally. Even in Wyoming, the program drew great interest, particularly in men's dormitories at the University of Wyoming! Those men born on the particular day drawn would be either subject to the draft or less likely to be drafted, depending on where in the order their birthdate fell. Those with a "high number" were unlikely to be called while those whose birthdates were among the first 50 or so drawn could count on hearing from Uncle Sam.

1. Drawing, December, 1969

The first lottery of the Vietnam era, it applied to all men born between 1944 and 1950. September 14 was the first number drawn. April 24 was #2.

2. Drawing, July, 1970

The second drawing applied only to young men born in 1951. The first date drawn was July 9; second was Dec. 24.

3. Drawing, August, 1971

Men born in 1952 were the only ones subject to this lottery. First date drawn was Dec. 1; second was Jan. 25.

4. Drawing, February, 1972

The final drawing for draft numbers during the Vietnam era, it applied only to men born in 1953. First date drawn was March 6; second, oddly, was March 7.

In 1998, the Philippine ambassador to the United States demanded the return of the "Bells of Balangiga," Spanish colonial church bells seized in the Philippines in 1901 by American forces after the bells had signaled a surprise raid on them. The bells were placed at what became F. E. Warren Air Force Base. Veterans' organizations became involved and the matter went to Congress for resolution. The bells remain in place (2010) at Warren despite numerous resolutions by the Philippine congress for their return.

Wyomingites Killed in World War II

Of the 35,000 Wyoming residents who served on active duty in World War II, 1,095 were killed in action. A complete list may be found in T. A. Larson, *Wyoming's War Years*. (Cheyenne: Wyoming Historical Foundation, reprint, 1993).

Wyomingites Killed or Missing in the Korean War
July 16, 1950-Dec. 31, 1953*

Allen Anderson, Sheridan
Clifford E. Baker, Big Horn
Ted U. Barnes, Goshen
Kenneth R. Barnhill, Platte
Neil B. Baxter, Sheridan
Malcolm Lloyd Budd, USMC, Big Piney
Leonard W. Clark, Sweetwater
James E. Clay, AF, Laramie
Ray P. Cowdin, Carbon
Courtenay C. Davis, Laramie
Donald L. Dewees, Albany
Paul R. Diana, USMC, Newcastle
Anthony Domingo Duram, USMC, Powell
Bill Elsom, AF, Cheyenne
Robert A. Finch, Fremont
Kenneth Finlayson, Fremont
Richard Friedlund, Washakie
Fred N. Garcia, Washakie
Joseph G. Garcia, Carbon
John N. Green, Sweetwater
Edward W. Harper, Sheridan
Thomas R. Harris, Sweetwater
Robert Hessenflow, Natrona
**Donald G. Hill, Fremont
Geroge B. Hittner, Carbon
John David Hoke, AF, Cheyenne
***John Lucius Horn, AF, Cheyenne
Roselio Jaramillo, Campbell
Kenneth C. Johnson, Fremont
James L. Jones, Park

Demaret Kirtley, Johnson
David N. Kuiper, Sheridan
Edgar J. Larson, Fremont
Robert I. Lewis, Sr., Park
Raymond J. Lieb, Platte
Charles E. Lunbeck, Sublette
Clinton McLaughlin, Uinta
Thomas Mitchelson, Sweetwater
Philip Patrick Neary, USMC, Lance Creek
Camerino Perea, Albany
Clifford F. Pratt, AF, Cheyenne
Charles E. Robb, Campbell
Lloyd G. Rogers, Laramie
Robert L. Roszek, Carbon
Helmar O. Rusth, Park
Russell Everett Smith, USMC, Bosler
William Sonnamaker, Sheridan
John A. Swanson, AF, Torrington
Ervin John Taylor, USMC, Laramie
Maynard M. Thompson, Washakie
Clark M. Tilton, Sheridan
Edward E. Toner, Sweetwater
Darold D. Urbanski, Park
Pablo J. Vigil, Sweetwater
Freeman Wadsworth, Laramie
Elmer L. Wells, Crook
Leland Henry Wolf, AF, Cheyenne
Samuel L. Wolfe, Big Horn

* *All were soldiers in the U. S. Army unless otherwise indicated.*
** *Hill was the first Wyoming soldier killed in Korea, July 11, 1950.*
*** *Horn was the last Wyomingite killed in Korea, Dec. 31, 1953*
List courtesy of Wyoming State Archives, State Parks and Cultural Resources Dept.

Wyomingites Killed in the Vietnam War, 1965-1972

1965

Carlton J. Holland. Casper, Army
Robert W. Grove, Casper, USMC
David G. Lucas, Rawlins, USMC
Alma J. Stumpp, Afton, USMC
Ernest E. Taylor, Kaycee, Army

Name, Hometown, Service Branch, listed by year killed

1966

Robert F. Guthrie, Cheyenne, Navy
Craig S. Blackner, Lyman, USAF
Samuel L. Dellos, Worland, Army
Barry A. Hansen, Evanston, USMC
Gary E. Bartz, Cody, Army
Leonard D. May, Medicine Bow, Army
Philip O. Robinson, Sheridan, Navy
Michael R. Beck, Cheyenne, USMC
Weldon D. Moss, Ethete, USMC

Gilbert B. Bush, Laramie, Army
Douglas T. Patrick, Casper, Army
Robert L. Shuck, Newcastle, Army
James F. Barnes, Laramie, Army
1967
Curtis T. Ando, Powell, USMC
Norman L. Moore, Riverton, USMC
Alva R. Krogman, Worland, USAF
Pablo Patino, Powell, Army
Joseph L. Hart, Afton, USAF
Jerry D. Byers, Casper, Army
Dennis W. Smith, Basin, Army
Larry L. Warnock, Buffalo, Amry
Daniel R. Laird, Wheatland, USMC
George R. Harrison, Clearmont, Army
Raymond E. Benson, Glendo, Army
Walter Washut, Jr., Sheridan, USMC
William B. Esslinger, Cheyenne, USMC
Harold L. Gibson, Greybull, Army
Timothy J. Saunders, Jackson, Army
Kenneth L. Brown, Sheridan, Army
William B. Graves, Douglas, Army
Bruce A. Jensen, Green River, USAF
Lawrence D. Torrez, Cheyenne, USMC
Robert R. Rogers, Gillette, USMC
Merrell J. Clayburn, Jackson, Army
Terrance H. Larson, Cody, Army
Pedro R. Montanez, Lovell, Army
Douglas E. Rogers, Green River, USMC
1968
Orville D. Cooley, Range, Navy
Edward McNally, Jr., Cheyenne, Army
Stephen W. Stark, Rock Springs, Navy
William D. Selders, Cody, USMC
Dennis D. King, Green River, USMC
Elmer D. Lauck, Torrington, Army
Walter E. Handy, Casper, Army
Leslie J. Lantos, Ten Sleep, Army
Richard S. Brown, Laramie, Army
Frank M. Darling, Cheyenne, USMC
James E. Pantier, Laramie, USMC
Charles W. Reberg, Casper, Army
Vernon W. Nix III, Casper, Army
Richard L. Endicott, Casper, Army
Richard M. Martin, Encampment, Army
Allen L. Faler, Riverton, Army
Joseph A. Padilla, Cheyenne, Army
Gary D. Fox, Sheridan, Army
Kenneth W. King, Sheridan, Army
Robert E. Barnes, Casper, Army
Terry L. Fetzer, Cody, Army
Edward R. Braun, Cheyenne, Army
Charles S. Roy, Rock Springs, Navy
Richard P. Cazin, Evanston, Army
Bennett E. Evans, Green River, Army
Edward L. Lawton, Thermopolis, Army

Elton G. Anderson, Lovell, USMC
Dale W. Johnson, Auburn, Army
Donald L. Ford, Sheridan, Army
William J. McAtee, Hanna, Army
Henry E. Maul, Worland, Army
1969
Dennis B. Farris, Cheyenne, Army
Victor R. Landes, Cowley, Army
Donald B. Schroeder, Clearmont, Army
Richard J. Sweeney, Casper, Army
Edward B. Steele, Douglas, Army
John W. Koberlin II, Cheyenne, Army
James L. Barton, Greybull, USMC
Candelario P. Bustos, Rock Springs, USMC
Leroy R. Cardenas, Casper, Army
Joseph B. Walker, Lovell, Army
John W. Aldrich, Sheridan, Army
Lonnie A. Dykes, Buffalo, USMC
William M. Wilson, Boulder, Army
Robert F. Maurer, Green River, Army
Dennis R. Wartchow, Jackson, Army
Richard P. Powers, Powell, Army
Lester McCabe, Fort Laramie, Army
Larry R. Owens, Lusk, Navy
Craig T. Marrington, Gillette, Army
Albert O. Wayman, Jr., Evanston, Army
Steven Boal, Upton, Army
Richard T. Kastner, Casper, Army
Walis W. Garst, Weston, Army
Robert E. Romero, Rock Springs, Army
1970
Roger L. Scott, Powell, Army
Edward C. Haggerty, Riverton, USMC
William T. McCormick, Thermopolis, Army
Ernest C. Balland, Cheyenne, Army
Roy J. Snyder, Fort Washakie, Army
Joe W. Green, Buffalo, Army
Ronald R. Stewart, Glenrock, Army
Robert G. Crichton, Burlington, Army
Donald W. Chipp, Jr., Rock Springs, Army
1971
Thomas W. Skiles, Buffalo, Army
Richard E. Tabor, Cheyenne, Army
John A. Cukale, Jr., Rock Springs, Army
Earl E. McCarty, Meeteetse, Army
Benjamin E. Slagowski, Evanston, Army
Gary J. Fuqua, Cody, Army
Randall J. Glasspoole, Riverton, Army
Robert L. Morganflash, Moorcroft, Army
Stephen E. Slocum, Thermopolis, Army
Emil M. Miltnovich, Rock Springs, Army
1972-75
Dennis C. Cressey, Cheyenne, USAF
Harry B. Coen, Riverton, Army
Lawrence G. Evert, Cody, USAF

Wyomingites Killed in
the Iraq-Afghanistan War, 2003-2010*

Therrel Shane Childers, Powell, USMC, 2nd Lt., March 21, 2003
Brendon Reiss, Casper, USMC, Sgt., March 23, 2003
Joe Mayek, Rock Springs, Army, PFC, April 14, 2003
Michael Deuel, Army, Spc., June 18, 2003
Leif E. Nott, Cheyenne, Army, Capt., July 30, 2003
Robert Lucero, Casper, Wyoming National Guard Capt., Sept. 25, 2003
Chance R. Phelps, Dubois, USMC, PFC, April 9, 2004
Kyle Burns, Laramie, USMC, LCpl., Nov. 11, 2004
Brian Bland, Newcastle, USMC, SSgt., Jan. 26, 2005
Mike Parrott, Wyoming National Guard, SSgt., Nov. 10, 2005
James Joseph Arellano, Cheyenne, Army, PFC, Aug. 17, 2006
Jason Corbett, Casper, Army Cpl., Jan. 15, 2007
Scott A. Miller, Casper, Army, Pvt., June 9, 2007
Brian M. Long, Burns, Army, SSgt., June 10, 2007
David Julian, Evanston, Army SSgt., March 10, 2008
Tyler E. Pickett, Saratoga, Army SSgt., June 8, 2008
Bruce Hays, Cheyenne, Wyoming National Guard, Captain, Sept. 17, 2008
Ryan L. Zorn, Upton, Army SSgt., Nov. 16, 2009
Jacob A. Ross, Gillette, USMC, LCpl., March 24, 2010

* List current to June 1, 2010. Several other soldiers killed in the war had Wyoming connections. They include: Brud J. Cronkite, Army, Sgt., May 13, 2004, grandparents lived in Torrington; Collier Barcus, July 8, 2004, spent part of his life on ranch near Powell; Jason Edward Obert, civilian security guard, April 21, 2005, former resident of Sheridan; Seferino J. Reyna, Army, Spc., Aug. 7, 2005, son-in-law of Sheridan residents; Robert W. Ehney, Army, Sgt., April 23, 2006, former resident of Casper; Eric M. Barnes, Airman 1st Class, June 10, 2007, once stationed at Warren AFB.

A survivor of Custer's command at the Little Big Horn is buried at Rawlins. Lansing A. Moore (b. Sept. 27, 1846), was assigned to the 7th Cavalry and rode with the unit commanded by Custer to the Little Big Horn in June, 1876. On the day of the battle, he was sent back to pick up some packs, thus missing the massacre. After discharge from the army, Moore operated a freight team between Rawlins and Lander. Later, he worked as a guard at the state penitentiary. He died July 27, 1931.

MINERALS

1st mining district in Wyoming organized: 1865 at South Pass City

Mineral royalties: Wyoming ranked first in the country in receipt of federal mineral royalties in 1998 with $217.4 million. In 1987, it was $153.5 million. Federal bonus payments in 1998 amounted to an additional $5.8 million.

First trona mines in Wyoming: Opened in 1948. Wyoming produces nearly the entire world's trona. The mineral is used in detergents and glass production.

Only iron factory in Wyoming: Sheridan Iron Works, established in 1910, was the only operating iron factory in the state during the years from 1924-1945. During World War II, the factory produced bronze clutch plates for army trucks and metal parts for hand grenades.

Unusual Mineral Discoveries

1. Gold in a Chicken

A gold nugget the size of a grain of wheat was found inside a chicken in a Casper meat market in 1928. The discovery set off a minor "gold rush" to the chicken farm.

2. Wyoming Diamonds

A 6.2-carat gem-quality diamond was unearthed south of Laramie in the Kelsey Lake project in November, 1993, by Redaurum Red Lake Mines, Ltd. It was the 268th diamond larger than two millimeters discovered in the area. More than 100,000 diamonds of gem and industrial quality had been found in Wyoming as of December 1993. In the spring of 1996, the company opened a mine just inside the Colorado border from Albany County. Diamonds were first discovered in Wyoming by Dr. M. E. McCallum, south of Laramie in 1975. Only one other state, Arkansas, has deposits of diamonds.

3. Soaking

Natural Epsom Salts Company formed near Douglas in August 1916, to transform the salts from a natural salt lake 20 miles southwest of Douglas into a commercially viable product. The project to extract the sulfate of magnesia apparently was not successful. The company was dissolved in 1927.

Early Mineral Discoveries in Wyoming

1. Gold, South Pass City (1842)

A Georgia-born miner found gold in the area in 1842, but he was killed by Indians before he could profit from his discovery. Later, prospectors found gold in 1855 and 1860, but the discoveries aroused little interest until 1867. The gold rush to the area caused South Pass City to grow to more than 4,000 people. The only important gold strike in Wyoming, the deposit proved not to be as important as similar strikes in Montana and Idaho about the same time.

2. Gold, Centennial (1876)

Great excitement was raised by the discovery, but rich veins petered out. In 2000, the Wyoming Geological Survey announced new discoveries there.

3. Silver, Lusk (1879)

The settlement next to the discovery was first called "Silver Cliff" and a mill was built there in 1884.

4. Copper, Hartville (1881)

For a time, the primary town was "Copperopolis." The town of Hartville was named for one of the main investors in the copper mining operation, Major V. K. Hart. In 1898, the

The University of Wyoming operated off-campus facilities in Afghanistan (1952-73) and Somalia (1964-70). The centers emphasized training in agriculture.

iron ore deposits were brought to the attention of Colorado Fuel and Iron Company. The firm leased and purchased 72 claims in 1901 and began mining the iron ore for shipment to its Pueblo, Colo., steel mill. The town of Sunrise was founded two years later by the company. The mine was served by the Colorado and Wyoming Railway which connected to the CB&Q and Colorado and Southern lines at Guernsey, six miles from the mine. The "block-caving" method was used extensively after 1940. The mine closed in the 1980s and the townsite was abandoned.

5. Copper, Rudefeha, Sierra Madres (1896)

The discovery was made by Ed Haggarty who named the company's town after the first two letters in the last names of the principals in the mining operation: John Rumsey, Robert Deal, George Ferris and Haggarty. Copper production from the Encampment area amounted to more than 23 million pounds from 1899 to 1908.

6. Trona, Green River (1902)

Westvaco Chlorine Products Company dug a 1,600-foot shaft and a processing plant in an 11-foot-thick trona bed in 1947. The first FMC shaft was dug the next year. Stauffer, a soda ash producer, came in 1962.

7. Limestone, Laramie Range (1912)

Located 36 miles northwest of Cheyenne, the mine was operated by Great Western Sugar Company. In 1926 the company began underground mining. In 1928, the Monolith Portland Midwest Company opened a quarry 12 miles southwest of Laramie. Later, in 1945, the firm opened another quarry a few miles east of Laramie.

8. Taconite (Iron Ore), South Pass (1962)

U. S. Steel operated the taconite mine, located 30 miles south of Lander, from 1962 until it was closed permanently in 1983.

9. Phosphate, Twin Creek (1947)

The San Francisco Chemical Company opened Wyoming's first large-scale phosphate mine west of Sage in 1947. A second mine for the mineral opened the next year near Kemmerer.

Locations of 10 Lost Mines in Wyoming

1. Bald Mountain

A "lost mine" somewhere in Sheridan County.

2. Thoroughfare Butte

It is said that the Cabin Creek lost mine is on the Park County butte.

3. Big Horn Mountains

Lost Cabin mine, the most famous of all "lost" mines in Wyoming, supposedly was discovered by Swedish miners who later died in Indian raids.

4. Centennial-Albany area

The Downey lost mine is said to be somewhere in the mountains.

5. South Fork, Yellowstone River

Dutchman's Lost Mine, a mythically rich lode, is said to be lost in this area.

6. Medicine Bow area

James Shaw's lost mine is located near the town, according to legend.

Cody hosted its first ever national convention in June, 1939, when the BPOE Does held the organization's 18th annual convention in the northwest Wyoming town. Some 200 delegates attended. On June 24, 1939, Carl Downing's first-ever "Pup Rodeo" performed for 625 people, including the Does. It was the beginning of Cody's "Nite Rodeo," held nightly each summer.

7. Lander area

Old Ike's lost mine is the best known in the southern Fremont County area.

8. Alcova

The Lost Shovel mine was located somewhere near the Natrona County site, possibly under the waters of the reservoir.

9. Arminto

A second "lost mine" in Natrona County is known as the Lost Soldier mine.

10. Sierra Madres

The Carbon County mountains are said to be the location of the Old Shoe lost mine.

BENTONITE

1. Uses

Native people used the clay to suck dirt and oils from buffalo hides. The substance can bind and absorb ten times its own weight. Later, wrinkle cream and cosmetic mud packs were made from bentonite. In the 1980s, the primary use was as a drilling lubricant in the oil fields. It is used in crayons and animal feed and to make golf greens and to line landfills. The most important use in recent years is in the manufacture of cat litter.

2. Production

Wyoming production of bentonite was 1.8 million tons in 1986, down from 4.8 million tons in 1981. Production rose in 1996 to more than four million tons, mostly as a result of cat litter sales. The industry employs 680 workers in Wyoming with estimated sales of $200 million in 1996.

3. Cat Litter Plants

Texan Dennis Markel and a partner developed a clay-based cat litter and, in 1987, began selling Everclean, made from the clay mixture. Soon after, chemist and Amcal International Corp. executive John Hughes viewed a demonstration of the new product in Chicago. He immediately recognized that Markel's clay mixture was not nearly as suitable as bentonite. After working with the substance, Hughes won a patent in 1991 for a bentonite grind effective as a cat litter.

4. Bentonite Companies

A division of cat litter inventor John Hughes' company, American Colloid, produces cat litter from its Colony, Wyo., plant. Black Hills Bentonite mines the mineral near Ten Sleep and processes it in Worland. The company also operates a plant in Casper. Bentonite, Corp., a division of Dresser Industries, processes bentonite near Lovell. Cat litter brands Scoop Away, Fresh Step Scoop, Tidy Cat Scoop and Everclean all contain Wyoming bentonite.

5. Early Bentonite Deposits

The mineral was mined as early as 1888 in the Rock River area. Bentonite deposits near Lovell, Worland and Colony have been used since the early 1990s as American primary source for cat litter.

A Reno-based company, Guardian American Minerals, Inc., found two diamonds within a core sample near the Sweetwater-Uinta County border in 1996. Diamonds already had been identified in the southern Laramie Mountains, the Medicine Bow Mountains, Seminoe Mountains, the Sierra Madre Mountains and the Green River basin. Diamonds were first found on the Wyoming border with Colorado in 1976 by Dr. M. E. McCallum. In 1996, a diamond mine was opened just south of the Wyoming border in Colorado. Only one other state, Arkansas, has proven diamond discoveries.

TRONA

1. Uses for Trona
Trona is used to produce glass, fiberglass, cleansers, detergents, pulp and paper, aluminum, baking soda, refined sugar, pharmaceuticals.

2. Employment
Trona employees represent about 19.5 percent of mining employment in Wyoming. Trona mines employed 3,102 Wyomingites in 1997, down slightly from the 3,290 employed in 1996. In 1970, there were just 1,070 trona workers. Peak employment came in 1981 when 3,995 Wyoming people held jobs in the industry. The number declined to 2,600 in 1986 and rose to 3,050 by 1993. In August 1993, 480 workers, members of the United Steelworkers, went on strike against General Chemical Company trona facility near Green River.

3. Trona Companies
More than 90 percent of the United States soda ash comes from Wyoming and 25 percent of the world's supply. In 1999 five companies operated trona mines and plants west of Green River. They were FMC, General Chemical, Rhone-Poulenc, Solvay Minerals, and Tg Soda Ash, Inc. According to the U.S. Geological Survey, Wyoming has reserves of 127 billion tons of trona. The five firms produced 9.2 million tons in Wyoming in 1992, up from 6.2 million tons in 1982. Production was 9 million tons in 1996. In 1999, five mines in the Green River basin produced 10 million metric tons of trona. In May 1993, Casper businessman John Wold announced plans for an underground trona mine in Sweetwater County.

4. Taxes and Prices
Trona companies paid total taxes (on all including production, property, sales and use) in 1991 of $33.8 million. Trona, from which soda ash is made, was $59.29 per ton in 1989. By 1994, the price had declined slightly to $47.23 per ton. The 1996 price was just over $50 per ton. The price of soda ash (1993) was about $75 per ton, up from $65 per ton in mid-1980s. Peak price was in 1980 at $93 per ton. The federal mineral royalty rate increased from 5 to 6 percent on renewed leases and from 5 to 8 percent on new leases in 1996. The royalty rate on Union Pacific lands was eight percent in 1996.

5. Trona Museum
The town of Lyman is the site of the only museum in the world specifically featuring trona. The Trona Mining Museum of Bridger Valley, located upstairs in the Lyman Town Complex in Lyman, Wyoming, has interpretive exhibits and displays on the history of the trona industry in Wyoming. The museum was owned by the town, but on Feb. 5, 1998, the museum was turned over to the Uinta County Historical Society.

6. Early Exploration
George B. Graff and Lamont DuPont inspected soda deposits in Natrona County in the summer of 1876. "Natrona" takes its name from trona.

A cube of coal measuring six feet by 5 1/2 feet by 4 1/2 feet, was sent from Cumberland No. 2 mine to the St. Louis World's Fair in February, 1904, as one of the entries demonstrating Wyoming mineral wealth.

URANIUM AND RADIOACTIVITY

Leading producer of uranium: Wyoming continued to lead the nation in uranium production in 1988, producing 45 percent of all uranium in the U. S. in that year (2.1 million pounds). The last mine closed production in Wyoming in 1992.

1st uranium found in Wyoming: Silver Cliff, near Lusk, in 1918.

1st uranium boomtown: Jeffrey City, built for Western Nuclear in April 1957

1st underground uranium mine: Phelps Dodge's Green Mountain mine, Crooks Gap, opened in January, 1956 (closed in 1967).

1st load of ore shipped from Lucky Mc Mine, Gas Hills: Sept. 24, 1954

1st processing mill at Gas Hills opened: 1960

1st processing mill at Shirley Basin opened: 1962

Radon: A 1992 study indicated that as many as 40 percent of Wyoming homes may have had dangerous levels of radon. It is created from decay of uranium into radium and then into radon.

1st Wyoming miner to receive a check under the Uranium Victims Compensation Act (1992): John Adkinson, Riverton

Employment in uranium industry: Between 1980 and 1984, more than 5,000 jobs were lost in Wyoming in the uranium industry. It was one of the most intense economic downturns in state history.

Uranium spot market prices: $48.50 per lb., in 2009. All-time low price was $7 per lb. (Jan. 1995); $12 per lb. (Jan. 1996); $10 per lb. (July 1999). The price per pound in the early 1980s was $40 and once sold for a record of $138 per pound.

Newest uranium mine: Ur-Energy was to open a uranium mine called Lost Creek ISR project, just outside Bairoil, in 2010.

6 Uranium Discoveries in Wyoming

1. Lusk, 1918

2. Red Desert, 1936

3. Black Hills in Crook County, 1949

4. Pumpkin Buttes, southern Campbell County, 1951
   The discovery was made in the autumn by USGS geologist J. D. Love.

5. Gas Hills, eastern Fremont County, 1953
   The discovery was made on Sept. 13, by Neil McNeice while he and his wife Maxine were hunting antelope and prospecting. The site was 50 miles northeast of Rawlins, 50 miles south of Moneta. McNeice had worked for Sinclair Oil Company from 1928 until he opened his own machine shop in Riverton in the fall of 1947. He filed the claim for the Lucky Mc in late September, 1953. Within a month of McNeice's filing, 140 claims had been staked by others nearby. By the end of 1954, 7,000 claims had been filed.

6. Big Horn Mountains, east of Ten Sleep, 1956
   The discovery met with little success. After a short boom in which dozens of prospectors descended on the area, the excitement dissipated. By 1958, only three claims were still active in the area.

The first portable nuclear plant built by the Air Force was placed on Warren Peak (6,600 feet), six miles north of Sundance. The P M-1 plant, designed to power the radar installation, was dedicated Sept. 18, 1962. It provided power previously furnished by generators which had burned 1.1 million gallons of fuel oil yearly. The nuclear plant, the first and to date (2010) the only non-academic one ever operated in Wyoming, was closed down in 1969.

7. Jeffrey City area

After years of inactivity, a joint venture in 1996 between Kennecott Energy and U. S. Energy planned to open the new Jackpot Mine near Jeffrey City.

8. Douglas

Highland uranium project near Douglas produced 900,000 lbs. in 1995 and an estimated 1.2 million planned for 1996. The project was operated by Power Resources. A second area facility, owned by Rio Algom Mining Corp. of Toronto, was the Smith Ranch project. In the late 1990s, a new processing plant was planned.

Some Radioactive Clouds Carried Over Wyoming

Nuclear tests in Nevada often took place on days when the radiation would drift away from populated areas of California, Nevada and Arizona. Thus, atomic testing often occurred when winds would carry the debris over Wyoming, an area the AEC considered lightly populated. One author concludes that Wyomingites may have been exposed to higher levels of radiation during the period than Eastern Europeans were during the Chernobyl nuclear accident in the USSR in April, 1986. The date of the tests and the towns over which the clouds passed are listed.

1. Oct. 22, 1951

The cloud moved over from Rawlins to Red Bird (Niobrara County).

2. Nov. 29, 1951

Passed over Church Buttes, Farson, Rawlins, Medicine Bow, Guernsey.

3. April 1, 1952

Passed over Rawlins, Wheatland, Hawk Springs.

4. May 7, 1952

Clouds from this test are believed to have produced intense local fallout. At the time the clouds were passing over the state, snow and rain was falling. The clouds entered Yellowstone Park, drifted at 10,000 feet over Powell, Deaver, Frannie, Parkman, Sheridan, Rocky Point, Colony. Three clouds from the same nuclear test passed over southern Wyoming on the same day.

5. May 25, 1952

Baggs, Dixon, Mountain Home, Woods Landing, Buford, Cheyenne, Carpenter.

6. June 1, 1952

Yellowstone National Park.

7. May 19, 1953

Frontier, Diamondville, Kemmerer, Fontenelle, Farson, Yoder.

8. June 4, 1953

Riverside, McFadden, Rock River, Douglas, Newcastle, Four Corners.

9. Feb. 18, 1955

Beulah, Aladdin, Sundance, Moorcroft, Powder River, Natrona, Rawlins.

The Wyoming speed limit was 75 miles per hour on interstates, 60 on all other roads, until March 3, 1974, when President Richard Nixon declared that for "energy conservation," the limit had to be dropped to 55 mph on all roads. A dozen years later, the 65 mph limit was placed on interstate roads but 55 mph remained in place for all others. On Nov. 28, 1995, President Bill Clinton signed the bill repealing the 55-mph speed limit and states were given the opportunity to determine the limits. Wyoming raised the speed limit on interstates to 75 mph immediately after authority was given and to 65 mph for primary roads.

10. March 29, 1955

Baggs, Saratoga, Bosler, Iron Mountain, Meriden, Albin.

11. May 15, 1955

Wamsutter, Red Desert, Jeffrey City, Gas Hills, Moneta, Lysite, Hyattville, Greybull, Shell, Kane, Lovell.

12. June 2, 1957

Canyon, Cody, Manderson, Ten Sleep, Sussex.

13. June 18, 1957

Cokeville, La Barge, Bairoil, Muddy Gap, Casper, Clareton, Newcastle, Osage, Four Corners.

14. July 5, 1957

Smoot, Halfway, Merna, Burris, Hamilton Dome, Winchester, Worland, Upton, Four Corners.

15. July 15, 1957

Red Desert, Creston, Shirley Basin, Douglas, Lance Creek.

16. July 19, 1957

Old Faithful, Canyon, Tower Junction.

17. July 24, 1957

Daniel, Pinedale, Crowheart, Wind River Reservation, Thermopolis, Lucerne, Kirby, Ten Sleep, Buffalo, Weston, Colony.

18. July 25, 1957

Yellowstone Park.

19. Aug. 7, 1957

La Barge, Atlantic City, Gas Hills, Bill.

20. Aug. 18, 1957

La Barge, Atlantic City, Gas Hills, Bill

21. Aug. 30, 1957

Cokeville, Bondurant, Valley.

22. Aug. 31, 1957

Etna, Freedom, Merna, Fort Washakie, Ethete, Kinnear, Riverton, Moneta, Hiland, Waltman, Powder River, Natrona, Bill.

23. Sept. 28, 1957

Old Faithful, Canyon, Silver Gate.

24. July 6, 1962

Marbleton, Boulder, Big Sandy, Lander, Hudson, Hiland, Waltman, Powder River, Natrona, Bill, Redbird.

Source: Richard Miller, Under the Cloud, published in January, 1987, utilizing official government reports.

In the 2002 dark-satirical movie "Learning Curve," a substitute teacher kidnaps insolent and violent high school students and holds them captive in cages, forcing them to learn with the threat of electrical shocks. At one point in the movie, the substitute teacher asks a student to name the capital of Wyoming. The student first answers "Comanche" but then realizes the correct answer is "Cheyenne" and avoids a zap.

MISS WYOMING

1937:	Mary Ann McLaughlin, Riverton	1985:	Tamara Jo Dereemer, Horse Creek
1941:	Patricia Marie Snyder, Cheyenne	1986:	Lacy Reeves, Laramie
1947:	Dorothy June McKay, Cheyenne	1987:	Terrilynn Marie Hove, Casper
1948:	* Carol Held, Lusk	1988:	Wendi Willis, Laramie
1949:	Esther Macleod, Sheridan	1989:	Alisa Mavrotheris, Cheyenne
1950:	Lenore Hoffman, Cheyenne	1990:	Carolie Howe, Chugwater
1951:	Patricia Seabeck, Casper	1991:	Laurie Biggs, Cheyenne
1952:	Ruth A. Francis, Casper	1992:	Stacy Dawn Cenedese, Cheyenne
1953:	Elaine Lois Holkenbrink, Torrington	1993:	Deborah Maston, Wheatland
1959:	Linda Lou Phillips, Laramie	1994:	Trisha Rae Ramirez, Cheyenne
1960:	Sharon Irene Luond, Cheyenne	1995:	Dana Marie Lane, Cheyenne
1961:	Mary Ray Orr, Sheridan		+Dawn Frantz, Casper
1962:	Gretchen Lea Stainbrook, Jackson	1996:	Rebecca Darrington, Gillette
1963:	Cody Marie Neville, Byron	1997:	Jeffie Ventling, Laramie
1964:	Joan Alser Selmer, Cheyenne	1998:	Mindy Jo Baughman, Rock Springs
1965:	Trudy Brower, Freedom	1999:	Elaine Dabney, Lander
1966:	Susan Lynn Liveri, Douglas	2000	Kimberly Wilkerson, Gillette
1967:	Patricia Ann Martinez, Torrington	2001:	Erin Empey, Casper
1968:	Carol Ann Ross, Burns	2002:	Beth Holland, Gillette
1969:	Sandra Ann Grim, Casper	2003:	Tamara Kocher, Gillette
1970:	Jane Hutchins, Cheyenne	200r	Megan Reichert, Dayton
1971:	Marsha Crandall, Rock Springs	2005	Heather Jackelen, Jackson
1972:	Annette Klipstein, Cheyenne	2006:	Jenleigh Sawatzke, Cheyenne
1973:	Pamela Jo Hill, Casper	2007	** Jennifer McCafferty, Scottsluff, Neb.
1974:	Cheryl Johnson, Cheyenne	2008	Courtney Gifford, Sheridan
1975:	Trish Long, Laramie	2009	Anna Nelson, Rock Springs
1976:	Carol June Wallace, Jackson	2020	Alicia Grove, Rock Springs
1977:	Jeanne Uphoff, Cheyenne		
1978:	Kim Pring, Cheyenne		*1st runner-up, highest finish by a Miss Wyoming
1979:	Karla Ann Singer, Cheyenne		** UW student
1980:	Susan Pennington, Casper		+ In Novembr 1995, Dawn Frantz, Casper, be-
1981:	Keri Lyn Borgaard, Cheyenne		came Miss Wyoming when Dana Lane, the origi-
1982:	Janie Hertzler, Cheyenne		nal winner, stepped down for personal reasons.
1983:	Heather Wallace, Cheyenne		The first runner-up was ineligble due to having
1984:	Ann Warren Easterbrook, Laramie		been married so, Frantz, as second runner-up, re-
			ceived the crown.

MISS WYOMING USA

No Miss Wyoming USA has ever won the national competition. Only semi-finalist from Wyoming was Beth King (1986)

1997:	+Stacy Cenedese, Cheyenne	2006:	Kristin George, Casper
1998:	Megan Wiggert, Cheyenne	2007:	Robyn Johnson, Sheridan
1999:	Arnica Bryant, Cheyenne	2008:	Cassie Shore, Casper
2000:	Rebecca Smith, Jackson	2009:	Cynthia Pate, Casper
2001:	*Heather Jackelen, Rock Springs	2010:	**Claire Schreiner, Gillette
2002:	Jeannie Crofts, Cheyenne		+ Previously Miss Wyoming, 1992.
2003:	Jamie Gorman, Cheyenne		* Later Miss Wyoming 2005.
2004:	Katie Rudoff, Green River		**Finished in the top 15.
2005:	Abby Norman, Laramie		

The only Wyoming winner of the National Junior Miss contest was Karen Morris in 1974.

MISS INDIAN AMERICA*

1951: Lucy Yellowmule, Crow*
1954: Arlene Wesley, Yakima
1955: Mary Louise Defender, Yanktonais Sioux
1956: Rita Ann McLaughlin, Sioux
1957: Sandra Mae Gover, Pawnee
1958: Ruth Larsen, Blackfeet
1959: Delores Racine, Blackfeet
1960: Vivian Arviso, Navajo
1961: Brenda Bearchum, Yakima/ Walla Walla/Cheyenne
1962: Ramona Soto, Klamath
1963: Williamette Youpee, Sisseton- Yankton Sioux
1964: Michele Portwood, Arapahoe*
1965: Marcele Sharron Ahtone, Kiowa
1966: Wahleah Lujan, Taos Pueblo
1967: Sarah Johnson, Navajo
1968: Thomasine Ruth Hill
1969: Margery Haury, Chey.-Arapaho
1970: Virginia Stroud, Cherokee
1971: Nora Begay, Navajo
1972: Louise Edmo, Shoshone-Bannock
1973: Maxine Norris, Papago
1974: Claire Manning, Shoshone-Paiute

1975: Deanna Harragarra, Otoe-Kiowa
1976: Kristine Harvey, White Mtn. Apache
1977: Gracie Welch, Mohave-Yavapai
1978-79: Susan Arkeketa, Otoe-Creek
1980: Melanie Tallmadge, Winn. Sioux
1981: Jerily Lebeau, Chey. River Sioux
1982: Vivian Juan, Papago

*Miss Indian America was chosen annually during All-American Indian Days, held each summer in Sheridan from 1953 to 1983. Lucy Yellowmule was chosen queen of the Sheridan-Wyo Rodeo for 1951 so, technically, Arlene Wesley was Miss Indian America I. In 1984, All-American Indian Days moved to Bismarck, N. D. *Source: Our thanks to Dale E. Kinley, Sheridan, for this information.*

Little America, located west of Green River, was opened by S. M. Covey in 1932 as a refueling stop along U. S. Highway 30. It was named after Admiral Richard Byrd's camp on the South Pole, first established in January 1929. (The original Byrd site set adrift on an iceberg in 1963). Inside the main location and just inside the front door of the Little America convention center complex in Cheyenne are emperor penguins. Emperor penguins are the largest of the penguin family. To connect the site to its namesake in Antarctica, Covey wanted a live mascot. A Captain Lysfadt who had accompanied the Byrd party to the Antarctic, shipped Covey a specimen that was about three feet tall and weighed about 140 lbs. However, before reaching the Wyoming site, the penguin died. Covey had it stuffed and put on display and it became the symbol of Covey's business.

MOUNTAINS

Highest mountain in Wyoming: Gannett Peak, 13,804 feet (only four states have higher mountains). It was named for Henry Gannett of the USGS.

Lowest elevation in Wyoming: Along the Belle Fourche River in Crook County, 3,100 feet.

Mean elevation: 6,700 feet (second highest in the U. S., just 100 feet lower than the mean average in Colorado)

Most frequently climbed peak in Wyoming: Probably Mount Washburn (10,243 feet) in Yellowstone. Thousands "climb" the peak to the fire lookout station during the summer months.

Mountain on Wyoming license plate (2008): The Teton Range was the background on the plate issued in 2008. For the license plate issued for 2001, Devils Tower was featured in the background. Sugarloaf Mountain in the Medicine Bow Range just beyond Centennial was the background on the plate issued in 1993. The 3M Company designed that plate.

1st person to ski from the top the highest peaks on all continents: Kit DesLauriers, Teton Village, on Oct. 18, 2006. DesLauriers established the mark after skiing down, Mount Everest, the world's highest mountain..

First Climbs of Wyoming Peaks

1. Washakie Needles (12,518 feet)

It is said that the mountain was first climbed by Chief Washakie when he was a young man. He climbed the peak in search of eagle feathers.

2. Gannett Peak (13,804)

The first recorded climb by a white American of a Wyoming peak also was the first climb of Wyoming's highest mountain. The climber was explorer Capt. B. L. E. Bonneville, 37, who scaled the peak in September 1833.

3. Mount Woodrow Wilson (13,502)

John C. Fremont and his African American aide Janisse climbed the peak on Aug. 15, 1842, during the first Fremont expedition through Wyoming. Fremont believed the mountain to be the highest in the vicinity, but he was in error. It is only 11th highest, 300 feet lower than nearby Gannett Peak.

4. Grand Teton (13,771)

N. P. Langford and James Stevenson made the climb on July 29, 1872. Langford, the first superintendent of Yellowstone National Park, was 40 years old when he climbed the peak. Army surgeon Charles H. Kieffer and two soldiers of the 6th Cavalry climbed the mountain in September 1893. The leader of the third successful expedition to the top in 1898, W. O. Owen, incorrectly claimed the honor of being the first to climb the Grand Teton. He disputed the Langford-Stevenson claim and ignored the Kieffer climb altogether. The various "first climbs" still are a mtter of dispute by historians.

5. Inyan Kara Mountain

The northeast Wyoming landmark was climbed for eons by Native Americans. The first recorded climb by white Americans was made by Gen. George A. Custer and several of his soldiers on July 23, 1874, two years before his fatal, last expedition to Montana.

6. Fremont Peak (13,745)

Eight members of the Hayden survey party climbed the mountain on Aug. 7, 1878. In the climbing party were F. V. Hayden and photographer William H. Jackson. It was assumed for many years that Fremont had climbed the peak that bore his name, but experts now believe Fremont climbed nearby Mount Woodrow Wilson instead.

7. Cloud Peak (13,167)

W. S. Stanton of the U. S. Army Corps of Engineers climbed the highest peak in the Big Horns in 1887. Stanton was not the first climber. At the top, he found evidence of a Native American bivouac made some years earlier.

8. Devils Tower

Willard Ripley and Will Rogers, two local ranchers, made the first climb using wooden pegs on July 4, 1893. The first free climb (without benefit of pitons or pegs) was made by Fritz Wiessner, Lawrence Coveney and Bill House in 1937. They made the climb in four hours, 46 minutes.

9. Mount Moran (12,605)

Dr. L. H. Hardy, Ben C. Rich and Father Bennet McNulty used sticks and two short auto shovels in making the first climb of the famous peak. They accomplished the feat on July 27, 1922.

10. Teewinot (12,605)

Legendary mountaineers Fritioff M. Fryxell and Phil Smith, both Park Service rangers, made the first climb of Teewinot on Aug. 14, 1929.

11. Mount Owen (12,928)

Fryxell, Smith and two others climbed the last major unscaled peak in the Tetons on July 16, 1930.

12. Laramie Peak (10,372)

Probably scaled countless times by native people and early settlers, the first reported climb was made by W. O. Owen in September 1889.

13. Pilot Peak (11,708)

The peak on the Montana-Wyoming border was first climbed by Hollis Mees, a ranch outfitter, and Robert McKenzie, a highway surveyor, on Aug. 12, 1932.

10 Highest Mountains in Wyoming

1. Gannett Peak (13,804)

The peak was named for Henry Gannett, chief topographer of the U. S. Geological Survey for many years.

2. Grand Teton (13,771)

The only mountain outside the Wind River Range among the state's ten highest peaks, the Grand Teton is the state's best known mountain.

3. Fremont Peak (13,745)

4. Mount Warren (13,742)

The mountain was named for U. S. Senator Francis E. Warren.

5. Doublet Peak (13,636)

6. Mount Helen (13,620)

The Wind River peak was named in 1901 for area resident Helen Fisher.

7. Turret Peak (13,600)

8. Mount Sacajawea (13,569)

Located between Fremont Peak and Mount Helen, the mountain was named for the woman who helped guide the Lewis and Clark expedition.

9. Dinwoody Peak (13,520)

The peak was named for Lt. William A. Dinwiddie, who had been stationed at Fort Washakie with the U. S. Cavalry. When the peak was named, Dinwiddie's name was inadvertently misspelled. The first recorded climb was made by A. E. Bent, E. P. Jackson and J. Wyman, Jr., on Aug. 24, 1922.

Famous Antarctic explorer Laurence Gould (b.1896, d. 1995) had a vacation home near Jackson. Gould, trained as a geologist, accompanied Richard E. Byrd to the South Pole in the 1920s and taught for many years at Carlton College and the University of Arizona..

10. Jackson Peak (13,517)

The peak was named for photographer William H. Jackson (not for Andrew Jackson, David Jackson, the Rev. Jesse Jackson or Michael Jackson!)

Some Famous Mountain Climbers

1. Fritioff Fryxell

The first National Park Service ranger in America, Fryxell first climbed the Grand Teton in 1926. Later, he made 14 first ascents of other Teton peaks, including Teewinot and Mount Owen. He wrote the first Tetons guidebook, *The Teton Peaks and Their Ascents.*

2. Finis Mitchell

Mitchell, born in Ethel, Mo., in 1901, started climbing mountains when he was just eight years old. He climbed 267 major peaks of the Wind River Range, including eight of them during the summer before his 80th birthday. He wrote a guidebook of the Wind River Range in 1975, in its 9th printing in 1993. He retired in 1969 from the Union Pacific Railroad where he worked as a carman in Rock Springs. During the Depression, he owned and operated a Sublette County hunting camp and worked for Game and Fish. He died Nov. 13, 1995, in Green River.

3. Paul Petzoldt

Born Jan. 16, 1908, Petzoldt first climbed the Grand Teton in 1924. He was wearing cowboy boots. Among Petzoldt's numerous climbing achievements are the first winter ascent of the Grand Teton (1936) and the first ascent of the Grand Teton's north face (1936). In 1934, he made a double traverse of the Matterhorn in one day. In 1938, on a climbing trip to K2 in the Himalayas, he set a record for most time above 20,000 feet without artificial oxygen. Founder of the Western Outdoor Leadership School in Lander (March 23, 1965), Petzoldt developed mountaineering voice signals (1924-1928), the sliding middle man snow climbing technique (1925-1928) and other climbing innovations. He died in Maine Oct. 6, 1999.

4. Glenn Exum

Born in Idaho in 1911, Exum was 18 when he first climbed the Grand Teton, alone, without ropes and wearing leather-cleated football shoes. This was the "Exum route," used by most Teton climbers today. From 1946 to 1978, he operated the School of American Mountaineering and a guide service in Grand Teton National Park. During the academic years from 1934 to 1971, he was music supervisor for the school system in Kellogg, Idaho, and was widely involved in music education. In 1935, he became the first American to make a solo climb of the Matterhorn. A glacier in Antarctica has been named for Exum who made his home in Moose following his retirement from Idaho schools. He died in Littleton, Colo., on March 17, 2000.

5.-6. Orrin H. and Lorraine G. Bonney

The Bonneys were well-known climbers of Wyoming peaks, but their most enduring fame comes from their *Guide to Wyoming Mountains and Wilderness Areas*, first published in 1960. The work remains the most complete treatment of Wyoming mountains ever written.

7. Frank McClintock

McClintock became the youngest climber ever to make a first ascent of a Teton peak when on June 23, 1931, the ten-year-old climbed Mount McClintock, 10,960 feet, with his parents.

8. Robert McNamara

The Secretary of Defense in the Kennedy and Johnson administrations climbed Grand Teton in August 1963, with his wife.

9. William J. Stroud

"Rocky Mountain Bill" Stroud (b. 1854, d. Oct. 1, 1946) climbed most of the peaks in the Wind River Range. The USGS once called on him to help map one remote area. He guided them but refused to accept compensation. The survey named a peak, glacier, creek and lake for him. Stroud, a philanthropist, lived modestly in Rock Springs. Not one for fancy climbing attire, he wore the same business suit and hat to climb mountains that he wore to conduct business or visit friends. He was one of the builders of the Congregational Church, Rock Springs. His photographs of Wyoming outdoor scenes were exhibited nationwide. *Source: John R. Waggener, unpublished biography of Stroud, 2000.*

10. Todd Skinner

Outside Magazine called Skinner "arguably the most prolific and colorful rock climber in America." He was credited with making the world's first free ascent of a grade 7 climb. Born in Pinedale in 1958, Skinner graduated with a degree in finance from the University of Wyoming in 1982. He climbed on every continent. In December 1991, Skinner climbed many of the rock towers surrounding Halong Bay north of Hanoi, Vietnam. In order to make the climb of "Houlihan," a 50-foot rock wall with a 20-foot overhang at South Pass, Skinner spent nearly six months trying to master the "single-finger pull-up" needed to make the ascent. He led a team consisting of Mike Lilygren, Bobby Model and Jeff Bechtel on a climb of Trango Tower, a solid granite monolith with an elevation of 20,469 feet in the mountains of Pakistan. Skinner's account of the climb was published in *National Geographic*, April, 1996. On Oct. 23, 2006, Skinner was rappelling down from a new route up the face of Leaning Tower in Yosemite when a loop failed on his climbing harness. He plunged 500 feet to his death. .

11. Kit DesLauriers

On Oct. 18, 2006. DesLauriers (b. Albany, N.Y., 1969) became the first woman to ski from the summit of Mount Everest, but more significantly, she became the first person to ski from the highest peak on each of the seven continents. A graduate of the University of Arizona, she lives in Teton Village.

12. Jim Williams

Williams, a guide for Exum for many years, was the first person to guide all the classic "seven summits" within one year. He climbed Mount Everest in 2000 and led numerous expeditions to mountain ascents on all continents. The Jackson Hole resident was presented the Explorers Club Lowell Thomas award in January 2010.

9 Earliest Climbs or Attempts on the Grand Teton*

1. Michaud LeClaire (1843)

A long-time trapper in the region, LeClaire was the first recorded white person to attempt a climb of the famous peak.

2. N. P. Langford and James Stevenson (July 29, 1872)

The first recorded ascent of the peak.

3. Thomas Cooper (July 1877)

Cooper, from Cheyenne, climbed with two other men to determine whether Langford had made the climb the way he and Stevenson had claimed. The Cooper party found that such a route was possible, but they did not reach the summit.

4. A. D. Wilson (Aug. 20, 1878)

Chief topographer of the Hayden expedition, he made many first climbs of Wyoming peaks. With Harry Yount and A. C. Ladd in 1878, he failed to climb Grand Teton.

The first two millionth annual visitor to Grand Teton National Park entered Sept. 27, 1963.

5. William Baillie-Grohman (August 1880)

The English mountaineer climbed to within 1,000 feet of the summit before night fell and he was forced to retreat back down the mountain. A forest fire prevented a later attempt. The Englishman belittled the effort needed to make the climb, saying it was "easier" than minor peaks in the Dolomites. The comment was viewed by some as a classic "sour grapes" response to a personal failure.

6. Dr. Charles H. Kieffer and soldiers Riley and Newell (Sept. 10, 1893)

Kieffer, an army surgeon, and two 6th Cavalry soldiers known only as "Riley" and "Newell," made the second successful climb to the summit.

7. W. O. Owen (1891, 1897, 1898)

His first seven attempts ended in failure, but on Aug. 11, 1898, Owen, Bishop Frank Spalding and others did make it to the summit. Owen later claimed he was the first to climb the peak, disputing the Langford-Stevenson ascent of 1872. A marker, purchased by Owen's widow, was placed at the summit on July 29, 1929, in an attempt to immortalize Owen's claim after years of heated disputes.

8. Andy DePirro, Quin Blackburn, Dave DeLap (Aug. 25, 1923)

The young climbers were the first to scale the peak in 25 years.

9. Eleanor Davis (Aug. 27, 1923)

Davis became the first woman to climb the Grand Teton. She made the climb with Albert Ellingwood, an experienced Teton climber.

Unusual Happenings Concerning the Grand Teton

1. More than a Foot Higher

In October 1991, a government satellite calculation indicated that the Grand Teton was actually 1.4 feet higher than previous believed. The new elevation was given as 13,771 feet, 7 13/16 inches, give or take a sixteenth of an inch!

2. Barefoot Climb*

Carmen Ruthling made the barefoot climb in 1958 because her rented boots were hurting her feet.

3. Youngest Climber*

Seven-year-old Jeff Love made the climb to the summit on Aug. 16, 1958.

4. Fastest Climb*

J. Glidden of Ogden, Utah, made the solo round-trip from Jenny Lake to the top of Grand Teton and return in four hours, 11 minutes.

5. Descent on Skis

Bill Briggs of Jackson made the first ski descent of the Grand Teton on June 16, 1971. After falling three times and rappelling down one rocky ledge, Briggs ran out of snow at 6 p.m., near the last trail switchback. Rick Armstrong of Wilson skied and snowboarded the Grand Teton in the 1990s.

6. Most Photographed Mountains

The Tetons, now the most photographed mountain range in the world, was first the subject of pictures by William H. Jackson who shot the photos in 1872.

7. First Paraglider over the Tetons

Jon Hunt of Wilson holds the distinction of being the first paraglider over the Grand. The first tandem paraglide over the Grand Teton was accomplished by Rick Armstrong and Eddie Horny in August, 1998. In August, 1999, three paragliders were fined $1,000 each for illegally paragliding from Rendezvous Mountain into Grand Teton National Park.

*Sources: *Orrin H. and Lorraine G. Bonney. Guide to Wyoming Mountains and Wilderness Areas. (Chicago: Sage Books, 1960); newspaper items.*

Some Encounters with Devils Tower

1. 1st recorded sighting by a white American

Capt. William F. Raynolds noted in his journal on July 18, 1855, that he had seen what the Indians called "Bear Lodge Peak" at the time of his exploration.

2. Homesteading the Tower?

Several ranchers filed for homestead claims on the quarter section on which Devils Tower is located. The government denied the claims and finally withdrew the site from homestead entry in 1890. President Theodore Roosevelt signed an executive order designating it a national monument, the nation's first, in 1906.

3. 1st Recorded Climb

Picnickers watched local ranchers Willard Ripley and Will Rogers use wooden pegs to make the first climb on the Fourth of July, 1893. At the summit, the two men raised a 12-foot American flag which was ripped down by the wind later in the day. Pieces of it were sold to onlookers as souvenirs.

4. 1st climb by a woman

Rogers' wife made the climb in 1895, using her husband's wooden-peg ladder.

5. 1st climb without direct aid

Fritz Wiessner, Lawrence Coveney and Bill House made the first climb without "ladder" help in 1937. The climb took them four hours, 46 minutes.

6. 1st climb by a woman without direct aid

Jan Conn made the climb on July 2, 1948, accompanied by a male climber.

7. Stranded on top

George Hopkins parachuted (intentionally) to the top of Devils Tower on Oct. 7, 1941. The stunt turned serious, however, when he found he could not get down. For six days, he remained stranded until eight rescuers, led by Jack Durrence, reached him, despite the heavy rain and icy cold.

8. 1st "mass scaling"

Sixteen members of the Iowa Mountaineers climbed it in August 1948.

9. Most ascents in a short period of time

The Wyoming Mountaineers of Casper College hosted climbers from around the world who made 81 ascents of the tower from July 14 to July 22, 1956. The event marked the 50th anniversary of the creation of the national monument.

10. Annual Ascents

From 1937 to 1947, just 19 climbers ascended Devils Tower and ten made the climb in 1941 during the Hopkins rescue (see # 7, above). In 1956, for the first time the number jumped beyond 100 when 158 climbers made it to the top, 81 in one group (see #9, above). The tower averaged more than 100 climbers per year until 1970 when the total hit 216. Just seven years later, 1,098 people climbed it in one year. In the 1980s, the average annual number hovered around 1,500 making up more than 600 climbing parties yearly. After 1974, officials kept records of unsuccessful climbs, too. They numbered 3,303 in 1987, up from just 87 in the first year such records were kept.

11. Rescue

Rangers at Devils Tower National Monument were called upon to rescue Gene Hagerman, age 16 of Upton, from the east side of Devils Tower. in June 1951. The youth had climbed around a narrow ledge and had slipped down a chimney in the rock. A narrow

---

The Long, Long Trailer (1954), a quaint Lucille Ball/Desi Arnaz farce, begins and ends in the 'Laramie Trailer Court' (actually, a soundstage at MGM studios in Burbank, California). The claimed Wyoming/Colorado mountain footage was shot in Yosemite. The film was directed by Vincente Minnelli.

ledge had saved him from a 200-foot fall. His climbing companion, Arthur Burdick of Moorcroft, reported Hagerman's predicament to monument headquarters. A rescue party led by Seasonal Ranger Ed Fitch and composed of seasonal rangers were able to remove Hagerman from his precarious perch and lead him to safety.

12. Motion Picture Feature

In 1978 Devils Tower was the backdrop for the film, *Close Encounters of the Third Kind*. Director Steven Speilberg spoke of the filming in a January 1978, interview with *American Cinematographer*: "The weather here [Devils Tower] has been the only tricky thing. In the morning you work for four hours under a blue dome. Later, it clouds up. Then a half-hour later, it rains like crazy. Then a half hour after that, it hails. Then it clears up again. You cannot outguess the weather. You simply wait for the tantrum to pass."

12. Young Climber

Eleven-year-old Tyler Hollon climbed Devils Tower in July 1992. He was accompanied by his 16-year-old brother and a guide.

13. Political Climb

Rob Wallace, a candidate for the Republican nomination for the U. S. House, climbed Devils Tower in May 1994 to call attention to the neglect of national parks and monuments by the federal government.

14. Climbing Fatality

The first recorded climbing fatality on Devils Tower was when Scott Hardy, 16, of Wright, fell to his death from a climb in August, 1986.

15. Native American Sacred Site

In the spring of 1996, several Native American groups petitioned the National Park Service to keep climbers off Devils Tower because it was a "sacred place" for native people. A compromise, in which no climbing would be allowed during the month of June met with intense opposition from climbing groups.

Elected Wyoming State Officials, 2010

Governor	Dave Freudenthal (D)
Secretary of State	Max Maxfield (R)
State Treasurer	Joe Meyer (R)
State Auditor	Rita Meyer (R)
Supt. of Public Instruction	Jim McBride (R)

The "White Horse of Ishawooa" is not a living animal. It is a snow field in a pattern resembling a horse's head, seen on the mountain southwest of Cody in early summer. Old-timers say that once one can discern the horse's head, the high water mark for the year has passed.

MOVIES

1st motion picture star in Wyoming: William F. Cody, the subject of the first-ever Western film, *Congress of Rough Riders*, made by the Edison Company in Boston in 1893.

1st motion picture made in Wyoming: *Wyoming Roundup* filmed north of Rock River by Charles Camp. The first scene was shot Aug. 22, 1904, and the film was completed in six weeks.

1st film company organized in Wyoming: Cheyenne Feature Film Co., organized by C. B. Irwin and others in 1912. The firm made just one film.

1st filming of a rodeo in Wyoming: Cheyenne Frontier Days in 1902 by E. T. Nash of the National Moving Picture Co.

1st color motion picture made in Wyoming: A short film made in 1919 of a cowboy roping a bear near Cody. The same cinematographer shot color scenes of the Cody Stampede later the same year.

1st Wyoming resident to win an Academy Award: Wolfgang Breyer, cinematographer, Jackson, 1986.

1st Academy Award (Oscar) donated to a Wyoming museum: Barbara Stanwyck donated her "lifetime achievement" Oscar to the American Heritage Center, University of Wyoming. (Stanwyck, who died in 1990, also donated an Emmy award and other items, all on display at the AHC).

1st full-length feature film ever dubbed in a Native American language: Bambi, the Disney classic, dubbed into Arapaho, featured voices of Ethete residents, 1995.

Film Actors with Wyoming Connections

1. Burnu Acquanetta

Born on the Wind River reservation in 1921, Acquanetta was reared in Norristown, Pa. She signed with Universal Pictures in 1942 after a brief career in modeling in New York. The "sultry brunette" claimed she was from Venezuela and the studio dubbed her the "Venezuela Volcano." She appeared in several films, but never gained stardom. In 1949, she filmed an ad for a tobacco company. The footage, shot at Cheyenne Frontier Days, showed Acquanetta puffing on a cigar.

2. Glenn Close (b. Connecticut, 1947)

Close's connection to Wyoming is quite tenuous. She never lived in the state, but her father, Dr. William Close, lived in Sublette County where he moved after a medical career that included long stints in Africa.

3. Steve Cochran (Robert Alexander Cochran) (b. Calif., d. Guatemala, 1965)

Educated at the University of Wyoming, Cochran made his film debut in 1945. He often played insensitive lovers, appearing in films in the early 1950s. In 1948, he co-starred opposite Mae West in a revival of *Diamond Lil*. He formed his own film production company in 1953. Film credits included *Storm Warning* and *Jim Thorpe, All American*. He died aboard his yacht off Guatemala in 1965.

4. Harrison Ford (b. Chicago, 1942)

Ford lives near Jackson. He has starred in *Star Wars* and other films since the 1980s, including *Empire Strikes Back* (1980), *Raiders of the Lost Ark* (1981), and *Indiana Jones and the Temple of Doom* (1984). In June 2010 he married actress Clarista Flockhart.

5. Mildred Harris (b. Cheyenne, 1901, d. Los Angeles, 1944)

Harris was the daughter of a Cheyenne-based railroad superintendent. She began her film career at the age of nine. When she was 18, she married Charlie Chaplin, but the couple divorced in 1920. In the 1920s, she was one of the highest paid silent film stars. She made the transition to talking pictures as a character actress in the 1930s. She died in Los Angeles of pneumonia in 1944.

6. Isabel Jewell (b. Shoshoni, 1909, d. 1972)

The daughter of a prominent medical doctor, Jewell was born in Shoshoni in 1909. She debuted on Broadway in 1930 in the hit show, *Blessed Event*, and then went to Hollywood to star in the film version. From 1933 to 1946, Jewell appeared in 80 films, including *Tale of Two Cities* (1935), *Lost Horizon* (1937), *Gone with the Wind* (1939), *Northwest Passage* (1940), and *High Sierra* (1941). Her career faded in the 1950s. She was arrested in Las Vegas on bad check charges in 1959 and two years later, served a brief jail term for drunk driving. At her death in 1972, Jewell had not appeared in a motion picture for more than 15 years.

7. Harold Lloyd (b. 1893, d. 1971)

Lloyd's mother homesteaded south of Torrington near Hawk Springs in the 1920s. Lloyd, a well-known actor at the time, visited her there and helped her out financially. The McDonald brothers, who operated the Torrington theater, kept three or four reels of Lloyd films handy and showed them whenever Lloyd came back to visit his mother. *Source: Larry Armstrong, Torrington*

8. Tim McCoy (b. Saginaw, Mich., 1891, d. 1978)

McCoy ranched in Wyoming near Thermopolis when he was a young man. After army service in World War I, McCoy returned to Wyoming where he became adjutant-general of the Wyoming National Guard. In 1923, he signed on as technical advisor for the film, *The Covered Wagon*, and his career on the screen began. He appeared in dozens of movie Westerns before 1930. In that year, McCoy starred in the first-ever sound movie serial. He retired from film in the mid-1930s to travel with a "wild west show" but returned to the screen in 1940. After military service in World War II, he returned to ranching, but he continued to appear in minor roles on screen and television through the mid-1960s. He had a minor role in the 1965 film, *Requiem for a Gunfighter.*

9. Laurie Anders (b. Casper; d. 1992)

She had just one movie credit--a role in the 1953 film, *The Marshal's Daughter.*

10. Anne Archer (b. Los Angeles, 1950)

Archer starred in *Patriot Games* (1992) and other movies, including *Fatal Attraction* which also starred actress Glenn Close. Archer is the sister-in-law of Kevin McKinney, UW Sports Information director and "second voice of the Cowboys." Archer's husband, Terry Jastro, is the brother of McKinney's wife Nancy. Jastro was a producer for ABC.

11. Jim Beaver (b. Laramie, Aug. 1950)

Beaver was reared in Irving, Texas, the son of a minister. He played Happy Doug in the television series, *Third Rock From the Sun,* in 1996. He acted in many movies including *Silkwood, Sister Act* and *Magnolia.*

12. Wallace Beery (b. 1889, d. 1949)

Academy award winner Beery made two films in Jackson Hole, *Bad Bascomb* in 1946 and *Wyoming* in 1940. He owned a home on Jackson Lake near Signal Mountain. To protest establishment of "Jackson Hole National Monument," he rode in the well-publicized "cattle drive" across the monument in the mid-1940s.

13. Jeff Branion (b. Cheyenne, April, 1969)

He played Alex in the 2000 movie, *Dropping Out.*

14. Thomas Wilson Brown (b. Lusk, Dec. 27, 1972)

Brown had roles in the movies *Silverado* and *Honey, I Shrunk the Kids.* He also appeared on the television shows *Knots Landing* and *Days of Our Lives.*

15. Sandra Bullock (b. Virginia, 1964)

Bullock bought a home west of Jackson in 1999.

16. Don Coleman (b. Sheridan, 1893, d. 1985)

Coleman, who changed his name from Lloyd to Don in 1926, began his movie career in New York in 1924 in a film starring Rudolph Valentino. He moved to California the next year. At the height of his career (1928), he starred in six films. His career ended with sound movies. He and his wife (a concert violinist he married in 1927) moved to a ranch near Willits, Calif., remaining there until his death.

17. Joyce Coad (b. Laramie, April 14, 1917; d. Calif., 1987)

Coad acted in movies from 1926-33. She played the child Pearl in the 1926 version of *The Scarlet Letter,* a silent film. She was the daughter of Raymond Coad, born in Cheyenne in 1884.

18. Mickey Daniels (b. Rock Springs, 1917; d. Calif., Aug. 1970)

Born Richard Daniels Jr., he played in 87 films in a career spanning from 1922-46. He initially starred in *Our Gang* comedies after being signed for films at the age of 9 by Hal Roach. His last movie role was of Cicero Grunts in the 1940 movie, *Li'l Abner.* He died in San Diego, alone, in a cheap hotel, his identity unknown for 21 years.

19. Sallie Fisher (b. Wyoming, 1880, d. 1950)

Listed as appearing in the one film, *The Little Shepherd of Bargain Row* in 1916, Fisher's film career was entirely in the days before "talkies."

20. Bruce Kellogg (b. Thermopolis, 1910; d. California, 1966)

He acted in films from 1937-55, mostly bit parts in Westerns. He played the title character in the 1943 movie, *Deerslayer.*

21. George Lollier (b. Wyoming, 1907; d. Los Angeles, Nov. 1971)

Lollier acted in many films from 1933-42, but never as the leading man. He also worked as an assistant director and production manager in television productions in his later years. He was romantically linked with actress Dorothy Granger in the late 1930s.

22. Geoffrey Lower (b. Casper)

Lower is known to TV viewers as the reverend in the 1990s TV series *Dr. Quinn, Medicine Woman*, but he also acted in the 2000 movie *Timeshare.*

23. John McCabe (b. Cheyenne, 1879, d. Buffalo, N.Y., 1929)

The record shows that McCabe appeared in one film--a forgettable one titled *The Great Victory: Wilson or the Kaiser? The Fall of the Hohenzollerns*, in 1919.

24. Ralph McCullough (b. Laramie, 1895, d. 1943)

McCullough had an enduring film career, acting in 25 movies in the 1920s as well as numerous films in the 1930s and 1940s.

25. Robert Muratore

Born in Casper in 1968, Muratore was cinematographer for and played "Frenchy" in the 1996 movie titled *Cannibal: The Musical.*

26. Wayde Preston (William Erskine Strange) (b. Denver, 1929, d. Lovelock, Nev., Feb. 1992) Preston was reared in Laramie, graduated from Laramie High School and attended the University of Wyoming, majoring in pharmacy. After service in Korea and work as a park ranger in Grand Teton National Park, he went into film. He is best known to American audiences as the star of the 1950s TV western series, *Colt .45*, premiering Oct. 10, 1957. He left the series in 1960 and began a long movie career in Europe. He became wealthy, starring in a long series of "spaghetti Westerns" in the 1950s and 1960s. His adopted home had been Italy.

27. Maudie Prickett (b. 1915, d. April 14, 1976)

Maudie Doyle graduated from the University of Wyoming in 1935. She married Charles Prickett and began a career as a character actress in some 30 films and numerous television programs. Her credits include appearances on television shows such as the *Andy Griffith Show* (Aunt Bee's gossiping sister), *Hazel* (another maid), and *Bewitched.* A dozen of her movie credits were parts in Westerns.

28. Skeeter Bill Robbins (b. near Glenrock, 1875? 1887?, d. 1933)

Born Roy Robbins, he began his career with the Wild West Show. Later, he acted in many silent Westerns. He married Dorothy Morrell ("Prairie Rose"). Both rode the rodeo circuit while he acted in films into the early sound era.

29. Jesse Garcia (b. Rawlins, 1982)

His first film was *Quinceañera* (2006). He appeared in the 2009 film, *Locker 13*.

30. Joe Ryan (b. Crook Co., 1887, d. 1944)

Ryan worked with Buffalo Bill's Wild West Show when he went into film in 1910 as a rider. He was featured in a succession of serials from 1916-25.

31. Joe Siedow (b. Cheyenne, 1920, d. Houston, 2003)

Siedow's best known roles were in the 1974 cult classic, *The Texas Chainsaw Massacre* and its 1986 sequel.

32. Kathryn Trosper (b. Lander, March 18, 1915)

Trosper played the role of a reporter at Xanadu in what has been called the greatest movie of the 20th century, the 1941 film *Citizen Kane*.

33. Wally Wales (Floyd Taliaferro Alderson) (b. Sheridan, 1895; d. Feb. 1980)

Alderson was reared on a ranch near Sheridan. His film career began in 1915, but it was interrupted by service in World War I. When he returned, he played bit parts until 1925 when his name was changed by producer Lester Scott to Wally Wales. In his long career from 1921 to 1964, he appeared in more than 200 movies, mostly Westerns. He was billed as "Hal Taliaferro" in some of his early films.

4 Wyoming Directors

1. Malcolm Harding

Producer and director of the popular television mini-series, *Centennial*, Harding attended high school in Laramie. He also was producer of the TV series *Falcon Crest* (1981-82) and assistant director for *Towering Inferno* (1974) and *The Missouri Breaks* (1976).

2. Neal Hart (b. New York, 1879; d. Calif., April 2, 1949)

Hart came to Wyoming with a cattle drive in 1895. After service in the Spanish-American War and graduation from an Eastern college, Hart returned to the Manville area to work on ranches. From 1907 to 1913, he was town marshal of Manville, losing a bid to become the first sheriff of Niobrara County in 1911. He joined a Wild West Show in 1914 and appeared in Hollywood films, starring in a 20-episode serial in 1915. He made silent films in the 1920s, reverting to a supporting actor with the advent of sound. He produced, directed and wrote many of the films in which he starred. His best known work was *Butterfly Range*. For the serial *Scarlet Brand* (1926), he shot scenes at the Rawlins rodeo.

3. Gene Levitt

Levitt was the director and producer for numerous television shows such as *Maverick, McCloud, Combat, Fantasy Island, Barnaby Jones,* and *Hawaii 5-O*. He was editor of the *Branding Iron* at the University of Wyoming when he was a college student. He graduated from UW in 1941. He died of prostate cancer Nov. 15, 1999, at the age of 79.

4. Daniel Junge

Junge produced an award-winning documentary film titled *Chiefs* (2002) centered around a winning basketball team on the Wind River reservation. Two of his later films were short-listed for Oscar nominations in 2009 and 2010. He was born in Cheyenne.

6 Motion Picture Screenwriters from Wyoming

1. John McDermott (b. Green River, 1892, d. 1946)

He wrote many screenplays for silent films and early "talkies."

2. Florabel Muir (b. Rock Springs)

Muir wrote one screenplay, for the 1935 movie, *Fighting Youth.*

3. **Caroline Lockhart** (b. Illinois, 1871, d. Cody, 1962)

The colorful Cody editor also wrote screenplays. Three were produced--*The Man from the Bitter Roots* (1916); *Fighting Shepherdess* (1921); and *The Dude Wrangler* (1930).

4. Katharine Burt (b. New York, 1882; d. 1977)

The Jackson Hole resident, best known for short stories, wrote 12 screenplays for film. Samuel Goldwyn purchased her first screenplay in 1920.

5. Dee Linford (b. Afton, 1915, d. Santa Fe, August 1971)

Linford, a UW gradute, wrote episodes of TV westerns, including *Sugarfoot* and *The Virginian*. In 1955, the film, *Man Without a Star*, was based on his novel. It starred Kirk Douglas, Claire Trevor, Jeanne Crain and Richard Boone. It was directed by King Vidor.

6. Mark Spragg (b. Pittsburgh)

Spragg, better known as an author, wrote screenplays and television scripts for many years prior to turning to writing books. He and his wife Virginia co-wrote the screenplay, *An Unfinished Life*, based on his novel. Robert Redford starred in the film.

Some Films Supposedly Set in Wyoming

1. The Great Train Robbery (1903)

The father of the story film Edwin S. Porter was known as the father of the story film. His pioneering western, the one-reel, 10-minute long film, was shot on the East Coast (New Jersey and Delaware) rather than the Western setting of Wyoming.

2. The Squaw Man (1913)

It was the second film made by Cecil B. DeMille who had traveled through Wyoming with a theater company and originally planned to shoot the picture on location. Unfortunately, his deadline required that the filming be done during the winter, impossible to do in Wyoming with the story line, to say nothing of the technology. DeMille settled for a small hamlet in California at the end of the railroad tracks where the countryside reminded DeMille of Wyoming. The town was Hollywood and the rest is history.

3. My Friend Flicka (1943)

The film, featuring Roddy McDowell as the boy who loves the horse, was shot in the Bryce Canyon area of Utah, even though the setting for the book was the Remount Ranch of Laramie County. The remake, *Flicka* (2006), was partially shot in Sheridan County.

4. The Outlaws is Coming (1955)

Casper is supposedly the Old West town where the Three Stooges, stars of the film, serve as deputies. The film co-starred Adam West as the sheriff.

5. Man Without a Star (1955)

The film, based on Afton native Dee Linford's novel, was directed by King Vidor and starred Kirk Douglas and Jeanne Crain. Supposedly set on a Wyoming cattle ranch, the entire film was shot in southern California.

6. Top Gun (1956)

Not to be confused with the fighter pilot film of the 1980s, this earlier movie supposedly portrayed outlaws and lawmen in Casper during the 1870s. Historical facts were stretched considerably. Casper was not founded until 1888.

7. Heller in Pink Tights (1960)

"Members of a two-wagon traveling show fight for their lives, their pride and a living in 1880s Wyoming," said an ad for the film starring Anthony Quinn and Sophia Loren.

8. Mr. Horn (1979)

The film was also titled *Tom Horn*. Although it is loosely based on fact, the film was shot in California (where, apparently, most of the research on the story wasn't done). Among the numerous grievous errors is the presence of the Wyoming state flag in several scenes, no mean trick given that Horn was hanged 14 years before it was even designed. The film starred Steve McQueen.

9. Heaven's Gate (1980)

The most costly movie ever made when it was released in 1980, the film purportedly was based on the Johnson County Invasion. Any resemblance to historical facts in the film are purely coincidence. No part of the film was shot in Wyoming. The "Wyoming scenes" were made near Wallace, Idaho. the film proved to be such a box office bomb that few Westerns were made during the next decade.

10. Heartland (1979, 1982)

The film was based on the book, *Letters of a Woman Homesteader,* the story of Eleanor Pruitt Stewart's adventures on a Burnt Fork, Wyoming, homestead at the turn of the century. The film was made in Montana. Starring were Conchatta Ferrell and Rip Torn.

11. Unforgiven (1992)

Clint Eastwood's academy award-winning film was set in "Big Whiskey, Wyoming." The film was not made in Wyoming, however.

12. The Legend of Earl Durand

The story, loosely based on fact, stars Peter Haskell as the title character, Martin Sheen as a friend and Slim Pickens as the jailer. "Sublette City, Wyoming" was the supposed place where the action occurred.

13. Cowboy and the Lady (1922)

Partially filmed in Jackson Hole, the film included many scenes of downtown Jackson and local people who were "extras" in the movie. When the film premiered, Jackson residents laughed heartily at a scene where a train pulled into the "Jackson railroad station." No railroad has run into Jackson Hole.

14. Red Rock West (1991)

The film, starring Nicholas Cage and Dennis Hopper, supposedly depicted Red Rock as a town "somewhere in Wyoming." In actuality, all of the scenes were shot in the vicinity of Willcox, Arizona, by Black Crow Productions.

15. Wind River (1998)

The film starred Blake Heron, A Martinez, Karen Allen, Wes Studi, and Russell Means who played Chief Washakie. It was advertised as "a historical drama is based on the memoirs of Pony Express rider Nick Wilson."

16. The Jack Bull (1999)

John Badham directed the fictional tale of Myrl Redding, a horse breeder living in Rawlins in the late 1880s. The action moves throughout southeast Wyoming, culminating in a Cheyenne gripped by statehood fever. The film was shot in Canada, largely at the CL Ranch and the Heritage Park Historical Village in Calgary, Alberta.

17. An Unfinished Life (2005)

The film, based on the novel by Mark Spragg and starring Robert Redford, is set in Park County. The actual filming was not done in Wyoming, however. Most scenes were shot in Alberta and British Columbia, masquerading as the mountains of Wyoming.

18. Miracle at Sage Creek (2005)

"Two families overcome prejudice and tragedy in 1888 Wyoming when a specail Christmas miralce saves the life of a msall boy." The film starred David Carradine. It was filmed in Arizona even though "Sage Creek" was supposed to be located near Lusk. When the home video was released in 2007, it was retitled *Christmas Miracle at Sage Creek.*

19. Brokeback Mountain (2005)

The film, based on a short story by Annie Proulx, contained scenes supposedly set in the Big Horn mountains of Wyoming. No actual Wyoming scene was used. Most of the move was shot in Canada or near Messilla, N. M.

19. Shooter (2007)

Sniper Bob Lee Swagger, played by Mark Wahlberg, is called away from his mountain home in Wyoming to help track down a presidential assassin. Also starring Ned Beatty and Danny Glover, the action thriller was shot mostly in British Columbia.

20. Did You Hear About the Morgans? (2009)

The comedy is about an estranged couple who witness a murder and then must be relcated to the small town of Ray, Wyoming, in a witness protection program. The film starred Hugh Grant and Sarah Jessica Parker. The film was shot in New York City and Galisteo, New Mexico.

21. 2012 (2010)

An "end-of-the-world" film, the main character in the film and his children go camping in Yellowstone National Park. A series of catastrophes occur culminating in a super volcano eruption in Yellowstone, the ash supposedly reaching Washington, D.C., in seven hours. The film starred John Cusack, Amanda Peet, Danny Glover, George Segal and Woody Harrelson (who plays a radio deejay in Yellowstone).

3 Wyoming People You Wouldn't Expect to Find in a Movie!

1. Curt Gowdy

Gowdy, a nationally-known sportscaster from Wyoming (b. Green River, 1919), played a television commentator in the 1978 movie, *Heaven Can Wait*, starring Warren Beatty. He also played a baseball announcer in the 1988 movie comedy, *The Naked Gun*.

2. Gerry Spence

The well-known Jackson Hole attorney played a Wyoming preacher in the 1991 movie, *Ghosts Can't Do It*, starring Bo Derek and Anthony Quinn.

3. Al Simpson

The former senator played himself in the film "Dave," starring Kevin Kline.

Some Movies Filmed in Wyoming

1. Charge of the Light Brigade (1912)

The Edison Film Company shot the silent picture at Pole Mountain between Cheyenne and Laramie in the summer of 1912. Some of the action was filmed on the Terry Ranch south of Cheyenne, according to film historian William R. Huey.

2. The Indian Wars (1913)

William F. Cody starred as himself in the film made near Cody in September 1913. Other scenes were shot on the Pine Ridge reservation in South Dakota.

3. The Man From Painted Post (Handsome Jim Sherwood) (1917)

The film, referred to by two titles, starred Douglas Fairbanks. One of the earliest full-length feature films made in Wyoming, much of it was shot at the Lakeside Ranch, 30 miles southwest of Laramie in August 1917.

4. Triple Chevrons (1918)

The film, shot near Cody, was also called *Heart of the Wilds*.

5. Nanette of the North (1922)

The 15-episode serial, a science fiction story, was shot in Yellowstone.

6. The Cowboy and the Lady (1922)

Some scenes were shot in Jackson and local residents were "extras."

7. The Covered Wagon (1923)

Parts of the film were shot on the Wind River reservation. Tim McCoy served as technical advisor and, as a result, began a long career in Westerns.

8. Pony Express (1925)

Filmed in Laramie County, the movie set was visited by the U. S. Vice President in the summer of 1925.

9. War Paint (1926)

The film starred Tim McCoy and numerous local residents of the Wind River reservation area appeared as extras in the film shot in August 1926.

10. Our American Girl (1930)

Filmed near Casper, the movie starred aviatrix Kay Gordon.

11. The Big Trail (1930)

The cast included a young actor by the name of John Wayne. The film was shot in the summer of 1929 in Jackson Hole.

12. The End of the Trail (1932)

Sixty mounted National Guardsmen from Riverton and Lander served as extras in the Columbia Pictures film.

13. The Plainsman (1936)

Wyoming National Guardsmen, on maneuvers at Pole Mountain east of Laramie, appeared in the film. A few had minor roles in the Paramount release.

14. Bad Bascomb (1946)

Filmed in Jackson Hole, it starred Wallace Beery and Margaret O'Brien.

15. Bronc Rider (1951)

The Universal Studios film was shot at Cheyenne Frontier Days in 1951. Billed as "the most authentic rodeo movie ever filmed," it starred Chill Wills and Scott Brady.

16. The Big Sky (1952)

The film, based on the A. B. Guthrie story set in Montana, was partially shot in Wyoming.

17. Shane (1953)

The Tetons served as a magnificent backdrop to this Western classic starring Alan Ladd, Jean Arthur, Van Heflin and Brandon deWilde. Much of the film was shot on the Square G Ranch.

18. The Far Horizons (1955)

The story of the Lewis and Clark expedition, critics incorrectly thought the film was made "along the Lewis and Clark trail." Not so. The film was made in Grand Teton National Park. Fred McMurray was Meriwether Lewis; Charlton Heston was William Clark. Donna Reed starred in the unlikely role of Sacajawea.

19. Jubal (1956)

The movie, filmed on a dude ranch in the Tetons, starred Glenn Ford, Ernest Borgnine and Rod Steiger.

20. Spencer's Mountain (1963)

The film was based on the Earl Hamer book, but using the Tetons in the background, the film departed markedly from the story which took place in Virginia! The television series, *The Waltons*, based on the film and the book, was set more accurately, but less grandly, in the Virginia hills.

21. Cheyenne Autumn (1964)

Parts were shot in Wyoming. The movie premiered in Cheyenne.

22. Newcomers (1969)

The Walt Disney film, starring Ronnie Howard (at the time, a TV star on the Andy Griffith show) and Vera Miles, was made on the Twin Creek Ranch and the Teton Valley Ranch, both near Jackson, during the summer of 1969.

23. Wendigo (1975)

Filmed near Jackson.

24. Close Encounters of the Third Kind (1977)

The Columbia Pictures film cast Devils Tower in a central role.

25. Centennial (1978)

The Universal Studios production, based on the James Michener novel, was primarily filmed in Colorado, but several scenes were shot in Wyoming. Michener visited the Wyoming town of Centennial for the dedication of the public library in the 1970s.

26. The Mountain Men (1979)

A Columbia Pictures film starring Charlton Heston, much outdoor footage was of the Tetons.

27. Pursuit of D. B. Cooper (1980)

Several Wyoming locations were used in the Polygram Pictures film.

28. Any Which Way You Can (1980)

Clint Eastwood participated in a fist fight in the Jackson town square.

29. Endangered Species (1981)

Universal Pictures production was filmed in Buffalo. Locations included Main Street and the interior of a local home.

30. Star Trek, The Motion Picture (1982)

The Star Trek crew returned to Earth and among the sites pictured were the mountains in northwestern Wyoming.

31. Rocky IV (1985)

MGM/United Artists production starring Sylvester Stallone was filmed near Jackson. Fifty local extras were hired for the film.

32. Hyper Sapien: People from Another Star (1986)

The science fiction film, starring Sydney Penny, was about a Wyoming rancher who reluctantly granted refuge to three fugitive aliens.

33. Prison (1986)

Much of the film was shot at the old State Penitentiary in Rawlins. Numerous local people appeared in walk-on roles. The film premiered at "Movies 3" on March 3, 1988, in Rawlins.

34. Dream West (1986)

Richard Chamberlain starred in a film about John and Jessie Fremont.

35. Supergirl (1984)

Squaretop Mountain was shown in the film although most of the picture, starring Faye Duniway and Peter O'Toole, was filmed in England.

36. Wrong Guys (1987)

The New World Pictures production was made in Jackson Hole.

37. Leaving Normal (1992)

Christine Lahti and Meg Tilly starred in the story of a woman fleeing a brutal husband in Normal, Wyoming, who joined up with a waitress en route to claim a home left to her by a former boyfriend in Alaska. "Normal" in the film was actually the town of South Superior where the scenes were shot.

38. The Vanishing (1992)

The film, starring Kiefer Sutherland, used one scene of the highway tunnel west of Cody. Most of the film was made in the Seattle area, however.

39. Starship Troopers (1996)

Many scenes of the planet's "landscape" were shot in Hell's Half Acre, west of Casper. The film employed numerous local Casper people as extras.

In the posthumously published science fiction novel and stories by Douglas Adams, titled The Salmon of Doubt: Hitchhiking the Galaxy One Last Time, northern Wyoming is mentioned as the possible landing spot for an asteroid. It is not known if Wyoming was hit, however, because the novel was not completed at Adams' death.

40. Flicka (2006)

An adaptation of the novel, *My Friend Flicka* wirrten by Mary O'Hara in 1941, the film was partially shot on the Eaton Ranch near Sheridan. Alison Lohman and Tim McGraw starred in the film. A sequel, titled *Flicka 2*, was to be released in 2010.

41. Losing Lusk (2005)

The short film called "Losing Lusk" was a finalist in the Sundance Film Festival Short Film competition for 2005. It is 7 minutes long, featuring Ty Baker, a young man who was born in Lusk and then had to leave the town for employment elsewhere. The film was directed by Vance Malone, who was born in Casper and grew up in Glenrock. Malone, who also did the cinematography, works for a film production company in Oregon.

Mentioning Wyoming...References in Various Films

1. Away All Boats (1956)

In the film, the Jeff Chandler character said: "So you're a rabbit hunter from Wyoming."

2. Dog Day Afternoon (1975)

The Al Pacino character, when asked what foreign country he wanted safe passage to, answered, "Wyoming."

3. The White Buffalo (1977)

Frequent mentions were made of Wyoming in the film. At one point, a character mentioned the "roundup of stray cats in Cheyenne." The film starred Charles Bronson as Wild Bill Hickok.

4. Zuma Beach (1978)

The family planned a vacation in Yellowstone. The film starred Suzanne Somers and Mark Wheeler.

5. Any Which Way You Can (1980)

"I love the place and the people," said Sandra Locke about Jackson.

6. Assassination (1981)

The Jill Ireland character (the president's wife) told Charles Bronson that her name was spelled "Lara" because it was short for "Laramie." At one point in the film, Bronson's character went through Wyoming on a train, eluding a mob.

7. Side by Side: The True Story of the Osmonds (1982)

"I'm from Star Valley, Wyoming, the prettiest little corner of the world," Joseph Bottoms (as Frank Osmond) said at one point.

8. Fool for Love (1984)

Kim Basinger told Sam Shepard: "I'm not going to Wyoming? What's up there, a Marlboro man or something?"

9. Roxanne (1987)

"You could de-emphasize your nose if you wore something larger—like Wyoming," joked Steve Martin as the long-nosed fire chief.

10. Midnight Run (1988)

In one scene from the film, Robert DeNiro said: "I'm in Casper, Wyoming."

11. Nothing Underneath (1989)

The film featured Donald Pleasance as a Yellowstone park ranger who went to Milan, Italy, in search of his missing sister, a world-renowned fashion model from Wyoming. An Italian detective working the case frequently addressed the Pleasance character, "It's you, Wyoming."

12. Quigley Down Under (1991)

The main character played by Tom Selleck said he was from Wyoming and frequent references were made to the state.

13. Buckaroo Bonzai

A woman in the jail said: "I'm from Cody, Wyoming."

14. Bright Angel (1991)

The show starred Sam Shepard, Valerie Perrine and Lili Taylor. In the film, the Shepard character talked about living in Casper where another character (a prostitute) was going. "Casper, the friendly city," she said. She also said, "What a place. My brother said it was nicer than this." The story was about a young ranch hand who agreed to help a woman get her brother out of a Casper jail.

15. Canadian Bacon (1995)

"The missile countdown has started in Wyoming and Montana," one character says in the comedy about an attempt to start war between the U. S. and Canada.

16. Santa Fe (1997)

The main character, played by Gary Cole, said he was sole survivor of a mass cult suicide in Wyoming.

17. K-PAX (2001)

In this science fiction film starring Kevin Spacey and Jeff Bridgers, Sheridan is noted with a stickpin as a locatin of a slaughter house.

18. Deepwater (2005)

Film based on a novel by Matthew F. Jones, concerns the adventures of Nat Banyon, a hitch-hiker who dreams of opening an ostrich farm in Wyoming. The film starred Lucas Black and Peter Coyote.

19. Miracle at Sage Creek (2005)

Ike: "We're gonna get those steers into Lusk and sold before Christmas."

20. Broken Trail (2006)

Starring Robert Duvall and Prentice Ritter, the film tells the story of two Old West characters in 1896 saving five Chinese women from a life of prostitution and exploitation in Wyoming.

21. Year of the Dog (2007)

In the film starring Molly Shannon, a character played by John C. Reilly said about the death of his dog, "I shot her in Wyoming." He added, "It was a hunting accident." He was there hunting moose.

Some Movies with Wyoming in the Title

1. The Man from Wyoming (1924)

The black and white, silent Universal production was based on the William MacLeod Raine novel, *Wyoming: Story of the Outdoor West.*

2. Wyoming (1928)

Tim McCoy starred in this MGM picture filmed in 1925, but released three years later. The film featured all of the ingredients of a classic Western.

3. A Man from Wyoming (1930)

The film by Universal starred Gary Cooper as a Wyoming cowboy who served in World War I, rescued a pretty girl, and secretly married her. No scenes were shot in Wyoming.

4. Wyoming Whirlwind (1932)

A criminal called the "Wolf" stole a ranch payroll. It was found that the crook was the rightful owner of the ranch who was cheated out of it years earlier.

5. Wyoming Outlaw (1939)

John Wayne starred in the film wherein his character tried to figure out why a law-abiding man would shoot an outlaw in cold blood.

6. Wyoming (1940)

Wallace Beery starred in the western.

7. Wyoming Wildcat (1941)

Starring Tom Tyler and Billie Bennett, the film plot revolved around the adventures of a cowboy who rescued a young woman from a villain who tried to throw her off a cliff.

8. Home in Wyoming (1942)

The film, a western, starred Gene Autry.

9. The Wyoming Hurricane (1944)

Russell Hayden, who appeared in more than 75 movies from 1936-63, starred in this film also titled *Proved Guilty*.

10. Song of Old Wyoming (1945)

The film starred Eddie Dean and Al "Lash" Larue.

11. Wyoming Roundup (1947)

The western starred Whip Wilson.

12. Green Grass of Wyoming (1948)

The film starred Charles Coburn and Burl Ives. Most of the movie was filmed in Ohio. In fact, no scenes were shot in Wyoming. Gov. Lester C. Hunt heard about the filming and sent a bale of hay to the Ohio governor. Hunt said he wanted to be sure there was "some green grass of Wyoming in the movie."

13. Wyoming Bandit (1949)

The Republic Pictures film was made entirely in California.

14. Wyoming Mail (1950)

An imprisoned telegrapher keeps busy by Morse code. The film starred Stephen McNally and Alexis Smith. The film was shot entirely in California.

15. The Redhead from Wyoming (1952)

Maureen O'Hara starred in the film as the manager of a cattle clearing house who got into trouble before she married the sheriff. She tried to organize settlers to stop an unscrupulous politician's range war.

16. Wyoming Renegades (1955)

Butch Cassidy and the Sundance Kid are portrayed in the film starring Phil Carey and Gene Evans who played Butch. William Bishop played the Sundance Kid.

Films with Wyoming Places in the Title

1. Coaches Going to Cinnabar from Yellowstone Park (1899)

2. Lonesome Luke from London to Laramie (1917)

The silent film starred comedian Harold Lloyd.

3. John Ermine of Yellowstone (1917)

4. Devils Tower (1928)

5. Cheyenne Kid (1930)

6. Laramie Kid (1935)

Western star Tom Tyler attempted to capture the meanest outlaw of all, known as the "Laramie Kid," in this 1935 film.

7. Cheyenne Tornado (1935)

The western was about a cowpoke who assisted a sheepherder's family from the intimidation of a group of cattlemen. Cheyenne also appears in the name of other movies, including: *Cheyenne Autumn, Cheyenne Rides Again, Cheyenne Roundup, Cheyenne Warrior* and *Cheyenne Wildcat*.

8. The Sheriff from Medicine Bow (1948)

The Western starred Johnny Mack Brown.

9. Rails into Laramie (1954)

The film starred John Payne and Dan Duryea.

10. The Man from Laramie (1955)

11. Revolt at Fort Laramie (1957)

12. Cheyenne Social Club (1970)

The movie irretrievably destroyed the historic truth about the famous "Cheyenne Club." The real Cheyenne Club was not an elaborate gambling den and house of prostitution, but an exclusive club for wealthy cattlemen.

13. Casper (1995)

The movie, about the comic-strip friendly ghost, had nothing to do with the city of Casper except for the name. Nonetheless, the movie premiered in Casper in 1995.

6 Actors Who Played "The Virginian"

1. Dustin Farnum (1914)

Cecil B. DeMille directed the film.

2. Kenneth Harlan (1923)

3. Gary Cooper (1929)

4. Joel McCrea (1946)

5. James Drury

Drury played the role in the television series that ran from 1962-1970. Although he didn't play the title role, Drury had a bit part in the 2000 version starring Bill Pullman. Stewart Granger played one character in the series in 1970.

6. Bill Pullman (2000)

Produced for Turner Network Television, Pullman's version most closely followed the plot in Wister's novel.

Recent Foreign Films with Wyoming Titles

1. Requiem para Cheyenne (Spain, 1990)

2. Le Vent du Wyoming (France, 1994)

The title translates to The Wind From Wyoming.

3. O Tsalapentinos tou Wyoming (Greece, 1995)

The title translates to Like a Prairie Cock in Wyoming.

Some Films about Buffalo Bill

1. The Indian Wars (1913)

Buffalo Bill himself starred in the film, part of which was shot in the Cody area in 1913.

2. In the Days of Buffalo Bill (1922)

A serial produced by Universal Pictures, it starred Art Acord.

3. Buffalo Bill on the U. P. Trail (1926)

The Sunset Pictures film starred Roy Stewart.

4. Young Buffalo Bill (1940)

The film featured cowboy star Roy Rogers.

5. Buffalo Bill (1944)

The 20th Century Fox film starred Joel McCrea as Buffalo Bill.

Root's Opera House in Laramie sometimes had customers as rowdy as the characters motion picture actors were portraying on the screen. A young boy asked, "Any shooting in the show?" Came the reply, "Well, if you go in and if there isn't anybody shot, you ask Mrs. Root for your money back when you come out."

6. Buffalo Bill Rides Again (1947)

Richard Arlen appeared in the title role.

7. Cody of the Pony Express (1950, serial)

8. Pony Express (1953)

The Paramount film starred Charlton Heston as Buffalo Bill. The first film by the same title, a silent picture, was shot in Laramie County in July 1925.

9. The Plainsman (1966)

The film by Universal starred Guy Stockwell.

10. Buffalo Bill and the Indians (1976)

Paul Newman starred as Buffalo Bill in the unflattering portrayal of the famous scout in the United Artists production.

Film historian William R. Huey lists 32 films in which Buffalo Bill was portrayed. Huey' wrote, In Search of Hollywood, Wyoming (Cheyenne: Westmark Limited, 1985).

Movie Theaters in Wyoming Towns

1. Acme Theater, Basin

Located in Fraternity Hall, the theater was gutted by fire soon after it opened.

2. Dr. Hook's Picture Show, Big Piney

The first movies shown in Big Piney were screened in "Dr. Hook's Picture Show," located on the second floor above the town drugstore.

3. Bison Theatre, Buffalo

The theatre opened on Buffalo's main street in 1917. It closed in 1984. The first theatre in town, however, was the Theatorium, opened in 1909.

4. Casper theaters

A "movie room" was set up in the Odd Fellows Building on the northwest corner of Second and Wolcott in 1908. The first films in town were shown there. The Bell Theater opened the next year, but burned on Jan. 8, 1912. The Iris Theatre was the first specifically designed to show films. It opened Aug. 22, 1912. The building was demolished in 1962. The first motion picture theater in town equipped to show "talking pictures" was the Rialto Theatre, built in 1921. The first sound film was shown in Casper at the Rialto in August, 1928. At the beginning of the 1920s, Casper had six movie theaters, but just three by 1930.

5. Atlas Theater, Cheyenne

The first "penny arcade" in Wyoming opened in the Atlas Theatre, Cheyenne, about 1907. The Atlas had been constructed in 1887 as a vaudeville theater. The name was changed to the Strand Theater in 1930 and sound films were first shown there that year. The Strand closed in 1946. The building was converted into the "Pink Pony" nightclub until it, too, closed in 1961. A decade later, the building was purchased by the Cheyenne Little Theatre Players. Placed on the National Register in 1973, the Little Theatre Players presented melodramas there each summer.

6. WYO Theatre, Cheyenne

Named the Princess Theatre and built for vaudeville, it opened May 29, 1918. Soon after, the theater was redesigned for showing films. In 1950, it reopened as the WYO Theater.

7. Paramount Theatre, Cheyenne

Designed by Cheyenne architect William Dubois, it first opened Aug. 26, 1905. Known as the Capitol Avenue Theater, the structure burned in 1915. Soon rebuilt, the name was changed to the Paramount and the theater was fitted for sound movies in 1930. A second fire damaged the Paramount in April 1981.

Robert Redford attended the reburial ceremonies for John "Jeremiah" Johnson whose body was reinterred at Old Trail Town near Cody June 8, 1974.

8. Lincoln Theatre, Cheyenne

The first sound movies in Cheyenne were shown at the Lincoln Theatre in early 1929.

9. Strand Theater, Evanston

Opened in 1918, the theater hosted vaudeville performers and other live entertainment along with serving as a movie theater. On May 7, 2007, the structure was destroyed by fire.

10. Hanna Opera House

Films, plays and musical programs were booked in the Hanna Opera House. Fire destroyed the building just one hour after the community Christmas program concluded in 1926.

11. Rainbow Palace, Jackson

The first sound movies in Jackson were shown there in 1931.

12. Root's Opera House, Laramie

The first movies in Laramie were shown in the building after owner Chauncey Root installed a screen and projection booth.

13. Empress Theater, Laramie

Opened in 1912, the theatre was remodeled in 1939 and renamed the Fox Theater, reopening Sept. 13, 1939. It closed in the 1970s, after operating briefly as an art theater. After years of neglect, the pigeon-infested structure was demolished in 2009 by the City of Laramie.

14. Wyo Theatre, Laramie

Built in 1925, the theatre was known as the Crown Theater until 1950 when it was renamed by a new owner.

15. Hyart Theatre, Lovell

The theater was built in 1950 by Lovell businessman Hy Bischoff and designed to seat an audience of up to 1,000 people. Bischoff's daughter Loretta operated the theater until 1992 when it was closed. In 2004, she sold the theater for $10 to a community group. The group refurbished the structure and it was officially reopened Nov. 13, 2004, with 900 people attending the feature film, Spider Man.

16. Lyric Theater, Powell

Built in 1919 as a vaudeville venue, the theater changed to silent films soon after it was opened. It was remodeled in 1948 and, again, in the middle 1990s.

17. Acme Theatre, Riverton

Belle Mote, a Riverton businesswoman, opened the theater in 1920.

18. Strand Theatre, Rawlins

Opened in 1921, the theater was remodeld in 1950 and the name was chnaged to the Fox Theater. It closed in 1984.

19. Star Theater, Rock Springs

The first movies shown in Rock Springs were screened at the Star, located on K Street and Pilot Butte Avenue. The building was razed in later years.

20. Wyo Theater, Sheridan

The WYO first opened in 1923 as the "Lotus" theatre. It closed in 1982. For next seven years, local people attempted to reopen it by raising popular subscriptions. Eventually, $1.2 million was raised and the art deco theater reopened on Nov. 10, 1989. Concerts, plays, and special performances are given there.

Sources: Theater files, Wyoming State Museum; Thomas G. Paul, Hollywood Grand: A Look at Wyoming's Movie Theaters. (Privately printed, 1988); newspaper clippings from a variety of newspapers.

MUSIC

1st piano in Wyoming: Mrs. Edwin Pierce brought a piano overland by ox team from Iowa to California in 1864. She stopped en route at South Pass on Aug. 29 and played her piano. Her diary noted, "It seemed good to hear it once more."

1st piano in Wyoming (brought specifically to be played in the state): The piano was ordered by Judge William A. Carter, post sutler at Fort Bridger.

1st organ installed in Wyoming: Congregational Church, Cheyenne, 1876.

1st Wyoming High School Music Festival held: 1936

1st ballet written about a Wyoming subject: *The Lynching of Cattle Kate*, written and choreographed by Patricia Tate and first performed at the University of Wyoming in June 1989. The work was the first ballet based on a Western subject since Aaron Copland's 1942 ballet "Rodeo."

1st bagpipes in Wyoming: Owned by Murray Noble, Rock Springs, 1891.

1st public concert by the Casper Symphony: February 1948, at NCHS.

Wyoming ranks 50th among the states in the number of composers and musicians living in the state. In 1990, they totaled just 73. California had 22,919.

Largest band to march in Rose Parade, Pasadena, Calif.: The 510-member Wyoming High School All-State Marching Band on Jan. 1, 2000, was the largest band to appear in the 111 years of the parade. Members represented 47 high schools.

"Wyoming" in Music

1. **"The Ballad of Nate and Nick"**
   The song was written and recorded in the 1950s by Burl Ives. It was the musical story of the Johnson County Invaders' attack on the KC ranch cabin and the murder of Nick Ray and Nate Champion.
2. **"Song of Wyoming"**
   Written and recorded by John Denver in the 1970s.
3. **"Hartville Rag"**
   A song played by fiddlers in Platte County using just one fiddle string.
4. **"We Are Wyoming"**
   The official state centennial song was recorded by Tom Stanko at the Mountain West Recording Studio in Thermopolis in 1989. The words and music were written by Stanko, Don Jackson and Ken Garrett.
5. **"The Old Double Diamond"**
   Written by Aspen, Colorado, composer Gary McMahon in 1970, the song is about the Dubois area ranch now known as the Thunderbird Ranch. McMahon lives in Colorado. His songs have been recorded by many Western artists.
6. **"Oh Why, Oh Why, Did I Ever Leave Wyoming?"**
   The words and music of the song were written by Morey Amsterdam.
7. **"Johnson County War"**
   The song about the 1892 incident was written by Chris LeDoux.
8. **"Ballad of the West"**
   The "epic ballad" was written and performed by Bobby Bridger, a Louisiana native who is a distant relative of mountain man Jim Bridger.
9. **"Do Drop In"**
   The Charlie Daniels tune referred to going to Wyoming via Omaha.
10. **"...through the badlands of Wyoming"**
    Line from Bruce Springsteen's song, "Nebraska," the title cut on his album.

Marian Anderson, the famous contralto, appeared in concert in February 1954, at the University of Wyoming.

11. "Wild Horses"

The Garth Brooks song included the phrase: "From a phone booth in Cheyenne/ I made a promise to Diane..."

12. "Wyoming A Hundred Years Ago"

Song written and performed by the Grizzlies for the first time in 1990.

13. "A Night in Wyoming"

Music by David Broza (b. Israel, 1955) and lyrics by Wyn Cooper, the song was sung by Broza on his album, "Stoned Doors," released in 1995.

14. "Women Gonna Be the Death of Me"

Country singer Ray Kennedy sings in the song from his album, "What a Way to Go," the line "I was waylaid by a widow from Wyoming..."

15. "The World's Greatest Rodeo"

The official song for the centennial of Cheyenne Frontier Days was written by Les Bowron and Ken Barbe. It was recorded in Casper Music's recording studio by Bowron, Barbe, dentist Kent Neubert and Pizza Hut manager Jim Henry. In 1996, Bowron retired from the legislature to pursue song-writing full-time. In 2010, he was living and working in Nashville. In June 2008, one of Bowron's songs was played on The Young and the Restless TV daytime serial.

16. "Yellowstone Coming Home"

The song was the last one written by John Denver before his death in an airplane crash off the California coast in 1997.

Some Noteworthy Musical Performances in Wyoming

1. Madame Ernestine Schumann-Heink's concert

The Wagnerian contralto sang before 6,000 people at the Wyoming State Fairgrounds in Douglas on July 4, 1924. The internationally known opera diva's performance was sponsored by the American Legion as a fund raising event for the construction of the Douglas airport.

2. New York Symphony Orchestra

The orchestra played at the Empress Theater in downtown Laramie on the evening of May 2, 1917. The concert opened with Overture to "Carneval" by Dvorak.

3. Neil Young's "Cheyenne Flood" benefit concert

When singer/songwriter Neil Young heard about the disastrous aftermath of the Aug. 1, 1985, Cheyenne flood in which 11 people died and many more were made homeless, he offered to perform at a benefit concert for the flood victims. His concert was given on Aug. 29, 1985. He was made an "honorary citizen" of Wyoming on Nov. 12.

4. Mannheim Streamroller's Yellowstone benefit concerts

The classical/New Age group from Omaha played a series of benefit concerts for the Yellowstone Library and Museum Association for helping the park recover from the disastrous fires of 1988. The group performed in Seattle on April 13, 1990, and elsewhere in the West during early 1990. The group also performed in Boston (July 10, 1991) and recorded an album called "Yellowstone."

5. Garth Brooks concerts

Brooks played to a packed house at the University of Wyoming Arena-Auditorium on June 5, 1992. He also performed in Casper and at Cheyenne Frontier Days. In a Dec. 11,

---

The John Philip Sousa band appeared in concert in Rock Springs for the first time on Oct. 13, 1904. The performance was in the Rock Springs opera house .

1999, interview on TNN, Brooks said performing at the 100th anniversary of Cheyenne Frontier Days was one of his greatest musical accomplishments.

6. "Winter Moons"

The musical written by Jarod Shaffer Tate and choreographed by Patricia Tate was performed statewide during 1992. Narrator for the ballet musical was Rodney Grant who played Wind in His Hair in the film, *Dances with Wolves*.

7. "Cello Festival"

The concert made up of 26 cellists was organized by UW visiting professor Darilyn Manring in November 1991. Playing to a full house at the University of Wyoming Concert Hall, it was the largest single-instrument cello concert ever held in Wyoming.

8. Centennial Singers

Established in 1986 by Bruce W. Bishop, the 30-member company had 15 singers. The group has conducted annual tours of the region, performing various musical programs. All participants were University of Wyoming students.

9. Fort Washakie Drum and Bugle Corps

Initially, 24 young Arapahoe and Shoshone men, aged 12-16, enrolled in the group formed in 1938. Later, another dozen joined the corps sponsored by the Women's Club of Fort Washakie. The first public appearance was in the Lander Fourth of July parade in 1938. The group performed at Cheyenne Frontier Days and for the National Convention of Elks Lodges in St. Louis in 1939.

10. Wyoming High School All-State Marching Band (1999)

The 510-member band represented 47 high schools from 68 communities in the state when it performed in the January 1, 2000, Rose Parade in Pasadena, Calif. It was the largest organized band to appear in the 111-year history of the event.

11. Hamilton Street Express

The 38-voice vocal jazz/gospel ensemble is made up of students in Converse County High School, Douglas. In 1992, the group won the Gold Microphone award, designating it as the "most outstanding high school vocal jazz ensemble" at Downbeat Magazine's National Musicfest in Oakland, Calif. The choir also won awards at numerous regional jazz festivals. Since 1992, the choral group has performed on tour in the Midwest and Northwest part of the country with nearly 150 performances in 14 states. Other high school choral groups also have gained national attention over the years, including high school choirs in Cody in the 1960s and 1970s.

12. Wyoming Gamelan

Balinese music can be heard at the concerts of the Wyoming gamelan. A gamelan is an orchestra of tuned percussion instruments: metallophones, gongs, kettle gongs and drums. The Wyoming gamelan, founded in 1996, is played by University of Wyoming students, faculty and community members, under the direction of Balinese gamelan master I Made Lasmawan and UW Professor Rod Garnett

Members of the 1st Univ. of Wyoming Orchestra, 1898

1. Ross Moudy	5. Harry Breitenstein	9. Harry Lee
2. John Frazee	6. Will Schilling	10. Hattie Fox
3. Charles Gilmore	7. Millie Thompson	11. Robert Merz
4. Harry Hanson	8. Prof. W. Merz	

On July 13, 2003, legendary singer/songwriter Bob Dylan performed in concert in Casper at the Casper Events Center. The Eagles performed there on May 26, 2004. One of the original members of the band, Randy Meisner, was born in Scottsbluff, Neb., in 1946. As a child, he lived for a time in Platte County, Wyoming.

Music Halls, Now....

1. Casper Events Center
Dozens of nationally known groups performed in the Events Center in the 1980s and 1990s. Among them were: Van Halen (October 1986), the Jets (June 7, 1988), Graham Nash (1984) and Bob Dylan (March 26, 2000).

2. Cheyenne Frontier Days
Night show performers have included Kenny Rogers, Willie Nelson, the Beach Boys (in 1988) and other top-name recording artists. Earlier, big bands played there, including Lawrence Welk in 1951.

3. Central Wyoming Fair, Casper
Usually, big-name acts highlight the evenings' entertainment. In 1976, Loretta Lynn sang at the fair.

4. Wyoming State Fairgrounds, Douglas
Nationally known musical groups have performed at the late summer fair. In 1989 the rock group Starship and country singer Charley Pride headlined.

5. University of Wyoming Arena-Auditorium
Numerous national groups have performed at the university, usually as part of the annual homecoming festivities each fall. One of the largest concerts featured country singer Garth Brooks on June 5, 1992. Elton John performed there in a benefit concert in support of legislation against hate crimes in June, 1999. He did an encore concert there a decade later.

6. University of Wyoming Concert Hall
Since its completion in the mid-1970s, the concert hall has been home to the University Orchestra.

7. Grand Teton Music Festival Hall, Teton Village
Internationally known composers and musicians have participated in the annual summer festival. In July 1989, the New York Philharmonic performed at four concerts in the hall.

8. University of Wyoming Arts and Sciences Auditorium
Built by the PWA during the depression era, the auditorium has hosted performances by groups which have included Zubin Mehta and the Los Angeles Philharmonic. In 1993, the university administration canceled a proposed concert by the Seattle "grunge" group, Pearl Jam, fearing the unruly reputation of the group's fans who had been known to damage concert sites.

9. Cheyenne Civic Center
Completed in 1981, the auditorium has a capacity of 1,496. Musical events, plays and lectures are performed in the facility. In 1989, the Wyoming centennial postage stamp was unveiled in ceremonies at the civic center. In 2007, the "Wyoming quarter" was officially introduced there by representatives of the United States Mint.

10. Cam-Plex Heritage Center, Gillette
Numerous musicians have appeared in concert in Cam-Plex since the structure opened, including Canadian singer Anne Murray on Oct. 12, 1992.

... and Then

1. Garden Spot Pavilion, Elk Mountain
The hotel hosted "big bands" in the 1930s and 1940s for weekend dances including Les Brown's band, Tommy Dorsey and Benny Goodman.

2. Cheyenne Opera House

Programs included numerous traveling opera and theater companies and such performers as Lily Langtry and Harry Lauder. Edwin Booth, the noted Shake-spearean actor and brother of presidential assassin John Wilkes Booth, appeared as Hamlet with a traveling company in the 1880s.

3. Cady Opera House, Sheridan

Touring musical groups in the late 19th century appeared in Sheridan at the Cady Opera House. Built in 1893, the third floor stage was destroyed by fire in 1906. A 1983 fire gutted the second floor. Once called the "Helvey Hotel," the building was restored in the 1980s.

4. Root's Opera House, Laramie

The theater later became a motion picture house, but in early-day Laramie, musical groups frequently appeared there. Other towns had similar "opera houses," including Evanston and Rawlins. Towns along the main line of the Union Pacific frequently attracted concerts from groups stopping off en route between performances on the West Coast and the East.

Some Wyoming Musicians
A Representative Sample in All Genres

1. Paul Arnoldi, Singer/Composer

The Laramie native wrote and recorded an album in the early 1980s called "Highroads." He attended Harvard in the 1960s and moved to Berkely, California, performing there in various venues. He moved to Montana in 2008.

2. John Perry Barlow, Composer

Barlow, born in Jackson in 1947, wrote lyrics for the San Francisco-based band, "The Grateful Dead." His credits include "The Music Never Stopped," a minor hit for the group in 1976. Barlow, a former rancher, lives in Pinedale and operates a national firm via computer hookups from his Pinedale headquarters. He is a co-founder of the Elecronic Froniters Foundation, a group advocating total internet independence. In July, 1999, he appeared on national television talking about his friend, John F. Kennedy, Jr., who died in an airplane crash. Young Kennedy once worked on Barlow's ranch. Barlow's father, Norm Barlow, was a state legislator, president of the State Senate and influential in the Republican party.

3. Spencer Bohren, Singer/Guitarist

Born in Casper in 1950, Bohren moved to New Orleans in the middle 1970s where he played what he called "New Blues," a form of jazz. He performed from Finland to Cody. His album, "Born in a Biscayne," was released in 1988. His 1989 recording, "Snap Your Fingers," was named album of the week in western France. Three of his CDs have been released in recent years--"Vintage," "Dirt Roads," and Carry the Word." Bohren has been called a "singer from the West who feels at home in the South." He and his family lived in New Orleans. Their family home suffered considerable damage in Hurricane Katrina.

4. Merrill Bradshaw, Composer/Arranger

Bradshaw, a professor of music at Brigham Young University, was born in Lyman in 1929. He wrote numerous instrumental works for orchestra, choral pieces, an oratorio and hymns.

Words from the writings of Tim Sandlin, Jackson Hole author known as the "literary voice of grunge," are included in song lyrics sung by Sonic Youth and Hole.

5. Neil Diamond, Singer

Diamond (b. Brooklyn, N.Y., Jan. 24, 1941), lived in Cheyenne for two years as a young boy. His father, Kieve Diamond, was stationed with the army at Fort Warren from 1945-47 and the family, including Neil and his younger brother, lived in Cheyenne. Neil remembered learning to ride a horse and aspiring to be a cowboy before his father's enlistment expired and the family returned to Brooklyn.

6. Theota (Sody) Clampett, Composer

Clampett, born in Buffalo in April 1931, wrote scores for television programs and cartoon shows, including the "Theme for Beany and Cecil." Her husband, Robert Clampett (b. San Diego, 1913, d. Detroit, 1984), was a pioneer in animation. Hee worked for Warner Brothers until he left in 1946 to start his own animation studio "Beany and Cecil," produced by his company, debuted in 1961 and ran on ABC for five years.

7. Ernest Hagen, Composer/Conductor

The long-time conductor of the Casper Symphony and instructor at Casper College also composed rhapsodies and opera works.

8. John Hagen, Musician

Formerly of Casper, Hagen toured with Lyle Lovett and his Large Band in 1992. A cellist, he appeared with Lovett on *Tonight Show* and *Late Night with David Letterman* (1992) and in such venues as Red Rocks (2006). He also appeared as cellist in the film *Bob Roberts* in 1992 and on albums since 1987. His father was Ernest Hagen *(above)*.

9. Paul Hanselmann, Composer/Director/Singer

Former director of choral music in Cody, Hanselmann managed the Chicago Opera House for several years. He later lived and worked in the Laramie area.

10. Marie Montabe Horton, Composer

A Nebraska native, Horton lived in Laramie where she wrote the pageant play, *Gift of the Waters*, presented annually at Thermopolis. She also wrote a number of songs.

11. Joseph Diamond, Composer/Singer/Instrumentalist

Born in Cheyenne in 1944, Diamond wrote for the Roger Wagner Chorale and for Walt Disney Productions. He wrote the *Juvenile Jury* theme, "My Trip Up to the Moon," and "Music is the Life I Sing."

12. Anne Guzzo

The Laramie-born composer holds the Ph.D. in theory-composition from the University of California, Davis, and teaches music composition and theory at the University of Wyoming. Her compositions have been played worldwide. Among her numerous other credits, she scored the Wyoming PBS series, *Wyoming Voices* (2005), a three-part documentary film on Wyoming history.

13. George W. Hufsmith, Composer

Hufsmith began composing music in 1939. Many of his compositions are orchestral and choral works, but his best known is *Lynching on the Sweetwater*, an opera he wrote for the Bicentennial in 1976 about Cattle Kate and Jim Averell. In 1993, he published a book on the lynching.

14. Don Jackson, Composer/Vocalist

A Thermopolis bank president and former state legislator, Jackson recorded his first album, *Hearts Shadow*, in 1986. The ten songs on the album range from country to rock and jazz. Five other Wyoming musicians accompanied Jackson on the album. He co-wrote *We Are Wyoming*, the official song of the state centennial in 1990. He published more than 300 songs, 60 of which have been recorded by other artists, including John Anderson, Charlie McCoy, Don King and the London Symphony Orchestra. He died in February 2009.

15. Jim Jones, Casper Trooper Founder

Jones started the drum and bugle corps in 1957. He served as director for 30 years.

Under his direction, the Casper Troopers won several national titles, performed at World Fairs and before two U. S. presidents. In 1972, he founded Drum Corps International, made up of the best 25 drum and bugle corps in the United States. It sets the standards and rules for drum corps competitions and trains judges. Jones died in June 1994.

16. George E. Knapp, Composer/Director

Knapp, a native of West Virginia, was director of music at the University of Wyoming for many years. As a composer, he was noted for many songs, including his arrangement of the Wyoming State Song.

17. Leo Kottke, Guitarist/Composer

Kottke, born in 1946, is well known for his guitar instrumentals. He recorded 15 albums between 1969, when he began his professional career, and 1990. During his childhood, he lived in 12 states. In elementary school, he attended Pioneer school in Cheyenne. He makes his home in St. Paul, Minn.

18. Chris LeDoux, Composer/Singer/Instrumentalist

LeDoux moved with his family to Cheyenne from Denison, Texas, when he was 15. He graduated from high school in Cheyenne and earned a rodeo scholarship to Casper College. He traveled the circuit as a professional rodeo cowboy and, in 1976, won the world title in bareback riding. When his rodeo career ended, he and his family moved to ranch near Kaycee. His music credits included "A Cowboy Like Me," "Too Tough to Die," and "What More Could a Cowboy Need." His story was told in a book on rodeoing, *Gold Buckle Dreams*, in 1987. He was nominated for a Grammy for the hit single duet with Garth Brooks, "Whatcha Gonna Do With a Cowboy?" as best country vocal collaboration. LeDoux, who recorded for Liberty, was featured on TNN on Feb. 8, 1993, cable network special "Chris LeDoux and Suzy Bogguss—Ropin' and Rockin'." He underwent surgery for a liver transplant in 2000 and died in Casper on March 9, 2005.

19. Darilyn Manring, Cellist

Manring, who studied music at Yale, taught cello at the University of Wyoming in the early 1990s and now teaches in Connecticut and performs professionally. She has appeared with a number of major orchestras. While teaching music at UW, she organized the largest all-cello orchestra in concert in state history.

20. Lesley Manring, Opera Singer

Lesley Manring (sister of Darilyn, above) sang opera in Germany for many years before returning to the United States. She teaches vocal music at the University of Northern Colorado. Father of the Manring sisters, Darryl, is, a Lusk native who taught music at Illinois State.

21. Beth McIntosh, Folk/Jazz Singer/Composer

She has released four albums. Her first, *Grizzlies Walking Upright*, was released in 1991. The contemporary folk/jazz musician was a resident of Wilson. Comfortable in all genres, she performed with many other musicians, including Emmylou Harris and Leo Kottke. In 2004, she studied Celtic music in Scotland and it has influenced her later work.

22. Gary Mascaro, Dance Choreographer

Born in Casper in 1949, Mascaro was an award-winning choreographer in Los Angeles at the time of his death Dec. 2, 1992.

23. Danny Rogers, Singer/Guitarist

Rogers and his brother Will formed a band in 1977 and by 1981, were touring the United States performing country music. After three years with the Saw Mill Creek band,

---

Singer John Denver was sued in October 1995 for a runway incident at the Jackson Hole Airport on May 31, 1994. The propeller of Denver's plane taxied into the side of a plane owned by David V. Coyle who sued Denver for "negligence" in the mishap.

the Rogers brothers formed their own band in 1990, naming it the Chugwater Band for their hometown. Rogers joined the Bar J Wranglers in Jackson in 2007.

24. Tom Rush, Singer/Songwriter

Rush (b. N.H., 1941), who lives in the Jackson area, gained famed in the 1960s as a folk singer/songwriter. *Rolling Stone* credited him for ushering in the "era of the singer-songwriter." In 1980, he formed his own independent record label, the first to be established by a musical performer. He was a central figure in the folk revival of the 1980s and 1990s. He performed the works and promoted the careers of friends including Joni Mitchell, Jackson Browne and James Taylor. In 2009, his 22nd album, "What I Know," was released. He moved to Wyoming in the 1980s.

25. Scott Schuele, Vocalist

A former Boy Scout in Sinclair, Schuele released an album in 1985. It held the top spot on the album charts in Germany for many months.

26. Maggie Simpson, Singer

Simpson's style ranges from acoustic folk to blues. She has released two studio albums, *OK Cafe* (1999) and *Angel of Thunder* (2004). Maggie is the daughter of Pete and Lynne Simpson of Laramie.

27. Jeff Troxel, Guitarist

Troxel, a native of Cody, won the U. S. Flatpick Guitar championship in 2003. A graduate of Berklee College of Music in Boston and the University of Southern California, he thas taught music at Northwest College and Central Wyoming College. He specializes in jazz and acoustic guitar. Troxel has recorded several albums and has written books on playing the guitar.

28. George B. Vest, Organist

Born in Sundance in 1888, Vest served for many years as the organist for the Pantages Theatre in San Francisco. Later, he was a noted circus organist. He died in Los Angeles in 1961.

29. Allan A. Willman, Concert Artist/Composer

From 1946 to 1974, Willman chaired the music department at the University of Wyoming. His compositions were performed by the Boston Symphony Orchestra, the Chicago Civic Orchestra and others. During his musical career, he worked as an arranger for CBS and NBC.

30. Lynn Wright, Episcopal Minister, Dubois

Wright was a professional musician before he entered the ministry in 1980. He wrote the song "Sweetwater" and recorded an album, "Lynn Wright from Wyoming," in 1987. He was Episcopal priest in Jackson and from 1993 to 2003, he played ragtime piano at the Silver Dollar Saloon in Jackson. In 2003 he retired to West Virginia.

Sources: Newspaper articles; biographical dictionaries; and Curtis Snook and David Tomatz, Wyoming Composers, A Bicentennial Review. (Laramie, 1976).

Noteworthy Annual Music Festivals in Wyoming

1. Grand Teton Music Festival

The annual festival attracts dozens of musicians and thousands of music lovers each summer. It began in 1961. Traditionally, the festival orchestra plays concerts on Fridays and Saturdays while Tuesday through Thursday, small ensembles perform. The season runs from late June to early August.

A Douglas man was blown off a hay wagon by high wind. He landed in a nearby river, suffering minor injuries, according to a story in the Lusk Herald, April 20, 1933."

2. Old Time Fiddle Contest

Shoshoni hosted the annual event for more than 30 years beginning in 1973, but the festival moved to Thermopolis where it continues to be held the last weekend in May. Fiddlers from throughout the country attend the summer festival. Bob Meredith served as emcee for the first 20 years of the event that attracts some 100 participants annually.

3. "Drums Along the Rockies"

The annual drum and bugle corps event was held in Casper in 1996 where it had originated 30 years before. The event was also hosted by Casper in 1989.

4. Western Arts Chamber Musical Festival

Originated by David Tomatz and Werner Rose, music professors at the University of Wyoming in 1972, the event was held annually at UW for many years.

5. State Music Festival

The annual event has been held for high school musicians since 1936.

6. Big Horn Mountain Festival

The festival, held annually in Buffalo, began in 2004. Featuring a variety of acoustic genres, primarily bluegrass, the festival commonly hosts the State Mandolin and Banjo championships.

7. Beartrap Summer Festival

The event, held annually on Casper Mountain, started in 1994. Commonly held in early August, the festival features bluegrass music.

8. Oyster Ridge Music Festival

The event was first organized in 1993 by Keith Chasteen, a Forest Service workers who wanted to find a home for the newly-created Wyoming State Flatpick Guitar champikonship. The State Fingerpick Contest was added in 1998. The free festival, held on the Triangle in downtown Kemmerer, attracts some 3,000 people and participants include nationally renowned guitarists.

Actor in Wyoming: Sammy Davis, Jr.

The late Sammy Davis, Jr., was one of the best known members of Hollywood's "rat pack." A child performer on Vaudeville, burlesque and night clubs since infancy, Davis was inducted into the army in 1943. He was stationed at Fort Warren near Cheyenne.

The experience, which included having to undergo basic training twice, had positive and negative aspects. He was influenced there by an African-American sergeant who gave him remedial reading lessons and lent him books. Previously, Davis, who grew up on the theater circuit, had read nothing but comic books. He also experienced bigotry, however. "I had scabs on my knuckles for the first three months in the Army," he wrote in his autobiography, *Yes I Can* (New York: Farrar, Strauss, 1965). Not specifically mentioned was the disturbance occurring on Christmas Eve, 1943, between Blacks and Whites in downtown Cheyenne.

Davis was not involved in the incident. For the remainder of his two years in the army, Davis directed and produced camp shows at army bases throughout the country, including at Fort Warren.

In *Roughing It*, Mark Twain paid the following compliment to the meal he ate at Green River station: "We had breakfast—hot biscuits, fresh antelope steaks, and coffee—the only decent meal we tasted between the United States and the Great Salt Lake, and the only one we were really thankful for..."

The Official University of Wyoming Song:

The Brown and Yellow by Dr. June E. Downey

Where the western lights long shadows
Over boundless prairies fling,
And the mountain winds are vocal
With thy dear name, Wyoming.
There it is, the brown and yellow
Floats in loving loyalty,
While the college throws its portals
Open wide to all men free.

Chorus:
And so our songs we bring,
Our Alma Mater sing,
To her our hearts shall cling,
Shall cling forever more.

"Cowboy Joe"

(More familiar than the official university song, "Cowboy Joe" is sung frequently during sports events at the university. Until recent years, freshmen were expected to know it before the first home football game of the season).

He always sings
Raggy music to the cattle
as he swings
back and forward in the saddle
on a horse--a pretty good horse!
He's got a syncopated gaiter
and you ought to hear the meter
to the roar of his repeater;
how they run-yes run!-

when they hear him a comin'
'cause the western folks all know
he's a high-falootin', rootin', tootin',
son-of-a-gun from ol' Wyoming,
Ragtime Cowboy,
Talk about your Cowboy,
Ragtime Cowboy Joe.
'C'! 'O'! 'W'! 'B'! 'O'! 'Y'! 'S'!
COWBOYS! COWBOYS!

Wyoming State Song

Lyrics by C. E. Winter Music by G. E. Knapp

1st verse: In the far and mighty West,
Where the crimson sun seeks rest,
There's a growing splendid State that lies above
On the breast of this great land;
Where the massive Rockies stand,
There's Wyoming young and strong, the state I love!
Chorus: Wyoming, Wyoming!
Land of the sunlight clear!
Wyoming, Wyoming!
Land that we hold so dear!
Wyoming, Wyoming!
Precious art thou and thine;
Wyoming, Wyoming!
Beloved state of mine!

Singer Johnny Cash performed several times in Wyoming, including in a concert at UW on Oct. 7, 1973. In his life story, Cash told of riding into Wyoming from Colorado while his wife June drove the car. As they passed the stateline south of Cheyenne, Cash was inspired to write the song, "Over the Next Hill" that he finished in the few minutes it took before they stopped in Cheyenne.

NAMES
Most Popular First Names in Wyoming*

2009		1994:		1979:		1969:	
Boys:	**Girls**	**Boys**	**Girls**	**Boys**	**Girls**	**Boys**	**Girls**
Wyatt	Isabella	Austin	Ashley	Michael	Jennifer	Michael	Michelle
William	Madison	Jacob	Emily	Jason	Amanda	Robert	Lisa
Aiden	Ava	Tyler	Jessica	Joshua	Melissa	John	Kimberly
Jacob	Emma	Michael	Amanda	Christopher	Heather	James	Melissa
Mason	Alexis	Joshua	Samantha	David	Sarah	David	Jennifer
Noah	Elizabeth	Christopher	Taylor	John	Jessica	Scott	Amy
Hunter	Addison	Zachary	Megan	James	Michelle	Brian	Julie
Logan	Olivia	Matthew	Brittany	Matthew	Amber	Jason	Mary
James	Abigail	Brandon	Kayla	Ryan	Amy	Jeffrey	Christine
Brayden	Taylor	Cody	Sarah	Robert	Crystal	Richard	Stephanie

2004		1989:		1974:		1964	
Boys:		**Boys**	**Girls**	**Boys**	**Girls**	**Boys**	**Girls**
Michael	Madison	Michael	Jessica	Jason	Jennifer	John	Lisa
Hunter	Emma	Christopher	Ashley	Michael	Heather	David	Mary
Jacob	Alexis	Kyle	Sarah	Christopher	Amy	Michael	Tammy
Ethan	Elizabeth	Joshua	Amanda	Robert	Stephanie	Robert	Brenda
Joshua	Hannah	Mathew	Brittany	John	Angela	James	Susan
Ryan	Abigail	Tyler	Jennifer	James	Michelle	Mark	Laura
Alexander	Emily	David	Samantha	David	Kimberly	William	Karen
Logan	Taylor	Andrew	Elizabeth	Brian	Mary	Scott	Julie
Tyler	Grace	Jacob	Danielle	Matthew	Tina	Richard	Lori
Wyatt	Ashley	Daniel	Kayla	Justin	Melissa	Kevin	Linda

1999:		1984:	
Boys:	**Girls:**	**Boys**	**Girls**
Michael	Taylor	Michael	Jennifer
Austin	Hannah	Matthew	Jessica
Tyler	Madison	Christopher	Amanda
Joshua	Emily	Joshua	Ashley
Jacob	Samantha	Ryan	Sarah
Ryan	Elizabeth	David	Heather
Cody	Sierra	Justin	Stephanie
James	Alexis	Daniel	Nicole
Matthew	Ashley	James	Amber
William	Brianna	John	Megan

* Most numerous baby names for children born in Wyoming. Absolute numbers are fairly small. For instance, to gain most popular for 2009, "Wyatt" was given to 42 babies and Isabella to 36. Michael, 1st in 2004, slipped to 27th in 2009. Hannah, number 5 in 2004, fell to 18th in 2009. **Source:** *Social Security Administration, "Popular Baby Names"*

Nicknames of Some Well-Known Wyoming People

1. "The man without a hat"

The nickname was given to Cheyenne news photographer Francis Brammer by humorist Will Rogers. Brammer, *Wyoming Eagle* photographer for a half century, shot pictures in all weather. Even on the coldest days, he never wore a hat. He once told a *Capitol Times* reporter that he had quit wearing the hat years before Rogers gave him the nickname. He was rabbit hunting and he shot a small brown-eyed bunny. Bram said the rabbit, as it lay dying, gave him a look as if to say, "Why?" He removed his hat and he said he cried. He left it there and vowed never to replace it--or shoot a gun again.

2. "The last hired gun"

Range detective Ed Cantrell was given the nickname by writer James Conaway in an article by that title in *Harpers*, August 1987.

3. "White robe"

The name was given to the Rev. John Roberts, Episcopal priest on the Wind River Indian Reservation from 1883-1929. Native American parishioners gave him the nickname.

4. "The extremely tall senator and the equally bald senator"

Nicknames given to Senators Al Simpson and Malcolm Wallop by the *Casper Star-Tribune*'s irreverent columnist Dan Gearino in 1986.

5. "Wyoming's Mr. Big"

Newspaper publisher Tracy S. McCraken, so nicknamed by *Time* magazine in a 1954 story. McCraken, owner of a chain of Wyoming newspapers, was a powerful figure in state politics. For many years, he was a leader of the Democratic Party in Wyoming.

6. "Mr. Republican"

Newspaper publisher J. B. Griffith, Sr., of Lusk, who was in some respects, the Republican counterpart of the Democrats' McCraken. Like McCraken, Griffith never served in an elective office, although he was commissioner of public lands from 1939 to 1943. Some years after the elder Griffith's death, his son, James B. Griffith, Jr., served as state treasurer and state auditor.

7. "The Grand Old Men"

Joseph M. Carey, Francis E. Warren and John B. Kendrick, so called by historian T. A. Larson. All three men served terms as governor of Wyoming and in the U. S. Senate. They were the main political figures in the first 40 years of statehood.

8. "The Great Sagebrush Senator"

Nickname applied to Sen. John B. Kendrick (b. Texas, 1857; d. Nov. 6, 1933) by Wyoming admirers who respected his attention to Wyoming issues.

9. "The Builder"

University of Wyoming President Arthur Griswold Crane, so nicknamed because of the new campus structures built during his tenure from 1922 to 1941.

10. "The Marlboro Man"

Darrell Winfield, Wyoming rancher, was among those who posed for the popular cigarette commercials in the 1970s.

11. "Boom, Boom"

Sportswriters applied the nickname to University of Wyoming football halfback Eddie Talboom. In 1950, he was UW's first All-American selection. After a career as a coach and in business, Tallboom moved to Florida where he died in 1998.

1 2. "The Gentleman Bandit" and "The White-Masked Bandit"

Bill Carlisle, who robbed four trains in Wyoming from 1916 to 1919, was so nicknamed by newspapers when it was disclosed that the robber, whose identity was then unknown, robbed only men on the trains. The white-masked bandit allowed women to keep their money, rings and other valuables. After capture and years in prison (and one unsuccessful escape), Carlisle was released and pardoned. He moved to Laramie and began operating a motel on the southwest corner of 30th and Grand, where the present Aspen Square is located. Carlisle died in Pennsylvania in 1964.

13. "Sundance Kid"

Nickname for Sundance resident Harry Longabaugh, a late 19th century minor outlaw. He spent time in the Crook County Jail for theft early in his life. His greatest fame came with release of the film, *Butch Cassidy and the Sundance Kid.*

14. "The man in the barrel"

Name self-applied by Harry Yesness, Casper clothier. The nickname began with an Elks initiation in which Yesness was required to walk down Center Street clad only in a barrel. A fountain in the shape of a man in a barrel occupied a prime spot on the sidewalk in front of his store for many years.

15. "Cheap John"

Lost Springs merchant in the early part of the century who never washed his shirt. He claimed the cost of laundering it, ten cents, exceeded the price for a new one.

16. "Uncle Pete"

The name applied by employees and others to the Union Pacific Railroad, sometimes affectionately and other times, derisively.

17. "Iron Jaw" Lewis

Teamster on the Salt Creek-Casper route in the first decade of the century, perhaps so called because of his conversational abilities or his ability to take a punch in the chin.

18. "Post Hole Jack"

Name given to Jack McGrath, manager of the B. B. Brooks ranch near Casper in the early part of the century. Brooks told his manager he would be gone ten days and he expected McGrath to dig post holes until he returned. Brooks, however, was delayed and did not return until three weeks later. He found McGrath following instructions, still digging postholes!

19. "Mohawk Dutchman"

President Theodore Roosevelt applied the name to rancher R. S. Van Tassell in 1908. A wealthy cattleman well past 80 years old, Van Tassell accompanied Roosevelt on his famous ride from Laramie to Cheyenne. The tiny Niobrara County town is named for him.

20. "Buffalo Bill"

The most famous nickname applied to any Wyomingite, "Buffalo Bill" was applied to William F. Cody after 18 months from 1867-1868 when he supplied buffalo meat to workers on the Kansas Pacific Railroad. During the period, Cody killed 4,280 buffalo.

21. "Pahaska"

The Indians called William F. Cody "Pahaska" or "Yellow Hair." In later years, Cody applied the name to his lodge, Pahaska Teepee, at the east gate of Yellowstone.

22. "MOM"

Name applied to Leslie A. Miller, Joseph C. O'Mahoney and Tracy McCraken, frequent dining companions at the Plains Hotel in Cheyenne in the 1930s. The three men, governor, U. S. Senator and publisher respectively, were leaders in the Democratic Party in Wyoming during the New Deal.

23. "Great American nail picker"

Nickname Democrats applied to Francis E. Warren, meant derisively. When Warren first came to Cheyenne, he offered to chop wood for A. R. Converse on the site of the wealthy banker's new home. Warren finished the task and then picked up nails around the house. When Warren campaigned, he spoke often of the incident with pride, prompting the Democrats' nickname, a take-off on Lincoln's nickname of "rail-splitter."

24. "Blanket"

The Indian name for "Old Gabe"—Jim Bridger. The origin of the nickname is unknown. Other trappers called Bridger the "Old Man of the Mountains" even though Bridger was just 30 years old when he was given the name.

25. "Jerky Bill"

Nickname given to Douglas cowboy who some writers have called the greatest bronc rider ever. He rode with Buffalo Bill's Wild West Show to Europe and elsewhere in the 1880s. Physically handicapped by cerebral palsy, Bill was not deterred from performing riding tricks and riding bucking broncs. As editor W. S. Kimball wrote: "He was the most rhythmically graceful figure on a desperately bucking horse I have ever known, and could do more stunts and with greater ease."

The former secretary to Hawaii's Queen Liliuokalani became an insurance agent in Laramie in 1895.

26. "Persimmon Bill"

Nickname of outlaw Bill Chambers. After stealing horses from the Indians, Chambers killed and robbed an army officer who was sent to return him to justice. An entire army company gave chase, but Bill eluded them. He continued to rob stagecoaches along the Cheyenne-Deadwood route and led a gang of horse thieves who lived along the Cheyenne River.

27. "Shadow Catcher"

Nickname given to famed photographer Edward S. Curtis, who spent a lifetime photographing Indians of the West.

28. "Tie-Down" Brown

The nickname was given to the Worland area rancher because of his ability tying down and branding neighbors' cattle—for himself. Tie-Down Flats, 12 miles south of Worland, is named for him.

29. "Preaching Lime"

Name for Lime Huggins, an early-day Kemmerer bartender who claimed patrons of his bar could drink and then "repent from sinning and get the whole thing over at once."

30. "Soapy Dale"

Tie-drive foreman on the Medicine Bow River in the 1880s. He gained the nickname after being held in a small-town jail. Officials forgot he was there. The only "edible" item in his cell was a bar of soap. "Soapy" became so hungry that he had eaten the soap by the time officials "remembered" him.

31. "Butch" Cassidy

Robert Leroy Parker's nickname, gained in 1892 for his brief stint as a butcher in a Rock Springs meat shop. He adopted the last name of Cassidy from a boyhood influence, rustler Mike Cassidy. Some sources indicate that Cassidy was the name of his employer at the Rock Springs butcher shop.

32. "Happy Jack"

Jack Hollingsworth hauled wood for the Union Pacific in 1865. He lived along the right-of-way, west of Cheyenne along present-day "Happy Jack Road." He was there when the railroad came through. It is said that he "laughed a lot." A Casper lawman in the early 20th century was also known as "Happy Jack."

33. "Cattle Kate"

Nickname given to lynching victim Ella Watson by Cheyenne newspapers after her death. The 170-lb. woman was lynched along the Sweetwater River with companion James Averell in 1889, when she was just 27 years old.

34. "Wyoming's historian"

Title earned by Dr. T. A. Larson (b. Jan. 18, 1910, Wakefield, Nebr., d. Jan. 26, 2001, Santa Ana, Calif.), author of the definitive history of Wyoming (1965, 1977) and professor of history at the University of Wyoming from 1936-1976. Following his retirement, Larson was elected to the Wyoming legislature, serving from 1977-85.

35. "Dad"

Nickname for C. H. Worland, founder and first resident of Worland. He operated a store which began in a dugout in the side of the Big Horn River bank before there was a town on the site.

36. "Voice of the Cowboys"

For many years the nickname was applied to sportscaster Larry Birleffi (b. Hartville, 1918, d. Cheyenne, September 2008), who covered University of Wyoming sports events, calling every UW football and basketball game from 1947 to 1986 . In recent years, Dave Walsh holds the distinction.

The Sheridan Elks Lodge, chartered in 1900, is the oldest in the state.

37. "Mr. University"
Nickname of Ralph McWhinnie (b. near Douglas, 1898) who served as registrar at the University of Wyoming from 1920 until his retirement in 1963. McWhinnie died Nov. 6, 1995.

38. "Fiddler Joe"
Mexican herdsman Joe Hurtado spoke little English, but he often walked about the streets of Lander with his fiddle and bow under his arm. During conversations, he would illustrate a point by playing his violin. He also was known as "Tornado Joe."

39. "Woodbox Jim"
Nickname of J. W. Evans, Gillette's first city marshal, the name was applied when he was a cowboy for the 4J ranch. One night, he drank excessively and in a drunken stupor, fell into the woodbox.

40. "Bear"
Ten Sleep area pioneer rancher George "Bear" McClellan gained his nickname because he loved to hunt bears and then tell wild stories about his adventures hunting them. The Canadian-born rancher was sometimes referred to as "Bear George."

41. "Suspender Jack"
The nickname of John McGee, a former rider with Buffalo Bill's Wild West show, who returned to his native New York about 1900 to work as a city policeman and, later police administrator. He was a strong supporter of Theodore Roosevelt and made speeches throughout the Northeast in 1912 for Roosevelt's Progressive (Bull Moose) Party.

Some Wyoming Place Nicknames

1. "Oil Capital of the Rockies" — Casper

2. "Magic City of the Plains" — Cheyenne
Charles V. A. Arnold, editor of the *Leader*, applied the name in 1867.

3. "Gem City of the Plains" — Laramie
The name apparently was originated by James Hayford, Laramie editor in the late 19th century.

4. "Garden City" — Basin
The name originated with an active tree and shrub planting campaign begun by the city in 1910.

5. "City of Roses" — Lovell
Lovell gained its nickname, the "Rose City," from the rose parks at each end of town. Lovell's "Rose Doctor," Dr. W. W. Horsley, began the plantings. He came to Lovell in 1924 and practiced medicine for 45 years. An expert on roses, he was president of the American Rose Society for 12 years and Lovell parks director for 31 years.

6. "Apple City" — Lander (also "Push Root City")

7. "Switzerland of America" — Star Valley

Fred "Jeep" Molnar (b. 1937) was given his nickname at birth, three years before Willys-Overland began building its famous Jeep in 1940. Nonetheless, in February 1989, Chrysler Corporation, who acquired the "Jeep" with its acquisition of American Motors in 1987, threatened to sue Molnar for using the name "Jeep's Bar and Restaurant" on signs at the establishment he had run for 15 years in Alpine, a town of less than 100 people in western Wyoming. The company claimed Molnar was violating federal trademark law by using "Jeep" in the name. Molnar refused the company's ultimatum. Chrysler reluctantly backed down, agreeing that Molnar could continue using the name.

NATIVE AMERICANS

1st reservation created in Wyoming: Wind River Reservation, under the terms of the Fort Bridger Treaty, July 3, 1868, signed by General William T. Sherman for the government, Chief Washakie and Narkok, a war chief, for the Shoshones.

1st Arapahos on the Wind River Reservation: In 1878, the U. S. Army escorted 900 Northern Arapahos to the reservation to take up "temporary" residence there.

Controversy over joint occupation of Wind River reservation: After years of complaints from Chief Washakie, who had given permission for the "temporary placement" of Arapahoes on what was then called the Shoshone reservation, the federal government finally admitted the placement wasn't "temporary." In 1891, the U. S. government asserted that the Arapahoes actually had equal right to the land. In the 1920s, the U. S. Court of Claims awarded the Shoshones $2,050,000, but allowed offsets so that total to the tribe was just $793,000. After more years of controversy and extensive litigation, n January 1937 the U. S. Supreme Court awarded judgment to Shoshones for sharing the lands of the Wind River reservation with the Araphaoes. The Supreme Court ordered a new trial over damage amounts in Court of Cliams. The Shoshone tribe eventually received a cash settlement in the matter in 1939, the reservation was renamed "Wind River reservation" and the Arapahoes received a cash settlement from which a portion was used to purchase Arapaho Ranch.

First woman elected to Shoshone council. Mrs. Mary Mead, daughter of Napoleon Kinnear, elected in Feb. 1935. Her mother was Shoshone. Mead, a teacher on the reservation, graduated from UW.

Area and population: The Wind River Reservation has an area of 2.3 million acres and an estimated population of about 8,000.

1st casino on Wind River reservation: In July 2005, the 10th Circult Court of Appeals ruled for the Arapaho tribe in a case against the State of Wyoming where the State, in 2000, sued to stop the tribe from opening a casino.. The Arapaho tribe's first casino opened soon after in what was called the 789 Bingo and Casino. On April 29, 2008, the tribe's new modern casino opened south of Riverton. Little Wind Casino also was opened by the tribe.

1st Shoshone casino: Shoshone Rose Casino, opened in Sept. 2007.

Primary Tribes Once Occupying Wyoming

1. Arapaho

They probably subsisted on farming in the Red River Valley of present-day Minnesota until the Sioux forced them southwest across the Missouri River. They formed a permanent alliance with the Cheyenne who also were pushed west by the Sioux. Later, the Arapaho divided into two groups. The Southern Arapaho drifted south while the Northern Arapaho stayed in what is now southeast Wyoming where they were living at the time of White exploration. Their name probably derives from what the Cheyenne called them, "blue cloud men." They called themselves "our people."

2. Blackfeet

The tribe occupied northwestern Wyoming around 1800. Thousands died in epidemics in 1781, 1837 and 1869. The worst was in 1837 when two-thirds of the population of 9,000 died of disease. After the early 19th century, the remaining Blackfeet in Wyoming migrated north to join fellow tribesmen in Montana.

3. Cheyenne

The Cheyenne occupied the northern portion of Wyoming until about 1832 when a large part of the tribe moved south to the Arkansas River area of Colorado. The remaining group, known as the Northern Cheyennes, were rounded up by the army after the Custer defeat in 1876 and forced to move south to share a reservation with their southern cousins. The conditions were so terrible that two years later, Little Wolf and Dull Knife led 300 Cheyennes north 1,500 miles to their homeland. *(See Dull Knife, p. 330).* Finally, after continued army harassment, the Indians were allowed to stay in 1884.

4. Crow

At the time of the first White exploration into Wyoming, the Crow dominated the northeast and central portions of what is now the state. They had come to the region about 1500 from the northeast. Known as the Absarokas ("bird people"), they were famous for their flamboyant horsemanship and distinctive clothing designs using porcupine quills. They remained generally on peaceful terms with the Whites. Many served as army scouts during the "Sioux wars" era because the tribe had been ancestral enemies of the Sioux.

5. Kiowa

The Kiowa once occupied the Black Hills area on the Wyoming-South Dakota border at the time of the first white explorations in the early 1700s. In the late 18th century, they were displaced by the Sioux and the Cheyenne.

6. Shoshone

The Shoshone (also spelled Shoshoni) tribe arrived in what is now Wyoming about 1400. They came into the area from the southwest and by the early 18th century, they had horses, earlier than any other Wyoming area tribe. These Eastern Shoshones are a relatively small branch of a much larger tribe which occupied much of the Great Basin ranging as far north as Montana. Many early travelers identified them as "Snakes" because in sign language, they were identified by a serpentine motion of the hand, index finger extended. The early explorers misunderstood that the correct translation was "grass lodges" or "grass house people."

7. Sheepeaters

The main occupiers of Yellowstone during the historic period, they had a population of no more than 400 by the end of the 18th century. Actually, they were a small Shoshone branch, so called by other Shoshones because of their diet of sheep. Togwatee, who guided Sheridan in 1882, was a Sheepeater. The Yellowstone group was banned from the park following the "Sheepeater War" of 1879. It was fought mostly in Idaho.

8. Sioux

The Sioux (Lakota) were formerly woodlands people who occupied lands in northern Minnesota until they began migrating southwest in the 18th century. By 1765, they had displaced the Kiowa and Cheyenne in the Black Hills. In 1822, they joined the Cheyenne in driving out the Crow from eastern Wyoming north of the North Platte. The tribe consisted of seven major divisions, three of which resided in what is now Wyoming. The Oglala were the best known. Crazy Horse and Red Cloud were principal leaders of this sub-tribe. Spotted Tail led the Brule Sioux, the second largest sub-group. Sitting Bull was a Hunkpapa Sioux, from the third largest sub-group.

Tribal Populations

Tribe	1800	1980	
Cheyenne	3,500	3,000	
Crow	4,000	5,000	
Arapaho	6,000	3,700 (Northern)	3,000 (Southern)
Gros Ventre	2,500	3,000	
Eastern Shoshone	2,000	3,000	
Sioux (total)	25,000	40,000 (in 7 divisions)	
Oglala		3,600	5,000
Hunkpapa		2,900	5,000
Brule		3,000	8,000

"Wyoming on My Mind" sung by Charlie Daniels was the Western Music Association's song of the year in 1999.

Some Significant Native Americans in Wyoming's Past

1. Black Bear (Waltoma), Northern Arapaho

He was a principal chief of the Northern Arapahos and played a prominent role in the Indian wars in Wyoming. In 1868, he signed the Fort Laramie treaty, but two years later, he was killed by white miners. CC

2. Black Coal, Northern Arapaho

He was called Tag-ge-tha-the (Shot-off-fingers) because of his three missing fingers. Born in 1843, he became head chief after the death of Medicine Man in the winter of 1871-1872. He was wounded in the Bates Battle (Battle of Snake Mountain) on July 4, 1874, when American soldiers and their Shoshoni allies attacked his village. He served as a scout with General Crook's expedition against the Sioux in 1876 and went to Washington in 1877 as part of a delegation to request that the Northern Arapahos be allowed a reservation in their Wyoming homeland. Black Coal was one of the first Arapahos to convert to Catholicism. He encouraged younger Arapahos to learn new ways, sent his son to boarding school, and earned praise as the "hidden hero of the Rockies" from the Rev. John Roberts, whom he helped to establish a government school. When Black Coal died in 1893, the Arapahos erected a stone obelisk "in honor of a brave and honest man." CC

3. Black Elk, Sioux

Born in the Powder River basin in December 1863, Black Elk was reared in northeast Wyoming until the death of Crazy Horse in 1877 prompted his family to flee with Sitting Bull to Canada. From the age of nine, Black Elk knew he had "mystical powers." He discovered it when he became very ill and lay unconscious for several days. During that time, he had visions of what he and his people would face in coming years. As time passed, he became recognized as an important mystic and medicine man. He returned to Wyoming in the 1880s and met William F. Cody. He accompanied Buffalo Bill to Europe with the Wild West Show, appearing before Queen Victoria and other notables. In 1932, he told his story to writer John Neihardt who published the book, *Black Elk Speaks: The Life Story of a Holy Man of the Oglala Sioux.* He died in 1950.

4. Sherman Coolidge, Northern Arapaho

His Arapaho name was E-tus-ch-wa-ah (Swiftest Runner). He was captured as a child when Americans attacked Chief Black Coal's camp in 1870. An army surgeon named the boy "William Tecumseh Sherman," and when Capt. Charles A. Coolidge adopted him, he became known as Sherman Coolidge. He received an education in white schools, graduated from Seabury Divinity Schools and was ordained in 1884. He assisted the Rev. John Roberts at the Episcopal mission on the Shoshone (later Wind River) reservation from 1884 until he left the reservation in 1910. Coolidge was a founding member of the Society of American Indians in 1911. His white wife, Grace, wrote a novel, *Teepee Neighbors*, based on her experiences on the reservation. CC

5. Crazy Horse

Born in the Powder River country about 1841, Crazy Horse was the son of an Oglala medicine man and a grandson of Spotted Tail, the Brule chief. He participated in all of the major battles against the army, including Red Cloud's war and the Fetterman fight. Despite his fearless attacks against often insurmountable odds, he was never wounded, confirming his belief that as long as he wore a red hawk feather, he would never be in

The Arapaho tribe opened the first casino in Wyoming shortly after the 10th Circuit Court of Appeals struck down the State of Wyoming's ban on such an opening in 2005. Two years later, the Shoshone tribe also opened a casino on the reservation.

danger. When Red Cloud retired, Crazy Horse took over the leadership of the warriors who raided surveying parties and attacked Crook's forces in March 1876 and three months later at the Battle of the Rosebud. Crazy Horse and Gall led the attack on Custer's forces in the Battle of the Little Bighorn. The army pursued Crazy Horse's forces until May 1877, when he surrendered with about 1,000 Indians. After several listless months on the reservation, Crazy Horse went to Spotted Tail Agency. He was coaxed into returning in September 1877, taken prisoner at Fort Robinson, Neb., and killed when he appeared to be attempting an escape.

6. Dull Knife, Northern Cheyenne

Born near the Rosebud about 1810, Dull Knife was so named because in combat with an enemy Indian carrying a buffalo hide shield, his knife could not pierce it. Dull Knife and Little Wolf led the Northern Cheyenne on their 1,500-mile return from the Indian territory in the fall of 1878. A signer of the 1868 Fort Laramie treaty, Dull Knife thought he and his people could remain in their home territory in what is now eastern Wyoming. After the Custer fight, however, the army forced their removal to what is now Oklahoma and, following two years of hardship, he and Little Wolf led 300 Cheyenne north toward home. They managed to elude 10,000 soldiers for most of the journey, but eventually, most were captured and sent to Fort Robinson, Neb., for processing back to Oklahoma. Dull Knife led an escape from the fort and took refuge with the Sioux. They did not succeed in escaping completely, but on their recapture, they were sent to their own reservation in the Rosebud Valley. Dull Knife died in 1883.

7. Herbert Burwell Fowler

Born in Cheyenne in 1919, Fowler graduated from the University of Wyoming in 1942. Four years later, he received his M.D. degree from the University of Michigan. He returned to the West where he pioneered mental health programs among Native Americans. He died suddenly in 1977 in Portland, Oregon, just before he was to receive an award for the significant work he had done for his native people.

8. Friday, Northern Arapaho

In 1831, an Arapaho boy named Warshinun who had been separated from his tribe was found by Thomas Fitzpatrick. Fitzpatrick called the boy Friday (the day of the week he found him) and took him back to St. Louis. There, Friday attended school and lived among whites for several years, becoming fluent in English. When he returned to his people, he fulfilled an important role as an interpreter and intermediary in the Arapahos' increasing dealings with the United States. As military conflicts escalated, Friday argued for peace and he consistently tried to maintain amicable relations with the Americans. He served as a scout for General Crook in the 1876 campaign against the Sioux. The next year, he accompanied the Northern Arapaho delegation to Washington, D. C., in an attempt to secure a reservation for the tribe in Wyoming. He died in 1881. CC

9. Hollow-Horn Bear, Sioux

Born in Nebraska in 1850, Hollow-Horn Bear was a Sioux chief who led the forces against Fort Phil Kearny in 1866 and the attack on Capt. William Fetterman's troops near there. In 1873, he went onto the reservation with Spotted Tail and by 1880, he was an official of the Indian Police on the Rosebud Reservation. He arrested Crow Dog for the murder of Spotted Tail in 1881. A primary Sioux spokesman in the 1880s, he died of pneumonia in 1913. Eleven years later, his likeness appeared on a 14-cent stamp.

10. Hump, Sioux

Born in 1848, he joined with Hollow-Horn Bear in leading the attack on Captain Fetterman's troops in 1866. A decade later, he led his own warriors against Custer and Crook. In the 1880s, he fled to Canada, but returned in time to warn his people against participating in the "ghost dance." He died in 1908.

11. Iron Tail, Sioux

The Oglala Sioux war chief was named when his mother saw hunters chasing buffalo and the animals' tails stood upright as though made of pieces of iron. After fighting Indians and whites, Iron Tail became friends with William F. Cody in the 1880s and went to Europe with the Wild West Show. James Earle Fraser, designer of the "Indian head" nickel, used Iron Tail as one of three models for the coin. Iron Tail contracted pneumonia in Philadelphia and, knowing he was close to death, elected to return to his homeland to die. Iron Tail died on a train in Indiana, en route to the Black Hills.

12. Chief Joseph, Nez Perce

Chief Joseph led 750 of his people on a 1,500-mile trek on an unsuccessful attempt to escape from reservations. His party came within 40 miles of reaching a safe haven in Canada, but army troops surrounded them and he was forced to surrender Oct. 5, 1877. "I will fight no more forever," he purportedly told the soldiers. He returned to the Colville reservation in Washington where he died in 1904 at the age of 72. The 1877 journey took Chief Joseph's Nez Perce through Yellowstone National Park, into Sunlight Basin and to Montana. Dead Indian Hill east of Sunlight Basin is named for one of Chief Joseph's warriors whose body was found there.

13. Plenty Coups, Crow

Primarily associated with southern Montana where he was born in 1849, Plenty Coups scouted with Crook against the Sioux in 1876. He was one of the first of his people to turn to agriculture and when he died in 1932, he deeded his home in Pryor, Montana, to the U. S. Government. He became principal chief of the Mountain Crow in 1904.

14. Red Cloud, Sioux

Born Sept. 20, 1822, on the North Platte River, Red Cloud was named for the fiery meteorite which hit in the vicinity on the day of his birth. A non-hereditary chief of the Sioux, Red Cloud gained his position by his intrepid feats against other tribes. In the 1860s, he led the Sioux who closed down the Bozeman Trail to white traffic. He led the Sioux forces against Fort Phil Kearny and in the so-called Fetterman Fight. In 1868, he was induced to agree to the Fort Laramie treaty which promised no white incursions into the Sioux hunting grounds. Consequently, he did not participate in the Little Bighorn battle against Custer. Because of his policy of acquiescence, he was removed as chief in the 1880s. Blind and sick, he died in 1909 on the Pine Ridge reservation.

15. Sacajawea (b. 1784, d. 1812? 1884?)

Born a Shoshone in the Rockies (probably Wyoming), Sacajawea was captured by the Crows at the age of 12 and sold to the Hidatsa on the Missouri River in present-day North Dakota. She was then sold to fur trapper Toussaint Charbonneau who later took her as one of two wives. In 1804, Lewis and Clark hired Charbonneau as a guide. He took his wife and young son Baptiste along. During the course of the journey, Sacajawea became an important intermediary between the explorers and the native population. At one point, she was reunited with her brother, a Shoshone chief who initially posed a danger to the party. Sacajawea accompanied the party to the Pacific, arriving there on Nov. 7, 1805, and returned with the Manual Lisa party to the Upper Missouri. Sacajawea's death remains a matter of controversy. Some sources believe she died in 1812. (Clark's diary indicates this was the case). Others contend she changed her name to Porivo and lived on the Wind River reservation until her death at nearly 100 years old.

16. William Shakespeare, Arapaho

Born on Wind River reservation, his original name was "Strikes Again," but it was changed when he attended St. Stephens Mission as a youth. Later, he attended school at Carlisle, Penn., and Haskell Institute in Kansas. After service in World War I in Europe, Shakespeare appeared for more than three decades in motion pictures. He acted in 14 films and had featured parts in *Covered Wagon, Oregon Trail, Northwest Passage* and *Black Hawk*. In the early 1920s, he traveled to Europe with actor friend Tim McCoy and 22 Indians. In later years, he studied linguistics and researched various forms of sign language used around the world.

17. Sharp Nose, Northern Arapaho

Sharp Nose served as a scout for General Crook in 1876 and in Mackenzie's campaign against the Cheyennes in the winter of 1876-1877. He was known as Crook's "head soldier" and impressed army officers as a formidable warrior. Capt. John Bourke wrote that "He handled men with rare judgment and coolness, and was as modest as he was brave." Sharp Nose was often photographed wearing his army uniform. He went to Washington, D. C., in 1877 as part of the delegation to request a Wyoming reservation. After settling on the Wind River reservation, he served as second in rank to Black Coal. Sharp Nose became head council chief when Black Coal died in 1893. Sharp Nose died in 1901. CC

18. Sitting Bull, Hunkpapa Sioux (b. 1834, d. 1890)

The Hunkpapa chief, the most famous of numerous Indians who had the name, was opposed to white encroachment on Indian lands and stayed active in the Sioux wars from the 1860s until after the Battle of the Little Bighorn. Sitting Bull is said to have predicted Custer's demise in a vision he received a few weeks before the battle. Following the two years in custody, he joined Buffalo Bill's Wild West Show for one season in 1885. He remained suspicious of whites and when the "ghost dance" movement began to spread on Sioux reservations in 1890, Indian police thought his arrest might quell the troubles. In the melee, Sitting Bull, his son and several others died in a hail of bullets. A few days later, the army massacred Big Foot's group at Wounded Knee.

19. Sitting Bull, Oglala Sioux (b. 1841, near Fort Laramie, d. 1876)

This second Sitting Bull (no relation to the above) worked as a telegraph operator along the Overland Trail in the 1860s. He spoke and read English fluently. Following the Sand Creek massacre, he and Crazy Horse answered the call for help from the Cheyenne. He assisted in the attack on Julesburg, Colo., in January 1865, and took part in the Fetterman fight the next year. He accompanied Spotted Tail and Red Cloud to Washington in 1875 to argue the Indians' case for the Black Hills. The next year, after he refused to be coerced into luring Crazy Horse back into white hands, he was killed by soldiers.

20. Spotted Tail, Brule Sioux

Born in 1823 near Fort Laramie, Spotted Tail was named for a raccoon given to him by a trapper when he was a young boy. Not the hereditary chief of the tribe, Spotted Tail gained the position from his skill as a warrior. He signed the Fort Laramie treaty of 1868. A decade later, he opposed the government negotiators' attempts to obtain a Black Hills treaty which he believed was not in the best interests of his people. He spoke, read and wrote English well and remained influential among many tribal members. On Aug. 5, 1881, he was murdered by Crow Dog, a disgruntled rival.

21. Two Moon, Cheyenne

Born in 1847, the Cheyenne chief was a leader of a camp on Powder River attacked by the Reynolds expedition in March 1876. Later in that year, Two Moon led the Cheyennes against Custer at the Little Bighorn. His account of the battle was told to writer Hamlin Garland and published in *McClure's Magazine* in 1898. Two Moon surrendered to General Miles at Fort Keogh. Later, he served as an army scout. He remained friendly with whites for the rest of his life. He visited President Wilson in 1914. Two Moon died at his home in Montana in 1917 at the age of 70.

Non-agricultural business loans on the Wind River Reservation went from zero in 1999 to 18 in 2000.

22. Washakie, Shoshoni

Washakie, born about 1804, was the son of a Umatilla father and a Shoshoni mother. He grew up along the Green River valley. He was not the hereditary chief of the Shoshones, but he became chief in 1842 on the death of the previous chief from an apoplectic attack. A signer of the Fort Bridger treaty, he maintained friendly relations with whites throughout his life. In the 1870s, he fought with the army against his tribe's traditional enemies, the Sioux, the Blackfeet and the Cheyenne. When he died in February 1900, he was buried in the military cemetery at Fort Washakie, the army post named in his honor.

23. Yellow Hand, Cheyenne

The son of Cheyenne chief Cut Nose, Yellow Hand was born in 1850 and died in 1876 in a duel with William F. Cody a month after Custer's defeat at the Little Bighorn. The duel took place near what is now the Wyoming-Nebraska border. Both men began the combat on horseback, but after Yellow Hand shot and missed, Cody shot Yellow Hand's horse from under him and grazed the Indian. The fight continued on foot with Cody drawing his knife and stabbing Yellow Hand who died at his feet. Newspapers advertised the event as "the first scalp for Custer" although Cody reportedly did not scalp the Cheyenne, but merely removed his war bonnet. There is controversy over whether the victim was "Yellow Hand" or "Yellow Calf."

CC: Indicates entries written by Dr. Colin Calloway, now at Dartmouth College but formerly on the faculty of the University of Wyoming Department of History, who teaches and writes on the history of Native Americans.

Interesting People Listed in Wyoming Census, 1880

Wyoming people counted for the 1880 census listed enough strange occupations to make one wonder what kind of place Wyoming was in those days. There were fewer people in the territory than now live in Laramie, but a look at the census shows the territory had a diverse population. Take some of the entries for Cheyenne's city jail. The four prisoners' occupations were listed as a soapmaker, a sailor and two painters. (Unless he operated a canoe on Crow Creek at flood stage, the sailor probably was not employed in his occupation in Cheyenne before he was jailed).

Counted as occupying hotel rooms in Cheyenne were members of the Vampire family. John, Jan, Mary and Otto Vampire listed their occupations as "traveling thespians," but it's anyone's guess what kind of show they presented!

At least six people in the territory were listed as "fossil hunters." Four were scientists digging at Como Bluff near Medicine Bow. One-third of the entire population of Owl Creek in 1880 were druggists. Living near the two men was an "ornamental plasterer."

A few names are recognized today. For instance, James Averell, remembered for being lynched along with "Cattle Kate" on the Sweetwater in 1889. Where was he and what was he doing nine years earlier? Serving time for an unspecified offense in the Carbon County Jail in Rawlins.

Few people were listed as unemployed although some folks were just barely counted. Take, for instance, the 29-year-old man on the Popo Agie River in Fremont County. The notation next to his name said: "Gunshot wound—must die from its effect."

There weren't many people who listed Wyoming as their place of birth. An exception was a four-year-old boy at Powder River. His name? Wyoming Smith.

Fur companies in the early 19th century in Wyoming often outfitted their employees with what was called "possible sacks" or "possibles." These were sacks in which as many as six or seven beaver traps could be carried along with ammunition, some tobacco, an extra pair of moccasins or other small articles. The sack was made of dressed buffalo hide. The reason the name was applied to the sack is not known.

NEWSPAPERS

1st newspaper published in Wyoming: *Fort Bridger Daily Telegraph*, published by Hiram Brundage, the telegrapher at Fort Bridger. The first issue is presumed to have been published on June 24, 1863. Subscription rates were $1 per month or $10 per year. Only two issues are known. Wyoming is the only state in which the first newspaper published was a daily. An earlier publication, The *Chugg Water Journal*, was handwritten by officers at Fort Laramie in 1849.

1st "moving" newspaper: The *Frontier Index*, which was also called the "Press on Wheels," was published at the rail head of the Union Pacific Railroad as it was being built westward. Publishers, brothers Legh R. and Fred K. Freeman, moved the press by railcar, locating it in a tent office in several "towns" along the route. *(See Wyoming Newsmakers, below).*

1st newspaper published north of the North Platte River: *Buffalo Echo*, Aug. 2, 1883, published by T. V. McCandish

1st newspaper published in the Big Horn Basin: *Bonanza Rustler*, June, 1889, edited by Joe De-Barthe. Later, the publication moved to Basin. It is the predecessor of the *Basin Republican-Rustler*. **Wyoming was the last state to get a printing press in the lower 48 states.**

Only private printing office in America authorized to print blank forms for the U. S. Land Office: The *Colony Coyote* newspaper, published from 1911 to 1930 in Crook County.

1st woman newspaper editors in Wyoming: Gertrude and Laura C. Huntington, editors of the *Platte Valley Lyre* in Saratoga. The first issue was published in June, 1888.

Youngest editor in Wyoming: Probably 12-year-old Edwin Smith of Evanston who published a monthly newspaper called the *Cottontail* in 1924. A subscription sold for 25 cents per year.

Wyoming Press Association organized: May 15, 1877, in Cheyenne. The first president was Herman Glafke, editor of the *Cheyenne Daily Leader*.

1st linotype in Wyoming: *Cheyenne Daily Sun*, Feb. 4, 1893.

1st newspaper to go on line on the Internet: *Casper Star-Tribune*, 1994.

1st Wyoming newspaper to switch to "desktop" publishing: *Wyoming State Journal* (Lander) in 1985 when it installed its first Apple Macintosh computer. The paper was one of the first in the world to go to computerized desktop typesetting. The *Journal* also was the first paper in Fremont County to print in more than one color (Dec. 7, 1939).

Wyoming Newsmakers

1. Bill Barlow

Merris C. Barrow (b. Canton, Pa., 1857) wrote under the name of Bill Barlow. He founded the *Douglas Budget* in June 1886, also edited *Sagebrush Philosophy*, a monthly magazine which contained witty western sayings.

2. Wallace R. Biggs

Considered the dean of Wyoming journalism, Biggs came to the University of Wyoming in 1946 to teach journalism in the English department. Two years later, he launched the university's journalism department, which he headed for 20 years. He founded the Wyoming High School Press Association, served as manager for the Wyoming Press Association for more than 15 years, and founded the *Roundtable*, a periodical for the American Society of Journalism School Administrators, and served as its editor. He was advisor to student publications at UW. He established the Wyoming Clipping Service, a business that he and his wife Jan ran for more than 30 years. He died in 1987.

3. Larry Birleffi

Known as "the Biffer," Birleffi has been in the sports news business for more than 50 years. He started working as a sports writer for the *Laramie Daily Bulletin* while still a student at UW in 1936. At one time, Birleffi's radio work made him the "Voice of Cowboy

Dorothy Johnson, the Montana author of *A Man Called Horse, The Man Who Shot Liberty Valance* and other western stories, studied writing under H. G. Merriam at the University of Montana. Merriam, a UW graduate, was Wyoming's first Rhodes scholar.

Sports." He wrote a column for the Cheyenne newspapers and appeared on a sports segment called, "Biff's Corner" on KGWN-TV, Cheyenne, until shortly before his death in September 2008. He was a native of Hartville.

4. Francis Brammar

The photographer for the Cheyenne newspapers for about 50 years received the Burt Williams Award from the National Press Photographers' Association in 1975. Brammar's photo subjects included Franklin Roosevelt, Will Rogers, Harry Truman, and Andrei Molotov (who came through Cheyenne on the train). Brammar, a native of Nevada, was a self-taught photographer. He died in 1986.

5. Milton B. Chilcott

Publisher of the *Sheridan Press* from 1969 to 1988, his name was honored by the establishment of the Chilcott Freedom of Information Award of the Wyoming Press Association. He was instrumental in getting the first open meetings law passed by the state legislature. The *Sheridan Press* took the Sheridan County commissioners to court when they were not publishing names and salaries as required by law and the newspaper won the case. When the Sheridan police chief closed police reports to the public and press, Chilcott's paper again went to court and, while the newspaper lost in district court, the decision was reversed and the paper prevailed in the Wyoming Supreme Court. He died in 1993.

6. Dean Conger

Born in Casper, Conger attained a photography director position with *National Geographic* magazine. Conger received his journalism degree from the University of Wyoming in 1950. He worked for the *Denver Post* before joining the *Geographic* staff in 1959. In 1961, he was named magazine photographer of the year.

7. Hugh Downs

The journalist who hosted ABC's "20/20" news program, once worked, during his youth, on a ranch near Laramie. He also has enjoyed vacations in Wyoming. In 1992, during a visit to the University of Wyoming campus where he got to meet journalism majors and other students, Downs donated his collection of personal and professional papers concerning his distinguished career to the UW American Heritage Center. Downs is listed in the *Guinness Book of World Records* as the person who has appeared more hours on television than anyone else in world history.

8. Robert "Red" Fenwick

Fenwick wrote for the *Denver Post* for nearly 40 years as a reporter and columnist. Born in Evansville, Ind., in 1909, Fenwick was reared in Converse County where his father was a railroad telegrapher. At 19, Red joined the cavalry and served for two years. Later, he headed a CCC camp in Yellowstone, worked as a lineman for a telephone company and served as press secretary to Sen. H. H. Schwartz in Washington, D. C. His first newspaper job was with the *Greybull Standard*. In the late 1930s until 1942 when he joined the *Denver Post*, he was city editor for a Casper newspaper. He received numerous writing awards during his career with the *Denver Post*. He died in Cheyenne Nov. 4, 1982.

9. Legh R. Freeman

Freeman, a native of Virginia, came to the west as a "galvanized Yankee." Following his capture by Union forces in the Civil War, he volunteered for frontier duty and was assigned to Fort Kearney, Nebr., where he became interested in the newspaper business. At the end of the war, he and his brother started the *Frontier Index*, a newspaper they published at the "end-of-tracks" towns along the Union Pacific Railroad as it was being laid west. The paper met its end when a mob attacked its tent offices at Bear River City near present-day Evanston. Legh Freeman escaped from the mob. They did not reopen the *Index*. Freeman returned to publishing newspapers in Montana, Utah and Washington.

10. Jean Godden

Elected to the Seattle City Council in 2003, Godden was a columnist for the *Seattle Post-Intelligencer* until 1991 when she moved to the *Seattle Times*. Godden, a native of Connecticut, was reared in the Big Horn Basin and graduated from Powell High School.

11. Curt Gowdy

The nationally known sports broadcaster did his first play-by-play at the Pine Bluffs-St. Mary's football game in 1943. He attended school in Cheyenne and the University of Wyoming where he played basketball. He has broadcast many noteworthy sports events in his career including serving as announcer for the first Super Bowl, describing Hank Aaron's 715th (and record-breaking) home run, and the UCLA domination of the NCAA basketball tournaments in the 1960s and 1970s. He was host of "American Sportsman" for many years. In 1981, he was inducted into the Broadcasters Hall of Fame. He died in February 2006.

12. Bill Hosokawa

Hosokawa served as editor of the *Empire Magazine*, supplement of the *Denver Post*, and worked as a *Post* columnist. He also wrote a column for the *Rocky Mountain News* (1992). He began his journalism career as editor of the *Heart Mountain Sentinel*, a newspaper published in both English and Japanese, at the Heart Mountain Relocation Center in Park County in the early 1940s. He died Nov. 9, 2007.

13. Bruce M. Kennedy

The publisher of several newspapers in Wyoming and Montana, Kennedy wrote the definitive book about community journalism called *Community Journalism: A Way of Life*, published in 1974 and used extensively in American journalism schools. A native of Basin, he began his career as a "printer's devil" at the *Basin Republican Rustler* while still in high school. Editor of the student newspapers at the University of Nebraska, he worked at weeklies in Wyoming and Nebraska, eventually bought the *Greybull Standard* and expanded his newspaper chain with top-quality papers. He died in a car accident in 1992.

14. Dorothy Kilgallen

Kilgallen, a celebrity reporter in New York, was a panelist on the TV game show, "What's My Line?" in the 1950s. Her father, James Kilgallen, served as editor of the *Laramie Boomerang* in 1913. She was born earlier that year in Chicago, but lived with her family in Laramie until she was 2. According to a 1979 book by Lee Israel, she made her theatrical debut at the age of 15 months in Laramie in an Elks Club production of "One Thing After Another." Dorothy, billed as "Tootsie," burst into impromptu tears during the first act, but regained her composure for the second act. The family moved from Laramie in 1915. As a reporter, she covered the "Lindbergh baby" kidnapping trial and interviewed numerous movie stars. In 1965, she died of what was said to be too much alcohol and pills. Perhaps it was suicide, though some rumors suggest her death could have been connected in some way with her last interview. It was of Jack Ruby, the assassin of Lee Harvey Oswald, and the material remained unpublished in a folder that was later destroyed.

15. Lou Kilzer

When he was a reporter for the *Minneapolis Star-Tribune*, Kilzer shared the 1990 Pulitzer Prize for Investigative Reporting for a story in which he and another reporter uncovered corruption in the St. Paul fire department. He won a Pulitzer in 1986 for public service while he was reporting for the *Denver Post*. He returned to the *Denver Post* in 1994 as investigative editor. Later, he moved to the *Rocky Mountain News* as investigative reporter. He is author of two books: *Hitler's Traitor* and *Churchill's Deception*. A native of Basin, he graduated from Yale in 1973.

16. Charles Levendosky

The editorial page editor of the *Casper Star-Tribune*, Levendosky is known for his strong commentaries in defense of civil liberties. He has received recognition for that effort, including the H. L. Mencken Award for best column in the nation in 1987. Gov. Sullivan named Levendosky, a poet, as the state poet laureate in 1988, an unpaid honorary position he held until 1995.

17. Ernest Linford

Linford served as head of the UW Journalism Department from 1967 to 1971. He had earlier been head of the editorial page of the *Salt Lake Tribune*. Born in Afton in 1907, he also worked as editor of newspapers in Cheyenne and Laramie.

18. Joe McGowan

A native of Sheridan and a former UW journalism student, McGowan went to work for Associated Press in Boston. He worked in AP bureaus in Indianapolis, India and Peru. In the 1990s, he was bureau chief of the Associated Press in Denver. He was the first American to interview Fidel Castro after he took power.

19. Doug Mellgren

Mellgren, who was a journalism student at the University of Wyoming and worked for the *Medicine Bow Post* in the 1980s, is an Associated Press reporter working out of Norway. In the 1990s, his reporting beat has taken him into the former Soviet Union, where he has visited the once-secret atomic cities and, from Riga, wrote about the first diplomat to recognize the independence of Latvia, Lithuania and Estonia. Mellgren also worked as editor for the *Douglas Budget*.

20. Asa S. Mercer

Mercer, (b. Princeton, Ill., 1839) was publisher of the *Northwestern Live-stock Journal* in the 1890s. He had served as the first president of the University of Washington in 1861. In an attempt to increase the population of marriageable women in the Puget Sound area, he organized the "Mercer Girl" scheme in the 1860s. His effort to bring Eastern women to Seattle was the basis for the 1960s television series, *Here Come the Brides*. Later, Mercer edited a newspaper in Texas, before coming to Wyoming. He wrote one of the most controversial books in Wyoming history, *Banditti of the Plains*, an "expose" about the Johnson County Invasion. The book began as a series of articles in his paper. In October 1892, he published a confession by George Dunning, who had been one of the gunmen hired to invade Johnson County. The confession described the invasion planning and the murder of Nate Champion and Nick Raye. Following publication of the newspaper account, Mercer was arrested and charged with criminal libel. His printing office was seized, he was jailed and copies of his newspaper were withheld from the mail by the Cheyenne postmaster who declared them "obscene." The book, published two years later, told the story. Mercer moved to Hyattville where he ranched until his death in 1917.

21. L. L. Newton

Editor of the *Wyoming State Journal* (Lander) in the 1940s, Newton stood alone in opposing the detention of Americans of Japanese descent in the Heart Mountain camp in Wyoming during World War II. He editorially argued that the move amounted to unconstitutional violations of the internees' rights as Americans. Other state newspapers, more favorably disposed to the federal government action, responded by questioning Newton's "sanity."

22. Edgar Wilson "Bill" Nye

A native of Maine, Nye (b. Shirley, Me., 1850) came west as a young man and located in Laramie where he worked for a local newspaper, practiced law, and served as a postal clerk. In March, 1881, Nye founded the *Laramie Boomerang*, naming the newspaper for his mule. His witty writing soon gained him a national following. Following the sale of his interest in the *Boomerang*, he became well known as a lecturer nationally, appearing with such figures as the poet James Whitcomb Riley. In his career, Nye wrote 14 books containing his humor.

23. James R. Simon

A Walt Disney wildlife photographer, Simon received his bachelor's and master's degrees at the University of Wyoming. Following military service during World War II, he became director of the newly-established Jackson Hole Wildlife Park. When it became a part of the Grand Teton National Park, he went to work for Walt Disney Productions. He died in 1973.

24. Rone Tempest

Tempest, whose father was a career military officer and his mother, a pioneering woman journalist, graduated from the University of California, Berkeley. In a long career with the Los Angeles Times, he was both a national and foreign correspondent, covering stories on six continents. He was part of a team covering the disastrous wildfires in southern California. The articles resulted in winning the Pulitzer Prize in 2004.. He was a lecturer at the Graduate School of Journalism of the University of California, Berkeley, from 2000-07. He returned to Wyoming and became editor of WyoFile, a non-profit web-based non-partisan public affairs news service, supported by foundations and donations. In 2010, WyoFile's investigations included an in-depth story on the Wyoming connections to the Department of the Interior's Minerals Management Service (MMS) and how that agency became captive to oil company interests. He lives in Lander.

25. Debbie Thunder

A member of the Northern Arapaho tribe, Thunder was editor of the *Wind River News* on the Wind River reservation. Later, she was a reporter for the *Casper Star-Tribune*. She was the first Wyoming person to be chosen for a fellowship through the Howard Simons Fund for American Indian Journalists in 1992.

26. Robert C. Warner

A professor of journalism at the University of Wyoming, Warner principally taught photography. A native of Converse County, he received numerous press and photography awards during his career, including being named one of the first four national winners of the Society of Professional Journalists' Distinguished Campus Advisors awards. Warner taught photography and journalism. He wrote a book, *The Fort Laramie of Alfred Jacob Miller*. He died in December 1988.

16 Oldest Wyoming Newspapers Still Being Published

1867: Wyoming State Tribune, Cheyenne. The paper began as the Cheyenne L e a d e r in July, 1867. The Tribune's first issue was printed in 1884 and it later merged with the Leader. On April 4, 1994, the Tribune and the Eagle merged into a morning newspaper.

1880: Rock Springs Rocket-Miner

1881: Laramie Boomerang (March 11)

1885: Wyoming State Journal (Lander)

1886: Lusk Herald (May 20)

  Douglas Budget

1887: Sheridan Press (as the Post on May 19; it became the Press in 1930).

1888: Saratoga Sun (June 7 as the Platte Valley Lyre)

1889: Basin Republican-Rustler (June 1 as the Big Horn County Rustler)

Alan Steen was held hostage in Beirut, Lebanon, for almost five years. In August 1992, he was hired to teach journalism at Casper College. He had been the second-to-last American still being held before his release on Dec. 3, 1991.

Newcastle News Letter Journal

Rawlins Daily Times (as Rawlins Republican; present name in 1946).

1890: Buffalo Bulletin (Oct. 9)

1891: Casper Star-Tribune (June 17, first issue of Star-Tribune's earliest ancestor, the Natrona County Tribune)

Green River Star (March, as the Advertiser; name changed to Star, 1894).

1899: Cody Enterprise (Aug. 31)

1900: Kemmerer Gazette (began in December as Kemmerer Camera; merged with Republican in 1912; present name adopted in 1924).

Source: Nancy Shelton, Wyoming Press Association

Most Common Names for Wyoming Newspapers

News (5): Jackson Hole News, Northern Wyoming Daily News (Worland), New-castle News Letter Journal, Gillette News-Record, Wind River News

Gazette (3): Guernsey, Kemmerer, Weston County (Upton)

Independent (3): Star Valley (Afton), Glenrock, Thermopolis Independent-Record

Times (3): Sundance, Rawlins, Platte County Record-Times (Wheatland)

Tribune (3): Powell, Casper Star-Tribune, Wyoming State Tribune (Cheyenne)

Post, Star, Herald, Guide, Journal and Pioneer (2 each)

Among the more unusual names for newspapers are the Basin Republican-Rustler, the Laramie Boomerang and the Pinedale Roundup.

Editors of the Wyoming Student/Branding Iron

The first University of Wyoming student publication was published in 1890 as a magazine. In 1912 it became a newspaper known as the Wyoming Student. In 1923, the name was changed to the Branding Iron.

Wyoming Student Editors

1912: Agnes Wright	1916: D. G. Shingler	1919: Charlie Young
1913: John E. Anderson	1917: Marie Mulligan	1920: Frank J. Kershisnik
1914: Margaret E. Mullison and Eda Laughlin		1921: Olga Moore
1915: M. V. Spicer	1918: Ted Olson	1922: Monte Warner

Branding Iron Editors, 1923-1929

G. Edward Pendray	Julian Snow	Shelly Thompson
Elmer R. Kissack	W. D. Fletcher	Elmer E. Johnson
Hazel Bowman	L. J. Burns	Ernest Newton
Ralph E. Conwell	Harry Mills Astin	Dean G. Nichols

Branding Iron Editors, 1930-1939

Elmer E. Johnson	Leo H. Wuesthoff	Virginia Pratt
Victor Rizzi	Charles D. Thompson	Burton DeLoney
M. P. Vogt	Bob White	George Henry
W. F. Himmelreich	Joe Jacobucci*	Ted Sherwin
George Holtorf	Ernest Hilton	Charles Smith
Douglas Tibbitts	Jerry W. Housel	

*Jacobucci was fired as a result of the "Yellow Sheet" incident, an April Fool's Day issue printed in 1936 which failed to amuse university officials who confiscated most of the copies and fired the editor.

> Passage through the Powder River country became so hot for the overland Astorians that one of their dogs died of heat exhaustion in August, 1811.

Branding Iron Editors, 1940-1959

George Johnson	Ruth Adams	Ralph Parlett
George Henry	Richard Redburn	Paul Holtz
William Lytle	Bill Schwiering	Warren Mack
Gene Levitt	Cal Queal	Dan Doherty
Bill Shutts	Don Shanor	Charles Coleman
Roy Peck	Don Thompson	Dick Bohrer
Jack Moses	Bill Schwiering	Diane Larson
Lila Mae Hoffman	Warren Carlson	Geoff Cole
Patty Tobin	Virginia Evans	Dick Perue
Ethel Sorgen	Jane Embrey	Don Bettis
Betty Johnson	Dave Mobley	Sandy Faus

Branding Iron Editors, 1960-1980

Russ Fawcett	Lee Catterall	Monica Miller	Karl Distad
Dave Bonner	Jim Coates	L. Mark Bowman	Rick Bush
Dick Evans	Claire Strid	Cheryl Malcom	Brian Kennedy
Gary Harvey	Mike Bryan	Ric Moser	Steve Prosinski
Sharon Suchta	Carl Lovell	Patrick McKenna	Ann Kennedy
Kathy Karpan	Larry Armstrong	Karl Swanson	Lollie Hernandez
Jack Cox	Philip White, Jr.	Stan Worster	Debra Baker

Branding Iron Editors, 1980-

Regular Term	Summer	Regular Term	Summer
1981: Nancy Tuma	-	1996: Gabrielle Studenmund	Kelly Milner
1982: Betty Specht	Emily Quarterman	1997: Jake Sherlock	Jamie Lewis
1983: Matt Winter	Truda Kinniburgh	1998: Shannon Rexroat	Staff-edited
1984: Jeff Thomas	Timothy Harms	1999: Jay O'Brien	John Eisel
1985: Agnes Kubik	Holly Pieper	2000: Heather Gierhart	
1986: Brad Bonner	Melinda Merriam	2002: Michael Owens	
1987: Chad Baldwin	Randy Bunney	2003 (Apr.-May):Jeremiah Johnke	
1988: Dana Smith	Erika Knudson	2003: Kevin Wingert	
1989: Kerry Lehto	Rebecca Alexander	2004: Kevin Wingert	
1990: David Eisenhauer	Le Templar	2005 (Fall): Tony C. Yang	
1991: Mark French	Linda Fantin	2006: Lindsey Lipska:	
1992: Wendy Pederson	Janet Montgomery	2007: Justin Joiner	
1993: Rob Jarosh	Rachel Keating	2008:Hanna Bush	
1994: Steve Bahmer	Scott Brown	2009: Hanna Bush	
1995: Vanessa Hastings	Kelli Stringer		

Newspaper Circulation, 1870*

800: Cheyenne Weekly Leader **400:** South Pass News (published Wed. and Sat.)
500: Cheyenne Daily Leader   **288**: Laramie City Sentinel (daily)
500: Wyoming Tribune (Cheyenne daily)
There were only five newspapers publishing in Wyoming in 1870.

Although he was not generally associated in the public mind with Wyoming, a member of Eisenhower's Cabinet did have a Wyoming connection. Fred Seaton served as Secretary of the Interior in the Eisenhower administration. Prior to that appointment, Seaton had owned and operated newspapers and radio stations in Nebraska, Wyoming and Kansas. In 1946, he purchased a majority interest in the Sheridan Press. Despite the ownership, Seaton never lived in the state.

Medicine Bow Post Student Editors*

Spring 1989:	Geoff Woodman	**Spring 1992:**	Da Nece Koenigs
Summer 1989:	Michelle Kodis	**Summer 1992:**	Le Templar
Fall 1989:	Jim Davis	**Fall 1992:**	Lisa Yeager
Spring 1990:	Eric Blomfelt	**Spring 1993:**	Hillary Duesler
Summer 1990:	Marci Hoff	**Summer 1993:**	Troy Chaney
Fall 1990:	Cary Berry	**Fall 1993:**	Wendi Frank
Spring 1991:	Stacy Bowers	**Spring 1994:**	Toby Marlatt
Summer 1991:	Dennis Cheatham	**Summer 1994:**	Pamela Dickman
Fall 1991:	Dan Mulholland	**Fall 1994:**	Don Pounds
		Spring 1995:	Shannon Stahl

The Post was founded in 1977 and donated to the University of Wyoming Department of Journalism by the Roberts family in 1989. Students edited the newspaper which both served the reading public in the community and taught students the duties and responsibilities involved in practicing community journalism. The University of Wyoming discontinued publication in 1995 and liquidated the newspaper's assets.

Wyoming Newspaper Hall of Fame

The Wyoming Press Association recognizes prominent newspaper people through the Wyoming Newspaper Hall of Fame, initiated in 2003. New honorees are inducted dkuring the WPA's annual summer meetings in June.

Initial Inductees (2003)
Milton Chilcott, Sheridan Press
Bruce Kennedy, Sage Publishing
Phil McCauley, Casper Star-Tribune
Tracy McCraken, Wyoming Tribune-Eagle
Roy Peck, Riverton Ranger.

Inductees (2004)
Chuck Harkins, Casper Star-Tribune
Fred McCabe, Jackson Hole Guide
Walter Biggs, UW professor and WPA executive director.

Inductees (2005
Bob Peck, Riverton Ranger
Ted O'Melia, Rawlins Daily Times
Cora Wanamaker, Rock Springs Rocket (1908).

Inductees (2006)
Francis Brammar, Wyoming Tribune-Eagle photographer
Jim Hicks, Buffalo Bulletin
Robert Warner, UW professor and photographer

Inductees (2008)
Bill Hosokawa, Denver journalist
Dick Perue, Saratoga Sun
J. E. Hanway, Casper Tribune

Inductees (2009)
T. Douglas Reeves, Wyo. Tribune-Eagle

Wedding cows? Is that a wedding gift that rural Wyoming folks like to give...or was it a "typo"? The words were in a newspaper article several years ago and show why even one letter can be important. The words appeared in the following sentence: "The couple exchanged wedding cows." Probably, "vows" was the intended word.

Presidents, Wyoming Press Association, 1877-Present

1877: Herman Glafke, Cheyenne Leader
1881-82: E. A. Slack, Cheyenne Sun
1883-85: J. H. Hayford, Lar. Sentinel
1885-88: Not known.
1889-90: M. C. Barrow, Barlow's Budget
1890-96: Not known.
1896-97: W. E. Chaplin, Laramie Republican
1900: E. A. Slack, Cheyenne Leade
1901-02: J. F. Crawford, Saratoga Sun
1903: W. C. Deming, Cheyenne Tribune
1904-07: W. E. Chaplin, Laramie Republican
1908: Frank Barrow, Sheridan Post
1909: Fred Winchester, Thermopolis Ind.
1910: J. W. Cook, Lander Clipper
1911: A. J. Mokler, Natrona Co. Tribune
1913-15: S. G. Hoplins, Wheatland Times
1916: A. H. Maxwell, Wyo. St. Journal
1917-23: Not known
1924: Ted Wanerus, Cheyenne Leader
1925-29: Ross Alcorn, Rawlins Repub.
1930: C. Stan Greenbaum, Laramie
1931: P. P. Anderson, Basin Rep. Rustler
1932: Tracy S. McCraken, Wyo. Eagle
1933: J. B. Griffith, Lusk Herald
1934: Earl Hanway, Casper Trib-Herald
1935: L. P. Loomis, Torrington Telegram
1936: L. L. McBride, Sheridan Press
1937: Ernest Shaw, Cody Enterprise
1938: C. Watt Brandon, Kemmerer Gazette
1939: George Houser, Guernsey Gazette
1940: Dave Richardson, Rock Springs R.
1941: Ralph Blackledge, Sheridan Press
1942. Stan Greenbaum, Laramie Rep.
1943: E. L. Newton, Wyo. State Journal
1944: O. B. Koefer, Wyoming Tribune
1945: E. T. Childers, Riverton Review
1946: Din Alcorn, Rawlins Times
1947: Gerald Bardo, Lusk Herald
1948: Ted O'Melia, Rawlins Times
1949: Hugh Knoefel, N. Wyo. Daily News
1950: Jack Perry, Casper Tribune-Herald
1951: Frank Taylor, Kemmerer Gazette
1952: Carl Rott, Sheridan Press
1953: R. R. Allbaugh, Lar. Boomerang
1954: Frank Hicks, Buffalo Bulletin
1955: Roy Peck, Riverton Ranger
1956: Adrian Reynolds, Green Riv. Star
1957: Russell Stout, Rawlins Times
1958: Max Call, Star Valley Ind.
1959: Earl Hanway, Casper Trib-Herald
1960: Robert Johnson, Rock Spr. Roc.
1961: James Griffith, Jr., Lusk Herald
1962: Curt Whaley, Powell Tribune
1963: Robert Peck Riverton Ranger

1964: Lee Call, Star Valley Ind.
1965: James Hull, Laramie Boomerang
1966: Mike Vukelich, Cody Enterprise
1967: Richard Redburn, Sheridan Press
1968: Roger Budrow, Wyo. State Jour.
1969: C. Richardson, Rock Springs R.
1970: Harvey Balison, Basin Rep. Rust.
1971: Bernie Horton, Wyoming Eagle
1972: Jack Nisselius, Gillette News-R.
1973: Milton Chilcott, Sheridan Press
1974: Chet Mariner, Pinedale Roundup
1975: Ron Brown, Wyo. Tribune-Eagle
1976: Dave Bonner, Powell Tribune
1977: Thomas Howard, Casper Star-T.
1978: R. R. Perue, Saratoga Sun
1979: Robert H. Tyler, Riverton Ranger
1980: William Sniffin, Wyo. St. Journal
1981: J. Doug Reeves, Wyo. Trib.-Eagle
1982: James F. Hicks, Buffalo Bulletin
1983: Ted Duffy, Laramie Boomerang
1984: Michael Sellett, Jackson Hole N.
1985: Robin Hurless, Casper Star-Trib.
1986: Pat Schmidt, Thermop. Ind.Rec.
1987: Mike Lindsey, Saratoga Sun
1988: Eric Adams, Basin Rep. Rustler
1989: Diane Bonner, Powell Tribune
1990: Lee Lockhart, N. Wyo. Daily N.
1991: Ron Van Ekeren, Lar. Boomerang
1992: Diane Essington, Pinedale Round.
1993: Dave Peck, Lovell Chronicle
1994: Mary Hicks, Buffalo Bulletin
1995: Mike McCraken, Wyo. Trib.-Eagle
1996: Ron Franscell, Gillette News-R.
1997: Dave Perry, Rawlins Daily Times
1998: Angus Thuermer, Jackson Hole N.
1999: Gary Stevenson, Saratoga Sun
2000: Robert H. Hicks, Buffalo Bulletin
2001: Tom Mullen, Newcastle N-L-Journal
2002: Scott Walker, Wyo Tribune-Eagle
2003: Matt Adelman, Douglas Budget
2004: Jim Wood, Platte Co. Rec.-Times
2005: Ann Franscell, Gillette News Rec.
2006: Curt Moberg, Sundance Times
2007: John T. Malmberg, Cody Enterprise
2008: Toby Bonner, Powell Tribune
2009: Thomas Dewell, Jackson Hole N&G
2010: Jeff Robertson, Lusk Herald

Executive Directors, WPA

George Houser (volunteer) to 1951
Wallace Biggs, 1951-1969
Nancy Shelton, 1969-1996
John Coykendall, 1996-1998
Jim Angell, 1998-present

Top Ten Wyoming News Stories of the 20th Century*

1. Treatment of women. While the state has the nickname, "Equality State," equality for women during the century was rarely "equal." As historian Roy Jordan said, "There's been no conviction or commitment to women's rights throughout our whole history."
2. Booms and busts in the mineral industry
3. Wyoming's relationship with the federal government
4. Poor treatment of minorities
5. World War II and its impact on the state
6. Abandonment of efforts to attract settlers and concentration on tourism
7. Poor treatment of Native American tribes in Wyoming
8. Identification of Wyoming with the image of the cowboy
9. The "colonial" aspects of the Wyoming economy
10. School finance disputes
* Panel was selected by AP writer Robert W. Black. Members included Dr. David Kathka, Dr. Bob Righter, Mark Junge, John Albanese, Don Hodgson, Patty Myers, Dr. Michael Cassity, Loren Jost, Mike Massie, and Dr. Roy Jordan.

Top Ten Wyoming News Stories of the Decade, 1980-1989*

1. Forest fires char one million acres in and around Yellowstone National Park (1988)
2. Economy booms, then busts (1980-1989)
3. Cheyenne teenagers Richard and Deborah Jahnke kill their abusive father (1982)
4. A husband-wife terrorist team holds a Cokeville school hostage (1986)
5. Rep. Dick Cheney becomes Secretary of Defense (1989)
6. Floods kill 12 people in Cheyenne (1985)
7. Black-footed ferrets make a comeback from virtual extinction (1986-1989)
8. The state is ordered to revamp its property tax system (1987)
9. U. S. Secretary of State James Baker and Soviet Foreign Minister Eduard Shevardnadze meet in Jackson Hole (1989)
10. Lovell physician Dr. John Story is convicted of sexually assaulting several of his patients (1985)
*Top stories selected in December 1989, by Associated Press member newspapers and broadcast outlets in Wyoming

Top Wyoming News Stories, 1990*

*As selected by Associated Press member papers and broadcast outlets.
1. Execution date set for Mark Hopkinson
2. Death of former Gov. Ed Herschler (Feb. 5)
3. Sullivan, Simpson, Karpan win in 1990 Elections
4. Thousands celebrate Wyoming Centennial
5. Laramie woman charged with child abuse for drinking alcohol while pregnant
6. Wyoming reservists called to service in "Operation Desert Shield"
7. State's economy shows mixed condition
8. Legislature designates Martin Luther King, Jr.-Wyoming Equality Day
9. Mother, three children murdered in Thermopolis; juvenile taken into custody
10. Crook Co. rancher John Dorrance fights with Game and Fish over exotic game ranch

---

The Wyoming State Society, was formed in 1977 in Washington, D. C. Similar organizations hold annual events in California and Arizona.

Top Wyoming News Stories, 1991*

As selected by Associated Press member papers and broadcast outlets.

1. Reapportionment plan overturned by federal court
2. Budget crisis strikes state government
3. Sen. Al Simpson's comments on Clarence Thomas-Anita Hill hearings
4. Guilty plea of Thermopolis youth in murder of mother and three brothers
5. Continued federal efforts to plan for wolf return to Yellowstone
6. Congress rejects attempt to raise grazing fees
7. Wyoming soldiers fight in Persian Gulf War
8. Amtrak returns passenger service to Wyoming
9. Kern River Gas Transmission Co., builds natural gas pipeline to California
10. Crook County rancher John Dorrance tries to legalize exotic game farming

Top Wyoming News Stories, 1992*

As selected by Associated Press member papers and broadcast outlets.

1. Mark Hopkinson executed (December); 1st execution in Wyoming since 1965
2. Legislature reapportions itself into districts
3. Some Fremont County residents try for a monitored retrievable storage site for nuclear waste in Fremont County
4. Legislators debate funding shortfalls in budget session
5. Large and small school districts battle over education financing system
6. Congress debates grazing fee increases
7. Demonstrations favor a stalking bill in Wyoming
8. Justice Walter Urbigkit ousted from Supreme Court in retention election
9. Federal officials investigate shooting of "wolf-like" animal in Yellowstone
10. Voters approve term limitation initiative

Top Wyoming News Stories, 1993*

As selected by Associated Press member papers and broadcast outlets.

1. Four schoolchildren injured in Sheridan by gunman, shooting randomly. Gunman shot self. Sept. 17, 1993.
2. District judge decided school funding was unsound. Judge Nick Kalokathis, after one-month trial of lawsuit by Green River, Rock Springs, Evanston and Campbell County schools against state. Schools alleged more state money per student went to small schools than to large. Ruling November, 1993, the judge said the state constitution did not guarantee equal funding for all districts.
3. Interior Department failed in an attempt for grazing reforms. The agency proposed raise of $1.86 per aum to $4 per aum, but Congress did not agree.
4. In Sept., Malcolm Wallop announces retirement from U. S. Senate.
5. Gunman-neighbor shoots two in Goshen County March 21; he is later shot by his sister-in-law. Gunman Ray Esquibel lived, sentenced to life in prison.
6. U.S. Fish and Wildlife Service released report on wolf reintroduction in Yellowstone.
7. 4-month strike by 480 workers at General Chemical's trona plant near Green River. Picket line violence July 31. Mediated agreement reached in November.
8. Torrington police officer Lt. Harley Mark killed in car accident in Sept. while searching for jail escapee.
9. Dick Cheney announced he would not be a candidate for the Senate (Dec.)
10. AP investigates Wind River BIA police brutality.

Top Wyoming News Stories, 1994*

As selected by Associated Press member papers and broadcast outlets.

1. Republican Party sweep of the 1994 elections in Wyoming. The governor and the four other top offices were won by Republicans and Republicans Craig Thomas and Barbara Cubin won their respective races for the U. S. Senate and U. S. House of Representatives.
2. Voters reject legalized gambling and also reject a proposed ban on most abortions.
3. Deaths of five Douglas teenagers, killed by a train at a local crossing in August. Noah Stavnes,

Jeremy Stavnes, Ryan Willson, Tiffany Rabun and Jennifer Coziahr were riding in a car hit by the train at an unrestricted crossing.

4. Continuing debate over rangeland reform and grazing fees.

5. Efforts to return wolves to Yellowstone National Park

6. The growing concern over the rise in the number of children bringing firearms to school.

7. State Board of Land Commissioners impose two-year moratorium on sales of state lands

8. Senator Malcolm Wallop retired from the Senate after 18 years of service.

9. The continuing debate over the constitutionality of school finance.

10. UW student John Candelaria shot and killed in May on the corner of 15th and Ivinson on the Laramie campus by Robert Lovato, the first murder ever committed on the UW campus.

Top Wyoming News Stories, 1995*

As selected by Associated Press member papers and broadcast outlets.

1. The Wyoming Supreme Court rules that the state's education funding system is unconstitutional and orders that the state comply with the Constitution by July 1, 1977.

2. U. S. Senator Al Simpson announces his retirement from the Senate at the end of his third term in 1996, setting off a flurry of activity among candidates.

3. Fourteen Canadian wolves are released into Yellowstone National Park to become acclimated to their new home

4. Two men are trapped hundreds of feet underground when a trona mine collapses in Sweetwater County; one rescued, the other dies.

5. Two convicted murderers, including a man convicted of killing his stepmother and three brothers, escape from the Wyoming State Penitentiary.

6. A Fremont County sheriff's deputy is shot to death as he returns a Boy's School escapee to the institution in Worland.

7. Gov. Jim Geringer produces his first budget, compiled through his "strategic planning" process.

8. Wyoming officials continue concern over planned gold mine in Montana near Yellowstone National Park.

9. President Clinton golfs, floats and shops his way through Jackson, bringing with him hordes of reporters and sightseers.

10. Mae Wardell, 83, survives for eight days after her car slides off a highway and gets stuck in mud.

Top Wyoming News Stories, 1996*

As selected by Associated Press member papers and broadcast outlets.

1. State Sen. Mike Enzi defeats former Secretary of State Kathy Karpan for U.S. Senate seat vacated by Sen. Al Simpson.

2. Jessica Dubroff, a seven-year-old seeking to become the youngest pilot to fly across the United States, is killed in a single-engine Cessna crash shortly after taking off in Cheyenne. The crash also killed her father and flight instructor.

3. President Bill Clinton announces a deal to halt building of a gold mine near Yellowstone National Park.

4. Levi Todd Collen is sentenced to three life terms in prison for raping and killing Berry Bryant of Riverton. Both had been students at Northwest College, Powell, at the time of the murder.

5. Widespread late-season forest and range fires cause damage statewide.

6. The legislature struggles with the impact of the Supreme Court's ruling on education finance.

7. The State Land Board renews a moratorium on the sale of state lands.

8. University of Wyoming head football coach Joe Tiller leaves to accept the head coaching job at Purdue University.

9. Nine people are killed when a C-130 transport plane crashes near Jackson. The plane was carrying vehicles used by President Clinton's entourage during his vacation in the Jackson Hole area.

10. State and county officials struggle with the question of whether to allow access to public lands to build the Express oil pipeline.

An oil company owned, managed and operated entirely by women drilled for oil near Douglas in 1922. The Women's National Oil and Development Co., was headed by Mrs. Maybelle Remore and headquartered in Seattle.

Top Wyoming News Stories, 1997*

As selected by Associated Press member papers and broadcast outlets.

1. Legislature agrees on plan for education finance reform, only to have it challenged immediately by 31 school districts and the Wyoming Education Association. A state district judge approved part of the plan and rejects the remainder.

2. Several wolves shot as the population of predators in Yellowstone National Park continues to grow faster than expected. A federal judge declares the reintroduction program illegal and orders the wolves removed, but puts the order on hold pending an expected appeal.

3. Amy Wroe Bechtel disappears near Lander while jogging.

4. Lawsuit over the winter use of Yellowstone National Park results in agreement to study closing segment of snowmobile trail for three years.

5. Correctional officer Wayne Martinez killed by three inmates in an unsuccessful escape attempt.

6. Joint public-private task force recommends elimination of Department of Commerce and relocation of economic development activities into a new quasi-government agency.

7. Marty Olsen, found guilty of murdering three people in a Worland bar, becomes first person in Wyoming in ten years to be sentenced to death.

8. Truck driver Keith Jesperson, convicted serial killer, returned to Wyoming to face murder charge two years after admitting to a murder in the state.

9. Mesa Airlines announces halt to service to five Wyoming towns in attempt to gain federal subsidies for continuing service to those communities.

10. U. S. Department of Agriculture panel recommends that cattle in six Wyoming counties be tested for brucellosis before sale.

Top Wyoming News Stories, 1998*

As selected by Associated Press member papers and broadcast outlets.

1. University of Wyoming freshman Matthew Shepard lured from a Laramie bar, kidnapped, tied to a fence east of Laramie, and savagely beaten. He dies in a Fort Collins hospital five days later. Police arrest two Laramie men for the murder. The case brings national attention as a "hate crime," committed because Shepard was gay.

2. Christen Lamb, an 8-year-old Laramie girl, is kidnapped and murdered while visiting her grandparents' home at Powell. A man living across the street from her grandparents is arrested, tried, convicted of the murder and given a life sentence.

3. Legislature fine-tunes the education funding formula in an effort to comply with a 1995 Wyoming Supreme Court ruling that lawmakers provide equal educational opportunities to Wyoming students. More than half of the state's school districts continue litigation over the matter.

4. Two penitentiary prisoners convicted of the murder of Wayne Martinez, a corectional officer, during an escape attempt. One is sentenced to life; the other is given the death penalty, but appeals the case.

5. An outbreak of E. coli sickens residents and visitors in western Wyoming. Outbreak is traced to the water supply in Alpine.

6. Gillette math teacher Cheryl Trover shoots and stabs her husband then lies to officials that an intruder committed the crime and kidnapped her. When police doubt her story, she commits suicide.

7. Wyoming Business Council is created to stimulate state's stagnant economy.

8. Two Green River teenagers push a third teen off a cliff, then take their own lives. The two are apparently motivated by the despair of one over his breakup with a girl.

9. National Park Service decides against closing a 14-mile snowmobile trail in Yellowstone National Park as part of a winter use study.

10. The federal government and environmental groups appeal a 1997 judge's order to remove wolves reintroduced to Yellowstone National Park. The judge had stayed the order, pending appeals, a process which nearly runs its course by the end of the year.

Top Wyoming News Stories, 1999*

As selected by Associated Press member papers and broadcast outlets.

1. Conclusion of the murder case that focused national debate on violence against homosexuals and the effectiveness of bias crime laws. Aaron McKinney and Russell Henderson were tried separately for the murder of 21-year-old University of Wyoming student Matthew Shepard.

2. Year-long struggle by state officials to address the budget shortfall, estimated at one time to be as much as $127 million.

3. First statewide standardized testing of 20,000 school students in Wyoming. The tests, criticized for errors, showed that two-thirds of students performed poorly in mathematics and from 40-60 percent, depending on grade level, failed to measure up in reading and writing.

4. Park Service proposal to ban snowmobiles on a road to Old Faithful in Yellowstone National Park.

5. Legislature's responses to the school funding formula.

6.-7. (tie) Threats received by several Wyoming schools in the wake of the Columbine High School shootings

6.-7. (tie) Investigations of the Wyoming National Guard involving improper loans of equipment and a false promotion.

8. Lawsuit over the funding formula for Wyoming's community colleges.

9. Former Casper youth soccer coach charged with ten counts of child pornography.

10. State's continuing problems with methamphetamines with 20 labs found making the illegal substance, up from 12 in 1998.

Top Wyoming News Stories, 2000*

As selected by Associated Press member papers and broadcast outlets.

1. Wyomingite Dick Cheney elected vice president of the United States
2. Wildfires rage from June to October
3. Snowmobiles banned in Yellowstone, Grand Teton National Parks
4. Coalbed methane industry continues boom
5. Oil industry rebounds
6. Wyoming Business Council troubles lead to resignation of CEO
7. Ban proposed on new roads in national forest roadless areas
8. Marilyn Kite becomes first woman appointed to Wyoming Supreme Court
9. Legislature considers variety of new taxes
10. Education officials express dismay with drop in Wyoming Comprehensive Assessment System (WyCAS) test scores for most school grade levels

Top Wyoming News Stories, 2001*

As selected by Associated Press member papers and broadcast outlets.

1. National terrorist attacks brought concern to entire state, particularly with respect to airport security.

2. Eight UW runners died in crash wth drunken driver, south of Laramie on Highway 287 on Sept. 16. They were riding in a Jeep Wagoneer that collided head-on with a large pickup truck. Killed were Joshua Jones, Kevin Slaverson, Nicholas Schabron, Shane Shatto, Morgan McLeland, Kyle Johnson, Justin Lambert-Belanger, and Cody Brown. Driver of the other vehicle Clint Haskins, convicted and sentenced to prison for driving drunk and causing the accident.

3. Wyoming Supreme Court ordered changes to K-12 funding formula. On Feb. 23, the court ordered the legislature to devise a better system for paying for new shool buildings and to come up with a statewide tax or similar method to fund $563 million in repairs. On Oct. 2, the court backed away from the earlier ruling by saying that the legislature remained in charge of funding school building construction to standards it deemed fit.

4. Dick Cheney, former U. S. Representative from Wyoming, is sworn in as vice president

5. Army Ranger Spec. John J. Edmunds, 20, killed in helicopter crash in Pakistan. He grew up in Cheyenne.

6. Wyoming's energy industry continued to bolster the state's economy with natural gas, oil and coal prices rising. The legislature had a $695 million surplus, making it possible to put away $200 million in the Permanent Mineral Trust Fund and provide $47 million to school districts to fund teachers' wage increases.

7. Drought continued through much of Wyoming. Most places in the state received below-average precipation and experienced warmer temperatures than normal for the second year in a row. Crop losses from drought were estimated at $6 million for the year. Many reanchers sold cattle early as stock ponds dried up.

8. Snowmobile ban set aside by NPS on June 29. The Clinton administration banned snowmobiles in Yellowstone and Grant Teton national parks, but the NPS lifted the ban to settle a lawsuit brought by snowmobile groups. The settlement required the NPS to conduct a new study of the impact of the vehicles on the parks.

9. Coal bed methane boom in Wyoming continued Methane trapped in coal seams in the Powder River Basin continued to be exploited during the year. About 230 billion cubic feet were produced, a 54 percent increase over 2000. Lack of pipelines continued to cause concerns..

10. Hot dry weather ushered in another summer of fire in Wyoming. A lightning-caused fire on July 29 closed the east entrance of Yellowstone for 11 days. Some 150 mountain homes near Jackson had to be evacuated the previous week due to fire southwest of town. Near Alpine, 40 homes were evacuated due to another fire. Several structures burned in separate fires in the Black Hills in the northeast.

Top Wyoming News Stories, 2002*

As selected by Associated Press member papers and broadcast outlets.

1. Dave Freudenthal is elected governor, defeating Eli Bebout by 3,762 votes. A former aide to long-time governor Ed Herschler and U. S. Attorney in the Clinton administration, he was the only Democrat to win statewide office in the November election.

2. West Nile Virus, a disease spread by mosquitoes, strikes in Wyoming

3. Drought continues throughout the state. In the northwest part of the state, light mountain snowpack led to spring and summer drought.

4. Kaycee flooded, many homes and businesses destroyed. FEMA refuses support, claiming the number of damaged homes and buildings did not meet its criteria for a disaster.

5. Clint Haskins, driver of a large pickup that struck a van in which eight University of Wyoming runners were riding, killing all eight of them, is sentenced to prison for vehicular homicide. Authorities proved Haskins was drunk at the time of the accident, south of Laramie on Highway 287 in September 2001.

6. Legislature passes a law that reduces blood-alcohol limit

7. A man is convicted in the Lisa Kimmell case. The young woman was killed in 1988 and the case finally was solved using DNA evidence gathered from a car buried on the property of the convicted man near Moneta.

8. University of Wyoming changed football coaches. Vic Koenning was fired and Joe Glenn, a very successful coach at Northern Colorado and the University of Montana, was named to succeed him.

9. Crime news was the next biggest story with such incidents as a serial rapist in central Wyoming.

10. Snowmobiles and whether they should be allowed in Yellowstone or Grand Teton national parks again brought controversy in Wyoming during the year.

Top Wyoming News Stories, 2003*

As selected by Associated Press member papers and broadcast outlets.

1. Death of Wyoming soldiers in Iraq (five killed as of Jan. 1, 2004)

2. Man charged in murder of Lisa Kimmell, 15 years after her body found in Platte River

3. Prosecutor prosecuted: Kevin Meenan, Natrona Co. DA for 17 years, resigned in Dec. after pleading guilty to forgery and theft from step-children.

4. (tie) Brucellosis found in Sublette County cattle herd in Dec. 2003.

4. (tie) Legislators and game officials crafted wolf management plan

6. State projects as much as $1 billion surplus for following year due to energy price rises

7. Snowmobile ban in Yellowstone approved by court; state appealed

8. 9 die, 393 sick from West Nile virus outbreak in state

9. Martin's Cove leased to LDS church

10. State in 4th straight year of drought

10. (tie) Newcastle firefighter killed; Anndee Huber killed when truck overturned en route to fire

---

"A country editor, having worked hard for 30 years, retired with a nest egg of $50,000. He explained his good fortune this way: 'I attribute my ability to retire with $50,000 to the fact that I worked hard and saved every cent—and to the death of an uncle who left me $49,999.50.'"
—Lusk Herald item, more than 50 years ago.

Top Wyoming News Stories, 2004*

As selected by Associated Press member papers and broadcast outlets.

1. Deadly crash: Fiery pileup on I-80 near Buford kills seven and injures 29 others. Thirty-six vehicles were involved in the chain reaction collision in heavy fog on August 19.

2. Malpractice Voters defeated a proposed constitutional amendment that would have let the legislature consider limits on awards in malpractice cases, such as for pain and suffering. The amendment, crafted during a special session of the legislature, was designed to reduce doctors' liability insurance and keep doctors in the state.

3. Brucellosis: An outbreak of the disease meant livestock producers would continue to face stringent testing requirements for the following year.

4. State budget surplus: A resurging mineral industry was largely responsible for a record $1.22 billion state surplus. The bulk of it, $462 million, was spent on a backlog of school and prison construction needs. About $252million or 20 percent, was put in permanent or short-term savings.

5. Wolves: Wyoming sued the federal government on April 22 over rejection of the state's wolf-management plan. The U. S. Fish and Wildlife Service said Wyoming's plan would have allowed too much uncontrolled killing of wolves, but state officials thought such a move was necessary to control the growing wolf population.

6. Term Limits: On May 4, the Wyoming Supreme Court ruled it unconstitutional for voters to impose term limits on state lawmakers through a 1992 ballot initiative. Severn incumbents freed to run again were returned to office, while four others retired even though the limit no longer was operative.

7. Snowmobiles: On Oct. 15, U. S. District Judge Clarence Brimmer struck down a Clinton administration phase-out that had been invoked by another judge in an earlier case.

8. Lisa Kimmell: A case that had baffled investigators for more than a decade was solved with Dale W. Eaton sentenced to death for the rape and murder of 18-year-old Lisa Marie Kimmell who disappeared in 1988 near Casper. Her body was later found in the North Platte River. Eaton's car was unearthed near Moneta and DNA from Kimmell was found in the vehicle.

9. Dormitory fire: A fire gutted Northwest College's Bridger Hall on March 30. The incident raised the issue of whether the state ought to help fund sprinkler systems in college structures. The governor included $3 million in the budget for assisting with such modifications.

10. Iraq War: Marine LCpl Kyle Burns of Laramie, Army PFC Collier Barcus, who spent time on a Wyoming youth ranch, Marine PFC Chance Phelps, who grew up in Dubois, and Army Spec. Billy Watts of Cody were all killed in Iraq during the year.

Top Wyoming News Stories, 2005*

As selected by Associated Press member papers and broadcast outlets.

1. Wright tornado

On the afternoon of August 12, a tornado with winds estimated at from 113-130 mph struck the sourthern Campbell County town, killing two people and destroying 60 homes. Killed were Etienne Iriberry, sr., 53, and Connie L. Allen, 97. Almost 60 other homes were damaged in the storm.

2. Resignation of Trent Blankenship as State Supt.

Blankenship, elected in 2002, resigned in June to accept the psotion of supt of the North Slope Burrough School District in northern Alaska

3. Hathaway Scholarships

The Wyoming state legislature created a $400 million trust fund to pay for scholarships for Wyoming high school graduates who attend Wyoming community colleges or the University of Wyoming. A special task force developed rules for implementing the program during the summer and fall.

4. New Prison

Lawmakers approved construction of a new medium-security prison at Torrington. Rawlins and Riverton both objected, claiming that most of the economic benefits would accrue to neighboring towns in Nebraska.

5. Budget surplus

The 2005 state legisalutre had an estimated $1.2 billion surplus to work with during the session. It was estimated that the amount would be $1.8 billion by the end of the year.

6. Death of Stan Hathaway
The former governor died at his home in Cheyenne on Oct. 4 after a long illness. He was 81. Hathaway served two terms from 1967-1975.

7. E-bingo
Laramie County District Judge E. James Burke ruled on Jan. 5 that electronic bingo machines were illegal gambling devices. Within days, bingo parlors were closed down throughout the state. Legislative attempts to revive electronic bingo failed and the House passed a bill specifally banning the use of electronic bingo devices.

8. Arapaho Casino
In July, the 10th Circuit Court of Appeals upheld a prevous ruling tht the state of Wyoming had negotiated in bad faith when it refused to allow for a casino on the Wind River reservation. The ruling allowed the Arapaho tribe to continue with plans for a Las Vegas-style casino on the reservation.

9. Death of Chris LeDoux.
Country music star and world champion bareback rider Chris LeDoux died March 9 of compications from liver cancer. He was 56. The 1976 PRCA bareback champion earned a loyal following by passing out tapes of his music at rodeos. He lived in Kaycee.

10. Education Audit
Just days after Blankenship resigned, an audit of his department revealed possible nepotism, poorly documented budgets, apparent circumvention of state purchasing rules and improper reimbursements for training. Blankenship dismissed the audit findings claiming their were politically motivated.

Top Wyoming News Stories, 2006*

As selected by Associated Press member papers and broadcast outlets.

1. Barbara Cubin's razor-thin win over Gary Trauner for her seventh term in Congress.
2. The legislature approve bill introduced by State Rep. Ann Robinson (D-Natrona) to remove the sales tax on food. Local governments would be reimbursed for lost revenues. $50 million set aside for first two years.
3. The legislature's creation of the Hathaway scholarship program, providing funds to graduating seniors from Wyoming high schools to attend college
4. Jackson Canyon range fire that started Aug. 14 and burned 10,000 acres on Casper Mountain, forcing evacuation of many homes
5. Gov. Dave Freudenthal's election victory over Ray Hunkins
6. Hiring of Tom Buchanan as University of Wyoming president
7. The federal appeals court dismissal of Wyoming's lawsuit against the federal government over how wolves should be managed after removal from the Endangered Species Act
8. Murder-suicide of three students in Laramie in July
9. GOP campaign advertisements backfiring on the party concerning use of the state airplane
10. Wyoming's energy boom prompting recruitment of workers from Michigan where unemployment was high.

Top Wyoming News Stories, 2007*

As selected by Associated Press member papers and broadcast outlets.

1. The death of Sen. Craig Thomas, R-Wyo., and the subsequent appointment of U.S. Sen. John Barrasso, R-Wyo. Thomas, who had been Wyoming's senior senator, died in June at age 74 after a fight with leukemia. Born in Cody, Thomas entered Congress in a special election in 1989 to replace Dick Cheney after he was named defense secretary by the first President Bush. Gov. Dave Freudenthal chose Barrasso, a Casper surgeon and state senator, to succeed Thomas from a list of three finalists selected by the Wyoming Republican Party. The state party had winnowed the list down from more than 30 people who had expressed interest in the Senate seat.
2. Progress toward removing wolves from protection under the federal Endangered Species Act
The U.S. Fish and Wildlife Service has pushed to remove wolves from protection in Wyoming, Montana and Idaho. The federal agency this year said it could accept a Wyoming plan for how to manage wolves in the state once federal protection is lifted, possibly as soon as 2008.
3. U.S. Rep. Barbara Cubin's announcement in November that she would not seek re-election in 2008
Cubin, 59, is serving her seventh term in Congress. She has missed more than half of her votes in Congress this year. She has spent much of her time in Wyoming tending to her husband, who has

been ill for many years with an immune disorder.

4-5-6. There was a three-way tie for the fourth-place story of the year -- the decision by Wyoming Republicans to move up their presidential delegate selection process to Jan 5, to be among the first in the nation; the death of Robin Munis, 40, who was shot by her husband, an Army-trained sniper, as she sang on stage at a Cheyenne bar; and the Wyoming Cowgirls winning the WNIT Championship.

Top Wyoming News Stories, 2008*

As selected by Associated Press member papers and broadcast outlets.

1. Cynthia Lummis Defeats Gary Trauner for House Seat

Lummis, the former state treasurer, defeated Trauner, the Democratic nominee, by a 53-42 percent margin. Trauner had come very close to defeating incumbent Barbara Cubin two years earlier.

2. Wolf Delisting--and Relisting

In March 2008, wolves were removed from the Endangered Species list. However, a few months later, after numerous wolf hunting events were proposed, Montana's federal district judge ordered that the wolf be relisted as endangered. The October order effectively blocked wolf hunts.

3. University of Wyoming head football coach fired

Joe Glenn, who had completed three seasons with losing marks after registering initial success with the program, was fired as head coach. He was replaced by Dave Christensen, a former assistant at the University of Missouri.

4. Obama's Big Win in Wyoming's Democratic County Caucuses

Led by huge margins in Teton and Albany counties, Barack Obama's supporters gained a huge win in the caucus race against Hillary Rodham Clinton. Obama appeared at rallies in the state prior to the March county caucuses, including one in Laramie where almost 10,000 people came to hear him speak--the night before the county caucuses. In the fall general election, the counties giving Obama the largest margins in the caucuses were the two counties where he scored electoral majorities, losing the state's three electoral votes to Republican John McCain.

5. Former Campbell County Fire Chief Sentenced to Prison Term

Gary Scott, former Gillette fire chief, entered guilty pleas in district court in March on ten counts of taking children across state lines and molesting them. He was sentenced to a 24-year prison term in October.

Top Wyoming News Stories, 2009*

As selected by Associated Press member papers and broadcast outlets.

1. The economic recession hits Wyoming. Energy companies curtail operations in the state as some fuel prices drop. Wyoming's unemployment rate increases to 7.4 percent in October, the highest in more than 20 years.

2. The U.S. Fish and Wildlife Service decides to leave gray wolves in Wyoming on the endangered species list while delisting them in Idaho and Montana. Wyoming files suit in response.

3. Gov. Dave Freudenthal orders $230 million in budget cuts for fiscal year 2010, or about 10 percent for all state agencies, as energy prices and state government revenues fall.

4. A second year of normal- to above-average precipitation helps fill Wyoming reservoirs and propels the entire state out of drought conditions for the first time in nine years.

5. Former Wyoming state trooper Franklin Ryle is sentenced to 15 years in prison for the January kidnapping of a truck driver in what prosecutors say was an aborted murder plot.

6. Health officials detect swine flu in Wyoming and say it contributed to several deaths.

7. Tie: Hundreds of Wyoming Army National Guard members deploy to the Middle East in the spring; The Environmental Protection Agency opens its only investigation in the nation into potential effects of hydraulic fracturing on water wells; The University of Wyoming selects Laramie County as the site for a $100 million plant being built by Wyoming and General Electric Co. to research ways to use Wyoming coal more cleanly.

8. About 900 small earthquakes shake Yellowstone National Park in the last days of 2008 and first days of 2009.

9. Tie: Former Wyoming Gov. and U.S. Sen. Clifford Hansen dies Oct. 20; The U.S. Fish and Wildlife Service's Wyoming field office says it opposes any wind energy development in Wyoming's sage grouse core habitat areas before demonstration that it can be done with no impact on the birds.

National Newspaper Association Awards

Many Wyoming newspapers have won national awards through the National Newspaper Association. Since 1975, recipients of the top general excellence awards have included the *Jackson Hole Guide*, the *Jackson Hole News* and the *Green River Star*. Multiple first-place award winners in various categories have included the *Douglas Budget, Green River Star, Jackson Hole Guide, Jackson Hole News, Medicine Bow Post, Sheridan Press* and *Wyoming State Journal*. Best contest years for Wyoming newspapers have included 1987 when Wyoming newspapers won 38 national awards and 1979 when they won 25. Four Wyoming newspapers received National Newspaper Association awards in 1994. The *Jackson Hole Guide* won seven awards; the *Green River Star* and the *Jackson Hole News,* two each; and the *Cody Enterprise*, one.

Journalism Stories: A Potpourri

1. Awards Named

The Wyoming Press Association annually gives Wyoming journalists awards for excellence. Among the awards are the Milton Chilcott Freedom of Information Award, named in honor of the late *Sheridan Press* publisher, and the Wallace Biggs Award, named in honor of the long-time UW journalism professor.

2. Battle for Jackson Hole

A story titled "The Battle for Jackson Hole" in the November 1990 issue of the *Washington Journalism Review* featured the two competing weekly newspapers, the *Jackson Hole News* and *Jackson Hole Guide*. The *News* was founded in April 1970, competing with the *Guide* founded decades earlier. Both papers consistently won national and state awards for their quality. The two papers merged in 2002, but Jackson had a third paper, *Planet Jackson Hole* that continued to compete. Kemmerer and Casper were the only other Wyoming towns which had two separately owned competing newspapers by 2002.

3. Blank Page Protest

When a proposal to eliminate the journalism department at the University of Wyoming was being considered in the spring of 1988, the campus newspaper, the *Branding Iron*, protested the idea by publishing one issue of the paper with a blank front page and a one-line protest message. Chad Baldwin was the editor.

4. Blooper of the Year

On the Dec. 28, 1991, CNN show called "Capital Gang," commentator Marty Schram said the "Blooper of the Year 1991" was Sen. Alan Simpson's accusations about CNN reporter Peter Arnett during the Persian Gulf War. Guest and humorist Mark Russell added, "And the apology [from Simpson] had more amendments to it than the U. S. Constitution."

5. Cameras in Court

With the approval of Chief Justice Robert Rose, the Wyoming Supreme Court opened its proceedings to cameras in 1981. The Supreme Court led the way because no district court in Wyoming at the time allowed cameras. Presently, district courts allow cameras in the courtroom only if the judge approves it.

6. Coattail Effect

Following the destruction of his *Frontier Index* newspaper office in Bear River City on Nov. 20, 1868, editor Legh Freeman barely escaped from a mob. A doctor told of see-

The American Heritage Center holds the Hugh Downs collection, the papers of the famed ABC-TV newsman. Downs once worked on a ranch near Laramie when he was a youth. The Guinness Book of World Records lists Downs as the person having the greatest number of hours (10,037) on U. S. national commercial television. He was host of the Today Show and Concentration. Until 1999, he co-hosted "20/20."

ing Freeman leaving town: "He was spurring his mule so fast that you could have played checkers on his coattail."

7. Columnists

One of the longest regular running columns in Wyoming was written by Bruce Kennedy, president of Sage Publishing Company, and ran from 1957 until his death in 1992. Notable Wyoming columnists include Joan Barron of the *Casper Star-Tribune*, Kirk Knox of the Cheyenne Newspapers, Carolyn Tyler of the *Riverton Ranger* and syndicated columnist Bill Sniffin. Knox died in November 2005, at the age of 85.

8. Environmental Paper

High Country News, the national environmental paper, was started in Lander by Tom Bell. It is now published in Colorado.

9. FAX Newspaper

In 1990 in a March issue of *Editor and Publisher* magazine, University of Wyoming journalism student Curtis Claar made news for starting a newspaper that was circulated mainly through FAX machines. His monthly *Z88 FAX News* newspaper, originating in Casper, was directed to users of the Cambridge Z88 laptop computer.

10. Final Frontier

Three Wyoming journalists submitted applications to NASA for the Journalist-in-Space program before NASA abandoned the program following the Challenger disaster in 1986. Bill Sniffin of the *Wyoming State Journal*, Robert Roten of the *Laramie Boomerang* and David L. Roberts of the *Medicine Bow Post* applied for the coveted seat.

11. Media Hotline

A Freedom of Information hotline, serviced by Casper attorney Michael Krampner, was established in 1987 for reporters seeking information on issues such as access to meetings.. The committee that developed the hotline was a joint venture of the Wyoming Press Association, the Wyoming Chapter of the Society of Professional Journalists, the Wyoming Association of Broadcasters, with help from the Wyoming Press Women.

12. "I DO."

Editor Robert Caston proposed marriage to his future wife, Gayle, in a column in the *Saratoga Sun* in the early 1980s.

13. Japanese Language Newspaper

The *Heart Mountain Sentinel*, published in English and Japanese, was the newspaper at the Heart Mountain Relocation Center in Park County, published during World War II.

14. Juvenile Names

Names of juveniles can be printed in Wyoming newspapers in connection with violations of municipal ordinances, illegal possession laws or for misdemeanor traffic violations. Courts can withhold names of juveniles in felony cases.

15. Law and Newspapers

Wyoming lawyers and politicians frequently owned newspapers. Among the lawyers owning interests in papers were Alex T. Butler (*Casper Tribune*, 1889) and Robert R. Rose (*Kemmerer Camera*, 1916). In 1931, the two newspapers in Jackson were edited by the only two lawyers there. William Simpson ran *The Grand Teton*, founded to fight the establishment of the national monument. Teton County attorney Wilford Nelson edited the *Jackson's Hole Courier*. Sen. John B. Kendrick owned newspapers in Sheridan, Newcastle and Cheyenne. Sen. F. E. Warren owned interests in numerous Wyoming papers, as his personal papers, held in the American Heritage Center, indicate.

16. Post Swap

In 1982, a reporter exchange was made between the *Washington Post* and the *Medicine Bow Post*. David L. Roberts, *Medicine Bow Post* editor, switched places for two weeks with Chip Brown, a *Washington Post* feature reporter.

17. Pulitzer Finalist

Though no Wyoming newspaper has yet won a Pulitzer Prize (to 2010), two papers have come close. In 1985, the *Casper Star-Tribune* was nominated for its reporting on natural gas issues. It was one of three finalists for the Pulitzer Prize for public service. The *Wyoming State Journal* (Lander) was nominated in 1977 for reporting about abuses committed by the Dubois police department.

18. Reservation Paper

The *Wind River News* is the only newspaper in Wyoming published on an Indian reservation. The paper, founded in 1977 at Jeffrey City, moved to the Wind River reservation and published its first issue on April 7, 1983. Jeff Schier was the first editor. Other editors included Tom Bell, Geoff O'Gara, and Debbie Thunder.

19. Scholarly Journal

Journalism Educator, a scholarly journal established in 1946 by the American Society of Journalism School Administrators, was edited by UW journalism professor Bill Roepke from 1976-1983 in Laramie. He taught at UW from 1967-1986. He died Feb. 6, 2005.

20. Student Publications Award

The UW Student Publications Award, named in honor of Michael D. Lindsey, Wyoming newspaper publisher, recognizes "people for their exceptional contributions to the cause of better quality" UW student publications. Recipients have included Michael D. Lindsey (1986); Milton B. Chilcott (1987); Doug Killian (1988); Robert C. Warner (1989); David L. Roberts (1990, 1992); Robert Peck (1991); Dana Dreinhofer (1994); David Eisenhauer and Bernard Ourth (1996).

21. Tenure at Newspapers

Many people have worked at Wyoming newspapers for decades. P. P. Anderson served as publisher of the Basin newspaper for more than 55 years. George Hopkins published the *Big Piney Examiner* for 51 consecutive years, 1917-1958. Jack Pierce worked for the *Cody Enterprise* for 49 years, 1933-1982. J. R. Parrish published the *Newcastle News Letter Journal* for 50 years. Nerwin O. Reed had been publisher of the *Glenrock Independent* from 1939 until his death in 1996--57 years. Russ Allbaugh, who retired as *Laramie Boomerang* publisher in 1992, had been on the job there since 1945. Melvin and Esta Baldwin stayed 43 years with *Uinta County Herald* in Evanston before selling in 1988. Don Kominsky was with the *Kemmerer Gazette* for more than 40 years, where printer/writer Guido Bott worked for 53 years and Frank Taylor for almost as long. Robert Peck served more than 40 years as publisher of the *Riverton Ranger*. Miriam Bremer returned to the *Lingle Guide* and *Guernsey Gazette* in 1992 after a short break. She had worked for the *Lingle Guide* for more than 40 years, from 1948-1989.

22. Trump Story

Bruce Kennedy noted in a January 1991 column: "In the middle of the big flap over Donald and Ivana Trump's breakup, *Gillette News-Record* editor Ron Franscell took a call from an editor at the *Chicago Tribune*. The guy and columnist Mike Royko had just made a bet: Royko claimed the Trump story was an East Coast story and no one cared a hoot about it out West. 'Call it,' Royko insisted. So the guy stuck his finger on Wyoming and called Gillette. Royko was right, it was NOT playing out West. 'How did he know that?' the guy wailed."

G Edward Pendray, a journalist who went on to help found the American Rocket Society, was a co-author with Kenyon Nicholson of a fictional one-act play. Titled "The Organ," it was copyrighted in 1926. The play begins in the front yard of a homestead in eastern Wyoming. The story centers upon the sale of an organ at an auction and one woman's spirited efforts to discourage her neighbors from bidding on it, so she can keep it for her son. Pendray was reared on a ranch near Van Tassell.

23. Wet Trunk

New York publisher Horace Greeley traveled through Wyoming by stagecoach in 1859. When the coach crossed the Sweetwater River at one of the many fords, Greeley's trunk fell off into a deep pool of water. He said he lost "several white shirts."

24. Wyoming in Cartoons

Probably the best known cartoonist in Wyoming is Jerry Palen whose cartoons feature ranch life. He owns "Laffing Cow Press" of Saratoga. The firm publishes cookbooks and books of cartoons. Best known editorial cartoonist in the 1990s was Joe Kearney of the *Casper Star-Tribune*. Some newspapers used "mascots" for one-line jokes: the *Casper Star-Tribune* had "The Old Grouch" on its front page; the "Bow Dog" was used by the *Medicine Bow Post*; and the *Hanna Herald*, in reference to the graveyard shifts of the coal miners, used the "Graveyard Grinch." The *Buffalo Bulletin* had "Sagebrush Sven."

25. "Ex-lamb-licker"

Columnist O. H. "Jack" Flagg, in an article in a December, 1912, issue of the *Wind River Mountaineer*, called State Senator William Madden of Fremont County an "ex-lamb-licker." Angered by the remark, the 250-pound Madden encountered the paper's editor, 143-pound Henry Wendt, in the lobby of the Fremont Hotel. "I'll teach you to say stuff about me in your newspaper," Madden said as he struck Wendt, knocking him down and out cold.

26. Newest Newspapers

High Plains Sentinel, Wright, became a member of the Wyoming Press Association in 2003 as the newest paper in state. The *Cowboy State Free Press* and *WyoFile* both started in 2008 as web-based news services.

27. Book on War Reporting

Reporting the War: Freedom of the Press from the American Revolution to the War on Terrorism, was published by Palgrave Macmillan in 2007. The author is John Byrne Cook, a resident of Jackson since 1982, who previously wrote historical fiction.

Newspaper Families

Of the four large newspaper chains in Wyoming as of 2006, three continued to be owned or controlled by Wyoming families. Those families have included descendants who continued the newspaper ownership, assumed their own papers or otherwise stayed in the newspaper business.

1. Cheyenne Newspapers, Inc.

Tracy S. McCraken (1894-1960), initial owner, *Wyoming Eagle* (1926); *Laramie Boomerang* (1938); and others. Tracy's son, Robert McCraken (1924-1989); and Robert's children, Mike McCraken and Cindy McCraken Marek (*Cheyenne Eagle and Tribune*). Mike is publisher of the *Eagle/Tribune*.

2. Sage Publishing Co.

Bruce M. Kennedy (1929-1992), initial owner, *Gillette News-Record* (1970); *Cody Enterprise* (1971); *Greybull Standard* (1978), and others. Bruce's children, Brian Kennedy (*Hungry Horse News*, Montana); Ann Franscell (*Gillette News-Record*); and Bob Kennedy (*Cody Enterprise*).

3. The Peck Newspapers

Roy Peck (1922-1983) and Robert Peck (1924-2007), initial owners, *Riverton Ranger* (1949), *Shoshoni Pioneer* (1980), and others. Roy's son, David Peck (*Lovell Chronicle*); Robert's son, Christopher Peck (*Spokane Spokesman-Review*, Washington); and Robert's son, Steven Peck (*Riverton Ranger*).

Laramie Boomerang founder and humor writer Bill Nye kept a stuffed bird on his desk. It had a duck's body and a hawk's head.

Some Celebrated Libel Lawsuits

1. Territory v. Wilson (1873)
The first libel case was brought against Posey S. Wilson by Judge Joseph W. Fisher on June 20, 1873. Wilson and the *Omaha Herald* were named as defendants in the criminal libel action which ended with Wilson paying a fine for contempt. The action was appealed to the State Supreme Court which affirmed the conviction.

2. A. A. Anderson v. Meeteetse News (early 1900s)
Anderson, head of the Yellowstone Forest Reserve, initiated a plan which limited the use of the forest, despite the bitter opposition of sheepmen. The editor of the *Meeteetse News* was particularly critical: "Mr. Anderson can by a single stroke of his diamond-bedecked hand put out of existence that noble animal that clothes his unclean body." Anderson sued for libel. The *News* apologized and the case was settled.

3. Hahn v. Famous Lasky Players Corp. (1923)
The suit was brought by Virginia Hahn, the granddaughter of Jim Bridger, who sued the film company for "defaming" Bridger in the motion picture, *The Covered Wagon*, filmed in 1922. Bridger was portrayed as a drunken lout. The parties settled the case, reportedly for $5,000, in May 1924.

4. Goppert v. Lockhart (1926)
Cody Enterprise editor Caroline Lockhart published an editorial criticizing what she saw as harsh treatment meted out to suspected bootleggers. Ernest Goppert, the county attorney, sued unsuccessfully for libel.

5. Spriggs v. Cheyenne Newspapers (1943)
John J. Spriggs, a perennial candidate for Supreme Court justice, was the subject of Associated Press Cheyenne bureau chief Burton Thompson's story in which Thompson reported the disbarment proceedings brought against Spriggs. Even though the statement was true, Spriggs objected to the sentence in which the reporter pointed out that it hadn't been the first time such an action had been taken. The suit was brought against both AP and the Cheyenne Newspapers where the story appeared. The trial was held in Federal district court in Casper. Spriggs lost the case.

6. Wataha v. CBS (1977)
In 1977, Paul Wataha, the mayor of Rock Springs, sued the network, reporter Dan Rather, other media outlets and program producers for libel. CBS had broadcast an episode, "Our Town," which focused on crime and corruption in Rock Springs. Wataha later dropped the $63 million lawsuit after a series of out-of-court settlements were reached with some of the defendants.

7. Casper Star-Tribune v. Natrona County Airport Board (1979)
The airport board unsuccessfully sued the newspaper for libel after the board members were exonerated of charges of wrongdoing in 1976.

8. Pring v. Penthouse Magazine (1981)
Attorney Gerry Spence represented Kim Pring, the former Miss Wyoming who brought the libel suit against *Penthouse* for a story it ran about a Miss Wyoming who engaged in all kinds of deviant sexual activities. The six-person federal jury returned a verdict against *Penthouse* for $26.5 million, but the judge reduced the amount to $14,035,000. A 10th Circuit Court panel overturned the verdict in 1982 and the U. S. Supreme Court denied certiorari.

Peter Manigault, publisher of the Evening Post in Charleston, S. C., owned a ranch near Parkman in Sheridan County. When he died in June 2004, he was recognized for setting aside much of the land in a conseration easement.

Some Cases of Censorship

1. Asa S. Mercer, Northwestern Livestock Journal, 1892

When Mercer published the full confession of gunman George Dunning in his weekly newspaper in October 1892, he was arrested, charged with criminal libel and jailed. His printing office was seized and the Cheyenne postmaster withheld copies of the paper containing the confession on the grounds that they constituted "obscene matter" and were, therefore, unfit to be carried by the U. S. Mail. Big cattlemen were particularly angered by Mercer's article because before that time, his newspaper was always favorable to them. The confession later appeared in Mercer's book, *The Banditti of the Plains.* Although the book was not favorably received by many people, it did not face the same attacks as Mercer's newspaper. No formal attempt was ever made to either ban the book or destroy copies of it.

2. University of Wyoming "Yellow Sheet"

On April 26, 1934, UW *Branding Iron* staff and editor Joseph Jacobucci put out a "satirical edition" of the paper called "The Ironing Board." In it, various campus personalities were lampooned. The lead article referred to the university president, dean of students and the president's secretary as "father, son and holy ghost." Of the 1,200 copies printed, only a handful circulated. Jacobucci was fired as editor and suspended from UW and the staff was fired and replaced.

3. "Five Nude Studies," University of Wyoming, March, 1936

"The fig leaf has now come to the university campus," an article in the *Nation*, March 18, 1936, noted. "From an exhibition of American painting at the University of Wyoming, five nude studies....were removed by order of the president, Dr. Arthur Griswold Crane." The paintings were first placed in a room "for adults only" and then removed altogether. Crane was quoted as saying that his objection wasn't because the paintings depicted nudes but because "they were ugly and out of taste for an educational exhibit."

4. Textbook controversy, University of Wyoming, 1947

The University of Wyoming Board of Trustees voted to require submission of all textbooks for board approval. Proponents of the measure contended that the measure was needed to keep "subversive" materials from being used in the classrooms. Most university professors and students protested the unprecedented attempt to abridge academic freedom and the faculty elected a committee to attempt to reverse the board's position. (Committee members included Dr. Gale McGee who was elected to the U. S. Senate in 1958). After student demonstrations in support of the faculty and the eruption of a national uproar over the plan, the trustees reversed their position in January 1948.

5. Cartoon in Campbell County High School newspaper, 1983

Student editors wanted to use a cartoon by nationally syndicated cartoonist Don Wright satirizing the so-called "Moral Majority." Jay Carson, the school principal, prohibited its publication, claiming the cartoon "ridiculed the conservative viewpoint." Judy Worth, English teacher and the paper's advisor, sued the district over Carson's censorship. She did not seek any monetary damages, only an order that the district rewrite its publication policy. The district settled the case, agreeing to change the policy and, additionally, paying Worth $51,000 for removing her as advisor in retaliation for her lawsuit. The case was settled before the U. S. Supreme Court decision in the Hazelwood case in 1988 which would seem to allow such censorship by a school official.

Is editing a newspaper safer than running a bank? Evidently it was for a former editor in Platte County. For many years early in this century, Ira Middaugh edited the Wheatland World newspaper. He left the newspaper business and became a banker in Park County where he was killed in a bank robbery.

6. "60 Minutes," Western Wyoming College, 1986

John Collins, political science instructor at WWC, wanted to show an episode of the CBS series in order to stimulate interest in politics among his students. The episode, "Our Town," had been broadcast in 1977 and focused on crime and corruption in Rock Springs. Paul Wataha, former Rock Springs mayor, heard of Collins' plan and exerted pressure on school officials to keep the instructor from showing the clip. School officials pointed out, however, that the program never had been found to be libelous. Besides, Collins did not intend to discuss the merits of the program. In fact, he had distributed materials attacking the program.

7. John Updike, Rabbit Run, Medicine Bow, 1987

When a Medicine Bow English teacher included the book on a voluntary reading list given to his high school class, the Carbon County District No. 2 board ruled that the well-known novel could not be included, even on a voluntary reading list. Later, in retaliation for the teacher's attempts to reverse the censorship, the board refused to renew his contract.

8. Alston Chase, Playing God in Yellowstone, 1987

The controversial work was not sold in Yellowstone National Park in 1987 because, the author alleged, the content was critical of park administrators.

9. Dungeons and Dragons, Saratoga, 1987

In 1987, religious zealots attempted to have the game and similar materials banned from the Saratoga school library. They contended such games somehow favored "Satanism." The same board had shown its susceptibility to such pressures because it was the same one involved in the *Rabbit Run* case (#5, above).

10. AMAX news blackout, 1988

In April 1988, AMAX coal company imposed a "news blackout" on the *Casper Star-Tribune*. The company was angry with the paper's report of a layoff of 110 workers in the Gillette area. Reporter Liz Brimmer heard that miners had received notice of the layoff on April 7. When she called company officials, they demanded she wait for the company press release on the matter. When she refused and the *Star-Tribune* printed the story, the company said it would give no news to the paper. The firm rescinded the order two weeks later.

11. Jane Whitson, "Ten Lanes and the Tetons," Jackson, 1990

The collage showed a ten-lane highway leading to the Tetons which was cut out of a $20 bill. The work had been donated by the artist to a silent auction sponsored by the Jackson Hole Alliance for Responsible Planning, but it was withdrawn by auction organizers when a member found it "offensive."

12. AIDS film, Deaver, 1992

A tenured Rocky Mountain Middle School teacher was dismissed by the school board for "insubordination" in July 1992 for showing students an AIDS education film and allowing them to read "non-approved" literature. School officials also charged the woman with allowing students to read a Jack Kerouac poem and the novel, *Summer of '42*.

Some Casper students in 1919 became very well versed on the U. S. Constitution. According to a newspaper report from that year, "several students in Casper High School organized a 'soviet council' and went on strike because they were not satisfied with the manner in which the school is conducted." Their activities landed them in front of the school board. The board ordered them to memorize the U. S. Constitution before they could be "restored in good standing in the school." The board also stipulated that the memorization had to be "accomplished outside of school hours."

13. "Virgin", Green River, 1992

The book by James Patterson was held in the collections of the high school library in Green River. Several parents objected to the book even though it was neither assigned reading nor included on any voluntary reading list.

14. "More Scary Stories," Rock Springs, 1992

The book was written by Alvin Schwartz for young children. The real "scary story" is that some parents objected to having the book on the shelves of the library in a Rock Springs elementary school. Apparently, the attempted censorship was based on some religious objection to the subject of the book.

15. Political correctness, University of Wyoming, 1994

When a university organization for ethnic groups objected to a column written from the conservative viewpoint on reverse discrimination, university officials tried to intimidate the *Branding Iron* staff into publishing a refutation letter immediately in the next issue, even though the paper's policy stated that letters would be published in the order in which they were received. There was a backlog of letters about other issues which, in the opinion of editor Rob Jarosh, should be published in the order they had been received. The administrators countered by ordering an advertisement for an entire page in which the organization's letter was included along with comments about the newspaper's alleged "racist" policies. The ad called for students to boycott the *Branding Iron*. The UW administration, which had funded the group's ad, later apologized, saying they didn't know what would be put in the ad and didn't endorse the call for a boycott. The "boycott" failed to materialize in any significant way.

16. Newspaper Not Litter

In September, 1994, the Wyoming Supreme Court ruled that distribution of a newspaper did not constitute littering. The case was brought in Laramie against a free distribution paper called the *Ad-viser*. Laramie Municipal Judge Ron Copenhaver had found the publisher guilty of four counts of littering, under a muncipal ordinance. A district court upheld the ruling, but the Supreme Court reversed on a 4-1 decision. The ordinance violated the First Amendment, according to the court. It did the *Adviser* no good. The paper had gone out of business before the case went to the highest court.

17. "Swearing," Star Valley schools, 1995

In March, 1995, the Star Valley school board decided to remove two books from its high school English curriculum because they contained "swearing." Superintendent of Schools J. Allen Lowe said of the decision, however, "We're not people who burn a lot of books."

18. LCCC President's Trip to Costa Rica

In the spring of 2010, a state district judge temporarily barred the Wyoming Tribune-Eagle from publishing an article outlining irregularties alleged to have been committed by LCCC administrators and students while on a college-sanctioned trip to Costa Rica. Following protests from the Wyoming Press Association and many media advocates, the judge lifted the order three days later and the article was published in May 2010.

Why were the highly partisan Wyoming newspapers of the 19th century always so vicious about political opponents? Most towns had two or more competing papers and each relied heavily on city, county and legal advertising. When the candidate supported by a newspaper won an election, he would see that the ads over which he had control went solely to the paper that backed him. According to U. S. District Judge T. Blake Kennedy, who had been active in early-day state politics, every politician in those days knew that the primary task after getting elected was to "apportion funds to hungry newspapers."

PEOPLE
Representative Citizens of the Past and Home Counties*

Albany: Thurman Arnold, lawyer; Mary Bellamy, legislator; June Downey, teacher; E. B. Long, Civil War historian; Samuel H. Knight, teacher/geologist; T. A. Larson, historian; Ernest Linford, journalist; Dr. Grace Raymond Hebard, historian/teacher; Walter Edens, teacher/historian; Gale McGee, U. S. Senator

Big Horn: Judge P. W. Metz; W. S. Collins, entrepreneur; H. C. Lovell, rancher; B. F. Wickwire, rancher; Bruce Kennedy, publisher

Campbell: Edward Gillette, surveyor; Alonzo Clark, governor

Carbon: George Ferris, miner; Dr. Lillian Heath Nelson; August Grimm, hotel builder; Dr. John Osborne, physician/politician.

Converse: Malcolm Campbell, sheriff; "Coyote" Smith, photographer

Crook: Nels Smith, governor; Rod Guthrie, lawyer/judge

Fremont: Sacajawea; J. B. Okie, sheepman; Chief Washakie; Esther Hobart Morris, judge; Noyes Baldwin, entrepreneur; Charles Stough, sheriff; William Bright, legislator; L. L. Newton, editor; Roy Peck, editor/politician; Robert Peck, editor/politician; Clara Jensen, historian/preservationist; Black Coal, Arapaho leader; Yellow Calf, Arapaho chief

Goshen: J. K. Rollinson, writer; John Hunton, Fort Laramie sutler/rancher; Stan Hathaway, governor.

Hot Springs: J. D. Woodruff, rancher; Col. Jay Torrey; Tim McCoy, actor

Johnson: F. S. G. Hesse, rancher; Red Angus, sheriff; Judge C. H. Parmerlee; Jack Flagg, editor; Frank Lucas, editor/politician; Verna Keays, flag designer

Laramie: Willis Van Devanter, Supreme Court justice; Tracy McCraken, publisher; W. C. Deming, publisher; Daze Bristol, columnist; Warren Richardson, businessman; John Charles Thompson, editor; Francis E. Warren, politician

Lincoln: Annie Richey, rancher; P. J. Quealy, miner; Susan Quealy, activist; Ed Herschler, governor

Natrona: Edness Kimball Wilkins, legislator; Minnie Mitchell, state official; Fred Goodstein, oilman; C. H. King, merchant; B. B. Brooks, governor; Verda James, legislator; H. A. "Dave" True, Jr., oilman; Peggy Simson Curry, poet/author; Tom Stroock, politician/oilman; Warren Morton, politician/oilman; Craig Thomas, politician..

Niobrara: Frank A. Barrett, politician; J. B. Griffith, publisher; George Gibson, merchant/town promoter; A. A. Spaugh, rancher

Park: Paul Stock, oilman; A. A. Anderson, artist/rancher; William F. Cody; Caroline Lockhart, editor; William R. Coe, businessman; Milward Simpson, politician

Platte: C. A. Guernsey, rancher; Alexander Swan, rancher

Sheridan: Malcolm Moncrieffe, rancher; Henry Coffeen; Dr. Will Frackelton; J. D. Loucks, pioneer; Elsa Spear Byron, photographer; Bill Gollings, artist

Sublette: P. W. Jenkins, rancher; Joe Budd, rancher

Sweetwater: Archie Blair, pioneer; Chris Bunning, Rock Springs mayor; William Gottsche, rancher/philanthropist; Teno Roncalio, politician/lawyer.

Teton: W. C. DeLoney, pioneer; William Simpson, lawyer/editor; S. N. Leek, photographer/guide; Harrison Crandall, photographer; Olaus Murie, naturalist; Margaret Murie, naturalist; Mary Mead, rancher; Conrad Schwiering, artist; Clifford P. Hansen, governor/senator.

Uinta: Judge W. A. Carter; Thomas Blyth, businessman; Clarence D. Clark, politician; Elizabeth Arnold Stone, historian; Louis Vasquez, fort founder

Washakie: Tom Daggett, editor; William Bragg, writer; C. H. "Dad" Worland

Weston: Frank Mondell, politician; Grace McDonald, lawyer; Keith Thomson, politician; Mabel Brown, historian/magazine publisher.

The list clearly is not exhaustive; simply representative. All are deceased. Most are credited to county where they either lived the greater number of years or where they became best known. With little thought, the list easily could be doubled.

King Hussein of Jordan (d. Feb. 7, 1999) and his wife Queen Noor were frequent vacationers in Jackson Hole in the 1980s and 1990s. The queen's sister lived in Jackson. The royal couple from the Middle East country were often seen shopping around town

Birthplaces of Some Well-Known Wyomingites

Alabama: Al Kincaid, former UW football coach, b. Tuscaloosa, 1946; Warren Morton, gubernatorial candidate, b. Birmingham, 1924=2002; William Hill, Supreme Court justice, b. Montgomery, c. 1948.

Arizona: Katherine S. "Casey" Herschler, former First Lady, b. near Springerville; Raphael Lillywhite, artist, b. Woodruff, 1891-1958; Gen. Samuel C. Phillips, NASA official, b. Springerville, 1921-1990.

Arkansas: Cecil M. Shaw, state superintendent of public instruction, b. Paris, 1923-1995; Pershing Geiger, sculptor, b. 1920-1996.

California: Paul Carlin, postmaster general, b. San Diego, 1931; Robert Roripaugh, author/poet, b. Oxnard, 1930; Charles J. Belden, photographer, b. San Francisco, 1887-1966; Dave Walsh, "voice of the Cowboys," b. San Diego; Cong. Barbara Cubin, b. Salinas, Nov. 30, 1946; Tom Throop, activist, b. Bakersfield, 1947; Phil Dubois, UW president, b. Oakland, Oct. 17, 1950.

Colorado: Sen. Al Simpson, b. Denver, Sept. 2, 1931; Conrad Schwiering, artist, b. Boulder, 1915-1986; Agnes Wright Spring, historian/writer, b. Delta, 1894-1988; Paul Stock, oilman, b. Florence, 1894-1972; Bill Daniels, founder of 1st cable TV system, b. Greeley, 1920-2000.

Connecticut: William J. Fetterman, soldier, b. Cheshire, 1833-1866; Edward Gillette, state treasurer/surveyor for whom town named, b. New Haven, 1854-1936; Keith Goodenough, state senator, b. Winstead, 1956.

Delaware: J. M. Carey, first U. S. Senator and gov., b. Milton, Jan. 1845-1924.

D. C.: Edith K. O. Clark, superintendent of public instruction, b. Sept. 1881-1936; John Wideman, author, b. June 1941

Florida: Frank Bowron, Casper attorney, b. Umatilla

Georgia: John Bozeman, trailblazer, b. Pickens County, Jan. 1837-1863; John C. Fremont, explorer/army officer, b. Savannah, 1813-1890; Benny Dees, former UW basketball coach, b. Mount Vernon, 1937; Joby Wright, former UW basketball coach, b. Savannah, Sept. 5, 1950

Idaho: Bill Gollings, artist, b. Pierce City, 1878-1932; Clarene Law, legislator, b. Thorton, 1933.

Illinois: Harry Jackson, sculptor, b. Chicago, April, 1924; William Dubois, architect, b. Chicago, 1879-1953; Tracy McCraken, publisher, b. Evanston, 1894-1960.

Indiana: Elwood Mead, water engineer, b. Patriot, 1858-1936; Gene Gressley, archivist/historian, b. Frankfort, June, 1931.

Iowa: William F. Cody, b. LeClaire, Feb. 1846-1917; Grace Raymond Hebard, historian, b. Clinton, July 1861-1936; Aven Nelson, UW president/botanist, b. Summerville, 1859-1952; Paul Petzoldt, mountain climber, b. Union County, Jan. 1908-1999; Larry Lehman, Supreme Court justice, b. Iowa City, 1945; Matilda Hansen, legislator, b. Paullina, 1929; Steve McClain, UW coach, b. Orient, 1962.

Kansas: Katherine Morton, supt. of public instr., b. Brown Co., 1879; H. C. Lovell, rancher; Ev Shelton, UW coach, b. Cunningham, 1899-1974; Harrison Crandall, Teton artist/photographer, b. Newton, 1887-1970.

Kentucky: William Sublette, fur trader, b. 1799-1845; John Hoback, mountain man, b. 1745; W. J. Hardin, black legislator, b. 1830; W. C. Deming, publisher, b. Olivet, 1869-1949.

Louisiana: Manuel Lisa, fur trader, b. New Orleans, 1772-1820.

Maine: Bill Nye, newspaper editor/humorist, b. Shirley, 1850-1896

Maryland: Alfred Jacob Miller, artist, b. Baltimore, Jan. 1810-1874; Struthers Burt, rancher/author, b. Baltimore, 1882-1953.

Massachusetts: Francis E. Warren, governor/senator, b. Hinsdale, June 1844-1929; Joseph C. O'Mahoney, U. S. Senator, b. Chelsea, Nov. 1884-1962; Frederic H. Porter, architect, b. Salem, 1890-1976.

Michigan: Tim McCoy, actor/Wyoming National Guard adjutant general, b. Saginaw, 1893-1978; Edward Grigware, artist, b. Caseville, 1889-1960; M. D. Houghton, artist, b. Otsego, 1846-1919.

Minnesota: Ed Jennings, UW president, b. Minneapolis, 1937; Olaus Murie, ecologist, b. Moorhead, 1889-1963.

Mississippi: George Duke Humphrey, UW president, b. Ivey, Tippah Co., Aug. 1897-1973.

Missouri: Nellie Tayloe Ross, governor/mint director, b. St. Joseph, 1876-1977; Tom Horn, gunman, b. 1861-1903; J. C. Penney, merchant, b. 1875-1971; Bob Schuster, lawyer, b. St. Louis, 1945.

Montana: Lynn Simons, state supt. of public instruction, b. Havre, 1934; Leonard McEwen, judge, b. Great Falls, 1925.

Nebraska: Gale McGee, senator, b. Lincoln, 1915-1992; Stan Hathaway, governor, b. Osceola, July 1924-2004; Mike Sullivan, governor, b. Omaha, Sept. 22, 1939; Dick Cheney, congressman/Secy of Defense/VP, b. Lincoln, Jan. 30, 1941; T. A. Larson, historian, b. Wakefield, Jan. 1910-2001

Nevada: Francis Brammar, news photographer for 50 years, b. Wadsworth, 1900-1986

New Hampshire: DeForest Richards, governor, b. Charlestown, Aug. 1846-1903; Col. E. H. Kimball, publisher, b. Center Sandwich, 1842.

New Jersey: John Wold, congressman/geologist, b. East Orange, 1916; Wilson Clough, teacher/author, b. 1894-1992; A. A. Anderson, artist, 1847-1940; Mary O'Hara, author, b. Cape May, 1885-1980.

New Mexico: George Baggs, rancher for whom town named, date/place unk.; Floyd Esquibel, legislator, b. Mora, 1938.

New York: Malcolm Wallop, former U. S. Senator, b. New York City, 1933; Robert I. Russin, sculptor, b. NYC, Aug. 1914-2007; J. H. Hayford, publisher/judge, Potsdam, 1828-1902; Tom Stroock, oilman/former ambassador, b. NYC, 1925-2009.

North Carolina: George W. Baxter, territorial governor/rancher, b. 1855-1929

North Dakota: Roy Peck, Riverton publisher/legislator, b. Rugby, May 1922-1983; Gladys Powelson Jones, artist/author, b. Rydes, 1909-2004.

Ohio: George Crook, army officer, b. Dayton, Sept. 1829-1890; Caspar Collins, soldier, b. Hillsboro, Sept. 1844-1865; Joe Tiller, former UW football coach, b. Toledo, Dec. 7, 1942

Oklahoma: Terry Roark, former UW president, b. Okeene, 1939; John J. McIntyre, congressman/judge, b. Dewey Co., Dec. 1904-1974; Michael Golden, Supreme Court justice, b. Enid, 1942; Vic Koenning, UW football coach, b. Owasso, 1960.

Oregon: Charles Scott, legislator, b. Klamath Falls, Aug. 1945

Pennsylvania: Owen Wister, author, b. Germantown, 1860-1938; M. C. Barrow ("Bill Barlow"), publisher, b. 1857-1910; Susan Anderson, journalist, b. Pittsburgh, 1945.

Rhode Island: William A. Heath, Rawlins inventor, b. Providence

South Carolina: James Stilman, 1st teacher at South Pass City; Irene Devin, state senator, b. Sumter, 1943.

South Dakota: Nels Smith, governor, b. Gayville, 1884-1976

Tennessee: William Ross, governor, b. Dover, Dec. 1873-1924; T. T. Thornburgh, army officer, b. New Market, d. 1879.

Texas: John B. Kendrick, governor/senator, b. Jacksonville, Sept. 1857-1933; Joe LeFors, U. S. Marshal, b. Paris, 1865-1940; Ewing T. Kerr, federal judge, b. Bowie, Jan. 1900-1992

Utah: Butch Cassidy, outlaw, b. Circleville, 1866- ? ; Rupert Weeks, artist, b. Garland, 1918-1983.

Vermont: W. W. Peck, territorial judge, b. Burlington, 1819-1899; John L. Grattan, soldier, b. about 1830-1854.

Virginia: Jim Bridger, mountain man, b. March 1804-1881; John Hunton, pioneer rancher, b. Madison Court House, 1839-1928; J. E. Stimson, photographer, b. Culpepper Co., 1870-1952.

Washington: Bill Hosokawa, editor/author, b. Seattle, 1915-2007; Eugene Phelps, dude ranch owner, b. Whatcom Co., 1884-1944; Margaret Murie, author, b. Seattle, 1903-2003; Mike Enzi, U. S. Senator, b. Bremerton, 1944.

West Virginia: Jesse Leo Reno, soldier for whom Fort Reno named, b. Wheeling, 1823-1862; Peg Shreve, legislator, b. Spencer

Wisconsin: Paul Roach, UW athletic director/coach, b. Spring Green; Joe Cardine, Supreme Court justice, b. Prairie du Chien, 1924-1998; Deborah Hardy, historian, Milwaukee.

Wyoming: Crazy Horse, warrior, b. Powder River Basin, 1849-1877; Black Elk, Indian medicine man, b. near Little Powder River, 1863-1950; Jackson Pollock, artist, b. Cody, 1911-56; Thurman Arnold, lawyer, b. Laramie, 1891-1969; Samuel H. Knight, b. Laramie, 1892-1975.

This list includes several individuals who never resided in the state, but because their names were applied to Wyoming towns or landmarks, they are included. Dates of death are included, when known. The 1890 census indicated that the most common birthplace of Wyomingites was in the state of New York. By 1910, Iowa had become the most common birthplace of Wyoming residents.

Height of Some Well-Known Wyomingites

9'6": The Inflatable Cowboy (former UW mascot)
6'11": Eric Leckner, former UW/NBA basketball player
6'10": Theo Ratliff, former UW basketball player, now in the NBA
6'8": Josh Davis and Ugo Udezue, both former UW basketball players
6'7": Al Simpson, former U. S. Senator
6'5": Fennis Dembo, former UW basketball player; Marcus Bailey, former UW basketball player
6'4": Man-Afraid-of-His-Horses; Gov. Nels Smith; Charlie Irwin, showman and cowboy (he weighed 450 lbs.).
6'3": Roman Nose, Cheyenne chief
6'2": William Sublette, trapper and trader; Earl Durand, mountain man; Chief Joseph, Nez Perce chief; Matthew Fox, TV/movie actor
6'1": Tom Horn, gunman; Bill Carlisle, train robber; William F. Cody.
6' : Stub Farlow, Lander cowboy; Nancy Hill, pioneer, died 1847 along trail
5'11": Esther Hobart Morris, 1st woman justice of the peace
5'10": Chief Washakie
5'6": Vernon Baker, Wyoming-born Medal of Honor winner in World War II
5'5": Philip Sheridan, army general for whom Sheridan is named

To a Different Drum:
Anecdotes about Interesting Wyomingites

1. Charles Jesse "Buffalo" Jones, buffalo hunter, game warden

Born in Tazewell Co., Ill., in 1844, Jones attended Wesleyan University and in the 1860s, became a buffalo hunter furnishing meat to railroad workers in Kansas. Young William F. "Buffalo Bill" Cody was involved in similar employment at the time. Jones founded Garden City, Kansas, then left Kansas for the Rockies. He established the first herd of "cattalo" (cattle crossed with buffalo) and, from 1902-05, he served as game warden in Yellowstone National Park. A friend of President Theodore Roosevelt, Jones led an expedition to British East Africa (Kenya) in 1910 to lasso and capture game animals for American zoos. In 1914, he led another expedition to the Congo to capture live gorillas. He died in Topeka, Kansas, Oct. 1, 1919.

2. E. T. Payton, newspaper editor/mental health reformer

Payton's career is impossible to summarize in one paragraph. He was present either as a participant or reporter in numerous incidents in Wyoming history including the Johnson County Invasion, the so-called Red Bank murders of the daughter and son-in-law of a Wyoming governor, and the posse chase of Butch Cassidy's gang after the Wilcox train robbery. A prolific and talented writer, Payton founded the first newspaper in Thermopolis (the second in the Big Horn Basin). Committed to the new state mental hospital in Evanston on several occasions, Payton worked actively to improve the conditions for patients. He wrote two accounts of his hospitalizations. Thermopolis old-timers remembered Payton for riding his horse backward, carrying a parasol while his horse wore his hat and necktie.

3. William B. Boyd, Crook County schoolteacher and homesteader

Boyd taught school east of Seely in 1916 and he was known for his "nocturnal" ways. His contract was not renewed after his first year in which classes began at 4 p.m. Later, he lived on a homestead along the Little Missouri, feuded with neighbors and lived on rabbits and fish. He spent much of his time nude. He tried riding a hog one time, was thrown off and his leg broken badly, requiring a metal plate to hold it together. Some months later, Boyd decided the plate was unnecessary, removed the screws with a pocket knife and took the plate off without either anesthesia or painkiller. In the early 1960s, he went to Missouri for cancer treatment and there, he was struck and killed by a car while he carried a burlap sack on one of his nocturnal journeys.

4. Frank Sykes, Crooked Creek rancher, Big Horn County

Sykes homesteaded by himself in the area before the turn of the century. Stories about his eccentricities are numerous, including his habit of going nude on days he tanned leather. "No visitors today. Tanning," the sign on his gate would announce. He ate but one thing at any one meal. One day, it was potatoes and a neighbor stopped in time for dinner. Sykes cooked with rancid bear grease and the neighbor could hardly stand bear grease when it was fresh. "I'll just have coffee," the neighbor announced politely. Sykes demanded he have some potatoes. The man reluctantly complied, choking down a small helping. When he finished, Sykes insisted he have more. When the man refused, Sykes pulled out his pistol. "Go ahead and finish those spuds because you're going to eat potatoes just like that horse of yours is eating my hay," Sykes snarled. The neighbor ate, but ever after, potatoes were his least favorite food. *Source: Rose Vida Bischoff Black. Lovell—Our Pioneer Heritage. (Salt Lake, 1984).*

5. Thomas A. Pickerell, "pack rat" and mail pilferer, Platte County

In March 1930, law enforcement officials and national guardsmen trudged through two feet of snow to Pickerell's cabin in Fletcher Park near Laramie Peak where they discovered a huge cache of stolen merchandise. Pickerell, a long-time mail carrier, had stolen thousands of articles from the mail over the years. His cabin was full of goods and he cached part of the loot outside. Items included almost anything that was mailable, ranging from children's toys to automobiles.

6. "Boxcar" Murphy (James H. Norman), raffle ticket salesman, Park County

Norman gained his nickname after falling asleep in a boxcar that ended up stopping in Powell in the middle 1960s. "Boxcar" carried a cane which he would twirl with a twist

---

St. Joseph's Children's Home at Torrington opened in 1930 on a 93-acre tract of land acquired by the Roman Catholic Church in 1924. The Episcopal Church-operated Cathedral Home near Laramie dates from 1910.

of his wrist while walking down the street. Sometimes, he would blow loudly on a police whistle as he strolled. A fixture hitchhiking Park County roads in mid-century, "Boxcar" sold thousands of raffle tickets on a chance to win a rifle which he carried with him. It is not known if he ever awarded the prize or if a drawing ever took place. His favorite route seemed to be between Cody and Powell and, on the way, he would dispense advice and tell stories to the driver who gave him a lift—and, often, try to sell him a raffle ticket. Once, a Powell resident spotted him along the road and he stopped to give "Boxcar" a lift. As he pulled to a stop, "Boxcar" disappeared into the brush and returned carrying the carcass of a deer! As he tossed it into the back seat, he said, "Thanks."

7. George W. K. Posvar, perennial political aspirant, Casper

Posvar once filed for statewide office giving his address a vacant lot in Casper. He frequently ran for statewide office, but never gained a party nomination.

8. Lou Polk, dance hall "hostess," Casper

Lou operated a dance hall in Casper in the 1890s. One night she was kidnapped by her jealous house mate Dagae Lee and taken outside town. He thought she should quit gaining the attentions of other men. She demurred; he cut off her nose to "make her less attractive." She survived the savage attack and a Casper doctor unsuccessfully tried to sew the nose back on. As an alternative, the resourceful doctor fitted Lou with a hand-carved wooden nose, held to her face by a pair of eyeglasses. Few people could judge the success of the novel carving, however, because Lou never appeared in public without wearing a veil over her face.

9. M. C. Barrow ("Bill Barlow"), newspaper editor, Douglas

Barrow learned printing in Nebraska, but came to Laramie as a postal clerk in the 1870s. He returned to printing and newspapering in 1879 and worked for both Laramie papers and the *Rawlins Tribune*. In 1886, he moved to the future town site of Douglas and named the new paper "*Bill Barlow's Budget*" for the pen name he adopted. He dispensed political advice from the pages of the *Budget* and also ran for public office. He served two terms as mayor of Douglas and was elected a delegate to the Constitutional Convention. Barrow was not a "party man." He switched political parties, gaining the enmity of one while never dispelling the suspicions of regulars in the other.

10. Clement S. "Ben" Bregough, rancher, Albany County

An Englishman who lived on the Laramie Plains far from any town, Bregough boxed with bears and used Siberian wolfhounds to chase coyotes. His grave, once far from any-where, can be seen from I-80 near Arlington.

11. John E. Johnson, tie hack and ranch hand, Sublette County

Johnson, a bachelor Finn, made beautiful cabinets. During his last illness in 1960, he was taken to Big Piney. He hadn't washed since the sauna had closed 30 years earlier. It is said that when the nurses scrubbed him down, the shock of the experience caused his demise. His housemates were trapper Charlie Stone and "Little Gus," a fellow Finn known for making whiskey from potato peelings.

12. Christopher "Kit" Castle, judge, Evanston

A California '49er, Castle came to Evanston in 1872 after avoiding authorities who wanted to question him about the suspicious deaths of two men in California and another two in Helena, Montana. Castle became Justice of the Peace in Evanston. When he adjourned court, all of the officers and many onlookers would cross the alley to Pete Downs' saloon for the afternoon. "Finance was not one of his strong points and at one time a committee was appointed to examine his books." They were turned over with cheerfulness. After fruitless work, the puzzled committee told him they could make neither head nor tail of his reports. "He answered that he was hoping that they might, as he could not." *Source: Elizabeth Arnold Stone, Uinta County: Its Place in History. (Laramie, 1924), p. 103.*

13. P. G. Murphy, "fisherman" and vegetable dealer, Albany County

Murphy, an Albany County rancher, was working on a dam when his son-in-law was dynamiting fish. A stick of the unexploded dynamite floated downstream instead of sinking as they usually did. Murphy was the surprise recipient when the thing finally exploded near his dam. To teach the son-in-law a lesson, he turned him in to the sheriff. Murphy was surprised when the officials implicated him in the illegal activity and jailed the two men together. Murphy sold vegetables in Laramie. One day Mrs. Edward Ivinson, wife of the prominent banker, yelled down from her window, asking him what he had for vegetables that day. Murphy's answer echoed throughout the neighborhood. He said he had carrots and other vegetables and "ma'am, I have rutabagas as big as your thigh." He sold the whole load right there. *Source: Robert Burns, et al. Wyoming Pioneer Ranches. (Laramie, 1954), p. 137.*

14. "Doc" Chambers, musician and raconteur, Cody

One of the numerous interesting characters from Cody country, Chambers won the title of "Wyoming's Ugliest Man" in 1959. He journeyed to Hollywood where he appeared on the Art Linkletter show, telling the story about being so ugly, he was hired as a scarecrow and the crows were so scared, they brought back corn they stole four years before. Chambers came to Cody in 1928, worked as Cody's first mail carrier when door-to-door service was initiated and, later, gave osteopathic treatments. He played in bands in Cody, Greybull and Sheridan. He had put himself through osteopathy school by playing the banjo.

15. Harry Luckinbill, rancher, Rock River

Luckinbill lived in a railroad boxcar converted into a comfortable home far north of Rock River and miles from any railroad tracks. An expert at braiding horsehair rope, a skill he learned from prisoners at Rawlins, he once raised several dozen young coyotes who lived with him in his home. When the animals had grown, they lived outside in a specially constructed pen, but they were nearly as tame as dogs. One often tried to untie Luckinbill's shoe. The coyotes had been abandoned as pups and he said he raised them, not as pets, but for their pelts.

16. Grant Jones, Doublejack editor, Dillon

A graduate of Northwestern University, Jones worked for newspapers in Chicago, St. Louis and Denver, before coming to the Carbon County mining town of Dillon to start his own newspaper at the turn of the century. The paper was often full of surprising characters like a bird who would swallow itself to hide from enemies and a mountain-climbing beast whose right legs were both shorter than its left ones so it could stand comfortably in the mountain territory. Drinking and drugs frequently interfered with Jones' great talent as a writer. On one occasion, he went on a drunken spree and did not collect any news for the week's issue. He simply reprinted the previous week's paper and ran a line at the top of the front page: "We received so many compliments about last week's newspaper that we decided to publish it again." Jones died very young for a combination of whiskey and morphine in 1903. Had he lived, he might have become as famous as Laramie writer and humorist Bill Nye.

17. Joe O'Brien, rancher, Niobrara County

One night, O'Brien's pickup became stuck in a stream bed during a torrential downpour. He hiked through the dark to a nearby ranchhouse. The ranchers fed him supper and he accepted their invitation to stay the night. The next morning, following a big breakfast, O'Brien was asked if he would like more coffee. "No, I'd better not," he said. "Cecil [his wife] is down in the pickup and, as it is, she's going to be plenty mad about having to sit down there all night."

An estimated 720 whistle blasts of trains passing through Newcastle daily—at 20 minute intervals.

18. George Rainsford architect/rancher, Cheyenne/Chugwater

The New York-born architect was not popular with neighbors who called him "Lord Rainsford" for his arrogance. At one point, Rainsford challenged God to prove He existed by hitting Rainsford with a lightning bolt. God did not accept the challenge; Rainsford was not hit.

19. John Sargent

Sargent, the "black sheep" of a wealthy Maine shipping family, came to Jackson Hole in 1886, joined by Robert Hamilton, a former schoolmate and descendant of Alexander Hamilton. They built a lodge near Leek's Camp and opened it as a dude ranch they called "Merry Mere." Four years later, Sargent brought his wife and young child to the lodge. In 1891, Hamilton disappeared while on a hunting trip with Sargent. His body was later found in the Snake River, his horse nearby. Some suspected Sargent of foul play. In 1897 soldiers skiing past Sargent's place heard a woman's screams. They reported it to authorities who found Mrs. Sargent badly beaten. She later died and Sargent was tried for her murder. After he was exonerated of the murder, he married again. His second wife is said to have roamed through the woods naked except for mittens on her feet, playing her violin left-handed and eating peanuts. Local people speculated that Sargent deprived her of clothes so she would not leave. Eventually, however, her family returned her to Philadelphia where she was institutionalized. Sargent, without funds and alone, committed suicide in the spring of 1913. The AMK ranch was built on the site years later. *(From "Strange Music at Merry Mere," by Esther Allan. Teton Magazine 9 [1976]. Used by permission of Gene Downer, editor.)*

20. Herbert Huncke, derelict, drug addict, founder of "Beat Generation"

Huncke, "a hustler and hooligan who gave the Beats their name and William Burroughs his first fix," (as *Time Magazine* described him, Aug. 19, 1996), hardly qualifies as a "Wyomingite." Although he was born in Greenfield, Mass., in 1915, lived in Chicago and, later, on the streets of New York City, Huncke had a close Wyoming connection. He was the grandson of prominent Laramie Plains rancher Col. E. J. Bell. "My mother was 15 when she married, the daughter of a wealthy cattle baron in Wyoming who was many years his wife's senior," Huncke wrote in his 1990 autobiography titled *Guilty of Everything.* "My grandmother...was a young, good-looking woman who had sort of been Queen Bee of Laramie." His father was a Chicagoan who delivered a car to Bell's ranch, met the daughter and they eloped. Huncke, a derelict in every sense of the word, died Aug. 9, 1996, in New York. His obituary called him "the hipster who defined 'Beat'." Another called him "a character in the works of his cronies Allen Ginsberg and Jack Kerouac."

21. Don Porter, "The Ladder Man"

Porter, born in Ohio, in 1915, was known in Laramie in the 1970s for sitting on a ladder in various spots around the downtown. He became a familiar sight in Laramie and, soon, he was referred to as "the Ladder Man." He was a veteran of the U. S. Army during World War II. On the afternoon of July 6, 1979, Porter was seated on his familiar ladder placed near the Laramie train depot. Suddenly, he stood up and walked into the path of an on-coming train. He died at the scene. A music group, the Son of Jerel, performed a song titled "Ladder Man." *Source: Albany County Library column, Laramie Boomerang, Aug. 13, 2000, p. 5.*

In August, 1929, 16-year-old Seattle student Wilbur Huston (b. Cheyenne, 1913), won the Edison award given annually to the brightest student in America interested in science. Huston's father had been the Episcopal priest in Cheyenne before the family moved to Seattle. The prize included a four-year scholarship to MIT. Huston later lived in Florida.

Languages Spoken at Home by Wyomingites*

According to U. S. Census, 1990.

1. Spanish

In almost 13,800 Wyoming homes, Spanish is the primary language spoken by those in the household.

2. Native American languages

A dozen different Native American languages are spoken in Wyoming homes. According to the 1990 census, 1,521 households listed Arapaho as the primary language; Shoshoni, 321; Dakota, 194; "American Indian," 104; Navajo, 89; Cheyenne, 25; Blackfoot, 22; Ute, 17; Comanche, 15; Cherokee, 13; Apache, 9; and Cree, 6. The figures show 23,809 people over the age of five speak a language other than English at home.

Citizen of the Century Finalists, 1999*

Agriculture: H. A. "Dave" True
Business: H. A. "Dave" True
Community Service: Olaus and Margaret Murie
Education: George Frison
Fine and Performing Arts: Peggy Simson Curry
Government: Al Simpson
Heathcare, Science and Technology: Samuel Knight
Military: Rudolph L. Esmay
Minerals, Oil and Gas: John Wold
Religion: Rev. John Roberts
Sports: Milward Simpson

Dr. Samuel Knight was the "Citizen of the Century." The list was chosen by committees, based on nominations and votes from the general public in a poll conducted by the Friends of the American Heritage Center, University of Wyoming, Win Hickey, chair.

Deaths by Counties, 2006

1. Laramie, 723
2. Natrona, 659
3. Fremont, 396
4. Sheridan, 312
5. Sweetwater, 253
6. Park, 250
7. Campbell, 198
8. Albany, 196
9. Big Horn, 141
10. Carbon, 137
11. Uinta, 131
12. Goshen, 122
13. Platte, 99
14. Lincoln, 94
15.-17. Johnson, Washakie, Converse, 79 each
18. Weston, 76
19. Teton, 69
20. Hot Springs, 53
21. Sublette, 49
22. Crook, 44
23. Niobrara, 36
Total Deaths: 4,275

"C. W. Berry declares he has purchased an automobile and warns all who take a shot at him will be prosecuted to the full extent of the law, run over and not allowed to ride." Laramie Boomerang, 1900.

International City

Since its earliest days as a center for coal mining, Rock Springs had the distinction of being one of the most ethnically diverse towns in America. A sign on the north edge of town reads: "Rocks Springs: Home of 56 Nationalities." In 2005, Rock Springs was listed as 36th of all ZIP codes in the country for percentage of first-ancestry Slavic residents. It was 49th on the list for percentage of first-ancestry Basque; 59th for Slovene; and 97th for Yugoslavian.

Wyoming's First Business Computer

Wyoming's first business computer was an IBM 1401 card system, installed in September 1960 at the Casper office of Pan American Petroleum Company (now part of BP). Vince Siren, a graduate of the University of Wyoming, was the first full-time computer programmer. Siren recalls that the computer was about four feet by four feet and stood seven feet high. It had 4,000 characters of memory and was connected by cables to a card reader-punch and to a 132-character printer.

Initially, the 1401 was used for accounting applications--lease records, oil and gas revenue and joint interest accounting. Magnetic tapes and additional memory were added later, as were engineering, geological and geophysical applications.

Other University of Wyoming alumni on the programming staff were Woodford (Woody) Jones, who later assumed responsibilities as a programming manager for the LDS Church in Salt Lake City, and Marvin Hollenbeck, who later became the data processing manager for the Rocky Mountain Division of Pan American in Denver.

Company Shares of Oil/Gas Production in Wyoming (1990)

OIL		GAS	
Amoco (now BP)	18%	Exxon	20.7%
Marathon	15%	Amoco	19.0%
Chevron	6%	Chevron	15.6%
Exxon	5%	Enron Oil and Gas	4.6%
Kerr-McGee	3.6%		
Conoco	3.5%		

Cowboys' Wages	1885: $100 a month, room and board, horse and equipment
	1890: $40 a month, food, horses and equipment
	1985: $500-$600 a month, room and board
	1996: $800 a month (average cowboy wage was $6,300 annually)

The Jewish Oil Company was formed in Torrington in 1916 "to raise $10,000 with which to drill for oil near Allen."

PETROLEUM

1st printed mention of Wyoming oil: "In this neighborhood, the captain [Bonneville] made search for the great tar springs, one of the wonders of the mountains...the men hastened to collect a quantity of it to use as an ointment for the galled backs of their horses and as a balsam for their own pains and aches." —Washington Irving, *Adventures of Captain Bonneville*, 1837.

1st recorded discovery of oil in Wyoming: An oil spring near Hilliard was well known when Fort Bridger was established in 1842.

1st recorded sale of oil produced in Wyoming: 1863. Oil from Oil Mountain Springs, 20 miles west of Casper, was sold to Oregon Trail travelers as lubricant for wagon wheels.

1st oil refinery in Wyoming: Casper, 1895

1st oil field in the world to be powered by electricity: Salt Creek field

1st oil refinery in the Big Horn Basin: Northwest Oil Refinery, Cowley, 1910, closed in 1923.

1st successful wildcatter: Mike Murphy, an ex-gold prospector, who drilled the discovery well at Dallas Dome in 1883-1884. The well found oil at 300 feet in the Chugwater formation.

1st town in Wyoming heated by natural gas: Greybull, 1908.

1st 3-inch welded pipeline in the world: Salt Creek, 1920.

Largest gasoline-producing refinery in the world (1922): Standard Refinery, Casper

Most complete oil monopoly: Just two companies, Standard Oil (Indiana) and Ohio Oil, controlled 97 percent of all oil production in Wyoming in 1922.

Companies/operators producing oil in Wyoming (2007): 475.

Companies/operators producing natural gas in Wyoming (2007): 288.

1st high-octane aviation fuel plant in Wyoming: Frontier Refining Company's high-octane unit, Cheyenne, built for $8 million, dedicated April 14, 1944.

Proposal made to legislature to build a state-owned refinery: 1931.

High gasoline prices and politics: The problem became a campaign theme for Leslie Miller's run for governor in 1932 and Nels Smith's campaign in 1938.

1st natural gas in Laramie: Feb. 14, 1933 by Rocky Mountain Gas Co., the first valve opened by Virginia Husted, wife of Ward W. Husted, the 1st manager.

Wyoming had 45 operating **gas plants** in 2007 processing 97% of the state's gas production.

Natural gas wells (2007): 27,400 wells produced gas. Of that number, 17,300 were coal bed natural gas wells.

Oil well drilled at greatest elevation: When it was completed in the summer of 1957, the Richfield Oil Co., well at 10,785 feet on Carter Mountain, 22 miles from Cody, held the North American mark for several years.

The Interstate Compact for Conservation of Oil and Natural Gas was formed in 1935 but Wyoming did not join until 1955.

First crude oil pipeline: 1911. In 2010, 89 companies operated 22,700 miles of pipelines in Wyoming carrying oil, natural gas or petroleum products.

Newest pipeline: The 904-mile pipeline from Opal to California. The Kern River Gas Pipeline transports 700 million cubic feet of natural gas per day.

Oil wells in Wyoming (1993): 14,000 wells, 10,000 miles of pipelines, 56 gas plants, four refineries. The state had nine operating refineries in 1981.

Oil wells in Wyoming (2007) 10,300 producing wells. Of those, 3,112 oil wells were drilled in 2007. According to the Petroleum Association of Wyoming, oil was found by 152 or 4.9 percent; natural gas by 2,875 (92.4 percent0 and 85 (2.7 percent) were dry holes. Almost half of wildcat wells struck gas or oil in 2007.

Wyoming had an estimated 5,000 stripper wells on federal land (1992). A stripper well is one producing 15 barrels or less daily.

Wyoming led nation in oil production on federal lands in 2006: 33.7 million barrels or 63.7% of the state's annual production. In 1994 oil production on federal lands was 47.7 million barrels or 40.1% of United States total.

Average daily production of oil per well (2007): 12 barrels

The 10,000-acre U.S. Department of Energy facility located within the Naval Petroleum Reserve No. 3 (also known as Teapot Dome Oil Field) about 35 miles north of Casper, Wyoming, has developed the first geothermal energy plant in Wyoming. It uses hot water from oil drill holes.

Wyoming led nation in natural gas production on federal lands in 2006: 1.5 billion mcf of natural gas (71.3% of the state's annual porduction) came from federal lands. In 1994: the total was 475.7 trillion cubic feet or 26.6% of U. S. total. State received $1.1 billion in federal mineral roaylties in 2006, up substantially from the $162.6 million in royalties from the production on federal lands in 1994.

Wyo. oil production: 104 million barrels (1990); 130 million barrels (1986). Wyoming was the 4th in proven reserves of crude oil among the states in 2008 with oil produced in 20 of the state's 23 counties. Platte, Teton and Goshen were the only counties where there was no oil or gas production in 2008.

Average daily production of natural gas per well (2007): 237 mcf.

Operating oil rigs in Wyoming (2007 monthly average): 74. The high point for operating oil rigs since World War II was in 1981 when an average of 192 rigs operated each month.

Wyomingites employed in oil/gas (2008): 30,000, with a payroll estimated at $2.2 billion annually. Federal mineral royalties paid by oil/gas producers in Wyoming: $491.2 million.

In 2007, sales of crude oil production totaled 53.4 million barrels, up 3.7% from 2006.

Natural gas sales (2007): 2,254 trillion cubic feet up 9.5% from 2006.

State royalty payments received from oil produced on state lands: $145.5 million (2007)

Nationally, Wyoming ranked **5th in production of crude oil** and 2nd in natural gas production during 2007. In 2007 Wyoming recorded its highest level of natural gas production, 2005 marked the lowest level of crude oil production since 1954. 1970 was the year of highest crude oil production in the state, producing 141,546,503 barrels.

Oil production by counties (2007): Park County was the leading crude oil producer in 2007 followed by Campbell and Sublette Counties. Sublette County was the largest natural gas producer, with Campbell, second; and Sweetwater, third.

Split estate: 44 percent of Wyoming surface is privately owned land and about one-half of that is owned over split estates (where the surface owner is not the same as the subsurface owner).

Average Price of Self-serve Unleaded Regular Gasoline

Dec. 15, 1992: $1.082 in Wyoming
Jan. 20, 1993: $1.037 per gallon. (national average $1.103 per gallon)
Jan. 1, 1996: $.95 per gallon (Cheyenne)
June 30, 1996: $1.13 per gallon (Cheyenne)
Jan. 1, 1999: 94 cents per gallon (lowest price in 20 years)
July 1, 2000: $1.67 per gallon (highest price on record to that time)
July 1, 2004: $1.98 per gallon
July 1, 2008: $4.11 per gallon (highest price on record to that time)
July 1, 2010: $2.49 per gallon

12 Significant Oil Discoveries in Wyoming

1. White Oil Spring, Uinta County (1866)

John C. Piere (or Fiere) reported to Judge W. A. Carter at Fort Bridger that he had found oil in a spring near the fort. He had experience in Pennsylvania oil fields and offered to develop the property for Carter. Some 150 barrels of the oil were sold to the Union Pacific Railroad. Judge C. M. White dug a large hole next to the spring in 1867 and skimmed off the accumulated oil. Most was sold to Salt Lake City tanners. White began drilling but quit the next year at 480 feet. Later, the Evanston Oil Company tried at the site, but failed to make a significant find.

2. Carter Oil Spring, Uinta County (1868)

In 1868, while tunneling for coal, oil was found on the site. The 8-19 gallons per day seeping to the surface were sold to the Union Pacific Railroad for locomotive lubrication.

Oil was first found at Quealy Dome, west of Laramie, in 1934. Kyle and Art Yarter of Laramie sunk a test on a section of land and brought in a gusher with a capacity of 490 barrels in first 13 hours. "Oil found on Quealy ranch near Laramie," Wyoming Eagle, Dec. 7, 1934, p. 12.

3. South Fork of Twin Creek, Fremont County (1867, 1885)

Frederick Lander reported finding oil there in 1867 while "building" his road. The site was not developed until 1885 when the Union Pacific claimed the land for its coal. The so-called Clark Well, produced a dark, heavy oil.

4. Dallas Dome, Fremont County (1883)

The first flowing well in Wyoming came in at Dallas Dome. Driller was Mike Murphy (b. Virginia) who had worked as a surveyor in Nebraska, followed gold rushes to Pike's Peak, Montana and South Pass City, and operated a store in Rawlins (1871-1876). Later, he served in the legislature.

5. Bonanza, No Wood Creek, Big Horn County (1884)

The first oil discovery in the Big Horn Basin, seepage was noticed in the area by pioneers. W. S. Collins drilled the first well there in 1888.

6. "Discovery Well," Natrona County (1887)

The first discovery in the county was made just northwest of Casper. Cy Iba reportedly found oil in the Seminoe Mountains as early as 1851, but this well was the first commercial producer in Natrona County.

7. Shannon Field, Natrona County (1903)

The field was found by a company headed by Philip Shannon. Soon after the first well came in, a London syndicate paid $350,000 for the entire field, a huge sum at the time.

8. "Stock Gusher," Salt Creek, Natrona County (1908)

Oil had been found two years earlier at Salt Creek, but in 1908, H. E. "Dad" Stock struck the first gusher in the field one mile northwest of Midwest. The oil erupted over the crown of the derrick and saturated the prairie.

9. Big Muddy, Converse County (1915)

In August 1915, the first producing well came in, 40 barrels per day at 985 feet. Major development was made the next year by Parker and Whitside.

10. University Well, Big Muddy, Converse County (1916)

The first discovery of oil on University of Wyoming land was made at Big Muddy. As a result of the find, the university was able to construct new buildings including the library (now the Aven Nelson building) and the Half Acre Gym.

11. Elk Basin, Park County (1916)

J. T. Hurst was the locater of the Elk Basin field.

12. Lance Creek, Niobrara County (1918)

The Ohio Oil Company brought in "Discovery Well" on Oct. 6, 1918. Drilling had begun in February.

3 Deep Wyoming Producers, 1948-1976

1. West Poison Spider Field

At 14,309 feet deep, it was the deepest producing well in the U. S. in 1948.

2. Superior Oil's wildcat well near Barnum

Oil was struck at 18,702 feet at the deepest producing oil well in the U. S.

3. Union Oil Company's well at Hell's Half Acre

The well hit oil at 22,241 feet, the world's deepest producing well in 1976.

4. Two Deepest Wells (2008)

The deepest well ever drilled in Wyoming was a dry hole that had been drilled to 25,764 feet. The deepest producing well was drilled to 24,877 feet for natural gas.

The first refinery in Cody was built by the Texas Company (Texaco). Soon after it closed in 1933, Cody businessman George T. Beck built a small refinery in the spring of 1933. Later that summer, two other local businessmen named "Orchard and Brown" built a third refinery, according to a July 20, 1933, article in the *Cody Enterprise*.

4 Wyoming Pipelines

1. Lance Creek to Denver (1938)
2. Fort Laramie to Salt Lake City (1939)
3. Casper to Wood River, Illinois
Five companies sold their interests in Platte Pipeline Company and its 940-mile pipeline system to Express Pipeline, Ltd., of Canada, Jan. 15, 1996. Included in the sale was the 20-inch in diameter main line along with 335 miles of gathering system pipes and tank storage of 3.8 million barrels.
4. Express Pipeline (1996)
In 1996, Express Pipeline, Ltd., of Canada, began construction of a 785-mile pipeline from Canada to Casper. Wyoming producers objected that such a pipeline would damage the industry in Wyoming, but it got state approval in 1996.

10 Oldest Producing Oil Fields in Wyoming

1. Dallas Dome, Fremont County (1883-1884)
2. Spring Valley, Uinta County (1900)
The discovery was made by a firm hired by the Union Pacific Coal Company to drill for water for the town of Spring Valley. Earlier, the firm brought in an artesian water well for the town of Piedmont, six miles away. Because oil and not water was found, the company had to haul water to Spring Valley in tank cars.
3. Garland, Park-Big Horn Counties (1906)
4. Greybull, Big Horn County (1907)
5. Lander Field, Fremont County (1909)
6. Oregon Basin, Park County (1912)
7. Lamb Field, Big Horn County (1913)
8. Grass Creek Field, Hot Springs County (1914)
9. Little Buffalo Basin, Park-Hot Springs Counties (1914)
10. Elk Basin Field, Park County (1916)

1st Casper Oil Refineries

1. Pennsylvania Oil and Gas Refinery, S. Center Street, 1895
Established by the company to refine oil freighted by wagon to Casper from the firm's six wells in Salt Creek.
2. Belgo-American Oil Refinery, east of Highland Cemetery, 1903
The refinery was sold to the Franco-Wyoming Oil Company in 1912 and that firm merged with Midwest Oil in 1914, the refinery becoming the Midwest Refinery. Midwest merged with Standard on Oct. 21, 1921.
3. Standard Oil Refinery, southwest Casper, March, 1914
By 1922, the refinery was the largest in the world, producing 615,000 barrels of gasoline per month and 170 barrels of kerosene. Standard, by that time, had two Casper refineries and one in Midwest.
4. Texaco Refinery, three miles east of Casper, 1922
5. White Eagle Oil Refinery, 1923.

A constitutional amendment allowing for a severance tax on minerals, including oil and gas, went on the ballot in Wyoming in November, 1924. Some 39,109 voted for it; 27,795 were opposed. The measure lost because the "yes" votes didn't exceed half of the votes cast in the general election—84,820. A severance tax finally passed in 1969.

Oil Refineries Existing in 2010

1. Sinclair Oil, Sinclair

The refinery was started in 1923 as a 10,000-barrels-per-day plant by the Producing and Refiners Company (Parco). The refinery was sold along with all of the rest of the company's properties (including the town of Parco) at a bankruptcy sale on April 12, 1934, conducted from the Carbon County Courthouse steps. Consolidated Oil Company, controlled by Harry Sinclair, was the successful bidder. The town's name soon was changed from Parco to Sinclair. In 1969, Sinclair Oil merged with the Atlantic Richfield Company (ARCO) and the refinery was sold to Pasco, Inc., in 1972. The present Sinclair Oil Corporation, owned by Earl Holding's Little America, purchased the refinery in 1976. The refinery's capacity (1999) was 60,500 barrels per day. The firm also owns the Evansville refinery *(below)*.

2. Frontier Refining Co., Cheyenne

Established in 1937 by M. H. Robinson and C. U. Bay as the Bay Petroleum Company, it was renamed Frontier on June 12, 1940. Husky Oil bought the refinery in February, 1968, but sold it to an independent group on Feb. 28, 1986. The name reverted to Frontier Refining Company.

3. Little America Refining, Evansville

The refinery is owned by Sinclair, the privately-held corporation owning Little America.

4. Wyoming Refining, Newcastle

The refinery was initially owned by Gray Oil Company. Later, it was owned by Sioux Oil Company and Tesoro. In 2010, it was held privately by Denver-based Hermes Consolidated, Inc.

5. LaBarge Gas Processing Plant

Not a refinery as such, but the Exxon facility is a huge gas processor. Wyoming had 45 operating natural gas plants in 2008.

6. C&H Refinery, Lusk

Certified by Guiness' Book of World Records in 2000 as the world's smallest refinery, it was opened in 1933 by partners Roy Chamberlain and Jim Hoblit, both former employees of Ohio Oil Company in the Lance Creek oilfields that had been booming in the 1920s, but declining by the early 1930s. The firm purchased a pair of refining stills that had been made by Erie City Iron Works in the 1850s, during the earliest years of the oil industry in America. The refinery operated at a capacity of 190 barrels per day and continued operating until 1978. In 1998, the abandoned refinery was sold to Zahir Khalid, a businessman from Pakistan. The first production run in the refurbished plant was made in June 2000 and, soon after, the facility was placed on the National Register of Historic Places.

Three Crowns Golf Course on Former Refinery Site

The giant Amoco (Standard) Oil Refinery along the North Platte River pumped and refined 48,000 barrels of oil per day until it closed in 1991. The 340-acre site was determined, by the Wyoming Department of Environmental Quality, to be highly polluted. In preparation for a lengthy trial, a structure was built to serve as the courtroom. Before trial, the site owner, BP Products North America, that had merged with Amoco, entered into a consent decree with the State, establishing the terms of the environmental cleanup. The site was excavated, capped in fill dirt and topped with a foot of sand. The company then installed a "remediation system"--a series of wells--that continues to collect and purify contaminants in the groundwater. Robert Trent Jones Jr., designed the golf course on the site. The municipally-owned Three Crowns Golf Course opened May 20, 2005. The course name comes from the three grades of gasoline Standard once refined on the site. Also on the tract is a business park, the historic headquarters for Standard Oil and the Oil and Gas Conservation Commission building, opened April 12, 2004.

Greatest Oil-Producing Fields in Wyoming, 1999-2007
(in barrels per year)

2007 Oil Production by Field
1. Jonah — 3,661,499
2. Salt Creek — 2,958,145
3. Pinedale — 2,729,087
4. Oregon Basin — 2,496,632
5. Lost Soldier — 2,061,289
6. Spring Creek S. (Dis 1929) — 1,568,596
7. WC (Discovered 2000) — 1,524,551
8. Elk Basin — 1,309,861
9. Hamilton Dome — 1,306,444
10. Garland — 1,296,925

2006 Oil Production by Field
1. Jonah — 2,769,255
2. Salt Creek — 2,558,216
3. Oregon Basin — 2,536,623
4. Pinedale — 2,220,993
5. Lost Soldier — 1,986,177
6. Spring Creek South — 1,452,616
7. WC — 1,430,217
8. Garland — 1,412,906
9. Elk Basin — 1,369,208
10. Hamilton Dome — 1,316,659

2005 Oil Production by Field
1. Oregon Basin — 2,634,298
2. Jonah — 2,365,385
3. Salt Creek — 2,350,591
4. Lost Soldier — 1,961,786
5. Pinedale — 1,890,598
6. Garland — 1,408,798
7. Elk Basin — 1,387,889
8. Painter Reservoir E. — 1,369,906
9. Hamilton Dome — 1,294,328
10. Hartzog Draw — 1,199,611

2004 Oil Production by Field
1. Oregon Basin — 2,680,693
2. Jonah — 2,177,550
3. Lost Soldier — 1,898,197
4. Salt Creek — 1,762,994
5. Painter Reservoir E. — 1,615,198
6. Elk Basin — 1,494,766
7. Pinedale (Discovered 1955) — 1,443,596
8. Garland — 1,381,124
9. Hartzog Draw — 1,363,882
10. Hamilton Dome — 1,333,317

2003 Oil Production by Field
1. Oregon Basin — 2,799,369
2. Jonah — 2,254,479
3. Lost Soldier — 1,856,321
4. Painter Reservoir E. — 1,840,000
5. Salt Creek — 1,824,859
6. Elk Basin — 1,605,826
7. Hartzog Draw — 1,532,743
8. Hamilton Dome — 1,429,096
9. Garland — 1,356,188
10. Grass Creek — 1,118,119

2002 Oil Production by Field
1. Oregon Basin — 2,943,046
2. Jonah — 2,204,878
3. Salt Creek — 2,032,829
4. Lost Soldier — 1,945,056
5. Painter Reservoir E. — 1,852,365
6. Hartzog Draw — 1,741,382
7. Elk Basin — 1,555,981
8. Hamilton Dome — 1,532,638
9. Garland — 1,426,148
10. Grass Creek — 1,067,051

2001 Oil Production by Field
1. Oregon Basin — 3,153,252
2. Painter Reservoir E. — 2,496,540
3. Lost Soldier — 2,124,291
4. Salt Creek — 2,098,733
5. Hartzog Draw — 1,948,730
6. Jonah — 1,892,388
7. Elk Basin — 1,671,812
8. Hamilton Dome — 1,590,677
9. Garland — 1,518,998
10. House Creek — 1,288,929

2000 Oil Production by Field
1. Oregon Basin — 3,442,149
2. Painter Reservoir E. — 2,961,598
3. Hartzog Draw — 2,257,865
4. Salt Creek — 2,079,425
5. Lost Soldier — 1,949,726
6. Garland — 1,688,817
7. Elk Basin — 1,683,800
8. Hamilton Dome — 1,671,629
9. House Creek — 1,544,899
10. Jonah (Discovered 1977) — 1,253,883

1999 Oil Production by Field
1. Oregon Basin — 3,549,138
2. Painter Reservoir E. — 3,281,116
3. Hartzog Draw — 2,297,211
4. Lost Soldier — 2,069,721
5. Salt Creek — 2,035,281
6. House Creek — 1,911,111
7. Garland — 1,725,879
8. Elk Basin — 1,724,068
9. Hamilton Dome — 1,710,641
10. Grass Creek — 1,280,494

Source: Wyoming Oil and Gas Conservation Commission (2009)

In 1973 a Chaparral Resources American Quasar wildcat oil well on the Patterson Ranch north of Glenrock blew out and caught fire. Red Adair's firefighters were brought in to control it.

Some Well-Known Wyoming Oil People

1. Hugh E. "Daddy" Stock (1861-1935)

Born in Pennsylvania, Stock was a fourth-generation oil man. He brought in his first well near Florence, Colo., and later hit an Oklahoma gusher that made him wealthy. He soon lost it in a series of dryholes. Early in the 1900s, his son advised that he should look into Salt Creek in Wyoming. He took claims of 3,000 acres in the area, struck oil immediately, and sold out for $3.25 million. He died in Glendale, Calif., Feb. 1, 1935. *(Source: Cody Enterprise, Feb. 6, 1935, p. 4).*

2. Paul Stock (1894-1972)

Born in Florence, Colo., in 1894, Stock was the sixth of seven children. In 1902, Hugh Stock (his father) and his brother James began drilling at Salt Creek. Three years later, at the age of 15, Paul Stock quit school to begin work as a roughneck for the firm. After stints in Cuba and Mexico, Paul Stock returned to Wyoming as a contract driller north of Casper. After World War I service, he worked in oil fields in Oklahoma and Texas. He moved to Cody in 1923 and used the first rotary rig at Oregon Basin and Byron. He became president of the family company that merged in 1944 with Texaco. Stock became the largest individual shareholder in Texaco. In 1958, he formed the Stock Foundation that generously funded educational and civic causes statewide. He died in 1972.

3. Clarence Richardson (1867-1961)

Reared in Cheyenne, Richardson began as a journalist and later, a mining speculator. In the 1890s, he invested in Wyoming oil becoming one of the first developers at Salt Creek oilfield. In 1916, his company discovered oil at Big Muddy near Glenrock. He died at the age of 94 in 1961.

4. Glenn E. Nielson (1903-1998)

Nielson was born in Alberta, Canada. His first career was in sheep ranching and he moved to the U. S. in 1935, to Montana, to raise sheep. He lost much of the herd to disease so he began selling fuel for a Cut Bank, Montana, refinery. He moved to Cody and, in 1937, with the help of two partners, purchased a local refinery. He eventually became sole owner. The firm expanded rapidly in the 1950s and 1960s, building pipelines and establishing retail outlets. Later, the firm went into offshore and natural gas development. He retired in 1978 after losing control of the company in a hostile takeover. He died in 1998.

5. H. A. "Dave" True (1915-1994)

Born in Cheyenne, True graduated from Montana State in 1937. He went to work for Texaco and 11 years later, went into business on his own. After a series of discoveries in northeast Wyoming, the company began diversifying in the 1960s. At the time of his death, his company employed 600 people statewide.

6. Fred Goodstein (1897-1983)

Goodstein's father founded American Pipe and Supply Co., in 1912. In 1923, Fred Goodstein established the Casper branch of the scrap iron firm. In the 1930s, he invested in oil fields at Salt Creek and Lance Creek. He organized Rocky Mountain Pipeline that carried oil to Denver. At the time he died in 1983, his fortune was estimated at some $300 million.

7. Kenneth S. Deffeyes (1931-   )

A petroleum geologist and emeritus professor at Princeton, Deffeyes moved with his family to Casper in 1944 and graduated from Natrona County High School in 1949. He went to work for Shell after graduation from Colorado School of Mines, served in the army, earned the Ph.D. from Princeton and rejoined Shell in 1958. In 1962 he joined the faculty at the University of Minnesota, moved to Oregon State and to Princeton in 1967. He became well known as author of *Beyond Oil, The View from Hubbert's Peak* (2005).

Trucks passing through Wyoming ports of entry reached 3 million for the first time in 2006.

PHOTOGRAPHERS

1st photographer in Wyoming: John C. Fremont shot the first photographs in Wyoming on Aug. 1, 1842, at Independence Rock. Unfortunately, he could not produce an image on any of the polished, silver-plated copper sheets used in the process which had been invented only three years before by Louis Daguerre in France.

1st photograph made in Wyoming: Probably, those made by a man named Jones, a professional photographer who traveled west on the Oregon Trail in 1851. It is not known if any of his photos survived, however, because Jones was killed by Indians on Boxelder Creek in present-day Converse County and his equipment was destroyed.

1st use of color photography by a Wyoming photographer: Charles Belden displayed his color photos at the Panama-Pacific Exposition in San Francisco in 1916, just nine years after the process was invented in France.

1st photographer of the Tetons: The most photographed mountains in the world were first recorded on film by William H. Jackson, a member of the Hayden expedition in 1872. His photos of Yellowstone also were the first.

1st use of aerial photography in Wyoming: Charles Belden, who was both an accomplished photographer and pilot, made aerial scenes while helping the state game and fish department conduct a statewide wildlife census by air in the 1920s.

Most photographed building in Wyoming: The Clark Moulton family's barn, now owned by the National Park Service, in Grand Teton National Park. The structure is said to be the most photographed building in the entire United States.

Best Press Photographs, Wyoming Press Association: *(See listing later in this section)*

Some Well-Known Wyoming Photographers

1. William H. Jackson

Jackson owned an Omaha photographic studio when he was hired by the Union Pacific Railroad to make photographs along the line in Wyoming in 1870. The next year, he accompanied the Hayden Expedition to Yellowstone where he became the first to photograph wonders there. He was first to photograph Mammoth Hot Springs on July 21, 1871. Jackson's scenes gained widespread public attention for Yellowstone. Congress made it America's first national park in 1872. Jackson lived to be nearly 100 years old. He visited the state for the Oregon Trail Centennial at Independence Rock in 1939 when he was in his 90s.

2. T. J. Hyne

The Chicago photographer accompanied the Barlow-Heap party to Wyoming in 1871 and shot pictures in Yellowstone the same year Jackson was there. Unfortunately, all of his work was destroyed in the Great Chicago Fire.

3. A. J. Russell

Russell served as official photographer for the construction of the Union Pacific Railroad, making some 200 photographs using 10x13 inch wet plate collodian negatives. With four assistants, Russell also made 600 stereoscopic views of the railroad.

4. Charles E. Belden

Born in California, Belden came to Wyoming to manage the Pitchfork Ranch owned by the father of a college classmate. Belden later married the daughter of the ranch owner. In 1909, he and Eugene Phelps (his classmate and future brother-in-law) became the first American automobile tourists in Russia. His best known photographs are of cowboys, cattle and ranch scenes made during his long career as a working cowboy and ranch manager. His work appeared in national publications. He died in Florida in 1966. In 1992, 1,500 Belden photographs went on display in the Charles Belden Western Photography Museum in Meeteetse.

5. J. E. Stimson

Born in Virginia in 1870, Stimson apprenticed to his uncle in an Appleton, Wisc., photo studio in the late 1880s. He came to Cheyenne in 1889 and lived there for the rest of his life. Stimson photographed in every part of Wyoming and along the route of the Union Pacific Railroad in other states while he was contract photographer for the railroad. More than 7,560 of his glassplate negatives were purchased by the State Historical Department in 1953 where they became the foundation for the department's photo collection.

6. M. D. Houghton

Houghton was born in Michigan in 1845. Known also as an artist for his sketches of towns and ranches, he was active mostly in Carbon County around the turn of the century. He moved to Spokane, Wash., where he died in the flu epidemic of 1919.

7. C. D. Kirkland

Kirkland is best known for his scenes of cowboys on the open range. He was born in Ohio on the Fourth of July, 1857, and came to Cheyenne at the age of 20. He operated a studio there until 1895 when he sold to W. G. Walker and moved to Denver. Three years before he left Cheyenne, Kirkland incorporated the "Kirkland Lithium Paper Company" for the manufacture of photographic papers. He died in Denver Aug. 23, 1926.

8. David D. Dare

Dare's career reads like a novel. He came to Cheyenne as a postal clerk in 1874, soon opened a drug store, and drifted into photography. Later, he sold furniture and paintings, and in the late 1880s, opened a bank in Cheyenne. In 1892, his banks in Cheyenne and San Diego collapsed. Dare absconded to the Middle East, where it is said he organized a railroad. Later, he was seen selling rugs in Athens. Apparently, he was killed by bandits in Armenia.

9. Steven N. Leek

Leek, born in Canada in 1858, ranched and operated a guide service near Jackson where he came about 1890. He guided famous celebrities on vacations in the Tetons and made photographs of the mountains. He is credited with taking the first motion pictures of the Tetons. His motion picture photography of wildlife was innovative for the time. The American Heritage Center has a Leek collection.

10. Arthur Rothstein

The famed photographer was employed by the Farm Security Administration in the 1930s when he traveled through Wyoming shooting photographs.

11. George "Coyote" Smith

Smith came to Wyoming and the Glenrock area in 1897 with $1 in his pocket. He trapped coyotes, averaging 300-350 per year, along with wolves, bobcats and muskrats. From the teens until the late 1920s, he shot photographs in the area, including early "cheesecake" shots and scenes of Big Muddy oil field. His collection was rediscovered in the early 1980s in a chicken coop on a ranch near Glenrock.

12. Charles S. Baker

Baker worked on a whaler, sailed to Asia with Commodore Perry, and served as a bugler for the Union Army during the Civil War. With a partner named Johnson, he set up the "Union Pacific Photograph Car," well known as a moving portrait studio in the West. In 1878, he opened a studio in Evanston, but he shot photographs throughout the region. He died Oct. 28, 1924.

Harold Floreen, a meteorologist with the U. S. Weather Bureau in Cheyenne, was honored in September 1933 by the Bureau for 55 distinctive photos of clouds he had taken while working for four years in Cheyenne. The Bureau kept a dozen of the photos for future publication.

13. J. C. H. Grabill

An early photographer of Native Americans, Grabill made numerous photographs of Wyoming towns. His picture of Lusk, taken on Sept. 1, 1886, is the first ever made of that town. Many of his photographs are held in the collections of the National Archives and Library of Congress.

14. F. S. Hiscock

Born in Michigan, Hiscock began a photo studio in Cody in 1904. He was particularly famous for his postcard scenes.

15. Francis Brammar

Born in Nevada, Brammar came to Cheyenne as a young man and accepted a job with the *Wyoming Eagle*. For the next 50 years, he was the *Eagle* photographer. He died in the early 1980s. An extensive collection of his photographs is held by the Wyoming State Museum.

16. Elsa Spear Byron

The daughter of a Sheridan area rancher, Byron (b. 1896) shot photographs of northern Wyoming and southern Montana scenes in the early 1900s. Her first camera was a Brownie that she received when she was 11. Along with photographing Crow Indians and "cowboy scenes," she worked as a mountain guide and also worked with the Sheridan County Historical Society when that organization operated Trail End, now a state historic site. Her work was widely published and exhibited. She died in Sheridan in 1993 at the age of 97.

17. Harrison Crandall

The Jackson photographer (b. Newton, Kansas, 1887, d. 1970) is particularly known for Teton scenes. He studied art in Los Angeles and established a homestead near Jenny Lake in 1921. He sold the homestead which became part of the national park. He operated the art/photo concession at Jenny Lake for 34 years.

18. Dean Conger

A Casper native, Conger graduated from the journalism school at the University of Wyoming. In the 1970s, he was chief photographer for *National Geographic Magazine*. In 2000, he was living in retirement in Colorado.

19. Brent C. Petersen

A native of Laramie, Petersen was photo editor of *Parade Magazine* in the early 1980s.

20. Jack Richard

Richard (b. 1909) worked as a newspaper photographer and operated a photo studio in Cody for many years. In 1989, he donated his collection of some 160,000 prints to the Buffalo Bill Historical Center. He died in 1992.

21.-22. Frank T. Nakako and Charles August

The two men operated a photo studio in Rock Springs, opening in 1919 as the "New Studio." They specialized in portraits of area residents and daily scenes from Rock Springs. Nakako studied photography in his native Japan for six years. He came to America in 1905 and worked in Seattle and North Platte before coming to Hanna, Wyoming, in 1909. After ten years in Hanna, he relocated his photo studio to Rock Springs. Later, he bought the Commercial Hotel in Rock Springs. From 1923-1927, he was president of the 500-member Japanese Association of Rock Springs. In the 1920s, he occasionally visited Japan, according to reports in the Rock Springs newspapers.

23. George Butler

Butler operated a photo studio in Newcastle for many years. In 1996, his collection was donated to the Anna Miller Museum, Newcastle.

24. Svenson-Ludwig studio, Laramie

Svenson opened a studio after the turn of the century. In the 1930s, his son-in-law, "Doc" Ludwig, took over the business. The two chronicled Laramie for a half century.

25. Mabel Graham McIntosh Souther, Ucross

Souther came to the Big Red Ranch at Ucross in 1897 when her husband was hired as the ranch manager. For the next two years, she took numerous photos of ranch scenes and activities. The couple returned east and Souther died in 1962 at the age of 98. She had left many of the photographs, however, with ranch hand Ed C. Brown who gave them to the American Heritage Center, UW, in 1959.

Picture of the Year by Photographers of the Wyoming Press Association

1975:	Dick George, Wyoming State Journal
1976:	Richard Murphy, Jackson Hole News
1977:	Bob Woodall, Jackson Hole Guide
1978:	Richard Murphy, Jackson Hole News
1979:	Mark Rohde, Jackson Hole Guide
1980:	Randall Stalker, Glenrock Independent
1981:	Dave Stump, Jackson Hole Guide
1982:	Bill Willcox, Cody Enterprise
1983:	Carl Berger, Hanna Herald
1984:	Bill Willcox, Jackson Hole Guide
1985:	Richard Murphy, Jackson Hole News
1986:	Mary Gerty, Jackson Hole News
1987:	Fred Yates, Sunday Tribune-Eagle (Cheyenne)
1988:	Fred Yates, Sunday Tribune-Eagle (Cheyenne)
1989:	Fred Yates, Sunday Tribune-Eagle (Cheyenne)
1990:	Bill Willcox, Jackson Hole News
1991:	Stan Hoskins, Green River Star
1992:	Garth Dowling, Jackson Hole News
1993:	Travis Heying, Gillette News-Record
1994:	Garth Dowling, Jackson Hole News
1995:	Garth Dowling, Jackson Hole News
1996:	Travis Heying, Gillette News Record
1997:	Dewey Vanderhoff, Cody Enterprise
1998:	Dan Cepeda, Casper Star-Tribune
1999:	Jim Evans, Jackson Hole News
2000:	David O'Connor, Jackson Hole Guide
2001:	Larry Brinlee, Wyoming Tribune-Eagle
2002;	Erin Krivanec, Douglas Budget
2003:	Bradley Boner, Gillette News-Record,
2004;	Robert Hendricks, Casper Star-Tribune
2005:	Sarah Beth Burnett, Casper Star-Tribune
2006:	Ken Blackbird, Cody Enterprise
2007:	Brendan Burnett-Kurie, Douglas Budget
2008:	Keith Domke, Riverton Ranger

Photographer Charles Belden sent a telegram from his Pitchfork Ranch to a newspaper during the winter of 1933: "Sixty degrees below zero registered on government thermometer at Pitchfork for the first time in history. Cowboys had to roll cigarettes with their mittons on and we had to feed the chickens Prestone to keep the eggs from freezing. Yours for higher temperatures. Charles Belden."

POETRY

1st book of poems published in Wyoming: William Lightfoot Visscher's book, *My Village Home*, published by the Cheyenne Sun in 1885.

1st poem by a Wyoming poet entered into the Congressional Record: Stephen W. Downey, as Wyoming territorial delegate (1879-1881), submitted the poem.

State Poet Laureates

1. E. Richard Shipp, Casper

Although the position was not officially sanctioned, Shipp was accorded the honor in the late 1920s. A lawyer who published numerous literary works, Shipp was called the "state poet laureate" in his obituary when he died in May, 1932.

2. Mae Urbanek, Lusk

Urbanek was appointed state poet laureate by Gov. Frank Barrett. Urbanek, a journalist trained in the Midwest, ranched with her husband north of Lusk. Her versatility as a writer is demonstrated by a career of writing non-fiction and fiction articles, poetry and history. She compiled the definitive work, *Wyoming Place Names*, which remains in print more than 30 years after it first appeared. She died in Lusk in 1995.

3. Peggy Simson Curry, Casper

Curry (b. Dunure, Scotland, 1911, d. Casper, 1987) was the first person whose appointment to the honorary post was made with Senate approval. Gov. Ed Herschler appointed her Jan. 14, 1981. She held the title at the time of her death.

4. Charles Levendosky, Casper

A poet and columnist for the *Casper Star-Tribune*, Gov. Mike Sullivan named him the state's poet laureate on Feb. 8, 1988. He died in Casper in March 2004.

5. Robert Roripaugh, Laramie

Roripaugh became state poet laureate in 1995. He was appointed by Gov. Jim Geringer. Roripaugh taught in the Department of English, University of Wyoming, until his retirement in 1995. His family ranched near Lander.

6. David Romtvedt, Buffalo

A poet and musician, Romtvedt published several books of poems including: *Moon* (1984); *YIP* (1991); and *A Flower Whose Name I Do Not Know* (1992). He was named Wyoming's poet laureate by Gov. Dave Freudenthal in August 2004.

Some Poems About Wyoming

1. "Wyoming Circuit" (7 poems) by William Stafford

Printed in *Northwest America Magazine*, May, 1979, p. 26, included are poetic descriptions of the Ten Sleep area and Cody. Stafford, who died in the early 1990s, was a well-known Oregon poet.

2. "May Time in Wyoming" by Donald Drummond

Poem published in the Drummond book, *The Mountain*. (Chicago: Swallow Publishing, 1971).

3. "Buffalo Bill's" by e. e. cummings

A short piece was included in the poet's *Poems: 1923-54*. (New York: Harcourt Brace, 1955).

4. "Wyoming Wind" by Robert Roripaugh

One of a number of poems about Wyoming in Roripaugh's book, *Learn to Love the Haze*. (Vermillion, S. D.: Spirit Mountain Press, 1976). Roripaugh, who was reared in Wyoming, is a retired professor of English at UW and state poet laureate.

5. "Battle of Platte Bridge Station" by Wendell H. Maynard

The narrative poem is one of several in the Raceland, Kentucky, poet's book, *Bannack and Other Poems*. (Philadelphia: Dorrance, 1976).

6. "Wyoming" by Maurice Morris

The poem (c. 1923) used a "place names" approach to poetry. A copy is held in the American Heritage Center, Thurman Arnold collection.

7. "Opium Peddling" by Allen Ginsberg

Ginsberg wrote the poem about the Wyoming prairies, even though the subject matter is unclear from the title. The piece was published in the University of Wyoming *Branding Iron*, April 23, 1971.

Some Wyoming Poets: A Sample

1. Alan Swallow (b. Powell, 1915, d. 1966)

A 1937 graduate of the University of Wyoming, Swallow held the Ph.D. degree from LSU. From 1946 to 1954, he taught writing at the University of Denver. He left DU to devote his full attention to his publishing house, Sage Books, which he founded and ran part-time beginning in 1940. He published works by numerous young poets as well as established writers. His own works of poetry included *XI Poems* (Prairie Press, 1942), *The Remembered Land* (1946), and *The Nameless Sight: Poems, 1937-56.* (1956).

2. Wilson Clough b. New Jersey, 1894, d. Laramie, 1991)

Clough started his distinguished career as an English professor at the University of Wyoming in 1924. His poetry books included *Brief Oasis* (1954) and *Past's Persisting* (1971).

3. Peggy Simson Curry (b. Scotland, 1911, d. 1987)

Curry was a University of Wyoming graduate and long-time writing teacher at Casper College. She published novels and two books of poetry, *Red Wind of Wyoming* (Swallows Books, 1955) and *Summer Range* (Dooryard Press, 1981).

4. Richard F. Fleck (b. Penn., 1937)

Fleck came to teach English at the University of Wyoming in 1965. His book of poems, *Bamboo in the Sun* (Sannomiya Press, 1983), resulted from a year's stay in Japan. Other works are *Palms, Peaks and Prairies* (Golden Quill, 1967), and *Cottonwood Moon* (Jelm Mountain Press, 1979). He later taught in Colorado.

5. Donald F. Drummond (b. Ohio, 1914)

Drummond, emeritus professor of English at the University of Missouri, was reared in the Big Horn Basin where his father, a minister, served a congregation. His books of poetry include *The Grey Tower* (Swallow, 1966), and *The Mountain* (Swallow, 1971). Many of his poems were set in Wyoming.

6. Joseph Langland (b. Minn., 1917, d. New York, April 9, 2007)

A University of Wyoming professor of English from 1948-1959, Langland accepted a professorship at the University of Massachusetts, Amherst. Among his many books of poems are *The Green Town* (Scribner, 1956), *Poems in Progress* (University of Washington Press, 1964), and *Any Body's Song* (Doubleday, 1980). Wyoming is the setting for several poems.

7. Charles Levendosky (b. New York, 1936, d. Casper, March 14, 2004)

From 1981 to 1988, Levendosky was arts editor and a columnist for the *Casper Star-Tribune*. Earlier, he served as director of the Wyoming Council of the Arts poetry programs. *Distances* (Dooryard, 1980), *Wyoming Fragments* (Buffalo Point Press, 1981), and *Nocturnes* (Dooryard, 1982) are among his published books.

The Jackson Hole Review began publication in the spring of 2009 to showcase the local artists, writers and poets of Jackson Hole.

8. Theodore Gostas (b. Montana, c. 1940)

Gostas, an artist and writer, is a graduate of the University of Wyoming. Following his capture by North Vietnamese troops in the battle for Hue during the Vietnam War in 1968, Gostas was a prisoner of war in Hanoi. Soon after his release, he wrote a book of poems about that experience, *Prisoner*, which was published in 1974. He lived in Cheyenne and in North Dakota in the 1980s and in the 1990s, in Sweetwater County.

10. Henry Pacheco (b. Cheyenne, 1947)

After service in the Marine Corps and study at the University of Wyoming, Pacheco became an English professor in New Mexico. Among his published works is *The Kindred/ La Familia* (Totinem, 1972).

11. James Galvin (b. Chicago, 1951)

A resident of Tie Siding in 1991, a poem he wrote about Albany county appeared in the *New Yorker*, March 11, 1991. He also published a book of poems, *Imaginary Timber*. He is probably better known as an essayist and novelist.

12. Jon F. Glade

Glade, a native of Riverton, was formerly editor of the *Owen Wister Review*, University of Wyoming. He has published numerous poems. Glade's book, *Photographs in a Jungle (1990)*, is a collection of poetry about his experiences as a soldier in Vietnam.

13. Craig Arnold (b. 1967, d. April 2009)

Arnold taught in the MFA Program at the University of Wyoming. His first book of poetry, *Shells*, won the 1998 Yale Series of Younger Poets award. His second collection was titled Made Flesh. He was working on a book about volcanoes when he apparently fell to his death on Kuchinoerabu-jima, a remote Japanese island in April 2009.

14. H. L. "Harvey" Hix (b. 1960)

Hix is a professor and director of the creative writing MFA program at the University of Wyoming. Hix was one of five finalists in 2006 for the National Book Award in poetry.

15. Verna Grubbs (Ann Winslow)

Winslow taught poetry at the University of Wyoming from 1936-1960. A founder of the College Poetry Society in 1931, she was instrumental in inviting nationally renowned poets to give readings at UW. During her retirement, she lived, a virtual recluse, on the outskirts of Laramie with prize Samoyed dogs. She died in Fayetteville, Ark., in 1974.

*This group is merely representative of the diversity of poets from Wyoming. Numerous others are listed in Eva Floy Wheeler, Wyoming Writers (1982).

Robert Louis Stevenson Crosses Wyoming, 1879

"On August 30, 1879, Robert Louis Stevenson stepped off the train in Oakland, Calif., completing a 23-day, 6,000-mile land and sea journey to reunite him with the married woman he had fallen in love with two years earlier." So begins the story of the famous Scottish author's experiences in the American West, chronicled in "Robert Louis Stevenson's Year in California," by Douglas MacGowan, *The Highlander* 38 (July-August, 2000).

Later, the woman divorced her husband and married Stevenson in May, 1880. While traveling to California, however, Stevenson had contracted "a lingering ailment" while crossing Wyoming. His recovery was slow, but by the time the couple returned to Edinburgh, Scotland, in the summer of 1880, he was healthy once again. Later, Stevenson wrote three books about his adventures in the American West. He returned across Wyoming to California in 1888, stopping briefly while en route to the South Pacific where he spent the remaining six years of his life.

Singer, songwriter and poet Rod McKuen was guest celebrity and performer at the Riverton Rendezvous Hot Air Balloon festival in June 2001. He gave a concert and reading at Central Wyoming College attended by more than 600 people.

POLITICS AND GOVERNMENT

Gubernatorial Election Results, 1890-2006

1890:

F. E. Warren (R)	8,879	55.4%
George Baxter (D)	7,153	44.6%

1892:

John Osborne (D)	9,290	55.3%
Edward Ivinson (R)	7,509	44.7%

1894:

W. A. Richards (R)	10,149	52.6%
W. H. Holliday (D)	6,965	36.1%
Lewis Tidball (P)	2,176	11.3%

1898:

DeForest Richards (R)	10,383	52.4%
Horace C. Alger (D)	8,989	45.4%
E. W. Viall (P)	431	2.2%

1902:

DeForest Richards (R)	14,483	57.8%
George T. Beck (D)	10,017	40.0%
H. Breitenstein (Soc)	552	2.2%

1906:

Bryant B. Brooks (R)	16,317	60.4%
Stephen Keister (D)	9,444	35.0%
William O'Neill (Soc)	1,236	4.6%

1910:

J. M. Carey (D)	21,086	55.6%
W. E. Mullen (R)	15,235	40.2%
W. W. Paterson (S)	1,605	4.2%

1914:

John Kendrick (D)	22,387	51.6%
Hilliard Ridgely (R)	19,174	44.2%
Paul J. Paulson (S)	1,816	4.2%

1918:

Robert Carey (R)	23,825	56%
Frank Houx (D)	18,640	44%

1922:

William Ross (D)	31,110	50.6%
John W. Hay (R)	30,387	49.4%

1924 (Special):

Nellie T. Ross (D)	43,323	55%
E. J. Sullivan (R)	35,275	45%

1926:

Frank Emerson (R)	35,651	50.9%
Nellie T. Ross (D)	34,286	48.9%

1930:

Frank Emerson (R)	38,058	50.5%
Leslie Miller (D)	37,188	49.5%

1932 (Special):

Leslie Miller (D)	48,130	50.8%
Harry Weston (R)	44,692	47.2%

1934:

Leslie Miller (D)	54,305	58%
A. M. Clark (R)	38,792	41.3%

1938:

Nels Smith (R)	57,288	59%
Leslie Miller (D)	38,501	40.2%

1942:

Lester Hunt (D)	39,599	51.3%
Nels Smith (R)	37,568	48.7%

1946:

Lester Hunt (D)	43,020	53%
Earl Wright (R)	38,333	47%

1950:

Frank Barrett (R)	54,441	56%
John McIntyre (D)	42,518	44%

1954:

Milward Simpson (R)	56,275	50.5
William Jack (D)	55,163	49.5

1958:

J. J. Hickey (D)	55,070	48.9
Milward Simpson (R)	52,488	46.6
Louis Carlson (I)	4,979	4.5

1962:

Cliff Hansen (R)	64,970	55%
Jack Gage (D)	54,298	45%

1966:

Stan Hathaway (R) 65,624		54.3%
Ernest Wilkerson (D)	55,249	45.7%

1970:

Stan Hathaway (R)	74,249	63%
John J. Rooney (D)	44,008	37%

1974:

Ed Herschler (D)	71,741	56%
Dick Jones (R)	56,645	44%

1978:

Ed Herschler (D)	69,972	51%
John Ostlund (R)	67,595	49%

1982:

Ed Herschler (D)	106,424	63%
Warren Morton (R)	62,119	37%

1986:

Mike Sullivan (D)	88,879	54%
Pete Simpson (R)	75,841	46%

1990:

Mike Sullivan (D)	104,638	65%
Mary Mead (R)	55,471	35%

1994:

Jim Geringer (R)	118,016	59%
Kathy Karpan (D)	80,747	40%

1998:

Jim Geringer (R)	97,235	55.6%
John Vinich (D)	70,754	40.5%
Dave Dawson (Lib.)	6,899	3.9%

2002:

Dave Freudenthal (D)	92,662	50%
Eli Bebout (R)	88,873	47.9%
Dawson (Lib.)	3,924	2.1%

2006:

Dave Freudenthal (D)	135,516	70%
Ray Hunkins (R)	58,100	30%

Senate Election Results, 1946-2008

Senate

1946

Joseph O'Mahoney (D)	45,843	56.2
Harry B. Henderson (R)	35,714	43.8

1948

Lester C. Hunt (D)	57,953	57.1
E. V. Robertson (R)	43,527	42.9

1952

Frank Barrett (R)	67,176	51.6
Joseph O'Mahoney (D)	62,921	48.4

1954

Joseph O'Mahoney (D)	57,845	51.5
William H. Harrison (R)	54,407	48.5

1958

Gale McGee (D)	58,035	50.8
Frank Barrett (R)	56,122	49.2

1960

Keith Thomson (R)	78,103	56.4
Ray Whitaker (D)	60,447	43.6

1962

Milward Simpson (R)	69,043	57.8
J. J. "Joe" Hickey (D)	50,329	42.2

1964

Gale McGee (D)	76,485	54%
John Wold (R)	65,185	46%

1966

Cliff Hansen (R)	63,548	51.8
Teno Roncalio (D)	59,141	48.2

1970

Gale McGee	67,027	56%
John Wold	53,279	44%

1972

Clifford P. Hansen	100,604	71%
Mike Vinich (D)	40,695	29%

1976

Malcolm Wallop (R)	84,810	55%
Gale McGee (D)	70,558	45%

1978

Al Simpson (R)	82,908	62%
Ray Whitaker (D)	50,456	38%

1982

Malcolm Wallop (R)	96,690	57%
Rodger McDaniel (D)	72,453	43%

1984

Al Simpson (R)	146,373	78%
Victor Ryan (D)	40,525	22%

1988

Malcolm Wallop (R)	90,326	50.3
John Vinich (D)	89,161	49.7

1990

Al Simpson (R)	100,784	64%
Kathy Helling (D)	56,848	36%

1994

Craig Thomas (R)	118,754	59%
Mike Sullivan (D)	79,287	39%

1996

Mike Enzi (R)	114,116	54.1
Kathy Karpan (D)	89,103	42.2
W. David Herbert (L)	5,289	2.5

2000

Craig Thomas (R)	157,316	77%
Mel Logan (D)	47,039	23%

2002:

Mike Enzi (R)	122,710	71.6
Jan Corcoran (D)	48,570	28.4

2006:

Craig Thomas (R)	135,174	66.6
Dale Groutage (D)	67,671	33.4

2008:

Mike Enzi (R)	189,946	75.8
Chris Rothfuss (D)	60,631	24.2

2008 (special)

John Barrasso (R)	183,063	73.4
Nick Carter (D)	66,202	26.6

House of Representatives, 1950-2008

1950

William Harrison (R)	50,865	54.5
John B. Clark (D)	42,483	45.5

1952

William Harrison (R)	76,161	60.1
Robert R. Rose (D)	50,559	39.9

1954

E. Keith Thomson (R)	61,111	56.2
Sam Tully (D)	47,660	43.8

1956

E. Keith Thomson (R)	69,903	58.2
Jerry O'Callaghan (D)	50,225	41.8

1958

E. Keith Thomson (R)	59,894	53.6
Ray Whitaker (D)	51,886	46.4

1960

William Harrison (R)	70,241	52.3
Hepburn Armstrong (D)	64,090	47.7

1962

William Harrison (R)	71,489	61.4
Louis A. Mankus (D)	44,985	38.6

1964

Teno Roncalio(D)	70, 693	50.8
Wm H. Harrison(R)	68,482	49.2

1966

Wm H. Harrison(R)	62,984	53%
Al Christian (D)	56,442	47%

1968

John Wold (R)	77,363	62%
Velma Linford (D)	45,950	37%

1970

Teno Roncalio (D)	58,456	50.3
Harry Roberts (R)	57,848	49.7

1972

Teno Roncalio (D)	75,632	52%
William Kidd (R)	70,667	48%

1974

Teno Roncalio (D)	69,434	55%
Tom Stroock (R)	57,499	45%

1976

Teno Roncalio (D)	85,721	56%
Larry Hart (R)	66,147	44%

1978

Richard Cheney (R)	75,855	59%
Bill Bagley (D)	53,522	41%

1980

Richard Cheney (R)	116,361	69%
Jim Rogers (D)	53,338	31%

1982

Richard Cheney (R)	113,236	71%
Ted Hommel (D)	46,041	29%

1984

Richard Cheney (R)	138,234	74%
Hugh McFadden Jr.(D)	45,857	24%

1986

Richard Cheney	111,007	69%
Rick Gilmore (D)	48,780	31%

1988

Richard Cheney	118,350	62%
Bryan Sharratt	56,527	38%

1989 (Special Election)

Craig Thomas (R)	74,258	52%
John Vinich (D)	60,821	43%

1990

Craig Thomas (R)	87,078	55%
Pete Maxfield (D)	70,977	45%

1992

Craig Thomas (R)	113,882	58%
John Herschler (D)	77,418	39%

1994

Barbara Cubin (R)	104,426	53%
Bob Schuster (D)	81,022	41%
Dave Dawson (Libert.)	10,729	5%

1996

Barbara Cubin (R)	116,004	55.2
Pete Maxfield (D)	95,724	40.8
Dave Dawson (Lib)	8,255	3.9

1998

Barbara Cubin (R)	100,687	57.8
Scott Ferris (D)	67,399	38.7
Steve Richardson (Libert)	6,133	3.5

2000

Barbara Cubin (R)	141,848	66.8
Michael Green (D)	60,638	28.6
Lewis Stock (Lib)	6,,417	3.

2002

Barbara Cubin (R)	110,229	62.6
Ron Akin (D)	65,961	37.4

2004

Barbara Cubin	132,107	55
Ted Ladd (D)	99,989	42
Lewis Stock (Lib)	6,581	2.8

2006

Barbara Cubin	93,336	48.3
Gary Trauner (D)	92,324	47.8
Thomas Rankin (Lib)	7,481	3.8

2008

Cynthia Lummis (R)	131,244	55.1
Gary Trauner (D)	106,758	44.9

Wyoming Members of Congress Born in Wyoming

1. Robert D. Carey, Cheyenne
2. Edward Crippa, Rock Springs
3. J. J. "Joe" Hickey, Rawlins
4. Milward Simpson, Jackson
5. Clifford P. Hansen, Teton County
6. Keith Thomson, Newcastle
7. Teno Roncalio, Rock Springs
8. Craig Thomas, Cody
9. Cynthia Lummis, Cheyenne

9 Unusual Political Disputes

1. Bucking horse license plate

When the insignia of the cowboy on the bucking horse was first added to the Wyoming license plate in 1936, Laramie lawyer Nellis Corthell taped paper over the design. He contended that the symbol was nothing more than a stunt dreamed up by Cheyenne merchants to promote Cheyenne Frontier Days in the rival city. In 2000, People for the Ethical Treatment of Animals (PETA) wrote to the governor, protesting the license plate as representing "cruelty to animals."

2. Declining a new post office building

In 1932, the town of Riverton formally declined the U. S. Post Office offer to build a new $70,000 building in town. The Lions Club sponsored the resolution, claiming the structure was not needed. The post office was built six years later.

3. Saying "no" to nuclear

In 1974 Sublette County residents protested plans by El Paso Natural Gas and the Atomic Energy Commission to use nuclear explosions to stimulate natural gas fields near Pinedale. The protests succeeded and the company and agency decided against such action.

4. Yellow stripes

The biggest controversy in the 1959 legislature involved the federal government's threat to cut off highway funds if Wyoming did not change the color of the highway stripes from yellow to white. Legislators, arguing that yellow could be seen better in ground blizzards, pointed to the dispute as an example of government interference in local matters.

5. Early "sagebrush rebellion"

The 1929 Wyoming legislature passed the following titled resolution: "Memorializing the President and the Congress to cede to the states all unappropriated and unreserved public lands together with sub-surface minerals and other natural resources." It predated the Nevada-based "Sagebrush Rebellion" by nearly 50 years.

6. Cattle drive protesters

Two months after Jackson Hole National Monument was created by presidential order, 40 armed riders, including actor Wallace Beery and then-Teton County commissioner Clifford Hansen, staged a cattle drive across monument lands to protest the designation. The May 1943, protest gained national publicity. Five years later, the presidential proclamation was withdrawn and some of the lands were added to Grand Teton National Park.

7. MRS spells nuclear waste dump

In the early 1990s, most Wyomingites polled opposed locating the "temporary" waste site in Wyoming. Fremont County supporters, however, said it would bring needed jobs to their county. After Gov. Mike Sullivan opposed any federally funded project, two Fremont County legislators, State Sen. Bob Peck and State Rep. Eli Bebout proposed a privately financed venture.

8. Nuclear incinerator in Idaho

Jackson Hole residents organized in September, 1999, to keep the Department of Energy from activating a nuclear incinerator at the Idaho Falls federal nuclear facility. Jackson attorney Gerry Spence offered to represent the group. Actor Harrison Ford was in the group. Early in 2000, the Department of Energy said it was dropping plans for such a project.

9. Barbara Cubin in 2006 Debate

On Oct. 22, 2006, after a televised debate between between incumbent U. S. Rep. Barbara Cubin, her Democratic opponent Gary Trauner, and Libertarian candidate Thomas Rankin, Cubin walked up to Rankin, who had multiple schlerosis and in a wheelchair: "If you weren't sitting in that chair, I'd slap you across the face."

U. S. Senators from Wyoming, 1890-2010

Seat A

Joseph M. Carey (b. Del., 1845, d. Cheyenne, 1924)	1890-1895
Francis E. Warren (b. Mass., 1844, d. D. C., 1929)	1895-1929
+Patrick Sullivan (b. Ireland, 1865, d. Calif., 1935)	1929-1930
Robert D. Carey (b. Cheyenne, 1878, d. Cheyenne, 1937)	1931-1937
Harry H. Schwartz (b. Ohio, 1869, d. Casper, 1955)	1937-1943
E. V. Robertson (b. Wales, 1881, d. 1963)	1943-1949
Lester C. Hunt (b. Ill., 1892, d. D. C., 1954)	1949-1954
+E. D. Crippa (b. Rock Springs, 1899, d. Rock Springs, 1960)	1954-1955
Joseph C. O'Mahoney (b. Mass., 1884, d. D. C., 1962)	1955-1961
Keith Thomson (b. Newcastle, 1919, d. near Cody, 1960)	++
+J. J. Hickey (b. Rawlins, 1911, d. 1970)	1961-1963
Milward Simpson (b. Jackson, 1897, d. Cody,	1963-1967
Clifford P. Hansen (b. Teton Co., 1912, d Jackson, 10/20/2009)	1967-1979
Alan K. Simpson (b. Denver, Colo., 1931)	1979-1997
Mike Enzi (b. Bremerton, Wash., 2/1/1944)	1997-

Seat B

Francis E. Warren (b. Mass., 1844, d. D. C., 1929)	1890-1892
*Clarence D. Clark (b. N. Y., 1851, d. Evanston, 1930)	1895-1917
**John B. Kendrick (b. Texas, 1857, d. Sheridan, 1933)	1917-1933
Joseph C. O'Mahoney (b. Mass., 1884, d. D. C., 1962)	1933-1953
Frank A. Barrett (b. Omaha, 11/10/1896, d. Cheyenne, 5/30/1962)	1953-1959
Gale McGee (b. Lincoln, Neb., 1915, d. D. C., April 9, 1992)	1959-1977
Malcolm Wallop (b. New York City, 1933)	1977-1995
Craig Thomas (b. Cody, 2/17/1933, d. Bethesda, Md;, June 4, 2007)	1995-2007
+John Barrasso (b. Reading, Pa., 7/21/1952)	2007-

+Appointed to fill unexpired term and elected to fill out term in 2008.
*A vacancy occurred for two years from 1893-95. A. C. Beckwith was appointed to the seat but did not serve. **Kendrick was first senator popularly elected (not chosen by legislature). ++Thomson was elected in Nov. 1960 but died a month later before being seated.*

U. S. Representatives from Wyoming, 1890-2010

Clarence D. Clark, Evanston (b. N. Y., 1851, d. Evanston, 1930)	1890-1893
Henry A. Coffeen, Sheridan (b. Ohio, 1841, d. Sheridan, 1912)	1893-1895
Frank W. Mondell, Newcastle (b. Mo., 1860, d. D. C., 1939)	1895-1897
John E. Osborne, Rawlins (b. N. Y., 1858, d. Rawlins, 1943)	1897-1899
Frank W. Mondell, Newcastle (b. Mo., 1860, d. D. C., 1939)	1899-1923
Charles E. Winter, Casper (b. Iowa, 1870, d. Casper, 1948)	1923-1929
Vincent Carter, Cheyenne (b. Pa., 1891, d. Albuquerque, 1972)	1929-1935
Paul Greever, Cody (b. Kansas, 1891, d. Cody, 1943)	1935-1939
Frank O. Horton, Saddlestring (b. Iowa, 1882, d. Sheridan, 1948)	1939-1941
John J. McIntyre, Douglas (b. Okla., 1904, d. Cheyenne, 1974)	1941-1943
Frank A. Barrett, Lusk (b. Omaha, 1892, d. Cheyenne, 1962)	1943-1951

William Henry Harrison, Sheridan (b.Ind., 8/10/1896, d. Fla., 1990)	1951-1955
Keith Thomson, Cheyenne (b. Newcastle, 1919, d. Cody, 1960)	1955-1960
William Henry Harrison, Sheridan (b. Indiana, 1896, d. Fla., 1990)	1961-1965
Teno Roncalio, Rock Springs/Cheyenne (b. Rock Springs, 1916)	1965-1967
William Henry Harrison, Sheridan (b. Indiana, 1896, d. Fla., 1990)	1967-1969
John Wold, Casper (b. N. J., 1916)	1969-1971
Teno Roncalio, (b. Rock Spr.ings, 1916, d. Cheyenne, 3/30/2003)	1971-1979
Dick Cheney, Casper (b. Lincoln, Neb., 1941)	1979-1989
Craig Thomas, Casper (b. Cody, 1933, d. Bethesda, Md., 6/4/2007)	1989-1995
Barbara Cubin, Casper (b. California, 11/30/1946)	1995-2009
Cynthia Lummis (b. Cheyenne, Sept. 10, 1954)	2009-

Vote in the Election for Permanent State Capital in 1904

Cheyenne: 11,781	Casper: 3,610	Sheridan: 122
Lander: 8,667	Rock Springs: 429	

The Constitution stipulated that a permanent site could be chosen only if a town won a majority of all votes cast in the election. Consequently, Cheyenne remains only the temporary capital of the state.

Residence of Wyoming Senators and Representatives

Natrona County (8): Winter, P. Sullivan, Schwartz, Wold, Cheney, Thomas, Cubin, Barrasso

Laramie County (5): J. Carey, Warren, Carter,* O'Mahoney, Lummis

Sheridan County (4): Coffeen, Kendrick, Harrison, Wallop

Park County (4): Greever, Robertson, M. Simpson, A. Simpson

Carbon (2): Osborne, Hickey*

Converse (2): McIntrye, R. Carey

Sweetwater (2): Crippa, Roncalio*

Weston (2): Mondell, Thomson*

Albany: McGee **Campbell:** Enzi **Fremont:** Hunt **Johnson:** Horton (Saddlestring) **Niobrara:** Barrett **Teton:** Hansen **Uinta:** C. D. Clark

*Roncalio and Thomson were practicing law in Laramie County at the time of their election; Carter and Hickey were in Laramie County serving in public office when they were elected. No residents of the following counties have served in Congress: Big Horn, Crook, Goshen, Hot Springs, Lincoln, Platte, Sublette, Washakie.

Governors

1st Wyoming native to be elected governor: Robert Carey, 1918

1st University of Wyoming graduate to be elected governor: Milward Simpson, 1954.

1st governor to serve more than two terms: Ed Herschler, elected for a third term in 1982.

1st governor to resign from office to accept a seat in the United States Senate: Francis E. Warren, 17 days after he became Wyoming's first state governor in 1890. It started a tradition. Kendrick, Hunt and Barrett resigned after being elected to the Senate; Hickey resigned to accept appointment to the Senate. Other governors elected to the Senate after serving as governor were Robert Carey, Milward Simpson and Cliff Hansen.

1st governor to have a veto overridden by the State Legislature: Mike Sullivan, 1991

Only governor elected as a Democrat even though he remained a registered Republican: Joseph M. Carey, elected in 1910.

> "D. R. Clay says that the temperance organization at Carbon is thriving nicely, and the saloons are doing as well as ever, so all parties are satisfied."—Rawlins paper, 1880s.

7 Wyoming Governors Born in Wyoming

1. **Robert D. Carey** (Cheyenne, 8/12/1878)
2. **Milward L. Simpson** (Jackson, 11/12/1897)
3. **J. J. "Joe" Hickey** (Rawlins, 8/22/1911)
4. **Clifford P. Hansen** (Teton County, 10/16/1912)
5. **Ed Herschler** (Kemmerer, 10/27/1918)
6. **Jim Geringer** (Wheatland, 4/24/1944)
7. **David Freudenthal** (Thermopolis, 10/12/1950)

Residence of Wyoming Governors*

Laramie Co.: (6) Warren, J. Carey, W. Ross, N. Ross, **Emerson, Miller
Converse Co.: (2) DeForest Richards, **Robert Carey
Carbon Co.: (2) Osborne, Hickey
Natrona Co.: (2) Brooks, Sullivan   **Park:** **Milward Simpson
Big Horn: W. A. Richards   **Platte:** Jim Geringer
Fremont: Lester Hunt   **Sheridan:** **John B. Kendrick
Goshen: Stan Hathaway   **Teton:** Clifford P. Hansen
Lincoln: Ed Herschler   **Weston:** Nels Smith
Niobrara: Frank Barrett

Acting governors are not listed.

**Governors are credited to the county in which they resided at the time they were elected.*
Several claimed different residences during the course of their careers. Frank Emerson lived in Sublette, Converse, Big Horn and Washakie counties, but was elected governor after serving in Cheyenne as state engineer. Milward Simpson was a native of Teton County and, for a time, lived in Hot Springs County. Robert Carey was born in Laramie County, but had ranching interests in several counties. John B. Kendrick once worked as a cowboy in Niobrara County.

13 Out-of-State Politicians with Wyoming Connections

1. **Gov. John Sparks, Nevada** (b. Mississippi, 1843)
    Sparks ranched in Wyoming in the 1870s. Later, he moved to the Reno area where he ranched until 1903 when he became governor. He was re-elected and died in office in 1908. The town of Sparks, Nevada, was named for him.
2. **Gov. Simon Bamburger, Utah** (b. Germany, 1847)
    Bamberger operated a general store at Piedmont, Uinta County, in the 1870s. A Democrat, he served as governor of Utah from 1917-1921. The first Jewish governor of that state, Bamberger died Oct. 6, 1926. He was buried in Salt Lake City.
3. **Tom Sturgis, fire commissioner, New York City**
    Sturgis had been a Laramie County cattle baron whose Union Cattle Company failed after the winter of 1886-1887. Sturgis left Wyoming, went to New York City where Theodore Roosevelt, then chairman of the civil service board, appointed him commissioner.
4. **Senator Sheridan Downey, California**
    Downey was born in Laramie in 1884 and attended Laramie schools. Following graduation from the University of Michigan Law School in 1907, he returned to Laramie to practice law. In 1913, he moved to Sacramento, Calif., and in 1938, he was elected to

It wasn't until 1969 that a severance tax was passed. The sales tax has been in effect in Wyoming since 1935, but introduced that year at the rate of two percent with no "county options" or other "extras."

the U. S. Senate from California as a Democrat. He served two terms. He did not seek re-election in 1950 and died Oct. 25, 1961.

5. Gov. Howard Pyle, Arizona

Pyle was born in Sheridan March 25, 1906. A Tempe, Ariz., businessman, he served as governor of Arizona from 1951 to 1955. He was a Republican.

6. U. S. Rep. Richard Hanna, California

Hanna was born in Kemmerer in 1914. He moved with his parents to Long Beach, Calif., when he was nine years old. Educated in California schools and a graduate of the UCLA law school, he was elected to Congress in 1962 from California's 34th district. After 12 years in office, he retired in 1974. Four years later, he was sentenced to prison for his involvement in a bribery scheme engineered by Korean lobbyist Tongsun Park. He died in Tryon, Polk County, N.C., June 9, 2001.

7. U. S. Rep. Robert Matsui, California

Athough Matsui was born in California in September, 1941, as an infant and young child, he lived in Wyoming. His residence was hardly voluntary, however. He and his parents were sent by the government to the Heart Mountain Relocation Center in Park County because they were Americans of Japanese descent. After the war and their release from internment, Matsui and his family returned to California. Matsui graduated from the University of California, Berkeley, and the law school there. He practiced law in California before he was elected to Congress for the first time in 1978. Matsui still represented California's 5th Congressional District at the time of his death on Jan. 1, 2005.

8. Commerce/Transportation Secretary Norman Mineta

A former California congressman, Mineta, too, lived àt Heart Mountain Relocation Center where his parents had been sent at the beginning of World War II. A former mayor of San Jose, Calif., he served in Congress for 21 years. In June, 2000, he was nominated Secretary of Commerce by President Bill Clinton. In January, 2000, he was appointed Secretary of Transportation by President Bush and retired in 2006.

9. Senator Tom Harkin, Iowa

Born in Iowa in 1939, Harkin spent several years of his youth in Rock Springs where he lived with relatives and attended elementary school from 1950-1952. Coincidentally, Harkin was a student in the same grade school former Secretary of State Kathy Karpan attended. He visited Rock Springs in 1991 when he was a candidate for the Democratic nomination for President and mentioned his associations with Wyoming during the 1992 primary election campaign.

10. U. S. Rep. David Minge, Minnesota

Minge (b. Clarkfield, Minn., 1942) taught constitutional and administrative law at the University of Wyoming for seven years. Minge, a Democrat, was elected to Congress for the first time in 1992 by a margin of 569 votes. He won re-election handily, however, with 57 percent of the vote against his Republican opponent in the 1994 general election. He served on the Agriculture committee and on the Science committee of the House. He was defeated in 2000 by 400 votes.

11. Senator Tom Coburn, Oklahoma

Coburn (b. Casper, March 14, 1948) was reared in Oklahoma, practiced medicine in Muskogee, Okla., and successfully ran for Congress in 1994 as a Republican. He retired from the House in 2000, but in 2004, he was elected to the U. S. Senate.

12. U. S. Rep. Brian Baird, Washington

Baird, who holds the Ph.D. in psychology from the University of Wyoming, was

---

The Wyoming Livestock Board administers cattle and horse brands for Wyoming. Cost to renew a brand was $300 for a ten-year renewal (2009). The Board hired 57 full-time and 34 part-time brand inspectors. More than 28,000 brands were registered statewide.

elected to the U. S. House from the 3rd District of Washington in 1998. He announced in 2009 that he would not seek re-election in 2010.

13. Texas State Sen. Wayne Connolly

Connolly, the brother of former Texas governor and Cabinet official John Connolly, served in the Texas legislature from 1965-73. Following retirement, he moved to Cody where he died on Dec. 20, 2000.

Books about Politics by Wyoming Authors

1. Almanac of American Politics

Worland native Grant Ujifusa is co-author of the biennial *Almanac of American Politics*, published every two years since 1972. A graduate of Harvard University, Ujifusa is also senior editor of *Reader's Digest*.

2. The Equality State: Government and Politics in Wyoming

The book, used in high school civics classes and college political science courses, was written by Gregg Cawley, Janet Clark, Michael Horan, Maggi Murdock, Alan Schenker and Oliver Walter. The book was published in 1988. Cawley, Clark, Horan and Schenker were political science professors at the University of Wyoming; Murdock was dean of UW-Casper and Walter was dean of the UW College of Arts and Sciences.

3. State Government: Politics in Wyoming

The 1981 book was written by Tim Miller, formerly a political science instructor at Northwest College, Powell.

4. Government and Politics of Wyoming

The book, last published in 1974, was written by John B. Richard, formerly chair, UW political science department. The textbook was used for a decade.

5 Wyomingites in the President's Cabinet*

1. Stan Hathaway, Secretary of the Interior, 1975

Born and educated in Nebraska, Hathaway served two terms as Wyoming governor prior to his appointment to the Cabinet. Hathaway, the first Cabinet officer from Wyoming, was appointed by President Gerald Ford. His appointment was confirmed by the U. S. Senate by a vote of 60-36 after contentious hearings. Hathaway held the job six weeks. Due to ill health and frustration with bureaucracy, he resigned and returned to Wyoming where he re-entered law practice. He died in 2005.

2. James Watt, Secretary of the Interior, 1981-1983

Born in Lusk in 1938, and educated in Wheatland and at the University of Wyoming, Watt was appointed to the Cabinet from Colorado where he worked as a lawyer. Following his service in the Cabinet, he returned to Wyoming. In 2010, he lived and worked in Jackson and Sedona, Arizona.

3. Paul Carlin, U. S. Postmaster General, 1985-1986

Born in California, Carlin was educated at the University of Wyoming. In 1953, he was NCAA All-American in track. Technically, after 1971, the postmaster general was no longer considered a presidential cabinet officer. The President appoints nine members of the Board of Governors of the Postal Service who chose the postmaster general. Nonetheless, because of the historical role as a Cabinet office, the postmaster general is included here.

When Allen Campbell was elected to the legislature in 1965, he became the first Wyoming legislator elected whose mother also had served in that body. Mrs. Lettie Campbell served from Lincoln County in the 1931 session.

4. Richard Cheney, Secretary of Defense, 1989-1993

Cheney was nominated to the post by President George Bush after the Senate refused to confirm Bush's choice of former Senator John Tower. Cheney had been President Gerald Ford's chief of staff from 1975-1976 and congressman from Wyoming from 1978 until he resigned to become Secretary of Defense. His appointment was confirmed by the Senate March 17, 1989. When the Clinton administration came into office, Cheney returned to the private sector and, in 1996, he became chief executive officer of Halliburton Co., Dallas, Texas. On July 25, 2000, Republican presidential nominee George W. Bush designated him as the Republican vice presidential candidate. He and Bush were re-elected in 2004. He was the only Wyomingite ever elected Vice President of the United States.

5. Norman Mineta, Sec'y of Commerce, 2000; Sec'y of Transportation, 2001

Mineta (b. San Jose, Calif., 1931) was appointed from California. When he was a young man, he lived in Wyoming--but not voluntarily. He and his parents were interned at Heart Mountain Relocation Camp in Park County. He attended school at Heart Mountain, but returned to California when the war ended. He served for 21 years in Congress, representing the 13th district of California.

Two other Cabinet officers have listed Wyoming as their residences, but like Mineta, they were residents of another state when appointed. Charles Duncan, Secretary of Transportation in the Carter administration, owned the TE Ranch near Cody and listed Wyoming as a residence. James Baker, Secretary of State in the Bush administration, bought the Tibbals Ranch on Silver Creek near Boulder, Sublette County, soon after the 1988 general election. He changed his voting residence to Wyoming in early 1990. He returned his voting registration to Texas in 1994. Both Duncan and Baker were appointed while residents of Texas.

Unusual Incidents on the Campaign Trail

1. "I left it on the airplane!"

When Democratic presidential candidate Adlai Stevenson made a campaign stop in Cheyenne in Sept. 1952, he had been asked to talk about issues important to the oil and gas industry, a subject about which he was quite unfamiliar. With the help of campaign aides and Wyoming Sen. Joseph C. O'Mahoney, Stevenson drafted a speech for delivery on the topic. His plane landed in Cheyenne and Stevenson went to the site of where he was to give the speech, leaving the speech notes on the plane. He talked about his childhood memories of visiting Wyoming instead of the more substantive issues that he had been urged to address.

2. Orange bombardment

When Milward Simpson was campaigning for election to the U. S. Senate in 1940, he was pelted with oranges at a campaign stop in Hanna. Simpson was not deterred. The former star UW athlete simply hurled the oranges back at the hecklers who had thrown them. Even though Simpson came out even in the orange toss, he lost the election.

3. Dropping in for dinner

Frank Hadsell, a candidate for Carbon County sheriff in the 1880s, was campaigning in the town of Carbon when he fell through the roof of a dugout occupied by a Finnish family. The falling body narrowly missed six startled Finns who were eating supper. Hadsell was not hurt, but he lost the election.

The first amendment ever to be voted on by Wyoming voters failed to pass. In 1899, both Houses of the legislature authorized an amendment that would have allow county bonding. Only 5,435 voters in November, 1900, favored the measure with 2,170 against. Most voters, nearly 18,000, didn't bother to vote. According to the Wyoming Constitution, an amendment must gain the majority of votes CAST IN THE ELECTION in order to pass. Not voting equates with a "no."

4. Sorry, Wrong State

When Percy Metz ran for Big Horn county attorney in 1908, the 25-year-old candidate traveled the entire county. One day, he stopped to help some men work on the roof of a ranch building. He spent the day on the job, had dinner and handed out his campaign cards at the end of the day. The ranch owner looked at the card and told him that while he would like to vote for the young man, "you've been campaigning in Montana."

5. Smear campaign

One of the dirtiest attacks in Wyoming political history was made by the Democrats in the 1918 gubernatorial election when party ads accused Robert Carey, the Republican candidate and son of a former Democratic governor, of being influenced by a "unregenerate offspring of Hunland." The ad accused Carey of promoting "Hun Kultur" at Careyhurst, his Converse County ranch. Carey had employed a German alien on the ranch briefly in 1914, but the man was neither sympathetic to the Kaiser nor influential with Carey. Despite the negative campaign ads, Carey won the election.

6. Another smear campaign

The Republicans furnished the dirty attack in the 1954 senatorial campaign by accusing Joseph C. O'Mahoney, the Democrat, of being "a foreign agent." O'Mahoney, a lawyer, once represented a Cuban business client, but the Republican charge suggested something far more sinister at a time when anti-Communist witchhunts were in full swing. Despite the attacks, O'Mahoney won narrowly.

7. Boxer shorts auction

In 1987, the Campbell County Republican Party held a fundraiser. One of the items auctioned off was a pair of Sen. Al Simpson's boxer shorts. Campbell County Democrats, in the 1990s, sponsored an annual "donkey dump" contest.

8. Church campaigning

Jim Griffith, former state auditor and treasurer, often campaigned on weekends and stopped for church services where he was campaigning. On one occasion, he stopped for church in Jeffrey City. At the appointed hour, only four people came and the minister had not yet arrived. One person asked Griffith's wife if she could play the pump organ which she had to admit she could not. Griffith claimed he was relieved when the minister finally walked in 15 minutes late. "The fellow who looked like he was in charge was giving me the eye, and I was fearful I was going to...be asked to say something," Griffith wrote. *Source: Jim Griffith, A Funny Thing Happened on the Way to the Wyoming Capitol. (Lusk, 1988).*

Well-Known Wyomingites
Who Lost Primary Election Races

1. Tim McCoy, actor

McCoy ran unsuccessfully for the Republican nomination to the U. S. Senate in 1942. A native of Michigan, he ranched near Thermopolis, served a term as state adjutant general and then went to Hollywood where he made numerous Westerns. After his unsuccessful quest, McCoy never sought elective office again.

2. Ewing T. Kerr, federal judge

Kerr ran for the U. S. Senate in 1954, but lost to William Henry Harrison in the Republican primary by a vote of 22,257-10,601. The next year, Kerr was appointed by President Dwight Eisenhower as U. S. District Judge for Wyoming.

3. Kenny Sailors, basketball star

Sailors was ranching near Jackson when he ran for the U. S. Senate in 1962, but lost in the Republican primary to Milward Simpson by a vote of 30,124-20,383. Simpson went on to win the general election.

4. Frank Barrett

Barrett is the only person in Wyoming history to be have been elected governor and to both houses of Congress. In 1960, however, he lost to U. S. Rep. Keith Thomson for the Republican nomination to the Senate. Barrett, an incumbent two years earlier, had lost a narrow general election in 1958 to Democrat Gale McGee. Thomson won the general election, but died before he could take the Senate seat.

5. Gerry Spence, lawyer

Spence ran unsuccessfully for the Republican nomination to the U. S. House of Representatives in 1962. He lost to incumbent Cong. William Henry Harrison in the Republican primary 31,443-18,911.

6. William Henry Harrison

The incumbent five-term congressman was defeated in the 1968 Republican primary by Casper geologist John Wold by a vote of 23,590-22,522. Harrison, who had moved to Wyoming in 1937 to buy the XL Ranch near Dayton, was 72 at the time he lost. Wold defeated Democrat Velma Linford in the general election.

7. Ed Herschler, governor

In 1970, four years before he was elected governor, Herschler ran in the Democratic primary for nomination to the congressional seat. He lost to Teno Roncalio by a margin of 26,309-11,238. Roncalio went on to win the general election over Republican Harry Roberts by a mere 608 votes. The Roncalio-Roberts race was the third closest congressional election in state history.

8. Malcolm Wallop, senator

Wallop sought the Republican gubernatorial nomination in 1974, but lost in a four-way race to State Sen. Dick Jones. Jones was defeated by Ed Herschler in the general election. Two years later, Wallop successfully challenged Sen. Gale McGee for the U. S. Senate.

Popular Vote in Wyoming for Presidential Candidates
(from the largest percentage to the smallest, 1932-2008)

Candidate	% of vote	Year	Candidate	% of vote	Year
1. Reagan	70.5	1984	11. Ford	59.3	1976*
2. Nixon	69	1972	12. Dole	57.5	1996*
3. W. Bush	69	2004	13. Johnson	56.6	1964
4. W. Bush	68**	2000	14. Roosevelt	56.1	1932
5. McCain	65	2008*	15. Nixon	55.8	1968
6. Eisenhower	62.7	1952	16. Nixon	55	1960*
7. Reagan	62.6	1980	17. Roosevelt	52.8	1940
8. Bush	60.5	1988	18. Truman	51.6	1948
9. Roosevelt	60.6	1936	19. Dewey	51.2	1944*
10. Eisenhower	60.1	1956	20. Bush	39.9	1992*+

Won majority in Wyoming, but lost nationally.
**Lost popular vote nationally, but won electoral vote.*
+In Wyoming, Clinton gained 34.3% and Ross Perot had 25.8% of the vote.

6 Wyoming Campaign Slogans/Ads

1. "Popular government at popular prices"

Suggested by Will Rogers for C. B. Irwin who considered running for governor in 1934. The slogan was never used because Irwin was killed in a car accident in March, 1934, before he could announce for the race.

2. "Wyoming's wealth for Wyoming's people"

The 1966 campaign slogan for Ernest Wilkerson, Democratic candidate for governor. Even though Wilkerson lost the race, the campaign created a climate of support for mineral severance taxes which were finally adopted in 1969.

3. "McGee for Me"

Senator Gale McGee used the slogan for three successful campaigns. When his fourth campaign used the slogan, "He Has Clout," in the 1976 election, McGee was defeated.

4. "Me and F. E."

The slogan was used by Francis E. Warren, the state's Republican leader and most popular vote-getter in the first third of the century. The "me" was variously Joseph M. Carey (before he broke with Warren in the middle 1890s) and Cong. Frank Mondell.

5. "The man without arms who has a family on his hands."

Used during the campaign of Henry Code, Uinta County coroner, who had lost both arms above the elbow in an accident early in life. Code operated a repair shop in Evanston and served as county coroner from 1886 to 1892.

6. A toilet on a horse

When Senator Malcolm Wallop ran against incumbent Sen. Gale McGee in 1976, his ad campaign was widely heralded as one of the most imaginative ever done. In one ad, making fun of government regulations requiring on-site restroom facilities for workers, a horse was shown carrying a toilet. After the election, all of the television networks showed the ad as an example of how difficult concepts could be simplified by using images.

14 Wyoming Ambassadors

1. John A. Campbell (b. Ohio, 1835, d. D. C., 1880)

The first territorial governor served as Consul to Switzerland, 1877-1880.

2. Thomas Moonlight (b. Scotland, 1833, d. Kansas, 1899)

The last territorial governor, Moonlight was Minister to Bolivia from 1893 to 1897.

3. Jacob Blair (b. West Virginia, 1821, d. Utah, 1901)

The former Wyoming territorial justice was Minister to Costa Rica from 1868-1873.

4. Frederic deBillier

The owner of a cattle ranch in Wyoming, deBillier lived in Wyoming from 1879 to 1892. From 1908 to 1924, he held diplomatic posts in Iran, Greece, Bolivia, and Peru.

5. Robert D. Coe (b. N. Y., 1902)

Coe, who owned a ranch southwest of Cody, served as U. S. Ambassador to Denmark from 1953 to 1957. He was a career State Department employee whose father, William R. Coe, was a well-known businessman and philanthropist.

6. J. Butler Wright (b. N. Y., 1877, d. 1939)

Wright, a career diplomat, served as U. S. minister to Hungary (1927-30), envoy to Uruguay (1930-34), minister to Czechoslovakia (1934-37) and U. S. ambassador in Cuba from July, 1937 until his death. Early in his career, following six years in banking in New York City, Wright operated a Wyoming ranch for two years. Later, when he was in the State Department, he owned a ranch near Cody and visited there frequently.

7. Nelson T. Johnson (b. D. C., 1887, d. Dec. 3, 1954)

A career diplomat, Johnson married Jane Thornton Beck of Cody in 1931while he was serving as U. S. ambassador to China. He served in that post from 1929 to 1941. Later, he was U. S. ambassador to Australia from 1941 to 1946. He and his family made frequent visits back to his wife's hometown.

8. Gale McGee (b. Nebraska, 1915, d. 1992)

Former Sen. McGee was U. S. Ambassador to the Organization of American States (OAS) in the Carter administration from 1977 to 1981.

9. Francois Dickman (b. Iowa, 1924)

Dickman was reared in Laramie and graduated from the University of Wyoming in 1947. A career diplomat, he served as Ambassador to the United Arab Emirates from 1976 to 1979 and U. S. Ambassador to Kuwait from 1979 to 1983. Following his retirement from the State Department, he joined the political science faculty at the University of Wyoming.

10. David Nicholas (b. Gillette, 1941, d. Kiev, Ukraine, 2005)

The former Albany County legislator was appointed U. S. representative to the North Atlantic Treaty Organization (NATO) alliance in 1989. Later, he accepted appointment as director fo the OSCE project office in the Ukraine. He died in Kiev while serving in that post, in March 2005.

11. Tom Stroock (b. New York, 1925, d. Casper, December 2009)

President George Bush nominated the veteran Natrona County legislator to become U. S. Ambassador to Guatemala in 1989. He served until 1992.

12. Mike Sullivan (b. Nebraska, 1939)

Sullivan's appointment as U. S. Ambassador to Ireland was confirmed by the Senate on Oct. 21, 1998. A former governor of Wyoming, Sullivan was appointed by President Bill Clinton. Sullivan was the first sitting governor to endorse Clinton for the presidency in 1992.

13. Jeanine Mathew Jackson (b. Sheridan)

Jackson, a native of Sheridan, served as U. S. ambassador to the African nation of Burkina Faso. A graduate of Hastings College (Neb.), she was in the foreign service for 21 years before her appointment on Feb. 21, 2006. She was replaced Aug. 4, 2009.

14. J. Thomas Dougherty (b. Casper)

Dougherty, a graduate of Brown University, was a career State Department employee when he was appointed to succeed Jackson (*above*) as U. S. Ambassador to Burkina Faso in the summer of 2010.

Wyomingites in Various Federal Agencies

1. U. S. Civil Service Commission

Cheyenne newspaperman W. C. Deming (b. Mt. Olivet, Kentucky, 1869, d. Cheyenne, 1949) served as president of the commission from 1923 to 1930. He was publisher of the *Wyoming State Tribune* from 1901 to 1937.

2. U. S. Bureau of Reclamation

Elwood Mead (b. Ind., 1858, d. D. C., 1936), a former territorial and state engineer, was appointed to the post of director of the USBR in 1924. During his term, construction was started on Hoover Dam and the resulting lake behind it was named Lake Mead in his honor. Floyd Dominy, (b. Neb., 1909) formerly a resident of Campbell County, served as bureau director from 1959-69. Following graduation from the University of Wyoming in 1932, Dominy taught school near Gillette for a time. He joined the USBR in 1946. He celebrated his 100th birthday in Virginia (2009).

3. Federal Power Commission

Claude Draper (b. Cheyenne, 1875) served as commissioner from 1930 to 1941. A Republican, he was formerly a ranching partner of R. S. Van Tassell.

4. Environmental Protection Agency

Ann McGill Gorsuch (b. Casper, 1942) served a controversial term from 1981-83 as director of the agency in the Reagan administration. She was forced to resign in 1983 following a confrontation over release of documents to Congress. Shortly before her resignation, she married BLM director Bob Burford.

432 Wyoming Almanac

5. National Endowment for the Humanities

Lynne Vincent Cheney (b. Casper, Aug. 14, 1941), was appointed to the post by President Ronald Reagan when her predecessor, William Bennett, became Secretary of Education. She also served in the Bush administration. Celeste Colgan, Cheyenne, served as her deputy.

6. U. S. Fish and Wildlife Service

John Turner (b. Jackson, 1942), a former Teton County state senator, was appointed director of the service in 1989, serving in the post through the Bush administration.

7. U. S. Maritime Commission

Admiral Emory S. Land (b. Colorado, 1879, d. 1971), a University of Wyoming graduate, served as director of the commission from 1938 to 1942. Later, he directed the War Shipping Administration. An annual Land award was given to the best scholar-athlete at UW for many years.

8. Department of the Treasury

Nellie Tayloe Ross (b. Missouri, Nov. 29, 1876, d. D. C., 1977), the former Wyoming governor, was appointed director of the mint by Franklin Roosevelt in 1933. The first woman to hold the post, she retired in 1953. Bradley Buckles, a UW graduate, was head of the Bureau of Alcohol, Tobacco and Firearms in the Treasury Department from 1999-2004.

9. U. S. Department of the Interior

Stan Hathaway was Secretary of the Interior, briefly, in 1975, appointed by President Gerald Ford. James Watt (b. Lusk, 1938) served as President Ronald Reagan's Interior Secretary from 1981-1983. Thomas L. Sansonetti of Gillette (b. Hinsdale, Illinois, 1949) was appointed solicitor of the department in March, 1990, by President George Bush. Robert R. Rose, Jr., (b. Evanston, Ill., 1915) was Assistant Secretary of the Interior for Mineral Resources in 1951-1952, in the final months of the Truman administration. Kathy Karpan (b. Rock Springs, 1942) was appointed director of the Office of Surface Mining Reclamation and Enforcement by President Bill Clinton in May, 1997. She took office Aug. 4, 1997, and served in that capacity until April, 2000, when she was transferred to Deputy Assistant Secretary for Land and Mineral Management. Several Wyomingites served in the George W. Bush Interior Department, including Johnnie Burton, head of Minerals Management Service, and Randall Luthi, also head of that sub-agency.

10. Bureau of Indian Affairs (Dept. of the Interior)

Larry EchoHawk (b. Cody, 1948) was appointed to head the Bureau of Indian Affairs in the Obama administration. He graduated from the University of Utah Law School in 1973. After private practice in Utah, he became general counsel to the Shoshone-Bannock tribes in 1977, serving in that capacity until 1985. Elected to the Idaho House of Representatives in 1982, he served until 1986 when he became prosecuting attorney for Bannock County, Idaho. In 1990, he was elected Idaho Attorney General, the first Native American in the United States to be elected attorney general of any state. He ran for governor in 1994 but lost in the general election. On May 20, 2009, the U. S. Senate confirmed his nomination and on May 22, he was sworn in as head of the Bureau of Indian Affairs in the Obama administration's Interior Department.

11. U. S. Department of Defense

Pete Williams (b. Casper, 1952) served as Defense Secretary Dick Cheney's press secretary. He appeared frequently on television during the Persian Gulf War. Frederick Morris of Cody headed the Hog Island shipyard, the nation's largest, during World War

Francis E. Warren served the longest term in Congress of any Wyomingite. He served 34 years. The shortest "term" was that of Senator-Elect Keith Thomson who died one month and one day after the election, before he was officially sworn into office.

I. Bryan Sharratt, a former candidate for Congress from Wyoming, was named Deputy Assistant Secretary of the Air Force by President Clinton in April, 1994. UW graduate Les Brownlee, class of 1962, served as Secretary of the Army from 2003-2004.

12. Federal Election Commission

Scott E. Thomas (b. Buffalo, 1953) was appointed to the non-partisan commission in 1986 by President Ronald Reagan. He was reappointed for a second six-year term by President Bush and a third term by President Clinton Sept. 2, 1997. A graduate of Stanford and Georgetown, he joined FEC as attorney in 1977. Later, he was assistant to the commissioner. In 1987, 1993 and 1999, he was commission chair.

Miscellaneous Political Facts

1. Closest legislative races in Wyoming history

In November, 1944, Democrat Andy Martin and Republican Ernest F. Shaw received the same number of votes for a legislative seat from Park County. Shaw's election was conceded by the legislature. In 1994 Republican candidate Randall Luthi and independent candidate Larry Call each received 1,941 votes for a seat in the legislature from northern Lincoln County. The tie was broken on Nov. 16, 1994, with a drawing broadcast nationally on NBC's Today Show. The law requires that, in the case of a tie, candidates draw lots. To avoid any appearance of unfairness, Gov. Mike Sullivan recommended that ping-pong balls be used instead of paper. Secretary of State Kathy Karpan drew the ball marked with Luthi's name from Gov. Sullivan's battered hat, giving Luthi the victory.

2. 1st election by mail

Wyoming law first allowed voting by mail in January, 1995. In August, 1995, the law was utilized in the state for the first time in a special election for the board of directors of Dubois Fire District.

3. Only Rock Springs resident to serve as U. S. Senator

E. D. "Ted" Crippa, appointed to serve out an unexpired term in 1954, holds the distinction. Even though Rock Springs always has been overwhelmingly Democratic, Crippa was a Republican.

3. Lord-Legislator

Only one former Wyoming legislator also served in the British House of Lords. He was Oliver Wallop, the 8th Earl of Portsmouth. Wallop was the grandfather of U. S. Senator Malcolm Wallop.

4. 1st legislative special session

The session was called by Gov. Robert Carey in January, 1920, to ratify the woman suffrage amendment to the U. S. Constitution.

5. Wyoming Socialists

In the 1932 general election, the Socialist Party nominated candidates in Wyoming for congress and governor. W. W. Wolfe, the congressional candidate, polled 1,428 votes of the 88,000 cast. A. O. Blow, the candidate for governor, did slightly better with 1,647 votes of 92,000 cast. Their best showings were in Platte County where Blow received 503 votes; Wolfe, 370.

6. Wyoming Communists

The Communist Party held a convention in Wyoming in July, 1936. Their presidential

---

Wyoming's then U. S. Sen. Malcolm Wallop sold a house in Arlington, Va., in 1986 for $902,700, the highest selling price for any home in that county that year. With the proceeds, Wallop bought a townhouse in Georgetown.

candidate, however, received only 71 votes statewide. A prominent editor of the largest Communist Party newspaper on the West Coast, based in San Francisco, had once worked as a shoemaker in Cody before World War I.

7. 1st geologist elected to the United States Congress

The distinction belongs to John Wold (b. New Jersey, 1916), a Casper Republican, elected to the U. S. House of Representatives from Wyoming in 1968.

8. Biggest legislative fight

In the 1913 legislative session, the Republicans held a 30-27 edge in the House of Representatives until two of their members decided to defect to the Democrats. On Jan. 20, 1913, fights broke when one of the defectors announced he was rejoining the Republicans. In exchange for his return to the Republicans, Martin Pratt of Park County received party support for speaker. The Democrats were so angered at Pratt's treachery that Speaker Pro Tem William Wood of Crook County rushed the speaker's rostrum and claimed the chair. Pratt threw him from the platform, the chair landing on top of Wood. After a quarter hour of shouting, peace was restored when some legislators began singing a humorous song.

9. Friend of the First Family

For two years, 1964-1966, Dr. Brent Eastman of Evanston dated Lynda Bird Johnson, the daughter of the sitting U. S. President. The two met in 1964 when Eastman was a guide on a river cruise in the Tetons for the president's family. Later that winter, Lynda Bird stayed with Eastman's family in Evanston during a ski vacation. In 1966, Eastman was an intern at the University of California Medical Center in San Francisco. The next year, Lynda Bird married Charles Robb, now a U. S. Senator, in a White House ceremony.

11. Contested Congressional races

The closest contest for Wyoming's lone House seat was in 1896 when John Osborne defeated Frank Mondell by just 266 votes. Only a few more than 20,000 votes were cast. In percentage terms, the closest House race was in 1970 when Teno Roncalio defeated Harry Roberts by just 608 votes out of more than 115,000 cast. Malcolm Wallop's 1,165-vote margin over John Vinich in 1988 was the closest contest for a U. S. Senate seat.

12. 1st Asian Indian elected to a state legislature

Nimi McConigley, who represented House District 59, Natrona County, was the first Asian Indian elected to any state legislature. Reared in Madras, India, she came to Wyoming in 1976. From 1988-1993, she was news director of KGWC-TV Casper. In 1996 she unsuccessfully sought the Republican nomination for the U. S. Senate.

13. Closest race for a county office

There have been numerous ties for various county offices through the years. In one such tie, William Watt and Thomas O. Miller, both Lusk lawyers, tied in the election for the Niobrara County attorney in July 1946 with 317 votes each. The two men drew slips of paper from a hat. On the eighth try, Watt pulled out the winning slip and became county attorney. (In heavily Republican Niobrara County, winning the primary often was tantamount to winning the office). His son, James Watt, later served as Secretary, U. S. Department of the Interior. Miller was Wyoming Attorney General from 1957-1959.

14. Only Wyomingite Chair of Young Republican National Federation

In Indianapolis, on July 4, 1975, Jack Mueller of Cheyenne was elected national chairman of the Young Republican National Federation. He served a two-year term which included service on the Executive Committee of the National Republican Party. He is the only Wyomingite to date elected as national chair in either party.

The U. S. House of Representatives approved two of four articles of impeachment against President Bill Clinton in 1998. Wyoming Congresswoman Barbara Cubin voted to approve all four. When the U. S. Senate voted on impeachment on Feb. 12, 1999, both Wyoming senators, Craig Thomas and Mike Enzi, voted to convict and remove Clinton.

Presidential Visits to Wyoming

All but two of the U. S. Presidents since Grant have visited Wyoming. (The exceptions are Grover Cleveland and Benjamin Harrison. Oddly, Harrison was president when Wyoming became a state and his son lived in the capital city of the neighboring state of Montana. A grandson, William Henry Harrison, served in Congress from Wyoming for five terms, 1951-1955, 1961-1965 and 1967-1969). Seventeen presidents visited the state during their terms of office. Several others came to Wyoming either to campaign for themselves or other candidates or to relax and enjoy the scenery.

1. U. S. Grant

Grant stopped in Wyoming while enroute to the West Coast during his second term. He spoke at a Cheyenne banquet given in his honor. It was not his first visit to Wyoming. Grant had traveled through when he was in the army.

2. Rutherford B. Hayes

Grant's successor the presidency, Hayes addressed a small crowd in Cheyenne from the depot platform in 1880.

3 James A. Garfield

Garfield crossed Wyoming by horse from Montana when he was an army gneral in 1872. He was moving to his new assignment at Fort Leavenworth, Kansas. Garfield's term was too short for a return visit to Wyoming. He was assassinated and died eight months into his term.

4. Chester A. Arthur

Among the more forgettable presidents, Arthur spent the most time in Wyoming of any 19th century chief executive. In August, 1883, he and a large contingent took the train to Green River and then rode cross-country to Yellowstone. During his visit, a single horse courier kept him in touch with world and national affairs with one mail delivery per day. Always the immaculate dresser, Arthur compromised between style and cowboy regalia during his two-month Wyoming vacation. His costume often consisted of a business suit, knee-length leather leggings, a heavy watch chain and a sailor cap.

5. William McKinley

McKinley merely peered out of the train window while his railway car passed through the state back to Washington, D. C. The president was visiting the West Coast when he received word that his wife had become seriously ill. The urgency necessitated a non-stop return on the shortest route, the UP line across Wyoming.

6. Theodore Roosevelt

Probably the most popular presidential visitor, TR made speech stops at several stations from Evanston east to Laramie and as far north as Newcastle in the spring of 1903. In Laramie, he spoke from the front steps of Old Main and then took a circuitous 65-mile horseback ride over the summit to Cheyenne. Roosevelt had been in Wyoming in the 1880s, when as a North Dakota rancher, he visited the Cheyenne Club and Buffalo twice. In 1900, he made speeches in the state including talks at Green River, Rawlins, Medicine Bow, Laramie and Cheyenne. He returned to Wyoming in 1910, two years after he left the White House.

7. William Howard Taft

Taft campaigned widely throughout the state in 1911. He gave formal speeches in Laramie on Oct. 4 and Rock Springs on Oct. 5, among the numerous appearances. On Oct. 20, 1911, he spoke in Newcastle from the steps of the newly constructed Weston County Courthouse.

8. Woodrow Wilson

In the fall of 1919, Wilson embarked on a national speaking tour to promote American entry into the League of Nations. By the time he arrived in Cheyenne on Sept. 24, he had spoken in nearly 40 cities during a three-week period. After a warm reception at the depot, he visited Fort Russell (now Warren Air Force Base) and gave a speech at the Princess Theater in downtown Cheyenne. "He had a look of almost inexpressible weariness," the Cheyenne newspaper reported, "and he has deep llines around his eyes." The next day, Wilson gave a speech in Pueblo, Colo., and at its conclusion, he collapsed from exhaustion. He returned non-stop on the train to Washington, D. C., where he suffered a stroke a few days later. He was incapacitated for the rest of his term.

9. Warren G. Harding

Harding rode through Wyoming on the way to Alaska in June, 1923. He made brief stops at Cheyenne and Laramie and then took a short sightseeing tour of Jackson Hole and Yellowstone in early July. On July 18, he made tahe first visit to Canada by an American president. Five weeks after he left Wyoming, Harding died in San Francisco. The train carrying his casket crossed southern Wyoming, returning the president's body to Washington. The train stopped for 27 minutes in Cheyenne where a crowd estimated at 10,000 came to the depot to pay respects on the Sunday afternoon of August 5, 1923.

10. Calvin Coolidge

Coolidge spent summers in South Dakota and came into Wyoming from time to time for short sightseeing excursions. In August, 1927, he vacationed in Yellowstone, passing back and forth through Cody.

11. Herbert Hoover

Hoover stopped in Cheyenne the night before his defeat in the 1932 election. In the election the next day, Hoover gained 43.9 percent of the vote in Wyoming, losing to Franklin Roosevelt by the biggest margin ever recorded to that time.

12. Franklin D. Roosevelt

FDR campaigned in Wyoming in 1932 and, as president, visited the state on three occasions. He gave a speech to 10,000 people assembled at the depot in Casper in September, 1937. Later that month, he stopped in many towns and visited the Tetons and Yellowstone.

13. Harry Truman

Truman "whistle-stopped" through Wyoming during the 1948 campaign. Large crowds met his train at depots throughout the state and Truman spoke to several of the assembled crowds from the back platform of his train. In Cheyenne, he spoke from the front porch of the Governor's Mansion on June 6, 1948. Sometimes, his train simply stopped for crew changes or refueling, Truman waved from the rail car platform. On May 9, 1950, Truman was in Casper. He spoke at NCHS auditorium and attended the dedication for Kortes Dam. As a former president, he rode a stagecoach down Casper's 2nd Street in July, 1953.

14. Dwight Eisenhower

Ike campaigned in Wyoming in 1952. His wife Mamie once lived in Denver, Colo., where they visited frequently during his presidency. He never traveled north to Wyoming. Before he was president, Eisenhower was in Wyoming. In 1919, he led an army motorized unit across country, through southern Wyoming, to show the need for better highways.

15. John F. Kennedy

Before he was president, Kennedy spoke to a party fund raiser at Casper June 14, 1958. During his presidency, JFK spoke to the largest crowd ever assembled to hear a speaker in Wyoming. The Sept. 23, 1963, speech was made in the fieldhouse at the University of Wyoming. Kennedy was assassinated less than two months later.

16. Lyndon B. Johnson

LBJ toured Wyoming many times when he was a senator from Texas. Soon after he

---

A news item on April 17, 1935, noted that the Canyon Hotel in Yellowstone would make "an ideal summer White House."

became vice president, Johnson again visited the state. He gave speeches at Cheyenne in 1962 and Casper in July, 1963. During the 1964 campaign, President Johnson spoke to a crowd of 4,000 people at Casper on Oct. 12. He was given a jade cuff-link set and his wife received jade earrings.

17. Richard M. Nixon

While he was vice president, Nixon made campaign visits to Wyoming in 1954, 1956 (when he spoke on Main Street in Sheridan), 1958 (at Casper on Oct. 17), and 1960. He also gave a campaign speeches in Wyoming, for Barry Goldwater on Oct. 22, 1964, and for state Republican candidates two years later. He did not visit the state during his presidency, however.

18. Gerald R. Ford

Ford's associations with Wyoming were numerous. Ford, of all presidents, had the closest family ties to the state. His grandparents were pioneers in the central part of the state and Ford worked in Wyoming during the summers in his college years. In 1978, he visited briefly in Casper where he met several people who had known his grandparents, Mr. and Mrs. C. H. King. After he was President, he visited UW in May 1984.

19. Jimmy Carter

Carter and his wife vacationed in Jackson Hole in August, 1978.

20. Ronald Reagan

Reagan made a campaign stop in Casper in 1976. He gave a speech in Cheyenne at Story Gymnasium in October, 1982, when he was president. After he left the White House, Reagan and his wife Nancy vacationed in Jackson Hole. In July, 1992, they were guests at the Lost Creek Ranch. During one day's visit, they shopped in Jackson stores.

21. George Bush

In July, 1988, during the Democratic Party's convention, Vice President Bush fished near Cody. Four years later, when the Democrats were meeting in convention at New York (1992), President Bush visited at the ranch owned by Secretary of State James Baker in Sublette County. Bush also made brief visits to Jackson Hole and Yellowstone in the summer of 1989 and in 1990 for the state centennial.

22. Bill Clinton

Of all modern-day Presidents, President Clinton probably spent the longest time in Wyoming when he vacationed in Jackson Hole for 17 days in August, 1995, and again in 1996. The President played golf at the Jackson Golf and Tennis Club. Clinton, his wife Hillary and daughter Chelsea rafted down the Snake River. The first family were guests at the summer home of Sen. Jay Rockefeller. The Clintons participated in at least one "official" event during their Wyoming vacation. They participated in a ceremony commemorating women suffrage. About 450 people attended the event. When he was a candidate, he made a campaign appearance at the Cheyenne airport during the 1992 election campaign. He often had visited the state when he was governor of Arkansas. Clinton also vacationed in Jackson Hole in August, 1996, where he finished writing a book.

23. George W. Bush

During the 2000 campaign, Bush appeared with Dick Cheney in Casper.

24. Barack Obama

Obama campaigned in Wyoming in 2008. He appeared before a crowd of close to 10,000 at the Arena-Auditorium at UW the night before the Democratic Party county caucuses in March 2008.

A bit more than ten percent of Wyoming homesteaders were single women, according to a study by historian Paula Bauman who studied homesteads in six eastern Wyoming counties. They made up 11.8 percent of 6,500 homesteaders.

This and That About Politics

1. Nominating the Candidate

At the 1960 Democratic National Convention in Los Angeles, the Wyoming delegation was the last to vote on the first ballot. Sen. John F. Kennedy had 10 1/2 of the 15 votes pledged to him. However, in order to keep from going into a second ballot, during which delegates pledged to Kennedy could have been released to vote for someone else, Kennedy needed the other 4 1/2 Wyoming votes. At the urging of Ted Kennedy, who was standing in the delegation, and without polling the delegation, Tracy McCraken, chairman of the Wyoming delegation, cast all 15 votes for Kennedy. It gave Kennedy the nomination. Even though the nomination was a foregone conclusion, Wyoming's delegation was designated to cast the deciding vote for George W. Bush in the 2000 Republican National Convention. Gov. Jim Geringer, the delegation chair, announced the vote, but the event lacked the drama of the 1960 convention which allowed Kennedy to escape a second ballot and deny his chief challenger, Sen. Lyndon B. Johnson, a chance to pick up delegates pledged to Kennedy only on the first ballot.

2. Model constitution

In January 1993, the Federal Election Commission recommended to Romania that they model their election code after that of Wyoming.

3. Fresh Faces

In the 1911 legislature, of 56 House members, 48 were freshmen. In 1993, there were 35 new legislators in the House and Senate.

4. 1st Woman State Senator

Dora McGrath (b. North English, Iowa, 1868; d. Thermopolis, 1949) of Hot Springs County was elected to the State Senate in 1930, becoming the first woman elected to the Wyoming State Senate. (Mary Bellamy, Albany County, had won election to the State House of Representatives in 1910). McGrath had come to Wyoming in 1887, settling with her husband near Fort Fetterman in Converse County. The couple moved to Thermopolis about 1900.

5. Smallest Precinct

The smallest voting precinct in Wyoming in 1996 was a two-household precinct in Laramie County. The two houses are in a county pocket surrounded by the Cheyenne city limits. The area cannot be combined with non-contiguous county land.

6. National Campaigns

In the days when presidential candidates utilized railroad transportation as a primary means of campaigning, Wyoming often hosted candidates from both major parties as well as nearly all minor parties. For instance, Socialist Party candidate Norman Thomas spoke in Laramie and in Cheyenne to a crowd of some 1,000 people on Oct. 12, 1932. During the same campaign, Democratic candidate Franklin D. Roosevelt campaigned from the train in the state. In November, Cheyenne was the final railroad stop for President Herbert Hoover in his unsuccessful reelection campaign.

The 10th Circuit Court of Appeals ruled against Robert Brewster's claim that all land north of Boulder, Colo., to the Canadian border and from the Pacific Ocean to the Atlantic belonged to him. Brewster claimed he was a direct descendant of Plymouth Colony founder William Brewster who had been given all of the land by the King of England. The federal court concluded in 1990 that the statute of limitations had run on his claim. The case was first filed in federal district court in Wyoming.

7. Untimely Death

George W. Tanner, the county clerk of Lincoln County, was seeking reelection to the post he had help for nine terms in 1934. The night before the general election, Tanner died. His wife was quickly nominated to replace him and stickers were printed for the ballot. Mrs. Tanner won by 500 votes.

8. Vice Presidential Nomination

When Richard Cheney was nominated for vice president at the 2000 National Republican Party convention in Philadelphia in July, 2000, he became the first Wyomingite ever nominated for Vice President by any national party (and the only Wyomingite elected to national office). Names of two prominent Wyomingites had been mentioned as possible choices in earlier years but neither gained the nod. Sen. Al Simpson was on the senior George Bush's list for a vice presidential running-mate in 1988, but Sen. Dan Qualye of Indiana was chosen. Sen. Joseph C. O'Mahoney's name was mentioned as a possibility to run with Franklin D. Roosevelt in 1944, but the nomination went to Sen. Harry Truman of Missouri.

Artist in Wyoming: Albert Bierstadt

Artists frequently accompanied explorers and adventurers to the West in the 19th century. Baltimore painter Alfred Jacob Miller accompanied Sir William Drummond Stewart to the rendezvous in 1837.

Twenty-two years later, in 1859, Frederick Lander led his third expedition from Fort Kearny in Nebraska to South Pass, attempting to find easier routes for travelers. He brought with him artist Albert Bierstadt.

Born in Germany, Bierstadt came to America with his parents when he was two years old. He returned to his birthplace of Dusseldorf, Germany, to study painting in 1854. Bierstadt returned to America to paint landscapes in 1857. The trip west with Lander was his first American expedition.

Two other artists traveled with the Lander party, a Boston man named F. S. Frost and Henry Hitchings, an illustrator.

When Lander's party reached South Pass in early summer, the three artists went into the Wind River Mountains to paint and draw. Most of Bierstadt's works featuring Wyoming scenes were inspired by this trip.

An exhibit, featuring huge canvases of the Wyoming scenes, opened in 1860. It brought him immediate fame.

In 1863, while the Civil War was raging in the East, Bierstadt came West again. This time he traveled with a party led by Fitz Hugh Ludlow. They followed the Overland stage route, passing through what is now southern Wyoming. The party stopped at Fort Halleck, in the shadow of Elk Mountain, and continued on west through what is now Sweetwater and Uinta counties.

The height of Bierstadt's fame came in the 1870s when he was proclaimed the country's greatest painter. By the late 1880s, however, his style lost its popularity. He died in New York City in 1902.

Within a half century of his death, however, his paintings once again gained favor. Several of the monumental works are held in the collections of the Buffalo Bill Historical Center in Cody where they are on display in the Center's Whitney Gallery of Western Art.

In August 1922, Charles W. Barton, brother of Bruce Barton (the famous Madison Avenue advertising man), purchased the *Natrona County Tribune* for $350,000. A year later, unable to make the payments, he returned the paper to publisher J. E. Hanway who had sold it to him. Hanway merged it with the *Casper Herald* in December 1925.

Officers of the Wyoming State Legislature, 1890-2009

Senate President	Speaker of the House
1890: W. R. Schnitger, Laramie Co.	Oliver P. Kellogg, Crook Co.
1893: Frank Mondell, Weston Co.	L. C. Tidball, Sheridan Co.
1895: George W. Hoyt, Laramie Co.	Jay L. Torrey, Fremont Co.
1897: George E. Abbott, Laramie Co.	A. D. Kelley, Laramie Co.
1899: John McGill, Albany Co.	Levi R. Davis, Weston Co.
1901: Edward W. Stone, Laramie Co.	Jerome S. Atherly, Albany Co.
1903: Charles A. Guernsey, Albany	Jerome S. Atherly, Albany Co.
1905: E. E. Levers, Uinta Co.	Lyman B. Cooper, Converse Co.
1907: O. H. Brown, Uinta Co.	Scott K. Snively, Sheridan Co.
1909: Edward T. Clark, Laramie Co.	C. H. Hayden, Big Horn Co.
1911: J. M. Schoob, Big Horn Co.	L. R. Davis, Crook Co.
1913: Birney H. Sage, Laramie Co.	Martin L. Pratt, Park Co.
1915: Edward W. Stone, Laramie Co.	James M. Graham, Fremont Co.
1917: Joseph W. Todd, Johnson Co.	W. K. Jones, Laramie Co.
1919: Thomas G. Powers, Goshen Co.	E. J. Sullivan, Natrona Co.
1921: W. W. Daley, Carbon Co.	L. R. Ewart, Park Co.
1923: Simon Skovgard, Big Horn Co.	J. D. Noblitt, Lincoln Co.
1925: Lewis H. Brown, Sweetwater	J. C. Underwood, Laramie Co.
1927: Perry W. Jenkins, Sublette Co.	A. W. McCullough, Albany Co.
1929: Frank O. Horton, Johnson Co.	M. L. Bishop, Jr., Natrona Co.
1931: Clarence Gardner, Lincoln Co.	Charles B. Mann, Big Horn Co.
1933: Roy H. Cameron, Crook Co.	William M. Jack, Natrona Co.
1935: N. A. Pearson, Sheridan Co.	Henry D. Watenpaugh, Sheridan Co.
1937: W. B. Saunders, Campbell Co.	Herman F. Krueger, Park Co.
1939: H. H. Horton, Albany Co.	Herbert B. Fowler, Weston Co.
1941: Earl Wright, Sweetwater Co.	Carl Robinson, Lincoln Co.
1943: R. H. Nichols, Natrona Co.	Richard J. Luman, Sublette Co.
1945: George A. Cross, Converse Co.	Walter W. Hudson, Goshen Co.
1947: E. J. Zoble, Natrona Co.	Homer Oxley, Goshen Co.
1949: George Burke, Park Co.	Herman D. Mayland, Big Horn Co.
1951: Robert J. Rymill, Goshen Co.	Frank C. Mockler, Fremont Co.
1953: Floyd W. Bartling, Converse	David Foote, Sr., Natrona Co.
1955: R. L. Greene, Johnson Co.	T. C. Daniels, Converse Co.
1957: Earl T. Bower, Washakie Co.	Lee E. Keith, Johnson Co.
1959: Norman Barlow, Sublette Co.	Jay R. House, Carbon Co.
1961: Albert C. Harding, Crook Co.	Joseph L. Budd, Sublette Co.
1963: Charles G. Irwin, Converse Co.	Marlin T. Kurtz, Park Co.
1965: Andrew McMaster, Niobrara	Walter B. Phelan, Laramie*
	Edness Kimball Wilkins, Natrona Co.

Phelan died during his term and Wilkins became speaker.

1967: Richard R. Jones, Park Co.	William F. Swanton, Natrona Co.
1969: Earl Christensen, Weston Co.	Verda I. James, Natrona Co.
1971: Dr. Pete Madsen, Sheridan Co.	Ward G. Myers, Big Horn Co.
1973: Dick Tobin, Natrona Co.	C. H. Davis, Campbell Co.
1975: J. W. Myers, Uinta Co.	Harold Hellbaum, Platte Co.
1977: L. Donald Northrup, Park Co.	Nels J. Smith, Crook Co.

When Sen. T. W. Ferry, president pro tempore of the U. S. Senate, signed the certificate of election of Rutherford B. Hayes after the contested election of 1876, he did so with a quill pen made from the eagle feather of a Wyoming bird. The pen, given to Sen. Ferry by Judge J. W. Kingham of Laramie, also had been used to sign the verdict in the first trial in the nation on which women sat as jurors in Laramie in 1870.

1979: L. V. Stafford, Johnson Co.
1981: Donald Cundall, Goshen/Platte
1983: Edward Moore, Conv./Niobrara
1985: Gerald E. Geis, H.S./Washakie
1987: John F. Turner, Teton/Sublette
1989: Russell Zimmer, Goshen/Niob.
1991: Diemer True, Natrona Co.
1993: Jerry B. Dixon, Weston Co.
1995: Boyd Eddins, Lincoln Co.
1997: Robert Grieve, Carbon Co.
1999: Jim Twiford, Converse Co.
2001: Hank Coe, Park
2003: April Brimmer Kunz, Laramie
2005: Grant Larson, Teton
2007: John Schiffer, Johnson
2009: John Hines, Campbell

Warren Morton, Natrona Co.
Bob Burnett, Albany Co.
Russell L. Donley III, Natrona Co.
Jack Sidi, Natrona Co.
Patrick H. Meenan, Natrona Co.
Bill McIlvain, Laramie Co.
W. A. "Rory" Cross, Converse
Douglas Chamberlain, Goshen
John P. Marton, Johnson Co.
Bruce A. Hinchey, Natrona
Eli D. Bebout, Fremont Co.
Rick Tempest, Natrona
Fred Parady, Sweetwater
Randall Luthi, Lincoln
Roy Cohee, Natrona
Colin Simpson, Park

Some Messages Sent by Wyomingites

1. Tents and Chaplains

When troops being mobilized for service in the Spanish American War, Gov. W. A. Richards of Wyoming sent a telegram to Gov. Alva Adams of Colorado: "Battalion constituting Wyoming's quota mustered in at maximum. Have several chaplains left over. Do you want any of them?" Evans replied with a six-word answer: "Long on chaplains, short on tents."

2. A Gatling gun?

Lt. Col. A. G. Brackett, stationed with the 2nd Cavalry at Camp Stambaugh (near present-day Lander), sent a message to the Department of the Platte army headquarters on July 19, 1873: "[I would like] one Gatling gun...what kind of ammo will it require as I have not seen a Gatling gun and know nothing about it." He then ordered "a year's supply" of ammunition, "whatever amount that may be."

3. Fire!

Mrs. J. M. Carey stayed at home in Cheyenne with the two Carey children while her husband represented Wyoming in the U. S. Senate in the early years of Wyoming statehood. One day, the children accidentally started a fire on the third floor of the palatial Carey home. Mrs. Carey called the fire department and then telegraphed her husband: "House is on fire. What should I do?" Carey sent back the terse telegram: "Put it out."

George W. Pike and a partner rode into Gillette one afternoon, dusty and thirsty after hard days seeking out "slicks"—unbranded cattle that they could claim with a rope and their own brand. They entered a saloon, asked the bartender if he would give two broke cowboys a free drink and, after he obliged, drank up and left. A few minutes later, two men with their faces covered with bandannas entered the saloon and ordered the keeper to empty the till. Soon after, Pike and his partner re-entered the saloon, excited about hearing that the place had been robbed. Eyewitnesses told them about what had happened and Pike and his partner bought drinks around—in cash. When the two men left the Gillette bar late that night, the bartender had as much in the cash drawer as he had before the robbery, but the liquor was gone.
Source: Warren J. Grove in *Pages From Converse County's Past*. (Casper, 1988), p. 526.

POST OFFICES
Interesting Facts about Wyoming Post Offices

1. First post office

The Fort Laramie post office was established on March 14, 1850. It was the first in Wyoming. The second post office was opened Aug. 6, 1850, at Fort Bridger, exactly three days before the Salt Lake City post office began operation.

2. Largest number of post offices statewide

In 1930, 392 post offices were operating in Wyoming, a record number. There had been 16 in 1869 when the territory was formed and 200 in 1890 at the time of statehood. In 1980, only 199 post offices still operated in Wyoming due to mergers and consolidations over the previous two decades.

3. Highest post office, odd location for a post office

The Holmes post office in Albany County, ten miles west of Albany, was the highest in elevation in the state at 9,500 feet. The post office of Little America is located in a motel room in the complex.

4. Fast mail service

A person mailing a letter from Fort Leavenworth, Kansas, to Fort Laramie in 1858 could expect it to take an average of 12 days to reach the addressee. When the Pony Express began in April 1860, a letter made the journey from Missouri to California in about eight days, on average.

5. Most post office closures

When the Pony Express suspended operation in 1861, half of the post offices in Wyoming (two of four) closed. The closures hit Deer Creek station, present-day Glenrock, which had opened in 1859 and the South Pass City post office, opened in early 1861.

6. Longest ride in Pony Express history

Fifteen-year-old William F. Cody claimed to have set the record for the longest ride by one Pony Express rider when he traversed 322 miles. (Other longer rides are on record, however). When Cody arrived at Three Crossings, his original destination, he found that the eastbound rider had been killed by Indians so he continued on to the next station, Rocky Ridge, then retraced his route to his home station at Red Buttes. Cody later became famous as a buffalo hunter, scout and showman.

7. Smallest town with a post office

Lost Springs, with a 1990 population of nine people, was the smallest incorporated town in the United States with a post office.

8. Oldest active mail carrier in the United States

Until shortly before his death in 1993, Don Taylor of Lusk delivered mail six days a week to 23 rural patrons on a 70-mile route. He started in 1943 when the regular carrier was called to wartime service. When he was 93, Taylor was featured on national television for his longevity as a mail carrier.

9. Special cancellation

On Valentine's Day, 1996, the Hartville post office used a special "Hearts" cancellation, authorized by the U. S. Postal Service. The town's population is 78.

When area ranchers lynched Ella Watson ("Cattle Kate") and James Averell on the Sweetwater River in 1889, it was not only the first hanging of a woman in Wyoming. It also was the first time a postmaster had been lynched in the territory. Averell had been appointed the first postmaster of "Sweetwater" post office when it opened on June 29, 1886. The post office barely survived Averell's lynching. It closed just 13 months after the infamous hangings near Independence Rock.

Wyoming on Stamps, 1898-2009

1. Fremont on the Rocky Mountains (1898)

The first stamp to portray a Wyoming scene was a five-cent stamp issued on June 17, 1898, showing John C. Fremont climbing a Wyoming peak. The issue commemorated the Trans-Mississippi Exposition in Omaha that year.

2. Beacon on the Rocky Mountains (1928)

The five-cent airmail stamp was issued on July 25, 1928.

3. Old Faithful (1934)

The "National Parks" issue included the five-cent stamp with an engraving of Old Faithful. The geyser was the subject of a second stamp in 1972 issued to commemorate the Yellowstone centennial.

4. Pony Express (1940)

The three-cent stamp was issued April 3, 1940.

5. Wyoming Statehood (1940)

A three-cent stamp featuring an engraving of the Wyoming state seal was issued July 10, 1940, in honor of the 50th anniversary of statehood.

6. Pronghorn antelope (1956)

Although the locale is not specifically identified on the three-cent stamp, Wyoming has the largest population of pronghorn in the world, thus it portrayed one of these Wyoming residents.

7. Devils Tower (1956)

The three-cent stamp commemorated the creation of Devils Tower National Monument, the nation's first national monument. The stamp was issued Sept. 24, 1956.

8. Pony Express Centennial (1960)

A second stamp honored the Pony Express. Issued July 19, 1960, the four-cent stamp was issued to commemorate the centennial of the service.

9. Amelia Earhart (1963)

The eight-cent airmail stamp honors the Kansas native who gained worldwide fame by her flying exploits. Earhart vacationed in Wyoming and, at the time of her disappearance somewhere in the South Pacific, her summer home was under construction near Meeteetse.

10. Chief Joseph (1968)

The Indian leader is principally identified with Idaho and Montana, but the route of his escape from the army took his group through northwestern Wyoming. The six-cent stamp was issued on Nov. 4, 1968.

11. John Wesley Powell (1969)

Powell began his famous trip down the Colorado River on the Green River in Wyoming. Also, the town of Powell was named for the explorer and proponent of irrigation. The Powell six-cent stamp was issued Aug. 1, 1969.

12. Big Horn sheep (1972, 1981)

An animal "resident" of Wyoming, the big horn sheep, was honored with its likeness on an eight-cent stamp in 1972 and an 18-cent stamp in May 1981.

13. Wyoming State Flag (1976)

The state flag 13-cent stamp was in the flag series issued by the post office to commemorate the nation's bicentennial. The Wyoming flag stamp was issued Feb. 23, 1976.

Jack Rosenthal designed three stamps: Buffalo Bill stamp in 1988; Wyoming Statehood Centennial stamp in 1990 and Oregon Trail stamp in 1990. He served on U. S. Postal Service Citizens' Stamp Advisory Committee from 1985-1993 and as chairman for his last three years on the committee.

14. Wyoming State Flower and State Bird (1982)

Wyoming's meadowlark and Indian paintbrush were depicted on stamps issued in the "states series" of flowers and birds.

15. Crazy Horse (1982)

The famous 19th century Native American became the first human native of Wyoming to be honored with his own stamp. The stamp was issued in 1982.

16. William F. Cody (1988)

The "Buffalo Bill" stamp was issued in Cody on June 6, 1988. The 15-cent postcard stamp was the first to be dedicated in Wyoming in 48 years—since the statehood stamp was issued in 1940. The stamp, which featured an engraved portrait of Cody, was designed by Casper resident Jack Rosenthal. It was one of the most popular stamps ever issued by the postal service.

17. Wyoming Statehood Centennial (1990)

The post office issued a 25-cent stamp for Wyoming statehood in 1990. The Conrad Schwiering painting, "High Mountain Meadows," is shown on the stamp designed by Jack Rosenthal of Casper. (Rosenthal is the only Wyoming resident ever to serve on the U. S. Postal Service's official committee charged with selecting events to commemorate). Jonathan R. Leal, a 6th grade student from Glendo, won the design competition for the official cachet. The stamp was unveiled before a joint session of the Wyoming legislature held in the Cheyenne Civic Center on Feb. 21, 1990.

18. Shoshone War Bonnet (1990)

The first day of issue for the stamp was at the Buffalo Bill Historical Center, Cody, on Aug. 17, 1990.

19. Buffalo Bill, Sacajawea (1994)

Issued as part of the legend of the West stamp sheet was issued Oct. 18, 1994, in Laramie, Tucson, Ariz., and Lawton, Okla. The sheet included 20 designs with original art by artist Mark Hess. The stamps featured Buffalo Bill, Sacajawea and other western historical figures.

20. Buffalo Bill Cody (2000)

One of the Great Americans Series, the stamp sold for 15 cents.

21. Greetings from Wyoming (2002)

The stamp was part of the Greetings Series and sold for 34 cents.

22. Grand Teton National Park (2006)

The stamp was sold for 98 cents.

23. Painting by Jackson Pollock (2010)

The Cody native's painting was featured on a stamp as part of a series honoring the Abstract Expressionists. It sold for 44 cents.It was the largest postage stamp ever issued by the United States Postal Service.

Number of Wyoming Post Offices by ZIP Code Prefix

820—	24	Cheyenne	826—	21	Casper
821—	1	Yellowstone NP	827—	18	Gillette
822—	22	Wheatland	828—	14	Sheridan
823—	14	Rawlins	829—	21	Rock Springs
824—	24	Worland	830—	6	Rock Springs
825—	10	Riverton	831—	18	Rock Springs

In the four years from 1940 to 1944, the U. S. Post Office sold more than 50 million Wyoming statehood stamps commemorating the 50th anniversary of statehood. More than 48 million had been sold between July 1, 1940 and June 30, 1941. The denomination? Three cents.

QUOTES

Some Interesting Statements Made by Wyomingites

1. *"The little red schoolhouse is redder than you think."* —Milward Simpson, 1947, referring to the common belief that subversive materials were used in some schools.

2. *"I am a firm believer in laughter. I think if Bad Luck came along, he would take to his heels if some one laughed right loudly."* —Elinore Pruitt Stewart, **Letters from a Woman Homesteader**, which first appeared in **Atlantic Monthly**, 1913-1914, and later published in a book.

3. *"You sons-of-bitches!"* —Indians, sent as decoys at Fort Phil Kearny to taunt troops of Capt. William Fetterman into crossing Lodge Trail Ridge. The taunts worked. Fetterman, disregarding warnings, ordered his command to pursue the Indians. Fetterman and his entire command were wiped out when they fell into the trap.

4. *"There are a lot of sacred cows in Wyoming, and cows are one of them."* —Pete Williams, now a reporter for NBC-TV, formerly press secretary to Dick Cheney and KTWO-TV newsman, quoted in the **Wall Street Journal**, Aug. 4, 1988.

5. *"We raise cattle for respectability, and sheep to pay the bills."* —Vivienne Hesse of Buffalo, quoted by Neil Morgan, **Westward Tilt**. (New York: Random House, 1963), p. 257.

6. *"Cheyenne is proud to be the nation's number one target for enemy missiles."* — Worth Story, Cheyenne mayor, on Feb. 2, 1958, when F. E. Warren Air Force Base became the home of Atlas ICBMs.

7. *"One does not sell the earth upon which the people walk."* —Crazy Horse, arguing against Indian ratification of treaties forfeiting hunting lands to the government.

8. *"You know very well that you're not asking him [Ronald Reagan] things so you can get answers. You're asking him things because you know he's off balance and you'd like to stick it in his gazoo."* —Sen. Al Simpson, berating the White House press corps for asking President Reagan questions at "photo opportunities," March 18, 1987.

9. *"Red brick."* —Sen. Al Simpson, when asked what his church preference was, quoted in the Denver Post, Oct. 28, 1989.

10. *"My brother...conveyed his sympathy to me when he learned that I had failed of re-election. 'The people gave and the people taketh away; blessed be the name of the people.'"* —Gov. Nellie Tayloe Ross, on her 1926 election loss.

11. *"As a region we [the West] suffer too greatly, still, from our common plagues: distance, isolation, colonialism of dependence upon what is the fashion outside our region, the movement of our people elsewhere."* —Alan Swallow, Powell-born poet/publisher in "A Magazine for the West," **Inland** (Autumn, 1957).

12. *"You done good."* —Gov. Nels Smith, to the graduating class of the University of Wyoming, 1941.

13. *"They never treated me this well when I was their congressman."* —Republican Vice Presidential nominee Dick Cheney, formerly a Wyoming congressman, on the enthusiastic reception he received with Presidential nominee George W. Bush at Natrona County High School on July 29, 2000, their first campaign stop after the nominating convention.

14. *"Cody, I think we died with Custer."* —Gen. Nelson A. Miles, after waking up on a sofa the morning after a late-night talking and drinking session with William F. Cody. Cody had slept on a table in the Chicago hotel bar.

15. *"The bitterness was fairly overwhelming."* —Dennis Erickson, University of Wyoming football coach for one season (1986), on his departure from Laramie to Washington State. Later, he took the head coaching position at the University of Miami. Later, he coached the Seattle Seahawks, Oregon State and Arizona State.

16. *"It's a poor imitation of a cow."* —Stockman John Coble, justifying why he shot holes in the Paul Potter painting, "The Young Bull," hanging on the wall of the Cheyenne Club, 1885.

17. *"If the sunrise is as fine a sight as the sunset, it must be a grand sight indeed."* —Bill Nye, writing about his habit of sleeping late in the mornings.

18. *"Ladies and gentlemen—Col. William F. Cody—Buffalo Bill—will shoot the glass balls off his horse."* —Nervous Wild West Show announcer to the crowd attending the London performance for Queen Victoria, November, 1890.

19. *"With what a dull, sickening thud do our gods go glimmering."* —Douglas editor Bill Barlow, on news that Buffalo Bill wanted a divorce from his wife so that he could marry an English actress, 1906. The divorce was not granted.

20. *"They [the legislature] may brace up and do some good later on, but up to the present writing, they are a heterogeneous mob of discordant spirits."* —Territorial Gov. Francis E. Warren, to the Secretary of the Interior, 1886.

21. *"[The commission] has every kind of mix you can have...a black, a woman, two Jews and a cripple."* —Interior Secretary James Watt, remarking on his department's special commission on coal leasing, Sept. 21, 1983. His remark, intended as a critique of "quotas," caused a furor.

22. *"I would make it a criminal offense for anyone to parade under the banner of liberalism who was not conscientiously and even religiously devoted to the ideal that in an industrial democracy, freedom of opportunity is the great value that must be preserved above all others. Unless this freedom is preserved, no other freedom will be secure."* —Lawyer/author Thurman Arnold, Laramie native, quoted in Seldes (ed.) **The Great Quotations**. (N.Y.: Pocket Books, 1967).

23. *"We saved the lake!"* —A local wag, commenting on National Park Service firefighting efforts in Yellowstone in the summer of 1988 when Yellowstone Lake proved to be the only effective fire break.

24. *"Once we were happy in our own country and we were seldom hungry, for then the two-leggeds and the four-leggeds lived together like relatives, and there was plenty for them and for us. But the Wasichus [whites] came, and they have made little islands for us and other little islands for the four-leggeds, and always these islands are becoming smaller, for around them surges the gnawing flood of the Wasichu; and it is dirty with lies and greed."* —Wyoming-born Black Elk, **Black Elk Speaks**, to told to John Neihardt. (New York: Morrow, 1932), p. 9.

25. *"When people speak of 'seeing life' out here, I think they must allow a wide latitude in the interpretation of the phrase. My own experience in Cheyenne would lead me to infer that 'seeing life' means seeing a good deal of death."* —Newspaper correspondent James Chisholm, dispatch to the **Chicago Times**, March 27, 1868.

26. *"When D-9s are outlawed, only outlaws will have D-9s."* —Bumper sticker seen in Gillette following an incident in which a man stole a D-9 caterpillar tractor and rammed numerous homes and cars with the vehicle, causing nearly $200,000 in damage.

27. *"I can hear the whizzing of steam on the Sweetwater, and the whirrings of car wheels through South Pass are a foregone conclusion."* —Artist Alfred Jacob Miller, on the inevitability of development of the wilderness of Wyoming in 1837. The statement is quoted in Robert C. Warner, **The Fort Laramie of Alfred Jacob Miller.** (Laramie: University of Wyoming Press, 1979).

28. *"I love Wyoming. I like its sagebrush and sand, its cactus, horned toads and*

Armpit, Scoop Shovel and Bed Tick are the names of three Wyoming "towns." Armpit is in Sweetwater County, Scoop Shovel in Uinta and Bed Tick in Converse.

ticks as well as its hills, valleys, mountains and streams, and its glowing sunshine. I like it because it is hard, rough and unyielding and because one must make a fight to gain its favors and because one can appreciate the good things of Wyoming so much better after the struggle of conquest, than as though they came without effort." —Pioneer Big Horn Basin settler J. D. Woodruff, speech to the "Pioneer Reunion," Wyoming State Fair, September 1921.

29. *"I saw, each year, the increasing hordes of automobile tourists sweep the country like locusts."* —Jackson Hole dude rancher and author Struthers Burt, article in The Nation, 1926.

30. *"There are a lot of expectations from the fans at Wyoming. But they are fair folks. All the fans expect is a WAC title, the Final Four championship, the NBA title and a win over the Russians."* —University of Wyoming basketball coach Benny Dees, Nov. 11, 1987, after his team was chosen as the favorites to win the WAC title in 1987. Dees resigned in 1993 and accepted the coaching position at Western Carolina.

31. *"I'm the best lawyer I know."* —Jackson attorney Gerry Spence on CBS Television, March 18, 1990.

32. *"Wyoming made dinosaurs famous because Wyoming showed the world that they were huge and were of a wide variety."* —Dr. Robert T. Bakker, University of Colorado paleontologist and advisor to the film **Jurassic Park**, at a public program in Laramie, March 1991.

33. *"We'll live on wind pudding and rabbit tracks, my dear, for there's lots of both."* —Goshen County homesteader to his young wife when asked "How are we going to survive out here? What are we going to eat?" The phrase became the title of a book on Goshen County history as explained by Dorothy Fifield

34. *"I'd rather eat road kill."* —State Sen. Barbara Cubin, Natrona County, on her dislike for campaigning door to door, 1992.

35. *"We've spent a lot of money, but we haven't got a thing to show for it."* —Retired Air Force Gen. Brent Scowcroft, in 1986, on the MX missile system. Each of the 50 missiles placed into silos in Wyoming weighed 90 tons and stood some seven stories high. Scowcroft served as President George Bush's national security advisor from 1989-1993.

36. *"The Jews are getting away with murder tonight."* --UW basketball coach Ev Shelton during a championship game against CCNY in Madison Square Garden in December, 1946. He later apologized.

37. *"Wyoming doctors should not wait on Hillary baby to come up with a national health care plan."* —Cong. Craig Thomas to the winter meeting of the Wyoming Medical Society, February 1993. He later apologized for the disparaging reference to the First Lady, Hillary Rodham Clinton.

38. *"If I hadn't known Carey from the time he stepped off the train in 1869, a green boy, up to the present, and hadn't figured inside the inner circles so much with him in political affairs, he might have possibly fooled me once in a while, for he surely is the most monumental hypocrite, the most seductive and successful hypocrite, and the most infernal liar—when necessary—that God ever permitted to live and whom I have been permitted to meet."* —F. E. Warren on J. M. Carey. The two men started as friends and political allies but after Warren lined up legislators to repudiate Carey in 1894, they began a rivalry that lasted for 20 years.

39. *"If we older men and women who have known freedom could live for another 50 years, we would probably free our state of this leper's touch [the federal government], but can we leave with our children and grandchildren that intensity of conviction necessary to carry on any crusade. Even with evil, once established, there is a static condition that is difficult to overcome.... Also, the host of bureaucrats have intermarried with our people* *(and there is no law against this) and Jones' uncle is superintendent of a national park, Smith's nephew is in the forest service, Brown's brother-in-law is with the Taylor grazing people, and anything that roots with the family tree is difficult to dislodge."* --Charles Myers, President, Wyoming Stockgrowers Association, address to annual meeting, 1942.

40. *"Our intent is not to tear it [the building] down to make a parking lot, but just to clear the area and park on it."* —Cheyenne Mayor Don Erickson, April 13, 1979, referring to the city's decision to tear down the Castle Dare carriage house. The building was demolished in the summer of 1993.

41. *"Three states will be fenced off as a white trash penal colony."* —Hunter Thompson, **Generation of Swine** (1988), predicting the future for Wyoming and two other states.

42. "People of Wyoming have not properly attended to their own advertising. They have allowed outsiders to gain their knowledge of the state through reading lurid tales of the barrenness of our deserts, the outlawery of our citizens and the general undesirability of everything pertaining to the state...[they] have gained their estimate of Wyoming by being swindled." --Wyoming Board of Immigration, Annual Report (1911).

42. *"I'll be the first one to tell you that we were wrong. Fighting the expansion of the park made good sense at the time, but clearly Grand Teton National Park has been a Godsend to this valley and gift to the citizens of the country."* —Clifford P. Hansen, former Wyoming governor and U. S. Senator, who helped lead the fight against park expansion in the 1940s. Hansen's comments were made to a Jackson Hole reporter in December 1995 when Hansen was 83 years old.

43. *"I don't care who the coyotes sleep with. My concern is what they eat."* —State Rep. Marlene Simons (R-Crook), on a State Department of Agriculture proposal to neuter coyotes rather than shooting them, in the *Weston County Gazette*, Jan. 18, 1996.

44. *"You couldn't round up half a dozen good cowboys in all of Wyoming."* --Pioneer saddlemaker Thomas Cobry, Cheyenne, told the *Wyoming Eagle,* January 18, 1996. He added that the "good ones were all dead" and the useless ones were in Hollywood or in rodeo troupes. "I'm afraid he'll be extinct before long," Corbry concluded. "Not Six Good Cowboys in State, Says Pioneer Here," *Wyoming Eagle*, March 29, 1935, p. 2. The *Casper Tribune-Herald* commented later: "...lots of people will hope he is mistaken. If true, it means that much of the glamor and romance still nursed by Wyoming has passed from the scene along with a dwindling population of pioneers." Quoted in "With Wyoming's Editors," *Wyoming Eagle*, April 12, 1935, p. 9.

Descriptive Passages About Wyoming

1. *"The water from this river [Clear Creek] which comes from the mountains a little ways off, is clear, excellent, and very cold, while that of the Powder river is so muddy that the savages have to hollow out a place on the bank in order to procure water for drinking."* — Francois Larocque. Journal entry, August 1805," in R. Hazlitt, ed., **The Journal of Francois Antoine Larocque,** in J. W. Hakola, **Frontier Omnibus**. (Bozeman: MSU Press, 1962).

2. *"Wyoming is the friendliest state I've ever been in, even friendlier than Texas or Nevada."* —John Gunther, **Inside U. S. A.** (New York: Harper, 1947).

3. *"Slide out of dark in the eddy of clean air*
   The smoke goes up from the high plains of Wyoming"
   —Archibald MacLeish, "American Letters," in **New and Collected Poems, 1917-76.** (Boston: Houghton Mifflin, 1976), p. 164.

"I wasn't born in Wyoming, but I got here as fast as I could."
--Bumper sticker phrase attributed to Don and Janet Wittrup of Cheyenne.

4. *"It is my opinion that we enclose and celebrate the freaks of our nation and our civilization. Yellowstone National Park is no more representative of America than is Disneyland."* —John Steinbeck, **Travels with Charley.** (New York: Viking, 1962), p. 145.

5. *"Now, as we crossed the North Platte River and ran on toward Rawlins in May, over the road were veils of blowing snow. This was Wyoming, not some nice mild place like Baffin Island—Wyoming, a landlocked Spitsbergen—and gently, almost imperceptibly, we were climbing."*—John McPhee, "Annals of the Former World," **New Yorker,** Feb. 24, 1986, p. 39.

6. *"Even the bison, to some extent, keeps pace with the seasons, cropping the pastures of the Colorado only till a greener or sweeter grass awaits him by the Yellowstone."* —Henry David Thoreau, **Walden.** (London: Scott, 1886), p. 317.

7. *"Big crowds of businessmen, fat businessmen in boots and ten-gallon hats, with their hefty wives in cowgirl attire, bustled and whooped on the wooden sidewalks of old Cheyenne; farther down were the long stringy boulevard lights of new Cheyenne."* —Jack Kerouac, **On the Road.** (New York: Viking, 1957).

8. *"It was a gala day for Rawlins for the great circus was there with all of its sideshows and clowns and the small boys and girls were out in their best gowns for they did not have the chance to see one every day and the town was so far away that nothing came that way very often."* —George D. Brown, **From Coast to Coast.** (Privately printed, 1923). (The author described himself as "the only man to drive a single horse across the continent.")

9. *"It [Rock Springs] seems to be a mining town. I went to a saloon, got a glass of beer, and had a fine wash in warm water... It seems to be the wild and woolly west with a vengeance."* —Jack London, diary entry for April 17, 1894, in Richard W. Etulain (ed.), **Jack London on the Road.** (Logan: Utah State University Press, 1979), p. 38.

10. *"Wyoming is cattle and sheep and range."* —Neil Morgan, **Westward Tilt.** (New York: Random House, 1963).

11. *"Then the Pass and down below the miracle of Jackson Hole—the milky winding of Cottonwood Creek and the Hole (and the wild west enchantments and bad-men legendries) terrific—and so down to it—and into Jackson—the square of Old West now beduded."* —Thomas Wolfe, **A Western Journal**. (Pittsburgh: University of Pittsburgh Press, 1951), p. 44.

12. *"Gillette, Wyoming, is a raw jumble of rutted streets and sprawling junkyards, red mud and dust, dirty trucks and crowded bars, faded billboards and sagging utility lines, and block after block of house trailers squatting in the dirt like a nest of giant grubs."* —James P. Sterba, **New York Times,** April 11, 1974.

13. *"The only thing Evanston is near is the Overthrust Belt. And that is three miles. Straight down."* —Joel Garreau, **Nine Nations of North America.** (New York: Avon, 1982), p. 293.

14. *"The scale of the storm, the immense quantities of snow it dumped minute after minute, forced me to remember that Laramie was just one more skimpy circle of wagons huddling against the wilderness."* —John Wideman, **Brothers and Keepers.** (New York: Holt, Rinehart, 1984), p. 5.

15. *"Many people in Wyoming refuse to boast about the grandeur of the state. They do not want to encourage migration of newcomers... They want to keep the mountains and prairies and rivers as free as possible of the excrescence of urban progress. Tourists are welcome because they come and go, gracing the state with their money and their departure. I hardly blame the natives. I even hope they succeed."* —Bill Moyers, **Listening to America.** (New York: Dell, 1971), p. 155.

16. *"Tourists need not go to the Alps or Greenland to see snow. Let them come to South Pass and patronize home institutions...there are places there where the snow is ten* *feet deep for miles, the crust hardly bearing a man."* —Caspar Collins, letter from Sweetwater Station to his mother, April 15, 1865.

17. *"At a time when states are competing to attract new companies by promoting their high-tech advantages and even pursuing their own foreign-trade agendas, there is a nagging perception here that Wyoming may be permanently left behind, a raw-material artifact in the post-industrial age—the West Virginia of the Rockies."* -Eugene Carlson, "Wyoming Has No Trouble Attracting Tourists, But Luring Industry Runs Into Problems," **Wall Street Journal,** Aug. 4, 1988.

18. *"You'd have to drive for a week to round up enough guys for a bowling league... Their [Wyoming's] politicians are honest. The last time they caught one stealing, I think they hung him from a tree and sang hymns."* —Mike Royko, **Chicago Tribune,** Dec. 31, 1987, p. 3.

19. *"I viewed Wyoming weather as a crime;*
    I viewed it then that way. I went away."
—Donald Drummond, "May Time in Wyoming," in **The Mountain.** (Chicago: Swallow Press, 1971).

20. *"Today the Laramie plains are all under fence. There is a great university in Laramie. The town itself is clean, respectable, undistinguished, and extraordinarily dull."* —Thurman Arnold, **Fair Fights and Foul.** (New York: Harcourt, Brace, 1965), p. 15.

21. *"Because those days were gone, the old brave innocent tumultuous eupeptic tomorrow-less days...a new time, a new age, millennium's beginning; one vast single net of commerce webbed and veined the mid-continent's fluvial embracements; New Orleans, Pittsburgh and Fort Bridger, Wyo., were suburbs one to the other inextricable in destiny."* —William Faulkner, **Requiem for a Nun.** (New York: Random House, 1950), p. 104.

22. *"I hear the echoes reverberate through the grandest scenery in the world*
    I cross the Laramie plains, I note the rocks in grotesque shapes, the buttes,
    I see the plentiful larkspur and wild onions, the barren, colorless, sage-deserts,
    I see in glimpses afar or towering immediately above me the great mountains,
    I see the Wind River and the Wahsatch mountains...." —Walt Whitman, "Passage to India," **Leaves of Grass.** (Philadelphia: David McKay, 1892), p. 317.

23. *"On the 26th of May [1832], the travelers encamped at Laramie's Fork, a clear and beautiful stream, rising in the west-southwest, maintaining an average width of 20 yards, and winding through broad meadows abounding in currants and gooseberries, and adorned with groves and clumps of trees."* —Washington Irving. **The Adventures of Captain Bonneville.** (New York: Putnam's, 1895), p. 44.

24. *"[W]hen we had reached Pacific Springs, the Wind River mountains appeared in marvelous majesty. It was one of the sights of the journey. The huge purple hangings of rain-clouds in the northern sky set off their vast proportions, and gave prominence, as in a stereoscope, to their gigantic forms and their upper heights, hoar with the frosts of the ages."* —Sir Richard Burton, **Wanderings in Three Continents.** (New York: Dodd, Mead and Co., 1901), p. 165.

25. *"Powder River [town] is little more than a Texaco station and a bunch of pronghorn antelope looking at it."* —James Conaway in **Harper's**, August 1987, p. 58.

26. *"It [Red Desert area] was the loneliest land for a grave!"* —Mark Twain, **Roughing It.** (Hartford: American Publishing, 1872).

27. *"...we have in sight of South Pass City. The hotelkeeper, the postmaster, the black-*

In the spring of 1876, a critic said of Laramie: "The town was called Laramie City for the reason that the looks of Laramie herself would never have suggested the appellation." The same critic noted: "The altitude was high; the assessed valuation low. Liquor was plentiful and water scarce."

smith, the mayor, the constable, the city marshal and the principal citizen and property holder, all came out and greeted us cheerily, and we gave him good day." —Mark Twain, **Roughing It.** (Hartford: American Publishing, 1872), chap. xii.

28. *"At the Green River station we had breakfast—hot biscuits, fresh antelope steaks, and coffee—the only decent meal we tasted between the United States and the Great Salt Lake, and the only one we were really thankful for."* —Mark Twain, **Roughing It.** (Hartford: American Publishing, 1872), chap. xii.

29. *"One year, the snow was so deep early in the month that Maurice couldn't get up to the Big Horns to cut our customary Christmas tree and we found a huge tumbleweed, sprayed it with glitter and decorated it."* —Betty Evenson, **Fifty Years at the Bright Spot.** (Hiland, Wyoming, privately printed, 1990).

30. *"We were short-cutting across old Wyoming dirt roads and hardly altered our 55-mile-an-hour pace. But the scene did not change. It was like being in a trance—traveling strenuously, but getting nowhere. So this was Wyoming, I thought, a secret, hidden world unknown to the rest of the country, serene and calm, with a slow heart beat."* —Mary O'Hara (1885-1980), author of **My Friend Flicka** and **Green Grass of Wyoming,** who lived on the Remount Ranch in Laramie County for a time.

31. *"Stately pine woods fringe either lip of the gorge which is—the Gorge of the Yellowstone. All I can say is that, without warning or preparation, I looked into a gulf 1700 feet deep, with eagles and fish-hawks circling far below. And the sides of that gulf were one wild welter of colour...neither pen nor brush could ever portray its splendours adequately..."* —Rudyard Kipling, **From Sea to Sea.** (London, 1889)

32. *"Winter looks like a fictional place, an elaborate simplicity, a Nabokovian invention of rarefied detail. Winds howl all night and day, pushing litters of storm fronts from the Beartooth to the Big Horn Mountains. When it lets up, the mountains disappear."* —Gretel Ehrlich, **Solace of Open Spaces.** (New York: Viking, 1985).

33. *"Have you ever been to Cheyenne, Wyoming? As far as I'm concerned, it's the pits of the earth. It is just terrible...It's like the crossroads to nowhere."* —Alaska State Rep. Ramona Barnes (R-Anchorage), on the floor of the Alaska legislature and widely quoted April 3, 1992. Barnes had been in Cheyenne on a state-paid convention trip. Retorted Secretary of State Kathy Karpan, *"I suppose we can always get a cheap shot by some obscure Alaska legislator."*

34. *"One of the most influential steps in finding my portrayal of the character of the Virginian began when I traveled to Medicine Bow, Wyoming."* —Actor/Director Bill Pullman, on preparing for his 2000 TNT movie, **The Virginian**.

35. *"You're not going to use the story, Mr. Scott?" "No, sir. This is the West, sir. When the legend becomes fact, print the legend."* —Dialogue in **The Man Who Shot Liberty Valance,** film based on story by Dorothy Johnson.

36. *"I was happy in the belief that I would meet with the embodiment of that type [cowboy] in its natural environment. I was doomed to disappointment, for all the cattlemen and cowboys I saw were like the hired hands back East."* —Glendolene Kimmell, the school teacher embroiled in the Tom Horn case in the early 1900s, who came to Wyoming to teach school in July, 1901.

37. *"The miners once struck against a boss who snored frightfully, fearing that the jar would cause a disaster. No one ever sings or sneezes in Carbon and that place boasts the best behaved children in the world."* --**Cheyenne Daily Leader**, Dec. 16, 1888, describing the problems inherent in living in a coal-mining town where six miles of tunnels underlaid the townsite and the crust was only six inches in some places.

Metallica appeared in concert at the Casper Events Center on March 30, 2004.

RADIO

1st radio messages heard in Wyoming: "Will reach Honolulu tomorrow," a radio message broadcast from a ship in the Pacific, picked up on a radio set by Edgar Edwards and John Scott, Lander, on March 20, 1912. On Jan. 29, 1913, Frank O. Robinson, Sheridan, heard ship messages from the Pacific.

1st radio station in Wyoming: KFA (later KFBU), Laramie, first on the air on Feb. 3, 1926. *(See below)*.

Two radio pioneers in Wyoming: Gilbert Hall and Dr. L. G. Van Slyke (*Electrical Experimenter*, Dec. 1917).

1st national broadcast of Cheyenne Frontier Days: CBS radio, 1931.

1st satellite transmission of KUWR public radio signal: Jan, 10, 1997, to Jackson.

Stations in Wyoming: 76 stations (AM and FM) were broadcastiing in Wyoming in 2010.

Voice on concourse trains in Denver International Airport: Pete Smythe, well-known Denver radio/TV personality, who was born in Glenrock in 1922. He died May 8, 2000.

Osgood file: On Aug. 12, 1987, Charles Osgood chided Wyoming Supreme Court Justice Walter Urbigkit for using the word "conclusory." The justice, acknowledging that it was not a word, nonetheless said it could be used in his courtroom. Osgood's criticism was not perfect either, however. In the broadcast, he mispronounced Urbigkit's name.

Earliest Radio Stations by City (in order of founding)

1. Laramie KFA (later KFBU)

The first broadcast station in Wyoming, KFA Laramie, went on the air Feb. 3, 1926. The station was established with funds from Mrs. E. H. Harriman, widow of the Union Pacific Railroad chairman. Bishop N. S. Thomas of the Episcopal Church urged the donation after telling Mrs. Harriman of a storm between Laramie and Cheyenne which nearly cost railroad crews their lives. The station, installed in the Cathedral basement, broadcast a daily weather forecast at 12:30 p.m. Late in the decade, the station was shut down after an employee was accidentally electrocuted. The equipment, however, was taken over by the University of Wyoming and returned to service in January 1929, as KWYO.

2. Casper KDFN

The station began broadcasting at 8 p.m. on Jan. 2, 1930. The first program was broadcast from the Townsend Hotel and featured Tony Kent, "King of the Ivories," followed by Earl Frye's orchestra, The Oilers. D. L. Hathaway, formerly of Denver, was station manager. The station broadcast on frequency 1210 AM from the transmitter and antenna atop the Townsend. Later, the station moved to offices in the 200 block of North Lennox. The station's call letters were changed to KSPR. When the company owning Channel 2 television went on the air, it bought the radio station and changed the call letters again, this time to KTWO.

3. Sheridan KWYO

KWYO began broadcasting July 8, 1934. The first program began with a trumpet fanfare. On June 13, 1935, the station stayed on the air for 36 straight hours during the height of the Sheridan flood. The first sports broadcast predated the station by three years. On Jan. 1, 1931, an "announcer" spoke into the telephone long-distance from Denver University Stadium where he watched the Wyoming state champion Sheridan football team play the Colorado champion Fort Collins team. W. A Dennis talked to John W. Carney who repeated what Dennis told him to an audience at the Orpheum Theatre. The "broadcast" was arranged by the Sheridan Press. Incidentally, Sheridan lost to Fort Collins 69-14.

In December 1956, KBBS in Buffalo began running a weekly Sunday morning programs in the Basque language, featuring Basque music, news and talk. The program was a regular feature for 40 years.

4. Rock Springs KVRS

The station began broadcasting on June 21, 1938. The programming for the first day's broadcast consisted entirely of local talent.

5. Cheyenne KYAN

KYAN began broadcasting in October 1940. The station, the first in Cheyenne, closed almost six months later following the opening of KFBC in December 1940. The second station, owned by Tracy McCraken who also owned the two daily newspapers in Cheyenne.

6. Powell KPOW

KPOW began broadcasting in 1941. It was the first station in the Big Horn Basin and the seventh and last station opened in Wyoming before World War II.

Later Radio Stations in Wyoming (by year of first broadcast)

1946: KWOR Worland (March 7), KVOC Casper (Oct. 1)

1947: KRAL Rawlins and KODI Cody

1948: KOWB Laramie, KOVE Lander and KWRL Riverton (July 11)

1950: KGOS Torrington and KRTR Thermopolis

1952: KVWO Cheyenne

1953: KASL Newcastle and KLUK Evanston

1955: KTHE Thermopolis

1956: KBBS Buffalo and KATI Casper

1957: KIML Gillette and KWIV Douglas

Stories about Wyoming Radio Broadcasters and Stations

1. Curt Gowdy

Well-known sportscaster Curt Gowdy (b. Green River, 1919, d. Florida, 2006) began his broadcast career doing "color" for high school football games in Cheyenne for the local radio station in the early 1940s.

According to his autobiography published in 1966, Gowdy's first "play-by-play" job was covering the district championship between Cheyenne St. Mary's and Pine Bluffs in a six-man football game.

As he wrote about it years later, there were no yard markers on the field nor were there any numbers (much less names) on the football jerseys. Seated in the open on a couple of soap boxes, Gowdy wrote that he "hoped for the impossible—that the teams would stay within sight, between what would have been the forty-yard lines, if there had been any lines." Unable to identify the players, he spread the "glory" around, keeping track of the score by noting when the offensive team jumped for joy.

It was such a cold November day that only 15 people showed up to watch the game. Having no seating, the 15 simply walked along the side lines and watched, intermingled with the respective coaches and teams.

"I've done the World Series and Olympics and football bowl games in the years since," Gowdy wrote. "I never see a big crowd without thinking of the 15 hardy souls who went out on a cold November day in 1943 to watch St. Mary's of Cheyenne play Pine Bluffs High School for the six-man football championship of eastern Wyoming."

In 1945, the Green River native left Wyoming to take a radio broadcasting job in Oklahoma City. In 1949, he joined the New York Yankees, working with Mel Allen. Later,

Nellie Tayloe Ross was the first Wyoming governor to speak over a Wyoming radio station when she spoke urging support for the American Legion on KFA Radio, Laramie, on Feb. 26, 1926.

he went on to network television, concentrating mostly on basketball and baseball and hosting *The American Sportsman* series for almost 20 years. Following his retirement, he moved to Florida. Until 2000, he owned KOWB radio in Laramie and remained closely identified with his home state. His son, also involved in television, married former Miss Teen America and TV actress Karen Morris from Cheyenne. He died in Florida in 2006.

2. Kerm Kath

Kath received his first broadcast license when he was barely 21. In 1956, he bought the six-year-old station, KGOS in Torrington, and operated it until his death in 1982.

3. Steve Lawrence

Lawrence said he was hired in 1970 to read the morning news by station owner Jeanette Esponda Maxwell because he delivered the Casper Star-Tribune every morning in town and, thus, up early anyway. Lawrence was renowned for his dedication to high school sports. A graduate of Cheyenne Central High School, he later attended Sheridan College and Marquette University, returning to Wyoming and KBBS. Lawrence's broadcast calls of Buffalo High School sports became legendary over 40 years. He broadcast a football game from Kemmerer from the back of a pickup; a play-by-play in Thermopolis by standing on the hood of a car. Lawrence died suddenly in June 2008 at the age of 58.

4. Joe and Mildred Ernst

The Ernsts began broadcasting in Thermopolis in 1955. Thermopolis had two radio stations and to augment their KRTR radio station, they opened the first television station in the Big Horn Basin, KRTR-TV.

5. KWRR, Wind River Radio

The 50,000-watt FM station, KWRR, was started in the 1990s as a station to serve the Wind River Indian Reservation. The station received a Department of Commerce start-up grant designed to encourage radio broadcast to isolated communities, the last one awarded in the program. The broadcast tower is located on Boysen Peak.

6. Radio Montanesa (KOCA), Laramie

The station is a low-power FM broadcaster providing a Spanish-language variety format to listeners in the Laramie area. Founded in 1999, the station went on the air in December 2002. On May 1, 2003, the station began broadcasting 24 hours daily.

Wyoming Association of Broadcasters Hall of Fame*
Initial inductees (2003)

Curt Gowdy	Roy Barnes, Powell	Larry Birleffi, Cheyenne
Jeanette Maxwell, Buffalo	Alice Bubeck, Casper	Kerm Kath, Torrington
Jack Rosenthal, Casper	Tony Kehl, Riverton	

Inductees, 2004

Joe and Mildred Ernst, Thermopolis	Bob Wilson, Sheridan	Roy Mapel, Gillette

Inductees, 2005

Ray Lansing, Cheyenne	Gene Benson, Laramie	Bill Grove, Cheyenne
George Kay, Casper		

Inductees, 2006

Jim Carroll, Kemmerer	Steve Lawrence, Buffalo	Carl Occhipinti, Cheyenne

Inductee, 2007

Will Sims, Casper

Inductees, 2008

Roger Sedam, Cody	Ken Keating, Laramie

Inductees, 2009

Dale Smith, Riverton	Alan Harris, Green River

Located in the UW Arena-Auditorium

RAILROADS

1st train in Wyoming: Union Pacific. The tracks entered Wyoming in 1867 and the transcontinental line was completed on May 10, 1869.

1st train through Wind River Canyon: October 1913

1st railroad line connecting Denver to Billings via Wyoming: When the Casper-Orin portion of the CB&Q line was completed on Oct. 18, 1914.

Last passenger train to Sheridan: Aug. 24, 1969

Last passenger train pulled by a steam locomotive: May 1, 1971, Cheyenne to Laramie.

1st adoption of time zones: Nov. 18, 1883. Railroads were the primary proponents for their establishment. Previously, more than 80 different time changes were possible on one coast-to-coast rail trip.

Royal railroader: When Queen Marie of Romania visited Wyoming in 1926, Union Pacific officials gave her an opportunity to "drive" a locomotive on the main line.

Worst train wreck in Wyoming history: Sept. 27, 1923, wreck of CB&Q train No. 30 from Casper to Denver. Wooden trestle over Cole Creek was washed out, train smashed into creek bed with more than 30 people killed.

Largest operating steam locomotive in the world: Challenger 3985, built in 1943, and retired from service in 1959. It was fired up again in January 1981 and run frequently by the Union Pacific Historical Society.

Largest steam locomotive ever built: The 4000s, which include "Big Boy," the 8444. None are operating, but one is on display in Holiday Park, Cheyenne.

Amtrak ended passenger service to Wyoming in 1983, but returned June 17, 1991, for regular service, but permanently suspending operations to depots in Wyoming in 1995.

Summer excursion runs were made regularly by the Laramie-North Park Railroad which operated from West Laramie from 1990 until 1995. In the spring of 1996, the railroad suspended operations and the owners sold the rails for scrap.

Last Treagle train: Sept. 29, 1979. The annual event, carrying advertisers and celebrities from Cheyenne to a UW football game in Laramie, had been sponsored by Cheyenne Newspapers, Inc.

Last railway mail car to cross Wyoming: 1968

Museums in depots: Many exist in Wyoming. Best known is the Transportation Museum, housed in the former UP Depot at the end of Capitol Avenue in Cheyenne. The Medicine Bow Museum was opened in 1980 in what had been the town's UP Depot.

1st Trains in Wyoming Towns

1. Casper: Chicago and Northwestern, 1888.

2. Gillette: Burlington, Aug. 10, 1891.

3. Sheridan: Burlington, Nov. 18, 1892.

4. Buffalo: Burlington, Feb. 28, 1918.

5. Centennial: Laramie, Hahn's Peak and Pacific in April 1907. The line went bankrupt in 1912 and the court sold it for its creditors two years later. The rails were in place until the 1990s when they were pulled up and sold for scrap.

6. Saratoga: Saratoga and Encampment Valley Railway, August 1907. The line went into receivership the next year.

7. Lusk: Fremont, Elkhorn and Missouri Valley Railroad, July 13, 1886.

Locomotives on Display in Wyoming Towns

1. Challenger 3985

The largest operating steam locomotive in the world, the Challenger 3985 was built in 1943, and retired from service in 1959. The locomotive was fired up again in January 1981. Rebuilt and maintained by a group of volunteers, the locomotive is housed in Cheyenne in what remains of the Union Pacific roundhouse in the UP railyards.

2. "Big Boy" (8444)

The largest steam locomotive ever built, the 4000s include "Big Boy," which is an 8444. None remain in operation although one is on display in Holiday Park, Cheyenne.

3. 4-8-4 Steam Locomotive

A gift to the city of Sheridan, the 4-8-4 locomotive, across the street from the Sheridan Inn, was built in 1940.

4. UP 535

The locomotive is a landmark in LaPrele Park in Laramie. Built in 1903, the 2-8-0 consolidated was converted from coal to oil in 1950. The Union Pacific donated the locomotive to Laramie in 1959. In 2010, the locomotive was scheduled to move to a new location next to the Laramie depot on Front Street.

5. Locomotive and Cars

A locomotive and six cars are on display west of downtown Douglas.

6. Snowplow 900098

The plow, used along the Union Pacific, is now on display near the Recreation Center in Hanna.

7. Engine 105, Wyoming Railroad

The locomotive ran on the Buffalo to Clearmont line from 1917-1946. Following its retirement, it was moved to the Buffalo City Park and put on display.

Cabooses Now Used for Other Purposes

In the 1980s, cabooses were replaced on trains with "FREDs" (end of train device or ETD containing a reflector, a battery, a strobe and various sensors). As a result, many communities in Wyoming received cabooses. A few include:.

1. Medicine Bow

The caboose is displayed next to the Medicine Bow Museum, a building which served as the town depot until the early 1980s.

2. Laramie

The city's "welcome center" on South Third Street is an old caboose. The caboose was scheduled to move to a new location next to the Laramie depot in 2010.

3. Torrington

A railroad caboose stands on the grounds of the Homesteader Museum, south of Torrington. The museum building was once the railroad depot.

4. Lusk

A Burlington Northern caboose served as the office of the town's chamber of commerce.

Some Less Known Railroads in Wyoming

1. U. S. Steel railroad

The company built the 77-mile railroad line from Winton, near Rock Springs, to the mining company's taconite plant near Atlantic City. Construction required four steel overpass bridges. The first train ran on the proprietary line in 1962. The last train used the tracks in October 1983. In the ensuing years, the tracks were pulled up and many of the concrete ties were removed.

2. Burlington Northern route, Donkey Creek to Orin Junction

Still the longest new stretch of track built in America since World War II, the railroad

The railroad depot and other buildings representing Medicine Bow, Wyoming, in 1879, were part of the sites once seen by tourists taking the Tour Tram at Universal Studios in California.

company spent $110 million to build the 126-mile line to connect the mines of Campbell County to the main BN line to the south. Unit trains continue to use the route, hauling millions of tons of coal from the Powder River Basin to connecting routes across central and southern Wyoming.

3. North and South Railway

Constructed in 1922, by September of the following year, daily trains ran on the 41-mile long route from Midwest to Ilco (a railroad stop near Casper). The railroad owner, C. W. Haskill, initially planned to build the tracks all the way to Miles City, Mont., 322 miles in total. The firm went bankrupt in 1924, however, and the tracks remained in place, unused, until they were pulled up in 1935 and sent as scrap iron to China.

Great Train Robberies

1. Wilcox train robbery, June 2, 1899

Two men flagged a Union Pacific train and, with revolvers drawn, ordered the engineer to cut the engine and express and baggage cars loose and to pull across the bridge beyond Wilcox station and stop. The two men dynamited the bridge to prevent the arrival of the second section of the train, due in ten minutes. They forced the engineer to run the train two miles west, then looted the express cars of an estimated $60,000 in unsigned bank notes. Almost 100 pounds of dynamite was found near the scene the next day. The robbers rode north, escaping into Montana. The robbery was attributed to Butch Cassidy and Flat Nose George Currie although there was no evidence of the culprits' identities.

2. Overland Limited near Cheyenne, April 4, 1916

It was the second of four train robberies by Bill Carlisle, the so-called "gentleman bandit." It was 13 below zero on Feb. 4, 1915, when Carlisle robbed his first train. Three miles beyond Rock Springs, he ordered all men to place their wallets in a bag. (He never robbed a woman, hence his nickname). He pulled the air brake, jumped off into the snow and escaped with $52.35, rings and watches. On April 4, he robbed the Overland Limited and the railroad raised their reward offer from $1,000 to $6.500 for his capture. Posses scoured the state while he wrote letters to the *Denver Post,* boasting that he would rob another train which he soon did near Laramie. After this robbery, Carlisle was captured and sent to prison in April 1916. He escaped from the Rawlins penitentiary in November 1919, and robbed another train near Medicine Bow before he was captured. Carlisle served 20 years in prison. After his release, he ran a gas station and motel on the east edge of Laramie until shortly before his death in 1964.

3. Portland Rose near Dana, 1934

An ex-convict named Lovett tried to rob the Portland Rose, the Union Pacific's sleek overland limited, near the Carbon County station in 1934. He derailed the engine, baggage car and one coach. Unfortunately for Lovett, the coach was filled with Marines in transit to West Coast duty. Before he could get the loot, Lovett fled with the Marines in hot pursuit.

Two Fatal Wyoming Train Wrecks in 1906

1. Union Pacific, Nov. 17, 1906

A head-on collision of two trains, between Green River and Granger, killed eleven people, including the crews of both locomotives.

2. Chicago and Northwestern, March 19, 1906

Ten men were killed and another 16 injured when the train tried to crossed a creek channel 26 miles northwest of Casper where a culvert had been washed out earlier in the day. A heavy, wet snowfall hampered rescue workers.

RANKINGS

...how Wyoming ranks nationally in various areas in relation to other states...

1st Coal production (2009); production of bentonite (2009); most antelope; percentage of mobile homes, 18.8% of all housing (1988); average annual vehicle-miles of travel per person, 17,735 miles (2008); suicide rate, 20.4 (2006). most gun owners per capita, 59.7% (2006)

2nd Per capita federal grants, $3,917 per person (2009); mean elevation, 6,700 feet; percent of population 3 or over in school, 31.1% (1993); percentage of hunters with firearms of population, 25.8% (1995)

3rd Number of sheep, 1.1 million; state-local revenues from federal sources, 28.1% (1996); underage percentage of teen drinking (2006); lowest per capita tax burden, $3,714 (2005); divorce rate, 6.1 (2001); economic competitiveness (2002)

4th Population change from 1970 to 1980, up 41.6 percent; death rate from firearms, per capita, 18.8 (2002); per capita state spending (2008)

5th Toxic chemical releases, per capita, 23 lbs. (1995); per capita state and local sales tax collections, $2,069 (2007)

6th Land owned by the federal government, 48.6 percent of state; personal income per capita, $45,705 (2009); gross per capita state product, $47,728 (2004)

7th Least time of residence needed to get a divorce (two months)

8th Land area owned by the federal government, 30,477,000 acres; average teachers' pay (1985, a decade later, Wyoming was 35th in teacher salaries and, in 1997, Wyoming was 41st)

9th Area, 97,804 square miles; percentage of households with computers (2005); bank deposits per capita (2001)

10th Annual average number of earthquakes, 6; percentage incidence of severe depression (2007)

11th Total persons per household, 2.68 (1993)

12th Alcohol consumption, per capita, 2.46 gal. (1994); average annual lowest temperature, 11.9 degrees

13th Percentage of residents of Hispanic origin, 5.68 percent (1990)

14th Per capita spending for police protection, $319 (1993)

15th Average paycheck, all workers, $18,322 (1984). In 1996, Wyoming had slipped to 45th in average pay, all workers; percentage of Hispanics in total population, 5.8% (1994)

16th Percent of the work force self-employed, 8.2 percent (1989); percent of labor force in unions (2002)

17th Best educated (2005); Percentage of voting age population registered to vote, 69% (1994)

18th Per capita personal income (1929)

19th Federal personal income taxes, per capita, $2,223 (1995)

20th Average annual pay, $18,969 (1986); per capita state debt, $1,661 per person (1993)

21st Area covered by inland water (1970)

22nd Acreage of state parks, 123,486 acres (1980)

23rd Percentage of non-elderly without health insurance (2003); Median age, 36.2 years (2005)

24th Average number of tornadoes annually: 9; percentage of population in poverty, 11.9% (1996); median age, 35 years (1996)

25th	Cost of living (1996); percentage 5-year increase in prisoners (1996)
26th	Average unemployment benefits, $181 per week (1996)
27th	Percentage of agnostics in population (1990); percent of adults who smoke, 22% (1995)
28th	Percentage of residents 25 or older with a college degree, 24.6% (2005). Percentage of residents with a BA degree, 18.8% (1994)
29th	Rate of violent crime (1980)
30th	Health index, 21 factors (2005); Murder rate per capita, 5.3 per 100,000 population (1986); overall rating for "quality of life" poll by American Mercury (1931); "Nest Egg" index of savings (2006)
31st	Child abuse rate per 1,000 children, 12.3 (1993); potato production, 536,000 cwt (1986)
32nd	Deaths per 100,000, 456.6 (1996); violent crime rate per capita, 293.1 offenses per 100,000 pop. (1986)
33rd	Number of cattle, 1,350,000 (1987); per capita state debt, $2,303 (2007)
34th	Percentage of people who are church members, 44.1 percent; percentage of people on food stamps, 6.9% (1996); percentage of children in poverty, 14.8% (1996)
35th	Per capita personal income, $21,245 (1996); Medicare recipients per capita, 137 (2004)
36th	"Homeless" persons, per capita (1994); total govt. farm subsidy payments, $29 million (1986); crime rate, 4,575 crimes per 100,000 population (2002)
37th	Corn production, 5.8 million bushels (1986); lawyers per capita, 1 lawyer for every 458 people (2005)
38th	Water area, .6 percent of total area; crime rate (1995); patents issued, 52 (1996)
39th	Average tuition and fees for higher education, $2,144 (1996); percent of births to unwed mothers, 27% (1996); cigarette taxes per pack, 60 cents (2007)
40th	Religiosity per capita--church attendance, membership, (2007), Birth rate, 13.1 per 100,000 (1996)
41st	Violent crimes per capita (2004); Average teacher salary, $31,721 (1997)
42nd	Unemployment, 6.8% (2009); Percentage of population holding advanced degrees, 7.6% (2006); total state revenues (1985).
43rd	Rate of violent crime, 254.1 per 100,000 (1995); percentage of African-Americans (1990); air passengers per capita (2001)
44th	Admission to the Union (1890); percent of population not physically active, 21% (1995)
45th	Average annual pay, $22,264 (1996); Value of prime military contracts awarded to state businesses, $125 million (1985)
46th	Average salary for university professors, $44,800 (1997); awards from federal stimulus funds, 25 (2009).
47th	Number of residents aged 65 or older, 38,000 (1980); percent of females in population, 49.7% (1996); exports per capita, $1,313.58 (2005).
48th	Total veterans of World War I, II, Korea and Vietnam, 67,000 (1980); gasoline tax, 14 cents per gallon (2007); per capita physicians (2001)
49th	Tax burden on high income family, $3,063 (1996); egg production, 4.5 million dozen (1986); population per square mile, 5.1 (2000).
50th	Population, 544,270 (2009 estimate); number of defense installations, 1; average value of farmland, $136 per acre (1989); resident undergraduate tuition, 4-year university, $3,726 (2009)

ROCKS

3 Big Pieces of Wyoming Jade

1. 3,600 pounds

The piece, the largest single chunk reported, was taken to the West Coast. It was the property of Chang Wen Ti of Los Angeles.

2. 3,366 pounds

For many years, this gigantic jade piece decorated the lawn of Bert Rhoades, Lander. It was found by Verla Rhoades in 1943.

3. 2,495 pounds

Alan Barnham, a Lander grocer, found the piece near Jeffrey City. He sold it to Joseph Kraft, cheese tycoon, who gave it to the Chicago Museum of Natural History in 1940.

Some Wyoming Rocks Containing Historical "Graffiti"

1. Independence Rock

The granite outcropping, more than a mile in circumference, reaches to a height of 136 feet above the surrounding area. Discovered by Robert Stuart's party in 1812, it became known as "Independence Rock" in 1830 when mountain men celebrated the Fourth of July there. Father DeSmet called it the "Great Register of the Desert."

2. Register Cliff

The chalky limestone formation, located three miles south of Guernsey, rises about 100 feet above the valley. Many of the names carved on the cliff date from the 1840s and 1850s, during the peak years of Oregon Trail travel.

3. Names Hill

The oldest inscription is dated "1822." On the rock is chiseled the name "James Bridger—1844." If it is authentic, the inscription must have been done for Bridger because he was unable to read or write even his name.

4. Sandstone bluffs, North Platte River Crossing

The earliest inscription is of a pioneer in 1847. The site is near Saratoga.

5. Old Balance Rock

Travelers wrote their names on the unusual formation which is one mile from the site of the Sulphur Springs Stage Station in Carbon County.

Other Noteworthy Wyoming "Rocks"

1. Pilot Butte

The large formation guided mountain men in the Green River basin after 1812.

2. Split Rock

Split Rock served as a guide to travelers on the Oregon Trail. The cleft in the mountain, which acts as a compass point, can be seen from both east and west.

3. Teapot Rock

When white men first saw the formation, it resembled a teapot, but erosion have taken caused the "spout" to fall away. When oil was discovered nearby at the turn of the century, the oil field was called "Teapot Dome." During the scandals of the Harding administration, the name became synonymous with scandal.

4. Wyoming quartzite

A piece of the stone, quarried near Hartville, was selected by state geologist Ray Harris in 1988 as the Wyoming stone used in the construction of the Bicentennial of the Constitution monument in Philadelphia.

5. Blackest decorative stone in the U. S.

A stone quarry opened in northern Albany County in 1991 which produced the blackest decorative stone in the United States. The black granite, taken from a quarry at the Kennedy ranch, was called "Wyoming Raven."

RUMORS AND HOAXES

1. Jackalope

The mythical animal was "created" by Ralph Herrick, a Douglas taxidermist, in 1934. The Douglas Chamber of Commerce claims the first sighting was made in 1829 by a mountain man named Roy Ball. The unusual animal has the body of a rabbit and the horns of a deer. A larger-than-life concrete sculpture stands on the main street of Douglas. In March 1994, two Douglas boosters carried jackalopes in their suitcases to present to municipal officials in a Japanese town. Japanese customs agents were reluctant to allow the strange-looking stuffed beasts into the country!

2. Colter Stone

In 1931 William Beard, a Jackson area farmer, plowed up a stone inscribed "John Colter 1808." Found just west of the Tetons, the stone started a continuing debate over its authenticity. J. Nielson Barry suspected the work was a practical joke by Al Sibley, the cook on the 1871 Hayden expedition.

3. Great Diamond Hoax of 1872

Two miners delivered diamonds to a California bank and told officials they had been found in what is now southwestern Carbon County. Clarence King, a government surveyor, heard of the "discovery" and uncovered the hoax. He knew the area had been "salted" when he found a dozen rubies with each diamond, lying on the ground. The miners profited from the scheme ($300,000 or more) which they had set up with $35,000 in cast-off gems.

4. Hair-growing Oil

Sheepherder Barney Bansman reported discovering an amazing oil pool near Bridger Creek in May 1897. He claimed oil from the pool, when applied to a bald man's head, would cause hair to grow. Practical joker Lem Harold of Muskrat Creek heard of the "magic" oil. He surreptitiously emptied half of the contents from several bottles and refilled them with urine. "When these bottles sold just as well and reportedly produced the same amazing results, Harold couldn't keep the secret. He boasted to his friends that he was a walking gold mine, and Bransman's sales suddenly fell off," wrote Karen Love about the incident in "J. B. Okie, Lost Cabin Pioneer," *Annals of Wyoming*, Fall, 1974.

5. Seventh Cavalry Rifles

On July 19, 1959, Lusk furniture dealer George Gibson announced the discovery of several frontier army rifles in a cave north of Lusk. The "discovery" brought national press attention. Only later, when even the hometown newspaper was fooled, Gibson divulged that the "discovery" was a stunt he had dreamed up to promote the "Legend of the Rawhide" pageant held later in that month in Lusk.

6. Cardiff Giant

During the 19th century, P. T. Barnum and other circus promoters displayed huge alabaster figures which were claimed to be petrified giants. One example, the Cardiff Giant, had several imitators. A copy owned by a small Western circus was left behind in Cheyenne when the circus was forced to leave town quickly, just ahead of creditors. The huge figure laid for many years in "Talbot's Grove" in what is now the northwest side of the city.

7. Fear of Indian Attack

On Nov. 4, 1887, Dayton law officers chased a drunk out of town. Because it was a cold night, the man set fire to a haystack, thinking it would keep him warm. Several men en route to Sheridan saw the burning stack near the town 20 miles northwest of Sheridan and concluded that Dayton had been attacked and sacked by Indians. They hurried to Sheridan and sounded the alarm. Public buildings were barricaded and citizens waited in vain for the "attack" the never came. (In a strange coincidence, however, a Crow leader named Sword Bearer was killed by Indian police that night near the reservation agency in Montana, miles from the scene of the supposed "attack.")

8. Caspar Collins' portrait

A photograph of a young soldier, believed to be Lt. Caspar Collins for whom the town of Casper is named, turned up some ten years after Collins' death at Platte Bridge Station. For almost a century, it was thought to be Collins' likeness and from it, statues were designed and oil paintings made. According to Chuck Morrison and Irving Garbutt, authors of *Casper Centennial Book* (1990), the photograph was not of Collins. The name of the soldier depicted in the picture is unknown.

9. Various Political Rumors

Wyoming politics has a habit of spawning regular rumors. For instance, it was rumored that Secretary of State James Baker's change of voting residence from Texas to Wyoming was so that he could run as fellow Texan George Bush's running mate in 1992. (Baker did register to vote in Sublette County, but he was neither the VP nominee nor did he seek a Senate seat from Wyoming. Ironically, eight years later, Dick Cheney did change his registration from Texas to Teton County to run for vice president under George W. Bush).

10. "Invasion" rumors

When Buffalo residents were told that Cheyenne-based cattlemen and Texas hired guns were descending on their town in April 1892, it was not a rumor. Neither is it mere rumor that "greenies" have sniffed out some of Wyoming's best fishing holes. Other "invasion" tales have not turned out to be true. For instance, in the 1960s, businessmen in various towns armed themselves after hearing rumors of invading parties of "Hell's Angels." University officials during the so-called "Black 14" incident in 1969, believed rumors that busloads of "Black Panther Party" members were en route to Laramie from around the nation. For a time in the 1980s, rumors flew about neo-Nazis possibly relocating en masse or followers of various Far Eastern religious leaders were starting colonies in the state. None turned out to be true.

11. Indecent Name?

In the fall of 1991, the "Committee to Restore Decency to Our National Parks" sent 70 letters to various officials demanding that the Grand Teton be renamed because of its indecent reference to female breasts (in French). Governor Mike Sullivan, Cong. Craig Thomas and Jane Fonda were among those who responded, defending the name of the mountain. Later, it was revealed that the "committee letter-writing campaign" was actually a prank engineered by *Spy Magazine*, the New York-based satirical magazine.

12. Pop Can Scare

In the rash of hoaxes involving the finding of syringes in pop cans in the summer of 1993, three such reports were made by Wyoming people—one each in Rock Springs, Casper, Washakie County. The U. S. Attorney had authority to charge them for making false claims, but no one was arrested.

13. Frank Hopkins' ride, Texas to Vermont, 1886

The totally ficticious story fooled historians for years, even the Disney company that based a movie on the story, thinking it was true. The fictitious account claims that Hopkins rode Joe, a small, seven-year-old stallion, in what was longest official endurance race in the United States, the 1,799-mile race was sponsored by California silver baron E. J. "Lucky" Baldwin and Richard K. Fox, owner of the *Police Gazette*. Hopkins' claim was that, on Joe, they averaged 57.7 miles per day and made the entire distance in just 31 days.

A rock formation in the median between lanes of Highway 30 east of Rock River has the outline of very large rabbit. Local people have dubbed it "Harvey."

SADDLES

Some Well-Known Wyoming Saddlemakers

1. Edward H. Bohlin (b. Sweden, 1895, d. 1980)

Many famous saddlemakers worked in Wyoming over the years. One of the most famous was Edward H. Bohlin. Born in Sweden, Bohlin came to the United States in 1910 and, seven years later, established a saddle shop in Cody, across the street from the famous Irma Hotel. After gaining fame from his craftsmanship, he moved to California where he became known as "saddlemaker to the stars." Many Western film stars rode Bohlin saddles.

2. Don King (b. 1923, Douglas, July 28, 2007, Sheridan)

King began making belts in Palm Springs, Calif., in 1938. His first job in saddle shop was in 1939 in Patagonia, Ariz. After service in Coast Guard during WWII, he returned to Sheridan for apprenticeship with Rudy Mudra. (Mudra had started own saddlery in 1933, closed in 1955). King opened his own shop in a converted garage in Sheridan on Jan. 1, 1947. King was instrumental in developing the famous "Sheridan-style wild rose pattern." He bought a ranch the next year near Sheridan and moved his shop there where he also engaged in ranching until 1953. He was asked to make trophy saddles for Rodeo Cowboy Association in 1959. His King Saddlery business began in 1963 on Main Street of Sheridan in room at the back of Pioneer Sporting Goods. It moved to its present location in 1973. His Western Museum opened in a converted warehouse next to the shop in 1989 where some 500 saddles were on display. Prince Bandar of Saudi Arabia, their ambassador to the United States, bought a King saddle in 1988 when he visited the store. King made a leather-crafted wastebasket for Queen Elizabeth in 1984.

3. Chester Hape

The Sheridan maker made PRCA trophy saddles from 1976-1989. He started making saddles in the late 1950s.

4. Otto Ernst (b. Kansas, 1872, d. Sheridan, 1938)

The Sheridan saddlemaker's shop was in the business for 73 years. Otto Ernst started making saddles in Sheridan in 1900, went into partnership with John Buckley, bought Buckley out in 1907, and brought his brother John into the business. He died in 1938 and his son Ernest and Otto's brother John took over the shop. Ernest died in 1974 and the shop closed in 1975.

5. E. L. Gallatin (b. St. Louis, 1828, d.

Known as the "Father of the Western Stock Saddle," Gallatin was the father-in-law and teacher of Frank Meanea *(below)*. He built saddles in Denver, but sold out in 1873 and moved to Cheyenne. Gallatin and his nephew originated the distinctly Cheyenne saddle.

6. Frank Meanea (b. Missouri, 1849, d. Cheyenne, 1928)

Meanea began his career repairing harness for the Union Pacific Railroad's construction teams and wagons as the railroad was being constructed west in the late 1860s. In 1868, he came to Cheyenne and stayed there the rest of his life. He started in the shop of E. L. Gallatin and, eventually, took over Gallatin's operation. Meanea used exclusively saddle trees made by his brother Theodore Meanea. Meanea pioneered saddle catalogs. At the time of their first publication, about 1900, his shop employed 22 craftsmen. As the open-range cattle industry declined, so did Meanea's business. By the middle 1920s, only one man still made saddles with Meanea. When Frank Meanea died at the age of

---

Samuel Cowley, son of Mathias Cowley for whom the town was named, died in December, 1934, in a gunfight with outlaw Baby Face Nelson. Cowley was a federal agent.

79 in 1928, he left a legacy of quality and saddles used by riders in every state and many foreign countries. Artist Charles M. Russell and author Owen Wister both preferred Meanea saddles. The saddles are increasingly rare and highly collectible. *Source: James R. Laird, The Cheyenne Saddle. (Cheyenne Corral of Westerners, 1982).*

7. All-Western Plastics, Inc., Lusk

The firm made and sold plastic saddles in the 1940s.Founded by William B. Vandegrift, All-Western made their saddles of plastic , using various color combinations. Working cowboys declared them impractical, but they became a hit novelty item. Only about 65 of them were made and sold and the operation moved to Scottsbluff, Neb., in the early 1950s. Roy Rogers bought one of the plastic saddles when he was concerned that riding Trigger in the 1952 Tourament of Roses parades in Pasadena could result in rain damage to his valuable Edward Bohliln saddle. The Rogers saddle was to be sold at auction in 2010 with an estimated worth of $30,000. Examples of the saddle are held in various museums, but also highly prized by saddle collectors. According to one news account, Cheyenne rancher and auctioneer Tom Harrower owned many of them.

—

Wyoming Legislature Passed Federal Income Tax

When the 1913 session of the Wyoming legislature got underway in January, 1913, the income tax amendment to the U. S. Constitution (16th Amendment) was under consideration by several other state legislatures. The amendment lacked just one ratifying state from becoming part of the United States Constitution.

Wyoming legislative leaders tried to gain the honor of having Wyoming be the 36th and deciding state to ratify. The record is silent as to what substantive arguments were made by proponents and nothing indicates that those opposed argued very forcefully against it. The race was on for the publicity of being the state pushing the amendment "over the top."

The ratification was introduced on February 3, passed both houses of the legislature under expedited rules and moved quickly to the governor's office for his signature.

Meanwhile, the Delaware legislature also was ratifying the amendment. Both states ratified the amendment on the same day and, thus, both were awarded the coveted distinction.

In 1933, a coalition of ranchers and farmers in the State House of Representatives tried to initiate a state income tax. The 23, called "the farm bloc," failed to gain support from the rest of the legislature. State revenues had been flat since the middle 1920s. Cities and counties were in serious need of funds to pay for public assistance because one in five Wyoming workers were jobless. In 1935, the legislature adopted a sales tax as a "temporary measure" for helping the cities and counties. In 1937, it was reinstituted, but as a permanent tax. The rate was 2 percent.

In--holdings (privately-owned lands) still exist within the boundaries of Grand Teton National Park. A house on less than an acre within the park was sold in 2007 for $1.9 million. The State of Wyoming owns school sections within the boundaries of the park. In 2010, the properties, consisting of about two square miles of land, were valued at about $125 million. In the spring of 2010, Gov. Dave Freudenthal threatened to put the land up for sale to private parties if the Department of the Interior, wanting to incorporate the lands into the Park, wouldn't pay the price the State believed the property was worth.

SCHOOLS

1st school in Wyoming: Fort Laramie, taught by the Rev. Richard Vaux, post chaplain, 1852.

1st school building in Wyoming: Fort Bridger, built by W. A. Carter in 1860 for his six children.

1st graduate of any educational institution in Wyoming: Morton H. Hanna who graduated from Cheyenne High School, c. 1875. Other sources state Miss Frankie Logan and Miss Ella Hanna were the first graduates of Cheyenne High.

1st university in Wyoming: University of Wyoming, established in 1886.

1st community college in Wyoming: Casper College, established in 1945.

1st kindergarten in Wyoming: Casper, started by Adah Turner, c. 1901.

1st mandatory attendance law passed: 1873, required three months of school for children age 7-16.

1st territorial teachers' institute: May 2, 1874, in Cheyenne.

Total teachers in Wyoming: 6,567 (2008). The number was 6,887 in 1999, down from about 7,300 in 1989. Of the total (1999), 1,939 were high school teachers.

Graduating seniors from Wyoming high schools: 5,600 in 1987; 6,137 in 1995; 6,348 in 1999; 6,093 in 2008.

High school graduation rate: 79.3% in 2008-9 compared to 76.5% in 1998-99.

Residents who are high school graduates: 91.9% (2005), ranking Wyoming second among the 50 states. The total was 87.9 percent in 2000; 77.9 percent in 1990, the fourth highest percentage in the nation.

School districts: 56 districts statewide in 1990; 48 school districts in 2010.

Total classroom buildings (K-12): 498 in 1999.

Total school fieldhouses/sports complexes (1999): 84

Public school enrollment in Wyoming: 86,519 in 2007; 91,883 in 1999; 100,314 in 1994.

Teacher pay: Average for all teachers was $43,255, ranking 29th in the nation (2007). The average starting salary for a teacher in Wyoming was $31,481, ranking 24th in the nation (2007). In 1998-99, Wyoming ranked 41st in the nation in average salaries for teachers, $33,500.

Years of teaching experience, statewide average: 14.75 years (2008)

5 alternative high schools in Wyoming: Casper, Rock Springs, Riverton, Cheyenne, Laramie. Laramie's opened in Sept. 1993. SixteenWyoming high schools have 600 or more students; eight high schools have fewer than 50 students.

National Science Teachers' Assoc. Top Science Teacher in U. S.: Jeb Schenk, Thermopolis, received $10,000 with award (1996)

School Funding (2008-09): Local sources, $501.5 million; county sources, $153.6 million; state sources, $846 million; federal sources, $102.3 million.

School Funding (1998-99): Local sources, $271 million; county sources, $54.6 million; state sources, $330 million; federal sources, $47.2 million.

Total revenues for education: $1,603,488,087 (2008-09); $780,881,961 (1998-99):

Total expenditures education expenditures (2009): $833,837,000.

Total expenditures per student: $12,841 (2008-09); $6,711 (1997-98).

Total expenditures specifically for instruction (2009): $268,940,000.

Average ACT test score in Wyoming: 20.0 in 2009; 21.4 (1999, same as 1996-98). National average was 20,9 in 2009; 21.0 in 1999.

Districts with the highest ACT (2008-09): Teton #1 (21.6); Park #1 (21); Albany #1 (20.2); Niobrara (20.2); Uinta #6 (20.2).

No. of students taking buses regularly to school (2009): 33,889

1st Schools in Wyoming Towns

1. South Pass City

First teacher in the mining boom town was James Stilman in 1870, who taught even before taxes were collected to pay his salary.

2. Cheyenne

Taught by Stephen Scriber, the school was located on the present site of the City-County Building. The first classes were held in 1868. The school building was dedicated on Jan. 5, 1868, when the temperature was -20 degrees.

3. Casper

Mrs. Adah E. Allen was the first teacher of the first private school to open in Casper on March 5, 1889. Miss Anna Weber taught the first classes in first public school established July 6, 1889. The public school opened in the Congregational Church, Durbin and First Street. The first actual building constructed for a school in Casper opened in January 1891, with 50 students.

4. Laramie

Miss Eliza Stewart opened the first school on Feb. 15, 1869.

5. Evanston

The first school opened on July 8, 1871, above a saloon on Front Street between 7th and 8th. Eight pupils attended. The first teacher was A. H. Parsons.

6. Sheridan

Clara Works Moehler taught the first school classes in Sheridan in 1882.

7. Lusk

The first classes were taught on Sept. 6, 1886, by Mrs. O. P. Goodwin.

8. Basin

The first school opened in March 1897, almost as soon as the town was platted, in the second floor of the building housing county offices. The building burned in 1899. The first actual school building was a one-room structure of logs and mud built in the fall of 1899. Miss Clara Orbin was the first teacher.

9. Cowley

Built by Andrew Willis in January 1901, the first school in Cowley was taught by Eliza Black. She had 30 students in various grades.

10. Afton

The first school was a one-room log cabin with a dirt roof and floor built in 1887. In the winter of 1887-88, William B. Burton came from Evanston to become the first teacher. He had 15 pupils.

11. County school, Goshen County

The first erected county schoolhouse in Goshen County opened in 1891, one mile north of Torrington. Mona Farnell was the teacher. Prior to that time, school was taught in homes and on ranches.

12. Jackson Hole

First classes were held in the home Sylvester Wilson in 1894 with about 12-15 students attending. The first schoolhouse was built in 1896.

13. Thermopolis

The first school opened in 1898 in a garage on the corner of 5th and Big Horn. Joe McGill was the first teacher.

12. Shell

The first "Shell Creek school" in the Big Horn County community was opened in an old stable with the manger serving as seating. The blackboard was made of a pair of rubber boots, split and nailed to the wall.

13. Arminto

Minnie Mitchell, the first teacher, later was elected Wyoming state auditor and treasurer.

A Florida school board in 1991 announced they were banning the novel My Friend Flicka by Mary O'Hara from the school library. The book, about a 10-year-old Wyoming boy and his wild colt, had been written in 1941. Apparently, the sensitivities of the board had been damaged by the mention of "damn" in one passage and reference to a female dog as a "bitch."

Wyoming Teachers of the Year, 1964-2000

1964 Letha L. Dickinson, Riverton	1988 Janice Truchot, Sundance
1965 Lawrence Bays, Wheatland	1989 Mark Levitt, Green River
1966 Pearl Bader, Ten Sleep	1990 Rod Laird, Saratoga
1967 Ann Halseth, Rock Springs	1991 Bette Sample, Newcastle
1968 Helen Horsley Kienlen, Worland	1992 Joan Barker, Green River
1969 Karl D. Allen, Thermopolis	1993 Judy McBride, Laramie
1970 Janette Plott, Sheridan	1994 Sharon Yovich, Laramie
1971 William H. Malloy, Thermopolis	1995 Joan Brummond, Cheyenne
1972 Margaret Blacker, Laramie	1996 Pamela Moore, Evanston
1973 Helen Meldrum, Buffalo	1997 Kevin Tennant, Gillette
1974 Maxine Torbert, Sheridan	1998 Mary Ellen Krisko, Worland
1975 Margaret Mecca, Thermopolis	1999 June Moore, Laramie
1976 Rosalee Ammons, Osage	2000 Bernie Schnorenberg, Sundance
1977 Jeanne Curran, Rock Springs	2001: Cindy Gulisano, Lingle/Ft Lar.
1978 Steve Campbell, Riverton	2002: Marcia Patton, Casper
1979 Mignon Hill, Laramie	2003: Eric Stemle, Evanston
1980 Elizabeth Shelton, Big Horn	2004: Jack Patrick, Saratoga
1981 Lois Horn Sackman, Riverton	2005: Debi L. Gaines, Saratoga
1982 Robert Hilgenfeld, Rock Springs	2006: Carol Kirkwood, Laramie
1983 Ann Tollefson, Casper	2007: Mark Nethercott, Star Valley
1984 Charlotte Levendosky, Casper	2008: Eileen Yager Johnson, Laramie
1985 Bob Meredith, Shoshoni	2009: Alice King, Gillette
1986 Marcine Miller, Ranchester	
1987 Lois Distad, Casper	

Some Schools Named for Wyoming People

1. Kelly Walsh High School, Casper

Walsh came to Casper in 1927. He served as school principal form 1936 to 1958 when he was named assistant superintendent. A lifelong musician as well as an educator, Walsh played the clarinet in numerous bands and orchestras. He retired from the school district in 1971 and died in 1992.

2. Dean Morgan Junior High School, Casper

Morgan was a long-time educator in Casper schools. He served as superintendent of schools. The new school was named for him in December 1956.

3. Velma Linford Elementary School, Laramie

The school on Laramie's west side was named for the former State Superintendent of Public Instruction who taught for 20 years at Laramie High School. A native of Afton, she lived in Washington, D. C., at the time of her death in 2002.

4. Carey Junior High School, Cheyenne

Named for Joseph M. Carey, former governor and U. S. Senator, the structure stands on property once owned by Carey. A part was donated by Carey heirs to the district in 1957.

5. Hebard School, Cheyenne

Alice Hebard, after whom the school was named, taught primary grades at Johnson

The fieldhouse at the high school in Lander was renamed for the late Bob Carey who taught from 1965-84. It was officially dedicated Dec. 2, 1995. He was the only coach to have state championships in boys (1968) and girls (1978) basketball. The football stadium at Natrona County High School in Casper was renamed in 2003 in honor of Dick Cheney, an NCHS alumnus.

School in Cheyenne for 33 years. She was the sister of Dr. Grace Raymond Hebard, a professor at the University of Wyoming for many years.

6. Goins Elementary School, Cheyenne

The school was named for Jesse L. Goins (b. Tenn, 1894, d. Cheyenne, 1964) who was principal of Corlett school from 1923-30, principal of Cheyenne High School from 1930-1938 and then superintendent of schools in Cheyenne until his retirement in 1954. The school was named for him in 1957.

7. Verda James Elementary School, Casper

The school is named for the long-time Casper educator and legislator. She was the first woman to serve as Speaker of the Wyoming House during a regular legislative session.

8. Whiting School, Laramie

The school, built in the early 1920s, was named for Betsy Whiting who held the record for service in Laramie schools having taught for 35 years until her retirement in 1911. She was the second teacher in Laramie.

9. Slade School, Laramie

The school in north central Laramie was named on Dec. 6, 1954, for Albert A. Slade, the founder of the national Future Teachers of America organization. He came to Wyoming because of his health in 1916 and served as superintendent in Cody and Casper. In 1938 in Laramie, he founded the small club which later expanded into the national FTA. He died in Fort Collins in 1971 at the age of 94.

10. Ralph Witters Elementary School, Thermopolis

Witters was a long-time principal in Thermopolis.

11. Glenn Livingston Elementary School, Cody

Livingston was a long-time school administrator.

2 School Auditoriums Named for Wyoming People

1. John F. Walsh Auditorium, NCHS, Casper

Walsh was a drama teacher at Natrona County High School for 29 years.

2. Wynoma Thompson Auditorium, Cody High School

Thompson taught speech and drama at Cody High School for many years.

State Spelling Bee Winners*

1980: Sandra Haggard, McCormick JH, Cheyenne
1981: Kevin Kauffman, Twin Spruce JH, Gillette
1982: Norman Reese, Douglas Middle School
1983: Lisa Hills, Torrington Middle School
1984: Amy Ksir, University Prep, Laramie
1985: Angela Miller, Ten Sleep School
1986: Matt Carvallo, Pinedale
1988: Claudia Woodman**
1989: Tally Neilson, Cody Junior High
1990: Charlotte Bright, McCormick JH, Cheyenne
1991: Jason Jett, Davis Middle School, Evanston
1992: Jason Jett, Davis Middle School, Evanston
1993: Jordan Nelson, McCormick JH, Cheyenne
1994: Tom Edrington, 8th grade, Kemmerer
1995: Cheyenne Hamilton, 8th grade, Heritage Christian, Gillette
***1996: Tyler Clayton, Centennial Junior High, Casper; Zach Bigalke

1997: LaDonna Johnson, Zach Bigalke
1998: Clayton Thomas, Lacelliese Witowski
1999: Tom Lennon, Clayton Thomas
2000: Jordan Hilton, Laramie; Tamara Kuehn, Jackson
2001: Adriana Johnson, Hawk Springs; Brent "Tony" Tremeling, Jackson
2003: Steve Lerner, Cheyenne
2004: Jennifer Black, Cheyenne
2006: Kelly Sullivan, Riverton
2007: Sarah J. M. Lehmitz, Torrington
2008: Catherine Cloetta, Jackson
2009: Sage Weber, Laramie+
2010: Taylor Ballek, Buffalo

*Until 1933, the spelling bee was held at the Wyoming State Fair. Until 1990, Wyoming winners did not automatically advance to the national contest unless they entered and won the Colorado title in a contest sponsored by the Rocky Mountain News. The policy changed in 1990 when the state contest was officially sponsored.

**No names of winners are available for years prior to 1980 or for 1987.

***Beginning in 1996, two contestants were entered from Wyoming. In 2000, 248 contestants from around the nation competed in the National Spelling Bee.

+State spelling bee hosted at the University of Wyoming for first time.

Wyoming Geography Bee winners, 1989-2010

1989: Jonathan Caspersen. Cheyenne
1990: Jeremy Braithwaite, Green River
1991: Jeremy Braithwaite, Green River
1992: Tom Whitney, Casper
1993: Michael Anselmi, Rock Springs
1994: Jeremy Lindsey, Cheyenne
1995: Aaron Moss, Riverton
1996: Patrick Schmiedt, Midwest
1997: Paul McVey, Casper
1998: Jonathan Abresch, Worland
1999: Ian T. Wallace, Ranchester

2000: Adam Towler, Laramie
2001: Adam Towler, Laramie
2002: Philip Michael, Cheyenne
2003: Doyle Evins, Douglas
2004: Doyle Evins, Douglas
2005: James Mothersbaugh, Casper
2006: James Mothersbaugh, Casper
2007: Kirsi Anselmi-Smith, Rock Springs
2008: Hunter Collins, Jackson
2009: Kirsi Anselmi-Smith, Rock Springs
2010: Zachery Dubisz, Alpine

Misc. Items About Education

1. Oil from Salt Creek School Section

When Wyoming gained statehood in 1890, the federal government provided land grants for many purposes. The greatest land grant was for maintaining public schools and the state received every Section 16 and 36 in each township. These "school sections" were leased by the state, in accordance with fee requirements in the State Constitution. One section was located in the middle of the Salt Creek Oil Field, north of Casper. Oil royalties from the one section brought in $4.7 million from 1924-34. An estimated 17.8 million barrels came from wells on the section during that decade with the best years, 1924 and 1925 at a time agriculture in Wyoming was suffering from drought and depression.

2. Demise of a High School

Jeffrey City High School graduated two students in May 1993 from a school of 9. K-12 had a total of 42 students in 1993, the smallest K-12 in Wyoming. In 1995-96, the entire school had but 33 students. Mindy McIntosh was the only graduate of Jeffrey City High School in May, 1997--and the last. The school closed at the end of the year due to lack of students.

3. Children in School for 32 Years

Dixie and Scott Bertagnole of Mills had children attending Mills Elementary School for 32 consecutive years. The youngest of 13 children graduated from sixth grade in May 1992.

4. Recognized School in 1992

In 1992, *Redbook* magazine asked education experts to rank the best American schools. Big Piney was designated the best in Wyoming. "Big Piney's challenging academic program helps send 73 percent of its 167 students to college and earns college credit for 100 percent of those taking AP exams," the article about the ratings noted *(April 1992, p. 70)*.

5 Arbitrary School Closing

In the most arbitrary action in recent school board history, Carbon County School District #2 board of trustees ordered the Medicine Bow High School and Junior High School closed in 1998. The board, dominated by members from Saratoga, a rival community, voted 5-4 for closure. Community members sued to restore the school, but lost in district court. "The board's action demonstrated that any school in a consolidated district can be closed," Phil Roberts, counsel in the case, said. "Carbon District #2 board members must have known that when a school closes, a town is in jeopardy. While they killed Medicine Bow, they also created extreme hardship on families still living there with school children. Ultimately, the school census in the district declined, a result of the board's myopic act."

6. Student Bus Drivers

Washakie County School Dist. No. 1 (Worland) is the only district in the U. S. having student school bus drivers. In 1990, the district had to gain a waiver from new federal child labor laws to keep the student drivers. Driving requirements are the same for the student drivers as for adult school bus drivers, including licensing and training in CPR.

National History Day
Wyoming State Historical Society

Wyoming History Day is a competition open to students from grades 6-12 in which they write essays, produce documentaries, construct exhibits or develop websites on a historical subject relating to the national theme. Students compete in districts and winners go on to state competition, held in Laramie each April.

The first Wyoming History Day was actually held as several regional contests only in 1980. The following year, the first state event was held, hosted by Western Wyoming College in Rock Springs. Wyoming was the first state west of the Mississippi River to participate and, for many years, winning students traveled to Washington, D. C., for the national finals by bus. Recent winners now go by airplane, accompanied by teachers, parents and other chaperones. The event continues to be an important way for the Wyoming State Historical Society to promote history among Wyoming young people.

Over the 30 years of the competition, there have been thousands of winners at regional contests, hundreds at the state finals and numerous Wyoming winners in the national contest. Students compete against students from the other 49 states. An estimated 500,000 students participate from throughout the nation at the various levels.

In 2010, **Blake Shields** of Cheyenne finished 9th nationally in the junior individual documentary. **Rachael Troxel** of Lander finished 12th in the same category. In the junior individual exhibit category, **Rachel Graham** of Riverton finished 10th. In junior group

On Sept. 12, 1994, Heidi Pexton and Christina Trujillo became the first two Wyomingites to be inducted into the AmeriCorps program. Both served as tutors for at-risk students at Laramie County Community College.

performances, the Lander team of **Louisa Austin** and **Montana Sannes** came in 10th. **Morgan Corney** of Jackson took 14th place nationally for senior individual exhibits.

In 2009, **Robert Coulter** of South Elementary School in Lander, won the national first place award for Junior Individual Documentary

5 High Schools in Wyoming in 1895*

1. Cheyenne   3. Evanston   5. Sundance
2. Rawlins   4. Buffalo

There were no other high schools in the state in 1895.

Wyoming School Teachers by Subject Areas
(full-time equivalents, 1999-2000)

Mathematics	363	Language arts	452
Science	361	Physical Ed.	298
Social Studies	331	General	356
Foreign Language	145	Fine/Perf. Arts	328

Wyoming Science Teachers Association
Lifetime Achievement Awards

2010 - Tim Maze, Art Orr, Rosanne Riley, Becky Stewart
2008 - Gloria Becker, Carolyn Hicks, Gail Moravek.
2007 - Roger Abelson, Judy Ellsworth, Pete Ellsworth
2006 - James (Jim) Boal, Windsor Copley, Stan Strikes
2005 - Elizabeth Horsch, Frank Stofflet, Dana Van Burgh

The National Senior Spelling Bee started in Cheyenne, Wyoming in 1996. Sponsored by the Wyoming AARP, it is open to contestants 50 and older. Maria Dawson is the only contestant to ever win two back to back titles at the National Senior Spelling Bee.

SCULPTURE

Largest foundry in Wyoming: Eagle Bronze. Monty and Beverly Paddleford started the Lander-based foundry where huge moumental bronzes are cast, many through the "lost-wax" method. More than 50 people were employed there (2009). Among the firm's works are the sculptures placed in the Dallas civic plaza and the "Carolina Panther" statue in the North Carolina stadium.

City Acquisitions: From 2002-2009, the City of Sheridan Public Arts Committee sponsored outdoor sculpture exhibits. During the period, the city acquired 32 sculptures for placement in parks and other public downtown areas.

Some Well-Known Wyoming Statues

1. Lions, entrance to Kendrick Park, Sheridan

The sculpture pieces were part of the 1915 World's Fair. They were bought by Sheridan meat market owner Peter Neiter and donated to the city in 1919. Each is 56 inches high, cast in bronze and weighs 600-800 pounds. The figures are modeled after Chinese lion-dogs.

2. Lady Justice (1911)

The Weston County Courthouse sculpture by an artist whose name is not known was dedicated in 1911. A similar statue of Lady Justice once stood above the cupola at the top of the Niobrara County Courthhouse in Lusk. The statue was removed in the 1920s because its weight caused structural issues. During World War II, the statue was consigned to a scrap metal drive.

3. "Buffalo Bill, the Scout" (1924)

Sculpted by Gertrude Vanderbilt Whitney, the statue is the best known equestrian work in the state. The dedication ceremonies were held on the Fourth of July, 1924. Cody's main street, Sheridan Avenue at its western point, ends at the statue.

4. Kistler Fountain, Sinclair (1927)

Erected in 1927, the circular fountain basin featuring the front quarters of lions facing forward was erected in honor of Frank E. Kistler, founder of Parco (renamed Sinclair).

5. "Robert Burns" (Nov. 11, 1928)

Henry Snell Gamley (1865-1928), Scotland's foremost sculptor, made the bronze statue of the Scottish national hero. The work was commissioned by Mary Gilchrist (b. Scotland, 1839, came to Wyoming, 1875) for $20,000 and dedicated in Nov. 11, 1928. Because of the sudden death of the artist, the Scots did not want his works to be exported. Nonetheless, because the Burns statue had been commissioned, fully paid for, and cast in Paris, it was shipped to Wyoming. It is located in a small park where Pioneer and Randall avenues connect with 26th street in Cheyenne and stands on a pedestal designed by Cheyenne architect William Dubois. The inscription from Burns reads:

"From scenes like these old Scotia's grandeur springs,
that makes her lov'd at home and rever'd abroad,
Princes and lords are but the breath of kings,
An Honest Man's the noblest work of God."

6. "Bust of Lincoln" (1959)

The bronze work by Robert Russin was first located at the highest point of the Lincoln Highway (U.S. Highway 30) and moved to its present site between Laramie and Cheyenne at the highest elevation reached by Interstate 80 in 1968. The bust, cast in Mexico, weighs 3 1/2 tons and stands 12 1/2 feet high atop a 30-foot marble column. The bust was removed from the column for several months for cleaning and put back in place on April 3, 1992.

7. "Esther Hobart Morris" (1960)

The statue, dedicated Dec. 15, 1963, faces down Capitol Avenue from the front of the Wyoming State Capitol. It is a copy of Wyoming's first entry in Statuary Hall in the United States.Capitol, dedicated April 6, 1960. The work was sculpted by Avard Fairbanks.

8. "Elk" (1962)

Russin also sculpted a life-sized elk for the Elks section of the Sheridan cemetery. It was commissioned by Frederic and Harriet Thorne-Rider and dedicated in 1962.

9. "Man and Energy" (1973)

The cast bronze piece by Robert Russin was placed in front of the Casper Area Chamber of Commerce.

10. "Prometheus" (1974)

Robert Russin's polished bronze stands in front of the Natrona County Library.

11. "Cowboy" (1976)

The work by Bud Boller is located in George Washington Memorial Park in Jackson.

12. "Story Teller" (1977)

Dick Greeves (b. St. Louis, 1934) sculpted the statue in bronze. The statue stands in front of the Sheridan County Fullmer Public Library. Greeves came to Wyoming in 1949 and worked in and exhibited from a studio in Fremont County.

13. "Sacajawea" (1980)

Harry Jackson (b. Chicago, 1924) sculpted the work which occupies a courtyard in the Plains Indian Museum, Buffalo Bill Historical Center, Cody. It was dedicated on the Fourth of July 1980. Copies of the work were placed at the University of Wyoming and Central Wyoming College, Riverton.

14. Fountainhead" (1980)

The steel sculpture in front of Casper City Hall was by Robert I. Russin.

15. "Indian Totem" (1980)

The work by Peter Toth (b. 1947) was dedicated Sept 28, 1980, on the grounds of the Washakie County Courthouse.

16. "Caspar Collins" (1982)

The bronze equestrian statue by Pershing Geiger (b. Arkansas, 1920, d. Casper, 1995) measures 11 feet, 5 inches tall and weighs 2 1/2 tons. Geiger received a commission of $94,000 for the work which stands in front of the Casper All Events Center.

17. "Sentinel of the Plains" (1982)

L. M. "Bud" Boller, Jr., a native Shoshone sculptor made other works including this bronze antelope sculpture in Lander, placed in Antelope Park in September 1982.

18. "Serenity" (1984)

The bronze work by Dolores Fausett was dedicated on the grounds of the Wyoming State Hospital in September 1984.

19. "Sheepman" (1984)

Carl Jensen's work stands in front of the Campbell County Library in Gillette. The sculptor is a Wheatland resident.

20. "L'Esprit de Femme" (1984)

The two outdoor panels depicted various female figures. Commissioned by the State of Wyoming for placement outside the Wyoming Women's Center, the work by Terry Kreuger was dedicated in November 1984.

21. "Up Front" (1985)

The sculpture by Peter M. Fillerup (b. 1953) stands in front of the Veterans Home of Wyoming, west of Buffalo. It was commissioned in 1984.

22. "Betrayed" (1985)

The sculpture of the angry bear, created by James L. Jellus, stands in front of the Ranchester Municipal Building in Ranchester.

23. "The Spirit of Wyoming" (1986)

Sculptor Edward Fraughton worked for more than two years on the work depicting a cowboy on a bucking bronc. Until 2000, the sculpture was located on the plaza between the State Capitol and the Herschler state office building in Cheyenne. Fraughton won a 1978 statue competition. His similar work was dedicated July 8, 1991, in Jackson.

24. "Order and Disorder" (1986)

The sculpture, a large opaque round ball with the inside painted and viewable, was executed by Dick Termes, holder of the MA in art from the University of Wyoming. The unusual sculpture is in the courtyard at the Wyoming Law Enforcement Academy, northwest of Douglas. The artist used what had been a large glass ball used as a Union 76 gasoline sign, painted it from the inside and then mounted the piece on a platform.

25. "Gift of the Smoking Waters" (1987)

The largest sculpture ever cast entirely in Wyoming at the time of its completion, the work is 14 feet tall and weighs 2,400 pounds. By Gerald Shippen of Lander, it stands in Hot Springs State Park, Thermopolis. It shows Chief Sharp Nose offering the buffalo horn of water to James McLaughlin, representing the United States government. Washakie stands next to them holding a peace pipe. The sculpture was dedicated on July 25, 1987.

26. "Pony Express" (1988)

The Harry Jackson work stands in front of the Cody Chamber of Commerce. It is the first public equestrian monument in the world in which the horse is shown standing on one leg. The unique sculpture was dedicated July 10, 1988.

27. Black-footed Ferrets (1990)

The sculpture of two black-footed ferrets is located on the corner of Water Avenue and State Street in Meeteetse. Mike Scoville was the sculptor of the piece dedicated in 1990 and commemorating Meeteetse as "the home of the blackfooted ferret."

28. "The Irrigator" (1990)

Wheatland sculptor Carl Jensen executed the bronze work honoring irrigation, important to the Wheatland area's economic history. The statue, on the Platte County Courthouse grounds, was commissioned to mark Wyoming's centennial and dedicated June 23, 1990.

29. "The Miner" (1990)

The work by Gary Prazen was commissioned by the United Mines Workers of America Local 1307 for the organization's centennial in 1990. It is located in the Miner's Memorial Park, Diamondville.

30, Jackalope" (re-dedicated, 1990)

The painted fiberglas depicts a large sitting jackalope, an animal "invented" in Douglas. The piece by an unknown craftsman was rededicated on Statehood Day, July 10, 1990, in the center of Douglas' main street.

31. Elk (1991)

The statue, four times the size of a real elk, was erected in June 1991 in front of a Jackson museum. The 1,500-lbs. bronze was by Idaho sculptor Danny Edwards. Sculpture placement raised a question about whether or not the statue was a "commercial sign." It would violate an ordinance for size if it had been so defined.

32. "Over the Top" (1991)

The work by Danny D. Edwards was cast locally in Lander at Eagle Bronze Works. The huge elk stands in front of the Pronghorn Lodge on Lander's main street.

33. "Story Book" (1993)

The sculpture, located in front of the Laramie County Library, was done by a Loveland, Colo., sculptor and dedicated May 3, 1993.

34. "Lane Frost" (1993)

By Chris Navarro (b. 1956), the 15-foot-high statue of Frost is located at Frontier Park in Cheyenne. The rodeo cowboy died in a bullriding accident on July 30, 1989.

35. "Pioneer Women" (1993)

Burke Rutherford was the sculptor of the eight-foot bronze commemorating pioneer women in Worland and Washakie County. The piece, dedicated Sept. 12, 1993, was placed on a pedestal in the city park near a similar piece depicting the digging of the area's irrigation canals.

36. Johnson County War statues (1994)
L. Michael Thomas of Buffalo was commissioned in 1993 to create two three-quarter life-sized statues commemorating the Johnson County War. The First National Bank of Buffalo made the commission. Titled "Living on the Edge," the two statues were dedicated on July 9, 1994.

37. "Tense Moments" (1995)
The sculpture of an eagle swooping for a rabbit is located in a Gillette park. The work, one of several by noted Gillette sculptor Don Marquiss, was dedicated in October, 1995.

38. "Thunder on the Plains" (1997)
Mike Flanagan bronze sculpture is located in downtown Sheridan.

39. "Chief Washakie" (1999)
The sculpture is Wyoming's second in Statuary Hall in the U. S. Capitol. Dave Mc-Gary, Ruidoso, N. M., formerly of Cody, was chosen as the sculptor of the piece in design competition in August, 1999. It was dedicated in September, 2000, in ceremonies in the U. S. Capitol.

40. "Lewis and Clark expedition" (1999)
John Kuchera spent 12 years sculpting the 60 figures from metal depicting the Lewis and Clark expedition. The works were shown on KTWO-TV Nov. 12, 1999.

41. Mounted cowboy and steer (1999)
The statue is in the boulevard of Broadway in downtown Thermopolis. Both pieces were sculpted by Carl Jensen. The steer is branded "88" and the base is decorated with area brands.

42. Mountain sheep (1999)
The sculpture, executed by Bill Davis of Cody, is one of several statues on the campus of Northwest College, Powell. The sheep statue is in the lobby of the Science-Math Building.

43. "Washakie — Chief of the Shoshone" (2000)
The work by R. V. Greeves is one of more than 20 outdoor sculptures on the grounds of the Buffalo Bill Historical Center in Cody. Greeves also sculpted a monumental work of Crazy Horse that was placed on the BBHC grounds in 1997.

44. Martin Luther King Jr. (2000)
The bust weighing 300 pounds, was placed in Martin Luther King Park in west Cheyenne. The work, by Lupe Barajas, local sculptor, was dedicated Aug. 26, 2000. Barajas also sculpted the large baseball mitt bronze installed near the three baseball diamonds in Cheyenne's Brimmer Park in 2001.

45. "CY Right of Way" (2002)
The sculpture by J. C. Dye is located at the corner of CY Avenue and Wyoming Avenue. It was the first of the "gateway" sculptures commissioned to welcome visitors at various roads leading into the city of Casper.

46. "Carolina Panther" (2003)
The sculpture piece decorates the home stadium of the NFL football team in Charlotte, N. C. The sculpture was crafted in Lander in the Eagle Bronze foundry.

47. "Man Made Energy" (2005)
Seth Vandable was the sculptor who created the two-and-a-half time life size bronze monument depicting four prominent local oilmen (Fred Goodstein, Mick McMurry, Dave True, and John Wold) working on the floor of a drilling rig. Installed in the summer of 2005, the bronze sculpture stands at the north exit of Hat 6 Road on I-25 east of Casper.

48. Grinnell Plaza sculptures (2004-2007)

Works by several sculptors are located at the site.

49. "Circle of Friends" (2005)

The sculpture by K. E. Crain is located at the Sheridan/Fulmer Library.

50. "Jim Bridger" (2008)

The 8½ foot tall statue of Jim Bridger was unveiled and dedicated on August 8, 2008 at Fort Bridger State Historic Site. The statue by Lander sculptor David Clark was commissioned by the Fort Bridger Historical Association in 2004 and cast at Eagle Bronze, Lander. Clark was a 1977 graduate of Green River High School. His statue of John Wesley Powell is at the entrance of the Sweetwater County Museum and dedicated in 2003.

51. "Three Mule Deer" (2008)

The 13-foot bronze sculpture of three mule deer, created by local Cheyenne artist Guadalupe Barajas, was installed at the Wyoming governors' residence in October 2008.

52. "Last of the Buffalo" (2009)

The bronze by Michael B. Coleman is at the entrance of the Draper Museum of Natural History. It joins 22 other outdoor sculptures at the Buffalo Bill Historical Center in Cody.

10 Sculptures on War Memorials

1. "Spanish American War Memorial" (1899)

The 1899 legislature appropriated $1,000 for the sculpture honoring the memory of Wyoming volunteers who died in the Spanish American War. The statue stands on the southeast corner of the State Capitol grounds.

2. "Doughboy Monument" (c. 1920)

The work is in Bunning Park, Rock Springs, and is dedicated to Rock Springs men who died in World War I. In recent years, vandals broke the hand and rifle off the sculpture and defaced the plaque.

3. "Uinta County War Memorial" (c. 1920)

Sculptor of the bronze figure is not known. The piece, on a tall base, is on the grounds of the Uinta County Courthouse.

4. Sweetwater County War Memorial (1923)

The work by E. M. Viquesney (1876-1946) is located in Bunning Park, Rock Springs. The bronze statue was dedicated Mayk 30, 1923.

5. Albany County War Memorial (1924)

Originally, the sculpture was located in the middle of the intersection of 2nd Street and Garfield in downtown Laramie. The statue was moved to the Albany County Courthouse grounds after numerous mishaps with vehicles knocking the piece from its base. It was dedicated at its current location in 1924.

6. First World War Memorial Cross (1924)

On July 4, 1924, the First World War Memorial Cross was dedicated on the grounds of St. Matthews Episcopal Cathedral.

7. Vietnam Women's Memorial (1993)

Green River native Robert Desmond was one of two artists selected to design the Memorial, placed in the Mall National Park in Washington, D. C., in 1993. He collaborated with Eileen Rose Barry of East Islip, N. Y., on the project which incorporated concepts from both competition winners. Desmond, a landscape architect, lived in Arlington, Mass.

8. Native American War Memorial (incomplete)

Lander sculptor Lynn Burnette Sr., Lander, designed the memorial for the Native American War Dead Memorial Foundation in Iowa. A heroic statue was planned as part of a proposed $1 million memorial.

9. Wyoming National Guard monument, Cheyenne (1994)

Cheyenne sculptor Dan Garrett won the commission to execute the privately funded monument honoring Wyoming's guardsmen, located on the northwest corner of the Barrett Building block on 24th and Central Avenue in Cheyenne. It was dedicated June 18, 1994.

10. Vietnam War Soldier, Big Piney (2008)

The statue by Tom White is located in Plainview Memorial Veterans Cemetery, Big Piney, Wyoming. It was dedicated in November 2008.

10 Sculptures on College Campuses in Wyoming

1. "Benjamin Franklin" (1956)

The sculpture by Robert Russin, located south of the Arts and Sciences Building on the campus of the University of Wyoming, was presented to the university by three Cheyenne philanthropists, the Richardson family--Warren, Clarence and M. Valeria.

2. "Dinosaur" (1964)

The work is actually a reconstruction of a giant tyrannosaurus rex, a huge dinosaur which once roamed Wyoming. Legendary geology professor Samuel Knight directed the construction of the model made from copper plates. It was dedicated April 11, 1964.

3. "University of Wyoming Family" (1983)

Robert Russin's sculpture is a seven-foot circular, interlocking figure of a father, mother and child. It was made from white Italian marble and placed in the center of "Prexy's Pasture" on the university campus in 1983.

4. "The Trapper" (1986)

The welded sheet metal work by Ross Welfl was dedicated on the campus of Northwest College in Powell in 1986.

5. "A Lasting Legacy" (1990)

The iron and stainless steel sculpture was designed by Sandra L. Rieb and sculpted by Leland J. Vetter. It was dedicated in 1990 on the grounds of Eastern Wyoming College.

6. "Fanning a Twister" (1990)

Cody sculptor Peter Fillerup sculpted the 14-foot-high bronze statue of Steamboat, the famous bucking horse and an unidentified rider. The work was commissioned by Jeff and Greg Taggart of the Taggart Co., Cody, and placed on the grounds of the Arena-Auditorium at UW. It was unveiled during the homecoming celebration on Oct. 13, 1990. Fillerup also sculpted the statue of "Liver-eating Johnson" on Johnson's grave in Cody.

7 "Rising Promise" (1991)

The bronze sculpture was executed by Fremont County sculptor Gerald Shippen. Dedicated Sept. 28, 1991, on the lawn of the Arts Center at Central Wyoming College, the sculpture was entirely made on the CWC campus. Shippen also sculpted "Gift of the Smoking Waters" (*previous page*) and "Statue of Justice" for the Lincoln County Courthouse, Kemmerer.

8. "Spirit of the Thunderbird" (1995)

The 15-foot bronze sculpture, dedicated during 50th anniversary ceremonies at Casper College in September, 1995, was done by Chris Navarro, a Casper College graduate.

9. "Catching the Spirit" (2004)

The sculpture of an eagle preparing to catch prey was created by Vince Valdez. It is at the front entrance of Laramie County Community College, Albany County branch.

10. "Socrates" (2009)

The sculpture by Jerry Palen in front of the University of Wyoming College of Law building was dedicated in September 2009. He also did the two bronzes along the airport parkway in Cheyenne, the girl with a kite and the boy with the airplane.

SHIPS

1st steamboat on Wyoming waters: Although evidence is contradictory, the El Paso in the spring of 1852 is said to have steamed up the North Platte River as far as present-day Guernsey Dam.

1st boat on Yellowstone Lake: The Annie, named for Anna L. Dawes, daughter of U. S. Senator H. L. Dawes of Iowa. The boat was brought from Salt Lake City and assembled on the lake.

1st steamboat on Yellowstone Lake: The Zillah, a 40-ton sightseeing vessel, was transported in pieces to the park and reassembled during the winter of 1888-89. The boat, once used on the Great Lakes, carried a maximum of 125 passengers and operated on Yellowstone Lake until about 1916.

1st steamboat on the Green River: Said to be the first steamboat used for commercial purposes in Wyoming, the Comet was launched amid much fanfare at Green River on the Fourth of July, 1908. Sandbars caused the vessel to run aground frequently and after several trips down the river into Utah, the Comet became a sightseeing vessel in the Green River area only. Sometime in the 'teens, the hull of the abandoned vessel was sunk into the river at Green River.

1st ferry across the Big Horn River: Operated by J. D. Woodruff, the ferry operated near present-day Thermopolis.

1st scenic float trips on the Snake River: Started in 1956 by the Grand Teton Lodge Company.

River rafters: Barker-Ewing of Jackson began rafting the Snake River in 1963 with 140 passengers. The partnership broke into two companies in 1985 and in 1995, the two firms carried their millionth rafter. The combined businesses carried about 40,000 passengers annually.

Caribbean scuba diving vessel: Casper residents Clay McCardell and Sarah Moody owned a 100-foot diving vessel based in St. Marteen. It was named the top overall scuba vessel in a reader's survey made by *Scuba Diving* magazine in 1995.

Noteworthy Voyages by Wyomingites

1. 1st successful navigation of the Amazon River, South America

Piotr Chmielinski of Casper and Joe Kane of San Francisco paddled the 4,200 miles from Aug. 29, 1985 to February 1986. The support team was Zbigniew Bzdak of Casper and Kate Durrant, London. The trip began atop 17,800-foot Mt. Mismi in the Peruvian Andes, the Amazon's source, and ended in the Atlantic Ocean past Marajo Island. Five previous expeditions had made attempts, but failed, three fatally. One 50-mile stretch of whitewater rapids had never before been run.

2. Cody to St. Louis by water

In the summer of 1904, the Holms brothers of Cody took a boat down the Shoshone River into the Big Horn, then the Missouri and Mississippi Rivers to St. Louis. Although fur trappers made similar voyages, this was the earliest such boat trip on record between the two places by non-trappers.

3. Fastest trans-Atlantic boat crossing

Jeff Brown of Jackson was crewman on the Proud Bird, a $6 million, 110-foot boat built in 1988 by speed racer Tom Gentry. The boat broke the trans-Atlantic mark by making the run in three days, eight hours, 40 minutes.

4. 1st successful navigation of the Green-Colorado River system

Major John Wesley Powell commanded a three-boat flotilla down the river system. The expedition left the town of Green River only two weeks after Union Pacific tracks had reached the point in 1869. Powell's "flagship," the Emma Dean, was an oak boat built in Chicago. Powell's historic trip down the river and through the Grand Canyon has been the subject of several books and motion pictures. The Wyoming city of Powell was named for him as well as Lake Powell on the Colorado River behind Glen Canyon Dam.

The kayak runs along the North Platte River in west Casper contain 17 million tons of rock. Construction of the course was completed on July 15, 2003.

5 Ships Named "Wyoming"

1. U. S. S. Wyoming (1859)

Named for the Wyoming Valley of Pennsylvania, the first Wyoming was launched in January 1859 and remained in service until 1882.

2. U. S. S. Wyoming (1900)

The second Wyoming was a monitor launched in 1900 at Vallejo, California, and assigned to duty along the coast of Panama until 1904. After a cruise to the Seattle area and back to Central America, the ship was converted to oil fuel in 1908, the first ship so fitted in the U. S. Navy. Renamed the U. S. S. Cheyenne, the ship was finally decommissioned in 1926 and sold for scrap in April 1939.

3. Wyoming, six-masted wooden schooner (1909)

The Wyoming, launched in 1909, was the largest wooden vessel ever built. The ship was named for the state because Gov. B. B. Brooks made private investments in wooden shipbuilding during the time he was governor, including a vessel named for him launched two years earlier. The Wyoming was built by the Percy and Small shipyard in Bath, Maine. The ship carried coal fromVirginia to New England ports until it was sold in 1917 to the French government for hauling war materials to Europe. In 1921, the ship was sold again and returned to service as a collier. The ship disappeared in a hurricane off Cape Cod on March 12, 1924. Nothing was ever found of the ship or its crew of 15. *Source: Francois M. Dickman, "America's Largest Wooden Vessel: The Six Masted Schooner Wyoming," Annals of Wyoming 66 (Spring-Summer, 1994).*

4. U. S. S. Wyoming (1911)

The battleship was launched from Philadelphia and became the flagship for the Atlantic Fleet in 1912. During World War I, the ship escorted other vessels in the British Isles. From 1926-1927, the ship's executive officer was Commander William F. Halsey, Jr., the future fleet admiral. Until World War II, the ship served mostly as a training vessel for midshipmen and members of ROTC units. During the war, the old battleship served as a gunnery training ship. An estimated 35,000 navy gunners learned their craft aboard the Wyoming during World War II and the ship set a record for firing the most ammunition of any Navy ship. The ship was decommissioned in August 1947, and sold for scrap to Lipset Company of New York on Dec. 5, 1947. During his navy career, Jimmy Carter served as an officer aboard the Wyoming. The hull number of the Wyoming was BB-32.

5. U. S. S. Wyoming (1996)

The second-to-last Trident nuclear missile submarine, the U. S. S. Wyoming was launched on July 13, 1996, from New London, Conn. The 560-foot, 18,000-ton vessel is homeported from Kings Bay, Georgia. Gov. Jim Geringer and other state dignitaries attended the launching ceremonies, held in the Dealey Center auditorium at the Naval Submarine Base because of inclement weather caused by the remains of Hurricane Bertha.

U. S. Navy Ships Named for Wyoming Towns

1. U. S. S. Sheridan

An attack transport, the Sheridan was used at Tarawa, Okinawa and elsewhere in the Pacific during World War II where the vessel earned six battle stars. Sold in 1947, the

---

In May, 1957, Wyoming descendants of individuals who had come to America on the Mayflower organized as the Wyoming chapter of the Mayflower Society. Ward Husted of Laramie was elected the group's first governor.

Sheridan was renamed the American Scientist. The ship was damaged by an explosion in July 1969, and later scrapped.

2. - 5. U. S. S. Cheyenne (five different vessels)

1st: A tug launched in 1885, it was used in Cuba in 1898; sold in 1900.

2nd: Launched as the U. S. S. Wyoming on Sept. 8, 1900, the ship was renamed on Jan. 1, 1909. It was the first U. S. Navy vessel to be converted to fuel oil. It was decommissioned in 1926 and sold in 1939.

3rd: The name was assigned to a Light Cruiser late in World War II but the contract for the vessel was canceled in August 1945.

4th: Launched in 1945, the vessel was named the U. S. S. Cheyenne on Nov. 20, 1962. Still in service, the tanker carries a civilian crew.

5th: The last of the Los Angeles class nuclear submarines, the U. S. S. Cheyenne was launched April 1, 1995, at Newport News, Va. Ann Simpson, the wife of U. S. Senator Al Simpson, struck the vessel with a champagne bottle, officially launching it. The vessel was commissioned in August, 1996.

6. U. S. S. Green River

A land troop ship, the Green River was launched April 28, 1945, in Texas. The ship was decommissioned in 1946 and sold in 1958.

7. U. S. S. Laramie

An oil tanker, the Laramie was launched in 1921 and served in the Atlantic in World War II. The ship was sold in 1947.

8. U. S. S. Casper

The Casper, a patrol escort, was launched Dec. 27, 1943, at Kaiser Shipyard, California. The vessel served in weather patrol in the Pacific during World War II. It was decommissioned in 1946 and sold in May 1947.

9. U. S. S. Worland

An escort vessel launched in December 1943, at Chicago, the Worland operated from Pearl Harbor during World War II. Later, the ship was a patrol craft on the Great Lakes. Named the Worland on Feb. 15, 1956, the vessel was struck from the Navy list in 1964. It became a training/research ship near Wilmington, N. C.

10. U. S. S. Manderson Victory

Launched Sept. 23, 1944, the Manderson Victory served in Okinawa during World War II. The Navy leased the ship to private interests as a freighter in 1966.

U. S. Navy Ships Named for Wyoming Natives

1. U. S. S. Mills

Named for Lloyd J. Mills, a naval aviator killed in World War II in the Aleutians. Mills was born in Rock Springs July 3, 1917. The ship, an escort vessel, was launched May 26, 1943. The Mills saw service in the Mediterranean and after World War II, in China. She was retired in 1946, but recommissioned in 1957, serving in Antarctica in 1964. Since 1968, the Mills has been a naval training ship at Baltimore.

2. U. S. S. Eisele

Named for George R. Eisele, a Seaman 2nd Class killed on the U. S. S. San Francisco at Guadalcanal on Nov. 12, 1942. Eisele was born in Gillette May 15, 1923. The ship, a

---

Sacajawea's likeness is on the dollar coin, first minted in 2000. Randy 'L Teton of Fort Hall, Idaho, posed for sculptor Glenna Goodacre of Santa Fe who executed the portrait of the Wyoming woman who had accompanied Lewis and Clark west..

destroyer escort, was launched June 29, 1943, serving in the Pacific in World War II. The ship was sold in 1948.

3. U. S. S. Washakie

A large harbor tug, the Washakie was launched Feb. 13, 1944, and named for the Shoshone chief born in Wyoming about 1800. The ship served in the Central Pacific in World War II, and from 1953 to 1975, it was assigned to Mayport, Florida. The name was struck from the naval list in 1975.

4. U. S. S. Sacajawea

A harbor tug, the vessel was bought from Brazil by the Navy in 1942 for service at Charleston (S. C.) harbor. After the war, the Sacajawea was sold to foreign buyers. Sacajawea, the Shoshone woman who accompanied Lewis and Clark on the expedition west, may have been born in Wyoming.

5. U. S. S. McInerney

A guided missile frigate commissioned in 1978, the ship was named for Adm. Francis X. McInerney who was born in Cheyenne in 1899. A Naval Academy graduate, McInerney commanded the allied destroyer forces in the Battle of Coral Sea during World War II. Later, he was captain of the battleship U. S. S. Washington. During the Korean War, he commanded all naval amphibious forces in the Far East. He retired in 1955 and died in 1956.

3 Ships Named Yellowstone

1. U. S. S. Yellowstone (1917)

The first Yellowstone was a freighter launched at Oakland in December 1917. The ship carried supplies to Europe, but the war ended before she reached port on her maiden voyage. After two more trips to Europe, the Yellowstone ran aground in the Azores and sank on Dec. 10, 1920. All 45 members of the crew were rescued.

2. U. S. S. Yellowstone (1945)

A destroyer tender, the second Yellowstone was launched at Tacoma, Washington, April 12, 1945. The ship became part of the Atlantic Fleet where it was recognized as the "Old Faithful" of the fleet for the next 28 years. The ship cruised the Mediterranean ten times before it was decommissioned in September 1974 and sold a year later.

3. U. S. S. Yellowstone (1979)

The latest Yellowstone, also a destroyer tender, was launched at San Diego on Jan. 27, 1979. The ship is part of the Pacific Fleet.

Beaver Dick Leigh, pioneer Jackson Hole, kept a daily diary. His biography quoting the exact spelling: "I am the son of Richard Leigh formely of the Britesh navey and grand son of James Leigh formly of the 16-lancers england. I was borne on January 9th in 1831 in the city of Manchester England. Come with my sister to philadelphia usa when i was 7 years old. went for the Mexcin war at close II'48 atched to E co [company] 1st infantry 10 months when come to rocky mountains and here i die."

SNAKES
9 Species of Snakes Inhabiting Wyoming

1. Prairie Rattlesnake
Snakes have been seen swimming in Pathfinder and Seminoe reservoirs.
2. Rubber boa
A rare, brown-colored snake found in northwest Wyoming.
3. Plains hognose
4. Yellowbelly racer
5. Smooth green snake
6. Gopher snake
7. Bull snake
In 1992, it was reported that a Florida herpetological center was selling bull snakes taken from the Thunder Basin area for $80 each to be sold as pets. Up to 1,000 a week were being sold and the Wyoming Game and Fish Department asked for authority to stop the practice.
8. Garter snake
9. Pale milk snake
Source: George Baxter and Michael Stone. Reptiles and Amphibians of Wyoming. (Cheyenne: Game and Fish Commission).

Amazing Snake Stories

1. Tobacco Juice and Snake Eyes
Mountain man Jack Stillwell and a partner hid from hostile Indians in a buffalo wallow in what was otherwise a flat prairie. Both men were afoot so they were able to keep low enough to stay out of sight of the mounted warriors. Suddenly, a huge rattlesnake crawled into the wallow and headed straight for them. They both froze, knowing that any attempt to kill the snake would alert the Indians of their presence. The snake continued its uncomfortable course until Jack hit on an idea. He had been chewing tobacco all day and as the snake moved closer, he let fly a mouthful of tobacco juice which splashed all over the snake's head. Temporarily blinded and confused, the snake turned around and crawled out of the wallow. The Indians soon dispersed and Jack and his partner walked to safety, both glad Jack had a disgusting habit and good aim.

2. Under a bunk with a skunk
The following news item appeared in the *Lusk Herald*, Oct. 8, 1886: "The boys of the CR ranch got after a skunk the other day when the animal took refuge under one of their beds which had been taken to a shed for comfort during the summer. In pulling the bed around to get at the animal, a rattlesnake was disturbed from his slumber and came crawling out of the blankets. The reptile was 4 1/2 feet in length and was ornamented with 15 rattles."

3. Bouncing off hard hats
The highway construction crew building I-25 near Chugwater in the 1960s had to dig a large cut through a rocky hillside. In the course of digging, the crewmen happened upon a snake den loaded with rattlers in various states of hibernation. There were more snakes than they could kill with shovels, so the foreman thought of a novel way to eliminate the

For many years, a rattlesnake skin measuring 8'4" long has hung above the cash register at the Mint Bar, Sheridan. The bar also has on display a pair of whitetail deer heads, the antlers locked together.

reptiles. Why not dynamite the den? A worker set the charge and the blast brought cheers from the rest of the construction crew, huddled behind nearby rocks. Suddenly, long scaly things started falling out of the sky, bouncing off the workers' hard hats. The dynamite sent the snakes skyward, but in doing so, it managed only to wake many of them. As the scrambling construction workers discovered, a snake awakened by a dynamite blast and a long fall from the air is not in the best of moods.

4. A snake and the keys

In July 1984, Mary Howe of Basin went outside to pull weeds in her garden, but before leaving the house, she clipped her keys to her bra strap. Near her porch, she reached to pull a weed and a rattlesnake struck, hitting her in the chest. The fangs penetrated her blouse and embedded in the keys. Howe reacted instinctively—she made a grab and caught the snake in the back of the head. Giving a mighty pull, the snake came loose, leaving two large holes in the blouse. Now, the elderly lady had hold of a snake and couldn't let go. Going into the house, snake clutched tightly, she tried to call the Basin police but couldn't get through. So, she put the snake's head between the cabinet door and the cabinet frame, grabbed a butcher knife and whacked off its head. After her experience, Howe told the reporter: "I'd advise everybody, men and women alike, to carry their keys on their bra straps." The story about the incident was written for the *Basin Republican-Rustler* by Marlys Good. Paul Harvey and national media ran the unusual story.

5. Extinct Snakes

The midget faded rattlesnake, once numerous in Flaming Gorge area, was probably wiped out by 1992.

6. 29 Rattles, 7 Feet Long

Wyoming newspapers reported in August, 1932, that Thomas Green had killed a rattlesnake seven feet long, "as thick as a man's arm," and having 29 rattles. The snake was found in Johnson County.

4 Species of Wyoming Turtles

1. Western spiny softshell

The turtle can grow up to 18 inches long in Wyoming waters.

2. Snapping turtle

3. Box turtle

4. Western painted turtle

The Wyoming Toad: An Endangered Species

The Wyoming Toad, formally known as the Bufo hemiophyrys baxteri (the latter name, in honor of former UW professor George Baxter), is believed to have inhabited the Laramie Basin since the last ice age. In the 1970s, the species was still numerous, but the population declined sharply in the early 1980s. Only 100 adult Wyoming toads remained on earth and the species was designated endangered in January 1984. The two-inch long, black and green spotted amphibians lived on the shallow edges of a privately-owned lake southwest of Laramie. In 1990, the owners of the lake sold 1,800 acres, including the lake site home of the toads, to the Nature Conservancy. The conservancy promised to protect the amphibian. The Wyoming Game and Fish Department began a captive breeding program for the Wyoming toad at the department's Sybille research center in the summer of 1989. Biologists conducted a "toad roundup" in 1990 in which 80 adults and 200 hatchling toads were found. By 2009, a number of other captive breeding programs were underway at varoius research centers and zoos, including the Toledo Zoo (Ohio), the St. Louis Zoo, Detroit Zoo, Philadelphia Zoo and Saratoga National Fish Hatchery (Wyoming).

STATE SYMBOLS

1st American flag raised over Wyoming: John C. Fremont raised a 26-star U. S. flag atop Mount Woodrow Wilson, Wind River Range, Aug. 15, 1842. The flag, designed by Fremont's wife, included more than the usual stars and stripes. Mrs. Fremont included an outline of an American eagle within the design.

1st state flag: Before 1916, the state flag was simply the state seal printed in the center of a blue field. It was the flag carried by Wyoming National Guardsmen to the Philippines in the Spanish American War. The present state flag featuring the figure of the buffalo was drawn by Verna Keyes for a DAR sponsored contest in 1916.

Statues in the U. S. Capitol Statuary Hall: Esther Hobart Morris, placed in April, 1960; Chief Washakie, placed in September, 2000.

State Flower: Indian paintbrush (Castillija linariaefolia), 1917.

State Bird: Meadowlark (American icteroid), 1927.

State Tree: Cottonwood (Populus Sargentii), 1947.

State Motto: "Equal Rights," adopted in 1955.

State Stone: Jade, 1967.

State Song: "Wyoming," words by Charles E. Winter, music by George E. Knapp, 1955.

> *1st Verse:* In the far and mighty West,
> Where the crimson sun seeks rest,
> There's a growing, splendid state that lies above
> On the breast of this great land;
> Where the massive Rockies stand,
> That's Wyoming young and strong, the state I love!
>
> *Chorus:* Wyoming, Wyoming! Land of the sunlight clear!
> Wyoming, Wyoming! Land that we hold so dear!
> Wyoming, Wyoming! Precious art thou and thine!
> Wyoming, Wyoming! Beloved state of mine!

State Mammal: Bison, 1985.

State Fossil: Fossilized fish Knightia, 1987.

State Fish: Cutthroat trout (Salmo clarki), 1987.

State Reptile: Horned toad. In 1993, Larry Hodgson's 3rd grade class at Gertrude Burns School in Newcastle began a campaign to make the horned toad the official state reptile.

State Dinosaur: Triceratops. The choice was made by a vote of 650 Wyoming schoolchildren in the spring of 1994. Wyoming was the first state to choose an official state dinosaur.

Wyoming now has a nearly full complement of state symbols.

In 1991, the legislature failed to designate an official state insect. The bipartisan bill to make the Pailio glaucus (tiger swallowtail butterfly) the official insect failed in committee.

Unlike several other states, Wyoming has no official state dog (Virginia's is the foxhound), state dance (Washington's is the square dance), state neck wear (Arizona's is the bolo tie), or state food (New Mexico's is chili and frijoles). Such omissions may allow future state legislatures to debate adoption of several more state symbols....

Legend has it that the name "Hole-in-the-Wall" was first used by cowboy Alfred Smith, a resident of the area, when he signed the guest register at the Occidental Hotel in Buffalo and put the phrase down as his address.

STREETS AND HIGHWAYS

1st graveled road in Wyoming: Douglas Good Roads Club spread gravel on chuckholes in roads in the Douglas area about 1910.

1st paved road in Wyoming: Probably, a short stretch of highway north of Casper used by trucks and wagons en route to the Salt Creek oil field before World War I.

1st contract awarded for interstate construction in Wyoming: Sept. 26, 1956, for a 10.1-mile section north of Cheyenne on I-25 between the Whitaker Road interchange and the turn-off to US 85.

Last segment of Interstate highway completed in Wyoming: 26.5 miles of I-25 between Casper and Kaycee, opened Feb. 2, 1982.

1st painting of stripes at highway curves: On August 16, 1932, the Wyoming Highway Commission determined that orange would be color to paint stripes at highway curves.

1st Wyoming town to seek a highway bypass to divert traffic away from downtown: Jackson, 1965.

1st federal appropriation for highway construction in Wyoming: $61,200 awarded in 1917.

1st road from Cody to Yellowstone National Park: Northfork road, 1900. In 1996, a five-year project began to rebuild the highway which had not been rebuilt since the 1930s. Estimated cost was $50 million.

2nd least traveled stretch of Interstate highway in the United States: I-25 between Buffalo and Casper, fewer than 2,500 vehicles per day, according to the U. S. Department of Transportation, Nov. 24, 1995.

Average per capita miles traveled on interstate highway routes: 17,735 miles, highest per capita in the nation (Oct. 2008)

Speed limit: In 1974, in light of the "energy crisis," President Richard Nixon ordered reduction in speed limits. The legislature reduced the limit on Wyoming highways to 55 mph. Raising national speed limits was authorized by the Bill Clinton administration in 1995. On Dec. 8, 1995, the Wyoming limit was raised to 75 mph on interstates and 65 mph elsewhere.

Wyoming's busiest interstate highway (1999): 14,365 cars per day used I-25 south of Cheyenne. This was an increase from 13,815 the previous year.

Wyoming's busiest urban highway: The I-80 viaduct in Cheyenne, counting 19,917 vehicles in an average day in 1999.

Highest single-day total vehicles on a Wyoming highway: 32,164, counting motorcycles en route to Sturgis, S. D., on Aug. 11, 1999, on I-90, east of Beulah.

Worst highway in state for big game animal fatalities: Highway 22 from Jackson to Wilson, Highway 390 from Wilson to Teton Village. At least five moose were killed during winter of 1992-1993 along the highway.

Most dangerous intersection: More accidents were recorded at the corner of Converse and Dell Range in north Cheyenne than at any other in Wyoming (1999-2009)

5 Wyoming Streets with Unusual Names

1. "Straight and Narrow Drive" --Evanston
2. "Obie Sue" --Worland
3. "Hog Eye" --Gillette
4. "Hobbit Hole" --Douglas
5. "Ram's Horn" --Dubois

Street Name Derivations in Various Wyoming Towns

1. Company Officers

Cody's north-south streets are numbered, but most of the older east-west streets were named for partners in the Shoshone Irrigation Company, formed by William F. Cody and George W. Beck in 1897. Partners included Nate Salisbury, Bronson Rumsey, Henry Gerrans

> The sign outside Upton says: "Best Town on Earth." Signs with that statement have been erected there since at least 1903.

and George Bleistein, among others. The town's main street, Sheridan Avenue, was named for the town where the company had been formed. Worland's streets, including Coburn, Culbertson and Howell, were named for several officials of the Hanover Canal Company.

2. Survey Crewmen

Many of the original Cheyenne streets were named for members of Gen. Grenville Dodge's survey party. Several streets, including the one named for Dodge, were renamed as years passed. Dodge was renamed "Warren Avenue" in honor of Sen. Francis E. Warren. Ferguson was changed to "Carey Avenue" in honor of Senator/Governor Joseph M. Carey. Eddy became "Pioneer Avenue" while Hill was renamed "Capitol Avenue." Present Central Avenue was known as "Ransom."

3. Explorers and Generals

Laramie's original east-west streets are named for explorers or military heroes. They include Garfield, Custer, Kearney, Lewis, Clark, Canby, Gibbon, Fremont, Ord, Russell, Steele, Sanders, Sully and Fetterman. Ivinson Avenue was once known as "Thornburgh" in honor of T. T. Thornburgh, killed by Indians south of Rawlins in 1879. The name was changed in the 1920s to honor Laramie banker Edward Ivinson whose home was located on the street. Numerous other towns have streets named for military officers and explorers. Both Rock Springs and Green River have streets named for Major John Wesley Powell. General John J. Pershing, hero of World War I and husband of Senator F. E. Warren's daughter, has streets named for him in Cheyenne, Lusk and Riverton. In Pinedale, streets are named for trappers Colter, Ashley, Bonneville, Stuart, Sublette and Bridger.

4. Trees

Numerous towns have streets named for trees. Lusk, Glenrock, Douglas, Rock Springs, Medicine Bow, Rawlins, Sundance, Wheatland and Kemmerer each have "tree streets." The main street in Pinedale is "Pine Street."

5. U. S. Presidents

At least nine Wyoming towns have honored presidents by naming streets for them. They include Afton, Casper, Douglas, Green River, Laramie (West Laramie), Pinedale, Riverton and Rock Springs. Sheridan has five streets named for Presidents: Washington, Harrison, Cleveland, Jackson, and Jefferson.

6. Main Street

The ubiquitous symbol of middle America, "Main Street" is present in no fewer than 11 Wyoming towns. These include Buffalo, Evanston, Kemmerer, Lander, Lovell, Newcastle, Riverton, Saratoga, Sheridan, Sundance and Torrington. The primary business street in Lusk is often called "Main Street" but its official name is "Cedar Street."

7. States

Streets in Lovell, Meeteetse, Medicine Bow, Basin and Green River are named for states. Most common are Wyoming, Montana, Colorado and Utah.

8. Government Officials

Gillette has streets named for Governors Brooks, Miller, Osborne, Emerson and Kendrick. Long-time congressman Frank C. Mondell was honored by street names in Thermopolis and Meeteetse. Evanston has streets named for 20 Wyoming governors, including recent holders of the office Hathaway, Herschler and Sullivan. Cheyenne renamed two of its streets for hometown government officials F. E. Warren and Joseph M. Carey. Lusk renamed a street for Frank Barrett, a Lusk resident who served as U. S. Representative, Governor and U. S. Senator. Simpson Avenue in Cody honors the late Sen./Gov. Milward

---

The first two snowmobiles in Casper were owned by Bob Adams, Natrona County Parks manager, and Frank Hazelton, Texaco mechanic (1960).

Simpson whose home was located on that street. Laramie streets in Family Housing (many of the units demolished in 2010) were named for university officials including former UW president and Wyoming governor Arthur G. Crane and botanist/UW president Aven Nelson. UW alumnus Emory S. Land and U. S. Senators Kendrick and Warren are honored with streets in that area, too. Laramie's Willett Drive is named for the town's first city manager, D. B. Willett, who was named to the post in January 1943. In Sept. 1993, the Torrington Town Council renamed a street for Police Lt. Harley Mark, killed in a car wreck Sept. 6 while searching for an escapee. The street is west of Pioneer Park in Torrington.

9. Letters of the Alphabet

This arrangement is relatively common in Wyoming. For instance, Torrington's major north-south streets are designated by letters. Newcastle uses an unusual variation on lettering. The name of nearly every street begins with either a "w" or "s." One set runs parallel to the other. Laramie's east-west streets were originally designated by letters of the alphabet. Starting from "Center Street" (now University), the streets were to the north: North A (Fremont), North B (Clark) and to the south, South A (Ivinson), South B (Grand). They were renamed for explorers and generals about 1900. The streets in Point of Rocks, although few in number, start with letters from A to Z--one street is Arwood, a second is Zanoni. The third street in town is named "Halter and Flick." In Sheridan, the "high school hill" streets are named alphabetically: Adair, Bellevue, Clarendon, Delphi, Exeter, Florence, Greystone, Highland, Idaho, Jackson and Kentucky.

10. Indians or Indian Tribes

Common names include Arapaho, Shoshone (or Shoshoni), and Washakie. Lander, Thermopolis and Glenrock are among the towns having streets named for Indian tribes. In 1992, the Wyoming Transportation Commission voted to rename the 141-mile stretch of state highway between Fort Washakie and Rawlins as the "Chief Washakie Trail."

11. Pioneers

Numerous towns honor pioneers or pioneer families with names of streets. They include Buffalo (Holland, Angus and Gatchell), Wheatland (Cole and Gilchrist), Casper (Wolcott, Kimball and Durbin), Jackson (Simpson, Deloney, Hansen, Pearl), and Lander (Amoretti). Thermpolis also has Amoretti Street. Sheridan's first streets were named for pioneers—north and south (Brooks, Gould, Scott) and east and west (Burkitt, Works, Loucks, Brundage and Grinnell).

12. Other Towns and Counties

Sheridan Avenue, Cody's main street, is named for the town of Sheridan where the idea of the town was hatched by William F. Cody and George Beck. A neighborhood in northeast Cheyenne has streets named for Rawlins, Rock Springs and other Wyoming towns. Also, Cheyenne has streets named for Wyoming counties but only alphabetically from Albany through Platte. A neighborhood in north Torrington has streets named for a number of Wyoming counties. Streets in southwest Evanston are named for several Wyoming towns. Green River has streets named for Chugwater, Sundance and Saratoga.

The "Elkhorn Arch" located over Afton's main street is the world's largest. It spans 75 feet across Washington Street (Highway 89) in the middle of downtown. The top of the arch is 24 feet high and made of 3,011 antlers. Two smaller walk-way arches are included in the structure. The work was inspired by Newell and Blanche Gardner who collected and donated more than half of the antlers. Gardner, the local game warden, persuaded the Wyoming Game and Fish Department to donate the remainder. The smaller side arches were designed and built by Gardner in 1956. The street arch was completed by community volunteers in the summer of 1958.

13. "Cute" Names with Absolutely No Connection to the Area

Modern subdivision developers are often guilty of naming streets whimsically for the way the name sounds—how it may convey status or "character" to an otherwise undistinguished subdivision. Nearly every Wyoming town has been victimized by this practice in recent years. Do homes on such streets sell better or are there no names of local pioneers, native groups, historic figures, grand events or fallen heroes left to honor?

3 Holiday Periods with Most Fatal Traffic Accidents

1. Fourth of July (19) 2. Labor Day (15) 3. Thanksgiving (14)

Figures from the Wyoming Highway Department, 1980-84 totals. The occurrence of the most fatal accidents in one holiday period was when eight people were killed during the 1981 Fourth of July holiday. Six people died in car accidents during the Thanksgiving holiday, 1984.

Some Items about Travel

1. Ike and the Trucks

Just after World War I, the U. S. Army sent out a truck convoy to determine the condition of coast to coast vehicle travel. The 42 trucks, five passenger cars, assorted motorcycles and ambulances left Washington, D. C. on July 7, 1919, and arrived in San Francisco on Sept. 6, 1919. In the contingent was a young lieutenant colonel, Dwight D. Eishenhower, who remembered the experience more than 30 years later when he authorized the Interstate highway system.

2. Oregon Trail travel

Of Oregon Trail travelers, only 362 were killed by Indians between 1840-60. The worst year was 1851 with 60 killed. In 1851, 37 people drowned during the year, attempting to ford the Green River. It took an average of 121 days to reach Oregon. Exactly 487 miles of the Oregon Trail passes through what is now Wyoming.

8 Towns Named Wyoming

Wyoming, N. Y.	Wyoming, Michigan	Wyoming, Minn.
Wyoming, Iowa	Wyoming, Illinois	Wyoming, Delaware
Wyoming, R. I.	Wyoming, Penn.	

The Weston County museum district was the first to be created in Wyoming. Voters authorized creation of the district on June 13, 1996.

TAXES

1st Wyoming sales tax : 1935 was 2 percent.

1st sales tax increase: 1965, when the rate went up to 2 1/2 percent with an additional 1/2 percent city option. The state rate went to 3 percent in 1967.

1st county in Wyoming to pass optional lodging tax (2%): Teton County, 1986.

Federal money: Wyoming receives $1.11 for every dollar in taxes it sends to the federal government (2005) Tax payments were $4.2 billion, but the state received $4.8 billion from the federal government.

Mineral Severance Tax

Severance taxes are applied to the value of the mineral "at the point where the production process is complete, before processing and transportation." Thus, the severance tax is assessed on the value of the mineral product at the mine mouth or oil drilling site, regardless of whether it is produced on private, state or federal land. The tax is not based on the sale price the product which would include costs of shipping.

The first severance taxes were enacted in 1969 with a one percent rate on all minerals. Initially, the tax was based on the valuation of the prior year's production with payment due July 1 of each year. In 1981, the assessment was made on the current year's production.

The rate rose, across the board on all minerals in 1973, rose to three percent. From 1974, the rates for various minerals divurged. For instance, in 1974, oil, gas and trona (with the exception of stripper oil wells) were assessed at four percent, but the coal rate rose to 4.4 percent. Over the following four years, the rates for oil, gas and trona stayed at 3% while the rate for coal rose to 4.8% in 1975, 9.7% in 1976, 10.1% in 1977, and 10.5% in 1978. .In 1984, the rate on coal produced from underground mines was reduced to 7.25% while the surface coal rate remained at 10.5%. Both rates were reduced in 1987--underground coal to 5.25% and surface coal to 8.5%. In 1993, the rates were again reduced--to 3.75% on underground coal and 7% on surface coal. The rates on oil and natural gas remained consistent at 6% throughout the period to 2010.

The State of Wyoming received total severance tax revenues in 2006, for the first time in excess of $1 billion. The Wyoming severance tax is not a royalty. (Minerals produced on state lands provide a royalty to the state just as to any landowner).

The tax rate for all coal mines was one percent in 1970, rising to three percent in 1973; 4.4% in 1974; 4.8% in 1975; 9.7% in 1976; 10.1% in 1977; and 10.5 percent until 1984 when it was reduced for underground-mined coal to 7.25 percent. In 1987, the rate for strip-mined coal was reduced to 8.5 percent and the next year, the underground coal rate dropped to 5.25 percent. In 1993, the coal rate dropped to 7 % on surface coal and 3.75% on underground coal and that rate continued into the new millenium..

Oil has been taxed at rates from one to six percent, depending on the type of recovery. For all oil below $20 per barrel, the 1999 legislature dropped the rate to just 4 percent. The base rate went back up to six percent in 2004, but remained at four percent for stripper wells (those producing less than 15 barrels per day.

Natural gas had been taxed at six percent from 1980-85. The tax was reduced to 5.5 percent for most production in 1985 and dropped to four percent in 1999. In 2004, the rate returned to six percent. From 1976, the trona rate remained steady at 5.5 percent until 1999 when it was cut to just 4 percent. Crude oil and natural gas production paid $666 million in severance taxes, about 76% of all the severance taxes paid by minerals produced in 2006. The overall total of $803.6 million coming from severance taxes in 2007 represented 39.7 percent of all state revenues.

Trona is taxed in 2010 at a rate of four percent. Uranium, once taxed at 5.5 percent, went down to one percent in the late 1990s. The rate in 2010 was 4 percent.

Severance tax revenues are distributed to a variety of funds including: General Fund,

Permanent Mineral Trust Fund, schools, cities, towns, highways, counties and water development. The Permanent Mineral Trust Fund was created by constitutional amendment in 1974. Severance taxes of 1.5 percent on most minerals was designated for deposit in the fund. Until 2001, significant "ear-marking" was made, i.e., severance tax revenues from various sources were designated for specific funds. The legislature changed the process in 2001 so that while the Permananet Mineral Trust Fund continues to receive the constitutionally mandated 1.5% rate, the rest of the funds are sent to the Severance Tax Distribution Account where up to $155 million annually is distributed to nine separate accounts, the remainder above that amount distributed one-third to the state General Fund and two-thirds to the state Budget Reserve Account. The nine accounts include funding for cities and towns, counties, water projects, and highways. In 2006, cities and towns received $16.1 million of the $155 million while water accounts received the greatest amount, $23.6 million. More than $406 million went into the Permanent Mineral Trust Fund in 2006; $240 million in the general fund; and $280 million in the budget reserve account. The value of the Permanent Mineral Trust Fund (corpus) is approximately $3 billion (2009).
Source: Legislative Service Office report

Mineral Severance Tax Revenues in Recent Years
(in millions of dollars)

	Coal	Oil	Gas	Trona	Others	TOTAL
2002:	109.7	54.6	128	6	1	299,433,961
2003:	122.3	68.1	230	7.5	1.2	4299,26,222
2004:	133.3	71.6	349.7	7.8	1.2	563,566,928
2005:	148.9	101.1	465.9	9.1	1.6	726,656,854
2006:	180.8	133.8	673.4	9.8	3.2	1,001,076,918
2007:	182.4	131.3	3993	12.5	2.1	727,600,000
2008:	187.9	134.7	457	12.7	2.1	794,400,000

Calculating the Mineral Severance Taxes

How much money does the State get in severance taxes from a trainload of coal? Much Wyoming coal is shipped by rail to public utility power plants around the country, 100-tons per car. A train may have as many as 100 cars. If the coal is valued at $8 per ton (as recent quotes indicated), and with the severance tax rate at 7 percent of the value of the coal as determined at the mouth of the mine, the State of Wyoming would receive 56 cents per ton or about $56 for each carload of coal. (Until 1986, the tax was 10 1/2 percent, but the 2 percent coal impact tax expired in 1987; an additional 1 1/2 percent capital facilities tax expired in 1993). For hauling the coal, railroads may charge $40-45 or more for each ton of coal shipped--$4,500 per carload. The state gets just a bit more than that amount, about $5,600, for the entire trainload while the railroad receives $450,000 for hauling that one trainload of coal! With the mines receiving $8 per ton, the railroads getting $45 or more per ton for shipping and the State being paid just 56 cents per ton in taxes, it is clear that a small percentage-point increase in severance taxes would have negligible impact on the power bills paid by Midwest utility customers, who are the ultimate payers of Wyoming's severance tax. A minute change in freight rates, however, could have a substantial impact.

Even though the measure had strong support from farmers and ranchers in the legislature, the House defeated the bill for a state income tax in a special session on Dec. 21, 1933. The vote was 24-36.

TELEPHONES

1st telephone exchange in Wyoming: Cheyenne, March 22, 1881. C. F. Annett installed the system which handled calls from all 40 telephones in town.

1st long-distance telephone call in Wyoming: Feb. 24, 1878, when phones were hooked to railroad telegraph wires and Bill Nye, editor of the *Laramie Boomerang*, spoke to E. A. Slack, editor of the *Cheyenne Sun*.

1st long-distance telephone line placed into service: Cheyenne to Laramie, the line began operating on Feb. 25, 1882.

1st transcontinental telephone line through Wyoming: Completed Jan. 1, 1915. The first New York to San Francisco public call was placed on Jan. 25, 1915.

1st telephone yellow pages in America: Printed in Cheyenne, it actually was only one "yellow page." The innovation was the subject of a telephone company ad shown on television in 1988.

1st dial operation exchange in Wyoming: Laramie, 1921. The exchange prefix was "FRanklin-5."

1st consolidated telephone system in Yellowstone Park: Prior to May 31, 1958, two separate systems operated in Yellowstone, one by the National Park Service and the other operated by the Yellowstone Park Company. Mountain States Telephone and Telegraph took over operation of the merged system.

Smallest Wyoming town connected with fiber optic telecommunication cables: Lusk. The system went into service on Oct. 16, 1993.

1st international telephone calls from Rock Springs: Introduced in February, 1927, to the city, home for many immigrants. The charge was $84 for three minutes and $29 for each additional minute.

1st long-distance telephone call from Jackson: Sept. 5, 1933. Prior to that time, no phone lines went out of the valley.

1st telephone line from Casper to Thermopolis: 1903.

First Telephones in Wyoming Areas

1. North of the Platte River
A line connected the Frewen Ranch on Powder River with a store 20 miles away, 1881.

2. Carbon County
The Rawlins exchange went into operation in October 1900, with 50 subscribers. The first dial system in Carbon County opened in Hanna, Sept. 2, 1953.

3. Casper
The first local calls on the exchange were placed on March 22, 1902. The first dial phones in Casper were introduced exactly 50 years later in 1952. Douglas and Casper were connected by phone lines in June 1902 with the first day of service celebrated by allowing free calls between the two towns.

4. Afton
The first telephone line was a Mountain States Telephone and Telegraph Co., line brought from Montpelier, Idaho, in 1902. The first phone call was made by Mrs. Archiso Corsi to her husband in Montpelier to tell him to come home because their daughter was not expected to live.

5. Green River
The first telephone exchange was opened in March 1911.

6. Chugwater
In 1883, the Swan Land and Cattle Company connected phone lines to their ranches and, by utilizing existing barbed wire fences, created a line to Cheyenne.

7. Upton
A 48-year franchise was given to Ranch and Home Telephone Co., Oct. 28, 1909.

8. Powell
First telephone service came to Powell in the winter of 1916-17. The Project Telephone Company had 200 customers by 1920.

Mean travel time to work: Wyoming, 17.8 minutes, (US average is 25.5 minutes)

TELEVISION

1st television programs seen in Wyoming: July 18, 1952, broadcast from KWGN, Channel 2, Denver.

1st Wyoming television station: KFBC, Channel 5, Cheyenne, began broadcasting March 21, 1954.

1st television program broadcast nationally from Wyoming: Probably, the Arthur Godfrey Show, featuring young vocalist Pat Boone, broadcast from Cheyenne Frontier Days in the summer of 1956.

Highest microwave relay tower in the world: Carter Mountain, 12,000 ft., placed on the peak by a company owned by Tom Mitchell and Roy Bliss, Worland, in 1956,

1st cable microwave system in the United States: Casper, December, 1953, begun by Bill Daniels. His firm later became TCI.

1st television program seen in the Big Horn Basin: Worland, May 1953. The program originated in Billings and was fed to the community hall by microwave relay. Some 300 people attended the viewing conducted by Tom Mitchell and Roy Bliss.

1st cable television system in the Big Horn Basin: Worland, 1954. By late summer, the system had 100 subscribers paying $5 per month.

1st privately owned microwave system in the United States: Casper, August, 1962. The microwave handled seven television channels.

1st television news man in Wyoming: Kirk Knox on KFBC-TV in 1954 when the station was on the air daily from 5:30 p.m. to 11 p.m.

1st federal anti-trust action against media concentration in the United States: Case brought in 1963 by the Justice Department against Cheyenne Newspapers, Inc., owners of the two dailies, the only TV station, the cable TV system and one radio station in Cheyenne.

1st public television station in Wyoming: KCWC-TV Riverton, went on the air on May 10, 1983, channel 4.

In 2009, 62 cable television systems operated in Wyoming, serving 91 communities and some 101,000 homes, according to the Wyoming Cable Television Association, the industry trade group.

3 Pioneer Television Stations in Wyoming

1. KFBC-TV Cheyenne

The station went on the air July 18, 1952. At the time, Cheyenne was the smallest city in America with a local television station. The station was owned by Tracy McCraken, owner of both Cheyenne newspapers and a local radio station. The call letters referred to "Frontier Broadcasting Company," the corporate owner that later started a station in Scottsbluff, Neb. The McCrakens sold the station in 1987 to Stauffer Communications and the call letters were changed to KGWN-TV. In 1996, as a result of a merger, the station was bought by Benedek Broadcasting. When Benedek took bankruptcy in 2001, the station was bought by Chelsey Broadcasting. It was bought by Sagamore Hill Broadcasting in 2003.

2. KTWO-TV Casper

The Channel 2 Casper station went on the air March 8, 1957. The station was sold by MDM Broadcasting to Eastern Broadcasting in June 1994 for $13 million. The station later was owned by Grapevine Broadcasting among a string of many owners. In 2009, following the bankruptcy of station owner Equity Broadcasting, the station was purchased by Silverton Broadcasting.

3. KWRB-TV Thermopolis/Riverton

Pioneer television broadcasters Joe and Mildred Ernst started the station which broadcast from a tower on Boysen Peak. Broadcasts began Dec. 22, 1957. In 1980, the call letters became KTNW and, in 1984, KFWY for two years. In 1989, it became KFNE.

Wyoming on Vintage Television

1. NBC News (1987)

A feature segment on August 11, told the story of 85-year-old Finis Mitchell who still climbed in the Wind River Mountains.

2. 20/20 (1987)

The August 27, 1987, segment on sexual assault and murder noted the Jahnke case from Cheyenne in which teenagers Richard and Deborah Jahnke were convicted of murdering their father, an IRS agent, at their home northwest of Cheyenne.

3. ABC Evening News (July 1, 1988)

Wyoming, the last state to raise the drinking age back to 21, was the subject of a news report on bar patrons and owners.

4. Democratic National Convention (July 18, 1988)

Actress Ally Sheedy read a letter written by Joelen Dawn Barkley, South Elementary School, Lander, during a segment about what children felt about America's future.

5. 48 Hours (1988)

CBS reported on the life of rodeo cowboys at Cheyenne Frontier Days.

6. Network news programs (July to early Sept. 1988)

Nearly every evening's broadcast included stories or references to the forest fires in Yellowstone. No fewer than two dozen on-site stories were broadcast from the scene by each of the three major networks. CNN covered the fires extensively.

7. Hour Magazine (1988)

Fran Lebowitz, author and satirist, said to host Gary Collins that since parents and teenagers can't get along, teenagers "should be sent to a place like Wyoming to grow up."

8. ABC Evening News (Aug. 3, 1988)

Wyoming's underpopulated jails were profiled.

9. 20/20 (1988)

The Sept. 2, 1988, program contained a segment on the "Wyoming Hotshots," the Big Horn National Forest firefighers who were called in to help extinguish the huge Yellowstone fires.

10. Murder She Wrote (Feb. 5, 1989)

Mason Adams, the guest star on the episode titled, "The Search for Peter Kerry," said at the end of the program: "I just got off the phone after talking to a woman in Laramie, Wyoming..."

11. Murder She Wrote (Dec. 17, 1989)

The episode was about a woman returning to Cabot Cove, Maine, and attempting to blackmail the local mayor. During a conversation between characters, the woman's hair style is complimented as looking up-to-date "for someone coming from Casper, Wyoming." A second character responds: "Well, it's because she had her hair done in New York before she came here." The Casper woman (who was murdered) was not popular in Cabot Cove. Said one character, "Who can believe an outside agitator from Wyoming?"

12. Eight is Enough (rerun shown March 31, 1990)

A female character told the family that her Montana sheepherder friend was a "graduate of the University of Wyoming history department."

13. Jeopardy (April 5, 1990; Jan. 15, 1993; Jan. 5, 1994)

Wyoming was one of the categories on the popular quiz show in 1990. In double jeopardy in 1993, the $1,000 answer was "This Wyoming senator is probably best known as author of the 1986 Immigration Reform Act." The "question" was "Who is Al Simpson?" On the 1994 program, "Cheyenne" was the answer to a Wyoming question. Wyoming answers frequently have appeared on the board during the 15 years since these shows aired.

14. Tonight Show (Oct. 3, 1990)

Laramie attorney Becky Klemt appeared on the program. Johnny Carson, who had trouble pronouncing her name, invited her on the show because she had written a funny letter in answer to a pompous California lawyer who had turned down a request to help Klemt collect a $4,240 child support settlement.

15. NBC Nightly News (Nov. 15, 1990)

A segment aired on the anti-smoking campaign conducted in Gillette schools.

16. Quantum Leap (January 3, 1991)

"Bye, bye, Wyoming. Hello Colorado," a family says as it travels west on vacation. The Quantum Leap character who "leaps" from person to person through the ages is a young boy member of the family.

17. Quantum Leap (March 20, 1991)

The character Sam finds himself in the late 1970s as a dancer in a disco. At the disco, he encounters a deaf girl who wants to be a dancer. He "sees" that if he does not help her, she goes down a road to ruin. The deaf girl is described as having been "raised in Wyoming" and attended "the Cheyenne School for the Deaf." At one point, a character says of her, "She should be on a bus to Wyoming." With Sam's help, she succeeds in an audition, gets a role as a dancer and her future is changed for the better.

18. Prime Time Live (June 13, 1991)

In a segment called "Chances with Wolves," the ABC program was on the issue of wolf reintroduction in Yellowstone. While the reporter seemed well prepared to talk about the subject, in one scene, an antelope was identified as an elk.

19. Over My Dead Body (June 20, 1991)

"Want to go to Wyoming?" a movie star says to the main female character in the TV show. The movie star tells her he has a "pad" there. Later, the other main character Max (played by Edward Woodward) says to his female co-detective: "Make him take you to Wyoming. It's got the Tetons, Old Faithful, Mount Rushmore..." She interrupts, "That's in South Dakota." Max says, "It's right next door."

20. World Uplink (July 27-Aug. 2, 1991)

The Fuji Television Network of Japan broadcast from several sites in Wyoming to viewers back in Japan during the week. Segments were broadcast from Cheyenne, a ranch near Meeteetse, Old Trail Town at Cody, Old Faithful in Yellowstone and a campground in Jackson for the 90-minute daily program.

21. This Week with David Brinkley (Aug. 25, 1991)

Secretary of State James Baker was interviewed about the U. S. policy toward the Soviet Union following the failed "hardliner" coup attempt. Behind Baker was Fremont Lake. He was vacationing at his nearby ranch. Brinkley commented on the "gorgeous place" where Baker was for the interview.

22. Evening Shade (1991)

The doctor in the show found a Wyoming thimble for their thimble collection. The character played by Burt Reynolds is amazed by the feat.

23. Designing Women (Nov. 4, 1991)

In the CBS program filmed during the debate over the Clarence Thomas/Anita Hill matter, Sen. Al Simpson is lampooned by the main characters. "Alan Simpson refers to this as this sexual harassment crap," one character says. Later, "I'll tell you the person I can't stand is that Bart Simpson." Another character says, "You mean, Alan Simpson?"

24. Rescue 911 (Dec. 17, 1991)

The CBS series segment featured the rescue of a Wyoming Highway Department employee after an avalanche caught his truck on Teton Pass in 1988. Featured were employees of the highway department, sheriff's deputies, and volunteer firemen who participated in the rescue.

25. Murphy Brown (Jan. 6, 1992)

Murphy, as the news anchor, said: "Now we go to Wyoming." The fictitious news segment featured the problems of "Harvey the grizzly bear" in Yellowstone National Park.

26. Good Morning America (Jan. 17, 1992)

Lusk mail carrier Don Taylor was featured. He was the oldest mail carrier in the United States, age 94. (Taylor died in 1993 at the age of 95, still active as a mail carrier at the time of his death).

27. Democratic Candidates' Debate (Feb. 29, 1992)

Senator Tom Harkin of Iowa says to a questioner in the debate held in Denver that he understands the West. He mentions he grew up in Wyoming.

28. Unsolved Mysteries (March 4, 1992)

The program featured a Powell woman, Ethel Sheme, who had been searching for years for her sister's two daughters and son. Following broadcast of the story, the family was reunited in Hardin, Montana. The children had been left with a baby-sitter in Seattle in the early 1950s.

29. General Hospital (June 12, 1992)

Wyoming is noted on the program. Many episodes of the popular daytime series were written by University of Wyoming history professor Dr. Deborah Hardy, daughter of the show's creators.

30. CBS Morning News (June 24, 1992)

Elementary school children from Whiting and Washington schools in Laramie were featured signing "Oh, What a Beautiful Morning."

31. Amazon: Journey to the Lost World (Oct. 26, 1992)

Featured on the ESPN program were two Wyoming climbers, Paul Piana and Todd Skinner (Pinedale) and their climb of Aratitiyope, a shark-fin shaped mountain rising above the Amazon jungle.

32. Top Cops (Fall 1992)

Produced by a Canadian TV company, the episode was on two Evanston police officers who tracked down the killer of fellow officer Phil Mensing in April 1988. The program aired in the fall of 1992.

33. Rescue 911 (Jan. 5, 1993)

The episode related the story of a snow tubing accident at Happy Jack, east of Laramie, on Feb. 13, 1988, in which Shauna Williams was paralyzed.

34. Prime Time Live (Jan. 21, 1993)

ABC reporter John Quinones reported on the REA as an "outdated agency." A former REA official in Torrington was interviewed..

35. Dr. Quinn, Medicine Woman (April 10, 1993)

Orson Bean, playing the role of a customer in a barber shop, reads from a newspaper: "Listen to this. In the Territory of Wyoming, they want to pass a law to give ladies the right to vote." The barber replies, "It will never happen."

36. The Price is Right (April 19, 1993)

Jeff Myers of Cody won $5,000 in furniture on "The Price is Right," March 10, 1993. The show aired April 19, 1993

37. Jeopardy (Jan. 15, 1993; June 16, 1993)

The 1993 program had "Who is Al Simpson?" as a $1,000 question to the answer, "This senator is best known for sponsoring immigration reform." On the June program, one category included clues about Dick Cheney as secretary of defense and Wyoming's Teapot Dome, for which the 1920s scandal was named.

Former NFL coach and sports broadcaster John Madden announced in January 1994, that he planned to establish his hall of fame in Medicine Bow. He made the announcement while taping his All-Madden Team for broadcast on CBS. The hall was never built.

38. Good Morning America (July 14, 1993)

Three-day cattle drive featured in the neighborhood of Hamilton Dome.

39. MASH

One episode of the popular television series showed President Harry Truman speaking at the University of Wyoming Ballroom in May 1950.

40. Sunday Morning (Sept. 19, 1993)

Charles Kuralt narrated the story ("Imagine a Herd") about the proposal to place 1,000 copper buffalo outside Lander. Sculptor was Bob Burkes. Secretary of State Kathy Karpan and Lander publisher Bill Sniffin were interviewed.

41. Now (Aug. 18, 1993)

The first broadcast of the show, on Aug. 18, 1993, featured a story on Gerry Spence and his defense of Idaho white supremacists charged with murder. The show was moderated by Katie Couric and Tom Brokaw.

42. The Stuff of Dreams (November 1993)

The PBS documentary series featured a segment on spider silk research done at the University of Wyoming, in episodes aired in November 1993. Randy Lewis, UW professor of molecular biology and research director of the project, was interviewed for the program. Lewis, a native of Powell, has taught at UW since 1980.

43. Murder She Wrote (Nov. 7, 1993)

"I thought Victor, WY was for Victor, Wyoming [sic]. But is was actually Victor Way," the name of a race horse, Jessica Fletcher (Angela Lansbury) said during the episode. It was an essential clue to solving the case.

44. Murphy Brown (Nov. 8, 1993)

Sen. Al Simpson appeared on the episode. "I saw her push a nun once," was one of the lines that Simpson, and newspeople Charles Kuralt and Linda Ellerbee each repeated.

45. This Old House (Nov. 21, 1993)

The episode featured Anderson Lodge, west of Meeteetse. Filming took place in July 1993. The lodge, built in 1903, was being restored by a crew from the Forest Service and volunteers. It had slid off its foundation. Norm Abram, one of the show's hosts, fell off a mule on the return trip from the lodge. He was unhurt.

46. Bob Hope Christmas Show (Dec. 15, 1993)

Ryan Yarborough, the UW receiver who was the NCAA all-time leading yardage leader, appeared on the annual NBC show.

47. Perry Mason Mysteries (Dec. 17, 1993)

"So I started singing in clubs in Wyoming—in Casper—that's where I'm from," a character says in the new Perry Mason Mysteries episode of Dec. 17, 1993. It was the first show which didn't have Raymond Burr as Mason. Paul Sorvino starred as the attorney. Barbara Hale, the last of the original Perry Mason cast, starred as secretary Della Street.

48. Larry King Live (Dec. 31, 1993)

The first caller asking guest Jay Leno a question was from Gillette.

49. 20/20 (March 11, 1994)

Reporter Lynn Scherr narrated a report on self-esteem building in children. Laramie children were featured at the Childrens' Museum.

50. Unsolved Mysteries (June 15, 1994)

The tiny mummy found in 1932 on Pedro Mountain was featured.

The Virginian, the first 90-minute TV western, premiered on Sept. 19, 1962. Based on the Owen Wister novel set in Medicine Bow, the NBC-TV version starred James Drury and Lee J. Cobb. Hugh O'Brien, star of Wyatt Earp, appeared in the first episode.

51. Jan. 17, 1994: Covering the LA area earthquake, Peter Jennings, noted the humor shown by scientists in the aftermath. He said one had a poster with the advice: "Before an earthquake, place yourself in a safe place...like Wyoming."

52. Brotherhood of the Rose

The TV mini-series was based on the book and starred David Morrill. In one scene, a "hideout in Wyoming" is pictured.

53. The Simpsons (1994)

One episode centered around a brand of "smokes" called "Laramie cigarettes."

54. Northern Exposure (Sept. 12, 1994)

"I have two kids. Becky lives in Lander, Wyoming. She's a teacher." The words were spoken to "Ed," one of the characters on the popular TV series.

55. Larry King Live (Jan. 14, 1995)

Wyoming lawyer Gerry Spence, who made numerous appearances on the CNN evening talk show, substituted for King as the guest host. The subject was the O. J. Simpson trial. Spence later had his own weekly show on CNBC.

56. Prime Time Live (Nov. 29, 1995)

A segment featured grizzly bears in the Rockies. Experts criticized the piece for inaccurately characterizing grizzlies as deliberate "man-eaters."

57. Murder She Wrote (Feb. 27, 1996; rerun on July 26, 1996)

In an episode shot in Jackson Hole, Jessica Fletcher solves the mystery of the murder of a young man with a secret. "They say you can see the whole world from the Tetons," one character says.

58. Reform Party Convention, all networks (Aug. 11, 1996)

Ross Perot, in his acceptance speech for the nomination, noted the differences between how health care is managed in Los Angeles as compared to "a small town in Wyoming."

59. Dr. Quinn, Medicine Woman (Oct. 26, 1996)

The character Sully is offered a job in Wyoming. "Wyoming? That's so far away," replied Dr. Quinn. Later she asked, "What does this Yellowstone National Park look like?" Sully, concerned with protection efforts for the park, then notes, "What if nobody stands for the land?" Dr. Quinn agrees to accompany him, but later in the episode, they decide to remain in Colorado Springs.

60. Chicago Hope (Dec. 9, 1996)

The doctor character played by Mark Harmon said: "Trust me. I'd be a lot happier back in Wyoming."

61. 20/20 (January 11, 1997)

John Stossel talked about religious lawsuits filed by people in prison, noting that prisoners in Wyoming who were "Luciferians" had sued.

62. Larry King Live (Oct. 22, 1997)

Gov. Jim Geringer was a panelist on the CNN program. He spoke of his protests about a web site featuring the activities of serial killers.

63. Public Eye (Oct. 22, 1997)

The show hosted by Bryant Gumbel contained a segment on the disappearance of Amy Wroe Bechtel. The broadcast was the same night as #62 above.

64. Network News Programs (October, 1998)

Frequent reports were broadcast from Laramie where Matthew Shepard, a gay UW student, had been murdered. Networks also did broadcasts from Shepard's funeral in Casper.

65. Crazy About You (1999)

The PBS production of the Gershwin musical includes a line: "I haven't seen him lately. Maybe you should try Wyoming."

66. 48 Hours (July, 1999)

Author Gretel Erhlich had been struck by lightning in Wyoming and her story was featured in the CBS news program.

67. Dateline NBC (Dec. 1, 1999)

The show featured the story of Larry "Sissy" Goodwin of Douglas. Goodwin is married with two children, works at a power plant and prefers dressing in woman's clothes.

68. Tonight Show (Dec. 20, 1999)

On Jay Leno's "headlines" segment, he showed two items from the UW Branding Iron. The first indicated that police had been asked to help remove a bicycle from a bike rack because the "owner" had lost his combination. The next item, showed that a few minutes later, police received a report of a stolen bicycle from the same rack!

69. Clinton's Final State of the Union Address, all networks (January, 2000)

President Clinton mentioned the Matthew Shepard murder: "...a young man murdered in Wyoming just because he was gay."

70. Diagnosis Murder (April 6, 2000)

In the CBS drama series starring Dick Van Dyke, a character says, "You think they just went out and found an actress with a goiter the size of Wyoming."

71. Television News, (July 25, 2000)

All networks carried George W. Bush's announcement that he had chosen Dick Cheney as his running mate when Bush made the statement, "I didn't pick Dick Cheney because of Wyoming's three electoral votes." The assembled reporters laughed and Bush added, "Although we're going to work hard to earn them."

72. American Experience (Sept. 4, 2000)

The program about the 1897 journey of the army bicycle corps from Fort Missoula, Montana, to St. Louis, described the trip along the Burlington Railroad route across northern Wyoming through Sheridan, Gillette, Moorcroft and Newcastle, in June, 1897.

73. Tonight Show (Oct. 4, 2000)

Jay Leno's featured guest was Rulon Gardner, Afton native who had won the Olympic gold medal for wrestling in Sydney, Australia. The segment included a shot of Afton townspeople in the school gymnasium congratulating Gardner.

74. Lehrer News Hour (Nov. 17, 2000)

Reporter Ray Suarez interviewed a number of students from Laramie County Community College about the close presidential election.

Wyoming in Some More Recent Television Programs

1. South Park (Nov. 12, 2003)

Cartman, asserting the world is coming to an end, says the astreroid about to hit earth is not the size of Texas, but about the size of Wyoming.

2. Wyoming Voices (Wyoming PBS, Dec. 5 -6, 2004)

The three-part documentary, produced and directed by Deborah Healy Hammons, summarized all of Wyoming history. The musical score for the series was composed by Anne Guzzo of Laramie and performed by the Cheyenne Symphony.

3. Monk (NBC, April 20, 2008)

The detective Monk is found, after suffering amnesia, in Wyoming. "He was dropped off in Wyoming," is a line in the show

---

"Captain Five" was the stage name for the host of KFBC-TV Cheyenne's afternoon children's program in the 1950s, so named for the channel on which the station broadcast.

4. Extreme Make-Over (ABC, Dec. 21, 2008)

The TV crew worked on a new house for Dan and Dawn Miller and their family in Cheyenne. They blew up the old house because radon gas was leaking from the ground into it and making their children sick. They were building the new house on this episode.

5. Don't Fence Me In (Wyoming PBS, 2009)

Jackson documentary film makers Bonnie Kreps and Charlie Craighead interviewed-Wyoming women and compiled stories about women's lives in the Equality State.

6. NOW (PBS, April 10, 2009)

The program featured a story on "clean coal" technology being developed in Wyoming.

7. Yellowstone: Battle for Life (BBC, 2009)

The BBC documentary revealed the survival struggle of wolves, buffalo, bears, antelope, and other wildlife in Yellowstone National Park.

Wyoming in Some Made-for-TV Movies

1. LBJ: The Early Years (TV movie, starring Randy Quaid and Patti LuPone)

A senator tells Johnson about Sen. John Kennedy's run for the presidency. "He's gonna fly out to Cheyenne, Wyoming, to eat chicken dinner."

2. Bigfoot (1987)

The film, shot in northwest Wyoming, was made for television.

3. Swallows Come Back (1987)

Film locations for the HBO production included the HF Bar Ranch near Buffalo and other locations in Johnson and Sheridan counties.

4. Lakota Moon (1991)

The Fox network's mini-series was filmed near Jackson. Many of the extras were from the Wind River reservation.

5. Assassination (1981)

Charles Bronson and Jill Ireland starred. The female character's name was "Laramie," so named for the Wyoming town, as the character explains.

6. Prophet of Evil: The Ervil LeBaron Story (TV movie, 1993)

Evanston is one place in the film starring Brian Dennehy and William Devane.

7. Headline: Starkweather (April 22, 1993)

The film was based on the murder spree of Charles Starkweather and his girlfriend, Carol Fugate, which brought them into Wyoming. They were captured near Douglas.

8. Glass Coffin (1993)

In Raymond Burr's last made-for-television Perry Mason movie, Burr says at one point, "The victim was from Cheyenne, Wyoming."

9. To Save the Children (1994)

The film, starring Richard Thomas and Robert Urich, dramatizes the incident in which a man and his wife took students and teachers hostage in the Cokeville school in 1986.

10. Dream West (1986)

Sun Classic Pictures/CBS-TV movie was shot near Jackson and Gillette. Richard Chamberlain starred.

11. Wild Horses (1985)

The CBS television movie, filmed in Sheridan County and other Wyoming locations, starred Kenny Rogers and Pam Dawber.

12. Without Warning (Oct. 30, 1994)

An object from outer space (meteor) hit in the Thunder Basin area, supposedly obliterating a Wyoming town.

13. Bright Angel (1990)

Dermot Mulroney and Lili Taylor starred in the story about a young ranch hand who agrees to help a woman get her brother out of a Casper jail.

14. Chiefs (PBS, April 1, 2003)

A documentary about the Wyoming Indian boys basketball team, the film follows the Chiefs from their heartbreaking finish in 2000 to their state championship in 2001. Cheyenne East graduate Daniel Junge directed the film, which took first place at Robert De Niro's TriBeCa Film Festival in New York the previous year.

15. Johnson County War (2002)

The film aired in August 2002 on the Hallmark Channel. It starred Tom Berenger and Flecter Humphrys.

16. Taking Chance (2009)

The film, made for HBO, tells the true story of Lt. Col. Mike Strobl as he accompanies the body of 19-year-old Marine Chance Phelps from where he was killed in Iraq in 2004 to his burial place in Dubois, Wyoming. The film starred Kevin Bacon as Strobl. It premiered on HBO on Feb. 19, 2009.

17. Searching for Cloud (2009)

The film, made for the PBS Nature series, is about a palomino horse growing up in the wild horse refuge northeast of Lovell in the Pryor Mountains. Director Ginger Kathrens made two earlier films about the horse, both for PBS.This third installment premiered on PBS on Oct. 25, 2009.

18. Matthew Shepard Story (2010)

The Lifetime network movie titled "The Matthew Shepard Story" starred Stockard Channing and Sam Waterson as Shepard's parents.

Television Personalities with Wyoming Connections

1. Larry Wilcox

Born in San Diego, Wilcox was brought as an infant to Rawlins where he lived with his divorced mother and grandparents on an area ranch. After graduating from Rawlins High School, Wilcox joined the U. S. Marine Corps in 1967. Following his discharge in 1970, after Vietnam service, he returned to California and eventually went into acting. Wilcox starred in two series. He was the rancher-owner of Lassie in the show's last two seasons of syndication in the early 1970s. He played Officer Jon Baker, the "serious cop," in *CHiPs* which premiered Sept. 15, 1977.

2. Karen Morris-Gowdy

A former national Junior Miss (1974) and Queen of the Senior Bowl (1975), she starred in *Ryan's Hope* on daytime television for six years. A Cheyenne native, she married TV producer Curt Gowdy Jr., the son of sportscaster Curt Gowdy.

3. Red Skelton

Skelton was a native of Indiana but his wife Georgia was born in Glenwood Springs, Colo., and reared in Casper. The couple visited Casper in 1945 shortly after their marriage. In the mid-1950s, Skelton had his own television program. Later, the couple divorced after a family tragedy. Georgia Skelton died, a suicide, on May 10, 1976.

4. Matthew Fox (b. Crowheart, July 14, 1966)

Fox was reared on a ranch near Crowheart. After attending Deerfield Academy, he gained a football scholarship to Columbia University. After earning a degree in economics, he worked on Wall Street before auditioning to do television commercials. From there, he played the oldest brother Charlie in the Fox TV series "Party of Five." Fox was on *People* magazine's 1996 list of "50 most beautiful people in the world." He gained wide acclaim for starring as Dr. Jack Shephard, the surgeon in the long-running ABC-TV saga, *Lost*, that ran from 2004 to May 2010. In 2006, he hosted an episode of *Saturday Night Live*.

Sean Martinez, Guernsey native, and his ex-girlfriend from Iowa were featured in an episode of "Second Chance" on the Learning Channel, in March 2004.

5. Jim Siedow (b. Cheyenne, 1920, d. Houston, 2003)

Siedow worked in radio in Chicago and directed theatre productions in Houston. He appeared in several made-for-TV movies, but his most famous role was as Drayton Sawyer in the cult hit, *The Texas Chain Saw Massacre* (1974).

6. Wayde Preston (William Erskine Strange) (b. Denver, 1929; d. Nevada, 1992)

Preston was reared in Laramie, graduated from Laramie High School in 1947 and attended the University of Wyoming, majoring in pharmacy. He starred in the 1950s TV western "Colt .45." Later, he starred in films in Europe.

7. Curt Gowdy

Born in Green River in 1919, Gowdy played basketball on the University of Wyoming national championship team in 1943. For 20 years, he hosted "The American Sportsman." He was inducted into the Baseball Hall of Fame in 1984, the first Wyoming native to be so honored. Curt Gowdy State Park, 25 miles west of Cheyenne, was named in his honor in 1971. He died Feb. 20, 2006.

8. Kevin Kiley

The ESPN sportscaster attended the University of Wyoming and played football for the Cowboys in the early 1970s.

9. John Barrett

Barrett, born in Cody in 1959, hosted a series on fly fishing for ESPN. The show premiered in April 1990. It is called "Fly Fishing the World."

10. Dr. Deborah Hardy

The retired University of Wyoming history professor is the daughter of the husband-wife team who created the soap opera, *General Hospital*. Dr. Hardy wrote many of the episodes for the popular day-time television program.

11. Barbara Bragg

Bragg's father, Bill Bragg, was a Wyoming historian and writer who served in the legislature from Natrona County. A native of Wyoming, she has appeared in *Guiding Light, One Life to Live, All My Children* and *American Playhouse* (PBS) and numerous New York City productions. She appeared in a one-woman stage show titled "True West Girl" in 2010 at the Santa Monica Playhouse and on other California theater stages.

12. Garro Ellis

Former UW football player Garro Ellis appeared on the daytime soap opera called *Bold and Beautiful* on Jan. 11, 1994, on CBS. Born in Torrington, he moved to Lingle with family at age 3. He played football at UW from 1985-86, as a walk-on. "My goal was to get paid to perform. I've achieved that goal," he said.

13. Geoffrey Lower

Born in Casper in March 1963, Lower graduated from Natrona County High School and attended the University of Nebraska, transferring to acting school in New York and began a career on Broadway. In 1883, began six seasons starring on the weekly television series, *Dr. Quinn, Medicine Woman*. He played the minister, Rev. Timothy Johnson.

14. Jeff Deist

Deist, a native of Rawlins, was a University of Wyoming theatre graduate. In the winter of 1994-95, he starred in "Earth 2" as an "alien life form." He also acted in other science fiction films and worked in special effects and make-up departments at various studios.

15. Jim J. Bullock

Born in Casper in 1955, Bullock was co-host of "The Jim J. and Tammy Faye Show" and played Monroe Ficus on the TV sitcom "Too Close for Comfort" starring Ted Knight.

16. Otis Carney

Born in Chicago in 1923, Carney, a former advertising writer, wrote episodes for many TV series, including *Dragnet, Adventure Showcase* and *GE Theatre*. He also wrote 17 books and novels. He moved his family to the Cora, Wyoming, area to ranch in the 1960s where he operated a ranch for the next half century. Carney died in Arizona on Jan. 1, 2006.

17. Pete Williams

Williams, born in Casper, is a graduate of Natrona County High School (1971) and Stanford University (1974). He worked for KTWO-TV in Casper from 1974-85. He has been covering the Justice Department and the Supreme Court of the United States as the judicial reporter for NBC's Washington bureau since March 1993. Prior to that position, he worked as press secretary for Dick Cheney in Congress in 1986 and when Cheney served as Defense Secretary in the first Bush administration, Williams was press secretary for the Department of Defense.

18. Robin Russin

Born in Laramie, Russin was a Rhodes scholar and later earned the MFA from UCLA. He has been a screen writer and also a producer on both independent and TV movies. In television, he wrote, produced and directed numerous segments and specials for *America's Most Wanted* and *The Prosecutors*. He was Senior Producer of the hour-long ABC primetime series, *Vital Signs*.

19. Freddie Prinze Sr. (b. 1954, d. 1977)

Prinze starred in *Chico and the Man*, and made guest appearances on *Tony Orlando & Dawn Show* and the *Dean Martin Comedy Roast* during 1975 and 1976. While vacationing in Wyoming, he met Katherine Cochran, a 26-year-old former cocktail waitress. They married in August, 1975, and had a child they named Freddie James Prinze on March 8, 1976, in Albuquerque, N.M. The senior Prinze died Jan. 29, 1977, at the height of his TV fame. Freddie Prinze Jr. went on to become a leading man in numerous films in the 1990s and 2000s, including *I Know What You Did Last Summer* (1997), *She's All That (1999)*, and guest starred on TV shows, including *Friends, Boston Legal* and *24*.

20. Darren Dalton (b. 1965, Powell)

Dalton's film career began in 1983 in *The Outsiders*. He appeared in *Red Dawn* and in the made-for-television film *The Brotherhood of Justice*. He made numerous guest appearances on television, including *Highway to Heaven*, *Quantum Leap*, and *Alien Nation*.

"60 Minutes" Programs Featuring Wyoming Subjects

1. Oct. 23, 1977: Our Town

The story about "crime and corruption" in Rock Springs was narrated by Dan Rather. The story was shown again on Sept. 3, 1978.

2. Oct. 30, 1977: High Noon in Cheyenne

The follow-up on the Rock Springs story focused on allegations of corruption in state government.

3. April 12, 1981: Oil Boys and Indians

The story was about Wind River reservation Indians being cheated on oil pumped from reservation wells.

4. Jan. 24, 1982: The Best in the West

Profile of Jackson lawyer Gerry Spence, the program was repeated June 13.

Geoffrey O'Gara is a Wyoming Public Television producer and host of Capitol Outlook and Wyoming Chronicle series. He is the author of *What You See in Clear Water: Indians, Whites, and a Battle Over Water in the American West* (2002) and *A Long Road Home* (1989).

5. Jan. 22, 1984: Dirty Little Secret

The segment told the story of Richard and Deborah Jahnke, charged with the 1983 murder of their father in Cheyenne. The piece was repeated July 28, 1985.

6. March 25, 1984: A Sporting Chance?

Debates surrounding the annual national park elk hunt were explored.

7. March 17, 1985: Brother's Keeper?

The profile of author John Wideman, University of Wyoming English professor, who had written a best-selling book, *Brothers and Keepers*, which told of the story of his brother, a prisoner in the Pennsylvania State Prison doing a life sentence for murder. The program was repeated July 21.

8. March 23, 1987: Small-Town Doctor

The story was about Dr. John Story of Lovell and the charges made against him by several of his female patients.

9. March 18, 1990: Who Killed Ernestine Perea?

The story about the arrest and conviction of a Wheatland man, Martin Frejas, for the July 1984, murder of his common-law wife. Throughout the trial, he maintained his innocence, contending that the woman had committed suicide. Later, forensics experts confirmed she had indeed committed suicide, but only after Frejas had served more than two years in the Wyoming State Penitentiary for a crime he did not commit.

10. Oct. 31, 1993: Nuclear Nightmare?

Newsman Ed Bradley traveled to Russia for a story about nuclear missiles there still aimed at the United States. At one site, he learned that the target of one of the missiles he was looking at was Warren AFB, Cheyenne. Later, the program showed pictures of F. E. Warren Air Force Base.

11. Oct. 30, 1994: Congressional Pensions

U. S. Senator Al Simpson was interviewed on the question of congressional pensions. He defended the pensions, noting that had he continued living and working as a lawyer in Cody, he would have "retired in leisure."

12. Oct. 24, 1998: Kennewick Man

Lusk native and UW graduate Doug Owsley appeared on "60 Minutes" on Oct. 24, 1998. He is the Smithsonian's chief anthropologist. He was involved in the controversial examination of the so-called "Kenniwick man," a skeleton of a human uncovered along the Columbia River and estimated to be thousands of years old. The nature of the skeleton suggested Caucasian features.

13. Nov. 10, 2004: Diplomas for Sale

The episode looked at "diploma mills" selling diplomas from various mailboxes around the country. One such operation the program featured was "Hamilton University" located in one room of an old motel in Evanston, Wyoming.

14. Feb. 9, 2005: Showdown in Wyoming Over Gas

The episode focused on coal-bed methane drilling in the Powder River Basin and how landowners who don't own the sub-surface often are at the mercy of drillers and owners of the below-ground mineral interest.

For updates on the TV section and other rapidly changing sections of Wyoming Almanac, consult the webpage at: www.wyomingalmanac.com

---

Betty Evenson, romance wrter and long-time owner and oeprator of the Bright Spot Cafe, gas station and post office in Hiland, appeared on the Phil Donahue show in 1973. She also was on the program, *To Tell the Truth*, in 1973. She sold the Bright Spot in 1974 to Carla and Robert Steelman and moved to Casper where she died in 1997.

YOU KNOW YOU'RE FROM WYOMING IF...

(a 30-point checklist*)

1. ...you've never met any celebrities.
2. ...your idea of a traffic jam is ten cars waiting to pass a tractor on the highway or waiting for cattle to cross the dirt road.
3. ..."vacation" means driving through Medicine Bow or going to Veedavoo.
4. ...you've seen all the biggest bands ten years after they were popular.
5. ...you measure distance in minutes.
6. ..."down south" to you means Colorado.
7. ...you know several people who have hit a deer.
8. ...your school classes were cancelled because of cold.
9. ...your school classes were canceled because of heat.
10. ...you've ridden the school bus for an hour each way.
11. ...you've ever had to switch from "heat" to "A/C" in the same day.
12. ...you only own 3 spices: salt, pepper, and ketchup.
13. ...you know what's knee-high by the Fourth of July.
14. ...stores don't have bags; they have sacks.
15. ...you see people wear cowboy boots and hats at funerals and weddings.
16. ...you see a car running in the parking lot at the store with no one in it, no matter what time of the year.
17. ...you carry jumper cables in your car.
18. ...you install security lights on your house and garage and leave both unlocked.
19. ...you think of the major four food groups as beef, pork, beer, and Jell-O salad with marshmallows.
20. ...you know what "cow tipping" or "Jackalope hunting" is.
21. ...you design your kid's Halloween costume to fit over a snowsuit.
22. ...driving is better in the winter because the potholes are filled with snow.
23. ...you think sexy lingerie is tube socks and a flannel nightie. (And what, pray tell, is wrong with a flannel nightie?)
24. ...the local paper covers national and international news on one page but requires six pages for sports.
25. ...you think that deer season is a national holiday.
26. ...you know which leaves make good toilet paper.
27. ...you find -20 degrees F "a little chilly".
28. ...you know all four seasons: Almost Winter, Winter, Still Winter, and Construction.
29. ...you know that Yellowstone is in Wyoming, not Montana.
30. ...you know that Wyoming is in the United States, not Canada.

*Courtesy of Lorraine Saulino-Klein, Laramie

In June, 1996, Spy Magazine ranked the states in the order of annoyance. Wyoming ranked 43rd. Most annoying (1st) was Texas; least annoying (50th) was New Jersey.

Maj.Gen. Carla Hawley-Bowland, a native of Casper, was the first female physician in the U.S. Army who rose to the rank of general.

The first travel service in Wyoming was Cheyenne Travel Service which was started in 1948 by Larry and Eileen Uphoff.

THEATER

1st theater troupe in Wyoming: The California Minstrels, a soldier troupe, performed at Fort Bridger in 1863. Admission to the show was 50 cents.

1st community theater group in Wyoming: Cheyenne Little Theater Players, organized in 1927.

1st play set in a Wyoming location: Probably, *The Scouts of the Plains*, written in four hours by Ned Butnline in December 1872.

Best known Wyoming playwright: George Abbott (b. 1889, d. January, 1995) who lived in Cheyenne as a youth. Abbott wrote *"Damn Yankees"* and numerous other Broadway plays. He died in New York at the age of 107. Actress Carol Channing said Abbott "gave musical theater its quality."

Wyoming Performances by Famous Actors/Companies

1. P. T. Barnum

Barnum's show first came to Wyoming in 1870 with performances in June of that year along the Union Pacific line. In July, 1880, Barnum's circus again followed the railroad route and gave performances in Wyoming towns.

2. Oscar Wilde

The English playwright and actor toured America in 1882. He made a brief appearance in Cheyenne on March 23, 1882.

3. Edwin Booth

Booth, the foremost Shakespearean actor of his day, played Hamlet on stage at the Cheyenne Opera House on April 18, 1887. His brother, John Wilkes Booth, assassinated Abraham Lincoln.

4. Sarah Bernhardt

The "Divine Sarah" appeared in a play called *Fedora*, presented in the Cheyenne Opera House on the evening of June 2, 1887.

5. Lily Langtry

Lantry, known more as a "famous beauty" and mistress of English royalty than for her acting ability, appeared in a stage production of *A Wife's Peril* at the Cheyenne Opera House on June 4, 1884. While in Cheyenne, she stayed at the home of Moreton Frewen, an Englishman who had extensive ranch holdings in the Powder River Basin at that time.

6. W. C. Fields

Fields worked with a traveling theater company just after the turn of the century. The company made frequent trips on the railroad west to California, stopping to perform at Union Pacific towns along the way. He appeared at the Cheyenne Opera House on Jan. 30, 1902.

7. Cecil B. DeMille

Renowned as a movie producer, DeMille toured Wyoming in 1902 with a theater company. A decade later, he planned to make his first film, *The Squaw Man*, in Wyoming. Due to time pressures, the film had to be completed during the late fall of 1912 and DeMille was well aware of the unpredictability of all weather in Wyoming. He decided to film in the southwest at a location that could pass for Wyoming. Flagstaff, Ariz., was singled out as one possibility. When DeMille arrived there on the train, he nixed the choice because it "did not look like Wyoming" to him. Consequently, the film company stayed on the train, riding to the end of the line in Los Angeles. There, DeMille located a barn he could rent in the tiny nearby hamlet of Hollywood. DeMille's film was the first motion picture ever made in what became the movie capital of the world.

8. Fred Allen

Later, a well-known radio personality, Fred Allen appeared at various theaters in Wyoming on the vaudeville circuit. He was a juggler and a comic.

Thayne, Wyoming, was the first place anywhere to host cutter races.

9. Bob Hope

The comedian entertained at the Casper Air Base in February 1942. In the spring of 1963, he appeared in Laramie and received an honorary doctorate from the University of Wyoming. He also performed at UW in the early 1970s as a headline attraction for homecoming.

10. William Demarest

Best known for his co-starring role on the television series, *My Three Sons*, Demarest played various Wyoming theaters while on the vaudeville circuit. He once told a reporter that he remembered his appearance in Cheyenne very well. "Cheyenne was still a pretty rough town in those days. I clearly remember being robbed of my wallet just a block from the Princess Theater."

11. Sammy Davis, Jr.

Davis, a child performer on Vaudeville, burlesque and night clubs since infancy, was inducted into the army in 1943. He was stationed at Fort Warren near Cheyenne. The experience, which included having to undergo basic training twice, had positive and negative aspects. He was influenced there by an African-American sergeant who gave him remedial reading lessons and lent him books. Previously, Davis, who grew up on the theater circuit, had read nothing but comic books. He also experienced bigotry, however. "I had scabs on my knuckles for the first three months in the Army," he wrote in his autobiography, *Yes I Can* (New York: Farrar, Strauss, 1965). For the rest of his tour, Davis directed and produced camp shows at army bases throughout the country, including Warren.

12. The Lone Ranger

A promotional tour brought the radio star to Cheyenne June 29-July 1, 1948. One episode of the serial was broadcast from radio studios in Cheyenne and the Lone Ranger autographed pictures for local children.

13. Blue Man from Wyoming

Pete Simpson (b. Eugene, Oregon) became a Blue Man in 1995. The group that began in experimental theater has appeared on television and in memorable TV ads as well as continuing to play to large live theater audiences in America and Europe. A graduate of the University of Wyoming and the National Theater Conservatory in Denver, Simpson performed with the Boston and New York casts and then went to Amsterdam to open the Blue Man production there. In the spring of 2010, he took a three-month leave from the group to serve as guest artist in the University of Wyoming Department of Theater and Dance. During his time as guest faculty, he appeared in the lead role of Hamlet with his father, Dr. Pete Simpson, playing the role of the ghost of Hamlet's father. Along with his role as a Blue Man, the younger Simpson has appeared on stage and in various television roles, including an episode of *Law and Order* in 2001.

14. William Missouri Downs (b. Bay City, Mich.)

Downs teaches theatre at the University of Wyoming. He has written textbooks on screen-writing and theater performance, including *The Art of Theatre* (2006). He also has written award-winning plays. Prior to joining the faculty at the University of Wyoming in 1993, he was a staff writer for television production firms. Among his credits, he wrote for 23 episodes on the NBC sitcom, *My Two Dads*.

At least ten Wyoming communities had "community theater" groups performing plays in the first decade of the 2000s. Included were Cheyenne Little Theatre Players (1930), Casper Stage III (1980); Sagebrush Theatre, Evanston (1981); Gem City Players, Laramie (1980); Sheridan Civic Theatre Guild; Platte County Players, Wheatland (1977); Gillette Community Theatre.

Wyoming on Stage: Plays Set in Wyoming

1. "May Cody; or Lost and Won" (1877)

The play was written by Major A. S. Burt.

2. "Viva Vance; or Saved by the Sioux" (1877)

The play by Will L. Visscher starred Buffalo Bill Cody. It was a stage play produced before Cody began his "Wild West Show."

3. "Wild West or Life Among the Red Men and Road Agents on the Plains and Prairies" (1883)

The play, "an equine dramatic exposition on grass, or under canvas," featured "the adventures of frontiersmen and cowboys." The author was William F. Cody who copyrighted the play Dec. 22, 1883. Cody used the story line for his Wild West Show.

4. "A History of American Civilization" (1886)

Written jointly by Nate Salisbury and William F. Cody, the play was "a drama of Wild West deeds and exploits." It was used in conjunction with Wild West for many performances by Cody's show.

5. "Wyoming: A Play in Three Parts" (1905)

Edgar Allin Martin of Cody copyrighted the play Oct. 19, 1905. He wrote two other copyrighted plays: *Bridegroom's Reverie* (1901) and *Man from Out There* (1908).

6. "Cheyenne: A Drama in Four Acts" (1906)

The play was copyrighted by Mattie Keene of New York.

7. "A Cheyenne Romance" (1910)

The musical melodrama in one act was written by Robert Blaylock of Iowa.

8. "Oh, Wyoming" (1960)

The musical was written by novelist Mary O'Hara. The show premiered at the Lincoln Theater in Cheyenne in 1960. Later, the film version was called "Top of the Big Hill."

9. "Shirley Basin" (1984)

The play premiered in Colorado Springs in November 1984. Written by Jack Gilhooley, it is about some women residents of Shirley Basin who struggle to survive in the isolated boomtown during a relentless winter. The play opened off-Broadway in New York in 1988.

10. "A Starry Night in Casper" (1986)

Written by S. I. Diamond, the play opened Jan. 24 and closed March 9, 1986, at the Beverly Hills Playhouse (Calif.). The play included a plane crash scene, a starlet who falls in love with a Wyoming cowboy, and a pilot who returns from the dead.

11. "Cleo and the Coyotes" (1990)

The original Western musical comedy premiered Dec. 31, 1990, in Casper. It was written by Brenda Simpson, with music by her and Jim Wyatt. The two were co-authors of *Wyoming, You're Heaven to Me.*

12. "Laramie Project" (2000)

The play, based on more than 200 interviews of Laramie residents made in the wake of the murder of Matthew Shepard, was written by Moises Kaufman. The play opened in Denver on Feb. 26, 2000, and moved to New York and other cities.

According to an article in a Laramie newspaper in October, 1913, a man was sent to jail for "mutilating an actress' clothes." His pet monkey went to jail with him. The monkey's offense was not indicated.

4 Wyoming Theaters and Companies

1. Cheyenne Opera House

It opened May 25, 1882, with a performance by the Comley-Barton Opera Company of a French comedy, *Oluette*. More than 850 people attended the performance.

2. Rock Springs Opera House

The magnificent theater opened in 1889, but burned to the ground in December 1894. A later structure, the Grand Opera House, renamed the Union Opera House when the local labor organizations purchased it, operated until it lost out to motion picture theaters.

3. Sheridan Civic Theater Guild

The Rainmaker was the first production presented by the guild. The play opened Feb. 28, 1957.

4. Cheyenne Little Theater Players

Three one-act plays were presented by the Players on May 7, 1930, opening night. The Cheyenne Little Theatre Playhouse on Windmill Road and Pershing Boulevard, opened in 1968. In 1971, the organization purchased the Atlas Theater in downtown Cheyenne.

4 Wild West Shows

1. Buffalo Bill's Wild West Show and Congress of Rough Riders

The first performance was held in Omaha in 1883. The show traveled throughout the nation, played a command performance for Queen Victoria in London on May 4, 1887, and, in 1893, performed at the Chicago World's Fair. The stars included Sitting Bull (for one season) and Annie Oakley who became a national institution during her more than two decades with Cody's show. The show played frequently in Wyoming. For instance, it was in Cheyenne on Aug. 9, 1902. The show was not a financial success for Cody. After a series of reorganizations, the remains of the show were sold at auction in 1913.

2. Irwin Brothers' Wild West Show

Charlie Irwin of Cheyenne was the guiding spirit behind the 1920s revival of the Wild West Show. Like its predecessor, the Wild West Show failed financially. Irwin was killed in an auto accident in March, 1934.

3. Tim McCoy's Wild West Show

McCoy, a movie star and former Wyoming adjutant general, opened the show in Chicago in 1938. In the next 21 days of performances, the show is said to have lost more than $300,000. The last performance ended in Washington, D. C., on May 4, 1938. McCoy returned to motion pictures.

4. Montie Montana's Wild West Show

The show opened July 31, 1971, in Nebraska, moving to West Coast cities that fall. In Phoenix, the show was sued by Ringling Brothers for infringing on "Buffalo Bill's Wild West Show and Congress of Rough Riders," a name it claimed. Montana's lawyers prevailed in the lawsuit and the show continued only to close for the time in early 1974.

The Davis Ranch near Wilson during the winter of 1936-37 had such heavy snowfall that the clotheslines were buried. Consequently, the family hung clothes out to dry on the telephone lines, according to the *Jackson's Hole Courier*, April 2, 9, 1936

TIME

Record Terms of Service

State District Court: Judge Percy W. Metz of Basin became the youngest person in the United States to serve as a district court judge when he was elected to the bench in 1913 at the age of 29. Five years earlier, he was the youngest county attorney in the United States at the age of 24. He served as district judge for 37 years (1913-1950), a Wyoming record. Two other men had similarly long tenures on the bench. Judge Sam Thompson served 36 years (1928-1964) and Judge James H. Burgess served 34 years (1916-1950).

Federal District Court: From statehood until 1955, only two men served as U. S. District Judge for Wyoming. Judge John A. Riner held the position from 1890 until 1921, a period of 31 years. Judge T. Blake Kennedy was appointed to succeed Riner and he served until 1955, 34 years. Kennedy's replacement was Judge Ewing T. Kerr who, in 1989, surpassed Kennedy's mark with 34 years of service. When he died in 1992, he was still on the bench, but in senior status.

Wyoming Supreme Court: Until 1958, the court was made up of just three justices. The record is held by Fred Blume, who was elected in 1921, and served on the Supreme Court until 1963 (42 years). Charles Potter, elected to the court in 1895, served until 1927 (32 years). Other lengthy tenures were posted by Ralph Kimball (1921-1952) and William Riner (1928-1955).

U. S. Senate: Francis E. Warren (R-Wyo) had the longest service in the U. S. Senate when he died in office after serving 37 years and four days. The mark was surpassed by Sen. Carl Hayden (D-Ariz) who served from 1912-69.

Congress: Frank Mondell served 12 terms in Congress from 1899-1923. Had he sought re-election instead of unsuccessfully challenging Sen. John B. Kendrick in a Senate election, he would have become Speaker of the House. No Wyomingite has held that position.

Governor: Ed Herschler is the only person ever elected governor for three terms. First elected in 1974, he served until 1987.

Secretary of State: Thyra Thomson served six terms, 24 years, from 1963-1987. She holds the record of service for that post as well as for all five statewide elected positions.

Legislature: Elton Trowbridge, Carbon Co., served for 34 years (1939-1973).

Mayor: Russell Staats retired in 1985 after serving 54 years as mayor of Chugwater, a state record.

State Offices: Many state employees have held positions for several decades. *Some of the most notable in terms of continuous service include:*

State Engineer: L. C. Bishop, 18 years (1939-1957)

State Examiner: Norris Hartwell, 25 years (1941-1966)

Adjutant General: R. L. Esmay, 34 years (1929-1963). The mark is a record for any adjutant general in the United States.

Deputy State Treasurer: Charles B. Morgan, 41 years (1913-1955). Total years in the treasurer's office: 45. Morgan served under 12 state treasurers. In 1955, he resigned and ran for the top post. He was elected and served until 1959 when he retired. He died in 1965.

Wyoming Highway Patrol director: Col. William Bradley, 24 years (1941-1965)

Librarian: John Slaughter served as territorial librarian from 1873 to statehood in 1890, during which time he was also territorial superintendent of schools. From 1890 to 1892, his daughter Minnie held the post of state librarian. Slaughter was reappointed to the position in 1892 and served until 1903 for a total of 28 years.

President of the University of Wyoming: Dr. Arthur G. Crane held the post from 1922 to 1941. Dr. George Duke Humphrey was university president from 1945-1964. Each man served 19 years.

State Hospital Medical Director: Dr. Charles Solier served as director of the Evanston facility for 39 years.

Medical Practice: Dr. George P. Johnston (1863-1956) practiced medicine in Cheyenne for 60 years. During that time, he delivered about 11,000 babies.

Law Practice: Many lawyers have practiced in Wyoming in excess of 60 years. Thomas Nicholas, at his death in 1993, had been a member of the Wyoming State Bar for 73 years. He began his practice soon after he received his law degree with the first graduating class at UW College of Law in 1920.

Newspapers: N. O. Reed was publisher of the *Glenrock Independent* for 57 years (1939-1996). George W. Hopkins, Jr., published and edited the *Big Piney Examiner* for 51 consecutive years (1917-1968). Francis Warren (b. 1915) retired in Sept. 1997, after nearly 70 years as a pressman for the *Laramie Boomerang.*

Sugar Beet Campaigns: John D. Fink, Jr., of Lovell worked 52 consecutive beet campaigns for Great Western Sugar Company from 1932-1986. (There were no campaigns in 1941 and 1984).

Railroad Station Agent: E. R. Maris was the Newcastle railroad agent for 49 years, 7 months. He took the job the day the station opened, Nov. 18, 1889.

Organization President: Dave Flitner, Greybull, was elected to his 23rd consecutive term as president of the Wyoming Farm Bureau Federation in Dec. 1992.

Organization Treasurer: Alf Diefenderfer, Sheridan, was treasurer of the Sheridan Elks Club for more than 61 years (1899-1961).

Weather Observer: John Kortes, a rancher near Leo, Carbon County, was honored by the weather service in March, 2000, for having served as an observer for 70 years. He served for an additonal five years, retiring in 2005. He started recording the daily readings in 1930. He was only the third person in U. S. history to serve as a weather observer for 70 years. He died in Casper at the age of 101 in May 2009.

In Three Centuries: Zora Tubbs Lewenthal (b. Casper, March 29, 1898) celebrated the beginning of the 21st century, one of the few Wyomingites to live in three centuries. Her father had been Justice of the Peace and Casper hotel owner.

Sports referee: Andrew "Moose" Marosok, Sheridan, refereed in 34 consecutive state basketball tournaments and other events for 43 years.

Contents of Time Capsules

1. Supreme Court Building, Cheyenne

"Buried" inside the wall in 1937, the copper-lined box was opened in January, 1987. It contained state documents from 1937, old newspapers, official photographs, family pictures and phonograph records. Also enclosed was an essay written by Jack Gage, then Superintendent of Public Instruction.

2. St. Mark's Episcopal Church, Laramie

The cornerstone was laid in 1886. The contents included a Bible, the *Book of Common Prayer*, a report of the territorial governor to the Secretary of the Interior in 1885, church publications, five newspapers, a premium list of the First Annual Fair of Wyoming, a map of the territory, a history of the parish and other items.

3. Casper City Hall

The cornerstone was laid in August 1918, when the building was constructed and the cornerstone contents were emptied when the structure was demolished in 1960. Inside were found various official papers, old coins and numerous old newspapers. One newspaper

Average interval of eruption of Old Faithful Geyser is 78 minutes. Until earthquake activity in recent years, the average was 65 minutes (from 30-120 minutes).

was not represented. The *Natrona County Tribune* editor had criticized the quality of the construction so the town officials omitted including a copy of his paper in the cornerstone.

4. Old Main, University of Wyoming

The cornerstone was laid Sept. 27, 1886. Contained inside were copies of official reports, city ordinances and the Bible.

5. Territorial Prison, Laramie

A box containing chewing tobacco, a hand-crafted eyebolt, a letter and picture, was found by Rick Kagel of Soderberg Masonry, during reconstruction of the prison in May 1989. The box had been hidden by a prisoner near the top of a wall in the north wing. Items inside the box dated from 1873, the first year the prison was used.

6. United Methodist Church, Cheyenne

A copper-coated tin box was placed in the church cornerstone when it was laid Nov. 27, 1890. A century later, the contents were opened before the congregation. Items inside included a gold-edged Cambridge Bible, a book of Disciplines of the Methodist Episcopal Church, copies of church publications and several Wyoming newspapers, pen and ink drawings of downtown Cheyenne and the state capitol building and other small items. The box was replaced with a new stainless steel container in which were placed numerous modern publications, messages to future members of the congregation and a U. S. flag used during President George Bush's trip to Frontier Days in 1990.

7. Medicine Bow

Items from local families were placed in the time capsule to be opened in 2033. However, it was opened at a ceremony in 2009, 25 years after it was placed and not 50 years. The time capsule had been held in a safe in the Medicine Bow Museum.

Time Capsules Still in the Ground

1. Centennial

Buried on July 4, 1976, while a raging fire destroyed a nearby lumber mill, the capsule was opened July 10, 1990, the 100th anniversary of statehood.

2. Cheyenne

Buried in the ground next to the sidewalk in front of the State Supreme Court Building in July, 1976, the capsule is to be opened July 4, 2076. The capsule was donated by Reynolds Aluminum Company.

3. University of Wyoming

A time capsule was buried in the center of Prexy's Pasture in 1986 as part of the university's centennial celebration. It is to remain buried for the next 100 years.

4. St. Paul's United Church of Christ, Laramie

A time capsule was placed behind the cornerstone in 1990, the 100th anniversary of the first services held at the historic Laramie building. The contents included centennial materials, church artifacts and letters written to the congregation who will worship in 2090 when the time capsule is to be opened.

5. Eleanor Chatterton Kennedy/Joe & Arlene Watt Centennial Complex, UW

In 1991, each county was invited to provide items for inclusion in the time capsule buried at the new facility. Among the counties responding were: Campbell (framed photographs of centennial quilts); Fremont (a commemorative plaque); Johnson (paperback books about the Johnson County War); Niobrara (map and program for the Legend of the Rawhide pageant); and Sheridan (King's Ropes hat and local newspaper). Also enclosed was a copy of the book by Emmett D. Chisum, *Memories of the University of Wyoming.*

6. Downtown Park, Evanston

The time capsule, buried in front of the rebuilt Joss house in the historic downtown mall, was sealed Dec. 15, 1990. It is to be opened in 2040.

TREES AND PLANTS

Wyoming State Tree: Cottonwood (Populus Sargentii), adopted by legislative act in 1947.

Wyoming contains 9.7 million acres of national forest lands.

1st forest reserve established in Wyoming: Yellowstone Park Timber Reserve, 1.2 million acres of forests bordering the park on the east and the south, created by order of Pres. Benjamin Harrison on March 30, 1891, under the terms of the Forest Reserve Act passed by Congress. Teton Forest Reserve, containing much of what is now Grand Teton National Park, was set aside by Pres. Grover Cleveland Feb. 22, 1897. The Medicine Bow Forest Reserve was created May 22, 1903.

1st ranger station in the United States: Wapiti Ranger Station in the Shoshone National Forest, west of Cody, built in 1903.

1st forest ranger in Wyoming: John Reid (b. 1846). He later served as Laramie municipal judge.

1st tie drive in Wyoming: On the Laramie River in 1868. Each tie hack made 20-25 ties per day which were used by the Union Pacific Railroad on the first transcontinental rail line.

1st tie drive on the Wind River: J. D. Stewart of Dubois organized it in 1906.

1st major tree planting on UW campus, Laramie: A group of citizens planted 160 trees on the campus on Arbor Day, 1897, "to soften its frontier aspect."

Beautification Awards: The city of Gillette was awarded the National Arbor Day Foundation's Lady Bird Johnson award in 1991 for planting 810 trees along major roads since since 1984. Sheldon Barney of Green River was presented with the Lady Bird Johnson Award on April 29, 2000, by the National Arbor Day Foundation. He received the award for his work from 1989-1999 planting trees between Rock Springs and Green River. Barney began the work soon after retiring from Mountain Fuel in 1988.

1st botanists in Yellowstone: G. N. Allen and Robert Adams, Jr., Hayden expedition, 1871. Adams later served as U. S. minister to Brazil and in Congress from 1893-1906.

Largest plant museum: The Rocky Mountain Herbarium and the Wilhelm G. Solheim Mycological Collection, in the Aven Nelson Memorial Building, UW campus, house more than 540,000 dried plant specimens and 50,000 fungal specimens. The herbarium expanded in the early 1980s with the addition of 125,000 botanical specimens from the U. S. Forest Service Herbarium. In 1994, a conservatory addition to the Aven Nelson Building was built.

1st orchard in Uinta County: An apple orchard planted by Hans Davidson near present Millburne about 1905.

Rarest plant species: Yellowstone Park contains more than 1,000 known species of plants. Rarest is probably the Yellowstone sand verbena, a flower known to grow only on two miles of Yellowstone Lake shoreline. Also rare is Ross' bentgrass, known to grow in only three geyser basins along the Firehole River.

Bacterial species: A bacterial species that prefers a low temperature was named for Laramie. "Clostridium laramie" was identified by UW Food Microbiology Laboratory researchers in 1994.

The Last "Tie Drives"

1. Medicine Bow River

The Union Pacific Railroad quit using hand-hewn ties, making the tie drives obsolete. The last drive down the Medicine Bow River was held in 1940.

2. Laramie River

More than 300,000 ties went down the river to the Laramie tie plant in 1939, the final run of its kind.

3. Wind River

The last year was 1947 when 150,000 ties were floated. All were machine-sawed. Just seven years earlier, it took 75 tie hacks from 25-35 working days to fashion the 308,000 ties for the 1940 drive.

Russian thistles, commonly known as "tumbleweeds," can be used for human food, according to H. D. Harrington, plant specialist and author. He claims boiling the young shoots makes for "one of the very best potherbs we have ever eaten."

Some Well Known Wyoming Trees

1. Tree in the Rock, 17 miles east of Laramie on I-80

In 1868, the tracks of the Union Pacific Railroad were laid next to the pine tree (Pinus flexilis) which appeared to be growing out of a rock. Firemen on passing trains drenched the tree with buckets of water as the trains passed. The tracks moved to the south about 1900. Now, the tree is between the east and west lanes of the interstate highway.

2. Largest Petrified Tree

A 3,600-pound petrified log was found in the Puddle Springs area near Lander in the summer of 1954. Log owners, the Green River Oil and Uranium Company, sold it for $3,000.

3. Octopus Tree, University of Wyoming campus

The peach leaf willow (Salix sp.) was planted by Aven Nelson in the 1890s. When the tree was small, a horse-drawn mower clipped the top branches so that limbs grew outward instead of upward. For many years, the tree was a favorite rendezvous point for lovers. It stood southwest of Old Main. The tree died and was removed in the 1970s. An oil painting by Donald Wiest in the permanent collections of the University of Wyoming Art Museum depicts the famed tree.

4. Camp Monaco Tree, Shoshone National Forest

A spruce, with the inscription, "Camp Monaco 1913" painted onto it during the hunting trip of Prince Albert of Monaco and William F. Cody, died of heat exposure in the Clover-Mist forest fire, northwest of Cody, during the summer of 1988. In January, 1994, officials removed a six-foot chunk of the tree on which the inscription was painted. The job was done in about four hours with a chain saw to cut down the tree and a helicopter to lift it out. Tree rings indicated the tree's age was about 400 years. The rescued portion will be on display at the Buffalo Bill Historical Center in Cody.

5. Cottonwood "Specimen Tree"

A plains cottonwood, believed to be the largest such tree in the world, was the inspiration for designating the cottonwood as the State Tree in 1947. The huge tree was located on the Clyde Cover ranch near Thermopolis. In 1955, the tree was destroyed in a fire.

6. Wyoming's Largest Tree

The largest cottonwood tree in Wyoming is believed to be one on the Flying X Ranch in eastern Albany County, planted in the late 1880s by homesteader Arthur Dover. In 1908, Tom McGill purchased the ranch and watched after the tree. In 1990 the Wyoming Chapter of the Society of American Foresters named it the "Wyoming Centennial Tree." It measures 31 feet in circumference, has a height of 64 feet and has a crown spread averaging more than 100 feet.

7. "Steinerocaulis"

A fossilized tree, the shoots of which were first discovered by Dick Steiner of Worland in 1961, was named for the discoverer in 1991. Steiner was hunting for an ancient plant when he came across the petrified shoots of the tree near Greybull. The fossilized remains are estimated to be more than 160 million years old. Steiner had sent samples of the agatized wood to paleobotanists, but they could not identify the species. Consequently, BYU professor William Tidwell named the tree for him. "They weren't fruits and seeds [as scientists originally thought], they were short shoots. I figured there was a significant difference," Tidwell said, "and we ended up making a new genus."

The Green River Women's Club collected 970 lbs. of dandelions taken from local lawns in the late spring of 1932. Some 20 women entered the contest to see who could gather the most. Linn Switzer won first prize for turning in 352 lbs. *Source: "Dandelion drive here nets total 970 lbs." Green River Star, June 10, 1932, p. 1. (contest ended June 6, 1932).*

5 Worst Years for Forest Fires

1. 1988: The worst fires in Yellowstone National Park's recorded history burned 995,000 acres within the park borders, more than one-third of the park's area. Including the fires in adjoining areas, more than 1.2 million acres burned.

2. 1937: One fire set the mark for the most deaths from any forest fire in Wyoming. On Aug. 21, 1937, forest ranger Alfred G. Clayton and 14 members of the CCC died when the Blackwater fire unexpectedly changed direction, trapping them against a cliff. A monument next to the highway 36 miles west of Cody points to the location of the fire disaster.

3. 1931: Fires were particularly numerous that year in the Wind River Range.

4. 1889: Drought, following extreme winters, caused the fire season to be the worst in the early history of Wyoming.

5. 2000: Drought caused serious fires, particularly in the Wind River and Owl Creek ranges.

Some Plants Used by Indians

1. Cottonwood

Medicine men used the cooked sap in treatment of broken limbs. When the sap reached the consistency of honey and the broken limb had been set, the medicine man spread the sap liberally over the arm or leg and then wrapped it tightly. Once the substance hardened, the wrapping became as hard as a plaster cast. After a month, the cast would begin to disintegrate, in time for the limb to have healed.

2. Bedstraw (Galium borcale)

The plant, used for bedding, also was a source for purple dye.

3. Sagebrush

Indians used the plant primarily for its yellow dye. It was used medicinally as an eyewash to relieve eye inflammation.

4. Elephanthead (Pedicularis groenlandica)

The plant was a prime source of salves for wounds.

5. Wintergreen

The substance was rubbed on insect bites to relieve the itch.

6. Yarrow

Another plant used for wound salves.

7. Blueflax (Lewis flax or Linum lewisii)

Indians in Wyoming made fishnets and cords from the plant.

8. Blue camas

Indians roasted the bulbs for food. Another camas, the mountain death camas (Zigadenus elegans) was the most deadly plant known to native people.

9. Cattail (Typha latifolia)

The plant was used for bedding, for emergency food and for dyes. During World War II, Wyomingites gathered cattails for use in life preservers.

4 Endangered Plants in Wyoming*

1. Colorado Butterfly plant (Gaura neomxicana)

The rare biennial herb was first listed as threatened in 2000 by the U. S. Fish and Wildlife Service and the critical habitat was designated Feb. 10, 2005. The only known Colorado butterfly plants are mostly on private land within a small area in southeastern Wyoming, western Nebraska, and north-central Colorado. With less than 50,000 reproducing individuals, only 10 of the 14 current populations are stable or increasing.

2. White Bark Pine

Whitebark pine trees can live up to 1,000 years. They grow at elevations up to 12,000 feet in conditions too harsh for most trees. In the summer of 2010, the U. S. Fish and

Wildlife Service announced the species would be placed on the endangered list because of the devastations from the mountain pine beetle and a rare fungus. Aerial surveys in 2009 showed beetles nearly wiped out some whitebark forests, including some along the eastern edge of Yellowstone National Park.

3. Ladies'-tresses (Spiranthes diluvialis)

The plant is found is small numbers in eight states, including Wyoming, but according to some reports, the largest concentration consists of 500 plants. The plant was first listed as threatened January 17, 1992.

4. Desert Yellowhead (Yermo xanthocephalus)

In 2002, the Federal government listed the desert yellowhead as threatened and, in 2004, an area of 360 acres surrounding the only known population was designated critical habitat. The sunflower species was discovered by botanist Robert Dorn in 1990 in southern Fremont County while he was conducting a survey of other rare plants. Dorn recognized that it was a new species and applied the name in 1991. Only 15,000 flowers exist on five acres in the one location where Dorn initially made the discovery.

*Listed on the Endangered Species List or proposed for listing.

11 Other Rare Plants in Wyoming

1. Antennaria arcuata

Known as meadow pussy-toes, it is no longer listed as a candidate for the endangered species list. The plant occurs in only 23 reported places in Wyoming, primarily in southern Fremont County on the northern edge of the Red Desert, but surveys in the middle 1990s found some 100,000-130,000 individual plants in 15 of the populations and several new populations were found in 1997.

2. Lesquerella Fremontii

Known as the Fremont bladderpod, the plant lives on rocky limestone slops in southern Fremont County.

3. Arabis pusilla

Known as Small Rock Cress, the plant has a TNC Natural Heritage ranking of extreme rarity and a state rank of critically imperiled. The plant is known to grow in only one small area in the southern Wind River Range in Fremont County.

4. Artemisia Porteri

Also known as Porter's sagebrush, the plant grows in the vicinity of South Pass and in the geographical center of the state along the Fremont-Natrona county line.

5. Townsendia microcephala

The Cedar Mountain Easter Daisy grows in one area in extreme southwestern Sweet-water County. It has a TNC Natural Heritage ranking of extreme rarity.

6. Thelesperma caespitosum

The Green River Greenthread grows in only one area in Wyoming in western Sweet-water County.

7. Physaria dornii

Dorn's Twinpod, first identified by Robert Dorn in 1992, is found in two locations in the Rock Creek Ridge area of Lincoln County.

Cheyenne publisher W. C. Deming presented the University of Wyoming with $6,000 in 1943 from which awards would be made over the next 20 years to successful farm shelterbelts and windbreaks. Because some prizes were not awarded and the contest was suspended because of World War II for a period, the last awards were made in October, 1969. First place winners that year were Elmer E. Fabricius of Burlington in the "irrigated division" and David J. Bredthauer, Lusk, in the "dryland division." Edith Champman of Lander received the "home beautification" award and a special award was given to Peter J. Owens, Lusk, for "caring for trees along a county road."

8. Draba pectinipila

Comb-hair Whitlow-grass grows on the Beartooth Plateau in northern Park County.

9. Sullivantia Hapemanii

The plant grows in shady canyons on both sides of the Big Horn Mountains.

10. Penstemon caryi

Known as Cary's beardtongue, the flowering plant grows mostly along the west slopes of the Big Horn Mountains in Big Horn and Washakie counties.

11. Cryptantha subcapitata

Owl Creek miner's candle is a plant that grows along the slopes of the Owl Creek range in southern Hot Springs and northern Fremont counties.

Source: Endangered and Threatened Plants in the United States. (Washington: Smithsonian, 1978); Fertig, Refsdal and Whipple. Wyoming Rare Plant Field Guide. (NPWRC, 1994),

One Well-Known Wyoming Botanist

1. Aven Nelson, (b. Iowa, 1859, d. Colorado Springs, 1952),

Nelson, one of the first five faculty members at UW, stepped down as UW president in 1922 to return to his first love, botany. He founded the Rocky Mountain Herbarium at UW in 1893. In his later years, with his second wife Ruth, he traveled widely, identifying new plants and conducting botany research. In *Botanical Companions: A Memoir of Plants and Place* (2005), author Frieda E. Knobloch writes about their lives centered on botany, where "work, nature, and companionship walked together." Phacelia Anelsonii, or more commonly know as Aven Nelson's Phacelia, is an annual forb/herb of the genus Phacelia. It is found throughout the United States, but grows widely in California, Nevada and Utah.

Killed by an Elephant...in Wyoming

Elephants are as rare around Medicine Bow now as they are anywhere else in Wyoming. But there in 1903, an elephant went on a rampage.

Alias Kalby was a Turk employed by a traveling circus. On May 24, 1903, as the circus caravan traveled east from Rawlins, Kalby was tending the elephants, a job he had held for several years. One elephant, according to later newspaper reports, was "very attached to Kalby."

The *Laramie Boomerang* reported what happened: "Kalby was in the car with the elephant trying to pacify him as he became more and more unruly and without thinking of his danger, he passed between the side of the car and the towering flank of the giant brute. In an instant the elephant threw his weight against the man and crushed him furiously against the strong iron-lined side of the car...So furious was the elephant that it was a long time before anyone could approach near to him or induce him to release his pressure upon the mangled body of the keeper."

The train's next stop was Medicine Bow. There, the man's remains were taken from the train and the Carbon County coroner was summoned to conduct a coroner's inquest. The jury returned a verdict of "death from misadventure."

Because the man had no survivors in this country, his body was buried in the Medicine Bow cemetery following a short funeral service. Apparently, it was organized by other Turks who were employed by the circus as keepers and tenders.

While the Turk buried in Medicine Bow might be the only person in a Wyoming cemetery killed by an elephant, he may not be the only victim of such beasts in the state's history. Might an incalculable number of Wyomingites in "cave man days" have been victims of mammoths that roamed the state? If so, where their bodies might be buried is anyone's guess....

UNIVERSITIES AND COLLEGES

1st building on the University of Wyoming campus: Old Main, cornerstone laid Sept. 27, 1886, opened for classes in the fall of 1887.

1st student body, UW: 42 students, taught by 5 professors and 2 tutors (1887).

1st alumni association in Wyoming: University of Wyoming Alumni Association, organized in 1895 with 15 members.

1st graduate school in Wyoming: UW, established in 1899.

1st summer school at UW: 1905, 27 students enrolled.

1st student newspaper at UW: *"Wyoming Student,"* published from 1899-1923 when the name was changed to the *Branding Iron*. The publication was a weekly until 1973 when it became a daily.

1st law school in Wyoming: University of Wyoming College of Law, opened in September 1920.

1st recipient of the George Duke Humphrey Distinguished Teaching Award, University of Wyoming: Dr. William T. Mulloy (1964)

1st homecoming game, University of Wyoming: 1922

1st community college in Wyoming: Casper College, first classes held Sept. 17, 1945, with 156 students enrolled. Classes were held on the third floor of NCHS. The college moved to its current location in 1955.

1st national debate champions from UW: Pat Hacker and Mike Anselmi, 1967. The national collegiate champion debaters then faced the USSR team in a debate exhibition in Toronto, Ontario. The topic was: "Resolved: The United States should immediately withdraw its forces from Vietnam." There was no winner declared in the exhibition match.

1st serving of beer in the Student Union, UW: 1976

1st American Indian graduation ceremony at the UW: May 7, 1993

1st UW professor elected to the legislature: Dr. T. A. Larson was retired when he was elected in 1976. Jim Rose, an engineering professor, was elected in 1998.

President's home, 1306 Ivinson, was added to University of Wyoming plant in 1949. The house was sold in 1995.

1st college of pharmacy in Wyoming: UW College of Pharmacy, formed in 1948.

Percent of state population, age 25+, holding a bachelor's degree or higher, 2005: 24.6%, 28th among the states.

Openings of Wyoming Colleges

1. Casper College, Sept. 17, 1945

The college opened with 73 daytime students and 83 evening students. Classes were held in the west wing of the third floor of Natrona County High School. The college had 17 faculty including Maurice F. Griffith, the 29-year-old dean. Land for the present site was obtained in 1951 and the first buildings opened there in the fall of 1955. *Source: Kevin S. Anderson, Spirit of the Thunderbird: The Growth of Casper College. (Casper College, 1995).*

2. National Outdoor Leadership School (NOLS)

NOLS was founded in Lander in May, 1965, by well-known mountaineer Paul Petzoldt. By 1999, approximately 50,000 people had taken NOLS courses. The organization, still headquartered in Lander, has nine branch schools and offers courses in Australia, Kenya, Patagonia, India and numerous other places. Famous graduates include John F. Kennedy Jr., who enrolled in the NOLS Kenya program in the late 1970s.

3. Wyoming Catholic College, Lander

The college was incorporated on July 11, 2005 with the first class of 34 freshmen admitted in the fall of 2007.The site for the college was selected in the fall of 2004 on land which included a 600-acre tract donated by Francie Mortenson. While construction plans were under way, courses were taught at the interim site in Holy Rosary Church. Founding board of directors were: Bishop David L. Ricken,Cheyenne; Dr. Robert K. Carlson, Casper; Father Robert Cook, Casper; Harry Flavin, San Antonio; Kate McDonnell, Chicago; Victor Riley, Cody. Father Cook was appointed the first president of the college.

Some Defunct Wyoming Colleges

1. Wyoming Collegiate Institute, Big Horn

Chartered in March 1890, and founded in 1892 as "Wyoming College and Normal School," the Institute graduated its first and only class in May 1897. The four graduates were the only people to receive degrees from the school. They were: Sula L. Sackett (later Mrs. T. J. Gatchell), Edna M. Jackson (later Mrs. Carver), James Malcolm White, and Carl L. Sackett. Sackett later served as U. S. Attorney for Wyoming for many years. The school closed its doors in 1898 because of financial problems.

2. Wyoming Agricultural College, Lander

In January 1891, the legislature authorized an agricultural college. The voters approved such an institution in the general election of 1892. According to the ballot measure, the site for the college had to have "an elevation of more than 5,500 feet above sea level." Lander was designated the site for the college, but an economic depression soon after the 1892 election stalled further progress on the school until 1903. On June 17, 1903, Philip Wisser died, leaving his estate, amounting to more than $17,000, for establishment of a Lander college. Trustees were selected who chose the campus site. On Feb. 2, 1905, the board hired a president and faculty Five days later, the legislature rescinded their 1891 act. The case went to court. and the Wyoming Supreme Court, ruled on Jan. 31, 1906, that the college act had been repealed by the legislature. Lander would not become home of "Wyoming State University."

3. Cody Military College and International Academy of Rough Riders

The school was organized in 1901. William F. Cody was president of the college and General E. V. Sumner was in charge of college operations. The school's aim was to teach all aspects of military science. According to the promotional brochures, "[Such] an institution is made useful, if not necessary, by the great changes in military tactics which the past ten years have recorded." The school failed to compete with established institutions, however. Col. Jay L. Torrey, organizer of the Spanish American War unit known as "Torrey's Rough Riders," considered establishing a similar school at Embar, Hot Springs County. He hired Capt. H. H. Austin, the former president of Big Horn Academy, but the school never became a viable operation.

4. Jireh College, Jireh

Several dozen members of the Christian Church of Dayton, Ohio, formed the farming colony of Jireh in 1908 in what is now Niobrara County. The college cornerstone was laid Oct. 21, 1909. Classes began in 1910. At its peak, Jireh College enrolled 65 students. Gov. John B. Kendrick addressed the four graduates at commencement in 1913. The school closed in 1918 and, a short time later, the financially strapped colony also failed. Jireh's most famous student was G. Edward Pendray who was scientist, author and Westinghouse Electric official.

5. Yellowstone College, Himes (across the river from Lovell)

Dr. Virgil V. Phelps, a Yale Ph.D., founded the college on the banks of the Big Horn River in the fall of 1912. The school graduated just one class—four students—before it closed June 13, 1913. One student, Alma Chronholm Fry, received a B. A. degree from the school. Two gained associate of arts degrees and one, a public school diploma. The campus consisted of "one medium-sized cabin." Dr. Phelps planned for a modern brick structure for the school, but the college closed before the new building was completed.

6. Cheyenne Business College, Cheyenne

One of a number of business colleges to operate in the state in the first half of this century, the Cheyenne school lasted the longest of any of them. It opened in 1905 and closed 30 years later, a victim of the "Great Depression."

7. Big Horn Academy, Cowley

The academy opened in 1911, but its collegiate department never became active. The academy remained a preparatory school after it moved to a new building in December 1917. Later, the building was bought by the school district and converted into Cowley High School in the fall of 1924.

8. Wyoming Correspondence School of Penmanship

One of the numerous schools established to teach specific skills to high school graduates, the school was founded in 1911 by H. T. Kubota of Kemmerer. He operated the school as the only "faculty" member until its closure in the 1920s.

Some Interesting Donations

1. Charles Clay (1887)

The Laramie man donated 300 books to the University of Wyoming which formed the beginnings of the University library collection.

2. Ferdinand LaFrentz (1888)

The Cheyenne-based cattleman who later became an Eastern financier sold ten copies of a book of his poems titled "Cowboy Stuff" for $5,000 per book. He then donated the proceeds to Lincoln Memorial University, Cumberland, Tenn., in order for that institution to build a dormitory.

3. Philip Wisser (1903)

The Lander man willed $17,000 for establishment of the Wyoming Agricultural College at Lander. The college was never built. (See "Defunct Wyoming Colleges," above)

4. John E. Higgins (1926)

When the Glenrock hotel operator and financier died, his will left $500,000 to the State of Wyoming for construction of a teachers' college at Glenrock. The legislature passed enabling legislation for the school in 1927, but Gov. Frank Emerson vetoed the measure. The bill was re-introduced in the 1929 session by State Sen. Leonard Smith of Converse County, but this time, it did not pass the legislature. The college was never built.

5. William and Caroline Gottsche (1944)

The Sweetwater County ranchers willed $750,000 to build the Gottsche Rehabilitation Center in Thermopolis, originally planned as a center for the treatment and rehabilitation of polio sufferers. Their only daughter Margaret had died from the effects of the disease at the age of 14. Gottsche came to the Rock Springs area in 1882 and, in 1890, married Caroline, a native of Rock Island, Ill. The Gottsches ran 50,000 sheep on their ranch. He also served as bank president and state senator from Sweetwater County. He died in 1939, but their joint gift became effective on his wife's death five years later.

6. Roy Montgomery (1949)

The Campbell County man gave half of his estate to the State of Wyoming to assist blind citizens. The corpus of the trust (1999) was some $3.56 million. Groups helping the blind as well as individuals may apply for help. The trust buys magnifying readers, computers, assistive devices for those who apply and qualify. *(Source: Jack F. Mueller, chair, trust's advisory board).*

7. William R. Coe (1956)

The Coe estate left more than $1.8 million to the University of Wyoming for construction of a new library and establishment of an American Studies program. As a result of the donation, the university named the new library for Coe. The Cody resident's estate also funded American Studies programs at Stanford, Yale and Simpson College in Arkansas.

8. Count Frederic Thorne-Rider

The New Jersey-born Sheridan County resident pledged $250,000 as a challenge match for construction of Sheridan College. Thorne-Rider Commons on the Sheridan College campus is named for him and for Harriett, his wife who died July 5, 1956. The gift to the college was one of numerous donations to Sheridan civic and cultural organizations, including the sculptured bull elk that stands over the Elks section of Sheridan Muncipal Cemetery. Thorne-Rider died in May, 1963.

9. Joe and Arlene Watt (1967-1993)

The prominent ranching couple donated nearly half a million dollars to the university from 1967 to 1992 with another half million donated in 1993 in honor of Professors H. T. Person and Gene M. Gressley.

10. Chasey Kuehn (1975)

Kuehn, whose father invented the creosoting process, was a New York-based businessman who began vacationing in the Dubois area in the 1950s. Although he never attended UW, he took an interest in the institution. When he died in the middle 1970s, he left a substantial endowment to the university for developing programs in business history.

11. Clarence Siebold (1980, 1985)

The Cheyenne man donated a collection of nearly 1,000 dictionaries in all languages to the University of Wyoming in 1980. Five years later, his estate left $400,000 as an endowment to the university.

12. John E. Rouse (1986)

The owner of the One Bar Eleven Ranch, located 18 miles from Saratoga, donated 5,000 acres of ranch land and an Angus cattle herd to Colorado State University in 1986.

13. Lowell A. Morfeld (1987)

Morfeld donated the 61-room motel, restaurant and lounge known as Sundowner Station to Central Wyoming College's Foundation in 1987. The manager of the facility reports to the executive board of the CWC Foundation. Morfeld's donation was valued at more than $1 million.

14. Edwin Flittie estate; Edwin Dunn bequest (1989)

Funds from the two separate donations were used to purchase a Bosendorfer concert grand piano with computer playback features for the University of Wyoming music department in December 1989. A very few of the Austrian-made pianos are in use.

15. Medicine Bow Post (1989)

Publisher David Roberts donated the newspaper to the university for use as a community journalism laboratory. The university had a journalism department at that time. The university used the facility as a lab for journalism students until 1995 when it was closed.

.16. Ralph "Roy" Whitney (1998)

In 1998, Whitney donated several million to convert a portion of the old Chem-Zoo building into an extension for the Health Sciences college at the University of Wyoming. The president and CEO of a private equity investment banking firm in New York, Whitney lives in Wheatland. The gift was made in honor of Whitney's wife Fay, a UW nursing professor and national leader in the training of nurse practitioners.

17. Curtis and Marian Rochelle (1999)

Curtis Rochelle (b. Lusk) graduated from UW in 1941. A long-time resident of Carbon County, he served as a UW trustee from 1983-1989. In 1999, Rochelle and his wife Marian donated $4.2 million to the university for construction of the "Rochelle Athletics Center," a complex of weight rooms, classrooms and offices for the UW athletic department. The structure also houses the UW Athletics Hall of Fame.

18. Allen Cook (2005)

Cook operated a 91,000 ranch in southeastern Wyoming. He donated 4,700 acres of it to the University of Pittsburgh for geology and paleontology program in 2005. The university honors program administered what was called the Allen L. Cook Spring Creek Reserve.

19. Mildred and Claude Kissick (2006)

The Kissicks gave $200,000 for the Rozet school in Campbell County, part of which was to be used to fund scholarships for Rozet alumni continuing on to college.

20. Robert and Carol Berry Center for Biodiversity and Conservation (2007)

The building, under construction at UW in the summer of 2010, will house more than 40 botany and other physical science scholars. It was built with a $10 million gift from Wolf Creek Charitable Foundation for the University of Wyoming, of which Robert Berry was trustee. When the gift was made in 2007, it was the largest single cash gift in UW history.

21. Marian Rochelle and her daughter April Brimmer Kunz

The two prominent women donated $1 million for completion of the UW College of Law expansion. The new addition was dedicated in 2009. In March 2009, the addition was the locale for the first hearing of cases of the 10th Circuit Court of Appeals ever held in Wyoming.

22. Dick and Lynne Cheney (2008)

The Cheneys donated more than $5 million for the University of Wyoming international program. The funds were to be used for scholarships and travel as well as for reconstruction of a portion of the former Student Health Center at UW for the new International Programs offices.

Wyoming Rhodes Scholars, 1905-Present

1. H. G. Merriam, B. A., University of Wyoming, 1905.

The state's first Rhodes scholar (and in the first class of Rhodes scholars ever named), Merriam later became head of the Department of English at the University of Montana. A prolific writer and editor, he was given an honorary degree from UW in 1962. He died in 1980.

2. Edward N. Roberts, B. A., UW, 1911

Roberts had a long career as research chemist for Standard Oil.

3. Esper W. Fitz, B. A., UW, 1911.

4. Frank G. Swain, UW, 1915.

Swain was chosen to attend Oxford in 1913. He served for many years as a California Superior Court judge in Los Angeles.

5. Seymour S. Sharp, B. A., UW, 1915

A Sheridan High School graduate, Sharp was elected to Oxford just as World War I began. He joined the army before graduating from Oxford, serving in one of the first American combat units. After the war, he returned to Wyoming and became assistant state engineer. He resigned his state position in 1924 and moved to Saratoga where he began a career as a private engineer. On July 4, 1953, Sharp drowned in the North Platte River while conducting a survey for a water line.

6. Horace N. Willcox, B. A., UW, 1917

7. Charles B. Coolidge, B. A., UW, 1920.

8. Frederick W. Layman, B. A., UW, 1921

Layman practiced law in Casper for many years and retired to Arizona.

9. S. Glenn Parker, B. A., UW, 1922.

Parker was elected to Oxford, but did not attend. He graduated from the UW College of Law and became the law school's first graduate to serve as a district judge and a member of the Wyoming Supreme Court. He served in the army in both World War I and II and became a district judge in 1949. He was appointed to the Supreme Court in 1955 and served for more than two decades. After he retired from the court, he practiced law in Cheyenne until his death at the age of 90 in April 1989.

10. Joseph Dexter Bennett, elected from Yale, 1924.

Bennett died in February 1953.

11. George T. Ross, B. A., UW, 1926.

Ross, the son of two governors (William B. Ross and Nellie Tayloe Ross) lived and worked in Washington, D. C., until his death in the early 1990s.

12. Herbert B. Woodman, B. A., UW, 1925.

Woodman served as board chairman of the New York-based firm of Interchemical company. Named a Rhodes scholar in 1927, he returned to graduate from Harvard Law School. He became president of Interchemical in 1947. In 1961, as presdient of New York's Economics Club, he presided at a dinner the club gave for Soviet Premier Nikita Khruschev.

13. Robert E. Burns, B. A., UW, 1929.

Burns was a partner in the New York law firm of Burns, Lobato and Adams.

14. John Paul Scott, B. A., UW, 1930.

Scott, the author of several books in his field, was professor of psychology at Bowling Green University in Ohio. He was honored in 1990 as an Arts and Sciences College Distinguished Alumnus. A founder of the Animal Behavior Society, he died March 26, 2000, in Toledo, Ohio

15. Lawrence H. Rogers, 1931.

Rogers attended the U. S. Military Academy and was named a Rhodes scholar while he was a cadet.

16. Robert M. Muir, B. S., UW, 1938.

Following his term at Oxford, Muir pursued a career in botany. He was a professor of botany at the University of Iowa.

17. Robert W. MacVicar, B. S., UW, 1939.

Named a Rhodes scholar, MacVicar did not enter Oxford because of World War II. Formerly vice president of Oklahoma State University, he served as president of Oregon State University until his retirement in 1986.

18. Daniel C. Jordan, B. A., UW, 1954.

Jordan was a piano major in the music department at UW. Later, he lived and worked in Massachusetts.

19. Jack O. Horton, Jr., 1960.

Horton, a native of Sheridan, graduated with a degree in geology from Princeton in 1960. From 1973 to 1977, he served as assistant secretary of the interior for land and water. He died of leukemia in Denver in February 1981, at the age of 43. At the time, he was serving on the Princeton Board of Trustees.

20. Gary Cathcart, B. S., UW, 1961.

A Cheyenne native, Cathcart was a student in mathematics at the time he was named a Rhodes scholar.

21. John Sadler, 1960

22. Marvin Henberg, B. A., Washington and Lee, 1971

Henberg, a native of Wyoming, was appointed president of the College of Idaho in July 2009.

23. John Ausink, 1976

24. Robin Russin, Rhode Island School of Design, UCLA, 1979

Russin taught screenwriting at UCLA and, later, at the University of California, Riverside. He has written for film, theater and television. His work, *On Deadly Ground,* starred Steven Seagal and Michael Caine.

25. Michael Fleming, 1982

Fleming was a native of Casper.

26. Ken Crouse, Princeton, 1987.

Crouse, a native of Casper, graduated from Kelly Walsh High School in 1983.

27. Janice Hudgings, Swarthmore, 1991.

Hudgings was the valedictorian of her class at Kelly Walsh High School in 1987.

28. Geraldine Wright, UW, 1994.

A botany major at the University of Wyoming, Wright spent a summer working at the largest tropical biology station in the world in Costa Rica. She also completed an internship in the British Museum of Natural History following a semester's study in London in 1992. After gaining the Ph.D., she was a post-doctoral fellow at Ohio State.

29. Jessica Mellinger, UW, 1999.

Mellinger, a Sheridan native, was a member of the UW golf team when she was named one of 32 Rhodes scholars nationwide in December, 2000. She was a double major in English and molecular biology with an interest in a career in medicine. In 2010 she was in the medical school at the University of Wisconsin, Madison.

Some Distinguished Scholars from Wyoming

1. Henry M. Wriston (b. Laramie, 1889, d. 1978)

Wriston graduated from Wesleyan University and received a Ph.D. in history from Harvard in 1922. He taught history at Wesleyan from 1914-1925 and served as president of Lawrence College from 1925-1937. From 1937 until his retirement in 1955, he was president of Brown University. He was also president of the Council on Foreign Relations from 1953-1964 and prominent in numerous other academic and civic organizations.

2. Ralph Aubrey Young (b. Cheyenne, 1901, d. 1980)

A professor at the Wharton School, University of Pennsylvania, until 1945, Young later became director of research and statistics for the Federal Reserve Board. He wrote numerous books on banking and finance.

3. Rensis Likert (b. Cheyenne, 1903)

Likert was director of the Institute for Social Research at the University of Michigan from 1949 until his retirement. A professor of psychology and sociology, he developed the "Likert scale" used extensively in public opinion polling. He was born in Cheyenne where his father worked for the Union Pacific Railroad.

4. Ed Bryant (b. Hat Creek, 1918)

Bryant, owner of a private economic consulting firm in Washington, D. C., once served as economist for the Department of Commerce. He has written several books on economics and statistics.

5. Alexander Schildt (B. A., University of Wyoming, 1964)

Schildt, a former president of Eastern Washington University, served as chancellor of the University of Houston.

6. Sister Irene Woodward, (b. Laramie)

Woodward served as president of Holy Names College, Oakland, Calif., in the 1970s. She held a doctorate from Catholic University of America.

7. Marvin Henberg

Henberg, a Wyoming native, became the 12th president of the College of Idaho in Caldwell, Idaho, in July 2009. Previously, he taught philosophy at Linfield College, Oregon, and at the University of Idaho. He graduated from Washington and Lee University in 1970 and earned the Ph.D. from the University of Texas in 1976.

Interior Secretary J. A. Krug, in a notice approved Oct. 3, 1946, authorized the opening of 7,720 acres on what had been Heart Mountain Relocation Center between Powell and Cody.

8. Marlan Scully (b. Casper, 1939)

Scully is a physicist best known for his work in theoretical quantum optics. A professor at Texas A&M University and Princeton University, he wrote more than 700 scientific articles, as well as standard textbooks such as "Laser Physics" He attended public schools and Casper College, finishing his undergraduate studies at the University of Wyoming and Rensselaer Polytechnic. He earned his PhD under the guidance of Willis Lamb at Yale University in 1965. The Scully-Lamb quantum theory of the laser was the first theoretical treatment which yielded the laser photon statistics, the laser linewidth, and all higher order photon correlations. It was later extended to explain behavior of the single photon maser.

9. John August List (Ph.D., University of Wyoming, 1996)

List earned his Ph.D. from the University of Wyoming in 1996. Now a professor of environmental and energy economics at the University of Chicago, from May 2002 to July 2003 he served as Senior Economist, President's Council of Economic Advisors for Environmental and Resource Economics, where he worked on multi-national market institutions to address climate change and the Clear Skies Act.

Deans/Presidents of Casper College

Maurice F. Griffith, 1945-1958	Dr. Lester T. Vierra, 1988-1990
Dr. George L. Hall, 1958-1961	Dr. A. LeRoy Strausner, 1990-2005
Dr. Tilghman H. Aley, 1961-1979	Dr. Walter Nolte, 2005-
Dr. Lloyd H. Loftin, 1979-1988	

Community College Presidents since 1990

Central Wyoming College

Jo Anne Y. McFarland	1989 –

Eastern Wyoming College

Guido E. Smith	1984 -1990	Jack L. Bottenfield	1995 –2007
Roy B. Mason	1991 –1993	Shari Olson	2007- 2008
Charles J. Engbretson (interim)	1994 –1995	Tom Armstrong	2008-

Laramie County Community College

Timothy G. Davies	1985 - 1991
Charles Bohlen	1992 – 2006
Darrel L. Hammon	2006 –

Northwest College

Philip Kendall	1989 -1991	Frances M. Feinerman	1999 –2002
John P. Hanna	1992 –1997	Miles La Rowe	2003 –2008
Mark S. Kitchen (interim)	1998	Paul Prestwich	2008-

Sheridan College Northern Wyoming Community College District

Stephen J. Maier	1988 - 2006
Kevin Drumm	2006 - 2010

Western Wyoming Community College

Tex Boggs	1988 - 2008
Karla N. Leach	2008-

The diary of Edward Robb Ellis, once held in the collections of the American Heritage Center, University of Wyoming, was the longest diary in the world with more than 18 million words. The mark was surpassed in the late 1980s when a Dayton, Wash., man claimed the record with a 23 million-word diary to which he continues to add more than 4,000 words per day. The Ellis diary is now held in the New York Public Library.

University of Wyoming Presidents

1. John Wesley Hoyt (1887-1890)

Hoyt served as territorial governor from 1878 to 1882. An unusually talented and well-educated man, Hoyt had degrees in both medicine and law. In 1887, he was appointed the first president of the University of Wyoming, a position he held until 1890. In his later years, Hoyt crusaded for creation of a "national university" in Washington, D. C., but his efforts were unsuccessful.

2. Albinus Alonzo Johnson (1891-96)

3. Frank Pierrepont Graves (1896-98)

Graves was the youngest president in the history of the University of Wyoming. He was appointed in 1896 at the age of 27. Two years later, he resigned to accept the presidency at Washington State University.

4. Elmer E. Smiley (1898-1903)

5. Charles Willard Lewis (1903-04)

6. Frederick Monroe Tisdel (1904-08)

7. James DeLoss Tower (March 28-May 8, 1908)

8. Charles Oliver Merica (1908-12)

After leaving UW, he briefly headed a training school in Minnesota and then edited an Indiana newspaper until his death in 1918.

9. Clyde A. Duniway (1912-17)

Duniway came to UW from Montana where he was second president of the University of Montana. He resigned from UW to become president of Colorado College where he served until 1924, going on to an administrative post in Eng-land. Later, he was a history professor at Carlton College where he retired in 1937. He was son of legendary suffragist Abigail Scott Duniway who edited *The New Northwest*, a suffragist newspaper, and a nephew of Harvey Scott, pioneer editor of the *Oregonian* (Portland).

10. Aven Nelson (1917-22)

Following his service as president, Nelson returned to the classroom where he already had a long career as a botanist, teacher and researcher.

11. Arthur Griswold Crane (1922-41)

Crane had one of the longest tenures of any University of Wyoming president. In 1941, Gov. Nels Smith, a long-time political foe, ordered the Board of Trustees to fire Crane. Not fired, he was eventually forced to resign. Five years later, Crane was elected Secretary of State and in 1949, he became acting governor when Gov. Lester Hunt was elected to the U. S. Senate. During Crane's tenure as university president from 1922 to 1941, the enrollment rose from 548 students to more than 2,200. Because of his university building role, he was called "Crane, the builder."

12. James E. Morrill (1942-45)

Morrill left UW to become president of the University of Minnesota.

13. George Duke Humphrey (1945-64)

Following his retirement, Humphrey was given an office in the American Studies wing of the library. He remained in Laramie until his death.

14. John T. Fey (1964-66)

Fey left UW to return to the insurance industry where he became president of National Life Insurance Company. He retired in 1982 as President and CEO of the Equitable Life Assurance Company.

15. John E. King Jr. (1966-67)

The president of Kansas State Teachers' College, Emporia, resigned following a vote of no confidence from college deans. He later became a dean of education at Southern Illinois University.

16. H. T. Person (1967-68)

Person, former dean of engineering at UW, was brought out of retirement to serve as interim president until Carlson's selection.

17. William D. Carlson (1968-78)

Following his resignation, Carlson became director of the USDA Office of Grants and Program Systems, Washington, D. C.

18. Hugh B. McFadden (1978-79)

19. Edward H. Jennings (1979-81)

Jennings, who had come to Laramie from the University of Iowa, resigned to accept the presidency of Ohio State University in 1981.

20. Donald L. Veal (1981-87)

Veal resigned in 1987 to become chief executive officer of a private research firm in Boulder, Colo.

21. Terry P. Roark (1987-97)

Roark announced his retirement in May, 1996, indicating that he planned to stay at the university as a professor of physics and astronomy. In the spring of 2000, he was named interim president at Montana State University, Bozeman.

22. Philip L. Dubois (1997-2005)

Dubois (b. Oakland, Calif., Oct. 17, 1950) came to UW in April, 1997, from the University of North Carolina, Charlotte, where he had served as provost and chief academic officer. He left UW to return to become president at UNC Charlotte in 2005.

23. Tom Buchanan (2005-   )

Buchanan was Vice President for Academic Affairs when Dubois departed, becoming acting president in 2005. Chosen as the university's permanent president in 2006, Buchanan had close ties to the University of Wyoming. He came to Wyoming as a student and earned the M.A. degree in geography prior to earning his Ph.D. from the University of Illinois. After teaching at Penn State and Illinois, he returned to UW in 1979 and joined the faculty in the Department of Geography, eventually becoming an associate dean and vice president. His wife Jacque is a native of Thermopolis.

Controversies at UW

1. "White Mule Boomerang," 1926

Three UW students were suspended and the campus minister was fired after an underground mimeographed newspaper was circulated on campus accusing President Arthur Crane of not effectively enforcing Prohibition on campus.

2. Student Protest, 1931

A short-lived student strike was called Dec. 4 to protest the activities of President Arthur Crane during and after the engineers' ball. The president left the dance, went outside and went from car to car in the parking areas, brandishing a flashlight in an attempt to determine whether "any hanky-panky" was occurring in the vehicles. He told some students, "You come out here for all your drinking and petting. You ought to go to First Street where you belong." His "moral crusade" apparently failed, but so did the strike. After Crane called in police, students returned to classes after two days and Crane apparently stayed out of darkened parking lots.

3. "The Ironing Board" (also "Yellow Sheet"), 1934

The "special issue" of the *Branding Iron*, vol. 39, #29, was published April 26, 1934. Edited by John Jacobucci, the articles mercilessly lampooned school officials. Of the 1,200

Wyoming Technical Institute was sold by Mike Schutte to Macmillan in 1986, who then sold it to Phillips Colleges, who then sold it to MJB Acquisition Company, in Dec. 1992.

copies printed, only 500 circulated and fewer avoided confiscation by an angry President Arthur Crane. Jacobucci was suspended and law student Jerry Housel was selected as editor.

4. Censorship of Books, 1947

On Oct. 25, the UW trustees voted to examine textbooks to determine "whether they are subversive or un-American." Faculty and students viewed the action as an attack on academic freedom. The trustees had the support of the labor unions, many chambers of commerce, the Denver newspapers, and the Cheyenne newspapers (owned by trustee Tracy McCraken). The controversy continued through the fall and early winter until a meeting between faculty members and trustees was held at the Plains Hotel on Jan. 20, 1948. The trustees dropped their plan.

5. Panty Raid, 1961

What began as a pre-finals week prank turned violent when an estimated 350 male students gained entrance to the Kappa Delta sorority house on the night of May 9, 1961. The intruders took 45-50 pairs of panties, ten slips, 20 girdles, and five blouses. The mob broke windows in Hoyt Hall before police, using clubs and smoke bombs, finally gained control over the situation. Two students were arrested and several suffered minor injuries.

6. Anti-War March, 1969

More than 700 Wyoming students participated in a march as part of the nationwide Vietnam moratorium. The event was overshadowed by the "Black 14" incident which began two days later.

7. "Black 14" incident, 1969

Fourteen African American football players were dropped from the team by Coach Lloyd Eaton early in the season. The 14 players had wanted to wear black arm bands to demonstrate against the racial policies of the LDS (Mormon) Church in a game against church-owned Brigham Young University. At the time, Wyoming was ranked 14th in the nation and had won the first four games of the 1969 season. Six of the "Black 14" were starting players. After the stormy meeting with Eaton at which he refused to compromise on the issue, he summarily dismissed them, causing a national incident. The university officers and the Board of Trustees backed Eaton and the players were not reinstated despite the First Amendment implications. The team, minus the black players, defeated BYU 40-7 and San Jose State 16-7 a week later. They lost the remaining four games. Several of the black players transferred to other universities. Eaton resigned after the next season when his team managed just one win. Several black players brought suit against him and the university, but the courts ruled against them.

8. Flagpole Incident, 1970

Two days after the Ohio National Guard shot anti-war demonstrators on the campus of Kent State, hundreds of Wyoming students marched to the campus flagpole on Prexy's Pasture to demonstrate their shock over the incident. With the support of University President William Carlson, Gov. Stan Hathaway ordered highway patrolmen and national guardsmen to end the demonstration. A confrontation was avoided, however, by the cool-headed intervention of Laramie law enforcement officers. After an all-night vigil around the flagpole, the student demonstrators dispersed and the flag was left flying. Unlike the "panty raid" incident of nine years earlier, the 1970 peace demonstration caused no damage or injuries to students or law officers.

Actor Harrison Ford donated a conservation easement for his ranch in December 1993. The 379 acres along the Snake River in Jackson Hole, combined with another parcel for a total of 768 acres, was covered by easements granted by owners Ford and his wife Melissa Mathison to the Jackson Hole Land Trust. It held 9,791 acres in 91 projects (December 1998).

9. Elimination of baseball and the doctorate in history, 1996

The trustees accepted UW administration recommendations to eliminate the baseball program and the history doctorate, both supposedly as a means of "cutting costs." Both moves were contested as unwarranted. The baseball team beat Grand Canyon College 24-5 in the last game of the 1996 season and the last game of UW baseball after 57 years of the sport on campus. The Department of History lost almost a dozen quality students to other institutions in the U. S. Neither action contributed appreciably to the stated goal of "cutting costs."

10. Reassessment of UW Physics Department

In 1999, the administration recommended that the graduate programs in physics at UW be eliminated. After protracted discussions and protests, the trustees placed a temporary moratorium on admissions to the program, pending review.

11. William Ayers Lecture on Campus, 2010

Ayers was scheduled to speak at UW, but campus officials abruptly cancelled the speech, citing security concerns. After a court hearing on the matter brought by a UW student, U. S. District Judge William Downes ordered the university to allow Ayers to speak. *(See p. 265).*

UW Student Union Directors

1. Burton Deloney (died in the Battle of the Bulge in WWII)
2. Elton Davis (acting)   5. Walt Miller   8. Jack Harrison   11. Bill Furth
3. Dessa Tippetts (acting)   6. Bob Justis   9. Maury Seaman   12. Darcy DeTienne
4. Edna Tichac Schilz   7. Larry Clark   10. Greg Tatham

Some Titles of University of Wyoming Theses Written by Wyoming Political Figures

1. "Highway Acceleration in Wisconsin: A Case Study in Executive-Legislative Relations," by Richard B. Cheney, 1966.

Cheney, vice presidential nominee in 2000, former Wyoming congressman and Secretary of Defense in the elder George Bush's administration, wrote the thesis for the M. A. degree in political science at the University of Wyoming.

2. "A Political Biography of Jack R. Gage," by Kathleen M. Karpan, 1975.

Among other offices, Gage served as Secretary of State from 1959-1961, the office Karpan held from 1987-1995.

3. "The Women of the Intermountain States in Literature" by Velma Linford, 1935.

Linford served as State Superintendent of Public Instruction from 1954-1963. Later, she was an official with the Johnson administration's VISTA program in Washington, D.C. She died in Washington in 2002.

4. "Sacajawea's Role in Western History" by William F. Bragg, Jr., 1953.

Bragg, who died in 1988, wrote several books on Wyoming history. An instructor and public information officer at Casper College, he was well known for his lectures on Wyoming history. He served in the legislature and as president of the State Historical Society.

"Manufacturing Consent: Noam Chomsky and the Media," a 1993 Canadian documentary, begins when linguist professor Noam Chomsky is being interviewed about "Thought Control in a Democratic Society" by Marci Randall Miller at KUWR Wyoming Public Radio in Laramie. Chomsky is also shown in the documentary giving a speech at the University of Wyoming.

Yearbook Editors, University of Wyoming, 1909-1989*

1909: Leslie B. Cook	1946: Leota Carson	1966: Ann Christensen
1912: L. A. Goines	1948: Ann Schmidt	1967: Wendy Young
1915: Seymour S. Sharp	1949: Bill Quinn	1968: Judy Poage
1918: Ben Appleby	1950: Ted B. Chapman	1969: Jacque Boyd
1921: Milward Simpson	1951: Russ Patterson	1970: Betty Millsaps
1922: Murray S. Klain	1952: Carl Kubo	1971: Sue Svenson
1923: Bates Booth	1953: Jacque Janssen	1973: Rich Alford
1924: Herbert Woodman	1954: Bob Smith	1975: Gwendolyn Haynes
1925: George F. Guy	1955: Thomas W. Love	1976: Kym Stogsdill
1926: J. M. Bruner	1956: Claude P. Mapes	1977: Rick Bush
1927: T. Eldon Boyd	1957: Sharon Dickensheets	1982: Renee Middleton
1928: Shelby Thompson	1958: Don Ricks	1983: Bill Dube
1929: Alice Moudy	1959: Carole J. Donley	1984: John Batenhorst
1930: William Holland	1960: Peggy Blackwell	1985: Shelby Bonner
1931: Elmer Modeer	1961: Donna Evans	1986: Megan Woods
1932: Lawrence Burley	1962: Robert Marshall	1987: Sheri Zapp
1933: Ernest A. Gould	1963: Ann Siren	1988: Sheri Zapp
1942: Jean Ann Dunn	1964: Larry Vering	1989: Sheri Zapp
1945: Elinor Thomas	1965: Ron Salvagio	

Yearbooks were not published after 1989.

George Duke Humphrey Distinguished Teaching Award Recipients, University of Wyoming*

1964: William T. Mulloy	1987: Jason Lillegraven
1965: L. Floyd Clarke	1988: Robert Jenkins
1966: T. Alfred Larson	1989: Barbara Baumgardner
1967: Jean F. Messer	1990: Richard Ewing
1968: Eric J. Lindahl	1991: Deborah Hardy
1969: Everett D. Lantz	1992: E. George Rudolph
1970: Frank J. Trelease	1993: Stephen Miller
1971: Donald L. Blackstone	1994: Conrad Kercher
1972: Charles P. Seltenrich	1995: Harold L. Bergman
1973: Francis M. Long	1996: Dennis Knight
1974: Sara Jane Rhoads	1997: David Jaeger
1975: Verne J. Varineau	1998: A. Duane Porter
1976: Richard A. Pasewark	1999: Myron Allen III
1977: Samuel W. Harding	2000: Maggi Murdock
1978: Gabor Vail	2001: Art Snoke
1979: Reid C. Miller	2002: William McLean
1980: Harold P. Aley	2003: Cedric Reverand
1981: E. Leon Borgman	2004: James I. Drever
1982: Thomas R. Preston	2005: Randy Lewis
1983: William C. Guenther	2006: Narina Nunez
1984: Robert S. Houston	2007: Jeff Lockwood
1985: George S. Frison	2008: Carol Frost
1986: John Wideman	2009: Bryan Shader

Named for UW president, 1945-64

Presidents, Associated Students, University of Wyoming
(ASUW was organized in 1912)

1937: Burton DeLoney
1938: David Hitchcock
1939: Ernest Wilkerson
1940: Teno Roncalio
1941: Darwin Solomon
1942: Don Shanor
1943: Jean Ballantyne
1944: Lyell Knight
1945: Lyell Knight
1946: Thomas Bell
1947: Glenn Daniel
1948: Robert Murphy
1949: John Callahan
1950: Walt Urbigkit
1951: Bill Brown
1952: Dean Borthwick
1953: Paul N. Carlin
1954: Dick Brown
1955: Bob McDonald
1956: Jerry Hand
1957: Bob Ralston
1958: Ron Mathewson
1959: Pat Smyth
1960: Colin Kaltenbach
1961: Brent Eastman
1962: Frank Mendicino
1963: Mike Golden
1964: John Hursh
1965: Gary Mathews

1966: Bill Keefe
1967: Keith Hanson
1968: Robert Hanscum
1969: Hoke MacMillan
1970: Bob Archuleta
1971: David F. Berry
1972: Calvin Rerucha
1973: Steve Miller
1974: John Sullivan
1975: Gary T. Coles
1976: Bruce L. Lawton
1977: Owen L. Stone
1978: Randall B. Luthi
1979: Martha J. Brown
1980: Martell Hilderbrand
1981: Lynn Nannemann
1982: John Eisenhauer
1983: Don Rissler
1984: John Eisenhauer
1985: Robin Kerr
1986: Rich Jamieson
1987: Greg Akers
1988: Lisa Skiles
1989: David Miller
1990: David Miller
1991: Travis Gentry
1992: Travis Gentry
1993: Julia Yates
1994: Matthew Ward

1995: Sam Krone
1996: Jason Thompson
1997: Scott Neu
1998: Jesus Rios
1999: Nathan Hammons
2000: Kara Calvert
2001: Warnell Brooks
2002: Keith Sapp
2003: Jack Edwards
2004: David Willms
2005: Jon Hughes
2006: Travis Jordan
2007: David Kiren
2008: Kelsey Day
2009: Matt Haigler

Student senators have included: Larry Birleffi (1938), Robert Rose (1939), Pete Simpson (1952), Al Simpson (1953), Mike Sullivan (1959).

Information provided by Patricia Diehl, administrative secretary, ASUW; update courtesy of Lorraine Lupton.

3 UW Dormitories Named for Faculty Women

1. Downey Hall

The university dormitory, part of the Washakie Center complex, is named for Laramie native Dr. June Etta Downey (b. July 13, 1875, d. Trenton, N.J., Oct. 10, 1932). Dr. Downey graduated from UW in 1898 and then went on for a Ph.D from the University of Chicago (1907), returning the next year to teach at UW. She was a senior member of the psychology and philosophy faculties at her death.

2. White Hall

The dormitory, at 12 stories, one of the tallest buildings in Wyoming, was named for UW history professor Laura White (b. Bloomington, Ill., d. 1948). She came to UW in 1913 and, the next year, became department chair at the age of 26, remaining in that capacity until her death in July, 1948.

3. McIntyre Hall

Also 12 stories, the dormitory stands across Washakie Center from White Hall. It is named for Clara McIntyre, prominent UW English professor.

In 1964, more than 800 young men went through fraternity "rush" at UW. Four years later, the number had dropped to just 250.

Christmas Celebrations in Pioneer Wyoming

Christmas was celebrated in the early days in Wyoming much like it is today with family dinners, parties, church services and school programs.

In Cheyenne in 1877 the ladies of the African Methodist Church reportedly cooked a Christmas dinner for church members and friends. "About 250 presents hung upon the tree," the paper reported.

The Presbyterian Sabbath School in Cheyenne elected their new officers for the coming year, according to the same 1877 Cheyenne newspaper. Elected secretary-treasurer was photographer-banker D. D. Dare who several years later fled to the Near East after two banks in which he had an interest failed.

The Evanston newspaper mentioned a Christmas present given to the local judge. It was a "magnificent gold cane," the judge told the Evanston editor.

It is difficult to determine just how "merry" Christmas was at Fort Laramie in 1877. One writer in a letter to the editor wrote: "Good old Christmas was fitly celebrated in Fort Laramie. . . .Every window in the Post was brilliantly illuminated with a dozen candles each, the quarters were decorated with evergreen... Wine flowed freely, and many a hearty toast was drank to the happiness of old friends...."

A second letter written several days later offered a different view. "Seeing the brief but improper item in your columns (about Christmas at Fort Laramie). . .the would-be correspondent gives not only an improper description, but a selfish account of the whole affair. But few evergreens were seen, the only being in the Band quarters. The tree was nine inches high (when placed on a bunk) and was decorated with old cigar stumps. Our would-be correspondent does not for an instant speak of the quality of the wine which flowed so freely. I have not the least doubt but some of that wine is flowing yet."

There was less debate on the festivities at Laramie that year. The "Wanless Hose Company" sponsored "a grand ball at a hotel Christmas night." Near present-day Newcastle, prospectors celebrated Christmas with the news of an oil strike close to Jenney's Stockade.

Festivities near Lander in 1877 were probably similar to those reported the next year. An 1879 newspaper reported that the "Fifth Cavalry held a grand military ball on Christmas Eve." The report added that "Lander.. .was well represented by 'the fair.'"

On Christmas Day, 1878, a huge Christmas tree decorated with "glittering tinsels and golden winged images" highlighted the program at the Indian agency near Lander. Presents were handed out by Santa Claus who "sprang out in his suit of furs and robes.' After the gifts "all assembled again and listened to the reading of the sermon by the agent."

The Christmas tree at Lander was not the first one raised in Wyoming, however. Nineteen years earlier in 1858 missionaries at Deer Creek (near present-day Glenrock) chopped down a spruce tree in the nearby hills and decorated it. That evening they entertained members of Capt. W. F. Raynolds' topographic expedition and Indians with violin music, Bible readings and German Christmas carols.

The Christmas tree was a standard part of celebrations in the 1870s. Residents of Rock Springs held a Christmas party at their one-room schoolhouse in 1878. The Christmas tree was decorated with cranberries and popcorn strung by the school children. According to one account, gifts were distributed. "Occasionally some old hardened sinner crouching in a seat at the rear of the building would be startled and surprised when Santa Claus, calling him by name, announced in ringing tones a gift for that man. When the child acting as Santa's messenger carried the prize to him, his old eyes would moisten and often tears trickled down his cheeks.. .The knowledge that someone cared for him."

A 2006 PBS documentary called "Two Days in October," historically describes events at two locations on the same two days in October 1967. One part of the documentary tells about a major battle (massacre) of American soldiers in Vietnam and another part describes the early protest of students on the campus of Unversity of Wisconsin-Madison over the recruitment efforts of Dow Chemical (maker of napalm), which sparked a riot and ongoing campus protest. The documentary is based upon the 2003 book *They Marched Into Sunlight* by David Maraniss, Pulitzer Prize-winning author and Washington Post journalist. Maraniss noted at the end of the book that Dick Cheney was attending University of Wisconsin at the time of the protest. Maraniss wrote: "During his years at the University of Wisconsin, political science graduate student Richard Cheney wanted nothing to do with Vietnam. He supported the war, but did not want to serve in it, and was barely interested in it one way or another. He and his wife, Lynne Cheney, were on campus during the Dow demonstration in October 1967, but only vaguely remembered the protest, nothing more than Lynne's recollection of a mime troupe prancing in white face."

Misc. Items about Wyoming

1. Do You Have a Pencil?

Harry O. Kapp was the pumping crew boss at Elk Basin oil field in northwestern Wyoming in the early days. Whenever his men hadn't been to town for three weeks or so, they would often begin to argue over religion or other matters. According to an account in the official history of Ohio Oil, for whom Kapp worked: "On such a foray, one of the men, a Kentuckian named Charlie Gingrich, who was on the small side physically and sensitive about it, decided that he needed a fist fight for the good of his soul. In a saloon, he took out a vest pocket notebook, and thumped it on the bar. 'I have here,' he said, 'the names of everybody I can lick in this town.' A six-foot, four-inch driller from another company took up the challenge. 'Is my name there?' he asked. 'Indeed it is, sir,' Gingrich replied. The driller seized Gingrich by the lapels with one hand and lifted him off the floor, saying, 'Why you little weasel, you couldn't lick me in a million years.' Gingrich knew when he was overmatched. 'In that case, sir,' he gasped, 'I'll strike off your name. Have you a pencil?'"

2. Cats on a Train

In the early days when the railroad was the chief mode of transport across the United States, the Wyoming newspapers along the Union Pacific line frequently made mention of unusual cargo. In one such case in December, 1899, the *Laramie Boomerang* noted that "a cargo of cats en route from Newark, New Jersey to Manila, goes west over the Union Pacific" this week. The federal government apparently sent the cats to catch Philippine rats. According to the news story, the cats were to protect the government warehouses in the Philippines from rodents. "Frederick W. Butler of Newark, who is engineering the scheme has 500, cats of all sizes, ages, colors and pedigrees, which he is taking to the Philippines to wage war on the rats and mice there." *Laramie Boomerang, Dec. 22, 1899.*

3. The Wyoming Quarter

More than 3,200 people submitted design suggestions for the "Wyoming quarter." Most suggested the bucking horse from the license plate--by an overwhelming majority. The Wyoming coin commission, appointed by the governor to determine the guidelines for the coin and accept the final design, was chaired by former Casper broadcaster Jack Rosenthal. The United States Mint gave each state the opportunity to choose its own design for the obverse of the quarter, one per state, released as a series in the order of statehood. The first coin with the unique back was Delaware's, minted in 1999. As the 44th state to be admitted to the Union, Wyoming was late in the coin series. The Wyoming quarter was officially released on Sept. 4, 2007. The official ceremony launching the coin was held at the Cheyenne Civic Center. Ed Moy, director of the U. S. Mint, attended. NBC correspondent Pete Williams served as the master of ceremonies and the University of Wyoming band played several numbers. Over the course of the mint run, 564.4 million of the coins were made.

4. Casper Sword-swallowing

The 2003 book *Esquire Presents What It Feels Like*, contains stories by people who have experienced strange events, One story titled "What It Feels Like to Swallow Swords" is by Brad Byers, a 43-year-old performer. Byers talks about the feeling of swallowing swords, of how the swords go down his esophagus and are so close to his heart that he can feel and see the swords move in time to his heartbeat. "I don't usually get nervous because then the esophagus will close up. But I got freaked out once. I was performing in Casper, Wyoming, at a shopping mall grand opening. At that time, I used to let people push the sword down my throat. I've always had women do it. But this time I chose a big, burly guy. He tried to act macho, but I noticed his hands were shaking a little bit. I knelt down on one knee and let him push it down. Then I gave him the stop signal, which I told him I would do, and I think to compensate for his feeling afraid, he pushed too far. The sword went down farther than I've ever felt before. I felt a stretching sensation in the bottom of my stomach. It was like a balloon being stretched too deep by a pointed object. I had to pull his hand off. I withdrew the sword and there was no blood so I thought I was okay and I finished the act with seven swords. When I pulled them out, they were covered with blood. Now I have people withdraw the blade from my mouth instead of pushing it down. You can't pull out a sword too far."

"Please hold on. This train is approaching concourse...." was the message played to passengers in the Denver International Airport trains in the early 2000s. It was the voice of radio announcer Pete Smythe, a native of Glenrock, Wyoming, who died in May, 2000

VISITORS
Well-Known People Who Vacationed in Wyoming

1. Archibald MacLeish, poet and Librarian of Congress (b. Ill., 1892, d. 1982)

When he was 12 years old, MacLeish spent the summer on a ranch in the Big Horns. From 1939 to 1944, he served as Librarian of Congress.

2. Eleanor "Sissy" Patterson, newspaper owner, author (b. Ill., 1884, d. 1948)

Patterson, editor and later owner of the *Washington Herald and Times*, came to Jackson Hole in 1916. Later, she purchased property east of Jackson where she built the Flat Creek Ranch. She spent summers there until 1934. At the time of her death, she was planning a return trip to Wyoming which would have been her first return to the state in 14 years.

3. Amelia Earhart, pilot (b. Kansas, 1898, d. 1937?)

In 1937, Earhart chose the site for a cabin on Wood River near Meeteetse which was to be her summer home. Later that year, she was lost in the Pacific in an unsuccessful attempt to fly around the world.

4. Frederic Remington, artist (b. N. Y., 1861, d. 1909)

Remington was a frequent guest at Buffalo Bill Cody's TE Ranch. He was in Cody at the dedication of the Irma Hotel and drew sketches of the occasion.

5. Mary O'Hara, author (b. N. J., 1885, d. 1980)

The noted author wrote several books while living in Wyoming. Her husband Helge Stuve-Vasa, whom she married in 1922, ranched in Laramie County. The couple divorced in 1947.

6. Ty Cobb, baseball player (b. Georgia, 1886, d. 1961)

Cobb had completed his fifth and final season as player-manager of the Detroit Tigers when he came to hunt big game in Wyoming in 1926. Another Hall of Fame baseball star, Tris Speaker, hunted with Cobb that fall. Max Wilde, a Cody outfitter, guided their hunt.

7. Tallulah Bankhead, actress (b. Alabama, 1903, d. 1968)

Star of such films as *Dark Victory* and *Little Foxes*, Bankhead enjoyed vacationing near Cody. In the 1930s, she was a regular guest at the Pitchfork Ranch.

8. John D. Rockefeller, oil magnate (b. New York, 1839, d. 1937)

Rockefeller's family were frequent visitors to Wyoming. His son, John D., Jr., purchased large holdings in the area. Most became part of Grand Teton National Park. Young Rockefeller's first trip to Wyoming was in July 1926.

9. George Eastman, inventor (b. New York, 1854, d. 1932)

The inventor of the dry plate film and founder of Eastman Kodak was a summer guest in Jackson Hole about 1900. Outfitter Steven Leek served as his wilderness guide during the visit. In 1905 he was a Cheyenne Frontier Days guest.

10. Eleanor Roosevelt, First Lady (b. New York, 1884, d. 1962)

Mrs. Roosevelt and sons Jimmy and Elliott were guests at the CM Ranch near Dubois in 1925. The sons stayed all summer at the boys' camp at the ranch.

11. Dale Carnegie, author (b. Missouri, 1888, d. 1955)

The author of *How to Win Friends and Influence People* vacationed frequently in Wyoming with his family.

12. Wallace Beery, actor (b. Missouri, 1886, d. 1949)

The famed character actor was a Pitchfork Ranch guest in the 1930s. Later, he bought property in Jackson Hole and participated in an "illegal cattle drive" to demonstrate against Jackson Hole National Monument in the 1940s.

13. Dom Pedro, Emperor of Brazil

The first royal head of state ever to visit the United States, Dom Pedro rode through Wyoming on the train en route to California and returned in the summer of 1876. Westbound, he stretched his legs at the Cheyenne depot. A buffalo bull on the tracks in Utah delayed his return trip, causing his train to pass through the state during the night. A Cheyenne newspaper reporter was allowed aboard to view the sleeping monarch and he wrote: "[Dom Pedro] arrived here at 4:30 this morning. He didn't climb down out of his royal car and saunter about the city in search of sights, he was still dreaming of his far-off palaces when the train reached the Magic City."

14. Jack London, author (b. 1876, d. 1916)

London was unemployed and en route east to join "Coxey's army" when he came through Wyoming on the Union Pacific in April 1894. London kept a journal of the trip in which he commented about Wyoming.

15. Thomas Edison, inventor (b. Ohio, 1847, d. 1931)

After viewing a solar eclipse at Rawlins and traveling west by train to California, Edison returned to Carbon County to fish for six days at Battle Lake and Big Muddy. It was his first vacation in 16 years. His visit is commemorated by a marker with a slightly exaggerated legend.

16. William Jennings Bryan, orator/politician, (b. Ill., 1860, d. 1925)

Bryan fished in the Saratoga area for ten days in 1901, the guest of former governor John Osborne. He returned for another vacation there in 1904. He made many other visits to Wyoming in his three unsuccessful presidential campaigns.

17. Gene Tunney, boxer (b. 1897, d. 1978)

Tunney defeated Jack Dempsey for the world heavyweight title in September 1926. He retired from the ring undefeated two years later. In the 1930s and 1940s, he often visited friends in Laramie. On these occasions, he frequently stayed at the home of safari companion, Richard Cooper of Laramie.

18.-19. Thomas Wolfe, author (b. N. C., 1900, d. 1938)

The author of *Look Homeward, Angel* crossed Wyoming by train in 1935. From June 20 to July 2, 1938, he took a whirlwind tour of the West with an editor from the *Portland Oregonian* and an Oregon tourism official to demonstrate the "possibility of making an automobile trip of the West in limited time and on a limited budget." On June 27, the party toured over the Tetons and to Old Faithful Inn in Yellowstone. The next day, they made a trip to Yellowstone and then went north through Montana. Wolfe contracted pneumonia in Seattle soon after the trip and died from the disease on Sept. 15, a bit more than two months after the trip.

18.-19. Clark Gable (b. Ohio, 1901, d. 1960) and **Carole Lombard** (b. Ind., 1908, d. 1942), **motion picture stars**

The couple stopped for lunch at Joe Delco's Cafe in Casper in October 1941, returning from a bird hunting trip in South Dakota. Early the next year, Lombard died in an airplane crash near Las Vegas, Nevada.

20. George H. W. Bush, U. S. Vice President/President (b. Mass., 1924)

Bush fished west of Cody on the North Fork of the Shoshone River in July 1988, during the Democratic National Convention. Bush was nominated by the Republicans the next month. As president, he celebrated his 65th birthday in Yellowstone on June 12, 1989. On July 17, 1992, Bush was guest at a barbecue in Jackson Hole.

21. Thomas E. Dewey, politician (b. Mich. 1902, d. 1971)

The former New York governor and unsuccessful Republican nominee for president in 1944 and 1948 came with a 700-person entourage to the Hoodoo Ranch near Meeteetse during the 1948 campaign. There, he and his party were guests of Wyoming Sen. E. V. Robertson.

22. John Burroughs, naturalist (b. N. Y., 1837, d. 1921)

The former school teacher and national bank examiner (1873-1884) was already well known for his work in conservation when he visited Yellowstone Park with President Theodore Roosevelt in the spring of 1903.

23. Ernest Hemingway, author (b. Ill., 1899, d. 1961)

Hemingway frequently visited in Wyoming. It is said that he completed the manuscript for *The Sun Also Rises* while he was staying at the Sheridan Inn. During a trip through Wyoming in July 1944, his wife became ill and underwent emergency surgery in a Casper hospital. On other occasions, he fished and hunted in the Cody area and stayed in Laramie as a weekend guest of his African safari companion, Richard Cooper, whose home now houses UW American studies.

24. John Dos Passos, author (b. 1896, d. 1970)

From Oct. 21-31, 1930, Dos Passos vacationed at the Lawrence Nordquist ranch northwest of Cody. He came at the invitation of his pal Ernest Hemingway.

25. Slim Pickens (Louis B. Lindley Jr.), actor (b. Calif., 1919, d. 1983)

The film and television actor owned a cabin at Boulder Lake. The home became an issue in a case appealed to the Wyoming Supreme Court in 1989. Actor/singer Rex Allen sued Pickens' estate for negligence, claiming Allen had fallen on the steps of the Pickens cabin and injured an eye. Pickens' estate prevailed in the lawsuit.

26. Bernard Baruch, financier (b. 1870, d. 1965)

Baruch held the dubious distinction of having been robbed in Wyoming. In the summer of 1915, he was a passenger in the last stagecoach in Yellowstone to be held up by a stage robber. He lost $50 to the armed gunman in the incident.

27. Wendell Wilkie, presidential candidate (b. 1892, d. 1944)

Wilkie campaigned for president in 1940. During the summer, he visited Cheyenne and rode in the Frontier Days parade. Later, at Frontier Park, he was soaked by a downpour and forced to leave the show early.

28. J. Danforth Quayle, U. S. Vice President (b. 1947)

Quayle was vice president when he vacationed on Senator Malcolm Wallop's ranch near Sheridan from Aug. 17-21, 1989.

29. Lady Bird Johnson, former First Lady (b. Tex., 1912, d. 2007)

In September 1991, Lady Bird Johnson, widow of President Lyndon Johnson, attended a weekend meeting in Jackson of the National Wildflower Research Center, which Mrs Johnson had founded to study, promote and re-establish wildflowers and other native plants.

30. Gen. H. "Hap" Arnold, Army Air Force commander (b. 1886, d. 1950)

Arnold made a brief Sunday morning stop at Casper Army Air Field on July 11, 1943. He gave medals to combat veterans and watched a parade held in his honor. He departed later the same day. That evening, a B-24 on a training mission crashed 30 miles north of the base killing all eight crewmen aboard.

31. J. M. Studebaker, Wagon Builder (b. 1833, d. 1917)

Studebaker rode the stagecoach from Cheyenne to Deadwood in 1877. On April 26, he reportedly stopped at Hat Creek station in present Niobrara County. At the time of his visit, he was a "partner in the nation's largest wagon builders." Years later, his family formed an automobile manufacturing company and the cars were named for the family.

32. Col. Robert McCormick, Chicago Tribune publisher (b. 1889, d. 1955)

McCormick and a party of friends flew to Thermopolis in the summer of 1935 to enjoy the hot springs. His plane was piloted by famed aviator H. A. Collison who was killed two months later when the United Airlines plane he was flying crashed ten miles west of Cheyenne, killing all 12 people aboard. McCormick's flight was without incident.

Congress passed a resolution recognizing the UW Cowgirls Basketball team that won the NIT on March 31, 2007. House Resolution 384 passed on July 23, 2007.

33. Tanya Tucker, Singer

Country singer Tucker spent a week on a fishing and horse-packing vacation in the Cody area in August, 1995. The vacation was marred by accusations made against the 36-year-old Tucker by a Montana woman who claimed that the singer had assaulted her in a Cody bar. Tucker denied the allegations.

34. William MacLeod Raine, Writer (b. 1871, d. 1954)

The Denver-based writer of westerns visited the Thermopolis area in August, 1923, to gather material for his fiction. The *Thermopolis Independent*, Aug. 17, 1923, reported that Raine had "visited the tie camp at DuNoir" while the tie drive was in progress down the river. Among his works was the novel, *Wyoming* (1907).

35. Malcolm Stevenson (Steve) Forbes

Forbes visited Wyoming in 1950s with his family. They vacationed near Whitegrass Ranch in Jackson Hole. His mother Roberta insisted on having the car stopped just at the Wyoming border so she could get out and walk over, becoming the first family member to step on Wyoming soil.

36. Lamar Hunt (b. 1932, d. Dec. 13, 2006)

The man who coined the term, "Super Bowl," often vacationed in the Cody area on the family's ranch, the Hoodoo, purchased by his father H. L. Hunt in 1948. At the age of 26, he was a founding member of the American Football League. After the leagues merged, it became the AFC of the NFL. The Lamar Hunt trophy goes to the AFC winner annually.

37. David Brinkley, Television Journalist (b. 1920, d. 2003)

In "David Brinkley: A Memoir," the 1995 Brinkley autobiography, is a photograph of the Brinkley family, taken at a dude ranch in Wyoming.

38. John F. Kennedy Jr. (b. 1960, d. 1999)

Young Kennedy spent time on the John Perry Barlow ranch in Sublette County in the middle 1970s when he was a young man. In Oct. 1996, Barlow attended Kennedy's small private wedding on a South Carolina island. The two remained friends until Kennedy's untimely death in an airplane crash in July, 1999.

39. Unknown Eastern tourist, c. 1880

A passenger, stretching his legs on the depot at Rock Springs and pointing to miles of open country, reportedly asked the station attendant, "Of what earthly use is this awful, desolate area?" The attendant replied, "Well, it helps hold the two ends of the country together."

European Visitors to Wyoming

1. Sir William Drummond Stewart, Scottish nobleman

Stewart paid William Sublette $500 so that he might accompany Sublette west in 1833, making Sublette the first hunting guide in Wyoming history. Four years later, Stewart returned to Wyoming for another hunting vacation, bringing with him the famed Baltimore artist Alfred Jacob Miller.

2. Sir George Gore, English nobleman

Gore, of Sligo, Ireland, conducted a two-year big-game hunt from 1853-1855 from his headquarters at Fort Laramie. In his party, he had 40 people, 112 horses, 50 hunting dogs, and six wagons.

3.-4. Lord Randolph Churchill and his bride Jenny Jerome Churchill

The couple visited in Wyoming at the Powder River Basin ranch home of Moreton Frewen, a close friend and brother-in-law of Mrs. Churchill. Their son Winston was 11 years old when Frewen married Clara Jerome, the sister of Winston's mother.

Salt Creek was the first oil field in the world to be totally powered by electricity (1924)

5. Sir Charles Wentworth Dilke, writer/adventurer (1789-1864)

Sir Charles commented on his trip through Wyoming by stagecoach, noting that he was "certain nothing but domesticated Himilayan yaks" could survive in Wyoming.

6. Queen Elizabeth

The queen spent two days, Oct. 15-16, 1984, visiting in Sheridan. She was the guest of Sen. Malcolm Wallop's sister, Lady Porchester, who is married to the queen's horse manager. Three years later, when a reporter asked Prince Charles if there was anyplace he would like to see during his United States tour, he commented, "Well, I've heard that Wyoming is very nice."

7. Grand Duke Alexis of Russia

The Grand Duke came by train to Wyoming in January 1872, following an autumn buffalo hunt on the Nebraska plains. After a brief stop in Cheyenne, marred by a minor rail accident, the Grand Duke continued by train to Denver.

8. Albert, Prince of Monaco

In September 1913, he hunted with Buffalo Bill in the northern Absarokas. It was Cody's last hunt. The camp site was named "Camp Monaco" and a historical monument marks the site.

9. Gilbert Leigh, nobleman

Leigh, an Irish nobleman-turned-cowboy, fell off a limestone cliff near Ten Sleep on Oct. 23, 1883. He was out hunting big horn sheep when a blizzard struck. He became disoriented and apparently did not see the edge of the cliff.

10. Noel Coward, playwright (1899-1973)

Coward vacationed at the Valley Ranch southwest of Cody.

11. Louis Agassiz, naturalist (1807-1873)

The Swiss-born naturalist rode the Union Pacific across southern Wyoming in 1868 while the tracks were still under construction. He visited Green River "Station" and was a guest of Judge William A. Carter, the sutler at Fort Bridger.

12. Sir Richard Burton, nobleman/author (1821-1890)

Burton, not to be confused with the 20th century actor by the same name, traveled by stagecoach across Wyoming in 1860. His journal of the trip, published after his return to England, contained several unflattering descriptions of the Wyoming portion of his trip.

13. Rudyard Kipling, author/poet (1865-1936)

The famous British Empire author wrote of his Yellowstone vacation in 1899: "Today I am in Yellowstone Park, and I wish I were dead...the tourists—may their master die an evil death at the hand of a mad locomotive!—poured into that place with a joyful whoop..."

14. David Niven, actor (1910-1983)

Niven visited the home of the Richard Cooper family in Laramie from time to time. He appeared in numerous films and television shows. He donated his papers to the American Heritage Center, University of Wyoming.

15. Marie, Queen of Romania

The Rumanian queen traveled throughout the state in November 1926. She was greeted with bouquets of flowers in Casper on Nov. 9. Other "royal visitors" have included the King and Queen of Belgium and the King of Hawaii.

16. Eduard Schevardnadze, Soviet foreign minister

The Soviet official met with then-Secretary of State James Baker in a pre-summit meeting in Jackson Hole on Sept. 19-20, 1989. Later, when the Soviet Union disbanded, Schevardnadze became president of the Republic of Georgia, serving from 1995 until 2003 when he was pushed out by the "rose revolution."

WATER

Wyoming's first wild and scenic river: The 20.5 miles of Clark's Fork in Park County, dedicated Aug. 31, 1991. In May 1993, the BLM announced two other rivers met the criteria, after an examination of 135 rivers in the Cody resource area. They were the Lower Clark's Fork and Porcupine Creek In April 1992, the U. S. Forest Service approved a resource management plan which designated sections of 28 rivers in the Bridger-Teton National Forest for Wild and Scenic designation. Included in the total of 602 miles of streams were the Gros Ventre River and the Hoback River.

1st state to claim state ownership of water: Wyoming, in Article 8, Wyoming Constitution, 1890.

1st state engineer: Elwood Mead, who also served as territorial engineer. Lake Mead, formed behind Hoover Dam, is named for him.

1st "automatic water system": The town of Battle, now a ghost town in Carbon County, had the first gravity flow automatic water system in the world when it was installed in 1898.

1st high school indoor swimming pool: Natrona County High School, 1929.

Number of lakes in Wyoming: 3,400, including ponds and reservoirs.

Miles of fishing streams in Wyoming: 15,846 miles

Deepest Lake in Wyoming: Fremont Lake, 607 feet deep, making it the seventh deepest lake in the continental United States.

Largest natural lake in Wyoming: Yellowstone Lake, 137 square miles with 110 miles of shoreline. The lake is 7,733 feet in elevation, the highest large lake in the United States.

Largest back country lake in the lower 48 states: Shoshone Lake in Yellowstone, 8,050 acres. The lake has no road access.

Highest lake in Wyoming: A tiny, ice-covered lake near the 13,000-foot summit of Downs Mountain, south of Dubois.

Fastest rising river (natural, not resulting from dam discharges upstream): In 1923, the waters of the Wind River near Riverton rose eight feet in less than two hours.

Highest waterfall in Wyoming: Lower Falls of the Yellowstone River drops 308 feet. The Upper Falls is 109 feet high.

Largest outdoor swimming pool in Wyoming: 1.2 million gallons, George Washington Memorial Park pool, Buffalo, opened in 1984. Originally, the pool was dirt-bottomed and filled with creek water. The citizens of Johnson County raised $85,000 to rebuild it in 1982.

Strongest "fire water": In the 1930s, visitors to the town of Arvada, Sheridan County, were often shocked to see local citizens opening water faucets, striking a match and setting the water afire as it flowed from the tap. After the "demonstration," the Arvadan would drink the water. The artesian well furnishing water to the town also seeped natural gas, hence the possibility for pyrotechnic displays.

Evaporation: The pool below "Fountainhead," a statue by Robert I. Russin, in front of the Casper City Hall, must be refilled daily on hot days. Evaporation of two inches or more per day will cause the fountain to automatically shut off.

Municipal water: South Superior, population about 280, in January, 1996, began receiving clean, potable water for the first time since 1981. An analysis that year showed that the old water supply system contained high levels of radioactivity. The water supply had been sold to the city in the 1960s by the Union Pacific Coal Company. The company constructed the cast-iron pipe system in the 1940s and the radioactive materials had built up in the pipes over the years.

River Sources

1. Belle Fourche River: 290 miles long

The river begins in Campbell County, east of Pine Tree about 15 miles southwest of Reno Junction, and ends in South Dakota where it flows into the Cheyenne River. The name is "beautiful fork" in French.

2. Big Horn/Wind River: 461 miles long

The Wind River begins in the southern Absarokas just south of Yellowstone Park at

The 11,000-acre Monolith Ranch, south of Laramie, was acquired by the City of Laramie in 1981 for future water development. The ranch properties came with senior rights to many streams as well as 14 groundwater permits on the ranch.

the 9,700-foot level. At Riverton, it joins with the Popo Agie River, 60 miles long. The name changes to the Big Horn River just as the river exits Wind River Canyon at "Wedding of the Waters." The Wind River, to that point, is 110 miles long while beyond it, the Big Horn River flows for another 351 miles.

3. Green River: 730 miles long

The river originates in Green River Lakes and ends when it joins the Colorado River in Utah. It was named, not for its color, but for a St. Louis partner of William Ashley, the man who named it.

4. Niobrara River: 431 miles long

The name means "running water" in Sioux. The river begins west of Manville in Niobrara County. It flows into the Missouri River at the Nebraska-Iowa-South Dakota border.

5. North Platte River: 680 miles long

The river begins in North Park, Colorado, and joins the South Platte in Nebraska where the combined Platte River flows on for another 310 miles before emptying into the Missouri River. Washington Irving called it "the most magnificent and useless of rivers." The word "Platte" is French for "flat." The river vexed boatmen because of its shallows.

6. Powder River: 486 miles long

The river originates with the confluence of the North, Middle and South forks in Johnson County, about four miles east of Kaycee. It empties into the Yellowstone. As the saying goes: "Powder River, Let 'er Buck, A mile wide and an inch deep, Too thick to drink, To thin to plow." The slogan is attributed to "Missouri Bill" Shultz. According to E. J. Farlow, Missouri Bill and some cowboys on a trail drive to Casper had never seen Powder River. As they neared the river, Farlow told them they should be ready to cross Powder River. Missouri Bill, thinking it would be a broad expanse, turned his horse loose. "This damn buckskin couldn't even wade a river," he said. When they got to Powder River, there was nothing but a few water holes. The rest was dry. Missouri Bill, astonished, talked about it for days. When the herd arrived in Casper, he went to a saloon. "Boys, have a drink on me. I've crossed Powder River." As the night progressed, he said he had "swum" Powder River. As he drank, he shouted, "Powder River is up; come and have another drink." Finally, "Powder River, let 'er buck." *Source: John C. Thompson, "In Old Wyoming," Wyoming State Tribune, Feb. 4, 1945.*

7. Shoshone River: about 100 miles long

The South Fork rises near Shoshone Pass on the Park-Fremont county line. The North Fork begins on the southwest slope of Stinkingwater Peak, ten miles northeast of Pahaska Teepee and flows 51 miles to Buffalo Bill Reservoir where it joins with the South Fork to form the Shoshone River. The river empties into the Yellowstone River.

8. Snake River: 1,038 miles long

The river rises in southern Yellowstone Park and flows into Idaho and then into Washington where it joins the Columbia River.

9. Sweetwater River: 175 miles

The river begins on the southern slopes of the Wind River mountains. Oregon Trail travelers forded it up to nine times on their journey west. More than 15 miles of the river's length is now under Pathfinder Reservoir. Along that portion, Jim Averell and Ella Watson ("Cattle Kate") were lynched in July, 1889.

A small furry mammal that scurried through the prehistoric forests of tropic al Wyoming during the dinosaur age was officially named in November, 1998, for Brent Breithaupt, at the time, UW Geological Museum director. The 140-million year old mammal was designated "Ctenacodon brentbaatar." The mammal was named by Dr. Robert Bakker, famed paleontologist who had worked with Breithaupt on many digs.

10. Yellowstone River: 671 miles long

The river begins on the northeast side of Yount's Peak, southeast of Yellowstone Park. (It does not begin in Yellowstone Lake as is commonly believed). The Grand Canyon of the Yellowstone (or "Fourth Canyon") is 24 miles long and ends at Lamar Junction where the Lamar River enters the Yellowstone from the east.

River Agreements Between Wyoming and Other States

1. Colorado River Compact (1922)

Wyoming gained a seven percent share of the waters, as measured at Lee's Ferry, Arizona. The terms of the agreement gave the "upper basin states" of Wyoming, Colorado, New Mexico and Utah one-half of the flow to be divided among them while the "lower basin states" of California, Nevada and Arizona divided the other half. Combined with Wyoming's water law that specifies ownership in all waters lies with the state, any effort to steal Wyoming water from the Green River for trans-basin diversion to the Colorado Front Range seems nearly impossible. Nonetheless, threats to the state's waters continue from many quarters, including drought-stricken cities of the Southwest.

2. North Platte Compact

The North Platte decree, issued in 1945 and affirmed by the U. S. Supreme Court, apportioned water between Wyoming, Nebraska and Colorado. The court modified the decree in 1953. It was challenged by Nebraska in October 1986. A special master, appointed to rule on the issue, sided with Wyoming and the case returned to the U. S. Supreme Court in January 1993. Disputes still occur, particularly in drought years, between the two states.

3. Belle Fourche River Compact (1944)

Ten percent of the water was reserved for Wyoming while the rest was granted to South Dakota.

4. Snake River Compact (1949)

Wyoming's share of the Snake River is approximately four percent of the flow with Idaho receiving the remaining 96 percent.

5. Yellowstone River Compact (1950)

Litigation among the states continues as the Yellowstone is also part of the Missouri River system. Recently, tribal claims from the Wind River reservation, based on rights retained by the tribes and conceded in the Fort Bridger Treaty of 1868, have caused lawsuits among users. The U. S. Supreme Court ruled for the tribes although later purchaser/users of Indian lands did not succeed in gaining similar priority.

6. Laramie River

Litigation over the waters of the Laramie River continued between Wyoming and

A "first" for Wyoming women occurred in March of 1919. "For the first time in Wyoming history, women appeared in court in men's attire," the Cheyenne newspaper reported. The two women were employees of the Union Pacific Railroad who had gained their jobs during World War I while many men were in the armed forces. They were called as witnesses in a trial before Judge W. C. Mentzer. Because their work required them to be so dressed and their appearances were to be brief but during working hours, the judge allowed them to testify in their work clothes. The attire of the two, Bessie Parker and Eunice Banks, gained little attention from anyone else, however. As the Cheyenne newspaper reported, "The appearance of women in male attire ceased to attract attention" during the war years when it was common clothing for women working in war industries.

Colorado for many years. Because the river is part of the North Platte system, Nebraska also became involved at times. The U. S. Supreme Court decided an early case of Wyoming v. Colorado in 1922, but ancillary issues continued to bring the two states into court for many years.

Depths of Wyoming Lakes
(at deepest measured point)

1. Fremont Lake: 607 feet
2. Flaming Gorge Reservoir: 437 feet
3. Yellowstone Lake: 309 feet (average depth is 139 feet)

10 Most Common Names for Streams in Wyoming*

1. Spring Creek (38)
2. Cottonwood Creek (30)
3. Beaver Creek (29)
4. Willow Creek (28)

5. Bear Creek (25)
6. Dry Creek (23)
7. Horse Creek (21)
8. Sand Creek (18)

9.-10. Rock Creek and Sheep Creek (each 17)

Source: Dee Linford, Wyoming Stream Names. (Cheyenne: Wyoming Game and Fish Department, 1975). The USGS Geographic Names Information System (1996) contains entries for 126 Spring Creeks, 66 Cottonwood Creeks, and 53 Willow Creeks--the three leading names for streams in their system.

Senior Water Rights in Various Areas

1. Southwestern Wyoming

The Black's Fork water right to irrigate 11 acres held by Edgar N. Carter dates to 1862. Myers Land and Livestock Company holds a water right on the Bear River dating from May 1, 1862. A Smith's Fork right to irrigate 155 acres, held in the name of Madge Coburn, dates to 1864.

2. Green River

The most senior right apparently was for the "Green River Water Works," a water right for 4 cfs dating from 1871. The UPRR also holds early rights.

3. Jackson Hole

S. N. Leek had a water right to Little Gros Ventre or Flat Creek, a tributary of the Snake River via Adams Canal to irrigate 132 acres. The right dates to Sept. 24, 1896. The Jackson Hole pioneer was well known as a photographer and "protector" of the Jackson Hole elk herd.

Women served on a jury for the first time in American history in Laramie in 1871. The first case was Territory v. John DeGair and the five women on the jury along with the seven men serving found DeGair guilty of assault. In the second trial, Territory v. William Gale, the jury that included three women, returned a not guilty verdict. Gale had been charged with receiving stolen goods. In the first murder trial on which women sat on the jury, Littleton Lawrence was found guilty of manslaughter in the death of Pressley Wall. Four women served on that jury. Harry Oaks and Henry Miller were charged with horse/mule theft. The six women on the jury found Oaks guilty, but not Miller. Women served on juries in three other cases during the term: Territory v. Herman Miller (assault, guilty); Territory v. William Van Scoy (assault, guilty); and Territory v. Peter Perrin (assault, not guilty).

WOMEN

Percentage of businesses owned by women (2002): 24.4 percent
Businesses owned by women (2002): 12,900, generated $1.1 billion in revenues.
Employer firms owned by women (2002): 2,500, an increase of 13.0 percent since 1997.
Self-employed women (2002): 17,300 or 42.2 percent of the state's self-employed persons in 2006, a decrease of 9.1 percent from the previous year.
Sources: U.S. Dept. of Labor, Bureau of Labor Statistics; U.S. Dept. of Commerce, Census Bureau.

1. First woman voter: Mrs. Louisa Swain, Laramie, September, 1870

2. First woman justice of the peace: Esther Hobart Morris, South Pass City, Feb. 17, 1870. Appointed to the position by the county commission, she served for almost 8 1/2 months. She was the first woman judge in America.

3. First woman district judge: Elizabeth Kail, Lander, appointed Oct. 6, 1982.

4. First woman to serve as a State Senator: Dora McGrath, Thermopolis, 1930.

5. First woman to serve as State Representative: Mary G. Bellamy, Democrat, Laramie, 1910.

6. First woman speaker of the Wyoming House of Representatives: Verda James, Republican, Natrona County, 1969.

7. First woman elected mayor: Susan Wissler, Dayton, 1911

8. First women members of the University of Wyoming Board of Trustees: Mrs. Mattie Quinn of Evanston and Dr. Grace Raymond Hebard, Cheyenne, both appointed in 1891.

9. First woman elected governor: Nellie Tayloe Ross, a Democrat, who took office Jan. 5, 1925. She was the first woman governor of any state and first woman to direct the U. S. Mint.

10. First woman elected to the U. S. Congress from Wyoming: Barbara Cubin, (b. Nov. 30, 1946, Salinas, Calif.), a Republican, first elected in 1994. As of 2010, no woman from Wyoming has served in the U. S. Senate.

11. First woman state treasurer: Minnie Mitchell, appointed to complete her husband's term in 1952.

12. First woman state auditor: Minnie Mitchell, elected in 1954.

13. First woman admitted to the Wyoming State Bar: Dr. Grace Raymond Hebard, Laramie, Dec. 14, 1914. She had been admitted to practice before the district court at Laramie in November 1898.

14. First woman admitted to the Wyoming State Bar who actually practiced law: Grace MacDonald Phillips, Newcastle, April 19, 1920.

15. First woman to argue a case before the Wyoming Supreme Court: Laura Bicknell Harris, Casper, in 1927.

16. First woman director of the State Department of Corrections: Judy Uphoff, appointed in 1991.

17. First woman president of the Wyoming Board of Agriculture: Carole Bardin, Sublette County, April, 1992.

18. First woman elected to statewide office: Estelle Reel, Cheyenne, elected State Superintendent of Public Instruction in 1894. She was the first woman in any state elected to statewide office.

19. First town in America to be governed entirely by women: Jackson. From 1920 to 1921, the town of Jackson had a woman mayor, town council and town marshal. Grace E. Miller served as mayor while the council members were: Mrs. Rose Crabtree, Mrs. Don Haight, Mrs. William DeLoney and Mrs. C. R. Van Vleck. Pearl Williams was town marshal. Mrs. Crabtree defeated her husband Henry for her council seat.

20. First all-woman fire department in the United States: Dayton, 1942-1945.

21. First woman postmaster: Susan R. Johnson, Cheyenne, March 3, 1880. She was the widow of attorney E. P. Johnson for whom Johnson County was named.

22. First woman appointed to the attorney general's staff: Ellen Crowley, 1958.

23. First woman elected county attorney: Nancy Guthrie Hinckley, Big Horn County, 1978.

24. First woman State Attorney-General: Gay Vanderpoel Woodhouse, appointed Nov. 25, 1998.

25. First woman officer in the Wyoming National Guard: Major Wanda Banta, commissioned in 1973. (Katherine Teague Durnford, who served as private secretary to Gov. Joseph M. Carey from 1913-1915, was legally entitled to the rank of major in the National Guard although she never served with the guard in an official capacity).

26. First woman president of the Wyoming Press Association: Diane Bonner, Powell Tribune, elected in 1989.

27. First woman named to Wyoming Coaches Hall of Fame: Pat Brown, Basin High School gynmastics coach, so honored on July 29, 1987. She began serving as the school's gymnastics coach in 1966.

28. First woman press agent in the United States: Said to be Mary Jester Allen, who served in that position for Buffalo Bill's Wild West Show in 1898.

29. First woman in the nation appointed chaplain of a men's prison: Mrs. E. E. Slosson, Laramie. She served five years from about 1891. Her husband later edited the *New York Independent and Science Service*.

30. First woman to operate a cattle ranch in Wyoming alone: Mrs. Michael Heenan, South Pass City area, 1872. She ran the Circle H Ranch.

31. First woman winner of the Wyoming Golf Championship: Dr. Grace Raymond Hebard, Laramie, 1902.

32. First recipient of a University of Wyoming honorary degree: Carrie Chapman Catt in 1921. UW is unique in having a woman as its first honorary degree recipient.

33. First woman to head a university psychology department in the United States: Dr. June Etta Downey, University of Wyoming.

34. First white woman in the Big Horn Basin: Said to have been Mrs. Martha Bull Waln (b. in England in 1860, died in 1944) who came to the Ten Sleep area in 1881.

35. First woman appointed superintendent of Indian education: Estelle Reel, appointed by President McKinley in 1898. She resigned as Wyoming's state superintendent of public instruction to accept the position. She served for 12 years.

36. First women newspaper editors in Wyoming: Laura and Gertrude Huntington, two sisters who began editing and publishing the *Platte County Lyre* in Saratoga in June 1888. Caroline Lockhart edited the *Cody Enterprise*, beginning about 1920. Cora Wannamaker edited the *Rock Springs Rocket* just before World War I.

37. First woman to hold a cattle brand in her own name: Eliza Montgomery Kuykendall, wife of a founder of the Wyoming Stockgrowers Association. In the fall of 1866, she brought cattle from Leavenworth, Kansas, through Wyoming to southwestern South Dakota. Her brand was recorded in by the county clerk in Cheyenne as the "rolling M."

38. First woman brand inspector in the United States: Holly Green, (b. Big Piney), appointed to part-time position in 1983, full-time in 1988, as of 1996, her duties covered the Big Piney area.

39. First woman officer of the Wyoming Highway Patrol: Bonnie Coppock, commissioned in 1979.

40. First woman sergeant in the Wyoming Highway Patrol: Karolyn Hughes, appointed to the position in December, 1999.

41. First woman bill poster in the world: Mrs. Helen Root of Laramie. Known as "Sissy" Root, she operated Root's Opera House in Laramie following the death of her husband. A bill poster changed letters on the theater's marquee and placed new signs on billboards.

42. First woman court reporter in Wyoming: Mary I. Webster Rennie, Laramie.

43. First woman in America elected county assessor: Mrs. Jesse Kirby (b. Iowa, 1890, d. N. M., c. 1960), Campbell County, 1920.

43. First Wyoming-born woman priest in the Episcopal Church: Gail Keeney-Mulligan, ordained in 1984. Prior to attending divinity school, she graduated from Rock Springs High School, Casper College and the University of Wyoming. In 1989, she was serving churches in the state of New York.

44. First woman bailiff: Mary Atkinson, Albany County, appointed in 1870.

45. First woman inducted into American Polled Hereford Association Hall of Fame: Snead Davis, Saratoga rancher, in 1993. She owned ranches near Saratoga and in Florida.

46. First woman to fly single-engine aircraft around Sugar Loaf Mountain, Rio de Janeiro: Lorna Kooi Simpson, (b. Chicago, 1900, d. Jan. 25, 1995).

47. First woman to serve as Receiver of Public Monies, United States Land Office: Julia Mary Cross, Douglas, c. 1920.

48. First woman supervisor of Bridger-Teton National Forest: Sandra Key, appointed in February, 1995.

49. First woman to coach a boys' high school basketball team: Mary Jane Davis, Cambria, 1920s.

50. First woman fire lookout in Wyoming (2nd in the U. S.): Lorraine Lindaley of Centennial, Medicine Bow Lookout Station, summer of 1921.

51. First woman firefighter in Wyoming to reach rank of company officer: Ann Pond, Laramie, April, 2000.

52. First woman partner in an oil and gas land-leasing business in Wyoming: Shirley M. Dymond (1924-1997) in firm of Stroock, Rogers and Dymond, Casper

53. First woman ever elected to Shoshone Tribal Council: Mary Kinnear Mead, elected Feb. 4, 1935. A teacher, she was a graduate of the University of Wyoming.

54. First woman county librarian in America: Mrs. E. Mason Smith, a widow who came to Cheyenne in the 1870s.

55. First woman appointed to the Wyoming Supreme Court: Marilyn Stebner Kite, appointed March 30, 2000.

56. First woman superintendent of Yellowstone National Park: Suzanne Lewis, appointed in 2001.

57. First woman director of the U. S. Forest Service: Abigail Kimbell, appointed in 2007, was forest supervisor of Big Horn National Forest from 1997-99.

58. First woman to command the Wyoming Army National Guard: Col. Kathy Wright, May 6, 2010.

59. First woman to serve as a U. S. District Judge for Wyoming: Nancy Freudenthal, sworn in on June 1, 2010.

Wyoming's First Ladies: The Governors' Wives

1. Helen Warren	8. Eula Kendrick	15. Margaret Miller	22. Winifred Hickey
2. Aurelia Barber	9. Ida Houx	16. Marie Christensen Smith**	23. Leona Gage
3. Harriet Richards	10. Julia Carey	17. Emily Hunt	24. Martha Close Hansen
4. Elise Richards	11. Ina Belle Lucas	18. Laura May Crane	25. Roberta "Bobbi" Hathaway
5. Stella Chatterton	12. Nellie T. Ross*	19. Alice Barrett	26. Kathleen "Casey" Herschler
6. Mary Brooks	13. Zennia Emerson	20. Mabel Rogers	27. Jane Sullivan
7. Louisa Carey	14. Lucy Clark	21. Lorna Kooi Simpson	28. Sherri Geringer
			29. Nancy Freudenthal

*Also served as governor **First native-born first lady.*

YELLOWSTONE

Some Interesting Facts about Yellowstone

1. Volcanic eruption

In 1991 a University of California geologist predicted a giant volcanic eruption in Yellowstone within 100,000 years. The geologist, Dr. Don DePaolo, claimed the eruption would occur in the giant caldera, an area 40 by 25 miles containing the hot springs and geysers. Were such an eruption to occur, it would rival the largest ever known, including that of Krakatoa in Indonesia in 1883. Ash from the eruption encircled the earth, bringing on what was known as the "year without summer." Sunsets around the world were colored for two years from the ash. The possibility inspired apocalyptic documentaries and figured into a popular motion picture in 2009 titled "2012."

2. Thermal features

Yellowstone National Park contains an estimated 10,000 individual thermal features, ranging from geysers to hot springs and mud pots.

3. Research in the Park

In 1999, Yellowstone National Park granted 275 research permits, allowing roaming scientists to "study everything from people's attitudes to the smallest and most primitive forms of life on Earth," said John Varley, who oversees cultural resource management and science in the park.

4. Into Outer Space

In July 2000, micro-organisms took a trip into space in a NASA rocket to test the theory that primordial life may have hitched a ride on a meteorite to Earth eons ago. According to CNN.com writer Richard Stenger, "Hundreds of millions of microbes took the suborbital flight, including some discovered in hot springs in Yellowstone National Park." The rocket was launched from White Sands Missile Range in New Mexico.

5. Undeveloped area

More than 95 percent of the 3,400 square-mile park remains undeveloped, offering sanctuary to wolves, grizzly bears, beetles and microbes that are believed to be among the oldest creatures on earth.

Yellowstone in Film

1. *Yellowstone: Battle for Life* (BBC, 2009)
2. *Secret Yellowstone* (National Geographic, 2007).
3. *Wolves: A Legend Returns to Yellowstone* (2007)
4. *Nature: Christmas in Yellowstone* (2006).
    Nature photographer Tom Murphy's visual documentation of the park.
5. *Firestorm: Last Stand at Yellowstone* (2006).
    Feature film about the 1988 fire starring Scott Foley.
6. *Live in Yellowstone: Music in High Places* (2003)
7. *Yellowstone* (2002)
8. *Yellowstone: The World's First National Park* (2001)
9. *Yellowstone: America's Sacred Wilderness* (2001)
10. *Discovering Yellowstone* (2000)
11. *Yellowstone: Fabric of a Dream* (2000)
12. *Yellowstone IMAX* (1994)
13. *Yellowstone: Imprints of Geologic Time* (1992)
14. *Yellowstone* (1939).
    A feature film starring Henry Hunter as a park ranger.

WYOMING SPORTS

Top 11 Athletes in Wyoming in the 20th Century*
* Selected by *Sports Illustrated* Magazine in 2000

1. Boyd Dowler, football
2. Lance Deal, hammer throw
3. John Godina, shot put
4. Ken Sailors, basketball
5. Tom Browning, baseball
6. Jerry Hill, football
7. Jim Crawford, football
8. Richard Babka, discus
9. Curt Gowdy, baseball coverage
10. Mike Devereaux, baseball
11. Karen Budge, skiing

University of Wyoming Athletics Hall of Fame

Inaugural Inductees, 1993

Dick Ballinger, Wrestling, 1958-60; Fennis Dembo, Basketball, 1985-88; Mike Dirks, Football, 1963-67; Jerry Hill, Football, 1958-60; Glenn "Red" Jacoby, Athletic. Dir., 1946-73; Jay Novacek, Football/Track, 1982-84; Kenny Sailors, Basketball, 1941-46; Ev Shelton, Basketball Coach, 1939-59; Johnny Winterholler, Baseball/Basketball/Football, 1936-39; National Championship Basketball team of 1943 (inducted as a team)

Inductees, 2nd Year, 1994

Paul Carlin, Track, 1951-53; George Duke Humphrey, Pres., 1945-64; Everett Lantz, Wrestling Coach, 1937-65; Flynn Robinson, Basketball, 1963-65; Mary Shea, Volleyball, 1980-83; Kenneth Sturman, Football, 1937-39; Eddie Talboom, Football, 1948-50; Bowden Wyatt, FB Coach, 1947-52; Bill Strannigan, Basketball/Baseball/Football, 1940-42, 1959-73; 1950 Skyline Champion Football Team

Inductees, 3rd Year, 1995

Jack B. Aggers, UW trainer, 1958-84; John C. Corbett, Football/Basketball Coach, 1915-39; James L. Crawford, Football, 1954-56; Robert S. Devaney, Football Coach, 1956-61; John J. Kosich, Baseball/Football, 1946-49; Patricia Miller-Davis, Track, 1980-82; Dewey McConnell, Football, 1949-51

Inductees, 4th Year, 1996

Larry Birleffi, "Voice of the Cowboys"; Michele Hoppes, Basketball, 1984-87; Charles Bradley, Basketball, 1984-87; Mark S. Miller, Swimming, 1985-88; Jim Kiick, Football, 1965-67; Milward Simpson, Football/Basketball/Baseball, 1917-21; Glenn "Bud" Daniel, Baseball Coach, 1951-61, 1963-71

Inductees, 5th Year, 1997

Joe Alexander, Rodeo, 1968-69; C. Keith Bloom, Basketball/Footballl, 1947-50; Stig Hallingbye, Skiing, 1974-77; Ronda K. Munger, Volleyball, 1984-87; Joseph N. Nzau, Track, 1977-82; 1967 Sugar Bowl Football team

Inductees, 6th Year, 1998

Curt Gowdy, Basketball, 1940-42; Joe Mastrogiovanni, Football, 1953-55; Bob Jingling, Baseball, 1952-55; Kathy Romsa, Track and Field, 1983-85; Eric Leckner, Basketball, 1985-88

Inductees, 7th Year, 1999

Darcy Cudaback White, Volleyball, 1986-89; Tony Windis, Basketball, 1957-59; John Pilch, Basketball, 1947-49; Paul Roach, Athletic Director/Coach, 1986-96 Galand Thaxton, Football, 1984-87; Paul Toscano, Football, 1965-67

Inductees, 8th Year, 2000

Jim Brandenburg, Basketball Coach, 1978-87; Lee Kizzire, Four-Sport Letterman, 1934-36; Amy Burnett, Basketball, 1992-95; Larry Nels, Football, 1967-69; Bill Ewing, Baseball, 1974-76; Curtis & Marian Rochelle, Special Achievement

Inductees, 9th Year, 2001

Nick Bebout, Football, 1970-72; Joe Capua, Basketball, 1954-56; Ken Cook, Special Achievement; Charles "Mickey" Dunn, Track/Field, 1949-51; Bill Garnett, Basketball, 1979-82; Jean Jackson, Administration; !956 Football Team

The UW ski club won national Nordic titles in 2003 and 2004.

Inductees, 10th Year, 2002

Greg Brock, Baseball, 1976-79; Mitch Donahue, Football, 1987-90; Christine Fairless, Basketball, 1986-89; Margie McDonald, Basketball Coach, 1975-83; George "Moe" Radovich, Basketball Coach, 1950-52; Reginald Slater, Basketball, 1989-92

Inductees, 11th Year, 2003

Ken Fantetti, Football, 1975-78; Norma Hughes Scifres, Swimming, 1990-92, 1994; William "Dutch" Witte, Basketball/Football Coach, 1930-39; John Wodny, Cross Country/Track, 1986-90; Ryan Yarborough, Football, 1990-93; Bill Young, Sports Information Dir./Ass't Athletic Director,1960-81; 1959-60 Wrestling Team

Inductees, 12th Year, 2004

Reese Andy, Wrestling, 1994-96; Leon Clark, Basketball, 1963-66; Marcus Harris, Football, 1993-96; Bill Levine, Football, 1961, 1963-64; Jimmi Jo Martin Ripsam, Rodeo, 1988-90; Pat Rabold, Football, 1984, 1986-88

Inductees, 13th Year, 2005

Ryan Butler, Track/Field, 1995-96; Phil Dickens, Football Coach, 1953-56; Joe Dowler, Wrestling Coach/Administrator, 1973-87; Ann Melander, Skiing, 1984-85; Theo Ratliff, Basketball, 1992-95; Vic Washington, Football, 1965-67; 1989 Cowgirl Volleyball Team

Inductees, 14th Year, 2006

Ryan Christopherson, Football, 1991-94; Jerry DePoyster, Football, 1965-67; Stan Dodds, Basketball, 1968-70; Robert "Bob" Hammond, Sportswriter; Milo Komenich, Basketball, 1940-43; Stacey Ward Straley, Skiing, 1979-84; 1966 Cowboy Baseball Team

Inductees, 15th Year, 2007

Brenda Graham Gray, Track/Field, 1980-84; Elsie Jo Bonger, Football Secretary, 1962-78; Jerry Jester, Football, 1953-55; Dave McCleave, Golf, 1989-92; Dick Sherman, Basketball, 1963-66; Randy Welniak, Football,1985-88; 1968 National Champion Ski Team

Inductees, 16th Year, 2008

Thomas "Rupe" Garrison, Track, 1987-91; Walker "Sonny" Jones, Football, 1948-49; Geir Kvemmo, Skiing/Track, 1977-80; Brian Lee, Football, 1994-97; Dave Myers, Wrestling, 1989-92; Steve Scifres, Football, 1994-97; 1978-79 Women's Basketball Team

Inductees, 17th Year, 2009

Jesseca Cross, Basketball/Track/ 1994-97; Sean Fleming, Football, 1988-92; Gene Huey, Football, 1966-68; Quincy Howe, Track, 1999-02; Mike Jackson, Basketball, 1980-83; Al & Pete Simpson, Special Achievement; 1961 National Champion Rodeo Team

Inductees, 18th Year, 2010

Staale Engen, Skiing/Track; 1971-74; Jerry Frude, Wrestling, 1959-60, 1962; Steinar Hybertsen, Skiing, 1973-75; Bob Jacobs, Football, 1968-70; Chuck Lamson, Football, 1960-62; Karen Sanford Gall. Track & Field, 1979-82; 1966 Cowboy Football Team

Wyoming Sports Officials Association Hall of Fame

Inducted in 1993
Fred Brownlee, Powell
Art Hill, Casper
Ed Strube, Casper
Bob Huelle, Lander
Bob Porter, Riverton
Glenn Phillips, Cheyenne
Inducted in 1996
Ron Hirst, Cheyenne
George Jelaco, Rock Springs

Inducted in 1994
Howard Dunbar, Chey.
Bill Hileman, Sr., Casper
Paul Kipper, Laramie
Quincy Tarter, Casper
Adolph Vellner, Casper
Harold Thornton, Glenrock

Joe Perea, Cheyenne
Joseph Lynn Williams, Jackson

Inducted in 1995
Carol Jeaco, Rock Spr.
Herman Boner, Casper
Warren Capellen, Kem.
Ed Jolovich, Thermop.
Paul Smith, Worland

Herman Stumpf, Cheyenne

The National Horseshoe Pitching Championships were held in 1996 in Gillette. There were 1,536 entrants.

Simpson Award Winners

Named for late Gov/Sen. Miward Simpson, the awards are given to the best boy and best girl high school athletes annually.

Boys	Girls
1976: Robbie Cragoe, Riverton	Debbie Norman, Buffalo
1977: Gerald Mattinson, Rock Springs	Mary Faure, Worland
1978: Mike Mees, Cody	Margaret Gonzalez, Torrington
1979: Lance Deal, Natrona	Jan Brownall, Lander
1980: Tony Turner, Central	Kathy Van Heule, Worland
1981: Allyn Griffin, Kelly Walsh	Brandy Brown, Rock Springs
1982: Marty Eliopulos, Central	Mila Rogers, Sheridan
1983: Tom Basye, Jackson	Joan Ragitsch, Kemmerer
1984: Mark Farmer, Powell	Shelly Marlyst, Riverton
1985: Jon Cogdill, Kemmerer	Francie Faure, Worland
1986: Mike Lansing, Natrona	Shelly Thacker, Riverton
1987: Cory Bruce, Green River	Jenelle Brown, Riverton
1988: Ben Gose, Riverton	Tricia Montgomery, Riverton
1989: Dale Reed, Snake River	Jamie Crawford, Greybull
1990: John Godina, Central	Dusti Hladky, Gillette
1991: Matt Stock, Central	Marcee Owens, Natrona
1992: Blaine Phillips, Sheridan	Becky Kopsa, Sheridan
1993: Lee Vaughn, Cheyenne East	Jesseca Cross, Powell
1994: Gregg Sawyer, Burns	Anne Stohrer, Buffalo
1995: Corte McGuffey, Riverton	Kerri Maxfield, Lyman
1996: Justin Hopkin, Burlington	Kristy Johnson, Powell
1997: Brett Keisel, Greybull	Ana-Marie Ortega, Green River
1998: Brady Poppinga, Evanston	Cheryl Ann Harmon, Green River
1999: Sundance Wicks, Gillette	Elisa Butler, Wright
2000: Jeff Martini, Sheridan	Elizabeth Brown, Thermopolis
2001: Scott Muir, Rawlins	Kelsey Wicks, Gillette
2002: Clint Oldenburg, Gillette	Katie Cox, Big Horn
2003: Mike Aimone, Kemmerer	Kristen Newlin, Riverton
2004: Alex Obrecht, Central	Angie Hellbaum, Wheatland
2005: Zeb Whipp, Lander	Megan McGuffey, Cheyenne East
2006: Chris Prosinski, Buffalo	Tahnee Robinson, Lander
2007: Brendan Ames, Central	Hillary Carlson, Cheyenne Central
2008: Stephen Michel, Laramie	Kristen Scheffler, Lovell
2009: Tommy Earl, Natrona	Emily Moore, Gillette

Wyoming Coaches Hall of Fame

Initial Inductees (1984) *posthumously inducted
Jack Aggers, Glenn "Bud" Daniel, Everett Lantz, Bob Robertson, Jack C. Allen, John Deti, Shad Martoglio, Burt St. John, Bill Bernatow, Robert Doerr, Lloyd McCullough, Ev Shelton*, Okie Blanchard, Gene Dozah, Jim McLeod, Marvin Strauch, Keith Bloom, Lloyd Eaton, Sandy Michelena, Bill A. Strannigan, Bob Bolles, Swede Erickson, Wilford Mower*, Glenn Burgess, Harry Geldien, Don Nelson, Phil Treick, Hank Cabre*, Art Hill, George Bud Nelson, Spike Vanoy*, Bob Carey, Dallas Hoff, Melvin Nelson, Spiro Varras, Thomas Confer, Bruce Hoffman, Pete Petronovich, B. B. Ted Weaver, Fran Connor, Glenn "Red" Jacoby*, Jerry Quinlan, Don Weishaar, Bob Cook, L. A. Kohnke*, Jack Rafferty Jr., J. Lynn Williams, Jim Wiseman
Inducted, 1985: Jerry Barrus, Walter Milliken, Denny Brown, Milt Riske*, Jerry Campbell, Carl Rollins. George Carmin, LeRoy Sinner, Duane Freeman, Dario Soto, David Gorman, LeRoy Sprague, Walter Gray, Jim Storey*
Inducted, 1986: Dennis Anderson, Earl Grey, Joe Bush*, William Hileman, Joe Dowler, Richard Macht, Ron Estes, Ken Rochlitz

Inducted, 1987: Patricia Brown, Brock Hileman, Layne Kopischka

Inducted, 1988: Gary Johnson, Brent Williams, Jerry Pierontoni

Inducted, 1989: Bill Bolles, Jim Rooks, Joanne Ball-Harvey, Richard Price, Rich Yeaman

Inducted, 1990: Gene Andrews, William McIntosh, Gary Campbell, John C. Miller Jr.,Sherry Douglas, Edwin Reed, Bill Hileman Beecher Ed Strube, John McDougall

Inducted, 1991: Tom Brown, Mick Lehner, Jerry Dalton

Inducted, 1992: John Arciniega, Richard Fullmer, Richard Cotton

Inducted, 1993: Chuck Wells, Lew Roney, Jerry Lane

Inducted, 1994: Barry Miller, Rich Scherry, Diane Moser

Inducted, 1995: Bruce Keith

Inducted, 1996: Terry Berg, Bob Matson, Bruce Gresley, Paul Roach, Wayne Hartman

Inducted, 1997: Ed Cook, Sheila Syvrod, Todd Dayton, Joe Stohrer

Inducted, 1998: Kay Fackrell, Mike Moon, Keith Francik, Doug Reachard, Mike Harris, Don Vail

Inducted, 1999: Dan Close, Harvey Daulton, Delwin Skipp McCrary, Steve Mischke

Inducted, 2000: Dean Sims, Wayne Roadifer, Gary Nickal, Ron Laird, Mike Carey

Inducted, 2001: Ron Nelson, Pat Kirk, Van Hokanson, James Fowler, Raymond Candelaria, Ray Bieber

Inducted, 2002: Briant Teichert, Arthur Redman, Sr., Verl Petsch, Robert Linford, Orville Hess, Jim Eldridge, Doug Bartlett

Inducted, 2003: Kevin Williams, Mark Wilkinson, Dale Ross, Grant Patik

Inducted, 2004: Randy Walker, Ken Swartz, Wendy Schuler, Sheryl Levi, Larry Heslep, Allen Finch, Joel Eskelson, John Deti

Inducted, 2005: Norm Sedig, Kendra Roeder, Linda Brown

Inducted, 2006: Ted Schroeder, Craig Prine, Mike Lopiccolo, Richard Hoopes, Bert Dow, Terry Burgess

Inducted, 2007: Steve Smoot, Walt Berling

Inducted, 2008: Scott B. Smith, Tom Schrupp, Kathryn Hamer-Smith, Glenn Freeburg, Don Dinnel

Inducted, 2009: Robert Urbach, Bart Trautwein

Wyoming Sports Hall of Fame

The Wyoming Sports Hall of Fame, (WSHOF) honors athletes, coaches, fans, and members of the sports media who have made an impact on their sport in Wyoming. These individuals are not required to have attended the University of Wyoming, nor must they be from the Cowboy State originally. The first class was inducted in June of 2000 at the Parkway Plaza in Casper. The Wyoming Sports Hall of Fame is run entirely by volunteers and relies upon sponsorships and donations to continue the wonderful tradition of celebrating the best of the best in sport. Plaques for each inductee are currently displayed at the Casper Events Center, however, it is the board's vision to one day have a facility to house a more in-depth display.

2001: Boyd Dowler, Football; John Deti, Sr., Coach; Kenny Sailors, Basketball; Mike Devereaux, Baseball; Lew Roney, Track/Coach; Jerry Hill, Football; Tom Browning, Baseball; Curt Gowdy, Broadcasting; "Swede" Erickson, Coach; Joe Alexander, Rodeo

Athlete of the Year: Rulon Gardner, Afton, Olympic Wrestler

Lifetime Achievement Award: Homer Scott, Jr.

2002: Jim Crawford, Football; Jay Novacek, Football; Keith Bloom, Coach; Chris LeDoux, Rodeo/Entertainer; Bill Strannigan, Basketball/Coach; Lance Deal, Track and Field; Tom Wilkinson, Football; Sherry Douglas, Coach; Jesseca Cross, Track and Field; 1943 Wyoming NCAA Basketball Team

Athlete of the Year: John Godina, Cheyenne, Shot Put

Lifetime Achievement Award: Art Hill, Coach

2003: Kandy Holmes-Hartman, Golf; Harry Geldien, Coach; Fenis Dembo, Basketball; Bruce Hoffman, Coach; Paul Roach, Coach; Dewey McConnell, Football.

Athlete of the Year: Marcus Bailey, Cheyenne, Basketball

Lifetime Achievement Award: Larry Birleffi, Broadcaster

2004: Bill Smith, Rodeo; Jack Aggers, Athletic Trainer; Mark Miller, Swimming; John Deti, Jr., Coach; Mike Lansing, Baseball; John Burrough, Football

Athlete of the Year: Barb Metz Lindquist

Lifetime Achievement Award: Mike Schutte

2005: Lew Lepore, Golf; Ronda Munger, Volleyball; the Skinner Family; Tony Windis, Basketball, Layne Kopischka Swimming

Athlete of the Year: Kelly Timberman

Lifetime Achievement Award: George Kay, Broadcaster

2006: Jim Benepe, Golf; Warren "Cappie" Capellen, Four-Sport letterman, UW; Robert Ranck, Boxer; Ken Rochlitz, Basketball Coach; St. Stephens basketball team, 1958-61.

Athlete of the Year: Shauna Smith

Lifetime Achievement Award, Bob Hammond.

2007: Joe Dowler, UW Wrestling Coach; Phil Kiner, Trap Shooter; Mila Rogers-Stender, UW Basketball; Fritz Shurmur, Football Coach; Jim and Margie Fassler of World for starting Girls Meet of Champions of the Year track meet

Athlete of the Year: Bret Kiesel, Greybull, Pittsburgh Steelers defensive end.

Lifetime Achievement: Jim Core, Wyoming State Golf Association

2008: Stan Dodds, Basketball, Rulon Gardner, Olympic Wrestler, Kosta Tsandes, Cheyenne Frontier Days rodeo,

Athlete of the Year: 2006- UW Cowgirl Basketball team

Lifetime Achievement: Milward Simpson family.

2010: Cynthia Clinger, Star Valley Basketball; John Godina, Shot Put champion; Wally Goodwin, Collegiate Golf Coach, (resident of Banner); Gregg Sawyer, Basketball/Track

Athlete of the Year: Tyler Cox, Gillette wrestler.

Lifetime Achievement: Margie Hunt McDonald, Coach/Broadcaster

Wyoming Outdoors Hall of Fame

The hall "recognizes individuals who have made significant lasting contributions toward conserving Wyoming's wildlife heritage through volunteer service, environmental restoration, political and individual leadership, the arts, educational activities and visual and written media."

2004 (initial inductees)

Curt Gowdy, Broadcaster who hosted American Sportsman TV show

Olaus and Mardy Murie, Pioneer Environmentalists and Ecological Scientists

D. C. Nowlin, State's first Game Warden

Theodore Roosevelt

Calvin King, 1st Wildlife Biologist in the Big Horn Basin, 1956

Frank and Lois Layton, Eagle Rescuers

2005:

Tom Thorne and Elizabeth Williams, Game Biologists

George Bird Grinnell, 19th century Conservationist who owned a ranch in Wyoming

Paul Petzoldt, Mountaineer and founder of the National Outdoor Leadership School

James Simon, Game Department Official

2006: Frank and John Craighead, Wildlife Researchers

Tom Bell, founder of High Country News

Floyd Martin Blunt, founder of Sybille Research Station

Sam Mavrakis. Advocate of Outdoor Issues and Education

2007:

Hans Kleiber, Sheridan area artist/naturalist

Finis Mitchell, Mountain Range explorer

Chuck Ward. Game Warden, Educator

Meg and Bert Raynes, Non-game Bird Conservationists

2008:

Jim Bridger, Mountainman

William Barlow, founder of the Powder River Basin Resource Council (1973)

Fred Eiserman, Fisheries manager

Bill Grunkemeyer, Wildlife Photographer/Videographer
2009:
Col. William D. Pickett, (Alabama, 1827; d. Kentucky, 1917) Boone and Crockett Club officer
Terry Cleveland, Game and Fish director
Olin Sims, (b. Riverton, 1960, d. Dec. 7, 2007), McFadden area rancher/conservationist

5 Years of Top Sports Stories from the 1990s

The Associated Press suspended the "Top Sports Stories" project in the middle 1990s because of member disinterest in running the end-of-the-year feature.

AP Top Sports Stories 1991
1. Joe Tiller completes first year as UW football coach
2. Spate of injuries strike UW sports
3. Possibility of professional baseball returns to Wyoming
4. Mitch Donahue signs with the SF 49ers.
5. UW basketball record team compiles strong record, loses in tourney.

AP Top Sports Stories 1992
1. Paul Westika, a Sheridan High School wrestler, is paralyzed in a match at Riverton (Feb. 8)
2. Sheridan wins third straight high school football title
3. Ryan Yarborough finishes the season with a school record for receptions, career yardage and touchdowns
4.-5. (tie) Wyoming football team finishes season at 5-7
Quein Higgins, UW basketball player, reinjures knee in game against Russian Nationals

AP Top Sports Stories 1993
1. Benny Dees resigns as UW basketball coach; Joby Wright hired for the job
2. UW finishes the football season with a 8-3 mark but lost to Kansas State 52-17 in the Copper Bowl
3. Ryan Yarborough sets three NCAA records: 4,357 yards receiving; seven 200-yard games receiving; 27 consecutive games with a reception
4. Sheridan wins third straight high school football championship
5. Gillette basketball team wins state title after chalking up 31 consecutive wins

AP Top Sports Stories 1994
1. Ryan Christopherson's record-breaking season for the University of Wyoming football team. He finished his career as leading rusher in UW history with 2,906 yards. He led the Western Athletic Conference and finished tenth in the nation in rushing at the end of the regular season.
2. Ryan Yarborough's move to the NFL New York Jets. Yarborough, who set the UW record for receiving with 4,446 yards, 239 receptions and 42 touchdowns, scored his first pro touchdown against Minnesota.
3. Undefeated Wyoming Indian basketball team (21-0) upset 65-57 in state tourney by Tongue River (12-9)
4. Big Horn barrel racer Sharon Kobold's performance in the National Finals Rodeo. She placed in all nine rounds and finished second over-all for the year.
5. Resignation of Campbell County High School football coach Paul Colgate. The veteran coach was not rehired by the superintendent.

AP Top Sports Stories 1995
1. Three Lyman parents offered money to their sons to injure opposition football players in the game against Glenrock. Glenrock won 14-6.
2. Paul Roach retired as University of Wyoming athletic director.
3. None of the No. 1 ranked teams season end won the state basketball titles.
4. Wyoming basketball star Theo Ratliff was drafted in the first round of the NBA draft by the Detroit Pistons. He was the 18th player chosen overall.
5. John Scott was hired to replace Paul Colgate as football coach at Campbell County High School. Colgate had resigned under fire the previous year.

In 1934 a black Bighorn ram was seen on the headwaters of Crystal Creek in the Tetons.

Miscellaneous Items about Wyoming Sports

1. In 1925, the Marlatt family of rural Goshen County won the "World Championship of Brothers" title in baseball. All nine players on the team were Marlatt brothers.

2. In 1992, the Laramie Jubilee Days committee held a contest to name the bull, known only as No. 722, the son of legendary Mr. T. They received more than 900 entries from 47 states.

3. Brent Weigner, Cheyenne, was the top American finisher in the 1998 Himalayan 100-mile stage race. He finished in sixth place overall in the grueling event.

4. In 1993, a 22-year-old man wanted for forgery in Oklahoma lied to Laramie Vigilantes Senior Babe Ruth baseball team officials about his true identity and claimed he was only 17 and, therefore, eligible to play for the team. The ruse was discovered only after police arrested him on an outstanding warrant.

5. Polo was played at Wyoming forts in the 19th century, but the first polo field in Wyoming was Big Horn Polo Field, started by Malcolm Moncreiffe around the turn of the century in Sheridan County.

6. The Wyoming Cowgirl Basketball team got into its first NCAA Tournament but lost the opening round game to the University of Pittsburgh Panthers 63-58 at the Pit in Albuquerque.

7. Led by WNIT Most Valuable Player Hanna Zavecz, the Wyoming Cowgirls won their first WNIT Championship with a 72-56 win over the Wisconsin Badgers in March 2007. More than 15,000 fans attended the game in the Arena-Auditorium in Laramie.

8. Wyoming has 15,846 miles of fishing streams, 297,633 acres of fishing lakes and 3,400 lakes, ponds and reservoirs holding 90 varieties of fish, 42 of which are game fish

9. Dave Walsh, sportscaster, is a 9 time winner of the Wyoming sportscaster of the year. In 2010, he begins his 27th year as the "Voice of the Cowboys".

10. Georgia Graves, Douglas, is one of Wyoming's most famous bowlers. In 1996, she won fourth in the nation in the National Senior Citizens' Bowling tourney in New York.

11. In the summer of 1997, two former University of Wyoming football players, Mark Brook and Tyrone Williams, played for the Rhein Fire in the World League of American Football championship.

12. Domenic Mediate, born in Sheridan, was selected by the Columbus (Ohio) Crew in the 2005 Major League Soccer draft. Later, he played for DC United. He is a distant cousin of PGA golfer Rocco Mediate.

.

Joe and Linda Fabian of Wheatland finished fourth in the world in their division at the 2000 United Country and Western Dance Council world dance championships in Nashville. They represented Wyoming in the 2001 championships in Edmonton, Alberta, and continued to participate in national dance events through the first decade of the new century.

BASEBALL

1st mention of baseball in Wyoming: "Men amuse themselves frequently when off duty by playing baseball." Post Surgeon's report, Fort Laramie, October 1868. A South Pass City team played a team from Atlantic City on the 4th of July 1870. On the same day, the Fort Sanders team defeated a Laramie city team 43-26. According to accounts, "several hundred dollars was staked on the outcome."

1st organized team in Cheyenne: "Eclipse baseball team challenged Denver," the *Cheyenne Daily Leader* reported on June 19, 1870.

1st Wyoming team in an organized baseball league: A Colorado state baseball league made up of eight clubs was organized in Pueblo in January 1910. Teams represented seven Colorado cities and Cheyenne. Damon Runyon, later a famed sports writer, served as the new league's first president.

1st professional baseball team in Wyoming: Cheyenne Indians of the Western League, pre-World War II years.

1st Minor League team in Wyoming (2001): The Casper Rockies baseball team became a member of the Pioneer League in 2001. With the name changed to the Casper Ghosts in 2007, the Ghosts are the only team in minor league baseball to wear glow-in-the-dark baseball caps. They are affiliated with the Colorado Rockies and play at Mike Lansing Field in Casper.

1st Wyoming-born major leaguer: Bob Harris, born in Gillette in 1916.

1st major league hit by a Wyoming-born batter off a pitch thrown by a Wyoming-born pitcher: Mike Deveraux's double off fellow Casper native Tom Browning on Sept. 9, 1987. Deveraux's hit was one of only two Browning allowed in the game which his team (Cincinnati) won 4-1 over the LA Dodgers.

1st paid woman baseball umpire: Amanda "Mandy" Clement who umpired from 1904-1910. A native of Hudson, S. D., Miss Clement umpired games in Wyoming and four other states. In the 1920s, she taught physical education in Wyoming schools. She returned to South Dakota in 1929.

Oldest baseball park in the West: Pioneer Park, Cheyenne, claims the title.

Best team in Wyoming history: Arguably, the semi-pro Cheyenne Indians of 1923. The team ended the season with a record of 28 wins and just one loss.

Oldest active softball umpire in U. S. (1995): Harvey Jepsen, Jackson, age 75.

Rocky Mountain Rookie League incorporated: Summer, 1992, teams in Fort Collins, Grand Junction, Greeley, Pueblo; Laramie and Cheyenne; Scottsbluff and North Platte.

Mountain Collegiate Baseball League started: Summer, 2010, with 4 teams: Cheyenne (Grizzlies), Fort Collins (Foxes), Greeley (Grays) and Laramie (Colts). This is a summer league affiliate of the National Baseball Congress. The league uses wooden bats and the league champion is invited to compete in the NBC World Series held in late July in Wichita, Kansas.

Wyomingites in Major League Drafts, 1989-2010

1989 Major League Draft: One player from Wyoming drafted. Brad Erdman, former Casper Cardinal player, drafted by the Chicago Cubs in the 17th round, June 6, 1989.

1991 Major League Draft: Outfielder Steve Hazlett (20th round, Minnesota), shortstop Ron Warner (21st round, St. Louis), pitcher/first baseman Rigo Beltran (30th round, St. Louis), and centerfielder Mike Eicher (40th round, Montreal). June 11, 1991.

1992 Major League Draft: Four UW players were drafted by the major leagues in June 1992, the most in the school's history. Drafted were pitcher Mike Lopez (9th round, Detroit), Jason Kummerfeldt (15th round, Cincinnati), pitcher Joe Carrillo (22nd round, St. Louis), and catcher Jeff Horn (47th round, Minnesota).

1994 Major League Draft: Pitcher/outfielder Kirby Drube, Gillette, drafted by Los Angeles Dodgers.

1995 Major League Draft: Pitcher Josh Kalinowski, 18, Casper, drafted by the Colorado Rockies in the 37th round.

1996 Major League Draft: Catcher Josh McAffee, Rock Springs native, drafted by the Arizona Diamondbacks, first round. (He moved to Farmington, N.M., as a high school student in order to play high school baseball.)

1997 Major League Draft: Pitcher Rocky Kirk, a 1997 graduate of Kelly Walsh High School, was drafted in the 28th round by the Colorado Rockies.

1998 Major League Draft: Kirk, who had opted to pitch for Cochise College in Arizona rather than turn pro, was drafted in the 33rd round, again by the Rockies. Casper native Jason Pruitt, who had moved to Tucson in 1986, was drafted by Baltimore in the 16th round.

1999 Major League Draft:
James Ralph, University of Wyoming, was drafted in the 15th round by the Baltimore Orioles.

2010 Major League Draft:
Patrick Farrell, catcher from Cheyenne who played at Regis University, was drafted by the New York Mets in the 32nd round; Dusty Harvard, centerfielder from Casper, who played at Oklahoma State, was drafted by the Chicago White Sox in the 34th round.

Recent Major League Players from Wyoming

1. Mike Deveraux, b. Casper, April 10, 1963, Outfielder

Deveraux, for several years, was the starting centerfielder for Baltimore. He played American Legion baseball with the Casper Oilers and starred in track and field at Kelly Walsh High School. He attended Arizona State University on a baseball scholarship and signed with the Los Angeles Dodgers in 1985. For two seasons, he played with San Antonio of the Texas League and put in one year with Albuquerque of the Pacific Coast League. After the 1988 season with the Los Angeles Dodgers, he was traded to Baltimore early in the 1989 season and to the Chicago White Sox in 1995. On Aug. 25, 1995, he was traded to the Atlanta Braves. During the 1995 league championship series, Deveraux was named the most valuable player, leading the Braves to the NL title. He also starred in Atlanta's victory over Cleveland in the World Series. During the 1996 off-season, Deveraux was signed as a free agent by Baltimore, the team with which he began his major league career. He had a lifetime major league batting average of .257 and 77 homeruns at the close of the 1993 season. Before the 1994 season began, he signed a multi-year contract for more than $3 million, making him one of the highest paid Wyomingites in any walk of life at that time.

2. Tom Browning, b. Casper, April 28, 1960, Pitcher

Browning, who signed a four-year contract with Cincinnati in November 1990 for $12.48 million, holds the distinction of pitching a perfect game, the only one thrown by a Wyoming-born pitcher in the major leagues. He finished that season (1988) with 18 wins and three losses and an earned run average of 3.41. (His perfect game was the first in the history of the Cincinnati Reds and only the 14th in major league baseball history.) Browning started his major league career with the Reds in 1984 with his first major league win on Sept. 9, 1984. The next year, he chalked up 20 wins for the Reds. He won the third game of the 1990 World Series against Oakland. On July 1, 1992, he ruptured a ligament in his left knee in a collision with the catcher when he tried to steal home against Houston. He was out for most of the season. In May 1994, in a freak accident, he broke a bone in his pitching arm while on the mound. He signed a free agency contract with the Kansas City Royals in 1995. After attempting a comeback with the Royals, he retired in 1996 before the season began. His lifetime record was 123 wins and 90 losses with an ERA of 3.94 in 11 seasons.

3. Mike Lansing b. Rawlins, April 3, 1968, Infielder

Lansing played shortstop on the Wichita State NCAA championship team of 1989. He led the NCAA in stolen bases and was named first team All-American. A 1986 graduate of

Natrona County High School, Lansing was drafted by the Expos in June 1990. He was the regular second baseman for the Expos. At the end of the 1993 season, he had a lifetime batting average of .287 in 141 games. His three homeruns in 1993 included the first ever hit against the Colorado Rockies in their home opener in Denver in April 1993. He was a regular starter in 1995 and 1996. By the All-Star break in mid-season, 1996, he was leading the National League in doubles with 22. He was traded to the Colorado Rockies before the 1998 season, but due to injuries, he didn't play up to his potential in the first two years. After some success as the lead-off hitter with the Rockies, he was traded to Boston during the regular season, 2000.

4. Jeff Huson, b. Aug. 15, 1964

An infielder, Huson is not a Wyoming native but he played his college baseball at Wyoming. In 1993, he played the entire season for the Texas Rangers. In early 1994, he was injured and sent back to the AAA league for rehabilitation. In 1995, he signed and played with the Baltimore Orioles. After another stint on the disabled list in 1996, he was called up in July, 1996, by the Orioles. He retired with the Chicago Cubs in 2000. In recent years he has been post-game commentator for the Colorado Rockies on FSN.

5. John Buck b. Kemmerer, July 7, 1980, Catcher

Buck was drafted by the Houston Astros in the 1998 amateur draft. He began his Major League baseball career as a catcher with the Kansas City Royals in 2004. He played six seasons with the Royals and then signed a free agent contract with the Toronto Blue Jays on December 13, 2009. In 2010, Buck was an active player with the Blue Jays.

Former Major Leaguers from Wyoming

1. Greg Brock, b. McMinnville, Ore., 1957

Brock played college baseball at the University of Wyoming and drafted by the Dodger organization in the 1979 amateur draft as the team's 13th selection. He started with the Los Angeles Dodgers in 1982. He was traded to Milwaukee in 1987.

2. Dennis DeBarr, b. Cheyenne, 1953

Debarr, a left-handed pitcher, appeared in 14 games for the Toronto Bluejays in 1977. He had just one decision, a loss, and struck out ten batters.

3. Jan Dukes, b. Cheyenne, 1945

A left-handed pitcher, Dukes played for the Rangers in 1972. He appeared in 16 games, ending his brief major league career with an earned run average of 2.70.

4. Dick Ellsworth, b. Lusk, 1940

Ellsworth's longest stint was eight years with the Chicago Cubs from 1958-1966. Later, he pitched for Philadelphia (1967), Boston (1968-69), Cleveland (1969-70), and ended his career in 1971 with Milwaukee. He had a lifetime record of 115 wins and 137 losses, struck out 1,140, and had an earned run average of 3.72.

5. Bob Harris, b. Gillette, 1916

The first native Wyomingite to play in the majors, Harris started with Detroit in 1938. The right-handed pitcher was traded to the St. Louis Browns in 1939 and to the Philadelphia Athletics in 1942. His baseball career ended there. From 1943-1945, he served in the armed forces. His major league mark was 30 wins and 52 losses, 205 strikeouts and an earned run average of 4.95.

6. Rick Sofield, b. Cheyenne, 1956

Sofield was an outfielder for the Minnesota Twins from 1979-1981. He appeared in 217 games, hit nine homeruns and had a career batting average of .243. After his playing career ended, Sofield went into coaching. From 1988-94, he was head baseball coach at the University of Utah. In 2010, he was coaching college baseball in South Carolina.

7. Dan Spillner, b. Casper, 1951

Spillner, a right-handed pitcher, started in 1974 with the San Diego Padres with a 9-11 record and 4.01 ERA. He led the team as a rookie in wins that year. From 1978- 1984, he pitched for Cleveland. He was traded to the Chicago White Sox in 1984 and retired from baseball the following year.

8. Bill Wilkinson, b. Greybull, 1964

Wilkinson pitched for the Seattle Mariners in 1985, and 1987-1988. His first major league win was on June 16, 1987. The Greybull native had a brother Brian in the minor leagues, drafted by the Mariners in 1987.

9. Art Howe, b. Pittsburgh, 1946

Howe played collegiate baseball at Wyoming. He started in major league baseball with the Pittsburgh Pirates in 1974, hitting a single on his first at-bat on June 10, 1974. The versatile infielder was traded, after two years, to Houston where he played second base and first base. He concluded his playing career with Houston in 1983 when he was placed on the disabled list. In February 1989, he was named Astros manager. When the team ownership changed at the end of the 1993 season, Howe was fired along with the general manager and other team officials. His team had finished third in NL West in 1993 with mark of 85-77. After one season coaching with the Colorado Rockies, Howe became general manager of the Oakland A's in 1996 and in 2000, led the team into title contention. At the end of 2002, he left the A's to become manager of the New York Mets. His two seasons were rocked by changes in upper management and a losing record on the field. He was fired at the end of the 2004 season. After a brief coaching stint with the Philadelphia Phillies, Howe joined the Texas Rangers as a coach. He reitred from major league baseball in 2008.

10. Bucky Jacobsen, b. Riverton, 1975

Jacobsen played baseball at Lewis and Clark College. He was drafted by the Milwaukee Brewers in the 1997 Major League Draft. Released by the Brewers in 2002, he was signed by St. Louis, but became a free agent the following year. Jacobsen played the 2004 season as a first baseman/designated hitter for the Seattle Mariners. In 2005, due to a knee injury, he was released from the Mariners. He later signed various minor league contracts before retiring from baseball in 2007. In 2010, he was working as a broadcaster for the Fox affiliate in Seattle, doing post-game coverage of the Mariners games.

11. Rigo Beltran, b. 1969

When Beltran played at Wyoming, he was called one of the most versatile players in team history. He pitched, played first base and was a good hitter. Drafted by the St. Louis Cardinals in 1991, Beltran pitched for their AAA farm club in Louisville from 1994-96. In 1997, he played for the Cardinals in 35 games. He was traded to the Mets the following year and to the Rockies in 1999. Later that year, he returned to the Mets where he pitched in 21 games. He closed out his major league playing career with Montreal in 2004. In 2009, he was pitching coach for a minor team in Carolina.

Wyomingites in the Minor Leagues

1. Mark Lee

Lee played baseball for the Casper Oilers American Legion team. Drafted by the Chicago Cubs, he was pitching for Iowa in AAA, a Cubs farm club, in 1994. He signed with Baltimore in 1995. In 1996, he pitched for Norfolk, the AAA farm team for the Mets.

Mike Lansing hit a 3-run homer in the eighth inning of the first home game played by the Colorado Rockies on April 9, 1993. Lansing's team, the Montreal Expos, defeated the Rockies 11-4. Five years later, he was traded to the Rockies and played in Denver for the next two years.

2. Brad Erdman, b. 1970

The former Casper Cardinal player was drafted by the Chicago Cubs in the 17th round of the 1989 Major League draft. He was a catcher and, in June 1994, he was with Daytona, a Chicago Cubs A farm team. In June, 1996, he was with the Iowa AAA farm team of the Chicago Cubs. He retired from baseball at the end of the 1996 season.

3. Jason Kummerfeldt , b. 1969

Drafted by Cincinnati in the 1992 Major League draft, Kummerfeldt played collegiate baseball at Wyoming. In 1994, he was pitching for the Reds' class A farm team, Winston-Salem. In 1996, he was with the independent Duluth-Superior team in the minor leagues. After retiring from baseball, he went into private business in Billings.

4. Steve Hazlett, b. 1970

A former University of Wyoming outfielder, Hazlett was drafted in 1991 in the 20th round by Minnesota. In 1994, he was assigned to the Twins' farm team in Nashville (Class AA). In 1996, he was an outfielder for the Salt Lake City AAA Twins farm team. His last season was in 1998 with the Orlando team in the Florida League.

5. Ron Warner, b. 1968

The former Cowboy shortstop was drafted by St. Louis in the 21st round of the 1991 draft. From 1994-96, he played third base for the Cardinals' farm team in Arkansas (Class AA), playing a total of nine seasons in the Cardinal farm system. In 2001 he began a long career in minor league coaching. From 2007-09, he was head coach for the Springfield Cardinals of the Texas League.

6. Jeff Horn, b. 1970

The former Cowboy catcher was drafted in the 47th round by Minnesota in the 1992 draft. In 1994, he was the catcher Fort Myers, the Twins' A farm team. In a nine-year career in the minors, he played for nine different teams.

7. Mike Moses, b. 1971

The former University of Wyoming pitcher, Moses was drafted by Cincinnati. He pitched for the Reds' farm team, Charleston, S. C., (Class A), in 1994, his final year in professional baseball.

8. Eric Mapp, b. Casper, 1972

Selected by the Cincinnati Reds in the 19th round of the 1995 Major League draft, he played collegiate baseball at Lamar. The Casper native was playing for Billings in the rookie league in 1996, his final year in professional baseball.

9. Josh Kalinowski, b. Pasco, Wash., 1976

The 1995 graduate of Natrona County High School was signed by the Colorado Rockies in May, 1997, and assigned to their Portland farm club. He had pitched Indian Hills Community College, Centersville, Iowa, to a fifth place finish in the national Junior College World Series in 1997. After playing for minor league teams in the Rockies organization, he underwent shoulder surgery in April 2004. After a year with Bridgeport, he retired and returned to Casper where he entered the real estate business.

10. Ben Phillips, b. Belle Fourche, S. D., 1975

The Sheridan athlete pitched for Howard Junior College in Texas in 1996 when he was signed by the New York Yankees. He was sent to Tampa and Norwich, the Yankees AA farm club, in 1998. He closed out his professional baseball career in 2000 with Elmira.

While on a hunting trip to the Casper area in 1954, baseball star and broadcast announcer Dizzy Dean stopped for a few drinks at the Wonder Bar. Word spread of his presence and, soon, fans began lining up, asking him for his autograph. He gave $20 to a waitress to buy as many baseballs as possible. He signed them and gave them away to his fans. Source: "Historic Casper, Wyoming," booklet by the Casper Historic Preservation Commission, c. 1993.

Some Facts on University of Wyoming Baseball

1. 1st UW baseball team

Baseball began as a varsity sport in 1938. Over the next 56 years, the team lettered 462 athletes. The baseball program was eliminated by the UW Board of Trustees in 1996.

2. Most Winning Coach at UW

Glenn "Bud" Daniel coached for 20 years. Under his direction, the team won four Mountain State Conference titles and one WAC Northern Division title. In 1956, he led the Cowboys to the team's only appearance in the College World Series.

3. Baseball Field

Cowboy Field opened in 1964.

4. End of Baseball

After 56 years as a competitive sport at the University of Wyoming, the trustees voted in January 1996 to eliminate the baseball program. The decision was very unpopular among Wyoming sports fans and citizens. Ironically, the 1996 team finished with one of the best records in UW baseball history. The team defeated Grand Canyon College 24-5 in the last game of the 1996 season--and final game for the sport at UW.

Recent Wyoming Baseball Winners*

^ For earlier records, see earlier editions of Wyoming Almanac.

American Legion Championship Games

2000: Torrington 13 Cheyenne 2	**2005**: Cheyenne 9 Laramie 3
2001: Cheyenne 7 Casper 2	**2006:** Cheyenne 19 Laramie 9
2002: Cheyenne 7 Gillette 2	**2007:** Cheyenne 11 Gillette 8
2003: Cheyenne 7 Casper 6	**2008:** Gillette 12 Cheyenne 0
2004: Cheyenne 26 Laramie 16	**2009:** Cheyenne 17 Gillette 11

Little League State Champions

1992: Torrington	**1998**: Laramie	**2004:** Gillette
1993: Rock Springs	**1999**: Green River	**2005**: Gillette
1994: Torrington	**2000**: Laramie	**2006:** Laramie
1995: Laramie	**2001**: Laramie	**2007**: Laramie
1996: Rock Springs	**2002**: Laramie	**2008**: Laramie
1997: Laramie	**2003**: Laramie	**2009**: Laramie

Most state titles: Laramie (16), Riverton (7)

National Little League Playoffs: 1987: Wyoming All-Stars 8, Nogales, Ariz. 2 It was the first time a Wyoming team won the first round game in the Little League tournament. They were eliminated in the second round by Albuquerque 14-0. In 1997 Western Regionals, the Wyoming team, Laramie, took third, the highest by a Wyoming team to that date. Laramie was fifth in 1995; Rock Springs, fifth in 1996.

Cowgirls Win National Title, 2007

The Wyoming Cowgirls basketball team won the WNIT championship in 2006-07 by defeating Wisconsin 72-56 before a crowd of 15,462 at the UW Arena-Auditorium on March 31, 2007. It was the first ever national title for the Cowgirls. The Cowgirls beat defending champion Kansas State 89-79 in triple OT to reach the championship game. In 2008, the Cowgirls gained an at-large berth in the NCAA tournament, but lost to Pittsburgh 63-58 in the opening round. In 2010, the Cowgirls won the first two games of the WNIT, beating Nevada 74-53 and Texas Tech 68-57 in OT, but lost to BYU in the third round 67-63.

BASKETBALL

1st University of Wyoming basketball game: UW beat Laramie town team 17-8 in 1905.

1st UW intercollegiate game: UW v. Colorado State College(now UNC),Greeley, 1909.

1st UW national basketball championship: 1943

1st UW Women's WNIT Championship: 2007

1st game played in the Arena-Auditorium: Feb. 20, 1982 against Air Force. More than 15,000 fans attended the game.

1st Wyoming high school basketball tournament: 1918, in Laramie. University Prep defeated Laramie for the title. Milward Simpson, then a UW player, was the Prep coach.

1st professional basketball team in Wyoming: Wyoming Wildcatters(CBA), 1982- 1988. The franchise, declared "defunct" by the CBA, moved to Cedar Rapids, Iowa, after the team lost the 1988 CBA championship series to Albany four games to three.

Longest high school basketball winning streak: 50 straight by Wyoming Indian Chiefs, 1983-1985. The streak was snapped Dec. 13, 1985, when the team lost to Lovell 74-57. The St. Stephens boys' team and the Lander girls' team each won 46 straight games.

Longest high school basketball losing streak: 63 in a row by Kemmerer. The streak ended with a win in December 1989. On Dec. 16, 2006, the Rawlins girls basketball team won a game. The next win came three seasons later on Feb. 2, 2010, over Newcastle snapping the longest consecutive game losing streak in girls' basketball.

1st coed high school basketball team in U. S.: Jeffrey City High School team in 1991- 92. The high school enrolled just 12 students that year. Consequently, drastic action had to be taken to field a team. Three girls and three boys suited up for the first game of the season against Wyoming Indian in December 1991. No team was fielded in 1990-91.

1st national title won by a Wyoming high school team: The Gillette Force, a team made up of Gillette High School girls, won the Basketball Congress International national tournament in Phoenix, Ariz., in the summer of 1996. The team won seven straight games including a 63-49 win over San Diego All-Stars to win the title.

Wyomingite and former owner of Los Angeles Lakers: Bill Daniels (d. 2000), cable TV magnate who started as an insurance agent in Casper in the 1950s before beginning his cable TV business in 1958.

Los Angeles Lakers owner and native Wyomingite: Dr. Jerry Buss, a Kemmerer native and UW graduate, is the principal owner of the 2010 World Champion Los Angeles Lakers.

Men's basketball attendance record at UW: 16,089 on March 2, 2002, when the Cowboys defeated Utah 57-56 to win the Mountain West regular season title.

Well-Known Wyoming Basketball Players

1. Kenny Sailors

Sailors was unanimous choice for All-American in 1943. He won the Chuck Taylor award as the outstanding basketball player in the nation the same year. He repeated as All-American selection in 1948. He was regarded as one of the "inventors" of the jump shot. He played with various NBA teams from 1946-51.

2. Milo Komenich

Komenich, the tall center, was one of three All-American selections on the national championship Wyoming team of 1943. From 1947-50, he played professional basketball with Fort Wayne and Anderson.

3. Jim Weir

Weir was the third Cowboy to be chosen an All-American in 1943.

4. George Livingston

In 1949, Livingston was the first UW basketball player ever drafted by a team in the NBA--the Baltimore Bullets. He later played for Philadelphia (1951).

5. Bill Strannigan

Strannigan starred for the Cowboys from 1941-1943. Later, in 1959, he was named head coach for his alma mater. In 14 seasons, his teams won 179 games.

6. Moe Radovich

Like Strannigan, Radovich was an All-American selection at Wyoming who later became head basketball coach at the university.

7. John Pilch

Pilch was Wyoming's leading scorer from 1947-1950. He was selected to the All-American team in 1949. The former Thermopolis High School star went on to play professional basketball with the Sheybogan Redskins and the Minneapolis Lakers in 1951-52. He died in 1991 at the age of 66.

8. Joe Capua

All-American selection in 1956.

9. Tony Windis

Windis was an All-American in 1959. He played one season in the NBA with Detroit (1959-60). He later coached basketball at Rawlins.

10. Flynn Robinson

Robinson came from Elgin, Ill., to play basketball at Casper College, transferring to Wyoming in 1963. In the next three seasons, he set school scoring marks that were not broken for a generation. After his college career, Robinson went on to play in the NBA for nine seasons, first with Cincinnati (1966-67), then with the Milwaukee Bucks (1968-70) and the famed 1971-72 Los Angeles Lakers, a team that won a record 33 straight games enroute to a 69-13 record. He closed out his NBA career with San Diego in 1973-74. In the 1990s, Robinson lived in California. An avid saltwater fisherman, he worked with a program to introduce disadvantaged children to fishing and ocean ecology.

11. John Johnson

Johnson played at Northwest Community College from 1966-1968. He went to the University of Iowa where he was an All-American in 1970. He played for Cleveland, Portland, Houston and closed his NBA career on the NBA champion Seattle Sonics in the late 1970s. In the 1980s and 1990s, he coached high school basketball in Bellevue, Wash. He moved to California in 2007 where his son Mitch was starting guard for Stanford.

12. Bob Lackey

The Evanston, Ill., native starred at Casper College from 1968-1970, leading the Thunderbirds to a fourth place finish in the National Junior College Athletic Association championships in 1970. Twice, he won All-American honors. He went on to Marquette where he gained the nickname "the Black Swan." Following his collegiate career, he played in the NBA for the New York Knicks and the New Jersey Nets. Lackey died in June 2002 of cancer. He was 53.

13. Charles Bradley

Bradley was drafted by the Boston Celtics in the first round of the NBA draft in 1981. He set several University of Wyoming all-time marks. He was an assistant coach at Wyoming, San Diego State and BYU before accepting the head coaching job at Metro State (Denver) in 1994. He then moved to the head coaching position at Loyola Marymount, but resigned after a disappointing record in 2000.

14. Bill Garnett

Garnett, a Bradley teammate, also went to the NBA in the first round. He was WAC player of the year in 1982. Drafted by the Dallas Mavericks, he also played for the Indiana Pacers during the last years (1984-86) of his NBA career.

15. Chris Engler

Engler, the 7-foot center for the 1981 and 1982 Cowboys, played professional basketball with a number of teams in the decade of the 1980s, including the Golden State Warriors (1982-84), New Jersey, Chicago and Milwaukee (1984-85), Portland, Milwaukee and New Jersey (1986-87), closing out his NBA career with New Jersey (1987-88). In

1989, he played for Rapid City of the CBA. Engler later taught social studies in Stillwater, Minn., schools.

16. Eric Leckner

The talented Wyoming center on the 1987 and 1988 WAC championship team, Leckner was picked by the Utah Jazz in the first round of the 1988 NBA draft. The 17th choice over all, Leckner started for the 1989 division-winning team. Later, in 1993-94, he played center for the Philadelphia 76ers as backup to former BYU star Shaun Bradley. He was traded to Detroit and in 1996, he played center for the Pistons. He played for the New York Knicks in 1996-97 and ended his NBA career with the Washington Wizards in 1997.

17. Fennis Dembo

Wyoming's all-time leading scorer, Dembo was drafted by the Detroit Pistons in 1988. He played in 1989, but he saw limited action in the Piston's four-game sweep of the Lakers for the 1989 NBA title. His contract was not renewed in 1990. In 1993, he was playing for Rapid City Thrillers of CBA. In 1994, he played professional basketball in Argentina. He retired from basketball in 1998, worked briefly in Alabama and moved to San Antonio. In the early morning hours of Easter Sunday, 2003, Dembo confronted a burglar who had broken into his house. He shot and killed the man. No charges were filed, but the incident gained national attention. Dembo continued to work for the San Antonio Water District and, in 2009, took engineering courses at a San Antonio area college.

18. Mike Manns

The Sheridan College star set a school record with 47 points against Miles City on Feb. 18, 1989. He went on to play at Towson State in his native state of Maryland.

19. Robbie Jackson

One of the best high school players in Wyoming history, Jackson scored 62 points for Kelly Walsh High School on March 13, 1986, in the first round of the state tournament in a game against Green River. Kelly Walsh won the game 72-70.

20. Reginald Slater

The 1992 WAC player of the year, Slater set the UW record for career rebounds and, at the conclusion of his Cowboy career, he was fourth all-time in scoring. He was leading scorer in 1991-92 with an average of 17.9 points per game, 11.3 rebounds. Following his college career, in the summer of 1992, he signed with Magia de Huesca, Huesca, Spain. In the 1995-96 season, he played with three NBA teams (Denver, Dallas and Portland). In 2000, he was playing for the Minnesota Timberwolves of the NBA.

21. Tim Breaux

A Cowboy star in the early 1990s (class of 1992), Breaux played for the Sioux Falls Skyforce of the CBA in 1993. He moved to the Houston Rockets of the NBA and played from 1994-96. He closed out his NBA career after one season with Vancouver (1996-97) and Milwaukee (1997).

22. Reggie Fox

The former Cowboy standout played for Quad Cities of the CBA when the team played for the 1994 CBA championship against Omaha. In 1995, he signed with the CBA Sioux Falls Skyforce. He holds the UW career record for three-point field goals (165) and attempted three-pointers (405).

23. Theo Ratliff

Drafted 18th overall in the first round of the NBA draft in 1995 by the NBA Detroit Pistons, Ratliff was leading the team in blocked shots in 1996. In 1999-2000, he was starting for the Philadelphia 76ers. He has since played for the Atlanta Hawks, Portland Trailblazers, Boston Celtics, Minnesota Timberwolves, San Antonio Spurs and currently with the Charlotte Bobcats. While a collegian, the 6' 10" Wyoming player became the NCAA's second greatest shot blocker in history with a career total of 425. With 144 blocks in the 1994-95 season, he set an all-time Wyoming and WAC single-season mark. He was named to USA Men's Under 22 Team in June 1993. In 2001, he was selected to play in the All-Star game.

24. Amy Burnett
Burnett starred at UW from 1992-1995, averaging 16.4 points per game. The 5'10" native of Huron, S. D., set the WAC career scoring mark with 1,768 points. She had 34 career "double-doubles" and in the 108 consecutive collegiate games in which she played, she fouled out only once.

25. Jay Straight
Straight led Wyoming in scoring from 2001-04. His 1,550 points for his career ranks him among Wyoming's all time best scorers. In 2010 he was on the roster for Fort Wayne of the Developmental League.

26. Anthony "Buckets" Blakes
Blakes played and graduated from UW in 2000. He played a couple of seasons in Europe and, in 2020, was entering his 8th season with the world famous Harlem Globetrotters.

27. Brandon Ewing
Ewing starred at UW from 2004-2008, where he led the Cowboys in scoring in all four years. A native of Chicago, Ewing made first team all MWC his senior year while making second team in his sophomore and junior year and third team his first year at Wyoming.

28. Hanna Zavecz
Zavecz starred at UW from 2004-2008, averaging 14.1 points per game. The 6' native of Melbourne, Australia, was an All-Mountain First team selection for three seasons and ended her collegiate career with 1,736 points.. In the WNIT Championship game against Wisconsin in 2007 she was named the MVP. In 2010, she was a starting forward on the 2010 Champion Bulleen Melbourne Boomers (Australia WNBL).

29. James Johnson
An outstanding player at Cheyenne East, Johnson was a All-State first team selection in both his junior and senior year. He was considered one of the nation's top players coming out of high school in 2007. He played two seasons for the Wake Forest Demon Deaco and led Wake Forest in rebounding for his only two seasons. Instead of completing his college playing career, he entered the NBA draft in 2009. He was drafted in the first round by the Chicago Bulls. His father Willie was a seven-time world kickboxing champion.

30. Jaycee Carroll
Carroll had an outstanding high school career at Evanston High School. As a senior, he set the Wyoming state record for average points per game at 39.4. In a game against Green River, he scored 56 points. He was named the Wyoming Gatorade Player of the Year in both his junior and senior years. He chose to play at nearby Utah State in Logan where he set numerous school records and was a two-time honorable mention All-American. He scored a total of 2,507 career points to become the second highest all-time scorer in the State of Utah, just 35 points behind former Utah Utes star Keith Van Horn. In 2010, he was playing professional basketball in Europe.

Well-Known Wyoming Basketball Coaches

1. Ev Shelton
Shelton chalked up 328 wins as University of Wyoming coach for 14 seasons (1940-59). His teams lost 201. In 1943, he led the Cowboys to their only national championship. Shelton's teams won eight Skyline Conference titles and appeared in four NCAA championship tourneys.

2. Bill Strannigan

Strannigan graduated from UW in 1940 after starring in basketball, baseball and football. The first of three former Wyoming basketball stars who later became head coach (Moe Radovich and Benny Dees were the others), Strannigan became head coach at Wyoming in 1959. In 14 seasons, his teams compiled a record of 179-187.

3. George "Moe" Radovich

Radovich, a native of Hot Springs County, coached at UW from 1973-76, compiling a disappointing record of 24-55 in three seasons. He had played basketball at UW and one season with Philadelphia in the NBA (1952-53).

4. Dan Devoe

Devoe coached at UW for two seasons from 1976-78, compiling a mark of 29-25. After the 1978 season, he moved to Tennessee where he was head coach for the next 11 years. After compiling a record of 211-158 with the Volunteers, he left for a one-year stint at Florida in 1989.

5. Jim Brandenburg

Cowboy coach for nine seasons from 1978 to 1987 (176 wins, 97 losses), Brandenburg was named WAC coach of the year three times. His 1981, 1982 and 1987 teams played in the NCAA tournament. His 1986 club lost to Ohio State in the NIT championship game. He resigned from Wyoming at the end of the 1987 season to accept the head coaching job at San Diego State. In 1993, he was fired at SDSU after his teams suffered disappointing seasons. In five years there, he was 52-87 with just two wins and 26 losses in his last year.

6. Benny Dees

Dees was named Cowboy coach on April 2, 1987. A 1958 graduate of UW, he had played basketball for the Cowboys in the 1950s. He resigned as head coach at the University of New Orleans after two seasons to accept the Cowboy job. He compiled a mark of 104 wins and 77 losses for the Cowboys with a career overall record of 171-114. Following disappointing tournament performances in 1992 and 1993, Dees resigned on March 8, 1993, to accept the head coaching position at Western Carolina, Cullowhee, N. C. Two years later, on May 9, 1995, he left Western Carolina to accept a school principal position in Mount Vernon, Ga.

7. Joby Wright

Wright coached at Miami (Ohio) before accepting the head coaching position at Wyoming on April 4, 1993. The first African-American to be head coach of the University of Wyoming basketball team, his injury and eligibility-plagued team compiled a record of 13 wins and 15 losses in 1993. In four seasons, his teams compiled a record of 53-60. He resigned after the 1997 season on March 3.

8. Larry Shyatt

After just a single season at UW (1997-1998) with a record of 19-9, Shyatt moved to Clemson. His first-year team made it to the NIT, but in his second year, the Tigers suffered one of their worst seasons in history. Shyatt sued to avoid terms of a contract he had signed with UW that called for surrender of bonus monies should he leave before completion of the contract. The courts upheld UW in the matter. He has been an assistant coach at the University of Florida since 2004.

9. Steve McClain (b. Aug. 15, 1962)

McClain was hired as UW's 19th basketball coach on April 22, 1998. In his first season, 1998-99, McClain led the Cowboys to a 18-10 record and an appearance in the NIT. A native of Orient, Iowa, he is a 1984 graduate of Chadron State (Neb.) He was head coach at Hutchinson (Kans.) Junior College for three years and coached them to a national title in 1994. He became an assistant coach at TCU where he worked under Billy Tubbs for four years. He became an assistant coach at Indiana University in 2010.

10. Oscar "Swede" Erickson (b. Norfolk, Nebr., 1921, d. Casper, 1999)

Erickson retired in 1986 after coaching at Casper College for 28 seasons. His Thunderbird teams compiled 638 wins (just 220 losses, 74.3 percent winning average) and nine regional titles during his career as well as a second place in the national JUCO tournament. He coached 38 players who went on to Division I basketball and three who became professional players in the NBA. The Casper College gym was renamed in his honor. Following his retirement, he served as CC athletic director and NJCAA president. Later, he served as Natrona County commissioner. He died August 3, 1999, in Casper.

11. Willard Witte

With 134 wins and 51 losses, Witte holds the highest win-loss percentage, .724, of any of the early University of Wyoming coaches. He coached the Cowboys from 1930 to 1938.

12. Pat Rafferty

Rafferty, a Buffalo native, was head basketball coach at Casper College from 1986-1988. He left Casper to become head coach at Northern Arizona University. In 1992, he accepted a position as assistant coach at Drake University in Iowa. During his career, he coached at Midland College and worked as a scout for the Minnesota Timberwolves' organization.

13. Rick Samuels

Named head basketball coach at Eastern Illinois in 1980, Samuels was a former Laramie resident and University High player. He is the son of Pete and Ina Samuels of Laramie.

14. Bob Hanson

A 1959 graduate of LaGrange High School, Hanson went on to play basketball at the University of Wyoming. Hanson was elected president of the National Basketball Coaches Association in 1996. Now an assistant coach at Kansas State, he began his coaching career at Rawlins High School. He coached at Hiram Scott College before going on to a 25-year career as head coach at University of Nebraska, Omaha.

15. Jerry Dunn

Although Dunn is not a Wyoming native, the Penn State head basketball coach played basketball at Casper College for two years. He was hired as the Nittany Lions head coach in 1995 and held that position for eight years. In 2007 he became an assistant coach at the University of Michigan.

16. Bruce Hoffman

Hoffman coached at Sheridan College for 34 years. There, he compiled the most wins of any coach in JUCO Region IX with a record of 651-395. He retired in 1999.

17. Tom Asbury

The former UW basketball star was 85-87 in five years as head basketball coach at Kansas State. He resigned under fire in 2000. After four seasons as an assistant coach at Alabama, he became the head basketball coach at Pepperdine University in 2008.

18. Hank Cabre

Cabre coached at Northwest College, Powell, most of his career. His teams included a national JUCO fourth place finish. Several of his players went on to NBA careers including John Johnson. The gym at Northwest is named for him and he was a charter posthumous entry in the Wyoming Coaches Hall of Fame.

UW athletic director Red Jacoby told a young assistant coach that he was nearly hired in 1959 as the head basketball coach at Wyoming. Jacoby's choice, however, was overruled by UW President George "Duke" Humphrey who preferred UW alumnus Bill Strannigan for the job. The young runner-up, Dean Smith, went on to the University of North Carolina where he coached until his retirement in 1999.

19. Steve Aggers

Aggers was head coach at Loyola Marymount from 2000 to 2005. A native of Laramie, he is son of former UW trainer Jack Aggers.

20. Joe Legerski

He was named Wyoming's sixth women's basketball coach on May 1, 2003. The Rock Springs native previously spent 12 years as a assistant head coach under Utah's legendary coach Elaine Elliott. Since arriving at UW he transformed the women's team into a championship caliber team, winning the WNIT in 2007 against Wisconsin. He has since guided the Cowgirls to several NCAA and NIT appearances.

UW Cowboys in the Tournaments

1942: Wyoming lost to Arkansas 52-40 in the regional semi-finals.

1943: NCAA championship, Wyoming beat Georgetown 46-34. The Cowboys beat Oklahoma 53-50 and Texas 58-54 to advance to the championship game. Following the tournament, the Cowboys defeated the NIT champion St. Johns, the only time the NCAA and NIT champions have met in a post-season contest.

1947: Wyoming lost to Texas 42-40 in the West Regional Semi-Finals.

1948: The Cowboys were eliminated in the semi-finals by Washington 54-47.

1949: For the third year in a row, the Cowboys dropped a close West Regional semi-final game, this time to Oklahoma A&M (now Oklahoma State) 40-39.

1952: Wyoming beat Oklahoma City College 54-48 to advance to the Far West championship, but lost to Santa Clara 56-53.

1953: Again, the Cowboys played Santa Clara, lost and then were eliminated by Seattle University 80-64.

1958: The Cowboys again met Seattle University and lost 88-51.

1966: The Cowboys recorded their worst tournament defeat when John Wooden's national champion UCLA beat Wyoming 109-60 in the West Regional opener.

1967: NIT. Wyoming lost to Villanova 77-66.

1968: NIT. Wyoming, invited to the NIT for the second straight year, again lost. Army prevailed 51-49.

1981: After a brilliant opening win 78-43 over Howard, the Cowboys lost in the final seconds of the second round contest to Illinois 67-65.

1982: The Cowboys dropped USC 61-58 to advance against Georgetown, a team Wyoming had not played since the 1943 national championship. This time, however, the Hoyas were victorious 51-43.

1986: NIT. Wyoming beat Texas A&M, Loyola Marymount, Clemson and Florida to advance to the NIT championship game against Ohio State which they lost to the Buckeyes 73-63 in a nationally televised game at Madison Square Garden.

1987: Wyoming dropped Virginia 64-60 in the first round of the West Regionals and then beat heavily favored UCLA 78-68 in the second round. In the West Regional semifinal, the Cowboys were stopped by UNLV 92-78.

1988: After the strong finish in 1987, the Cowboys under new head coach Benny Dees returned to the West Regionals but lost to high-scoring Loyola Marymount 119-115 in the highest scoring NCAA tournament game ever.

1991: After a 20-12 season, the Cowboys played Colorado at Boulder in the first round of the 1991 NIT. The Cowboys lost 83-75. The game set an attendance record at Boulder.

1998: At the end of Larry Shyatt's only season as Cowboy coach, the Pokes went to the NIT, losing to Gonzaga 69-55.

1999: Coach Steve McClain's first season ended with a record of 18-10 and a NIT bid. The Cowboys beat USC 81-77 in Round 1 and lost to Oregon 93-72 in the second round.

2002: After finishing the season at 22-9, Wyoming defeated #6 Gonzaga 73-66 before losing in the 2nd Round of the NCAA Tournament to #3 Arizona 68-60.

2003: Finishing the regular season with a 21-11 record, Wyoming was named to the NIT. Beating Eastern Washington 78-71 in the first round, they lost the second round game to the North Carolina Tar Heels 90-74.

3 Wyoming Wildcatter Coaches

1. Jack Schalow

The first Wildcatter coach, Schalow ran the team from its founding in 1982 to 1985. He had been a successful coach in Washington.

2. Bill Klucas

Klucas coached the Wildcatters for just one season and, after compiling a mark of 21 wins and 27 losses, he was fired.

3. Cazzie Russell

A former University of Michigan star and NBA player, Russell coached the team from 1986 until the franchise departed Casper after the 1988 season. Russell's 1988 team lost the league championship to Albany four games to three.

Some Historic Highlights, JUCO Basketball

1. 3rd in the Nation

Casper College Thunderbird Women finished 3rd in the nation in 1996 with a record of 28-6. The T-Birds defeated Utah Valley State College 62-54 for the third place finish. Dianne L'Ami was named to the all-tournament team.

2. 7th in the Nation

Casper College Thunderbird Women finished 7th in the nation in 1992.

3. 7th in the Nation

Eastern Wyoming College basketball team won the division crown and came in 7th in national JUCO tournament in 2004.

Wyoming Cowboys Drafted by the NBA

George Livingston (1949)	Ed Huse (1956)	Charles Bradley (1981)
John Pilch (1950)	Tony Windis (1959)	Kenneth Ollie (1981)
Jerry Reed (1950)	Flynn Robinson (1965)	Bill Garnett (1982)
Loy Doty (1950)	Leon Clark (1966)	Chris Engler (1982)
Keith Bloom (1950)	Mike Eberle (1968)	Mike Jackson (1983)
Cliff Hagg (1952)	Harry Hall (1969)	Tony Martin (1984)
Moe Radovich (1952)	Carl Ashley (1970)	Eric Leckner (1988)
Ron Rivers (1954)	Willie Roberson (1971)	Fennis Dembo (1988)
Harry Jorgensen (1955)	Stan Boyer (1975)	Theo Ratliff (1995)

The first state high school basketball tournament was held in Laramie in 1918. Milward Simpson, later governor and U. S. Senator, coached the University Prep team that beat Laramie for the championship. The title team members were Oliver Knight, Sam Neff, Harmon Bailey, Kenneth Burke, Carl Simmons, Dick DeKay and Robert Thompson.

University of Wyoming Individual Scoring Leaders

Early Records compiled by Bob Burns, courtesy of UW Office of Sports Information, 1988, 1994.

Year Player	Pts. Games	Year Player	Pts. Games	Year Player	Pts. Games
1910: Oscar Prestegard 76	5	**1946**: Milo Komenich	372 26	**1978**: Doug Bessert	343 27
1915: Fulton Bellamy 42	2	**1947**: Jimmy Reese	327 28	**1979**: Charles Bradley	392 25
1916: Fulton Bellamy 20	1	**1948**: John Pilch	264 27	**1980**: Charles Bradley	459 24
1917: Harry Craig 73	5	**1949**: John Pilch	377 35	**1981**: Charles Bradley	577 30
1918: Milward Simpson 58	5	**1950**: John Pilch	415 36	**1982**: Bill Garnett	544 30
1919: Bob Burns 75	9	**1951**: Moe Radovich	505 37	**1983**: Anthony Martin	377 29
1920: Bob Burns 112	10	**1952**: Moe Radovich	413 35	**1984**: Anthony Martin	436 30
1921: Robert Fitske 75	8	**1953**: Bill Sharp	385 27	**1985**: Rodney Gowens	417 29
1922: William Smyth 85	11	**1954**: Bill Sharp	346 28	**1986**: Fennis Dembo	577 34
1923: Don Thompson 58	9	**1955**: Harry Jorgensen	377 26	**1987**: Fennis Dembo	689 34
1924: Bill Lester 50	7	**1956**: Joe Capua	637 26	**1988**: Fennis Dembo	653 32
1925: Cyril Fox 55	12	**1957**: Tony Windis	457 26	**1989**: Robyn Davis	586 30
1926: Oz Koerfer 113	15	**1958**: Tony Windis	545 26	**1990**: Reginald Slater	485 29
1927: Don Harkins 145	13	**1959**: Tony Windis	463 19	**1991**: Reginald Slater	613 32
1928: "Oz" Koerfer 167	21	**1960**: Terry Happel	413 24	**1992**: Reginald Slater	518 29
1929: Bob Outsen 222	9	**1961**: Earl Nau	421 25	**1993**: David Murray	384 28
1930: Jim Jiacoletti 142	14	**1962**: Curt Jimerson	454 26	**1994**: David Murray	474 28
1931: Les Witte 274	23	**1963**: Flynn Robinson	682 26	**1995**: LaDrell Whitehead 417 28	
1932: Les Witte 238	20	**1964**: Flynn Robinson	666 26	**1996**: LaDrell Whitehead 513 29	
1933: Les Witte 234	23	**1965**: Flynn Robinson	701 26	**1997**: LaDrell Whitehead 390 18	
1934: Les Witte 323	27	**1966**: Leon Clark	582 26	**1998**: Jeron Roberts	532 28
1935: Willard West 124	16	**1967**: Harry Hall	535 26	**1999**: Ugo Udezue	575 28
1936: Lew Young 194	19	**1968**: Harry Hall	542 27	**2001**: Marcus Bailey	521 17.4
1937: John Winterholler 115	14	**1969**: Carl Ashley	488 28	**2002**: Danta Richardson 578 18.1	
1938: Lew Young 229	17	**1970**: Stan Dodds	539 26	**2003**: Jay Straight	424 15.7
1939: Lew Young 220	20	**1971**: Willie Roberson	482 24	**2004**: Jay Straight	505 18.
1940: Willie Rothman 158	15	**1972**: Rod Penner	436 26	**2005**: Brandon Ewing	423 13.2
1941: Bill Strannigan 200	19	**1973**: Ron Crowell	313 26	**2006**: Brandon Ewing	616 19.9
1942: Milo Komenich 222	19	**1974**: Ron Crowell	460 26	**2007**: Brandon Ewing	517 17.2
1943: Milo Komenich 551	33	**1975**: Stan Boyer	405 26	**2008**: Brandon Ewing	612 18.5
1944: No team (World War II)		**1976**: Pat Flanigan	341 27	**2009**: Afam Muojeke	269 16.8
1945: George Nostrand 169	17	**1977**: Joe Fazekas	350 26		

High School Basketball in Wyoming, 1995-2010

1995 State High School Basketball Championships

Boys
4A Gillette 42 Casper Natrona 40
3A Buffalo 59 Rawlins 48
2A Rocky Mtn. 75 Greybull 60
1A Burlington 67 Hulett 55

Girls
Gillette 63 Sheridan 44
Lyman 48 Rawlins 37
Tongue Riv. 63 Wyo. Indian 53
Cokeville 56 Burlington 51

1996 State High School Basketball Championships

Boys
4A Gillette 87 Cody 71
3A Buffalo 72 Powell 60
2A Greybull 74 Lovell 56
1A Snake River 61 Burlington 51

Girls
Gillette 76 Green River 53
Lander 49 Buffalo 47
Lusk 38 Wind River 36
Encampment 56 Cokeville 47

1997 State High School Basketball Championships

Boys
4A Gillette 56 Evanston 54 (OT)
3A Rawlins 45 Worland 31
2A Rocky Mountain 68 Wyo Indian 67
1A Cokeville 57 Shoshoni 55

Girls
Gillette 88 Green River 68
Douglas 68 Mountain View 51
Tongue River 71 Dubois 57
Southeast 54 Albin 52

1998 State High School Basketball Championships

Boys
4A Central 58 Rock Springs 50 (OT)
3A Powell 68 Buffalo 64
2A Rocky Mtn. 77 Lusk 65
1A Farson-Eden 69 Burlington 50

Girls
Gillette 81 Kelly Walsh 43
Mountain View 48 Douglas 46
Tongue River 63 Wright 60
Burlington 49 Cokeville 35

1999 State High School Basketball Championships

Boys
4A Gillette 63 Laramie 53
3A Douglas 50 Powell 46
2A Riverside 53 Rocky Mtn. 40
1A Kaycee 72 Burlington 71

Girls
Natrona 76 Gillette 61
Wheatland 56 Buffalo 36
Lusk 52 Burns 33
Big Horn 62 Kaycee 27

2000 State High School Basketball Championships

Boys
4A Gillette 76 Kelly Walsh 51
3A Star Valley 61 Lyman 52
2A Riverside 71 Wyoming Indian 65
1A Snake River 54 Burlington 52

Girls
Natrona 87 Gillette 84 (2OT)
Star Valley 60 Powell 59
Lovell 64 Rocky Mountain 55
Cokeville 48 Burlington 42 (OT)

2001 State High School Basketball Championships

Boys
4A Casper Natrona 60 Evanston 50
3A Star Valley 68 Douglas 63
2A Wyoming Indian 77 Lusk 66
1A Burlington 61 Southeast 50

Girls
Gillette 63 Casper Natrona 57
Wheatland 43 Thermopolis 37
Big Horn 63 Greybull 33
Cokeville 68 Albin 51

2002 State High School Basketball Championships

Boys
4A Gillette 76 Sheridan 49
3A Douglas 43 Star Valley 41
2A Lovell 78 Lusk 71
1A Chugwater 69 Arvada/Clermont 63

Girls
Gillette 74 Sheridan 45
Thermopolis 46 Star Valley 43
Big Horn 38 Sundance 37
Little Snake River 55 Burlington 50

2003 State High School Basketball Championships

Boys
4A Gillette 64 Casper Natrona 55
3A Thermopolis 66 Kemmerer 60
2A Lovell 63 Lusk 50
1A Burlington 60 Kaycee 56

Girls
Sheridan 62 Gillette 61
Thermopolis 48 Star Valley 42
Wyoming Indian 75 Pine Bluffs 48
Burlington 57 Albin 48

2004 State High School Basketball Championships

Boys
4A Evanston 58 Casper Natrona 48
3A Thermopolis 70 Kemmerer 61
2A Wright 78 Wyoming Indian 53
1A St. Stephens 69 Little Snake River 61

Girls
Gillette 56 Cheyenne East 41
Douglas 42 Thermopolis 39
Wyoming Indian 59 Lusk 55
Encampment 43 Burlington 35

2005 State High School Basketball Championships

Boys
4A Casper Natrona 47 Rock Springs 38
3A Lander 53 Thermopolis 39
2A Wright 52 Lovell 49
1A St. Stephens 79 Hulett 67

Girls
Cheyenne Central 41 Cheyenne East 39
Douglas 59 Star Valley 41
Tongue River 64 Lovell 39
Encampment 53 Guernsey-Sunrise 44

2006 State High School Basketball Championships

Boys
4A Cheyenne East 62 Cheyenne Central 49
3A Buffalo 59 Lander 44
2A Greybull 42 Lovell 41
1A Burlington 49 St. Stephens 47

Girls
Gillette 54 Cheyenne Central 39
Lander 57 Douglas 26
Tongue River 55 Lovell 51
Lingle-Ft. Laramie 32 Encampment 31

2007 State High School Basketball Championships

Boys

4A Casper Natrona 63 Laramie 54
3A Star Valley 50 Mountain View 39
2A Lyman 59 Tongue River 54
1A St. Stephens 52 Burlington 46

Girls

Sheridan 45 Casper Natrona 39
Jackson 34 Buffalo 27
Tongue River 49 Big Horn 43
Arvada-Clearmont 57 Burlington 36

2008 State High School Basketball Championships

Boys

4A Gillette 68 Rock Springs 53
3A Lander 49 Newcastle 44
2A Lusk 69 Sundance 63
1A Encampment 40 Southeast 38

Girls

Cheyenne Central 58 Gillette 55
Jackson 46 Torrington 37
Big Horn 47 Tongue River 32
Southeast 47 Arvada-Clearmont 29

2009 State High School Basketball Championships

Boys

4A Casper Natrona 62 Kelly Walsh 43
3A Buffalo 36 Kemmerer 33
2A Wyoming Indian 69 Lusk 61
1A Southeast 41 Burlington 37

Girls

Gillette 67 Rock Springs 39
Jackson 43 Powell 29
Big Horn 47 Mountain View 36
Burlington 46 Southeast 44

2010 State High School Basketball Championships

Boys

4A Casper Natrona 55 Gillette 47
3A Torrington 42 Buffalo 39
2A Wyoming Indian 52 Southeast 51
1A Burlington 61 St. Stephens 48

Girls

Cheyenne East 49 Laramie 35
Jackson 49 Powell 42
Tongue River 55 Big Horn 38
Burlington 43 Kaycee 40

Interstate All-Star Basketball Series

An annual two game series between Montana and Wyoming boys' all-stars began in 1975.

2006: Wyoming 90, Montana 84
2007: Montana 100, Wyoming 93, Wyoming 80, Montana 63
2009: Montana 117, Wyoming 94, Wyoming 90, Montana 86 (2OT)
2010: Montana 114, Wyoming 53, Montana 91, Wyoming 75
Annual Series against South Dakota All-Stars began in 1992
2004: South Dakota 113, Wyoming 105, Wyoming 80, South Dakota 68
2005: South Dakota 111, Wyoming 99, South Dakota 121, Wyoming 107
2007: South Dakota 95, Wyoming 92
2008: Wyoming 127, South Dakota 95, Wyoming 129, South Dakota 108
2009: Wyoming 90, South Dakota 80 (OT)
2010: Wyoming 114, South Dakota 80, Wyoming 99, South Dakota 88

Interstate Girls' All-Star Basketball Series

Annual Series against South Dakota began in 1993

2004: Wyoming 108, South Dakota 90, Wyoming 116, South Dakota 97
2005: Wyoming 99, South Dakota 92 (OT), South Dakota 84, Wyoming 76
2008: Wyoming 93, South Dakota 88, South Dakota 84, Wyoming 79
2009: Wyoming 79, South Dakota 74
2010: Wyoming 81, South Dakota 61, South Dakota 78, Wyoming 68
Annual Series against Montana All-Stars began in 1997
2006: Wyoming 71, Montana 67, Wyoming 89, Montana 81
2007: Wyoming 73, Montana 68, Montana 84, Wyoming 81 (2OT)
2008: Montana 84, Wyoming 74, Montana 79, Wyoming 70 (OT)
2009: Montana 83, Wyoming 76, Montana 83, Wyoming 76
2010: Montana 92, Wyoming 85 (OT), Montana 95, Wyoming 73

FISHING

1st fishing licenses issued in Wyoming: 1919

Game and Fish Department established: 1921 under the present name, but the agency had been known as the "fish commission" in the territorial period.

1st stocking of Yellowstone lakes: 1890, when lake trout were introduced from Lake Michigan. Years later, when fish were decimated in Lake Michigan, the Yellowstone descendants of original transplants were re-introduced to their natural home.

Wyoming has 15,846 miles of fishing streams, 297,633 acres of fishing lakes and 3,400 lakes, ponds and reservoirs holding 90 varieties of fish, 42 of which are game fish.

1st daily limit on fish caught in Yellowstone set: 1920 (20 fish per day)

Planting fish in Wind River lakes: During the Depression, Finis Mitchell and his brother used horse trains to pack rainbow, cutthroat, brook and brown trout into 314 of the 4,000 lakes in the Wind River range. The descendants of the fish have spread to more than 700 bodies of water in the range.

Wyoming State Record Fish

(as of June 1, 2010, as compiled by the Wyoming Game and Fish Department)

1. **Brook Trout,** 9 lbs., 11 oz., 24 1/2 inches long
   Caught at Green River Lake, Sublette County by Max Long (1976)

2. **Brown Trout,** 25 lbs., 13 oz., 34 1/4 inches long
   The fish had a girth of 25 1/4 inches. Caught at Anvil Draw, Flaming Gorge Reservoir, by George Rose (1982)

3. **Cutthroat Trout,** 15 lbs., 32 inches long
   Caught at Native Lake in Sublette County by Alan Dow (1959)

4. **Golden Trout,** 11 lbs., 4 oz., 28 inches long
   Caught at Cook Lake in Fremont County by C. S. Read (1948) The oldest record in Wyoming, it is also a world record holder recognized by the International Game Fish Association.

5. **Lake Trout (Mackinaw),** 50 lbs., 46 inches long
   Randy Calkins, Green River, caught a 50-lb., 48-inch-long Lake Trout at Flaming Gorge in March, 1995. The fish, estimated to be 20 years old, had a girth of 32 inches. A 46-inch lake trout, also weighing 50 pounds, was caught at Jackson Lake in Teton County by Doris Budge in 1983. By weight, they are the two biggest fish ever caught in Wyoming.

6. **Ohrid Trout,** 14 lbs., 4 ozs., 30 inches long
   Caught at North Platte River in Natrona County by Kim Durfee (1986) Holds the world record, recognized by the International Game Fish Association.

7. **Rainbow Trout,** 23 lbs., 35 1/2 inches long
   Caught at Burnt Lake in Sublette County by Frank Favazzo (1969)

8. **Largemouth Bass,** 7 lbs., 14 oz, 21 1/2 inches long
   Caught at a stock pond in Sheridan County by Dustin Shorma (1992). The previous record was 7 lbs., 2 oz., caught from Stove Lake in Goshen County by John Tetters in 1942.

9. **Smallmouth Bass,** 5.94 lbs, 21 inches long
   Caught from the Flaming Gorge Reservoir by Bubba O'Neil of Evanston on April 27, 2003. The previous mark was 5 lb., 8 oz., bass caught by Lonnie Zimmer in 1993 from the Tongue River in Sheridan County.

10. **Bluegill,** 1.47 lbs., 10.3 inches long
    Caught at the Lake View North Pond, Platte Co., by Brad Artery (1988)

11. **Black Bullhead,** 2.9 lbs., 15 1/4 inches long
    Caught at Ten Sleep Pond, Washakie County by Brian Rygwalski (1987)

12. Carp, 34.15 lbs., 35.4 inches long

Bobby Brown of Harrison, TN caught the record-setting carp from the Pilot Butte Reservoir on September 28, 2005 The previous mark was 30.23 lbs. caught from the Buckboard Marina dock at Flaming Gorge Reservoir by Mike Bozner in 1999.

13. Channel Catfish, 27.99, 38 inches long

Don Ackerman of Rock Springs caught the big fish at Flaming Gorge Reservoir on April 27, 2005. The previous record was 24.19 lbs., 34 1/4 inches, caught a farm pond in Platte County by James Hayes in 1993.

14. Flathead Catfish, 22.46 lbs., 34 inches long

Dallas Stanton of Glenrock caught at the North Platte River on April 18, 2004.

15. Utah Chub, 1.26 lbs., 13 inches

Caught at Flaming Gorge Reservoir by Dave Franke of Rock Springs on May 14, 2005.

16. Black Crappie, 2.34 lbs., 15 inches long

Edward Hausauer caught the big fish in 1997 from Boysen Reservoir. Previous record was 2 lbs., 3 oz., length not stated, caught in Crook County by Mardell Palmer (1983)

17. White Crappie, 2 lbs., 45 oz., 16.35 inches long

Caught at Glendo Reservoir in Platte County by Terry Young of Douglas on August 31, 2009. Previous record of 2.3 lbs., caught at Kleenburn Ponds (known locally as Acme Strip Pits) in Sheridan County by Russell W. Korp (1991)

18. Freshwater Drum, 11 lbs., 14 oz., 26 inches long

Caught at Glendo Reservoir in Platte County by Rich Detry of Westminster CO on June 23, 1993. The previous record was 7.94 lbs., 25 inches long, caught at Keyhole Reservoir in Crook County by Michael Feurt in 1989.

19. Gizzard Shad, 1.20 lbs., 14.375 inches long

Tom Durst of Casper caught this fish at Glendo Reservoir in Platte County on December 12, 2007.

20. Goldeye, 1.32 lbs., 16 3/4 inches long

The fish was caught by Jim Williams of Gillette from the Powder River in Campbell County in 1996. The previous mark was 14 ozs., 13.4 inches long, caught at the Crazy Woman drainage in Johnson County by Darren Bordeaux (1986)

21. Grayling, 2.36 lbs., 19 5/8 inches long

The fish had a girth of 10 12 inches. Caught at Meadow Lake in Sublette County by Robert Doak of Rock Springs (1983).

22. Green Sunfish, .82 lbs., 9.6 inches

Caught by Doug Nixon of Lovell on May 30, 2006 at Lovell Lakes in Big Horn County.

23. Ling, 19 lbs., 4 oz., 44 inches long

Caught at Pilot Butte Reservoir in Fremont County by K. E. Moreland (1965)

24. Tiger Muskie, 29.37 lbs., 49 inches long

Caught at Grayrocks Reservoir, Platte County by Frank Rubrecht of Rawlins on June 2, 1992. By length, it was the biggest fish ever caught in Wyoming. The previous record was 26.78 lbs., 46.5 inches long, caught by Bob Higgins from Grayrocks in 1991.

25. Perch, 2.2 lbs., 16 inches long

Caught at Mayland Pond in Big Horn County by Mike Miller of Greybull on February 9, 1991

It is amazing who one might encounter while fly-fishing on a Wyoming stream. In July 1928, novelist Ernest Hemingway, staying in Sheridan that summer and writing *A Farewell to Arms*, took time out to fish on Shell Creek. There, he encountered another fly fisherman, author Owen Wister. The two men had never previously met although each knew of the other's work.

26. Northern Pike, 27.4 lbs., 47 inches long

Robert Hockett of Newcastle caught the record fish from Keyhole Reservoir in Crook County on October 27, 2004. Michael McCrary caught the previous record fish from Keyhole Reservoir in 1998. Previous mark was 26 lbs., 44 oz., 43 inches long.

27. Pumpkinseed, .62 lbs., 8.7 inches long

Anthony Wendtland of Sheridan caught this record fish from a farm pond near Big Horn on June 24, 2009.

28. River Carpsucker, 12 lbs., 10 oz., 28 inches long

Caught by Garhart Stephenson of Lander on Boysen Reservoir on June 15, 2005.

29. Rock Bass, 1.76 lbs., 13 inches long

Randy Reece of Sheridan caught this record fish on May 12, 2007 at a Sheridan County farm pond. It surpassed the old mark of 1.29 lbs., 11 inches caught by Shelby Holder in 1996 also from a Sheridan County farm pond.

30. Kokanee Salmon, 5.73 lbs., 26 inches long

The record fish was caught by Brian Ekx of Evans CO at Flaming Gorge Reservoir on June 14, 2009. The previous record was held by Mary Robinson, Fort Collins, at Buckboard Crossing, Flaming Gorge, Aug. 1, 1996.

31. Sauger, 7.5 lbs., 26.5 inches long

Tom Durst of Casper caught this record fish at Boysen Reservoir on January 7, 2007. Brad Berg, Riverton, had the previous record sauger of 7.4 lbs., 26.2 inches long from Boysen Reservoir on March 14, 1999.

32. Splake, 12.74 lbs., 30 1/2 inches long

This fish, caught by Christian Van Kirk of Fort Laramie from Libby Lake on September 11, 2004. The previous record was held by Zach Connor from Hog Park Reservoir, Carbon County, with the previous mark at 11.52 lbs., 30 inches long.

33. Shovelnose Sturgeon, 10.2 lbs., 40 inches long

Chris Marshall of Gillette caught this record fish on the Powder River June 1, 2000. The previous record of 7.6 lbs., 36 inches was also caught on the Powder River by Allen Gorzalka (1993)

34. Longnosed Sucker, 2.19 lbs., 18 inches

The large fish was brought in by Darrell Meineke. He caught it from Little Goose Creek, Sheridan County, in 1998. Previous mark was 1 lb., 2 oz., 14 inches long, caught from the Big Laramie River by Scott Miegs in 1993.

35. Utah Sucker, 8.4 lbs., 28 inches

Caught on the Snake River near Alpne by Mike Cullimore of Thayne on June 5, 2003

36. White Sucker, 3.78 lbs., 20 1/2 inches

Steve Newton of Worland caught the fish from the Big Horn River, Washakie County, on March 4, 2000. It narrowly surpassed the previous mark of 3.69 lbs., 19.8 inches long, caught at Alsop Lake in Albany County by Peter Kuhn in 1992.

30. Walleye, 17.42 lbs., 34 inches long

Caught at Boysen Reservoir in Fremont County by Stan Seivewright of Casper on December 28, 1991, it is a world record for the largest fish taken through the ice, recognized by the Freshwater Fishing Hall of Fame. The previous Wyoming record was 15 lbs., 5 oz., caught from Seminoe Reservoir by Marty Petersen in 1988.

31. Whitefish, 4 lbs., 4 oz., 21 inches long

Caught at the Snake River in Teton County by Dennis Jennings (1977)

According to the Game and Fish Department, if you catch what you think might be a record fish, get it weighed as quickly as possible on a certified scale such as the ones in post offices or grocery stores. The weighing must be witnessed by two people or a professional fisheries biologist. All entries must be caught on hook and line.

Some Unusual Fish Stories

1. Eagle Claw

Fisherman Ernie Hirsch was putting up a metal roof on his Jackson home in June 1992 when he was startled by a loud thud on the new roof. A few seconds later, a large cutthroat trout flopped to his feet. Suspecting a prank, he saw no one around except an eagle hovering overhead. There were talon marks on the fish.

2. Thumbs Up

Robert Lindsey of Green River lost his right thumb in July 1991 in a boating accident in Flaming Gorge Reservoir. The propeller of the boat motor also cut off his index and middle fingers, but they were recovered and reattached. The thumb was presumed lost. Six months after the accident on Feb. 13, 1992, a fisherman discovered the digit inside a six-pound lake trout. According to news reports, "It is believed the thumb was preserved in the water by saponification, which occurs in moist dark places and prompts flesh to take on a chemical condition like soap." County officials believed the fish ate the thumb within 24 hours before it was caught. The statistical likelihood of such an occurrence was compared to the odds in winning a national lottery.

Noteworthy Fishing Expeditions in Wyoming

1. Crook's Army, 1876

Capt. Anson Mills and two enlisted men in Crook's army caught 146 trout in one day from Goose Creek, near present-day Sheridan, after the Battle of the Rosebud. It is estimated that in two weeks, Crook's troops caught as many as 15,000 fish from the stream.

2. Thomas Edison party, 1878

The famous inventor came to the area to view a solar eclipse but he also went fishing on the Big Muddy in Carbon County in August 1878. He and his party reportedly caught 3,000 trout in six days.

3. Webb Hayes, 1879

Hayes, the son of President Rutherford B. Hayes, came to Carbon County to hunt and fish in 1879. Game was plentiful and so were fish. The party of fewer than a dozen men caught 1,200 fish. Major T. T. Thornburgh, later killed by Indians at Milk River, caught 56 fish in 32 minutes from Battle Creek.

4. President Chester A. Arthur, 1883

The President vacationed in Yellowstone for three weeks during the summer, during which time he was virtually out of contact with official Washington. He caught a total of 105 lbs. of fish, according to press reports. On one occasion, he caught three fish in one cast, weighing a total of 4 1/4 lbs.

5. William Jennings Bryan, 1904

Bryan had the opposite luck experienced by Edison and Thornburgh. During his vacation in the Saratoga area, the perennial unsuccessful presidential candidate was just as unsuccessful in fishing. He did not catch a single fish during the vacation. Later, he hunted unsuccessfully for ducks, but he did not leave empty handed. An area guide arranged for him to shoot two tame ducks in a ranch yard near town.

6. Ernest Hemingway, various times

Hemingway fished frequently in Wyoming. In the summer of 1930, he fished on Clark's Fork and declared it the "best fishing in the world." Later that summer, he was in an auto accident in Montana. In 1928, he was fishing on Shell Creek when another famous author, Owen Wister, came by with a fly rod.

A common practice before World War II by the Game and Fish Department was to give sports clubs tiny fish to plant in streams in their area. For instance, in 1933, the G&F gave the Lovell Rod and Gun Club some 60,000 fry for planting. A similar number went to a Wheatland club.

7. Jimmy Carter, 1978

Carter went fishing while he vacationed in Jackson Hole in August 1978.

8. George Bush, 1988

While he waited for the Democrats to nominate his eventual opponent in their convention in Atlanta, the then-vice president and James Baker, his future Secretary of State, fished in the Cody area and camped four miles north of Pahaska in Sam Berry Meadows. Press reports indicated that Bush caught and released a number of trout during the four-day vacation.

9. J. Danforth Quayle, 1989

Vice President Quayle vacationed at Malcolm Wallop's Sheridan County ranch in August 1989. During the four-day vacation, the vice president caught "one or two fish," according to press reports.

Rare and Endangered Fish in Wyoming

1. River shiner

The native fish from the minnows family was once found in the North Platte River near Torrington. It is common in the Mississippi River and elsewhere, but probably is now extinct in Wyoming.

2. Orangethroat darter

The rare native species is a member of the Perch family. In Wyoming, it is found only in Lodgepole Creek, Laramie County.

3. June sucker

A native fish, now presumed extinct, the only one ever found in Wyoming was caught by Dr. Olaus Murie from the Snake River near Jackson in 1927. The specimen is now held in the collections of the University of Michigan Museum.

4. Humpback sucker

No humpback sucker has been seen in Wyoming since 1962. The native fish, which once inhabited the Green River, is now presumed extinct.

5. Suckermouth minnow

A native rare and endangered species, the minnow is common in South Dakota and Texas. In Wyoming, it is found only in the Laramie River and in Lodgepole Creek, Laramie County.

6. Colorado squawfish

This member of the minnow family was once native to the Colorado River drainage. After construction of Flaming Gorge Dam, the fish has not been seen in Wyoming. It probably is extinct.

7. Leatherside chub

Another member of the minnow family, the leatherside chub is a native, rare and endangered fish.

8. Bonytail

The bonytail, a member of the minnow family, still inhabits the Bear River and the Snake River, but it is now extinct from its native home in the Green River.

9. Sturgeon chub

Common in the Missouri River drainage, the fish is found only in the Powder River and Big Horn River in Wyoming.

10. Honeyhead chub

A common fish in some eastern states, this variety of chub now lives only in the Laramie River drainage.

The Wyoming Racquetball Hall of Fame was established in 1988 by the Wyoming Racquetball Association. The first inductee was Mario Ibarra.

11. Kendall Warm Springs dace

The 85-degree waters of the springs provide the only known habitat for the fish, barely two inches long when fully grown. The fish spends its entire life in the spring pools. At breeding time, the males are purple and the females are green. The springs are located 26 miles north of Cora in Sublette County.

12. Finescale dace

Montana Lake in Crook County and the Niobrara River are the only remaining natural habitat for this native fish, common in northern lake states.

13. Northern pearl dace

Found only in the Niobrara River drainage.

14. Shovelnose sturgeon

The fish, now considered rare and endangered, was commonly found in Wyoming prior to 1900, primarily in the North Platte River and Powder River. Two were caught from the Powder River near Arvada in recent years and a few have been seen in the Big Horn and Greybull Rivers in the late 1980s.

15. Colorado River cutthroat trout

The cutthroat, the only native trout in Wyoming, lives in many Wyoming waters, but this variety is found only in the headwaters of the Little Snake River in Carbon County, now designated a fish preserve by the Game and Fish Department.

Source: George T. Baxter and James R. Simon, Wyoming Fishes. (Cheyenne: Game and Fish Department, 1970). The authors identified 78 species of fish in 14 different families. This list is selected from their book.

12 Wyoming Homes for Catfish

1. Flaming Gorge (stocked in 1981)

2. Big Sandy Reservoir (stocked in 1983)

3. Big Horn River (native)

4. Nowood River (native)

5. Beck Lake, Park County (stocked in 1986)

6. Glendo Reservoir

7. Grayrocks Reservoir

8. Laramie River

9. Powder River

10. Pickett Lake

11. Hawk Springs Reservoir

12. Clear Creek, Johnson Co.

The State Fish Hatchery near Story is the oldest in the state. It was opened in 1907. Five million trout eggs, primarily rainbow, are hatched there annually.

FOOTBALL

1st football team in Wyoming: Rock Springs town team, 1888
1st University of Wyoming game: 1893, UW beat Cheyenne HS 14-0.
1st UW intercollegiate game: 1895, UW beat CSU 34-0.
1st UW conference championship: 1949, Cowboy mark was 9-1
1st game in War Memorial Stadium: 1950, UW beat Baylor 7-0
1st UW home attendance above 10,000: 1950, UW v. Baylor
1st UW home attendance above 20,000: 1959, UW v. Air Force
1st UW home attendance above 30,000: 1983, UW v. Air Force
Only university in the U. S. where the football stadium capacity exceeds the town population: UW War Memorial Stadium, with a capacity of 33,500, in Laramie with a population of 28,000.
1st Shrine football game (high school all-stars): 1974.
Longest high school losing streak: Greybull, 1978-1983. The string ended with a win over Red Lodge, Mont., 40-14. In 1987 the Farson high school team picked up its first win since 1956, but the sport was not played annually during the period.
Most memorable game in UW football history: Fans have various favorites, but two seem particularly memorable to the editors. On Sept. 24, 1988, the Cowboys scored 31 points in the fourth quarter to defeat Air Force 48-45. It was one of the greatest comebacks in NCAA history. In 1972, Arizona State came to Laramie to play a UW team. The Cowboys shocked the nationally ranked Sun Devils 42-40.
Most disputed game: Probably, UW v. Denver on Thanksgiving Day, 1955. Wyoming led 3-0 with eight seconds left in the game. A Denver player returned a kickoff to the 30-yard line, was tackled, went down and the whistle blew ending the play. The man with the ball lateralled to another player who was tackled at the two but fell into the end zone. DU was awarded the touchdown, winning 7-3.
Another disputed game: UW v. CSU, 1966. UW was leading when the CSU quarterback either passed the ball or pitched it to another player, but the ball bounced on the ground. The whistle blew, the Cowboys went to the huddle. A CSU player grabbed the ball and ran it in for a touchdown. The officials claimed that the play was not a forward pass, and thus, could be advanced. They also denied that the whistle had been blown. The 12-10 defeat was the only Cowboy loss of the 1966 season.
1st ever high school football game played at night under artificial lighting: Casper High School v. Midwest High School, November 1925.

Some Professional Football Players from Wyoming

1. Boyd Dowler, b. Rock Springs, 1937
Born in Rock Springs where his father was a high school coach, Dowler starred at Cheyenne High School in the middle 1950s. He played his college football at the University of Colorado where he was the Buffaloes quarterback from 1956-1958. He was picked in the third round of the NFL draft in 1959 by the Green Bay Packers and became NFL rookie of the year. He went on to star for the Packers for the next 12 seasons as wide receiver. During his career, he helped the Packers to five division championships and wins in Super Bowl I and II. He retired from football in 1971. Later, he worked as a scout for the Atlanta Falcons.
2. Nick Bebout, b. Riverton, 1951
Bebout was an offensive tackle during his football career. A graduate of Shoshoni High School, he played at the University of Wyoming and was drafted in the sixth round of the 1973 NFL draft by Atlanta. Later, he played for the Seattle Seahawks, after the 1976 expansion draft.
3. Dennis Havig, b. Powell, 1949
Havig played fullback for Powell High School and played college football at the University of Colorado, on the starting team from 1968 to 1970. He was drafted as a guard in the 1971 NFL draft by the Atlanta Falcons where he played for five seasons before being traded to Houston in 1976. He wrapped up his pro career with Green Bay.

4. Don Westbrook, b. Cheyenne, 1951

Westbrook graduated from Cheyenne Central and played college football at the University of Nebraska. He was selected in the sixth round of the NFL draft in 1975 by the Baltimore Colts. He played for Baltimore and, later, for Philadelphia in the World Football League. He signed with Tampa Bay in 1976 and played for the New England Patriots the following year.

5. Jerry Hill

Born in Lingle, Hill was named the "player of the century" at the University of Wyoming in the centennial year of Wyoming football (1993). He starred for the Cowboys from 1958-60 and then became well known as a running back in the NFL for the Baltimore Colts. After a successful career with the Colts, Hill became a marketing specialist and, for a time in the 1980s and early 1990s, worked with the UW athletic department in the promotions area.

6. Tom Wilkinson, b. Iowa, 1943

He came to Greybull with his parents when he was two. He played both football and baseball during high school in Greybull and scouted for both sports during his senior year in high school. Quarterback for the University of Wyoming, he gained his greatest fame in the Canadian Football League, first with the Toronto Argonauts (1967-70) and then quarterbacking Edmonton to Grey Cup championships in 1975, 1978, and 1979, and as backup in 1980 and 1981 championship seasons. He was the first player to be honored on the "Wall of Fame" at Commonwealth Stadium, Edmonton, in 1982. Following his retirement from pro football, he coached for the University of Alberta.

7. Don Bracken, b. Thermopolis, 1962

Bracken graduated from the University of Michigan where he punted for the Wolverines. In 1984, he became punter for Green Bay of the NFL. He signed with the LA Rams in 1992 and 1993.

8. Win Croft

Croft played high school football at Lovell and college football at Utah in the early 1930s. From 1934 to 1936, he played for St. Louis, Brooklyn, Green Bay and Pittsburgh of the NFL.

9. Jay Novacek

An All-American at the University of Wyoming in 1984 when he caught 33 passes for an average of 22.5 yards that year (ending his UW career with 83 receptions for 1,536 yards and four touchdowns), he was drafted in the sixth round by the Phoenix Cardinals. He played for the Cardinals for five seasons before being signed by Dallas as a Plan B free agent in 1990. In 1992, Novacek became the first tight only and only the second player in Dallas Cowboys history to record three consecutive seasons with 50 or more receptions. He caught 74 passes for 694 yards for Dallas in 1992. He played in the 1993, 1994 and 1996 Dallas Super Bowl victories. In his 12 years in the NFL, he caught 422 passes for 4,630 yards and 30 touchdowns. He retired in the summer of 1997.

10. Dave Edeen

A Cheyenne native, Edeen was an All-WAC player at Wyoming. In 1990, he was signed by the NFL champion San Francisco

11. Tom Massey

Massey, a native of Basin, signed a pro contract with the Denver Broncos as an offensive center in 1967.

12. Allyn Griffin

A native of Casper, Griffin starred at Kelly Walsh High School before beginning his collegiate career for the Wyoming Cowboys in 1981. He led the team in receiving in 1984 and 1985. In 1986 he was drafted by the Detroit Lions in the 8th round of the NFL draft.

Two weeks before the regular season began, he suffered a ruptured disk in his back in a practice session. The injury abruptly ended his NFL career. He returned to Laramie to continue his education. He was campus president of the Associated Black Student Leaders in 1990. After a decade in various jobs, he became a counselor and football coach for a Christian boys' ranch near Prescott, Wash. His team made it to the state playoffs in 2004.

13. Mike Dirks

Dirks, who played professional football for 11 years, was at UW in the Sugar Bowl year (1967 game in Jan. 1968). UW led nation in rushing defense 42.3 yards per game. Dirks was named to the All-America first team by Football Writers and *Look Magazine*. He played four years in the NFL with the Philadelphia Eagles. He then spent seven years in the CFL in Canada with the Winnipeg Blue Bombers for three years, briefly with WFL team in Chicago, and Saskatchewan Roughriders on their Grey Cup team in 1976. He retired two years later, returned to his hometown of Monticello, Iowa, for 7 years. Later, he moved to Cedar Rapids, Iowa.

14. Pat Ogrin

The former Cowboy standout played for three years with the Washington Redskins and two years with the Denver Gold of USFL. A lineman, in 1988, at age of 30, Ogrin came out of retirement to play with Pittsburgh Gladiators of the Arena Football League.

15. Ryan Yarborough

Yarborough set the season mark for catches (86) and total yards (1,351), leading the nation. In his senior year in 1993, he set the NCAA record for receiving with 4,357 yards. He set two other NCAA marks. He gained 200 yards or more receiving in seven games and went 27 straight games with a reception. He was drafted by the New York Jets, but played sparingly his first two years in the pros. On July 28, 1996, he was traded to Green Bay, but opted to retire.

16. John Burroughs

A native of Pinedale, Burroughs started playing collegiate football at Washington State, but transferred to Wyoming where he was a starter as defensive end and defensive tackle for three years. He was drafted in the seventh round of the NFL draft in 1995. He signed with the Atlanta Falcons in 1995 as a linebacker. He played in the NFL for seven seasons with three teams: Atlanta, Minnesota and St. Louis. In 1999, he appeared in the Super Bowl, playing for Atlanta against the Denver Broncos.

17. Adam Archuleta

Born in Rock Springs Nov. 27, 1977, Archuleta played collegiate football at Arizona State. He was drafted in the first round of the NFL draft in 2001 by the St. Louis Rams, the 20th pick overall. During his career, he played for the Rams, Washington Redskins, and Chicago Bears. A linebacker in college, he switched to strong safety in the NFL. He took free agent status in 2008.

18. Chris Cooley

Cooley, born in Powell July 11, 1982, graduated from high school in Logan, Utah, and went on to play for his hometown university, Utah State. In his senior year, he led the NCAA in receptions by a tight end. He was drafted in the third round of the 2004 NFL draft by the Washington Redskins. He was named to the Pro Bowl in 2005, 2007 and

Former UW football player Conrad Dobler was called "Pro Football's Dirtiest Player" by *Sports Illustrated* in July 1977. A starting guard for the St. Louis Cardinals, Dobler was an all-pro selection from 1976-78 and NFL Offensive Lineman of the Year in 1981. In 2010 Dobler lived in Missouri where he suffered from health problems due to sports injuries he sustained as a player. He has had 32 knee surgeries and eight knee replacement operations. He sometimes needs a wheelchair to get around, according to press accounts in early 2010.

2008. His best year was in 2005 when he broke the franchise record for most receptions by a tight end. In 2007, he set an NFL record for scoring six or more touchdowns by a tight end during each of his first four years in the pros.

19. Jack Snow

Born in Rock Springs in 1943, Snow graduated from high school in California. He played for Notre Dame as a star receiver from 1963-65. Drafted by the NFL Minnesota Vikings in the first round (8th pick overall), he was traded to the LA Rams before the season began. He played for the Rams for the next ten seasons, setting receiving marks for the team. Following his retirement from the NFL, he sold real estate and in 1982, rejoined the Rams as a receivers' coach. In 1992, he became a broadcaster/radio analyst for the team. In 2005, he developed a staph infection and died Jan. 9, 2006. His son, J. T. Snow, played major league baseball.

20. Sean Fleming

Fleming completed his football career as Wyoming's all-time scorer with 324 points. He holds all UW placekicking record which include field goals made (57) and extra points made (153). He also set a record of 59 straight PAT's made in 1988. He was drafted in the first round of his native Canadian CFL draft by the Edmonton Eskimos. In his 16 seasons with Edmonton, he played in five Grey Cups and was named the MVP of the 81st Grey Cup (1993) in Edmonton's victory over the Winnipeg Blue Bombers 33-23. He also kicked the winning field goal in overtime at the 93rd Grey Cup in 2005 against the Montreal Alouettes, won by Edmonton 38-35.

21. Scottie Vines

One of Wyoming's most versatile athletes who played wide receiver on the Cowboy football team and as a guard on the Cowboy basketball team. He played wide receiver from 2004-06 with the NFL's Detroit Lions.

22. Malcom Floyd

In 2010, Floyd is a wide receiver for the San Diego Chargers. He attended the University of Wyoming from 1999-2003. As a sophomore, Floyd was first-team all-conference selection by *Football News* and *Sporting News*. He finished his career at Wyoming with 186 catches for 2,411 yards abd 14 touchdowns. He signed as a free agent in 2004 with the Chargers. He caught his first touchdown against Kansas City which was also the current quarterback Philip Rivers' first NFL touchdown pass. His older brother Malcolm (same name, but spelled differently) also played in the NFL with the Houston Oilers.

23. Adam Goldberg

Goldberg started 44 of 45 games as a tackle for the Cowboys. He was honorable mention All-American and two-time first team All-Mountain West Conference honoree. He signed on as a free agent with the Minnesota Vikings in 2003. He was traded to the St. Louis Rams in 2006. During the 2008 season he was the only offensive lineman in the NFL to start at four different positions. He begins his 7th season in 2010 as a member of the Rams.

24. Patrick Chukwurah

A three-year starter for the Cowboys, he racked up 245 tackles and 27 sacks. As a senior, he earned first team All-Mountain West honors in 2000. He was drafted in the 5th round by the Minnesota Vikings. In the season opener in 2001, he became the first rookie linebacker to start since Roy Winston in 1962. He later played with the Houston Texans, Denver Broncos and Tampa Bay Buccaneers. In 2009, he was signed by the Florida Tuskers of the United Football League in the new league's initial season.

25. Aaron Elling

A graduate of Lander Valley High School, Elling was a two-time Soccer All-State player. He began his football career at the University of Wyoming as a placekicker. He made honorable mention All-Mountain West in 1999 and second team in 2001. He was signed as a free agent in 2002 by the Minnesota Vikings, but he also spent time with the Tennessee Titans, Baltimore Ravens, Atlanta Falcons, Jacksonville Jaguars, and Cincinnati Bengals. He signed with the Oakland Raiders in 2008.

26. Casey Bramlet

Bramlet was born April 2, 1981 in Casper. He was an all-state quarterback at Wheatland High School. He began his college career at Wyoming where he set new records in career passing yards (9,684), touchdown passes (56) and completions (767). He was drafted in the 7th round of the 2004 NFL Draft by the Cincinnati Bengals. In February 2005, the Bengals allocated Bramlet to the Hamburg Sea Devils of NFL Europe. Bramlet started all ten games of Hamburg's inaugural season. In 2006 he was signed by the Washington Redskins, but in January 2007, the Redskins allocated him back to NFL Europe. On June 23, 2007, he led the Hamburg team to a 37-28 victory over the Frankfurt Galaxy in World Bowl XV. Bramlet was named as its MVP. He later signed with the Miami Dolphins, San Diego Chargers, Baltimore Ravens and, finally, with the CFL Winnipeg Blue Bombers. His father Tom and brother Corey played for UW. Corey also played in the NFL Europe with the Amsterdam Admirals in 2007.

27. Brett Keisel

Born September 19, 1978, in Provo, Utah, he was a three-sport athlete at Greybull High School. He was USA Today Wyoming Player of the Year in his senior year in 1996. He went on to college at Brigham Young University where he finished his career wtih 66 tackles and 9 quarterback sacks. Keisel was selected by the Pittsburgh Steelers in the 7th round of the 2002 NFL Draft. He has played with the Steelers since 2002 as a standout defensive end. He played in two Super Bowls (XL XLIII).

28. Brady Poppinga

Poppinga, born in Evanston September 21, 1979, graduated from Evanston High School where he was named Wyoming's Athlete of the Year as a senior. He led Evanston to a 9-1 record and a 4-A State title. He played collegiate football at Brigham Young University. In each of his playing years at BYU he was named All-Mountain West first team. He was selected in the fourth round of the 2005 NFL draft by the Green Bay Packers. A few years ago, he signed a five-year $17 million extension through the 2012 season with the Packers. Poppinga comes from an athletic family. His father Dennis played tight end for BYU from 1968-71. His brother Casey played at Utah State, brother Kelly played linebacker at BYU and has signed an NFL contract with the St. Louis Rams. His sister Tara played volleyball at Utah State.

29. John Wendling

Born June 4, 1983, in Cody, Wendling was a standout athlete at Rock Springs High School. He was a three-year All-Conference selection at safety and a first-team All Mountain West player in 2006. He was also a four-time Academic All-Mountain West (2003-06) selection. Wendling was drafted in the 6th round of the 2007 NFL draft by the Buffalo Bills. He was considered one of the NFL's top special teams players.

30. Brock Ralph

Born July 16, 1980, in Raymond, Alberta, Canada, he played wide receiver at UW. He has played since 2003 in the Canadian Football League with Edmonton, Hamilton and the Winnipeg Blue Bombers. He is on the active roster of Winnipeg for the 2010 season. His brother Brett retired in 2010 with the Calgary Stampeders.

31. Devin Moore

Moore was born October 6, 1985, in Indianapolis, Indiana. He was a four-year letterman running back at UW. In his senior year (2008) he was a first-team All-Mountain West choice. He was ranked #7 in the NCAA for all-purpose running averaging 167.3 yards per game. He signed a free agent contract with the Seattle Seahawks in 2009. In January 2010 he signed a free agent contract with his hometown Indianapolis Colts.

32. Derrick Martin

Born May 16, 1985, in Denver, Colorado. Martin was an outstanding player at Denver's Thomas Jefferson High School. He played safety at UW where he made 24 starts and finished his abbreviated college career with 134 tackles and 6 interceptions. He was selected in the 6th round of the 2006 NFL Draft by the Baltimore Ravens. He played with the Ravens from 2006-08. In September 2009, Martin was traded to the Green Bay Packers. He is presently the starting strong safety for the Packers, entering the 2010 season.

33. John Chick

Born November 20, 1982, in Gillette, Chick played defensive end at Utah State in Logan. He was signed as a undrafted free agent by the Houston Texans in 2006. He moved to the Canadian Football League and played three seasons with the Saskatchewan Roughriders. In 2009 he won the Most Outstanding Defensive Player Award presented by the CFL. He signed a contract with the NFL Indianapolis Colts in 2010.

Numerous NFL players had been on the University of Wyoming football team including Dave Hampton, Jim Kiick, Conrad Dobler, Vic Washington, Jerry DePoyster, Lawrence Gaines, Mitch Donahue, Rob Bohlinger, Ryan Christopherson, Steve Scifres,and Tyrone Williams. A number of other Wyomingites came to the state following a professional football career including Russ Thompson (Chicago Bears), Lusk; and Richard Ackerman (various NFL teams, 1981-1988), Laramie.

The Best Football Teams at the University of Wyoming

1. 1967

Ranked fifth in the nation by UPI and sixth by AP, the 1967 Cowboys finished the regular season with a perfect 10-0 mark. The team lost 20-13 to LSU in the Sugar Bowl, Wyoming's only appearance in that post-season event. UW led the nation in rushing defense in 1967 for the second year in a row.

2. 1956

Led by Jim Crawford, the nation's leading rusher with 1,104 yards, the Cowboys finished with a perfect 10-0 record. The team went on to defeat Texas Tech in the Sun Bowl 21-14.

3. 1950

Outscoring opponents 343-53 behind the scoring heroics of Eddie Talboom, the 1950 Cowboys had a 9-0 mark, capped by a 20-7 win over Washington and Lee in the Gator Bowl. Talboom scored 15 touchdowns, passed for eight more and kicked 40 extra points during the season.

4. 1966

The perfect season was marred by a fluke play which resulted in a 12-10 loss to Colorado State, giving the Pokes a season record of 9-1. The team led the nation in rushing defense and wrapped up the season with a 28-20 win over Florida State in the Sun Bowl.

5. 1959

The Pokes outscored opponents 287-62. The only loss came to Air Force 20-7 in the second game of the season.

6. 1949

The team led the nation in scoring average and shut out opponents in six games. The only loss was a 32-7 humbling to Baylor. The team scored the most points in modern Cowboy history in a 103-0 win over Colorado State College.

Wyoming in Bowl Games

1. Gator Bowl (1951)

Wyoming beat Washington and Lee 20-7 in the school's first-ever bowl appearance. The Cowboys never trailed in the game.

2. Sun Bowl (1956)

Cowboys beat Texas Tech 21-14 in the El Paso event.

3. Sun Bowl (1959)

The Cowboys defeated Hardin-Simmons 14-6.

4. Sun Bowl (1967)

Wyoming kept a perfect bowl mark with a 28-20 win over Florida State.

5. Sugar Bowl (1968)

Probably the best team in Wyoming football history, the 1967 Cowboys shut out LSU and led 13-0 in the first half. The Tigers came back in the final quarter and downed the Pokes 20-13 in the New Orleans classic.

6. Fiesta Bowl (1976)

In Fred Akers' final game as Cowboy head coach, the team lost to Oklahoma 41-7. Akers accepted the coaching job at Texas prior to the game and did not return to Laramie with the team.

7. Holiday Bowl (1987)

The Cowboys led Iowa 19-7 at half-time, but could not hold off a Hawkeye rally. Iowa won the game 20-19.

8. Holiday Bowl (1988)

Wyoming faced the unenviable task of trying to stop Oklahoma State's Heisman Trophy winner Barry Sanders. Meanwhile, the Poke offense sputtered to just two touchdowns in a 62-14 loss.

9. Copper Bowl (1990)

In the Cowboys' first appearance in the Tucson event, the team lost narrowly to California 17-15.

10. Copper Bowl (1993)

The 8-3 Cowboys again appeared in the Copper Bowl. This time, the team fell to Kansas State 52-17.

11. Las Vegas Bowl (2004)

Quarterback Corey Bramlet threw a 12 yard pass to John Wadkowski with 57 seconds remaining to preserve a 24-21 win over the UCLA Bruins.

12. New Mexico Bowl (2009)

Freshman quarterback Austyn Carta-Samuels threw three touchdown passes including a 13-yard strike in double overtime to David Leonard to give Wyoming a 35-28 win over the Fresno State Bulldogs of the WAC. It was Wyoming's first appearance in a bowl game since the Las Vegas Bowl in 2004.

Former Wyoming Players in the Super Bowl

Former UW football players have been in 11 of the 43 Super Bowls.

1.-2. Mark Smolinski and Jim Hill, Super Bowl III (1969)

Smolinski played for the New York Jets and Hill started for the Baltimore Colts in the game played at Miami. Hill also played for the Colts in Super Bowl V.

3. Joe Williams (1972)

Williams played for the Dallas Cowboys in Super Bowl VI in January, 1972.

4. Jim Kiick (1972, 1973, 1974)

Kiick, teamed with Larry Csonka, led the Miami Dolphins backfield in three consecutive Super Bowls, VI, VII, VIII.

5. Aaron Kyle (1978, 1979)

The former UW star was on the Dallas Cowboy team for Super Bowls XII and XIII.

6. Guy Frazier (1982)

Frazier was on the Cincinnati Bengal roster for Super Bowl XVI.

7. Jay Novacek (1993, 1994, 1996)

Novacek's third appearance in the Super Bowl in 1996 for the Dallas Cowboys tied a former UW Cowboy mark for single-player appearances with the three Super Bowl appearances by Jim Kiick.

8. Brett Kiesel (2006, 2009)

Kiesel, from Greybull, played for the Pittsburgh Steelers in Super Bowl XL against Seattle and XVIII against the Arizona Cardinals. Pittsburgh won both Super Bowl games.

Wyoming Membership in Sports Conferences, 1938-2000

1. Mountain States Conference (1938-1961)

Formed in 1938, the league included seven original members: BYU, Utah, Utah State, CSU, Denver, Wyoming and Colorado. CU withdrew in 1947 to join the Big Eight. New Mexico and Montana were added in 1951 and Denver University withdrew in 1960. In its final decade, the league was known as the "Skyline Conference."

2. Western Athletic Conference (1962-1998)

The six original members of the WAC in 1962 were ASU, Arizona, Utah, BYU, New Mexico and Wyoming. CSU and UTEP were added in September 1967 and ASU and Arizona departed in June 1978 to join the Pac-10. At the same time the two Arizona teams left, San Diego State joined the league followed by Hawaii in July 1979 and Air Force in July 1980. Fresno State was added June 12, 1991, for full participation the next year. In June 1994, the league was expanded and organized into four quadrants. Wyoming, CSU, Air Force and UNLV are in one quadrant; Texas Tech, Tulsa, SMU and Rice in another; BYU, Utah, New Mexico and UTEP in the third; and Hawaii, San Diego State, Fresno State and San Jose State in the fourth. In 1998, before Wyoming and others left the conference, the WAC had the most teams of any major conference in the country.

3. Mountain West Conference (1998-

High travel expenses, lack of television coverage and infrequency of playing against traditional rivals led eight members of the WAC to leave and form their own conference. Wyoming, Colorado State, Air Force, Utah, Brigham Young, San Diego State, UNLV, and New Mexico formed their own conference and, in 1999, began playing in the newly named Mountain West Conference. Texas Christian University became an official new member beginning in the 2005-06 season. The WAC remained intact with Hawaii, Fresno State, San Jose State, Tulsa, Texas Tech, SMU, Rice and UTEP staying in the conference. In June 2010, the Utah Utes departed the MWC for the PAC10.

Cowboy Football All-Americans*

1. Eddie Talboom, Halfback, 1950
2. Dewey McConnell, End, 1951
3. Jim Crawford, Halfback, 1956
4. Mike Dirks, Tackle, 1967
5. Jerry DePoyster, Kicker, 1967
6. Bob Jacobs, Kicker, 1969
(Am. Football Coaches' Assoc.)

7. Dennis Baker, Offensive Tackle, 1977
8. Ken Fantetti, Linebacker, 1978
9. Jack Weil, Punter, 1983
10. Jay Novacek, Tight End, 1984
11. Ryan Yarborough, End, 1993
12. Marcus Harris, wide receiver 1995
13. Brian Gragert, punter, 1996

*First team All-American selections chosen either by a major wire service, Football Writers Association or Kodak.

Academic All-Americans, UW Football

1951: Fran Miknis　　**1987:** Pat Arndt　　　　　　**1997:** Korth, Wedel,
1965: Bob Dinges　　**1994:** Ryan Christopherson. Brian Lee **1998:** Brian Brown
1967: George Mills　　**1995:** Joe Cummings　　　　**2004:** Trenton Franz
1973: Mike Lopiccolo　**1996:** Jay Korth, Cory Wedel　**2006:** John Wendling

In January 1996, eight Wyoming football players were named to the WAC all-academic team, the most of any WAC school and a record for UW. They were Joe Cummings, Jeremy Gilstrap, Shane Glasser, Jay Korth, Brian Lee, Erek Noland, Kelley Pratt, and Cory Wedel.

Some Noteworthy Wyoming Football Coaches

1. Paul Roach

Roach was athletic director when he took over the football program in 1987 following the departure of Dennis Erickson to Washington State. He was the first person in history to be both UW football coach and athletic director. During the next two seasons, Roach's teams won conference titles and gained bids to the Holiday Bowl. The oldest major college head football coach, Roach won conference coach of the year honors in his first two seasons. A native of Wisconsin, Roach was assistant coach at UW from 1962-1970 and an assistant with John Madden's Oakland Raiders. Later, he coached for the Green Bay Packers and Denver Broncos in the NFL.

2. Bob Devaney

Devaney had a career winning percentage at Wyoming of 78 percent (35 wins, 10 losses, 5 ties). He coached the Cowboys from 1957 to 1961 when he was hired for the head coaching job at Nebraska where he closed out his career as athletic director after leading the Cornhuskers to football prominence. (The sports complex at Lincoln is named for him). Devaney retired as Nebraska Athletic Director in 1992. His UW teams won four conference titles. The 1958 team beat Hardin-Simmons 14-6 in the Sun Bowl.

3. Phil Dickens

Dickens coached the Cowboys from 1953-1956 and had a career 73 percent record (29-11-1). His last team at Wyoming was undefeated. The 1955 team beat Texas Tech 21-14 in the Sun Bowl. Dickens left UW in 1957 to accept the head coaching job at Indiana University.

4. Bowden Wyatt

Wyatt coached Wyoming from 1947 to 1952 and compiled a 70 percent mark (39-17-1). His 1950 team finished the year undefeated with a Gator Bowl victory over Washington and Lee. Wyatt later coached at the University of Tennessee.

5. Lloyd Eaton

Eaton coached the Cowboys from 1962 to 1970 and his teams won three conference titles. His career mark of 63 percent (57-33-2) included two bowl appearances. His 1967 team was undefeated in regular season play and ranked fifth in national polls. Eaton resigned in 1970 following the so-called "Black 14 incident" which tarnished UW's football reputation in 1969. He worked as a scout for several pro teams and then retired to Kuna, Idaho.

6. William McMurray

The most successful of the early-day UW coaches, McMurray had a career mark of 56 percent with 15 wins, 10 losses and one tie.

7. C. H. "Okie" Blanchard

Known as "Wyoming's winningest coach," Blanchard amassed 31 state high school titles during his 35-year career. Blanchard was a member of the Wyoming and National High School Sports Halls of Fame. Cheyenne's football stadium was named for him in 1971. He died in 1989.

8. Vic Koenning

A native of Owasso, Okla., Koenning came to UW from the University of Memphis where he was defensive coordinator for six seasons. He was UW defensive coordinator for four years when he was elevated to head coach in 2000 on the departure of Dana Dimel. Koenning was an all-Big 8 linebacker for Kansas State University where he graduated in 1982. He was UW's 29th head football coach and one of the youngest at 39 years old when he was named head coach.

9. Joe Tiller

A native of Toledo, Ohio, Tiller came to UW in 1990. His Cowboy teams were 39-30-1, including a 10-2 mark his final year at UW in 1996. In 1996, he led Wyoming to the WAC title game against BYU and a final AP national ranking at #22. That was their last top 25 ranking.

10. Joe Glenn

Glenn became head coach at UW in 2003. Popular with the fans, he was renowned for playing "Cowboy Joe" on the piano. On Dec. 23, 2004, he led UW to its first bowl victory in 38 years--a 24-21 win over UCLA in the Las Vegas Bowl. The following year, however, the Cowboys went 6-6. In 2007, the Cowboys dropped four straight at the end of the season to finish at 5-7. Despite a historic win over Tennessee at Knoxville (13-7), the 2008 team finished with a mark of 4-8. Glenn was fired the day after the final game of the season, a 31-20 home loss to CSU. He was 30-41 in six seasons as UW head coach.

11. Dave Christiansen

Christiansen was named Wyoming head football coach starting the 2009 season. In his first year he led Wyoming to a 7-6 record including an exciting New Mexico Bowl win over highly regarded Fresno State of the WAC. The victory was Wyoming's first bowl win since the 2004 Las Vegas Bowl against UCLA.

12. Steve Zenisek

Zenisek, a 1977 graduate of Pinedale High School, coached Central Washington University to the NAIA Division II championship game in 1995. Central tied Findlay (Ohio) for the title. That same year, Zenisek was named NAIA coach of the year. His record was 30-12-1 in four seasons as head coach.

"Departing" Wyoming Football Coaches

1. Fred Akers (b. 1938, Arkansas)

The first sell-out in the history of War Memorial Stadium brought in an excess of 33,000 fans to the UW-BYU contest for the WAC lead on Nov. 11, 1990. Akers "deserted" UW after two seasons (1975-76) to take the head football coaching job at Texas, previously occupied by his mentor Darrel Royal. Wyoming fans were outraged because the university had given Akers a sizable pay bonus just before he announced his departure. After lackluster seasons at Texas, Akers teams had a combined record of 86-31-2 over ten seasons. He left after the 1986 season to coach at Purdue University where his teams had a record of 12-31-1 in four years. He was fired following the 1990 season when the Boilermakers went 2-9.

2. Pat Dye (b. 1939, Georgia)

Rivaling Akers' abrupt departure, Pat Dye coached the Cowboys but one season (1980), compiled a 6-5 mark and then skipped off to become head coach at Auburn. While at Auburn, his teams were 99-39-4 over 12 seasons, including a mark of 11-1 in 1983 and a win in the Sugar Bowl. Following NCAA investigations over rules violations, Dye resigned in 1992. In November 2005, the surface at the Auburn stadium was named Pat Dye Field. That same year, he was inducted into the College Football Hall of Fame.

3. Dennis Erickson (b. 1947, Everett, Washington)

The most traveled head coach in UW history probably was Dennis Erickson. Erickson came to Wyoming after serving as head coach at the University of Idaho from 1982-85. Erickson left Wyoming in 1987 to take what he called the "only position" he couldn't refuse—the head coaching job at Washington State University, Pullman. His single season mark at UW (1986) was 6-6. In 1989, he resigned from WSU and told Pullman fans he was taking the "only position" he couldn't refuse—the head job at the University of Miami. Wyoming athletic director Paul Roach, disgusted with coaches using the UW job as a stepping-stone elsewhere, became head football coach, to the delight of Cowboy fans also tired of opportunistic coaches. After six seasons with Miami and soon after his team was placed on three years of NCAA probation, he was named head coach for the NFL Seattle Seahawks in January 1995. Fired there, he moved to Oregon State in 1999, staying until 2002. The following year he was back in the NFL with San Francisco, but after two seasons, he was fired in 2004. In 2006, he was back as head coach at Idaho where his team finished 4-8. After only ten months at Idaho, he took the job as head coach at Arizona State University in 2007, coaching the Sun Devils to a 10-3 season and appearance in the Holiday Bowl. His mark from 2007-2009 at ASU was 19-18.

4. Bowden Wyatt (b. 1917, d. 1969)

Wyatt was lured from Wyoming after six seasons to coach at the University of Arkansas. After two seasons there, he moved on to the University of Tennessee where his Volunteer teams compiled a mark of 49-29-4 in eight seasons. Wyatt was Cowboy coach from 1947-52 and had a mark of 39-17. He was elected to the College Football Hall of Fame in 1972 as a player (he had been a standout end at the University of Tennessee) and again in 1997 as a coach.

5. Robert S. "Bob" Devaney (b. 1915- d. 1997)

Devaney came to Wyoming after being an assistant coach at Michigan State. He left Laramie for Lincoln and the University of Nebraska in 1961 after five seasons at UW. He turned the Nebraska program into a national power house. His Husker teams were 101-20-2 over 11 seasons including two national championships. In 1967, while he was still football coach, he became the school's athletic director serving in that capacity until 1993. His influence on Cornhusker sports was so great that the new sports complex was named for him.

6. Phil Dickens (b. 1915, d. 1983)

Dickens came to Wyoming from the head coaching position at Wofford. Dickens coached at UW for four years (1953-56) and then moved to Indiana University in 1956. He was 29-11-1 at Wyoming and 20-41-2 with the Hoosiers. His final season at Bloomington was in 1964. In his collegiate playing career, he was an All-American tailback at the University of Tennessee.

7. Fritz Shurmur (b. Michigan, 1932, d. Wisconsin, 1999)

Shurmur's departure after four disappointing seasons (15-29 from 1971-74) was involuntary. His very successful tenure as defensive coordinator under his predecessor Lloyd Eaton led to similar positions in the NFL. In 1989, he was defensive coordinator for the Los Angeles Rams. During that year, he purchased a "retirement home" in northern Wyoming. In 1991, he was defensive coordinator for the Phoenix Cardinals of the NFL. Later, he accepted the defensive coordinator's position for the Green Bay Packers, a position he held during Green Bay's 1995 season culminating in the Pack's appearance in the NFC championship game. He was defensive coordinator when the Packers won the Super Bowl in 1997 and the next year when the Packers lost to Denver in Super Bowl XXXII. Soon after accepting the defensive coordinator's position with the Seattle Seahawks in 1999, he developed cancer and died later that year in Wisconsin.

8. Bill Lewis (b. Philadelphia, 1941)

Like Shurmur, Lewis left following three disappointing seasons (14-20-1 from 1977-79). He was hired as assistant coach at the University of Georgia from 1980-89. Later, he became head coach at East Carolina (1989-91) and then went to Georgia Tech where he was head coach from 1992-94. From 1996-2004, he was a defensive coach for the Miami Dolphins. In 2005 he joined Notre Dame as the coach for defensive backs.

9. Al Kincaid (b. Alabama)

Kincaid was a star quarterback at Virginia Tech while a collegiate player. His first coaching jobs were in high schools, moving to Alabama as an assistant under Bear Bryant and, later, as assistant to Pat Dye at UW. On Dye's departure, Kincaid was named head coach. He had a career mark at Wyoming of 29 wins and 29 losses in five seasons (1981-85). When his contract at UW was not renewed after the 1985 season, he worked for a sports consulting firm, served as recruiting coordinator for the University of Alabama, and then became head coach of Arkansas State. Following his second year there, he was reassigned to another position in the Arkansas State athletic department. His Arkansas State teams had a record of 4-17-1 in two years (1990-1991). In the late 1990s, he became an assistant coach at Temple.

10. Joe Tiller (b. Toledo, Ohio, 1942)

Tiller played football at Montana State where he later worked as an assistant coach to Jim Sweeney, who later was the head coach at Fresno State. Tiller accepted the UW job in 1990. His Cowboy teams were 39-30-1, including a 10-2 mark his final year at UW in 1996. Tiller was named the head coach at Purdue in 1997 and led the Boilermakers to winning seasons in all but two years (mark of 87-62) and ten bowls in 12 years, including eight straight bowl appearances from 1997 to 2004. He retired as Purdue coach in 2008. He and his wife now live near Buffalo, Wyoming.

11. Dana Dimel (b. Columbus, Ohio, 1962)

Dimel, hired in November, 1996, came to UW from Kansas State where he had served as an assistant coach. When he was hired, he was 34, youngest football coach ever at UW. He resigned after three seasons at UW (22-13) to coach at the University of Houston. In three seasons, his Cougar teams went 8-26. In 2001, Houston went 0-11, the first winless season in the school's history. From 2006-08, he was an assistant coach at Arizona. In 2009, he moved to Kansas State as coach of the runningbacks.

12. Vic Koenning (b. Owasso, Oklahoma, 1960)

As a defensive standout at Kansas State, Koenning played two years of pro football (in the USFL at Oklahoma) before becoming an assisant coach at the University of Memphis in 1986. After ten years at Memphis, he was hired as defensive coordinator at UW in 1997. In 2000, after Dimel moved to Houston, Koenning was named Cowboy head coach. His teams went 5-29 in three seasons, including 1-10 in his first year (2000). He was fired at the end of the 2002 season. In 2002, he was hired as assistant coach at Troy, moving to Clemson as defenisve coordinator in 2005. After being passed over as Clemson head coach, he resigned in 2008 and took an assistant job at Kansas State. In December 2009, he was named defensive coordinator at the University of Illinois.

13. Joe Glenn (b. Lincoln, Nebraska, 1949)

Glenn was head football coach at Doane College in Nebraska at the age of 27, the youngest head coach in the country. After four seasons and mark of 21-18-1, he was hired as an assisant coach at the University of Montana for five seasons. In 1987, he moved to the University of Northern Colorado where in 1989, he was named head coach. In the 11 seasons he was head coach at UNC, his teams went 98-35 and two Divi-

---

In the first-ever 1A, 9-man football playoff, Hanna defeated Midwest 41-14 (1989)

sion II national championships (1996 and 1997). He returned to Montana as head coach in 1998 and in the next five years, the Grizzlies were 39-6 and I-AA champions in 2001. He became head coach at UW in 2003. On Dec. 23, 2004, he led UW to its first bowl victory in 38 years--a 24-21 win over UCLA in the Las Vegas Bowl. The following year, however, the Cowboys went 6-6. In 2007, the Cowboys dropped four straight at the end of the season to finish at 5-7. Despite a historic win over Tennessee at Knoxville (13-7), the 2008 team finished with a disappointing mark of 4-8. Glenn was fired the day after the final game of the season, a 31-20 home loss to CSU. He was 30-41 in six seasons as UW head coach.

Shrine Football Games, 1974-2009

Best players from teams playing in the north half of the state play best players from teams in the South. All high school divisions participate.

1974: South 37 North 0	1987: North 22 South 15	2000: North 26 South 3
1975: North 21 South 16	1988: South 31, North 14	2001: North 24 South 20
1976: South 14 North 7	1989: North 31 South 7	2002: North 28 South 7
1977: North 6 South 6	1990: South 18 North 17	2003: South 20 North 10
1978: South 12 North 0	1991: South 29 North 19	2004: North 17 South 6
1979: South 7 North 0	1992: South 20 North 20	2005: North 10 South 0
1980: North 6 South 3	1993: South 36 North 15	2006: South 24 North 20
1981: North 19 South 18	*(1st held in Casper)*	2007:.South 20 North 17
1982: North 39 South 7	1994: South 20 North 13	2008: North 16 South 10
1983: North 24 South 0	1995: South 10 North 7	2009: North 27 South 26
1984: North 26 South 22	1996: South 41 North 13	**North: 17 wins**
1985: South 37 North 15	1997: South 18 North 15	**South: 17 wins**
(sudden death overtime)	1998: North 18 South 7	**2 ties (1977, 1992)**
1986: South 26 North 10	1999: North 26 South 19	

Some Football Fields Named for Former Coaches

1. Okie Blanchard Stadium and Riske Field, both in Cheyenne
Cheyenne's oldest football stadium was named for "Wyoming's winningest coach" in 1971. The football field at Cheyenne Central was named for long-time football coach Milt Riske.

2. Deti Stadium, Laramie
Named for John Deti, the long-time Laramie High coach who led Laramie to conference and state titles over a long career. Deti's son coaches the Plainsmen.

3. Harry Geldien Stadium, Casper
Named for the long-time football coach at NCHS.

4. Wiseman Field, Torrington
The stadium was named for THS coach Jim Wiseman.

5 Worst Road Trips in Major-College Football

(according to Sporting News)

1. Fayetteville, Arkansas (University of Arkansas)
2. Laramie, Wyoming (University of Wyoming)
3. Pullman, Washington (Washington State University)
4. State College, Pennsylvania (Penn State)
5. Honolulu, Hawaii (University of Hawaii)

About the Laramie trip, the Sporting News wrote: "It is one of the longest bus trips in college football. Most teams fly into Denver and take a grim three-hour bus ride."

> The first-ever ESPN Thursday night NCAA football game was played Sept. 1, 1988, in Laramie. UW defeated BYU 24-14.

High School Football in Wyoming, 1994-2010

High School Football Championships, 1985
4A Casper Natrona 14, Cody 13
3A Evanston 47, Torrington 8
2A Shoshoni 18, Seton 7
1A Big Horn 7, Wright 6

High School Football Championships, 1986
4A Sheridan 44, Rawlins 14
3A Jackson 17, Douglas 16
2A Lusk 38, Big Piney 0
1A Cokeville 21, Big Horn 7

High School Football Championships, 1987
4A Rock Springs 14, Laramie 13
3A Powell 7, Wheatland 3
2A Lovell 14, Upton 6
1A Cokeville 14, Meeteetse 12

High School Football Championships, 1988
4A Cheyenne Central 26, Evanston 9
3A Torrington 6, Worland 0
2A Big Piney 28, Upton 14
1A Cokeville 35, Big Horn 0

High School Football Championships, 1989
4A Cheyenne Central 32, Rock Springs 0
3A Worland 16, Jackson 14
2A Cokeville 46, Burns 0
1A Hanna 41, Midwest 14

High School Football Championships, 1990
4A Sheridan 35 Central 30
3A Torrington 20 Star Valley 6
2A Thermopolis 21 Lovell 20 (OT)
1A Cokeville 20 Sundance 6
1A, 9-man Lingle 35 Dubois 20

High School Football Championships, 1991
4A Sheridan 27 Gillette 8
3A Cody 25 Star Valley 7
2A Thermopolis 6 Lovell 0
1A Cokeville 34 Pine Bluffs 6
1A, 9-man: Midwest 6 Big Horn 0

High School Football Championships, 1992
4A Sheridan 27 Gillette 9 (Sheridan's 25th consecutive win over two years)
3A Star Valley 34 Torrington 13
2A Thermopolis 28 Buffalo 13
1A Rocky Mountain 10 Wind River 7
1A (9-man) Burlington 46 Hulett 6

High School Football Championships, 1993
4A Sheridan 42 Evanston 7
3A Star Valley 14 Lander 12
2A Kemmerer 27 Buffalo 6
1A Cokeville 40 Rocky Mountain 22
1A (9-man) Meeteetse 23 Hulett 20

Three inches of snow fell in Laramie on June 25, 1958.

High School Football Championships, 1994
4A Laramie 30 Natrona 9
3A Riverton 33 Lander 27
2A Kemmerer 16 Thermopolis 6
1A Cokeville 17 Pine Bluffs 8
1A (9-man) Burlington 36 Hulett 20

High School Football Championships, 1995
4A Sheridan 21 Laramie 15
3A Star Valley 32 Lander 14
2A Mountain View 27 Buffalo 0
1A Rocky Mountain 32 Lusk 20
1A-2 Cokeville 34 Guernsey 0

High School Football Championships, 1996
4A Natrona 7 Sheridan 0
3A Star Valley 35 Torrington 0
2A Buffalo 33 Thermopolis 6
1A Moorcroft 9 Lusk 6
1A-2 Cokeville 26 Hulett 3

High School Football Championships, 1997
4A Evanston 25 Sheridan 20
3A Riverton 23 Star Valley 20
2A Mountain View 29 Thermopolis 9
1A Rocky Mountain 32 Lusk 20
1A-2 Wind River 18 Upton 0

High School Football Championships, 1998
4A Gillette 14 Laramie 7
3A Riverton 9 Star Valley 7
2A Big Piney 27 Lovell 8
1A Rocky Mountain 48 Pinedale 26
1A-2 Cokeville 12 Upton 7

High School Football Championships, 1999
4A Casper Natrona 13 Gillette 10
3A Riverton 14 Douglas 6
2A Lyman 16 Mountain View 6
1A Lusk 28 Pinedale 16
1A-2 Southeast 33 Cokeville 14

High School Football Championships, 2000
4A Gillette 28 Laramie 7
3A Rawlins 39 Powell 14
2A Big Piney 44 Mountain View 28
1A Lusk 34 Sundance 7
1A-2 Southeast 41 Big Horn 20

High School Football Championships, 2001
5A Rock Springs 22, Gillette 19
4A Worland 6, Star Valley 0
3A Big Piney 24, Mountain View 14
2A Southeast 14, Luak 7
1A Cokeville 26, Normative Services 14

High School Football Championships, 2002
5A Rock Springs 36, Gillette 14
4A Worland 17, Star Valley 14
3A Glenrock 35, Mountain View 0
2A Lusk 31, Big Horn 0
1A Cokeville 54, Guernsey-Sunrise 0

High School Football Championships, 2003
5A Casper Natrona 28, Gillette 3
4A Worland 23, Buffalo 13
3A Glenrock 13, Lovell 6
2A Big Horn 29, Lusk 8
1A Cokeville 14, Southeast 13

High School Football Championships, 2004
5A Green River 20, Casper Natrona 0
4A Buffalo 31, Lander 10
3A Big Piney 14, Mountain View 10
2A Big Horn 52, Upton 22
1A Guernsey-Sunrise 20, Cokeville 18

High School Football Championships, 2005
5A Central 27, East 14
4A Buffalo 17, Star Valley 14
3A Kemmerer 37, Glenrock 12
2A Sundance 40, Wright 0
1A Upton 55, Guernsey-Sunrise 6

High School Football Championships, 2006
5A Gillette 16, Cheyenne East 14
4A Powell 37, Douglas 25
3A Big Piney 21 Tongue River 18
2A Southeast 8, Riverside 6
1A Guernsey-Sunrise 14, Cokeville 12

High School Football Championships, 2007
5A Cheyenne East 24, Evanston 14
4A Jackson 10, Buffalo 6
3A Kemmerer 22, Glenrock 0
2A Riverside 21, Big Horn 20
1A Southeast 28, Guernsey-Sunrise 12

High School Football Championships, 2008
5A Gillette 23, Green River 21
4A Douglas 34, Buffalo 21
3A Glenrock 18, Kemmerer 0
2A Burns 41, Big Horn 12
1A Southeast 12, Burlington 0

High School Football Championships, 2009
4A Sheridan 40, Cheyenne Central 15
3A Douglas 44, Cody 14
2A Thermopolis 22, Glenrock 20
1A Southeast 27, Lingle-Fort Laramie 20
1A-6-man Guernsey Sunrise 76, Kaycee 16

Cavalry: Wyoming's First Pro Football Team

The first professional football team in Wyoming began play in 2000 as an expansion member of the Indoor Football League. They were known as the Casper Cavalry. Despite a 9-5 season they fell in the playoffs to the Black Hills Machine. In 2001 the Cavalry joined the National Indoor Football League and became known as the Wyoming Cavalry. The team played in the inaugural Indoor Bowl, losing to the Mississippi Fire Dogs, which was coached by Brett Favre's father Irvin. Since 2008 the Cavalry has been in the American Indoor Football League. The Cavalry made it to the first two AIFL Championship Bowls but lost to Florence (2008) and Reading (2009).

GOLF

1st woman to win the state golf championship: Dr. Grace Raymond Hebard of Laramie who won the title in 1902.

1st golf course in Wyoming: The record is unclear. Cheyenne had a golf course in the 1890s. Several individuals built golf courses near their ranches in the early days, including A. A. Anderson at the Palette Ranch in the Meeteetse area, and J. B. Okie at his "Big Teepee" near Lost Cabin. Both laid out courses before 1917.

1st Wyoming native to win a Professional Golfers' Association (PGA) tour event: Jim Benepe of Sheridan who won the Western Open in July 1988. He finished with a ten under par to win the $162,000 top prize. In November, 1989, he bogeyed the final hole in the Australian PGA tournament and lost by one stroke.

1st U. S. Golf Association championship event held in Wyoming: The U. S. Amateur Public Links Championship, Jackson Hole Golf and Tennis club, July 1988. Jeff Rafferty, Buffalo, was the lone entry from Wyoming of 159 golfers.

1st University of Wyoming golf All-American: Dave McCleave, UW senior, named to the Golf Coaches Association All-American team in June 1992.

Most tourney wins by Wyoming collegiate golfer: Dave McCleave, winner of five college tournaments and the first UW golfer in the 51-year history of college golf at UW to appear in NCAA golf tournament (1992)

1st Wyoming team to win National Junior College Golf Tourney: LCCC won the national title at the tourney held in Midland, Texas, June 7, 1991.

1st Wyoming Secretary of State to shoot a hole-in-one: Kathy Karpan on July 18, 1991, at the Niobrara Country Club, Lusk

Big Prize: John Oja won a new $24,000 Ford pickup when he shot a hole-in-one in a Rock Springs golf tournament in July, 1992. Tourney organizers hired Jackie Legerski to serve as witness at the second hole. When Oja and the three playing with him prepared to tee off, Legerski told them to make a hole-in-one so she could stop watching. At that point, Oja slapped in the ball with a five-iron.

"Playable days": From 1981-1991, the Buffalo golf course compiled the number of "playable" days on the course. Of 183 days in the "golf season" from April 1 through Sept. 30, the high was 178 days in 1987; the low, 149 in 1984.

Tragedy: Mark Doherty, 21, a former Cheyenne Central golf star and Weber State golfer, died when he fell in downtown Ogden, Utah, in a parking lot, May 14, 1988.

Oddest golf "shot": Kemmerer High School student shot during state tournament by a pellet gun fired by a former Jackson student, Jackson golf course.

"First" Golf Courses in Wyoming Towns

1. Casper

The first golf course was opened to play in June 1924. That same August, the course hosted the Wyoming Golf Tournament.

2. Rock Springs

The first course was laid out in the winter of 1923 when snow still covered the ground. The site was ten miles south of town on Kent's Ranch. Two years later, "Dead Horse Canyon" golf course was laid out in an area where horse carcasses were once dumped. The two clubs merged in 1927 and, after a short period as "Boulder Golf and Country Club," reverted to the "Dead Horse" name. Early day golfers were said to have carried "snake irons" in their golf bags.

3. Laramie

The Red Jacoby Golf Park in Laramie started in 1958 as a "Laramie Community Municipal Golf Course." A group leased land from the Union Pacific and in the spring of 1958, laid out a nine-hole course. In the spring of 1968, the course was turned over to the University of Wyoming with the stipulation that it remain a municipal course. Nine more holes were added soon after. In the fall of 1973, the course was named in honor of Glenn J. (Red) Jacoby, who had died that spring during his 27th year as UW athletic director.

State High School Golf Championships, 1998-2009

Boys	Girls		Boys	Girls
1998: Evanston	Cheyenne Central		**2005: 4A:** Chey. Central	Gillette
1999: 4A: Sheridan	Natrona		**3A:** Buffalo	Kemmerer
(in play-off with Central)			**2A:** Lovell	Lusk
3A: Lander	Buffalo		**2006: 4A:** Chey. Central	Sheridan
2000: 4A: Rock Spr.	Gillette		**3A:** Lander	Buffalo
3A: Worland	Buffalo		**2A:** Tongue River	Lusk
2001: 4A: Kelly Walsh	Gillette		**2007: 4A:** Chey. Central	Gillette
3A: Worland	Powell		**3A:** Lander	Cody
2A: Sundance	Lusk		**2A:** Lusk	Thermopolis
2002: 4A: Kelly Walsh	Gillette		**2008: 4A:** Sheridan	Gillette
3A: Worland	Lander		**3A:** Douglas	Lander
2A: Lusk	Lusk		**2A:** Lusk	Thermopolis
2003: 4A: Sheridan	Gillette		**2009: 4A:** Evanston	Cheyenne Central
3A: Lander	Star Valley		**3A:** Cody	Lander
2A: Lusk	Lusk		**2A:** Kemmerer	Moorcroft
2004: 4A: Chey. Central	Casper Natrona			
3A: Star Valley	Star Valley			
2A: Lovell	Lusk			

Wyoming State Amateur Winners, 1994-2009

Men's	Women's
1994: Todd Griffin, Rock Springs	Mary Ann Morrison, Dubois
1995: Todd Griffin, Rock Springs	Lori Savoy
1996: Dave Balling, Cody	Mary Ann Morrison, Dubois
1997: Dwayne Lewis, Cheyenne	Beth Purcell
1998: Mike Urbachka, Sheridan	Maureen Humphries
1999: Kyle Landon, Casper	Jessi Santesson
2000: Mike Urbachka, Sheridan	Laurie Wasson
2001: Mike Urbachka, Sheridan	Jessi Santesson
2002: Mike Urbachka, Sheridan	Jennifer Tucker, Casper
2003: Ashdon Woods, Lander	Jennifer Tucker, Casper
2004: Ashdon Woods, Lander	Jennifer Tucker, Casper
2005: Keegan Bradley, Jackson	Jennifer Tucker, Casper
2006: Todd Griffin, Casper	Mikala Henzlik, Laramie
2007: Mike Urbachka, Cody	Kaelee Aegerter, Laramie
2008: Steve White, Jackson	Jessi Waring, Casper
2009: Gabe Maier, Cody	Kelsey Podlesny, Green River

Wyoming Men's Pro/Am Open Golf Champions, 2000-2010

	Professional	Amateur		Professional	Amateur
2000:	Travis Williams	Ryan Prew	**2006:**	Kane Webber	Michael May
2001:	Travis Williams	Bill Fowler	**2007:**	Luke Antonelli	Justin Howell,
2002:	Matt Schalk	Anthony Giarratano			Klint Krieger
2003:	Steve Schneiter	Bill Fowler	**2008:**	Travis Williams	Josh Creel
2004:	Steve Schneiter	John Hornbeck	**2009:**	Mike Northern	Justin Howell
2005:	Jeff Klein	Keegan Bradley	**2010:**	Nathan Lashley	Gabe Maier

Some UW Golf Highlights

1999-2001: UW golfer David Hearn qualified 3 straight years for the NCAA Regional Tournament, the only UW golfer to accomplish that feat. After leaving UW he joined the the PGA Nationwide Tour.

2010: UW golfer Gabe Maier became only the fifth Cowboy to qualify for the NCAA Regionals. A graduate of Cody High School, he was an Academic All-MWC selection while at UW.

HUNTING

1st game law in Wyoming: Passed by Congress for the territory in 1869.
1st elk hunting regulations adopted: 1871.
1st non-resident hunting regulations passed: 1886, when non-residents were prohibited from killing big game.
1st non-resident licenses issued: 1895. A law passed four years later made it illegal for non-residents to hunt without a guide.
1st state appropriation for feeding game animals: 1909.
Game commission established: Actually, the State Fish Commission had been in existence since 1878. Its jurisdiction was extended to game in 1895.
1st State Game Warden: Albert Theophil Nelson, appointed in 1899 soon after the legislature authorized the position. Nelson lived in Jackson Hole.
1st Lander one-shot antelope hunt: The first such event, consisting to two teams, was held in 1940, as a result of challenge between Harold Evans of Lander and Hank Dahl of Golden, Colo., as to who could shoot a pronghorn with just one bullet. The event became annual in 1945.
Two Wyoming towns named for game wardens: Hudson, named for Daniel E. Hudson, the state game warden from 1911-1914 and Wilson, named for Hudson's successor, Nate Wilson.

15 Fabled Hunts

1. Sir George Gore, 1853-1855
During a two-year hunt in Wyoming, Gore's entourage of 40 people shot 2,500 buffalo, 40 grizzly bears and thousands of other game animals.

2. Tex Eastwood, 1854
Trappers harvested beaver pelts by the thousands in the first third of the 19th century, however, the animals were still plentiful in the 1850s. Eastwood, a pioneer Green River Valley trapper, caught 600 beaver in 1854 season.

3. Indians near Savery, 1858
Jim Baker once claimed that he remembered seeing buffalo so thick during the fall of 1858 near present-day Savery that the Indians stayed three weeks in the area and never had to go more than 300 yards to shoot a buffalo.

4. Edward Shelley, 1862
The gentleman nephew of poet Percy Shelley hunted in Wyoming during 1862 while the Civil War was raging in the east. On September 21, he shot an elk on the Greybull River, but before he could reach the carcass, wolves devoured it. Two days later, according to his diary, he shot another elk and four antelope.

5. John Hunton and Little Bat Grenier, 1875
The two men claimed to have shot 97 elk one day in December, 1875.

6. Yellowstone poachers, 1875-1877
In two years, illegal hunters killed more than 7,000 elk within the park for their hides and antlers. The carcasses were either left for carrion or used for baiting bear, wolves and wolverines.

7. Captain Coates and John J. Clarke, 1881
Coates, the commander of Fort Steele, went with guide Clarke on a sage chicken hunt in September, 1881, at Pass Creek, Carbon County. Between them they bagged 310 sage chickens.

George Storer, chairman of the board of Storer Broadcasting Co., owned several ranches in the Saratoga area in the 1950s. In 1960 he built a championship 18-hole golf course and planted 7,000 trees on it. Four years later, he opened the Old Baldy Club on the site. After Storer's death, a corporation of several members was formed to purchase the club from his estate in October, 1976. The club is now run by a five-member board.

8. Lt. A. R. Jordan and five soldiers, 1881

The six men left Fort Laramie to hunt game on November 19, 1881. Within a few hours' ride from the fort, they bagged ten elk, six black-tailed deer and one buffalo.

9. Moreton Frewen and guests, 1881

Frewen was an Englishman who ranched in the Powder River Basin. His diary for Oct. 5, 1881, tells of accompanying two guests on a hunt. They "killed 95 wild duck, mallards, shovellers, widgean and teal within a mile of the house." Guests included Randolph and Jenny (Jerome) Churchill, parents of Winston Churchill who left the future prime minister of Britain at home while they visited Jenny's sister, Frewen's wife Clara.

10. Moreton Frewen, 1884

One afternoon in late summer, Frewen spotted, from his ranch house window, one of the last surviving buffalo in the wild. "I ran into the hall, not even half dressed," he wrote in his diary, "picked an Express rifle out of the rack and broke the poor brute's shoulder, killing him ten minutes later on the flat a quarter of a mile away."

11. Colorado hunters, 1885

A soldier wrote to a friend from Fort Fetterman in 1885: "One outfit killed 42 elk in one day. These outfits are from Colorado and are shooting everything from a Jackrabbit up to Elk...Two years more and Elk will be as scarce as Buffalo."

12. Theodore Roosevelt, 1892

The future president and five companions hunted elk near Two Ocean Pass in the fall of 1892. Roosevelt reported shooting 13 elk, removed their tongues for food and their heads and antlers for trophies and left the meat to rot. He also shot two bighorn sheep. According to an account of his trip in *Century Magazine* (1892), Roosevelt killed ruffed grouse to eat because he and his companions did not like the taste of elk even though some had been freshly killed. In Cheyenne at the time, elk meat sold for 13 cents a pound and hotel restaurants were accused of trying to pass it off as beef, a more expensive meat.

13. W. Seward Webb, 1897.

Webb, a railroad magnate, hosted a hunt near Jackson Lake in 1897. His party included four "sportsmen," five guides, a U. S. Army general, 24 enlisted men and a camp crew. The party was photographed by Benjamin Sheffield.

14. Ned Frost, 1900

The Cody area guide once killed and dressed 32 deer before breakfast to feed the highway crew building the Cody Road to Yellowstone.

15. Prince Albert of Monaco, 1913

In September, Buffalo Bill took Prince Albert hunting in the Northern Absarokas west of Cody where the prince shot a large brown bear. He had it stuffed and sent back to his castle in Monaco. It was Cody's last big game hunt.

Big Game Licenses and Numbers

1. Moose

Odds of receiving a license were approximately 15-1 (2000). Wyoming has more Shiras moose than anywhere on earth. About 600 of them live in Jackson Hole.

2. Big Horn Sheep

Two million of the animals roamed Wyoming in 1800, but the numbers were down to fewer than 3,000 in 1940. Today, the number is about 6,000. Hunting seasons for them were established in 1937. In 1988, a Wyoming hunting tag sold at a charity auction for $32,000.

3. Mountain Goat

Mountain goats are not native to Wyoming. Fewer than 100 make their home here. In 1988, eight tags were issued, six to resident hunters. The chances of having one's name drawn for a goat permit are about one in 210. The animals are found principally along the east boundary of Yellowstone.

4. Elk

The state ranks fifth in elk population with about 71,000 animals. In 1986, 44,000 hunters went afield to hunt elk, shooting about 14,000. The Jackson elk herd of 15,000 animals is the largest in the world. It had a similar population in 1911. The Yellowstone herd, until the fires of 1988, numbered approximately 5,000. In 1914, there were 35,000 elk in the park, but almost 25,000 of them were killed in the hard winter of 1920. The National Park Service killed 4,309 elk from the herd in the winter of 1961.

5. Wild Turkey

The birds inhabit the Black Hills in northeastern Wyoming. Hunters winning the drawings for permits could hunt them from Nov. 1-30 and were limited to one turkey per hunter. Morgan Ellsbury, a Sundance high school student, bagged the 21-lb. record-breaker on May 17, 1999. The record started in 1997.

Record Trophies*

1. Whitetail Deer

The Wyoming record deer, 191 5/8 points, was shot by Dean Ross of Laramie, Oct. 4, 1986, on the Laramie River.

2. Mule Deer

The state record was taken by an unknown hunter in Hoback Canyon many years ago. The trophy is in the collections of the Jackson Hole Museum. The animal holds the second-highest Boone and Crockett score in the country. *Other trophy mule deer:* Gary L. Albertson, Uinta County, 1960; Robert V. Parke, Teton County, 1967; Herb Klein, Split Rock, 1960; Al Firenze, Sr., Lincoln County, 1969; John E. Myers, Lincoln County, 1968; Ora Magurn, Crook County, 1957; Monte J. Brough, Lincoln County, 1968.

3. Moose

The world record Shiras moose was killed near Green River Lake in 1952 by John M. Oakley. The trophy, displayed in the Jackson Hole Museum, contains 15 points on each side and has a maximum spread of 53 inches. Richard Jones of Banner shot the Pope and Young Club archery record Shiras moose on Sept. 15, 1987, near Bull Creek. The rack had a spread of 55 inches and rated out at 185 points. *Other trophy Shiras moose:* Arthur Chandler, Fremont County, 1944; Alfred Berol, Atlantic Creek, 1933; Kenneth Booth, Jackson, 1969; Curt Mann, Sublette County, 1972; Robert C. Neely, Sublette County, 1959; Isabelle Perry, Teton County, 1961.

4. Elk (Wapiti)

The rack from the state's record elk is held by the Jackson Hole Museum. The elk was shot by an unknown hunter in the Big Horn Mountains in 1890. Nerwin Martin of Powell shot the largest elk ever taken in Wyoming in a century in 1991. The rack, rated by Boone and Crockett at 418 7/8, had a spread of 50 inches and a height of 60 inches. It was shot north of Cody. On Oct. 15, 1994, Tim Metzler of Powell shot an elk in Sunlight Basin that scored 400 4/8 points. *Other trophy elk:* Douglas Spicer, Teton Co., 1972; Cecil Atkins and Ott Maynard, Jackson Hole, 1947; Roger Linnell, Fremont Co., 1955; Edwin Shaffer, Big Horn, 1946; Thomas Yawkey, Thoroughfare Creek, 1936; Floyd A. Clark, Big Horn Co., 1976; Jerry F. Cook, Converse Co., 1965.

When the old Post Office building on Third Street in Laramie was torn down in 1956 to make way for a bank parking lot, art students from the University of Wyoming carved statues from the stone that once served as window sills. Many of the distinctively elongated scuptures are in private collections in the Laramie area.

5. Mountain Lion

Wyoming's record mountain lion is displayed in the Museum of Natural History in Washington, D. C. It was shot in the Wind River mountains by M. Abbott Frazier in 1892. *Other trophy mountain lions:* Win Condit of Saratoga shot three record mountain lions near Saratoga between 1954 and 1967.

6. Black Bear

C. W. Redshaw shot the record black bear in Lincoln County in 1976. *Other trophy black bears:* J. P. V. Evans, Gallatin River (on display in Museum of Natural History, Washington, D. C.), 1914; Charles R. Nixon, Lincoln Co., 1973.

7. Grizzly Bear

Grizzlies from Alaska dominate the list of record-holders. The record grizzly in the lower 48 states is one whose remains were picked up at Eagle Creek in 1961 by Loren Lutz and Harry Sanford.

8. Big Horn Sheep

Wyoming's record was shot by a man named Crawford in the Wind Rivers in 1883. *Other trophy sheep:* Oris Miller, Dinwoody Creek, 1954; Dale McWilliams, (finder), Park Co., 1975.

9. Bison

The national record bison is one scored by Boone and Crockett at 136 4/8 held in the collections of the Fishing Bridge Museum, Yellowstone. The animal was shot in the park by S. Woodring in 1925. The span between the horns measures 35 3/8 inches. *Other trophy bison:* H. A. Moore (finder), Park Co., 1977; George Burnap, Jr., (finder) Big Horns, 1953; C. C. Basolo, Jr., Gillette, 1963; Lee L. Coleman, Yellowstone, 1958; Lord Rendlesham, Wyoming, 1892; Prince Abdorreza Pahlavi, Gillette, 1967.

10. Pronghorn

The Boone and Crockett Wyoming record is held by the trophy animal shot in Carbon County in 1964 by J. Ivan Kitch. The horns are in excess of 16 inches long. *Other trophy pronghorn:* Fred Starling, Rawlins, 1967; Allen Douglas, Weston Co., 1943; Mary Kircher, Rawlins, 1961; John T. Peddy, Ferris Mountains, 1957; Roy Vail, Laramie Co., 1958; Terry N. TenBoer, Fremont Co., 1974.

*Source: Boone and Crockett Club, Alexandria, Virginia; news articles. Like any records of this type, these may change after any season.

Some Unusual Incidents Involving Hunting

1. Crowheart and a fight over hunting lands, 1866

When the Shoshones and the Crow disputed hunting rights in what is now northwest Fremont County, it was decided that the two leaders would duel to decide the victor. Washakie, the Shoshone chief, defeated the Crow chief Big Robber and to celebrate the victory, Washakie removed Big Robber's heart, hence the naming of Crowheart Butte.

2. Waln-Strong murders, 1888

A huge piece of Pennsylvania granite marks the spot along Monument Creek in Carbon County where Morris Waln of Philadelphia and C. H. Strong of New York City, were murdered by their hunting guide, Thomas O'Brien. Robbery was the apparent motive. Officers found the bodies and trailed O'Brien, but he was captured some weeks later in Colorado and sentenced to prison there for horse theft. Before he could be returned to Wyoming to stand trial, he died in prison. The marker was shipped west from Pennsylvania by Waln's sister and erected Dec. 23, 1889, on the spot where he died.

The 25th annual National Bow Hunt was held in September, 1994, at the Duncan Ranch, southeast of Glenrock. The Wyoming team, made up of Edgar Bobo, Randy Ivie and Lou Waters, won the "C team" title.

3. Jailing of Red Cloud, 1894

Red Cloud, his son and another man were arrested and jailed in Casper for hunting without a license. They were released without penalty for the first offense, but were re-arrested soon after on the same charges. In order to pay the $80 fine and court costs, Red Cloud was forced to sell his meager possessions consisting of a horse, a battered wagon and the harness.

4. Jackson Hole skirmish, 1895

The incident stemmed from a dispute between nine Bannack Indian families and 26 Jackson Hole residents over the terms of a treaty allowing for Indian hunting in Jackson Hole. The excitement brought national attention and bitter feelings for years.

5. Lightning Creek Fight, 1903

The last Indian-white fatal battle in Wyoming history, the incident occurred in October, 1903, after Billy Miller, Weston County sheriff, was informed that 25 Sioux Indians from South Dakota were illegally hunting game in the area. Miller and a 13-man posse caught up with the Indians at Lightning Creek, Converse County, and a gunfight ensued. Five Indians and two whites (including Sheriff Miller) died in the battle.

6. "Tarzan of the Tetons," 1939

Earl Durand of Powell was accused of poaching an elk west of Cody in March, 1939. He was arrested and held in the Park County Jail, but when he was being fed lunch, he struck a deputy with a milk bottle and escaped. He eluded authorities in Sunlight Basin for several days and then slipped through the dragnet and into Powell where he attempted to rob the First National Bank. He was gunned down by citizens in a shootout that also killed the bank teller. The national press gave him the inaccurate nickname, presumably because "Tarzan of the Absarokas" would have been correct but lacked the proper "ring."

7. Gored by a Deer Antler

The only hunting fatality in Wyoming in 1995 came in November when a Worland man died after being gored by the antlers of a deer he had shot and was dragging through rugged country. The man bled to death.

8. Celebrities Shooting

The 2nd annual Buffalo Bill Celebrity Shootout was held in September 1995. Shoot-ers in the event included Jerry Mathers (*Leave It to Beaver*), James Drury (*The Virginian*) and Denver Pyle (*Dukes of Hazard*). The initial event in 1994 was broadcast by ESPN.

9. Lander One-Shot

The event is held on the opening day of antelope season. Gen. Norman Schwarzkopf and actor Jamison Parker (who starred in *Simon and Simon*) were among the celebrities participating in the 1993 Lander One-Shot Antelope Hunt. Actor Robert Stack partici-pated in 1998. Earlier hunt participants included Roy Rogers, Tex Ritter, Steve Allen and Charlie Daniels. The winning team in 2009, the German Aristos, was made up of Count Erbach, Count Duerkeim and Prinz Hohenlohe. The Colorado team, led by Gov. Bill Rit-ter, came in second. The Past Shooter Club was formed in 1955.

10. Dick Cheney's Famous Quail Hunt

On Feb. 11, 2006, Cheney, then the U. S. Vice President, shot Harry Whittington, a 78-year-old Texas lawyer, while the two were hunting on a Texas ranch. Cheney shot at a quail, not realizing that his friend was in the vicinity. Whittington survived and the incident was ruled an accident.

OLYMPIC GAMES

Wyoming Athletes in the Olympic Games, 1990's

1. Lane Deal

Deal (b. Riverton, 1961), won the silver medal in the hammer throw in the Atlanta Olympics. A 1979 graduate of Natrona County High School, he competed in college for Montana State.

2. John Godina

Godina, (b. Fort Sill, Okla., 1972), graduated in 1990 from Cheyenne Central High School. He attended UCLA on a track and field scholarship, won the silver medal for the shot put. He also competed in the discus throw but did not qualify for a medal.

3. David Zuniga

The Worland-born wrestler competed for the United States in the featherweight division. He won preliminary matches but was not a medalist. In high school, he was state champion for three years (1984-86). He attended Utah State and the University of Minnesota.

4. Ryan Brieske

The Gillette boxer was an alternate on the U. S. Olympic boxing team.

Wyoming Athletes in the Summer Olympics, 2000, 2004, 2008

1. Rulon Gardner, Afton, wrestling, gold medal (2000), bronze (2004)

Gardner, born in Afton in 1971, was the American sensation in the Sydney, Australia, games held in September, 2000. Sportscasters said he had no chance for victory against world champion wrestler Alexander Karelin of Russia who had never lost in 200 international matches and allowed just one point in ten years. Nonetheless, on Sept. 27, 2000, Gardner faced Karelin, one of the most famous men in Russia, in the finals of the Greco-Roman super heavyweight match. Gardner won 1-0. It was regarded as one of the biggest upsets in Olympic history and Gardner became an instant hero. His previous best had been a fourth place finish in the 1993 NCAA wrestling championships when he wrestled for the University of Nebraska. Following his return to America, the Star Valley High School graduate appeared on the *Tonight Show* with Jay Leno on Oct. 4, 2000. In February 2002 he was stranded overnight in sub-freezing temperatures as the result of a snowmobile mishap. The incident caused him to lose toes, but he went on to win the bronze medal in the 2004 Olympics in Athens, despite the missing toes. In February 2007, he and two other men survived an airplane crash into Lake Powell. The men had to swim for more than an hour to safety on the shore where they spent the night awaiting rescuers. During the 2008 Olympics, Gardner served as a color analyst for television broadcast of the wrestling events.

2. Heather Moody, Green River, water polo team, silver medal (2000); bronze (2004)

Moody received a warm welcome back to her hometown in October, 2000, after her team won an Olympic silver medal in Sydney. She was team captain of the American team in the 2004 Olympics. The team won the bronze medal. In September 2001, she became the first American water polo player to sign to play the sport professionally. She signed with a top European club in Greece. In 2007 she became the coach for the US Women's National Water Polo team. The team lost in double-overtime in the championship contest. She was assistant coach of the USA Women's National Water Polo team at the Beijing Olympics in 2008.

3. John Godina, Cheyenne, shot put, Silver and Bronze medal

Godina participated in three Olympic Games (1996, 2000, 2004) winning the Silver

Medal at the 1996 summer games in Atlanta and the Bronze Medal at Sydney, Australia in 2000. He was the first American in 72 years to make the Olympics in both the shot put and discus in both 1996 and 2000. He attended Cheyenne Central High School and later starred at UCLA, He has also won the Gold Medal for the shot put at the World Championships in 1995, 1997 and 2001.

4. Lance Deal, Casper, hammer throw, Silver medal

Deal won the Silver medal in the hammer throw in the 1996 Summer Olympics at Atlanta. He competed at three other Olympics (1988, 1992 and 2000). A three-sport All-State athlete at Casper Natrona High School, he went to college at Montana State.

5. Ryan Bolton, Gillette, men's triathlon

Bolton competed in the first Olympic triathlon at the Summer Games in Sydney. He was a three-sport athlete at Campbell High School in Gillette and later ran cross country and track for the University of Wyoming. He continued to compete in triathlon events. In 2002 he won the Ironman Triathlon at Lake Placid, New York.

6. Dawn Ellerbe, Laramie, women's hammer throw

Ellerbe was a four-time NCAA champion and six-time All-American at the University of South Carolina. She came to the University of Wyoming to complete a master's degree in Communications. While at UW, she was an assistant coach of the Cowgirls track team where she coached eight All-Americans and three MWC champions.

7. Jesseca Cross, Laramie, women's hammer throw and shot put

Cross competed in the hammer throw and shot put at the 2000 Summer Games in Sydney. A native of Laramie, she attended the University of Wyoming on a basketball scholarship. In 2007, she coached volleyball at Northwest College, Powell.

8. Scott Usher, Grand Island, NE, swimmer

Usher was the first Wyoming swimmer to qualify for the Olympics. He placed 7th in the 200 meter breaststroke at the 2004 Olympic Games in Athens, Greece. Still holds the Mountain West Conference records in th 100 and 200 yard breaststroke. He missed by .64 seconds from qualifying for the 2008 Olympics during Olympic trials, finishing third in the 200-meter breaststroke.

9. Jennifer Nichols, Cheyenne, archer

Nichols, born in Cheyenne in 1983, represented the United States in archery at the 2004 and 2008 Summer Olympics. At age 15, she won the National Youth Archery competition. In 2007, she won the gold medal in the individual competition in the Pan American games in Brazil. In June 2010, her team set a record in the Archery World Cup competition in Turkey for mixed team competitors.

Wyomingites in the Winter Olympics*

1. Resi Stiegler (b. Jackson, 1985)

Stiegler placed 11th in the combined Alpine and 12th in the slalom in the 2002 Olympics in Turino. A season-ending knee injury in Nov. 2009 kept her from competing in the 2010 Winter Olympics at Vancouver. Her father, Pepi, won silver in 1960 and gold and bronze in the slalom and giant slalom at Innsbruck in 1964.

2. Darin Binning (b. Rock Springs, 1966)

Binning was the only Wyomingite in the 1988 Winter Olympics in Calgary. He finished 42nd in the biathlon and 9th as a member of the biathlon team. He lived in Pinedale.

3. Tommy Moe (b. Missoula, Montana, 1970)

In the 1994 Winter Olympics in Lillehammer, Norway, Moe won the gold in the men's downhill and a silver medal in the Super G. At the time of the Olympics, Moe lived in Alaska, but he now lives in Wilson.

At least 20 Wyomingites have competed in the Winter Olympics since 1936.

RODEO

1st organized rodeo in Wyoming: Rodeos were held at both Lander and Dayton during the summer of 1893. Stub Farlow organized the Lander event which continues as the oldest annual rodeo in the state. The Dayton rodeo, organized by Shorty Jennings, did not continue as an annual event.

1st Cheyenne Frontier Days: 1897. The rodeo was held on just one day in September and, therefore, it was initially known as "Frontier Day."

1st Wyoming High School Rodeo championships: 1955, in Saratoga.

1st Cody Stampede Rodeo: 1920. Occasional rodeos had been held on the Fourth of July in Cody as early as 1903.

1st Cody Nite Rodeo: The rodeo, held nightly during the summer months, began on June 24, 1939. Known as "Carl Downing's Pup Rodeo," its first performance was for the national convention of the BPOE Does.

1st Laramie River Rendezvous: The University of Wyoming-hosted annual collegiate rodeo began in 1944.

Greatest bucking bull of all time: Probably "Mr. T," who threw 188 cowboys during a five-year period. He was ridden for the first time by Marty Staneart of Sanger, Calif., on July 30, 1989, at Cheyenne Frontier Days. Only two other cowboys stayed on the required eight seconds to get a score—Raymond Wessel and Ty Murray. Owned by Hal and Pete Burns Rodeo Company of Laramie, Mr. T was retired in July 1991. He died at the age of 16 on the ranch where he spent the last four years of his life near Red Bluffs, Calif., in March 1994.

Longevity: Casper College rodeo coach Dale Stiles coached the team for 38 years. He died in March 1994, at the age of 73.

Longest Collegiate Rodeo winning string: Casper College won four consecutive national championships from 1963-66. CC finished second in 1978 and third in 1983. The string is an overall collegiate record. In sports competition among all colleges, no junior college has come close to matching such a mark.

1st national collegiate team title won by UW: 1961. Team members included Frank Shepperson, Clara Wilson, Al Smith, Sally Shepperson, Fred Wilson, Jerry Kaufman, Leon Cook and Fred Wilson.

1st woman saddle bronc rider in a PRCA event: Gywnn Turnbull of Laramie, spring 1987.

1st woman to win Frontier Days wild horse race: Tracy Robinson tied for the title in 1981.

1st Miss Frontier: Jean Nimmo Dubois, crowned in 1931.

1st African-American cowboy to win a Frontier Days event: Probably, Nollie Smith who won the wild horse harnessing and hitching contest in 1913. Smith later became a well-known American diplomat.

Some Rodeo Cowboys from Wyoming

1. Joe Alexander

Reared on a ranch near Cora in Sublette County, Alexander finished his 13-year professional rodeo career in 1982 after winning five world bareback championships and reaching the National Finals Rodeo in each of those 13 years. At Cheyenne Frontier Days in 1974, he set a record in bareback with a score of 93. On the collegiate level, Alexander starred at Casper College where he led the team to two national titles in 1965 and 1966.

2. Bill Smith

Considered one of the all-time saddle bronc riders, Smith from Cody, won two National Championship titles in 1971 amd 1973.

3. Hank Franzen

The 1978 college all-around and bull riding champion at Casper College, Franzen now operates Powder River Rodeo Productions, a rodeo stock company, from a ranch near Wright.

4. Chris LeDoux

LeDoux rode the rodeo circuit for several years, winning the world bareback riding championship at the National Finals Rodeo in Oklahoma City in 1976. He attended Cheyenne Central High School and Casper College. He retired from rodeo competition in 1984. He became a famous song composer and performer singing most of his own works. In 2000, he had liver transplant surgery, recovered and returned to performing and in 2006, he was inducted into the Pro Rodeo Hall of Fame in Oklahoma City. He made his home near Kaycee. He died March 9, 2005, from a form of cancer. A bronze statue in city park in Kaycee was dedicated in his honor in June 2010.

4. Dave Brock

The PRCA Rookie of the Year in 1972 won the world calf roping championship in 1978. He was a member of the Casper College rodeo team in the early 1970s.

5. Marvin Garrett

Garrett was the only Wyoming cowboy to win a world championship in the decade of the 1980s. He won world titles in 1988 and 1989. His winnings in the bareback events in 1989 were $105,931. He was top rookie bareback rider in 1984. Following recovery from a serious injury suffered in an airplane crash, he returned to the rodeo circuit, taking fourth overall in 1997.

6. Bob Harris

A Gillette team roper, Harris and his roping partner, Tee Woolman of Plano, Texas, won the National Finals Rodeo event in Las Vegas in 1991. Later, Harris teamed up with Doyle Gellerman for the team-roping title in the late 1990s.

7. Larry Sandvick

The Kaycee cowboy was a leading money winner on the pro circuit in 1999 and 2000. He first qualified for the National Finals Rodeo in 1992, qualifying every year after (to 2000). He was fifth, overall, and champion in bareback in 1997. He bought a ranch in western South Dakota in 2000.

8. Kelly Wardell

Formerly of Moorcroft, but living in Bellevue, Idaho, he placed fourth nationally in bareback in 1997.

9. Lynn Wiebe

A native of Ottertail, Minn., she competed for Central Wyoming College. In 1998 and 1999, she won the college all-around title and also the goat-tying title.

10. Jason Miller

Miller, from Lance Creek, won the World Title for steer wrestling at the National Finals Rodeo in Las Vegas in 2007.

11. Kaleb Asay

Asay, from Powell, was named the Rookie of the Year in the saddle bronc division for 2008. He attended Casper College and is the younger brother of Kanin, also on the pro circuit.

12. Dusty Tuckness

Tuckness, from Meeteetse, is a world-renowned bullfighter (rodeo clown). His job is to protect bull riders from harm. He has worked many of the top rodeos.

Others include Enoch Walker, Cody; **J. D. McKenna**, Sheridan; **Ralph Buell**, Sheridan; **Nick Harris**, Gillette; **Ike Rude**, Buffalo; **Frank Shepperson**, Midwest, **Kanin Asay**, Powell, **Kelly Timberman**, Mills. **Seth Glause**, Rock Springs, **Chet Johnson**, Gillette/Lusk, **Bobby Welsh**, Gillette, **Jhett Johnson**, Casper

Wyoming Cowboys Who Won All-Around at Frontier Days
(for the period 1938-2000)

1. **Nick Knight**, Cody (1938)   3. **Warren Wuthier**, Buffalo (1965)
2. **Buck Rutherford**, Cheyenne (1954) 4. **Harold Baumgardner**, Chey. (1984)

Cowboys from 15 states won the all-around title at Cheyenne Frontier Days in the past 50 years.

UW dropped mandatory male student participation in ROTC in 1965.

Wyomingites Who Were Miss Rodeo America

1. **Marilynn Scott Freimark** (1956)
2. **Sandy Meyer Brazile** (1984)
3. **Stacy Talbott Sinclair** (1991)

Talbott's family ranched west of Laramie. She was a student at the University of Wyoming.

4. **Michele Green Mackey** (1993)

Green, from Lander, was selected Miss Rodeo America, Dec. 7, 1993. She was a senior at Northwestern Oklahoma State University.

Some Rodeo Highlights

1. **Youngest Winner**

Kera Washburn of Cody was the youngest rodeo competitor ever to win a national rodeo title. She was nine years old when she won the Northern Rodeo Association barrel racing title in 1993.

2. **Collegiate Rodeo**

The University of Wyoming women's team won national championship in 1990 and 1991. Two members of the UW women's team won national titles in those years. Jimmie J. Martin, Longmont, Colo., won all of UW's points in 1990. She was all-around cowgirl. Lori Rhodes, Hamilton Dome, won the national goat-tying title in 1991. In 1996, the UW women finished second in the College National Finals rodeo, held that year in Bozeman, Montana. UW's Brenda White won the national breakaway roping crown. In the men's events, Todd Suhn of UW won the national steer wrestling title in 1996. Bryel Zancanella of UW finished second in breakaway roping in the Collegiate National Finals for two years in a row (1998-99). UW's James Tarver took second in calf roping in 1999. Lynn Wiebe, Central Wyoming College, won the 1998 and 1999 all around titles at the CNFR. Will Farrell of Lander (representing Chadron State) took the bull-riding championship at the 1999 CNFR held in Casper.

3. **Bucking winner**

Kadafy Skoal, a bucking horse owned by Powder River Rodeo Co., of Natrona County, won PRCA bucking horse of the year honors in 1990.

4. **College Rodeo**

Gillette College won the girls team title at the 2010 National High School Rodeo held in Casper in June 2010.

4 Fatalities at Cheyenne Frontier Days

1. **Floyd Irwin** (1917)

The son of showman Charlie Irwin, Floyd Irwin was killed in a pre-rodeo roping contest in 1917.

2. **Eddie Burgess** (1923)

Burgess, a Creek Indian roper, died in 1923 after his horse fell on him during the roping competition.

3. **Reva Grey** (1938)

Gray died when her horse collided with another and she fell under them.

4. **Lane Frost** (1989)

Frost, a 25-year-old bull rider from Quanah, Texas, was killed on July 30, 1989, when he was gored and trampled by a bull. He had been the 1987 World Champion bull rider. Later, a statue was cast and placed at Frontier Park in his memory and a movie was made about his life.

SKIING

1st NCAA team championship won by a University of Wyoming ski team: The UW team won the NCAA crown in 1976 and repeated the feat in 1985. It is the most national titles won by UW in any team sport. The university ski team finished fourth in the national finals in both 1989 and 1990; 6th in 1992.

U. S. Pro Ski Tour "Pro Challenge": 70 professional skiers competed in January, 1993, at Jackson Hole Ski Area. It was the first time in 10 years a US Pro Ski Tour event was held in the Tetons.

Costs: Ski areas pay lease fees to U. S. Forest Service. Rates have varied over the years and depended on the amount of Forest Service land each resort used. Grand Targhee Ski Resort paid $160,000 in 1992; Jackson Hole Ski Area, $358,727; Snow King Resort, $8,354 for 1990-91.

14 Wyoming Ski Areas

1. Jackson Hole/Teton Village (Tetons, 12 miles from Jackson)

Aerial tramway and five chairlifts service the towering 4,139-foot mountain, the largest in the United States. In 1991, *Snow Country* magazine listed the ski area in the top 25 ski resorts in the United States. Development began in 1965.

2. Grand Targhee (Tetons, 42 miles northwest of Jackson)

The site averages 500 inches of snow per season and artificial snow-making is almost never done. It has runs of 2,200 vertical feet and up to 2 1/2 miles long.

3. Snow King Mountain (Tetons, Jackson)

The mountain towers over the town of Jackson which lies at its northern base. Chairlift from Jackson is up 1,571 vertical feet. From 1992-95, more than $7 million was invested for a new base lodge, ice rink and triple chair lift.

4. Sleeping Giant (Absaroka Mountains, 48 miles west of Cody)

Near east gate of Yellowstone Park, the ski area closed in 2004. A foundation raised more than $1 million to reopen the ski area. Skiing resumed there in January 2010.

5. Big Horn/Greybull (Big Horn Mountains, 35 miles east of Greybull)

A ski touring terrain surrounds the ski slopes of 650 vertical feet. The ski area closed in 2008 when the U. S. Forest Services disapproved of the condition of the leased site on U. S. Forest lands.

6. Powder Pass (Meadowlark) (Big Horns, between Worland and Buffalo)

Lift rises from the shore of Meadowlark Lake. Five runs, 600 vertical feet.

7. Sundance Mountain (Black Hills, 10 miles from Sundance)

The ski area has eleven runs. The owners were involved in litigation that went to the Wyoming Supreme Court in 2006 when they denied access to Union Telephone company's towers on the top of the peak. The site commonly is confused on the internet with Sundance ski area in Utah, the site of Robert Redford's annual film festival.

8. Hogadon Ski Area (Casper Mountain, 11 miles south of Casper)

Operated by the Casper Parks and Recreation Department, 60 acres of trails and runs, 8,000 feet in elevation. The city of Casper acquired it in 1975 and, in 2009, the city provided almost $200,000 to operate the facility.

9. Snowy Range Ski Area (Snowy Range, 32 miles west of Laramie)

Two chairlifts, 12 ski runs. It once had the confusing name, Medicine Bow Ski Area, thus attracting disappointed out-of-state skiers to the town of Medicine Bow, many miles from the actual site. The area opened in 1959. The ski area passed through bankruptcy in the 2000s and was owned for several years by a bank. It was sold in the summer of 2010.

10. White Pine (Wind River Range, 10 miles northeast of Pinedale)

Lift serves vertical rise of 1,000 feet. The ski area operated from 1960-1989 under special use permits from the national forest. In 1996, the forest service approved a master

Jamaica's bobsled team trained near Evanston for the 2002 Winter Olympics in Salt Lake City.

plan for redevelopment of the ski area by Wind River Resorts, Inc. The ski area reopened in the winter of 1997 and a new lodge was opened in 1999.

11. Snowshoe Hollow (Wyoming Range, 1 1/2 miles east of Afton)
Small family-oriented winter sports area.

12. Pine Creek (Wyoming Range, 6 miles east of Cokeville)
Owned by Lincoln County, the ski area is leased out to private operators. Chairlift rises 1,200 vertical feet, runs up to a mile long. The lodge is a refurbished railroad depot.

13. Eagle Rock (Uinta Range, 15 miles east of Evanston)
Chairlift and tows rise 430 vertical feet. The Uinta Range is America's only major east-west mountain range.

14. Antelope Butte (Big Horn Mountains, 30 miles east of Greybull, 300 acres).
The resort closed in the 2000s due to financial problems.

Some Ski-Related Items

1. Skiers and dogs
Avalanche rescue dogs Coup, Rage and Barley helped ski patrol and sheriff's rescue crews find skier Robert "Drew" Dunlap after he was buried by an avalanche near Jackson April 2, 1992. Dunlap survived after being hurled down hundreds of feet, plunging off two cliffs and being buried in snow for 1 1/2 hours. Rescue dog Coup frantically began digging right over Dunlap's head where he had made a small air pocket in front of his face. Dunlap suffered only a minor knee injury.

2. Big sale
Jackson Hole Ski Corporation was sold in July 1992 to a company controlled by John L. "Jay" Kemmerer III, of the Kemmerer family for whom the Wyoming town was named. The resort was purchased from a corporation controlled by founder Paul McCollister and a major shareholder, Dutch oil trader John Deuss of Deepwater Investments. McCollister, who had founded the corporation in 1963, became locked in a lawsuit with Deuss over control after Deuss bought into it in 1987.

3, Skiing down mountains
Kit Deslauriers, Teton Village, became the first person to ski from the top of Mt. Everest on Oct. 18 2006. She also skied the highest peaks in North America, Europe, South America and Antarctica.

State High School Skiing Championships. 1995-2010

Boys Alpine	Girls Alpine	Boys Nordic	Girls Nordic
1995: Jackson	*Jackson (4th title)	**1995:** Kelly Walsh	Lander
1996: Jackson	Laramie	**1996:** Natrona	Lander
1997: **Jackson	Jackson	**1997:** Natrona	Lander
1998: Natrona	Laramie	**1998:** Natrona	***Lander
1999: Jackson	Laramie	**1999:** Natrona	Jackson
2000: Jackson	Jackson	**2000:** Jackson	Natrona
2001: Jackson	Jackson	**2001:** Natrona	Jackson
2002: Jackson	Jackson	**2002:** Kelly Walsh	Lander
2003: Jackson	Jackson	**2004:** Lander	Pinedale
2004: Cody	Jackson	**2003:** Pinedale	Lander
2005: Cody	Jackson	**2005:** Jackson	Natrona
2006: Natrona	Jackson	**2006:** Jackson	Jackson
2007: Natrona	Jackson	**2007:** Jackson	Jackson
2008: Jackson	Jackson	**2008:** Jackson	Jackson
2009: Jackson	Pinedale	**2009:** Lander	Natrona
2010: Jackson	Jackson	**2010:** Cody	Lander

* 4th consecutive title. ** 9th consecutive title ***6th consecutive title

High school alpine skiing in Wyoming began in 1964. Six teams competed except for a brief period when Worland had a team.

SOCCER

State High School Soccer Championships

Boys' events 1st held in 1986; girls in 1988

Boys	Girls
1988: Cheyenne East	Cheyenne East
1989: Cheyenne East	Casper Natrona
1990: Cheyenne Central	Casper Natrona
1991: Cheyenne Central	Casper Natrona
1992: Cheyenne East	Cheyenne Central
1993: Central 5 Riverton 2	Sheridan 3 Cheyenne East 0
1994: Gillette 1 East 0	Kelly Walsh 2 East 1
1995: East 2 Central 1	East 2 Central 1 (in overtime)
1996: Natrona	East 2 Kelly Walsh 1 (OT)
1997: Buffalo 2 Riverton 1	Natrona 4 Central 0
1998: Kelly Walsh 2 Central 0	Central 4 Casper Natrona 3
1999: Central 1 Kelly Walsh 0	Casper Natrona 4 Sheridan 1
2000: Laramie 1 Kelly Walsh 0	Casper Natrona 2 East 0
2001: Cheyenne East 2 Rock Springs 0	Cheyenne East 2 Gillette 0
2002: Kelly Walsh 1 Cheyenne East 0	Cheyenne East 2 Gillette 0
2003: Kelly Walsh 1 Cheyenne East 0	Casper Natrona 1 Cheyenne East 0
2004: Cheyenne East 3 Laramie 1	Casper Natrona 1 Cheyenne Central 0
2005: Kelly Walsh 2 Cheyenne East 1	Kelly Walsh 1 Cheyenne East 0
2006: Cheyenne Central 5 Gillette 2	Buffalo 3 Laramie 1
2007: Kelly Walsh 1 Cheyenne Central 0	Cheyenne Central 1 Cheyenne East 0
2008: 4A: Laramie 1 Kelly Walsh 0	Laramie 2 Cheyenne East 0
3A: Cody 2 Buffalo 1	Jackson 5 Worland 1
2009: 4A: Cheyenne Central 3 Natrona 1	Laramie 1 Gillette 0
3A: Cody 5 Buffalo 1	Jackson 2 Buffalo 0
2010: 4A: Laramie 2 Sheridan 0	Laramie 2 Gillette 0
3A: Buffalo 1 Cody 0	Jackson 1 Buffalo 0

Eight students/members of the University of Wyoming cross-country team--Cody Brown, Kyle Johnson, Josh Jones, Justin Lambert-Belanger, Morgan McLeland, Kevin Salverson, Nick Schabron, & Shane Shatto-- were returning from Colorado on Highway 287 near Tie Siding, 17 miles south of Laramie, when their vehicle was struck by a pickup driven by a drunk driver. The eight cross-country team members all died in the accident on Sept. 16, 2001. A memorial was unveiled in Sept. 2002 at the spot south of the fieldhouse where the squad began a daily run that usually traversed the sage-covered high plains surrounding Laramie. It includes an 8-foot-by-5-foot rounded slab of pink- and gold-colored granite taken from near the crash site. Eight smaller boulders, 2-feet to 3-feet in diameter, lie alongside, plus flowers, trees, grass, soil and a gravel walkway. Cinders from the university track are embedded in the concrete curbing. There are two park benches and a plaque designed by teammate Joel Hess that reads, "Come Run With Me."

SWIMMING

State High School Swimming Championships

	Boys	Girls			Boys	Girls
2009:	4A Laramie	Gillette		**2004:**	4A: Laramie	Cheyenne Central
	3A: Lander	Jackson			3A: Lander	Jackson
2008:	4A: Gillette	Gillette		**2003:**	4A: Laramie	Cheyenne Central
	3A: Lander	Jackson			3A: Lander	Lander
2007:	4A: Gillette	Gillette		**2002:**	4A: Kelly Walsh	Gillette
	3A: Lander	Jackson			3A: Lander	Newcastle
2006:	4A: Gillette	Gillette		**2001:**	4A: Green River	Laramie
	3A: Lander	Lander			3A: Lander	Newcastle
2005:	4A: Laramie	Gillette		**2000:**	4A: Laramie	Laramie
	3A: Lander	Jackson			3A: Lander	Newcastle

Some Noteworthy Swimmers from Wyoming

1. Layne Kopischka

Kopischka was Laramie High swim coach for 20 years. His boys teams were 267-10-1 in dual meets and won 12 state team titles. His girls' teams finished 148- 9-1 with six state championships. (He coached the girls team for 12 years). In 1984, he was named national swim coach of the year. He retired in 1988 and died July 12, 1992. His daughter Shauna won four straight state diving titles (1988-92).

2. John Green

Green, a 1987 Sheridan High School graduate, was named swimmer of the year by the National Junior College Athletic Association in May 1989. Green won three individual events and participated in three relays in the NJCAA championship. He swam for Indian River Junior College, Florida.

3. Mark Miller

Miller was an All-American swimmer throughout his collegiate career at UW in the middle 1980s. Following graduation, he became swimming coach at Campbell County High School. In 1989, he was ranked 18th in the U. S. in the 100-yard and 200-yard breaststroke and 200-yard individual medley.

4. Tamra McCullough

She starred for the 1989 University of Wyoming swim team and set records in the 100-yard and 200-yard breaststroke and 200-yard individual medley.

5. Scott Usher

Usher was the first Wyoming swimmer to qualify for the Olympics. He placed 7th in the 200 meter breaststroke at the 2004 Olympic Games in Athens, Greece. He still holds the Mountain West Conference records in th 100 and 200-yard breaststroke

TENNIS

Wyoming State High School Tennis Championship

	Boys	Girls			Boys	Girls
2009:	Chey. Central	Jackson		**2000:**	Jackson	Gillette
2008:	Gillette	Jackson		**1999:**	Casper Natrona	Jackson
2007:	Gillette	Kelly Walsh		**1998:**	Gillette	Jackson
2006:	Gillette	Casper Natrona		**1997:**	Casper Natrona	Kelly Walsh
2005:	Casper Natrona	Cheyenne Central		**1996:**	Chey. Central	Kelly Walsh
2004:	Gillette	Sheridan		**1995:**	Chey. Central	Cheyenne Central
2003:	Casper Natrona	Sheridan		**1994:**	Kelly Walsh	Cheyenne Central
2002:	Jackson	Cody		**1993:**	*Chey. Central	Cheyenne Central
2001:	Jackson	Gillette			*8th consecutive title	

TRACK AND FIELD

High Jump: UW's Bud Hamilton set high jump mark of 7'3" (school mark), Jan. 15, 1993, at an indoor meet in Laramie.

Decathlon: Gregg Sawyer, Burns High School, finished fourth in decathlon at US Track and Field Junior Championships, Baton Rouge, La., July 27-28, 1993.

1st University of Wyoming student to be named NCAA Woman of the Year in track and field: Shelly Thacker-Coventry, a Riverton native, in 1991.

3 "Throwing" Stars

1. John Godina

Godina, while a student at Cheyenne Central set the high school record in discus and shot put in 1990. At UCLA, he won the shot put and discus at Junior Pan Am Games. On March 11, 1994, as a senior at UCLA, broke the NCAA shot put record of 65' 8 3/4" at the NCAA Track and Field Finals. He won the silver medal for the shot put in the 1996 Summer Olympics. The first American to compete in both shot put and discus since 1924, he narrowly missed a medal for the discus. He won the bronze medal in the 2000 Olympics.

2. Lance Deal

Deal lived in Eugene, Oregon, but he is a native of Casper. In 1992, he qualified for the 1992 Summer Olympics in the hammer throw by finishing second in the event at the Olympic Trials at New Orleans, with a throw of 262 feet, 3 inches. Deal competed in the same event in the 1988 Summer Olympics. He was the world record holder in the event in the early 1990s. On March 4, 1995, he set a world mark for the 35-lb. shot with a throw of 84 feet, 10 1/4 inches, in Atlanta. In 1995, he won the Mobil Indoor Grand Prix for the second time in three years. He won the silver medal for the hammer throw in the 1996 Summer Olympics. He also participated in the 2000 Olympics, but did not place.

3. Ryan Butler

Butler, while a senior at the University of Wyoming in 1996, won the 35-lb. weight throw in the NCAA Indoor Track and Field championships in Indianapolis. His throw of 71 feet, 1 1/2 inches, was more than two feet better than the second place finisher. He placed fifth in the nation in 1995.

Wyoming State High School Track and Field Records
Record to June 2010

	Mark	Date	Name	School
100 Meter Dash:				
Boys:	10.50	2008	Stephen Michel	Laramie
Girls:	11.91	1996	Arnetta Simpson	Cheyenne Central
200 Meter Dash:				
Boys:	21.39	2008	Stephen Michel	Laramie
Girls:	24.10	1998	Arnetta Simpson	Cheyenne Central
400 Meter Dash:				
Boys:	47.63	2009	Mario Harris	Casper Natrona
Girls:	54.78	1990	Shanelle Porter	Cheyenne East
800 Meter Run:				
Boys:	1:51.92	2006	Bob Hewitt-Gaffney	Gillette
Girls:	2:10.93	2006	Stacy Slight	Cody
1600 Meter Run:				
Boys:	4:15.84	2009	Dominick Robinson	Gillette
Girls:	4:52.12	2001	Alicia Craig	Gillette
3200 Meter Run:				
Boys:	9:25.70	2010	Garrett Zans	Rock Springs
Girls:	10:33.15	2001	Alicia Craig	Gillette

110 Meter Hurdles:
Boys:	13.73	2007	Brandan Ames	Cheyenne Central

100 Meter Hurdles:
Girls:	14.36	2001	Shaunna Smith	Sheridan

300 Meter Hurdles:
Boys:	37.25	2009	Taylor Villegas	Casper Natrona
Girls:	43.25	2001	Shaunna Smith	Sheridan

4x100 Meter Relay:
Boys:	42.24	1993	Cheyenne East	Cheyenne East
Girls:	48.30	2006	Gillette	Gillette

4x400 Meter Relay:
Boys:	3:20.98	2001	Gillette	Gillette
Girls:	3:57.17	2006	Cody	Cody

4x800 Meter Relay:
Boys:	7:56.17	1994	Rock Springs	Rock Springs
Girls:	9:30.85	2005	Cody	Cody

High Jump:
Boys:	7-00	1995	Chaarlie Clinger	Star Valley
Girls:	5-07	2008	Cate Brus	Cody

Pole Vault:
Boys:	16-00.25	2008	Justin Gebicki	Cheyenne East
Girls:	11-09.	2010	Anna Bales	Cody

Long Jump:
Boys:	24-06.75	2007	Brandan Ames	Cheyenne Central
Girls:	19-06.	2009	Emily Moore	Gillette

Triple Jump:
Boys:	48-09.50	2008	Stephen Michel	Laramie
Girls:	39-07.50	2006	Emily Moore	Gillette

Discus Throw:
Boys:	210-04	1990	John Godina	Cheyenne Central
Girls:	159-02	2010	Baillie Gibson	Casper Natrona

Shot Put:
Boys:	63-01	1990	John Godina	Cheyenne Central
Girls:	48-09	2010	Baillie Gibson	Casper Natrona

VOLLEYBALL
Wyoming High School Volleyball Champions

Year	Team	Year	Team	Year	Team
2000:	4A: Gillette	**2004:**	4A: Cheyenne East	**2008:**	4A: Casper Kelly Walsh
	3A: Wheatland		3A: Star Valley		3A: Powell
	2A: Big Horn		2A: Pine Bluffs		2A: Big Horn
	1A: Cokeville		1A: Little Snake River		1A: Cokeville
2001:	4A: Casper Kelly Walsh	**2005:**	4A: Casper Kelly Walsh	**2009:**	4A: Green River
	3A: Rawlins		3A: Star Valley		3A: Wheatland
	2A: Sundance		2A: Pine Bluffs		2A: Big Horn
	1A: Cokeville		1A: Guernsey-Sunrise		1A: Burlington
2002:	4A: Casper Kelly Walsh	**2006:**	4A: Cheyenne Central		
	3A: Star Valley		3A: Wheatland		
	2A: Lusk		2A: Sundance		
	1A: Burlington		1A: Burlington		
2003:	4A: Cheyenne East	**2007:**	4A: Casper Natrona		
	3A: Star Valley		3A: Wheatland		
	2A: Pine Bluffs		2A: Big Horn		
	1A: Little Snake River		1A: Hulett		

WRESTLING

1st Wyoming wrestler to win an Olympic gold medal: Rulon Gardner, 2000 Olympics
1st Wyoming high school wrestler to be named all-American: Jack Donahue, Sheridan (1990)
Donahue wrestled in the 125-lb. division in the first-ever national championship matches held at the University of Pittsburgh. Justin Martin, also of Sheridan, was the only other Wyoming participant in the tournament.
Famous wrestling personality living in Cody: Eric Aaron Bischoff (born May 27, 1955) is a professional wrestling booker and producer, He was executive producer and, later, president of World Championship Wrestling (WCW). With an amateur background in martial arts, Bischoff also competed as an in-ring performer, and is a former WCW Hardcore Champion. He wrote an autobiography, titled *Controversy Creates Cash*, that was published in 2006.

Some Well-Known Wyoming Wrestlers

1. Rulon Gardner
   The Afton native is the only Wyomingite to win a medal in the Olympic games in wrestling. In September, 2000, he defeated three-time Olympic champion Alexander Karelin of Russia to gain the gold medal. The 29-year-old Gardner was internationally recognized after the victory with television appearances and a special welcome home to Afton, featured on network television nationwide.

2. Dick Ballinger
   Ballinger won the national title at 167 lbs in 1960; he finished second in same weight class in 1958. He was the first UW wrestler to win a national title.

3. Jerry Frude
   UW wrestler Frude won second place in the NCAA in 147-lb. class in 1959.

4. Craig Walters
   In the decade of the 1980s, Walters had the best NCAA finish of any UW wrestler, a fourth place in 1988.

5. Reese Andy:
   Andy, in the NCAA 177-lb. class, finished second after losing in the championship in a 3-2 decision to a West Virginia wrestler in March 1994. A UW sophomore, Andy allowed an escape with 49 seconds left which meant the difference in the contest. In 1996, he lost to Les Gutches of Oregon State by a 8-2 count in the 177-lb. championship. He became the second Cowboy wrestler ever to become a three-time All-American.

6. Gil Sanchez
   A 1981 Cheyenne Central graduate, Sanchez was an All-American wrestler at the University of Nebraska. In 1992, he was named head wrestling coach at Clemson University in South Carolina.

7. Ray Sanchez
   The brother of Gil Sanchez, Ray Sanchez won four consecutive state championships and compiled a record of 93 wins with no losses or ties for Cheyenne Central. Later, after a collegiate career at UW and wins in various amateur matches, he went into coaching at the high school level at Greeley West. He quit coaching in 1976, earned an advanced degree and entered administration in the Denver and Jefferson County public schools. He retired in 2005.

8. Greg Gagne
   Gagne, a professional wrestler in the 1980s, played football at Wyoming during the previous decade.

UW men's rugby team lost to California for the national collegiate title in 2000 The team had a mark of 22-2-1, the best since the team was formed in 1972. The club sport at UW continued to win national recognition into the 2000s, but never as close as the national runner-up crown .

9. Jack Taylor

Taylor wrestled against world champion Stanislaus Zbyszko of Poland in Boise, Idaho, on Nov. 14, 1921. The Pole won the match in two falls, the first after 21 minutes and six seconds and the second, after ten minutes, 10 seconds. Later that year, Zbyszko, Taylor and others wrestled exhibition matches in Sheridan.

10. "Young Pistol" (Tracy Smothers)

"Young Pistol" appeared in a match on TBS World Championship Wrestling in January 1992. The Wyoming wrestler lost the match to "Heavy Metal Hammer."

11. Kevin Jimenez

Jimenez won the National Junior College wrestling title in the 190-lb. bracket in 1996. He wrestled for Northwest College, Powell.

12. Joe LeBlanc

LeBlanc was UW's first freshman to be named an All-American wrestler. From Meeker, Colo., LeBlanc placed 4th at the 2010 NCAA Wrestling Tournament and 9th place in 2009. He was the 2010 and 2009 Champion in the Western Wrestling Conference.

Wyoming High School Wrestling Team Champions, 2000-2010

Year	4A	3A	2A
2000:	Green River	Worland	Lusk
2001:	Green River	Worland	Lusk
2002:	Green River	Torrington	Lusk
2003:	Gillette	Star Valley	Cokeville
2004:	Gillette	Star Valley	Wright
2005:	Gillette	Torrington	Moorcroft
2006:	Gillette	Star Valley	Cokeville
2007:	Gillette	Star Valley	Cokeville
2008:	Gillette	Powell	Cokeville
2009:	Gillette	Powell	Cokeville
2010:	Gillette	Douglas	Greybull-Riverside

Mike Roberts, play-by-play announcer for University of New Mexico football, started KMER, the radio station in Kemmerer. Lured from a job in Scottsbluff, Nebr., he went to the "tri-cities" of Kemmerer, Frontier and Diamondville, where he was asked to locate the new radio transmitting tower. He chose a location in a swampy area where radio reception was superb, causing the FCC to visit often, wondering how the signal reached into Nebraska and surrounding area. He left Kemmerer after experiencing a temperature of 31 degrees on July 4th. *Source: Radio interview by Dave Walsh, Oct. 13, 2007.*

WYOMING ON THE WEB

1. Wyoming on Google

In June 2010, Google indicated some 68 million results for a search in which the name "Wyoming" was used. In comparison, in 2001, an America Online NetFind for the subject "Wyoming" provided 15,638 matches. the online auction website.

2. Wyoming Items for Sale

For mid-July 2010, eBay items related to "Wyoming" on sale numbered 14,780, including WPA era paintings of Wyoming and a vintage 1953 Wheaties Wyoming bicycle license plate. (By comparison, on the Fourth of July, 2001, there were 662 items relating to Wyoming for sale on e-Bay).

3. Wyoming Truth or Rumor

At the Snopes.com website, a search in July 2010 showed that information about 19 "Wyoming" subjects was deemed as truth or rumors.

4. Sports site

Collegefanz.com provides information about University of Wyoming sports as well as other universities and colleges of Divisions I, II and III, and the NAIA. Brandi Benson of Gillette is an anchor for the broadcast video for game coverage on the website, which was started by ESPN founder Bill Rasmussen.

5. Wyoming on Bing

A search of the topic "Wyoming" using the Bing search engine listed 99 million results in July 2010.

6. Wyoming Movies through Netflix

Netflix, the nationwide company that distributes movies and documentaries through mailed DVDs or by online viewing, has some "Wyoming" and "Yellowstone" titles, including "Country Roads: Wyoming," a 2005 workout video that uses a cross country adventure through Wyoming and the 1994 French film "Le Vent du Wyoming" ("The Wind of Wyoming").

7. Wyoming and a Movie Database

The Internet Movie Database lists 41 movie titles that contain the word "Wyoming" as well as the names of an actress named Layla Wyoming and a writer named Alan Wyoming.

8. Wyoming on YouTube

In July 2010, a search of "Wyoming" on YouTube provides 10,900 results, including videos of cattle drives, tornadoes, and a UW "Beer Song."

WEATHER

Wyoming's record highest temperature: 115 degrees recorded on Aug. 8, 1983, in Basin.

Wyoming's record lowest temperature: -66 degrees recorded on Feb. 9, 1933, at Riverside Ranger Station.

Record maximum annual precipitation: 55.5 inches, Grassy Lake Dam, 1945.

Record maximum precipitation in a 24-hour period: 6.06 inches, Cheyenne, Aug. 1, 1985.

Record maximum annual snowfall: 491 /1/2 inches (almost 41 feet), Bechler River, 1921-22.

Record maximum one-day snowfall: 38 inches, Burgess Junction, March 4, 1973.